P9-BJA-380

SIN AND FEAR

SIN *and* FEAR

The Emergence of a Western Guilt Culture 13th–18th Centuries

JEAN DELUMEAU

Translated by Eric Nicholson

St. Martin's Press,
New York

Originally published as Le Péché et La Peur.

Book design by Jaye Zimet

First published in the United States of America in 1990

Printed in the United States of America

ISBN 0-312-03582-9

Library of Congress Cataloging-in-Publication Data

Delumeau, Jean.
[Péché et la peur. English]
Sin and fear : the emergence of a western guilt culture / Jean Delumeau : translated by Eric Nicholson.
p. cm.
Translation of: Le péché et la peur.
Bibliography: p. 559
Includes index.
ISBN 0-312-03582-9
1. Sin—History of doctrines. 2. Theology—History.
3. Civilization, Modern. 4. minaissance. I. Title.
BT715.D443 1989
241'.3'09—dc20 89-12421
CIP

CONTENTS

TRANSLATOR'S PREFACE

Robert Burton, the seventeenth-century English scholar and author of *The Anatomy of Melancholy* (1621–38), avowed that "I know not wherein to do a more general service, and spend my time better, than to prescribe means how to prevent and cure so universal a malady, an epidemical disease, that so often, so much, crucifies the body and mind."[1] The universal malady in question is melancholy, that psychological affliction which disturbs not only lunatics, lovers, and poets, but also devout practitioners of religion and many others apt to suffer a guilty conscience. In many ways, Burton's copious and wide-ranging study anticipates the work of Sigmund Freud on precisely these syndromes of guilt, repression, and obsessional neurosis. Like his predecessor, but with far more depth and acumen, Freud perceived how the consciousness of guilt was a cultural as well as individual phenomenon. In *Civilization and Its Discontents* he writes, "may we not be justified in reaching the diagnosis that, under the influence of cultural urges, some civilizations, or some epochs of civilization—possibly the whole of mankind—have become 'neurotic'?" He then suggests that "an analytic dissection of such neuroses might lead to therapeutic recommendations which could lay claim to great practical interest."[2]

This English translation of Jean Delumeau's own wide-ranging and perceptive *Le Péché et la Peur* hopes to at least provide such interest, if not also its own therapeutic insights. Delumeau's cultural history of sin, which draws on Freud and makes ample citation of Burton, has contemporary diagnostic value to go along with its rich interdisciplinary analyses. As Professor Delumeau observes in his introduction, exaggerated attributions of guilt have enabled the late twentieth century to outdo preceding ones in the use of name-calling, repression, torture, and mass political violence. It should also be noted that this book is the sequel to Professor Delumeau's *La Peur en Occident* (Paris: Fayard, 1978), which has not yet been translated into English. It is also the second volume in a four-part series: This year, the author's study of early modern mentalities of security, *Rassure-Nous (devant les epreuves)*, will be published, to be followed by *L'Histoire du Paradis*. The current translation thus performs the valuable service of introducing English-speaking readers to the erudite work of Professor Delumeau.

Any responsible translation must acknowledge its inability to capture the full sense of the original. The French subtitle of this book, "La Culpabilisation en Occident," has obviously required a periphrasis in English. For the most part, such phrases as "guilt-instilling" and "the intensification of guilt" have been used to render the expressions *culpabiliser*, *culpabilisation*, and *surculpabilisation*. The same rule generally applies to the verb *sécuriser* and the noun *sécurisation*, which have been conveyed through "reassure" and "reassurance." As for the book's multitude of quotations, for the sake of uniformity they have been rendered into English by the translator (with a few exceptions, cited in the notes, that give information on the translated versions of Saint Augustine, Aquinas, Luther, Pascal, Freud, and so on). Unless otherwise noted, biblical quotations have been drawn from the Authorized King James Version. I would also like to thank Angela Armstrong, who painstakingly provided most of the original English texts cited in chapters 19 to 21.

Thanks are also due to Professor Delumeau himself, who provided various corrections and further assistance.

A special note of thanks and even more credit belong to Sara Matthews Grieco, who began the work on this translation and translated all of the introduction, chapter 1, and chapter 2. She also performed invaluable proofreading work and supplied references, books, and assistance. Credit also goes to Allen Grieco, for work on chapter 19, proofreading, and the translation of all the notes.

Appropriately enough, this translation was accomplished in four different countries, and even more cities. I therefore must express my gratitude to a variety of friends, colleagues, and others who have generously provided their time, support, and comments. These include the staffs of the Yale, Harvard, and UCLA university libraries, as well as of the British and Bodleian libraries. Special thanks for the use of their facility, and for their friendliness, go to the members of the Middle Common Room, Worcester College, Oxford University. I must also thank Pat Phillippy, Brandy Alvarez, and Julia Lupton not only for their advice, support, and friendship, but also for invaluable word processing assistance. I should also like to acknowledge my profound and ongoing debt to my advisors at Yale University, most especially Professor Thomas M. Greene, as well as Professor Natalie Zemon Davis and Professor George K. Hunter. As ever, the members of the Yale Renaissance Studies Program have been a constant source of support and encouragement. Last but never least, I give my deepest thanks and acknowledgment to my family, and to Carol Symes, for all their patience, generosity, commentary, and loving support.

Finally, the reader's attention should also be drawn to various books published on this and related subjects in the past five years, especially by Natalie Zemon Davis, Jacques Le Goff, Elaine Pagels, Jaroslav Pelikan, Christopher Hill, and David Underdown.

—ERIC A. NICHOLSON
Oxford, the city of Robert Burton, 1989

INTRODUCTION

A Cultural History of Sin

It might easily be thought that any civilization—in this case Western civilization from the fourteenth to the seventeenth centuries—which was besieged (or believed itself to be besieged) by a multitude of enemies—Turks, idolaters, Jews, heretics, witches, and so on—would not have had time for much introspection. This might have been quite logical, but exactly the opposite happened. In European history, the "seige mentality," which I have analyzed in a previous publication,[1] was accompanied by an oppressive feeling of guilt, an unprecedented movement toward introspection, and the development of a new moral conscience. The fourteenth century witnessed the birth of what might be called a "scruple sickness," a global phenomenon that soon reached epidemic proportions. It was as if the aggressivity directed against the enemies of Christendom had not entirely spent itself in incessant religious warfare, despite constantly renewed battles and an endless variety of opponents. A global anxiety, broken up into "labeled" fears, discovered a new foe in each of the inhabitants of the besieged city, and a new fear—the fear of one's self.

Expressing the feelings of the entire teaching body of the church on the fourteenth Sunday after Pentecost, Lefèvre d'Etaples commented on the Epistle to the Galatians (5:16–24) in these words: "All things considered, the life of a Christian in this world is nothing less than a continuous battle . . . His greatest adversary, however, is none other than himself. There is nothing more difficult for him to overcome than his own flesh and his own will, which are, by nature, inclined to all evil."[2] In much the same spirit Bourdaloue wrote: "It is no paradox, but rather certain truth when we say that our most fearful enemy is our own self. How is that possible? . . . I am . . . more dangerous to my own self than the rest of the world, for it is up to me and me alone whether or not I condemn my soul to death and exclude it from the Kingdom of God."[3] Both Lefèvre d'Etaples and Bourdaloue pushed to a similar extreme their interpretations of Saint Paul, according to whom a Christian must free himself from his evil instincts in order to rise above his baser nature.

This religious theme was the direct descendant of a long ascetic tradition. It was also linked to two other recurrent affirmations, which have been examined in *La Peur en Occident*. The first affirmation contended that a causal relationship linked the sins of mankind to a variety of collective punishments sent by an irate God.

Although bishops and preachers were most active in affirming this connection, they were not alone. Heads of state also considered wars to be a form of celestial chastisement for the faults of the people, and even doctors such as Ambroise Paré discerned divine wrath behind diseases such as plague and syphilis.[4] The authors of almanacs also shared and spread this conviction. An almanac of 1573, for example, gave the following warning, placing it in the mouth of God so as to be all the more convincing: "If you despise my prescriptions [*sic*] and commandments I shall turn my face against you and you will fall before your enemies . . . I shall send pestilence among you. I shall turn your sky to iron and your earth to stone so that the earth will not bear its fruit. You will eat the flesh of your sons and daughters."

Another almanac of 1578 reads: "Now, more than ever before, [God] is preparing to loose his anger upon our vices, daily afflicting us with war, torrents of blood, extortion, pillage, theft and oppression, and even with disease and unknown maladies."

A 1593 almanac joins the lugubrious chorus: "It is certainly our hideous sins and our lamentable and mad persistence in all sorts of evil deeds which have increasingly irritated our Good Lord."[5]

Insofar as these threats accompanied incessant appeals for conversion and penitence, they reinforced the second affirmation of the church, according to which Satan was omnipresent—and therefore also present in the heart of everyone. Were it not for the intervention of divine grace, every man and woman born after the Original Sin would have belonged to the demonic empire. In this respect, the remarks of Saint Catherine of Genoa (d. 1510) on mankind in general and herself in particular are as revealing as they are stupefying:

> *What is man by himself, without grace? A being more evil than the demon, for the demon is a spirit without a body while a man without grace is but a demon clothed with a body . . . I then thought that were God ever to withdraw his grace from me, I would be capable of all the crimes committed by the demon. I therefore judged myself to be even worse than Satan himself, and much more hateful. I then saw myself as a devil incarnate, and all this seemed to be so true, that if all the heavenly angels had come to tell me that I had even one good thing in me, I would not have believed them. For I clearly perceived that all that is good resides in God alone, whereas in myself resides only evil.*[6]

Thus reasoned a saintly widow who devoted herself to the poor and who was subject to visions. She so despised herself that she even avoided pronouncing her own name. A theatrical attitude? This judgment would be too hasty. Agrippa d'Aubigné confessed: "My head has a great many less hairs than sins" and, moreover, "My dreadful transgressions horrify me . . . growl in my ears, hiss like serpents in the night, constantly appear before my eyes like so many fearful specters, accompanied by the hideous image of death. Worse still, these are not the vain smoke of dreams but rather the living portraits of my very own deeds."[7] A contemporary, Saint Francis de Sales, used similar rhetoric in writing to Madame de Charmoisy: "Your faults are greater in number than the hairs on your head, greater still than the sands of the sea," and he invited Philotée to confess: "I am but an excrescence of the world, a sewer of ingratitude and iniquity."[8]

Such excesses of humility cannot be fully understood unless they are viewed in context—that is, within the parameters of the history of sin in the Western world, where they appear side by side with all the other fears and real or imaginary enemies described in *La Peur en Occident*. Among the multitudinous agents of Satan whom the men of God strove to track down and drive out of their hiding places, they could not omit the most secret and dangerous of them all. This agent was no other than each and every individual, insofar as he (or she) might conceivably relax his guard and lose control of himself. Seen in this perspective, the terrors that tormented early modern Europe before the discovery of the "unconscious" can be understood in terms of a much larger phenomenon. In addition to the "fear," the "dread," the "terror," and the "fright" occasioned by exterior perils of all kinds (natural or human), Western civilization was afflicted by two supplementary and equally oppressive causes for alarm: the "horror" of sin and the "obsession" of damnation. The church's insistence on both of the latter eventually led an entire society to condemn material life and daily concerns. Whence the inspiration for hymns such as this one, sung in the beginning of the eighteenth century by the congregations of Grignion de Montfort:

Leave your wood awhile, carpenter,
Put aside your iron, locksmith.
Set down your work, craftsman
Let us seek Grace.[9]

Then, more than ever before, did the West's religion of "anxiety" differ from the Eastern religions of "tranquility": Hinduism and Buddhism.[10] It is true that from the point of view of power politics, the dramatization of sin and its consequences reinforced clerical authority. The father-confessor became an irreplaceable figure whose unshakable status inspired the naïve and revealing affirmations of a canon from Bologna who declared, in 1602, that God sent three kinds of scourges to punish men for their sins: famine, war, and pestilence. No matter how serious famine might be, however, it was still the least terrible scourge of all, for whereas war and pestilence struck all men indiscriminately, famine spared the priesthood and therefore one could confess one's sins before dying. Famine also spared notary publics, so that one could draw up one's will, as well as princes, who were responsible for the welfare of the state.[11] It was certainly no accident that the father-confessor should have headed the canon's list, for it was he, after all, who opened and shut the doors of paradise. In the end, the only thing that really mattered was the aftermath of death.

It is precisely due to the importance accorded to this final objective that the history of guilt cannot be reduced to a mere history of clerical power. The two were most certainly connected, but the former extended far beyond the latter. Both Sigmund Freud and Carl Jung agree on the key role that all societies attribute to the notion of sin. Freud considers guilt one of the prime problems of civilization,[12] and Jung affirms that "There is nothing better for stimulating consciousness and awakening than a disagreement with one's self."[13]

No civilization had ever attached as much importance to guilt and shame as did the Western world from the thirteenth to the eighteenth centuries. This major fact cannot be underestimated, especially as any attempt to write the history of sin (that is, the history of a negative self-image) within a given period and a specific geographical area will inevitably involve the entire universe as it was then conceived. Any history of sin must also study the networks of relationships and attitudes that make up the collective unconscious. Similarly, it will shed light upon the society's conception of the individual and freedom, of life and death, of failure and harm. It must necessarily explore the society's conception of the relationship between man and God and investigate its image of divinity. Within certain limits, the history of sin also entails writing the history of both God and man. Is God more good or more just? This question provided an entire civilization with food for thought for several centuries.

Insofar as Western man was concerned, however, his intense guilt feeling led him to examine his own past, to know himself better, to develop his memory (if only through self-examination and "general confession"), and to explore his own identity. The notion of "bad conscience" developed at the same time as the art of the portrait and accompanied the rise of both individualism and the sense of responsibility. A connection surely exists among guilt, anxiety, and creativity.

At this point I feel it would be expedient to clarify my feelings on the subject at hand and state my own position as I see it.

First, the historian should not judge the past but make it understandable. Even though this book inevitably reflects contemporary thought, it aims, first and foremost, at being a historical record of an era that is rapidly receding into the past. It also aims at documenting a massive cultural phenomenon—a profound and widespread pessimism that permeated even the "optimistic" Renaissance. This observation occupies the first part of this study, where origins and causes are traced back in time according to the methods of "regressive" history. The entire second part is dedicated to the doctrine of sin and to an investigation of the world of fault and transgression as they were formerly perceived and practiced. The third part closes the circle, for doctrine automatically entailed pastoral diffusion: If preaching spread pessimism, pessimism also motivated preaching. In fact, neither ever ceased influencing the other.

The second point I would like to make concerns the relation of the historian to his research. It has long been obvious that historians cannot stand "outside" of their work. Voluntarily or not, they become involved in their investigations and commit themselves to their conclusions. I myself cannot hide my own feelings on the documents that are discussed here, and thus I prefer to say things clearly. I think that sin exists, I feel its presence in me. Furthermore, I cannot see how one can eliminate the idea of an Original Sin, whose scars we still bear. Freud felt this and tried to explain it, while both Bergson and Gouhier observed that "everything happens as if there were an original defect in man."[14] My book must therefore not be taken as a refusal of either guilt or the need for a consciousness of sin. On the contrary, I think it will shed light on the excessive sense of guilt and "culpabilisation" ("guilt-ification") (TRANSLATOR'S PREFACE) that has characterized Western history. By excessive "culpabilisation" I mean any of the arguments that inflated the dimensions of sin over and against those of forgiveness.[15] It is this very discrepancy—between fault and forgiveness—that furnishes the material for this book.

This discrepancy has long weighed heavy on the Western world. Pierre de Boisdeffre had his twentieth-century Goethe say:

> *Although redemption should have freed man from anguish, the church continues to insist upon self-examination, which the approach of death renders unbearable. There will be many called but few chosen, won't there? An "infinitely small number" says your Julian Green. Furthermore, subsequent generations have only aggravated the consequences of the Original Sin. God is only there to condemn and punish! What an atrocious interpretation of the role played by the Father! Hell, Purgatory . . . why are so many tortures inflicted in the name of love? He who has loved, be it only once in his life, is he not worthy of being loved for all eternity?*[16]

Such a terrifying image of God actually existed, and for centuries—whence the need to distinguish between a filial and reverential fear of God and a dread terror of God. My book will examine only the latter and will not question authentic Judeo-Christian maxims, such as: "Blessed is everyone that feareth the Lord" (Psalms 128) or "His mercy is on them that fear Him" (Magnificat). The following pages are, in fact, concerned only with exploring the gap that appeared between the fear of God and the dread of God.

The third and last point to be made is the following: We of the late twentieth century have more reasons than ever to exercise prudence when tempted to pass a verdict of "guilty" on the ecclesiastics of the past. Our era constantly speaks about liberating itself from guilt feelings without noticing that, in the entire history of guilt, the accusation of others has never been as strong as it is today. In a country as democratic as France, the Right and the Left accuse each other of unspeakable political sins. In states subjected to totalitarian yokes, the indictment of the adversary—capitalist or socialist, reactionary or progressive—has legitimized torture and led to the execution of millions and millions of people. In terms of excessive accusations of guilt we have—alas!—far surpassed our ancestors.

The historical inquiry that has resulted in this book would never have been completed were it not for the help of many friends who brought me texts and references, who proffered helpful suggestions and criticisms. I have therefore chosen to thank them in the course of this study and have quoted the names of those who so kindly furnished material in the notes. At the beginning of this book, however, I would like to express my profound gratitude to all my friends and colleagues, and in particular to Angela Armstrong and to Sabine Melchior-Bonnet, who were deeply involved in this project from beginning to end.

PART ONE

Pessimism and the Macabre in the Renaissance

CHAPTER 1

Contempt for the World and Mankind

AN OLD THEME

In the course of Christian history, both self-examination and an uncompromising attitude toward man and the world mutually reinforced each other—hence the need to resituate the fear of the self within the vast panorama of European pessimism.

The scorn for the world and the contempt for mankind propounded by Christian ascetics stemmed equally from the Bible (the Book of Job, Ecclesiastes) and from Greco-Roman civilization. This theme was particularly favored by Plutarch, for example, who quoted the *Iliad*'s comment that "Of all that moves and breathes, nothing is more wretched than man."[1] Similarly, a mosaic found in Pompeii affirms that *Mors omnia aequat*. The first centuries of Christianity also saw dualist anthropologies (Orphic, Platonic, and Stoic) grafted onto the biblical message by the great Cappadocian doctors, by Saint Augustine and by Boethius.[2] Even Eastern "hyper-spiritualism" infiltrated Christianity, where it modified the meaning of certain passages of Saint Paul, portrayed the body as a prison, and overrode the creation of man as described in Genesis.[3] When evoking the ineffable joy of seeing God face to face, Saint Paul (I Cor. 13:12, II Cor. 5:1–8) did not describe the experience as a return to an original state from which man had been excluded but rather as a progression beyond his present situation. Equally foreign to the Bible was the theme of the Fall into the sensible and the multiple, both of which notions derive from Platonism and its posterity. In conjunction with Christianity, these ideas led to a lasting nostalgia for a primitive, asexual man-angel, "spiritualized" and dedicated to pure contemplation. From this concept derived the opinion, expressed by Saint Augustine and generally accepted by the twelfth century, that man had been created in order to replace the angels who had fallen from the celestial city.

This failure to recognize man's objective reality and the authenticity of divine immanence was accompanied by a refusal, on the part of most theologians and moralists, of a specifically human life-style in favor of a type of existence that Robert Bultot calls—in a deliberate paradox—"angelical anthropology."[4] This failure was further reconfirmed by Saint Augustine's affirmations as to the "instability" of nature, since God is able to intervene at any moment.[5] And if nature has no internal solidity, how then could science ever aspire to understand her? Significantly enough, Montaigne was deeply struck by such reasoning. Bultot[6] has rightly pointed out that the doctrine of contempt for the world was derived from an ancient cosmology that condemned the earth on two accounts. According to this cosmology, the sublunar world is opposed to the ethereal part of the universe: the *corpora inferiora* (that is to say the lower part of the cosmos) to the *coelestia*. Under the earth's crust lies Hell. Consequently, if the earth occupies the lower and most "vulgar" part of the universe, it must be therefore be composed of an element that is much less noble than the other three (air, fire, and water). The entire Middle Ages adopted this cosmology, hence the temptation to think, like Macrobius (the fourth-century commentator of the *Dream of Scipio*), that any soul exiled from the celestial world could only be imprisoned on earth. Last but not least, this underestimation of nature was inseparable from a devaluation of the notion of time, another inheritance from the Hellenistic tradition. Worldly things are vain because they are fleeting.[7] Similarly, Montaigne considered that transitory things lacked consistency. As Claude Tresmontant correctly observed with refcrence to the church fathers:

> *The discovery of the meaning of time can hardly be possible unless a sense of temporality emerges out of reflection on the cosmic, biological and historical experience. Despite the fact that the church fathers had the Bible right in front of their eyes and found their inspiration in it, they had difficulty escaping the Neoplatonic scheme, which abolished real time. It was not until the modern era that reflection upon real time was able to break free from the old, mythical and cyclical system that Neoplatonism had bequeathed to Western philosophy.*[8]

By the fourth century the Christian theory of contempt for the world was already fully developed. Of course Saint Augustine's prolific writings sometimes painted a slightly less pessimistic picture: As pilgrims on this earth, wayfarers traveling to the true country, we are obliged to accept the intimate dependence that ties us to life. It has been said that *The City of God*, far from being a book on the flight from this world, is principally concerned with "our duty, within the framework of the mortal existence which is common to us all."[9] How to live in the world and still be detached from it—thus might one describe the book's professed object. In fact, neither admiration nor praise for nature are absent from Saint Augustine's work. The last chapters of *The City of God* are even dedicated to the "good things of this life" by which the Supreme Judge "tempers" the ills afflicting mankind:

> *What can I say about . . . the lively sparkle of light and the splendor of the sun, the moon and the stars, about the dark beauty of the forests, the colors and the scent of flowers, about the multitude of birds, so different in their song and plumage, about the infinite diversity of animals of which the smallest are the most admirable? . . . What can I say about the gentle breezes which temper the summer heats? And what about all the different types of clothing with which trees and animals furnish us? . . . And if all these things are naught but consolations for the wretched, condemned creatures that we are, and not the rewards of the Blessed, what then will God give to those he has predestined to life, if he gives these things to those he has predestined to death?*[10]

Despite their pessimistic overtones, texts of this sort show why a theology of human values has been found in Saint Augustine's work.[11] The wealth and nuances of Augustinian thought are, however, less important here than the simplification and dramatization they underwent in the hands of posterity, not to mention the fact that Saint Augustine himself was quite convinced of the "decrepitude of the world."[12] What was the use, therefore, of becoming attached to "vain and harmful" things that could only give rise to:

> *bitter worries, disorders, afflictions, fears, mad joys, dissensions, trials, wars, ambushes, rages, enmities, duplicities, flatteries, frauds, theft, pillage, treachery, pride, ambition, envy, homicides, parricides, cruelty, savagery, perversity, lust, rudeness, impudence, lewdness, debaucheries, adulteries, incests, and so many violations and effronteries against the nature of both sexes that one blushes to name them, sacrileges, heresies, blasphemies, perjuries, oppressions of the innocent, calumnies, deceptions, prevarications, robberies, and many other crimes which do not come to mind but which are nevertheless ever-present in this sad human life.*[13]

This overwhelming list also comes from *The City of God*, just two chapters before the passage quoted above. It refers to a series of biblical judgments passed on the "world" and the "times," judgments whose negative tenor cannot be ignored. For this reason it would be useful to dwell for a moment upon the ambiguity of the term "world," which has already been discussed in the preceding volume of this trilogy.[14]

For Saint Paul,[15] sin and death entered the world at the beginning of history, and ever since then the world has been in league with the mysteries of evil (Rom. 5:12). From the moment in which Adam relinquished the domain God had entrusted to him, Satan became the "prince" and even the "god" of the times (John 12:31, 14:30, 16:11; II Cor. 4:4). Man is therefore surrounded and even penetrated by a deceitful world, which is in opposition to the Spirit of God and whose wisdom is naught but folly (I Cor. 1:20). Its peace is but a sham (John 14:27) and its fashions pass away (I Cor. 7:31), as do its desires (I John 2:16). Its final result is despair, which leads to death (II Cor. 7:10). Jesus declared that he was not of this world (John 8:23, 17:14), no more than was his kingdom (John 18:36), and that the world hated him (John 15:18). Those Christians faithful to the message of the Beatitudes could not, therefore, hope for any treatment better than the one their Lord had to face. The world will rise up against them (John 15:18). They will be hated, misunderstood, and persecuted (I John 3:13; Matt. 10:14; John 15:18). As long as history lasts, this tension between the world and the disciples of Jesus will endure.

Despite these condemnations, biblical texts do not always paint the world in such grim colors. In spite of sin, the universe created by God continues to demonstrate the greatness and goodness of the Creator (Prov. 8:22–33, Job 28:25; Wisd. 13:3), and man will never cease admiring it (Ps. 8, 19:1–7, 104). It is, however, still unfinished, and it is up to Adam's children to perfect it by their labor (Gen. 1:28). Furthermore, although it is true that the world has been sullied by sin, it will be fully regenerated on the Last Day at the same time as humanity (Rev. 21:14): They will share the same fate for all eternity. Their mutual regeneration already began, in fact, with the coming of the Son of God. He "has taken away the sin of the world" (John 1:29), given his life for that of the world (John 6:51), reconciled all things unto himself, united a divided universe (Col. 1:20). The new humanity redeemed by the sacrifice of Jesus will not, however, attain its full stature until the end of time. Meanwhile, mankind must labor along a difficult path, painfully waiting to be reborn (Rom. 8:19, Eph. 4:13). At the end of this long ordeal, however, joy will burst forth in a world that will know neither hate nor sorrow. As for the disciples of Jesus, they are not of this world—neither yesterday nor today (John 15:16, 17:16). Nevertheless, they are still in the world (John 17:11). The Savior does not beg his Father to withdraw them but rather to keep them from all evil (John 17:15). Their mission is to spread the Good Tidings to the entire world and to shine there like so many stars (Phil. 2:15). Although they must renounce desire and reject that which might entice them away from God, their detachment does not exonerate them from the obligation to build a better world, nor does it excuse them from a just and appropriate use of worldly goods, in keeping with the requirements of brotherly love (I John 3:17).

The biblical term "world" is therefore ambivalent, as its meaning oscillates between two opposite poles. At times it designates the reign of Satan—which is opposed to that of God and which will eventually be conquered—and at times it designates both humanity and the earth on which men live. When used in the latter sense, the "world" is not condemned but rather subject to redemption. The children of Adam must renounce Satan rather than their destiny as men. It is this "world" that must evolve.[16] One of the enduring dramas of Christian history resided, in fact, in the confusion between the two meanings of the term "world" and in the spread of an anathema that was originally limited to the realm of Satan. This led to further confusion in that one could conceivably detach one's self from the world (that is, the domain of Adam's children) and even flee it, without having to despise it. *Fuga* is not necessarily synonymous with *contemptus*. In actual fact, however, the doctrine of detachment from the world most often ended up as an accusation of the world, insofar as the earth men lived on was also the earth they sinned on.

THE REASONS BEHIND "CONTEMPT FOR THE WORLD"

By the end of antiquity the doctrine of the vanity of the world (and the scorn it merited) found fertile ground in the monastic communities of Egypt and the East. This doctrine constituted a protest, on the part of the ascetics, against a Christianity that seemed to have grown overly lax. Later, throughout the Middle Ages, this same doctrine inspired the spiritual life of convents,[17] where the lives of the desert fathers were read with great fervor. A resurgence of a dualist myth has been discerned in the asceticism of monastic life, a myth that survived principally in Bogomilism and Catharism. According to this myth it was Original Sin that was responsible for having precipitated the soul into matter. The soul must therefore rehabilitate itself by "angelizing" itself. The expression "angelical life," which appeared frequently in everyday monastic language, was also familiar to the Cathars.[18]

Certain oppositions help to define the doctrine of *contemptus mundi*, since this doctrine was dominated by conflicts—between time and eternity, multiplicity and unity, exterior and interior, vanity and truth, earth and heaven, body and soul, pleasure and virtue, flesh and spirit. First and foremost, the world is vain because it is ephemeral. The monk Jean de Fécamp (d. 1078) confessed: "All that I see [that is, the exterior world] saddens me. Everything I hear about transitory things weighs upon me."[19] In one of his laments he elaborates upon Ecclesiastes, addressing the sinner in terms that will remain virtually unchanged right up to the moralizing literature of the fifteenth century:

> *Alas man, alas woman, alas unhappy man.*
> *Why do you love the goods and chattels of this earth, which will perish?*
> *Vanity of vanities,*
> *All that exists under the sun is vanity.*
> *Like the flower and the grass is the glory of this world.*
> *The world will pass, and so will desire . . .*[20]

A century later an English monk, Serlon of Wilton (d. 1171), deployed poetic virtuosity in expounding upon this same theme:

The world passes, fleeing like time, like the river, like the breeze . . .
The world passes, the name passes quickly, and the world with the name,
But the world passes more quickly than its name . . .
Nothing exists in the world but the world which passes . . .
The world passes; eliminate that which passes, the world passes . . .
The world passes, Christ passes not, adore Him who passes not[21]

It is obvious that the dramatic question *Ubi sunt*? (oft repeated in the Middle Ages in the wake of Saint John Chrysostom's treatise on the virtue of "patience") can best be understood in the context of this tradition. Not knowing the fate of certain individuals, we ask: "Where is such and such a prince? and we learn: he is dead. And where is such and such a glorious king?—He is gone. And such a friend?—He had departed. Where?—To appear before the Judge of Judges."[22] The *Ubi sunt* theme was repeated and embellished upon through the ages, attaining full growth long before it reached Eustache Deschamps and François Villon[23]:

Tell me, where is Solomon, once so great?
Or else, where is Samson, the invincible leader?
Where is the handsome Absalom, of the admirable face?
Where the gentle Jonathan, so worthy of love?

Where has Caesar gone, made an emperor?
Where the ostentatious rich man, always at table?
Tell me, where is Cicero, famous for his eloquence?
Or Aristotle of the supreme genius?[24]

An echo to this poem, which was written by the extremely mystical and pessimistic Jacopone da Todi (d. 1306), can be found in an anonymous hymn from the thirteenth century:

Where [is] Plato,
Where Porphyry,
Where Horace,
Where Darius,
Where Caesar,
Where Virgil,
Where Varro,
Where Pompey?

Where Alexander
The greatest of kings,
Where is the magnanimous
Achilles?
Is he with Helen,
The handsome Paris?
Where the bravest
Of the Trojans, Hector?

They have crossed
The kingdom of mortals
In the space
Of a single day.[25]

These staccato rhythms on the theme of the leveling effect of death—which cuts down even the greatest of men—were soon to undergo a highly successful iconographic transcription in the *danse macabre*. Long before this, however, the saintly monk Anselm of Canterbury (d. 1109) had drawn the following conclusion for the benefit of a nun, a conclusion imposed by the fear of passing time: "No one can love both earthly and eternal things at the same time: Say with the blessed apostle Paul, 'The world is crucified for me and I am crucified for the world,' and like this same apostle look at all transitory things as if they were dung."[26] In the same spirit the Camoldolese hermit Peter Damian (d. 1072)—prior to having the diocese of Ostia imposed upon him—concluded a sermon with an exhortation to "scorn all that is visible."[27]

While urging man to stay alert and keep ready, an anonymous poem from the thirteenth century compares life to a spider web that can easily tear or disintegrate. Fleeting and fragile, it cannot be built securely. Immediately after this comparison, the author—doubtless a monk—affirms:

In this world every man *Is lived in sorrow.*
Is born into affliction; *In the end it terminates*
And human life *With the suffering of death.*[28]

A link is thus established between the transitory nature of life and its sadness. This connection is a constant of the *contemptus mundi* and runs counter to Horace's *carpe diem*. Peter Damian incessantly decries the "miserable condition of man."[29] Jean de Fécamp affirms that life is very evil and unhappy ("*haec pessima vita, ista infelicissima vita*"—the superlatives are here fully exploited) and that man is "full of misery" and lives "in sorrow."[30] Around 1045 another monk, Hermann Contract, wrote an *Exhortatory Poem on the Contempt for the World* where he enumerates the worries, sadness, problems, sicknesses, fears, ills, and sufferings that fill existence. He also cites pell-mell the dangers and aggressions that persecute man: worms, serpents, beasts of all kinds, birds, cold, heat, hunger, thirst, water, fire, wind, earth, violence, thunder, lightning, accidents, poisons, deceit, discord, amputations, war, captivity, slavery, and countless diseases.[31] The same themes and the same pessimism are to be found in the work of the Benedictine Roger of Caen (d. ca. 1095), author of another *Carmen de mundi contemptu*. He points out that life is short and full of evils: It begins with the tears and wailing of the newborn child and continues with the sufferings caused by heat and cold, by hunger and thirst, by flies and fleas (who spare not even kings), by the exile and death of loved ones, by infamy and prison. Man is susceptible to unhappiness. Can one speak of health when illness is stronger? Can one speak of life since death ends it?[32]

Such gloomy thoughts were far from new. The book of Job compares man to a piece of worm-eaten wood and to a moth-eaten garment. "Man . . . is of few days, and full of trouble" (Job 13:28, 14:1). The Book of Wisdom put melancholy reflections on the first moments of existence into Solomon's mouth: "I also, when I was born, drew in the common air, and fell upon the kindred earth, uttering, like all, for my first voice, the self-same wail. In swaddling clothes was I nursed, and with watchful cares" (7:3–4). This theme is also found in Pliny's *Natural History*: "Man is the only [being] whom, at birth, nature throws naked upon the naked earth, immediately abandoning him to wailing and tears" (VII, 2).

In religious (and especially monastic) literature of the Middle Ages, the condemnation of human life took on larger proportions and attained a higher level of violence. Cardinal Lotario di Segni, who was to become Pope Innocent III, wrote a grim *De Contemptu Mundi, Sive de Miseria Conditionis Humanae*, where the very first chapter affirms that: "Man is born for work, for suffering, for fear, and—what is worse—for death."[33] But most virulent of all was perhaps Jean de Fécamp, who refused to become involved in an existence that he considered to be irremediably stained by vanity, sin and suffering: "Miserable life, decrepit life, impure life sullied by humours, exhausted by grief, dried by heat, swollen by meats, mortified by fasts, dissolved by pranks, consumed by sadness, distressed by worries, blunted by security, bloated by riches, cast down by poverty . . ."

Earth is a "vale of tears," a "desert," an "exile" that cannot be overdepreciated in comparison with the blessed life, the "sure life, tranquil life, beautiful life, pure life."[34] In an anonymous hymn of the twelfth century, a poet asks himself: ". . . Evil life of this world then/Why do you please me so?" And in order to better reject its temptations and illusions, he heaps it with abuse:

Fugitive life,
More harmful than any beast
. . .
Life which should be called death,
Which one should hate, not love
. . .
Worldly life, sickly thing
More fragile than the rose
. . .
Wordly life, source of labors,
Anguished, full of suffering
. . .
Worldly life, future death,
Permanent ruin,

Worldly life, evil thing
Never worthy of love
. . .
Worldly life, foul life
Pleasing only to the impious
. . .
Life, stupid thing
Accepted only by fools,
I reject you with all my heart.
For you are full of filth.
With all my heart I reject you
. . .
I prefer to undergo death,
O life, rather than serve you.[35]

We here find ourselves far from the Book of Wisdom (2:1–21), where a well-known passage definitely depreciates worldly life, but places this depreciation, most significantly, in the mouth of the ungodly: "For they say to themselves, with their misguided reasoning: 'Our life is short and dreary . . . The breath in our nostrils is a puff of smoke . . . Our life will pass away like wisps of cloud, dissolve like the mist . . . Yes, our days are the passing of a shadow . . .' This is the way they reason, but they are misled."

For the author of the Book of Wisdom, human life has a meaning, "Death was not God's doing . . . the world's created things have health in them, in them no fatal poison can be found, and Hades holds no power on earth."[36] He who has been just on earth will never perish. When earthly existence is turned toward God, it cannot be despicable. For Peter Damian, however, and for all the ascetics who thought as he did, life is quite the contrary. Earthly existence is an "exterior exile from which we are delivered by death in order that we might enter the interior country."[37]

The radical—and artificial—distinction between body and soul (the latter profiting from all that is denied to the former) logically led to the contempt and even condemnation of life on earth, which is continually compared to a dangerous sea.[38] One would therefore do far better to avoid it entirely. Furthermore, since hope lies only in the rewards of Heaven, the only worthwhile occupation (according to Peter Damian, for whom the layman is essentially a concupiscent creature) is contemplation, far from "worldly vanities" and "secular concerns."[39] To abandon the world in favor of the monastic life is equivalent to "leaving Sodom."[40] Lay society and corrupt society are synonymous,[41] hence the difficulty in finding one's salvation there.[42] According to Damian's writings (which are quoted here only insofar as they represent an entire current of thought), the suspicion cast upon all earthly tasks extends even to the priesthood. Rather than living in monastic seclusion, priests are far too "close to laymen, and fraternize with them in daily life. The majority of priests do not even manage to distinguish themselves from the disorderly morals and life-styles of their flock."[43] In short, the secular world has no meaning. The activities inherent to man's earthly condition belong to a vacuum of "anti-values,"[44] just as (in a more general sense) nature is emptied of its internal necessity[45] and all worldly pleasures are repudiated as being unhealthy.

Sexual pleasure is obviously the most ferociously attacked. A long Neoplatonic tradition, adopted by several of the church fathers, considered that the irrational nature of carnal communion reduced man to the level of an animal.[46] According to Saint Augustine, sexual relations in the Garden of Eden were bereft of lust, "like hands joining one another." Without sin—which perverts everything—man could have used his sexuality to procreate in like manner, rationally and deliberately, no matter what he used: his eyes, his lips, his hands, or his feet.[47] But "ever since he fell, through disobedience, from the state of glory in which he was created, he has become like the beasts and engenders like them."[48] The myth of primitive man not indulging in sexual activity (virginity would thus constitute a return to "true" human nature) was particularly dear to Saint John Chrysostom, Gregory of Nyssa, and Saint Athanasius,[49] and its career in Christian thought was long and successful. Peter Damian, for example, could not conceive of human sexuality as a simultaneously spiritual and carnal reality.[50] The embrace of those who love is always and can only be a corruption of the flesh. Sexual desire and its fulfillment are contaminating. Marriage is filth (*sordes*) from which only the blood of martyrdom washed Saint Peter. Even when strictly limited to the act of procreation, sexual communion represents a form of servitude and slavery. The monk Peter echoed Saint Augustine in evoking "our sordid and hideous origins." Marriage is tolerable only in view of procreation, the pains of childbirth constituting a justified penalty for sinful pleasure. Yet to deflower a virgin is still to "corrupt" her. Consequently, chastity is always preferable to marriage, especially as it is the first of the religious virtues. In the *De Contemptu Mundi* of the future Innocent III, marriage is condemned on similar grounds. The sexual act is a sin that sullies the child to whom it gives life:

> *Man is formed of dust, mud, ashes, and, what is even viler, of foul sperm . . . Who can ignore the fact that conjugal union never occurs without the itching of the flesh, the fermentation of desire and the stench of lust? Hence any progeny is spoiled, tainted and vitiated by the very act of its conception, the seed communicating to the soul that inhabits it the stain of sin, the stigma of fault, the filth of iniquity—in the same way that a liquid will corrupt if it is poured into a dirty vessel . . .*[51]

It is understandable that, given such teachers, the authors of confession manuals and handbooks cast a suspicious eye on marriage in particular and on sexuality in general.

Let us recapitulate the main themes of the *contemptus mundi*: the fleeting joys of life on earth engender eternal suffering (Roger of Caen); earth is an exile; "the love of the world is night" (Jean de Fécamp); flesh is a "dungeon" (Philip the Chancellor); man is the "son of putrescence" and will become "food for worms" (anon., eleventh century); the senses, "miserable condition of man," are the pimps of sin (Peter Damian). Those who wish to save themselves are invited to "spit on the rot of the world" (Peter Damian) and, if possible, enter a monastery; to live in this world is to inhabit "Babylon" (Saint Anselm).

Did the hatred of the "world" engender complacency in the ascetics who were brave enough to break away from it? Hypothetically, this might have happened, but exactly the opposite occurred. In fact, like Saint Augustine and the desert fathers, the monks of the Middle Ages equated contempt for the world with personal shame. Even the most Christian of clergymen would not dream of excusing himself from either a fundamental pessimism or a global feeling of sin. From this conviction came one of the dominant themes in religious poetry of the tenth to the thirteenth centuries: the tearful confession of numberless faults. Saint Peter Damian cries out, for example:

Neither the drops of the sea, nor the sands of the shore
Equal the infamy of my misdeeds:
In number, they exceed the stars and the [drops of the] rains,
In weight, the mountains . . .
The crushing savagery of all my faults
Gathers to subjugate me . . .

I weep for my soul, drowned in sins
And wounded by a thousand arrows shot by the Old Enemy . . .[52]

Sixty-four verses of Damian's *Rhyme of the Penitent Monk* feature similar confessions, all of which could easily have been written by any of the numerous monks who, between the tenth and the thirteenth centuries, despaired of the basic corruption of their soul. The following extracts from Henry Spitzmuller's rich anthology show to what extent this despair was not an isolated phenomenon but rather a shared concern: "Every day I sin, I err at every moment then / And often, like a dog, I lap my vomit / I surpass all creation in mortal vices / deadly sins" (Alphanus of Salerno).[53] "Roaring like a lion I weep for my sins" (Marborde).[54] "Knave, malingerer, prostituting my words, / [You are] envious, immodest, impure, treacherous, cruel, / Buffoon, trickster, scoundrel, violator of my brothers' love, / I have committed all the infamous deeds which defile the wretched" (Baudry de Bourgueil).[55] "I languish from the disease of sin, / I have no one to care for me" (Geoffroy de Vendôme).[56] On the day of the Last Judgment, "Where will I go / To escape /From the terrifying verdict? / By what means / Can I escape / from the ire of my Judge?" (Saint Bernard)[57] and so on.

There can be no doubt about this essential historical fact: This woeful vision of life was first developed and refined in monasteries, and subsequently in the convents of the mendicant orders. Later, this attitude was transmitted to the whole of society as a self-evident truth. Its three main components—hatred of the body and the world, the pervasiveness of sin, and an acute consciousness of fleeting time—found a new and striking illustration in a poem by the Franciscan Giacomino di Verona (written in the second half of the thirteenth century). Giacomino addresses both man in general and himself in the following terms:

In a very dirty and vile workroom
You were made out of slime,
So foul and so wretched
That my lips cannot bring themselves to tell you about it.
But if you have a bit of sense, you will know
That the fragile body in which you lived,
Where you were tormented eight months and more,
Was made of rotting and corrupt excrement . . .
You came out through a foul passage
And you fell into the world, poor and naked . . .
. . . Other creatures have some use:
Meat and bone, wool and leather;
But you, stinking man, you are worse than dung:
From you, man, comes only pus . . .
From you comes no virtue,
You are a sly and evil traitor;
Look in front of you and look behind,
For your life is like your shadow
Which quickly comes and quickly goes . . .[58]

A CONSTANTLY RECURRING THEME IN THE FOURTEENTH TO SIXTEENTH CENTURIES

The Mystics' Version

In the preceding pages I have drawn heavily upon the work of Robert Bultot, whose detractors have accused him of having exaggerated the pessimistic world view propounded by the contemplative orders of the Middle Ages.[59] It has been said that monastic rules and regulations did not necessarily lead to *contemptus mundi*. According to these critics, a refusal of the world certainly existed but was considerably tempered by its context. For example, medieval spirituality was also characterized by admiration for the universe (particularly strong in Saint Bernard) and eschatological optimism. Seen in this light, contempt for the world functioned less as a theory than as an exercise or guideline to humility. If denigration of the temporal world was considered a necessary attitude in monks—who aspired to eternal life and to a supreme love for God—it still did not stop them from becoming men of letters, from promoting the "twelfth century Renaissance," or from expressing an interest in medicine.[60] The historian of today should therefore not succumb to anachronistic temptations. The spirituality of yesteryear cannot be judged by present standards, nor can any culture be condemned in the name of another.

While all this is certainly true, I personally prefer Robert Bultot's interpretation. Of course, historians should try to avoid anachronism, but one still cannot ignore the fact that Lucien Febvre's famous saying—"History is the daughter of her times"—is equally valid. The past is always examined in terms of contemporary concerns, and it is nearly impossible to do otherwise. After all, historiography evolves with the renewal of the questions it asks, and these questions are always inspired by the present. True to their times, therefore, lay Christians are now studying monastic spirituality, a subject that has been long and jealously guarded by monks—hence the rosy picture generally presented. Today things have changed. Is this so terrible? The few texts presented in the preceding section prove, in fact, that *contemptus mundi* was not just an exercise in humility. It was theorized, generalized, enthroned as a universal truth. At the same time it tended to create an abyss between saintly and profane life.[61] "A theology of earthly reality based on the *Vanitas vanitatum* of Ecclesiastes could only result in a theology of denigration."[62] This monastic discourse spread far beyond the ranks of men for whom it had been intended, to the extent that it was held to be a general rule, valid for an entire civilization.

Through the course of centuries, the writings of Saint Augustine, the desert fathers, and the monks of the tenth to thirteenth centuries furnished the Catholic Church with a complete guide to the doctrine of *fuga mundi* as well as to a profound shame and fear of the self. It is vital to realize the homogeneity of this doctrine, its constant occurrence, and its long posterity. Furthermore, it is crucial to understand the novelty of such a widespread feeling of guilt and the expansion of monastic ethics, both of which might easily have been restricted to a small, heroic, and ascetic elite.

Innumerable texts denouncing the world were written by the spiritual leaders of Christianity from the beginning of the thirteenth to the end of the sixteenth century. Often written in colorful language, these texts perpetuated and even aggravated the existing confusion between the two interpretations of the word "world." Mystical flights from this world required the eradication of anything that might weigh down the soul and thus prevent it from reaching the Savior. Such exemplary detachment could be attained only by exceptional people and, in principle, was far beyond the reach of common mortals. Yet a certain number of works written by the greatest mystics actually had a far-reaching influence that, in turn, created even further confusion between the two "worlds": that is, that in which God had placed man in order that he fulfill his destiny, and the world as a synonym for sin. In one of his sermons Meister Eckhart (1260–1328?) declared: "Only that which is detached and separated from all creatures is pure, for all creatures are nought, and thus they are defiled."[63] To the young, prematurely widowed Queen of Hungary, he wrote similar advice: ". . . If you wish to find and maintain full joy and total consolation in God, take care to rid yourself of all other beings and to cast off all consolation which comes from them."[64] One of Eckhart's students, the Dominican Heinrich Suso (1295–1366), faithfully reflected his master's council in words attributed to "Eternal Wisdom": ". . . Lift your heart above the ooze and slime of carnal pleasures . . . all that the world has to offer cannot appease your desire. You live in a wretched vale of tears where pleasure is mixed with suffering, smiles with tears, joy with sadness, where no heart has ever found total joy, for the world deceives and lies . . ."[65]

In a sermon delivered to a monastic congregation, the Alsacian mystic Tauler (1300–1361), who also studied under Eckhart and who had a great influence on Martin Luther, declaimed: "Man by himself is nothing, at best he corrupts all that is good."[66] In her dialogue with God Saint Catherine of Siena also attacks the world in terms of a verse from Saint John (16:8): "he will reprove the world of sin, and of righteousness, and of judgment." When invited to open the eyes of "her body and her spirit" in order to view the world around her, what does Catherine see? "Criminal men sunk in atrocious poverty, deprived of light, the corruption of death in their souls, creatures of darkness and shadow. They go about singing and laughing, spending their time on vanities, on pleasures, in contemptible debauchery."[67] What disquieting and summary generalizations! Moreover, for Catherine, "no sin is as abominable as that of the flesh,"[68] and she cries out, as did Saint Paul, "unhappy creature that I am! Who will deliver me of my body, for in it reigns a perverse law that rebels against the spirit" (Rom. 7:23–24).

Saint Teresa of Avila is astonished that "God could bring himself to communicate with such abject earthworms in exile."[69] Heavily influenced by the *Confessions* of Augustine, she asserts (as do many other spiritual writers) that there is "no security in this life" and that "our life here below is naught but misery."[70] "O my Lord and my All," she cries, "how can you expect us to love such a despicable life?"[71] In evoking the "second mansion" of the interior castle, she describes good-willed people who are nevertheless "still concerned with their pastimes, with their business, with their pleasures and the gossip of the world." In fact, "the whole world" (note the generalization) "is filled with lies . . . in the midst of the pleasures proposed by the demon, there is naught but sorrow, problems, and contradictions."[72] The things of this world are "reptiles full of venom."[73] But even Teresa had trouble choosing between the world and God. For a while she even tried to reconcile strict obedience to religious rule with the more worldly occupations of the convent parlor. In order for her to progress on her mystical path, however, she was obliged to abandon such an impossible task. In her *Life* she confesses: "I behaved as if I wanted to reconcile two bitterly opposed adversaries: the pungent joys of spiritual life and sensual pastimes."[74]

In a passage of the "seventh mansion," Saint Teresa affirms that as soon as the soul "empties itself of all that is proper to creatures, in order to better love God," God himself "will then fill the soul with his own self."[75] Saint John of the Cross pushed this kind of affirmation to its limit. According to him, the only way that the soul may be restored to its real essence is to "create a vacuum between the self and all the other objects of creation."[76] The soul needs darkness in order to reach God. It must cease "feeding itself with its taste for things" and free itself from the five senses, remaining "in the dark, without anything"—"the cleansing of all that the soul might contain must be complete."[77] The soul must always attempt that which is difficult rather than that which is easy, that which is displeasing rather than that which is pleasing. It must always look for the bad in things rather than the good.[78] Two "opposites" cannot cohabit in the same person.[79] "A soul that is attached to the beauty of any other creature is supremely ugly to God. As a consequence, an ugly soul can never become beautiful, for ugliness never attains beauty."[80] "Compared with the grace of God, all of the graces and attributes of all beings are only supremely awkward and supremely displeasing."[81] Jean Baruzi has very aptly pointed out that the mystical poetry of Saint John of the Cross is closely related to the "volatilized" figures that appear in the paintings of El Greco.[82]

One of the darkest and most beautiful poems on the universal nature of evil was written in Spain (during its "golden century") by the Augustinian monk Luis de Léon (1528–1591). A Carmelite nun, Anne of Jesus, asked him for this poem, just as she had asked Saint John of the Cross to write a work that was later to be known as the *Spiritual Canticle*.[83] Late as they are, these works still convey a mystical vision of the universe. Luis de Léon's *Commentary on the Book of Job*, written on the eve of his death, was little known until it was finally published in 1779.[84] Yet Luis was a bit of a celebrity in his time. Not only was he one of the best-known professors of the Univerity of Salamanca, but he was also chosen for the honor of editing the official edition of Saint Teresa's works. A choleric and highly strung person, he was, however, often affected with melancholy, and at one point the suspicious Castilian Inquisition saw fit to imprison him for four and a half years in a narrow cell. He had supposedly contested the worth of the Vulgate, translated the *Song of Songs* into the vernacular, and fraternized with heretics. Once cleared of these three accusations, he was able to resume his teaching position at Salamanca, but by now his prison experience had taught him the meaning of despair. This ordeal most certainly cast a dark shadow upon his subsequent *Commentary* of the Book of Job, which, in itself, is one of the gloomier books of the Bible.

De Léon was not insensitive to the charms of nature. He praised the cool solitude of fields, pastures strewn with flowers, flowing streams, and starry nights. When compared with their Creator, however, these beauties could hardly rival the joys of Paradise to which the author aspired. He therefore refused to be fooled by the false attractions and smiling aspect of this world. Man himself is but a shadow. Job compares him to a flower, which a gust of wind can spoil in a moment. Although he seems to be an "immortal God," gifted with understanding, memory, intelligence, ability, and skill, he is nonetheless "a cut and faded flower, which cannot even hope to bear fruit." He is like to "a spider, which can be killed by a mere puff of air."[85] And as for human life, it is generally nothing more than "a continual loss of the self, a death which constitutes, in each and every instant, the very eve of death."[86] Although a topos, this theme was widespread in early modern Europe and had a strong influence on the collective mentality for a number of centuries.

De Léon was thus profoundly convinced of the contemptibility of the world, especially in his last poem, where he glosses the Book of Job with poignant sincerity:

He who walks a steep and stony path, constantly risking a precipitous fall, or who risks his life traveling through lands inhabited by brigands, naturally abhors the road he travels on. He wishes to see it end, and would never have taken that path had he been able to do otherwise. Life is a dangerous voyage, and should be equally despised. Since we are born in order to die, and since the ultimate end of life is death, an early death can only bring an early end to our suffering. Careful consideration of such an obvious truth can lead to one conclusion only—whence Silenus' famous saying: "It would have been best to have died at birth, and better still never to have lived."[87]

One wonders how the author of such a negative description of life did not end up committing suicide. Furthermore, de Léon continually reinforced his desperate vision of earthly existence with a multitude of arguments, such as "every hour of life has its pain." Even those who seem happiest suffer: "The rich, the refined, the big spenders, the great . . . all confess that they live in misery."[88] Such is also the fate of "those who hope to find spiritual peace in the treasures of Heaven. Who can describe the dangers of the paths they tread? Or the obstacles which the Demon places before them? Or the tricks, the subtle devices, the baited traps he sets to catch them?"[89] Unhappiness is everywhere, but nothing is more dangerous than a peaceful life, a paradox that is developed in the following terms:

When the sea of life is calm it should be all the more feared, for in the midst of calm lurks the storm. Its quiet and tranquil aspect hides waves higher than mountains . . . Life is like war . . . because it is so perilous . . . men deceive us, fate fools us, animals assail us, and the elements bring death more often than not. In fact, who would ever have guessed the number of invisible things that wage a secret war against us, or divine their number, their ingeniousness, their wiles, or their strength?[90]

As all is but vanity, wisdom is certainly not to be found in faraway lands: "distant and wealthy countries cannot give anyone peace of heart"[91] . . . De Léon obviously thought little of the frenetic overseas expeditions that thrilled the Iberian peninsula in his time. Earthly love and beauty also inevitably end in bitter deception: "He who falls in love with two bright eyes and golden hair pays for a meager hour with a thousand worries, brief joy with endless tears."[92] Even friendship is a form of treason: "The greatest friend . . . testifies to our great virtue when we are present, and in our absence tells of misdeeds we have never committed."[93] As if this were not bad enough, the past was as evil as the present is now, and the future will not be any better. "It is no use hoping that some new kind of earthly convenience will be able to satisfy the spirit so that man can live in pleasure and blessedness."[94] In the end of it all, the discouraging philosophy of this religious poet can be summarized in two sayings: We are all imprisoned in a "dark and narrow dungeon,"[95] and "all that is visible is but sadness and tears."[96]

A Philosophy for all Christians

Originally used by the mystic philosophers as a stepladder to God, the doctrine of contempt for the world began to spread beyond the small, elitist monastic circle at the end of the Middle Ages. It is significant that Cardinal Lotario's lugubrious *De Contemptu Mundi* should owe the majority of its 672 known manuscripts and 47 printed editions to fifteenth-century scholars,[97] not to speak of the fact that it was translated into Tuscan by two Florentine laymen and into French by Eustache Deschamps. The first of the Italian translators, Bono Giamboni, was a judge in Florence during the second half of the thirteenth century. Although his translation is rather a literal one, his prologue is particularly eloquent: "Whoever reflects upon all the adversities that are to be found on earth will find no good in them. The world is nought but misery, created by God for man in order that he suffer torment and tribulation, and there undergo punishment for his sins."[98] The second Italian translator, Angelo Torini, was a fourteenth-century cloth merchant who held several public offices in his lifetime. This married layman—survivor of the Black Death, contemporary of Boccaccio, and member of a flagellant order—wrote a *Brieve collezione della miseria della umana condizione* between 1360 and 1380, where he elaborated upon the cardinal's text. In the first part of the treatise he added two new subjects to Lotario's original: "How fetid and dark is our first resting place" and "On the number and intensity of the sufferings we undergo in that place and [there] inflict upon our mothers." In the second part he used both Lotario and Saint Gregory the Great's *Moralia in Job*, whereas the third part far exceeds the arguments presented in the cardinal's *Contemptu Mundi*. Although definitely inspired by the work of the future Pope Innocent III, Torini's book is more than a mere adaptation. It belongs, in fact, to a well-known tradition of anathemas directed against the world.

This tradition had a long posterity, extending far beyond the monastic circles of the thirteenth century. Lotario's book was translated (or adapted) not only into Tuscan and French, but also into English, Dutch, and Spanish. Petrarch, meanwhile, was torn between meditation on death and the desire for glory, and after him the ambition to find immortality through fame gained ground in elitist circles.[99] Nevertheless, the Tuscan poet also helped increase the audience of the *contemptus mundi*. In his *Trionfi*, for example (the Triumph of Love over Youth, of Chastity over Love, of Death over Chastity, of Fame over Death, of Time over Fame, of God and Eternity over Time), it was the Triumph of Death that most fired the imagination of artists.[100] Petrarch had an acute sense of the decadence of things, the decline of time, and the misery of the human condition. In his epic poem *Africa* he complains "Alas, man is born on earth for an unjust fate. All other living beings know peace, but man knows neither rest nor respite. He rushes anxiously toward death, year in and year out."[101] The self-examination that Petrarch called *De Secreto Conflictu Curarum Mearum*, consisting of a dialogue between himself and Saint Augustine, has also been considered a *De Contemptu Mundi*. Petrarch there chose the Bishop of Hippo as his guide and advisor, destined to lead the author along the path to the interior life by inciting him to reflect upon death and the ephemeral nature of all things.[102]

It is therefore not surprising that Erasmus, who greatly admired Petrarch, wrote (as did many others) his own *De Contemptu Mundi*. He wrote it as a youth, around 1488–89, in the convent at Steyn. He did not publish it until 1521, however, and two years later added a twelfth chapter that would seem to contradict the spirit of the preceding eleven.[103] Is it possible, as believe most Erasmus scholars (such as Pineau, Telle, and Hyma), that this young aspirant to literary glory had written this book only to "amuse" himself, "exercising" his talent on a suitable subject? This *declamatio*, which quotes Cicero, Horace, Seneca, Ovid, and others (a fairly new practise at that time), as well as the church fathers and the monastic tradition of the Middle Ages, might seem to be an anthology of platitudes. It compares the evils of the world where Satan reigns to the beauty and joy of God's Kingdom and affirms that natural man is subject to all vices. In repeating the famous theme *Ubi sunt*? it particularly stresses the themes of decrepitude and old age. The world—a tempestuous sea and *campus diaboli*—is represented as subject to arbitrary change and to the whims of *Fortuna*. An anathema is cast upon the "seductions of this world." Man can attain virtue only if he is "crucified by the world," as was ordained by Saint Paul. Salvation can be obtained only through internal peace. Where, other than in a cloister, can man find a haven of rest and contemplation that will permit him to escape the "world's tumult" and the "vicissitudes of fortune"? Erasmus did not remain in a monastery, however, and the whole of chapter 12 is an attack on monastic orders, accused of having lost their original purity. From this attack stems the conclusion that Erasmus might not have taken his *declamatio* on contempt for the world very seriously. It has also been suggested that he abandoned the ideals of his youth upon leaving Steyn. A third explanation has been proposed by both Samuel Dresden and Ernst Wilhelm Kohls, according to whom chapter 12 condemns convent life only in order to better present the merits of "monasticism in the world." This concept, which Erasmus discussed again, much later and with fervent enthusiasm in his *De Praeparatione ad Mortem* (1533), did not undergo any fundamental change between the beginning and the end of his career. In any case, it is significant that his *De Contemptu Mundi* was published at the height of his fame for, apart from the author's celebrity, the subject itself was sure to interest a large audience.

It is thus hardly surprising that a poet such as Ronsard should have drawn heavily upon this theme in his *Hymne de la mort*, a poem whose form is far more original than its content. Ronsard there compares man on earth to a "prisoner who, day and night, endures / handcuffs upon his wrists, cruel chains about his ankles." As he would have it, we are "true children of suffering and misery," ". . . naught but / Quickened earth, a living shadow . . ."[104] These statements could just as easily have been written by Cardinal Lotario himself.

Most probably it was the *Imitation of Christ* that was first responsible for introducing the philosophy of contempt for the world to a large public (I am speaking of the reading public, of course).[105] Generally attributed to Thomas à Kempis, the *Imitation* was written in the fifteenth century under the influence of the *Devotio Moderna*. Inspired by the mystical tradition, it also testifies to the influence of Jan van Ruysbroeck. Its success was enormous even before the invention of the printing press, and more than seven hundred manuscripts have survived to this day. It is therefore certain that its public included not only the secular clergy but also a much larger audience of pious laymen. The *Imitation*'s popularity lasted a very long time. There are no less than eighty-five *incunabula* known today and as many as two hundred printed editions from the sixteenth century.[106] It was translated into French as many as sixty times in the space of four hundred years, by authors such as Corneille, Gonnelieu (a seventeenth-century Jesuit preacher), and Lamennais. In Lamennais's version the more pessimistic passages were accentuated by commentaries far gloomier than the original text. It is nonetheless true that the first book of the *Imitation* is "a veritable *De Contemptu Mundi*, which harks back to the asceticism of Windesheim and insists, above all, on otherworldliness"[107]:

> *He who knows himself well, despises himself. The highest and most useful science is the exact knowledge and contempt of the self. All of us are weak but no one is as weak as you . . . (I, chap. 2)*
>
> *Flee the tumult of the world as much as you can, for it is dangerous to have anything to do with the things of this world, even if your intentions are pure . . . (I, chap. 10)*
>
> *Life on earth is truly wretched. Since eating, drinking, waking, sleeping, resting, working are subject to all the needs of [human] nature, life is truly a great misery and a terrible affliction for any pious man who would like to detach himself from*

earthly things and deliver himself from all sin . . . Woe to them who do not know their own misery, and even more woe to them who love this perishable life and its misery. (I, chap. 22)

The scorn for earthly life and the affirmation that it is but a sequence of ills and evils are not limited to the first book of the *Imitation of Christ*. In the third book the very same theme appears under the form of a quasi-suicidal question (the only refuge being in God): "How can one love a life filled with so much bitterness and subject to so many evils and calamities? How can one call life that which engenders so much pain and so much death?" (III, chap. 20).[108] Hundreds of thousands of readers meditated upon these words for several hundred years. Was not the *Imitation* "alongside of the Bible, perhaps the most frequently printed work of all time?"[109]

Another best-seller of religious literature was *The Great Life of Jesus Christ* by the Carthusian monk Ludolph of Saxony—a book that was destined to become one of Saint Francis de Sales's favorites. This work was written at the same time as the *Imitation of Christ*, and it was once thought (especially in the sixteenth century) that Ludolph had written both.[110] The Carthusian relates the life of Jesus, elaborating somewhat upon the Gospels. At times he interrupts his tale to make spiritual commentaries, and then he resumes the biography of Christ. These religious reflections are of primary interest to us here, especially as they are often more expansive than those of the *Imitation* and contain useful definitions aimed at the layman. Ludolph declares that there are basically two types of disciples who serve Christ: "necessary" ones and "supererogatory" ones. The former must take care not to love earth more than heaven, whereas the latter have a "real" obligation to give up everything (like the apostles) and practice voluntary poverty. "All Christians are not obliged to abandon everything, only those who are bound by vows of poverty. All of us, however, must renounce the world in our hearts so as to love God above all else."[111]

Elsewhere Ludolph makes an even more positive statement: ". . . Let us love man, and beware of the demon; let us pray for man, and strive against the demon."[112] Unfortunately, this apparently benign formula is much less encouraging when viewed in context, for the passage in which it appears also contains a merciless verdict against the whole of mankind:

"When He wishes us to know that man is the greatest danger on earth the Savior says: 'avoid man as if he were the worst of all evils' . . . Every wild beast has its own special way of doing harm, but man contains within himself all the types of harm possible. And what is more, man is worse than the devil himself."[113] To be sure, Ludolph means to say that when man is bad, he is worse than anything. But like many other Christian writers, he generalizes because of his pessimistic view of humanity. It is in this same spirit and with the same ambiguity that he writes: "If you are a Christian, says Saint Augustine, the world is your enemy,"[114] and ". . . Nobody can ardently aspire to future life if he does not first despise his present existence . . . Who most desires to reach the true country if not he who most suffers from the troubles and the pains of exile? What reasonable person would complain of his present state if this state were not a burden to him?"[115] Farther on is another maxim: "In this life, time belongs to the soul, not to the body."[116]

The success of Ludolph's *Vita Christi* was widespread and long lasting. It was translated into most European languages even before the invention of printing and was the very first book to be printed in Portuguese (in the year 1495).[117]

The *Spiritual Exercises* of Ignatius Loyola (written around 1522) was another "best-seller" and was especially popular among those who practiced religious retreats, laymen included. Loyola there suggests that one should beseech the Blessed

Virgin to bestow "knowledge of the world in order that [one] might loathe it and [thus detach one's self from] worldly and vain things."[118] Despite this categorical rejection of the "world," which is evoked with all of its usual ambiguity, the *Exercises* make a distinction that is often omitted in other spiritual works. Ignatius does not despise earthly things for the simple reason that they were made for man, who must use them for his salvation.[119] On the other hand, like the Dominican monk Louis of Granada, he declares war against the senses, the flesh, and the earth.

Louis of Granada was a successful author in his time whose career as a writer began with a translation of the *Imitation of Christ* into Castilian. His two-volume *Guía de los pecadores* (originally intended to be the third part of his *Treatise on Prayer and Meditation*) appeared in Lisbon in 1556–57. Its impact was long lasting (no less than 476 editions in different languages appeared between 1598 and 1904, ensuring it a correspondingly large audience),[120] which is what makes this book interesting for us here. In addressing the sinner (that is, every Christian), the fiery Dominican gives the following advice: "There where the sufferings of the world are to be found are also the favors of Heaven; there where nature resists, grace saves, for grace is stronger than nature."[121] All this on condition, however, that the body is treated "roughly and rigorously. Is not dead flesh preserved with salt and myrrh, which are bitter, in order that it not spoil and swell with worms? In like manner the body becomes tainted and filled with vice if it is treated with tenderness and delicacy."[122] Louis thus proposes a "holy hatred of the self"[123] and the mortification of all passions, which he calls the "sensory appetite." What exactly did he mean by "sensory appetite"? No less than "all affections, all natural emotions such as love, hate, joy, sadness, desire, fear, hope, anger and other such feelings."[124] This vast appetite was also defined as being:

> *the lowest part of our soul, and therefore that which renders us most like animals . . . that which debases us, which pulls us down to earth and estranges us from Heaven. It is all too often the source and origin of all the evils that exist in the world; therein lies the cause of our perdition . . . Therein lies the entire arsenal, the entire strength, the enitre ammunition of sin.*[125]

Caught up in his own reasoning, the ardent preacher then compares the sensory appetite with Eve. It is the Eve within ourselves, "the weakest part of our souls and the one most inclined to evil, the one through which the ancient serpent attacks our inner Adam." The inner Adam, on the other hand, is the superior part of our being "where reside both will and understanding." The drama of the Original Sin is thus continually reenacted throughout each person's life, moving up and down a hierarchy whose lower levels are permanently occupied by a black and malevolent villain. Such an analysis, which faithfully reproduces the misogynistic themes of ecclesiastical culture, entirely forgets that, according to Genesis, the Fall was caused by pride and defiance with respect to God rather than by the indulgence of the senses.

JUSTIFICATION BY FAITH AND THE NEED FOR DESPAIR

How does Protestant theology treat the *contemptus mundi* and the devaluation of man? In a certain sense, the world and life in the world are rehabilitated, in contrast to the above-cited monastic anathemas. First of all, the spirit and the flesh are no longer opposed in terms of the dualist system inherited from Neoplatonism. "It is absurd to take the word 'flesh' to mean the body," wrote Calvin. In commenting on the Epistle to the Galatians, Luther also observed that Saint Paul "does not use the word 'flesh' to describe wild sensuality, animal passion, or sensual appetite."[126] The body in itself is not evil as compared to the soul. From this affirmation stems a fertile reevaluation of "secular and carnal duties" that, as he points out, are criticized by the papists:

> *All Christian duties—such as loving one's wife, feeding one's children, governing one's family, honoring one's parents, obeying magistrates, etc.—which, according to them [i.e., the papists] are but secular and carnal duties, are in reality fruit of the Spirit. Blind men such as these cannot distinguish vice from that which is part of God's good creation.*[127]

Luther thus praised marriage, in total defiance of all prior ecclesiastical tradition. Once, in the midst of dinner, he exclaimed: "Is it possible to sufficiently admire conjugal union, which God has established and rules over, and from which both the human species and domestic institutions derive?"[128] Another *Tischreden* echoes the preceding one: "Marriage is the most beautiful institution created by God and the impious laws of the Pope are only a violent oppression of nature."[129] The Reformer also reproached the "Holy Fathers" (of the church) to have "written nothing worthy on the subject of marriage. All of them have been duped by vile celibacy, from which stem so many horrors, and they have not perceived the dignity and the eminence which both the Old and New Testament accord to marriage."[130] A few years later Luther argued this point again, declaring that "Procreation is a marvelously organized institution in all creatures, both male and female."[131]

This praise of sexuality is only part of an encompassing and enthusiastic admiration for all of Creation, which Luther calls the "pleasure garden of the soul" (because the soul may there "stroll among the works of God").[132] True to his cloth, Calvin also wrote a number of magnificent verses on the beauty of the universe:

> *[God] has manifested Himself [to mankind] in the beautiful and exquisite architecture of the sky and the earth, and daily shows and presents Himself there, so that man need but open his eyes to perceive his Creator. This is why the Prophet (Ps. 104:2) . . . compares the heavens to a royal tent, saying that God has wrapped it in water, that the clouds are His chariots, which He rides on the wings of the winds, and that both the winds and the lightning are His messengers . . . We cannot contemplate this artificial [i.e., masterly], well-ordered and regulated construction of the world without being almost confounded by its infinite light."*[133]

In another chapter of the *Institutes* Calvin wonders at the "multitude of stars, which could not be more delightful to see" and at the strength of He who simultaneously upholds "the great mass that is the universe" and yet "turns the world so gently."[134] God created all things "in view of man," and man himself has been a great success. "When, therefore, we perceive the admirable light of truth in books written by pagan authors, we should be chastened and remember that, although human nature has fallen from its original perfection and is quite corrupt, it is nonetheless graced with many of God's gifts."[135] In his sermons Calvin also points out that all men, including sinners, receive and conserve the "image of God," contrary to oxen, donkeys, dogs . . . and even stars, which do not share this privilege. From this resemblance man derives extraordinary dignity: "God . . . wishes to be magnified in the sky and on the earth, and in all of his doings, but most of all in man, for he has impressed his image upon us more than on all the rest. He certainly did not say of the sun, of the stars, or of any other creature, no matter how excellent it might be: I will here make a masterpiece in my own image and likeness."[136]

After reading these quotations, one might think that Protestant theology had eradicated the brand of pessimism (with regard to the world and man) that had characterized monastic literature. It so happened, however, that exactly the opposite occurred. Both Luther and Calvin had inherited a tradition that was not easily forgotten. It was thus in the wake of the many Catholic authors and preachers before him that Calvin saw fit to remind his congregation of the humble origins of man:

> *If God had formed us of the stuff of the sun or the stars, or if he had created any other celestial matter out of which man could have been made, then we might have said that our beginning was honorable . . . But when someone is made of clay, who pays any attention to him? . . . [So] who are we? We are all made of mud, and this mud is not just on the hem of our gown, or on the sole of our boots, or in our shoes. We are full of it, we are nothing but mud and filth both inside and outside.*[137]

This takes us back to where we began. As for Luther, he is of course convinced that the sexual act stems from a universal and inescapable need, just "like drinking, eating, spitting or defecating."[138] So why fight against it? In the end of it all, however, "it is a sin, and if God does not hold married couples responsible for it, this is only out of mercy."[139] Luther wanted to make very sure that no one got the wrong impression from his eulogy on marriage and thus he wrote:

> *In praising conjugal life, I deny having conceded to nature that there be no sin in it at all. On the contrary, I say that both flesh and blood, having been corrupted by Adam, are conceived and are born in sin . . . and that conjugal duty is never accomplished without sin. But God spares married couples through grace, because the conjugal order is his own creation. He preserves, by his own means, all the good with which he has blessed marriage, and this even in the midst of sin.*[140]

From the point of view of sin, Luther regarded marriage with a far more pessimistic eye than did the majority of the Catholic casuists. This was due to justification by faith, which divides humanity into two groups: the saved and the reprobates. Both groups commit deadly sins, and both of them are unworthy of salvation, but the faults of some of them will be—and are already—pardoned, whereas those of the others will not. In texts where the Reformers let their conception of the Original Sin sink into the background (or perhaps they even forget it for a moment?), they appear rather optimistic and inclined to a more humanist view of life. At times they even seem to want to rehabilitate man and the world. Yet as soon as they return to their fundamental doctrine, they are overtaken by pessimism. They accuse man of being a sinner, can find no excuse for him, and declare that the world is so rotten that there is no point in fleeing it in a (vain) attempt to find an unreachable purity through otherworldliness.

It was therefore in the sixteenth century, and specifically in Protestant theology, that the accusation of man and the world reached its climax in Western civilization. Never before had they been so totally condemned, and never had this condemnation reached such a large audience. Luther and his successors urged all Christians to "despair totally of themselves in order to be able to receive Christ's grace." "Having grown into a bad tree, [man] can only want and do evil."[141] Salvation lies in accepting the obvious—everything in and around us is bad. "World" and "devil" are synonyms. Luther's commentary on the Epistle to the Galatians is highly revealing.[142] There he says that the world is the "son" of the devil, which is why it is "all bad" and "filled with ignorance, hate, blasphemy, contempt of God, lies and errors, not to speak of gross sins such as murder, adultery, fornication, theft, pillage, etc."[143] When justification by faith is absent, only sin, filth, and hellfire can be found. With his usual vehemence, Luther refuses to accord any value to the actions of those who have not believed, who do not believe, or who will not believe. He declares: "There where the world seems to be better, it is twice as evil,"[144] and "Paul correctly calls this world evil, for where it is best it is really the worst."[145] These contradictory affirmations are then commented as follows:

> *. . . All that is in the world is subject to the devil's malice, for he reigns over the entire world. This is why the world is also called the devil's kingdom . . . No matter how many people there may be in this world, they are all subject to sin and to the devil. They are all the devil's subjects, for his tyranny holds all men captive . . . When Christ is absent, then the evil world and the devil's kingdom are present. All the spiritual and bodily gifts you possess—be they wisdom, justice, holiness, eloquence, power, beauty, or riches—are therefore but the instruments and slavish weapons of the devil's infernal tyranny. These he uses to make you serve him, to promote his reign and to increase his power.*[146]

This bitter diagnosis and irrevocable judgment belong to the history of European pessimism, to which Protestantism (above and beyond Luther's contribution) added a new dimension. And even if certain of Huldrych Zwingli's writings seem to partially rehabilitate man under the influence of the Renaissance,[147] other texts such as his *De Vera et Falsa Religione* (1525) remain excessively faithful to the Augustinian tradition, despite their humanistic veneer. Contrary to Erasmus, Zwingli considers man to be as incapable of free will as capable of making a rope out of sand or turning a devil into an angel. The Zürich Reformer's severity thus equals Luther's, as does his melancholy view of existence: "The life of a Christian resembles a ship cast here and there by a terrible storm. At one moment the sailors can just barely steer the boat, in the next they must run before the violence of the winds."[148] Zwingli accuses man of being impermeable to his own intelligence, like the cuttlefish, which creates a cloud of ink in order to hide from its pursuers: " 'Evil and unfathomable, such is the heart of man. Who can pierce its secrets?'[149] (Jer. 17:9), 'God regrets having made man (Gen. 6:5–9), for he is wicked from birth, desires only fame, pleasure and riches, and shows himself to be both deceitful and ignorant.' 'We are all hypocrites' (Isa. 9:12–20). The caverns and the hiding places of the human heart are so numerous that it is impossible to count them, just as it is impossible to measure the ocean or to clean the Augean stables. Man manages to camouflage his wickedness, but let no mistake be made: 'evil are his thoughts, and evil his heart.' "

The entire chapter of Zwingli's *De Vera et Falsa Religione* dedicated to man deals primarily with wickedness and egoism. He concludes with the following words: "Man is wicked from all points of view. Egoism dictates all of his thoughts and actions." No Christian can reach salvation without first recognizing his "treason and his wretchedness." It is only by "totally despairing of himself" (despair being at the heart of Protestant theology) that he will be able to discover "the vast pattern of (divine) mercy."[150] Another Reformer, Martin Bucer, wrote a catechism (1534) in which he affirms that even the most saintly of men must "consider all the good they have done to be no more than mud," for "our whole life long, sin continues to inhabit our flesh, where no good can be found."[151]

Calvin treats man and the world with equal harshness. He calls man an "apostate," a "monkey" (a strong insult at the time), a "wild and ferocious beast," "dung," and "rubbish."[152] In fact, as he points out, man's understanding is "completely subjected to stupidity and blindness, and his heart is given over to perversity."[153] It is certainly not by chance that the first book of the *Institution Chrétienne* opens with a discussion of man's fall from grace: "Our nudity reveals such a despicable mass that we are totally ashamed."[154] Man is "earth and dust," "worm and rot."[155] Experience certainly shows that "a seed of religion has been planted in everyone by the secret inspiration of God," but in no man does it "ripen, and the fruit never comes in season . . . ; everyone strays from the true knowledge of God, and there remains no solemn piety in the world."[156] Like Luther and Zwingli, Calvin believes that God can be reached only by following the path of despair: "No matter where we look, high or low, we can see only a curse that, spreading over all creatures and embracing the earth and the sky, ought to burden our souls with horrible despair."[157] To know one's self is to despise one's self, an attitude that is considered to be quite healthy: ". . . Self-knowledge progresses most when one is crushed and abashed by knowledge of one's own calamity, poverty, nudity and ignominy, for there is no danger that man can go too far in abasing himself." In this process of self-abasement man stands to discover "in God that which is missing in himself."[158] This doctrine is so central to Calvinist theology that it inspires the opening passage of the *Institution Chrétienne*:

> *. . . It is necessary that we be conscious of . . . our unhappiness, in order that we glean at least some knowledge of God. That is why consciousness of our ignorance, vanity, scarcity, infirmity—and even perversity and corruption—makes us realize that true clarity of wisdom, firm virtue, righteous wealth, and pure justice can be found nowhere else but in God . . . ; we can only wittingly aspire and reach out [to God] when we have begun to truly dislike ourselves.*[159]

All of the spiritual teachers whose pessimistic philosophy and growing audience interest us here generally discuss contempt for the self in association with endless lamentations upon the misery of the human condition and gloomy reflections upon the transitory nature of this world's meager satisfactions. Calvin points out that "Life in this world is full of worries and troubles. It is totally wretched. Nowhere is happiness to be found." The things of this world "are transitory, uncertain, frivolous, and mixed with infinite misery."[160] God does not want men to fall asleep in "restful peace," which would jeopardize their salvation, and therefore he exposes them to "wars, tumult, brigandage and other such abuse":

> *In order that they not aspire to decadent riches with excessive avidity, or grow complacent with the wealth they have, He reduces them to indigence, sometimes through the sterility of the earth, sometimes by fire, sometimes in other ways, or else He restricts them to mediocrity. In order that they not take too much pleasure in marriage, He gives them coarse or headstrong wives who torment them or who bear wicked children to humiliate them. He can also afflict them by taking their wives and children away. When He treats them gently in all things . . . He then uses illness and dangers to warn them, thus giving them a practical demonstration of the extent to which all mortal beings are fragile and of short duration.*[161]

At the end of this none-too-cheerful description on human existence, Calvin concludes with a reflection on the "battle" that is life: "There is nothing to look or to hope for in this world except war."[162]

The *Chrestiennes Méditations* of Théodore de Bèze (written around 1560)[163] faithfully reflect Calvin's conception of man. The first meditation (on the Psalm *Beatus vir*. . .) begins with a cry of distress: "Alas, poor, miserable and wretched creature, you who are never so unreasonable as when your blind reason leads you and your mad will pushes you, what path will you choose among the myriad routes which make up the labyrinth in which you were born and through which you have wandered aimlessly up until now?"[164] The second meditation (on the Psalm *Domine ne* . . .) echoes the preceding one and, like many other Protestant texts, plays on the necessary note of despair:

> *Alas, I who am more than miserable, assailed, pressed, forgotten on all sides, mortally grieved by my conscience, pierced through and through by the consciousness of infinite misdeeds, nothing is left to me but the profound abyss of despair. And as for my body, it is burdened with evil and plunged into mourning. Torment can there find nothing left to torment. What can I do, what can I say, where can I go . . . and who could help me anyway?*[165]

This entire series of meditations is filled with bitter reflections of the same stamp: "What am I, Lord, except corruption, injustice, and death?"[166] and "I have spoiled everything. I have destroyed everything and ruined it."[167] In his meditation on the Psalm *Miserere mei* . . . , Théodore de Bèze has David speak for all men: "From the moment in which . . . my mother conceived me and warmed me in her womb, vice lodged inside of me like a root, later to produce bitter and poisonous fruit . . ."[168]

Entire volumes could be filled with sixteenth-century Protestant texts that despair of man, his sin, and his unhappiness. In conclusion, I would like to quote two texts by John Knox, the man responsible for bringing Scotland into the Protestant fold. Knox here expresses the same mistrust of nature and reason as do Luther and Calvin, the same refusal to accord any value whatsoever to those who are not justified by faith. The first text is taken from *An Answer to a Great Number of blasphemous cavillations written by an Anabaptist*: "they neither have the glorie of God in their actions before their eies, neither yet mynd they to serve nor obey God's purpose and will. Sathan, in tempting man, studied nothing to promote God's glorie; man, in obeying the temptation, looked not to the counsell of God."[169]

The second text is taken from the *The Confession of Faith . . . Within the Realm of Scotland* (1561), which was approved and distributed by the civil authorities and therefore imposed upon the population: "For of nature we are so dead, so blind and so perverse, that neither can we feel when we are pricked, see the light when it shines, nor assent to the will of God when it is revealed . . . For of ourselves we are not sufficient to think one good thought."[170]

Let us briefly recapitulate the continuous and yet diversified path that has led us from medieval monastic anathemas against the world and man to the precepts of Protestant theology. The Reformers introduced certain changes without, however, deviating from the main road. For example, they no longer considered the senses to be the natural enemy of the spirit, for it is the spirit itself that is bad. The concept of flight from this world is therefore useless, for evil is as present in convents and monasteries as it is in the outside world; it is as deeply rooted in ascetic retreats as it is in social life. Sexuality is sinful, of course, but certainly no more so than the rest of our actions. There is no rational "upper story" in man, no intelligence that tries to put a bit of order into the agitation of the "lower stories." Without Christ's grace, which in any case is totally gratuitous, everything in man is destined to remain evil.

In its sixteenth-century form, the doctrine of justification by faith thus represents the logical (although extreme) end of the long and desolate road through pessimism. Incessantly repeated for more than a thousand years, the affirmation of the world's fragility, of its vice and its vanity, reached a vast audience. Man was but "dung" and "filth"—no wonder the result was despair. Yet it was exactly this despair that was destined to save those who, miserable and naked, abandoned themselves entirely to God.

ALONG THE BORDERS OF THE PROTESTANT WORLD: A RETURN TO OTHERWORLDLINESS

The official churches that emerged from the Reformation unanimously declined to interpret the doctrine of *contemptus mundi* in terms of *fuga mundi*. On the fringe of the Protestant world, however, the doctrine of flight from this world survived and flourished, for *fuga mundi* has long constituted a recurrent form of collective hostility toward society.

The religious nonconformists of the Middle Ages (the flagellants, the Brethren of the Free Spirit, and even Valdes's early disciples at the beginning of their apostolate) were not very well organized as a general rule and tended, on the whole, to imitate confraternity structures.[171] Their common goals invariably included the regeneration of the ecclesiastical institution. On the other hand, the Czech Church, or Communion of Brethren, adopted yet another form of differentiation with respect to both the church and society. These Brethren (who can be traced back to the year 1458) attempted to live their refusal of the world in terms of the ideals set out in the Sermon on the Mount. They were opposed to any law—be it human or ecclesiastical—that dealt with moral or dogmatic issues. As a consequence the Communion abandoned the church (considered to be inextricably bound up in a sinful society) and left it to its own fate. The alternative they eventually opted for took the form of rural communities composed entirely of volunteers who willingly embraced a rigorous discipline. Thus emerged, or rather reemerged, a "sect" type of organization such as Ernst Troeltsch has defined them, along the lines of similar sects (gnostic, montanist, novatian, donatist, and so on) that have repeatedly appeared since the dawn of Christianity.[172]

Writing in a context that might now seem a trifle dated, Troeltsch defined the opposition between church and sect in the following terms. The church is open to the masses and adapts itself to the world, disregarding "subjective sanctity in favor of the objective advantages of grace and redemption." This collusive relationship with the world quite naturally gave rise to radical reactions, one of which was monasticism. Yet the church managed to integrate the heroic and dualist asceticism of monastic life (which rejected the senses in order to better practice contemplation) insofar as it imposed and maintained the apostolic tradition, the sacraments, the priesthood, and the principle of succession. Sects are much like monastic communities in that they are made up of a relatively restricted group of volunteers who seek individual and interior perfection. On the other hand, sects not only establish a certain distance between themselves and society (they may even be downright hostile) but they also break with all churches and condemn them categorically. Sects also tend to reject apostolic tradition and succession, "referring their members directly to the supernatural, outside of any sociological synthesis. Their Christianity is nonsacerdotal, and they oppose subjective sanctification to objective sanctification [by the sacraments]." Ascetic sacrifices are not considered to be a contribution to the communion of saints or to the "treasure" of the church, but rather as a means to union with God, as a form of mutual aid and as a refusal of the world's traps and foibles. Finally, whereas the church lives in the present day, sect members often live in expectation of an eschatological outcome—a Last Judgment or a felicitous *millennium*—which would confirm their chosen status in the eyes of the sinful world.

The violent Anabaptists of Münster (who seized power in the year 1534) followed this pattern to a certain extent.[173] They totally repudiated the church and the society of their time, transforming the entire city into a kind of monastery where community of goods and "biblical" polygamy were practiced. They considered themselves to be the chosen people, the "sword" of the Lord whose duty it was to realize the *millennium*. Yet the dictatorship with which they ruled the new Jerusalem and their coercive support of the Divine Kingdom resulted in totalitarian solutions contrary to the "sectarian" spirit. Rather, it was the peaceful Anabaptists of the sixteenth and early seventeenth centuries who followed this "spirit" to the letter: Their declarations, regulations, and confessions of faith—issued by Swiss, German, Alsatian and Dutch groups—unanimously rejected corrupt Christianity. Grebel of Zürich, who was persecuted by Zwingli, declared that "true and faithful Christians are lambs in the midst of wolves, lambs for the slaughter. They must be baptised with anguish, affliction, tribulation, suffering and death" (letter to Müntzer, 1524).[174] This means, in effect, that the "true Christians" are but a small flock, hemmed in by impious masses who seek only to

> *save themselves by practicing lip service to faith, without searching for its true fruits . . . without charity and hope, and bereft of true Christian customs. They prefer their old ways, their personal vices and their common, ceremonial and anti-Christian customs of Baptism and Holy Communion. Thus do they despise the Word of God, submitting completely to the papist word and to the words of antipapist preachers, both of which are far from the divine word.*[175]

Thus did Grebel and his friends distinguish themselves from both the Catholics and the "antipapists" of their time, a distinction that meant they rejected the vast majority of their contemporaries. In the year 1527 the magistrates of Zürich passed a death sentence on one of Grebel's friends (who had escaped from prison); this sentence throws light upon some of the convictions held by the Anabaptists: "[Manz] and his followers have left the Church and have gathered seditiously in order to create a schism and constitute an independent sect under the guise of a Christian assembly."[176] This, in fact, was the Anabaptist goal as confirmed by the Schleitheim confession (1527). The Swiss and German Anabaptists responsible for this document had decided to create a "brotherly understanding between *some* of God's children," to distance themselves from "the abomination" (that is, the world), and to "behave well among themselves and before the pagans." The "pagans" were obviously all non-Anabaptists, globally condemned as being "those who do not obey the faith, who are not reconciled with God and do not wish to do his Will . . . They are a great abomination before God. Nothing can germinate or grow within them that is not abominable."[177] Hence the need to repudiate all Nicodemism and all participation whatsoever in official worship: "We cannot sit both at God's table and at that of the Demon,"[178] the Demon's table being Holy Communion as practiced in the more important churches.

This "chosen," "pure," and "converted" people wished to create new communities on the model of the primitive church. Being quite peaceful, however, these Anabaptists were not interested in imposing their doctrine on others but rather demanded the right to be different and even the right to secede from the rest of society, for they firmly intended to create a tangible difference between themselves and the sinful world "ruled by the devil." Their separatism was defined first and foremost by the rebaptism of adults, for they believed membership in the Christian faith should be voluntary and not the result of political or religious conformity. This baptism of free and responsible adults was, in fact, somewhat similar to the vows taken by novices, who usually assume a new name upon that occasion. Another parallel between monastic life and that of the Anabaptist communities lay in their strong internal cohesion. Menno Simons (d. 1561), who directed a number of communities in the Netherlands and in northern Germany, maintained a rule of strict excommunication, though this practice was considerably mitigated after his death. Simons believed that a church without an effective policy of apostolic excommunication (as opposed to sanctions on the part of the civil authorities) "would be like a city without walls or barriers, like a field without a fence, like a house without doors or walls."[179] In 1644 the Nonconformist divine John Goodwin pleaded for a "congregational way" (that is, a voluntary fellowship of true Christians) where excommunication would function as a kind of medicine to keep the churches pure. A contemporary of his, Roger Williams (founder of both Rhode Island and the city of Providence), hotly disputed this point with the Presbyterians of New England. Like all sectarian thinkers, he favored an intolerant church whose members should all be "saints."[180]

Another trait common to both religious orders and sects is the austere way of life they often adopt in order to distinguish themselves from the corruption of the world. Such was the case with the Anabaptists. In 1525 the Bernese group affirmed that "Food must be provided for the brothers whenever they gather in assembly. They should be served just soup or cabbage and a little bit of meat, for the Kingdom of Heaven does not consist of eating and drinking."[181] Regulations drawn up at an Anabaptist conference in Strasbourg (in the year 1568, later revised in 1607) decree that: "Tailors and seamstresses will follow simple and humble patterns and will make nothing ostentatious. Brothers and sisters . . . will have nothing ostentatious made."[182] Such directives stemmed from a general rejection of all worldliness, an attitude that was reinforced in Anabaptist communities from the sixteenth to the eighteenth centuries by their strict endogamic practice (in order to separate the pure from the impure). Thus the 1568 and 1607 regulations read:

> *Those who wish to enter into the state of matrimony will only do so with the knowledge and advice of both the officials and the Elders. They will also prepare themselves in the fear of God. It is equally seemly that they inform their parents [of their plans].*
>
> *. . . Believers should marry in God, and not with unbelievers. This goes for young ladies, young men and widowers [or widows].*[183]

The directives decided upon in Steinseltz in the year 1752 stipulate (section 2):

> *"Should a brother or sister have a relationship or marry with a* worldly person, *and later return to the assembly, begging (with regret and repentance) for readmission, they shall not be refused. This, however, shall be on condition that he or she bring their spouse, with whom they are joined before God and His Word. If this should be impossible, then they must separate, the repentant party making sure*

that the other be provided for, and praying God for their conversion and return to truth.[184]

Jean Séguy rightly describes such communities as "ghettos," as "closed civilizations dedicated to nonworldliness," and as "Anabaptist-Mennonite ethnic groups" where endogamy was the rule.[185] Their voluntary restrictions with regard to the world of the flesh also gave rise to a number of directives complementary to those outlined above. The first Swiss Anabaptists refused to take oath, to carry arms, to fulfill any civil task or appointment to the magistrature, to stand bail, to undertake any professional or commercial engagements with the world, and to have recourse to law courts. This was because they said they belonged to the Kingdom of Grace and Christ, and not to that of temporal law and the flesh.[186] In the course of time it became necessary to temper this intractable stance, and a casuistic debate developed around the question of what was permitted and what was not. According to the Confession of Dordrecht (1632), God "had created [State] Power or Authority, and established it in order to protect the good and punish evildoers."[187] Anabaptist groups nevertheless strove to preserve their identity and their autonomy vis à vis society by means of physical isolation (especially in the country), by counterfashions in clothes, by endogamy, and by strict discipline within the group.[188]

Anabaptism is only one small continent in the sectarian world that developed along the borders of Protestantism during the sixteenth century and afterward. The will to break with the sinful world was, in fact, a common denominator of all of the "regenerated" and "chosen" Christian congregations that aimed at creating "pure bodies of true believers governed by Christ rather than by a Prince." Even when the baptism of adults was not practiced, dissident separatists refused worldly concerns. The founder of the Quakers, George Fox (1624–1691), taught absolute religious egalitarianism (no ministers) and complete antisacramentalism (no baptism and no communion). He also advocated passive resistance and the abolition of the forms and practice of good manners. The taking of oaths, public office, and titles (such as those of nobility) were equally disposed of. His "Society of Friends" willingly adopted outmoded manners of dress and practiced endogamy.[189] Another more recent example is that of the Jehovah's Witness movement, founded in 1874. This group associates a very "liberal" theology (Christ is not God) with a very literal exegesis (every number in the Bible has an exact meaning), with millenary expectations and with an aggressive and radical attitude toward all churches, sects, and civil authorities. They have no priests but rather itinerant preachers. They also refuse military service and recognize no national banner.[190] This movement is but one more example of a refusal of the world based on fear of the world, of a deep pessimism, and anathema based on aversion.

C H A P T E R 2

From Contempt for the World to the "Danse Macabre"

"FAMILIARITY" WITH DEATH

The gradual expansion of the *contemptus mundi* doctrine from the fourteenth to the eighteenth centuries was largely due to the efforts of the church, even though its influence was felt far beyond the boundaries of religious life. One of the side effects of this doctrine was the particular attitude toward death that characterized European civilization at that time. Despite the number of books and articles that have appeared in recent years on the subject of death and dying,[1] the special relationship between contempt for the world and the concept of mortality deserves a second glance. Before going any further, however, I would like to express my great debt and gratitude to my predecessors, whose work I have drawn upon repeatedly in the course of my research on the fears of the past. In the context of this general synthesis, a reexamination of their findings throws new light upon this subject.

To begin with, certain methodological problems must be taken into account. For example, one certainly cannot attribute a widespread historical phenomenon —such as the obsessive preoccupation with death in early modern Europe—to a single cause. There were, as a matter of fact, several converging factors that influenced each other (factors that could have diverged just as easily) and that should be brought to the fore. In terms of the subject matter covered by this book and by the volume preceding it, two phenomena help to explain the role assigned to death in this period: (1) the long process of religious "culpabilisation" and acculturation that, originating in monasteries, spread out in concentric circles so as to reach larger and larger segments of the population, and (2) a profound pessimism, stemming from an accumulation of different types of stress, which dominated European thought (especially that of the elite) from the time of the Black Death to the end of the Wars of Religion.

Our investigation of this dramatic attitude toward death will lead us right back to *contemptus mundi*, but before setting out on our journey, it might be prudent to determine the exact meaning of the expression "familiarity with death" that is so often used by historians when discussing the customs and behavior of the past. An example from Montaigne will serve this purpose. In the first volume of his *Essays*, which is heavily influenced by stoic thought, Montaigne declares that men must be taught to die in order that they may learn to live. "One must always be booted and ready to leave," he wrote, and then went on to praise the Egyptians, who concluded all festive occasions "by showing a large image of death to the assembled company." Hence Montaigne's famous words of advice: "Let us remove [death's] strangeness and practice it instead. Let us grow accustomed to it, having no thought in mind as often as that of death."[2] This pedagogic approach thus sought to "tame" death—Montaigne used this very term himself.[3]

Although he often meditated on the end of life, Montaigne seemed to be quite unconcerned with the question of life after death. It was, in fact, salvation that most concerned the world in which he lived. This leit-motif of all religious thought at that time obliged man to think continually about death in order to avoid sin, for sin plus death could land him in Hell. Familiarity with death was therefore recommended, a forced and willful familiarity that, like that first advocated by Montaigne, involved a long struggle with one's self. One should always keep death in mind, just as one would always mount guard against an enemy who might suddenly appear. Significantly enough, the term "enemy" as a synonym for death appears in the same passage of the *Essays* quoted above: "let us learn to face it courageously, and strive against it."[4] On the other hand, Montaigne eventually discovered exactly how difficult it was to acquire familiarity with death by sheer willpower. As a result, he eventually renounced his early stoicism in favor of a "more relaxed"[5] attitude toward the inevitable. Yet even the heroic current that dominates the first book of *Essays* is interrupted, in chapter 20, by a naturalist stream of thought that essentially contradicts his stoic stance: "Death is the beginning of a new life . . . Nature compels us to it . . . Your death is one of the ordered pieces of the universe, it is a part of this world . . . You are in death while you are in life because you still exist, after death, even though you exist no longer in life."[6] In his third book of *Essays*, this hearthside philosopher ends up by canceling the last traces of his former stoic pose: "Let us not trouble life by worrying about death, nor death by worrying about life . . . If we have managed to live a calm and constant life, then we shall know how to die in like manner,"[7] and elsewhere: "It is certain that most people have suffered far more torment from preparing for death than they have from any other cause."[8]

Thus did Montaigne modify his original opinion, rejecting the heroic familiarity with death advocated by philosophers and preachers and founding his new position on the living example of the "common people." Peasants, for example, had a true familiarity with death that enabled them to live their last hours in a natural way. On this subject the third book of *Essays* contains observation of a quasi-ethnographic nature: "Let us look upon the poor people we see scattered about the land, their weary heads bent after their labors . . . how many of them desire death, and how many pass on with neither alarm nor affliction? That man over there who is digging in my garden, this very morning he buried his father or his son."[9] And, during the plague that struck the Bordeaux region in 1585: "What exemplary resolution was to be seen in the simplicity of all those people . . . Each and every one of them preparing themselves and waiting for death to come that very evening, or the next day. Their faces and voices were so little afraid. They seemed to have accepted this as a necessity, as an inevitable and universal condemnation."[10]

Montaigne also made the following observation: "I have never seen any of my peasant neighbors worry about the way in which they would spend their last hour . . ."[11] Prior to death "the common people need neither remedy nor consolation."[12] Natural death is here opposed to cultural death. According to Montaigne, the simple people think of death only when it comes to them, at which point they accept it calmly, as if it were a law of nature to which they have always been resigned. Such observations are moreover confirmed by the behavior of the nineteenth- and twentieth-century Russian peasants described by Philippe Ariès.[13] Like the farmers of sixteenth-century France, their attitude toward death and their actual manner of dying follow the pattern set by most traditional civilizations.

Such docile acceptance of this universal and immutable law has long been associated with belief in the survival of a "double." Any historical study of death must, in fact, pay due attention to the ethnographic aspects of dying, which have already been touched upon in the first volume of this series.[14] Like the members of many other civilizations, our ancestors found it difficult to accept the abrupt disappearance of those with whom they had shared their lives. Hence they believed in ghosts, which testify to the continuing presence of the dead—at least for a certain time. In other words, the dead took a long time to actually pass away. They only gradually disappeared from the world of the living. The Aztecs of precolumbian America furnish a good example of this type of belief. For Aztec civilization, the majority of the dead—that is, all those who were not cared for by the triumphant Sun or by the Rain God—had to walk the earth for four years before reaching the place where they would finally be dissolved.[15] Innumerable examples of belief in ghosts can be found the world over, not to speak of the European versions—such as those in Montaillou,[16] which are so well-known it is hardly necessary to mention them here.[17] This belief was so strong in our civilization that Christianity integrated it quite spontaneously and used it as part of the pedagogy of salvation. The *exempla* or edifying anecdotes narrated by preachers were chock full of apparitions of saints or souls from Purgatory (pleading that someone pray for them) and peopled by damned sinners (warning the living to avoid their bad example).[18] The convergence of a plurimillenary belief in ghosts and the Christian explanation given to them (ghosts are but souls in Purgatory) shows up clearly in a sonnet entitled "Des esprits des morts" composed by Ronsard's secretary, Amadis Jamyns (1540–1593):

> *The Shadows, the Spirits, the ghastly Images*
> *Of the Dead, burdened with sins, wander in the night:*
> *And to show the grief and the evil that afflict them*
> *They make the silence moan with their long and piteous voices,*
> *For they are deprived of the rapturous delights*
> *Which attend the soul, after death, in Paradise,*
> *Banished from the day, they make noise in the shadows,*
> *Begging for help for their shameful sufferings.*[19]

The results of an inquiry on belief in ghosts in the nineteenth century, carried out by a Polish ethnologist in his own country, were published in the volume preceding this one.[20] Since then other studies have appeared on the same subject, notably a survey of 175 oral statements gathered in Beauce, Québec, between 1972 and 1975. According to the authors of this survey, one has only to "step into the house of a worker, a young accountant, an elementary school teacher, an elderly couple, even a college student, to learn with some surprise that the belief in ghosts is still very alive in Beauce."[21] This was all the more true in the past.

Of course ghosts were feared to a certain extent, but at the same time they were not unfamiliar. Furthermore, as even the Beauce inquiry shows, the dead appeared only rarely in fearful guise, as specters or phantoms.[22] Many of them were even quite helpful and gave useful advice.[23] This brings us round to a conception of the universe as a place in which the death of an individual is secondary to the survival of the living community, and where both the living and the dead maintain social ties and solidarity. This concept, which is shared by many civilizations, has found its expression in ancestor cults and in the casual use of death images in everyday life.[24] It is for this reason, moreover, that one must be careful not to misinterpret the iconography of traditional cultures, no matter how lugubrious it might seem, nor misconstrue attitudes that appear to be quite morbid. Such manifestations simply testify to a true familiarity with death, a familiarity that found expression in a type of spectacle which seems horrible to us today.

Such intimacy with the dead can be found in China, where the bones of ancestors are carefully brushed clean, as well as in Madagascan[25] and Mexican funeral rites. At Imerina, where "life is sweet," the dead are periodically "turned over," for they get tired of always lying on the same side. In the middle of a large and joyous ceremony, composed of speeches, dances, and banquets, they are carried from the cemetery to the village, exhibited on a platform, and honored in different ways. Once the fête is over, they are wrapped in new shrouds and taken back to their tombs by a long and circuitous route so that they cannot find their way back to the village. Before they are put away again, they are requested to bless their descendants, who have done their duty toward them, by throwing a party and giving them new clothes. In Madagascar the traditional cosmology thus maintained a permanent alliance between the living and the dead. As a result, "the Malagasy are concerned with death, but not afraid of it. They know it to be inevitable, and therefore they do not fear it,"[26]

In another part of the world, the second of November marks an equally significant moment. On this day, bread shaped like a tibia is eaten throughout Mexico.[27] Bakeries and pastry shops fill their windows with skulls made of sugar whose eyes are of unnatural colors, red or green. Attached to the forehead is a strip of paper with a name written on it—to be offered to a friend who bears that same name. On the night of the second, the deceased's favorite flowers and sweetmeats are placed on his tomb, and aromatic copal is burned to make him happy while transistor radios bring him up to date on the latest tunes. Children turn gourds and pumpkins into death's heads, cutting out the eyes and nose and mouth and illuminating the whole from the inside with a candle, whose flame flickers eerily in the wind. At home, altars are set up for the dead on which food is placed. Prayers are then said in order that the deceased rest in peace and not come back to bother the living.[28] This ambivalence is typical of the dead—simultaneously near and far, frightening and reassuring—they are somehow everpresent.

Although the customs described above belong to non-European cultures, they help us to better understand our own past and our own macabre tradition—which seems far less dismal when compared with similar practices elsewhere. In other words, the European tradition was based neither on a morbid attraction nor on a lugubrious fascination, but rather on a certain complicity and familiarity with the dead combined with an apparent insensitivity and indifference to the banal reality of someone else's death. Burials were frequent, and ever since the triumph of Christianity graveyards have occupied a central position in villages, towns, and cities: Consequently, they became lively centers of public life. Philippe Ariès has described the key role they played in the communities of yesteryear.[29] In the Middle Ages, justice was served and edicts were proclaimed in cemeteries, and sometimes even the town bakehouse was to be found there. Anatole Le Braz has pointed out that in nineteenth-century Brittany the graveyard was used as a kind of auditorium: There the community made decisions, elected its municipal officers, listened to the mayor's secretary announce new laws, and read the notary's list of next week's sales.[30] In cities, cemeteries doubled as parks, marketplaces, fairgrounds, and dance halls. In seventeenth-century Paris, the famous *Cimitière des Innocents* served as a public shopping center, featuring bookstores, haberdashers, and drapers.[31] Anyone could stroll about there, buying, selling, drinking, procuring. No one seemed to mind that burials were going on at the same time, not to speak of the daily exhumations and the inevitable odors that lingered about the yard.

The church strove to repress this type of behavior, which, in its eyes, constituted a scandalous mixture of the sacred and the profane. In fact the church fought against all manifestations of familiarity between these two worlds, which it considered to be antithetical, with the result that councils and synods regularly tried to abolish all dancing, games, and commercial activities in cemeteries.[32] This ecclesiastical "allergy" to the carefree cohabitation of the living and the dead appears quite clearly in a text written by Martin Luther during the Wittenberg plague of 1527. According to Luther, it would have been far better to return to the customs of ancient Rome, where the dead were carried outside the city walls and cremated so that the "air stayed pure."[33] Moreover, a cemetery should be "a calm and quiet place, set apart and favorable to contemplation." Luther's proposal, which was finally adopted some three centuries later, was based on a preoccupation with Christian pedagogy. In such a "venerable and almost sacred place, where one would walk with respectful awe," one would naturally be led to "reflect upon death, the Last Judgment and the Resurrection, and pray." Furthermore, why not paint religious frescos on the walls? The Reformer then went on to compare his ideal cemetery to that of Wittenberg:

> *It is made up of four or five alleys and two or three squares, and there is no more common or noisy place in the whole city. Every day, day and night, everyone passes through, man and beast. All of the houses in the neighborhood have a door or a passageway opening onto the cemetery, and all sorts of things happen there, perhaps even things that it would be better not to mention. Thus the piety and respect due to the dead are reduced to nothing, and no one pays any more attention to them than they would to a cadaver just come from the knacker's yard. Not even the Turks would keep a cemetary in such a shameful fashion, yet we ourselves should find piety there, and meditate on death and on resurrection, and respect the Saints who are buried there.*

According to Luther, the cemeteries of his time by no means inspire visitors "to reflect upon death" or feel a "respectful awe." This observation throws further light upon much of what has been written on the "natural" way of experiencing death. In the past, another person's death was regarded with indifference; it shocked no one. Everyone was used to death, and nobody was surprised when it was their turn to go.

Seen in these terms, it is quite legitimate to compare the attitudes toward death decried by Luther with those of "primitive" peoples who, contrary to European civilization today, attribute little importance to the individual. The participatory mentality of such peoples prevents them from "experiencing death as a separation or as a kind of dereliction."[34] This attitude can doubtless also be credited with their good psychological balance and for the rare occurrence of psychosis and suicide. In archaic societies, death does not result in an acute sense of the absence of an irreplaceable person. I might also add that the antifeminist and clerical culture that asserted itself in Europe between the fourteenth and the sixteenth centuries may well have played a key role in eradicating a more serene concept of death. After all, women are less afraid of death than are men, for they feel closer to it. She who gives birth knows, far better than her male partner, the close relationship between life and death, and the necessity for both.

The once-popular idea that death, far from representing a point of rupture or a social scandal, is rather a normal event, necessary to the continuing rhythms of life, can be discerned in Saint Francis of Assisi's *Canticle of All Created Things*, written at the very end of his life (1225–26) when he was almost blind and ravaged by fever. In the last stanza, Francis invites the reader to meditate upon the "second death" (Hell): "Woe to those who die in mortal sin." Yet this reminder to ensure one's salvation before it is too late by no means prevents him from praising the Lord "for Sister our bodily death, from which no living man can escape." The saint then goes on to speak of "Brother Sun," "Sister Moon and the stars," "Brother Wind," "Sister Water," "Brother Fire," and "our Mother the Earth."[35] Thus death is reinstated in a cosmic kinship that automatically justifies it.

Literature of all periods has shown traces of this "natural" attitude toward death—with or without the preoccupation of salvation—for many people seem to have felt it both deeply and spontaneously. Ronsard, in his *Hymne de la mort* (which I shall refer to quite often, as it contains a number of pertinent elements),[36] comforts himself with the following reflections:

> *What is so terrible about Death? Is it such a calamity? . . .*
> *Remember that eternal matter remains,*
> *And that form changes and alters at all times,*
> *And that which is composite will fall apart of its own discord;*
> *Only that which is simple is exempt from death.*[37]

Like Ronsard, Rabelais firmly believed in the eternal and immortal soul. His vision of death, however, was rather different from the poet's in that he considered it to be a natural transition. Man passes on so that his descendants can have a chance at life, man follows man. The "hoary age" of old people "blossoms once again" in young children. The interruption of an individual's destiny is compensated by the continuity of man's collective fate. Procreation compensates for death, whence Gargantua's letter to Pantagruel: "Among the gifts, graces, and prerogatives with which the supreme and all-powerful maker God has endowed and adorned human nature from the very beginning, one of the most singular and excellent is that which permits man in his mortal state to attain a kind of immortality, and, in the course of transitory life, perpetuate his name and his seed, as happens with lineage issuing from us in legitimate marriage."[38]

THE COMPONENTS OF THE MACABRE

Above and beyond the material quoted above, what image of death haunted Europe at the time of Rabelais and Ronsard? Iconography, religious texts, sermons, and "insurance" (masses for the dead, indulgences, and so on) accumulated by the faithful in view of the hazards of the afterlife all seem to concur in painting a hideous portrait of death. Death is an interruption, a scandal, a danger. In his *Danse aux aveugles* (1405), Pierre Michault placed a sign bearing an important message in front of the ghostly reaper: "I am death, the enemy of nature."[39] Another "*rhétoriqueur*," Aimé de Montgesoye, attacked death in no uncertain terms in the course of his *Complainte de très haulte et vertueuse dame . . . Ysabel de Bourbon* (1465):

> *Master of horror! Mirror of vile deeds!*
> *Enemy of the works of Nature . . .*[40]

In evoking the mirror of death (as compared to the *Miroir de vie*), Jean Molinet (1435–1507) paints an equally gloomy picture:

Horrible spectacle, hateful mirage,
Proud vision, most fearful object,
Mortal signal, oh most lively specimen,
You are an impossible and contrary monster . . .[41]

For the poet Clément Marot, on the other hand, death is a god:

. . . Emaciated and ugly,
Who, with his cold and pestilential breath,
So wastes the air all around,
That the birds which fly above his head
Fall down from on high, and lie dead upon the earth,
Except for those which predict misfortune.[42]

The church played a key role in the gradual erasure of a "tame" image of death and the "natural" way of experiencing departure from life when it proposed meditation on death as a prime method of moral pedagogy. If Christianity did not invent the "death of the self," it was at least responsible for spreading this concept throughout an entire civilization. I have therefore retained Philippe Ariès's apt expression, "death of the self," as it so clearly states the break between the concept of individual fate as compared to the collective fate of the species. I shall, however, focus on an area Ariès neglected, that is to say on the "predecessors of the great macabre authors" of the fourteenth and fifteenth centuries. I do not think these authors should be "passed over" as being only "rare and not very eloquent."[43] On the contrary, contempt for the world, the dramatization of death, and insistence on personal salvation all emerged at the same time. This interdependence appears early on, in the sermons of Saint John Chrysostom for example, where the saint discusses the "vanity of vanities" of Ecclesiastes on no less than eight occasions, and the advice of Sirach (Ecclus. 7:4) four times: "In all that you do, remember your end and you will never sin." He also repeats the biblical aphorism: "Better . . . the day of death than the day of birth. Better go to the house of mourning than to the house of feasting; for to this end all men come" (Ecclus. 7:1–2).[44] Another treatise by Saint John Chrysostom—*On Patience*—bears the subtitle "the dead must not be bitterly mourned" and features an authentically macabre passage:

He whom I found charming yesterday is now laid out and fills me with horror. He who was like a part of myself now seems a stranger. He whom I only recently embraced, I would no longer even touch. I shed my tears on him for he is mine, but I flee his purulent matter as something foreign. Affection causes me to draw near his fetid corpse, but the corruption and the worms send me away . . . Where is his dear face? It is already tarnished. Where are his lively eyes? They have putrefied. His hair was like an ornament, but this ornament has vanished . . .[45]

Even before Saint John Chrysostom, Saint Ephrem delivered a sermon on "those who have fallen asleep in Christ" where macabre realism plays a similar role:

When we go to see the tombs where they are rotting and oozing, we point to them and say: Here lies so and so . . . this one was a king . . . that one was a captain . . . this one, a prince . . . here lies his nephew, there his daughter—once so fair—here the young dandy . . . [All have disappeared] . . . Then we call them by their names: Where have you gone to, brothers? Where do you live now? . . . Speak to us as you used to do before . . .

[And they answer]: We have left the ranks of men and now find ourselves here, in the place our deeds have earned for us! This dust . . . this ash, this rot . . . these tainted bones, these foul worms are but the bodies of the young men and women who once charmed you. This dust is the flesh you once hugged so tight. This decay is the face you once kissed with insatiable lust, day and night. This oozing stench is the the body you so hungrily embraced in sin. Therefore look, and see and believe, you who are dragging yourselves through a useless life. Do not let yourselves be fooled for long, young men and women, by the beauty of your youth. In life we too were what you are now, and we too spent our days in festivities. And now we lie here before you, dead and decayed . . .[46]

In terms of the macabre tradition, it is most significant that ecclesiastical literature from the Middle Ages up through the nineteenth century attributed a *Speculum peccatoris* ("Sinner's Mirror") to Saint Augustine. The author there declares that "Consideration of the brevity of life engenders contempt for the world" and then goes on to say:

Within the entire body of knowledge, is there anything that can increase man's vigilance, his flight from injustice, and his saintly behavior in the fear of God more than the realization of his [future] alteration, the precise knowledge of his mortal condition and the consequent thought of his horrible death, when man becomes a nonman? When a man falls ill, his illness feeds on itself, the heart vacillates, the head is paralyzed, the senses faint, strength is exhausted, the face pales, the complexion turns gray, the eyes cloud over, the ears become deaf, the nose rots, the tongue becomes heavy, the mouth falls silent, the body consumes itself and the flesh wastes away. Physical beauty then turns to stench and putrefication, man is reduced to ashes and transformed by worms.[47]

Certain manuscript editions of the *Speculum peccatoris* also feature a terse statement that was often quoted by other authors: "After man comes the worm. After the worm, stench and horror."

As might well be expected, the macabre descriptions that so frequently illustrate the *Vitae patrum* can be traced back to the Bible. The future Pope Innocent III dedicated a subsection of his *De Contemptu Mundi* to "the corruption of cadavers," where he proceeded to enlarge upon this theme by quoting heavily from the Scriptures: "Grubs and worms will have him as their legacy"[48] (Ecclus. 19:3); "Together now they lie in the dust with worms for covering" (Job 21:26); "The moth shall eat them like garments, the grub devour them like wool" (Isa. 51:8); "My life is crumbling like rotten wood, or a moth-eaten garment" (Job 13:28); "I tell the tomb, 'You are my father,' and call the worm my mother and my sister." (Job 17:14); "What, then, of man, maggot that he is, the son of man, a worm?" (Job 25:6).

This pedagogical insistence on the decomposition of the body—ostensibly aimed at inspiring the reader with contempt for the world—never weakened throughout the Middle Ages. The monk Andrew of Crete, who became archbishop of the island in the seventh century, advised his flock to meditate, as he did, in the vicinity of graves. To any person who might draw near he would say:

Do not run away . . . look upon this pitiful spectacle . . . Stay long enough to perceive these odors, which are not unfamiliar—they are ours. Manfully bear the stench that emanates from the decay, the evil vapors rising from the ooze. Stand fast before the wormy spectacle and the steaming putrification full of pus. You too are destined to be undone and become the food of devouring worms.[49]

In the early twelfth century, the Benedictine monk, Robert de Deutz (d. 1124), offered similar advice in his *Meditation on Death*: "Whoever you may be, go to the sepulchers of the dead . . . and they themselves will answer you. They will speak to your eyes until you have seen enough, and if they are recent bodies with a bit of sap still left in them, they will speak to your nostrils until you have smelled enough, and until you can stand it no longer."[50] A few decades later Adam Scotus (d. after 1210)—who was first a Premonstratensian, then a Carthusian, and finally the Bishop of Lincoln—addressed Saint John the Evangelist in the following words: "At the hour of my death, come to my aid, move the Judge to clemency, ward off the accusing demon. My fear stems from my sins, and not from any consideration of the future stench and putrefication of my body." "However," he then adds, "I am ashamed and I blush at the knowledge that my body is not even worthy of a fetid and ignoble grave. The infamy and the disgrace of my tomb will be far removed from the purity and the beauty of your sepulcher, for the stink of my horrible corpse will render my grave repulsive and swarming with worms, whereas your resting place will produce manna."[51] Another entry in the catalogue of monastic meditations on the corpse is provided by the *Speculum Monachorum* of Arnoul de Bohéries (end of the twelfth century), which was well known in the fourteenth and fifteenth centuries under the title *Speculum Bernardi*:

> *May the monk who finds life to be tedious [in the strongest sense of the word:* taedio affectus*] go and meditate on the stone upon which the dead are washed [in monasteries]. There he should imagine how those who are about to be buried are treated, how they are turned on their back, on their face, how their head wobbles, their arms dangle, their thighs stiffen, their legs splay out . . . how they are dressed again, and how they are sewn up, how they are taken away and placed in a grave, how they are covered with earth, and how they are slowly consumed by worms, like a rotten sack. The greatest philosophy consists in always thinking about death. If everyone carries this thought within him, wherever he may go, he will never sin.*[52]

Given the predominant images of the macabre theme, it is hardly surprising that the Jansenist Gerberon attributed a series of particularly gruesome questions to Saint Anselm, who had been one of the most enthusiastic promoters of *contemptus mundi*:

> *Speak, mortal flesh. Speak, worm, of decomposition. Wretched creature, why do you act so foolishly? What good is the glory of the flesh? Speak, man. Speak, dust. Decay, whence comes your pride? . . . Do you not know the law that rules the condition of man? The body comes from the earth, the seed comes from the body, blood comes from the seed, the body from blood. Just as man's body is formed in the womb, so will it rot in the bosom of the earth. The body engenders corruption, corruption engenders worms, worms create ashes, and ashes make earth. Thus the mother of the human body is the earth, and to the earth it shall return.*[53]

Saint Anselm did, however, write to Gunhild, the daughter of King Harold, when she had lost her lover, Alan the Red, and sought love once again in marriage with his brother:

> *You loved Count Alan the Red and he loved you. Where is he now? . . . Go lie down in the bed he now occupies, take his worms upon your breast, embrace his corpse, kiss his bare teeth, for his lips have been eaten away . . . Do you not fear that on account of you [God] will strike Count Alan the Black [brother of Alan*

the Red] with a similar death? Or, what is worse, that he abandon both of you, if you unite, to eternal death.[54]

The connection between monastic literature on the misery of man and the macabre is even more evident in a treatise incorrectly attributed to Saint Bernard: *Meditatio de humana conditione.*[55] Most probably written by Hugh of Saint-Victor,[56] this treatise was used by the future Innocent III when he composed his dark and gloomy diatribe against human pride. What is interesting for us, however, is the fact that it was once considered to be of such pertinence and of such pedagogic importance that for several centuries it was attributed to the founder of the Clairvaux order.[57] This treatise is best understood when compared with the earlier (or contemporary) texts cited above, for it provides a kind of key to the macabre sensibility that gradually spread out from monasteries to reach the secular world. The subtitle of this treatise ("After man, the worm. After the worm, stench and horror") gives the reader a foretaste of the text, which then goes on to outdo even the horrors promised on the title page:

> *According to the exterior man, I come from parents who made of me a condemned man* [damnatum] *before even I was born. Sinners begot a sinner in sin, and nourished him in sin. Wretches brought another wretch into the light of day. I received nought from them but misfortune, sin, and the corrupt body I wear. I hurry to those who have already departed through the death of their bodies. When I look at their graves, I see nothing but ashes and worms, stench and horror. That which I am now, they once were. What am I? A man born of a slimy humor, for at the moment of conception I was conceived out of a human seed. This foam then coagulated and, in growing, became flesh. After which I was thrown out into the exile of this world, wailing and crying. And here I am, already dying and filled with iniquity and abomination . . .*

Further on the author compares "the dignity of the soul" with "the baseness of the body," arguing his point in terms of the inherent corruption of the human condition:

> *This body, to which you are so closely attached, is nought but foam made flesh and covered with a flimsy garment. When it becomes a wretched and putrid corpse it will become food for worms . . . If you pay close attention to that which comes out of the mouth, the nostrils and the other apertures of the body, you will find no excrement more foul.*
>
> *Look, O man, at what you were before you were born, at what you are from birth to death, and at what you will be after this life . . . Formed out of foul matter, wrapped in base attire, you were nourished with menstrual blood in the maternal uterus, and your tunic was the second envelope . . .*[58]
>
> *Man is nought but fetid sperm, a bag of excrement, and food for worms . . .*
>
> *Why are you so proud, O man? Think rather that you were vile seed and coagulated blood in the womb. You were then exposed to the sorrows of this life and to sin, and in your grave you will provide pasture for worms. Should anyone boast of being dust and ashes, of having been conceived in sin, of having been born a wretch, of living in pain and of dying in anguish? . . . You spare no expense in fattening and ornamenting flesh which is soon destined to be devoured by worms in the grave.*[59]

On this theme, Lothair composed the following variation:

> *Man is conceived of blood corrupted by the heat of desire—the desire for death over which graveworms will preside. In life, he engenders lice and intestinal worms. In death, he will engender maggots and flies. In life, he produces dung and vomit. In death, he will produce stench and decay. In life, he fattens only himself. In death, he will feed a multitude of worms. What stinks more than the human corpse?*[60]

Both the "Meditation" attributed to Saint Bernard and the chapter on the corruption of corpses in Lothair's *De Contemptu Mundi* somewhat modify the conclusions drawn by Jean-Charles Payen in his article: "*Le 'Dies irae'* dans la prédication de la mort." Payen there affirms that "Death is present in all of the texts we have seen. Strangely enough, however, it generally appears in an almost negative light. It is never referred to directly . . . Nor is there any mention of the decomposition of the body—therefore, there is no macabre."[61] Yet a thirteenth-century German preacher used to recount the following apologue in order to convince his listeners of the need to confess each and every one of their sins: A woman once hid a severe fault from her confessor. An angel appeared to her, accompanied by a handsome child whose back was covered with worms and toads. The angel explained that her incomplete confession made her like this child.[62] Living on one side, she was already dead and rotting on the other . . . Bruno Roy has pointed out that, even before the fourteenth century, the theme of contempt for the world and macabre descriptions were by no means restricted to monastic circles. Above and beyond their frequent appearance in sermons, they were also used to teach grammar in schools. An entire chapter of Alain de Lille's *Summa de Arte Predicatoria* recommends the use of similar pedagogical devices and urges the reader to illustrate the biblical maxim "vanity of vanities, all is vanity" with a description of the terrors that haunt dying men and with reflections upon the theme *Ubi sunt?*[63]

I find it somewhat difficult to concur with Philippe Ariès, according to whom "The image of universal destruction dear to the Middle Ages before the fifteenth century . . . is dust and powder, and not the swarming corruption of worms."[64] This statement is definitely valid for the iconography of the early Middle Ages, but not for written documents, whose iconographic interpretation developed much later. Johan Huizinga was quite correct when he noted that, in the early Middle Ages, "Ascetics indulged in thoughts of ashes and worms. In religious treatises on contempt for the world they took great pleasure in describing the horrors of decomposition."[65] This observation was also quite valid in that the macabre was part and parcel of a number of popular and widely diffused works that highly resembled sermons. For example, M. Maccarone has shown that the success of Lothair's *De Contemptu Mundi* was hardly limited to the "macabre era." Out of 418 manuscripts, 34 percent date from the thirteenth century, 36.5 percent from the fourteenth (of which at least half from the first half of the century), and only 29.5 percent from the fifteenth century.[66] Furthermore, the text attributed to Saint Bernard shows that there was no contradiction in the monk's mind between worms and ashes, for both types of decomposition are there used for the same pedagogoical purposes. I really do not believe that the images skeletons and mummified bodies conjured up between the fourteenth and sixteenth centuries were in any way different from those of decaying corpses. All of these images contributed to a varied yet essentially homogeneous spectacle in the same horror-show. The writings of Bernard also draw the usual parallel between contempt for the world and a deep aversion to conception and gestation. The human seed is considered to be a foul fluid, which this monk (and Lothair after him) associates with excrement and other effluvia emanating from the body. Decay is within us. It is associated with carnal love and with death—two sides of the same coin—and will conquer us in the end. The decomposition of the body is a punishment (if it were not for sin Nature would never act that way). Similarly, the filth of the acts of conception and gestation constitute a punishment, as does the bloodied birth that casts us wretchedly upon the earth and condemns us to a lifelong exile.

One of the pet phrases of the monastic discourse on death and decay[67] was probably Arabic in origin: "That which I am now, they once were, and that which I shall be, they are now." This maxim appeared in both Peter Damian's funeral epitaph (1072)[68] and in Peter Alfonsi's *Disciplina Clericalis* (early twelveth century).[69] It was, in fact, sin that provided the link between the corruption of the flesh—living or dead—and the fear of the Judgment Seat that lurked at the close of every mortal's life. In the monastic version of the macabre, the fear of the *dies irae*, contempt for the world, and gruesome imagery (worms and ashes combined) joined together to create a coherent interpretation of life and death. In the *Meditatio* falsely attributed to Saint Bernard, for example, the author wails:

> *Woe is me, wretched creature that I am! When the Day of Judgment comes, the books in which all my acts and all my thoughts are written will be opened and presented to God. Then my head will hang in shame, burdened with my evil conscience, and I will stand before the Lord's Judgment, silent and distressed, remembering all of my misdeeds . . .*
>
> *Why do we so fiercely desire a life in which the longer we live, the longer we sin? The longer life is, the more numerous are our transgressions . . .*
>
> *It is all too true that the soul leaves the body in the midst of great fear and terrible pain. Angels come to fetch it, and bring it before the awesome Judge. Remembering the sins and misdeeds it has committed, both by night and by day, the soul trembles and wishes to escape. It requests a delay, saying: give me only one more hour . . . Demons with terrifying and horrible faces will terrorize it and chase it furiously, trying to catch it and hold it back—O terror and horror!—unless, of course, the soul is torn from their grasp . . .*[70]

Although the term "*dies irae*" was first made famous by the poet Thomas of Celano (d. 1250/60), it was not he who invented it. Long before Thomas, the wrath of God had haunted the guilty imagination of monks who read Zephaniah (1:15): "A day of wrath is that day! A day of distress and anguish, a day of ruin and devastation, a day of darkness and gloom, a day of clouds and thick darkness . . ." The Day of Judgment will judge not only the world in general but also each and every one of us. In quoting Zephaniah, Lothair heaps fuel on the fire and, after having equated physical filth with moral impurity, he whimpers at the thought of the day on which he will be brought to account: "The cruel day will come when, full of indignation, anger and rage, God will punish the earth, rendering it a desert and punishing all sinners."[71] Similarly Saint Bernard, who has also been accredited with a poem on the Last Judgment,[72] made use of a multitude of references to decomposition in order to convey the idea of sin (leprosy, impure discharges, devouring worms), and compared the sinner to the body of Lazarus, which smelled terrible after four days in the tomb.[73]

THE LONGEVITY OF THE MONASTIC CONCEPT OF DEATH

Having traced the progress of *contemptus mundi* from the monasteries to the wider reaches of the secular world, the long posterity engendered by this doctrine can be further demonstrated by a more specific investigation into the art and literature of subsequent centuries.

The ambivalence of the many manifestations of the macabre cannot be denied,[74] nor can one ignore the fact that, after 1350, its pedagogic and moral aspects were often neglected in favor of a morbid insistence on gruesome details. It seems that the traditional meaning of macabre imagery could even be reversed so that it constituted an invitation to enjoy life rather than the contrary. It would nevertheless be totally unjustified to discount the moral interpretation that was long associated with this theme, just as it would be a mistake to arbitrarily discount the influence of the medieval *contemptus mundi* on the concept of physical corruption current in the fifteenth and sixteenth centuries.

It was the considerable mass of literature on this theme that was doubtless responsible for the repulsive description of the (female) body as it appears in a poem composed at the beginning of the fifteenth century—*Der Ackermann aus Böhmen* (*The Plowman from Bohemia*)—where Death makes the following statement: the (female) body is "a repulsive object, a bag of filth, a foul food, a stinking sink, a repulsive bucket, a decaying carcass, a mildewed coffer, a threadbare sack, a pocket with a hole."[75] This description is practically identical to an earlier one, written in the tenth century by Odo of Cluny,[76] and it is also strikingly similar to the iconographic evocations of *Frau Welt* (Dame World), who is exquisitely beautiful in front and repulsively ugly behind. For the monastic world, woman could easily represent the ultimate in decay insofar as she incarnated a self-evident image of sin and death. As a matter of fact, antifeminism and the macabre were intimately linked, hence the importance of tracing the concept of death from the writings of the early Christian ascetics to the later manifestations of European culture as a whole.

A passage from Angelo Torini's book, *Brieve collezione della miseria della umana condizione*, illustrates one of the ways in which Lothair's *De Contemptu Mundi* was imitated and enlarged upon. Here the subject is one that was also exploited by the Pseudo Bernard: man's living body is already half rotten . . .

LOTHAIR (I, VIII, 1): *"Look at the grasses and the trees, they produce flowers, leaves and fruit, but all that you produce are nits, lice, and worms. The former give out oil, wine, and balm, but you, you exude saliva, urine, and dung. The former emanate pleasant odors, but you give off an abominable stench."*

TORINI (VXII, 17–19): *"What fruit do we bear? The pleasant and useful fruit that we produce and to which we give birth are nits, fleas, lice, and worms. These are created by our bodies and in our bodies, and they are continually born there. What aromatic spices and useful gums do we produce? The snot, spittle, and stool that continually exude from the different parts of our bodies. Which is why the blessed Bernard says: 'O man, if you stop to consider all which passes through and spills out of your mouth, nose, ears, and all the other orifices of your body, you will realize that there is no dung heap more foul.'"*[77]

The macabre poets of France contributed to the success of this theme while freely paraphrasing their sources. Eustache Deschamps's *Double lay de la fragilité humaine* (1383), for example, is a loose translation of Pope Innocent III's *De Contemptu Mundi*, which resumes the stereotyped comparison between plants and men, to the predictable detriment of the latter:

Shameful human condition,
Which always errs!

Trees bear fruit, flower and leaf:
You bear
Lice, worms, and nits.
Plants are laden with wine, oil, and balm:
You are laden with dung, urine, and spittle . . .[78]

A similar and equally unflattering comparison was made by Pierre de Nesson (1383–1440), Secretary to John I of Bourbon, who earned a nickname for himself as "the poet of death." In a versified paraphrase of the Book of Job, he wrote:

Alas! When the trees are in bloom
Beautiful and sweet-smelling flowers appear
And savory fruit, which can be eaten.
But you produce nought but filth,
Mucus, spittle, and decay,
Tainted and stinking excrement![79]

Such graphic disgust reappears elsewhere in the same poem:

Beware of natural lures
No matter how beautiful people may be
Nor how clean they may keep themselves,
You will see that each and every one of them
Passes stinking matter, continuously
Produced by the body.[80]

French poetry of this period also made a point of echoing the monastic aversion to conception, gestation, and birth. After all, what are we fed with when we are in the womb? According to Eustache Deschamps:

It is horribly bitter,
It is tainted blood,
Menstrual flow it is called,
Which then ceases to pour
From the mother.
It is well known that grass withers
That trees are confounded
And dogs go mad
At the mere touch of such matter.[81]

Insofar as this poem only confirms the female mysteries in order to better reject them, it communicates the eternal masculine aversion for menstrual blood, the age-old accusation of impurity and danger that has long been leveled against the female flow with all its attendant fears and taboos.[82]

Deschamps and Nesson insist on the "horror of birth" in much the same spirit as the Pseudo Bernard. Deschamps declares that, on that occasion, our flesh is "afficted with a filthy skin and sullied by blood . . ."[83] Likewise Nesson, having discussed "the great filth of conception," goes on to describe its end result:

You come out through a dirty and stinking passage,
Horribly enclosed
In a bloody envelope

Where a foul gut, full of filthy
Menses, is then cut . . .[84]

Having examined various monastic texts on the decomposition of the body, it hardly comes as a surprise when equally macabre and nauseating descriptions turn up in French poetry of the fourteenth and fifteenth centuries. In this respect at least, late medieval French poetry is a direct descendant of the monastic tradition. Eustache Deschamps, for example, commented on the biblical quotations used by the future Pope Innocent III in his description of a corpse:

You will have neither foot, member nor ear
Which is not contracted and distorted
You will be more hideous than a bear
Your resting place will be the earth
Worms will devour your entrails.[85]

Pierre de Nesson, who was well acquainted with Cardinal Lothair's *De Contemptu Mundi*, had a particular fondness for dead bodies. Faithful to his predecessor, he describes man in terms of "stinking decay"[86] and as a "bag of filth."[87] He also points out that "From the very day you die / Your filthy flesh will begin / To release a pungent stench."[88] Lothair was also paraphrased by another poet, Jean Meschinot (1420–1491), author of the *Lunettes des princes*. Having reminded his readers, as did most authors of his time, that all of the "passages" of the living body "expel horrors," Meschinot then goes on to describe the condition of the body after death:

When your stinking carcass is dead
Try to find someone to anoint your flesh
With sweet balm:
No one will do it, for the heart
Cannot bear to smell
Such an odor, nor can it accept it[89]

No matter how bizarre they might seem to us today, repulsive descriptions of this type constituted neither gratuitous games nor ghastly affirmations of the absurdity of life. All such poems were supposed to fulfill certain pedagogic functions and were generally considered to be quite edifying. Nesson's book was called the *Vigiles des morts*. It consisted of a series of prayers and an "Office for the Dead," which was supposed to inspire the reader with a desire for repentance rather than with despair: "So do well in your life / You who live, do not wait . . ."[90]

Following in the footsteps of their monastic predecessors, many fifteenth-century laymen composed veritable sermons on the decomposition of the body, using the "thou" or "you" characteristic of contemporary preachers.[91] An example of this is the *Pas de la mort* (*pas* here meaning "passage") written by Georges Chastellain (1405–1475), poet laureate of the dukes of Burgundy. The premature death of his beloved lady caused him to turn his initial horror of decay into a focus on Christian meditation.[92] In this case it was a personal tragedy that, once again, prompted the *contemptus mundi*:

Look at what doleful death does . . .
And the vile and filthy body
Which you will lose forever;

It will provide a foul-smelling meal
For the earth and its vermin.[93]

In this poem (as well as in the *Ballades de moralité* written by the same author), there appear "graves full of sorrow" and the "stinking decay"[94] of a body that will soon be reduced to "dung."[95] It is therefore only logical that "It is great folly to adorn that which will become food for worms,"[96] and that "[once you are dead] you will have no goods other than / Your grave and your shroud / And vermin to eat you."[97] Monastic themes thus appear over and over again in the products of an elitist culture where the Book of Job, Ecclesiastes, and their commentators were widely read. "Wherefore," exclaims Georges Chastellain, echoing Job, "were you of woman born / If only to die so dolefully?"[98]

Insofar as the entire elite of that time was familiar with the themes and variations of *contemptus mundi* and used them continually, it is hardly surprising that the *Ubi sunt?* motif can be found at practically every turn. Although this lugubrious question can be traced back to pagan antiquity,[99] Etienne Gilson has pointed out that medieval literature was solely inspired by its biblical renditions (Isa. 33, Bar. 3:16–19, St. Paul, I Cor. 1:19–20),[100] often as interpreted by Saint Augustine, by Prosper of Aquitaine (d. ca. 460),[101] and by Isidore of Seville (d. 636).[102] In later years this question was posed by authors such as Alain de Lille[103] and Saint Bonaventure,[104] and by a great number of preachers. It even appears in the *Imitation of Christ* and in Denis the Carthusian's *De Quatuor Hominis Novissimis*. Gilson has shown that, on the whole, European poetry of the thirteenth to fifteenth centuries (Italian, English, Irish, German, and Slavic) took up the refrain, which appears especially frequently in French poetry of this period. Eustache Deschamps uses it in four ballads (LXXIX, CCCXXX, CCCLXVIII, MCLXXV, MCCCLVII),[105] all of which feature the stereotyped list of famous figures from the past:

What has happened to David and to Solomon? . . .
King Arthur, Godfrey, Charlemagne? . . .
Where has stout-hearted Lancelot gone? . . .
Where is he who conquered Aragon? . . .
They are all dead. This world is a vain thing.
(Ballad CCCLVIII)

And elsewhere:

Alas! Where are the virtuous princes of old
Who conquered the earth . . .
David, Hector, Charlemagne, and Roland?
They are all dead. Go open their graves:
You will find dust there, for we all rot away.
(Ballad MCLXXV)

François Villon's *Grand Testament* is also heavily influenced by *contemptus mundi*, at least from the twelfth stanza on. Villon knew his Bible well and was acutely conscious of being a "lowly sinner," whence the references to Job and Ecclesiastes and the ever-present question *Ubi sunt?* which is here enriched with several new elements and unusual references to women.

Where are the gracious gallants
Whom I once followed,

Who sang so well, and spoke so well,
Who were so lovely in both words and deeds?
Some of them are dead and stiff,
Nothing is left of them now.[106] *(Stanza 29)*

Tell me where, in what country
Lives Flora, the beautiful Roman,
Archipiades and Thais
Her first cousin;
Echo . . .
Whose beauty was more than human?

Where is the wise Heloise . . .
The Queen who was white as a lily
Who sang with the voice of a siren . . .
Where are the snows of yesteryear?[107]
(Ballade des dames du temps jadis)

During his imprisonment the poet Jean Régnier (1390–1468) wrote another, somewhat more conservative version of *Ubi sunt?*: "Where is Arthur, where Hector of Troy? / Where are the valiant knights who cried Mountjoy?"[108]

The history of mentalities would do well to note the constant repetition of this theme, for neither authors nor readers ever tired of repeating the same obsessive truth. In Georges Chastellain's *Pas de la mort*, eight stanzas out of ninety-three confront the eternal question: "Where are they?"[109] Moreover, his *Passage of Death* is really much more a "Mirror of Death" (probably its true title) insofar as it belongs to a body of moralizing literature that centered on this word (*Spécule des pécheurs*, *Mirouer des pecheurs et pecheresses*, and so on).[110] All of these texts aimed at presenting man with a kind of mirror in which he might see the image of his body after death. As Jean Meschinot wrote in his *Lunettes*:

Prince . . .
Look at this vile image
Which lies upside down, so ugly!
Like this, you will be . . .[111]

Thus was the monastic discourse relayed and passed on via sermons and moralizing literature aimed at the general public. In particular, the question *Ubi sunt?* was well adapted to poetry and preaching: "Let us reflect on the world and its ways then / Let us reflect on our weakness / Let us reflect on ourselves that we may be saved."[112]

The withered and decomposing corpses that appeared in European art between the end of the fourteenth century and the end of the sixteenth also contributed to the spread of the same moral message. Particularly frequent in France, England, and the Germanic countries, these half-decayed bodies were portrayed with a ghoulish attention to detail. The cadaver depicted by François de la Sarraz, for example, is being devoured by toads that find the eyes, mouth, and genitals particularly appetizing (ca. 1390, near Lausanne).[113] The half-naked figure that represents Dr. Guillaume de Harcigny (d. 1393) in the Episcopalian Chapel of Laon is partially mummified and partially stripped to the bone, its modesty preserved by a skeletal hand covering its private parts.[114] The recumbent body of Cardinal Lagrange (d. 1402) is quite similar to that of the doctor. In addition to the visual meaning it conveys, it also bears a written inscription: "Wretched man, what reason have you to be proud? You are nought but ashes, and you will soon be like me, a foul corpse, food for worms."[115] The tomb of William II of Hesse (d. 1509), which lies in the church of St. Elisabeth at Marburg, shows its occupant in the process of being consumed by worms. Equally horrible are the reclining figures of Louis XII and Anne of Brittany at St. Denis. Emile Mâle wrote a colorful and accurate description of the king's body as it is depicted on the lower level of his tomb: "naked and hollow cheeked, his nose is pinched, his mouth open, his belly slit by the embalmer. His body is already horrifying and will soon be hideous, as gruesome as that of a dead beggar."[116] As late as the second half of the sixteenth century a number of artists applied the style and techniques of the Renaissance to the well-established tradition of detailed representions of the dead. The unfinished figure of Catherine de Medici, fashioned by Girolamo della Robbia in 1566, now lies in the Louvre[117] where a postmortem representation of Valentina Balbiani can also be found. Valentina's body was admirably rendered by Germain Pilon (between 1572 and 1584), who managed to suggest the emaciation of the corpse by subtly intermingling the strands of her hair with the folds of her shroud.[118]

From a statistical point of view, the presence of the macabre in the art of the past actually contradicts the current conception of the Renaissance. In fact, out of 264 tombs depicting some sort of corpse (some still exist today and some are only known to have existed), it is surprising to find that only 5 of these can be traced to the fourteenth century, whereas the fifteenth century accounts for 75 of them and the sixteenth century for no less than 155. The seventeenth century, on the other hand, shows a definite slacking off, as only 29 of such tombs are to be found.[119] Even more widespread are the *momento mori* to be found in churches, in prayer books, and on clocks of the fourteenth to sixteenth centuries. How many private houses, how many coats of arms, how many fireplaces in taverns and manor houses bore images or inscriptions relating to death? Once it crossed the threshold of the monastic world, the concept of *contemptus mundi* invaded the entire culture.

One of the more important aspects of *contemptus mundi* was, of course, fear of judgment (the Last Judgment or individual judgment), and as such it appears in all of the poems cited hitherto. Having paid homage to the theme *Ubi sunt?* in his *Fortunes et adversitez* . . . , Jean Regnier goes on to beg the Virgin to intercede for him: "On that great day, I humbly beseech you then / To help me, that I need not declare null / The sum total of my account before God."[120] Eustache Deschamps's description of the Last Day is even more terrifying. Although his *Double lay de la fragilité humaine* is, on the whole, quite mediocre, his poetic talent rises to the occasion when he describes the *dies irae* and the torments of Hell—where the damned "scream like madmen":

Who can escape the wrath
Of that great day, or endure
The perilous judgment
When the sky, the earth, and the sea
Will sear and burn together? . . .

Then [the damned] will suffer great pain
Great stench
And great tears
And they will clench their teeth
And suffer anguish and sadness
And great trembling
And heat
And many groans,

Wails
Hunger, thirst, and all kinds of languor . . .
Vermin and serpents shall assail them,
All torments
Will dwell with them
And ne'er depart again.
In fear
Will come God's judgment.[121]

In his *Pas de la Mort*, the "rhétoriqueur" Vaillant paraphrased a hymn by Thomas of Celano ("Well then, what will the sinner do / When that terrible day comes? . . .).[122] Far from restricting himself to a simple elaboration of his source of inspiration, Vaillant composed a curious poem full of wordplay and bizarre twists. Thus does the *Cornerie des anges* render the Judgment Day:

When the four angels sound their horns
Dolefully
He who is not sound
Will tremble, if he has no horn . . .
Let us pray God that each horn
Will sound the VII virtues that God proclaims
So loudly that we hear not the horn
Of Hell, where no good body rests . . .[123]

Earthly riches will be of no use to us on the day in which we will be brought to account—a prospect that obsesses the *contemptus mundi* enthusiasts, who lose no opportunity in expounding upon this basic truth. As Jean Meschinot pointed out: "What good will your riches and your possessions do you / Your great beauty, your friends, your knowledge / When you come up for judgment before God?"[124] Hence Jean Molinet begs the saints of Paradise to use their influence and plead on his behalf when he appears before the Throne:

[The throne of] the King who patronizes kings
Who reaps the good reapers
Who cudgels those who cudgel
Who gives to those who give[125]

All of these poems are really sermons in verse form, as can be seen in the dialogue between Death and the Man of the World, which concludes the *Lunettes des princes*:

Death	Man of the World
You will die	*When?*
Soon	*How cruel, alas!* *Where shall I go?*
You will rot away	*I need advice*
Go and confess yourself *I know nothing better.*[126]	

Seen in this light, meditation on death necessarily led to self-examination—another key theme in the monastic vision of life that had spread far beyond convent walls. Hence the accusatory tone of verses such as those by Georges Chastellain, in which the poet assumes the role of preacher:

> *For you then, human creature,*
> *It is time for you to tremble . . .*
> *Doubt not that you must die . . .*
> *Doubt not the Day of Judgment.*[127]

It is hardly possible to speak of "familiarity with death" when it obviously inspires such terror. Although the church insisted that man think continually about death, it certainly did not want him to become accustomed to the idea. Furthermore, it was unthinkable that man should get so used to the presence of death that it could pass by unheeded. In the eyes of the church, death was not supposed to be (or should no longer be) "tame." On the contrary, it was a perilous passage that could be safely undertaken only at the price of a lifetime of vigilance. Death must engender fear, and any means were useful to that end—be they evocations of ashes, decay and agony, the trumpets of the Judgment Day, or visions of Hell—so long as they prevented that fear from diminishing.[128]

DEATH AND CONVERSION

The Christian concept of death is inseparable from the idea of the ultimate goals of life (known as the *novissima* in Latin), for which the desert fathers are once again responsible. It was they who conceptualized the chronological progression: "death, judgment, Hell (or Paradise)."[129] It was also they who recommended meditation on death as a fitting preparation for eternity: thus their advice was indissolubly linked with the *contemptus mundi* philosophy. At Tabennisi, on the Nile, Saint Pachomius (d. 348) gave his monks the following advice: "Above all, let us always keep our last day before our eyes and let us always fear everlasting torment."[130] Saint Ephrem (d. 379), another monk from the East, was said to have given similar advice: "He often reminded his listeners of death and judgment."[131] When Saint Basil (d. 379) returned from Egypt, where he had gone to seek wisdom among the monks, an intellectual asked him "What is the definition of philosophy?" to which he answered, like Plato, "The first definition of philosophy is meditation on death."[132] On another occasion (in the course of a debate with two philosophers), Saint Basil exclaimed: "May your philosophy be to always think about death!"[133] Saint Macarius the Elder (d. 390) also urged reflection on the ultimate end of life. In his third degree of ascension toward God, he suggested that man should always keep the day of his death in mind and remember that he must appear before God someday and be judged—as well as remembering all of the torments reserved for sinners and the honors due to saints.[134] An equally imperative invitation to meditation on the afterlife appears in an exhortation composed by Evagrius (d. 399) and addressed to each of his monks:

> *When you sit in your cell, compose yourself and think about the day of your death . . . May the vanity of this world inspire you with horror . . . Think also about those who are in Hell . . . And yet again about the Day of Resurrection; try to imagine the divine, the terrible Judgment . . . Moan when you think about the punishments reserved for sinners, cry at the thought of their tears, and fear to share their ruin. Rejoice, however, at the thought of the rewards promised to the Just.*

Rejoice, exult and be glad . . . May your mind never lose sight of these things, if only to avoid all evil thoughts.[135]

Saint Augustine, who was profoundly influenced by monastic life and imposed both poverty and communal life on his followers, proffered similar advice: "God shows his great mercy in that he keeps us in ignorance of the day of our death. As you then think that you might die any day, you hasten to convert yourself."[136]

These texts testify to the tradition of *quotidie morior*, a doctrine that was initially practiced, and later taught, by the monasteries it originated in. According to this tradition, all of life should be a preparation for death. The fourth chapter of Saint Benedict's (d. 543) rule, for example, contains the following instructions: "Dread the Day of Judgment, fear Hell, desire eternal life with entirely spiritual ardour, keep the possibility of death ever before your eyes."[137] In the same vein, the sixth step of the "Ladder to Heaven" of Saint John Climacus (d. 600) contains two illuminating comparisons: "Just as bread is the most necessary of all foods, so meditation on death is the most important of all actions" and "Just as it is generally said that a vortex is deep water which cannot be sounded, for which reason it bears that name, so also does the thought of death produce in us unfathomable depths of purity and good works."[138]

Cistercian spirituality also adopted the concept of meditation on the end of earthly life and, although Saint Bernard did not attach prime importance to that subject, his successors tended to magnify the import of a few words uttered in the course of a sermon to his monks:

What are the ultimate ends of life? It is said that if you think about them, you will sin no more. They are death, judgment and Gehenna. What is more horrible than death? What more terrible than judgment? Can you conceive of anything more unbearable than Gehenna? What are you frightened of, if you do not tremble before this, if you are not terrified out of your wits, if you are not shaken by fear?[139]

Given the anguish that underlies such questions, it would seem that the transformation of the natural fear of death into a religious fear of judgment far antedates the fifteenth century (or even the seventeenth century), which is usually considered to be the turning point. As a matter of fact, monastic culture had achieved this transition long before, the final outcome of life being one of the spiritual exercises practiced by the Cistercian order. A *De vita eremitica* attributed to the Cistercian Aelred of Rievaulx (d. 1166) features some thirty chapters (47–77) on the subject of the past and the blessings of God, the present and the misery of man, the future and its companions: death, the Last Judgment and eternity . . . be it blessed or damned.[140]

The appearance of mendicant orders primarily devoted to preaching also helped spread the notion of *cogitatio mortis* to a wider segment of the population. In his *Second Letter to the Faithful* Saint Francis of Assisi wrote:

. . . Everyone should know that, no matter where or how a man dies, in mortal sin and without atonement (that is, if he could have atoned but did not), the devil will wrest his soul from his body and he will suffer such terrible agony and tribulation that no one can possibly imagine what it is like unless he himself has suffered so . . . Worms will eat his body and his soul in this brief sojourn on earth, and he will go to Hell where he will suffer torment without end.[141]

This advice shows up again in the Rule of 1223, in a paragraph on preaching: ". . . I exhort . . . my brothers . . .: to use chaste and well-chosen words in their sermons for the use and for the edification of the people—explaining vice and virtue, suffering and glory—and to be brief in their speech."[142] Like Saint Francis, Saint Bonaventure wrote a veritable apology for *contemptus mundi* in his *Soliloquium*. After discussing the wretchedness of the world, Bonaventure urges the soul to turn "toward lower realities, that it might understand the inevitable necessity of human death, the fearful equity of the Last Judgment and the intolerable harshness of infernal punishment."[143] The last chapter, however, manages to shift the reader's gaze toward the "joys of Heaven."

Alberto Tenenti has pointed out the important contribution made by the Dominican mystic, Heinrich Suso (1296–1366), to the long prehistory of the *Artes moriendi*.[144] Suso's *Little Book of Eternal Wisdom* (*Das Büchlein der ewigen Weisheit*) and his *Horologium sapientiae* (often considered to be a free translation of the former) both insist on the necessity of learning how to die and on the tragic end of any person who dies without adequate preparation. Thus, enlightened by the bedside spectacle of the death agony and by images of Hell and Purgatory, Wisdom's "servant" exclaims: "Oh! Lord . . . How frightened I am! I never realized that death was so close to me . . . I will look out for death every day, and I will look about me so that it cannot surprise me from behind. I want to learn to die, I want to turn my thoughts toward the other world. Lord, I see that my resting place is not here below."[145]

Tenenti has also pointed out that "the expression *scientia*, or *doctrina moriendi*, is not to be found before Suso."[146] Furthermore, it is revealing to note that chapter 21 of the *Little Book of Eternal Wisdom* (which features the passage quoted above) was often published as an *Ars Moriendi* (*Sterbebüchlein*) in the late fifteenth and early sixteenth centuries,[147] which in itself accounts for the far-reaching influence of this German Dominican on the subject of preparation for death. Later developments gave equal opportunity to both Dominicans and Franciscans to ensure the success of the *danse macabre*.[148] Both orders preached on the same goals in life, and both for the same pastoral reasons. A (Latin) sermon on "fourfold death" delivered by the Dominican missionary Saint Vincent Ferrer defines it as follows: the first type of death is spiritual (= sin) and must be fled; the second is physical death, against which certain precautions must be taken; the third is infernal death, which must be avoided; and the fourth is eternal death (= judgment and sentence), which is to be greatly feared.[149] Although the logic of this sequence leaves something to be desired, another Dominican, Johann Nider (d. 1438)—author of a famous work on demonology, the *Formicarius*—did a somewhat better job in his *Dispositorium moriendi*, where reflections on the ultimate goals of life are discussed in terms of the heavy scholastic structures of his time.[150] As for the Franciscan preacher San Bernardino di Siena (d. 1444), his sermon on the *Quatuor novissima* is followed by a homily on death, another on Judgment, a third on Hell, and two more on the misery of the human condition.[151]

The *Devotio Moderna* also made a substantial contribution to the techniques of meditation on death. According to Father Bourdeau, "this Northern school, which favored both methodical and emotional prayer, seems to have systematized meditation on the end of life."[152] In fact the *Fascicularius*—long attributed to Saint Bonaventure (a significant error) but actually written by Gerard of Zutphen (d. 1398)—includes a sequence of reflections upon death, Judgment, and Hell.[153] Similarly, in the *Imitation of Christ* all monks and Christians who wish "to make some progress" are invited to meditate upon the wretchedness of humanity, death, judgment, Hell, and Heaven.[154] Following in the wake of the *Imitation*, a Carthusian monk from the Netherlands, Denis of Rychel (d. 1471), wrote some two hundred works on mystical theology, including a *De Quatuor hominis novissimis*. This *De*

Quatuor inspired in turn a host of similar works, notably John Mombaer's *Rosetum*, written at the end of the fifteenth century. The thirty-fifth article of the *Rosetum* is a *Prologus generalis in quatuor novissima*, where the following resolution can be found: "I carefully carry these four considerations in my heart: my death, judgment, the black abyss, and bright paradise."[155] In the edition of 1503 no less than forty-five pages of commentary and development follow this statement. Finally, it was thanks to Garcia Cisneros's *Exercitatorio de la vida spiritual* (1510) that the type of meditation on death dear to the *Devotio Moderna* reached Saint Ignatius of Loyola, who then spread it far afield in his *Spiritual Exercises*.[156]

Gerson, however, had already been influenced by this current of thought at the beginning of the fifteenth century. The third part of his *Opusculum tripartitum* provided one of the primary sources for the *Ars moriendi*, which became successful after 1450. Another major source was the *Cordiale quatuor novissimorum*. Although this text was long attributed to Cardinal Capranica, it was most probably written in southern Germany at the time of the Council of Constance, drawing heavily upon Gerson's treatise. The author might have been a Dominican from Constance, which would mean that the initial circulation of the *Cordiale* would have reached two important circles: the fathers attending the council and the wide network of Dominican monasteries.[157] If this hypothesis is correct, both the *Devotio Moderna* and the Order of the Friars Preachers would have played a decisive role in launching the *Ars moriendi*.

Thanks to Roger Chartier, the astounding career of this "best-seller" can be traced through its multiple permutations.[158] As a "veritable crystallization" of Christian death (insofar as it considered itself to be a "technique" or "method" for ensuring a good death), the *Ars moriendi* originally appeared in two versions of differing lengths. The long version comprised six parts: advice on how to die well, the temptations of one's dying moments, what questions to ask a dying person, the prayers he or she should say, how the other people should behave, and the prayers that they should say. Most manuscripts and the majority of printed editions follow this version. The shorter version, on the other hand, sandwiches the temptations of the dying moments between an introduction and a conclusion. This version was the one used for the xylographic editions and for a small number of typographic editions.

The *Ars moriendi* were already quite successful in manuscript form. A search based on library catalogues turned up 234 volumes: 126 in Latin, 75 in German, 11 in English, 10 in French, 9 in Italian, 1 in Provençal, 1 in Catalan, and 1 in an unspecified language. Given the number of manuscripts that have survived, the *Ars moriendi* rates high after the Bible, of course, and after the *Imitation of Christ* (700 manuscripts), the *De Regimine principum* by Giles of Rome (about 300 manuscripts), and the *Roman de la Rose* (about 250). Yet the success of the *Ars moriendi* was largely due to the eleven woodcuts illustrating the shorter edition. These engravings showed the five temptations (infidelity, despair, impatience, vainglory, and greed) that, gathered around the bed of the dying person, were about to be chased away by five angelical "inspirations." From what we know today, it would seem that the *Ars moriendi* was the most widespread of all the block books (it comprises 15 percent of the thirty-three xylographic publications known today), and it is certain that the impact of these works was further strengthened by the number of similar prints that people stuck in coffers or on walls. One of Jerome Bosch's engravings—the "Death of the Miser"—is but a variation on the temptation of greed in the *Artes moriendi*.[159]

The invention of printing further expanded the influence of the *Ars moriendi* and served to acquaint the public at large with older works (such as Suso's *Horolo-*

gium . . . , Gerson's *Opus tripartitum*, and the *Cordiale* . . . *novissimorum*) that aimed at drawing the attention of the faithful to the issues of death and judgment. Sister O'Connor has found 77 incunabula editions of the *Ars moriendi*,[160] a number that is no doubt far less than the original count[161]: 51 in the long version and 26 in the short version, 42 in the vulgar tongue (which means they were destined for a lay audience), and 35 in Latin. The geographic distribution of incunabula production centers is also very similar to that of the contemporaneous *dance macabre*[162]: Paris (17 editions), northern Italy (14), southern Germany and the Rhineland (14), Leipzig (9), and the Netherlands (6). These 77 editions (or 97, according to Tenenti) meant some 50,000 copies in circulation (or 63,000, in the second hypothesis). These numbers are by no means as modest as they might appear by today's standards. If one takes into consideration the fact that no less than 85 incunabula editions of the *Imitation of Christ* have also been identified,[163] it becomes evident that these two works were more or less equally important in the second half of the fifteenth century. Of course it is true that the *Ars moriendi* (and therefore also the *Imitation of Christ* represented only 0.5 to 2 percent of the religious literature of that time, which seems relatively little. Nonetheless, this percentage increases to 3 or 4 percent as soon as it is grouped with other works dealing with the subject of preparation for death: the *Miroir de la mort* by Georges Chastellain, the *Pas de la mort* by Aimé de Montgesoye, the *Dictier pour penser à la mort* by Jean Molinier, the *Mirouer des pécheurs et pécheresses* by Jean Castel, the *Lunettes des princes* by Jean Meschinot, the *Complainte de l'âme damnée* by an anonymous author, and so on.[164] Tenenti has pointed out that the *Cordiale* . . . , which was first printed at Speyer in 1471, underwent forty-five further editions in Latin before 1500 and an equal number of translations. One of the primary reasons for this book's success was the striking iconography of its macabre illustrations.[165] Roger Chartier has observed that the *Ars moriendi* (and similar publications of the fifteenth century) can therefore be considered to have been "a major weapon for mass pedagogy,"[166] with the reservation that the most extensive distribution of works on "preparation for death" came later (in the seventeenth century). Furthermore, the impact of these books was substantially reinforced by preaching, which often discussed the same themes. In this respect Geilier's career is quite illuminating. Upon arrival in Strasbourg in 1478, Geilier delivered a series of sermons on the "art of dying." Shortly thereafter he translated into German and published in popular pamphlet form the last part of Gerson's *Opus tripartitum*, which addresses the exact same subject.[167]

Alberto Tenenti and Roger Chartier have both shown that, from 1530 to the end of the sixteenth century, the number of editions of *Artes moriendi* and other literature on "preparation for death" considerably diminished, especially in France. On the other hand, the Christian discourse on death had diversified noticeably. As these two authors have also pointed out, there are five Paris editions of the *Ars moriendi* for the years 1501 to 1510 but only four between 1511 and 1600. Moreover, out of the 15,000 editions published in Lyons during the sixteenth century, only two deal with the *Ars moriendi*. Bordeaux put out 711 editions in this same period, but not one "preparation for death." England also seems to have lost any interest in the art of dying: Only four editions are to be found, the last two having appeared in 1506. Northern and eastern Europe were a trifle more intrigued by this subject: five editions appeared in Sweden and Denmark between 1533 and 1580, and five anti-Protestant versions were printed in Dillingen (Bavaria) between 1569 and 1603. All of this is negligible, however, when compared with the two hundred editions of the *Imitation of Christ*.

It is nevertheless true that several works on "preparation for death" adopted a new style—a good death can be best prepared for by living a good life—and encountered considerable success. Josse van Clichtove's treatise, *De Doctrina moriendi . . . ad mortem foelicieter appetendam . . .* , was one of the most widely read, having been published eleven times in Latin (Paris and Antwerp) between 1520 and 1546 and translated into French in 1533. Erasmus's *De Praeparatione ad mortem* (1534) was even more successful, having appeared in fifty-nine Latin and vernacular editions in the second third of the sixteenth century, after which this work—written by a "blacklisted" author—would, quite naturally, have been rarely published. "Over and above these two classics, the inventory of publications on the 'art of dying' in sixteenth-century France and England features a limited number of titles."[168] Between Protestant meditations and Catholic directives, only a dozen titles appear in each country. In England, a treatise written by an Erasmian layman, Lupset (1534), underwent five editions in ten years.[169] In 1561 there appeared another treatise written by a Calvinist, Thomas Becon, which was republished eleven times in the sixteenth century and seven times in the first third of the seventeenth century.[170] In Catholic territory, the Jesuit production on death began to make itself felt with Father Juan Polanco's widely imitated booklet, *Method for Helping the Dying* (first Latin edition 1575),[171] and with Bellarmine's *De Arte bene moriendi* (1620). A total of 20 Jesuit titles on death appeared between 1540 and 1620, as opposed to 139 titles between 1621 and 1700, and 101 from 1701 to 1800.[172] This in itself confirms the comparatively slight production of the sixteenth century.

The diversification of the Christian discourse on death merits a more detailed examination for a variety of reasons, one of which is the fact that the particular emphasis of the *Ars moriendi* on the dying moments remained strong throughout the sixteenth century. A good example of this is provided by a well-known book —the *Agonia del transito de la muerte* (published in 1537 and at least five more times before 1575)—written by a Spanish layman, Alejo Venegas. After stating that the life of a Christian is "a long martyrdom ending in death,"[173] Venegas advises the reader to prepare himself well ahead of time for the "fearful and perilous passage."[174] He then observes that "agony" also means "struggle," not only because the unsuitable combination of elements that make up the body then release their conflicting components, but also because at that moment man enters into the greatest battle of his entire life—a "spiritual" battle that comprises so much "anxiety" and even "anguish" that "all of life's past afflictions are easier to bear than this one passage."[175] An intriguing analysis then follows, describing the tactics adopted by the Devil at the moment in which a stricken person is no longer defended by his five senses. It is then that the dying are most vulnerable:

"Before the five senses are lost, and no matter how tired an ill person may be, the Devil cannot attack in the same way as he will during the death agony when the use of the senses has vanished." Then, "the Devil sees that the patient is approaching radical dampness [death] and that little time is left to win him over." The Demon then recognizes that the agonizing person "is stripped of those instruments—the five senses—with which he might defend himself. For he well knows that these instruments were given to mankind in order that, with their aid, humanity might vanquish the Devil and win [Heavenly] Glory by submitting all of the senses to reason, and then subjecting both to faith." Which is why "the Devil attacks most strongly when he sees that life is ending and that the patient is least capable of resisting his artifices and his secret weapons.[176]

Everything hinges therefore on the moment on which the dying person seems to be totally defenseless and is yet more capable of sinning than ever before.

Venegas, by the way, cannot even conceive of extenuating circumstances according to which an individual on the point of passing away might be partially excused for giving in to temptation. As far as he is concerned, "the Devil would never tempt a man in the hour of his death if he did not think he could get him to sin once more, and then worse than all the other times he had caused him to sin in the course of his life . . . [He would never would do this] if he knew that the patient had already been sentenced and were incapable of sin once he had begun the death struggle." On the contrary, he would give up and go play his tricks elsewhere. But this is far from being the case: "The soul is not deprived of judgment and reason just because the five senses are out of order." In this ultimate moment, "the soul is more alive and more concentrated than at any other moment in its past life."[177] To add to the drama of the situation, Venegas believes that this battle takes place after the patient's will has been drawn up, and after he has made his confession and received the Last Sacrament[178]—as if these three remedies were totally incapable of protecting anybody against the Evil One. In the rest of his book, the author enumerates the temptations presented to the dying. There he enlarges upon the model provided by the *Artes moriendi*, increasing the list of classic temptations with solicitations proper to certain areas, to certain professions, to friends and family, and to the individual's own personality.[179]

Like many of the experts on death who lived at that time, Venegas believed that demons appeared to the dying in the course of horrible visions.[180] In this he concurs with Savanarola (*Predica dell'arte del bene morire*, 1496) and Raulin (*Doctrinale mortis*, 1518) in thinking that man is like a chessplayer, who can lose everything if he makes but one mistake at the end of the game.[181] This comparison helps us to understand the extreme importance given, in works on the art of dying, to the choice of a friend designated to help the dying person and to encourage him with wise advice and pious exhortations. It also helps explain the increasing importance attributed to the Last Sacrament (despite what Venegas thought) in that it instilled a feeling of security at the approach of death. Finally, the "chessplayer" concept is doubtless partially responsible for the multiplication of certain confraternities, in the course of the sixteenth century, that volunteered to pray for the dying and to sustain those condemned to death.

The conviction that the moment of death is the decisive "point" on which all the rest of eternity hinges was maintained throughout the age of humanism. Pietro da Lucca (*Dottrina del ben morire*, 1540) described man's end as "terrifying," and Erasmus himself had recourse to the traditional formula in the beginning of his *De Praeparatione ad mortem*: "Man's eternal happiness or eternal misery depends on this last act of our life, which can be compared to a drama. There the supreme combat takes place, when the Christian Soldier will gain eternal triumph, if he wins, or eternal dishonor, if he loses."[182] Death is a "catastrophe" in the strictest sense of the word—that is to say, a decisive event that determines the outcome of the individual's personal history. Montaigne expresses a similar point of view when he describes man's last day on earth: "It is the supreme day, the day which will judge all the others. As one of the Ancients [Seneca] has said, it is the day that will judge all my past actions."[183] In a Sunday sermon delivered at the beginning of the eighteenth century, Jean-Pierre Camus told his flock:

> *In order that we may teach ourselves to live righteously, we must always keep our end—which is death—in sight. The entire play will be judged from a sample, by a glance . . . The end is the best moment of a drama and the conclusion the best part of an epigram. Let us then see to both the ending and the conclusion, for they will balance the books on the basis of which we shall be judged.*[184]

The importance of temptation in works on "preparing for death" diminished noticeably in the course of the sixteenth century, but this partial disappearance only came about slowly. Clichtove's *De Doctrina moriendi* cites Cicero and Seneca, Saint Cyprian and Saint Ambrose, in order to reassure his reader with respect to death. Yet he also identifies no less than ten temptations that attend the passing of life, and dedicates the second and largest part of his treatise to them.[185] In Erasmus's *De Praeparatione ad mortem*, the space occupied by the question of temptation is much less (only a tenth of the book),[186] yet far from negligible. Like all of his contemporaries, Erasmus thinks that "the Enemy finds a favorable opportunity in a person's sufferings, in his terror of death, in his fear of Hell and in that natural weakness of the spirit, that sadness of the soul which is brought about by a serious illness."[187] The demon thus tries to topple the dying person's faith, to drive him to despair or to incite him to presumptiousness and instill in him the "fear of Purgatory." In Bellarmine's *De Arte bene moriendi*, temptation and the struggle against it account for five out of thirty-three chapters, or rather five out of seventeen, if one considers that the second part of this treatise is devoted to the approach of death, whereas the first addresses the Christian who is still in good health. According to Bellarmine, the dangers that threaten a dying person are the temptations of heresy, despair, and the hatred of God.[188]

As we shall see in a later chapter,[189] Catholic preaching never really abandoned the theme of the deathbed although it did tend to place a growing importance on two contrasting images: the atrocious death of the sinner and the serene and exemplary demise of the good Christian. Churchmen had long been convinced that the hardened sinner had little or no chance of reprieve *in extremis*. A chapter of Suso's *Büchlein der ewigen Weisheit* is dedicated to "that which is death without preparation." When he stands before the doors of Judgment, the sinner feels like a "beggar who is being chased away."[190] The Latin transcription of San Bernardino's sermons contains two adjacent homilies describing "the twelve perils threatening the sinner at the last moment" and "the twelve sufferings endured by the sinner at the hour of his death."[191] The dominant motif of these two descriptions of the deathbed is the sinner who, assailed by both physical pain and by anguish with regard to his fate, is incapable of behaving correctly. Devils torment him. His earthly ties prevent him from repenting. He already knows he is destined for Hell. In fact, as Tenenti has pointed out, the spiritual authors of the fifteenth and especially sixteenth centuries "tend to exclude any possibility of salvation for he who repents upon his deathbed only because he is afraid of judgment."[192] This attitude, in conjunction with the preceding conviction, helped reinforce the opinion held by spiritual leaders according to whom death must be prepared for throughout one's life—otherwise only the worst can be expected.

On the other hand, the death throes of a devout Christian are a spectacle worthy of contemplation, an example to be followed.[193] This edifying model, along with its characteristic traits—patience in suffering, ardent piety, supernatural joy in receiving the sacraments—can already be found in certain fifteenth-century humanist texts from Italy. In the course of the sixteenth century it gained greater currency thanks to the group led by Girolamo Cacciaguerra (a friend of Filippo Neri), who made no secret of the fact that he eagerly awaited the hour of his death. In the case of a devout person's demise, the dominant attitudes toward the dying moments are reversed. Death is no longer feared but rather looked forward to, for it leads to eternal bliss. This kind of death wish produced a strange poem around 1500: the *Canzone alla Morte*, composed by the humanist politician Pandolfo Collenuccio. Collenuccio cannot praise death enough. Throughout his poem he calls it "noble," "splendid," "generous," "compassionate," "gracious," "benign and valorous," and "timely and desired."[194] Is this a "desperate" poem, or an early foreshadowing of the romantic period? The key to this "song" lies in fact elsewhere, for certain passages (such as the following one) are clearly Neoplatonic:

White, pure and divine,
Our immortal soul enters our body
Where she divests herself
Of the light of her glory, walking
Between fear and desire, between
Suffering, vain joy, scorn and anger,
Running up against nature and the elements,
And buffeted by contrary winds.

As is often the case in Christian literature, themes of Neoplatonic hue are to be found within the monastic philosophy of *contemptus mundi*. Collenuccio declares death to be "generous" because it "lifts the dark veil of ignorance . . . , distinguishes the true from the false, the perpetual from the fragile, the eternal from the mortal." Furthermore, he declares that "the world is ungrateful" and phrases traditional questions in terms almost identical to those of Cardinal Lothair:

That which is falsely called life on earth,
What is it but fatigue, worry, privation,
Sighs, tears and moans,
Suffering, infirmity, terror and war?

Hence the reference to certain passages of the Bible: "Someone said, 'Happy is he who dies in swaddling clothes . . .' and others have said 'Happy is he who is not born.' " Here we find ourselves once again at the heart of the Christian discourse on death, as is further confirmed by the last verse of Collenuccio's poem, where he begs "He who, on wood, extinguished the rage of the horrible serpent" to sprinkle and purify him with his pacifying and beneficial blood:

Filled with bitter woe I beg for help.
May His infinite goodness right my errors:
I am the work of His hands.
Faithful minister of His goodness,
Gently lift the fatal thread
And open for me the holy and gilded doors
Which give out upon the heavenly harbor,
Dear death, so timely and desired.

This kind of death wish, here expressed by a man who had spent sixteen months in prison (twelve years before he wrote this poem, however)[195] and who was destined to die by execution, is quite similar to that described by Erasmus in his *De Praeparatione ad mortem*. Erasmus there echoes the "divine Psalmist"—"Free me from this imprisonment, that I might glorify thy name, O Lord" (Ps. 142)—as well as Saint Paul—"Life to me is Christ and death would bring me something more . . . I want to be gone and be with Christ" (Phil. 1:21–23). Such comparisons help us to better understand Bartolomeo d'Angelo's *Ricordo del ben morire* (1589), especially when he declares:

> *God fashioned the figure and the image of death with such artifice that whomsoever looks at it in the right way, that is to say with the eyes of reason and in the light of faith, will see it to be so beautiful and so useful that he will cry out: "O Death, it is so good to think on thee!" But whomsoever looks at it the wrong way, that is to say with only the eyes of the body, with the earthly senses and without the light of faith, so ugly and frightening will it seem that he will immediately cry out in a shrill voice, "O Death, how bitter it is to think of thee!"*[196]

This sort of fervent desire for death eventually led a number of seventeenth-century authors to describe their ideal of a beautiful and lucid death. These descriptions then created a model destined to long outlive its original function.[197]

The growing diversification of the discourse on the ultimate end of life eventually brought about a reduction in the number of its macabre components. Erasmus and Bellarmine, for example, refused to have recourse to terrifying images. However, as the rest of this book will show, this reduction did not lead to total disappearance. It was the Renaissance that invented the scene where Saint Jerome meditates in front of a skull, and, as an iconographic motif, the "saint and skull" (often associated with a water clock) was destined to enjoy great success. Although Clichtove excluded overly funereal elements from his text, he was nevertheless one of the first to feature, as a frontispiece to his *De Doctrina moriendi*, a skull with a tibia clenched between its teeth and, underneath, a spade, a pickax, some bones, and a tombstone. In December 1981 an *Office de la Vierge* dating from the year 1586 was sold at the Hôtel Drouot.* Originally commissioned by Henri III for the Parisian *Compagnie des confrères de la mort*, the fawn-colored morocco leather cover features an assortment of tears, a skeleton, shin bones, death's heads, candles, crosses, and aspergillums. Savonarola's *Predica dell'arte del ben morire* contained a number of suggestions that were also largely followed: The faithful should visit graveyards, attend burials, voluntarily assist dying relatives or friends, keep death images in the house (especially in the bedroom), wear spiritual "death glasses" (that is, treat each moment as if it were the last), and, finally, each time they look at their body, they should remember that it will soon rot and be reduced to dust and ashes.[198]

Faithful to the tradition followed by Savonarola, the canon Pietro da Lucca included similar advice in his *Dottrina del ben morire* (1540). According to him, the devout should make a point of attending deathbeds and funerals, visiting cemeteries, and meditating once or twice a week in front of a skull. He even provides the reader with an example of the type of conversation that can be had with a cranium.[199] The Franciscan friar Cornelio Musso (who was the best-known religious orator in Italy in his time) made identical demands. In an Ash Wednesday sermon delivered in Rome in the year 1542 and printed somewhat later, he urges his listeners to visit graveyards and dramatizes the struggle between two great champions, Nature and Death. He there describes death as being "cruel" and "powerful." Scythe in hand, "it hides behind men everywhere, on land, on sea, persecuting them, assailing them, killing them, burying them, reducing them to ashes."[200] In 1550 Innocenzo Ringhieri set his *Dialoghi della vita e della morte* in a cemetery where Death appears among the tombstones, armed with a scythe. In this case, however, Death acts as a guide to eternal beatitude.[201] It would seem that even though the most innovative of Renaissance treatises on the art of dying tended to reject morbid imagery, a macabre tradition flourished under the auspices of the church, where it was destined to enjoy a long and successful career.

In any case, death remained a dominant theme on all levels of religious teaching.

*Translator's note: A Paris auction house.

On a beam once belonging to an abbey in Cornwall, a fifteenth-century Breton inscription reads: "When I think about it, I find the subject I study to be most difficult: after our life in this world, the end of each and every person is death."[202] Another Breton composition, a *Mirouer de la mort* composed in 1519, contains the following verse: "When man contemplates death, judgment and cold Hell, he must tremble. He whose mind refuses to reflect is mad, seeing as he must die."[203] The idea of death must then guide our entire existence. Pietro da Lucca categorically affirms: "We have only been given this life in order to learn the art of dying,"[204] and, farther on, he states: "If you develop the habit of keeping death in mind, in all of your gestures and all of your acts, you will then be filled with the fear of the Lord and freed of all fear and laziness."[205] For Pierre Doré, "the first preparation for death which he [Jesus] taught us, is to meditate and think about death very often . . . [For] the Gospels teach us that Our Lord often thought about his death and often spoke about it."[206] In 1545 Michelangelo gave similar advice to friends: "In order to find and enjoy one's self, amusements and joy are not necessary, but rather the thought of death."[207] Even Erasmus—who was positively allergic to the macabre and whose professed goal, in the *De Praeparatione ad mortem*, was to help his readers overcome their fear of dying—still declared that "all life is but a march toward death."[208] Did not Plato himself define philosophy as a form of meditation upon death,[209] which "results in a kind of training for death"?[210] "Therefore we must practice the contemplation of death throughout our entire life"[211]—as noted above, Montaigne repeated this advice to himself throughout a good part of his own life.

Did Bellarmine, who believed that the best way to die like a Christian was to live like a Christian, think differently? In the second part of *De Arte bene moriendi* (which, it is true, was written with the seriously ill in mind), he makes a series of statements that apply equally to the sound in body: "To we who are only allowed to die once, there is no better path than the thought and contemplation of that which happens when one dies,"[212] and elsewhere: "Who then, if he is not entirely stupid and bereft of all judgment, would dare to leave this life if he has not learned beforehand, and with all possible diligence, how to die well . . ."[213] Thus did the religious thought of the time place death at the center of each and every individual's life, just as the village cemetery was placed at the center of communal life.

As has been repeatedly pointed out, this conception of death was developed by monks, and its diffusion was also largely due to monastic endeavor (Nider, Denis the Carthusian, Savonarola, Raulin, and so on). At the end of the sixteenth century and in the beginning of the seventeenth, it was again taken up by churchmen (particularly Jesuits, such as Polanco and Bellarmine) who, although they were not monks, nevertheless inherited a certain amount of monastic spirituality—hence the quasi-obsessive repetition of the principal themes of *contemptus mundi* in all Christian writings on death and even in the writings of laymen. The body is unimportant and life is but a dream (and often a bad one at that). In the letter mentioned above, Michelangelo advised his friends to meditate on death because that is the only thing which can prevent us from being "stolen" from our own selves "by relatives, by friends, by great masters, by ambition, greed, and by all those other vices and sins which steal man from himself."[214] Bartolomeo Arnigio, who wrote a *Discorso intorno al disprezzo della morte* in the second half of the sixteenth century, explains that death only attacks the less interesting part of ourselves, for it is not as if we really die.[215] Similarly, a monk from Fontevrault, Gabriel Dupuy-Herbault, declares in his *Miroir de l'homme chrestien, pour cognoistre son heur et son malheur* (1557): "[We] should pay little attention to our bodily needs, and none at all to the desires and covetousness of the flesh, but rather advise ourselves on how to deliver our soul (which is all our wealth) from this world, shrinking not from starvation, nor from the loss of our soul's enclosure, which is the body."[216] Bartolomeo d'Angelo's *Ricordo del ben morire* (1589) advises the Christian to start with the fear of death. Once he is possessed by this fear, he can conquer it by "contempt for the world and earthly things."[217] Given such an atmosphere, it is hardly surprising that the ex-monk Erasmus should have allotted considerable space to *contemptus mundi* in his *Preparation . . .* As I have suggested earlier[218] this work, which was written at the end of his life, throws retrospective light upon the *De contemptu mundi* written forty-five years earlier by the young humanist from Rotterdam. It comes almost as a surprise when the clichés of the monastic tradition turn up in the *Preparation*:

> *If one remembers all the stages of human life—foul conception, perilous gestation, pitiful birth, childhood exposed to a thousand maladies, youth sullied by so many vices, maturity afflicted by so many worries, old age tormented by so many ills—I do not think that any person, even one born under a lucky star, could be found who would accept the following proposition: that God should allow him to pass again through all the stages of his past life, following the same path from conception on, enjoying the same joys and suffering the same misfortunes.*"[219]

Erasmus then continues in the time-hallowed manner, paraphrasing Ecclesiastes ("More happy the day of my death than the day of my birth"), quoting Saint Augustine ("To increase in age is to increase in sin"),[220] and referring to the Book of Wisdom ("The corruptible body weighs the soul down, and the earthly envelope burdens the spirit with multiple worries").[221]

On first reading, Bellarmine's *De Arte bene moriendi* seems to stike a somewhat different note.[222] Jesuit that he is, he begins by carefully distinguishing between the different meanings of the word "world." The first definition generally designates the earth and those who inhabit it whereas the second refers to all forms of concupiscence (lust, greed, pride). One can therefore belong to the world (first definition) without loving it (second definition). In a radical departure from the monastic tradition, the author then declares that saints who are "truly dead to this world" can exist not only in convents and among the clergy, but even among laymen. Furthermore, one can be rich without being attached to riches—witness Abraham. This is why earthly goods—wealth, honors, pleasures—are not entirely forbidden to Christians on condition that they do not love them immoderately. Neither riches nor honors determine whether one is worldly or not. Hints of the laxness with which the Jesuits—confessors of the great men of Christianity—were to be accused of in later years show up here. A second reading of Bellarmine's text, however, disallows this first interpretation, for he himself has a certain amount of difficulty with the ambiguities of the word "world." When referring to I Corinthians 7:29,[223] an epistle written with the end of the world in mind ("the time is short"), he echoes Saint Paul in saying: "The faithful should love their wives, but moderately, as if they had none. If they must mourn the loss of their children or their wealth, they should do so moderately, as if they were not sad and had nothing to cry about . . . The Apostle orders us to act in the world as if we were guests or pilgrims, and not citizens." Bellarmine thus proposes an almost stoic model of behavior that is a direct descendant of the *contemptus mundi* tradition:

> *To live in the world and scorn its wealth is a very difficult thing to do. To see beautiful things and not love them, to taste the sweetness [of life] and not enjoy it, to despise honors, to deliberately choose the lowest place, to give high positions to others and, finally, to live in flesh as if we did not have it, such an existence*

> *might be said to be more angelic than human. Yet the Apostle wrote to the Church at Corinth, where almost everyone was married, and spoke to people who were neither clerics, nor monks, nor anchorites, but rather laymen, just as if someone were to say today: . . . "May all those who have a wife live as if they had none."*

And so on.

The "angelic" model proposed to all Christians—including laymen—appears here once again. Bellarmine is conscious of the heroic nature of the detachment he proposes and yet he believes that "if someone, with the help of grace, begins to love God truly for Himself, and his neighbor for God's sake, then will he begin to pass from this world. Once his love begins to grow, greed (that is, his taste for worldly things) will diminish and he will begin to be dead to the world." This conciliatory tone is nevertheless counterbalanced twice by the affirmation that: "this business [detachment from the world] is not a child's game" but rather a "very big and very difficult" affair. The Jesuit reminds his reader that "few will be saved"[224] and concludes with the following remark: "it is entirely impossible to live both for the world and for God, to enjoy both the earth and Heaven." For Bellarmine, as for all churchmen before him, earthly values have no real substance. Man is not a citizen of this earth.

THE LEGEND OF THE THREE LIVING AND THE THREE DEAD

When Guyot Marchant published his 1486 edition of the *Danse macabre des femmes*, he added to it the *Débat du corps et de l'âme* and the *Complainte de l'âme damnée*. These significant additions demonstrate the close links existing between the different aspects of the macabre at this time and their debt to the monastic tradition of *contemptus mundi*. The gist of the debate is as follows[225]: A hermit sees a corpse in a dream. Next to this lifeless body, the soul that has left it laments, accusing the flesh of having been the cause of the spirit's damnation. The body tries to protest its innocence, but in vain. The debate ends with the arrival of devils, who carry the soul off to Hell. This tale has often been attributed to Saint Macarius the Elder, who was one of the favorite characters of eastern Christian funeral lore.[226] It was said that one day, while walking with two angels, he came upon a stinking corpse from which he recoiled. The two angels then held their noses and drew back, not at the smell of the dead body but at the approach of Macarius. The saint asked why and was told that it was because his sins smelled worse than the cadaver. As early as the year 380, this legend was also associated with the story of the "Vision of Saint Paul." According to this tale, Saint Paul witnessed the separation of the soul from the body of both a saved and a damned person and even made a trip to Hell. This "vision" was extremely popular throughout the Middle Ages and was recounted in all of the vernacular languages (French, Provencal, English, Italian, German, Russian, and so on). As for the *Débat du corps et de l'âme*, it fuses the above-mentioned legends. The main text of this debate is an eleventh-century manuscript from the monastery of Nonantola, but the debate made its appearance in all of Europe (including Ireland, Norway, and Bohemia). The original Neoplatonic and gnostic tone was generally respected. In a monastic poem derived from the Nonantola version, the Latin author depicts the body as being the declared enemy of the soul: "I wanted to breathe / (says the soul to its bad companion) / But you did not give the the space to do so / . . . I wanted to fast but you foiled me with sickness / . . . I wanted to work / But you made me rest."[227] So well known was this debate that Jacopone da Todi even wrote a sermon on this theme in the form of a burlesque poem:

THE SOUL:	THE BODY:
Evil and filthy body,	*Help! Neighbors!*
Lustful and devious,	*The soul has flayed me*
You have always been deaf	*Without reason, bloodied*
To the question of my salvation.	*And beaten me.*[228]

The macabre found ample opportunities for expression in the reproaches made to the body by the soul. The famous poem *Pèlerinages*, written by the Cistercian monk Guillaume de Digulleville, features such a debate. In the "pèlerinage de l'âme séparée du corps" (the pilgrimage of the body separated from the body), the soul comes to a place full of bones and there finds its old earthly dress, which it scolds soundly:

Among several bodies there lying
I saw my own
Those bones that I once knew so well . . .
Are you, said I, that evil body
That very vile body, so filthy and so malodorus
Meat for worms and putrification,
That horrible and ugly creature?[229]

Given the emphasis on decomposition, it is understandable that the debate of the body and the soul should have sometimes become (in fifteenth-century England, for example) a debate of the body and the worms.[230] Furthermore, since de Digulleville's poem had a long and sucessful career from the fourteenth to the sixteenth centuries, it is hardly surprising that the theme of the argument between two adversaries should have appeared in Guyot Marchant's collection, which, after all, aimed at a large public. Even François Villon's fine *Debat du cuer et du corps* echoes this tradition. For Villon the heart is the conscience and the body is the fool.[231] The poet's description of the conflict between good and evil thus treads the well-worn path of tradition, as did the well-known opposition between reason and the perishable, animal part of man's being.

Before publishing his *Danse macabre des femmes* in 1486, Marchant had already published a reedition of his 1485 *Danse macabre*, along with "several new and pleasing tales" that include the debate of the three living and the three dead. This legend can best be understood in the context of the current pastoral theme of fear where, once again, the written text seems to have preceded visual expression (as was the case with monastic literature and tomb sculpture). In this case, striking similarities exist between this tale and a Byzantine hagiographic "novel," *Barlaam and Josaphat*, which, in itself, is the adaptation of a Buddhist legend.[232] Here is the plot of the "novel" as it is summarized by Louis Bréhier. In India, King "Abenner" is persecuting Christians. An astrologer tells the king that his son Josaphat will convert to Christianity, so he locks his son up in a marvelous palace where all worldly pleasures are offered to him. The young prince is soon bored, however, and the king lets him leave. While hunting one day, the prince meets a leper and a blind man, and then finally an old man who teaches him the vanity of the world and the benefits of meditation. Sometime thereafter a Christian hermit (Barlaam) disguised as a merchant manages to reach Josaphat and convert him. The king first reacts by banishing his son but ends up by becoming a Christian himself and giving half of his kingdom to Josaphat. When "Abenner" dies, Josaphat retires to the desert, where he again meets Barlaam. Several elements of this story recall the legend of Buddha: the encounter in the course of a hunt, the dialogue of the young prince with three people (who, if they are not yet dead, are certainly the closest living approximation), the role of the hermit who teaches the prince a lesson, and, finally, the lesson itself: a monastic invitation to contempt for the world.[233]

The oldest surviving Greek version of the "novel" dates from the eleventh century and is the translation of a Georgian text. The earliest known Latin translation dates from 1048, and, from then on, the story enjoyed a great vogue in Europe where it was translated in all of the languages of the continent. No less than sixty variants have been found, all of which inspired a quantity of iconographic works: door lintels, ambones, frescoes, tombs, coffers, psalters, and so on. Such popularity would explain the recycling of this legend in the tale of the three living and the three dead, which, in itself, owes a great deal to the numerous corpses appearing in the *Vitae Patrum*. The transformed tale seems to have first appeared in southern Italy at the end of the twelfth century, due to this area's contacts with the Greek world. In a fifteenth-century manuscript now in Ferrara, a Latin poem of forty-five verses contains the essential elements of the new story: traveling kings chance upon decomposing corpses in their open tombs. Certain historians trace this poem back to the twelfth century, and in some cases it has even been attributed to Saint Bernard.[234] Others believe the Ferrara manuscript to be the first version,[235] but this second opinion does not take into account the fact that this poem uses the oldest form of the legend: There is only one living person and, as yet, no real dialogues. Later on, the story gains in the telling. There are, more often than not, three "living" men suddenly confronted with three living cadavers who tell them: "That what you are, we once were. That what we are, you will be," a formula that the Latin poem also features. Confronted with such a ghastly spectacle, the three living men recoil in horror and decide to mend their ways.[236]

The legend again appears, at a relatively late date, in a fifteenth-century collection of *exempla*, those moralizing anecdotes used to liven up medieval sermons, which often included stories of ghosts and walking corpses in order to suitably impress the audience.[237] This mention, which is the only one to be found so far in *exemplum* literature, is interesting in itself and suggests that others may still be discovered. At any rate, the *Legend of the Three Living and the Three Dead* had the structure and the function of an *exemplum* enriched by subsequent variants and additions. The living are usually young nobles or princes dressed in beautiful clothing. They are sometimes of different ages, representing the three ages of life, and each one reacts to the horrible apparition according to his age: The oldest prays, the thirty- or forty-year-old pulls his sword, and the youngest turns away from the atrocious spectacle. The encounter happens most often during a hunt, which would seem to be a distant echo of the Byzantine tale. The horses rear, one of the hunters loses his dog in the confusion, another unleashes his falcon. The dead tend to be less clearly differentiated, although they often wear a crown or a mitre. It is not uncommon for them to appear in three different stages of decomposition, the most recently dead addressing the oldest of the living and the most decomposed addressing the youngest in order to better drive the lesson home. They are sometimes portrayed as lying in open coffins, as is the case with the Ferrara manuscript, but most often they are described as standing.

In literature as in iconography, the *Legend of the Three Living and the Three Dead* is often attributed to a hermit who recounts a vision sent to him by God. This is, once again, an indirect echo of the eastern origin of the story, for it is most probably Saint Macarius who is being referred to. The *Vitae Patrum* (which were translated into Italian by Domenico Cavalca around 1330), the *Debate of the soul and the body*, and the *Golden Legend* all underlined his strange familiarity with dead bodies. In the *Golden Legend*, for example, he was said to have once entered a cave in order to sleep. In this cave were buried many pagans, and he had taken the body of one of them to use as a pillow. Some demons then appeared to frighten him, and they called the body as if it were that of a woman, saying: " 'Get up and come bathe with us.' And another devil, who was underneath Macarius, acted as if it were he who were dead and said, 'I have a stranger on top of me, and I cannot get up.' Macarius, however, was not afraid, but rather beat the corpse, saying 'Get up and go if you can.' When the devils heard him, they fled, crying aloud: 'You have vanquished us.' "[238]

This long tradition had accustomed the clerics of the Middle Ages to associate Saint Macarius with cadavers. The link between tales of meetings between the living and the dead and the *Vitae Patrum* stories about Egyptian monks thus seems certain. It is even more obvious in an Italian panel of the late fourteenth or early fifteenth century that is now in the Crawford Collection (London). In a wild landscape of mountains and valleys, an area fit for pious meditation, are to be found fourteen hermits (among whom Saint Jerome, Saint Macarius, and Saint Pachomius) and their disciples. Between these groups appear five horsemen who, returning from hunting, have come upon three open caskets.[239]

The first written and painted references to the story of the three living and the three dead appear before the middle of the fourteenth century, a fact that again invites the historian to pay special attention to the prehistory of the macabre in Western Europe. Apart from the Ferrara poem, whose date of composition is open to debate, there exist four French poems composed at the end of the thirteenth century by Countess Marguerite d'Anjou's minstrel, Baudoin de Condé (1244–1280), by Nicolas de Margival (end of the thirteenth century), and by two anonymous poets. A fifth French poem lengthens this list as of the beginning of the fourteenth century: *Se nous vous apportons nouvellez*, which is written in dialogue form.[240] And soon appear other works, such as one Italian and four German poems that paraphrase Badouin's verse.[241] Like the monastic literature dedicated to contempt for the world and *momento mori*, all of these poems stress the gruesome decomposition of the body, combining visions of the skeleton with pictures of putrefaction to enhance the poem's effect. Baudoin writes:

Death and worms, they have done the worst
They could . . .
Behold, all three (of the dead)
Are without a hair on their head,
Without an eye in their forehead, nor mouth or nose
Nor sight nor prick . . .[242]

One of the anonymous authors also describes the "three disfigured . . . dead bodies":

The gaping holes of the eyes and the nose
The bones, all dry, legs, arms, feet and hands
All consumed and pierced by worms . . .[243]

The oldest representations of this dramatic tale are to be found in southern Italy and around Rome,[244] which further reinforces the hypothesis of its original link with the Barlaam story. A fresco in Santa Margherita de Melfi (near Foggia) that dates from the first third of the thirteenth century already shows the encounter between three young hunters and skeletons.[245] The same scene appears again around 1260 in the Cathedral of Atri (Abruzzo) where, against a backdrop of thick foliage, a hermit (Saint Macarius?) urges the living to repent. In the second half of the thirteenth century, the legend was painted on the back wall of the church of Poggio Mirteto (Monti Sabini region). This time, however, there is only one live person, a king, who stops in horror when confronted with three crowned corpses, each of which has reached a different stage of decomposition. Finally, at Montefiascone (near Orvieto), at the beginning of the fourteenth century, three riders sporting large bonnets have dismounted in front of a group of skeletons (only two are visible). Behind them, on a rock, a monk calls upon them to repent.

In France, Emile Mâle cites a miniature from the end of the thirteenth century that illustrates a manuscript copy of Baudoin de Condé's poem.[246] In Metz, a small painting from the early fourteenth century representing an encounter between the living and the dead used to grace the church of Notre-Dame de Clairvaux.[247] In England, a psalter that dates from around 1290 features an illustration of this same scene.[248] But it is only around 1350, and especially in the Campo Santo of Pisa, that this theme expresses its greater implications, which it will then carry to the farthest reaches of the Western world. The Pisan painter—Orcagna, Spinello, Traini?—created a forceful visual and semantic synthesis in which the encounter of the three living (at the head of a glowing group of horsemen) and the three dead is associated with Death, an emaciated hag with the wings of a bat, long hair, and claws on her hands and feet. Behind her are piled the bodies of those she has already struck down, and ahead of her can be seen a garden of wealthy young men and women amusing themselves with music and pleasant games. Death is preparing to take them.

Given the number of publications on this painting, it is not necessary to insist on the impact of this theme and its success in terms of the new sensibilities of the period. Nonetheless, several elements of this imposing fresco are often passed over, and it is precisely these elements that are of special interest with respect to classical texts on contempt for the world. One of these details is the battle between angels and demons for the possession of the souls of those just deceased. The judgment that then follows death gives meaning to all of the other elements of the composition. On the other side of the painting, in the upper left, monks are depicted living their peaceful and bucolic life, dividing their time among prayer, meditation on holy writs, and manual labor. They do not fear death, and it is by no means an accident that the painter placed the group of carefree young people in a symmetrical position, on the lower right-hand side. The pedagogical intention of this coherent composition cannot be denied. Nor can its monastic inspiration be passed over, all the more so as a hermit—again Saint Macarius?—is depicted unrolling a parchment from which he reads the *exemplum* of the three living and and the three dead.

If, therefore, it is true that an increased and even morbid attention is paid to mortal remains as of the middle of the fourteenth century, it is certainly an error to affirm (especially with reference to *Legend of the Three Living and The Three Dead* that this new vision "focused the senses on an object which, in itself, had no Christian meaning"; nor is it correct to assert that the macabre had raised "an insurmountable wall between earth and heaven."[249] It would be more correct to underscore the fact that, throughout Christian history, there have been two coexisting attitudes toward death. One of these attitudes spurned the macabre, and the other embraced it. Saint Thomas Aquinas gave the following advice in his *Summa theologica*: "There is no sense in thinking about death every time one desires something or does something . . . No more so than a traveler must, at every step, think of his final destination."[250] Later Pascal, quoting Saint Paul (Thess. 4:12), writes about his father's death: "We should no longer consider the body to be stinking carrion, because deceitful nature makes us see it so, but rather as the sacred and eternal temple of the Holy Spirit, as faith teaches us."[251] This attitude might now seem preferable, and closer to the spirit of the New Testament, but there is no denying the equally authentic and authoritative history of Christianity with its heavy reliance upon the fathers of the church and the hermits of the desert, upon the monks of the Middle Ages, Gerson,[252] and others.

By 1350 or thereabouts, the tale of the three living and the three dead spread by both written and iconographic means (frescoes, manuscript illuminations, sculptures) throughout Italy and—especially in the fourteenth century[253]—to France and England. Mâle mentions a good fifteen churches and chapels in different parts of France where representations of this legend are to be found. The latest of these is a painting dated 1554 in the church of Saint-Georges-sur-Seine.[254] This theme was especially popular with the illustrators of fifteenth-century French manuscript prayer books and the woodcut artists who illustrated Books of Hours. The Duke of Berry, who requested that this subject be represented in one of his Books of Hours (ca. 1400), also had it sculpted (in 1408) on the portal of the church chosen to house his tomb, the Church of the Innocents.[255] Only one hundred years ago there were still to be found, in England, a good fifty paintings from the fourteenth and fifteenth centuries that illustrated this legend. For the most part, they had been commissioned for the walls of humble chapels, and, as they shocked the sensibilities of nineteenth-century pastors, a good many of them were destroyed during the Victorian era.[256] Historian Philippa Tristam, who has pointed out the untimely demise of these paintings, has also observed that whereas only two complete written versions of this tale are known to exist in England—one a poem attributed to Audelay and the other to Henryson (both fifteenth century)—numerous texts refer obliquely to this story. It may therefore be assumed that simple allusions were more than adequate for a public familiar with this legend.[257] As for Switzerland, Germany, and the Low Countries, they also paid due homage to a theme that, by now, had become European in scope.[258] Dürer and Cranach both used it, and in the drawing attributed to Dürer (now in the Albertina, Vienna) it has assumed an anecdotal form. The corpses are no longer standing before the riders, they are violently attacking them. The horses rear, the hunters fall backward. This idea is not new to artists, but Dürer has exploited it with unusual force, showing grim death, rather than cadavers, that, "multiplied by three, attacks all three riders simultaneously."[259]

The richness of Dürer's genius should not, however, obscure the didactic function this tale usually fulfilled with respect to its various audiences. French poems from the thirteenth and beginning of the fourteenth centuries, Henryson's poem from the end of the fifteenth century, and most English mural paintings do not give the details of the encounter. The hunting scene is omitted or simplified to an extreme. The members of each group—the living and the dead—are practically identical.[260] On the other hand, the macabre realism is almost always emphasized because it is the vehicle of a moral lesson. This aspect of the story also remains important in its more elaborate expressions, such as the Campo Santo of Pisa, the Subiaco version, or the Guyot Marchant poem. In the tale told by Marchant, which he attributes to a solitary hermit, the words of the dead echo the menace of many a sermon delivered at his time:

The first of the dead declares: "You will have to receive death. A death that will be, alas, so painful, so bitter, so agonizing that those who die would never want to live again for fear of having to die, once again, such a death." The third accuses: "O foolish people, so poorly advised that I see you disguised in diverse clothing and robes and other things that you have stolen, you will be stinking carrion . . . When I see such faults and crimes . . . the great excesses, the great outrages that you impose on those who labor in the fields for you and who work, all naked and crying with hunger . . . I have no doubt that God will suddenly wreak such vengeance that you will have neither the time nor the space to beg Him for mercy."

The end of the tale is in full accordance with the moral lesson it was supposed to convey. The "three handsome men, all alive" pray before a cross that happens to be nearby, accept the warning they have been given, and make resolutions that even the hermit finds edifying. Equally significant is the fact that, at the Cemetery of the Innocents, at Ker-Maria and at Clusone (near Bergamo), the *Legend of the Three Living and the Three Dead* is to be found close to a dance of death. In the Church of Ennezat (Puy-de-Dôme), this legend has been painted on a wall opposite a Last Judgment, these two themes being closely associated at this time (as is also attested by the Campo Santo of Pisa).

Last but not least, the story of the three living and the three dead had the same function as those "mirrors" that contemporary literature placed before the terrified eyes of the public. In an English poem of the fifteenth century, *A Mirror for Young ladies at Their Toilet*, it is the image of the corpse that she will be that is reflected in the mirror. The image then cruelly declares to the beautiful young lady:

O maset wriche, I marke the with my mace.
Lifte up thy ieye, be-holde now, and assay!
Yche loke one me aught to put the in affray;
I wyll not spare the, for thou arte my pray.[261]

THE DANCE OF DEATH AND THE *DANSE MACABRE*

Guyot Marchant called his *danse macabre* "*Le Miroir salutaire*" (*The Salutary Mirror*) for he too understood the dance of death to be yet another, extremely convincing invitation to *memento mori*. As a matter of fact, the *danse macabre* cannot be fully understood unless it is put into the context of an entire body of penitential, pedagogic literature. Essentially, both the dance of death and the tale of the three living and the three dead are based on the same precept—vanity of vanities, all is vanity—and on the same denigration of earthly concerns that inspires *contemptus mundi*. And if the Ferrarese poem on the encounter between the living and the dead really dates from the twelfth century (which I believe may well be possible), then a number of its rhythmic verses can easily be considered as a precursor of the *danse macabre*. Should this be the case, this forty-five-verse poem would furnish proof of a common, monastic origin for both the danse of death and the *Dict des trois morts et des trois vifs*. So reads the poem:

6. *Weak or strong,*
Death gets them in the end,
Foolish or wise,
It gets them all equally.

> 7. *Death spares no one,*
> *Neither the rich nor the poor,*
> *Neither the miter nor the crown,*
> *Neither the bishop nor the prince.*
>
> 9. *It spares not age*
> *Nor honest folk*
> *Nor the young in the flower of youth.*
> *Everything it sees, it takes.*
>
> 33. *Here are worms and decay.*
> *Here the corpse which horrifies*
> *Whether you want it or not,*
> *Such is the end of all.*[262]

The prehistory of the *danse macabre* is still shrouded in mystery, as is the term "macabre," which appears only in the fourteenth century. The most plausible hypotheses traces this word to Judas Maccabee, who had bid the Jews pray for the souls of the dead. At a period in which the church was promoting belief in Purgatory, Judas Maccabee was also a focus of clerical propaganda, whence the passage of his name into contemporary language.[263] It was at this level of expression that Judas Maccabee became associated with ghostly legends. In the area around Blois, the spectral hunt of ghosts in search of a living prey was called the "*chasse maccabée.*" There was doubtless a link between the dance of death and folktales about dancing corpses and ghosts hunting the living.[264]

Around the year 1350, a Dutch monk who translated the French romance *Maugis d'Aigremont* added a revealing comparison to the original text. When Maugis had captured his enemy, King Antenor, and several of the king's knights, he tied them to a pole in the middle of his tent. The translator here adds his original comparison, for he notes that the prisoners thus formed a circle, "like a dance of death,"[265] a dance that was not meant to be a game but rather a form of constraint. In much the same fashion, the medieval inhabitants of Lower Saxony believed that, on Saint Thomas' day (December 21), the likenesses of those who were going to die in the following year could be seen dancing with the dead.[266] From the sixteenth century to the present day, both Swiss (Lavater) and German (Fehse) studies have established a link between the *danse macabre* and belief in ghosts who play music and dance at night, attracting the living within their circle.[267] This link seems probable, all the more so as Jean Wirth points out that not just the lower classes but even the elite of the Middle Ages and Renaissance believed in ghosts. The dance of death may have been, therefore, an erudite and clerical re-creation based on ancient customs and a widespread belief in a ghostly life after death.

Mâle argued that the oldest *danse macabre* may have been a mimed illustration of a sermon on death. Danced at first in church, it would have then been danced outside on a stage as a sort of morality play, as happened in Bruges in 1449 at the "*Hôtel*" of the Duke of Burgundy.[268] Later painted, engraved, or reproduced in manuscript illuminations, this dance became the "comic strip" that is still well known today. This account of the dance's evolution rings true, but it would be doubtless equally useful to look beyond the mimicry of sermons to even earlier dances that preachers would have Christianized and remodeled. These dances would have had all the more success given the widespread belief in ghostly balls. One thing is certain: People danced in both churches and cemeteries in the Middle Ages, especially on holidays such as the Feast of Fools, the Day of the Innocents, and so on, to the extent that the Council of Basel (section XXI, 1435) ruled against this practice. It would be useful to have a study on this subject. The legend of the Kölbigk dancers is well known. According to the Nuremberg chronicle,[269] a priest was celebrating mass on Christmas Eve in Kölbigk, in the diocese of Magdeburg. A group of eighteen men and women created a disturbance by singing and dancing in the neighboring cemetery. The priest went to reprimand them, but they made fun of him and continued their revels. The priest then called upon Heaven to condemn them to dance for twelve months. When the year was over, the Archbishop of Magdeburg ended their penance. Three of the dancers died on the spot, and the others did not survive them for very long.

A likely hypothesis is that the church revived a number of ancient dances and Christianized them, just as secular songs had been turned into hymns and canticles, the words being changed but the melodies remaining the same. Writing around the year 1400, Johann Bischoff, a Franciscan monk from Vienna, reported that there were as many as twenty dances performed by all social classes in his area during the Easter season. Unluckily for us, he described only two of them: one in which Christ leads the blessed into Paradise, and another in which the Devil leads into Hell all those who had transgressed against the Ten Commandments.[270] It is probable that at least one of these dances dealt with death. Mâle speaks about a document dated 1393 that describes a dance of death performed in the church of Caudebec.[271] And were there not also funeral dances, which are not only common to many other civilizations but are also supposed to have been practiced in medieval Aragon, where certain macabre traditions inherited from the Moors still survived? During certain coronation banquets held in honor of Aragonese kings in the early fifteenth century, pantomimes of death were performed. Even today, in Vergès (Gérone province), a dance of death is carried out during Easter week by young people dressed as skeletons and beating tamborines.[272]

To these observations on the development of the *danse macabre* must be added what is now known about the Catalan *Dansa de la Mort*, which must not be confused with the Castilian *Dança general de la muerte* (to be discussed later), nor with the 1497 Catalan translation of the song that accompanied the dancers of the Cemetary of the Innocents. The *Dansa de la Mort* gives a good example of the church's Christianization of old funeral rites, which, in this case, was carried out by monks. The text and the music of this dance are known thanks to a fourteenth-century manuscript—the *Libre Vermell*—that is now at Montserrat, having escaped destruction under Napoleon.[273] This dance has undergone a recent revival, having been performed at the church of Montserrat in 1973 and 1978 and, again in 1978, at Barcelona, Saintes, Etampes, Cologne, Kirchenheim, and Berlin during "Catalan weeks." Here are the somber lessons conveyed by the Latin text (*Ad mortem festinamus* . . .):

REFRAIN (tornada)*:*
Toward death we hasten,
Let us sin no more, sin no more.

VERSES (cobla)*:*
I wanted to speak of contempt for the world
So that that men would not be deceived by vanity.
The moment has come to leave the treacherous sleep of death,
The moment has come to leave the treacherous sleep of death.

Toward death we hasten . . .

Short life will soon be over:
Quickly death runs, and respects no one.

Death kills everyone. It feels sorry for no one
Death kills everyone. It feels sorry for no one.

Toward death we hasten . . .

If you do not convert, if you do not become humble,
If you do not change your life and do good deeds,
You will not be able to enter God's kingdom as a blessed soul
You will not be able to enter God's kingdom as a blessed soul.

Toward death we hasten . . .

When the trumpet sounds, the last day,
When the Judge comes
He will call the chosen to the eternal country
He will call and cast the damned into hell
He will call and cast the damned into hell.

Toward death we hasten . . .

How happy they will be, those who will reign with Christ!
They will see Him face to face.
They will sing: Holy, Holy is the Lord God of armies,
They will sing: Holy, Holy is the Lord God of armies.

Toward death we hasten . . .

How sad will be those condemned to eternal punishment!
Their torments will never end and will never consume them.
Alas! alas! wretched creatures! Never can you escape,
Alas! alas! wretched creatures! never can you escape.

Toward death we hasten . . .

May all the kings of this age and all the great of the earth
And all the clergy and all those in power
Make themselves small; And reject all vanity,
Make themselves small; and reject all vanity.

Toward death we hasten . . .

Dearest brothers, if we meditate properly upon the Passion of our Lord,
And if we shed bitter tears,
He will protect us like the apple of His eye
He will protect and will prevent us from sinning,
He will protect and will prevent us from sinning.

Toward death we hasten . . .

Holy Virgin of virgins, crowned in Heaven,
Be our advocate, intercede for us with your Son
And after this exile, be the mediator who will welcome us,
And after this exile, be the mediator who will welcome us.

Toward death we hasten . . .

The Montserrat *Dansa de la Mort* is not a real *danse macabre* insofar as it does not include dialogues between a living person (whose social category is generally clearly indicated) and Death or, more often, a corpse acting as Death's representative. Yet each one of these dances sheds light upon the other. The manuscript of the *Dança general de la muerte*, which is kept at the Escorial and which constitutes the earliest known text to describe an authentic Castilian dance of death, is full of Catalan, Aragonese, and even Arabic expressions. The link between this text and the earlier Catalan *Dansa de la Mort* thus seems irrefutable.[274] There would therefore seem to be a clear relationship in the kingdom of Aragon (and doubtless also elsewhere) among clerical pedagogy, old funeral dances, and the acculturation of the latter by the former.

The *Dansa de la Mort* was performed for pilgrims who had come to Montserrat. It was danced in the evening, in front of the church altar and out of any liturgical context, as a preparation for confession the next morning. It seems that the singers did not dance, but the dancers sang the last half-line of each verse with them, and everyone—singers, dancers, and pilgrims—sang the refrain together. The *Libre Vermell* also contains the earliest choreographic directions known in Europe, a precious and fragile testimony of a very ancient culture. The directions indicate a *ball rodó*—a circular dance—that is also to be seen on one of the Gothic capitals of the Montserrat cloister. Steps were to be taken, forward and back, the movement of the circle was to change both to the left and to the right, and little jumps, changes in the position of the body, and short halts, and so on, were all indicated.[275] Among the instruments that accompanied the singers and the dancers were the bagpipes, the *rota* (a kind of lyre), and the *samfoina* (Pan flute). The *Libre Vermell* also features, after the various verses of the song, a picture of a skeleton in an open tomb with the following inscription: "O Death, it is so bitter to think of you." Seven reflections then follow, which may have been sung by a chorus of all participants, or may have been sung by two groups, who addressed each other in turn:

Vile corpse that you will be. Why do you not fear sin?
Vile corpse that you will be. Why do you swell with pride?
Vile corpse that you will be. Why do you seek wealth?
Vile corpse that you will be. Why do you dress so ostentatiously?
Vile corpse that you will be. Why do you run after glory?
Vile corpse that you will be. Why do you not confess and repent?
Vile corpse that you will be. Do not rejoice in the pain of others.

Thus Monserrat's *Dansa de la Mort* mingles both popular tradition and Gregorian style, demonstrating the way in which a funeral rite of great antiquity could be used within the context of a moral lesson concerning salvation. There is little need to point out the explicit references, in the song, to contempt for the world, the Last Judgment, and, finally, the decay of the body.

The pastoral tradition of fear found as apt an expression in the *danse macabre* as it did in the other manifestations of piety discussed heretofore. Rather than recapitulating the history of these dances, however, I would rather point out the strong connections that existed between them and the teachings of the church. In the thirteenth century a religious order was founded that called itself the Order of Saint Paul, although its members were commonly known as the Brothers of Death. They wore a death's head on their scapular and greeted each other with the words: "Think of death, my dearest brother." When they entered the refectory, they kissed a skull at the feet of a crucifix and said to each other: "Remember our ultimate end, and you will not sin." Many ate facing a skull, and all of them were supposed to have one in their cell. The seal of the order features a death's head and the words: "*Sanctus Paulus, ermitarum primus pater; memento mori.*"[276] This "reminder" helps us to understand Vincent of Beauvais's statement that a poem written around the year 1190 by the monk Hélinant—*Vers de la mort*—was wildly successful and widely read in monasteries.[277] This poem already seems to describe a kind of *danse macabre*. Hélinant, a former troubadour and nobleman turned Cistercian monk, wishes to inspire his contemporaries with a healthy fear of death. He therefore requests Death to pay them a visit, to give them his greetings, and to frighten them out of their wits. First he sends this dark emissary to his friends, then to various princes, and then to the cardinals of Rome. On route to the eternal city, Death stops off to visit the Archbishop of Reims as well as the bishops of Beauvais, Noyon, Orléans, and so on. Like the authors of *danses macabres* who will follow him, Hélinant follows the order of earthly hierarchies in order to better point out the equality of all before death:

> *Death, you cut down to one same level*
> *As the king within his tower*
> *So the poor man under his roof.* (*Verse 21*)

Worms and hellfire await those who have made ill use of their riches and indulged in the joys of the flesh:

> *Well-fed bodies, delicate flesh*
> *Will wear worms and fire as a dress.* (*Verse 29*)

Hence this conclusion, which could easily be that of a sermon:

> *"Flee, pleasure! Flee, lust! . . .*
> *I prefer my peas and my gruel.*[278]

Toward the middle of the thirteenth century, Robert Le Clerc wrote a poem to which he gave the same title as Hélinant's poem—*Li vers de le Mort*—and which is also very similar to its predecessor. The poet first sends Death to Arras, where it visits both the great and the insignificant. Then it continues on to Rome, where it urges both Pope and king to repent.[279] One of the salient characteristics of the *danse macabre*, the participation of living representatives from all walks of life, appears even more clearly in a number of Latin poems known under as the *Vado mori* (I am going to die) series, the oldest of which dates from the thirteenth century.[280] The dramatic affirmation—"I am going to die"—is pronounced in turn by a king, a pope, a bishop, a soldier, a doctor, a logician, a rich man and a poor man, a wise man and a fool, and so on.[281] It might be also pointed out that a note of irony, which will increasingly accompany the theme of the dance of death, is already present here. No potion can save the doctor; the logician taught others to conclude, but death concludes for him; the voluptuary realizes that lust does not lengthen life . . .

Although manuscript copies of the *Vado mori* are to be found in all of the more important European libraries, it would seem to be of French origin. The thirteenth-century text, for example, does not mention the emperor. On the other hand, Mâle's belief that the *danse macabre* is of French origin no longer seems tenable.[282] In any case, the theory that the first poem of this type was written by Jean Le Févre no longer holds up, despite the fact that his *Respit de la mort* (1376) features the following statement: "I made a dance of Maccabee then / Who leads all people in his dance then / And brings them to the grave."[283]

Even if the fresco painted in 1424 on the walls of the Cemetery of the Innocents constituted an iconographic precedent, the dance of death was already well known. For example, a French chronicler, writing in 1421, expressed the misery of his age in terms of a *danse macabre*: "Fourteen or fifteen years ago began this wretched dance; and most of the nobility have died, by the sword, or by poison, or by other evil and unnatural deaths."[284] There were doubtless texts and images that antedated the fresco in the Cemetery of the Innocents. Hellmut Rosenfeld's hypothesis, according to which the first *danse macabre* poem was written at the Dominican convent of Würzburg in 1350, may therefore be correct. This poem, which was also illustrated, contains a series of Latin monologues spoken by the different characters (pope, emperor, cardinal, and so on) obliged to enter the deathly dance. In a mid-fifteenth-century manuscript now found in Heidelberg, this poem is accompanied by a more elaborated German text that is a real *danse macabre* with verse dialogues (quatrains) between Death and people of different social station. As always, it is the Pope and the emperor who begin the round. Having studied the internal details, Rosenfeld also dates this document from the middle of the fourteenth century.[285]

Is a lengthy investigation of the exact place and date of origin of the dance of death really worthwhile? It was long believed that the Castilian *Dança general* had derived from the Guyot Marchant's *Danse macabre*, published in 1485, which, in turn, had been inspired by the paintings and poems to be found in the Cemetery of the Innocents. Spanish scholars now tend to affirm the originality of this text, and even date it much earlier, from the early 1400s.[286] Many scholars—French, German, Spanish—display a touch of chauvinism in affirming different national origins for this theme. What is most important, however, is not the country that gave birth to the first *danse macabre* (since future discoveries will doubtless alter theories current today), but rather the fact that this theme was in the air, that it caught on and spread throughout the whole of Christian Europe in the course of the fourteenth century. It cannot be denied, of course, that the dance of death painted in the Cemetery of the Innocents had a great impact outside of France and especially in northern Germany. What is of utmost importance, however, is the fact that, in this period, a collective sensibility actively sought to express (in both iconographic and textual form) a theme that was already to be found in a number of current poems, legends, and conventions: the tale of the three living and three dead, the debate of the body and the soul, the *Vado mori*, and the church's transformation of ancient dances into mimed sketches of the highest pedagogical value.

At the present time, at least eighty representations of the *danse macabre* dating from the fifteenth and sixteenth centuries have been found or were known to have existed in Europe. Stained-glass windows, frescoes and sculptures, embroideries and tapestries—all techniques were used. Germany (including Alsace, Austria, Estonia, and Istria) accounts for no less than twenty-two of these representations; Switzerland, eight; the Low Countries, six; France, twenty-two; England, fourteen; northern Italy, eight. None date from before 1400, which is an indication that the written word once again preceded the image. On the other hand, some thirty other images were executed in the course of the seventeenth, eighteenth, and nineteenth centuries, mainly in Germany, Austria, and Switzerland.[287] This quick count obviously does not solve the problem of the actual diffusion of the dance of death, for countries such as Spain and Portugal, which neither painted nor sculpted this theme, still wrote about it, usually without illustrations.[288] Denmark and Sweden were also familiar with this theme, mostly thanks to books and engravings produced in Germany.[289] The importance of these manuscripts and, later, printed books often accompanied by illustrations must therefore be recognized for their role in spreading both the theme and the moral teachings of the *danse macabre* throughout Western and Central Europe. This is certainly the case with the German *Blockbücher* of the fifteenth century, whose name derives from the fact that each page of text and illustrations was carved from a single block of wood and then printed. This technique, which antedated Gutenberg's invention of movable letters in 1455, remained in use for another half century. The oldest of the *Blockbücher* dedicated to the *Toten Dantz* dates from 1465 and belonged to the current Palatine elector.[290] Two other block books that reached a large audience were printed at the end of the fifteenth century at Ulm (or Heidelberg?) and at Mainz.[291] There would therefore seem to be two main channels responsible for diffusing the text and the visualization of this theme throughout Europe, one French and the other German.

It was the vast audience reached by the *danse macabre* of the Cemetery of the Innocents (1424) that led scholars to believe in the French origin of this theme. Reproduced, with a certain literary and iconographic freedom,[292] by Guyot Marchant as well as by other publishers, such as Pierre Le Rouge and Antoine Vérard, these frescoes inspired a number of mural paintings. The dances of death to be found at Ker-Maria (ca. 1460), at La Chaise-Dieu (ca. 1470), at La Ferté-Loupière (late fifteenth century), at Meslay-le-Genet (before 1540), and so on, all have a debt, be it direct or indirect, to the Innocents.[293] A number of foreign representations also owe a great deal to the Parisian model, such as those to be found in London's Pardon Cemetery in 1430, Lübeck in 1463, and Berlin in 1484. On the other hand, it was both the text and the images of the Cemetery of the Innocents that were translated into Catalan in 1497 by the royal archivist Miquel Carbonell, who attributed the original authorship to a "doctor and chancellor of Paris by the name of Joannes Climachus, sive Climages."[294] This identification, which was only partly wrong, referred to Matthieu de Clémanges (d. 1434), a Parisian professor, whose works appear with those of Gerson in a manuscript dated 1429 that reproduces "the verses of the *danse macabre* as they appear in the Cemetery of the Innocents."[295] It is therefore hardly surprising that Carbonell's text is so close to that of Guyot Marchant, as the latter also transcribed the verses of that same cemetery in Paris.

If North German representations of the dance of death are strongly influenced by the French model, those that appeared in Switzerland, Alsace, south Germany, and even northern Italy were more influenced by the German *Blockbücher* tradition of fifteenth-century Würzburg. These two traditions converged in Basel, where two compositions (at the Dominican cemetery around 1440 and at Kligental around 1460/1480)[296] show traits belonging to both. It was also from Basel that the two traditions were relayed back to other parts of Europe. There are no dead musicians in Guyot Marchant's 1485 publication, whereas his second edition includes them. It has been suggested that he owed this innovation to the eclectic Basel model and, less directly, to German iconography.[297] To be sure, the *danses macabres* of La Chaise-Dieu, Lübeck, and Berlin (the last two being of French inspiration) place a dead musician under the preacher's chair. This is, however, doubtless due to the importance that had already been given to this motif in German-speaking lands. The novelty introduced by the Basel dances was the presence of two mummies playing a fife and a tambourine at the entrance to a charnel house. In a block book from 1465, a corpse plays the bagpipes in front of a pope. In the Ulm (or Heidelberg?) edition published around 1485, there is a macabre orchestra composed of three pipers and one trumpet player. Guyot Marchant had only to continue this tradition by inventing variants. His 1486 edition contains four dead musicians playing the bagpipes, a choir organ, a harp, and a piper-tambourine player. Furthermore, with respect to the role played by Basel in the diffusion of these themes, it was in this same city that Hans Holbein the Younger, originally from Antwerp, came to stay in 1515. There he published his *Small Alphabet* (1520) and his *Great Alphabet* (1521) where each letter appears in a scene taken from the *danse macabre*—in each scene a skeleton attacks a living person. These alphabets were, in fact, only preliminary studies for a larger work, which appeared at Lyons in 1538 under the title *Les Simulachres et historiees faces de la Mort.* And as for the greatest Swiss painter of his time, Niklaus Manuel Deutsch, his *Dance of death* (Berne) is also full of dead musicians, which seems only logical given the fact that he had spent his apprenticeship in Basel.[298]

The success of this theme at the end of the fifteenth and early sixteenth centuries and its reproduction by the greatest artists and printers of the time proves not only a public demand but also a public contribution to this very success. A fifteenth-century pack of cards from Holland represents thirty-four men of different social extraction from the emperor down to a modest valet as well as Life, blowing soap bubbles, and Death, of course.[299] A dance of death painted on the walls of Lübeck's Marienkirche (destroyed in 1942) also inspired several illustrated editions of the *Totentanz*, which were published in this same city in 1489, 1496, and 1520. The latter of these publications eventually inspired a Danish edition in 1536.[300] No less than sixteenth French manuscripts (dating mostly from the fifteenth century) reproduce the *danse macabre* of the Cemetery of the Innocents: fourteen reproduce the text only, two are enriched by miniatures, and six add a female counterpart: a *danse macabre des femmes*. As for the incunabula editions published by Guyot Marchant, Antoine Vérard, Pierre Le Rouge, and others, they were responsible for diffusing the two dances in French-speaking countries. At least fifteen different books were published in the years 1485 to 1500, first in Paris, then in Lyons, Troyes, Geneva, and Toulouse.[301] There are also twelve manuscripts still extant that feature the English variant of the dance in the Cemetery of the Innocents, despite the fact that Reformation England was rather hostile to the dance of death (the Pardon Cemetery version was destroyed in 1549 by Lord Somerset's order). And even at the end of the sixteenth century, numerous broadsheet editions of the *Dance and Song of Death* were still sold, where pictures (often taken from Holbein) and verses appeared on the same page. Holbein's *Simulachres* were, of course, highly successful: As many as eleven editions came out between 1538 and 1562, without counting numerous imitations and forgeries.[302] These few remarks, in addition to the observations made above, help measure the important place occupied by the *danse macabre* in the mentality and culture of Western and Central Europe in the fifteenth and sixteenth centuries.

The dance itself is usually a march or procession of all the different stations of human life toward death. Within this parade, each living person is being dragged along by an animated corpse or mummy, which often executes a lively dance step. This general structure did undergo many changes according to the period, the place, and even the room available. On the whole, the number of characters invited to join this sinister procession by a dead person, or by Death itself, increases in proportion to the dance's growing public. At Ker-Maria there are only twenty-three living dancers, whereas the original (?) Latin text and its German variant call for twenty-four. Lübeck and La Chaise-Dieu also respect this number, but Berlin increases the number of living participants to twenty-eight. According to Guyot Marchant, there were thirty at the Cemetery of the Innocents. The *Dança general* features thirty-three scenes coupling a live person and a corpse, whereas the *Blockbücher* of the end of the fifteenth century feature thirty-eight and the frescoes at Basel, which antedate both of these works, feature as many as thirty-nine. It is therefore understandable that Marchant should have reacted to the success of his 1485 publication by repeating the experience the following year with the added attraction of ten more male dancers and a dance of women. Holbein created forty scenes for the first edition of his *Simulachres* (1538) of which seven, however, represent the Creation, the Last Judgment, and Death's escutcheon rather than the traditional dialogue between a living person and a funereal partner. On the other hand, no less than eight new characters appear in the 1545 edition. The height of inflation seems to have been reached in the *Dança de la Muerte* published at Seville in 1520. In this work, which is basically a lengthly adaptation of the *Dança general*, fifty-eight members of the living argue vainly with Death.

The *danse macabre* adheres to a strict hierarchical order that must be read from left to right. It normally begins with the Pope and generally reserves the last place to the peasant or, in the case of the women's dance, to the mother and child—a scale of values that leaves no room for discussion. The clergy also generally go before laymen, either as a group or alternating with members of the laity. The first case is illustrated by the Berlin dance as well as by both of the late fifteenth-century *Blockbücher*: The ecclesiastics are grouped together, ahead of those representing secular society. The second case is more common: A clergyman and the cadaver with which he dances a sort of "polka" precede a layman and his own mummy. Thus the Pope comes before the emperor, the archbishop before the knight, the bishop before the squire. This rule remains inviolable only at the highest level, however. Below the nobility of the church and the sword, imagination takes over. In the fresco of the Innocents, there are five laymen between the monk (number 20) and the curate (number 26): a usurer, a doctor, a lover, a lawyer, and a minstrel. In the Dominican cemetery of Basel, only nine out of thirty-nine characters belonged to the church. Real differences are therefore to be found within the universal pattern. The Berlin dance allots a place to the innkeeper's wife. The Jew, the Turk, and a pagan man and woman are to be found only in the Basel dances. The *Dança general*, on the other hand, includes three contemporary Hispanic characters: the rabbi, the *alfaqui* (Muslim doctor), and the *santero* (sancutary attendant). True to their period and current social concepts, the dances also tend to underrepresent peasants and artisans. One exception to this rule is the *Dança de la Muerte* with its fifty-eight participants (twenty-five more than the *Dança general*). The newcomers are all from the lower social orders: shopkeepers, artisans, and vagrants. There is a tailor, a sailor, a shoemaker, a baker, a biscuit pedlar, a vagabond, and so on. Furthermore, this dance, like the *Dança general*, concludes with the mention of "all the others" who were not able to be included. This kind of remark is not to be found in most *danses macabres*, although the *Blockbücher* printed in the 1490s dedicates its thirty-eighth place to all those who were not already mentioned, a rather necessary memorandum given the fact that Death forgets no one.

Like artisans and peasants, women play a small part in the dance of death, with the obvious exception of Marchant's *Danse macabre des femmes*, taken from a rather poor poem penned by Martial d'Auvergne (d. 1508).[303] At times, women are even totally absent, such as in the Innocents dance, at Ker-Maria, and in the *Dança general*. At Lübeck their appearance is extremely discreet (two female characters out of twenty-four), as it is also at London (three out of thirty-five), Berlin (two out of twenty-eight), at La Chaise-Dieu (three out of twenty-four), and in the *Blockbücher* (three out of thirty-eight). On the other hand, their participation increases in dances inspired by the Latin and German texts coming out of South Germany (Würzburg), where four out of twenty-four places are allotted to women. In the Dominican cemetery of Basel, women occupy eight out of thirty-nine places, and in Holbein's *Simulachres*, eight out of thirty-four. Conversely, in the *Dança de la Muerte*, there are only three females in a total of fifty-eight participants. It would seem, however, that the anonymous author of this poem tried to repair his error by having Death deliver a solemn sermon to two heavily made-up young women who are forced into the dance ahead of the Pope.[304]

On the whole, the *danse macabre* was faithful to the dominant culture that created it, since it systematically undervalued women by simply omitting them, either totally or partially. When they do appear, it is a function of their social status, where they always occupy a secondary place with respect to man—such as the empress (in Germanic countries), the queen, the countess, and the bourgeois's or innkeeper's wife. Other token presences involve women's vulnerability with respect to death—the young girl, the old woman, the mother whom death tears from her children. To conclude, as regards the sociological composition of the dance of death, it is, on the whole, not very original. With the exception of a few details, the genius of the initial idea stopped with its realization. In most cases, it was the sterotype that prevailed.

Should this analysis be pushed in another direction and a distinction made between dances of the dead and the dance of Death? According to a few scholars, the dead pranced long before Death entered the round.[305] From this point of view, the fresco in the Cemetery of the Innocents would have been a "dance of the dead," since each participant was accompanied by his posthumous counterpart. Inversely, Holbein's *Simulachres* would represent the successful transformation of this sort of dance into a series of everyday scenes where Death plays a facile and multiform game with humans, winning every time. But is Holbein's series a true *danse macabre*? The reality of this theme was doubtless more complex. On the whole, authors, spectators, and readers seem to have continually associated both the dead and Death and assimilated them into one coherent lesson.

The theme of the mirror in which one sees the corpse one will eventually become is of great antiquity. It can be found in monastic writings and in the story of the three living and the three dead, which was often used as a powerful illustration of this theme. It is this same idea that is conveyed by the statues of corpses found in many churches, and by the image of a woman looking at herself in a mirror that is found in many manuscripts. Even Guyot Marchant called his dance of death a "*miroir salutaire.*" This probably meant that his readers understood the picture of the emperor, who declares "you must arm yourself with a pickax, a spade, and a shroud" while his dead partner carries these same objects, to mean that the sovereign would someday look just like his cadaverous escort. This is all the more probable as a number of didactic works written at the end of the Middle Ages featured the word "mirror" in their title: *A Mirror for Princes, A Mirror for Magistrates*, and so on. The Franciscans were especially fond of this term and used it in the sense of "moral lesson." The dead dancers of the *danse macabre* cannot, therefore, be too strictly identified with the persons they accompany. It would be difficult, otherwise, to explain the dead musicians who play under the preacher's pulpit, urging the living to join the funereal procession. The dead dance partners are rather delegates or representatives (with interchangeable instruments) sent by Death itself, who had become, by the end of the fifteenth century, an entirely formidable individual. It is this individual whom Hélinant sends to his friends, to princes and to bishops to inspire them with a healthy fear. It is this same individual who flies over the heaps of bodies depicted in the Pisan Campo Santo. It is Death again who, seated on a chariot, advances in all of its pride and invincibility in the numerous "Triumphs of Death" so dear to the fifteenth century, of which I will speak later. It is Death who stars in the German quatrains of Würzburg and in the Castilian *Dança general*. It is this same actor who converses with a peasant in a remarkable text dating from the beginning of the fifteenth century: *Der Ackermann aus Böhmen* (The Laborer from Bohemia).

This text, which is often considered to be the most beautiful example of German prose before Luther, survives in sixteen manuscripts and seventeen printed editions from the early fifteenth to the midsixteenth centuries.[306] It is thought to have been written by a schoolmaster and notary public from Saaz in Bohemia, Johannes von Tepl, who had lost his young wife in August 1400. The peasant, who speaks for the author, attacks Death vehemently, accusing him of being "the ferocious exterminator of all people, the evil persecutor of the entire world, the cruel assassin of all men . . . Sink into wickedness, disappear . . ." (chapter 1). With touching emotion he remembers his model wife, who had been so cruelly taken from him: "I was her love, she was my dear . . . the light of my eyes . . . my shield against all discomfort . . . my magic wand . . . my most precious treasure . . . She was good and pure" (chapters 4 and 9). For German literature at this time, this text provides a rare and lovely example of praise for conjugal love. Lord Death is not speechless, however, and comes up with apt arguments throughout the dialogue. Refuting the laborer's accusations, he becomes an arrogant prosecutor, calling his opponent an "imbecile" and confronting him with a "common sense" argument:

> *If, since the time in which the first man was formed of clay, I had not controlled the growth and the multiplication of people on this earth, of animals and worms in the deserts and on the wild heath, and of libidinous fish, all covered in scales, in the seas, no one could exist on account of the mosquitoes, no one would dare go outdoors because of the wolves; human beings, animals, all living creatures would eat each other because there would not be enough food; the earth would be too tight for them. (chapter 8)*

Lord Death then points out that he had taken the peasant's wife in the year 1400, which was a jubilee year. Her ascent into Heaven would therefore have been automatic (chapter 14). At any rate, the grim reaper claims to be one of "God's creatures" and declares he works for Him (chapter 16). When the peasant insists on defending every person's right to life and joy, Death replies by digging up the old misogynist argument: Woman is rot and filth,[307] and she is immoral (chapters 24 and 28). According to the usual scenario of contemporary debates, the two opponents end up appearing before the divine tribunal. God puts both of the speakers back in their places. The peasant's wife was not his by inheritance, but rather as a loan. Death boasts of his power, but this power was only given in fief: "He glories in a power he does not own." In the end, "every man is obliged to give his life to death, his body to the earth, and his soul to Us" (chapter 33).

Death appears again, hard at work, in a curious poem, *Le Mors de la pomme* which dates from the middle of the fifteenth century. Several passages of this poem were probably inspired by the images and inscriptions of a dance of death painted in the cloister of Amiens around 1450 (this painting was destroyed in 1817).[308] As for the dialogue between Death and the mother and child who is destined to die, this passage comes from the oldest literary versions (both Latin and German) of the *danse macabre.*[309] The link between the dance of death and the poem is therefore certain. Death is personalized in *Le Mors de la pomme*, having been born at the moment of the Original Sin. Armed with three arrows and the seal of God, it exercises total power over men. The poem describes Death at work: helping Cain kill Abel, striking down the Pope in the middle of his court, the knight in full combat, the young girl before her mirror, and so on. This same concept of a sovereign and implacable Death appears in Simon Vostre's *Heures* (1512). Following in the wake of the *Le Mors de la pomme*, the engraver working for Simon Vostre created variations and invented new themes. Death causes the mason to fall from his scaffolding, he helps the brigand to kill his victim . . . and the executioner to hang the brigand.[310] Mâle believes that Holbein knew these French works, for his *Simulachres* constitute a variant with respect to the classical model. His *danse macabre* is less of a dance and more of a series of scenes from ordinary life, like those that can be found in *Le Mors de la pomme* and Vostre's *Heures*, as well as a number of scenes that he invented: Death helps Adam work the earth, accompanies the empress on a walk, walks next to the laborer and drives his horses. Death, as personified in these more recent iconographic sources, had therefore a long prehistory and an active past. Furthermore, it is not really necessary to distinguish between dances of the dead and the dance of death insofar as the populations of the past did not make this distinction. There is even one explicit testimony to this effect. When John Lydgate, a Benedictine monk, came to France, he visited the Cemetery of the Innocents, discussed the significance of the fresco with Parisian monks, and translated the verses into English. He understood this *danse macabre* to be a dance of death, and so translated the inscriptions: "First Death says to the Pope . . ." "Death again says to the hermit . . ." and so on. For Lydgate, it was indeed Death who was speaking to the living.

Holbein took a certain amount of liberties with his *danse macabre*. For example, the term does not even feature in the title of his 1538 publication: *Les Simulachres et historiees faces de la mort, autant elegamment pourtraictes que artificiellement imaginees*. The term is also lacking in the Latin and Italian translations of his book, and appears only in certain German adaptations, where the expression *Todtentanz* can be found.[311] On the other hand, the Bernese *Danse macabre* painted by Niklaus Manuel Deutsch in 1516–20 (it was destroyed in 1660) is only partially true to its name. Here there is no longer a continuous and rhythmic procession of couples made up of a living person and his or her dead counterpart, but rather a gallery of different scenes. The characters are often grouped: The Pope is with a cardinal, the emperor with a king, a knight with a jurist, a soldier with a whore. Death appears only in the last scene, a scythe in one hand and a bow in the other, his quiver full of arrows. In front of the grim archer some twenty people of both sexes and all ages are strewn on the ground, pierced with arrows. On his left, hanged men dangle from a tree that has been split halfway down its trunk. There is also a major innovation: The painter has signed his work and has even represented himself with a paintbrush, palette, and handrest. He is in the process of touching up his work, oblivious to the fact that a skeleton, hourglass in hand, is coming to interrupt him.[312]

When Deutsch painted this composition, the Reformation had not as yet triumphed at Bern, although Luther's revolt had already begun and had reached a certain intensity. The violent anticlericalism of this painting is therefore due to a personality who would later embrace Protestantism and who made a point of writing his own inscriptions in Bernese dialect. At the moment of death, the bishop confesses: "Like a wolf, I devoured my flock . . ." Death cries out to a group of monks: "You are voracious wolves disguised as sheep." Death also tears the tiara and stole off a pope who is being carried, like an idol, on a sedanchair. It pulls the patriarch along mercilessly by his hatstrings, just as animals are dragged to the slaughter, and so on. Deutsch thus pushed this traditional satire of the clergy to a new limit. Similarly, Marchant's clergyman, "who ate the living and the dead," is told by a skeleton that he will be devoured by worms. A bit farther to the left, the dead companion of an abbot says: "Commend the abbey to God, it made you fat, you could not have done better, the fattest is the first to rot." Both Marchant's and

Deutsch's anticlericalism reveal a strong desire to have the church reform itself. This desire for reform does not, however, alter the fact that the *danse macabre* was a kind of sermon. This is visible even in its most important and artistically successful transformations. Holbein and Deutsch both integrate scenes representing the Original Sin and the Last Judgment. Holbein also adds the Creation and the Garden of Eden, whereas Deutsch represents Moses receiving the Ten Commandments and a preacher holding a skull.

These images, which frame more traditionally macabre episodes, translate the true meaning of the whole and help the viewer to avoid mistakes in interpretation.

CHAPTER 3

Ambiguity of the Macabre

THE *DANSE MACABRE:* A SERMON

The black humor that characterizes the dances of the dead (or of death) can be explained by the double lesson they wished to convey. The final hour arrives suddenly—hence the comic effect of surprise. It strikes equally both young and old, rich and poor—hence the ridicule aimed at those who believed themselves protected by age, rank, or fortune. But did this irony, underlined by the mocking smile of toothless cadavers, go so far as to constitute a form of social satire? This view has been affirmed too quickly.[1] Certainly death was less intimidating to the humble than to the prosperous. A constant feature of the macabre iconography of the fourteenth to sixteenth centuries, this trait appears in the fresco of the Campo Santo of Pisa, where a group of miserable folk implore Death, but to no avail, for he is already hurrying toward a group of wealthy and carefree youths. In the *Danse* of Guyot Marchant, the corpse who addresses the worker declares: ". . . In care and in pain / You have lived all your days / . . . With death you must be content / For it delivers you from great worry." Scene 38 of Holbein's *Simulacnres* depicts a living corpse showing compassion for a peasant. The corpse helps the peasant to cross his final furrow as the rays of the setting sun illumine the horizon behind the church. On the other hand, when macabre images (and notably dances) place the rich, the great, the young, and the clergy face to face with Death, this visitant always appears as a "criminal sergeant," executor of divine "commandments."

To what extent did the poor and the unfortunate interpret these images as a sort of future revenge? Did they see in them something other than the constant teaching of Christianity that opposed Lazarus's peaceful death to that of the evil rich man? Such is the message conveyed by a Strasbourg painting of 1474, where a beggar is received into Paradise and a glutton, surrounded by young women and musicians, is the prey of demons.[2] As was pointed out in my previous study, seventeenth-century missionaries to rural areas thundered against the abuses of the rich but, in contrast to numerous parish priests, they kept to the side of power in times of revolt.[3] This fact retrospectively clarifies certain aspects of the *danses macabres* insofar as they promise equality, but only after death. As for the present life, they carefully maintain existing hierarchies and order people accordingly. They do not, however, stigmatize these people (were they not so ordered by God?) but rather point out the laughable illusions that honors and money engender in the well-to-do. Although the *danses macabres* were not a denunciation of the deadly sins, they did consistently vilify two of them: pride and avarice (with its by-product, usury). Pride, of course, is the first of the capital sins. As for avarice, whose importance was constantly growing in a society increasingly attracted to luxury and money, it became one of the main targets of the confession manuals and other such handbooks.[4]

At the risk of going against traditionally accepted interpretations, it is worth insisting on the Christian pedagogy that the church wished to convey by means of the *danse macabre*. For Emile Mâle, once the dance is "stripped of its commentary, it does not retain, in fact, any strictly Christian character"[5] it is content to illustrate two truths that are not particularly religious: equality before death and the suddenness with which death strikes. In the same spirit, Johan Huizinga posed the question: "Can thought be truly pious if it clings so tenaciously to the terrestrial aspect of death?"[6] Extending these analyses and pushing them to their limit, Alberto Tenenti sees in the macabre of the fourteenth to sixteenth centuries (dances included) a dislocation of acquired values, an "overthrow of the Christian schema." Death is no longer a passage but an ending, a decomposition: "Those who previously considered themselves to be Christians now saw themselves as mortals." "An inversion of the traditional meaning of death plays itself out across the motifs that appear the most ascetic." These macabre sarcasms, which were only partially inspired by Christian sensibility, in reality bypass it.[7] Philippe Ariès contests Tenenti's opposition between a Christian High Middle Ages, which would have insisted on death as the anteroom to eternity, and the following period when it was supposedly laicized. He agrees, however, with his predecessor's view that during the fourteenth to sixteenth centuries "images of death and of decomposition signify neither the fear of death nor that of the afterlife—even if they were used for this purpose."[8] Jean Saigneux affirms that "the fifteenth century no longer even considered death as a consequence of sin." The concept of the dance of death "is still Christian, but in a fashion more external than real. The heart of man adheres to a vision that excludes all transcendence." "The theme of death and, in a more precise sense, that of the *danse macabre*, tends to substitute itself for that of hell."[9] For Corvisier, "the moralizing purpose of these works [the dances] ends up being secondary to a realistic expression of terror in the face of death and its inevitable association: the sour taste of life."[10] Jean Wirth argues that the *danse macabre* "is nothing but an unstable synthesis of popular beliefs, that is, pagan ones, and of a moral content incidentally tinged with Christianity."[11]

One cannot but be impressed by such a consensus. Hence the obvious question: To what extent did the macabre escape from its promoters? Historians, and especially French historians, have tended to "read" the macabre in both modern and lay terms, whereas it involved a discourse above all issued and propagated by the church. We have already surveyed the macabre's monastic roots. Let us now clarify its diffusion in the dances of the dead (or of death). Mâle and his above-mentioned successors certainly recognized the role that the mendicant orders played in this regard. And Mâle, in particular, attributed the invention of the *danse macabre* to these same orders: "They were . . . the ones who began to terrorize the crowds by speaking to them of death."[12] Further research, especially outside of France, has corroborated this view and will continue to provide a better assessment of the extent of the macabre phenomenon. For example, the *danse macabre* did not exist in Bohemia before the seventeenth century. This fact is doubtless a result of the role the Hussite movement played in this country. Jan Hus and his successors reproached the Catholic Church for having exploited the people's terror of Hell.

According to this reformer, priests implied in their sermons that the Pope and even they themselves could send Christians into the Inferno.[13] In a still more significant way, Jakoubek de Stirbra affirmed, in a sermon delivered in 1416: "Hell is destined for devils, not for men . . . it is the devil who enters hell, not the Christian."[14] Under these conditions, what use was it to frighten people with *danses macabres*? And, in fact, these dances appear only in Bohemia at the time of the Counter-Reformation.

It is thus worth repeating: The *danse macabre* was a sermon. Its purpose was didactic rather than aesthetic.[15] Is it any accident that the dance's origin has been attributed to Gerson?[16] The verses of the Innocents do, in fact, figure in a 1429 manuscript containing works by this great academician, who was famous in his own time as a preacher. It is therefore understandable that many have believed Gerson to be the inventor of the dance of death. The dance, however, is most likely older. In the Latin and German versions that Hellmut Rosenfeld dates back to the fourteenth century, the march of the living and the dead is framed by two preachers, the one opening, the other closing the funereal procession with a sermon. Moreover, the Latin manuscript, which has lost its illustrations, includes a final notice: "*Alius doctor* [the second preacher] *depictus predicando in opposita parte de contemptu mundi*."[17]

From the outset, then, the *Totentanz* is unambiguously presented as a sermon on this theme. Likewise, the fourteenth-century Catalan *Danza de la mort* begins with the following formula, clearly written by a man of the church: "I wished to treat of the contempt for this world . . ."[18] The preacher in his pulpit (sometimes called "the actor" or the "doctor") whose homily precedes the dance itself appears throughout the fifteenth and sixteenth centuries in both writing (Guyot Marchant, the *Dança General*, and so on) and in iconography (at La Chaise-Dieu, Basel, Strasbourg, Berlin, Lübeck, Reval, Ulm, Metnitz, and even Berne).[19] This constant feature is significant: The preacher plays a role comparable to that of the hermit who, unrolling his parchment, recounts the *exemplum* of the three dead and three living men. In addition, within the procession itself, reference is sometimes made to sermons on death. Such is the case with Marchant's text, where the corpse accompanying a Franciscan monk tells him: "Often have you preached of death . . ." Lydgate's English translation amplifies this challenge in the following way:

Sir Cordelier
to you myn hand is stretched
To this dance
you to convey and lede
Which in your preaching
have full oft taught
How that I am
most ghastful for to drede
All be that folk
take thereof no hede.[20]

A fourteenth-century Catalan Benedictine composed the words that accompany the *Danza de la mort*. Another Benedictine, Lydgate, impressed by the fresco and verses of the *Cemetery of the Innocents*, introduced the *danse macabre* to England. The dance at La Chaise-Dieu is to be found in a Benedictine abbey. The chapel of Ker-Maria belonged to the Prémontrés. The mendicant orders were therefore far from having a monopoly on the *danse macabre*. All the same, their role was essential. Certain dances explicitly refer to a "friar" who preaches on death—without, however, specifying his order. In the *Dança General*, Death, at the end of his first interruption, taunts his listeners: ". . . If you do not see the friar who preaches / At least pay attention to what he says in his great wisdom."[21] Prior to this passage the preacher intervenes, announcing the content of the poem. Soon Death resumes his speech to pointedly say: "Since the friar has preached to you / You must all do penance."[22] This *Dança General* is thus presented as a mendicant's sermon. It is sometimes possible to determine the identity of this actor's order. Rosenfeld used massive documentation to demonstrate how the first Latin and German texts originated from a Dominican convent in Würzburg. The preaching friars then contributed greatly to the diffusion of the theme, which the Franciscans eventually took over, somewhat modifying its spirit.[23] Indeed, the Dominicans, who probably initiated the frescoes in the Campo Santo of Pisa, also commissioned the Basel dances[24] as well as those in Strasbourg, Berne, Constance, and Landshut (in the seventeenth century). Thus the Dominicans would have first been promoters, and then active disseminators, of the *danse macabre*.

Yet there can be no doubt that the Franciscans gave them stiff competition. In the two *Blockbücher* of the 1490s, the eleventh living member of the procession—the good monk—is dressed as a Franciscan while the twelfth member—the bad monk—wears the Dominican habit. Since the time of their founder, the Franciscans had preached the *contemptus mundi*. In the *Fioretti*, there is a phrase that could illustrate the opening scene—the preacher in his pulpit—of several *danses macabres*: "Then Saint Francis entered the pulpit and began to preach wonderfully on the contempt for this world . . ."[25] Early on, the Franciscans associated images of death with ascetic preaching. On the walls of the Lower Church of Assisi, a fresco depicts Saint Francis displaying a crowned skeleton. An analogous fresco exists in the chapterhouse of Saint Anthony's Basilica at Padua. As of the last quarter of the thirteenth century, the Franciscan movement also seems to have been responsible for the emergence of the theme of bodily decomposition, both in painting (the church of Saint Margherita di Melfi) and in sculpture (the "tempter" of Strasbourg cathedral). The Franciscans also promoted the iconography of Jesus' tortured body.[26] At a later point—in the seventeenth century—the Franciscans (Capuchins included), in their cemetery chapels at Rome, Naples, Palermo, Evora, and so on, created pillars completely covered with tibias, as well as arches, vaults, rose windows, capitals, and entire altarpieces composed of skulls. They also furnished their underground galleries with standing cadavers, dessicated in their mortuary outfits and arranged by categories (the priests with their caps, the hanged with their ropes, and so on).

Returning to the dances of the dead, we read in the *Journal d'un bourgeois de Paris* that in the year 1429 Frère Richard, a well-known Franciscan friar, preached for eight consecutive days at the Cemetery of the Innocents "atop a platform nearly nine feet high, the charnel house as his backdrop, across from the Charronerie, at the site of the *Danse Macabre*."[27] In 1453 the Franciscans of Besançon, following the lead of their provincial chapter, had the *danse macabre* portrayed in the Church of Saint John.[28] In the Marienkirche of east Berlin, the preacher who speaks from the pulpit at the beginning of the mural is a Franciscan. The danses of Augsburg, Hamburg, Bad-Gundersheim, and Fribourg (eighteenth century) are also Franciscan. Rosenfeld perceives in these paintings a less scholastic, more Pietist and democratic spirit than that of the dances of Dominican inspiration: *Cupiditas* is denounced more strongly,[29] and the Cross on which Jesus hangs is placed either in the middle or to one side of the composition, thus explaining to the faithful that sin and death have been vanquished by redemption. This vivid reference to the crucifixion, which is characteristic of all the Franciscan dances in northern Germany, is also found in Italy: at Pinzolo (1519) and at Carisolo (1539).[30] A highly Franciscan touch likewise appears in an Italian poem of the late fifteenth or early sixteenth century, the *Ballo della Morte*.[31] Although largely inspired by the dance of the Innocents, the author, clearly a member of the order of Saint Francis, has included a lively critique of the High Church. An archbishop, who considers himself a saint, is sent to Hell. The cadaver that escorts him ironically says that "benefices are given to prelates in order for them to lead dissolute lives." The patriarch is entitled to even more serious threats: "Already," he is informed, "Satan shows his fangs." The bishop, who had saved a number of souls, nevertheless receives a biting reprimand from his ghastly companion, who declares: "I could wish myself the last of the minor friars . . . I will not forsake the certain for the uncertain." The bishop agrees—"you speak true"—and commends himself to divine mercy. The Franciscan, on the other hand, is privileged in all respects. He is qualified as "the servant of Christ," and Paradise is promised to him.[32] There is no doubt, therefore, that both Dominicans and Franciscans ardently competed to popularize the theme of the *danse macabre* with the clear intent of instructing the faithful. For their part, the Augustinians exploited the subject only slightly: A dance at Pinzolo (1539), in the Trentino, was painted on a wall adjoining the cemetery of a mountain church belonging to their order.

THE MACABRE AND THE RESURRECTION

Pierre Chaunu considers the literary and iconographic emergence of the decomposing cadaver to be linked "to a pedagogical intention indissociable from judgment (individual)." Previously, the church had especially emphasized the resurrection—body and soul—of all those baptized, and representations of the Last Judgment had evoked this complete resurrection. In contrast, the promotion of the "perished" pushed the final resurrection into the hazy distance and accentuated the judgment of each individual soul, immediately after death. In order that this "anthropology of disembodied souls might be deployed, the body had to be killed." The emergence of the macabre was thus inseparable from "the usury of the resurrection and of the Last Judgment."[33] Writing some months before Chaunu, Philippe Ariès developed the same thesis. He argues:

> *After the fourteenth century, the theme of the Last Judgment was not completely abandoned: We find it in the fifteenth and sixteenth centuries in the painting of Van Eyck and Hieronymus Bosch, in the seventeenth century still here and there (Assisi, Dijon). Yet, though it survives, it has lost its popularity and people no longer imagine the final end of mankind in this form. The idea of judgment therefore becomes separated from the idea of resurrection.*[34]

I agree with these two historians to the extent that, in the long run, the result of this clerical teaching was precisely what they emphasized: Christians eventually came to forget, or at least to underrate, this body-and-soul resurrection that constitutes the "profound originality of Christian thought," insofar as it promises "an entire lifetime beyond time."[35]

My reservations, however, pertain to both the shift in mentality and to the chronology that led to this obliteration of the original Christian message. Certain passages of my book were already written when Aaron Gurevic published his article "Images of the Afterlife."[36] He accurately points out that medieval religious literature, so rich in *exempla*, is filled with stories of ghosts who momentarily return to earth after the individual judgment that appointed them to either Heaven or Hell. Individual judgment is thus omnipresent in medieval ecclesiastical discourse. It coexists alongside of the preoccupation with the Last Judgment. The one does not exclude the other. There is no reason to diametrically oppose them. It is not worthwhile, therefore, to dissociate the macabre and the Last Judgment of all.

As I have already pointed out, the monastic discourse on the contempt for this world regarded the devaluation of the body from the perspective of the *Dies Irae.*[37] This view again appears in the literature of the macabre era in the writings of Jean Regnier, Eustache Deschamps, Georges Chastellain, and others. In the same way, the representation of Death as an irresistible rider or as a pitiless reaper often accompanied the iconography of the *Apocalypse* and the Last Judgment.[38] Finally and above all, Europeans painted, sculpted, described, and announced the end of the world (and hence the general resurrection) to a greater extent during the fifteenth and sixteenth centuries than in the High Middle Ages.[39] Obvious examples are the important compositions to be found at Albi, at Orvieto (Luca Signorelli), in the Sistine Chapel, at Beaune (Van der Weyden), at the Hermitage (Jan Van Eyck), and at Gdansk (Memling). Equally, and perhaps especially, important are the small change of provincial works devoted to the Last Judgment. In Normandy alone there are still three dating from the twelfth to the thirteenth centuries, six for the fourteenth century, six for the fifteenth, sixteen for the sixteenth, and one for the beginning of the seventeenth.[40] These figures are similar to those for the French Midi. Michel Vovelle writes, "For all that one may extrapolate an evidently residual supply from the numerical givens, the blossoming of Last Judgments did not occur until the fifteenth and early sixteenth centuries: forty-five out of fifty-six examples . . . ; the eleven earlier cases announce rather than develop the theme."[41] In Breton stained-glass windows, Last Judgments also increase in number during the sixteenth century.

Thus collective eschatology and the macabre did not compete with each other. On the contrary, they were in step, shoulder to shoulder, and together they declined during the seventeenth century. The last great Judgments are those of Peter Paul Rubens (1616 and 1620, both in Munich). By this time, the iconography of the macabre had already exhausted itself. Conversely, it is revealing that Frère Richard, who preached before the fresco of the Innocents, had specialized in apocalyptic predictions. These predictions spread throughout Europe in the period called the "Renaissance," and notably in such countries as Germany, France and England, where the *danse macabre* became popular. A remarkable correlation: Surviving "*transi*" tombs featuring dead or decomposing bodies are essentially located in countries where eschatological fever was strongest and most persistent during the fifteenth to seventeenth centuries. According to Kathleen Cohen, the geographical distribution of these tombs is the following: 57 in Germany, Switzerland, and the Low Countries, 61 in France, and 146 in England.[42] One notes the absence of Spain and Italy[43] where, as was discussed in *La Peur en Occident*, the different forms of fear were, on the whole, weaker than those current in other Western countries. In England, the fashion for "*transi*" tombs carried on the longest (until the first part of the seventeenth century). It was also in this country that apocalyptic anxieties —and hopes—remained current for the longest time.[44]

In the long run, both the Bull of Benedict XII, *Benedictus Deus* (1336) (which declared that the just obtain the beatific vision[45] at their death without having to wait for the resurrection), and the "officialization" of Purgatory and the immediate judgment of souls by the Council of Florence in 1439 and again by the Council of Trent, incontestably worked against the eschatology of the general resurrection.

These theological moves encouraged the growth of the custom of legacies for masses to be said in favor of souls in limbo and stimulated the multiplication of the *Artes moriendi*. At first, however, there was an identification between the macabre of the Last Judgment and the new theme of Purgatory. Vovelle has demonstrated this using several examples from southern France. The most astonishing among them is located in the chapel of the Penitents at Tourves, in the region of Var (second half of the sixteenth century). The background of the painting shows the fire and destruction of Jerusalem—a most apocalyptic panorama. The foreground and the center evoke the vision of Ezekiel: Skeletal remains recompose themselves into bodies. On either side of the central panel, two heads—one male, the other female—further confirm this resurrection of the flesh. Amid the field of bones, which is also a field of battle, the conquered figure of Death kneels before Christ. The macabre abounds in this naïve composition: There is Death with his flag, his skeletal cohorts bearing hourglasses, and, for good measure, in the upper portion of the painting, heavy foliage bears mitered skulls as fruit. Yet, at the center, this foliage opens up to reveal a luminous vision: An angel welcomes souls ascending from the flames of Purgatory.[46]

This painting closely associates general resurrection, Purgatory, and macabre iconography, and it is not an exceptional case. In Robert Mesuret's inventory of mural paintings to be found in southwestern France, there are three churches where Purgatory and the Last Judgment mingle in the same composition: at Birac, Montaner, and Pervillac. These three works all date from the fifteenth century.[47] To these iconographic examples should be added a number of contemporary texts that convey a veritable confusion between individual judgment and the Last Judgment. This potentially surprising confusion becomes quite understandable in the works of writers who, like Eustache Deschamps, believed in the imminent end of the world.

To come back to the *danses macabres*, we now face the difficult question of how they were understood. A fully satisfying answer will always elude us. How can we know what the numerous illiterate people of the time retained from images whose commentary they could not read? We do know, nevertheless, that the teaching church not only delivered visions of decaying cadavers to the public's more or less unwholesome curiosity, but also gave the faithful an explanation independent of the accompanying verses. Most of the dances included a preacher, who set their tone, while others added, before the dance itself, the fall of Adam and Eve. At La Chaise-Dieu, the serpent in the arch has a death's head. Both Niklaus Manuel Deutsch and Hans Holbein, following the example set by *Le Mors de la pomme* and the *Heures* of Simon Vostre, both inserted the Original Sin into their textual illustrations. To the last sequence of their dances, these two artists add the general resurrection. Elsewhere, the redemptive cross, victorious over death, figures prominently in dances of Franciscan inspiration such as those to be found at Hamburg, Berlin, Pinzolo, and Carisolo.

It is also worth recalling where frescoes depicting the dance of death were situated. Some appear in palaces: at Blois, Whitehall, Ferrara (Palazzo della Ragione), at Croydon (the archbishop's palace), and at Coira (Episcopal palace). But the majority were painted in churches, chapels, or cemeteries (at Paris, London, Basel, Kernascleden, Ker-Maria, Pinzolo, and so on), hence in places of preaching. For this reason they cannot be artificially isolated from the sermons that were given in the same locations. These early "comic strips" were, in fact, a constituent part of a generalized audio-visual instruction with respect to a global history of salvation. This same teaching presented death as the by-product of Original Sin, both of which were to be eliminated at the end of time.

In an unpublished study, the Romanian historian Pavel Chihaia attempts to relate the church's discourse on the macabre to the "ideology" that inspired it. Yet the latter always included the belief in human "everlastingness" in an otherworld beyond death. The provisional decay of the body, a consequence of sin, is the inevitable passage toward a resurrection of the purified flesh. For Saint John Chrysostom, Saint Gregory of Nysa, Tertullian, and others, the body will be reborn in the state that Adam enjoyed before the Fall. Readers may object that this final optimism did not appear in literature dedicated to the *contemptus mundi*, overrun as it was by pessimism and insisting on the decomposition of the flesh rather than on its eternal rebirth. This was undeniably the case. Yet this evangelism of fear, as terrifying as it was, did not cause the total disappearance of teaching with respect to the eternity of the reconstituted body. In the great Last Judgments of the fifteenth and sixteenth centuries—such as those of Hans Memling (Gdansk) or of Luca Signorelli (Orvieto)—there are scenes representing the resurrection of the flesh. This observation holds for all the Last Judgments of the period. To be sure, they were never as numerous as during the period characterized by the full efflorescence of the macabre. All the same, the faithful Christian who contemplated Jan Van Eyck's admirable altarpiece of *The Mystic Lamb* at St. Bavo of Ghent (its large dimensions make it highly readable) or Dürer's evocation of *All Saints* painted for an old person's hospice in Nuremberg[48], could only believe in fleshly resurrection. Such a destiny was made evident in both cases by crowds of the blessed, carrying palms and surrounding the divine lamb of the Trinity.

Kathleen Cohen rightly stresses the ties that, from the fourteenth to the sixteenth centuries, associated the representation of the macabre with a firm belief in resurrection.[49] Nicolas Flamel (d. 1418), author and copyist for the University of Paris, who prided himself on his learning, ordered for his wife at the Innocents, and later for himself at St.-Jacques, a funerary iconography readable on two levels, that of religion and that of alchemy. On his monument (now at the *Musée de Cluny*), the radiant sun and the full moon on either side a representation of Christ in majesty signify eternal life and, at the same time, the natural powers that by God's command, will transfigure the corrupt and putrefied corpse into an eternal body. Here decomposition is understood as a necessary stage leading toward an ultimate state of incorruptibility.[50] Adam's open tomb that, revealing his skeleton, was placed below the Cross of Christ, had for a long time been regarded as a double symbol for the punishment of sin and for the redemption that would bring about the resurrection of the flesh. This key provides an interpretation to works such as the central tympanum of Strasbourg Cathedral (end of the thirteenth century) and Masaccio's fresco of the Trinity (1435) at Santa Maria Novella in Florence.[51]

In funerary chapels, beneath the cross of Golgotha, the representation of a deceased person's body often replaced that of Adam's skeleton. The general meaning remained the same: temporary decomposition would be followed by a conclusive resurrection that was guaranteed by Christ's victory over Death. A tomb project drawn by Jacopo Bellini around 1440 presents a nude corpse below the cross. So that there would be no doubt as to the symbolism of the composition, the artist portrayed a lioness and her cub at the base of the tomb. According to a common belief, the lioness could bring her young back to life by licking them for three days.[52] In the Fugger chapel of Saint Anne of Augsburg, representations of two members of that illustrious family, Ulrich and George, lie below the resurrection of Christ and the Victory of Samson over the Philistines. These homogeneous illustrations, designed by Dürer, together signify that Death will one day die.[53] There are numerous parallel examples. Mâle described a stained-glass window representing the resurrection that, in his time, was located at St.-Vincent of Rouen and is now in the church of the Vieux Marché. At the base of the window, the donor's entire body is stretched out on the slab of the tomb. Worms already eat him. But he cries "Jesus, sis mihi Jesus" ("Jesus, Jesus, take my part"): in other words, "You who are risen, pardon me, and grant me resurrection."[54]

The theme of the resurrection accompanied a variety of macabre horrors. The funerary plaque of the abbess Jacquete de Rothais (d. 1525) at Beaumont-lès-Tours (known from a drawing) shows the deceased entirely wrapped in a shroud between the crucified Christ and the Virgin and Child. As in modern comic strips, an inscription issuing from the dead woman's head contains the words: "*Exspecto resurrectionem mortuorum.*"[55] Historians who have worked on the subject of death in the fifteenth century often and justly mention the portable polyptych of Strasbourg (ca. 1494, school of Memling, Musée des Beaux Arts),[56] whose images are particularly striking. It is composed of six small paintings of identical size representing the Christ of the Last Judgment in glory, Hell, the standing figure of Vanity, an upright cadaver, a skull, and the donor's coat of arms. The donor was a Bolognese who commissioned this work on the occasion of his wedding with a Flemish woman. The corpse, who smiles in triumph, his stomach opened by the embalmer and a toad on his genitalia, stands atop a tomb slab surrounded by bones. With the help of an unfurled banner—again anticipating the convention of the comic strip—he proclaims: "Behold the end of man. I have become as clay. I am like to dust and to ashes." Vanity, a young nude woman, is an embodiment of sin. The ensemble of the polyptych must have been particularly distressing to behold. There is no doubt, however, about its general sense. Under the skull one reads, written in very clear script, a Latin translation of Job (19:26): "After my awakening, he will set me close to him, and from my flesh I shall look on God." There is also a symbolic redoubling of this affirmation: The eye sockets are not totally empty. Two narrow slots in the middle of the sockets signify that, on the day of resurrection, these eyes will regain their sight.

The same lines from the Book of Job appear on a black velvet mortuary cloth from Evreux Cathedral. The embroideries portray a cadaver—the body of Adam? —gnawed by worms and placed at the foot of the cross. Below this "*transi*" the gothic inscription reads, "*Credo quod Redemptor meus vivit, et in novissima die de terra surrecturus sum et in carne mea videbo deum salvatorem meum*," which are the same lines as those quoted in Strasbourg.[57] In this light, it would be difficult to interpret the celebrated tomb of Ligier Richier (at Saint-Pierre of Bar-le-Duc) as anything other than a symbol of resurrection. In passing, it is noteworthy that the artist of this work became a Protestant and died in Geneva. Even in the eighteenth century, people found "this an inimitable work of art."[58] On the tomb of René de Chalons, a prince of Orange-Nassau who was killed at the siege of Saint-Dizier in 1544, there also stands a body whose skin is peeling off: It has disappeared from his head and from most of his chest. Moreover, the skin has holes, like old worn-out fabric falling into tatters. In his will, the prince had requested that he be represented as he might look three years after his death. Still, the deceased figure is standing, and holds out his heart to God, while his skull and his left arm are turned toward the light of eternal life.

Hope for the definite rebirth of the entire human being is conveyed by numerous double tombs of the period, whose lower levels show a more or less decomposed "*transi*" and whose upper levels display the same person alive, hands clasped together, the eyes turned toward heaven. "This cadaver that frightens us," writes Mâle, "is only a deceptive appearance. On the final day the body will regain its form in response to the call of God."[59] How then to interpret the desire of both clerics and laymen who asked to be portrayed as cadavers atop their sepulchers?

Was it morbid exhibitionism? Perhaps, but even more certainly it was a sincere act of humility. Accepting the lessons of the contemporary church, the future deceased thus acknowledged the degradation that would be wrought upon the skin of their sinful bodies. At the same time, they affirmed *coram publico* their belief in an otherworld of decay and ashes. In doing so, they offered a "mirror" to all those who gazed upon their tombs, thus facilitating the evangelistic efforts of the clergy.[60]

In this regard, the funerary monument of the judge François de la Sarraz (d. 1363), near Lausanne, is most revealing.[61] The nude corpse, beside whom two standing knights and two women pray, has his arms crossed across his chest. Two toads chew on his eyes, two others attack his mouth, and a fifth his genitalia. Long worms infest and devour his entire body. On his chest and his pillow, there are scallop shells. The toads most likely symbolize sins, the worms figure the remorseful conscience, and the shells express belief in resurrection. This ancient meaning of the scallop shell explains those that appear above the niches of praying monks on the sarcophagus of Jean de Beauveau (d. 1479) (once to be found at the cathedral of Angers and now lost) and those above the "*transi*" of Jeanne de Bourbon (d. 1521), which is now in the Louvre.[62] Sarraz's tomb also associates the humility of the sinner, the contrition of the Christian, and hope for the definite rebirth of regenerate man. The same keys—humility and hope—also help explain double portraits where one of two antithetical panels represents two fiancés in full youth joining themselves for life, and the other features the same figures as hideous cadavers, ravaged by worms and toads.[63]

THE MACABRE AND THE MISFORTUNES OF THE AGE

The macabre sermon—both text and images—participated in a Christianization movement that spread the monastic ethic through progressively wider sectors of the population and, at the same time, found itself confronted by an increase in wealth and a "passion for living," at least at the upper levels of society. I therefore disagree with Chihaia, who sees in the fourteenth- to sixteenth-century discourse on death an "internal crusade" against knights forgetful of their Christian ideals and attracted by a pagan life-style.[64] An "internal crusade" it certainly was, but one that sought to lead from the evil path all those who, in an advancing civilization, squandered their increasing wealth, whether they be noble or bourgeois. Hence the insistence of the church on *cupiditas*, in both confession manuals and the *danses macabres*. Innumerable *memento mori* inevitably called attention to people's appetite for pleasure and to their powerful love of life, which the church vainly attempted to control. More generally, the church's mission was to give a solid moral code to a society in which ethics and religion did not coincide. Among many other examples, evidence of this moralizing effort appears in a fresco by Pinzolo that comprises a dance of death on the upper level and, below, a depiction of the deadly sins.

Now, however, the question arises: Why this explosion of a morbid aesthetic as of the middle of the fourteenth century? Even a rapid overview of Western funerary iconography from the Greco-Roman era to our own times immediately reveals that the representation of decomposing bodies, of skeletons, and of *danses macabres* only dominated the scene for a relatively brief period of 250 to 300 years. In contrast, most images linked to the memory of the dead—among the Greeks and the Christians of the Late Empire and of the High Middle Ages as well as in the contemporary or precontemporary world bathe in a soothing or melancholy atmosphere that is often tinged with hope. In spite of the long prehistory that explains it, the macabre period thus appears as a parenthesis within the longer European time scale. Why, therefore, this violent and temporary rupture? Why, for a certain length of time, did a civilization open its tombs to reveal putrefying bodies? Why did it let itself become haunted by images of skulls, of bones, of rotten and nauseating flesh? Until the middle of the fourteenth century, these phantoms had been contained by psychological bulwarks. Suddenly these collapsed, not to be reestablished until three hundred years later. In short, what exactly happened?

The history of Europe itself supplies the answer. First of all, the West had forgotten the plague. When it returned with a vengeance in 1348 and devastated a good part of the continent for four years, a third of all Europeans perished. It continued to reappear periodically until the beginning of the eighteenth century. How could such a completely unexpected offensive fail to impress contemporary people? Moreover, just when these epidemics had started, bad harvests became more frequent, urban and rural revolts increased, the Turks accelerated their pressure, the Great Schism tore apart Latin Christianity (every Catholic whose prince refused obedience to the Pope was excommunicated), and civil and foreign wars ravaged France, Spain, England, Bohemia, and so on. Such is the panorama of Europe between the middle of the fourteenth and the middle of the fifteenth century. It is true that a lull then intervened, that the population, notably in France, began to increase again after the end of the Hundred Years' War. Yet one can too easily forget, due to the prestigious sound of the word "Renaissance," that the plague continued, that the Schism, patched up for a moment, reopened during the Reformation, that the German peasants rose up in arms in 1525, that the Wars of Religion afflicted France and the Low Countries during the second half of the sixteenth century, that these religious conflicts soon reached Germany and wreaked havoc there between 1618 and 1648, and that Elizabethan England lived under the fear of a Spanish invasion. Is it by chance than that a new generation of macabre poets—Agrippa d'Aubigné, Sigogne, Chassignet—emerged at the time of the Wars of Religion, that the dances of the dead pursued their iconographic career during the seventeenth century in Germanic countries, and that England, despite its conversion to Protestantism, continued to represent "*transis*" on tombs at the same time that ghastly murder scenes proliferated in its theater? Clearly, the chronology of the macabre is the same as that identified in *La Peur en Occident*, with respect to the Last Judgment, witches, Jews, and heresy. It belongs to the same global phenomenon that brings together the discourse of guilt, fear before accumulated misfortunes, and the omnipresence of violence.

Does not our own epoch help us to understand the beginnings of European modernity? The mass killings of the twentieth century from 1914 to the genocide of Cambodia—passing through various holocausts and the deluge of bombs on Vietnam—the menace of nuclear war, the ever-increasing use of torture, the multiplication of Gulags, the resurgence of insecurity, the rapid and often more and more troubling progress of technology, the dangers entailed by an overly intensive exploitation of natural resources, various genetic manipulations, and the uncontrolled explosion of information: Here are so many factors that, gathered together, create a climate of anxiety in our civilization which, in certain respects, is comparable to that of our ancestors between the time of the plague and the end of the Wars of Religion. We have reentered this "country of fear" and, following a classic process of "projection," we never weary of evoking it in both words and images. Mixing the present and a hypothetical future, science and fiction, sadism and eroticism, our fears for tomorrow and our experience of daily dangers, voyages into outer space and a paleontology of secondhand remnants,[65] we propagate violent, barbaric, dehumanized, and flashy stories with graphic imagery. In brutal cacophonies, we associate futurism and archaism, antediluvian beings and spaceships.

Such is the standard bric-à-brac of adult comic strips that the "United Humanoids" publish four times a year in *Screaming Metal*—and this is but one example among many. These morbid fantasias, rich in vampires and gray dawns, find expression in numerous books with provocative titles: *Advent of the Supermen*, *Black Galaxy*, *The Gardens of the Apocalyse*, *Anti-Worlds*, *Terminal Man* (and again) *The Dissociated Man*, *Disjointed Time*, *Futures Without Future*, *The Macabre Worlds of Richard Matheson*, and *We're All Afraid*. These last two titles recall the historical themes of the present study. Yesterday, as today, fear of violence is objectified in images of violence and fear of death in macabre visions. When the presence of corpses killed by plagues, famines, and soldiers becomes obsessive, the guilt-instilling sermon with its nauseating imagery will find a new audience. Untiringly connecting death and crime, sin and punishment, it seems confirmed by facts, and this very confirmation feeds and thus fills it with even stronger force. It speaks of fear to people who are afraid and, finally, it speaks their own fear.

There is debate over the place that the plague—and first and foremost the epidemic of 1348 to 1351—should occupy in European history. In the nineteenth and early twentieth century, there was a tendency to explain everything by the plague: the fracturing of the feudal system, the crisis of the church, and the progress toward the Renaissance and Reformation. Today, at least in France, certain historians seek to redimension the impact of the Black Death.[66] On the one hand, it is clear that the erosion of the feudal system and the deterioration of its socioeconomic organization had already begun. On the other hand, Western civilization continued its forward march despite this violent pandemic. Four main points help to clarify this debate. (1) Even if contemporaries overestimated the impact of the various plagues (and above all that of the Black Death), the severity of their recurrent outbreaks cannot be underestimated—the most sober statistics for 1348 to 1352 produce estimates of mortality between 25 and 40 percent, depending on geographic locality.[67] In a longer chronology, an instructive case is that of Paris, where between 1348 and 1500 the plague returned more than once every four years. (2) For the historiographer of *mentalités*, the actual figures of the losses matter less than the spiritual shock created by the singularly violent spectacles of disease and death. (3) The plague, henceforth installed in the West for more than three hundred years, was only the most dramatic element within a vast ensemble of calamities, all of which contributed their respective impacts between 1348 and 1648. (4) European civilization, accepting the challenge presented by so many handicaps, continued to innovate in every area,[68] although not even the sixteenth century possessed an optimism comparable to that of the Enlightenment or the second half of the nineteenth century. People of the Renaissance believed human history to be near its end. They did not conceive of the future in terms of moral or technological progress. Hence the need to introduce the notion (incidentally mentioned by Jacques Soustelle in regard to the Aztecs) of "active pessimism," which also applies to our own experience of the late twentieth century. A civilization can be at once dynamic and pessimistic. So it is with us. It is was also thus for our forebears, at the beginning of European modernity.

Millard Meiss has written that the Black Death was "a cultural event," especially in the domain of religious painting.[69] It inspired the well-known fresco of the Campo Santo of Pisa (ca. 1350), which conjoins the triumph of Death, the legend of the three dead and three living men, the Last Judgment, and Hell. Slightly later, the same scenes recur together in a composition painted by Orcagna for the church of

Santa Croce in Florence of which there remain only a few fragments. A funerary(?) painting of the second half of the fourteenth century by Giovanni del Biondo (in the Vatican) presents an iconography unprecedented in Tuscan art: The Virgin and child are surrounded by saints, beneath them lies a corpse devoured by worms and toads, an old bearded hermit points toward them, and a man and his dog recoil in horror.[70]

Another novelty dating from just after the Black Death is the representation of Christ on the Day of Judgment concerned only with condemning the damned. Previously, he had blessed with one hand and rejected with the other. But at the Campo Santo of Pisa, for the first time, he has only one active hand, the one that consigns the reprobate to Hell.[71] Several of Fra Angelico's compositions, and especially the Christ of the Sistine Chapel, repeat this dramatic gesture. Again, it is only after the Black Death that the image of sinful humanity struck down by the arrows of the plague spreads throughout Italy and beyond the Alps.[72] At San Pietro in Vincoli in Rome, a fresco commemorating the plague of 1476 shows Evil as a winged demon-skeleton aiming an arrow at the inhabitants of a town. A century later, among the macabre themes painted on the interior and exterior of the church of San Michele d'Oleggio, near Novara, one notices God striking the dead into their half-open tombs with his thunderbolts: a probable allusion to the plague of 1575–76.[73] Against these attacks, people would henceforth invoke, among others, Saint Sebastian, the transfixed martyr, whose cult suddenly grew after 1348. Finally, was it a coincidence that masses for the dead became more frequent after the middle of the fourteenth century?[74] In any case, it seems that the sight—endlessly renewed in times of plague—of open tombs and rotting corpses made public opinion more receptive to the macabre images of the sermons. And these latter unconsciously reflected the public's morbid propensity to look at dead bodies that had lost the habitual dignity of death.

The links between plague and the *dense macabre* were certainly numerous. Occasionally they are only implicit, but in other cases they are clearly evident. If Rosenfeld's hypothesis is exact, it is even possible to date to around 1350 the Latin poem and the German quatrains that, according to him, comprise the first written versions of the *danse macabre*: The Black Death would therefore have encouraged the clear formulation of a latent theme. In any case, the Latin text includes this complaint placed in the mouth of a child about to die: "Dear mother, the dark one snatches me from you / I must dance, I who can no longer walk"; and in the German text, Death invites the king to join "the dance of the deathly brothers."[75] Taking into account the now nearly certain dating of the fresco of the Basel Dominican cemetery (ca. 1440), it would be logical to establish a relation between this dance and the great outbreak of the plague that struck the town in 1439 (at the moment of the council) and which was described by Aeneas Silvius Piccolomini, the future Pius II.[76] Piccolomini describes how the piles of corpses were so impressive that "the fathers of the Council walked in distress and grew extremely pale." At Lübeck, the *danse macabre* of the Marienkirche was painted in 1463 before the plague reached the town in the following year. Yet the citizens knew that the disease was already present in the Rhineland—in Saxony, Thuringen, and Brandenburg—and therefore was already approaching the town.[77] As for the *danse macabre* of Berlin, it was painted in 1484 at the end of a pestilence.

Given this data, why not propose certain chronological parallels, at least as hypotheses? In the twelve years that precede the completion of the fresco of the Innocents (1424), Paris suffered three outbreaks of the plague: in 1412, 1418, and 1421.[78] The *danse macabre* of the cemetery of the Pardon in London, beside St. Paul's, dates from around 1440. Previously, the plague had swept through the

English capital in 1433, 1434, 1435, 1436, 1437, and 1438.[79] At the same time, the monk Lydgate, who adapted the verses of the Cemetery of the Innocents into English, composed a poem entitled "Dietary and Doctrine for the Pestilence."[80] At Clusona (near Bergamo), the composition that assembles the legend of the three dead and three living men, the triumph of Death, and the dance of the dead was painted in 1484. For the previous four years the plague had raged through Lombardy, and in 1485 it was more severe than ever.[81] Similarly, the *danse macabre* of Füssen (ca. 1600) followed upon epidemics in 1583, 1588, and 1598. It can thus be seen that the use of this iconographic theme is a sort of magic ritual, a way to either ward off imminent danger or to prevent the return of the plague. The depiction of the *danse macabre* was both a form of exorcism and a manifestation of repentance.[82] Thus understood, the danse can be compared to the bloody processions of flagellants to which the Black Death gave an unprecedented impetus.

To contemporary eyes, three characteristics of plague outbreaks would have been expressed by the *danse macabre*: divine retribution, the brutality of death, and the equalizing effect it had insofar as it brought the same fate to both rich and poor, young and old. Furthermore, a definite cause-and-effect relationship can be established between the slaughters caused by plague[83] and the success, from the fourteenth to the sixteenth century, of the iconography of the Triumph of Death. The theme must have been already current before the Black Death if an earlier date is assigned (which is not certain) to the *Allegory of Sin and Redemption* at the Siena Pinacoteca. Between scenes depicting on the left the Fall and on the right Christ overcoming Sin and Death, the latter, at the center of the piece, is portrayed as a winged dragon with a woman's head. With her scythe, she has already cut down hundreds of men and she heads toward a panic-stricken group who plead before Christ on the cross.[84] There are numerous resemblances between this work and the great fresco of the Campo Santo of Pisa, which is, of course, generally thought to have been inspired by the Black Death.

Without a doubt, in late fourteenth- and early fifteenth-century Italy, a country constantly visited by epidemics and besieged by wars (Petrarch describes it as "an unpiloted ship in a great storm") there arise striking representations of the triumph of Death. Two of them merit special atttention. At the monastery of the Sacro Speco (the Holy Grotto) of Subiaco, around 1363 to 1369, a Sienese artist figured Death as an old skeletal woman, hair blowing in the wind, mounted on a horse and facing three dead or living men. To the right, as at Pisa and in the fresco of Orcagna at Santa Croce in Florence, beggars exhausted by an overly bitter life vainly beseech her not to spare them. At the center and to the left, she uses her scythe to batter monks and nuns whom her horse is trampling underfoot. In her right hand, she holds a sword with which she wounds a young hunter.[85] The artwork is clumsy but redolent with meaning. The fresco of the Palazzo Sclafani of Palermo (ca. 1445), which had been transformed into a hospital some years earlier,[86] has an even greater power. Here the composition is already traditional: On one side are the beggars and the crippled who uselessly seek out Death, on the other are young women and musicians near a graceful fountain. Death, at the center, occupies the two levels of the composition. With a derisive sneer, mounted on a ghostly horse whose skeleton is sharply defined, she shoots her arrows at the oblivious youths. Her steed—nostrils quivering, neck stretched out, and mane flying—bestrides the cadavers piled up below him. An important detail: The arrows hit their victims especially in the ganglionic areas. There is thus a clear reference to the plague.

The link that a collective mentality established between the plague, the invincible power of death, and its personification as a rider appears in a schematic and exemplary fashion in two documents: a manuscript of the *Decameron* of 1427[87] and the cover of a Sienese account book for 1437. In that year, a "very homicidal" epidemic raged through the town from June to December. "Leading citizens and many others died." On the cover of the volume, an anonymous artist portrayed a triumphant Death with the wings of a bat—as at Pisa—riding a fast-moving charger that tramples prone corpses. At her side hangs a scythe, and she aims her bow at a seated group of people who are busy gambling.[88]

Death, the sinister and invincible rider, is a widespread popular image that also appears in a charcoal sketch by Dürer in the British Museum. Here the artist depicts him as a crowned skeleton, armed with a scythe and urging on an emaciated horse from whose neck hangs a bell. Dürer executed this drawing in 1505 while the plague was decimating Nüremberg.[89] The recurrence of plagues and wars in Europe of the fourteenth to the sixteenth century revived the credibility of the Apocalypse and gave a new career to the theme of the Four Horsemen. The frequent evocation of the Apocalypse in painting, tapestry, stained glass, manuscript illumination, and engraving led to a proliferation of images showing the horrible steed and his grim rider. Most often, the latter is figured as a living corpse who—sometimes with a sword and arrows, elsewhere with a lance and scythe—mercilessly cuts down human beings. Artists enriched this general theme with a number of variations. The oldest Netherlandish *Apocalypse* (a manuscript from around 1400) shows Death on horseback breaking through the heavy gate of a town, which shatters into pieces.[90] Hans Memling, on the other hand, presents the rider issuing from the mouth of a flame-breathing monster.[91] And Dürer, in his famous series engraved in 1497–1498, breaks from tradition by replacing the cadaver with a hideous and fleshless old man armed not with a scythe, but with a trident.[92]

Italy invented yet another figuration of the Triumph of Death. On a Santa Croce altarpiece painted in 1362 by Agnolo Gaddi, this version of Death rides a black steer that crushes dead bodies under its hooves. And when, in the middle of the fifteenth century, Italian artists illustrated Petrarch's *Trionfi* (composed from 1356 to 1374), they reused the bulls, attaching them to a chariot. In Petrarch's poems, the figure of Death who invites Laura to join the multitude of the dead is a lady dressed in black. She is neither on a horse nor in a chariot. Yet, in representations of the first of the *Trionfi* (that of love), Cupid is depicted standing on a flaming chariot drawn by four white horses.[93] Illustrators also placed Chastity, Death, Fame, Time, and Eternity on chariots. This innovation, which tied in with the Roman representation of Imperial triumphs, was highly successful and gave rise to numerous Triumphs of Death wherein bulls were attached to its chariot. This iconographic theme appears in frescoes and paintings, but it is more commonly found on chests (*cassoni*), tapestries, and as a manuscript illumination. Later, in printed editions of Petrarch, the skeleton-body of the implacable reaper was sometimes replaced by the Three Fates, or by at least one of them (Atropos).

Various important features are common to all of these Triumphs. First, there is an almost "baroque" refinement, with an accumulation of astonishing details, especially in the depiction of the chariots. One of these, in an illustrated manuscript of Petrarch's works, features three "stories" in Renaissance style with pilasters, cornices, garlands, and skulls placed in shell-lined arches. Death, a skeleton with the wings of a dragon and armed with a scythe, is seated on a skull that sports a tiara.[94] A sixteenth-century Bruxelles tapestry, based on Italian cartoons, shows the Three Fates riding the dragons that are hitched to the chariot of Death. Its wheels have skulls for their hubs and tibias for their spokes.[95] In these deliberately erudite and "sophisticated" compositions, artists enjoyed setting off the macabre by meticulous, pleasant, warm rural and/or urban landscapes. The exuberance of life thus tempers the frequent irony of the Death's heads. In general, Italy showed less predilection than France, Germany, and England for images of putrefaction. Triumphant Death is often a well-cleaned cadaver, an ancestor of the pedagogical anatomies that would flourish at the beginning of the next century. Despite clever morbid inventions, this learned and complicated iconography is thus less traumatizing than the rest of the contemporary production of the macabre. Its ingenuity suggests that it is a kind of game that anyone can play. The viewer relishes a ludic reading of the image that distances the spirit from its general meaning.

In this context, dates are of high importance. The Triumphs of Death inspired by Petrarch's poem flourished in the golden age of the Italian Quattrocento. During this period of equilibrium (1454–1494) among its five main constituent states, the Italian peninsula, despite plagues, lived one of the high points of its history. By its culture, wealth, and technological advancement, it was the prime mover and school of Europe. In sudden contrast, beginning with the "Italian Wars" of 1494, it seesawed into impotence and turmoil and passed under foreign control. The Petrarchan Triumph thus continued its course, not only in Italy but also in other countries, where it inspired both artists and poets. Marot (d. 1522) uses it in his *Déploration de Messire Florimond Robertet*:

I saw Death hideous and dreadful
Atop a chariot, mounted in triumph,
Under her feet a human corpse
Dead, upside down; with a dart in her hand,
Of mortal wood, feathered with the plumes
Of an old raven, whose cursed song
Foretells all evil; and the steel point was drenched
In the waters of Styx, Hell's grim river.
Death, in place of a venerable scepter
Held in her hand this fearful dart
Which was tinged and stained all over
With the blood of those whom she had visited.[96]

Although this theme persists in Italy and beyond the Alps at the end of the fifteenth and throughout the sixteenth century, it tends to lose its relative serenity. Quite often Death becomes, once again, "comparable to the most horrible figures created by the survivors of the plague of 1348."[97] Once more he spreads out her bat-wings or is accompanied by a horde of skeletons. This climate of rediscovered anguish is evident in the masque that was organized in Florence by Piero di Cosimo for the 1511 Carnival and described by Giorgio Vasari. The traditional iconography of the Triumph in antique style here expressed terror in so morbid a fashion that the public was not ready for the spectacle prepared for them:

Nothing like it had been seen or heard before. It was seen and interpreted at the same time. On an enormous chariot drawn by oxen, all black, and with white bones and crosses, a very large Death presided, holding a scythe and surrounded by closed tombs. At each station where the cortège halted to sing, the tombs opened up and there emerged figures in dark cloth on which were painted all the parts of the skeleton in white on a black background . . . All these dead figures, at the sound of harsh and muffled trumpets, rose up, and sitting on the side of the float, sang in a sad and languid voice this song, so well-reputed today: "Dolor, pianto, e penitenza." *Before and behind the float marched a great number of dead figures on certain horses carefully chosen to be the thinnest and most fleshless that could be found, all covered in black drapes with white crosses. Each one had four attendants*

> *dressed in shrouds with black torches, and during the entire procession, the group sang in strict time and in a trembling voice the* Miserere.[98]

Vasari notes that this macabre procession—which set a trend[99]—"filled the city with terror and wonder." This Florentine parade shows, in any case, how the classicizing version of the Triumph of Death was susceptible to a troubling transformation in an Italy that was once again uneasy, and in a city where the dramatic Savonarola episode had ended less than fifteen years earlier. Moreover, in Italy and elsewhere, the alternative iconography of the Triumph of Death continued, or even regathered its strength. At Clusona, near Bergamo, a synthesizing and, as such, highly pedagogical fresco regroups the principal elements of the iconography of death employed at that period. On the lower level the *danse macabre* proceeds, half farandole and half procession, while, above, the artist has depicted a quite unusual Triumph of Death that includes the legend of the three living and the three dead men. Above a tomb are placed three animate skeletons. The central one wears a royal crown and cloak, and two acolytes stand at its side. One, equipped with arrows, shoots at the three hunters who try to flee. The other aims a crossbow at a crowd of rich people—pope, kings, princes, bourgeois, and so on—who, on their knees, vainly offer presents to the implacable sovereign. Across the top of the fresco, Death broadly unfurls banners that announce: "Here arrives Death, bringing equal justice. I want only you and not your riches. I am most worthy to wear a crown, I who control everyone."[100] Some years later, the frontispiece of an edition of Savonarola's *Predica dell'arte del ben morire* (Florence, 1497) represents Death as a ghostly apparition, an ominous comet. A skeleton dressed in a flowing tunic, it flies across a wasteland where corpses lie next to dead trees. In one hand it holds a scythe, in the other a scroll that reads: "*Ego sum*": "Alone, I exist."

Pieter Brueghel the Elder was responsible for the most powerful evocation of a non-Petrarchan *Triumph of Death* (ca. 1562, in the Prado). This painting's message remains that of the *danses macabres* and of the legend of the three living and three dead men: pleasures, riches, and glory count for nothing once life is over. Yet the demonstration of this lesson is given through a hallucinatory nightmare-vision that embroiders upon the carnage and horrendous details of Bosch's repertoire: a wheeled coffin, a giant mousetrap, and living people herded into nets held by the dead. The composition reads from the left, where two skeletons sound the knell by pulling the ropes of a bell fixed to a desiccated tree. At the base of a ruined tower (which bears a clock), corpses in white winding sheets blow trumpets heralding the fatal day. Indeed, from this place an army of the dead sallies forth, at the foot of a cliff. There also appears a cart, filled with skulls, led by skeletons and drawn by a shriveled horse. At the center of the painting, the artist portrays the Triumph proper. Death, riding his skinny mount, mows down the living with both hands or pushes them toward a "mousetrap" whose door has been pulled open. The victims would like to flee but numberless cadavers block their path with tombstones. Death is also surrounded by armed skeletons who attack people making merry and playing music. Beside a deserted table, a young knight has drawn his sword and makes a desperate resistance. Brueghel has here given quantitative proof of Death's power, for dead figures far outnumber living ones. In a panoramic view, Brueghel also shows a thousand ways of dying: Death by disease (the plague?)—an emperor faints, a cadaver carries a stricken cardinal toward a ditch, and the cart laden with skulls recalls; the mortuary wagons of plague time; death by drowning in stormy seas or lakes death by war: Weapons, torches, and fires form a sinuous and nearly continuous line from one end of the painting to the other; death by accident: An unlucky soul falls off a rock. The sense of Death's irresistible and omnipresent power had never been conveyed with such fullness and imagination.

Similar to the concentration of the macabre in Brueghel's painting (which forms nearly a compendium in this regard) is the proliferation of deathly images in the iconography of the fifteenth and sixteenth centuries, where there is far too much from which to choose. Italian marquetry works portray *trompe l'oeil* skulls and water-clocks.[101] In an illuminated Book of Hours, Death methodically mows a blooming meadow and chops down trees while, all around him, the landscape (crossed by a stream and closed off by a hill) is sweet, colorful, and charming.[102] In another such book, Death is crowned, seated on a tomb, holding a dart as a scepter in one hand and a skull in the other (in place of a globe). Far off there are mountains and a town dominated by a great church.[103] An edition of Geiler's *Sermons* shows Death intruding on a private home. With one kick, he knocks down a woman who leans on her husband. Their child, meanwhile, vainly seeks protection near his mother.[104] The image of a skeleton bearing a coffin frequently occurs during this period. Here he enters a sick person's room. There he accosts an insouciant, mad person.[105] An anonymous German "*livre de raison*" (second half of the fifteenth century) includes a remarkable etching of a young man and death. The piece represents a skeletal old man, almost nude, who rests his hand on the shoulder of a young dandy. A snake slithers between the old man's legs, a toad draws near his feet.[106] A century later—in 1559—an artist of Chambéry, Gaspard Masery, dedicates two panels to the theme of the painter and death. On the left hand panel, Death—an animate corpse who holds a lantern and an upside-down compass—passes through a doorway. On the right, the seated painter, in his doublet, works on Death's portrait.[107]

There are many other objects that belong to this context, such as rosaries whose beads are shaped like skulls[108]; tarot cards that represent Death on horseback mowing down a king, a cardinal, a canon, a knight[109]; a copper engraving of a chess match between an old king and his victorious opponent[110]; and German terracotta medallions showing a woman and Death, a couple and Death, a learned man and Death.[111] These depictions, and the many others that could be added to this list, comprise the environment that nourished the rich macabre production of Holbein: his *Small Alphabet* (1520), *Great Alphabet* (1521), and *Simulacra* (1538). Such is also the context of Hamlet's famous question in the graveyard: "How long will a man lie i' th' earth ere he rot?"

THE MACABRE AND VIOLENCE

The armies of corpses that in Brueghel's painting, victoriously fight against living souls evoke their era's almost permanent state of violence. The macabre was linked with the plague. Yet it was also tied to war, the terrifying companion of Europeans from the time of the "*Grandes Compagnies*" until the end of the religious wars (1648). These wars were not exactly genocides. All the same, war was almost always present, with its continually renewed march of soldiers, atrocities, pillaging, and devastated harvests. With civil wars and rebellions doubling or filling in for foreign wars, contemporaries felt that armed violence would never leave them. For forty years, claims Eustache Deschamps in 1385, the curé had sung only the *Requiem*, "so much that he knew no other service." And he continues: "Without ever having peace, we will have war, war."[112] Moreover, Deschamps remarks, "Day by day, war marches forward."[113] He also addresses rulers: "Princes, I will complain to you of war,"[114] and he protests the abuses of mercenaries: "There is neither a room nor a larder, even if locked / Which they have not broken into . . ."[115] Hence the grim warning: "To wage war is nothing but a damnation."[116] Christine de Pisan, student and disciple of Deschamps, composed the *Lamentations sur les guerres civiles*. In his prison cell at Beauvais (1432–1433), Jean Régnier also cursed war:

There is nothing that war does not kill . . .
War is one great prison . . .
If war wants to seize
And detain all, it is for dinner-meat.[117]

A half century later (1477–79), the rhetorician Jean Molinet was witness to battles between the French and the Burgundians. In his *Ressource du Petit Peuple*, he strongly takes to task "the rectors of public affairs":

Powerful princes . . .
Who dominate, you who move the people,
Who decide, you who persecute men,
And torment souls and bodies . . .

What do ye who trouble the world
By unclean war and criminal assaults?
Fire cannons, stir up a great melée,
In a hundred years you will be putrid![118]

Certainly, it would be an untenable and antihistorical paradox to paint a uniformly black panorama of the years 1348 to 1648. Intervals of calm and recovery are often overlooked, and periods less warlike than others are left in shadow. There was Italy from 1454, to 1494, for example; France and Spain from the end of the fifteenth century to 1520, the Low Countries during the second half of the sixteenth century; and Elizabethan England.

There *was* a Renaissance. Europeans took advantage of every respite to spread and stimulate the growth of arts, letters, and technology—even if such advances moved from one country to another with invading soldiers. The use of the term "Renaissance" without variation, however, leads to a reverse simplification. "Renaissance" camouflages the revolt of *Los Comuneros* (1521), that of the German Peasants (1524–25), that of the "*Communes de Guyenne*" (1548), those of English Catholics or peasants in 1536, 1549, 1569. "Renaissance" hides the call for mercenaries for the Italian wars, the coming and going of soldiers in the peninsula, the sacks of Rome (1527) and Antwerp (1576). Above all, the term "Renaissance" neglects the most tragic aspect of the sixteenth and early seventeenth centuries: The religious conflicts that also entailed the persecution of Anabaptists (in Germany and the Low Countries during the 1530s), "iconoclastic furies," burnings of heretics, murderous conspiracies, organized massacres (Saint Bartholomew's Day), as well as pitched battles and sieges on a national (France 1562–1628) or European (Thirty Years' War) scale. Sadistic violence was the order of the day. The people of Luderon were smoked inside caves, monks were buried alive by the Gueux, English Catholics were disemboweled, some alive, with their hearts and viscera already torn out, children were roasted on the spit (in the Vivarais, ca. 1579) in the presence of their parents, and so on. And this is but a succinct selection.

Ronsard thus compares France (1562) to a merchant, harassed by a thief who is not satisfied to rob him but "beats and torments him, and with a dagger he tries / By a single wound, to sever the soul from the body / Then, seeing him dead, he smiles at his wounds / And leaves him to be eaten by mastiffs and wolves."[119] Sebastien Castellion also addresses France, wasted by religious struggle: "[God] strikes you with such a horrible and detestable war that I know not whether, since the world was created, there has been a worse . . . Your own children devastate and afflict you. They murder and strangle each other without mercy, with fine naked swords and pistols and halberds plunged into your lap."[120]

Agrippa d'Aubigné, who as a child witnessed a series of consecutive executions in the wake of the Amboise conspiracy, was scarred his entire life by the horrible spectacles of the Wars of Religion. The Fourth Book of his *Tragiques*, entitled *Fers et Feux*, recounts the massacres of Protestants. In the *Misères* (the first book of the *Tragiques*), he cries out "wasted France . . . is not earth but ashes," and he condemns the crimes of the soldiery:

> *I saw the dark mercenary crashing through*
> *The cottages of France, and like a storm,*
> *Carrying off what he could, raping the rest . . .*
> *There in a thousand homes one finds only flames,*
> *Carrion, dead bodies, or fearful faces.*[121]

Later, Germany would undergo similar spectacles during the Thirty Years' War. D'Aubigné's poetry is a good example of the link between military violence and a taste for the macabre. If, returning to the early sixteenth century and the Museum of Fine Arts at Basel, one opens the portfolios of drawings by Urs Graf, the Swiss Goya (ca. 1485–ca. 1527), this association becomes strikingly clear. Goldsmith, engraver, watercolorist, painter, and glassmaker, Graf nevertheless also served as a *landesknecht.* His paintings and engravings often form a chronicle—and a satire—of the military profession with all of its inhuman savagery and illusions,[122] while his drawings are filled with men of war and prostitutes whom the artist enjoyed comparing to fools. Before the viewer's eyes march insensitive brutes, banners widely unfurled and holding lances. They are dressed with baroque and almost ridiculous ostentation. One mercenary comes home loaded with loot, another is captured by a terrible horned and obscene devil. A third, who symbolizes the uncertainty of war, is sumptuously dressed on the right half of his body while the left half of his outfit is that of a beggar in rags. Here also is the macabre. Beneath a tree converse two soldiers, one young, the other old; to their left a seductive woman, holding a little dog, vies for attention, but on the tree a skeleton brandishes an hourglass surmounted by a raven. The message? Fighting men will more surely encounter death than pleasure.[123] Another scene shows a German *landesknecht*, obviously a braggart, who sits at one end of a table and discusses his pay with a recruiter, seated at the the other end and holding a sack (of écus) stamped with the arms of France. Between the two figures are a Swiss who serves as intermediary, an artisan, a clerk, and a merchant. Beside the recruiter is a fool. His counterpart is a skeleton who sharply strikes his knee into the recruiter's back. He carries a banner proclaiming that the king's money is not worth one single life.

In many instances Graf depicts scenes of execution. A woman—Saint Barbara—is decapitated by a soldier beside a lake. A vending woman passes indifferently, almost smilingly, past a soldier hanging from a tree. A confederate gets ready to cut off the head of a kneeling German mercenary. To the right, an unlucky soul is exposed at the pillory and two torture victims hang from the gallows, the body of one being already half-eaten and decomposed. Another pen drawing portrays a large battlefield where opposing infantries, cavalries, and artilleries confront each other. The dead are numerous: They are strewn across the ground, naked (they have already been stripped) and surrounded with broken drums, shattered weapons, and dead horses. Hit by a bomb, a house is in flames. On the left, however, a soldier indifferent to the fight is busy pouring a drink down his throat. To the right, two warriors hanging from branches are already being attacked by birds of prey—an anticipation of the scenes of hanging that Jacques Callot, a century later, would realistically render in his famous series of etchings: *Misères de la Guerre*.

Graf simultaneously conveys a sense of the insanity of the mercenary's profession and the attraction of a life of violence and adventure. Similarly, Hans Baldung Grien in 1503 and Dürer in 1510 also created striking images of the dialogue between the *landesknecht* and Death. The first puts a sad-looking soldier face to face with a mocking corpse who leans on a lance made of tibias.[124] The second evokes a conversation between a flamboyant soldier and a corpse dressed in a shroud who still sports long, disheveled hair. This latter figure presents an hourglass to his dandified companion.[125]

Even a rapid overview of the macabre of this period could not neglect the vast number of scenes representing martyrdom and massacre. The spectacle of violence produced a trauma that demanded expression through liberating "projections." If one could count all the martyrdoms of saints that were painted, sculpted, or engraved in Western and Central Europe between 1350 and 1650, the stupefying total would restore, in this respect, a certain continuity between Gothic, Mannerist, and Baroque periods. In this museum of horrors a prominent place clearly belongs to the Crucifixion of Isenheim, which features a "greenish Christ, looking as if he were already decomposing from torture, his skin riddled by wounds, his fingers twisted in pain, his face marked by an atrocious agony."[126]

Scenes of massacre often add a quantitative element to violence and sadism: The macabre comes across in a plural form. An example of this trend is the theme of *The Martyrdom of the Ten Thousand Christians* (ordered by a Persian king) that inspired Dürer, Niklaus Manuel Deutsch, Jacopo da Pontormo, and Perino del Vaga. In Dürer's work (1508), which was commissioned by Frederick the Wise,[127] a highly colored palette heightens the gruesome details. Innocent Christians are thrown off a cliff while others are bludgeoned, decapitated, whipped to death, stoned, or crucified. Deutsch's painting [128] is still more cruel. The bloody bodies of the victims are impaled on dead branches, as stiff and sharp as blades. Such works influenced Antoine Caron's highly mannerist composition, the *Massacre des Triumvirs* (1562)[129]—where decapitations are differentiated by means of a sumptuous archaeology—as well as all those paintings and prints that which show the various stakes, executions, and mass slayings that characterized the Wars of Religion.

Again, there is too much from which to choose. There are *autos da fé*, the punishment of the Amboise conspirators, the Saint Bartholomew's Day Massacre, and the sophisticated tortures inflicted on Dutch monks and English Catholics. It was inevitable that so much violence, added to the spectacle of the plague, should have compelled Westerners to represent death and executions. At Antwerp in 1587 there appeared (with an *imprimatur*) a *Théâtre des cruautés des heretiques* that is no more than an appalling collection of tortures.[130] Some years later in Rome, the Oratorian Gallanio, inspired by the preceding work, published his *Trattato degli instrumenti di martirio* illustrated by Tempesta, one of the leading Italian engravers of the end of the sixteenth century.[131] This erudite treatise is devoted to instruments of torture formerly employed by the pagans against the Christians, and was doubtless equally inspired by frescoes that the Jesuits of the Eternal City had commissioned from Pomarancio for both the Coleggio degli Inglesi (ca. 1582)[132] and the church of San Stefano Rotondo (ca. 1585). In the Coleggio, a series of paintings (now lost) narrated the history of England in terms of tortures: from Saint Edmund shot with

Danish arrows, to Fisher and More dying on the scaffold and Campion stretched on the rack. The thirty or more frescoes still to be found at San Stefano minutely describe scenes from *The Golden Legend* and narrate the history of Roman persecutions: Victor is thrown into a furnace; Corona is drawn and quartered; Martina is torn apart by iron nails; Vitus, Modestus, and Crescentia are cast into boiling lead. Some of the frescoes even feature as many as three tortures on different levels.

It is thus hardly by chance that death pervades French Senecan tragedies of the late sixteenth and early seventeenth centuries as well as the contemporary literature of England under Elizabeth and the first Stuarts. These literary works also integrate a major motivating force behind the violence of the time: revenge. This theme, so present during the struggles between Armagnacs and Burgundians, was reactivated in the sixteenth century by religious conflicts. In the High Renaissance, it continued to remain firmly rooted in popular sentiments. Most of Bandello's *Novelle* are tales of vengeance.

These pictorial, theatrical, and literary creations have "documentary" counterparts in the descriptions of executions that fill the chronicles and journals of the period. Huizinga notes, citing Molinet, that the citizens of Mons bought a bandit at a high price in order to enjoy the pleasure of seeing him quartered, "at which the people were happier than if a new sacred body had been revived."[133] Molinet also relates that, during Maximilian of Austria's captivity at Bruges in 1488, the citizens were courteous enough to install a torture platform within the royal prisoner's view in order to provide him with amusement.[134] Continuing Huizinga's line of inquiry, Michel Vovelle found records of two servants who were buried alive and five priests who were condemned to die of hunger in an iron cage exposed to public view in fifteenth-century Augsburg.[135] Executions accompanied by torture were considered to be just so many moral lessons, and children were brought to them so that they would be suitably edified. Felix Platter recounts how:

> *a criminal, having raped a seventy-year-old woman, was flayed alive with burning tongs. With mine own eyes I saw the thick smoke produced by his living flesh that had been subjected to the tongs. He was executed by Master Nicolas, executioner of Berne, who had come expressly for the event. The prisoner was a strong and vigorous man. On the bridge over the Rhine, just nearby, they tore out his breast; then he was led to the scaffold. By now, he was extremely feeble and blood was gushing from his hands. He could no longer remain standing, he fell down continually. Finally, he was decapitated. They drove a stake through his body, and then his corpse was thrown into a ditch. I myself was witness to his torture, my father holding me by the hand.*[136]

A German newsheet of 1603 describes the execution of two "diabolical good-for-nothings" aged fourteen and fifteen who were guilty of having poisoned their drunken father and uncle. The sheet specifies: "All the youths of the town were there to watch, convened by the civic authorities, because it is good to instruct young people by such examples." The account of the torture follows:

> *They began by stripping the two boys, then they whipped them in such a way that their blood abundantly covered the ground. Then the executioner stuck red-hot irons on their wounds, at which they screamed such screams that it is impossible to describe them. Next they cut off their hands . . . The execution lasted about twenty minutes. Boys and girls attended, as well as a great crowd of adults. In this torture, one and all admired the just judgments of God and learned from this example.*[137]

Literary works closely echoed these tragic scenes of daily life. Witness the particularly sadistic description of an execution that Thomas Nashe puts at the end of *The Unfortunate Traveller* (1594). The scene supposedly takes place at Rome, in an Italy that contemporary English people thought capable of all vices and horrors. The hideous inventions described below are qualified by the author as "Italianisms":

> *To the execution place was he [the Jew Zadoch] brought, where first and foremost he was stripped; then on a sharp iron stake fastened in the ground he had his fundament pitched which stake ran up along into the body like a spit. Under his armholes two of like sort. A great bonfire they made round about him, wherewith his flesh roasted, not burned; and ever as with the heat his skin blistered, the fire was drawn aside and they basted him with a mixture of aqua fortis, alum water, and mercury sublimatum, which smarted to the very soul of him, and searched him to the marrow. Then did they scourge his back parts so blistered and blasted with burning whips of red-hot wire. His head they nointed over with pitch and tar and so inflamed it. To his privy members they tied streaming fireworks. The skin from the crest of the shoulder, as also from his elbows, his huckle bones, his knees, his ankles, they plucked and gnawed off with sparkling pincers. His breast and his belly with seal-skins they grated over, which as fast as they grated and rawed, one stood over and laved with smith's cindery water and aqua vitae. His nails they half raised up, and then underpropped them with sharp pricks, like a tailors' shop window half-open on a holiday. Every one of his fingers they rent up to the wrist; his toes they brake off by the roots, and let them still hang by a little skin. In conclusion, they had a small oil fire, such as men blow light bubbles of glass with, and beginning at his feet, they let him lingeringly burn up limb by limb, till his heart was consumed, and then he died.*[138]

One might hope that such an accumulation of bloody details would suffice for the author and his readers, but this is far from being the case. A few pages later the story moves into a new description of tortures, so that the final moments of *The Unfortunate Traveller* are nothing but a series of refined executions.

After these striking excerpts, it is hardly necessary to insist upon the macabre's strong presence in Elizabethan and Jacobean literature. In the realm of theater, four plays do stand out notably and will serve here as representative examples: *The Revenger's Tragedy* (1607) and *The Atheist's Tragedy* (1611) by Cyril Tourneur, John Webster's *The Duchess of Malfi* (ca. 1616), and *The Second Maid's Tragedy* (anonymous) all of which date from the beginning of the seventeenth century.[139] For nine years the Revenger keeps the skull of his dead fiancée who had been poisoned by an old duke. His revenge consists of smearing poison on this skull, which the duke then kisses in the dark believing that he is kissing the face of a young woman. The Atheist is a French gentleman who has had his brother stoned to death in order to claim the latter's property. After a series of murders, suicides, and rapes (in a cemetery), the guilty man sees the ghost of his brother. He kills himself in trying to kill his nephew. The Duchess of Malfi is a widow whose brothers (a duke and a cardinal) stop her from remarrying. She therefore marries her steward Antonio. Duke Ferdinand then drives his sister mad by bringing her a cadaver's hand in the dark and telling her that it is Antonio's. He also forces her to look at dummies of Antonio and her children that have been made to look as if they were dead. The duke then sends all the mad people of the asylum to "her lodging: There let them practice together, sing, and dance / And act their gambols to the full o'th' moon" (IV. i. 126–8). Finally, he has her strangled. The last act is a general carnage. *The Second Maid's Tragedy* shows the mad love of the tyrant Giovanni for the dead queen whose decomposing body he has exhumed. He attempts to love her as though she were not a corpse. In general terms, these brief and brutal synopses convey only a feeble idea of all the murders, suicides, ghosts, rapes, and incests that were the daily bread of the late English Renaissance *Grand Guignol*. There the macabre and violence were everywhere.[140]

DIVERGING SIGNIFICATIONS

The course of this discussion has somewhat neglected the religious message that, in that period, was necessarily attached to the representation of death. This neglect stems from the fact that the religious message seems to be missing in a certain number of literary works. Yet this affirmation should not be carried too far. Even in the most classicizing depictions of the Triumph of Death, Christian evangelism is not always absent. For example: In two illuminated manuscripts of Petrarch's *Trionfi* and in two series of engravings devoted to the same subject, Death's chariot is surrounded by gesticulating demons who carry off the damned and angels who elevate the elect.[141] In another manuscript illumination, the horses that draw the lugubrious chariot are struck down when, in the *The Triumph of Divinity*, they find themselves face to face with the risen Christ.[142] In the painting that Lorenzo Costa painted in 1488–90 for San Giacomo di Bologna, the chariot of Death is surmounted by a great theophany where God the Father is enthroned between Mary and Christ, and all three are surrounded by concentric ovals of angels and saints. Just above Death's scythe a naked child, carried by two angels, symbolizes the soul's taking flight after death.[143] In the "*Déploration de Messire Florimond Robertet*," Marot associates a genuinely Christian lesson with the Italianate Triumph of Death. He there assigns Death a speech in which *contemptus mundi* crops up once again: "The soul is on high and the worthless body / Is nothing other than a base prison / In which the noble and gentle soul languishes"; and again: ". . . Without me, I who am Death, / You cannot pass into the life everlasting."[144]

Of course other Petrarchist figurations of the Triumph of Death would seem to be totally secular. Apart from the conventional white crosses that mark the black cloth, nothing would allow the untrained observer to guess that Christian iconography was involved. The only teaching these images propose is that of the omnipotence of the implacable deity. The same religiously neutral lesson is expressed by certain Triumphs of Death that are not inspired by any classical references. And even though it is located in a church, the Triumph at Clusona contains no reference to salvation. The three skeletons (the middle one crowned) who dominate the composition are simply invincible murderers, unmoved by any gift or supplication. In this case, however, both sermons and actual worship would have provided the congregation with the appropriate commentary—similar to the glossing that accompanied the majority of *danses macabres*. Brueghel's famous *Triumph of Death*, however, features neither angels nor devils, neither Paradise nor Hell. His portrayal is void of both redemption and resurrection. Here everything transpires as if we were thrown outside the Christian universe—an impression that is also given by his *Census at Bethlehem*.

The ambiguity of the macabre is thus a distinguishing characteristic of the period covered by this study, especially in the case of images without words which are susceptible to contrasting interpretations. There is a definite risk in reading too much into works that are primarily artistic and not necessarily concerned with sending out a message. Was Hans Baldung Grien, who took pleasure in showing lovely nude young women being embraced by Death, an "anti-Christian," a predecessor of Nietzsche?[145] It is difficult to confirm such a verdict. Rather than being deliberately subversive in its intentions, it seems preferable to detect, in the predominantly religious and moralistic corpus of the macabre, the often involuntary intrusion of dissident and discordant elements that, in several instances, managed to modify or even invert the traditional meaning.

In all likelihood, the proliferation of texts and images involving skeletons and corpses gave renewed vigor to ancient, pre-Christian beliefs concerning ghosts, dances of the dead in cemeteries, and "wild hordes" of prematurely deceased humans—by accident, hanging, or warfare—who ran about after their death, especially during Advent.[146] Yet the "wild horde" is also the nocturnal airborne procession of witches led by Diana or Herodias. In one of his rare paintings, Urs Graf amalgamates the two elements of the "horde"—ghosts (of either tortured or drowned people) and two nude divinities who unleash a storm and take command of the ride.[147] Lucas Cranach the Elder likewise evoked the "wild horde" in three paintings on the theme of *Melancolia* (ca. 1530), tightly meshing the fearful aspect of the "horde" with the erotic revels of Venusberg.[148]

As for Dürer, he frequently depicted Death as an old man: in his *Apocalypse*, in his *Knight, Death, and the Devil*, and in "The *Coat of Arms of Death*."[149] These monstrous old men can justifiably be seen as reincarnations of the "wild man" of old folk traditions. An inhabitant of the forests (and as such a representative of all the terrors those dark places once inspired) the "wild man" belonged both to the world of the living and to the otherworld. The explosion of the macabre would thus seem to have provoked a folkloric revival, assuredly compatible with and often joined to contemporary Christian discourse, but often removed from it, and in any case liable to a double reading.

Over and above the folkloric themes used by Urs Graf, what was the actual Christian content of his works? The macabre scenes he draws—hanging soldiers, corpses littering the battlefield, a live corpse tapping the knee of the mercenary ready to enlist—no doubt carry a moral lesson (the danger and folly of the military trade), but they are devoid of Christian reference. As for his *Flagellation* (of 1526), it is only a pretext for the presentation of a spectacle of torture treated with "calculated brutality." There exists no decisive proof that the victim is Christ.[150] Sadistic in spirit, such a work compares to Niklaus Manuel Deutsch's *Martyrdom of the Ten Thousand Christians* and, more generally, to the taste for violence that unblushingly developed in French and English theater of the late sixteenth and early seventeenth centuries. The universe of the morbid is here in full sway, and the macabre has no meaning other than itself. It is revealed in its pure state, without any Christian sense, desacralized.

In another direction—one already explored by various historians, such as Alberto Tenenti[151] and Jean Wirth[152]—the Christian lesson of the macabre (the *memento mori*) was transformed into an invitation with an inverse meaning (*memento vivere*). Did not the insistence on the theme of premature death sometimes become a stimulus for eroticism, and did it not signify a veritable "passion for living"? Such a paganizing interpretation is certainly convincing in regard to the work of the Beham brothers, whose irreligion troubled the Nüremberg authorities of Dürer's time and who resolutely used pornography in association with the image of death. As for the "funeral beds" drawn in the same period by another Nüremberg artist, Peter Flötner, they also comprise, by means of a surprising macabre iconography, a clear provocation to sensual pleasure.[153]

Can some of Hans Baldung Grien's paintings and drawings be understood in the same way? In the years 1510 to 1520, this artist often symbolized Vanity by a young and beautiful woman surprised by Death. He enriched this general pattern with diverse variations: for example, the skeleton or decomposing cadaver appears in the mirror in which the unfortunate woman is looking at herself. Occasionally the deathly figure holds an hourglass, or he places his hand on the victim's side, or pulls her by the hair, or detains her by the arm, or kisses her on the mouth. During this same period, contemporaries of Baldung treat of the same subject. In particular, a drawing by Deutsch presents a corpse lifting up a young woman's dress.[154] In theory, all these works wish to signify the fragility of the pleasures of this world and the ephemeral nature of beauty and youth.

Is there a pagan lesson to be discerned behind these fables? Such is Jean Wirth's interpretation of a later diptych by Baldung, now in the Prado. On one side—the shining classical one—appear three young female beauties reading a musical score. On the other side—somber and Christian—a young woman is clutched by an old woman who, in turn, is accompanied by a skeleton carrying an hourglass. It has been pointed out that the artist had connections with the "libertines" of Strasbourg. In the sixteenth century, however, "libertine" primarily meant being independent of religious orthodoxies. Was Baldung himself a "libertine"? He worked for Catholics, for Protestants, and for dissidents. He seems to have been moved by "successive faiths." Certainly he was an admirer of female beauty. Does that mean that he rejected Christianity? In the Prado allegory, on the Christian side, the lance of Death is broken and a crucifix appears in the sky. I ultimately agree with François G. Pariset that Baldung's works, of which many were religious, "convey multiple concepts," but "converge toward a Christian lesson that is more than a mere alibi."[155]

The case of Ronsard may, perhaps, help to clarify that of the German artist. This poet clearly displays various discourses on death that can even cohabit (not necessarily coherently) the same work, with the Christian lesson nonetheless prevailing over all the others. A faithful witness of his time, Ronsard was haunted by the idea of the fleetingness of Time: "You oaks, heirs to the silence of the woods, / Hear the sighs of my final speech / And be the present notaries of my will and testament,"[156] "Soon we shall be stretched out below the blade,"[157] and so on. He sometimes takes pleasure in describing the cadaver, "food for worms, / Jelly of veins and nerves," a "sepulchral shadow" that

No longer has spirit, nor reason,
Socket, nor joint,
Artery, nor tender vein
And no hair clings to its head.[158]

Since, however, invitations to quickly enjoy one's youth are contained in Ronsard's most beautiful lines—and these are the ones most easily remembered—it is all too easily forgotten that these verses constitute, in quantitative terms, only a quite modest element in the ensemble of his writings on death. In fact, a more important theme is the pessimistic and doubtlessly hedonistic affirmation that life is short ("Before their time your temples will flower"[159]; "Already I can see the storm of next winter."[160] Death "alone among the immortals / Wishes to have neither temple nor altar, / Nor is he moved by prayers or offerings"[161]—the same subject as appears in the macabre fresco of Clusona. In addition, Ronsard resumes the classic medieval themes of the meditation on death. The "*ubi sunt?*" is also present in his work:

Homer is dead, Anacreon,
Pindar, Hesiod, and Bion.[162]

And they no longer care to ask
About the good and the evil that was said of them.[163]

Are we more divine than Achilles or Ajax,
Than Alexander or Caesar, unable
To defend themselves from death, even though in war
They grasped and subjected almost the entire world?[164]

The *contemptus mundi* appears again in this *Hymne de la Mort.* The gifted poet thus renews a theme that could have been considered stale:

A great blessing, were we already dead,
If we would consider that we are nothing
But animate earth and living shadows,
Subject to pain, misery, and accident,
In truth, how we surpass in miserable ills
The rest, O heartbreak, of all animals!
Not otherwise does Homer equate us
To the winter leaf that falls from the tree,
Thus are we weak and wretched laborers,
Without rest receiving thousands on thousands of evils.[165]

These are statements that the desert fathers and the ascetic monks of the eleventh and twelfth centuries would not have disavowed. It would be also possible, taking them out of their context and aligning them with Du Bellay's *Complainte du désespéré*, to add them to the Renaissance dossier of pessimism and melancholy that occasionally swerved away from Christianity. Ronsard's work, however, must be regarded in its entirety. The poet certainly knew the temptation of paganism ("The true treasure of man is lusty youth, / The rest of our years naught but winter"[166]) and the desire to transcend death by fame.[167] Yet his macabre meditations finally led him back to the traditional pathways of the church. He contrasted the skeleton, "stripped of flesh, of nerves, of muscles, of tissue,"[168] with the soul, liberated by death, that "ascends to Heaven, its native home."[169] There, "exempt from all evil / From century to century [the soul] lives most happy and content / Near our Creator . . ."[170] Hence the advice: "let us have nothing to do with Circe's swine," so that one day the eternal "Ithaca" may be attained:

Laden with hope,
Poverty, nakedness, torment and patience,
Being the true children and disciples of Christ,
Who, living, showed us this way in writing,
And marked with his own blood this most sacred road,
Dying to deliver us from fear.[171]

At the end of this survey of the representation of the dead and death at the beginning of European modernity, the polyvalence of the macabre asserts itself. Its divergent meanings resist all reductionism, although its origins are no longer subject to doubt. The macabre derives from the ascetic contemplation of monks entirely turned toward the otherworld and who sought to convince themselves—and to persuade others—of the wicked character of our illusions here below. This ecclesiastical discourse then spread out of the monasteries through preaching and iconography—that is, through an evangelism of fear. The impetus behind this movement was the increasing luxury and growing aspiration for earthly goods in a civilization that, at least at its highest levels, moved from destitution toward ever-increasing comforts. The insistence on the macabre, in the wake of the *contemptus mundi*, thus stood within the logic of a vast enterprise of guilt-infliction aimed toward salvation in the afterlife.

Coinciding circumstances—epidemics, famines, and a rise in violence—favored the reception and enlarged the audience of the *memento mori*. Given the misfortunes of the time, this constantly repeated warning from the church seemed more justified than ever. It is also worth repeating the fact that the majority of the surviving written and iconographic records of the macabre from the fourteenth through the sixteenth centuries bear the undeniable imprint of the church, even if at times they integrate elements of pre-Christian folklore. These macabre images do not invoke a conception of life and death detached from Christianity. On the contrary, they urge penitence and detachment from worldly things such as honors, wealth, beauty, and carnal desire. This seems to be the dominant meaning of the texts and images that, for more than two centuries, stressed the brevity of life and the decay of the body in the tomb. And such is the sense, moreover, of the complex and fantastic itinerary that visitors were invited to take in the Parco di Bomarzo (province of Viterbo), which was laid out according to the directions of an Orsini prince toward the middle of the sixteenth century. A symbolic route through wilderness led the visitor to encounters with monstrous sculptures and unusual constructions. Along the pathway, the visitor could read inscriptions such as "Disdain worldly goods," "True delight comes after death," "Lord, guide my steps," and so on. The initiate's itinerary ended in a small temple preceded by a three-headed Cerberus and marked off by funerary stelae bearing skulls and crossbones. What an astonishing mix of the art of gardens with the lessons of *contemptus mundi*, a taste for the macabre and a fascination for the monstrous.[172]

Nevertheless, in a climate of anguish and morbidity, the allure of the macabre risked leading the people of the time (and it did not fail to do so) in two directions, each of which was ultimately opposed to the initial religious message. The first of these blind alleys was a taste for spectacles of suffering and death. This syndrome started with the crucifixions and flagellations of *The Golden Legend* and other saints' lives, eventually culminating in willfully pernicious scenes of tortures, executions, and slaughters. Departing from the moral and religious lesson, there was a gradual sliding into sadistic pleasure. The macabre eventually became exalted for its own sake.

The second detour away from the paths approved by the church consisted in the turning of the *memento mori* into a *memento vivere*. Since life is so short, let us hasten to enjoy it. Since the dead body will be so repulsive, let us hurry to gain all possible pleasure from it while it is still in good health. Here it is important to recall what took place during outbreaks of the plague.[173] Some people rushed off to churches while others greedily indulged in the worst debaucheries. This evidence proves that the macabre could be received as an invitation to eroticism—hence the ambiguity of Baldung's paintings and engravings. However, if some legitimate doubt exists regarding this artist's intentions (which may not have been so different from those of a Ronsard), there is none regarding those of Flötner and the Beham brothers. In all periods and civilizations, certain people interpret macabre spectacles as an incitement to take advantage of life while it lasts. Ancient bas-reliefs, sepulchral lamps, and goblets had long before associated skeletons with scenes of fleshly delight.[174]

In conclusion, I do not believe that one can globally detach the *memento mori* of the fourteenth to sixteenth centuries from either the religious concept that fostered it or the Christian preoccupation with the afterlife. It is true, however, that the macabre was laden with potential deviations and that these deviations were effectively produced in the direction of either violence or eroticism, the one being frequently linked to the other. The weapon of the macabre cannot be handled without danger.

CHAPTER 4

A Sinful World

"AN AGE OF TEARS, ANGUISH, AND TORMENT" (EUSTACHE DESCHAMPS)

Pushed to the front of the stage by three temporarily convergent forces—the church, the plague, and violence—the macabre of the fourteenth to the sixteenth centuries is a striking characteristic of the beginnings of European modernity, at least at the level of the dominant culture. And the macabre can be even better understood if it is placed within a larger context, a context that justifies the synthetic approach taken by the present study for it is often a highly gloomy setting, or at least can be perceived as such. If this context were to take the form of a painting, it might be entitled "All Goes Badly" (a formula of Eustache Deschamps), or better yet, "All Goes from Bad to Worse" (another affirmation of the same poet). Certainly throughout history and throughout the globe, discontented people have looked with nostalgia toward the past and have bitterly disparaged the present. If, however, this *topos* becomes ubiquitous during a certain phase of history, asserting itself as a leading component of the collective mentality, it then deserves particular attention.

I now aim to demonstrate, by widening the circle of this inquiry, that the diffusion of curses against the world and mankind outside of the monastic setting, from the early fourteenth century on, was inseparable from the grim view that contemporaries had of their own epoch. The "signs of the times" inspired an often disheartened evaluation of human nature and of life in this world. A situation of anxiety thus gave credit to the cultural dissemination of the guilt complex. These two phenomena reinforced each other and merged together. The two following chapters seek to clarify this historical encounter (which could just as easily not have happened) through an investigation of the pessimism of the Renaissance.

When the *Roman de Fauvel* (1310–14) argues that, in this corrupt world, everything seems to go wrong ("men have become beasts, they carry their heads along the ground"), it reasons in accordance with a very vague chronological logic. And this despite the satire written by those who wished to "thrash" Fauvel, thus expressing the protests of groups faithful to the spirit of Saint Louis and opposed to the politics of Philip the Fair. Likewise Tauler, in a sermon, is equally subject to generalization when he states that: "today the love of one's neighbor is truly extinct in all the countries of the world."[1] In the following poem, composed by the Austrian Cistercian Christianus of Lilienfeld (d. before 1332), this type of commonplace is still preeminent. The present to which he refers is not clearly dated; the poem could apply to any century:

If you desire to know why laughter flees me,
You might understand given the present situation:
The lamb has engendered the wolf who will enter in fury;
All good is gone, evil rages in a terrifying fashion . . .

Justice ebbs, law has collapsed; alas, why was I born? . . .

The fever of gluttony is beloved by all . . .
Everyone glories in being fat, no one in their leanness . . .

Fornication spares no one, oh suffering![2]

With the misfortunes of the second half of the fourteenth century—famines, plagues, the Hundred Years' War, civil wars and various revolts, the Great Schism, and the advance of the Turks—the banal generalizations are left behind. Those who witnessed these disasters and their effect on Christianity experienced the feeling of belonging to a time of unprecedented calamities, explicable only by the existence of a hideously sinful church and humanity. All things now appeared to be upside down, the climax of such a crisis seeming to be nothing less than the Last Judgment itself. A global connection must therefore be established (at least for certain diachronic sequences) between, on one side, eschatological fears and expectations and, on the other, the conscience of sin, contempt for the world, horror of the self, and a sharpened sense of the fragility of life.

Nicholas de Clamanges (1363–1437), who was a theologian from the Champagne region (first a rector of the University of Paris and then secretary to Benedict XIII in Avignon), is a good representative of the type of person who sank into pessimism and saw all things worsen. His works, which are here studied in a Protestant edition of the seventeenth century, include a *Livre de l'état corrompu de l'Eglise (Book of the corrupt state of the Church)*, a *Déploration sur la calamité introduite dans l'Eglise par le très abominable schisme (Condemnation of the Calamity introduced to the Church by the most abominable Schism)*, a treatise *Sur les prélats simoniaques (On Simoniac Prelates)*, and another on *l'Antéchrist, sa naissance, sa vie, ses moeurs et ses oeuvres (The antichrist, his birth, life, habits, and deeds)*.[3] This brief list of titles already reveals the fears and preoccupations of Nicolas de Clamanges, yet his avowals of anxiety, indeed of despondency, are no less numerous in his correspondence. He writes letters to Gerson on "the lamentable state of the Church,"[4] to a royal secretary on "the corruption of behavior among both laymen and ecclesiastics,"[5] to a clerk of the Paris Parliament on the vices "that God does not always correct with the same scourge, but which he does not cease to punish with his blows. If civil war abates somewhat, He then afflicts us with both plague and foreign wars."[6]

In opposition to the present state of the church, Clamanges describes a golden age when piety, holiness, and poverty flourished. If the priests' only treasure then was good works, this humble treasure was nonetheless rich and overflowing. They had no gold or silver goblets, they drank from earthen or tin receptacles. The high clergy had no need for the trappings of horses and armor, they did not march in processions preceded by a crowd of play actors, nor were they accompanied by youths with curled and effeminate hair, in outfits striped like the skin of monsters, with sleeves dangling to the ground—"almost barbaric" spectacles.[7] With the increase in the cost and abundance of ephemeral things—it was already a consumer society!—luxury and insolence were seen as having insinuated themselves into the church, religion had grown cold, virtue faded, discipline slackened, charity diminished, humility vanished, poverty and sobriety had become things of shame, and cupidity intensified. People were no longer satisfied with their own property, they no longer coveted only that of their neighbor, they sought to steal from the poor and to oppress them. In such a way did the church leaders behave, surpassing laymen in their greediness. Quite an example they set for the laity to follow![8]

Reading these accusations, one understands why the Protestants of the united provinces republished the works of Clamanges. What better testimony, they must have thought, of the corruption of a church that the Reformation was trying to clean up! Still, in this painful period of the Great Schism, were there no more saintly souls? In chapter 25 of his *De corrupto ecclesiae statu*, Clamanges answers that dissolution within the church had grown to such proportions that it was better to pass over those of good conduct: "They are far too few in number and influence" *(parvo nimis in numero atque momento sunt).*[9]

As a result, an impending punishment was prophesied in the *De Antichristo* . . .[10] Addressing princes, the ecclesiastical hierarchy, and all Christians, Clamanges predicts that great mishaps are gathering just above their heads. The perfidious Christian race has excessively abused divine patience. Christians will now therefore bear a heavy burden of scourges and retributions. The "great judgment is at our very doors." As proof he cites the advance of the Moslems, heathen executors of divine vengeance. The progress of this innumerable, bloodthirsty multitude will finally repay man's revolt against God, which not plagues, foreign wars, or the excess of internecine struggles could hold in check. Moreover—an added chastisement—the action of the "cruel beast" that is the Turk is compounded by that of the "other beast" of heresy, which notably raged in Germany[11] and in Italy. An ominous time is coming. "Everywhere will be fury, everywhere sorrow and violence, everywhere the image of death. Happy indeed are those who have rendered their souls before the advent of these tribulations and calamities."

In the France of Charles VI, Eustache Deschamps (1346–1406), a contemporary of Clamanges and a prolific though not brilliant poet, was a fine spokesperson for a generation traumatized by the Hundred Years' War and the Great Schism. In his work appear most of the pessimistic themes that Western culture was then cultivating. This work also merits special attention here as it constitutes a kind of melancholy synthesis that the tender love ballads of this ultimately misogynist writer do not contradict.[12] It is worth following the passage of his poems from commonplaces detached from any precise chronology to the bitter evocation of a present that only too readily inspires grief. Naturally, he regrets the loss of an idyllic past, even if at least one ballad attempts to be critical in this regard. Alluding to Nero and Ganelon, the poet recognizes that "many acted wickedly / In times past."[13] Yet such is not the dominant note in his work, which abounds with references to a vaguely defined golden age reminiscent of that of Clamanges. At that time "honor inhabited the world," and so did "sovereign wisdom," "generosity . . . valor and loyalty."[14] There had been an era in which the church was "in great triumph," when people did not grow proud and "Nobility fought for both . . . / These folk did not envy others."[15] The ancients, "by their great efforts / Conquered lands and realms, / And many founded great cities. / Now men of the present do not achieve what they did."[16]

The happy days of long ago contrast with the rapid aging not only of humanity but also of the earth itself, a belief that was widespread among the governing culture in early modern times and that has already been described in the first volume of this study.[17] Deschamps asserts that the seasons are out of sequence.[18] "The air is hot when it should be cold." Days are short when they should be long. In addition, trees are now "sickly and meadows bear only thistles." "People are puny"—a view that French Protestant apologists of the seventeenth century will reaffirm—"animals, birds are of weak health, / Fish are tiny, seeds meager and infertile / . . . Vines are worth little and yield less / They do not produce profitable drink. / The grain which is gathered, worsens beneath the roof / Or in the barn, and we only collect a small amount anyway." Nature is thus wasted, deprived of her living forces. Yet, worst of all, men are conducting themselves more and more badly. On this theme, the poet is tireless: "Today only madmen rule."[19] "There is no love except that of the fox."[20] "There is no news of virtue."[21] "People no longer believe in anything."[22] "Neither Hell nor Paradise interest anyone."[23] Like contemporary preachers, Deschamps attacks dishonest practices. He thunders at those who wear such scanty clothing "that they show their backsides like monkeys," and at women who "openly display their breasts."[24] Everywhere "vices and dissolute habits reign / The poor suffer, the rich are exalted, / The bad thrive, the good undergo punishment."[25] One only sees "Envy, disordering plots, / Hatred . . ." Hence divine punishments, "sudden deaths," deluges, snow, storms, ice, and "wars in all places."[26] It would be impossible to enumerate the complaints, reproaches, remorse, and cries of sorrow that resonate through Deschamps's work. To choose but a few haphazard examples: Ballad 185, *"Déploration des maux de la France"*; Ballad 193, *"Acte de contrition de Paris"*; Ballad 243, *"Sur les malheurs de l'Eglise"*; Ballad 255, *"Complainte du Pays de France."*[27] The major key is given by Ballad 375, *"Tristesse du temps présent"*:

> *Age of tears, anguish, and torment,*
> *Sad above all others, full of bitter pain . . .*
> *Without joy, full of the seven deadly sins,*
> *Empty of virtue, haughty with pride,*
> *Where each man languishes, comfortless . . .*
> *Today is the time of peril . . .*[28]

Since everywhere there is only "sadness and mourning,"[29] since the church has become a new "Babylon,"[30] since it has fallen under the reign of the moon, the evil star,[31] and since "all things run counter to good sense,"[32] it is clear that human history is nearing its end. Deschamps frequently expressed this conviction that was so strong in his period and that would persist until the middle of the seventeenth century. In Ballad 52 he prophesies: "The signs show that the body will die / Of this world that approaches its end, / Which can no longer last in this state."[33] In Ballad 126, he returns to the same theme: "Little by little the century declines, / Charity is gone and people kill each other, / Because the world is quite close to its end."[34] The time of the Antichrist has come, he says, because "all graces" are for sale in the church.[35] "Today is the time of tribulation,"[36] foreseen in Scripture. To the question—"How goes today's world?"—the answer is simple: "It certainly could not be worse."[37] Thus "the world is old, which advances toward its end,"[38] "The church and all things are in decline: / And so one can perceive / That the end is at hand."[39] An illustrious contemporary of Deschamps, Duke Jean de Berry, expressed the same sentiment when, in his old age, he chose for his motto: "The time will come,"[40] meaning both the time of his death and the death of the world.

Deschamps's student and disciple was Christine de Pisan, who was widowed at twenty-five and left with three children, deprived of protectors during the civil wars and forced to take refuge in a nunnery for a decade. Pisan was also a saddened witness to the sins and ills of her age. Her work resounds with the echo of these vicissitudes, particularly in her *Lamentations sur les guerres civiles*, her *Livre de mutacion de la fortune*, and in a letter dated February 1403 (old style) that was addressed to Deschamps. This letter, whose form is overrefined and burdened by punning rhymes, is not a masterpiece. What matters, however, is its theme—that of "all goes badly"—a theme on which Deschamps and Pisan could only have agreed:

O master! What a hard marvel
It is to see, in this time that endures
Lies and theft so rife
In cities, in castles in the courts
Of princes, by common practice,
In noblemen and commoners,
In the clergy and in every court of law . . .

. . . Everyone tries to gain,
By a great lust to own,
By fraudulent malice and a readiness
To deceive, and no one cares
To acquire virtuous profits . . . More than heaven, worldlings love the fat earth,
Crammed with dung and excrement.[41]

In such an atmosphere, is it any surprise that there emerged an exaggerated sense of man's physical, moral, and intellectual fragility? Among so many other voices there stands out that of the great poet and prose writer Alain Chartier (1385–1436), himself a contemporary of the Great Schism and the Hundred Years' War:

Sickly human creature
Born to labor and to pain
Dressed in a frail body
So feeble and so vain
Tender, fragile, uncertain
And so easily struck down

Your thinking strips you of virtue
Your mad sense hurts and kills you
And leads you to no wisdom.
You are born so poor
Only Heaven allows
You to live in health.[42]

Yet however numerous were the outcries of this type, they did not lead contemporaries to greater wisdom and virtue. Even if the Great Schism was resolved in 1417, other religious splits and other abuses ensued or continued, other wars broke out, and new Turkish armies threatened. The fifteenth century appeared to many to be the continuation of a decline and an accentuation of the "aging" of Christianity.

This attitude seems to have obsessed Germany at the end of the fifteenth and beginning of the sixteenth century. An anonymous book, contemporary with the

Great Schism and entitled *The Reformation of the Emperor Sigismund*, bemoans: "Our empire is sick, weak, and feeble." The dominant theme of this book is that "the world is afflicted" and that there is "no longer any order."[43] Nicholas of Cusa, presenting his treatise *De concordantiâ catholica* to the Council of Basel in 1433, delivered dark judgments on his time and his country. Around him he only saw "universal destruction," "total depravity," "overturned order," "mortal illness," and "deviancies." He also says that the world "is falling into decadence," that it is "sinking" and "going under," "declining," and "becoming perverse."[44] The world has "lost its center." Deprived of stability, men and things are carried along by centrifugal forces and scatter into the void. At the end of the fifteenth century, the Alsatian preacher Geiler de Kaisersberg complained (as had Nicolas de Clamanges eighty years earlier) that "Christianity is in ruins from top to bottom, from the Pope to the sacristan, from the emperor to the shepherd."[45]

The 112 chapters of *The Ship of Fools* (1494) (written by a layman!) incessantly repeat this same message: "The swords of papal and imperial power are rusted . . . justice is blind; justice is dead."[46] Avarice, mother of all vices, impels Christians to work on Sunday, or to revel. On holidays, instead of praying, "people kill time by speeding along in their cars"[47]—a translation that reflects a singularly modern habit. Blasphemy triumphs, and this claim recalls many other observations of this kind made by the men of the time.[48] "Be not amazed," Sebastian Brant declares, "if God, before similar outrages, causes the world to sink. Heaven may fall, or shatter into pieces, so great are the blasphemies on earth . . . The outrage is so huge that it has spread everywhere." The "degradation" of faith also grows greater every day, and "indulgence has lost any sort of price, no one wants it any more."[49] During this time, "the diabolical spirit of the sons of Mohammed" ravages the East and heads for Latin Christianity. "The enemy is at the gates. But everyone awaits death by sleeping."[50] The future looks bleak: "I very much fear that tomorrow things will be worse and that our future will be even darker."[51] Overloaded with fools who have not even equipped themselves with charts, a compass, or an hourglass,[52] the boat of Christianity is "tossed about on the waves,"[53] it "rolls and pitches and lists, the first whirlpool may seize it."[54] "If Jesus Christ himself does not climb into the crow's nest, we will soon plunge into the depths."[55] Brant also says that even "the mast is cracked; all is carried away. Swimming is impossible in the raging sea. The waves are too high to scale."[56] And, especially, the "great enemy"[57]—the Antichrist—now cavorts around the ship. "One can already see the scorpion moving."[58] He has "sent his messengers to earth and propagated error throughout the lands."[59] "The times have been turned inside out."[60] "The day of judgment draws near."[61]

Thus, a century later, Brant echoes Eustache Deschamps. Both speak the same language, regard the world in the same manner, predict the same outcome. Nevertheless, they are but two of many voices expressing a collective pessimism that will long continue. Exemplary in this regard are the positions held by Luther, Viret, and Bullinger that I discussed in my previous volume.[62] All the same, it is worth briefly reviewing Luther's frequently expressed conviction that the end of the world was at hand,[63] especially as his audience was enormous. One day he declared: "It is the final seal of the Apocalypse. It is going to break."[64] In fact, he was convinced that the Antichrist, whose extraordinary misdeeds were to precede the end of time, was busily at work. His spirit was the Pope and his body the Turk, the latter physically "ravaging, attacking, and vexing the Church of God," the former "spiritually" oppressing it.[65] For Luther, no doubt was possible: "The time of distress" announced by Saint John, "the like of which there had not yet been since there first were nations," was the sixteenth century in which he lived.[66] In these moments of despondency, Luther also wished for the end of time. In April 1544, when his sister Margaret was mortally ill, he wrote to a friend: "I would not be upset with our Lord if he carried off this Satanic time and century and I would wish that I and my family were quickly removed from hence, for I desire the coming of the day that will put an end to the furies of Satan and his followers."[67] In only slightly more restrained terms, Martin Bucer proclaimed in his *Das Ihm selbs niemand sonder anderen leber soll* ("Treatise on Loving One's Neighbor") ". . . In place of apostles we now have only false prophets, in place of educators only seducers . . . in place of pious princes and leaders . . . only tyrants, wolves, bears, lions, children [sic], and fools."[68] In the same spirit, Henri Estienne declares in his *Apologie pour Hérodote* (1566): "Our century is worse than all the preceding ones."[69]

At the same time, although for opposite reasons, the most zealous of Catholics did not think differently. Thus Guillaume Budé, in his *De Transitu Hellenismi ad Christianismum* (1535)—an angry work directed against the Reformation, which notably claims that "the overflow of errors" is growing each day—declares: "It is like a deluge of the Ancient Religion, which floods all the parts of the Christian world and which, little by little, drowns the difference between piety and impiety." Budé characterizes his century as being "depraved and deaf to the understanding of truth, having become not only hard as iron but heavy as lead." According to him, "religion and contempt for God are on equal footing . . . the ruin of good customs, the defeat of Christianity, the dishonor of literature, the destruction of virtue increase each day and spread like wildfire through the churches."[70] Hence a grim foreboding, expressed in a powerful phrase that could just as easily been written by Luther: "As for me, I am inclined rather to think that the final day has arrived, and that the world is already in decline, that it is already old and bereft of sense, that it intimates, forewarns, and announces its approaching end and its downfall."[71] In this fashion one of the most illustrious French humanists characterized the present and envisaged the future.

The above appraisals, spread out between Nicolas de Clamanges and Guillaume Budé and Henri Estienne, come mainly from men of the church but also from personalities moved by a profound religious concern. A link can therefore be made between this period's Christian preoccupations and its severe judgment with respect to a time deemed unfaithful to the Gospel. This association was naturally reinforced by the Wars of Religion, which, at the European level, augmented the pessimism of the most spiritually engaged Christians as well as those most worried about public order. Christianity goes from bad to worse: Such was still the opinion of Philip II and his counselors in the Low Countries who, in 1560, prohibited songs, farces, ballads, and comedies treating more or less of religion. Before they could be tolerated, but not any longer: ". . . And as the world was previously less corrupt, and as errors were then not as great as they are today, such a close interest was not taken in games, farces, songs, refrains, ballads, and other recitals, as is now necessary this present time, when wicked and damnable sects swarm day by day and increase in number."[72]

This text can be combined with the numerous affirmations of those who believed in the multiplication of blasphemies and witches in early modern Europe.[73] For Agrippa d'Aubigné, the cup is full and it is high time for God to finally punish sinful humanity:

Befoul the air, O heavenly avengers
With poison, venom, and flying pestilences! . . .
Breezes, no longer purge the air! Crack open, turn back, collapse!
Drown us instead of sprinkling us! Blaze without warming us!

Our sins are at the utmost height and, rising to heaven,
From above they pour out on all sides by the score"[74]

Hyperbolic exclamations from the vindictive pen of a persecuted Protestant? Without a doubt. Yet they are not isolated. Another French Protestant, Christophe de Gamon, in a poem published in 1609, considers that the world of his time is "a wood filled with lions, a filthy valley, / . . . where all is gloom." Also, "near at hand, Death menaces / The world, which, already old, bows its face toward the ground," and "lies down, sick with sinning, on a bed of torpor." Hence the prophecy: "O decrepit world! O listless world! You're done for, you're done for."[75] A prominent feature of these Protestant verses—as in those of Luther but also in those of Eustache Deschamps, Nicolas de Clamanges, and Sebastian Brant—is the link between a dark moral diagnosis of the present and the belief in the imminent end of the world. This association, moreover, works both ways. Farther on it will be seen how eschatological fevers swept through England and Scotland from the end of the sixteenth century to the 1660s. Consequently, it is no surprise that people laid heavy stress on the extraordinary sins of an age given over to the Devil that surpassed all preceding times in its moral ugliness. Edwin Sandys, Bishop of London and later Archbishop of York, wrote in 1583 to the Bishop of Chester: "When I look, venerable brother, at the course and condition of this world lost in impiety; what triumphs Satan obtains, how far and wide vice bears rule, how numerous and crowded are the assemblies of ungodly men, how weak, how withered, or rather how entirely gone from the earth is faith, is piety; it seems to me that we are now arrived at the last and ungodly times of this world, drawing near to destruction."[76]

In 1633 Thomas Adams, "the prose Shakespeare of the Puritans," goes still further in defining his time as the meeting-ground of "all the vicious customs of former ages . . . as the Kennels of a city run to the common Sewer." Before, one form of perversity had been dominant, then another. Now, however, "like so many land-flouds from the mountains, they meet in one channel, and make a torrent of united wickedness in these lower and latter days."[77]

Over and above the clerical dossier, the Italians of Machiavelli and Guicciardini's time passed a severe judgment on themselves and blamed their own sins for the misfortunes of their country from 1494 onward. Thus the Venetian Girolamo Priuli sees in Charles VIII's rapid triumph the punishment merited by Italian sodomy, a practice especially common in Naples.[78] In a minor key, the magistrate and storyteller Noël du Fail (1520–1591), who anxiously watched the growth of urban civilization, states that the world has become an "unruly boy, and that this "wicked century" is "an age as hard as iron." Making melancholic reference to the happy time of François I, he asserts that "the children of today seem no more than dwarfs compared to the ancients," no more than "longish semi-humans, thin like leeches."[79] In the *Histoires Prodigieueses* of Boaistuau, the French adaptor of Bandello, there is found an allusion—all the more interesting in that it is presented as a given—to our "centuries in which sin has more and more abounded."[80] Two years earlier, he had even more clearly denounced "such a century as ours, that is so corrupt, depraved, and steeped in all kinds of vices and abominations that it clearly seems to be the pit and sewer where all the filthy wastes of other ages and centuries have come to empty and purge themselves,"[81] which is the same analogy that Thomas Adams had made and which may well have been a topos. It is useful to recall that Boaistuau's *Histoires Prodigieuses* (which were far more thorough than his *Bref Discours* and whose intentions was opposed to that of *De l'Excellence de l'homme*) were read, imitated, copied (there were no less than sixty editions in fifty years), and were seen by moralists as being a model of their genre. The pages of this book caught and reflected the sensibility of an era.

A saddened observer of the Wars of Religion, Etienne Pasquier, filled his correspondence with alarmist formulas and severe judgments on the times: ". . . We hear of nothing but fires, wars, murders, and sackings of cities" (1562).[82] "We no longer live in the kingdom, we live in the empire, because all things are *getting worse*" (French "*empir*ant").[83] In his *Essais*, Montaigne avers that the good opinion of the people is "harmful," "especially in an age as corrupt and ignorant as this."[84] In 1582, Thierry Coornhert, an Irenist and notary from Haarlem, writes that "our days . . . can be counted among the very worst."[85] Shakespeare describes the world of his time as a "prison," "a goodly one, in which there are many confines, wards, and dungeons, Denmark [that is, early seventeenth-century England] being one o' th' worst" (*Hamlet*, II. ii. 245–247). A Spanish writer, Martin Gonzalez de Cellorigo, echoes him in 1600, declaring: "A time has come that we believe to be worse than was the past."[86]

THE DREAM OF THE GOLDEN AGE

The above citations comprise only a selection. Yet their sum total, which could be increased, tends to show that the dominant tone of the Renaissance was not necessarily optimism (as is often believed) but rather pessimism, even if the word was not then in use.[87] "Optimists" like Francesco Pico della Mirandola and Guillaume Postel were a minority. Still, it is true that the term "Renaissance" was itself employed by writers and artists to signify a resurrection of learning, letters, and good taste. People spoke of a "new golden age," especially in fifteenth-century Italy and in early sixteenth-century France and Germany. In 1547 the Florentine Giovanni Rucellai declared: "It is thought that since 1400 our era has more cause for contentment than any other since Florence was founded."[88] A short while later, Marsilio Ficino went even further: "It is undoubtedly a golden age that has brought back to light the previously almost destroyed liberal arts: grammar, eloquence, painting, architecture, sculpture, music."[89] In 1518 Ulrich van Hutten exclaimed: "O century, O studies, it is a joy to be alive."[90] Rabelais echoes him in having Gargantua declare: "I see the thieves, hangmen, adventurers, and stableboys of today more learned than were the teachers and preachers of my youth."[91] These enthusiastic appraisals, however, must be qualified in various ways. On the one hand, sixteenth-century Italians felt that the happy era which had more or less coincided with Lorenzo the Magnificent's government had long since passed. Henceforth, even a decadence of art could be expected. So thinks Vasari, for whom, after Michelangelo, there could only be a decline. On the other hand, the Renaissance era made highly important use of the theme of the golden age.[92] Upon closer examination, it becomes clear that the golden age was most often experienced and presented as an antidote to a bleak present. This global point of view includes even the numerous panegyrics composed by court poets, affirming upon each accession of a new ruler that his reign would bring the rebirth of the golden age. At the same time, this stereotypical adulation also expressed the widespread desire for change with respect to the difficult conditions of the time.

The dream of the golden age took multiple forms. The majority located this blessed time in a far-off, undated past, blending the terrestrial paradise of the Bible with that of Ovid's *Metamorphoses* and imagining an era of peace during which there was no fear, evil, or unhappiness. It has been mentioned, in passing, that Clamanges, Deschamps, and Noël du Fail all clung to this myth, and they were not alone. The *Ship of Fools* can be understood only with reference to a distant "once upon a time," when princes and ministers were "full of intelligence and rich in experience. In that age, scandal and outrage were punished and peace extended and reigned throughout the world."[93] Into the mouth of Folly Erasmus put the elegy of an era when men had only one guide, "the instinct of Nature." In the following famous passage, the critique of the "sciences" of the time (and especially of grammar) calls on a former system of reference that far outshines the modern one:

> *For what need was there of grammar when all spoke the same language, and had no other aim in speaking but that some one else should understand? What use for dialectic, where there was no battle of opinions ranged in contradiction to each other? What room for rhetoric, when no man cared to make trouble for his neighbor? Wherein was the study of law called for, when folk had not learned the evil ways from which, we must admit, our good laws arose. Then, moreover, they had too much piety to search out, with a profane curiosity, the secrets of nature; to investigate the dimensions, motions, and influences of the stars, or the hidden causes of things . . . But as the pristine simplicity of the golden age little by little slipped away, first the arts were discovered—by evil spirits, as I have told.*[94]

(Erasmus had earlier affirmed that the arts and sciences "crept in by stealth, along with other banes of human life.")

Coming from Folly, such a speech is undoubtedly ambiguous. Still, when aligned with numerous other like-minded texts of the period, this passage bespeaks a collective nostalgia sustained by a sad present. Marot is close to Erasmus in the rondeau (1525) that he devotes to "the love of the ancient age," a happy epoch when mutual affection took the place of science and law:

> *In the virtuous olden times a spirit of love reigned,*
> *Which without great art and gifts acted in such a way*
> *That a bouquet touched with profound love*
> *Made the entire round earth to be so touched . . .*
> *Now is lost that which love ordained:*
> *One only hears of false tears, of changes . . .*[95]

Another melancholy complaint about the vanished golden age is that of Don Quixote. In this case, moreover, it is a madman who speaks—that is, a pure heart lost in a world hardened by egotism. Long ago, "yours" and "mine" did not exist and Nature gave freely to all. At the end of this line of thinking stands Rousseau. Don Quixote also laments in this vein:

> *In that blessed age all things were held in common. No man, to gain his common sustenance, needed to make any greater effort than to reach up his hand and pluck it from the strong oaks, which literally invited him to taste their sweet and savory fruit . . . All was peace then, all amity, all concord. The crooked plow had not yet dared to force open and search the kindly bowels of our first mother with its heavy coulter; for without compulsion she yielded from every part of her fertile and broad bosom everything to satisfy, sustain, and delight the children who then possessed her.*

And the knight continues: In that blessed age women had no need for cosmetic luxuries. They clothed themselves simply, "without any search for artificial elaborations." "Nor had fraud, deceit, or malice mingled with truth and sincerity."[96]

Certainly, even in Cervantes's own time, some texts argued an opposite view. Jean Bodin wrote one of the most significant; in his *Méthode de l'histoire* (1566), an entire chapter sets out to demolish the theory of the golden ages, which in reality were "ages of iron." This systematic refutation seemed necessary to the author, who wrote that "this inveterate error has such deep roots that it now appears impossible to extirpate it," especially since it also has "an almost infinite number of adherents." This latter observation is crucial: Bodin was aware that he argued a minority view:

> *And thus were these famous golden and silver ages! Men lived scattered in the fields and woods like wild animals, and only possessed as their own what they could retain by force and by crime: much time was necessary in order for men to gradually progress from this savage and barbarian way of life to the civilized practices and a well-ordered society of the kind we find today . . .*

Moreover, if, as was widely accepted, "humanity was moving toward a general disintegration, we would have already reached that extremity of vices and dishonesty which was attained long ago."[97]

Even during the Wars of Religion, Bodin contrasts "the virtues" of his contemporaries and the justice prevailing in modern states to the cruelty and crimes of former centuries.[98] In addition, he extols the arts, letters, and discoveries of his time, according due merit to the compass and printing, which alone equal all the inventions of the ancients.[99] As innovative as these remarks appear, it is also necessary to qualify them. Bodin believed only in temporary eras of human progress, which are then followed by inevitable declines. For "nature seems subject to the law of the eternal return, where everything is the object of a circular revolution such that vice follows upon virtue, ignorance supplants wisdom, evil succeeds honesty, and mere darkness replaces errors . . ."[100] Ten years later (1580), Bodin paints an extremely bleak picture of his period in his *Démonamanie des sorciers*, which modern criticism has had trouble reconciling with the rest of the production of such a perceptive writer. Despite these exceptions, however, it still remains true that the Renaissance passionately dreamed of a lost paradise that held a never-ending attraction. Hence this astute observation of Eugenio Garin in regard to Italy at the end of the *Quattrocento*: "At the end of the fifteenth century, it is not hard to find these two themes brought together, even by the same author: On the one hand, the signs of the Antichrist and the imminent cataclysm, on the other hand, the golden age."[101]

The theme of the golden age necessarily calls attention to the myth of the Fountain of Youth, notably depicted in a painting by Lucas Cranach the Younger (1546; Berlin, Staatliche Museum) although, in 1530, the artist's father had already painted a *Golden Age* now in Oslo.[102] Upon plunging into the restorative waters, youth and vigor are restored. Time is obliterated and, with it, old age and death. In carts, wheelbarrows, on stretchers, even on the backs of other men, the sick, the old, and the lame are brought to the miraculous pool. Naked, bathing in the regenerative water, they emerge healed, young, happy, and ready for dances, feasting, and love. Faust's dream is here accomplished, but without the Devil's intervention. In the left half of the painting, the side of old age, the landscape is jagged and disturbing; to the right, the side of youth, nature smiles with leafy, fruit-laden trees.

The Land of Cockaigne sometimes included a Fountain of Youth, and it has, in fact, often been called the "golden ages of the poor."[103] This mythical land is always an alimentary paradise where nature gives freely and abundantly in a universe where there is no need to work for one's living. In addition, according to most surviving versions, the people of Cockaigne spend their time in perpetual revelry and make love without any moral anxiety. Clearly the Lands of Cockaigne comprised an evasion from a civilization normally characterized by poverty, miserable working conditions, and the rigorous sexual morality of religious authorities. The theme took shape during the thirteenth century, with *Li Fabliaus de Coquaigne*. The essential point for this study, however, is that Cockaigne had its widest diffusion during the sixteenth and seventeenth centuries. For this period, no less than twelve variants have been identified in French, twenty-two in German, thirty-three in Italian, and forty in Flemish.[104]

In their own way, the Lands of Cockaigne were utopias. This book aims neither to enumerate nor to analyze these utopias in detail, but only to point out that they featured among the favorite imaginary projects of Renaissance writers and architects. From Thomas More's *Utopia* (1516) to Campanella's *City of the Sun* (1623), Bacon's *New Atlantis* (1627), and Honoré D'Urfé's *Astrée* (1607–28), via Rabelais's Abbey of Thélème and Kaspar Stiblin's *De Eudaemonensium republica* (1553), from Filarete's *Sforzinda* (middle of the fifteenth century) to Antonio Doni's "solar city" (1552) and the *Christianopolis* (early seventeenth century) of the Lutheran Valentin Andreae (which is both a labyrinth and a barracks), there was a considerable construction on paper of these "radiant cities."[105] Unreal towns, artificial paradises, serious descriptions of worlds based on "principles different from those that operate in the real world," the utopias bear witness to how a substantial number of intellectuals experienced a cruel divorce between the aspirations of the time and its daily reality.[106] By their title alone, these utopias work as counterproofs within a history of Renaissance pessimism. Like Plato and Horace, More, Stiblin, Campanella, and Bacon all locate their happy land in a distant *somewhere else*, in a lost isle at the heart of an ocean that, if not always imaginary, was then necessarily difficult for the people of the time to access: equatorial seas, the Pacific or Indian oceans. In short, their point was that peace, harmony, and plenty are not at all within reach.

The same geography of the impossible explains why certain Europeans believed in the "American Mirage."[107] Newly discovered by the great Renaissance voyages, the peoples of America were assigned virtues that Europe had long since lost. Moreover, upon contact with civilization, these native American virtues vanished away. It has been rightly noted that "the golden age of utopia was linked to the history of the great maritime discoveries. Each travel narrative, embellished by the imagination, acted as a limited cultural shock, provoking a comparison that threw contemporary social structures into doubt."[108] The myth of the "noble savage" and the praise of primitivism that, during the sixteenth century, pressed this disillusioned outlook on modern times was not the exclusive property of Montaigne. His essay "On Cannibals" belonged to an entire current of thought. His opinion was not, however, that of the majority insofar as many Europeans (principally soldiers, administrators, and colonists) saw the overseas peoples as barbarians to be civilized and exploited. All the same, the "noble savage" idea is too important to neglect, especially in terms of a historiography of mentalities in which it should be reassigned its just place within the global intellectual context.

Yet various travelers, geographers, and writers of the Renaissance continued (from afar) to think that they had found the land of the golden age.[109] "The people of Cuba and the neighboring isles . . . for the most part, live in a golden age" (Pietro Bembo).[110] "The Tartars . . . adjacent to the realm of Cathay . . . lead the most simple life of the golden age, not seeking the honors and dignities of the world" (Jean Macer).[111] "It seems to me that what we see by experience in these nations [the Americas] surpasses not only all the pictures with which poetry has bedecked the golden age . . . but also the conception and even the desire of philosophy" (Montaigne).[112] "All the savages [of New France] live generally and everywhere in common . . . the life of the ancient golden age, which the holy apostles wished to bring back to us" (Marc Lescarbot).[113] Peter Martyr, Thevet, Léry, Montaigne, Charron, and many others insist on the nudity of the "savages," a nudity that is without immodesty. Furthermore, even where the climate does not permit this happy absence of clothing, people live according to the state of nature. They know not mine and thine. They do not covet riches. They are "in great familiarity and friendship" with each other. They know neither thefts or trials. If they practice war, they do so with courage, and if they are cannibals, it is with the full consent of prisoners carefully fattened for this final banquet. The "savages" have neither kings nor "absolute and sovereign" lords. All their laws are made such "that they do not contravene the law of nature." This natural law, moreover, seems to accord (at least outside of Canada and Iceland) with the "goodness" of the natives. In effect, their nudity is explained by a benevolent climate and their happy idleness by the abundance of all things. Ronsard, a great bard of the golden age ("And then there was not this word of Thine or Mine"[114]), merged most of these themes in his *Discours contre Fortune.* Here he addresses Villegaignon, sent to Brazil by Coligny, leader of the Huguenots, in 1555 with six hundred colonists, and reproaches him for trying to civilize a people who are

> *Innocently and completely untamed and nude,*
> *As naked in dress as they are stripped of malice,*
> *Who know neither the names of virtue nor vice,*
> *Of senate nor king . . .*
> *Who do not trouble the earth with sharp coulters,*
> *An earth which, like the air, is common to all . . .*
>
> *Live happy, you people without pain, without cares,*
> *Live joyously: I myself would wish to live so.*[115]

In the old world, everything has declined. The harsh weather and barely fertile soil correspond to the hardness of mankind. In addition, the striking contrast between "noble savages" and wicked Europeans allows the former to set an example for the latter. The "naked philosopher" of Cuba and the "barbarous theologian" of Nicaragua put to shame their invaders' cruelty and insatiable thirst for gold.[116] This lesson, however, is lost on sixteenth-century invaders. In the name of a false civilization, they blithely destroy the earthly paradises they had discovered.

The Protestant Bernard Palissy also argued that all things run backward in the old world. Frank Lestringant has recently drawn attention to this writer's *Recepte veritable, par laquelle tous les hommes de la France pourront apprendre à multiplier et à augmenter leurs thrésors* (1563).[117] This title inadequately describes the contents of a book that evokes the "Garden of Refuge" where one may "flee the iniquities and maliciousness of men, in order to serve God." To a limited extent, this book resumes the myth of the golden age. Palissy dreams of welcoming "Christians exiled in a time of persecution into a 'hilly' *locus amoenus*, filled with 'shady grottoes' protecting one from the fierce heat of the sun." In this circular garden, animals would wander at liberty while the sayings of divine wisdom would be expressed in the "letters" of leaves and the "scrolls" of branches.

WORLD UPSIDE DOWN, PERVERSE WORLD

Along with the regret for a lost golden age, the predilection for themes of folly and the "world turned upside down"—each being the offspring of the other—constitutes yet another indication of the pessimism of the Renaissance. Michel Foucault notes that "at the end of the Middle Ages, madness and the madman become major figures, in their ambiguity . . . In learned literature [as in popular customs], Madness or Folly is at work, at the very heart of reason and truth; . . . from the fifteenth century on, the face of madness has haunted the imagination of Western man."[118] Similarly, Jean-Claude Margolin has observed that: "The sixteenth century was, more than any other century (on account of its crisps of values and conscience) that of rites of inversion and the world turned upside down."[119] That which was impossible, or at least should have been, became real. This topos of *impossibilia* was not unknown to antiquity or the High Middle Ages.[120] The Renaissance, however, would see its proliferation. In fact, Folly could then be found everywhere: in princely courts (since the fourteenth century, apparently) where it mocks great lords; in card games, notably the tarot[121]; in carnival processions; in the Feasts of the Ass, of the Innocents, and of course that of Fools; in the paintings of Bosch, Brueghel, and their followers; in prints representing the "topsy-turvy" world and images of Aristotle (that is, "Reason") being ridden and whipped by Phyllis the prostitute; in critical essays of which the most famous are *The Ship of Fools* and *The Praise of Folly*, and so on. At the end of this series there are, among others, *Hospidale de' pazzi incurabili* (1589) by Tomaso Garzoni, Cervantes's *Don Quixote*, Quevedo's *La Hora de Todos* . . . (1628–39), and the *Criticon* of Baltazar Gracian (1651–57)—titles that are but signposts on the long conceptual road that travels through the upside-down worlds of Europe's nascent modernity.[122]

Nonetheless, and as it is often said, the Folly of the Renaissance is ambiguous. With its folkloric aspects and often distant origins, folly was a manifestation of health and not of melancholy. Carnivals, the Feast of Fools and that of the Ass, were moments of liberation. These crowded gatherings constituted a provisional vacation from normative reason and daily institutions. Their notably sexual and alimentary permissiveness, their momentary noisiness and violence, the license given to abusive speech, the inversion of hierarchies, the use of sacred rites for burlesque purposes, their masks and their travesties, all offered a "safety valve" for instincts that were repressed during the rest of the year.[123] The above points are perceptively discussed in a plea defending the Feast of Fools to the Paris Faculty of Theology in 1444. This remarkable text argues that:

> *Such a diversion is necessary, because folly, which is our second nature and seems inherent to man, can thus express itself at least once a year. Wine barrels will burst if one does not occasionally release the plug to give them some air. We men are but poorly jointed barrels that the wine of wisdom would cause to burst if this wine were to stay in a state of constant fermentation under the effect of piety and the fear of God. We must therefore give it air, so that it will not deteriorate. This is why we allow ourselves to be foolish for certain days, that we may then return with greater zeal to the service of God.*[124]

In a slightly different spirit, but using the same "safety valve" argument, the jurist Claude de Rubys writes at the end of the sixteenth century: "It is sometimes expedient to tolerate the people's making fools of themselves and rejoicing, given the fear that, by holding them too rigorously, one might drive them to despair."[125]

These "brief and joyous diversions" constituted a psychic and social "tonic." They also extended beyond fixed historical frames—here the Renaissance—and particular human groups—poor village or rich town.[126] At the same time, however great their presence has been throughout history, their expression from the fourteenth to the seventeenth centuries was conditioned by their rapport with Christian civilization. "The fool," writes Yves-Marie Bercé, "is like the mystic or the infant child. It is he whose empty head, innocent to the distractions of the world, can receive the breath of the Holy Spirit."[127] The choirboy temporarily wearing a miter and the crowned fool gave a lesson in humility to the powerful and the educated.[128] The Feasts of Fools, of the Innocents, and of the Ass were ecclesiastical at first, before they were driven out of the sanctuary. Likewise, carnival license erupted prior to the silence, the fasting, and gloominess of Lent. It was taken for granted that the carnival king would soon be vanquished by "Lady Sardine."[129]

With regard not only to youth abbeys and charivaris, but also to the noisy festivals that filled the calendar from December to Lent, recent studies have clarified how "license was not rebellious."[130] This formulation of Natalie Davis now receives general assent. Bercé notes that the "counterorder is still an order."[131] The *Lord of Misrule* is not a *Lord of Unruliness.* "Ridicule" is not necessarily "subversive" and caricature can be "instructive." The mocking routines of royal clowns did not question the institution of monarchy. Masking inversions comprised a "symmetrical image" of reality, and in addition these rites "remained well on the near side of theoretical inversion." As for youth tribunals and charivaris, they played "a safeguarding role for the future of the community by protecting its potential for fertility and renewal." Thus there is no need to separate folkloric festivals from rites of passage.[132] It is even possible to agree with Keith Thomas that they ultimately confirmed the structures, the established hierarchies, and the conception of time in preindustrial society. Burlesque activities were declared "legitimate" during a limited period and on precise occasions, and everyone agreed not to infringe certain boundaries of the calendar beyond which normal life was to resume.

This clarification of the "functional" character of carnival rites (in the widest sense) sensibly contradicts the thesis of Mikhail Bakhtin, who saw in them a revolt of popular culture against learned culture, a reversal of hierarchies, the temporary emergence of a truth rising up from below against official dogmas, a brief victory of the flesh over ascetism, and the rejection, one or more times a year, of routine, authority, and religious interdictions. The external liberty that characterized popular festivity was inseparable, Bakhtin thinks, from a momentarily recaptured internal liberty. A "positive" (that is, materialist) conception of the world triumphed, for the space of a few hours or days, over spiritualist constraint.[133]

This thesis is too systematic and thus hardly convincing. It is true, however, that festivals sometimes turned into revolts, that civil authorities feared anonymous violence more and more, and that they strove to enclose and harness folkloric rites in designating prosperous men of honorable reputation to be "abbots of fools."[134] It is especially true that churchmen (Catholics before 1520, Catholics and Protestants afterward) conveyed a growing antipathy toward all burlesque and even festive manifestations. In charivaris they saw an opposition to the remarriage of widows and widowers that was accepted by canon law. In carnival, the May Day festivities, and the bonfires of Saint John, they saw resurgences of paganism and occasions for scandal. In the Feasts of Fools, the Ass, and the Innocents, they saw an inadmissible confusion of the sacred and the profane that was sometimes repeated in the course of Fête Dieu processions.[135] In 1580 a Catholic priest of Bohemia, Vavrinec Rvacocsky, published a "Pleasant Meditation on Carnival's twelve sons, or the infernal patriarchs . . ." in which he shows how "the devils, during Carnival, pervert human nature as much as they can, so that, seizing hold of men, they take them off to hell."[136]

At the beginning of modern times, therefore, the church led an increasingly vigorous combat against collective public folly. This fight was only partly crowned by success. Still, as this was the era when the locking up of mad people began, the church's campaign reveals a peremptory diagnosis: folly equals sin. This equation was not accepted without reticence, even at the level of elite culture. In Erasmus's *Praise of Folly*, Folly plays many roles and presents many faces. Folly is the happy virtue of children and is synonymous with candor and humility.[137] These qualities pertain to both necessary terrestrial joys and to the Christian symbolism of the Feasts of Fools and the Innocents. Finally, Folly becomes a way of adhering to the Mystery of the Salvation, by abandoning "the wisdom of the wise and the prudence of the prudent." Citing the prophets, the Gospels, and Saint Paul, Erasmus concurs with the latter when he writes that "the word of the cross is folly for men who die."[138] A century later Don Quixote is not only presented as a kind of lunatic who is possessed by an *idée fixe*, but also as a sort of pure being who is generous and loyal, a man who has arrived too late in a world that has lost these qualities. Erasmus and Cervantes thus partially attempt, each in his own way, a true "Praise of Folly." Moreover, this praise could be transposed from the strictly religious plane to that of social and political protest. In seventeenth-century England, radical groups such as the Ranters and the first Quakers presented themselves as Christ's mad people and recalled how Jesus himself was somewhat eccentric. In 1640 Lilburne exclaimed that God "doth not choose many rich, nor many wise, . . . but the fools, idiots, base and contemptible poor men and women in the esteem of the world." Winstanley affirmed in 1649 that "the declaration of righteous law shall spring up from the poor, the base and despised ones and fools of the world."[139] In *The Praise of Folly*, however, another aspect of this discourse appears that is more in keeping with the common sentiment of contemporary elites: the assimilation of human faults to insane attitudes. Merchants, grammarians, theologians, preachers, courtiers, popes, cardinals, and bishops are the type of fools who do not know themselves and who do not realize that their absurd behavior leads them and humanity to unhappiness. More than half of Erasmus's book is devoted to these condemnations, which recall those of Sebastian Brant.

The Ship of Fools was published during carnival time (February 1494), and the author included a chapter condemning the same festival: "The idea that carnival is made for amusement is the invention of the devil or of folly itself . . . the cap with bells brings anguish and pain, but never rest."[140] Brant's work is perhaps the most striking illustration of an important cultural fact: the increasing use of themes of folly and the world upside down by intellectual circles, especially the church, for the purpose of instilling guilt. For them, folly and subversion were interchangeable. The reversed world is a perverse world.[141] Affirmations of this sort are legion in European writing between the end of the fifteenth and the middle of the seventeenth century. The great moralist Geiler de Kaiserberg preached at Strasbourg cathedral on the texts of *The Ship of Fools* and, following in Brant's footsteps, the humanist publisher Jodocus Badius published a *Stultiferae naves* ("Mad Ships") (1501), which continues the story of the fleet that Brant had abandoned after his first chapter. Badius thus launches six boats on the demented seas. The first is that of Eve, author of the Original Sin, while the other vessels represent the five senses and the follies to which they lead.[142] In a song of 1522, the Franciscan friar Thomas Murner, an enemy of Luther, declared that everything was ass-backward with

Christianity: "The legs are on top of the table, the cart before the ox." Churchmen lead the faithful astray, and civic authorities sleep.[143] At the dawn of the seventeenth century an Italian Dominican, Giacomo Affinati, published a work entitled *Il Mondo al rovescio e sosopra*.[144] The introduction of the French translation unambiguously claims: "the intention of the author is to show by vivid reasons that sin has introduced such confusion to the world that one may justly say that all things go backward there."[145] Having first evoked the golden age, Affinati observes that man has become an "ugly metamorphis of himself"[146] as a consequence of Original Sin. Disorder prevails all the way to the heavenly spheres, which, with God's permission, now let themselves run backward. Since Adam had acted "like a mad beast,"[147] all his descendants conduct themselves likewise. Affinati gives a decisive proof, drawn from his experience as a preacher: "We see every day . . . how the sense of hearing goes in such a contrary course to the straight path that people would rather run to hear a tumbler, a singer of sonnets, or a charlatan who sells paste for the hands, powder for the teeth and rat poison, than a skilled preacher."[148]

In turn, *La Hora de Todos* written by the diplomat Quevedo (who had studied theology), used fiction to demonstrate the reality and permanence of the inverted world. Men complain to Jupiter because Fortune allots blessings to the wicked and misery to the virtuous. Jupiter thus decrees an "hour" of truth during which situations will be reversed. At the end of this hour the rich, having become humble and without resources, repent whereas the formerly poor, who have now received wealth and honors, give themselves over to pride and vice. Hence, no matter what happens, the world remains upside down and contains a constant quantity of folly and sin.[149] The same bitter appraisal appears in the *Criticon* of the Jesuit preacher Baltazar Gracian.[150] This work describes the world as a deceptive facade where all is falsehood. Madrid is a city where "all runs backward": "Those who should be leaders because of their wisdom and knowledge are cast down, despised, forgotten, and humiliated. On the contrary, those who should be subjects because of their ignorance and incapacity, incompetent people who are without knowledge and experience, these are the men who govern."[151] Consequently, the author generalizes: "All goes backward . . . virtue is chased out, vice exalted, truth mute, three-tongued lies run rampant . . . books are without teachers and teachers without books . . . young people grow feeble and elderly folk rejuvenate . . . beasts play the man and men play the beast . . . young women cry and old men laugh; lions bleat and deer hunt; chickens cackle and roosters keep quiet . . ."[152]

Augustin Redondo connects the importance of the theme of the world upside down in Spanish literature of the late sixteenth and early seventeenth centuries to the "crisis" then afflicting the Iberian world.[153] This link cannot be doubted. His observation, however, needs to be enlarged: The considerable place given to folly in the discourse of literate European culture during some 150 years involves the crisis of an entire civilization,[154] an atmosphere of anxiety, and a pervasive feeling of guilt. John Donne cries out:

> *O age of rusty iron! Some better wit*
> *Call it some worse name, if aught equal it;*
> *The Iron Age that was, when justice was sold, now*
> *Injustice is sold dearer far.*[155]

The images of an inverted world clarify the texts. Assuredly, both verbal and visual productions maintain a sense of humor that derives from popular festivities and carnivalesque rites. The folly of the Renaissance caused laughter, hence artists and writers were encouraged to collect unusual details. The more strange touches they added, the greater would be their success. This was a constant feature of the genre, and it added more weight to the ultimate lesson[156] for, during the period covered by this study, the iconography of folly was never a gratuitous frivolity. It always both teaches and condemns. Doubts persist regarding *The Extraction of the Stone of Folly* (The Prado), which may not be an original Bosch, as well as his *Ship of Fools* (The Louvre) which some have called *Concert in a Boat.*[157] In any case, the two themes refer to popular comic motifs of the Low Countries. In this region, fools were portrayed with a stone in their head that needed removal, and it is likely that during festivals charlatans and quack doctors simulated the operation. On the other hand, the name the *Blauwe Schuit* (the blue ship) was used to designate those societies of "fools" that were prevalent in all European countries since the early fifteenth century.[158] Each painting, however, utilizes comedy for moralizing ends. The height of folly is that it congratulates itself; and yet this world turned upside down is a daily reality. As for the *Ship of Fools*, even if it should be called *Concert in a Boat*, it is clearly inspired by Brant's book, with all the pejorative connotations classically assigned to music by rigid contemporary moralists. The ship of sin and its apathetic passengers are headed for perdition. Moreover, these works become clear only when placed in a series, with the painter's *The Garden of Earthly Delights*, *The Haywain*, and *The Seven Deadly Sins*: All these compositions insist on the folly of sin and invite the viewer to ponder his ultimate end.[159]

As with Bosch's paintings, many of Brueghel the Elder's painted and engraved works were inspired by "carnivalesque" themes or popular rituals. Like other Flemish and Dutch artists, Brueghel also portrayed the operation on stones in the head. *Dulle Griet* (Mad Meg) evokes satires on the shrewish woman of fabliaux and farces. Engravings (known from seventeenth-century adaptations) alluding to the *Pilgrimage of Molenbeek* depict a local custom: Once a year, friends and family would force epileptics, hysterical women, and mad people to cross the bridge of Molenbeek, in the suburbs of Bruxelles.[160] *Temperantia* and other prints show a scene from popular theater: the fool with his baton who makes an unexpected or preposterous onstage reply to the other actors.[161] Finally, the engraving entitled *The Feast of Fools* evokes both the festivals of this name and the habitual excesses of carnival.

These depictions, however, have a predominantly bitter tone, especially in the case of *Dulle griet* (Mayer Van den Bergh Museum, Antwerp). With evident antifeminism, this remarkably painted nightmare prophecies what the world would become were it exposed to the violence of liberated and dominating viragos. Sword in hand, Meg the Shrew and her followers attack the men whom they have obeyed for too long.[162] At the bottom of the fire, the demented throng moves toward Hell. In *The Feast of Fools*, the balloons that carry haggard and staggering characters symbolize just so many deranged minds. The engraving of *Temperantia*, which includes in the upper left-hand corner a fool and two actors, teaches a lesson of moderation to all those who give themselves over to lechery, greed, and wastefulness, or who, on the contrary, sink into avarice ("*vivendum et nec volupatati dediti, prodigi et luxuriosi appareamus, nec avara tenacite sordidi aut obscuri existamus*").[163]

Still more revealing is the print devoted to *Elck* (Everyone) at the top of which a fool looks at himself in a mirror.[164] Playing on the double negative "Nemo non" and reusing the European theme of everyone equals nobody, Brueghel makes a simultaneously individual and collective accusation: We are all united in the anonymity of sin but no one is aware of his or her responsibility. *Elck* is the alchemist trying to fabricate gold, the merchant amid bundles of merchandise, the conquering soldier, the person who fights his neighor for a piece of cloth. The caption reads: "Everyone (*Nemo non*) only seeks his own interest. Everyone in all enterprises only seeks himself. Everyone on every occasion aspires to wealth. Everyone tugs for the longest end. All people have only one desire: to own."[165] More generally, the folly of sin creates chaos. This is also the lesson of *The Tower of Babel*, a theme of which Brueghel and others of his time were fond. Thus, despite enigmatic and controversial details, Bosch and Brueghel offer the same moral: Folly—that is, the daily behavior of men—deserves blame. Bosch, a comic and powerful preacher, calls folly the attachment to worldly goods. Brueghel, perhaps more humanistic and indulgent, would wish man to be reasonable since he is endowed with reason; but reason is a privilege that man rarely uses.[166]

The prints of the end of the sixteenth and early seventeenth centuries that represent the "world upside down" are also undoubtedly more moralistic than they might appear at first sight.[167] Assuredly, they accumulate amusing *impossibilia* for the sake of pleasure: boats atop mountains, men hunting game at sea, children beating their parents, women carrying swords and men holding distaffs, horses or asses riding peasants, paupers giving alms to the rich, the "rustic" mounted on a steed while the king, still wearing his crown, goes on foot. These inversions have an absurd logic. They provoke laughter because of their absurdity, and by ricochet they reestablish things in their proper place. An "emblem" published in 1616 reveals the pedagogical intentions that guided the production of these humourous images:

> *The world is upside down, I do not understand;*
> *The devil is in command, and the Lord beseeches him;*
> *The rich man cries, the poor man laughs;*
> *The mountain lies low, the valley in the clouds.*
> *The hare hunts the hound*
> *And the mouse chases the cat . . .*[168]

Finally, several prints (less popular perhaps) use the theme of the "overturned world" as an element in preaching. An example from 1576 has for its title "The Hypocrite and Tyrant keep the world upside down; Faith and Charity sleep. A witness to the time and all of us." In fact, one sees the terrestrial globe held down by an old woman, rosary in hand (Hypocrisy), and by a soldier carrying a heavy sword. Another print of 1635 shows the topsy-turvy world flanked by Democritus (who laughs) and Heraclitus (who cries). Inside the globe and upside down men fight each other, boats run aground, and so on. The text proclaims:

> *Behold this topsy-turvy world*
> *Too much given over to worldly things,*
> *Willing to die for a trifle,*
> *Beneath the shadow of blind pleasure.*
> *And Satan, who always waits and watches,*
> *Promises them marvelous treasures,*
> *Knowing that under such pleasure*
> *Lurks a deadly remorse.*[169]

And thus the reader remains very much within the framework of a guilt-instilling discourse.

The polemical use of themes linked to folly and the world upside down supplies further examples. The adversary is a dangerous fool who is responsible for the chaos into which society is plunging. During this period, when most heated debates took place in the field of religion, Catholics and Protestant accused each other of insanity. In 1522 Thomas Murner entitled his aggressive anti-Reformation pamphlet *The Great Lutheran Lunatic*. It is not Luther himself who is so named, but "the polyvalent incarnation of his imbecile sectarians, both lewd and greedy."[170] The book's argument is as follows. A Franciscan monk meets a gigantic fool, drawn on a sledge by eleven horses and other fools. This carnivalesque image here symbolizes the enormity of a fault.[171] Murner tries to exorcise the Great Fool whom he characterizes as a possessed man. This man resists, but admits that more fools reside in him than there were Greeks hidden inside the Trojan horse. In his head are erudite fools and preachers who encourage sedition, in his pocket those who "wash their hands in money and the goods of others" (an allusion to the secularization of church property), and so on. A purge administered to the Great Fool has no more effect than exorcism and the giant dies unrepentant. A grotesque burial follows, with family quarrels regarding the inheritance. Murner sensed the coming of the Peasants' Revolt (1524–25) and wished to make his contemporaries aware of the social dangers—and disorders—that the Reformation could engender. Furthermore, he considered that the Reformation's dismantling of the Sacraments constituted a serious menace. If marriage was no longer a sacrament, all repudiations became permissible. If a dying man could no longer count on extreme unction and the intercession of saints, he would die in anguish, defeated, alone, under the judgment of a terrifying God. Denouncing other grave dangers with an often scurrilous verve, Murner resolutely presented himself as a fool in the eyes of his contemporaries, thus creating a reversal of the classic roles of the time: The mad believe the wise man to be demented when he tries to protect them from the storm.

On the Protestant side, the theme of the world upside down was exploited for equally accusatory ends. Pierre Viret, in a book that carries the meaningful title *Le monde à l'empire* . . . , declares that "those who teach and lead others go the wrong way, all backward and inside out." He also states that "*empereurs*" have become "*empireurs*" (literally, "worseners").[172] Agrippa d'Aubigné employed the formula "*monde à l'envers, monde pervers*" to an even greater extent. Not surprisingly, he aims his criticisms at Catholics and sovereigns who persecute the Huguenots: "As in the world upside down / The perverse child whips his aged father" (*Tragigues* I. v. 235–236).[173] Likewise, kings, who should be fathers of their people, have become "bloodthirsty wolves" (I. v. 197–198). "The wise judge is dragged off to torture" (I. v. 233–235), "the places of rest are foreign places / The towns of the center are border towns" (I. v. 225–226). The entire century is nothing more "than a tragic history, / All their actions are farces and games [to the tyrants]" (II. v. 206–207). The sacred scepter is "in the fist of a powerless woman" (Catherine de Medici) (I. v. 734), and the Antichrist Pope has become "God on earth": He "dispenses law against the law," he "authorizes vice," he puts "Hell into Heaven and Heaven into Hell" (I. v. 1235–1244).

Another inverted world is that of the League, as stigmatized by the moderate Catholic authors of the *Satyre Menippée*. There one can see:

> *. . . the small made great; the poor, rich; the humble, proud and insolent. Indeed, those who once obeyed are now in command; those who borrowed, lend as usurers; those who judged are judged; those who imprisoned are put into prison; those who were standing are now seated. O marvelous fate! O great mysteries! O secrets of God, unknown to wretched mortals! Shop awnings are turned into halberds, inkstands into muskets; breviaries turn to shields, shoulder-cloaks to corslets, and monks's cowls to helmets and visors.*[174]

The polemical exploitation of the theme of folly—a well-known synonym of perversion in the domain of religious conflict—thus exemplifies the annexation of this theme by the ruling culture. As a footnote, it is worth emphasizing the fact that seventeenth-century English revolutionaries who presented themselves as "fools," in order to convince the world of its current lunacy and thus set it aright, unconsciously followed the example set by the religious elites. These were the groups who inflicted guilt on their contemporaries through the conjoined themes of folly and the world turned upside down.[175] In any case, this usage is far removed, not only from "the safety valve" or popular mayhem of carnival festivities, but also from the "functional" character of the comic celebrations that allowed youth to express itself, rites of passage to be accomplished, and time to flow according to a coherent rhythm. Folly, with its multiple negative connotations, became the favorite subject of a predominantly conservative and moralistic discourse.[176] The world upside down came to signify the destruction of cosmic, religious, or social equilibrium. Thomas Cromwell's publicist, Richard Morrison, edited a *Remedy for Sedition* after the 1536 uprising of the Pilgrimage of Grace where he declares, in a most revealing fashion: "Now, were it not by your faithe, a madde herynge, if the fool shuld say, I will wear a cappe with an ouche, as the heade dothe? If the knees shulde say, we will carie the eyes, eche of them an ear: if the heles wold now go before, and the toes behind?"[177]

In another key, Shakespeare's *Taming of the Shrew* shows the domestic disorder created by a disobedient wife who requires rough training so that the normal order of things and hierarchy of beings can be reestablished. This is one of the ways in which farce and the charivari could be transformed into a discourse on guilt. Even in festivals, folly and the upside-down world could be used as a means of righting disorderly situations (for example, as a critique of a stupid husband who is too submissive to his breeches-wearing wife). Humanist and clerical culture had, however, moved past this level of the banal regulation of domestic conduct. It had already extrapolated and dramatized the disorder of folly and inversion, wherein it perceived sin.

High culture tended to see folly at work everywhere in a diseased society. In this regard, two works by of the Italian canon Tomaso Garzoni are very informative. The *Teatro de' varii e diversi cervelli mondani* (1583) and the *Hospidale de' pazzi incurabili* (1589) claim to classify every type of folly in order of increasing evil.[178] The second of these books met with considerable success, having gone through eleven editions in thirty years. It inspired Lope de Vega's *Los Locos de Valencia* and was quickly translated into English (1600), German (1618), and French (1620), with the title *L'Hospital des fols incurables* . . .[179] This work reflects the need of an era not only to measure the gravity of its own folly but also to make an inventory of all its aspects. Certainly Garzoni's chaotic enumeration is tinged with humor, especially when he describes the rooms of the hospital where reside both the "amusing and clownish fools"[180] and the "merry, facetious, and amiable fools."[181] On the whole, however, the incurables of the hospice can be divided into two basic categories: those who are fools as a consequence of illness (these "idiot and vulgar fools"[182] will be forever incapable of learning the alphabet), and those who have become fools by their attachment to a passion (such as that for "the glory of the world").[183] The worst of these guilty fools ("the most accursed type of fool to be found in the world") is described by the author as being "reckless and desperate." This type is violent and rebellious. They are "an infinity of God's enemies that have been seen committing in our time every sort of rapine, violence, sacrilege, homicide, and rebellion that can be imagined . . . they are worthy of a thousand gallows."[184] Garzoni thus installs jesters, lunatics, and vicious fools all within the same building. To some extent, they are all dangerous, wherein this imaginary confinement recalls other confinements of the period. The book's preface expresses the dangers of foolishness in hyperbolic terms. Folly is:

> *. . . more deformed than Cadmus's serpent, more ugly than the chimera, more venomous than the dragon of the Hesperides, more harmful than the Monster of Corebe, more felonous than Theseus' Minotaur, more hideous to behold than three-headed Geryon. Being sent to the world only to vomit Hydra-like the flames of its venom, it must be described as being so terrible that its gaze alone makes everyone tremble with fear.*[185]

Farther on, Garzoni involuntarily sees Folly as an equivalent of the Death in the *danses macabres.* Like Death, it "cares not for kings or emperors, neither for men of war nor men of letters. In short, there is no respect that holds it back or that prevents it from striking the entire human race with sword and dagger."[186]

PROLIFERATION OF THE MONSTROUS

If so many fools inhabit the earth that the confusion reigning here rivals that of Hell (the chaotic place *par excellence*), then it is no wonder that the natural order of the universe itself would have seemed to have lost its "common sense". The sin of mankind extends to Nature, which seems touched with a "strange madness." This aberration affects "a thousand self-contradictory or imbalanced events" that God permits to happen for the instruction of mankind. What was originally diversity now perverts itself into absurd "mixtures": Here appears the "indecent" sow of a pig with the face of a man, there a fish with the head of a lion who cries like a human. These monstrosities are illustrations of sin. Such is the reasoning of the Dominican Giacomo Affinati, and, in this respect, his opinion speaks vividly for a belief widely held by his contemporaries.[187]

The abundant literature on monsters and prodigies of the late fifteenth to early seventeenth centuries must therefore be placed within the context of a generally pessimistic outlook on a time of extreme evil.[188] San Antonino di Firenze seems to have been the first to introduce a special treatment of monsters and monstrous breeds, in his *Chronicon*, printed in Venice in 1474 to 1479. His example was then profusely followed, notably by Filippo di Bergamo in his *Supplementum Cronicarum* (1st ed., 1483), and by Hartmann Schedel in his famous *Nüremberg Chronicle* (1493). Authors rummaged through the past to rediscover forgotten prodigies and soon composed works devoted especially to these aberrant cases. Such was a book by Joseph Grünpeck, the historiographer and astrologer of Maximilian I: *Prodigorum, ostentorum et monstrorum quae in saeculum Maximilianeum inciderunt, interpretatio* (1502). Twenty-one years later, Luther and Melanchthon published a book whose title was accurately rendered as "of two woonderful popish monsters, to wyt, of a popish asse . . . and of a monkish calfe." This tract had great success and was translated into English (1579) and French, the latter text being approved by Calvin himself.

Toward the middle of the sixteenth century, interest in prodigies and monsters greatly increased. In 1552 Conrad Wollfahrt (nicknamed Lycosthenes) published an edition of the *Prodigiorum Liber* of Julius Obsequens that, for the first time, did not drown this catalogue of extraordinary ancient Roman phenomena amid other, only slightly related classical works, such as Pliny the Younger's *Letters* or the *De viris illustribus*. At the same time, however, it was placed in a collective volume with two other texts: Polydore Vergil's *De prodigiis* and the *De Ostentis* of Joachim Camerarius I, which had already appeared in 1531 and 1532 and had not yet received much public attention. Through their association in Wollfahrt's edition, all three texts soon became well known. In a short four years (1552–55), Julius Obsequens and Polydore Vergil were edited or translated four times and Camerarius three times. Riding this wave, Lycosthenes brought out his *Prodigiorum ac ostentorum chronicon* (the fruit of twenty years' work), which he dedicated to the magistrates of Basel. Claiming to be informed by the best sources, he records, in minute detail, the "prodigies and ostentations that have appeared outside of the order, movement, and workings of nature, in both the upper and the lower regions of the world, from the beginning of time to our own day." At least four elements stand out in this vast anthology of disorder. (1) The confusion is so widespread that an entire gamut of synonyms is needed to designate the *portenta, prodigia, ostenta, miracula, signa,* and *monstra* it describes. The humanist penchant for repetition again indulges itself in the apparent prolixity of the phenonemon. (2) The first "prodigy" of history is —alas!—that of the cunning serpent who seduced Eve. (3) Eclipses, qualified as *defectiones solis,* are preeminently cosmic scandals that appear under exceptional circumstances (such as the crucifixion of Jesus). (4) "The world is full of rubbish," which is why strange phenomena should be interpreted as signs of God's power and anger toward sinful men.[189]

In 1560 Boaistuau published his *Histoires prodigieuses,* a book that, in effect, spawned an entire genre. The *Histoires* quickly gained exceptional success, at once attested by the considerable number of its reprintings and the numerous additions that increased the length of this text throughout the rest of the sixteenth century.[190] The *Histoires* were translated into Dutch and English while, in France, they were copied, adapted, and abundantly cited. Ambroise Paré, for one, drew on this book for a good number of his tales. Boiastuau's work was followed in 1567 by the *Tractatus de monstris* of the theologian and preacher Arnauld Sorbin (translated into French by Belleforest)[191] and by Paré's *Des Monstres et des prodiges* (1573). Furthermore, the same subjects were treated in two books that appeared in 1575, one by Loys Le Roy, *De la Vicissitude ou varieté des choses en l'univers,* the other by Frison Cornelius Gemma, *De Naturae divinis characterismis.* The latter work contains a complete list (with interpretations) of all the prodigies that had taken place in Belgium and its environs between 1555 and 1574. It must be pointed out, however, that at the end of the sixteenth and beginning of the seventeenth century there arose a critical attitude, heralded by Montaigne, which contended that monstrosity had a legitimate place in natural science. Monsters also cease to be considered "prodigies" in four notable works by Weinrich (1595), Riolan (1605), Liceti (1616), and Aldrovandi (not published until 1642).[192] In Germany, however, the tradition of the *Histoires prodigieuses* continued. In France, the fashion was maintained by "canards," which were published in increasing numbers during this period. Fify-seven of these publications appeared between 1529 and 1575, 110 between 1575 and 1600, and 323 between 1600 and 1631.[193] It can reasonably be assumed that the number of "prodigious stories" diffused by these texts was increasing at the same rate. Thus the people of the Renaissance took delight in descriptions of monstrous beings, in tales and catalogues of stupefying facts. They also felt that these extraordinary phenomena had increased only recently, just as had the number of witches and blasphemies. The link between the two seemed to be more than just fortuitous. Was not witchcraft the most evident proof that the world had been turned upside down?

Abundant testimony exists to the effect that contemporaries were convinced history had never produced so many monsters and prodigies. In 1508 Joseph Grünpeck affirmed:

> *We read that in the time of our ancestors, many prodigies appeared in the heavens and on earth, and frequently monstrous creatures . . . but could the times when these happenings took place compare to our time, in the frequency of events of this*

> *nature and in the amazement they cause? . . . It is a fact that nobody can dispute. It would be difficult to find and age when so many stupefying prodigies occupied mortals as much as they do today.*[194]

In an Advent sermon delivered at Wartburg, Luther uses many of these same images:

> *In the space of ten or twelve years, we have seen and heard such winds and such howlings—not to mention those things which then follow—that I can hardly believe that any earlier epoch heard such great and numerous winds and howlings . . . For our time sees the sun and moon lose their light at the same time, the stars fall, people become anxious and desperate, the great winds and waters roar . . . all these crowd together at once. Thus we also see comets, and recently many crosses have fallen from the sky and, amid it all, a new and unheard-of sickness has arrived, the French disease.*[195]

In short, the Reformer interpreted these events as just so many announcements of the imminent end of the world. Ten years later, Camerarius was just as confident that his readers would agree with him when he mentioned, pell-mell and in an assured tone, the "hideous monsters," "terrifying events of unknown cause," eclipses, comets, and other "unusual spectacles—flaming swords, crosses, lances," that anyone could notice in the skies.[196] For Melanchthon's son-in-law, Peucer, who published the *Commentarius de praecipuis divinationum generibus* (1553), no doubt was possible. In these times, eclipses are seen "more often and more hideous than in ancient times."[197] In 1557 the doctor Jean Fincelius dedicates a "complete list of the innumerable, miraculous, and terrifying signs" recorded in Germany since 1517 (the year of Luther's entrance on the scene) to the Duchess Marie of Pomerania. He there declares: "In reviewing the history of nations, one will never find so many miraculous signs as in our era. Hardly has one appeared but another one follows, which indeed proves that God has some great plan, and that we are destined to see great suffering in the Christian Church."[198]

Contemporary Germany was, without a doubt, the most fertile terrain for the proliferation of such horror stories. Lutheran preachers strongly upheld the authenticity of the most unlikely facts in order to lead people to repentance and into the fold of the evangelical church. A commentator on Revelations spoke, in 1589, "of the torrent of prodigies that have been spreading in Germany for fifty to sixty years in the dazzling light of the new Evangelist."[199] The Frenchman Belleforest also expressed the common sentiment: "the present time is more monstrous than it is natural."[200]

Such a view, moreover, gained support from the many "terrifying but true" births that filled the many chronicles and newssheets of the sixteenth century, thus inspiring contemporaries to believe that the world was indeed going backward. Were there not "babies born with two, three, or more heads; women giving birth to piglets or even donkeys; children born with a golden tooth, or even wide breeches, their necks surrounded by strawberries; some speaking or prophesying as soon as they are born"[201]? In 1563 a preacher of Hamburg commissioned the engraving of "the authentic image" of a calf born with two heads, two tails, and six feet."[202] In 1575 a pamphlet from Arnhem divulged the strange birth of a monstrous child "covered with shaggy hair," who started to walk immediately after birth and hid under its mother's bed. It had two horns on its head, the feet of a peacock, and the talons of a bird. In 1565 a Tübingen gazette related a stupefying birth that had occurred in a neighboring village, that of a child born without head or bones, with one ear on the left shoulder and its mouth on the right one. It was identified without hesitation as a creature of Satan and given over to the executioner, who chopped it up and threw the pieces into the fire. An abnormal quantity of wood and gunpowder, however, was needed in order to obtain full combustion. Happier than this monster's mother was a woman of Cleves who gave simultaneous birth to sixty-five children. In 1610 a famous German physician, one Dr. Schenk, brought out a memoir in which he recounted the birth of "ninety-six creatures, monstrous and bereft of reason."[203] Twenty-five years earlier the preacher Christoph Irenaeus had edited a volume of some seven hundred pages on "the existence, cause, and meaning of monstrous children": God himself created these babies to chastise the deviations of men.[204]

The relationship between monsters and prodigies on the one hand and sin on the other formed a commonplace in contemporary chronicles. Like San Antonino, many of their authors made reference to the Flood or to the Tower of Babel. In fact, the presumptuous building of the latter was punished not only by the confusion of languages but also by that of species—whence the appearance of strange and deformed beings.[205] Using medical comparisons, Cornelius Gemma established a general link between moral and natural disorder: Just as vicious maternal blood alters the paternal semen, so the evil committed on earth leaves its mark on the spirit of the world, which, in turn, transmits it to the elements and then to human bodies.[206]

It is therefore not surprising that the people of the sixteenth century associated heresy with monstrosity. Luther and his friends described calf-monks, pigs with priests' faces, and grasshoppers wearing priests' hoods. If the Tiber had thrown up a gruesome animal with "the head of an ass, the torso of a woman, the foot of an elephant for its right hand, fish scales on its legs, and a dragon's head at its backside," according to Luther it was because God wished to show his great anger toward the papacy.[207] On the Catholic side, much the same affirmations were made. A doctor, whose poem appears among the marginal pieces in Sorbin's *Tractatus de monstris*, asserts: "Before the time of heresies we did not see monsters disfiguring Gaul." Elsewhere, Sorbin goes even one better: When France was pious, he writes, the country "did not know what monsters were, whereas now it seems that it has taken on the look of an African wilderness, each day producing some new aberration."[208] Saxony, too, "ever since it was opposed to Christ by Luther's perfidious fraud, trembles beneath the proliferation of countless monsters."[209]

Like prodigies, these apparitions are both punishments and warnings of greater castigations to come. For the chronicler Nauclerus, writing at the end of the fifteenth century, comets, blades of fire, dragons in the sky, and children with multiple heads "show that God's wrath threatens mankind."[210] Luther was convinced that the calf-monk of Freiberg "presages for Germany an immense military catastrophe or even the Final Day."[211] Ronsard similarly avers that great calamities are imminent:

Since one sees so many lightning bolts
In calm weather, since one sees so many comets,
So many horrible planets
Threatening us: since amid the air
One sees so many flames flying so thickly . . .[212]

And elsewhere he returns to the same theme: When one sees:

. . . *So many new sects*
. . . *So many deformed monsters,*

Their feet on top, their heads below,
Stillborn children, dogs, calves, sheep, and cats
With double bodies, three eyes and five ears

How can one not perceive these "strange marvels" to be the harbingers of famine and war, "the certain messengers of change"?[213]

The question that inevitably comes to mind is how could the intellectuals of the Renaissance have reconciled this fear of the future with their oft-affirmed conviction that their era had seen the resurrection and growth of letters and the arts?[214] The answer is that what would seem contradictory today was not so at that time, as is shown in this significant passage from Guillaume Budé's *De Transitu*:

> *O miserable and catastrophic fate of our time, which has prestigiously restored the glory of letters, but which, by the crime of some and the misdeeds of many, is cursed with a sinister and inexpiable impiety! . . . Everything . . . has been mixed and tangled up, the highest with the lowest, Hell with Heaven, the best with the worst* [once again, the classic theme of the world turned upside down] . . . *as much as the study and the renown of letters have reached their apogee in this our time, so much also has the ship of our Lord found itself in the thickest of shadows and the dankest of nights. Worse still, this transport ship is now cracked by outrages and could . . . end up sinking, exposed as it is to the eyes of all and jeered at by hatred.*[215]

Luther, whom Budé had fought against, nevertheless expressed an opinion quite similar to that of the French humanist and even added a supplementary argument: Since humanity has arrived at "a summit,"[216] the Day of Judgment is near. This "summit" can be seen in many ways: Never had people built or planted so much, never had luxury been so great. "Never have men heard of such commercial activity as today's, which embraces the entire world." The arts are at a point unequaled since the birth of Christ. Knowledge grows by such giant steps that "today a youth of twenty knows more than twenty doctors knew previously."[217] Thus a sort of terminus has been reached. Moreover, and on the negative side of the analysis, "It is not only in temporal things that we have arrived at a summit," since "never have greater errors, greater sins, and greater lies reigned over this world."[218] The cup is full. In Loys Le Roy's book, *De la Vicissitude ou varieté des choses en l'univers*, the same two opposing feelings are to be found: pride in being born in a time of renewal and the conviction that menacing tomorrows are on their way. In fact, the author boasts of "this age in which we see nearly all the former liberal and mechanical arts restored with their languages, after having been lost for almost twelve hundred years, while other new ones have been invented."[219] Le Roy rejoices that the West has, "after twelve hundred years, recovered the excellence of good letters, and revived the study of the disciplines."[220] Only a few pages after this enthusiastic declaration, however, Le Roy expresses a more somber, indeed apocalyptic view:

> *I foresee internecine and foreign wars arising on all sides: factions and heresies that will profane all things divine and human, famines and plagues threatening mortals: the order of nature, the governing of celestial movements, and the concord of the elements falling apart, floods occurring on one side, excessive heat on the other, and most violent earthquakes.*[221]

Thus Le Roy, and many others, agreed that the Renaissance would not outlast its springtime.

On the subject of monsters and prodigies, the reasoning of the people (and notably of the elite) of the time was almost definitely as follows. Never had there been seen so many "strange things" and "miracles of nature." Such facts are the warning signals of God's anger, "to awaken our senses, slumbering in the delicious honey of worldliness."[222] People, however, do not care. Thus the worst is to be feared: Prodigies and monstrous happenings presage "our disaster."[223] A dark future was explained by an excess of earthly wickedness. At the same time, had not mankind always been wicked?

WICKEDNESS

In Marlowe's *Doctor Faustus*, Mephistopheles affirms: "Hell hath no limits, nor is circumscribed, / In one self place: but where we are is Hell, / And where Hell is there must we ever be" (II. 1. 513–515).[224] The word "humanist," to which we have habitually given an optimistic shading, often hides many things about the Renaissance, a period more sensitive to the sadness of life and more generally severe about humanity than is often thought. To Pico della Mirandola's *De Dignitate Hominis* it would be easy to oppose multiple proverbs then in use that bespeak a bitter and doubtless widely accepted philosophy: "The true name of man is Thief." "A good man is rare in this world." "Man is an enemy to other men and to himself." "All men are liars." "A man of good faith is considered to be most foolish." "The man who knows how to deceive is worth much." "Under the skin of a man lurk many beasts." "Man is a Hell that can no longer hold itself in." What was the profound reason for perversity? As expressed in the discourse of the "reversed" world, it was because: "Man is an upside-down man" (that is, on account of his Original Sin).[225] In *La Celestina* (1499), which has been called a vast *exemplum*, the complaint of Pleberio after his daughter's suicide contains an anathema against the world and the constant omnipresence of sin as part of the play's general conclusion:

> *In my more tender years I thought that both thou [the world] and thy actions were governed by order, and ruled by reason: but now I see thou art pro and con; there is no certainty in thy calms. Thou seemest now unto me to be a labyrinth of errors, a fearful wilderness; an habitation of wild beasts; a dance full of changes; a fen full of mire and dirt; a country full of thorns; a steep and craggy mountain; a field full of stones; a meadow full of snakes and serpents; a pleasant garden to look to, but without any fruit; a fountain of cares, a river of tears, a sea of miseries; trouble without profit; a sweet poison, a vain hope, a false joy, and a true sorrow. O thou false world! . . . thou promisest mountains, but performest mole-hills . . . Thou dost put out our eyes, and then to make us amends thou anointest the place with oil; thou breakest our head and givest us a plaster; after thou has done use a great deal of harm, thou givest us a poor cold comfort.*[226]

The love of Callisto and Meliboea was clearly impossible in this corrupt universe (our own) on which Machiavelli, bereft of any Christian spirit, passes his famous judgment in chapter 17 of *The Prince*:

> *For it is a good general rule about men, that they are ungrateful, fickle, liars and deceivers, fearful of danger and greedy for gain. While you serve their welfare, they are all yours, offering their blood, their belongings, their lives, and their children's lives, as we noted above—so long as the danger is remote. But when the danger is close at hand, they turn against you . . . People are less concerned with offending*

a man who makes himself loved than one who makes himself feared . . . men are quicker to forget the death of a father than the loss of a patrimony.[227]

These sour statements echo canto eight of Machiavelli's unfinished poem, *The Golden Ass*. An aged man turns into a pig and brags of his new state, underlining by contrast all the mishaps, weaknesses, and vices of his former condition. This laicized invitation to the *contemptus mundi* is clearly an offshoot of all the literature previously devoted to the theme:

Only man is born stripped of any kind of defense: he has neither leather-hide, nor quills, nor feathers, wool, silk, nor shell that would serve to shield him.

In crying he enters life, and so feeble and so plaintive are his first sounds that it causes nothing but pity to behold. If one examines the length of his life, it is certainly quite brief, compared to that enjoyed by a deer, a crow, or even a goose . . . You have at once ambition, luxury, tears, and avarice, the true itch of this existence that causes you so much distress. There is no animal whose life is so fragile, who is so possessed of such a great desire to live, who is subject to more fears and more rage.

A pig does not torment another pig, a deer leaves other deer in peace: there are only men who massacre men, who crucify and strip him bare.

Now consider if you could wish that I become human once more . . .[228]

Machiavelli embroiders upon a pessimistic meditation that had already appeared, though in a fragmentary and attenuated state, in earlier humanist writings. In his *De Ortu . . .* , Aeneas Silvius Piccolomini writes: "In truth, though man procures many blessings for his fellow men, all the same there is no scourge [*pestis*] that man does not inflict on his same fellow men."[229] More categorically, Leon Battista Alberti is convinced that "the nature of man is 'perverse, wicked, egotistical.' " Paradoxically, "wild beasts born to be ferocious and free from restraint do not harm each other except in crisis of fury. But we men, who are born to be sweet, kind, and sociable, we always seek to be rebellious, troublesome, and hurtful to others."[230] Such judgments lead to the perception that for the first time in history (that is, in fifteenth-century Italy) a purely lay theory of both the state and political practice was founded on the premise of human wickedness.[231] The lucid establishment of this relationship must have evolved chronologically until the period of Machiavelli. Yet it is quite certain that, during the time of the Florentine secretary and largely thanks to him, this political formulation stood out in full relief.[232]

Pietro Pomponazzi affirms the following in his *De Immortalitate Animi* (1516): "The majority of men, when they do something good, do it more out of fear of eternal punishment than in hopes of eternal happiness . . ." If they were drawn toward virtue by its very nobility, "even supposing the soul to be mortal, they would conduct themselves honestly. But this is hardly ever the case." Besides, ". . . human nature is almost totally immersed in matter, . . . man is as removed from intelligence as a sick person from a healthy person, a child from an adult, a fool from a wise man."[233] Working from the same diagnosis, Ludovico Guicciardini draws practical conclusions for use by governors: "If men were good or wise, those who command them could legitimately use kindness rather than severity. Insofar as the majority, however, is neither sufficiently good nor sufficiently wise, it is better to base one's rule on severity. He who sees things differently only deceives himself."[234]

It was Machiavelli who most clearly expressed the expediency of basing political action on the evidence of human wickedness and cowardice, affirming that bad faith would be more useful to the head of state than loyalty. The text is well known and must be included in any survey of Renaissance pessimism:

> *How praiseworthy it is for a prince to keep his word and live with integrity rather than by craftiness, everyone understands; yet we see from recent experience that those princes have accomplished most who paid little heed to keeping their promises, but who knew how craftily to manipulate the minds of men. In the end, they won out over those who tried to act honestly . . . Since a prince must know how to use the character of beasts, he should pick for imitation the fox and the lion. As the lion cannot protect himself from traps, and the fox cannot defend itself from wolves, you have to be a fox in order to be wary of traps, and a lion to overawe the wolves . . . Thus a prudent prince cannot and should not keep his word when to do so would go against his interest, or when the reasons that made him pledge it no longer apply. Doubtless if all men were good, this rule would be bad; but since they are a sad lot, and keep no faith with you, you in your turn are under no obligation to keep it with them . . . the man [has] succeeded best who knew best how to play the fox.*[235]

This political lesson assumes its full importance when one considers how much Machiavelli was read in the courts of Europe. The Protestant Innocent Gentillet, in his *Discours contre Machiavel* (1576), notes that the Italian author's books "could rightly be called the Koran of courtiers, so much do they esteem them, following and observing his teachings and maxims, no more or less than the Turks use the Koran of their great prophet Mohammed." Gentillet later specifies that, in France, from the death of Henri II "to the present, the name of Machiavelli has been and is celebrated and honored, as the wisest character in the world, and better understood in affairs of state, and his books held dear and precious by Italian and Italianate courtiers, as if they were the books of the Sibyls."[236] The same observation could have applied to contemporary England.[237]

The doctrine of justification by faith insisted on human perversity, but it also comprised a certain optimism since, in penetrating men's corrupt hearts, divine grace could transfigure them. For Machiavelli, however, this penetrating light does not exist. A similar illumination may have shone for Cornelius Agrippa (1468–1535), doctor of Louise of Savoy and later historiographer of Charles V before his year-long imprisonment on charges of necromancy.[238] Although he combatted Luther, he did share the latter's fideism. His appraisal of mankind, however, is as severe as that of Machiavelli. In his *De Vanitate* . . . , all social classes are purported to rely on cruelty and deceit. Nobles achieve their power only by warfare (another name for murder), by the prostitution of their wives and daughters to the sensual appetite of monarchs, or by base flatteries and the most abject servitude toward the great and powerful. They maintain themselves only by oppressing their inferiors, by defrauding the crown, or by selling their influence at court. Their life is an accumulation of vices.[239] Many religious functionaries regard their would-be vocation only as a means to lead a life of ease, and their image protects them against any investigation of their misdeeds and immorality.[240] Doctors are simpletons and charlatans who do more harm than good.[241] The men of law are corrupt, they pervert good laws and insinuate themselves into princes' councils while evicting titulary or hereditary counselors.[242] Merchants are deceivers and usurers.[243] Agrippa's biting accusations do not derive from any sort of democratic sentiment, for he reputes the lower classes to be superstitious and cruel. His contempt for the crowd even leads him to philosophical esotericism.[244] Monks commit an unpardonable sin when their sermons expose the debates of specialists to the general public. It is especially important to avoid attacking Luther in public sermons because this would lead to writing in the vernacular and to infecting one's own opinion with his heresy. Agrippa did not fear anything so much as the vernacular diffusion of both his thought and anticlericalism.[245] And as for the so-called natural "law," by which so many men regulate their behavior, it could be defined as follows: "Do not be hungry, do not be thirsty, do not be cold, do not exhaust yourself," "refuse all the works of penance," consider "as supreme happiness Epicurean pleasure."[246]

Thus rules egotism and the law of the mighty.[247] Agrippa pointedly observes that when noblemen put animal figures on their armor, they always choose predators.[248] He also repeats the ancient proverb: "Man is a wolf to man." Yet the complete phrase includes two parts that are at once antithetical and complementary: "*Nosce teipsum: homo homini Deus. Homo homini lupus.*"[249] The suppression of the first part is full of consequences, not the least of which is its revelation of a disillusioned anthropology. By extending the discourses of Machiavelli and Agrippa, one logically arrives at the saying cited by Thomas Nashe, "man is a devil to man,"[250] and from there to Hobbes. It matters little that the author of *Leviathan* (1651) avowed: "Fear and myself are a pair of twins," alluding to the fact that he was born prematurely as a consequence of the fear his mother felt at the approach of the "Invincible Armada." If Hobbes was able to construct the "monstrous" figure of an all-powerful state, the individual's only safeguard, it was because Machiavelli and Agrippa had preceded him along this path. Like them, Hobbes saw man as "a wolf to man," and only that. Describing the natural human conditions, he presents it as a "perpetual desire, without respite, for more and more power."[251] In the presocial state, everyone is a rival, since fundamentally all people are equal in body and spirit. From this equality of aptitude are born defiance and war. Hence the necessity of the state to guarantee human rights, for "during the time men live without a common power to keep them all in awe, they are in that condition which is called war; and such a war, as is of every man, against every man."[252] This laicized pessimism, which increased the era's Augustinian pessimism, would later influence Diderot and especially d'Holbach.[253]

CHAPTER 5

Fragile Humanity

THE DISAPPEARANCE OF REASON

Not only is man wicked but his intelligence, despite appearances to the contrary, is ultimately powerless. This second conclusion, as extremist as the first, was widespread during the High Renaissance. An entire current of thought from the fourteenth century on challenged the intellectual assurance of Aristotle and Saint Thomas and fought against the vanity of knowledge. Aquinas and his disciples had reconciled the universal and the particular, the general concept and concrete realities, groups and individuals. William of Ockham's nominalism, however, took issue with this conceptualizing, which gave consistency to "universals." On the contrary, the English Franciscan denied all reality, affirming that the same thing could not exist at the same time in diverse beings or objects. Concepts are only words. Only individual entities exist: These are knowable by intuition, either sentient or suprasentient. This critique invalidates scientific generalizations—on the other hand, it privileges experience—and all rational theology, construing notions such as common good, law, cause, and finality as purely mental constructs and giving to religion the sole support of faith.[1]

There were also elements of skepticism in the *De docta ignorantia* ("Of Learned Ignorance") of Nicholas of Cusa, who believed all human knowledge to be more or less arbitrary and compared the relationship between science and truth to that between a polygon and a circle that circumscribes it, their coordination being attained only in the infinite, beyond the reach of human spirit. For Nicholas, the only sure knowledge was that of the limits of reason.[2] A new step forward in the critique of knowledge was realized by Giovanni Francesco Pico della Mirandola, the nephew of the famous author of the *De Dignitate hominis*. His *Examen vanitatis doctrinae gentium et veritatis christianae disciplinae* (1520) borrowed material from Sextus Empiricus, who with Pyrrho was the principal representative of ancient skepticism. He simultaneously destroys the validity of the syllogism and of inductive reasoning, and he attacks metaphysics, the concept of causality, and knowledge gained by the senses. He exposes the innumerable difficulties that philosophy encounters in defining terms, knowing objects, and working correct demonstrations. Mirandola concludes that it is necessary neither to deny nor affirm, but instead to suspend one's judgment. Since reason does not prove religion, the latter can be based only on a revelation.[3]

Mirandola's book points to a collective anxiety in certain intellectual circles of his time. It was not by chance that doubts regarding the power of reason grew at the beginning of the sixteenth century. Together the questioning of past or modern authorities and the nascent Reformation led to at least a partial reactivation of ancient skepticism. This interrogation of the limits of human knowledge expressed a spiritual malaise and a feeling of intellectual discomfort present at the heart of Renaissance culture.[4] This uneasiness is tangible even within the rather optimistic thinking of Erasmus. In fact it has been shown how his *Praise of Folly* describes "the sciences" as an "invention" of "wicked spirits" who pushed humanity far from the golden age, and the book chides the "impious curiosity" that leads to "scrutinizing the secret mechanism of the world."[5] Thus Erasmus gives a new apology for "learned ignorance."

Amid the intellectual current that propelled the critique of learning, Cornelius Agrippa occupies an important place (though he had trouble reconciling this devaluation with the practice of magic). For many years Agrippa was considered to be a Neoplatonist immersed in esotericism. Only recently have the skeptical aspects of his work been made apparent, particularly as they appear in his *De incertitudine et vanitate scientiarum declamatio invectiva* (1531).[6]

In the book's opening chapter, Agrippa asserts: "Truth possesses so vast a liberty and so ample a dimension that no scientific speculation, no convincing sensory judgment, no logical argumentation, no evident proof, no demonstration by syllogism, no process of human reason can understand it. Only faith can arrive at truth."

The same author also affirms: "All the sciences are nothing but the decrees and opinions of men" (chap. 1). Not only are we incapable of establishing correct premises and deducing valid syllogisms from them, but we are also deceived by our own senses. All knowledge assuredly comes from the use of the senses but—resuming the Ockhamist critique—they do not bring certitude. The senses tell us nothing of a profound nature; they convey only the superficial and individual. Since sensations do not reveal general principles (chap. 7), any science built on concrete givens is fallacious.

Agrippa takes pleasure in stressing the contradictions between schools and devaluing the great authorities of the past, notably Aristotle (chaps. 44, 52, and 154). He remarks that the voyages of the Spaniards have destroyed the opinions of the earlier geographers (chap. 27). He proposes the hypothesis that unknown stars and planets may exist: This view would invalidate the astronomy of the period (chaps. 30–31). Moreover, the arts and sciences are often sources of evils, sins, and heresies. In itself, architecture is praiseworthy, but it overloads churches and builds engines of war (chap. 28). Rhetoric, uncertain in its very principles, comes to the aid of injustice, of bad faith and of heresy (chap. 6). Painting inflames passions and portrays obscene subjects (chaps. 24 and 25). As for neutral sciences—mathematics and cosmography—they are useless for health and happiness (chaps. 11 and 27). In any case, human life is too short to master what would be only one science (chap. 1). From these accumulated arguments, there results the position that if reason ignores its limits, great danger may ensue (chaps. 97 and 101). The only area of certainty is that of faith, because in this regard we can avail ourselves of a continuous revelation in Scripture.[7]

Agrippa's *De . . . Vanitate* most likely influenced Montaigne,[8] who also became familiar with Sextus Empiricus through a new Latin translation of his works by Henri Estienne (1562). Montaigne first read this edition in 1576, and marked the occasion by having a medal struck and reproducing the great skeptic's sayings on the walls of his house.[9] Other traditions, however, converge in the famous *Apologie de Raymond Sebond*, which constitutes an entire book within the *Essays*. The references to monastic texts on the *contemptus mundi* made earlier in this study help to situate and clarify Montaigne's disparagement and condemnation of mankind:

> *Man is the frailest and most calamitous of creatures, and yet all the same the most proud. He feels and sees himself placed here, amid the mud and dung of the world, bound and nailed to the extreme, in the deadest and most stagnant part of the universe, at the lowest level of the world and the farthest from the celestial vault, with the animals having the worst condition of the three.*[10]

Man is filth and degradation: "Who regards man without flattering him, he will see neither effect nor faculty that feels anything but death and the earth."[11] Montaigne also cites the words of Ecclesiastes, "Dust and ashes, what have you to glory in?"[12] which he had inscribed on one of the beams in his library. We are almost an insult to God. "How else could he suffer some correspondence and similarity to something as abject as we are, without extreme concern and wasting of his divine grandeur"?[13] Abjection indeed, because "we are made of inconstancy, irresolution, uncertainty"—themes to which Montaigne ceaselessly returns—and moreover "sorrow and pain, superstition, cares for things to come, both soon and after our life; ambition, avarice, jealousy, envy; unruled, frantic, and indomitable appetites, war, deceit, disloyalty, abuse, and curiosity."[14]

This list of deadly sins is more elaborate than that of his classical predecessor, and the above condemnations could have been signed, some centuries earlier, by Peter Damian or Cardinal Lothair.

Man has no superiority. "We are neither above nor below the rest."[15] "There is no animal on earth exposed to as many offenses as is man."[16] In contrast, animals are not "incapable of being . . . trained in our ways,"[17] and "if there are some animals less attractive than we, there are a great number of others who are more so."[18] "As for fidelity, there is no animal in the world so great a traitor as man."[19]

The senses of animals are often sharper than our own,[20] which we constantly abuse and "in which lie the great foundation of our ignorance"[21] and our erroneous "fantasies."[22] In the wake of Pyrrhonism, of Giovanni Francesco Pico della Mirandola and Cornelius Agrippa, Montaigne offers his own critique of sensory perception: "As for the error and uncertainty of the operation of the senses, everyone can provide as many examples as they like, so many are the faults and deceptions that they commonly work on us."[23]

Hence the impossibility of science, whose prodigious growth the author of the *Essays* did not in any way foresee. "It is likely that this great body we call the world is something quite other than we think."[24] Our minds cannot arrive at the knowledge of the movement of the planets, "nor can we imagine their natural conduct."[25] Science, however, is no better equipped to penetrate the mysteries of the earthly environment. "Our condition entails that the knowledge of that which we hold between our very hands is as distant from us, and as high above the clouds, as is the knowledge of the stars."[26] Similarly, we do not even understand our own bodies. For "if the soul knew something, it would above all know itself; and if it knew something outside of itself, it would be above all its own body and external shell."[27] It follows that "human science can maintain itself only by unreasonable reason, which is mad and frantic."[28] These affirmations temper overhasty judgments on Montaigne's modernity. More generally, our spirit is incapable of attaining truth. For truth is a "vagabond tool, dangerous and audacious."[29] The "view of our judgment" is no more capable of truth than is "the eye of the screech owl able to see the splendor of the sun."[30] "Philosophy is only a sophisticated poetry,"[31] and systems of thought contradict each other.[32] Thus Psalm 93 is correct in asserting that "The Lord knows the thoughts of men, and he knows that they are vain."[33] The infirmity of human intelligence thus prevents all access to definite knowledge.

With penetrating lucidity, Montaigne delineates all that science, legislation, and morality base on relative terms. In this regard he contributed key elements to modern thinking, without himself becoming a fully modern thinker. For Montaigne accorded the same negative connotations to this phenomenon of relativity as had the authors of treatises on the contempt for this world. "There is no constant existence, neither of our being, nor of objects. And we, and our judgment, and all mortal things ceaselessly glide and roll."[34] Montaigne does not allow for the contingent, the transitory—thus the temporal—to carry authentic value. For him relativity means variation, inconstancy, instability, vanity, and weakness, which he first will discover in himself: "During fasts I feel different than after a meal; if my health and the brightness of a fine morning make me smile, then I am a courteous man; if I have a corn that afflicts my toe, then I am gruff, unpleasant, and inaccessible."[35] "Nearly everyone," he adds, "would say as much if he considered himself in the way I do." In chapter 1 of *Essays II*, one furthermore reads: "We change as does that animal that takes the color of each place it visits; . . . there is only swaying and inconstancy."[36] Hence not only the fundamental inconstancy of man ("always being between life and death"[37]), but also the impossibility of any coherent and universal order. "That which is truth within these mountains, the people on the other side hold to be lies."[38] Truth should have "an equal and universal face."[39] Nonetheless, "there is nothing so subject to continual agitation as the laws."[40] "We hide ourselves in order to enjoy our women; the Indians enjoy them in public."[41]

As I have previously noted, an emphasis on the consonance between certain aspects of Montaigne's pessimism and monastic *contemptus mundi* exhortations relocates the *Essays* at the center of Christian history. Montaigne agrees with the church that the first and principal sin of man is "presumption"—that is, pride—"our most natural and original malady,"[42] by which we try to forget and disguise our misery. Certainly his skepticism owes much to the teachings of the Pyrrhonians, but as revised and adjusted by Saint Paul and Saint Augustine. Montaigne thus concludes that salvation resides at once in the recognition of the weakness of our judgment"[43] and in the humble acceptance of the Revelation that God freely gave us

> *simple and ignorant witnesses he chose from the crowd, in order to teach us of his admirable secrets. Our faith is not our acquisition, it is a pure present of the liberality of another. It is not by speech [= reason] or by our understanding that we have received our religion, it is by outside authority and command. The weakness of our judgment helps us in this respect more than strength, and our blindness helps us more than our insight. It is more by the action of our ignorance than of our knowledge that we are aware of this divine wisdom.*[44]

This fideist declaration recalls a good number of earlier or contemporary praises of "learned ignorance." How then to avoid bewilderment with the many aberrant interpretatons of Montaigne's religious thinking? For example, the rapid judgments of Sainte-Beuve: "Religion hardly touched him, nor ever altered him." "He is in the midst of non-Christian humanity." In the *Apology* . . . , "all is contrived, calculated, tortuous, speaking in apparent contradiction of that which the master concludes on his part and what he implies."[45] Sainte-Beuve also speaks of the "very pagan Rabelais"[46]—another summary appraisal, which Lucien Febvre has corrected. Sainte-Beuve's reading of Montaigne has been repeated up to the present day.[47] André Gide adopted it,[48] and it reappears in the writings of Hugo Friedrich, one of the leading Montaigne commentators of the last fifty years.[49] For him, the resemblance between the wish for man's humility, so striking in the *Essays*, and the theses of earlier Christian theology is only superficial. He is a "true skeptic" for whom religion is only "mortal and human."

It is worth recalling here that Montaigne translated, at his father's request, the *Theologia naturalis* of Raymond Sebond, a fifteenth-century Catalan (d. 1432), and found "this author's inventions excellent, his book's structure well managed, and his design full of piety." "He undertakes by human and natural reasons to establish and prove against the atheists all the articles of the Christian religion; wherein, to tell the truth, I find him so firm and felicitous that I do not think it is possible to do better in that argument, and I think that no one has equaled him."[50]

Thus Montaigne, in resuming the apologetic intentions of Raymond Sebond, in translating, glossing, and defending the work of this Catalan theologian—even if he disagrees with him over certain points—maintains an objective similar to that of Pascal in the *Pensées*. Both authors aim to fight "damnable atheism."[51] Montaigne could not foresee that his writings would become the bedside reading of libertines, when he had clearly wished—why accuse him of duplicity?—to demonstrate the necessity of Revelation and of grace. Faithful to a long Pauline and Augustinian tradition that he amplifies through a mercilessly Pyrrhonian critique of knowledge, he presents "man naked and empty," so that "recognizing his natural feebleness," he may become "cleansed to receive from on high some foreign strength, stripped of human knowledge and so more apt to receive the divine, obliterating his judgment to give more room to faith. The more we give and commit ourselves to God, and renounce ourselves, the more we become worthy."[52]

This statement thus conforms to the most constant Christian philosophy, indeed to mystic experience. It is true that a preoccupation with salvation is absent from the *Essays*. It is also true that a gap exists between the religious "speech" of Montaigne and his Epicurean "action." The latter fact explains the accusation of duplicity formulated by the authors of the Port-Royal *Logique* (Arnauld and Nicole) and the libertines' conviction that he must have camouflaged his true feelings. Why deny, however, any contradiction within the same personality? And what purpose do these impoverishing reductions serve?

While fearing Montaigne's morals and regretting the "foolish project" he had of depicting himself, Pascal is more correct in identifying the author of the *Essays* as "a humble disciple of the church, through his faith."[53] Such also was the view of the devout Mademoiselle de Gournay, Montaigne's spiritual daughter, who wrote in a preface to the 1595 edition of the *Essays*: "I thank God for supporting his church with such a powerful human pillar." Whoever would still doubt Montaigne's religion should consult the chapters that he devoted to "prayers" (Book I, 56) and to "Repentance" (Book III, 2). Therein one reads a moving praise of the Lord's Prayer ("the only prayer that serves me everywhere") and a challenge to the false regret provoked by "the catarrh" or "the colic," to which is opposed the true repentance moved by "respect for God." This Montaigne is a far cry from today's still most popular version of him.[54]

Furthermore, it is revealing that he was the friend of Pierre Charron (1541—1603). The latter, a lawyer and later a priest and preacher, devoted a treatise to *La Sagesse* (1601) in which he resumes and coordinates the arguments of the *Essays* on the misery and feebleness of man. Charron defines the human spirit as "a mass of darkness full of pits and prisons, a labyrinth, a confused and highly twisted abyss."[55] He also describes this spirit as a "wandering, changeable, distorting, variable implement . . . an instrument of lead and wax" that "folds in, opens out, agrees with everything,"[56] "ever in flux, and in the wrong and backward way, with lying as with truth,"[57] justifying almost anything: What is "abominable in one place is piety . . . elsewhere."[58] "There is no reason that does not have its opposite."[59] "Errors enter our soul through the same way and conduit as does truth," and we do not possess firm enough criteria to choose between the former and the latter. "Wisdom and folly are extremely close to each other. There is but a half-step between them . . . Melancholy belongs to each."[60] To these disillusioned considerations, Charron adds a condemnation of research and intellectual curiosity: "The pursuits of the human mind are without purpose, without form; their sustenance is doubt, ambiguity; it is a perpetual movement, without a break or a goal; the world is a school of questioning."[61] Two important conclusions thus ensue: (1) It is necessary "to bind up" and "pinion" men of "religions, laws, customs, sciences, precepts, threats, mortal and immortal promises"[62]; (2) Intellectual dullness is worth more than an excess of wit. "Quite intellectually mediocre people live in greater serenity than do the ingenious"—and here Charron contrasts the Swiss and the Florentines. "The refinement of minds does not bring wisdom"[63]: a new justification of "learned ignorance."

A rapid overview of these pessimistic arguments reveals their obvious defects. First, they tend to set all the disciplines on the same footing: architecture and astronomy, rhetoric and mathematics. These skeptics amalgamate science and philosophy, moral judgment and epistemological critiques. Man is disparaged for being both proud and incapable of attaining truth. Furthermore, this last point is not given any distinctions that would mark degrees of comparison. The scientific level is not separated from the metaphysical level. Finally, all that is temporal and fleeting is automatically imbued with negative connotations.

To draw attention to these members of a certain school of Renaissance thought is not to pass judgment on it; rather, it is to state that Giovanni Francesco Pico della Mirandola, Cornelius Agrippa, Montaigne, and Charron did not yet have the intellectual terms and methodologies that would have given them access to the universe of modern science. Certainly their critiques of Thomist and humanist optimisms achieved a salutary deconstruction. Their hostility toward generalizations led to a valorization of concrete experience. They did not foresee, however, the course science would soon be taking from this lesson of humility. It is only with Giordano Bruno,[64] apologist for reason, and also with Jean Bodin and Loys Le Roy[65] that the notion of relativity acquired positive qualities. Then the concept takes on a cosmic dimension: The horizon changes with the observer's own displacement; movement, time, and weight are not immutable; two objects are never identical—the old Ockhamite thesis—the earth is only a point within a limitless universe, and it lacks the circular perfection it was believed to possess. Nonetheless, for many of Bruno's predecessors and notably for Montaigne, the critique of knowledge and the insistence on relativity had the primary function of valorizing fideism and proving the necessity of Revelation.

Moreover, it would be an error to consider the skeptics' attempted humbling of man as a marginal sixteenth-century outlook. Quantitatively speaking, this viewpoint was probably as, if not more, important than the optimistic valorization that previous historians of the Renaissance have emphasized. For along with other contributing factors, the two Augustinian currents of the time were coalescing: that which remained Catholic (with Charron, for example) and that which opted for

Protestantism. During the period, the apology for rational thought did not predominate.

Given their immense influence, Luther and Calvin deserve quotation in this context. Both essentially thought that corrupt man retained a certain "natural light," the vestige of his splendor before the Fall. "That three and two make five is most clear in the light of nature," writes Luther, and he specifies that "the light of Reason is lit by Divine Light . . . it is a fragment and a beginning of the true light, in which it understands and glorifies Him who provided its light."[66] Calvin extends the praise of human intelligence and lets science retain its variables: "Shall we say that those who invented medicine were witless? Of the other disciplines, shall we think that they are follies?"[67] One can assimilate these affirmations with this other claim, found in Book 1 of *The Institutes of the Christian Religion*: ". . . Those who are expert and adept in science, even if they are not highly esteemed, are aided by this means, and are raised to more closely understand the secrets of God."[68] The two Reformers thus clearly differ from Agrippa and Montaigne in their analysis of the variations, shortcomings, and infirmities of the human mind and spirit.

On the other hand, Luther and Calvin aim to prove that the mind falters when it becomes mixed with metaphysics and religion. Incurably wounded, our reason "can no longer approach, nor prepare, nor set up its goal, to understand this truth of who the true God is, and what he wishes for and with us."[69] At the philosophical and religious level, the two Reformers repudiate Thomist optimism and oppose the terms "supernatural" and "natural" light. Without freely given grace and illumination of faith, man can only err, lose himself in his own contradictions, and raise idols. Calvin insists at length on the impossibility of reason to understand predestination: "If anyone feeds and stuffs himself with too much confidence and boldness" in this "labyrinth," he "will find no escape."[70]

Opposed to "supernatural light," "natural light" is thus given negative connotations by Luther: "flesh," "appearance," "world," "sin," "shame," "nature," "presumption," "free will,"[71] and so on. Two consequences ensue. First, the conviction that human reason is incapable of dictating a correct moral choice. Luther explains that reason may declare that one must do good and avoid evil, but it "does not succeed in telling us which things are good and which are bad." Thus reason is similar to the traveler who wishes to go to Rome but does not know which road to take.[72] Calvin, with a touch more nuance, concedes that "reason, by which man discerns good from evil . . . cannot be utterly destroyed." At the same time, it is truly "debilitated" and "corrupted" by Original Sin, so that "it only appears as a disfigured ruin."[73] There is no surprise, then, with the errors and variations of the human laws and judges later denounced by Montaigne. The second and crucial consequence mentioned above finds Luther, carried away by his ardor, bearing full tilt at reason with a number of peremptory generalizations and vindictive reprimands. He writes that "man [without grace] is but a liar and a vain being, such that he can only use this natural light against God."[74] Furthermore, why do we boast of this "natural enlightenment," so common to Jews and pagans, demons and the damned? These groups possess this illumination even "more clearly" than we, "so that they are all the more tormented by it."[75] Man, in order to reach God, would therefore not be able to too much mistrust his own reason, which Luther frequently qualifies in his sermons as "a harlot"[76] and "a beautiful whore."[77] Nature, when she debates against the Spirit with the help of "beautiful reason," is described by him as "snotty and shitten."[78] Taking issue with the Anabaptists and Zwinglians who, in the name of rationality and of appearances, denied real presence, Luther in his final Wittenberg sermon exhorted each of his listeners in these terms—it is a famous text:

> *Therefore, see to it that you hold reason in check and do not follow her beautiful cogitations. Throw dirt in her face and make her ugly . . . Reason is and should be drowned in baptism, and this foolish wisdom will not harm you, if you hear the beloved Son of God saying, "Take, eat; this is my body, which is given for you . . . If I hear and accept this, then I trample reason and its wisdom under foot and say, "You cursed whore, shut up! Are you trying to seduce me into committing fornication with the devil?" That's the way reason is purged and made free through the Word of the Son of God."*[79]

Once again it is clear that Luther vilifies reason only insofar as it works against the Gospel. In doing so, however, he moves toward devalorizing man, as part of a sixteenth-century project to which Machiavelli, Guicciardini, Agrippa, and Montaigne all contributed. Elizabethan and early Stuart literature also links such a devalorization to the widespread belief that an entire world was slowly dying out. Hiram Haydn writes that "it would have been very difficult, indeed, to exaggerate the extent of popular pessimism in England during the last years of Elizabeth's reign and the first of her successors." In spite of optimistic voices, "it remains true, with testimony a thousandfold, that the average, not unintelligent Englishman of the late sixteenth century did despair, not only of certain knowledge, but of the very continued existence of this world."[80] The same period did produce Francis Bacon, who in stressing the "false mirror" of human knowledge and the tricks of sensation defended experience and sent a message of hope to his contemporaries: "I am now therefore to speak touching hope."[81] Nevertheless, in the time of Shakespeare, Edmund Spenser, Sir Philip Sidney, and John Donne, anxiety prevails, with a melancholy regard for the fleeting of time and the passing of beauty: George Chapman, for example, writes that "Man is a torch borne in the wind; a dream / But of a shadow" (*Bussy D'Ambois* I. i. 18–19).

In the pessimistic works of Elizabethan literature, three themes are attached to the position of melancholy: (1) the critique of knowledge; (2) the seriousness of sin; (3) a foreboding of the ruination of the world. "What is this *knowledge*?" asks the jurist, diplomat, and poet John Davies (1569–1626):

> *What can we know? or what can we discerne?*
> *When* Error *chokes the windows of the mind;*
> *The diverse forms of things, how can we learne,*
> *That have bene ever from our birth-day blind?*[82]

Hence this disillusioned conclusion:

> *I know my soule hath power to know all things,*
> *Yet is she blind and ignorant in all;*
> *I know I am one of Nature's little kings,*
> *Yet to the least and vilest things am thrall.*
>
> *I know my life's a paine, and but a span,*
> *I know my Sense is mockt with every thing;*
> *And to conclude, I know my selfe a Man,*
> *Which is a proud and yet a wretched thing*[83]

One of the most accomplished writers of his time, John Donne (1572–1631) typifies an anxious generation. He was possessed with both insatiable curiosity and intense spirituality. Having moved from Catholicism to Anglicanism, he evolved toward fideism and found a solution to his anguish in the doctrine of justification by faith. This solution, however, included a dark judgment on sinful mankind:

> *A toad is a bag of poison, and a spider is a blister of poison, and yet a toad and a spider cannot poison themselves; man hath a drachm of poison, original sin, in an invisible corner, we know not where, and he cannot choose but poison himself and all his actions with that; we are so far from being able to begin without grace, as then when we have first grace, we cannot proceed to the use of that, without more.*"[84]

In a remarkable synthesis, Donne conjoins recent astronomical discoveries with the pessimism of Machiavelli and Montaigne, and places this combination within a panorama of the end of the world:

> *The new Philosophy cals all in doubt,*
> *The Element of fire is quite put out;*
> *The Sunne is lost, and th'earth, and no mans wit*
> *Can well direct him, where to looke for it.*
> *And freely men confesse, that this world's spent,*
> *When in the Planets, and in the Firmament*
> *They seeke so many new; they see that this*
> *Is crumbled out againe t'his Atomis*
> *'Tis all in pieces, all cohaerence gone;*
> *All just supply, and all Relation:*
> *Prince, Subject, Father, Sonne, are things forgot.*[85]

A world had fallen apart. Donne could not foresee what would eventually replace it.[86]

FATE

Is man perhaps inevitably wicked? Without a doubt, he is fragile. Such is the lesson taught by numerous early modern texts and images devoted to the theme of Fortune.[87] At the beginning of Monteverdi's *Il Ritorno d'Ulisse in Patria* (1641), Fortune, Time, and Love sing together, "Let us make man fragile."

For Ernst Cassirer, the major shift from the Middle Ages to the Renaissance consisted in the passage from confidence in God to confidence in man.[88] Eugenio Garin, however, is right to adjust this overly categorical affirmation in showing that the symbol of Prometheus does not necessarily best characterize the Renaissance.[89] The following discussion takes the line of this latter, more nuanced judgment. From a new vantage point, I will aim to highlight a wide collective anxiety—at least at the level of elite culture—about mankind's destiny, as well as a distressed interrogation into his liberty.

The Greeks and Romans had feared and honored Fortune (*Tyche* for the former, *Fortuna* for the latter). She was the inconstant and redoubtable goddess, mistress of personal destinies, readily attached and likened to the wheel and sphere. Among writers, her description became commonplace. The leading families believed they could appease her by joining her name to theirs (Fortuna Flavia, Fortuna Torquatiana, and so on). In their fight against paganism, the church fathers quite logically sought to destroy the belief in Fortuna's exorbitant power. Lactantius asserts: "She does not exist."[90] He could not see how chance could operate in an entirely rational world created by God. Saint Augustine ironically observes: If Fortuna is what she is said to be, that is, unstable and changing by definition, what good is there in maintaining her worship?[91] In reality, that which seems to occur by accident does so either by God's hidden plan or by our own free choice between good and evil.[92]

Saint Jerome also repudiates Fortuna and announces: "Having carefully considered the matter, it seems to me, contrary to the false opinion of certain others, that chance does not guide all things, and that inconstant Fortune does not toy with human destinies: Everything happens according to divine decisions."[93] A complementary similarity therefore exists between the three church fathers: If, in other passages, they seem to maintain the existence of Fortune, it is to classify her among the forces of evil.[94] Saint Thomas Aquinas later adopts the basic point of view of his predecessors and denies the philosophical possibility of chance. Glossing Aristotle's physics, he notes: ". . . once one attributes events that seem to take place by chance and accident—that is, independent of the intention of sublunar causes —to some higher cause that induced them, by reference to this latter cause they cannot be called fortuitous and random. This higher cause cannot be called Fortune."[95]

It is hardly surprising that Calvin launched a war on belief in Fortune. His idea of providence was too elevated to admit any place to chance. Those who affirm Fortune's existence, he says, are "apostates" who rebel against God. Our "monstrous idolatries" and our "nature inclined to error" blind us, even though "the order of human things argues so clearly for God's providence."[96] The Lutheran "*meistersinger*" Hans Sachs opines in the same way. Describing Fortune with a bridle in her mouth that is held by a celestial hand, he argues that good and bad times come by God's command and by virtue of his eternal prescience. Everything occurs for our own benefit.[97] Guillaume Budé, although an adversary of Protestantism, nevertheless reaches the same conclusion. Blaming fortune is to blame God. Men should not let events discourage or embitter them, but on the contrary perceive that they are accomplished by "the divine fates who are at the service of Providence in a certain and secret way. Nothing happens, has happened, or will happen without the high direction of He who from the beginning has been the author of every sort of cause, and who is always the judge of the movement of the heavens."[98] If, however, one wishes to say that Fortune exists, then it is necessary to specify that this "capricious" and "unbalanced" force is "helped" by "the world . . . and the flesh, that is to say desire and passion."[99] Budé thus doubly echoes the fathers of the church, who denied the possibility of chance but saw in Fortuna another name for temptation and evil.

The most official theology thus debunked the goddess Fortuna. In fact, however, she continued her career. She represents the exemplary—but not isolated—case of a less successful and less profound acculturation than one might expect. More or less Christianized, she traverses the Middle Ages without hindrance. Boethius (d. 524) was especially responsible for her survival. Certainly he affirms that God is the sovereign organizer, and therefore what we call "chance" is only the moving rim of the great wheel, at whose center is God.[100] Since no evil can emanate from God, good and bad fortunes are equally profitable to us.[101] In adversity, one must be patient—something that the ancient philosophers had already advised. In prosperity, one should not become attached to honor and glory, which are fleeting. Nevertheless, in his *De Consolatione* (written in prison), Boethius combines this Christian discourse with the accounts of Fortune he inherited from the pagan tradition. She is called the queen of the universe, "her versatile hand distributing variable lots."[102] Her blind power has two faces.[103] Who can hope to hang on to the movement of her wheel?[104] Her permanent activity is to keep spinning her wheel.[105] Boethius's influence was enormous up to the end of the sixteenth century. He had successfully promoted the images of blind Fortune and of the wheel she indefatigably turns.

Henceforth two different and ultimately contradictory discourses coexist on the subject of Fortune: One, of pagan origin, evokes the powerful mistress of human destinies; the other, a product of Christianity, corrects the first and reinstates it in a theology of salvation. Many authors will conglomerate these two languages. Even in the Middle Ages, however, the first often starts to act independently of the second. For example, this effect occurs within the famous *Carmina Burana* (thirteenth century), goliardic songs conserved in a manuscript from Beuren Abbey in Bavaria: Here the theme of Fortune's disconcerting power gives rise to four sequential developments: (1) "O changeable and slippery Fortuna!"; (2) "O Fortuna, your state changes as doth the moon: always you wax or wane"; (3) "Inconstant Fortune advances in ambiguous steps"; (4) "he who is too high (the king at the top of his glory), beware a fall."[106] During the Renaissance, Fortune will escape more and more from the Christian universe and in this very respect will become —or again become—extremely disturbing.

Although the allegory of Fortune is present throughout the Middle Ages, in both Honorius of Autun's *Ecclesiae* and the windows of churches,[107] she still occupies little space in the contemporary *chansons de geste* and analogous novels. Her return to prominence in Western civilization is due to certain major works, at once causes and witnesses of a change in the European psychological climate: the *Roman de la Rose* (second part), Dante's *Inferno*, and the books of Boccaccio and Boethius. In France, Jean de Meung had translated Boethius. In the wake of this best-seller, he did much to popularize the dual pagan/Christian conceptions of Fortuna. He affirms that God is all-powerful, that man is endowed with freedom of choice, and that divine foreknowledge does not imply necessity.[108] He tells Reason that "perverse and contrary" Fortune is often preferable to "kind and favorable" Fortune.[109] Fundamentally, however, de Meung exploits the description (which he did not invent) of Dame Fortune's ramshackle dwelling.[110] She is called "so perverse that she throws her wealth into the muck,"[111] and she is seen as totally disloyal, deceiving humans, troubling their spirits, bringing them vinegar when they are brokendown. Certainly she has no power over what is truly good, but she controls the property of this world and distributes it according to her whim.[112] Considering the long-term success of the *Roman de la Rose*, one can hardly overestimate the impact these developments had on the popular image of Fortune.

A similar remark holds for *The Divine Comedy*, the work that most fully integrated Fortune into the Christian universe and nevertheless greatly raised her mysterious power in European mentalities. In canto 7 of the *Inferno*,[113] Virgil explains to his companion that "He whose knowledge transcends all things," the Creator of the Heavens and of light, also installed Fortune as "minister general" and ordainer of any human greatness. From the higher regions, he calls on her to cause worldly goods to pass from people to people, from one family to another, and to alternately hand out power and subservience. Therefore men have no right to "accuse" and "crucify" Fortune. Hers is a divine task. Reason assists her.[114] Without hatred for anyone, moreover, she serenely continues to "turn her sphere." At the same time, this description has a second aspect: Subject to God, Fortune has complete power over men whose "knowledge cannot engage her in debate." She alters situations without considering the plans and distinctions made here below. She is as secret as the snake hidden in the grass. "She decides and she judges; she directs her kingdom as other divinities govern theirs." Finally, her vocation, her "necessity," is to make permutations continually give way to still others. She was created in haste and made to preside over change. Faced with the sovereign power of such a "divinity" (Dante does use this term), one must attempt humble submission to her decrees and a detachment from worldly belongings: Dante thus resumes a number of classical remedies. This Christian discourse, however, does not prevent Dante's poem from magnifying Fortune. Hence the reproach that the learned Cecco d'Ascoli (burned as a heretic in 1327) addressed to the author of *The Divine Comedy* in his encyclopedic *Acerba*: "You, Florentine poet, have sinned in claiming that necessity commands the distribution and destination of worldly goods. There is no fortune that reason cannot conquer."[115] In effect, Dante had made man minuscule before Fate.

Petrarch did not fear to speak in a different manner on this serious subject. In a letter written near the end of his life, he states, like Lactantius, Saint Augustine, and Saint Thomas: "I have always thought, in fact, that Fortune does not exist . . . Nothing happens without cause."[116] Analogous statements already appear in the second book of the *De Remediis utriusque Fortunae*. If, he says in both these texts, he has spoken of her at length in his other works, it was only to use the expression found "in everyone's mouth"—an admission that further clarifies collective thinking. Still, this period preferred Petrarch's classicizing evocation of Fortune. In his sonnets, he at once complains of the stars, of Fortune, of fate, and of death.[117] Especially in the prologue to the first book of *De Remediis*, he takes up the distinction of Valerius Maximus and of Seneca between Good and Bad Fortune, claiming that these two regents of human destinies are equally formidable. From the dialogues in this work that bring together Reason and Joy, Reason and Hope, Reason and Sorrow, it becomes clear that the list of evils that assail us is endless, that one has to fortify oneself against the blows of chance, that worldly goods are transitory, and that the only things of value are the consolations of wisdom. The *contemptus mundi* and Stoic morality thus converge to invite people to enjoy the most they possibly can from a universe where they receive a host of unlucky setbacks. Detachment: such is the lesson taught by the proof of human weakness in the face of fate.[118]

Boccaccio also speaks a double language on the subject of Fortune. As in Boethius and Dante, she is doctrinally Christianized. In his "commentary on Dante," the author states that only "poetic fiction" calls her a "goddess."[119] The *De Casibus nobilium hominorum et feminarum* presents her as she who is charged with punishing the proud. If men imagine her to be hard, blind, and senseless, it is because they cannot perceive the secrets of the heavens and are themselves blinded by their desire for possessions.[120] Therefore the necessity of detachment, which makes one indifferent to the disgraces of one's fate. Conversely, however, in the first chapter of the second book of *De Casibus*, Boccaccio writes a highly lively and troubling description of Fortuna:

> . . . *I was struck dumb with fear when I beheld her great stature and the wondrous form of her body. For she had burning eyes, and it seemed they threatened those who gazed upon her. Fortuna had a cruel and horrible face. She had rough, long hair that hung down from her mouth, and I think she had a hundred hands and as many arms, to give and take away riches from men and to cast them down and raise them on high. Fortuna's clothes were of divers colors. For no man knows her. Her voice was so harsh and so hard that it seemed her mouth was made of iron, so she could threaten all the greatest men of the world and put these threats into action.*"[121]

In addition, one is inevitably struck by the continual references to Fortune that swarm through Boccaccio's work. Howard Patch counted 250, or one every twenty pages, with a special development on this theme in each of his important writings. Without a doubt, Fortune acts as a convenient *deus ex machina* for Boccaccio when he recounts tales of love. Still, his emphasis on the goddess suggests the hypothesis that he used this name to designate the mysterious cause of numerous events for which no coherent explanation can be found. Fortune thus becomes, as in antiquity, she who "modifies all conditions here below," who forever turns her great wheel toward the left. "Deaf and blind, she does not listen to any prayer."[122] In Boccaccio, then, there exists an appreciable shift between his theoretical discussion of Fortune and his continual recourse to it as a highly disturbing theme. This evaluation likewise elucidates the comments of his successors on the same subject.

The High Middle Ages, as has been seen, were preoccupied by the relationship between liberty on the one hand and chance and fate on the other. All the same, Fortune, with all the problems she poses, was never evoked with so much frequency as between the middle of the fourteenth and the end of the sixteenth century. One would never complete a catalogue of the texts and images that were devoted to her during this period. She pervades the works of Eustache Deschamps, of Christine de Pisan (cf. her *Mutacion de Fortune*), of Martin Le Franc (*Estrif de Fortune et de Vertu*), of Pierre Michault (*La Danse aux aveugles*). She appears on the paving of the cathedral of Siena and on the coat of arms of the Rucellai family of Florentine bankers.[123] She is the protagonist of Virtue in a play presented before Lucrezia Borgia during the latter's entry into Milan in 1512.[124] She figures among the allegories in both a tourney at Bologna in 1490 and a Roman cortège of 1545.[125] Her ancient temple at Palestrina is ideally reconstructed in the famous *Hypnerotomachia Poliphili*, where the visionary narrator sees a great stepped pyramid topped by an obelisk on which is mounted a statue of Fortune in gilt metal, turning toward all the winds.[126] She is prominent in both *The Ship of Fools* (chap. 37) and *The Praise of Folly*. She also inspired Botticelli, Dürer, Burgkmair the Elder, Lucas van Leyden, Giovanni Bellini, and Veronese. One can locate three hundred instances of the word "fortuna" in the writings of Machiavelli.[127] As for Elizabethan literature, the speeches of the characters of Shakespeare, Marston, Chapman and others are filled with references to fortune.[128] When Philip Henslowe built a new and beautiful theater at the end of the sixteenth century in the north of London, he named it "The Fortune."[129] His choice is partly explained by the fact that in England, morality plays and "pageants" highlighted this goddess, whose image frequently appeared in the immensely popular contemporary emblem books. These collections of allegorical images, glossed by moralizing verses, enjoyed an enormous vogue during the period. For example, Alciati's emblems went through ninety-four editions between 1531 and 1600.[130] Moreover, a sample of five emblem books published in French or French translation between 1539 and 1588 provides fourteen representation of Fortune or of her twin, Occasio.[131] Josef Macek correctly writes that "the notion of fortune is a central Renaissance problem and one of the period's preferred topics of discussion."[132]

Since this issue had such a long background, it is not surprising that certain fifteenth- and sixteenth-century voices continued to echo or agree with the early church fathers, Saint Thomas Aquinas, Calvin, and Budé in saying that fortune does not exist as an autonomous power. Martin Le Franc teaches that all is in God's hands. If the events that affect us appear incomprehensible and occur by chance, it is because "God makes his decisions behind closed doors."[133] For Alain Chartier (*L'esperance ou consolation des trois vertus*), "it cannot be doubted that lordship and servitude are establishments of reasonable law, not at all the gift of fortune."[134] Pico della Mirandola, in his *Disputationes adversus astrologos*, affirms that apparently fortuitous events depend neither on celestial conjunctions nor on mysterious chance. "Nothing departs from divine providence," even if it is true that spiritual powers, both angelic and demoniac, bring good and bad fortune to men, with divine permission.[135] In Sir Philip Sidney's *Arcadia* (1590), Cecropia the atheist is refuted by his niece Pamela, for whom chance is an absurd notion. For by definition, Chance is variable and unstable—or else she would not deserve her very name. Since we see that the world is stable and obeys certain laws, how then could chance govern it? If chance alone had gathered all the world's pieces, the heaviest parts would be continually tumbling down. Wisdom governs the universe, and this providence excludes blind Fortune.[136] In *The Faerie Queene* (1590–96), Edmund Spenser likewise considers that over a superficial mutability there reigns a profound stability and a fundamental constancy.[137]

A theoretically similar conception in fact reassigns personality and power to Fortune—identifies her as the servant and "chambermaid" of God. Such is Dante's viewpoint, shared by an entire group of French authors of the thirteenth and fourteenth centuries (Jean de Condé, Watriquet de Couvin, Philippe de Beaumanoir, and so on). In the sixteenth century, Etienne Dolet's opinion was quite similar. He proposes that all the virtues of François I were incapable of counteracting bad luck: "over all order and human power, I saw how much the king suffered misfortune in every enterprise of his wars." He then defines destiny as

> *a daughter of all-powerful God, who, following the wish and command of her father, causes and carries out all that we call good and evil. And human beings receive these two things by the infallible will of God, which is rightly called Destiny: because Destiny is nothing other than the eternal order of things. However much Destiny may suit prudence and human virtue, nevertheless she is the one who reigns and has power over all our deeds.*[138]

Jean Céard correctly argues that this theologically debatable definition did not necessarily confirm, as Henri Busson had believed,[139] "an inflexible determinism which replaces Providence." On the contrary, it is possible to align Dolet's view with Dante's conception, though it is true that the French author accentuates both man's impotence and the rigidity of Destiny. Quite logically, for some individuals the executrix of God's will becomes the force that, if necessary, pushes men toward virtue. In the *Dis de Fortune*, Jean de Condé (d. 1340), explains that "Fortune cannot turn her place" without the "consent" of God, who uses this "worker" to "retrieve" hardened hearts.[140] Charles d'Orléans, for his part, has Fortune say: ". . . For a long time, God, sovereign king over all things, has ordered me to give punishments to the world."[141] Hence it is understandable that the sixteenth century most often interpreted Dürer's *Nemesis* as an illustration of Fortune[142] hence the erroneous title "The Great Fortune." This confusion makes sense, however, since Nemesis, like Fortune, rests her feet on a sphere. Her left hand holds a bridle and reins in order to curb excessive mortals, and her right hand a cup in order to reward the just.[143] An earlier Dürer engraving had depicted an amorous Fortune balancing on a globe, conveying at once her instability and her power over the world. This was the first female nude that Dürer engraved (1497).[144]

Since Fortune is in God's hands, and since "what we suffer is divine punishment" (Alain Chartier), common sense advises resignation in adversity and detachment from the wealth of this world. Moreover, many authors express the idea that if a mysterious force exists, which sometimes favors and most often opposes human will, it acts only in a limited sector: the sublunary world, a place of confusion situated between the crystalline order of the starry spheres and the underground disorder of hell. Christine de Pisan notably develops this theme in her *Livre de la Mutacion*, wherein she writes that Fortune cannot take from anyone "the higher treasures of the soul."[145] In another work, the *Chemin de long estude*, Pisan had said of the terrible goddess: "She cannot reach or take / Nor give, or acquire / Anything that is above the earth."[146] In his *Dialogo de Fortuna* (1521), the Italian Fregoso expresses the same conviction. He states that the stars and Fortune have power over bodies but not souls, over worldly passions but not virtue.[147] An ethical conclusion therefore arises, which had long been taken by the Stoics and then by the apologists for the *contemptus mundi*: Disdain the glories of a world that will soon be nothing but maggots and dust, be detached from all earthly ambition, aspire only to eternal values.

Pierre Michault's *La Danse aux aveugles* thus quite sensibly associates Love, Fortune, and Death in the same allegorical vision, as the three dancing masters who lead us in their fatal *rondes*. The macabre meditation logically encouraged a contempt for Fortune and her illusory gifts and treacheries. It was no accident that the apogee of the theme of Fortune coincided with the diffusion of the *danses macabres*. The dance at Beram (Istria, ca. 1474) is placed near a representation of the wheel of Fortune. Both images are in a cemetery. In the spirit of the preachers and catechizers of the period, these two symbolic languages had to teach the same lesson: detachment from worldy goods. Since, however, justice-loving Fortune humbles the proud, she recalls—even in her Christianized version—the classical Destiny, envious of overly glorious careers. The Renaissance seized on this confusion and often united in the same character God's servant who punishes the first of the deadly sin, and the envious goddess who cannot tolerate the excessive ascent of human beings. The goddess eventually regained the upper hand.

It is worth observing that Christine de Pisan reproaches herself in her *Livre de la mutacion* . . . for according too much terrestrial power to Fortune. In addition, she has Darkness admonish her in these terms: "I wish to reprove you for a certain part of your writings, in your book entitled *De la Mutacion de Fortune* . . . , when you attribute so much power to Dame Fortune, that you call her the great governor of all things that occur among people . . ."[148] These words resemble the above-cited admission of Petrarch and resume the personification and deification of Fortune, so prevalent during this period.

The goddess is frequently depicted with a wheel and sphere, images of her instability. It is not rare, however, for her to be portrayed wearing symbols of royalty. Pisan crowns her with a diadem. Jean Fouquet's frontispiece for *L'Estrif de Vertu et de Fortune* gives a crown and scepter to the latter figure. In Shakespeare's *Timon of Athens*, the poet says that "I have upon a high and pleasant hill / Feign'd Fortune to be thron'd." "With her ivory hand" she indicates her chosen favorites[149] (*Timon of Athens* I. i. 62–63; 70). An anonymous morality play of 1600, performed in London before the court, features Fortune atop a chariot drawn by kings.[150] Another frequently emphasized characteristic of the goddess is her disconcerting ambiguity. In Cesare Ripa's *Iconologia*, a manual that gathers together the majority of all existing Renaissance emblems, one may read: "One represents Fate [here equivalent to Fortune] as a bizarre woman, dressed in dark-colored robes, holding a golden crown in her right hand with a purse full of money, and in her left a rope" (for hanging humans).[151]

Borrowing several details from the *Roman de Fauvel*, Christine de Pisan had already stressed the two simultaneous faces of Fortune. The diadem placed on her head is adorned with jewels on one side, on the other with spikes and blades; her right hand holds a crown, her left a sword; one of her feet is in water, the other in fire; her palace presents two beautiful façades and two other blackened and ruined ones. Elaborating this theme, the Benedictine John Lydgate—who introduced the *danse macabre* to England—specifies that Fortune's cellar contains two types of barrels, some filled with sugar and spices and the others with gall.[152] Regarding Fortune's two-faced hypocrisy, writers and artists were inexhaustible. An engraving by Hans Burgkmair presents her with two heads. She sits on a throne, with one hand turning a wheel and the other dismissing people who fall into two blankets held respectively by humans and demons.[153] In its turn, a drawing in Jean Cousin's *Livre de Fortune* (1568) denounces the duplicity of the goddess. On the right side, she is lovely and luminous; her hand touches a young man who plays the lute and symbolizes happiness. On the left, she is dark and ugly, and her companion is a sick and hooded character who represents misery.[154] In the same spirit, the English writer Robert Greene (d. 1592) introduces an old man who owns an image of Fortune. She rests one foot on a fish with ever-changing reflections and her other on a chameleon. The inconstancy of the goddess continues to be expressed by the either multicolored or shifting mantle she wears in successive works by Fouquet (the illumination for *L'Estrif* . . .), Lydgate, and Robert White (*The Masque of Cupid's Banishment*, early seventeenth century).[155]

The Renaissance seems to have invented the association of Fortune and the ship whose sail is filled by a sometimes favorable and sometimes uncontrollable wind (at least since the classical statues of "Venus Marina" were not images of Fortune as such.[156] In any case, a long list of symbols served to clarify the capricious and inscrutable character of the formidable goddess. Giovanni Bellini shows her holding a globe; but it is a ball of glass. This idea is reused by a German painting of about 1530 now in Strasbourg. Budé, expressing not his own opinion but that of the masses, describes Fortune as a "player of dice, blind and deaf."[157] She is the classical *caeca Fortuna*, whose bandaged eyes henceforth suggest Night, the Synagogue, Infidelity, and Love.[158] Such is the teaching of Pierre Michault in *La Danse aux aveugles*: "Love, Fortune, and Death, blind and bandaged, / Each in turn make humans dance to their music." "Blind Fortune" intervenes in both *The Merchant of Venice* and *Coriolanus*.[159] In the Palazzo Ducale of Venice, Veronese places in one of her hands the emblems of state power and in the other a die. Finally—but is the list at an end?—Fortune is quite often confused with *Occasio*—opportunity, which demands hasty capture. In this case, her head is bald in back and only has hair in front. Boiardo (d. 1494), who in the *Orlando Innamorato* fuses the fairy Morgana, *Occasio*, and *Fortuna* into a single character, specifies how this composite goddess is quick to flee, having no hair in back and a dress that escapes those trying to clutch her.[160]

These accumulated symbols evoke a mysterious force, most often seen as disturbing. Hence the people of the Middle Ages and Renaissance more and more frequently associated Fortune with devouring Time (with a correspondence between her wheel and the successive ages of life), with the sinister and malevolent moon, with Death, Love, and Hypocrisy. Nonetheless, certain positive affirmations at least partially refuted this pessimism. One assertion as much Stoic as Christian is that virtue is stronger than chance. Poliziano pronounces anyone happy who looks at Fortune's frowning eyebrows without flinching, who placidly faces the rage of her storms and does not complain of the setbacks he suffers. Sure of himself and calm, "not only is he not governed by chance, but it is she who obeys him."[161]

Such an argument may seem primarily a defensive one. In its moments of optimism, however, the Renaissance went much farther, exalting human possibilities and disparaging all that seemed to obstruct free will. In this regard, there comes to mind Gianozzo Manetti's famous *De Dignitate et excellentia hominis* (1452), a work that sought to refute the *contemptus mundi* doctrine. It includes this rousing enumeration: "Because men have accomplished them, all the houses are ours, all the strongholds, all the cities and all the buildings on earth . . . Ours the paintings, the sculptures, ours the arts and sciences, etc."[162] Pico della Mirandola would soon resume this praise in both his *Oratio de dignitate hominis* (1486) and his *Disputationes adversus astrologos* (after 1492). In the second of these treatises, he exclaims: "The wonders of the spirit are greater than those of heaven. On earth there is nothing greater than man; and in man there is nothing greater than his spirit and his soul. When you raise them to their full height, you climb above the heavens."[163] As for the *Oratio de dignitate*, it shows that, alone here below, man is conditioned neither by space nor an essential being (nor of course, by Fortune). He creates himself by his activity and as a result dominates nature. He is the child of his works and of liberty.

In his *De Sapiente* (1509), the French Platonist Charles de Bovelles echoes Pico's theses on man's central position and on his exceptional prerogatives, though he stresses knowledge (*sapientia*) as the means to liberation.[164] Hence the book's engraved frontispiece, which illustrates Fortune face to face with Wisdom. The former is on the left, crowned, blindfolded, holding a wheel to which men cling in vain, and the latter is on the right, without a diadem, holding a mirror of wisdom. Significantly, Fortune sits on a moving globe and Wisdom on a square, solid chair. In a medallion, a fool proclaims: "[Fortune], we have made you a goddess and placed you in the heavens." A "wise man" answers him: "Trust yourself to Virtue. Fortune flees more quickly than a wave."[165] Elsewhere in the book the author develops this iconographic lesson with such phrases as "The wise man learns to tread on the feet of Fortune and not to hold her in awe,"[166] and "The wise are not exposed to Fortune's unstable wheel; they are above the vicissitudes of the times; they ceaselessly endure, with a safe, entire, and inviolate soul."[167] In this same line of thought that issues from Manetti and Pico, there should be placed an affirmation of Jean Bodin: "Human history derives from human will, which is always diverse and whose limits are unforeseeable. In fact, each day new laws, new customs, and new institutions are born."[168] Man is great because he is free.

This confident type of discourse, however, is quite rare during the period, and it is revealing that eminent humanists such as Leon Battista Alberti and Marsilio Ficino anxiously contemplated the relations between Fortune and liberty. Alberti opens his *Libri della famiglia* with a prologue that poses the question of Fortune's power. He writes that before the abundant reversals of situations that history offers:

> *I often sadly wonder if iniquitous and malignant Fortune is now so powerful over men that it might be possible for her to attack, with inconstancy and audacity, families rich in virtuous men, in fine and precious belongings desired by mortals, families possessed of great dignity, fame, praises, authority, and grace, that she might deprive them of all happiness, and reduce them to poverty, solitude, and misery.*[169]

Not satisfied with composing this reflection that explains why he is writing a treatise on the necessary family virtues, Alberti will later devote an entire dialogue to the theme of *Fatum et Fortuna*, "one of the most profound works of all ethical literature."[170] On the same subject, Ficino writes a letter in response to a request from the Florentine banker Giovanni Rucellai. At the beginning of this text, the Florentine philospher does not hide his embarrassment: "You ask me if man can divert his future or at least prepare some remedy for future things, especially for those that are called fortuitous. On such a matter my spirit, without a doubt, is divided between contrary opinions."[171] Still, these preliminary hesitations do not prevent these two authors from taking optimistic views of man's chances of controlling Fortune. After a rapid glance at ancient history and contemporary Italy, Alberti declares, in words anticipating those of Machiavelli,

> . . . *To acquire, increase, maintain, and conserve majesty and glory . . . Fortune is never worth as much as a good and saintly discipline of life . . . Contrary to the belief of certain fools, it is not within Fortune's power to easily vanquish those who do not wish to be vanquished. Fortune only conducts the game of those who submit to her . . . Families rarely fall into unhappiness* [treating here of political and economic decadence] *for any other reason than a lack of prudence and diligence . . . Fortune only wrecks and drowns beneath her enormous waves* [note nonetheless this allusion to her power] *those families who neglect themselves.*[172]

Elsewhere in his work, Alberti makes similar calls to the victorious battle with fate, notably in a line too often quoted out of context: "Have no doubts: by herself, Fortune has always been and will always be extremely weak and feeble when confronted with strong human opposition."[173] This observation therefore lies at the heart of the great Renaissance debate over the respective powers of Virtue and Fate, the former being understood primarily in the Italian sense of Virtù, a mixture of courage and intelligence. In his letter to Rucellai, Ficino recalls Alberti in teaching that "the prudent man has power over Fortune."[174]

It thus becomes necessary to fight this mysterious force. In chapter 25 of *The Prince*, Machiavelli gives this advice with the deepest conviction and the most striking analogies: "So with Fortune, who exerts all her power where there is no strength [virtù] prepared to oppose her . . . it is better to be rash than timid, for Fortune is a woman, and the man who wants to hold her down must beat and bully her."[175] Machiavelli thus vividly reuses the old adage that Fortune favors the audacious, a notion found in both the *Roman de Renart* ("Fortune assists the bold"[176] and the *Roman du Jouvencel* (fifteenth century): "They say that Fortune helps the daring man."[177]

Audacity, however, does not consist only in violating Destiny. It is equally the art of seizing the opportunities that Fortune offers. As Ficino aptly tells Rucellai, "One does best to make peace or a treaty with her, adapting our will to hers, and to go where she directs, in such a way that she need not drag us by force."[178] The Florentine banker did indeed act in this spirit, notably in marrying his son Bernardo to Nannina, the daughter of Piero de' Medici. For the façade of his palace in Florence, he commissioned a sculpted coat of arms containing *Fortuna Occasio* holding the sail of her ship and steering it toward a happy landing. He also ordered an engraving of a boat, wherein his son Bernardo appears as the mast and supports a sail billowing with favorable winds. Nannina is at the tiller and a caption explains: "I let Fortune carry me, with the hope of a happy outcome."[179] To sum up, the Renaissance, in its euphoric moments, clearly declared man to be stronger than Destiny, or it at least taught that Fortune "loves the mad, the foolhardy, the bold and courageous men, those who say as Caesar did in crossing the Rubicon: the die is cast."[180] Under favorable conditions, the Renaissance could believe that "Fortune governs half of our actions, but that even so she leaves the other half more or less, in our power to control," to quote Machiavelli's famous calculation.[181] People do have the chance to play a winning game.

Nevertheless, this idea was far from being the prevailing one. How else could astrology have held its place among the preoccupations of the time? To be sure, official theology continued to affirm with Saint Thomas Aquinas that "it is impossible for heavenly bodies to make a direct impression on the intellect and will; for this would be to deny the difference between intellect and sense" (*Summa Theologica* IIa–IIae, question 95, article 5; trans. by the Dominican Fathers, London, 1922, vol. 11, p. 202). For their part, the handbooks of the magic arts constantly repeated Ptolemy's formula, "The wise man will conquer the stars." The Neoplatonists and Ficino (in his *De Triplici Vita*) exalted the greatness of man, this speck of dust, who can, if he so wills, become the master and lord of a world that resembles him, of which he himself is the epitome.[182] As for the astrologers, convinced of their knowledge of the habits of the stars, the zodiac, climates, and planetary influences, they strove by prayers, rites, and talismans to oppose "cunning to strength (that of the stars), exorcism to menaces, craftiness to traps."[183] This attitude therefore parallels the one in favor of following the bias of Fortune.

All these more or less significant concessions to liberty should not conceal another reality, in other words the proliferation of images and writings devoted to the activity of the stars. During the Renaissance, astrological practice was common to both princely courts and the population at large.[184] Paintings, sculptures, tapestries, engravings, illumination, calendars, medals, books (even prayerbooks), carved and painted chests, costumes, and playing cards all attest to this enormous interest in the power of the stars and planets—an interest that contained a good deal of fear. The planets, it was believed, govern the liberal arts, the continents, empires, and individual temperaments. One reads in the 1529 Troyes edition of the *Grand Kalendrier . . . des bergiers*: "He who is born under the sign of Scorpio . . . will be a great fornicator." From the age of fifteen, "he will be bold as a lion, and lovely of form."[185] Many believed that syphilis had appeared in Europe as a result of a conjunction of Saturn and Jupiter on November 9, 1494.[186] A great flood was feared for 1524, since multiple conjunctions were due to occur that year in the water signs.[187] If the people of the fifteenth and sixteenth centuries continually sought answers from horoscopes and predictions and continually sought advice from astrologers, they did so because they judged that the stars gave them only a narrow space in which to operate.

This summary of the importance accorded to astrology enhances an understanding of the corrections that even the "optimists" of the Renaissance brought to their statements on the subject of Fortune. For example, in Zurara's *Cróñica dos feitos de Guiné*, there appears significant hesitation regarding the death of Captain Gonçalo de Sintra:

> *It seems to me that a great mystery is hidden beneath [this] event . . . The peril was so manifest . . . that, in this case, it could have been avoided, had this captain wished to heed counsel; but I willingly say that the celestial spheres had thus ordered things and that Fortune had blinded his reason to the extent that he could not foresee his misery. Even though Saint Augustine wrote many holy words that reject predestination and heavenly influences, it seems possible to discover authorities who maintain the contrary: for example, Job, when he says that God has imposed on us a limit that we cannot cross, and many other passages of Holy Scripture.*[188]

For his part, however much Alberti celebrates the *Virtù* that gives glory and prosperity to courageous and diligent families and nations, he nonetheless concedes that it cannot do everything. He cannot deny the role of Fortune in military affairs. Likewise, literary careers are subject to a thousand of her "assaults." Alberti, who belonged to a family of "merchants," also has words to say about great international trading concerns: When wool is shipped from Flanders to Florence, "is it beyond the reach of Fortune's arms?" How many perils, rivers, and difficulties there are to cross before it reaches safe harbor! "Thieves, tyrants, wars, the negligence and vices of middlemen, hazards of every kind are ever at hand."[189] The dialogue of *Fatum et Fortuna* is still more melancholic. The aged Theogenio, who expresses Alberti's outlook, curiously reiterates the traditional themes of the *contemptus mundi* on human misery from birth to death,[190] and for good measure specifies that "man is worse for man than all other calamities."[191] In such a context, Fortune is presented as a malevolent force. One can escape her power only by not expecting anything of her:

> *I recall having verified for myself and others a nearly infinite number of examples that have taught me not to trust myself to Fortune and not to owe her any obligation.*
>
> *I know her instability and perfidy and I conclude that he who wishes to have neither a liaison nor commerce with her cannot suffer any harm from her. The order of things, her frequent deceptions, the constant experience I have had of her mutability and inconstancy serve as my guides.*[192]

If one now returns, in its full context, to the conclusion of Ficino's letter to Rucellai, one finds more resignation than optimism. The final statement is the following:

> *One does well to fight Fortune with the weapons of prudence, patience, and greatness of spirit. One does still better to retreat from such a war and flee her, because men rarely emerge as victors and those who do succeed pay the price of wilting fatigue and a great deal of sweat. One does best of all to make peace or a treaty with her, adapting one's will to hers, and to go where she leads, in such a way that she need not drag us there by force. We will accomplish all that, if we know how to orchestrate our will, strength, and wisdom.*[193]

This ultimately ambiguous text thus concedes much to Fortune. As for Machiavelli's position on this subject, it is not expressed only in chapter 25 of *The Prince*, which too often has been exclusively excerpted. He returned to the same theme on many occasions, in particular in the *Capitoli* on "Occasio" and "Fortuna," and in several chapters of the *Discorsi*. Certainly Machiavelli never varied on certain key points: It is necessary to seize opportunity and "to adjust to circumstances."[194] Fortune "loves and chooses those who attack her, and unsettle her, who ceaselessly stay close on her heels."[195] Finally, fate "can do nothing to great men" who are "impervious to its blows"[196]: a hardly original Stoic proposition. On the other hand, the Florentine writer used adages that partially run against the affirmation that Fortune lets us govern nearly half of our efforts:

> *She overturns states and kingdoms from top to bottom, just as she pleases, and she snatches from just men the blessings she bestows on perverse men.*
>
> *This inconstant goddess, this mobile divinity often places unworthy men on thrones where deserving men never arrive.*
>
> *She uses her time as she wishes; she lifts us up, she throws us down without pity, without law and without reason.*[197]

> *Men who habitually live in great prosperity or in great misery merit less praise or blame than one thinks. Most of the time, one may see them thrown into ruin or greatness with an irresistible ease that heaven grants them, whether it takes from*

> *them, or offers them the chance to employ their Virtù*. Such is the way of Fortune: when she wants a great project to go well, she chooses a man of spirit and *Virtù*, such that he will be able to recognize the opportunity thus offered. Similarly, when she prepares the devastation of an empire, she gives leadership to men incapable of stopping the decline. If someone exists who would be strong enough to stop the fall, she has him eliminated or denies him all means of doing something useful.[198]

In this text, which extensively yields to an exterior determinism, *Virtù* plays only a supporting role to a capricious, unfathomable, and irresistible Necessity.

Most often, Renaissance culture feared Fortune, the evil goddess whom it is better to avoid than confront. Such is the lesson given by the paving of the cathedral of Siena (based on a cartoon by Pinturicchio, 1504–06): There one beholds the nude deceitful woman, holding a billowing sail, with one foot on a fateful ball, the other on a ship. A crowd of wise men turn away from a force that gives and removes the blessings of this world.[199] Many similar works make it clear that there was a common belief in Fortune's power during the sixteenth century. Budé asserts that Destiny, "at one time raised to heaven by human error," is "even today generally held to direct the highest as well as the most trivial affairs, and all those in between."[200] Calvin identifies the same reality and notes: "Concerning things that occur every day beyond order and natural process, the majority, and *quasi tous* imagine that Fortune's wheel turns and jostles men to and fro."[201] Machiavelli adds a precise clarification: In his view, the negation of free choice has won out during his period. In fact, he writes: "This opinion (that it is useless to sweat over mastering events, instead of letting them be governed by chance) has gained credit in our time due to the great revolutions we have seen and do see at all times"[202] This growing trend surely parallels that of faith in astrology. In any case, many proverbs attest to the collective regard for a simultaneously powerful, shifting, and malevolent Fortune: "Fortune quickly sets a man on high. Then she quickly throws him from the sky."[203] "Fortune changes like the moon. Bright today, but dark quite soon."[204] "Blind is Fortune, blind her followers."[205] "Against Fortune, strength there is none."[206] "Against Fortune the changing, every cart goes backward ranging."[207] "In Fortune no reason,"[208] and so on. Even Montaigne stressed "the inconstancy of the varying swings of fortune."[209] He cites and apparently reuses in his own way these disillusioned lines by Manilius:

> *The ill-advised may win; the wise may lose;*
> *Fortune cares not what cause prevails, or whose,*
> *But wanders in our midst, unheeding, free.*
> *Something beyond, whatever it may be,*
> *Commands and rules, and bends us to its laws*.[210]

Montaigne concludes that "events and outcomes depend for the most part, especially in war, on Fortune, who will not fall into line and subject herself to our reason and foresight." On the contrary, "she involves our reason also in her confusion and uncertainty."[211]

Human weakness in the face of destiny: Even more than Montaigne, contemporary Italian historians, such as Machiavelli, taught this lesson regarding the misfortunes of the peninsula from 1494 and throughout the first half of the sixteenth century. Italy's impotence, the coming and going of foreign armies across her territory, and the sack of Rome all aggravated the pessimism of saddened observers writing between 1530 and 1540.[212] In a still-unpublished *History of the Italian Wars* (in Latin), Girolamo Borgia announces in the introduction that he will describe ". . . the events of this changing epoch and the variations of Fortune." The prologue to Book 3 then specifies:

> *And if we see the changes of Fortune contained in every individual life, they are nowhere more evident than in the condition of states that undergo the inconstancy of things; how fragile are these kingdoms that foolish mortals so much admire and covet with so much energy . . . in a single state, the sovereignty changes five times in the space of three years. To those whom she will raise on high, Fortune will just as quickly show an undeniable tragedy.*[213]

Against such a force, *Virtù* cannot be of much use. The Florentine Francesco Vettori says as much in his *Summary of the History of Italy from 1511 to 1527*,[214] in which he frequently declares that "all human actions are subject to Fortune" and that she is constantly changing.[215] Taking the gonfaloniere Piero Soderini as his example, the author confirms that he was "good, intelligent, competent, and never let ambition and greed carry him outside of justice." He was the victim, however, of "bad Fortune (not his own as much as that of his unhappy city)."[216] Vettori also sees the case of the two Medici popes (Leo X and Clement VII) as conclusive. The first commits fault upon fault but "the more errors he made, the more Fortune favored him."[217] Conversely, Clement VII—the Pope of the sack of Rome—who had been a well-reputed cardinal, became "a poorly esteemed little pope," despite his good qualities. It was "Fortune who, after having given the French their victory at Ravenna, changed from being their tender mother to a cruel shrew, and did the same to Clement."[218]

In his great *Storia d'Italia*, Guicciardini is much harder than Vettori on Soderini, Clement VII, and on all his contemporaries, Charles V included. Nonetheless, the failings and weakness of leaders and peoples do not comprise for him the main reason for the peninsula's collapse, which was above all caused by Fortune. From the beginning of the work, he signals that "innumerable examples will clearly show to what degree of instability human things are subject, like a sea stirred up by the winds" and that rulers do themselves and their people a great worry to "forget the frequent variations of Fortune."[219] The classic expression of "the wheel of Fortune" naturally reappears many times in his work.[220] Historian Felix Gilbert writes that "the references to the power and influence of Fortuna are so frequent that it is evident that Guicciardini indeed meant to carry out the intention which he stated in the first chapter of the first book: to demonstrate the " '*spesse variazioni della fortuna.*' "[221] In other works, moreover, Guicciardini was still more categorical: "Even children, even the illiterate know that prosperity does not last and that Fortune changes." And again: "Neither fools nor wise men can finally avoid that which must happen. I have never read any saying that appears more apt than this: "*Ducunt volentes fata, nolentes trahunt*"[222] ("Destiny leads those who accept it and drags along those who don't").

Man's powerlessness before destiny, the absurdity of his fate: Such is the frequent affirmation of many characters from the late English Renaissance theater. Their opinions are not necessarily those of the authors. Yet they express—and this is what matters—an attitude widely held by mainstream culture. In Shakespeare's plays, Fortune, with her wheel and blindfold, is called "blind . . . turning, and inconstant" (*Henry V* III. vi. 29; 35–36).[223] She is described as "that arrant whore" (*King Lear* II. iv. 52),[224] as a "false housewife" (*Antony and Cleopatra* IV. xiii. 43),[225] "in her shift and change of mood" (*Timon of Athens* I. i. 85).[226] In the context of this study, these remarks appear to be clichés. Yet even their banality is significant.

Still more revealing are the complaints in the plays of Shakespeare's contemporaries, made by characters who seem to have thrown Christianity overboard. In Marston's *Antonio and Mellida*, Andrugio's disenchantment is complete: He states that "Philosophie maintaines that Natur's wise, / And formes no useless or imperfect thing . . . Goe to, goe to; thou liest, Philosophy. / Nature formes things unperfect, uselesse, vaine."[227] The "Paduan" Rinaldo in Chapman's *All Fools* declares:

Fortune, the great commandress of the world,
Hath divers ways to advance her followers.
To some she gives honor without deserving,
To other some, deserving without honor,
Some wit, some wealth, and some wit without wealth,
Some wealth without wit, some, nor wit nor wealth
But good smock-faces, or some qualities
By nature without judgment, with the which
They live in sensual acceptation,
And make show only, without touch of substance.[228]

In *Bussy d'Ambois*, another Chapman character, Monsieur, is more emphatic:

Now shall we see, that Nature hath no end
In her great works, responsive to their worths,
That she who makes so many eyes, and souls,
To see and foresee, is stark blind herself:
And as illiterate men say Latin prayers
By rote of heart, and daily iteration;
In whose hot zeal, a man would think they knew
What they ran so away with, and were sure
To have rewards proportion'd to their labors;
Yet may implore their own confusions
For anything they know, which oftentimes
It falls out they incur: so Nature lays
A mass of stuff together, and by use,
Or by the mere necessity of matter,
Ends such a work, fills it, or leaves it empty
Of strength, or virtue, error or clear truth;
Not knowing what she does.[229]

In the same spirit, Bussy opens the play by proclaiming that "Fortune, not Reason, rules the state of things."[230]

History needs to be the domain of nuances and not of systematization. From the preceding argument, it would be wrong to conclude that the entire era wallowed in pessimism; this would be an absurd generalization. All the same, this thorough dossier clearly demonstrates that there existed a widespread belief in a mysterious force far stronger than human liberty and more inclined to oppose than to favor it. During the Renaissance, Fortune was depicted as malevolent rather than benevolent. She was more often the "fortune of the sea," in other words the disturbing hazards of navigation, than fortune in our present sense of the accumulation of wealth. A rapid but significant quantification: Of fourteen representations of Fortune (or of "Occasio") taken from a survey of five emblem books published in Francefrom 1539 to 1588, none are positive[231]; nine are explicitly negative and five reflect on the instability of fate. The *Théâtre des bons engins* flatly reproaches "men blinded and misled by Fortune" and invites them to examine "how badly she leads you, / Toward stumbling into a narrow trap, / An abyss of evils and calamity."[232] In the *Hecatomgraphie*, Fortune answers the man who inquires after her attributes (broken mast, the sea, sail, ball, and dolphin beneath her feet):

> *They are to show my instability,*
> *That in me there is no security . . .*
> *Thus I am only at sea by chance.*
>
> *Thus my portrait-painter*
> *Wishes to express nothing else*
> *Than that mistrust swirls all around me.*[233]

At a deeper level, Fortune represented one of the aspects of the myth of the "dangerous woman."[234] As such, popular imagination associated her with the pallid and disturbing moon, with the turbulent waters that swallow things up, with the Fates who cut the thread of life. As well as this revival of a mainly pagan conception, however, there must be noted the Protestant notion of predestination. In his *on the Bondage of the Will*, Luther argues in bitingly epigrammatic style that

> *human will finds itself placed between God and Satan, and lets itself be led or pushed around like a horse. If God leads the will, it goes where God wills and where He wills, as Psalm 73:22 says: "I am for you a stupid animal." If Satan lays hold of the will, it goes where and how he wills. Hence, under these conditions human will is not free to choose a master; the two knights fight and contest over the possession of the will.*[235]

By two converging invitations, each widely diffused, the people of the Renaissance were thus led to doubt their free will. Hence the necessity of questioning the image of Prometheus that has been used too hastily to characterize the Renaissance.

MELANCHOLY

Sadness and the Renaissance: These two terms would seem mutually exclusive. Nonetheless, they were often close traveling companions.

It would be only natural that the contemporaries of the Black Death,[236] the Great Schism, and the Hundred Years' War were filled with melancholy. Huizinga based *The Waning of the Middle Ages* on the evident importance of this "general anxiety"[237] (at least at the level of written culture). Eustache Deschamps, who defined himself as a "melancholic man,"[238] claims that "All hearts have been seized / With sadness and melancholy."[239] Later in the fifteenth century, French and Burgundian poets and chroniclers continue in their dark depression. Jean Meschinot portrays himself as a "sad heart, feeble and vain," and admits: "Tears forever in my eyes / I see nothing but death and dying."[240] In his turn, Georges Chastellain presents himself as a "sorrowful man, born in eclipses of shadows, in dark spaces of lamentation."[241] His successor at the court of Burgundy chooses for his emblem: "La Marche has suffered so very much."[242] The duke himself, Philip the Good, regrets his life: Learning of the death of his one-year-old son, he cries out that "if it had pleased God that I had died so young, I would count myself happy."[243] The poetry of

Charles d'Orléans (d. 1465) and of René d'Anjou (d. 1480) is also dominated by "coldness" and "melancholy."[244] King René calls Sorrow his "next of kin."

Huizinga, citing certain of these avowals, opposes them to the humanist optimism of the early sixteenth century. Indeed!? Is the break between one epoch and another so clean? On the contrary, a great many historians and critics now confirm Europe's immense interest in melancholy during the years 1480 to 1650. Between these undoubtedly approximate dates, a vast panorama extends from Ficino to Burton.[245] At the center of this landscape, clearly, stand the black sun and gloomy angel of Dürer's *Melancolia I*. Other artists, however, also handled this theme: Among the most notable are Lucas Cranach the Elder's *Melancholia*, Cornelius Antonisz's *Melancolia*, the works of Matthias Gerung and those of Maerten van Heemskerck, Thomas de Leu's *Melancolicus*, a last *Melancolia* of Giovanni Bellini, and so on. An entire epoch thus devoted an inquiry to the nature and consequences of sorrow, from inquisitors to doctors through philosophers, artists, and poets. Saint Teresa commits an entire chapter of her *Foundations* to the question of "how Mother Superiors should treat melancholy nuns."[246] Hamlet is the epitome of the melancholic character.[247] The Spanish doctor Andres Velasquez published a *Libro de la Melancolia* (1585), and his compatriot Luis Mercado composed a similar treatise (1604). The famous doctor Alonso de Santa Cruz also edited (before 1613) a book entitled *De Melancholia*.[248] The work of André Du Laurens, doctor of Henri IV, *Discours de la conservation de la veue; des maladies melancholiques; des catharres et de la vieillesse* (1597), went through ten French editions until 1626, without counting various translations.[249] The success of Robert Burton's monumental treatise, *The Anatomy of Melancholy* (1621), is even more revealing: English readers so avidly read this book that it went through five editions before the author's death in 1640.[250] Starobinski aptly writes that "the Renaissance is the golden age of melancholy."[251]

The discourse on melancholy was another way of remembering the limits on free will—limits imposed by both the humors and planetary influences. From distant antiquity to the eighteenth century, an extended sorrow was considered to derive from a corrupt humor.[252] Hippocrates and Galen had clearly given this explanation, which was repeated an elaborated over the ages, notably by Constantinus Africanus (d. 1087), the first to revive the study of Greek medicine in Italy. In this regard, his *De Melancholia* comprised the link between ancient science and the medicine of the Renaissance. Along with Fernel,[253] Paré,[254] Bright,[255] Du Laurens, Burton, and so on, Africanus only slightly modifies the theory of the four humors, which are respectively blood, phlegm or mucus, choler or yellow bile, and the humor of melancholy—this term was derived from the Greek, meaning precisely "black bile."

In practice, the word "blood" has two meanings. Following Galen, Paré explains this duality with an analogy to new wine, where one can detect four different bodies: the dregs, at the bottom, are equivalent to black bile; the flowers at the surface of the juice represent choler, "the thinnest of the humors"; the greenness, or water content, resembles "phlegm"; finally, the wine itself, "fine, sweet, and pleasant," is like blood in the strict sense. Therefore, the blood that circulates through the veins and arteries is impure. It contains the three other humors in variable quantities, which nevertheless should not reach too high a level. Phlegm, being no more than "imperfect blood," should normally change into "good blood" by "our natural warmth." Yellow choler is progressively "drawn out by the gall-bladder," and melancholic humor by the spleen, an organ of dark color supposed to be the seat of black bile. Hence the table given by Paré,[256] with reference to the four traditional elements (air, water, fire, and earth).

Paré notes that "a certain quantity and proportion of these humors (of the blood in the general sense) being maintained, it gives health to the body: But if it becomes

HUMOR	ELEMENT/ NATURE	CONSISTENCY	COLOR/ COMPLEXION	FLAVOR	FUNCTION
Sanguine (blood)	Air: warm and moist, temperate	Medium, neither too thick nor too clear	Red and ruddy	Sweet	It primarily nourishes the muscles, is distributed through the veins and arteries, and brings warmth to the body.
Phlegmatic (phlegm)	Water: cold and moist	Variable	White	Sweet or sometimes flat: good water has no flavor	It nourishes the brain as well as the other cold and moist parts, tempers the blood, and helps to move the limbs and joints.
Choleric (yellow bile)	Fire: hot and dry	Thin and steady	Yellow or pallid	Bitter	It stimulates the expelling operation of the intestines and dilutes the phlegm inside them, for excremental as well as alimentary purposes. It nourishes the parts that are most like its own element.
Melancholic (black bile)	Earth: cold and dry	Sluggish, thick, and muddy	Black	Sharp and acid	It stimulates the appetite, nourishes the spleen and every other part of its own nature and temperature, such as the bones.

corrupted, it can bring on disease." In the right measure, "melancholy" is thus indispensable. If, however, it prevails in the organism, this imbalance of elements works to our detriment. Taking into account the correspondences then recognized between the humors on the one hand and the four elements on the other, the direction of the winds, the ages of life, the seasons of the year, and even the moments of the day, a system for the four major human temperaments and their predominant humors was established with great coherence:

1. The sanguine temperament, regarded as "the most perfect," corresponds to air, to Zephyr (the gentle and mild west wind), to springtime and youth. Its principal hours are between three and nine in the morning.
2. The phlegmatic temperament corresponds to water, to Auster (the rain-bringing south wind), to winter and old age. Its dominant hours are between nine in the evening and three in the morning.
3. The "choleric" temperament corresponds to fire, to Eurus (the hot and dry east wind), to summer and the time of maturity. Its most active period is between nine in the morning and three in the afternoon.
4. The melancholic temperament corresponds to earth, to the north wind (Boreas), to autumn, to "middle and first old age." In the day, its privileged hours are between three in the afternoon and nine in the evening. The Dutch doctor Lemnius explains that then "the liver purges itself, and throws out its scum, and all its excrement, which is then sent to the spleen: which entails that during the said hours a man's understanding is clouded, and with a thick black smoke, his spirit becomes downcast and vexed."[257]

While sanguine and choleric men have health, dynamism, and gaiety, phlegmatic and melancholic people share serious defects: The former are "sleepy, lazy, and fat, and white hairs come to them too soon," and the latter—again in Paré's words—are "sad, annoying, rigid, severe, and rude, envious, and timid."

As a malady, melancholy can be provoked either by the generative causes of a black humor or by a malfunctioning of one of the abdominal organs that together form "the hypochondrium": spleen, liver, gall bladder, bladder, uterus, and so on. This dysfunction then creates "that kind of madness which we properly call hypochondriac melancholy."[258] The main agent of this disorder, however, is the spleen, whose role is to absorb excessive black bile from the blood and liver. The spleen uses the richest part to nourish itself, releases a certain quantity into the stomach to stimulate the appetite, and then excretes the rest. If, however, through weakness or obstruction, it has not pumped melancholy out of the blood, it can then corrupt the entire body. Moreover, a spleen overcharged with black bile lets this escape and corrupts itself. Hot "vapors" ensue, comparable to those emitted by boiling water. These vapors then spread through the entire body.[259] In passing, it is noteworthy that traditional Chinese medicine established links between the spleen, earth, and morbid sorrow, and that contemporary energizing acupuncture maintains and employs this scheme.

For the Western doctor of the Renaissance, however, there existed a "melancholic matter": a thick fluid, a black and sticky tar, circulating slowly, whose excess needs to be removed from the body. If not corrected, this excess will make the individual heavy and sluggish and darken his or her spirit. Hence the importance of purgatives, notably hellbore, in the treatment of melancholy. The "*evacuatives*" have the effect of purging the corrupt humor. To them must be added "*alteratives*, that dilute, sweeten, and moisten the deposits of black bile, though without mobilizing them," and also "*comfortatives*, whose cordial and strengthening virtues give joy and vigor to the patient."[260] Thus melancholy is essentially an illness of the abdominal area, where black bile accumulates and from where toxic emissions travel to the brain. These vapors sometimes exit through the patient's mouth and therefore spread contagion. In this regard, a German stayed home during Holy Week to perform his devotion, because he feared the excessive quantity of "melancholic vapors exhaled by the crowd of contrite worshippers."[261]

This connection between contrition and melancholic vapors implies an alternative movement, from high to low, with the excess of black fluid thus resulting from a psychological process. Paré clearly identifies these two causes of melancholy, whose humor, he writes, "is made with heavily juiced and hard-to-cook food, and also with troubles and vexations of the spirit."[262] Likewise, Burton corroborates that "the body's mischiefs, as Plato proves, proceed from the soul," and he notes how Galen "brags, *1. I. de san. tuend.* that he for his part hath cured divers of this infirmity [melancholy] *solum animis ad rectum institutis*, by right setting alone of their minds."[263] Furthermore, theologians sustained an analysis inclined to perceive the activity of demons who sought to lead pious souls away from the divine service and into deep sadness.[264] Therefore the cure for melancholy could not be achieved only by means of a healthy diet and judicious purgations (in this regard coitus could not be neglected). The cure also came from the use of a diverse panoply of psychologically oriented methods: a balanced schedule of work and rest, of waking and sleeping, the enjoyment of music, smooth and light wines, fragrant perfumes, pleasing colors (Du Laurens recommends red, green, yellow, and white), merry tales, festive groups who will prevent the neurotic patient from remaining alone; but also the use of rough treatment, abuse, indeed more rigorous methods such as the whip or dungeon[265] supposed to act as "moral revulsion."

Among the actions operating from high to low, and in line with the many correspondences made since antiquity and notably reactivated by humanism, the planetary influences rank high. The Renaissance did not question the consonance between the sanguine temperament and Jupiter (and very often Venus), the choleric temperament and Mars, the phlegmatic temperament and the moon, the melancholic temperament and Saturn.[266] The least noble of the humors was thus governed by this redoubtable star, which took on the personality of the pagan divinity. He is certainly the highest of the planets, the oldest of the Olympians, the ancient king of the golden age. Yet he is also a dry and icy planet, the dethroned father of the gods, castrated and imprisoned in the bowels of the earth. Collective mentality thus associated him with old age and incapacity, with worries, suffering, and death.

In the *Picatrix*, a highly popular manual of magic and astrology, Saturn is described as "cold, sterile, gloomy, and pernicious." He is not only "wise and solitary," but he also "has more cares than anyone" and "knows neither pleasure nor joy." He may grant his children—those who are born under his sign—power and fortune, but at the price of generosity. If he gives them wisdom, it also costs them their happiness. Those who are under his influence, however, are most often poor peasants, cutters of stone or wood (Saturn had been the god of the earth), cleaners of latrines, ditchdiggers, beggars, or criminals. Such figures appear as his "children" in a German miniature of the fifteenth century that notably includes two melancholics in the upper corners and a hanged man at the center of the illustration.[267] In the Wolfegg *Hausbuch* (late fifteenth century), which devotes a page to each of the major stars, the "children" of Saturn are, apart from laborers, a condemned man being led to the gibbet, a knacker cutting up a horse, and a witch next to a cave where two prisoners have their hands and feet bound to an iron collar.[268] A

Lombard manuscript of the same period, *De Sphaera*, evokes in its turn the planets that preside at birth, govern temperaments, and cause sickness. Saturn is portrayed as thickly hirsute and bearded. He leans on a crutch and holds a sickle. This tool recalls that he is the patron of agriculture. The emphasis, however, is on his malevolent influence. He sustains infirmities, provokes misunderstandings, inspires gambling, causes quarrels, and prompts thievery. In fact the viewer sees burglars working in a wealthy mansion, a wrongdoer attacking a gentleman to rob him of his purse and, as background décor, a prison. The caption explains: "Saturn produces slow men [because the course of this planet is the longest], thieves, liars, assassins, peasants, boors, lowlifes, shepherds, paupers, and other people of no account."[269] In his *Temptation of Saint Anthony* (now in Lisbon), Bosch includes a "Saturnine cripple," chased by dogs.[270] It is one of the illustrations of evil on the earth. A sad destiny, then, for melancholics.

Nevertheless, as Erwin Panofsky[271] so remarkably demonstrated, Marsilio Ficino and the Neoplatonists, guided by both Aristotle and Plotinus, pursued a vigorous rehabilitation of Saturn and melancholy. Saturn is higher than Jupiter. He is spirit (*spiritus*), whereas Jupiter is only soul. The former encourages contemplation, the latter action. Saturn is thus the patron of those who apply themselves to reflection and meditation, melancholy being the aptitude for the investigation of the highest secrets.[272] Ficino, born under the sign of Saturn and forever anxious, spread the idea that genius is Saturnine. Pico della Mirandola confirms this notion, writing that "Saturn incarnates that intellectual nature that devotes and commits itself only to ruling, administering, and regulating the motion of things subject to it . . . Indeed it is said that Saturn produces contemplative men, while Jupiter gives to his children the offices of prince, governor, and administrator of peoples."[273]

Due to this theory, Pico, and more curiously, Lorenzo the Magnificent—the actual ruler of Florence—termed themselves Saturnians. Lorenzo doubtlessly owed much to an already ancient tradition when he assimilated melancholy and love sickness, an eternal theme elaborated by the poets of the *dolce stil novo*.[274] He similarly employed the image of the *figura sedens*, the solitary figure who meditates with head in hand. Both Petrarch and various German miniaturists had popularized this image, which reappears in the posture of the seated nymph in Luca Signorelli's *Education of Pan* (1488). Three main elements, however, deserve particular attention. First, this description: "The feeling of an incessant struggle, of a *lungo affanno* and a sorrow that reaches desolation, finds expression in many of Lorenzo's poems."[275] Next, the cause-and-effect relationship established between melancholic temperament and amorous passions: Lorenzo writes that

> *It is natural for lovers to take delight in sad thoughts and melancholy, that, amid sighs and tears, feeds their amorous hunger, and this even as they also feel the greatest joy and rapture. I believe that the reason thereof is that love, simple and constant, proceeds from a strong imagination and this movement is achieved with difficulty unless a melancholic humor predominates in the lover. For the lover's nature is to be always disturbed and ready to turn every event, whether favorable or adverse, into chagrin and passion.*[276]

Finally, a third characteristic must be underlined: Amorous melancholy itself passes into poetic meditation. The "holy lamps" that gleam in the eyes of the beloved lady are also the radiance of a higher spiritual reality. Thus the Ficinian universe reemerges.

All the same, the Saturnians of Florence were well aware that their presiding planet remained a distressing force, for it gave, according to each case, genius or illness, and occasionally the two together. The melancholic temperament was predisposed to be philosophic, poetic, and intellectual. This predisposition, however, brought risks, notably that of losing the very *spiritus* that enables the most noble thoughts. In his *De Triplici vita* (1489), "a hygiene manual for intellectuals,"[277] Ficino gives instructions for restoring the spirit, recommending the traditional means—purgations, physical exercise, the use of certain wines and fragrances—but adding a talismanic magic that, by means of stones, signs, images, and music, catches the *spiritus mundi* and so revitalizes the depressed intellectual. The influence of Apollo and Jupiter therefore works as an antidote against the malignant emanations that ambiguous Saturn never ceases to aim at his "children."[278] These "prayers" addressed to other planets, so they may balance Saturn's power, make the suppliant's "body" and "soul" capable of gathering the invisible matter—the *spiritus*—present in cosmic reserves, which is too quickly spent by the Saturnian's cogitations. In any manner of situation the Saturnian should not despair of his lot but rather take hold of his destiny: "These men escape Saturn's unhealthy influence, and so gain the ability to not only ascend to Jupiter but also are transported to the divine contemplation signified by Saturn."[279] For spirits dwelling in the sublime spheres of Heaven, even Saturn is a benevolent father.

Ficino gained considerable credit in cultivated circles. Within a century, his *De Triplici vita* was edited twenty-six times, of which thirteen were French, without counting the Italian, German, and French translations. Cornelius Agrippa, who curiously allied Pyrrhonism and Platonism, was a reader of Ficino and resumed the idea that geniuses are melancholic types, better equipped to capture Saturn's power. *Furor melancholicus* therefore means *furor divinus*. Nonetheless, Ficino had especially attributed this "frenzy" to intellectuals, the principal employers of the intuitive spirit (*mens*). On the other hand, he had put discursive reason (*ratio*), which operates in ethics and actions, under Jupiter's government, and *imaginatio*, which inhabits artists and artisans, under that of either Mars or the Sun.[280] Agrippa enlarged the notion of *furor melancholicus* and declared that Saturnine inspiration could stimulate all three mental faculties and thus sustain three types of geniuses: philosophers, theologians, and prophets have a surplus of *mens*; scholars and heads of state have an abundance of *ratio*; painters, architects, sculptors, and so on, are richly provided with *imaginatio*. In this vein, Raphael was described as being "melancholic, like all men of such high merit."[281]

Erwin Panofsky convincingly showed that Dürer's famous and enigmatic engraving of *Melencolia I* (1514)[282] can be understood only through a reading of Ficino via Agrippa. The "I" following *Melencolia* may be the first letter of the adjective "imaginativa." Saturn was characterized as the governor of Geometry. This science, personified by the great winged figure, in effect represents the arts that use measurements. Hence the nearby hammer and carpenter's nails, joiner's plane, mason's scale, jeweler's crucible, and the perspectivist's polyhedron. The art of drawing is figured by the *putto* busy with the engraver's burin. Several Saturnine elements attract the viewer's attention: the comet on the horizon; the dog and bat, two traditional animals of melancholy; and the keys and purse, since Saturn can give wealth and power but he is also known as a miser. In addition, Geometry's crown of planets and Jupiter's magic square, whose numerals always add up to thirty-four, are so many magic elements to stave off the eventually malignant influences of Saturn. Despite the hourglass, the composition gives an impression of immobility. The beam of the balance is horizontal, the clapper of the clock does not move. Head in hand, the silence of meditation accentuates the pensive air of Geometry. Finally, the work projects a sense of defeat. The *putto*, whose intense scribbling may signify manual dexterity, is contrasted with thought, the conceptualizing that searches with restless effort. Theory and practice are thus separated. The face of Geometry is wrapped in shadow. Her eyes contemplate an inaccessible horizon. Meditation is the simultaneous honor and torment of genius. Using the Saturnine key, Panofsky logically relates Dürer's engraving to Michelangelo's *Pensieroso* in the Medici chapel in Florence. The "open" composition of the statue of Giuliano is opposed to the "closed" composition of that of Lorenzo—Lorenzo II, Duke of Urbino (d. 1519). Giuliano is the extrovert, the magnanimous prince ready for action and holding a scepter. Lorenzo, the introvert, contrastingly embodies meditative melancholy. Like that of Dürer's Geometry, his face is darkened by shadow. His left index finger held to his lips expresses the silence of reflection. His elbow rests on a locked chest, adorned with a bat, which symbolizes parsimony.[283]

Ficino, Agrippa, Dürer, and Michelangelo contributed to a fashionable vogue for melancholy. Montaigne writes that "I am one of those most exempted from this passion (sadness), and I neither like nor esteem it." At the same time, he claims that "everyone has decided to honor it, as if at a fixed price, with particular favor. They clothe wisdom, virtue, conscience with it: a stupid and monstrous ornament."[284] This affectation was especially popular in Burton's England. The English writer of the time increased his appeal by assuming a melancholic stance, whether as the wounded lover or as the satirist aiming barbs at his apparently talentless and virtueless contemporaries.[285] Jaques, in *As You Like It*, is a good exemplar of the "Elizabethan Malady," in his desiring to "suck melancholy out of a song as a weasel sucks eggs" (II. v. 13).[286] He also praises folly, condemns human vanity, and proclaims life to be a drama of seven ages, at the end of which one returns to "second childishness and mere oblivion, / Sans teeth, sans eyes, sans taste, sans everything" (II. vii. 165–166).[287] When asked to explain his melancholy, Jaques responds: "It is a melancholy of mine own, compounded of many simples, extracted from many objects, and indeed the sundry contemplation of my travels, in which my often rumination wraps me in a most humourous sadness" (IV. i. 15–20).[288] He is one of those "malcontent travelers" who have traversed the globe and so have learned misanthropy and love for one's native country. In this regard, Du Bellay is Jaques's first cousin.*

Since he developed his melancholic feelings in Italy, Du Bellay's name takes on all the more relevance. For the peninsula played a double role in this context. Italy valorized melancholy—the malady of great spirits—and at the same time acted as a negative model, due to the vices that especially English travelers believed it to have. It became a school for misanthropy. From Italy, one returned disillusioned.[289] Yet the visit at least taught advantageous mannerisms. Burton is explicit on the diffusion of melancholy during his period: He writes that it is

> *a disease "so frequent," as Mercurialis observes, "in these our days"; "so often happening," saith Laurentius, "in our miserable times," as few there are that feel not the smart of it. Of the same mind is Aelian Montaltus, Melanchthon, and others; Julius Caesar Claudinus calls it "the foundation of all other diseases, and so common in this crazed age of ours, that scarce one in a thousand is free from it."* [290]

Farther on, Burton specifies how the syndrome has zeroed in on a certain social level: "this feral disease of melancholy so frequently rageth, and now domineers almost all over Europe among *our great ones*."[291]

*Translator's note: Jaques, however, does *not* appear to love his native country. See Rosalind's comments at IV. i 33–38.

In Elizabethan and early Stuart literature, melancholic characters are so numerous that they may be grouped into categories[292]: (1) Those who suffer from their uncompromising superiority and seek out solitude, such as Samuel Rowland's *Melancholic Knight*. (2) Melancholic villains, inclined to crime and vengeance, such as Shakespeare's Aaron in *Titus Andronicus*: "Madam, though Venus govern your desires, / Saturn is dominator over mine . . . Vengeance is in my heart, death in my hand, / Blood and revenge are hammering in my head" (II. iii. 30–31;38–39).[293] (3) Cynical melancholics who are tolerated and are sometimes amusing. Jaques and Timon of Athens occupy this category. (4) Melancholic intellectuals, whom Burton describes at length, he himself being one such figure. These individuals are easily spotted in the street, with their suffering look, their black clothes and clumsy movements. They have overworked their brains and are poor and undernourished.[294] (5) Amorous melancholics, to whom Burton devotes three sections of his Third Part[295]; jealous lovers are included in this group. In Elizabethan literature, melancholy is associated with love far more than it had ever been.[296] The Italian influence somewhat contributed to this trend. Still, the weight of medical explanations must be taken into account. In theory, amorous passion is especially strong in "sanguine" temperaments, which at least partially depend on Venus. Nevertheless, hot and dry humors, deriving for instance from the spleen's combustion of black bile, may also stimulate erotic impulses. Jacques Ferrand, in his work on the "maladie d'amour" (1612), clarifies how there exist "hot, stimulating, flatulent, and melancholic nourishments."[297] (6) Finally, there are the "religious melancholics" who occupy a special section in Burton's work. Religious melancholy includes all cases where the malady in its causes or symptoms—or both at once—is linked with religion. It manifests itself in immoderate penitence and mortification, in visions, the excessive fear of God, and so on.

The impressive size and success of Burton's book and the number of contemporary learned works on melancholy certainly prove that this sentiment was in style.[298] At the same time, they show that it was more than a mere fashion. The penchant for sadness in learned circles was not only a pose. It was fed by Neoplatonic philosophy that, in the manner of the *contemptus mundi*, systematically devalued the present world and aspired toward a purified universe. At the exact center of his *Theologia platonica*, Ficino places this revealing statement (included in a paragraph on the action of "black bile" on reason):

> *As long as this sublime spirit [ours] lives in an inferior body, our intelligence is, so to speak, tossed about from one side to the other, above and below, by a perpetual disturbance, and it will not cease from sleeping and wandering. All the movements, all the actions and passions of mortals are naught but the dizzy reelings of sick people, the dreams of men asleep, the delirium of the mad. Euripides rightly called our life "the dream of a shadow."*[299]

More generally, there is much more than superficial feeling in the fear of the passing of time, common to the *danses macabres*, to the Triumphs of Death, to Ronsard's finest poetry, and to a number of Shakespeare's sonnets:

> *Thy glass will show thee how thy beauties wear,*
> *Thy dial how thy precious minutes waste;*
> *The vacant leaves thy mind's imprint will bear,*
> *And of this book this learning mayst thou taste.*
> *The wrinkles which thy glass will truly show,*
> *Of mouthed graves will give thee memory.*

These lines from Sonnet 77 only serve to recall the numerous others in this vein written by the great playwright.[300]

Thus the melancholy of the period is better understood when explained by its own representatives. The impossibility of slowing the flight of time, omnipresent mortality, the world turned upside down, Fortune's hostility, the tyranny of the stars, and so on, all augment a sense of melancholy and encourage a strange diagnosis, frequently reappearing between the work of Ficino and that of Calderon: Life is a dream. The magistrate Pierre de Lancre, both humanist and demonologist, vividly and succinctly combines the vertigo and confusion that he experiences when faced with the fragility of beings and things: "The past is a dream, the future a dark cloud, the present but wind."[301] He sees a "furious wind of inconstancy" striking down "the leaves, flowers, and fruits of the plants of humanity."[302]

An entire book would not suffice to assemble all the citations that reveal the Renaissance elite's penchant for sadness. With rare audacity, Dürer portrays himself as a whipped and tortured Christ, "the man of sorrows" (1522).[303] Du Bellay writes a harrowing "Complainte du désespéré" wherein he declares: "I deserve to be called / The slave to all misfortune," and he accuses the "rigorous heavens" of having subjected his birth "to the insuperable power / Of such an unlucky star"[304]—Saturn, without a doubt. There is even romanticism in this admission of Camoens, an involuntary traveler to the Far East: "When, having escaped the maternal sepulcher, I saw the light of day, a fatal celestial influence immediately controlled me. They denied me the liberty I deserved. A thousand times fate showed me the best and, despite myself, I followed the worst."[305] The brutal and violent Agrippa d'Aubigné proclaims: "I search the deserts, the far-off rocks, / The trackless forests, the dying oaks."[306] And Mathurin Regnier avows at thirty, though he died before the age of forty: "My lovely days are turned to night / And my heart besieged with worry / Only awaits the tomb."[307] All these tear-jerking declarations presuppose a literate audience, eager to sympathize and at least partially given to admiring the melancholic temperament, that distinction of exceptional souls. Dürer portrayed the four humors with the apostles, and in this composition Saint John becomes the incarnation of "the melancholic." At a still more sublime level, Dürer and his imitators (such as Marcantonio Raimondi) show Christ exhausted and crowned with thorns, seated on a rock, his head in his hand, in the typically Saturnine pose of the *pensieroso*.[308]

This admiration of melancholy, however, remained limited, or at most coexisted with a much older and deeper rejection of an undesirable temperament. The connotations of melancholy were still primarily pejorative. The proverb books of the sixteenth century state that "Melancholy makes the healthy sick and causes the sick to die"[309]; "To be at law or melancholy is to bury life"; or again, "Flee melancholy, sadness, and madness." In his *Traicté de l'apparition des esprits* (1600), the Franciscan Noël Taillepied speaks without indulgence of "the senseless and melancholic . . . Saturnians who ponder and forge so many chimeras."[310] Saturn was certainly the patron of men of genius, but at the same time he was the star of "dark flames," sometimes likened to Devouring Time, and he remained the sinister god held responsible for taciturnity, old age, infirmities, and indigence. In a 1516 drawing by Baldung Grien, now at the Albertina in Vienna, he appears as a thin and disheveled old man whose misanthropic eyes stare blankly into the distance. Both iconography and astrology continued to present his malevolent aspects as well as his ill-favored "children": beggars or criminals, farm workers, cesspool cleaners, and ditchdiggers. Panofsky notes that the Neoplatonic Renaissance, "which succeeded in identifying Saturnine melancholy with genius, could not displace the popular belief that Saturn was the most malignant of planets."[311]

This affirmation, however, needs to be refined and extended.[312] For at the most educated level of culture, Saturn often retained his disturbing characteristics. A sinister old man, feeble and with a wooden leg, he was shown as castrated by Jupiter and/or devouring a child—scenes evoked by Marten van Heemskerck (*Melancholici*) and later by Rubens and Goya.[313] The sixteenth-century engraving by Heemskerck—an artist who lived in Rome—particularly reveals the ambiguity of Saturn in the elite's mental representations. The god, armed with Time's scythe and devouring the leg of an infant, has children who are geometricians, hanged men, land surveyors, and cripples.[314] A German humanist such as Conrad Celtis rebuked the Neoplatonic rehabilitation. Born under Saturn, he complained of a planet that "had wreaked such harm" on him and continued to consider it as an agent of misfortune, a patron of sorrowful men, workers, and monks. It is necessary to beseech him to leave his "deadly arrows" in the quiver.[315] The French engraver Thomas de Leu depicts the "Melancolique" (ca. 1600) with the double aspect of a suppliant woman and a restless sleeper, defined in the caption as a "gloomy and anxious" being living in constant fear. A "violent fury" runs from this character's black mouth, produced "by the mass of his black bile." Even in Italy, where Saturn's rehabilitation had taken place, a defiance persisted, of a star that could produce geniuses only if its "poison" was tempered by other stellar influences.[316] Italian artists did not fail to confirm this alarming diagnosis. An engraving by Leon Davent after Giulio Romano shows Melancholy as a young weeping woman. Another by Jacques Androuet de Cerceau, after Guiglielmo Porta (called Salviati), symbolizes it as a sorrowfully pensive woman, under whom run the following lines: "I warn you to beware of it (Melancholy) if you wish to lead a happy life."[317]

This suspicious appraisal of melancholy is also clarified by a frequent Renaissance confusion of vice and illness. For the numerous moralists of the period, reason and the passions were strictly opposed. In his treatise *De la sagesse*, Charron groups sadness with jealousy, cruelty, and fear. He accuses sorrow of being a "cowardly, base, and mean-spirited passion," which "tarnishes the face . . . dries out the bones . . . embitters our life and poisons all our actions." Charron goes so far as to call melancholy "the most peevish, harmful, and unjust passion." One must therefore learn to "hate and flee it with all [our] strength."[318] Although he was a medical doctor, Lemnius construes melancholy as one of the punishments God sends down on heretics who defy Him.[319]

A surplus of mischance: Melancholy broadly inherits the monastic condemnations of sloth or "acedia,"[320] this "extinction of the voice" of the soul, this spiritual torpor that especially strikes at ascetics, but by extension every Christian discouraged by the difficult struggle for salvation. During the entire Middle Ages, the theological definition of sloth had accorded with medical descriptions of melancholy. Theodulph of Orléans, a contemporary of Charlemagne, said of *Tristitia*: "It is weighed down with so much slumber, so much heavy silence. She walks snoring, becomes quiet in murmuring . . . *Tristitia* sleeps with her eyes open. Though silent, she thinks herself to be speaking a great deal," and so on.[321] Hugh of St.-Victor lists sorrow's companions as "despair, rancor, torpor, fear, sloth, complaints, pusillanimity"; "rancor" being defined as "a wasting and corruption of the forces of the body and soul, resulting from black bile or excessive laziness."[322] Sadness was thus common to both sloth and melancholy, as attested by the verses of *Inferno*, Canto 7. The *accidiosi* who were "sullen in the sweet air that is gladdened by the sun" are now confined in a "black mire" from which they will never escape.[323] Spiritual lethargy predisposes one to melancholy. Idleness predisposes one to melancholy. "You will always see the indolent heavy and melancholic," says the *Roman de Mandevie*.[324] In 1489 the Carmelite friar Battista Spagnuoli, called Mantuan, composed a poem entitled *De Calamitatibus temporum* (treating mainly of the plague that ravaged Italy in 1479), in which he makes a striking description of a "monster" named "Idleness":

> *And behold the mother of cares, incapable of the slightest activity, unable to accomplish the slightest task: Idleness, raised by the companions of Megaera, learnèd in apathy and mistress of sorrow [luctus]. Sitting all alone, her eyes on the ground, with an ill-looking frown, pale and disheveled, she scratches her lice-ridden hair with her crooked nails. Her face is dirty, her hands filthy, her disgusting beard sticky with slobber, and her nose forever dripping snot. She has the rickets: her back is hunched up and chest sunken, and beneath her thin torso lies a belly resembling a goatskin, as if she suffered from the dropsy; she has spindly legs and bony knees, though her swollen feet impede her gait, having joints afflicted by malignant gout . . .*[325]

Evidently, this "monster" is terrifying due to its ability to engender sorrow. This tragic evocation of idleness, a solitary figure, "eyes fixed on the ground and brows wrinkled," recalls the classical iconography of Melancholy. Conversely, various calendars and engravings of the late fifteenth and early sixteenth century, notably in Germany, symbolize the "melancholic temperament" with a woman who has ceased to spin and a man who sleeps, seated at a table, head resting on crossed arms.[326]

In fact, the science of the time at least partially qualified the idea that idleness and melancholy were inextricably linked. Laurent Joubert argues that the moon (which in theory governs phlegmatic temperaments) causes the falling sickness and "that type of folly called melancholy."[327] Burton resumes the debate on this subject. Although he enumerates a series of authors, beginning with Galen, who deny the possibility that phlegm could engender "melancholic matter," he also cites several others (Cardan, Melanchthon, and so on) who hold a contrary view. Melanchthon notably uses the term "*asinia*" to characterize the heavy and bestial variety of melancholy that leads to the degeneration of phlegm. Indeed, since the Middle Ages, the ass had regularly been used as a symbol of idleness.[328] The animal appears under this title in Ripa's *Iconologia*.[329] Lemnius may have the ass in mind when he describes the "cold melancholy" that affects "these sorts of men who . . . move but slowly," "doleful," "with lowered heads."[330] As for Burton, he agrees with Melanchthon[331] that too much sleep is dangerous to melancholics:

> *"yet in some cases sleep may do more harm than good, in that phlegmatic, swinish, cold, and sluggish melancholy which Melanchthon speaks of, that thinks of waters, sighing most part, etc. It dulls the spirits, if overmuch, and senses; fills the head full of gross humors; causeth distillations, rheums, great store of excrements in the brain, and all the other parts, as Fuchsius speaks of them that sleep like so many dormice."* [332]

Burton furthermore contends that sleep during the day, "upon a full stomach, the body ill-composed to rest, or after hard meats," will inspire "fearful dreams" and in turn create anguish.

The conflation of sloth and melancholy is rendered by both artistic and literary production. In Dürer's *Melencolia I*, various details borrowed from medieval portrayals of *acedia* have been identified.[333] It has also been shown that the artist made use of Giovanni Bellini's painting of *Acedia* as a dreamer seated on an aimlessly drifting boat. In the same spirit, the extremely melancholic Hamlet berates himself for his slowness—rather his idleness—in avenging his father. He calls himself a "John-a-dreams, unpregnant of my cause, / And can say nothing" (II. ii. 568–569).[334]

Thus the epoch frequently linked sloth and melancholy: As a result, the moralists were able to add the latter to the traditional list of deadly sins. Vice and malady therefore became entangled in a global instilling of guilt: Hence the idea that Satan plays on physical fragility to induce sinning. He works his way into the soul via the weak points of the body. Torpor and sullenness are thus the snares of the Devil. Saint Theresa explains this process in clear and explicit terms. She is well aware that melancholy is an illness that "overcomes" reason and that "they [the nuns] are not to blame; as madmen are not, whatever follies they commit." She also knows, however, that the "devil is seeking to make prey of many souls under color of this temper." He insinuates himself during the patient's lucid intervals. It is a terrible "artifice" of the Devil, and "the soul is [then] in great danger. Except [when] it is, as I say, a case of such entire loss of reason that the nun is constrained to do what she says or does when she cannot help herself."[335] Furthermore, nuns touched with melancholy should be kept occupied as much as possible: "the best remedy at the prioress's disposal is to give them plenty to do, so that they may have no opportunity for idle imaginations . . . it must also be arranged that they shall not spend much time in prayer, not even so much as others spend . . . also they must not be allowed to keep such prolonged fasts as the others."[336]

Likewise, Luther viewed melancholy as a demonic ruse. As he notes in *Table-Talk*,

> *All sorrows, illnesses and melancholy come from Satan . . . for God never saddens, frightens, nor kills us: He is a God of the living. Thus he sent his only Son that we might live for Him, who died to become the conqueror over Death. This is why Holy Scripture says: "Be joyous and filled with confidence"* [337] *The monks have rightly said: "The melancholic humor is a bath prepared by the devil."* [338]

Luther includes bad and disturbing dreams among the temptations of diabolic neurasthenia. As a parry against all forms of melancholy, he not only recommends prayer and religious chanting, but also a balanced and nonascetic life-style: "Whosoever may be tormented by sadness, despair or other heartaches, and has a worm gnawing at this conscience, first cling to confidence in the Holy Word, then eat and drink healthily, and seek the company and conversation of pious Christians."[339]

Meditating on his dead father's apparition, Hamlet similarly affirms that the Devil trips the lever of sadness to seize fragile souls: "The spirit that I have seen / May be a devil, and the devil hath power / T'assume a pleasing shape, yea, and perhaps, / Out of my weakness and melancholy / As he is very potent with such spirits, / Abuses me to damn me" (II. ii. 598–603).[340] Contemporary medicine supported Hamlet's view. Dr. Lemnius resolutely attributed illness to the humors. He explains, however, that "the demons, or aery spirits, who possess a deep knowledge and understanding of things . . . not only enter into the humors, but also incite human inclinations to all misdeeds . . . so that we read how Satan had maddened the melancholy Saul, and provoked him to carry out murders, treasons, and other most ill-sorted things."[341]

During the climatic period of the fear and hunting of witches, it is hardly surprising that the demonologists established a connection between melancholy and witchcraft. It was commonly said: "*In Saturni parte sunt diabolici.*" André Chastel, citing this formula, notes that Bosch pointedly used a witchcraft scene to frame his *Temptation of Saint Anthony* (Lisbon). For Saint Anthony embodied "in every way a saturnine figure of the church"[342]; he bears witness to the ongoing belief that melancholy involved sloth, thereby opening the doorway to the devil. It is true that those who defended witches (Champier, Wier, Godelmann) explained, in accord with traditional medicine, that an abundance of black humor clouded the mind with fantastic visions and that the abominations confessed by witches were often the sad result of their distracted condition. Nonetheless, these writers agreed that "the devil, that fine, crafty, and cunning enemy, gladly seduces members of the female sex, naturally inconstant due to their constitution, their fickle belief, their malicious, impatient, and melancholic character apt to be commanded by their affections." Such is Wier's description.[343] Institoris and Sprenger, active and significant agents of repression, are too orthodox to believe that the stars constrain people "in a necessary and sufficient manner." Instead, they argue for the operation of free will. Yet they do concede that "the variations of bodily dispositions do much to alter the affections and attitudes of the soul." Thus melancholics tend to be jealous.[344] "If anyone should dream of the earth, it is a sign of a melancholic predisposition."[345] The demonic tactic thus aims to further drown those personalities already susceptible to the melancholic passion.[346] These victims, in yielding to their natural inclinations, could be induced to experience the most disturbing visions.

Much later Goya, the heir to a long tradition, will symbolize this danger of the dream in his engraving "El sueño de la razon produce monstruos": The somnolent figure, head on his crossed arms, dreams of diabolical bats.[347] Melancholic reverie is the path to Hell: Such is certainly Lucas Cranach the Elder's intended message in the three paintings on Melancholy of 1528, 1532, and 1533.[348] These works are generally interpreted as antihumanist manifestos, Lutheran-spirited replies to the rehabilitation of the Saturnine genius attempted by Dürer in *Melencolia I*. In particular, two of Cranach's works—those of 1528 and 1532—clearly allude to details of Dürer's engraving: the pensive woman, the sphere, the scientific instruments, the dog (Saturnine beast), the naked infants. Here, however, these features emphasize the negative aspects of the melancholic temper. The two sad heroines refuse to touch the fruits and drinks placed at their side: However, as Luther said, food and drink are necessary in order to fight against neuroses. One woman appears to be completely idle; the other, nearly unconscious, whittles a staff reminiscent of a witch's wand. At the left of each of these two compositions (as also in the third), an airborne demonic processsion appears, featuring goats and nude people. Consequently, there can be no doubt as to the mortal danger one courts by giving oneself over to melancholy. Such a move is to stray from eternal salvation.[349]

Although the word "melancholy" is not mentioned in the work, it is worth considering that the anonymous author of *The History of Doctor Faustus* (*Historia von D. Johan Fausten*, 1587) wished, in a spirit not unlike Cranach's, to vilify the overambitious designs of the Saturnine intellectuals whom Ficino and Dürer had so highly praised. Faust is described as "superior to all men in his skill at debating," and he is a doctor of theology. He has "a proud head" and is nicknamed the "speculator." He is also an astrologer, mathematician, and medical doctor. Little surprise then if, "taking on the wings of the eagle, he sought to attain the ultimate limits of heaven and earth." Is it not a "melancholic fury" that seizes Faust in leading him to sign a pact with the Devil?[350] Faust shows yet another similarity to Saturnine types. At the end of twenty-four years of earthly triumphs given to him by Mephistopheles, the doctor is gripped by dark despair: "O desperate hope that I must renounce," he cries.[351] He deems it "too late" to return to God.[352]

The Renaissance habitually yoked melancholy with despair. Influenced by Prudentius's *Psychomachia*, the High Middle Ages had tended to associate anger and despair.[353] Though it did not completely disappear, from the thirteenth century on this association gradually gave way to the more psychologically realistic conjunction of *acedia* or *tristitia* and *desperatio*. Suicide as the consequence and illustration of a final lack of repentance was notably presented as a negative example, borne out by the lamentable ends of Judas and Pilate.[354] This act was therefore condemned for its despairing of divine pardon. Thus sloth again intersects with melancholy, whose ultimate expression is the wish to kill oneself. In the sixteenth and seventeenth centuries, when one needed a striking citation of extreme melancholy, one would draw on Plutarch and evoke "the daughters of the Milesians [who] fell into such reverie that they all sought to hang themselves and any effort made to prevent or divert them from this folly was utterly useless."[355]

The bond between melancholy and despair is evident in a Dürer engraving of about 1514–15. It is therefore nearly contemporary with *Melencolia I*, and it perceptibly corrects the latter's praise of Saturnine genius. Its title is "The Desperate Soul."[356] Dürer contrasts a healthy man with four other characters who represent the different humors, but who also all suffer from an excess of melancholy: The idea is that the latter mood can combine with the other humors and disrupt any sort of personality by pushing people to their own pathological limits. The melancholic man, "times two"—he is so both by nature and by illness—has a haggard face that emerges from shadow like a mask; the "sanguine" melancholic becomes, through an excess of mirth, a grimacing idiot; the "phlegmatic" melancholic is a nude woman drowning in slumber; finally, the "choleric" melancholic beats himself and tears out his hair: hence the engraving's title.

For the demonologists, however, this passage from melancholy to fatal despair occurred by means of "taciturnity." The Devil often succeeds in preventing his imprisoned minions from speaking and confessing. When necessary, he mistreats them so that they will remain quiet.[357] The drama of final unrepentance is played out at the heart of this inhuman silence, which the professional inquisitors sought to break.[358] Even if they succeeded, all was not yet won, for as the authors of the *Malleus Maleficarum* state regarding witches.

> *After the confession of their crimes under torture, they do everything possible to hang themselves; this is a truth that derives from our own practical experience. Thus, after their confessions, guards have always been posted with them, attentive to such desperate efforts. And when on occasion, through the negligence of the guards, they have been discovered hung by strings or veils, [it has been clear] that it was at the instigation of the enemy, so that they would not obtain pardon through contrition and sacramental confession.*[359]

Such is the demonologists' position; yet for the men of the church, final contrition and bitter despair totally excluded one another. This, then, is the most dramatic consequence of melancholy: the refusal of confession, which is a refusal of God and a "homicida animae," according to the saying of Augustine as quoted by Burton.[360] The English author, like most of his contemporaries, conflated physical and moral sickness. Citing Saint Gregory, he confirms that the Devil tempts everyone after their own temperament: If one is of a merry disposition, he will encourage that person to fornicate. If another is "pensive sad," he strives to lead the unhappy soul to "a desperate end." In this latter case, the melancholic humor "is *balneum diaboli*, the devil's bath": Burton reiterates a classic analogy.[361] He furthermore writes that

> *Black choler is a shoeing-horn, a bait [which the Devil uses] to allure them, insomuch that many writers make melancholy an ordinary cause and a symptom*

of despair, for that such men are most apt, by reason of their ill-disposed temper, to distrust, fear, grief, mistake, and amplify whatsoever they preposterously conceive or falsely apprehend.

To be sure, Burton follows other authorities in affirming that "melancholy and despair, though often, do not always concur." In more than one instance, "melancholy alone again may be sometimes a sufficient cause of this terror of conscience." As a result, overly troubled souls come to doubt divine pardon and even question the existence of God. Excessive meditation on man's final ends and the eternity of hell leads to vexation of the spirit. Melancholy and idleness once more encompass one another. Self-abusive fasts, prolonged solitude, and exhausting reflection on the hereafter may cause fatal dizziness. Burton then considers whether all suicides are damned like Judas and Pilate. His answer is complex, but ultimately benevolent: For those who "die so obstinately and suddenly that they cannot so much wish for mercy, the worst is to be suspected"; for those who took some time to die, charity leads one to believe that they had enough time to repent. Finally, "if a man put desperate hands upon himself by occasion of madness or melancholy, if he have given testimony before of his regeneration, in regard he doth this not so much out of his will as *ex vi morbi* [on account of his disease] we must make the best construction of it, as Turks do, that think all fools and madmen go directly to heaven."[362] This astonishing final pirouette reveals the progress of the medical notion of "extenuating circumstances," inserted into a discourse whose premises are guilt-instilling.

Burton's questions and hesitations belong to an epoch that deeply pondered the question of suicide. Montaigne devotes an entire chapter of his *Essays* (Book II, chap. 3, "A Custom on the Island of Cea") to this "malady peculiar to man, and not seen in any other creature, to hate and disdain himself," and to the "fantastic and irrational humors that have driven not only individual men but nations to do away with themselves" (an allusion to the Milesian virgins). It is therefore reasonable to consider whether suicides became more frequent during the Renaissance. Erasmus seemed to think so. In his dialogue *Funus*, he writes, "As we see so many people taking their own lives today, what would happen if there was nothing horrible about the thought of death?"[363] Sixteenth-century Germany was struck by several recurrences of local suicide epidemics.[364] In this regard, however, the evidence is too subjective for making definite conclusions. For this period, serious and possibly revealing statistics are and will no doubt always be lacking.[365] Taking account of religious prohibitions and the public degradation inflicted on the suicide's body, one may suppose that voluntary deaths were extremely rare. Estimates offered of the London *Bills of Mortality* (1629–1660) give a figure of 0.1 percent of death by suicide (11.3 percent in England during the year 1958).[366] The word "suicide," first used in Latin by seventeenth-century Casuits, did not appear in French until 1734.[367] On the other hand, the balance of surviving material suggests that the Renaissance was far more concerned with suicide than were the Middle Ages.

In a study of the vocabulary of the collection of *exempla* entitled *Alphabetum narrationum* (compiled ca. 1308–10), Jacques Le Goff and his team find that *desesperacio* only moderately concerned contemporary preachers.[368] This word appears in only eleven *exempla* and occupies only the twenty-eighth position (tied with many others). The frequency rating instead highlights the ten following words: *Demon* (77 *exempla*), *Mulier* (64), *Mors* (49), *Temptacio* (41), *Deceptio* (38), *Timor* (35), *Prelatus-Prelacio* (34), *Conemptus* (33), *Oratio* (33), *Penitencia* (33). The *exemplum* was a "mass-produced and widely consumed" cultural artifact, and thus reveals the major themes of an intense religious and moral acculturation.

Conversely, despair was a major preoccupation of early modern elite culture. Not only does it pervade Tasso's *Aminta*, or the character of Hamlet—who regrets that Christianity forbids suicide—but also the *Ars Bene Moriendi*, a genre that the printing press helped to make widely popular during the late fifteenth and early sixteenth centuries.[369] These texts always included a chapter on the struggle, at the moment of death, against the temptation to despair of divine pardon. "Nothing offends God so much as despair," proclaims a probably German edition of the *Ars moriendi* (ca. 1470).[370]

Suicide is one of the possible corollaries of *desesperacio*. Despair, however, could carry other motifs. During the Renaissance, it underwent a partial rehabilitation. After having written that "Not all troubles are worth our wanting to die to avoid them," Montaigne ends his chapter on "A Custom of the Island of Cea" by praising those men and women who took their own lives through the greatness of their souls.[371] For in such cases, the motivating factor is not despair but courage. Many Christian and pagan examples, as well as Stoic heroism, uphold this distinction. In *The Rape of Lucrece*, Shakespeare echoes Montaigne in his praise of she who "sheathed in her harmless breast / A harmful knife, that thence her sould unsheath'd: / That blow did bail it from the deep unrest / Of that polluted prison where it breath'd" (ll. 1723–1726).[372] For European literati, Lucretia was the object of unanimous admiration during the late sixteenth and early seventeenth centuries.

In fact, this period conducted a philosophical inquiry into suicide. In his *Epitres Morales* (1598), Honoré d'Urfé disparages the voluntary deaths of cowards but declares that "the act which Cato performed in killing himself, as he was Cato, did not involve cruelty, but courage and magnanimity."[373] Charron nearly plagiarizes Montaigne, in arguing that suicide "for a weak reason" must be avoided and in exalting those who took their own lives for a "great and important reason . . . one that was just and legitimate": for example, "in order to escape living at the mercy and whim of those who despise them."[374] Justus Lipsius, imbued with Stoicism, edited an unfortunately lost treatise, the *Thraseus*, in order to defend courageous suicides. Duvergier de Haranne—later Saint-Cyran—used the following explanation as the subtitle to his *Question Royale* (1609): "Wherein is shown under what extremities, principally during times of peace, the subject may be obliged to preserve the life of his prince by giving up his own." Still more clearly and extensively, John Donne writes a treatise on suicide, the *Biathanatos* (1608), based on some two hundred "authorities."[375] Donne challenges the view that all suicides result from despair (moreover, not all despair is sinful). He compares certain heroic suicides to the most noble martyrs and professes that in some cases, the man before death is "Emperor of himself." "And he whose conscience well tempered and dispassion'd, assures him that the reason of self-preservation ceases in him, may also presume that the law [that is, the prohibition against suicide] ceases too, and may doe that then which otherwise were against that law."[376]

Most notably in Elizabethan and Jacobean England, the theater of the time echoed this debate. First, it gave a considerable place to suicide. Between 1580 and 1600, as many plays including one or more suicides appeared as in the first eighty years of the century.[377] Between 1580 and 1625, no less than 116 characters kill themselves on the English stage (24 of whom are in Shakespeare's plays); 107 try to kill themselves (52 of whom are Shakespearean).[378] Of these 223 successful or failed suicides, 90, or 40 percent, are presented with praise (25 of these being Shakespearean). These instances are motivated by love, honor, or chastity. This impressive proportion reveals a collective regard for voluntary death as no longer a taboo subject. Still, this affirmation must be qualified by several considerations. In exact figures, there are more suicides in the Jacobean than in the Elizabethan theater—Shakespeare being excluded from this calculation. In general, however, the Jacobeans produced far more plays than the Elizabethans. Hence the average number of suicides per play and the proportion of accomplished suicides drops during this second period; on the other hand, despair with its variants—remorse and ruin—thereafter outstrips other motifs: love, honor, chastity. At a more general level, it must be added that Donne's work could not have had a major influence during its author's lifetime, since it remained unpublished. Meanwhile, Justus Lipsius himself destroyed the *Thraseas* wherein he defends the legitimacy of suicide: His prudence is revealing.

After all, voluntary, despair-driven death remained officially condemned. On the other hand, the conclusion of this study of melancholy has to emphasize the late Renaissance attraction to suicide. The case of Donne is illuminating. He praises heroic death but he is himself subject to serious discouragement. In the preface to *Biathanatos*, he writes that "I have often such a sickly inclination . . . whensoever any affliction assails me, mee thinks I have the keyes of my prison in mine owne hand, and no remedy presents itselfe so soone to my heart, as mine own sword."[379]

In this regard, the literature of the period and the theater in particular seem to have played the role of an outlet, or better, of *catharsis*. Psychiatrists have in fact shown that a writer can sublimate his or her tendency toward suicide in creating a work where this tendency is given free rein.[380] For the historian, the epoch's indisputable interest in suicide reveals a collective sadness—at least at the level of elite culture—that requires close attention. Sadness was not only a fashion, but a deeper *malaise*, a pointed disenchantment linked to a pessimistic regard for the world. In his description of the Hospital of the Incurables, Garzoni confirms that "we see an infinity of melancholic mad people."[381] Burton holds the same opinion: In the preface to *The Anatomy of Melancholy*, he intentionally mixes ethics and medicine, and he relentlessly depicts a universe where everything goes badly. In line with Sebastian Brant, Bosch, and the critics of the upside-down world, Burton unhesitatingly asserts that we are all melancholics:

> *And who is not a fool, who is free from melancholy?*
> *Who is not touched more or less in habit or disposition? . . .*
> *In whom doth not passion, anger, envy, discontent, fear, and sorrow reign?*[382]

Unhappiness exists because of evil. Each explains the other, due to the sin whose daughter is melancholy.

PART TWO

A Failure of Redemption?

CHAPTER 6

Focusing the Examination of Conscience

A THEOLOGY OF SIN

The five preceding chapters have highlighted a fact of immense but usually underrated importance: the dominant pessimism of early modern Europe. The appeal of the macabre, the sense that the world was going from bad to worse, and the conviction that humanity is fragile, all touched a large sector of the elite and left a deep imprint on the culture of the time. At the heart of this cultural "melancholy" lies the bitter certainty that humans are great sinners. Hence the need, in the second stage of this study, to explore the central tenets of the doctrine of sin.

Like all the other fears studied in the preceding volume, the fear of one's self, which crested during the early modern era, possesses its own long history. Early Christianity had placed sin at the center of its theology, a move that the Graeco-Roman religions and philosophies had by-passed. In *Oedipus at Colonus*, Laius's unhappy son and murderer says: "The bloody deaths, the incest, the calamities / You speak so glibly of: I suffered them, / By fate, against my will . . . In me myself you could not find such evil / As would have made me sin against my own . . . How could you justly blame it on me? On me, who was yet unborn, unconceived."[1] Reflecting at numerous junctures on the problem of moral failure, Plato—in *Gorgias*, *Meno*, and *The Laws*—has Socrates explain that "no one is willfully evil." The guilty man is the one who deceives himself: "Can anything be clearer than that those who are ignorant of evils do not desire them, but they desire what they suppose to be good when they are really evils, and they who do not know them to be evils, and suppose them to be good, desire good?"[2] For his part, Aristotle holds to an imperfect notion of liberty and an uncertain conception of duty. He attributes moral failure to error and clumsiness, and not to any violation of a divine order, any offense in the eyes of an impersonal God.

On the other hand, Stoicism made up for Aristotle's lack of reference of human actions to the divine order of things. Through the intermediary of Stoicism (and most notably via Cicero's *De Officiis*), the Greek terms for sin (*hamartia* and *hamartema*) were changed into the Latin *peccatio* and *peccatum*, and passed into general usage. The Stoics nonetheless saw God, the soul of the world, as an impersonal being, and moreover gave no ranking to virtue and vice: All failings are equal. Closer to Christianity were the mystery cults that flourished in the Graeco-Roman world at the time of the Gospels' early diffusion. Like the Christian message, these religions' doctrines laid stress on sin as a stain on the soul and an obstacle to salvation, while they also accentuated ritual purification more than the moral sense of human actions.[3] In contrast, Christianity, taking its cue from Judaism, cast sin as an opposition of human will to that of a personal God. This opposition not only shows itself in external actions but also in one's thoughts and feelings. Furthermore, this concept created the terms *peccator* and *peccatrix*, which did not exist in Classical Latin, and which progressively gained an extraordinary stature in the new Christian civilization.

The Old Testament presents Adam's sin as man's willful disobedience to a divine precept. Following this rupture—for which man alone takes the entire blame—sin enters the world: It will henceforth affect all human history, and notably that of Israel. The disobedient Israelites worship the golden calf, prefer meat to manna, and constantly deviate from the paths God traces for them. One after another, the prophets chastise them for their iniquities: violence, adultery, injustice, lies, and so on, which "open a chasm" between them and Yahweh. At the same time, the prophets will reveal the proportions and nature of sin: ingratitude toward a most loving father (Isa. 64:7), and infidelity, akin to that of a wife who prostitutes herself to all comers, neglectful of her husband's inexhaustible love (Jer. 3:7–12; Ezek. 16:23). These seers indicate the ways of conversion—confession, expiation, ashes, faith—that will merit pardon. They announce the coming of the Redeemer, dispenser of this pardon.

The New Testament gives no less a place to sin than does the Old. Jesus, the Servant, arrives among men and women not for the just but for the sinners (Mark 2:17). He "remits" sins, to the great scandal of the Pharisees. He tells the parable of the merciful father who daily watches the highway for the return of his prodigal son (Luke 15:11–32). Saint John says of Christ that He is "the Lamb of God, which taketh away the sin of the world" (John 1:29). Sin is the denial of the light (John 3:19–20) and of love (Matt. 7:12). The works of Satan and his servants are murder, deceit (John 8:44) and hatred (John 3:20). This hatred will lead to the murder of the Son of God (John 3:37). This death, however, followed by resurrection, is the victory over "the prince of this world" (John 12:31; 14:30; 16:33), "because your sins are forgiven you for His name's sake" (I John 1:12). He communicates the Holy Ghost to the apostles, in order that "Whose soever sins ye remit, they are remitted unto them" (John 20:23).

In his turn, Saint Paul gave a structured character to the doctrine of sin. After Adam's crime, man, cut off from Redemption, is "sold under sin" (Rom. 7:14), certainly still able to desire the good but not to "perform" it (Rom. 7:18). Man is inevitably bound unto eternal death, the "wages of sin" (Rom. 6:21; 7:24). In the letters of Saint Paul are already found the lists of moral failings (most likely derived from the Stoics' lists) that would inundate the West after the invention of the printing press. Among them, the most serious are, according to the apostle of the gentiles, idolatry, sexual misconduct, social injustice, and yet another form of idolatry: covetousness (Rom. 1:23–25; 7:7). Nevertheless, this black picture is rigorously made only to heighten, in contrast, the necessity and grandeur of Christ's redemptive mission. Original and personal sin become an integral part of a system of salvation, whose other component is justification. In the very place where sin was abundant, grace is now superabundant. The fault of Adam caused and permitted the redemption that triumphs over it. By faith and baptism, man becomes a "new creature" (II Cor. 5:17), even if, living in a mortal body, he sometimes falls again under the empire of sin and "obeys it in the lusts thereof" (Rom. 6:12). Through his redemptive death, Jesus, the primary being, passed from the fleshly to the spiritual condition (Rom. 8:32). He simultaneously overcame death and sin, and thus opened the path of eternal salvation to humanity.

Since before Saint Augustine, the message of biblical texts—with their emphasis on repentance—along with the difficulties and tensions within the church led to a continuous Christian meditation on sin. It will suffice here to recall a few signposts.[5] *The Pastor* of Hermas, edited at Rome toward the middle of the second century, is troubled by the multitude of failings that already disfigure the church: those of the apostates and the traitors, those of the impostors, those of the quarrelers, and those of the half-Christians whose conduct denies faith. Resuming the tone of the Jewish prophets, the author makes a heated call for repentance. Tertullian (d. ca. 220), a man of excess and rigor, writes two works of increasing vehemence (the *De Poenitentia* and the *De Pudicitia*) on guilt and the need to repent. In the second of these books, marked by Montanism, he nonetheless affirms that idolatry, shamelessness, and homicide are three unpardonable faults. Moreover, in the *De Spectaculis*, he evokes the healthy combat of the virtues against the vices: Shamelessness overturned by Chastity, Perfidy massacred by Good Faith, Cruelty felled by Pity, and Pride eclipsed by Humility.[6]

Clement of Alexandria (d. ca. 216) and his disciple Origen (d. 252) both refer to Christians who are tempted to forget that baptism does not guarantee an innocent life and that sin is the fruit of our freedom. At the beginning of the fourth century, the treatises on sin and penitence increase in number, notably in response to the Novatians, who denied all possible remission of sins committed after baptism. Lactantius (d. 325), in his *Divine Institutions*, urges putting oneself in the presence of He who will one day be the sovereign Judge and who is already the irrefutable witness of our most secret acts (*Judex et testis idem futurus*). However, He also is the only one who can remedy our corruption. Saint Ambrose (d. 397) compiles a treatise called *De Poenitentia*, and Saint John Chrysostom devotes nine homilies to the same subject, stressing the boundlessness of divine pardon. His Spanish contemporary Prudentius (d. ca. 415) composes a poem, the *Psychomachia*, which would later give medieval religious iconography one of its favored themes: the combat of the Virtues and Vices.[7] The following section pits Chastity against Lechery:

> *Chastity, a virgin . . . presents herself in the grassy field, ready to fight. She is resplendent in her magnificent armor. Lechery, a child of Sodom, equipped with the fires of her ruined city, attacks her, and at her face hurls an ember of pine, coated with pitch and burning sulfur . . . But without taking fright, the virgin severely batters the arm of the hot fury and the fiery features of the same sinister woman . . . Having disarmed the courtesan, Chastity places her blade on her enemy's throat, and lets it pierce straight through . . .*

And so on.

Similarly, Prudentius casts Pride as an unruly mounted warrior, who insolently taunts the unshakeable Virtues. Fraud, however, has dug a booby-trap in the battlefield, into which rider and horse suddenly fall. Humility has only to take up a sword offered by Hope and then slice off the head of Pride.[8] Remembering Prudentius's text, Romanesque and Gothic sculptors would vigorously portray these allegorical duels between Good and Evil.[9]

The science of sin took on a new dimension with Saint Augustine, who would henceforth reign as the master of this immense field. Christian theology would later adopt his famous definition: "sin is all action, word, or greed opposed to the eternal law."[10] Such behavior is *aversio a Deo* and *conversio ad creaturam*, repentance being the opposite step. The Archbishop of Hippo represents moral failing now as an attack on the Creator's work, now as an injustice that violates God's sovereignty over man and the world. In these two ways, the disorder of sin is an insult to God.

From Saint Augustine to Luther and Pascal, via Saint Gregory (d. 604), another "master of the science of sin," Hugh of St.-Victor (d. 1141), Abelard (d. 1142), Peter Lombard (d. 1164), the fathers of the Council of Trent and the neo-scholastics of the sixteenth and seventeenth centuries, Christian thought never refrained from scrutinizing sin, from focusing its definition, and from measuring its impact. Saint Thomas Aquinas, however, has the distinction of having achieved the most refined and ample of all medieval reflections on this question. His discussion of sin occupies a significant place in the *Summa Theologica*.[11] In addition, his *De Malo* addresses itself entirely to the same subject. Saint Thomas clarifies the philosophical notion of sin, which anyone can elaborate without having recourse to God. Aquinas agrees with the ancient philosophers that human will only desires the Good, whether real or apparent. He then integrates this conviction into a Christian schema. Indisputably, moral failure runs contrary to the rules of reason.[12] At the same time, theology locates in sin a more serious problem, since it opposes itself to the eternal law, the prime and sovereign measure of human action. The "angelic doctor" is thus led to cite and approve Augustine's definition that "sin is all action, word, or greed opposed to the eternal law."[13] He shows, however, that this definition also includes sins of omission. For "it is always for the amassing of wealth that the miser plunders others and does not pay his debts. Likewise, it is to satisfy his gluttony that the glutton overeats and does not fast when it is required to do so."[14] Sinful omission is thus a negation linked to an erroneous affirmation. This invitation to reflect on the sin of negligence, from now on clearly defined, did not fail—and has not yet ceased—to make a deep impression on Western conscience. Furthermore, Aquinas amplifies an insight of Peter Lombard and specifies that any misdeed is worse than vice, the latter only being a predisposition for wrongdoing, whereas sin marks the accomplishment of the action. Sin thus "gets the better of human habits, in the realm of good as well as of evil."[15] Independent of the disorder that it introduces to creation, sin tarnishes the guilty soul, which then loses its shining luminosity. More important, sin is a challenge to God. Doubtless, sin leaves divine dignity intact. On the other hand, this condition does not apply to the will of the sinner, who had wanted, if it were possible, to harm the Creator: Hence the infinite aspect of sin. "All sins are against God."[16]

Despite clarifications by Abelard and Aquinas, sermons and iconography continued frequently to confuse sins with vices. On the other hand, specialists in moral theology, striving for centuries to categorize the sins, successively attempted a number of distinctions: sins by excess and by default (a differentiation inspired by Aristotle); carnal sins and spiritual sins (Saint Gregory); sins of thought, of word, and of action (Tertullian, Origen, Saint Cyprian, and later Albertus Magnus, Saint Bonaventure, and Aquinas); sins against God, against one's self, and against one's neighbor (Peter Lombard); and so on. These different criteria of identification, however, were finally integrated into two great ensembles—not exclusive of the preceding ones—that came to have a long history: on the one hand, the list of the Deadly Sins, and on the other, the opposition between mortal and venial offenses.

Christian thought hesitated for a long time over both the meaning of the phrase "Deadly (literally, *Capital*) Sins"—major sins or sources of the others?—and their precise number. The Letters of Saint Paul and Saint John are explicit concerning each of these disputed questions. The former, following Ecclesiast (10:15), places special weight on cupidity, "the root of all evil" (I Tim. 6:10), and an "idolatry" (Col. 3:5). The latter groups "all that is in the world" under three headings: "the lust of the flesh, and the lust of the eyes, and the pride of life" (I John 2:16). All the while, there can be found in the early discipline of the church—for instance in the *Didache* and Tertullian's works—a list of sins whose remission could be obtained only by public penance: idolatry, blasphemy, homicide, adultery, debauchery, false witness, and fraud.[17] Later, Origen enumerates several wicked tendencies that serve as the prime movers of sins. To each of these he assigns a particular demon. At the same time, he reserves the expression "Deadly Sins" for certain particularly grave intellectual transgressions such as heresy.[18] With Evagrius Ponticus (d. 399), a monk of the Egyptian desert, both the list and the definitions become more precise. He in fact notes eight "malicious moods" or bad "generic thoughts" that respectively engender gluttony, fornication, avarice, sadness, anger, despair or *acedia*, vainglory, and pride.[19] This taxonomy has a hierarchical value. It indicates the order in which to combat these evil inclinations, with respect to the increasing resistance that each one offers to the action of the will. Still, were not gluttony and fornication the first temptations that monks would inevitably encounter? Furthermore, one must recall the importance accorded sadness and *acedia*, which together ambush undernourished ascetics. Thus elite individuals, dedicated to mortifying their souls, were the ones who most notably elaborated the list of the deadly sins. Thus Cassian (d. 432), in honor of the cenobites, resumes Evagrius's enumeration of the eight principal vices.[20] In his turn, Saint John Climacus (d. ca. 649), Abbot of Sinai and the author of the *Scala paradisi*, finding pride and vainglory to be too readily confused, reduces the principal vices from eight to seven.[21] As for Saint Gregory the Great (d. 604), he locates pride—*superbia*—outside this classification, since it is the "root of all evil" and "the Queen of the vices." He then lists the seven "Deadly Sins" as vainglory, envy, anger, sadness, cupidity, gluttony, and luxury.[22] In this group, envy-jealousy makes its appearance. On the other hand, Gregory includes within sadness spiritual idleness (*torpor circa praecepta*). Finally, for him, there exists a psychological connection and thus a family relationship between the seven vices in the order that he assigns to them. Henceforth, the classifications of the Deadly Sins acquired full acceptance in theological thinking. Albeit in a different order, Isidore of Seville (d. 636) uses Gregory's same group of vices, and he also puts pride at the top.[23] Alcuin of York (d. 804) prefers Evagrius's and Cassian's taxonomies,[24] but Peter Lombard (d. 1164) returns to Saint Gregory's, which is also the source for Aquinas's work in this area.[25]

In his list, Saint Thomas, like Saint John Climacus, merges pride and vainglory and substitutes *tristitia* (the breaking or disgust with spiritual goods) for *acedia*. Aquinas's series is therefore the following: vainglory, envy, anger, avarice, sadness, gluttony, and lechery. He connects the seven main categories of sins to erroneous goals: either the pursuit of an apparent but nonexistent good, or the flight from an apparent but nonexistent evil.[26] Moreover, he sets himself off from Saint Gregory on three points. Faithfully following Prudentius's *Psychomachia*, Gregory contrasts the Seven Deadly Sins with the Seven Gifts of the Holy Ghost. Saint Thomas does not maintain this opposition, for one does not sin in turning oneself from virtue, but in loving some transitory good.[27] Meanwhile, if he retains Gregory's proposed sequence, he does not establish such a logical passage from one sin to the next.[28] Finally, while for Gregory "capital" means "major," for Thomas the seven sins mainly deserve to be called "capital" because each is the root and head (*caput*) of the other sins that derive from them.[29]

Thus during Aquinas's period, and primarily thanks to him, the septenary of the Deadly Sins becomes definitively fixed. In the medieval context, this number of exceptional power should not come as any surprise. Gregory the Great had opposed the Seven Vices to the Seven Gifts of the Holy Ghost and had compared them to the Seven Tribes of Israel.[30] Hugh of St.-Victor explains that seven is the supreme human number, being composed of four, the number of the body, and three, the number of the soul. Human life is itself divided into seven ages that correspond to the seven virtues. These virtues combat the seven vices, and the seven requests of the *Pater* and the seven sacraments (whose list was determined in the twelfth century) play the same role.[31] The spiritual literature of the Middle Ages would henceforth use this magically potent number in every sort of way. There are the seven works of mercy, the seven psalms of penance, the seven canonical hours, the seven parts of the spiritual armor, the seven signs of the birth of Christ, and so on. Certain authors affirm that the divine blood running from the seven wounds washes the Seven Deadly Sins. A fourteenth-century wood engraving portrays Christ's blood submerging seven characters grouped around the cross, who symbolize the Deadly Sins. In the same spirit, a Flemish painting of 1460, preserved at the bishop's palace in Teruel, shows Mary surrounded by the same seven little people: The seven sorrows of the Virgin here wipe clean the Deadly Sins.[32]

Despite the career of this magic number, Romanesque and even thirteenth-century Gothic sculpture maintained an even number of Vices and Virtues. These latter figures—young women armed with shields and lances, who threaten or knock down their Vice opponent—appear in groups of no more than eight during the Romanesque period. Later, they increase to ten at Strasbourg cathedral, and to twelve at Amiens and Notre-Dame in Paris. The artists held to symmetrical arrangements.[33] All the same, in art as in literature, the number seven would eventually come into greater vogue for the Virtues as for the Vices: an index of the growing impact of scholastic speculation. If in the dark funnel of Hell, Dante does not arrange the circles of torments according to Aquinas's specifications—though such may have been his original plan—he does make the seven rising terraces of Purgatory correspond to the Seven Deadly Sins in order of the decreasing gravity achieved via the gradual ascent toward heaven.

Saint Thomas had also reflected on the penalty due for sin: In the *Summa theologica*, he writes that "All that rebels against the order of things must hope for a repression of the order itself, by He who is its sovereign." Now "human nature is primarily subordinate to its own reason, secondly to those who have either spiritual or temporal government, and thirdly to He who rules the universe." Sin disturbs each of these three orders: "Whence the sinner's triple pain: one comes from himself—remorse; another from other men; and the third from God."[34]

In this conception, the penalty for sin is not atonement (which is gained through penance), but the counterpart of the offense. This response reaffirms the triumph of order over disorder. God's justice wills that there be a penalty for sin, this being to the guilty life what reward is to the virtuous one. In this regard, and in more measured terms, Aquinas joins with Augustine, who had made this formidable claim in the *De libero arbitro*: "In order that the beauty of the universe not remain soiled, the disgrace of the crime must not remain without the beauty of vengeance."[35] The authors of the *Malleus maleficarum* would later remember this same statement.[36] The sinner is thus in debt toward God, and all crime necessitates its punishment (*reatus poenae*).[37] However, could the penalty not be somehow proportional to the gravity of the case? This question, constantly posed and debated through the ages, led to the other great distinction mentioned above, that between mortal and venial sins. It must be noted, moreover, that certain authors equated these mortal sins with the Deadly Sins.

Apart from an obscure passage of Saint John, one can hardly find any scriptural sources for the venial-mortal distinction. John writes that "If any man see his brother sin a sin that is not unto death, he shall ask, and he shall give him life for them that sin not unto death. There is a sin unto death: I do not say that he shall pray for it. All unrighteousness is sin: and there is a sin not unto death" (I John 5:16–17). The apostle identifies sin against the Holy Ghost (cf. Mat.: 12:31) and sin that leads to death. One can interpret it so. On the other hand, during the first centuries of Christianity, two levels of sin came to be distinguished in regard to the type of remission they each required. Their delimitation, however, varied according to the author (Tertullian, Origen, and so on) and the penitential regimes: Were these trangressions to be remitted by God or by the church? Do they or do they not lead to public penance and the intervention of the church, which readmits the sinner to communion with the faithful? Will the church delay or not delay their pardon up to the point of death?[38]

These doubts ended with Saint Augustine, who clarified the venial-mortal distinction in such a way that his version has dominated all later theology. He explains that venial sins—*crimina levia, quotidiana, veniala*—do not take away the life of the soul, which remains united with God. In these cases one loves the flesh and what is transitory, not against but outside of God. Such transgressions thus do not cause damnation and are remitted through prayer, fasting, and charity. In contrast, mortal sins—*crimina letalia, mortifera*—are incompatible with the grace that they extinguish. They cause the loss of the right to Heaven granted by baptism, and they can be remitted only by the church, by virtue of the keys given to Saint Peter. In this way Augustine establishes a lasting and absolute demarcation between those crimes that do or do not deserve the everlasting fire.[39]

Nevertheless, the question of the nature of venial sin continued to fuel debate. Saint Anselm and Abelard notably held disputes over this matter. Hence the great explanation of Aquinas, who confirmed and clarified the distinction established by Augustine. Saint Thomas sets forth how every voluntary act is necessarily shaped toward an end. In this regard, a venial sin is not applied to an evil end (if so, it would be mortal), but neither is it reducible to a good end (because then it would no longer be a sin). It follows that venial sins pass outside of the law (*praeter legem*) without actually opposing it, while mortal sin is totally directed against the law (*simpliciter contra legem*). The latter is thus a complete sin, while the former is an unfinished one. Assuredly, venial sin may be a disposition toward mortal sins, and its object is always "irregular," but it is not produced by "malice." Furthermore, an accidental sin is never mortal, and before the age of maturity a child commits neither mortal nor venial sins.[40] From the Middle Ages to recent times, many Catholic theologians and moralists thought that the division of sins by Augustine and Aquinas into the two great categories of "mortal" and "venial" had settled the question of moral evil. The orthodox world, however, paid the distinction little attention at a time when the Latin church gave it enormous importance and prescribed confession of all mortal sins.

With hindsight, it appears that the mortal-venial distinction took its full importance only during the Fourth Lateran Council (1215), which decreed confession of all "mortal sins." From then on, it became necessary to decide in each case whether each sin was mortal or venial.

THE PENITENTIAL REGIMES

At the same time that it was clarifying its doctrine of sin, the church organized, after much trial and error, the practices of confession and of penitence. Three penitential regimes succeeded one another over the centuries.[41] In ancient usage, the admission of sins was made to the bishop, in a form of which we are ignorant. It was doubtless not public, but it was a penitential process. Under the bishop's control, the community admitted the sinner into the rank of penitent, most often at the beginning of Lent, and reconsecrated him or her on Holy Thursday. Solemn rituals marked the admission into penance. During the stage of expiation, the sinners were consigned to an inferior place inside the church. The reconsecration was proclaimed before the united assembly, who prayed, cried, and moaned for the penitents. Even though reconsecrated, they forever remained under certain prohibitions: They were forbidden to have normal marital lives, to marry or remarry, to assume public responsibilities, to take legal action, to enter into commerce, to become a deacon, presbytery, or bishop. Clerics could not benefit from reconsecration. Others were authorized to acquire it but once in their lives. The faithful avoided penitence, and most often had recourse to it only near their death. In fact, this system, as Cyrille Vogel says, led to a "penitential void" and a "spiritual desert."

In the monastic milieu of the fourth and fifth centuries, the second penitential step was taken, and a new character appeared: the director or spiritual father, in whom the anchorites and cenobites could confide. Thenceforth, one is on the path toward private confession. The latter soon developed in Celtic and Anglo-Saxon monasteries, which seem to have never experienced ancient rituals of penance. Thus after the seventh century, the new penitential forms were gradually imported to the continent by British missionaries, who reached large segments of the European populace.

Nonetheless, until the middle of the twelfth century, confession was only one of the means for the remission of sins, along with prayer, alms, and fasting. The characteristics of the new penitential regime were the following: All sinners, lay or clergy, could be reconsecrated as many times as they had sinned. The sinner spoke in private to a priest (and no longer only a bishop). Pardon, however, was obtained only when penitential taxes (diverse mortifications, charity, and so on) had been accomplished. The entire process of reconsecration was secret. The special garments and their removed place during holy offices disappeared. Once penance had been performed, they were free of any prohibition. Public penance, however, remained for grave public sins. Indeed, the Carolingian Renaissance strove to restore its former importance.

The new system was called that of "penance by tariff." In fact, the confessor now appeared above all as a judge who investigated, held an inquiry, and pronounced the sentence after having evaluated the crimes. Thus there was a need for lists of cases with the corresponding penalties. These were the famous "Penitentials" that appeared in the British Isles during the sixth century, passed into the continent during the seventh, and remained in currency until the eleventh to twelfth centuries. They applied the principle of *contraria contrariis* and imposed fasting on the glutton, work for the idle, and chastity on the lecherous. In theory, the penalties were extremely severe. Thus the *Penitential of the Pseudo-Theodore* (ca. 690–740?) estimates four years of fasting for an act of fornication, forty days' fasting for the desire to do the act, ten years without food for a homicide in a fight, and eleven years of the same for perjury. Hence, if someone confessed to being guilty of all four of these misdeeds, the consequence would have been twenty-five years and forty days of fasting. Obviously, these punishments were inapplicable. As a result, and following the model of the German *Wehrgeld*, there was recourse to lists of equivalences (a one-year fast could be "bought off" through thirty-six days of continual fasting or by the recitation of three psalters or by a certain number of lashings), and especially to "ransoms" in the form of hard cash or of penitential masses that had a set price. Clearly, the rich could offer permutations unavailable to the poor, who were obliged to perform their own expiations. Moreover, the system of penance by tariff paid more attention to material offenses than to intentions, to concrete expiation more than contrition. It therefore arrived at its own impasse.

The remedy emerged from a psychological and religious evolution that also took shape in the monastic milieus, departing from Graeco-Roman antiquity in its emphasis on a new value: redemptive repentance.[42] In the ninth to eleventh centuries, Saint Nilus, Saint Romuald, Saint Peter Damian, and the apostles of the *contemptus mundi* fervently preached a dramatic and thoroughgoing conversion that they themselves had experienced.[43] Then, in the twelfth century, Abelard, Saint Anselm, and Hugh of St.-Victor laid stress on conscience, intention, needful shame, and the tears of Peter after he had denied John. These theologians of "contritionism" who highlighted the penitent's responsibility were also, quite logically, philosphers of human liberty.[44] A special citation of Abelard must be made here. For it was he, Jacques Le Goff writes, who "in a fully developed manner, displaced the center of penance from exterior penalty toward interior contrition, and opened to men and women, by the analysis of intentions, the field of modern psychology."[45] In this regard, he stood opposed to the more traditionalist Saint Bernard, who certainly emphasized the humbling of the confessee and salutary remorse, but declared that the sinner is inexcusable and that indifference or ignorance does not diminish the offense.[46]

During the tenth and eleventh centuries, the first prayers *pro petitione lacrimarum* (that is, tears of repentance) appeared, which recovered both a doctrine and practice of monks from the Orient. In the twelfth century, the Cluniac monk Pierre de Celle (d. 1183), at one time Bishop of Chartres, says that tears are the bread of the repentant soul: They put out the fire of the passions, smother the vices, cleanse away sins, soften the heart, spread good speech and action, disseminate virtues, and inspire God's mercy and benevolence.[47] Soon came the move from sweeping contrition to frequent confession. For centuries, however, there was continued stress on "compunction" (self-recognition as a sinner) and the idea was now promoted, against penance by tariff, that the confessee's inherent shame and humiliation in themselves comprised the expiation as such. Hence the passage to the third penitential regime, which granted absolution as soon as confession had been made. Expiation being accomplished with "confession," there was no longer any reason to defer pardon. From henceforth the focus would be placed on this confession itself (which ultimately designated the entire penitential process), and thus on the examination of one's conscience.

The regular practice of the latter, a proof of lucidity and moral rigor, logically necessitated the abandonment of "contritionism," which was "contradictory of the practice of frequent confession. It in fact assumed that penance was unusual enough that the penitent would be impressed by it; it also assumed the confession of grave sins, the recollection of which could be overwhelming to the confessee."[48] Thus the interiorization achieved by monks and theologians led the church, at the Fourth Lateran Council (1215), to impose on the faithful a practice (Canon 21) that doubtless was already being implemented in certain places:[49] annual obligatory confession for each Christian, to the parish priest. This decision was crucial for the history of mentalities, as well as of daily life (softened in practice, it is true, by the work of the mendicant orders and later by that of the Jesuits). Certain regional councils increased the imperatives of Lateran IV and imposed three annual confessions.

This evolution toward a culture of guilt intersected with another that tended, during the same period, to fix the theology of the sacraments and by ricochet to aggrandize the powers of the clergy. By the absolution given to the repentant sinner who desired self-improvement, the priest not only conferred pardon but also multiple favors that would help the penitent go on in his or her regained path of good life. Hence the man of God acquired truly substantial power, as he was the means by which the entire church acted as a mystical body and communion of saints. From then on he alone could give absolution (at the same time that the *chansons de geste* attest to a certain lay practice of confession), and this absolution is the direct source of remissions. Thus there existed, by means of the priest's action, a self-efficacy of the sacrament (*ex opere operato*). It was in this manner that Aquinas summarized the doctrine of penitence that would eventually become the official one.[50]

Did the precept of annual confession imply, in the spirit of the conciliar fathers, a doctrinal affirmation of the necessity of confession in general? Such does not seem to be the case. The majority must have continued to agree with the canonists of the time that aural confession is obligatory only in light of a tradition of the Latin church. Such is the reason why the Greek church, with its differing tradition, has not imposed confession, just as it has not constrained priests to celibacy and consecrates fermented rather than unleavened bread. On the other hand, after the generation of Saint Thomas, theologians characterized the duty of confession as a "divine right," that is, a divine institution, a view confirmed by the Council of Trent (session XIV, ch. V).

In taking its decision of 1215, the teaching church aimed at evident evangelical objectives. It not only wished to develop the practice of the examination of conscience, but also to permit the confessor to judge the religious knowledge of the faithful and to give him the opportunity to catechise, during the course of his interrogatory dialogue with the penitents. This was a singularly effective method of religious acculturation. In tandem, the obligation of annual confession henceforth gave the clergy a considerable device for applying spiritual pressure. Hence the second *Roman de la Rose*'s satiric portrait of Faux-Semblant, the hypocritical and enormously powerful confessor who admits: "And for the salvation of souls / I inquire of lords and ladies / And of everyone their obsessions, / Their characteristics, and their lives."[51] At another level, the new theology of penitence, by enlarging the priest's role, risked diminishing that of the sinner and his or her necessary contrition. With the accent placed so heavily on confession—the Council of Trent would later confirm the duty of reciting all mortal sins—it became difficult to also stress the intentions that had prompted the sinner's transgression. The new penitential system thus included a danger of formalism and legalism: Many people, without sufficiently preparing themselves for the reception of the sacrament through spiritual exercises, mainly sought to keep themselves in line with church doctrine. Therein lay yet another obligation from which, in the regime of "Christianity," there was no possible escape.

CONFESSORS' HANDBOOKS AND CONFESSION MANUALS

Canon XXI of the Fourth Lateran Council stimulated a spectacular rise in literature about sin. One can imagine how the parish priests—soon to be assisted by the mendicant friars—were gripped by genuine panic at the prospect of having regularly to interrogate and judge their flock at the tribunal of penitence. There was thus a need for writings that would enlighten and guide them in their weighty task. In addition, seeking to fight the routine of annual confessions, the more zealous men of the church and the ones most concerned to Christianize the masses undertook an intensive program of orienting people's minds toward guilt. They did so by relentlessly emphasizing the different categories of offenses, as well as the ontological seriousness of sin.

These two converging demands engendered multiple "confessors' handbooks" and "confessions manuals" that replaced the tariff lists of the preceding age. All the same, it is true that the obligation of annual confession decreed by Lateran IV only managed to confirm a movement already in progress, and that works marked by penitential evangelism were being composed before or around 1215. This is notably the case with Alain de Lille's *Liber poenitentialis*, composed in the final years of the twelfth century, and with similar works written around 1210–15 by Thomas of Chabham and Robert of Flamborough, two Englishmen in close contact with the Parisian university world.[52] Following this period, works on sin fall into two main categories. The first, in large and heavy volume format, are legalistic moral treatises that provide for the passing of exact judgments on acts admitted to in confession. Consequently, they also prescribe appropriate atonement and remedies that will prevent relapses.[53] These tomes have been given the general name of confessors' handbooks. The second, more concise and manageable, only give priest and penitent the indispensable guidelines for a good confession, whose purpose is to elicit the admission of every grave fault committed by the sinner. These treatises of diverse titles—at times also entitled "handbooks"—are commonly called confession manuals.

The model for the former group was conceived in the years 1220 to 1240 by the Catalan Dominican Raimond de Peñafort. His *Summa de casibus poenitentiae*, soon enriched by the glosses of another Dominican, gained considerable success. From the thirteenth century, condensed versions of it were edited and distributed. In the fifteenth century, various poets adapted it into verse.[54] In 1603 Rome published an edition two years after canonizing its author. Numerous Franciscans and Dominicans followed Peñafort's example up to the Great Schism. The place held by these orders in this domain should not be surprising. The Franciscans and Dominicans based their Christianizing missions on an ideology of guilt. Whether preachers or inquisitors—or both at once—they soon were authorized to confess despite the privilege supposedly granted to parish priests. It is therefore possible to take the beginning of the thirteenth century as a major caesura in the history of Christianity, since between 1210 and 1215 there occurred the creation of the Franciscans, that of the Dominicans, and the Fourth Lateran Council.

In a way, the "casuistry handbooks" came out as an international production: They were compiled in Spain, Germany, France, Italy, and elsewhere. Medieval borders, however, were blurry. In reality, all these Latin works emerged from a homogeneous context: that of the mendicant friars, for whom Europe was still missionary territory. In the period before 1378, the following are but the major productions of this new literary genre: the *Summa confessorum poenitentia* (ca. 1290) of the German Dominican John of Freiburg; the *Summa de poenitentia* (1295–1302) of the Franciscan Jean d'Erfurt, altered by another Franciscan, Durand de Champagne; the monumental *Summa Astesana* (ca. 1317) composed by the Franciscan Astesanus d'Asti; the shorter *Summa de casibus conscientiae* (1338) by the Dominican Bartolomeo di Pisa (hence the name of *Pisanella*); finally the *Supplementum* (1444) to the *Pisanella* edited by the Franciscan Nicolo d'Ausimo, who adds references to his predecessor's work, held to be too brief.

The first preoccupation of the handbook writers was to aid the confessors by explaining how to interrogate the penitent (notably on the Deadly Sins) and so simplify the diversity of special cases. They also explained how to guide the penitent through his or her examination of conscience, how to illuminate motives and circumstances, and thus how to evaluate the magnitude of an offense, and how to overcome obstacles (fear, shame, presumption, despair) to a good confession. Still, the authors of the handbooks, beginning with Peñafort, were canonists. They perceived the confessors as judges seated at a "tribunal" of penitence, and appointed by the church for "the judgment of souls." From their point of view, sin signified transgression of the law (divine, ecclesiastic, or civil), and their discourse operated around the two categories of "licit" and "illicit." Hence the massive supply of law in their works, and their constant references to legal texts: The resulting tone is often negative and repressive. The handbooks thus progressively drain off considerations of pastorship. They were less and less practical guides for the use of confessors and their congregations, and more and more autonomous works detailing a hard discipline: that of the "cases," itself tightly attached to canon law. This new science became an object for teaching and still more refined and exhaustive speculation. The number of examined "cases" snowballed, and learned authors attempted to settle these problems by drawing on an ever-growing number of authorities (*auctoritates*), demonstrations (*rationes*), and legal decisions (*jura*).

The Great Schism put a temporary halt to the production of these works. Around 1500, however, the genre returned with a vengeance,[55] with the "Summae" successively published by the Franciscans Battista de Salis (1480–90), Angelo de Chiavasso (1490s), and by the Dominicans Sylvester Prierias (ca. 1516), Giovanni Cagnnazzo de Taggia (1517), and the famous Gaetano (1525). With the exception of the last example, which was brief and relatively nonjuridical, these new Italian "summae" emphasize—despite certain evangelical touches—the erudition and technicalities of the period prior to the Great Schism. In this regard, Prierias's encyclopedic *Summa summarum* is particularly revealing. The author states that he has used the works of forty-eight theologians, 113 jurists, and eighteen other "Summaists." Cagnazzo, however, goes still further, as he gathers 20 percent more of cited authors and articles: an excess of learning that sought support from actual cases but had lost its contact with reality. These observations clarify Luther's hostility to canon law, which he called "The Adversary of God," and his stance, notably in *The Babylonian Captivity*, not against confession per se, but against the church's practice of it. For him, the sacrament of penance had become the most powerful weapon of the Roman hierarchy's domination.[56] Among the Roman negotiators with whom Luther could not reach agreement were none other than Gaetano and Prierias. In December 1520 the Reformer burned at the stake not only the Papal Bull "Exsurge Domine" but also Angelo de Chiavasso's *Summa angelica*, which he called the "Diabolica." To Luther, this work embodied all the defects of the Catholic penitential system. After the Council of Trent, a different spirit inspired a new, less legalistic casuistry. With canon law supplying less and less adequate answers to new situations brought about by major social transformations, reference started to be made not only to written laws but also to a moral law inscribed in the individual conscience. At the same time, the notion of extenuating circumstances was gaining currency.

Even if the massive standing of the law had increasingly influenced theology and the practice of penance, more clearly evangelical preoccupations can be found in the confession manuals themselves. From the thirteenth to the early sixteenth century, an enormous literature in this field developed, where numerous anonymous books mingled with the writings of famous people. Among the first group, the Anglo-Norman *Manuel des Péchés* (second half of the thirteenth century) occupies a special place.[57] In the second group, there stands out the *Somme Le Roi* (ca. 1280), a moral treatise designed to facilitate the examination of the conscience, which was written at the request of Philip III ("le Hardi") by his confessor, the friar-preacher Laurent.[58] Also noteworthy are the *Specchio della vera penitenza* by the Florentine

Dominican Giacomo Passavanti (d. 1357), the two complementary treatises (*Lumen confessorum* and *Modus confitendi*) by the Spanish Benedictine André d'Escobar (d. 1427), the *Specchio della confessione* and the *Renovamini* of the Franciscan San Bernardino di Siena (d. 1444), and three tracts by the Dominican San Antonino di Firenze (d. 1459): *Omnis mortalium cura, Curam illius habe*, and the *Confessionale*, which preceded his great *Summa theologica*. This last-named book constituted the first work of "moral theology" composed in Christian Europe aimed at a "guiding science of human conduct."[59] Beyond the Mediterranean countries, the main titles were the *De Confessione* of Henricus of Langenstein (d. 1397); the *Manuale confessorum* of the Dominican Johann Nider (d. 1438), also the author of the famous *Formicarius*, directed against witches; the *Tractatus de confessione* of Matthias of Cracow (d. 1410); and the Paris University chancellor Jean Gerson's *Miroir de l'âme* and *De la confession*, which in 1404 he added to the *Art de bien mourir* in a *Livre des trois parties*. Two intermediate works, between a handbook and a manual, merit special mention for the reception they garnered. These are the *Manipulus curatorum* of Guy de Montrocher, the fourteenth-century curé of Teruel, and the *Confessionale* of the Dutch humanist Godschalk Rosemondt, a contemporary of Erasmus and Luther.[60]

As with the "Summae of cases," the best-known of the confession manuals were often edited by members of the mendicant orders. This fact is yet another proof of their concern to take charge of the Christianizing mission. On the other hand, and as previously, this international production remained quite homogeneous, as it reflected the pedagogical obsessions that were then emerging in the most militant sector of the teaching church. Certain confession manuals were more particularly written for priests who strove to administer the sacrament of penance. Such is the case with San Antonino's *Confessionale* and Nider's *Manuale confessorum*, which both contain instructions for interrogating the penitent, the way to counsel this person, the penance to prescribe, and the manner of providing absolution. As for the *Tractatus* of Matthias of Cracow, it was composed primarily for those who confessed others in the religious orders: Hence the precise details regarding the transgression of vows and the rules of conventual life.

At the same time, other texts were expressly aimed at the general public of the faithful. The prologue to the *Manuel des péchés* clearly announces: "This is for the laypeople." Other authors specify that they write for those "who are not grammarians," "who are not of the clergy," or "for those who are neither lettered nor clerics."[61] These last formulas must be understood in the larger sense, as they seem to have embraced not only laypeople but also numerous parish priests whose familiarity with Latin was only slight. This double public was the most frequent target of the confession manual authors, a fact that explains their frequent recourse to the vernacular. Passavanti wrote his *Specchio della vera penitenza* in Italian and San Bernardino di Siena did the same with his two previously mentioned treatises. San Antonino published Latin and Italian versions of his writings on confession. The *Summa pacifica*, in reality more a manual than a summa, by the Franciscan Pacifico di Novara was originally composed in Italian. As for Gerson, although he translated them into Latin for an international audience, he first put out in French the *Miroir de l'âme, De la confession*, and the *Art de bien mourir*. Finally, numerous anonymous "confession formulas," in verse and prose, which proliferated during the fifteenth century, especially in England and Germany, were written in the vernacular.[62]

Signed or not, the confession manuals thus had a double usage for both the priest and the worshipper. In their didactic way, they taught how to administer and how to receive the sacrament of penance. Penitential doctrine and spiritual formation were provided, within a frame that encompassed three successive phases of the sacramental act: the preparation of the penitent (reception, exhortations), his or her confessions, and finally their consequences (the penance to be performed and the absolution).[63] Within this required procedure, however, the examination (by the confessor) and the confession (by the worshipper) attract the author's special attention. The examination of conscience was carried on with reference to the Seven Deadly Sins, to the Ten Commandments, to the five senses, and also occasionally to the twelve articles of the *Credo*. Certain manuals also invoke other parameters: the eight beatitudes, the six or seven bodily acts of mercy, the six or seven spiritual acts of mercy, the four cardinal virtues, the three theological virtues, and so on. Thus, as the number of written works increased, so too did the penitential inquiry expand its search for the often aggravating circumstances of sin, and multiplied the viewpoints by which transgression could be considered. San Antonino, Pacifico di Novara, and many composers of anonymous manuals took account of considerations relating to the professional status of the penitent and to his political duties.[64] Above all, however, the scholastic mania for subdivision, and its propensity to categorize, refine, and complicate, led, in particular with the anonymous works, to a prodigious inflation of the number of sins. This evolution touched, confirmed, and accentuated a larger movement that led a troubled civilization to be more and more inclined toward guilt. From then on, the interrogation of the penitent would be extraordinarily insistent, and the examination of the conscience equally meticulous. This extremism is evident in the *Confessio generalis brevis et utilis*, which enumerates, in order of increasing gravity, a number of different sexual crimes. The following chapter will more thoroughly discuss this issue, about which the church had always wished the faithful to be most vigilant.[65] The sixteen categories of sin were arranged in the following order: (1) the immodest kiss; (2) the immodest touch; (3) fornication; (4) debauchery, often understood as the seduction of a virgin; (5) simple adultery (when one partner was married); (6) double adultery (when both were married); (7) willful sacrilege (when one of the partners had taken religious vows); (8) the abduction and rape of a virgin; (9) the abduction and rape of a married woman (a more serious sin than the previous, being compounded with adultery); (10) the abduction and rape of a nun; (11) incest; (12) masturbation, first of the sins against nature; (13) improper sexual positions, even between married couples; (14) unnatural sexual relations; (15) sodomy; and (16) bestiality.

Certain handbooks were thus transformed into long lists of possible transgressions, which—as in the preceding example—took the name of *confessio generalis*. For Gerson and others, this term could designate a confession that applied to the penitent's entire life since "the age of reason" (about seven). In the fourteenth and fifteenth centuries, however, "*confessio generalis*" mainly referred to the long lists of sins provided for confessors, which they in turn explained to the penitents. In particular, these works featured refinements and detailed modifications of earlier writings.[66] One treatise entitled *Quia circa confessionem*, lists 153 sins of thought, word, deed, and omission. Another, the *Primo confitens debet*, identifies 168 crimes and 106 sinful deficiencies. A third, the *Confessio generalis exigit*, distributes sins on the basis of their opposition to the virtues, and thus locates 92 types of transgression. The *Tractatum praesentem* divides the examination of the Fourth through Tenth Commandments into three parts, each including an average of eight to ten sins. This notwithstanding, there ensues a list of Deadly Sins with their "offspring," and the enumeration of fifteen various other offenses. This supersophistication helps to clarify Luther's later protests against these "excogitations of charlatans," which torture the spirit "[in regard to] the mothers, daughters, sisters, parents, branches, and fruits of sins. Certain crafty and completely idle men have thus concocted a thoroughly absurd family tree, with degrees of consanguinity and relationship, so rich is the fecundity of their impiety and ignorance."[67]

From the end of the fourteenth century, certain authors add to the classic sins (Deadly, against the Commandments, those pertaining to the five senses, and so on), particularly rebellious offenses against Heaven (*clamantia in coelum*)—murder, sodomy, and so on—crimes of complicity (*aliena*), and sins against the Holy Spirit—commitment to evil or error, despair, and so forth. These increasingly exhaustive and overloaded lists clearly risked turning confession into a formalized and almost mechanical recitation of a certain number of excessively catalogued offenses. Nevertheless, it is necessary to perceive the underlying element of the teaching church's collective mentality: the fear of incorrect and sacrilegious confession, which deeply troubled Gerson,[68] and the conviction that God the Creditor kept an exact account of every sin and every debt. To escape such a rigorous judge, it would have been impossible to acquire too much guilt. For "it is an evil thing, most weighty and dangerous, to neglectfully forget one's sins."[69]

Careful self-scrutiny could be possible only if one knew all the ruses by which the Evil One, adapting his tactics to every single personality, could toy with one's best intentions and draw well-disposed but inadequately self-aware souls into sin. Hence Gerson composed (in French) a *Traité des diverse tentations de l'Ennemi*.[70] With great psychological acumen, this book clarifies the multiple traps whereby one becomes a sinner in believing one's self to be virtuous. To support his argument, Gerson studies no less that fifty-eight cases, or "temptations," by which this conversion of good into evil may happen almost without one's knowledge. At times the Enemy leaves off tempting one's soul for a certain period, and so one's vigilance becomes relaxed. He encourages a man to undertake "high and mighty works of virtue," knowing that these cannot be achieved and the victim will then founder in sorrow. To the latter he sends "very great and marvelous pains, in the semblance of devotions, so that the person takes full pleasure in such sorrow, and only wishes to love or serve God in order to acquire more such pain." This temptation is familiar to mystics. At other times, the Enemy sends happy thoughts to someone, not for the good but to prevent prayer, for example during mass. Or again, "repentant individuals desire in good faith never to sin again; and the Enemy then reminds them . . . of their frailty and how frequently they are entangled in sin." Gerson does not bother to consider pleasure. One of his other pamphlets, for example, teaches *Le profit de savoir quel est péché mortel et veniel*[71] ("The benefits of knowing deadly from venial sin"). Likewise, the *Traité des diverse tentations* aims to be reassuring and offers an appropriate parry for every Satanic trap. All the same, there is a sense that this refinement of introspection and ceaseless self-examination risked causing a sort of psychic paralysis. In any case, the moral works of Gerson, at least for their main audience, played a leading role in the history of sin in the West.

A few figures will clarify the measure of this guilt-instilling propaganda. The text of the *Somme le Roi* survives in a hundred or more manuscripts,[72] ten of which are English translations. Guy de Montrocher's *Manipulus curatorum* went through ninety-eight editions in the fifteenth and a dozen in the sixteenth century (in Paris, London, Venice, Louvain, and Antwerp). The *Summa angelica*, vilified by Luther, came out in twenty-four incunabula editions (printed in Venice, Lyon, Nüremberg, and Strasbourg) and twenty-three sixteenth-century ones. Gerson's *Opus tripartitum*, after sixteen fifteenth-century editions, had considerable success until the eighteenth century: French bishops continued to recommend its reading. It appeared in Flemish, Swedish, German, and Spanish translations, including a Mexican edition of 1544. Gerson's complete works were themselves printed ten times before 1521. Fifty-four manuscripts of his *De modo audiendi confessiones* have been discovered. The two "giants," however, of the ecclesiastical literature on sin were Andreas d'Escobar and San Antonino. The first author's *Modus confitendi* went through some eighty-six different fifteenth-century editions, published in twenty-three European cities, while his *Lumen confessorum* appeared in forty-eight different incunabula editions. As for San Antonino's *Confessionale*, in the fifteenth century it was printed 119 times in thirty-two cities.[73]

These works by famous authors, however, must be placed in context with the anonymous confessional tracts, disseminated by printing throughout Europe. For instance, just before Luther's period there appeared in Germany the *Peycht Spiegel der Sünder* ("The Mirror for the Confession of Sinners"), published in Nuremberg in 1510, and the "Manual for Parish Priests," which was published fifteen times in the fifteenth century and three more times between 1512 and 1514. The first, in the vernacular, addresses the reader: "Young confessor, I was entreated by many penitents to compose a short treatise on confession for layfolk"—nevertheless, the work is two hundred pages long. In contrast, the "Manual for Parish Priests" is in Latin, but in easy prose and a convenient format. During the years just prior to the Reformation, this book seems to have been bedside reading for many central German priests.[74] It must be repeated, however, that these works comprised only two elements of an enormous library, wherein are found manuscripts and early printed works, such as various "Mirrors of Sinners" and other guides to successful confession. Under the word "confession," a German catalogue has inventoried thirty-five different anonymous works published between the invention of printing and the year 1500. Particular mention should be made here of 100- to 200-line poems whose shared theme was "hasten your confession" (*poeniteas cito*). For the fifteenth century, six different versions of this pressing admonition have been identified. The most widely circulated, in 111 verses with commentary and interlinear glosses, bore the title *Libellus de modo poenitendi et confitendi*. Fifty-one editions of this work appeared between 1485 and 1520, six in Cologne and a dozen each for Paris, Antwerp, and Daventer.[75]

The church's encouragement of lay introspection necessarily called for the implementation of contemporary European vernaculars. Thus the Anglo-Norman *Manuel des péchés* was translated into English as soon as French began to be "too little understood" across the channel. Otherwise the book would have started to gather dust in curio shops. Hence its fourteenth-century adaptation into English by the monk Robert Mannyng, with the title *Handlyng Synne*, a poem of some 12,630 verses, enriched with tales and anecdotes.[76]

In France two works, the *Doctrinal aux simples gens* and the *Compost et Kalendrier des bergiers*, deserve special mention. Although produced in ecclesiastical contexts, these books were aimed at relatively large audiences and were thus written in the vernacular. There exist two *Doctrinals*[77]: a short version sometimes attributed to Gerson, sometimes to Guy de Roye, Archbishop of Sens (1385–90), then of Reims (1390–1409); and a long version, signed by a monk of Cluny (ca. 1388). The short version survives in twenty manuscripts, most of which belonged to laypeople. It was published only once, however, before 1800. On the other hand, the long text, which was translated into Provençal and English, is preserved not only in fifteen manuscripts but also in thirty-seven editions published between 1478 and the mid-seventeenth century. The four latest examples, with a text revised to suit Counter-Reformation taste, formed part of the "Bibliotheque bleue" of Toyes. Simultaneously, inspired by the *Somme le Roi* and Guy de Montrocher's *Manipulus*, the *Doctrinal aux simples gens* or the *Doctrinal de sapience* (long version) is a combined summary of the Catholic faith, a moral treatise, a guide for priests, and a book of devotion. A catalogue of truths of the faith but also of interdictions, it privileges ethics over dogma. Relentlessly emphasizing the Passion of Christ, this work invites human beings to suffer and detach themselves from a sinning world.

The more original *Compost et Kalendrier des bergiers* was published in 1491 by the printer-bookseller Guyot Marchant, also a priest-artist whose workshop was located behind the Collège de Navarre (the former site of the Ecole Polytechnique). The 1493 edition consulted here is fuller than the preceding one, and embellished with drawings by Antoine Vérard.[78] In short, the *Compost et Kalendrier* . . . is designed to be the common person's encyclopedia. The shepherd, who is the supposed editor of this illustrated almanac, gives his readers all sorts of useful information concerning new moons and eclipses, "the constitution and regimen of health," "the astrology of the signs, stars, and planets, and the physiognomy of shepherds." Moreover, an entire third of this highly didactic calendar focuses on "the tree of vices, the tree of virtues, and the symbolic tower of knowledge." With great refinement, the author identifies the eighty-seven branches of the Deadly Sins and further subdivides them by attributing three offshoots to each one: hence a total of 261 "branches." In turn, each of these blossoms with three distinct "bunches of foliage," making for an impressive total of 783 possibilities for falling prey to one of the Seven Deadly Sins. Quite logically, this long description of the Tree of Vices is followed by the illustrated evocation of the "pains of hell, comminatories of sin." The counterpart is "health-giving wisdom and the tree or field of virtues." At the end of this extremely detailed moral lesson, an involved scholastic diagram reveals the architecture of the "tower of wisdom," at whose summit stands a gibbet with a hanged man: Such is the punishment that awaits the "wicked." Like the *danses macabres*, one of which appears in its pages, the *Compost et Kalendrier* . . . makes an urgent plea for prompt confession:

> *O man in danger, know this for certain:*
> *If you nor seek nor quickly entertain*
> *A wish to make amends, in contrition,*
> *Someday quite soon, you shall then ascertain*
> *A man—thyself—in defeat and perdition.*"[79]

With or without illustrations, this universal almanac was continually reprinted during the next three centuries by editors who specialized in "popular" publications.[80]

SIN IN LAY LITERATURE

Side by side with the ecclesiastics, laypeople—such as Saint Louis[81]—also wrote at length on sin, and in similar terms. This syndrome appears as early as the thirteenth century, when the knight Jean de Journy composed at Cyprus a poem exclusively about confession. This work, the *Dîme de pénitence*, was imposed on Journy for the expiation of his sins, and he executed his task "joyously."[82] He explains that our flesh is a "spy," ready to ambush us, and that the human body never stops waging war on the soul, with an army whose captains are Envy, Anger, Avarice, and above all Pride and Arrogance. One can only "avenge" one's faults through penance, which includes contrition, confession, and atonement. "Amaritude," or contrition, is like a good washing that requires active heat and extended scrubbing of dirty linen. As soon as a man becomes aware of the extent of his errors, "at once he tells them, without delay." Thus he stirs up his faults, as a washerwoman mixes her laundry. Once confession to the priest has been made, the sinner willingly agrees to fast (the supreme weapon against the flesh) and to perform other penitential works: These will shatter the doors of the prison where the Enemy holds one captive. Less didactic, and more moving, are the *Congés* of Jean Bodel, poet and leper, which date from the early thirteenth century and may comprise the earliest literary confession in the French language.[83] The *trouvère* of Arras has sinned; he has improperly profited from life's pleasure. With a hideous malady, God now guides him to repentance and makes him enter into a "prolonged Lent" and a "laborious week" (that is, a Holy Week) that will continue until his death. He accepts this suffering, as an expiation that can only lead him to God:

> *Now the Lord requires me thus to endure*
> *The evil that wounds my heart,*
> *That by willingly accepting my pain I will be fit*
> *To present my soul to Him. (537–540)*

Rutebeuf, a contemporary of Saint Louis who suffered gambling debts and marital unhappiness, expresses a violent animosity toward the mendicant orders. Still, the church taught him the whereabouts of the road to heaven. This route, clearly mapped out in *Le Voyage de paradis*,[84] systematically bypasses the dwelling places of the deadly sins. Pity, the husband of Charity, instructs the poet to make his way to the House of Confession, while avoiding the dangerous residence of Pride, "friend to all other sins." Slightly below the House of Pride, reached by a narrow black valley, lies the House of Avarice, with its dark vassals; just beyond is the Home of Anger, "who is forever gnashing his teeth." Its frame is made of hatred and its fence of sorrow. At the bottom of a dark valley, where no light enters, Envy lies hidden, not far from Idleness, "the aunt of Sloth." A few steps away, at the inn of Chance, lives Gluttony, "the sister of Excess." Lechery is Gluttony's next-door neighbor, and whoever rides into her house comes out naked and shoeless. She destroys both body and soul, and charges a high price for her services. Any reasonable person must therefore avoid these evil places and proceed unswervingly toward the City of Repentance, where misfortune never befalls anyone. This city was founded after Christ's resurrection, on the day of Pentecost, in the very place where the Holy Ghost descended to inspire the apostles to convert the "perfidious" Jews. It is protected by four sturdy gates, called Memory, Fear, Hope-in-Our-Savior's-Compassion, and True Love. This last portal gives access to the House of Confession, where all is made pure.

In his great and innovative epic, the supreme literary achievement of the Middle Ages, Dante likewise follows this difficult route to Paradise. It is symptomatic that *The Divine Comedy* entirely bases itself on sin, since this powerful work not only evokes the provisional and definitive punishments of those who gave in to Satanic temptations but also the rewards given to the few select souls who resisted such evil. Canto I makes clear that the way to Divine Grace is blocked by three beasts: the *lupa* (avarice), the *lonza* (lechery), and the *lione* (pride). Dante is the inspired torturer of the damned but also of the elect souls in Purgatory. For he does not stop at describing the vile bath where the squatting Thaïs continually scratches herself, the tombs of fire where those who denied the soul's immortality are confined, or the hallucinating spectacle of the fomenters of discord, whose dismembered bodies keep walking through all eternity. He also assigns harsh torments to the future blessed souls, who for a time must be purified in Purgatory. In Hell, the wrathful are suffocated in the muck of the river Styx; those in Purgatory laboriously struggle for their breath in the thick smoke that completely engulfs their terrace. The simoniacs of the eighth circle are sunken upside down in the earth for which they were so greedy; and the misers and prodigals on the fifth terrace are tightly bound to the earth. In Hell, tongues of fire fall upon the sodomites; in Purgatory, a wall of fire impedes the lecherous on the seventh terrace, the heterosexuals as well as the homosexuals. Even if the poet, in the fiction of his otherworld voyage, gives himself convenient opportunities to take revenge on his enemies, *The Divine Comedy* must be placed at the center of the history of sin in the West. Its centrality is especially apparent from its wide diffusion—fifteen fifteenth-century editions, thirty in the sixteenth century—in Europe, which did not always coincide, however, with a genuine understanding on the part of the humanists.[85] In any case, Dante's masterpiece shows that from the fourteenth century on, even among laypeople, the formation of a guilt consciousness had become the main preoccupation of the ruling culture.

In a somewhat different vein, *The Canterbury Tales* demonstrate this growing mentality of guilt. This collection, put together around 1386 by a squire-poet who married a lady-in-waiting to the queen, knew Froissart, and heard Wycliffe's sermons, presents a vast group portrait of late medieval English society. Chaucer portrays great lords and knights, clerks and nuns, merchants and rustics, rogues and laborers, within the frame of the pilgrimage to Canterbury that annually attracted large crowds of the faithful. Nonetheless, the final tale—not always attributed to Chaucer—is a strongly didactic treatise on penance, placed in the mouth of a village parson.[86] The path to Salvation, this character declares, passes through penance, which resembles a tree whose root is Contrition. Confession forms its branches and leaves, and Atonement its fruit, with the understanding that Repentance involves not only actions but also intentions, not only deeds but words. "Contricion destroyeth the prison of helle, and maketh wayk and fieble alle the strengthes of the develes, and restoreth the yiftes of the Hooly Goost" (sec. 310). The Parson has read Aquinas, and reestablishes the latter's distinction between Deadly and venial sin. With Deadly Sin, "man loveth any creature moor than Jhesu Christ," whereas with venial sin, "man love Jhesu Christ lasse than hym mooghte" (sec. 357). Humans must beware the accumulation of venial sins: "A greet wave of the see comth som tyme with so greet a vilence that it drencheth the ship. And the same harm doon som tyme the smale dropes of water, that entren thurgh a litel crevace into the thurrok, and into the botme of the ship, if men be so negligent that they ne discharge hem nat by tyme" (sec. 362).

There then follows a detailed analysis of the Deadly Sins and the remedies for overcoming them. Pride has so many branches that "no man kan outrely telle the nombre of the twigges and of the harmes" (sec. 389). Envy, however, is "the worste synne that is. For soothly, alle othere synnes been somtyme oonly agains a special vertu; but certes, Envye is agayns all vertues and agayns all goodnesses" (sec. 487–488). As for Ire, "it is the develes fourneys, that is eschawfed with the fir of helle" (sec. 545). It destroys all spiritual things, just as fire destroys earthly things. Idleness weighs man down and is a mortal sin, since the Book says: Cursed be he who neglects to fulfill the service of God. Avarice, or the heart's concupiscence for worldly possessions, is an attitude of idolatry: "What difference is bitwixe an ydolastre and an avaricious man, but that an ydolastre, per aventure, ne hath but o maumet or two, and the avaricious man hath manye? For certes, every floryn in his cofre is his mawmet" (sec. 748). Gluttony has corrupted the world, as seen in the sin of Adam and Eve. It also has many branches, first among them Drunkenness, "the horrible sepulture of mannes resoun" (sec. 821). The parson, following Saint Gregory, then cites the other limbs of gluttony:

> *The first is for to ete biforn tyme to ete. The seconde is whan a man get hym to delicaat mete or drynke. / The thridde is whan man taken to muche over mesure. The fourthe is curiositee, with greet contente to maken and apparaillen his mete. The fifth is for to eten to gredily. / Thise been the fyve fyngres of the develes hand, by which he draweth folk to synne. (sec. 828–829).*

The branches of lechery, moreover, are the five fingers of Satan's other hand, ever desiring to lure people into "villanye":

> *The firste fynger is the fool lookynge of the fool womman and of the fool man, that sleeth, right as the basilicok sleeth folk by the venym of his sighte; for the coveitise of eyen folweth the coveitise of the herte. / The second fynger is the vileyns touchynge in wikked manere. And therefore seith Salomon that "whoso toucheth and handleth a womman, he fareth lyk hym that handleth the scorpioun that styngeth and sodeynly sleeth thurgh his envenymynge"; as whoso toucheth warm pych, it shent his fyngres. / The thridde is foule wordes, that fareth lyk fyr, that right anon brenneth the herte. / The fourthe fynger is the kissynge; and trewely he were a greet fool, that wolde kisse the mouth of a brennynge oven or of a fourneys. And for that many man weneth that he may not synne, for no likerousnesse that he dooth with his wyf, certes, that opinion is fals. God woot, a man may sleen hymself with his owene knyf, and make hymself dronken of his owene tonne . . . The fifthe fynger of the develes hand is the stynkynge dede of lecherie" (sec. 852–861)*

The Parson concludes his homily with advice on the means of confession and an invitation to avoid the four obstacles to penance: fear of expiation; the shame of declaring one's sins; the hope of a long life or of obtaining God's pity without effort; or conversely, the despair of divine mercy and one's own improvement. Clearly, this sermon, replete with unction, is an offshoot of earlier handbooks and other manuals of sins that were listed and briefly discussed above. "The Parson's Tale" allows, if not for the precise measuring, at least for the guessing at the propagation of the guilt-instilling wave that issued from monastic circles into an ever larger general audience. Likewise, *Handlyng Synne* was reused in the mid-fifteenth century by an English nobleman, Peter Idle, who compiled a book of *Instructions* for the benefit of his son. This collection has survived in eight manuscripts. In fact, Idle does not only address his son, but all Christians, whom he warns against "the worlde, the flesshe, the feende." He thus advises his readers to examine themselves by the light of the Ten Commandments and the Seven Sacraments, in order to shun the "dedly synne / Suche as mankynde daily falleth ynne."[87]

In France, the *Menagier de Paris* is a similar compendium of "instructions."[88] A rich and elderly Parisian burgher composed this work in 1393, for the use of his young wife as well as for others. For he writes to her, "I know, that after you and myself this book will be dearly held in the hands of our children and of our friends."[89] The text contains various historical reminders, useful information on the foods eaten by both the court and the Parisian populace, precepts on the art of managing a household, advice on gardening and how to choose horses, an extended cooking treatise, and another one, no less detailed, on hunting with the sparrow hawk. The book begins, however, with a moral lesson and a confession manual, founded on the soon-to-be classic list of Deadly Sins and the appropriate virtues for remedying them:

> *Now I shall show you . . . just how you may be sinful. First let us list the names and conditions of the Seven Deadly Sins, which are so vile that all other sins are dependent on them, and are called deadly for the death toward which the soul is taken when the Enemy succeeds in enslaving the heart to their laborious demands. And also, in order that you henceforth safeguard yourself from the said sins, I shall show and teach you the names and power of the Seven Virtues which are opposed to the seven aforesaid sins and are the fitting medicine and remedy against their dependent sins, called deadly; as soon as the virtue arrives, the sin completely goes away.*[90]

Naturally, each sin is subdivided into "branches." An austere moral ensues upon this enumeration, as the husband proposes, or rather imposes, a highly regulated existence on his young wife: no lying in bed, no excessive meals, no indecent caprices with her spouse:

> *The third branch of sloth is carnality. Carnality is the seeking after the desires of the flesh, as sleeping on fine beds, lying about for long periods of time, indulging in lazy mornings, as when one is lounging in bed and the bells have sounded out the mass, and one ignores it, rolls over, and goes back to sleep . . . the first branch [of gluttony] is eating before one should, that is, too much in the morning, or before one has prayed or gone to church and heard the word of God and his Commandments; for a person should have sense and discretion, and not eat before tierce [nine in the morning], if there is no need caused by sickness or weakness or any other constraint.*

The young wife is thus encouraged to admit to her confessor, "Many times have I drunk without being thirsty, for which my body has been damaged, disordered, and ill-disposed . . . ; meats also have I eaten, without the need or any hunger." At the "fifth branch of lechery," the following warning is made: "Every man may very greatly and in many different ways sin with his own wife," when the two spouses behave themselves "against the law, and in any other indecent manner."[91]

One of the chief characteristics of this period's intensive Christianization consists in the mass diffusion of a rule of life conceived by ascetics. Enlarged to meet the dimensions of an entire civilization, this Draconian ethic incorporates marriage only with reluctance—a point that deserves repeating—and holds secular pastimes in extremely low esteem. In the Middle Ages, married couples were prohibited from having sexual relations during times of collective penitence: Lent, vigils, novenas, and triduums. A fast without chastity was only a half fast. Joys of the table and of the bed were considered to be close partners. Franco Chiavaro writes that "a rapid estimate of these days [of prohibition] in the medieval calendar leads to the conclusion that for nearly half the year one had to abstain from amorous marital relations. If to this calculation are added the periods of menstruation and full pregnancy—three months before and forty days after childbirth—it must be concluded that for the greater part of the year, sex between spouses was forbidden."[92]

During the time when European modernity was taking shape, it is clear that the meditation on sin gripped the conscience of the cultivated elite and is notably expressed in poetic discourse. In a famous section of his *Pater*, the "rhetoriquer" Jean Molinet (1435–1507) thus develops the biblical verse *Debita nostra*:

By the false gaze, the greedy tongue,
A too gluttonous and begging mouth,
In speaking and in eating,
Our poor soul, dirty and vile,
Turns away from the course of reason.[93]

In his turn, François Villon confesses:

I am a sinner, I know it well,
Yet God wills not my death, but that
I should reform and live in righteousness,
I and others touched by sin.[94]

It is revealing that in the Germanic countries, Sebastian Brant's *Ship of Fools* (*Narrenschiff*) (1494) had extraordinary success. A few years later, Ulrich van Hutten would write that "few works, in all the history of literature and nations, have had such a sudden and profound effect."[95] The author was compared to Homer, Dante, and Petrarch. At the cathedral of Strasbourg, the preacher Geiler gave a hundred sermons whose themes were drawn from the *Narrenschiff*, and the book also inspired Murner, Fischart, Erasmus, and Sachs. The work was soon adapted into Latin and translated into French, English, Flemish, and other languages, becoming one of the greatest successes of the sixteenth-century book trade. The son of a Strasbourg innkeeper, having become a "doctor in both laws" at the University of Basel, Brant returned in 1500 (at the age of forty-two or forty-three) to his hometown, whose secretary he remained until his death in 1521. This married layman and father of seven children had read all the known Greek and Latin authors and held a lively admiration for Virgil. At one and the same time serious, irritable, pious, and pessimistic, he was thirty-five when he wrote his poem on sin. For such is the focus of the *Ship of Fools*: "Fools are those afflicted with vices, the senseless men who do not realize that their acts against divine law doom them to perdition."[96] Furthermore, Brant denounces with equal vigor venial sins—the mania for travel, disobeying doctors' orders, the custom of singing in the streets at night—and the more serious vices—pride, wrath, envy, and so on. Albeit in a disorganized manner, the Deadly Sins are thus vilified anew, amid diverse satires ridiculing charlatans, bureaucrats, brutish soldiers, and false scholars. Like a preacher, Brant castigates dancing:

. . . But later then I called to mind
That dance and sin are one in kind
That very easily 'tis scented:
The dance by Satan was invented
When he devised the golden calf
And taught some men at God to laugh
. . . The pagan Venus gives her hand
And purity is rudely banned[97]

The sin of omission merits special mention: "Some trees do burn in hell below / On which good fruit would never grow."[98] This gloomy picture of a mad and stumbling humanity appears within an entire eschatological panorama, a point stressed in *La Peur en Occident*: the end of the world looms on the horizon. Brant opines,

> *I'm tempted candidly to say:*
> *We do approach the Judgment Day,*
> *Since mercy's held in cold despite*
> *We're now approaching total night,*
> *Such things have never happened yet,*
> *The vessel sways, it may upset.*[99]

CHAPTER 7

The Realm of the Confessor

ENVY

The decision of the Fourth Lateran Council (1215) in favor of mandatory confession vastly enlarged both the power and the jurisdiction of the confessor, who had become a specialist in cases of conscience. A refined as well as massive casuistry profoundly altered mentalities within a civilization that was itself undergoing transformation.

Mireille Vincent-Cassy's study, *L'Envie en France du XIIIe au XVe siècle*, convincingly shows how the efforts of the church, combined with economic and social developments, brought about a collective awareness of this Deadly Sin that mainstream opinion had before only dimly perceived. Undeniably, envy had made an early appearance on the blacklist of major offenses drawn up by specialists in moral theology. Many people, however, confused envy with amorous jealousy, and before the thirteenth century, "except in a few cases, it was not genuinely distinguishable, neither in manuscripts, nor in sculpture, nor in painting. It was impossible to represent Envy, because its character was not fully defined."[1] Then, however, the synodal statutes of Angers (1216–19), which each priest of this diocese was supposed to possess, include this formula: "The confessor will inquire of the penitent if he grieves or has grieved over the advantages of his neighbor, or if he has been glad of his neighbor's misfortune."[2] For his part, Aquinas demonstrates that Lucifer and his demons have committed and still commit but two sins: Pride and Envy. It was through Pride that they disobeyed God. Their disgrace, however, consists in being torn by the pangs of envy, since on the one hand they behold in vain their paradise lost and on the other they are enraged to see humans reaching this place of happiness from which they are forever excluded. Hence they seek, by temptation, to prevent mortals from attaining the port of salvation.[3]

The Norman Cistercian Guillaume de Digulleville, who between 1330 and 1358 composed a three-part allegorical poem (the *Pèlerinage de vie humaine*, the *Pèlerinage de l'âme* and the *Pèlerinage de Jésus-Christ*), gives an evocative description of Envy. His protagonist the Pilgrim meets an old emaciated woman who creeps about like a snake. The two looks that flash from her eyes are "wrath at the joy of others" and "joy in others' adversity." On her back she carries Treason and Detraction. The first, an expert in deception, conceals a knife and a box of poison. She bites without barking and lurks in the grass like a snake that lies in wait for its prey. She is the worm-eaten plank that breaks under one's feet. "Detraction" holds the end of a dagger between her teeth, which stabs ears willing to heed her cruel lies. She has a bloodied face, like that of a wolf who has choked a lamb.[4] These descriptions take on their full importance with the recognition that de Digulleville's works, especially the *Pèlerinage de vie humaine*, maintained a great success until the sixteenth century and even beyond. Bunyan's *The Pilgrim's Progress* (1678–84), for many years the most popular book in the English-speaking world after the Bible, is an imitation of the *Pèlerinage de vie humaine*.

In surveying French chronicles, novels, poems, and satiric works of the thirteenth to fifteenth centuries and maintaining a more or less equal number of pages for each century, Vincent-Cassy traces an extremely infrequent thirteenth-century use of the word "envy" (also true for the twelfth century). Geoffroide Villehardouin, for example, uses the word only twice, and it is found only six times in the 1,500 quarto pages of the 1225 version of *Lancelot du Lac*, edited by Heinrich O. Sommer. For the first half of the fourteenth century, the situation hardly changes: not a single mention in Joinville, nor in Jean de Venette, and only two in the chronicler Guillaume de Nangis. In contrast, seventy-eight references to envy occur in the writings of Gilles li Muisis, abbot of Tournai, (ca. 1350). Meanwhile, envy is a keynote in the poetry of Eustachè Deschamps. The fifteenth-century authors Monstrelet and Chastellain employ the term 80 and 111 times, respectively.[5] It therefore appears that the Black Death, followed by the tragic events of the 1380s, pushed to a mass level an identification of envy that previously had been clear only in monastic circles.

A parallel study of the French iconography of envy during the same period leads to similar conclusions. Vincent-Cassy locates only three depictions of envy in the thirteenth and four in the fourteenth century, but forty-five in the fifteenth. Even if numerous reconstructions of churches were necessary after the Hundred Years' War, which may partially explain the last figure, the visual documentation can only confirm the onomastic research.[6] It would seem that an entire civilization, at least at the level of its elites, was acquiring a heightened awareness of the content and weight of envy. The same impression can also be gleaned from the principal words that the texts associate with envy. During the thirteenth century, the main connotation is slander; during the fourteenth, covetousness; during the fifteenth, hatred: a revealing progression, linked to the evolution of the European social context[7] and indicative of the ever-increasing gravity of this sin. For covetousness is added onto slander, and hatred onto both these sentiments.

To begin with, envy is a sin of the tongue, committed by weak and inferior people jealous of their social superiors, who thus avenge themselves of their subaltern status: This is the the level of slander. Then, in the second phase, money and the *haute bourgeoisie* introduce new social rapports. The clergy is the first group accused of covetousness. Especially the nobility and the *nouveaux riches*, however, with their sumptuous repasts and arrogant ostentation in dress, induce the poor to covet their possessions. The people desire the wealth of the well-to-do—hence the various fourteenth-century revolts and uprisings—while at the same time certain impoverished nobles denounce the parvenus' ostentatious life-style. Finally, at the far end of this development, when "the frequency of the word 'envy' explodes," there comes the association with hatred. The desire for power did in fact lead to implacable hostilities, among them the Great Schism of the West, the French and English civil wars, and the rivalry between the dukes of Burgundy and the kings of France. Men turn out to be each others' Cains. Envy, opposed to both love and charity—as Aquinas noted—is worse than death. It is a living damnation. The *Compost et Kalendrier des bergiers* distinguishes no less than 13 branches, 39 "boughs," and 117 sprigs of envy, and by the turn of the sixteenth century, European iconography widely diffuses images of the infernal torment that awaits people guilty of this sin: "The envious men and women are thrown into a frozen river, submerged to their nostrils, and above them blows the chilliest of winds; those who try to escape this wind must needs dive down into the said ice."

Thus runs one of the descriptions placed below the great Last Judgment of Albi, which resumes a theme found in the second edition of the *Compost et Kalendrier*. . . .

Would parallel inquiries into the other Deadly Sins reveal a process similar to these progressive stages of the internalization and enlargement of the notion of envy? It is quite possible to think so.

LUST

First, a survey of the case of lust. The official septenary places it in the final position. In the *Compost et Kalendrier* . . . , along the lines of gluttony, it is subdivided into only 5 branches, 15 boughs, and 45 twigs, whereas for avarice these figures become respectively 20, 60, and 180. This classification and this relative lack of interest in lust and gluttony comprise a legacy of the list long before established by Evagrius Ponticus, who advised desert monks to begin by overcoming gluttony and lust, in order to then attack, little by little and in order of increasing difficulty, the more resistant vices. At the beginning of modern times, however, lust takes on a gravity that contradicts its usual consignment to the end of the list for many directors of Christian conscience. An anonymous penance manual of the 1490s teaches that fornication is a sin "more detestable than murder or theft, which are not substantially evil." For, in certain cases of necessity, one is authorized to kill or to steal; but "no one can deliberately fornicate without committing a deadly sin."[8] To the authors of the *Malleus Malleficarum*, also written at the end of the fifteenth century, "the world is full of adultery and fornication, especially in the palaces of princes and wealthy men"; it is "the time of women" and of "mad love," marked by the unhappiness of all. Fire is therefore necessary to suppress the most grave of heretical perversions: witchcraft. Such is the price of reestablishing order, at least at the level of sexual morality.[9] In the *Doctrinal de sapience* (Troyes, 1604), a widely diffused work, lust is listed—surprisingly—as the fourth among the Deadly Sins, and is described as follows:

> *There is certainly no sin so displeasing to Jesus Christ as the sin of the flesh, which prompted Saint Augustine to say that many people who indulged in impure acts on the night of Jesus' coming into the world, thereupon died a sudden death. Likewise he remarks that during all the time of His passion, he never allowed his enemies to mingle the least reproach of this infamous vice among the great number of injuries, blasphemies, outrages, and calumnies they made Him suffer; it is the vice that gives greatest pleasure to the devil, since it is the most charming and most effective bait for luring souls into his traps . . . There is no sin whose entire circumstances are as deadly as those of the sin of impurity. A petty theft, a slight burst of anger, are only venial sins; but a lewd glance, an impure thought with the least complaisance, these are deadly sins that condemn you to the everlasting flames. Finally there is no vice that drags down such a prodigious number of souls into hell as impurity. Unhappy they who are of this number.*[10]

In its early seventeenth-century version, the *Doctrinal de sapience* expresses a rigor that had assumed a renewed severity toward the flesh at the time of the Counter-Reformation. Although it is true that the church had always severely judged extramarital sex, the practice of confession led directors of conscience to question—and increasingly to self-questioning by the penitents themselves—the sinfulness of certain activities even within marriage. In the long run, Catholic moralists distributed themselves among three major positions on this difficult subject: one, rigorist, which rooted itself in ancient doctrine; another, which gradually opened itself to understanding the conduct of married people; and finally a third, situated between the two others, which became the majority opinion.[11]

In the Imperial Greco-Roman world, several converging traditions—Stoic, Pythagorean, Neoplatonic—opposed the flesh and the spirit, marriage and love, and professed that "the sexual organs were given to man not for pleasure but for the preservation of the human race."[12] Christianity thus implanted itself in a culture that on the one hand accepted, indeed deified pleasure, but on the other, and in a contradictory way, condemned and denounced it, opposing it to sexual renunciation or at least the exclusive duty of procreation. The Gnostic movements, and then Manichaeism, increased the condemnation of sexuality still further, in such a way that Christian orthodoxy was compelled to establish its own differing position by proclaiming the legitimacy of marriage. Nevertheless, Christianity only did so in affirming the "concupiscence of the flesh" that comes from "the prince of this world." Inevitably present in the sexual act, this carnal knowledge could be justified only by procreation. In the *De bono conjugali*, Augustine defines the three "goods" of marriage: *proles, fides, sacramentum*. *Proles* signifies both procreation and the (Christian) education of children; *fides* means not only fidelity in sexual relations but also the act of accomplishing one's conjugal duty in every way; *sacramentum* (later translated as "sacrament") is the indissolubility of the matrimonial bond.[13] Augustine's analysis greatly influenced ensuing Christian thinking on marriage. It did not, however, say anything about amorous relations between man and wife, and did not cite Paul's letter to the Ephesians (5:25): "Husbands, love your wives, as Christ loved the church."

Over the centuries, the rigorist position on sexuality made constant reference to Saint Augustine, adding to his work if and when necessary. In his famous *Summa*, Raimond de Peñafort resumes the already-classic distinction of the three goods of marriage and declares that they "excuse sin." He then lists the four possible motivations of the conjugal act: the desire for children, paying the "debt" to one's spouse seeking a remedy to incontinence or avoiding fornication, and satisfying one's desire. The first two are without sin, the third is a venial offense, and the fourth is a deadly sin. The Dominican Guillaume de Rennes, who finished and glossed the *Raimundina* (with the result that many manuscripts of this work include Guillaume's glosses) elaborates on his predecessor's assessment: He judges that there is always some sin in the conjugal act when it is done for any motive other than procreation.[14] This last viewpoint was nevertheless at a remove from the teaching of Gregory the Great, who wrote to the Archbishop of Canterbury: "This pleasure (in the legitimate union of married couples) cannot be without fault. For neither in adultery, nor in fornication, but in legal marriage was born the man who says: 'Behold, I was shapen in iniquity; and in sin did my mother conceive me' " (Psalms 51:5).[15] Gregory's opinion appears again in the "supplement" that the Franciscan Nicoló de Osimo, the friend and collaborator of San Bernardino di Siena, added in 1444 to the *Pisanella*. According to Osimo, marital sex can be exempt from fault only if there is no "delectation of pleasure"; as this is almost never the case, it is therefore at least a venial sin.[16]

At the same time that he charts the famous distinctions between the four motivations for the conjugal act, Peñafort cites a pagan adage that identifies as an adulterer any man who is too desirous of his own wife, an appraisal then taken up by Augustine, Jerome, Gratian, and Peter Lombard (*omnis amator ferventior est adulter*). Clarifying—or perhaps darkening—Peñafort's thought, Guillaume de Rennes cites a twelfth-century rigorist, Huguccio, and concurs with the latter that to excite oneself with the hands, or the mind, or in using warm drinks "so as to more often copulate with one's wife"[17] is a deadly sin. In the *Directorium ad confitendum* (published in 1474) of Antonio di Butrio, a penitent is instructed to say: "I sinned in contracting marriage for the pursuit of pleasure . . . and not for procreation or in order to avoid fornication."[18] In the same period, Denys le Chartreux considers marital sex to be without sin only if the partners intend to have children, to pay their conjugal debt, or to flee fornication. According to this author, however, many married people commit Deadly Sin by an excessive quest for pleasure.[19] At the beginning of the sixteenth century, Godschalk Rosemondt's *Confessionale* includes a similar admission: "I sought to achieve fleshly pleasures in illicit ways and with excessive ardor. I thought too little of procreation, the good end for which marriage was primarily established."[20] Still, the most drastic opinion on this question belongs to Nicoló de Osimo, who reasoned that since only three legitimate motives allow married people to have sexual relations—procreation, the conjugal debt, and the avoidance of fornication—"it follows that in all other cases one falls into fornication, which is a deadly sin, since it violates the sixth commandment."[21]

Directors of conscience could not escape meditating on the legality of the various sexual positions. Only one—the man on top of the reclining woman—was then considered as "natural." To what degree, however, did one sin in the other positions, the spouses' genital organs still being united? Not surprisingly, the rigorists inclined toward a negative evaluation, especially when conjugal relations took place "in the manner of beasts." Guillaume de Rennes, John of Freiburg, Astesanus, Guy de Montrocher, Johann Nider, Rosemondt, and so on judged that especially in the last case, there was Deadly Sin if such a position was used for the aim of pleasure and not because of the woman's pregnancy or various infirmities.[22]

The most austere moralists naturally confirmed and sometimes reinforced the traditional taboos regarding the improper times and places for the act of love. For example, Nider considers that sex in a time of prohibition—the eve of church holidays, days of fasting or abstinence, and so on—is a serious sin of "intemperance." When it is done in a sacred place, the fault is venial, if there was no other possible place; in other cases, it is "suspect," and therefore more grave.[23] Astesanus teaches that sexual relations must be abstained from before communion. The same opinion occurs in the *Directoire des confesseurs* (uncertainly attributed to Gerson), which also prohibits sex on the days before festivals.[24] Nicoló de Osimo's *Supplementum* to the *Pisanella* is even more categorical. He writes, "It is certain that any matrimonial coitus, even for paying the debt, is an impediment to communion." Moreover, to avail oneself of marriage is a Deadly Sin, "when it occurs in contempt of the times and rules fixed by the church."[25]

Against the declarations of the severest censors of the sexual act, it is useful to place the opinions of those ecclesiastics who strove toward a fuller comprehension of married people. J. T. Noonan convincingly demonstrates that this more humane tendency grew, if but slowly, over the course of time.[26] The immense theological consideration of confession that led to the decision of 1215 produced, among other results, a more equitable appreciation of the practical conditions of sexuality in marriage. Written at the end of his life, Albertus Magnus's *Summa Theologica* includes an astonishing statement for its time: "There is no sin in conjugal rapports."[27]

Although this line is ambiguous, Albertus had consistently taught his pupil Thomas Aquinas not to be a prisoner of Augustinian pessimism. Certainly such pessimism is present in the work of "the angelic doctor." He does think that concupiscence, born of Original Sin, marks every man's sexual life, and that "in the union of man and woman, there is injury to reason." For "it [reason] is consumed by the vehemence of pleasure until there is no more potential for intellectual activity . . ."[28] On the other hand, Aquinas states that as conjugal coitus is good, it likewise holds true for the pleasure linked to marriage, which would have been still greater if man had not committed Original Sin.[29] Pleasure is thus recognized as a positive value, but totally linked to a procreative end.[30] During the same thirteenth century, an English Franciscan, Richard Middleton, offers a defense of "moderate pleasure" in validating, against Augustine and "general opinion," that "satisfying concupiscence and seeking moderate pleasure are two different things."[31]

What precisely is a "moderate" and therefore permissible pleasure? In his *Regulae morales*, Gerson explains that sexual pleasure is always licit whenever the married couple desires to have children, to pay the conjugal debt, or to avoid fornication; and if they seek only pleasure, there is no offense—or the offense is merely venial—as long as they "do not go beyond the limits of marriage."[32] According to many confessors, this last advice carries two conditions: "Do not be possessed with such mad passion that you would desire to make love with your partner even if you were not married; and in making love, do not think of anyone other than your legitimate partner." San Antonino di Firenze is of the same mind as Gerson.[33] Likewise Angelo di Chiavasso who, in a chapter on "the conjugal debt" in his *Summa*, considers whether the conjugal act performed "for the aim of pleasure" is a Deadly Sin, when for instance the desire is stimulated by thoughts, touching, or warm drinks, "so that lovemaking may happen more frequently." His answer is that the offense is venial, provided that there is no intention to behave in such a way outside of marriage.[34] Along the same lines, the *Sylvestrina* specifies that no matter how intense the appetite for pleasure, there is no Deadly Sin if the partners desire no one else but each other.[35]

At the end of the fifteenth and the beginning of the sixteenth century, two Parisian masters, the Frenchman Martin Le Maistre and the Scot John Mair, were courageous enough to go beyond the discreetly innovative viewpoints cited above. As Noonan shows,[36] the importance of their positions must be stressed, even if their contemporary impact was limited. Le Maistre declares, "Common sense tells us that it is permitted to unite for pleasure, just as I am permitted to eat lamb or mutton, and to prefer lamb if that pleases me . . . Aristotle herein sees no evil, provided that the practice is moderate."[37] Mair, who finds the majority of ecclesiastical moralists too severe, pursues the same track as Le Maistre. "No matter what they have said on the matter," he writes, "it is difficult to prove that a man has sinned if he has lain with his wife for pleasure." There is no more sin in making love for the sake of pleasure (within marriage, of course) than there is in "eating a fine apple for the pleasure that it brings." Moreover, it is completely legitimate to have sexual relations, for the health of both the man and woman: Aristotle recommends it.[38] Brave thinkers, Le Maistre and Mair had, it must be repeated, only a narrow contemporary audience.

Nonetheless, confessors were obliged to resolve the actual cases that penitents gave them. In addition, Christian directors of conscience had always thought that spouses were bound mutually to render their "conjugal duty." Saint Paul had in fact written to the Corinthians: "Let the husband render unto the wife due benevolence: and likewise also the wife unto the husband. The wife hath not power over her own body, but the husband: and likewise also the husband hath not power of his own body, but the wife. Defraud yet not one the other, except it be with consent for a time" (I Cor. 7:3–5). To what extent, however, should one push the license of one spouse's request and the consent of the other? Gerson argues that the conjugal debt may be refused for important reasons of health or to prevent a miscarriage. Still, "not all excuses are valid: certain sacred times or places do not exempt the partner from the obligation of paying the conjugal debt."[39] The *Compendium theologiae*, mistakenly attributed to Gerson, upholds the same opinion: The couple should not perform the sexual act in public. "But at any time, in any circumstances, leaving all other business aside, if one spouse knows that the the other is seized with dangerous desire, it is then needful to find out a secret corner and to pay the debt."[40] Berthold de Fribourg also maintains that couples must pay their conjugal debt, even in sacred places. Certainly the other spouse should attempt to dissuade his or her partner from demanding the payment in such inconvenient circumstances. If, however, such dissuasion fails, one must acquiesce. Moreover, to claim the debt in a sacred place in order to avoid temptation or for the sake of procreation does not constitute even a venial sin. It is then necessary, however, to reconsecrate the polluted area.[41]

As for sexual relations that at the time seemed "*contra naturam*," notably the position *a tergo*, are they inevitably sinful? Albertus Magnus had claimed that such positions prevent conception and reveal a deadly concupiscence, unless an overriding physical reason prohibits the normal position. More prudently, Aquinas had thought that in itself, the position does not always imply Deadly Sin. The *Angelica* is even less rigid. To be sure, it advises penitents against pursuing such acts. At the same time, it implores confessors not to be overhasty in labeling these acts as Deadly Sins: "Keep to this opinion: no matter how the act is begun and accomplished, if the seed is emitted into the appropriate orifice, in such a way that the woman may conserve it, there is not in the deed itself any deadly sin."[42] It is worth recalling that the *Angelica* had a mass audience.

Another question tormented confessors: May one have sexual relations during menses, and does the man sin if he demands, in full knowledge of his wife's condition, the conjugal debt? Ancient restrictions dating back to the Old Testament prohibited sexual activity during menstruation. In addition, medieval science held that conception was possible during the menstrual cycle and that the child would then risk being deformed. If, however, Guy de Montrocher, Gerson, and Nider considered sex during menstruation to be a Deadly Sin, the dominant tendency of the casuists was, despite their discouragement of such activity, to see it as only a venial sin.[43] The fourteenth-century Dominican archbishop Pierre de la Palud even goes so far as to declare sex during menses totally permissible. He was alone, however, in this position. He was also the first and for a long time the only authority to allow for the *amplexus reservatus*, or intercourse interrupted before ejaculation and ending without it.[44] His isolation in this regard points to an ecclesiastical mentality that condemned any sexual activity not directed toward procreation. At the least it must be noted, after this rapid overview of thirteenth through early sixteenth century attempts at "laxism," that the insistence on procreation led to a partial rehabilitation of sexuality and that the "permissible" progressively became "meritorious."[45] Thus, in the austere *Sylvestrina*, marital sex is called "meritorious" for several reasons. In paying the debt to one's spouse, one performs an act of justice. In desiring children that one will raise in God's love, one achieves an act of piety. And in preserving one's spouse from adultery, one displays charity.[46] Such an analysis was not restricted to its own time.

All the same, regarding even marital sex, the predominant tone of the confession handbooks and manuals was pessimistic. An anxious investigation perceived multiple opportunities for sin in conjugal relations, the confessors being persuaded that a great number of deadly transgressions, in particular acts "against nature," were committed by married couples. No doubt expressing a commonly held view, Saint Catherine of Siena, in a vision of Hell, claims that the only group of sinners who comprise a special class are "those who sinned in the estate of marriage."[47] A half-century later, San Bernardino di Siena, preaching on marriage, unhesitatingly asserts: "Out of a thousand marriages, I believe that 999 belong to the devil."[48] Assuredly, this is the exaggeration of a preacher who felt obliged to use a terroristic approach! At the same time, churchmen also believed it necessary to alert laypeople to the multiple moral dangers of marriage. To her confessor, who asks her why people are more severely punished in Hell for marital rather than other sins, Saint Catherine paradoxically responds: "Because they are not as conscious of them, and do not repent of them as much as for other sins, and therefore they succumb to such crimes more often."[49]

Reckoning from confession, the process of forming a guilt mentality in regard to sex took place in a complex way during this period. The hesitations of specialists, and their mutual differences of opinion, did not facilitate the task of confessors, nor of penitents, and could only have created an atmosphere of uneasiness. Thus the rigorists required sexual abstinence before communion. Others, however, permitted it, if the only goals were procreation or the conjugal "debt."[50] Similar disagreements also existed, it has been shown, on the subject of marital sex in sacred times and places, coitus *a tergo*, and during menstruation and pregnancy. Even if many authors tended to demote the gravity of such relations to the level of venial faults, doubts remained in the minds of both interrogators and interrogated. In any case, the examination of one's conscience imposed self-questioning about such behavior. To the scruples that may have spawned these differences of opinion were added those that engendered the wave of definite analyses. The notion of guilty pleasure is difficult to define. Where to locate the slippage from the desire to make love in order to avoid concupiscence and the desire to experience sexual pleasure in the same act? Moreover, the casuists frequently perceived deadly sin in the man's desiring his wife so violently that he would sleep with her even outside of marriage. In fact, however, this could only be an unreal case. In the heat of action, would the future penitent think that much about it? Furthermore, it has been noted how sins "against nature" greatly embarrassed the moralists, who often tended to enlarge this notion. Finally, in several confession manuals, penitents are asked to consider whether they have not sinned against chastity "through touch, embraces, kisses, and other indecent acts that may be deadly offenses in not agreeing with the sanctity of marriage." Thus writes Jacopo Foresti in his *Confessionale seu interrogatorium* (Venice, 1497)[51]; he was not the only one to pose such a question. In fact, many moralists had nothing but suspicion toward erotic stimuli.

Not only did the disputes among casuists, and the sheer volume of their questions, instill a consciousness of guilt, but so too did certain categorical affirmations, such as the obligation of performing one's conjugal "duty." Not until the middle of the sixteenth century and Domenico De Soto would there be any extenuation of this rule, to allow for parents facing the impossibility of raising any more children.[52] Before De Soto, this motive was always judged a Deadly Sin. Likewise and *a fortiori*, this judgment applied to any form of onanism or masturbation, on which a treatise often attributed to Gerson is thoroughly explicit. In this astonishing document, one reads that the confessor should "more and more openly exhort the penitent to tell the truth." If it is a young man, the confessor should speak to him "with a calm expression, so as to make it seem to him that the matter about which he is questioned is not indecent, but on the contrary something he can be at ease about." If, however, the young penitent refuses to confess, the feint should be abandoned, and direct questions employed. Such as, "[at the age of ten or twelve] have you not touched or rubbed your penis as children are in the habit of doing?"[53] Clearly, in the mind of the author of this treatise, such acts bring a risk of damnation, akin to the punishment of Sodom and Gomorrah.

This inquisitorial curiosity and such an excess of details are not commonly found in Gerson's work, nor in that of most authors of the manuals and handbooks. It would be a historiographical mistake to take this particular text as representative of the literature of confession. On the contrary, various influential authors—specifically Gerson, San Antonino, Sylvester Prieras—often advise the confessor to combine prudence and diligence and to stay within reasonable limits of discretion during interrogation. In a French manual of the fifteenth century written for priests, the confessor is encouraged to have a discreet attitude, as "he should keep his eyes on the ground." Otherwise, the penitent runs the risk of not daring to tell his "shameful sins."[54] This circumspection will go further, in consequently becoming more marked, under the urging of a San Carlo Borromeo, a rigorist to be sure.[55] Theodore N. Tentler is therefore right to argue against imagining the confession practice of the time to be an excessively realistic and indiscreet inquisition. Penitents were not constrained to give detailed accounts of their entire married sex life,[56] which furthermore did not interest the authors of the handbooks and manuals any more than the legal impediments to matrimony: religious vows, degrees of kinship, and so on. Finally, if problems of sexuality occupy an important place in works on confession, they do not overwhelm these texts. San Antonino allots seven times as much space to the commandment "thou shalt not steal" as to "thou shalt not commit adultery."[57]

Nevertheless, even when restored within its true limits, the ecclesiastical discourse on sex of the thirteenth through sixteenth centuries was quantitatively important. It censored morals and behavior but did not keep silent about them—in this regard, I concur, in going back in time, with the analysis of Michel Foucault. With both the means and mentality of the time, the church sought to forge a "science of sexuality." And "confession was . . . the general matrix"[58] that governed the production of this "science." Precisely because it was based on confessions, this production constitutes an important episode in the global development of the early modern guilt mentality. Le Maistre writes with good reason on the subject of the frequent prohibition of sex during pregnancy: "I ask myself what dangers they [my adversaries] expose the consciences of scrupulous spouses . . . [because] they condemn as deadly sinners whomsoever seeks the *debitum*, unless they be totally sure they are doing it to avoid fornication."[59] More generally, Christians were encouraged constantly to look into their own married sexuality. Did the partners deny the conjugal debt, excite their desire beyond the measure, pay no heed to sacred times and places, have sex during the menstrual cycle, seek pleasure for its own sake?: These were so many questions that married people had to ask themselves. Thus a double conclusion emerges: (1) "the casuistry of sins of desire, when applied to sexual impulses, provides opportunities for the imputation of guilt that none of the other deadly vices can match"[60]; (2) never had an entire civilization been subjected to such an investigation of sexuality, especially within marriage.

USURY AND AVARICE

It was mentioned above that the authors of the handbooks and manuals of the thirteenth through sixteenth centuries were less obsessed with sexual sins than might be thought *a priori*. The second part of San Antonino's *Summa*, primarily devoted to sins in their diverse categories, reveals the following distribution: cupidity (*avaritia*), twenty-five chapters; the duty of making restitution, eight chapters; pride, eleven; vainglory, nine; lust, fifteen; gluttony, eight; anger, eight; envy, nine; sloth, sixteen; lying and perjury, eight; vows and their transgression, two; infidelity, eleven. It is therefore cupidity and the duty to make restitution that far and away hold first place among the archbishop's preoccupations: 25 percent of the chapters and 32 percent of the pages in the 1571 Venice edition. It is true that this was a classic distribution, resumed, it is worth recalling, by the *Compost et Kalendrier des bergiers*. All the same, in this work, destined for a relatively modest audience, usury is but one of the twenty branches of "avarice." On the other hand, amid the developments that San Antonino attributes to this sin, there are six chapters covering some seventy-four pages on usury (only forty-nine on lust). During a time of economic expansion and the rise of commercial capitalism,[61] Christian civilization conducted an intense self-inquiry regarding the propriety of mercantile and banking transactions. In this domain, then, the making of a guilt mentality was also played out to the full.

As always, the guilt-instilling discourse drew support from ancient and venerable references. Exodus (22:25), Leviticus (25:35–37), and Deuteronomy (23:19–25) forbade the Israelites to lend at interest. In fact, the Book of Ezekiel (22:12) proves that usury was common in Jerusalem. For their part, Greco-Roman philosophers, particularly Plato and Aristotle, protested against lending at interest. In this regard, Aristotle's analysis must be recalled, given its long posterity in the scholastic tradition. According to "the Philosopher," the worst social activity is that of the moneylender, because he pretends to make a product from something sterile: coins. For the latter have no other function than to be a measure of things (*Politics* I, 10). The Middle Ages will likewise say: Money does not engender money. Nonetheless, despite this condemnation and the attacks of Aristophanes, Plutarch, Plautus, Cicero, and Tacitus against usurers, Greek and Roman legislation did not seriously challenge the legitimacy of lending at interest, trying at most to limit the maximum rate. Things would change with the arrival of Christianity.

Jesus had counseled to "lend, hoping for nothing again; and your reward shall be great" (Luke 6:35). This recommendation, however, did not condemn lending at interest, which both the Greek and Latin church fathers castigated unsparingly. Clement of Alexandria, Saint Gregory of Nazianzus, Saint Basil, Saint Gregory of Nyssa, Saint John Chrysostom, Saint Ambrose, Saint Augustine, and Saint Jerome together declare that the usurer reaps where he has not sown, that lending at interest amounts to taking other people's belongings, that the rich must freely lend to the poor, and that usury runs contrary to faith, religion, and natural law. Usury was also especially forbidden to clerics, and this prohibition was legally confirmed by the fourth-century and later church councils. On the other hand, it took until the reign of Charlemagne for civil legislation (the *Admonitio generalis* of 789) to proclaim a general ban on anyone, lay or clergy, who attempted to lend at interest for the sake of usury. Local councils and episcopal statutes then exploited and diffused this prohibition. Finally, the twelfth-century Decretum of Gratian (*Concordantia discordantium canonum*) and Peter Lombard's *Sententiae* repeat that there is usury whenever the moneylender requires, in money or in kind, something beyond the value of the original loan, such a practice being outlawed by the Fourth Commandment.

Despite these repeated condemnations, the definition of usury remained vague, the rational justification for its prohibition imprecise, and the distinction of its cases barely outlined. Moreover, the multiplication of currencies, economic growth, the rise of both land-based and maritime commerce, and the development of the Champagne trade fairs came to pose problems of increasing complexity: the merging and remuneration of capital; exchange and transfer, especially for the needs of the Holy See; and risks and damages in business enterprises. Furthermore, high interest rates—on the order of 30 to 40 percent annually—were commonly charged in the Italian merchant cities and by the "Lombards" of France.[62] Finally, in a noteworthy conjunction, the obligation of annual confession instituted in 1215 also obliged the moralists to study the various aspects of usury as much if not more than those of sexual activity.

Thirteenth-century casuists argue that as a rule, the usurer improperly sells time, something that belongs to all creatures. William of Auxerre (d. 1229) was apparently the first to propose this argument, in his *Summa Aurea*. He writes that

> *the sun is required to give of his own light; likewise the earth is required to give up all that it produces, and so too the water. But nothing gives of itself in a manner more true to nature than does Time: willy-nilly, all things have their time. Therefore, since the usurer sells that which necessarily belongs to all creatures, he injures all creatures in general . . . : this is one of the reasons for the church's prosecution of usurers. From which we conclude that it is they against whom God says: "When I shall retake time, when time shall be in my hands so that no usurer could sell it, then shall I judge according to my justice.*[63]

Innocent IV would reemploy this reasoning, which an early fourteenth-century Franciscan reader-general expressed in more concise form: The usurer sells time, which belongs only to God.[64]

Aquinas's intervention in the usury debate, however, was doubtless even more fundamental. Relying on a freshly rediscovered Aristotle, the "angelic doctor" confirms the illegality of any practice leading to the stipulation, in a loan (*mutuum*), of the payment of any sum beyond the principal. Any loan at interest is usurious, and draws not only the creditor but also the debtor into sin.[65] In effect, the usurer sells the use of that thing whose ownership he has transferred. One must not sell one's wine or wheat and at the same time the use of this wine or wheat, since then one sells the same thing twice.[66] Aquinas reinforces this point by resuming the Aristotelian analysis that money, a means of exchange or of measurement, can bear no fruit. Money should not engender profits[67]: The usurer is guilty of Deadly Sin.[68]

Such condemnation occasionally goes very far. If one sells above the just price because one awaits the buyer's credit as payment, there is "manifest usury." Such is also the case if the buyer spends below the just price because he will pay the sum before the delivery of the merchandise. "If on the other hand the seller, in order to be paid sooner, agrees to take something away from the just price, then there is no sin of usury."[69] Like all his predecessors, Aquinas does not distinguish between loans of consumption and loans of production. Among the former, moreover, he does not consider those that might be granted to someone wealthier than the moneylender; Aquinas is thus the heir of a Judeo-Christian moral tradition that saw loans as being given only to people in financial trouble: Such services should be free of charge. Only at the beginning of the sixteenth century will Jacques Lefevre d'Etaples (1455–1537), Calvin's precursor in this field, invent the expression "public economy," thus establishing its distinction from domestic economy.[70]

Like Aristotle, then, Aquinas considered money only in and of itself, independent of the multiple uses that can be made of it. He perceived only the metal and abstracted that which it could procure. Finally, he does not say a word about exchanges, which were on their way to gaining considerable importance. In most respects, Aquinas's teachings on usury did put a constraint on merchants, though by leaving some doors open, they did not achieve complete elimination. Certainly the "angelic doctor" only conceived of missed profits and indemnities of sacrifices made at the time of a loan independently of any explicit pact agreed upon at the beginning, and only from the time of the expiration of credit.[71] Not until after his time were the notions of *lucrum cessans* and *damnum emergens* enlarged and specified. If, however, Aquinas was not familiar with loans of *periculum sortis* (the risk run by committed capital), which the jurist Paul de Castro condoned in the late fourteenth century, his writings on "societies" or companies only condemned "leonine" loans. To him, it seemed normal that a merchant or artisan who traded or worked with an associate's money should share some of the profits with the latter.[72] A wide opening was thus provided for the *commenda* and incorporated societies.

Following Aquinas, scholastic works on usury sometimes enlarged and sometimes narrowed his critical domain. Nonetheless, and despite the varying amounts of space devoted to the subject, this sin was now fully described and strongly reproved. Aquinas affirms that "it wounds natural justice." William of Auxerre counts it more serious than homicide, since the latter can sometimes be legitimate, but usury (like lust) never is. Always "immoderate," it is a sin unto itself (*secundum se*): This diagnosis is found especially in the *Summa* of Astesanus. San Antonino perceives worsening circumstances in the continuation of moneylending transactions. The Ecumenical Council of Vienne (1311–12) decrees: "If anyone falls into the error of obstinately maintaining that usury is not a sin, he shall be punished as a heretic."[73] The preachers' *exempla* competed with each other in decrying the fate of usurers, who even on earth already lived in the company of devils.[74] Canon law excommunicated them and ordered their burial outside consecrated ground. In his treatise *De usura*, composed in the early fourteenth century, Robert de Courçon wishes that for penance, parishioners may undergo "instead of fasts, almsgiving, and ordinary satisfaction, the obligation of accusing usurers." Furthermore, he carefully determines the nine incriminating modes of practicing usury: by order, counsel, consent, praise, receipt, connection, silence, neutrality, and tolerance.

As in the domain of sexuality, rigorist positions are taken in that of usury.[75] Guillaume de Rennes, Peñafort's commentator, identifies as usurers the miller who lends to the baker in order to gain clientele and the teacher who pays his students to take his courses. The *Decretals* of Gregory IX (1239), which became a major part of canon law, condemn under the title *De usuris* a creditor's commission for the risks of maritime transport of the money he has lent. The commentary of Innocent IV (d. 1254) on these *Decretals* resumes this condemnation. Even if based on a risk, any *superabundantia* was considered usurious: This view therefore rejected the *periculum sortis*. The *Summa* of Goffredo da Trani (d. 1245) and those of Hostiensis (Henri de Suse, d. 1271) and of Bartolomeo di Pisa (d. 1347) brand as illicit any exchange operation that plays on the variation between currency values, and the same negative judgment applies to loans prolonged from one trade fair to the next (*de nundinis in nundinas*). Astesanus, who wrote his magnum opus around 1317, rightly perceived that multiple exchanges camouflaged loans. He also condemned loans as soon as the lender received more than he had lent. The *Angelica*, while tolerant in regard to sexuality within marriage, takes a rather rigorist stand toward monetary exchange. This work refuses to see the latter as a buying-and-selling transaction, and only allows for those that assist travelers or help to clear overseas debts. The ex-banker Pandolfo Rucellai (d. 1497), who became a Dominican and a disciple of Savonarola and whose former trade taught him that interest was often disguised behind an exchange rate, only grudgingly approved of real transactions, without which commerce would be paralyzed. He still advised any banker who wished to save his soul to leave his profession. Some decades later Francisco de Vitoria (d. 1546), a defender of the rights of Amerindians and one of the founders of international law, regarded an exchange contract as a licit *permutatio*, but justifiable only between distant places; within a kingdom they are usurious, since the resulting profit is not based on a transfer but on a loan. De Vitoria thus pays no heed to the diversity of currencies.

The Anglican Thomas Wilson (d. 1581) is even more severe, as he holds any unequal exchange to be usurious, fully realizing that exchange rates conceal the interest taken by the exchange brokers. As for the austere Pius V, his famous constitution on exchanges (1571)[76] condemned them not only when they are feigned, but even when, though real, they cover up a loan: thus with "deposits" that, in their sixteenth-century sense, were loans carried out by princes or private individuals under the guise of exchanges from one market to another. The Pope decided that, even in the case of late payment, interest cannot be "certain and determined" nor "measured by the date of maturity," but only adjusted to the distance from the place of payment. Pius V also protested against those "who hoard cash for the sake of altering exchange rates." Thus an entire rigorist movement running from Gregory IX and Innocent IV to Pius V aimed to hunt down and make guilty those moneylenders who charged interest.

On the other hand, the majority of church doctors resigned themselves to daily reality and absolved various practices that had become indispensable to European economic life. Hence, in a free loan, allowance was made for the *poena* imposed on the tardy borrower by the lender. The key issue remained that the delay and the *poena* were not to be foreseen at the start of the contract. In addition, the notion of *periculum sortis* justified maritime insurance, with a premium being paid to the insurer as in today's practice. This type of insurance is documented from the end of the fourteenth century.[77]

The Florentines and Siennese had been using letters of exchange since the late thirteenth century, and these eventually gained almost inevitable acceptance. The Franciscan Alessandro Lombardo (d. 1314), the fiery preacher Giovanni da Capistrano (1456), and the theologian Luca Pacioli, friend of Leonardo da Vinci and publisher of his famous *Summa de arithmetica* (1494), were consistent in their praise of the *ars campsoria*. They saw this as an essential institution for the maintaining of society, and as vital to commerce, Pacioli declares, as water is to navigation. The moralists disagreed, however, on the justifications for exchange. Some, such as San Bernardino, Lorenzo Ridolfi (d. 1442), Vitoria, De Soto, and Lainez, interpreted it as a *permutatio pecuniae*, that is, a conversion of local into foreign currency. Others, especially Baldo degli Ubaldi, a specialist in Roman law (d. 1400), Gaetano, Prieras, and later Diana, regarded such exchange as a buying and selling transaction like any other. Finally, others such as San Antonino and Azpilcueta, the uncle of Saint Francis Xavier, considered financial exchange as a contract *sui generis*, unknown to Roman law and requiring a new analysis. Furthermore, all these authors demonstrate that the money changer has a right to be compensated for his efforts and risks; San Antonino in particular expresses this opinion, and he also maps out a theory of value correctly founded on utility and rarity.[78] On the whole, these scholars allowed for exchange transactions only between one country and another. In 1585, however, Miguel Palacios, a professor at the University of Salamanca, accepted *permutatio* of exchange within the same state. Some years earlier Azpilcueta had thrown the Aristotelian theory of monetary sterility into doubt, observing that the merchant's money bears fruit in the manner of the sower's seed.

With moneylending at interest still forbidden, exchange operations frequently served to camouflage it, by means of variously named subterfuges: "Venetian exchanges," exchanges of "Lyon" and "Besançon,"[79] and exchanges "with recourse." In the "Venetian exchange," which San Antonino distrusted, the transaction occurred in the following way: Someone would borrow a sum of florins in Florence and undertake to pay them back after a certain time in Florence itself, but at the rate that they would then have in Venice. This system involved a *mutuum*, designed to bring in profit; hence, "even though it is called an exchange," there is usury, because the money has not left Florence, thereby making the case all the more suspect. The equally suspect exchange of "Lyon" or "Besançon" often featured a creditor in Florence, who would lend someone the Florentine equivalent of 100 Lyonnais écus au soleil, or 104 ⅔ Florentine écus. The debtor had to return the 100 écus au soleil at the next Lyon fair. This settlement, however, would not take place. Instead, a protest for nonpayment would intervene, and by mean of a backward exchange, the debtor would reimburse the 100 écus au soleil in Florence, or by this point 106 ⅔ Florentine écus. The status of currency at the Lyon fair (or at "Besançon") inevitably determined that the back-exchange would almost always work to the lender's advantage. The exchange "with recourse" merely perfected the preceding system, as the protest of nonpayment was bypassed and care was always taken to have letters of exchange conveyed from the exchange to the fair and back again; this practice was often omitted in the "Lyon" exchanges. Needless to say, many debtors were kept for a long time "on the exchanges": Having been unable to pay their debts at the first fair, they would suffer quarterly penalties through this game of coming and going.

Not only San Antonino but nearly all theologians before the permissive seventeenth-century casuists, Turi and Diana, reproved such exchanges, which were labeled as "dry." For his part, Pius V, by his 1571 constitution, condemned "dry exchanges," which gave the pretense of negotiation with another locality, while in fact the letters were not sent, or they were without being delivered, or they were both sent and delivered but not for a real payment.[80] Without a consistently established distinction between loans of consumption and loans of production, lending at interest, as well as discounting, remained illegal in the late sixteenth-century Catholic world. Those who engaged in such practices were in theory guilty of the Deadly Sin of usury.

All the same, casuistry was active on this subject. Certain latitudinarians continued to permit exchanges that were in fact "dry," under the pretext that there had been a buying and selling of cash (this rule also applied to trade fair currencies), and whenever they had followed a "just price"—in other words the going market rate and not one fixed in advance. The skillful cover-ups of the bankers, coupled with the theologians' disagreements, allow the continuation and growth of practices that were indisputably opposed to the spirit of canon law regarding usury. As the Dominican De Soto observed in the mid-sixteenth century: "This question of exchange, already abstruse enough in itself, is made increasingly obscure by both merchants and the contradictory opinions of church doctors."[81]

In any case, the church gave absolution to fixed interest payments, public loans, and the sale of offices—which it itself employed—either at the high level of the Apostolic Chamber or in the more modest context of any type of ecclesiastical person or institution. The fixed interest payment was a loan with interest legally disguised as a sales contract. For a lump sum, a creditor "bought" the right to levy an "annual and perpetual interest, until the time of repayment," assessed on certain properties nominated by the debtor.[82] Innocent IV determined that there was no usury as long as the interest payment did not exceed the normal revenue from a property whose value equaled that of the paid sum. Nonetheless, various casuists continued to examine this subject. Consequently, Martin V in 1425 and Calixtus

III in 1455 declared fixed interest payments to be legitimate only on condition of their being assessed on real estate, with a limit of 10 percent. Pius V, who fought "dry" exchanges, also tried to curb the practice of fixed interest payments. He proposed that the price of their repurchase must be the same as that of the original purchase: This scheme did not allow for inflation, and thus disfavored the creditor. In addition, he proclaimed edicts that denied creditors any recourse against tardy debtors.[83] All these restrictions, however, were abandoned by his successor Gregory XIII.[84] In practice, moreover, fixed interest payments had already been a key part of the Western economy for several centuries.

The fiction of buying and selling likewise allowed for the justification of public loans and their resulting annual interest payments. From the fourteenth century on, Italian cities such as Genoa, Florence, and Venice resorted to inevitable loans, which they were unable to pay back. As compensation, they decided to pay their creditors an annual and perpetual interest rate. The system was then perfected in two ways: one, the governments would issue nonbinding public loans with annual interest, and two, they would do so on a scale surpassing the municipal level, in pontifical *monti*, "rentes de l'Hotel de Ville de Paris," *juros* of Spain, and so on. By this means, the papacy borrowed 382 tons of fine silver between 1526 and 1606, and Spain, between 1515 and 1600, some 78 million ducats.[85] Before the standardization of these loans, however, certain casuists pondered the legality of the system. San Bernardino di Siena accepts the collection of a small interest on the money that a lender was constrained to pay the municipality. On the other hand, he maintains that one should not spontaneously buy credit from the *Monte*[86] in order to thereby acquire an annual bonus. To the objection that clerics engage in this practice, and that popes and cardinals are less intransigent than he, the great Franciscan preacher replies: "As long as there is a difference of opinion among theologians, there is doubt on the matter, and in such doubt, it is needful to refrain from action: It works against the salvation of the soul."

Furthermore, as Saint Thomas Aquinas argued, exposing oneself to committing a Deadly Sin is itself a Deadly Sin; it is enough to be exposed to buying the said credit, since doubt exists as to its legitimacy. Confronted with the same problem twenty years later, San Antonino takes a contrary position:

> *In doubtful cases, we must take the most sure way. This principle is true if it will endow our actions with the greatest possible perfection, but is hard to establish as a means of resolving all doubts in the realm of conscience. Otherwise, everyone would have to follow the religious life, since it is a more sure path than living in the world.*

As for credit on the *monti*, San Antonino confirms that "there is really very little doubt. Since the Church has not pronounced a definite ban, and many learned doctors deem it permissible, one's conscience may consider it legitimate."[87]

Such is the general doctrine of the "probabilists" in regard to bonds of public debt, a position that Pascal eventually fought against during the seventeenth century. Moreover, this doctrine assisted European governments that used and abused, especially in the sixteenth century, the system of issuing state loans.

At the edge of the dispute over public loans there developed that over pawnbroking, the former having provoked the latter. In the fifteenth century, Franciscan preachers such as Bernardino da Feltro not only waged war on usury but also propounded a concrete solution for alleviating debts incurred by the poor. Thus the terms of pawnbroking were created, by which loans were granted against deposits whose value was twice that of the amount loaned, with a small interest—often 5 percent—imposed for processing fees. The Dominicans and Augustinians often forcefully protested the collection of this percentage, and one Augustinian, in open hostility to Bernardino da Feltro, wrote a treatise entitled *De monte impietatis* (*Of* Im*pious Pawnbroking*).[88] Public welfare, however, overrode these objections, and pawnbroking establishments spread throughout Italy during the later fifteenth century and afterward beyond the Alps. The growth and legalization of this system worked directly in favor of the practice of state loans.

The sale of offices constituted a variant of this practice.[89] When pressed for money, a government would create and sell a certain number of offices, many of them useless, which carried an annual interest rate—10 percent, for example—paid out on determined profits. To cite two well-known cases, the fifteenth to sixteenth-century papacy and the French Ancien Régime monarchy made extensive use of this system, which, like state loans, diverted savers' money from productive investments and increasingly burdened the public debt. In any case, the sale of offices undoubtedly disguised, under the pretense of a buying-and-selling transaction, the loans at interest that certain individuals granted to certain governments.

Two other justifications, however, were added to the notion of buying and selling to authorize the taking of interest, particularly in the *monti*. These were the *lucrum cessans* (when a missed profit occurred) and the *damnum emergens* (when there was a fiscal loss). The thirteenth-century scholar Hostiensis was one of the first to approve the *lucrum cessans*, when someone refrains from trading to lend to someone else in need.[90] Early in the following century, this viewpoint was upheld by Astesanus, who also advanced the idea of the *damnum emergens*. During the fourteenth century, however, various authors, such as the nominalist Jean Buridan (d. ca. 1358), rejected both of these notions. All the same, the multiplication of *monti* led both San Bernardino and San Antonino to accept the *lucrum* and the *damnum* in cases of obligatory borrowings. For individuals under such circumstances were deprived of their money (*damnum emergens*), and they could not use it for diverse transactions (*lucrum cessans*). As practice came to confirm the theory, these two additional justifications to the buying-selling concept permitted buying bonds of public debt, fixed interest payments, and various offices with an untroubled conscience.

Looking at the situation in the late sixteenth century, one can affirm that lending at interest remained forbidden in Catholic countries and would continue so until 1830. Nevertheless, the notions of *periculum sortis*, *poena*, *lucrum cessans*, and *damnum emergens* removed guilt from many transactions that were in fact loans at interest. These loopholes, moreover, in bending official doctrine, operated on a grand scale in the financial markets, where especially kings and queens borrowed enormous sums for their political needs. For them as for commoners, the system of letters of exchange then permitted obtaining needed money on credit. On the whole, and taking into account the complexity of financial operations that confused more than one theologian, official morality was more relaxed toward "usury" than sexuality.

Even in this field, however, it would be a misunderstanding of early modern mentalities to neglect the rise of a guilt consciousness. If Calvin, breaking from scholastic tradition, allows for business loans in which "usury is no worse than a purchase,"[91] he nonetheless declares professional moneylending to be "unworthy of a Christian and honest man."[92] For his part, Luther relentlessly and violently stigmatized "usury," which he understood in a thoroughly medieval fashion and combatted during his entire career: in *To the Christian Nobility of the German Nation* (1520), in the treatise *Trade and Usury* (1524), in *The Great Catechism* (1529), in an instruction *To Pastors, for Preaching Against Usury* (1540), and also in *Table-Talk*. The Reformer is pained to admit that "the evil [usury] has made enormous progress and . . . has reached new heights in all countries."[93] He writes of "enthroned thieves, brigands, and highwaymen . . . they who, seated on their thrones, are looked up to as great lords and pious respectable citizens, who rob and pillage under a mask of honesty."[94] He states that he cannot understand "how one can annually turn 100 florins into 120, and even 200, and all this without working the land or farm animals."[95] Strictly faithful to the rigorist conception of lending, he confirms that "to exchange something with someone, and to make a profit from this exchange, is no deed of charity but outright thievery. All usurers deserve to be hanged. I call usurer anyone who lends at five and six percent."[96] He attacks those who "make no scruple to sell their wares on credit, at prices higher than they ask for cash purchases."[97] He takes complete exception to commercial companies: "Therein all is so groundless and unreasonable, with only greed and injustice pertaining, that one is unable to find anything that can be dealt with in good conscience. If these companies must survive, then justice and honesty must disappear. But if justice and honesty are to survive, then these companies must disappear."[98]

To be sure, in Germany as elsewhere, lending at interest continued, but early modern businessmen had undeniably troubled consciences. Hence the many donations willed to the church by Catholic merchants, to the special profit of the mendicant orders that frequently implanted in the cities, were closely linked to the rising bourgeoisie. Here the reaction of Fra Santi Rucellai, the banker turned Dominican, is revealing. In his treatise *De cambi*, he attacks "dry" exchanges and calls "Lyon" exchanges usurious. According to Rucellai, money changers risk losing their souls. A significant fact: In 1532, the merchants of the powerful Spanish colony at Antwerp sent their confessor to Paris to present diverse cases of conscience to the doctors of the Sorbonne. This was not the first time that they had addressed themselves to the Parisian theologians, for they allude to a previous consultation.[99] The general line of the Sorbonnistes' response is that interest from exchange is illicit and usurious and that the factor of time counts for nothing. Only the material expenses involved in the exchange may be legitimately entered on the books. This response was followed by the "particular" views of Francesco de Vitoria, an even more rigorist scholar who notably rejected any notion of *lucrum cessans*.

This severity becomes clearer when compared to Ludovico Guicciardini's comments, in his famous *Descrizione de Tutti i Paesi Bassi* (1567), on "deposits," or financial advances granted from market to market to both sovereigns and private individuals. He writes that the merchants "nowadays call, to cover over the infamy of the thing with a special title, this proceeding a 'deposit,' when one gives money to someone else for a certain time, on payment of a set and determined price and interest, that is . . . at the rate of twelve percent per annum."[100] One can infer from this judgment how scholastic doctrine still exerted a strong influence over merchants, who strove to ease their conscience by using transparently hypocritical stratagems. Pius V's global prohibition (1571) of "dry exchanges" particularly struck at the system of "deposits" or "exchanges from market to market," Doubtless, for a certain time and especially at Lyon, people continued to assess deposit rates on printed exchange references, on which they would scribble added figures at the last minute. The practice, however, had received a sizable blow, and bankers increasingly used the "exchange with recourse" (*ricorsa*), whose subtle movements of coming and going between town and marketplace confused the religious authorities more than ever. Hence there was hypocrisy, but at the same time a certain scrupulousness, which attests that mercantile mentalities did pay close heed to the ecclesiastical discourse on the sin of usury.

SLOTH

Both mercantile activity and the pressure of social and economic changes undoubtedly led Latin Christianity to discover the "Deadly" Sin of sloth. Judging by the French example, the words relating to indolence had a relatively rare usage in the Middle Ages: *Pereise, pareise, parece,* and *parecier* certainly existed, but only make sporadic appearances. It is true that words referring to idleness are more frequent.[101] The latter, however, was not always disparaged. As late as the sixteenth century, humanists opposed *otium*, or calm meditation away from the world's loud bustle, to *negotium*, which signified a fragmented agitation in sterile and exhausting occupations. As for the term *fainéant* ("idle, lazy"), often employed by Calvin and Montaigne, it rarely appears before their time.[102] Complementary support for these assessments comes from the revealing results of a survey that Jacques Le Goff and his research team have made of an early fourteenth-century collection of *exempla*. First place belongs to *Demon*, in seventy-seven *exempla*, *Mulier* occurs in sixty-four, and *Mors* in forty-nine: These figures are further confirmations of the fears studied in the preceding volume. In contrast, *Negligencia* is mentioned only six times; *Acidia*, five; *Ocium*, five; *Pigricia*, three; and its opposite, *Labor*, six.[103] During this period, then, work and sloth were not among the preachers' main preoccupations. These half-silences and quasi-absences evoke a civilization that was not obsessed with production.

All the same, from the time of the desert fathers, the church considered *acidia* a grave and quite Deadly Sin. *Acedie* meant spiritual torpor, dislike for religious exercises, and a disheartening sorrow that kept the soul from any desire to serve God or even live. Aquinas preferred to call this depression specifically "sadness" —*tristitia*—and defined it as an "emptiness of the soul," a profound "ennui" toward spiritual welfare, due to the physical effort the latter requires; he associates it with voluntary ignorance regarding religion, "by which one refuses to attain spiritual blessings, because of the pain that gives."[104] Having arrived in the fifth circle of Hell, Dante appears to recall Aquinas's analysis: In the black waters of Styx, he discovers, at the side of the wrathful, the *accidiosi* who "bore the mist of sluggishness in us: / Now we are bitter in the blackened mud."[105] On the other hand, the fourth terrace of Purgatory contains souls who feverishly agitate themselves and will henceforth atone for their earthly "loitering ways" and "lukewarmness" with this "zeal" and "present ardor." Their moroseness was therefore conjoined with their idleness. Nevertheless, they are primarily punished for their lack of zeal and love, and especially for their having yielded to despondency, like certain Hebrews who, after crossing the Red Sea, delayed in serving Moses and perished in the desert; so too the many Trojans who remained in Sicily instead of sailing on with Aeneas to Latium.[106] This depression is thus only a distant cousin of sloth in its modern sense. In passing, it is worth noting how much the medieval and early modern church fought the temptation for the faithful to despair: *Desperacio* occurs in eleven of the Le Goff team's *exempla*. The *Artes moriendi*, which rapidly grew in number during the early fifteenth century, would further emphasize the dying person's fight against despair at those crucial moments when, ruminating over sins committed on earth, he or she did not believe in being able to obtain divine pardon. This *desperacio* therefore appears as an extreme form of "acedie."

In its turn, "The Parson's Tale" places emphasis on *acedia*.[107] It is a deadly offense, for the Bible says: Cursed be he who does the service of God negligently. The Parson then specifies: "Outher it [the estate of man] is th'estaat of innocence, as was th'estaat of Adam biforn that he fil into synne, in which estaat he was holden to wirche, as in heriynge and adowrynge of God. / Another estaat is the estaat of synful men, in which estaat men been holden to laboure in preiynge to God for amendement of hire synnes . . . Another estaat is th'estaat of grace, in which estaat he is holden to werkes of penitence" (sec. 681–683). The sin castigated by the homily is thus a spiritual idleness, which in many cases can cause despair, but also somnolence, which deadens the body and soul; Negligence—"And how that ignoraunce be mooder of alle harm, certes, necligence is the norice"—Sluggishness (*tarditas*), which distances a man from God; and Sorrow, which causes the death of the soul. The virtue that counteracts sloth is *Fortitudo*, a mixture of courage, greatness of spirit, and constancy. This virtue must itself rely on meditating on eternal punishments, the joys of paradise, and keeping faith in the grace of the Holy Ghost.

Gerson, in his *Le Profit de savoir quel est péché mortel et véniel*,[108] uses the word *paresse*, but in the sense of "ennui with spiritual welfare" and "a lessened devotion to charity." Such a sin becomes deadly only if "it leads one to neglect doing one's obligation," or if "the ennui is such that it brings a displeasure with living, and one slides into despair." For Gerson, "paresse" is thus the French translation of "accidia." The key examples for his argument clarify this point: If someone, bound by either wish or command to say his or her "hours," willfully neglects to do so, or if, in reciting them, he or she consciously desists from thinking of God, a Deadly Sin has been committed. The same holds true for anyone who, without a "reasonable excuse," misses Sunday and compulsory holiday masses.

The importance of "sloth" in the *Compost et Kalendrier* . . . may appear surprising: 17 branches, 51 sprigs, 153 foliage bunches. Studied in detail, however, the concept is imprecise, embracing a diverse range of sins: "Bad thoughts. Ennui with goodness. Imprudence toward evil. Pusillanimity. Wicked desire. Breaking [= broken vows]. Impenitence. Infidelity. Ignorance. Vain sorrow. Cowardice. Idleness. Deviation [of the spirit from the straight and narrow path]. Obstruction of goodness. Dissolution." A catch-all sin, therefore, which was made to encompass not only things related to *acedia*—spiritual disgust, pusillanimity and cowardice, willful ignorance, despondency—but also diverse and apparently unrelated attitudes: evil desire, infidelity, curiosity, dissoluteness, and so on. "Idleness" comprises only one of the seventeen branches of this polymorphous sin, and corresponds poorly with modern usage. The successive definitions of its three sprigs are: "(a) Ceasing to do good. Namely, ceasing good thoughts, good words, and good works. (b) Seeking to do evil. Namely seeking concupiscence of the flesh, and concupiscence of the eyes. It is avarice, and the concupiscence of proud living. (c) Not resisting evil. For the love one has for evil. For the tedium one finds in good. For one's own self-negligence."[109] This passage thus makes a pell-mell condemnation of sins of omission and nonresistance to temptation and of initiatives toward evil. Moreover, the refusal to work is implied, rather than clearly expressed. This document therefore gains interest from its suggestion of the difficulty that ecclesiastical discourse formerly faced when attempting to conceptualize sloth.

Nonetheless, the Hebrew proverbs, an integral part of the Bible, incited those who tended toward sleep or drowsiness to observe the activity of the ant.[110] These proverbs describe how "The slothful man roasteth not that which he took in hunting."[111] "In all labor there is profit: but the talk of the lips tendeth only to penury."[112] "Slothfulness casteth into a deep sleep; and an idle soul shall suffer hunger."[113] "Yet a little sleep, a little slumber, a little folding of the hands to sleep: So shall thy poverty come as one that traveleth, and thy want as an armed man."[114] These sayings had a long posterity. Their spirit and sometimes their letter recur in popular French proverbs of the sixteenth century: "Forever poor is the idle man"; " "Lazy in youth, sick in old age." "He who sleeps until sunrise lives in misery until sundown."[115] These were clear warnings, but without any religious aspect. The church, turning its thought and guilt-instilling efforts first toward *acedia*, also found it difficult to pass from this idea to unwillingness to work and to making such a vast concept specifically mean both spiritual ennui and the refusal to undertake simple daily tasks. Three convergent paths eventually led to a synthesis.

The first highlighted the moral dangers of idleness, an old moral theme found in Ecclesiasticus and easily Christianized, but one that gradually led to the praise of work for work's sake. As an admittedly arbitrary point of departure, one can take the *Disciplina degli spirituali*, composed by the Pisan Dominican Domenico Cavalca (d. 1342). The author criticizes idleness and beseeches man to put his body to work, for it is a mulish servant who must not be given the slightest chance to be recalcitrant.[116] Furthermore, the idle man "puts himself in a state more vile than that of beasts, for the latter are allowed to eat. In contrast, the holy apostle Paul confirms that he who does not work has no right to eat." This admonition to "contemplatives who wish to do nothing, and live only from alms"[117] would often reappear in later times: during the Reformation, and in both the seventeenth and eighteenth centuries. Hence Cavalca's biting formulation: "If you are a man, go, work, and eat the bread of your own fatigue."[118]

Returning to the *Menagier de Paris*, it disjointedly groups with sloth, next to negligence, "carnality," and "despair," rancor, "heart's vanity," and presumption. Its conception of the fourth Deadly Sin thus remains quite confused. Nevertheless, the author lays stress on "idleness": ". . . The Gospel says that the life of an idle body is a deadly enemy of the soul, and His Grace Saint Jerome gives this assurance: Always do something, so the Enemy may not find you idle . . . and His Grace Saint Augustine says . . . that anyone capable of work must not be idle."[119]

It should be recalled, moreover, that this work was composed by a solid bourgeois gentleman for the sake of his young wife and that, in the contemporary masculine mind-set, idleness was a moral danger particularly threatening to the female half of humanity. A highly misogynistic sermon by San Bernardino, cited in the preceding volume, notably exploits this commonplace: "So long as you control your wife, she will not linger by the window, and neither this thing nor that will cross her mind."[120] The humanist, architect, but also "merchant"-class Leon-Battista Alberti uses the same language in his *Libri della famiglia* (1433–1443). For him, only constant activities can counteract the inconstancy, fickleness, and frivolity of women, and keep them from looking out the balcony. For women are naturally idle, and therefore must fight this defect; it is up to the husband to create the conditions that will prevent his wife from succumbing to indolence.[121] Still, inactivity harms everybody and can ruin one's health. Alberti is categorical on this point: "Inactivity fills the veins with phlegm, the blood becomes watery and pale, the stomach grows delicate, the sinews lazy and the whole body slow and sleepy. The mind by too much inactivity goes sour and murky. Every power of the spirit becomes weary and inert."[122]

The second route toward the global condemnation of sloth crossed the land of poverty, whose horror was more fully gauged after the early thirteenth century.[123] In the second *Roman de la Rose*, the poor man, at one time the image of Christ, gradually becomes an object of contempt, suspicion, rebuke, and fear. Similarly, Chaucer's Man of Law says, "Bet is to dyen than have indigence . . . All the dayes of poure men been wikke" (ll. 114, 118). The *Roman de Mandevie* of Jean Dupin (1302–1374) teaches that "[the poor man] will find it hard to climb the wheel of fortune . . . You will always see the shiftless man heavy and melancholy . . . He who lives idly will be mad everlastingly . . . If you wish to be prosperous, leave nothing off to tomorrow."[124] Alberti echoes these statements: "Even the gods dislike the poor . . . It is better to die than to live in poverty."

More precisely, there emerged the idea that poverty was not only pitiable but guilty. In the second *Roman de la Rose*, it is closely linked with sin. For Deceit and the other vices came into the world with Poverty and her son, Theft: "Evil the early day when she appeared, / For her arrival was the worst of all!"[125] Here it is instructive to return to the *Menagier de Paris*. Although its author condemns idleness, he remains confused over the notion of sloth. His own treatise, however, is modeled on the poem written in 1342 by the royal notary Jean Bruyant, entitled *Le Chemin de la Povreté et de Richesse*. If he has copied from the earlier work, he has done so, he says "to help me gain the diligence and perseverance that a new husband must have."[126]

Bruyant's poem may be taken as a major landmark in the secularization of sloth and the move toward a condemnation of poverty. Of this vice that causes so many ills, the poem says: "Laymen call it sloth / And Clerks call it accidia."[127] So much for the secularization. As for Poverty, it is certainly lamentable; it is "A lady who is neither esteemed / In this world, nor approved / She is but an old dog, in truth." She brings with her "all adversity, / Mischief, pain, and sorrow." Bruyant, however, sees poverty as the consequence of a voluntary choice. Every man, he lets it be known, finds two roads before him. The right-hand one, made of "diligence" and "perseverance," leads to wealth for anyone who holds to it. That on the "sinister" side, in contrast, leads to "anguish" and "distress." There one will find no "comfort, no help / No counsel, no hope, nor possessions; / But pain, sorrow, and misfortune." If the cap fits, wear it: "Therefore begone, away from the path / That lies before him" (One must leave the road that leads to poverty). Finally, the poor do not deserve compassion: "For such people, in faith / One should have little pity . . . / That they suffer want, it is only right." From then on the accusation is full blown, and for centuries, the same sweeping condemnation will mix together "ruffians, thieves, scoundrels . . . useless people of vile condition." Persons "without hearth or home," "inhabiting almost any place," would be called "vagrants" of "ill repute." These curses were the counterpart of the growing number of unemployed people in early modern Europe—now a well-studied subject, which hardly needs further emphasis.[128]

The third route toward the full identification of sloth is more difficult to delineate; it was staked out from a meditation on time, which may have originated in a phrase attributed to Saint Bernard: "Nothing is more precious than time . . ."[129] In the fourteenth century, the concept is clearly stated by Domenico Cavalca, who devotes two chapters of his *Disciplina degli spirituali* to "the loss of time" and the duty of "keeping track of time." As Jacques Le Goff has noted, Cavalca speaks in mercantile terms, associating time and spirituality and comparing wasted time to the sterile, buried talent of the Gospel parable.[130] God will ask a reckoning not only of the evil we will have committed but also of the good we will not have accomplished, due to the misuse of the days of our lives.[131] The author of the *Menagier de Paris* likewise affirms: "On the Day of Judgment, every idle person will have to recognize the time lost in idleness."[132] From these clearly religious considerations, there develops a growing secularization. At the turn of the fifteenth century, the owner of a manuscript of the *Elucidarium* alludes to time in a way characteristic of the behavior and mentality of a good Christian bourgeois.[133] Some years later the biographer of Gianozzo Manetti praises the sense of time he observed in the humanist. He recounts how Manetti liked to say that God calculates the time spent in eating and sleeping, and that on the Day of Judgment he will require an explanation not only of the months and years of our lives, but also of our days, hours, and briefest moments. Hence Manetti did not want to waste the slightest atom of time that had been given him.[134] At a time when mechanical clocks first appeared, when the cloth-producing towns regulated their activities by the chimes and apparatus of their belfry towers, when post-Petrarchan humanism was discovering history, and when there was also born the *Devotio moderna*, with its advice on how to pray in the right manner, people of the church, of business, and of letters together found out—doubtless with each other's reciprocal support—the price of each moment and the gravity of indolence.

This discovery, as well as the tentative efforts that preceded it, can be perceived in the *Summa* of San Antonino. Spiritual author that he was, he still conceived of sloth in a traditional way: It was a "sorrow," a "torpor" that so depressed the human soul that one was no longer motivated toward goodness.[135] Although he touches on idleness,[136] a vice that leads one to Hell and spawns a multitude of evils, he discusses it without any reference to daily work. He explains how Christ was indefatigable throughout his public life. Thus the Kingdom of Heaven is not rewarded to "the lazy and the negligent, but to they who beseech it through prayer, who seek it through reading and hearing holy scripture, and justly deserve it for their good works." Following Saint Bernard, the Florentine archbishop specifies that "to be occupied with God is not idleness and therefore a sin, but on the contrary the occupation of all occupations." He employs the term "*pigritia*," but mainly to designate a slowness to convert, confess, and properly behave oneself.[137] This director of conscience therefore has only spiritual, indeed ecclesiastical, objectives in mind. His treatment of sloth essentially concerns the various "negligences" that lull both clerics and laypeople in their religious pursuits: Prelates sometimes neglect to learn or fulfill the duties of their office; some religious people do not recite the canonical hours; certain of the faithful do not observe religious holidays, forget both confession and annual communion, do not go to sermons or hear them without listening or listen to them without putting them into practice.[138] After making these classic observations, however, San Antonino more strikingly acknowledges the inestimable value of time. Like Saint Bernard, he affirms: "Nothing is more precious than time, but nothing today has such a vile reputation." Furthermore,

> *"Do not make light of time spent in idle chat and futile endeavors . . . Time is so precious that in a single instant of his lifetime a man may obtain pardon and earn eternal life, just as the thief crucified with Christ attained paradise in a fleeting moment. Time is so precious that one would give all the treasures of the earth for one more minute of life in which to do penance and escape the torments of hell. Nothing pertains to us as much as time; whence these words of Seneca: all other possessions are foreign to us. Only the time is our own."*[139]

Nothing is more our own than time: a new claim, superseding the church's previous teaching that time belonged to God and therefore must not be sold nor be the basis for charging interest on a loan. San Antonino's affirmation is echoed in a dialogue from Alberti's *Libri della famiglia*:

> GIANNOZZO: *But, to put it in brief, there are three things that a man can truly call his own. They are such that nature gave them to you the day you saw the light, with the freedom to use them well or badly just as it pleased and suited you. These are things nature ordained should always remain with you and never leave you till your last day. One of these things, as you realize, is that*

moving spirit within us by which we feel desire and anger . . . Another such thing, as you realize, is your body . . .

LIONARDO: *And what is the third?*

GIANNOZZO: *Ha! A most precious thing. My very hands and eyes are not so much my own.*

LIONARDO: *Amazing! But what thing is this?*

GIANNOZZO: *It cannot be bound, it cannot be diminished. In no way can it be made other than your own, provided you want* it to be yours.

LIONARDO: *And at my will it can belong to another?*

GIANNOZZO: *And if you wish it can be not yours. Time, my dear Lionardo, time, my children.*[140]

This insistence on the value of each moment permits the movement from religious to secular time, from the time of salvation to the time of competition and profit-taking. Already, at the mid-fourteenth century, the Tuscan Paolo da Certaldo's otherwise medievally spirited proverb collection, *Il Libro di buoni costumi*, had included this advice: "If you are negligent in your work, tomorrow you will be no other than a poor man . . . Do not say: I will do it tomorrow. What you have to do, do it quickly."[141] In 1408 a notary writes to the merchant Datini: "I do not forget your saying: he who knows best how to use his time outstrips other men."[142] Alberti's work gathers these dispersed maxims into a clearly elaborated discourse:

GIANNOZZO: *And to waste no part of such a precious thing [time], I have a rule that I always follow: never remain idle. I avoid sleep, and I do not lie down unless overcome by weariness, for it seems disgraceful to me to fall without fighting or to lie beaten . . . I avoid sleep and idleness, and I am always doing something. To be sure that one pursuit does not crowd out another, and that I don't find I have started several things but completed none, . . . do you know, my children, what I do? First thing in the morning, when I arise, I think to myself, "What are the things I have to do today?" There are a certain number of things, and I run through them, consider, and assign to each some part of my time: this for the morning, this later today, and that this evening. In this way I find every task gets done in an orderly way, almost without effort.*

. . . The man who neglects things finds that his time escapes him . . . I would sooner lose sleep than lose time, that is, than let the right moment for doing something slip by. Sleep, food, and things of that sort I can catch up on tomorrow, and take care of my needs, but the moment for doing something that must be done, no.[143]

Elsewhere in the dialogue Giannozzo reiterates this statement: "If a man knows how to keep from wasting time, he knows almost everything. If he knows how to make good use of time, he can be lord of anything he pleases."[144]

This secularized time, which rejects any sloth, is thus conceived in terms of utility and profit. Franklin's famous dictum that "time is money" was first coined by the Italian Renaissance. Alberti must again be cited in this context, since he argues that to use time well is to enrich oneself: "If money supplies our needs, however, why trouble our minds with the management of other things?"[145] A little less than a century later, Guicciardini similarly writes: "Know for certain that, despite the brevity of human life, time brings gain to the man who knows how to capitalize on it, and now consume it in vain."[146] Thus theologians, humanists, and merchants concordantly discovered and proclaimed that time is man's most precious good. In particular, however, the secularized conception of time boldly outlined sloth as the wasting of human possibilities; and lay society furthermore drew the church from the condemnation of sloth to that of idleness, a seriously harmful vice for a society that increasingly stressed worldly activity, profit, and money. Sloth had only been an individual offense. Idleness, however, quickly took on the image of a public enemy.

Sebastian Brant was a faithful witness of this evolution. Chapter 97 of *The Ship of Fools*, of "Indolence and Sloth,"[147] resumes certain classic moral themes: idleness is the mother of all the vices; the devil "notes all idleness / And sows his seeds in wickedness." Other lines, however, have a more modern ring: "A lazy man is useless too / Except to be a bugaboo"; "He's happy who with pickax works"; "Good work God will always reward." Work is therefore valorized as an absolute good. Moreover, the opening of the chapter specifies that its satire is primarily aimed at valets and chambermaids. Still more revealing is chapter 63,[148] which attacks the "beggardom" that enriches a great number of people, including monks, sellers of relics, and dealers in "votive knickknacks." Brant concedes that misery sometimes forces unfortunate people to beg. This slight concession, however, does not balance out the long diatribe against false cripples, pickpockets, vagabonds, and other "pious dealers and pretenders. / No kermes but they thither fare." The section makes some disturbing generalizations, such as the following: "Full every beggar boasts a Moll, / She lies, cheats, plies her folderol." To sum up, Brant expresses, beneath an unaware and global condemnation of sloth, a fear toward the poor felt by early modern people of status:

Beggars I grant a deal of space
They're plentiful in every race
And evermore their numbers grow

Begging brings them many joys,
These toying, courting beggar boys,
For after they have spent their share
They're always beggars now as e'er,
They may go begging anywhere.
As beggars many men live high,
Who have more coin than you or I.

Despite this and other similar texts, a fair amount of time elapsed before idleness became the target of universal censure and was fully integrated into the guilt-instilling discourse. It is still *accidia* that is castigated in Bosch's painting of *The Deadly Sins* (Prado). The sin is symbolized by a monk sleeping beside a fireplace where a rosary hangs in vain. Luther fumed against idleness, but mainly with regard to monks. This critique led him to champion the crafts and the humble daily work of laypeople: One does not need to give up a trade in order to "slide into a convent." God "is not necessarily pleased . . . if you become an ascetic, a monk, a nun, a priest. That gratifies him much less than the most modest trade of the earth."[149] Like Scripture, the Reformer is sickened by indifferent people,[150] and he most often relates idleness to sloth, a mix of spiritual inertia and pride. In *The Great Catechism*, he takes a fully traditional approach to this theme, and like San Antonino emphasizes the allergy for preaching. He writes that

> *These delicate souls must be censured, who when they have heard a sermon or two, are tired and sated as if they already knew the the text themselves and no longer needed teachers. For such is the sin that until now has been counted among the*

> *deadly sins, the one called* acidia, *in other words idleness or repletion, an odious, pernicious wound, with which the devil bewitches and deceives innumerable hearts, to suddenly ambush us, and to secretly and yet again steal the Word of God from us.*[151]

Likewise, the Jesuit Canisius, who spread the Counter-Reformation in sixteenth-century Germany, continued to place *accidia* on his list of the Seven Deadly Sins. In contrast, shall it be said that Montaigne laid siege to laziness in the *Essays* "Of Idleness" and "Against Do-nothingness"?[152] To be sure, he sought to employ his leisure time for controlling and organizing his thoughts that would otherwise give birth to "so many chimeras and fantastic monsters."[153] He extols the diligence of emperors who died "standing" and admires the greatness of spirit of those who are "ever keeping the soul and body busied in fair, great, and virtuous things."[154] On the other hand, Montaigne is not preoccupied with a functional use of time and an obsession to avoid losing a single moment. While he declares "nonchalance" to be a "vice," he admits that it is one "toward which I clearly lean by temperament."[155]

It is not as well known that this temptation affected Calvin, whose work sums up a diverse number of earlier thoughts and condemnations of idleness. In *The Institutes*, he has sloth in mind when he discusses spiritual "nonchalance and pride." Such attitudes suppress one's "humility and reverence for God" and lead "into forgetting His graces."[156] Calvin, however, adopts the Renaissance discourse on time: ". . . Just as the brevity of the day must needs incite laborers to work and be diligent, in fear that night's dark shadows may interrupt their first efforts, so too, seeing how little time is given to our lives, should we beware of remaining idle."[157]

At the same time, work is a "law of nature," independent even of Original Sin: "God might well have sent us pasture for free, but it pleased him to make us work, that we might have care, that we might work, that everyone according to their estate should strive to do that which is appropriate . . . God . . . wishes not that we rest, that everyone wallow here and that we might forget what it is to work the earth, or to labor in other manners."[158] God does not want "us to be slack and idle like blocks of wood."[159]

God "does not wish one to rest": an imposing statement, which clarifies an entire civilization as well as the weight of its curse on idleness. When Brueghel the Elder engraves *The Seven Deadly Sins* (1556–57), he does not castigate "*accidia*" so much as idleness, which makes one poor. The caption reads: "Idleness. The lazy, the poltroons, and all these do-nothings are always provided with wind but never with money." The engraving also treats religious indifference and reluctance to pray, yet features people "hunting flies instead of working," and "do-nothings neither cooking nor spinning nor sewing." A man hunts after the fleas on a dog, while others gaze at storks flying by, and so on.[160] In this regard, the modernized version of the *Doctrinal de Sapience* (1604) speaks like Calvin, as it expresses a wide and integrated conception of idleness: It is at once "a dullness which makes us late and unapt to work," and "a contempt and distaste for spiritual things."

Even if he most likely does so unconsciously, the anonymous reviser of the old text of the *Doctrinal* synthesizes the messages of Aquinas, San Antonino, and Alberti. To be sure, he chides those who begin a good work and do not finish it, or those who have an aversion for virtuous people, or those who "idly and in all ways seek to either tell or listen to useless tales of amusement." He stresses, however, the value of time and the imperious necessity of never being inactive:

> *He who seeks after [idleness] is extremely mad, and will be consumed with misery and poverty . . . Job affirms that man is born for work, as the bird is for flying. The span of our life being short and precious, it is vital not to squander the slightest part of it. God has the fiercest punishments in store for the lazy; they are like servants whom one thrusts out into dark streets . . . they are trees, which, bearing no fruit, are cut down and thrown into the fire . . . Idleness makes a man completely incapable of anything: it makes him find thorns and problems everywhere. That which weighs less than a feather for the diligent man seems like a mass of lead to a lazy man. Laziness robs or steals from us the most precious thing in the world, which is time.*

Hence the advice: "One must look upon each new day as if it were the last of one's life: One must manage and organize one's time for sleep, for meals, and for all the works and chores of the day."[161]

This text remains directed toward teaching humility and preparation for death. Nonetheless, the author gives a more general lesson, insofar as he emphasizes the obligation to fully employ one's time and banish any idleness. This teaching involuntarily leaves piety behind and depicts poverty and misery as the logical outcome of laziness. A telling comparison can be made between this late *Doctrinal de sapience* and its 1478 edition (Paris, Bibliothèque Nationale), which only accentuates spiritual indolence, and even includes an apologue devaluing work. The anecdote (an *exemplum*) presents two artisans. One is an excellent worker; however, he is poor. His "close friend" is professionally inferior but nonetheless rich. Why? Because he regularly goes to church. He therefore advises his comrade to do as he does: "I want you to know that I have found no other treasure than the church, and I am sure that if you attend Mass you will be as rich as I. And so [the other] did grow rich, once he had gone to hear sermons at his church."[162] This "story" does not appear in the 1604 edition.

An entire social panorama looms behind this censure and the harsh discourse of the later edition (he who indulges in idleness . . . will be filled with misery). During a time when beggars and vagabonds were growing more numerous in Western society, unemployment and shiftlessness became clearly identified. Idleness threatened the established order, and the lazy and out-of-work were a dangerous class. It became prudent to imprison the itinerant poor in "workhouses" or, with mad people, in hospitals.

THE ICONOGRAPHY OF SIN

The rise of the bourgeoisie and an economic situation that created great numbers of beggars thus heightened public awareness of the grave consequences of being lazy. Put in context, however, this awareness was itself only one aspect of the wide-reaching emergence of a guilt mentality. With the accomplishment of this process, the church succeeded in imposing the system of the Deadly Sins as a collective mental category. When Charles VII solemnly entered Paris on November 13, 1437, the Virtues and Vices took part in his procession: "Then came the figures of the Seven Deadly Sins and the Seven Virtues, on horseback, and fully costumed according to their qualities. These figures followed the lords of the Parliament and of the Requestres. After them came the presiding judges."[163] A *Moralité de l'homme pécheur*, performed in Tours, printed by Vérard in 1481 and frequently reprinted, and another *Moralité de l'homme juste et de l'homme mondain*, likewise printed by

Vérard, in 1508, presented audiences with the combat of the Virtues and Vices, which reappears in the delightful short poem by Gringore (d. 1538) entitled *Le Château de labour.*[164] In this poem, Reason comforts a young distressed husband, telling him: Your only enemies are your own vices. Fight courageously against the Seven Deadly Sins, fearing not their lances and shields.

Between the fourteenth and sixteenth centuries, iconography also latched on to the theme of the Seven Deadly Sins. Previously, psychomachy had been performed in front of churches, but before the confessional experts' learned elucidations of the septenary had entered mainstream consciousness. When, in the first half of the fourteenth century, the fresco cycles of Giotto at Padua and the Lorenzetti at Siena arrange the Deadly Sins in sequence under arcades, they do so more as anticipations than as transcriptions. In contrast, portrayals of the Deadly Sins appear even on the façades of fifteenth-century bourgeois town houses: in Thiers, Orleans, Le Blanc, and Aguilar de Campo (Palencia).[165]

One of the main schema for depicting the vices—or sins—was the Tree of Evil, originally described in general by Saint Gregory and then in detail by Hugh of St.-Victor.[166] The basic idea, drawn from Ecclesiastes (10:6–18), is that all vices derive from pride, and, branching off from the same trunk, bear wicked leaves and fruits, which often are shown drooping toward the ground, while their counterparts in the trees of good are depicted as raised on high. This iconographic theme naturally had many variants. Sometimes Pride is at the root of the tree and the Devil at its summit, enthroned, his arms crossed, grinning a hideous grin. In other depictions, such as various fourteenth-century English wall paintings,[167] Leviathan and his followers form the roots of the tree. Each branch ends in the head of a dragon, from which there emerges a figure representing a vice. Pride is perched atop the highest branch. Or again, as in a French fourteenth-century miniature from the *Verger de soulas* (the *Orchard of Consolation*), the vices issue from the tails of dragons, which together form the roots of a tree surmounted by the Queen of Evil (*superbia*).[168]

Saint John Climacus provided another type of relationship between the vices, that of their being joined together like links on a chain. Mireille Vincent-Cassy observes that all fifteenth-century French murals of the vices show devils dragging along groups of sinners on enormous chains attached to their necks or waists, as they head toward Hell. For reasons as yet unclear, these paintings are restricted to the regions of the Alps and the river Lot. These unruly bands of vices often occupy an entire lateral wall of a church or chapel, and usually face a series of virtues painted on the opposite side. At Vigneaux in the high Alps, however, the fresco of the vices is located on the outside of the church, so that the inhabitants had no choice but to see it whenever they went about their daily village errands. The pedagogical intentions of these compositions and their patrons are obvious.

The image of the circle was also used to express the conspiratorial solidarity of the vices. During the twelfth century, it was used to illustrate a manuscript of Hugh of St.-Victor's *De . . . septenariis*[169] and to adorn bronze liturgical basins that include the names of the vices around the plate's edge.[170] Similarly, the rose windows of Notre-Dame de Paris and Auxerre enclose psychomachy within a circle dominated by God. The theme becomes further enriched. A fifteenth-century illuminated manuscript of *The City of God* portrays a town surrounded by a circular wall and divided into seven radiating quarters where warring figures symbolize the Deadly Sins and their opposed Virtues.[171] Two English wall paintings exploit the same image, and around a central figuration of Hell arrange the spokes of a wheel, separating the vices of the septenary into their own compartments.[172] An Augsburg engraving of 1477 features a water-wheel on which each of the sins appears as a bucket; in turning, it tips guilty souls into an infernal lake where monsters and demons await them.[173] Another German engraving, dated 1490, puts God at the center of a wheel. He is surrounded by concentric rings that bear the names of the vices and virtues.[174] Many of these themes become synthesized in Bosch's *Seven Deadly Sins* panel. The eye of God, whose pupil represents the risen Christ, surveys a circle, divided into seven sections, wherein each vice is labeled and evoked by an eloquent scene.

Christian moralists, casuists, and artists quickly perceived the link between the Seven Deadly Sins and the Beast of the Apocalypse. On a high-relief from Solesmes (fifteenth century), seven proud heads twist themselves around their own monstrous neck. Frère Laurent, author of the *Somme le Roi*, sees the exact image of the Deadly Sins in the seven heads of the Beast. It can be supposed that between the fourteenth and sixteenth centuries, when people beheld scenes of the Apocalypse, such as that engraved by Dürer, they perceived a correlation between the seven heads of the Beast and the seven vices described and classified by the experts.[175] The evolution of the theme led from the apocalyptic monster to the human body. Several English murals of the fourteenth and fifteenth centuries display a huge man on whose body one can see seven dragons covered with scales; each monster belches forth a small figure symbolizing a Deadly Sin.[176] Finally, in a new transference, a granite bas-relief at Saint-Léry (Morbihan, Brittany) shows a man attacked by seven animals at the points of the body most likely to commit the seven sins: pride bites the head, envy the right shoulder, lust the genitalia, and so on. The man is shown naked, for his nudity recalls Original Sin.[177]

Thus a new iconographic system associated the sins with certain animals. A literary tradition had already suggested this approach: The desert fathers, followed by Peter Damian, Rabanus Maurus, Honorius of Autun, and Vincent of Beauvais had compared the vices to animals. This assimilation also occurs in the *Hortus deliciarum*, the florilegium that Herrade von Landsberg (d. 1195) the abbess of the canonesses of St.-Odilde, composed for her nuns, as well as in a *Dieta salutis* falsely attributed to Saint Bonaventure.[178] All the same, if "the differentiated applications of animal symbolism to the range of vices appears quite early on, [they] were not truly systematized until the early thirteenth century,"[179] and especially during the fourteenth century: hence at the time of the church's great offensive to induce a guilt consciousness.

Whereas the beasts at the cathedrals of Chartres, Paris, and Amiens still have only a limited role in the psychodrama of the sins (a hare from which cowardice flies, the horse from which pride has a fall, and so on), a hundred years later the animal symbolism becomes precise. A manuscript (ca. 1390) conserved at the Bibliothèque Nationale and studied by Emile Mâle clearly delineates the relationships among sin, social status, and animal symbolism, and represents the vices, in a soon-to-be classic format, riding their particular animals[180]:

Pride = a king, riding a lion, and carrying an eagle
Envy = a monk riding a dog, and carrying a sparrowhawk
Anger = a woman riding a boar, and carrying a rooster
Sloth = a peasant riding an ass, and carrying an owl
Avarice = a merchant, riding a mole or a badger, carrying an owl
Gluttony = a youth riding a wolf, carrying a kite
Lust = a lady riding a goat, carrying a dove[181]

Other attributions were certainly accepted: for Pride, the peacock; for Lust, the billy goat; for Avarice, the monkey or toad; for Envy, the snake or greyhound. The crucial fact is that this animal symbolism for the Deadly Sins became widely accepted and easily recognizable. Mâle noted that it is frequently encountered in country churches,[182] as if it were the fitting instrument for the moral instruction of peasants. This type of iconography, however, transcended class and regional boundaries. A useful test case is the Viennese monk Mattias Farinator's *Lumen animae* (ca. 1330), a psychomachy between vices and virtues, embodied by armed knights riding animals. For example, Pride rides a camel (a swift animal), carries a shield decorated with a lion, and wears chain-mail featuring an eagle, and a helmet crested with a peacock. Transmitted via the *Livre des sept péchés mortels et des sept vertus* (Augsburg, 1474), the *Lumen animae* inspired engravers and tapestry weavers in late fifteenth- and early sixteenth-century Germany and Flanders.

It is worth taking pause at this devaluation of animals, brought on by their identification with the Deadly Sins. The process surely involves the important biblical teaching that places Adam at the center of creation and affirms that he alone was created in God's image: hence the need to establish a wide gap between him and other living creatures. Saint Bernard, for one, distrusted any Christian art that highlighted the bestiary and overexalted the animal kingdom. In the wake of this protest, late medieval theologians held that sinful people debased themselves to the level of animals. This analogy indicates the extent to which that level had fallen. There was thus a move away from an iconographic tradition that, especially in early Christian times, had been inclined to associate both flora and fauna with the message of the Gospels, in a kind of paradise regained. To clarify this point, I will cite two examples that speak for many others. The first, a fourth-century mosaic from the church of Tabgha (near Lake Tiberias), depicts the miraculous draft of bread and fishes but adds an aviary of ducks, herons, and peacocks, set amid an Egyptian-style lotus patch. Likewise, a great fifth-century mosaic from an Armenian chapel in Jerusalem is exclusively composed of animal and floral motifs, creating an atmosphere of tranquil happiness. Much later, this harmony of man and nature received one of its loveliest expressions in Saint Francis's "Canticle of the Brother Sun and Sister Moon."

During the rise of the European guilt mentality in the fourteenth to sixteenth centuries, however, inspirers of religious art instead tended to increase the distance between animals and men, for whom monkeys were now the caricature. Literature often followed suit. The early fourteenth-century royal notary who composed the *Roman de Fauvel* turns his title character into a symbolic ass or horse, who incarnates all the human vices in the six letters of his name: *F*lattery, *A*varice, *V*anity, *V*illainy, *E*nvy, and "*L*âcheté" (Cowardice), all men—pope, king, lords, priests, bourgeois, and peasants—having no other ambition than to "wipe Fauvel's ass." An entire symbolic system was thus called into question, indeed overturned in a negative direction: The peacock, which had once signified eternal life, was henceforth identified with Pride.

Since most people's minds were now preoccupied with the fear of Deadly Sin, artists contrived all sorts of representations for it. Some drew on history. In particular, the tapestry makers, who worked for a sophisticated clientele, habitually attached certain vices to famous characters: Tarquin, Holofernes, Judas, Nero, and Mohammed. These comparisons seem to have originated in Italy, where they were employed in several fourteenth-century manuscripts.[183] They soon crossed the Alps, since in 1396 Philip the Bold purchased an Arras tapestry on which emperors, kings, and other well-known figures symbolize the virtues and vices. Later, in 1488, Simon Vostre's *Les Heures à l'usage de Rome* shows the virtues triumphing over their most famous enemies: Faith overcomes Mohammed; Hope, Judas; and Justice, Nero. On the great Flemish tapestry at Granja,[184] around the enthroned figure of Justice there are grouped the great men who honored her, while at the bottom are gathered the ancient criminals and notorious rebels whom the heavens struck down.

Nevertheless, given the negative image of women the church then held, iconography did not fail to identify women with sin.[185] Although *Superbia* was doubtless the "queen of vices" atop the trees of evil, was she not also simply woman in general? In Guillaume de Digulleville's *Pèlerinage de vie humaine*, the traveler Everyman meets as many women as sins. As noted in *La Peur en Occident*,[186] many sixteenth-century French prints of the Deadly Sins personify sometimes five or even six of them with female figures. Still more striking and revealing are the veritable diagrams given by Woman-Vice images from fourteenth- and fifteenth-century Bohemia and Germany. A symbol of pride, crowned with peacock feathers, she embodies the sum total of the Deadly Sins through iconographic inventions familiar to contemporaries: One of her legs, in the form of a bird's claw, is labeled *acedia* and bitten by her other, serpentine leg, envy. In one hand she holds a bow (anger), and in the other, a horn of plenty (avarice), and so on. Thus the Woman-Vice is the synoptic image of all sin.[187]

Mâle aptly observed how fifteenth-century images of the vices outnumber those of the virtues not only in France but elsewhere, the church having primarily sought to teach the latter by degrading the former.[188] Paintings, sculptures, stained-glass windows, tapestries, illuminations, and printed illustrations all came untiringly to direct their iconography toward promoting the message of confession manuals, such as the *Miroir de l'âme pécheresse, Destruction des vices, Doctrine pour les simples gens*, and other works, among them the *Art de gouverner le corps et l'âme*, this message being that "there is no man, no matter how perfect, in whom this dire septenary must not strike fear . . . for the Seven Deadly Sins are like the seven heads of the hydra, which grow back as soon as they are cut off . . ."[189]

The fine wood-carved jubé (ca. 1480) in the chapel of Saint-Fiacre du Faouet (Finistère, Brittany), teaches the same daunting lesson: Facing the choir, a man, personifying both envy and theft, gathers fruit from someone else's tree; another vomits a fox: thus gluttony degenerates into drunkenness; a Breton bagpipe player symbolizes sloth, and so on. This is but one among a host of contemporary artworks portraying the Deadly Sins. To cite at random: a sculpted group by Peter Dell (Nuremberg); a Flemish tapestry at Zaragoza; and of course Bosch's painting at the Prado. Around the central divine eye runs the dreadful phrase *Cave, cave, Dominus videt* ("Beware, beware, God is watching"). The circle around the eye is divided into seven compartments, wherein vivid scenes evoke each of the vices. Thus Anger is portrayed by an overturned table and a woman who attempts to restrain a man armed with a knife. Bosch not only produced several versions of this work, but he again treated the theme of the Deadly Sins and their consequent infernal punishments in his Last Judgments of Bruges and Vienna. In its turn, the right panel of *The Garden of Earthly Delights* (Prado) reemphasizes the tortures suffered and justly deserved by each category of sinners, it being clear that the garden of delights at the left—a paradise for nudists inside a gigantic amusement park—represents hardly the earthly paradise but rather a world consumed with lust.[190] It may even be the case that in *The Temptation of Saint Anthony* (Lisbon), the seven figures surrounding the hermit symbolize the Deadly Sins. Another of Bosch's most famous works, *The Hay-wain*, ridicules the mad love for earthly things that makes one forget the only reality that matters: salvation. In Old Dutch, the word "hooi" (hay) allegorically signified the ephemeral nature of the human world. The ensemble forms a triptych whose caption might read: "Birth, diffusion, and punishment of evil." On the left, Original Sin is recalled; on the right, Hell appears, where demons drag in the hay-wain and all those who grasped at straws to satisfy their greed. Seated atop the enormous pile of hay, two lovers, fascinated by their guilty desire and charmed by a demonic melody, do not listen to the guardian angel, who turns toward Christ in discouragement. Around the hay, an image of fleeting gold, there jostle and grapple a pope, an emperor, monks, vagrants, and representatives of all social classes. The work's dominant chord is thus the double denunciation of lust and avarice.

Brueghel the Elder, in many ways Bosch's successor, himself depicted the Deadly Sins in a series of engraved prints.[191] These works reanimate Bosch's monstrous characters and infernal visions, as well as his mixture of sharp realism and terrifying fantasy. The female epitome of Gluttony drinks voraciously and tramples on a wild pig quarreling with a dog over some turnips. In the garden of love, or the space of lust, a nude woman couples with a fish-headed monster, and so on.

Artists occasionally symbolized one of the Deadly Sins in greater detail. I think here of the theme of The Tower of Babel, masterfully handled by Brueghel (Vienna, Kunsthistorisches Museum, and Rotterdam), but also exploited by other painters as well as manuscript illuminators.[192] It is easy to see why this subject seduced Renaissance artists, as it gave them the chance to reproduce the much-admired architecture of the Roman Colosseum and at the same time render contemporary building techniques, especially the cranes that could be seen towering over Bruges and Antwerp. To this reading, however, must be added another of a different order. Many fifteenth- and sixteenth-century people saw the Tower of Babel as the symbol of a pride that had received double punishment: the collapse of the upper stories, which dared to reach the heavens, and the confusion of languages. The latter signified the impossibility of communication between men who remained obstinate in their sin.

Early modern Europeans were constantly thrust into the presence of sin and its punishment. Even the compassionate and luminous Fra Angelico painted a scene of hell (in his *Last Judgment* at the convent of San Marco, Florence). Representations of the great rendering of accounts abounded, as well as vignettes of individual judgment, in which demons seek to tip the scales to the side of hell.[193] In this context, however, there can also be noted a sin curiously neglected by the classic septenary, one that contemporaries looked at with new fear (and enjoyment): malice, especially that which expresses itself through cruelty. This new predilection comes across in the fourteenth- to sixteenth-century iconography of not only Christ's crucifixion but also the painful stages of His Passion. No epoch in the history of Christian art had put so much diligence and excess into the portrayal of the hateful torturers who wound and crown Christ with thorns, savagely flagellate him, and renew their blows once he falls, exhausted, on the road to Calvary. "The Man of Sorrows"—the Devout Christ of Perpignan, the Crucified Christ of Isenheim, or the "Christ with a toothache" at the cathedral of Vienna—thus appears as the privileged victim of human malice, which enjoys torturing others. In pedagogical fashion, a triptych by Goosen Van der Weyden (1507; Musée des Beaux-Arts, Antwerp) places the cross at the center and, behind it, a painted ensemble of the instruments, cruelties, and betrayals of the Passion. The iconography of the time also conveyed the unleashed sadism of torturers against holy devotees of the faith. Their martyrdoms inspired artists just as much as that of Jesus.

During my visits to European museums—at Barcelona, Antwerp, Warsaw, and so on—I have often had the following experience (less so in Italy or in the case of Italian works): As I move from room to room, descending from the High Middle Ages toward the fourteenth to sixteenth centuries, I have observed that scenes of torture proliferate. The era is one of slicings, flayings, burnings, tortures with red-hot pincers. Western society thus tirelessly represented and denounced—but also no doubt savored—cruelty, which seems to have assumed new diffusion and dimensions between the time of the Great Companies and the Wars of Religion. It has been noted[194] that *The Golden Legend*, so frequently painted, illuminated, and then printed, constituted a veritable "torture manual." As witness: Saint Boniface has needles driven under his nails and Saint Quentin nails into his head, Saint Vitale is buried alive, Saint Blaise torn to pieces by nails, Saint Eupheme ground up by millstones, Saint Hippolyte tied by the feet with his hands bound behind his back to the tail of a horse, Saint Sebastian riddled with arrows until he looks like a porcupine, Saint Christopher forced to sit upon a red-hot metal seat. The Victoria and Albert Museum, London, owns a remarkable illustration of these tortures, which a German artist living in Valencia painted for a confraternity in the early fifteenth century. With a stupefying richness of detail it records all the tortures suffered by Saint George, "the great martyr." It seems incredible that the hero could have survived so many trials, since before being decapitated, he is ripped by sharp-toothed wheels, plunged into burning oil, and flayed on a table. His torturers had even begun to slice him up like an animal at the slaughterhouse.

In this area, events appear to have caught conceptualizing by surprise: A civilization discovered its own cruelty before moralists had the time to integrate malice—a sin just as major as the others—into their intellectual categories. The discourse of malice was more iconographic than theoretical; it is therefore justifiably ambiguous. The absence of malice or cruelty (both of which are not necessarily offshoots of anger) from the list of Deadly Sins is yet another proof that the guilt-instilling discourse had developed within the monastic world. This omission on the part of cloistered monks was natural . . . and all to their honorable credit. They could well have felt the temptations of pride, envy, jealousy, anger, and sorrow, of lust and gluttony. It is hard, however, to think of them as inordinately cruel: Hence they neglected to include malice in the list of major sins.

There remains the fact that, in a world radically divided between black and white, incessant and multifaceted warnings urged Christians, both with word and image, to hastily leave the world of perdition in order to find their way through the gate of salvation. A late fifteenth-century German retable, formerly in Gdansk and now at the Warsaw National Museum, clearly illustrates this insistent pedagogy with regard to the Ten Commandments. A series of compartments, each divided into two antithetical halves, makes point-by-point contrasts between virtuous attitudes and sinful conduct. One of these panels opposes the peaceful and devout attendance of a preacher's sermon to a sequence of frivolous pursuits, prominent among which are visits to taverns and dangerous groups of women. The preacher's homily can be readily assimilated with innumerable exposés on sin that were then being offered to the faithful, such as the following one, again taken from the *Doctrinal de sapience*:

> *Bear in mind . . . that it is most reasonable to constantly attack the Seven Deadly Sins, and put them to death, because they are just so many heads, which being brought down, will also bring the ruin and final demise of all other vices: they are the seven demons whom Jesus Christ chased from Mary Magdalene's body, whose flight dispersed and utterly defeated the rest of their legion. Finally, they are the seven enemies of the people of Israel, who must needs be conquered to gain entry to the promised land, which is heaven.*[195]

By the beginning of the sixteenth century, the Catholic Church believed that it had successfully identified the diverse forms of evil and the many paths of temptation. The church had focused the details of the required examination of conscience, to which the Christian must be devoted for life. Until the mid-twentieth century, these minutely elaborated moral guidelines would not be called into question. At the same time, in sermons and catechisms, the church strove for the assimilation of such teaching into the greatest possible percentage of the population. With the impetus of the preceding period, the sixteenth to nineteenth centuries would see the development of the most powerful mass imposition of guilt in history.

CHAPTER 8

Original Sin

ORIGINAL SIN AT THE HEART OF A CULTURE

The preceding pages have continually focused and refocused on a central explanatory concept: Original Sin. This chapter will now address the immense place Original Sin holds in the mental universe of early modern times.

To the question "Why does God let innocent people die?" a doctor of the Holy See, Bartolomeo Spina, gave the following answer in 1523: "He does so with just cause. For though they do not die because of the sins they have committed, they die still guilty of original sin."[1] This explanation's logic therefore proposes that animals do not suffer, since they have not sinned: Such is in fact the teaching of Malebranche, who used the doctrine of Original Sin to justify the Cartesian theory of animal-machines. He writes that if animals had any sensibility, "it would happen that, beneath a just and all-powerful God, an innocent creature would suffer from pain that would be both penalty and punishment for some sin." Thus he arrives at the following syllogism: Since animals have not tasted a "forbidden fruit," they cry without pain.[2] A rather unusual demonstration!

If Luther accuses reason of being "an accursed whore," it is because Adam's crime corrupted it. Lycosthenes emphasizes how the first "monstrous" event of history was caused by the diabolical snake who seduced Eve. Donne states that men are worse than toads and spiders, since as a result of the first sin they hide a reserve of poison in some "invisible corner" of themselves. This poison corrupts all human actions. The Puritan poet George Wither (d. 1667) sees rhetoric as a necessary concession to man's fragility and corruption; without Original Sin, men would not need rhetoric, which appeals to the senses. These latter have dethroned reason ever since the Fall.[3] Louis Tronson (d. 1700), a father superior of St.-Sulpice, taught his seminarists that "we must always wear [our garments] with profound feelings of penitence; for they are a continual sign of our crime. In the state of innocence, man had no need of clothes with which to dress himself, for a certain radiance of God's glory surrounded him, visible even on the outside, and so served as his clothing."[4]

A violently anti-Protestant French preacher of the sixteenth century, Simon

Vigor, accused Adam of heresy: ". . . Later [Eve] gave it [the fruit] to her husband Adam, who let his wife make a monkey of him, and he ate thereof: and so the world's first sin was heresy (I follow Tertullian here), because man preferred to believe his wife and the devil who lied to him, rather than God who had told him the truth."[5] In a work published in 1699, the Reformer Jacques Basnage also saw Adam as "the first heretic" of history. He writes that "he should have upheld the succession of God's doctrine . . . But although there was a pure light and holiness in the earthly paradise, enough to guide him, he let himself waver from the religion that was confided in him."[6] Likewise significant are the three following texts, purposefully chosen for the wide distances between their dates and intentions. The first concerns the birth of melancholy and was written by Saint Hildegard of Bingen (d. 1179), whose many works include a medical treatise, the *Causae et curae*:

> *At the very instant when Adam disobeyed divine order, melancholy coagulated in his blood, just as clarity vanishes when the light goes out, though the still hot oakum produces malodorous smoke. And so it was with Adam, for while his own light was being put out, melancholy curdled in his blood, which filled him with sadness and despair. Indeed, when Adam fell, the devil breathed melancholy into him, that melancholy which makes man fainthearted and unbelieving.*[7]

Nearly five hundred years later, Robert Burton extends this analysis by logically beginning his *Anatomy of Melancholy* with a discussion of Original Sin, which transformed man, "the miracle of nature," into a miserable being subject to illness, fear, unhappiness, and death: *Heu tristis et lachrymosa commutatio!*[8]

Similarly, in 1649, master Robert Mentet de Salmonet offers this explanation for the revolts of his century, especially in Great Britain:

> *The disobedience of the first man put death and disorder into the world . . . All living things then revolted against him and no longer recognized Adam's authority. He forthwith felt an even more dangerous rebellion within himself . . . : the elements making up his body, which for his sake had forgotten their natural enmity, resumed their prior hatred and did not cease warring against each other until this admirable edifice was reduced to dust. It is from this first internecine revolt that men became wolves, eating one another's flesh . . .*[9]

In the same spirit, a sermon prepared by Saint Vincent de Paul (and his secretary) for use by rural missionaries poses this unexpected question: If the first man had kept his state of innocence, would all of his descendants have been equally noble? The probable answer: There would have been superiors and inferiors, but the former would not have governed the latter "despotically," and they would not have looked down on them as servants. "Man only acquired this name [of servant] by his fall: had not man sinned in the first place, you would have no authority over any other . . . consequently, if you give commands to a servant, it is sin which permits you to do so." The sermon's conclusion is intended for the masters: "Your servants are men like you and you are sinners as they are."[10]

Unlike Islam, which, it should be noted, did not incline toward the macabre, Christian civilization placed the Fall at the center of its preoccupations and construed it as a catastrophe initiating all history.[11] Although the story of Adam and Eve's crime appears in the first book of the Old Testament (Gen. 3:1–24), ancient Judaism did not focus its theology on the first sin. Only during the earliest Christian era did certain noncanonical Jewish writings date the penalties that weigh upon humanity back to Adam; these texts, however, do not clearly describe the transmission of the sinful state from the first father to his ensuing line. In the Gospels and the Creed of Nicaea, Original Sin is not the issue. Rather, Jesus stresses "the sin of the world" and does not mention Adam. On the other hand, Saint Paul, in a famous passage from Romans (5:12–21) boldly highlights the role of Adam: By him, not only death but sin entered the world. Nevertheless, the aim of the Apostle of the Gentiles is mainly to show that grace prevails over sin and that Christ the Redeemer takes away the "condemnation" forced on humanity. Thanks to His sacrifice on the cross, "by the obedience of one shall many be made righteous": Hence Paul speaks a language of hope.

Until the late second century, the question of Original Sin remains obscure in the texts of the holy fathers and other Christian apologists. Henri Rondet writes that "the story of the fall did not obsess [the early Christians]. The dogma of Redemption was not founded on the sin of Adam as a primordial catastrophe."[12] The same author adds that "original sin was only part of the Christian faith, and in a rather general sense. The Genesis story was familiar: Adam and Eve had sinned, but what the exact nature of this sin was, what its exact consequences had been, and what place needed to be given to personal sin in the miserable state of the human race, were not things the church was preoccupied with *ex professo*."[13] A change, however, occurred during the late second and through the third centuries, when Irenaeus, Tertullian, and Origen, each in his own way, examined the crime of Adam, an event that became the essential concern of Augustine. The probable inventor of the expression "Original Sin," the Bishop of Hippo, achieved both a systematization and a dramatization of Christian doctrine regarding this problem. His argument against Pelagius and the latter's followers would henceforth play a decisive role in not only the history but the daily life of Latin Christianity. In contrast, the orthodox tradition did not interpret sin so much "as the major and fundamental category of the experience of salvation."[14]

Schematically, the system of sin according to Augustine—"an anti-Gnostic who become a quasi-Gnostic"[15]—is as follows: In the first state of rectitude and justice, Adam and Eve perfectly controlled the inclinations of their bodies, especially their sexual desires (this view resumes the Stoic ideal of the wise man controlling his passions). If Eden had not vanished, people would have engendered children "without any pleasure, or at least with a pleasure ruled and ordered by the will."[16] Adam and Eve were mortal by nature, but death did not penetrate into the earthly paradise. The animals went forth from Eden to die,[17] and our first parents escaped death by eating the fruits of the tree of life.[18] Their joy was perpetual and without shadow. They took pleasure in God. They were good. They were filled with ardent charity, sincere faith, and upright conscience.[19] But disobedience changed everything. Adam and Eve seesawed from eternity to time (the place of all degradation), from abundance to poverty, from stability to debility.[20] They not only became subject to pain and death, but they lost that subordination of the passions to the will that they had received as a special grace. Just as the animals revolted against man to the point that some now try to devour him, so man became a bundle of contradictory tendencies. Since that time "he has been divided, scattered, a stranger to himself."[21]

With the initial crime, there appeared ignorance and concupiscence. The latter especially shows itself in sexual excitement, which reason no longer controls: The result is that even a legitimate marriage is only the good usage of an evil thing.[22] We inherit this ignorance and concupiscence, yet we are also guilty of them. For at the time of his sin, Adam formed one single man with all his posterity; all of us were contained in him. The unity of the human race within Adam explains how the first offense was also our offense.[23] Hence Augustine's statement that sinning humanity henceforth comprised a "great mass of perdition,"[24] by itself incapable of true virtue. Baptism is the indispensable requirement for a regeneration that allows one to escape the "torment of eternal death," which effaces culpability without, however, removing the concupiscence and ignorance brought by Adam and Eve's disobedience. Thus "children who have not received baptism will suffer the effects of the sentence pronounced against those who will not have believed, and will be condemned."[25] The necessary baptism of children also gave Augustine the opportunity to specify that "grace is not given to all men, and those to whom it is given do not obtain it for the merit of their works, nor for that of their wills, which can be especially seen with children."[26]

The Council of Carthage (418), which condemned the Pelagians, confirmed Augustine's positions, in particular by declaring that

> *if someone says . . . that there exists in the Kingdom of Heaven, or elsewhere, an intermediate place where children without baptism live happily . . . , may he be anathema. In fact the Lord has said: "Whosoever is not reborn with water and the Holy Spirit shall not enter the Kingdom of Heaven"; also, what Catholic would hesitate to call a joint heir of the demon someone who has not deserved to be a joint heir of Christ? Whosoever will not be on the right will inevitably be on the left.*[27]

Behind this damnation of unbaptized children, one rediscovers the dramatic vision of a first crime, so monstrous that it must have logically brought offended divine justice to throw into Hell all sinning humanity, as embodied in Adam. Redemption, however, saves the elect from this tragic destiny.

This conception of Original Sin had such a profound impact that all future theological reflection on this problem in the Christian West was geared toward it, whether to lighten it (as with Aquinas, Erasmus, or Molina), or to darken it a bit more, as especially with Luther. Here, however, in the context of a historiography of mentalities, what matters most is that Augustinian pessimism gained both its strongest coloring and widest audience during the period highlighted by this study, the years 1400 to 1700. This development had its own counterreaction: Molinism, which not surprisingly became the favored target of the "anti-Pelagians" and refueled their melancholy. It is no exaggeration to assert that the debate over Original Sin and its diverse by-products—problems of grace, of free will or servitude, of predestination—came to be one of the prime obsessions of Western civilization, a concern of all people, from the theologians to the most modest peasants. The latter, after all, were caught up in the whirlwind of the Wars of Religion. Meanwhile, colonial missionaries hastened to baptize the New World Indians, so that at their death they would not join their ancestors in Hell.

Today it is doubtless somewhat difficult to measure the place that Original Sin held in people's minds and at all social levels. This place was certainly much greater than that now occupied by the notion of "class struggle," which was not really experienced by a large part of the European populace. It is also certain that in early modern Europe, Original Sin and its consequences were at front-and-center stage —a stage, moreover, that was deeply troubled. The Protestant Reformation was above all the proclamation of justification by faith, this being absolutely vital for fallen mankind. In his treatise *On Christian Servitude*, written in response to Erasmus's symmetrical *On Free Will*, Luther pays his adversary a strange compliment.[28] In the same manner, Bellarmine writes: "All the controversy between Catholics and Lutherans is about knowing whether the corruption of nature and especially of concupiscence in itself, insofar as it resides in just and baptized people, is strictly speaking original sin."[29]

Luther and Bellarmine were right. To be sure, the conflict between Catholics and Protestants grew in scale and across a variety of issues—ecclesiology, tradition, the sacraments, actual presence, fasting, and so on. The fundamental point, however, was what Dr. Martin Luther had identified as the major problem from the very beginning. Thus the *Augsburg Confession* (1530) expresses his highly Augustinian conception of Original Sin, immediately after he had proclaimed his faith in the Trinity.[30] The Council of Trent, convened in 1545, answered him in June of the following year, and then again in January 1547, by insisting on the role of human effort in the work of salvation. It was only afterward that Luther concerned himself with the sacraments: This is a revealing priority.[31]

One might think that the splitting of Latin Christianity into two mutually hostile camps would have clarified and fixed the theological positions on the gravity and consequences of Original Sin. Not at all. The constantly renewed interest in this problem and the truly inexhaustible inquisitions about it proved so strong that ever finer conflicts arose within each sect. The Catholics became divided between Jansenists and Molinists, and the Protestants between Arminians and Gomarists. In each case, the question was not only one of assessing the impact of Original Sin on human nature, but also of probing the mysteries of predestination. The Gomarists claimed that the decree of election or of condemnation predates the decision that determined Adam's Fall. The entire weight of Voltaire's global critique of Christianity would inevitably fall on Original Sin as it was then being taught.[32]

Images and words constantly presented this doctrine to the faithful. The iconography of this subject is ancient.[33] For example, the temptation and first sin already appear in a painting from the catacombs of Saint Januarius at Naples (second century), and then in the frescoes from Doura-Europos. Through the course of the Middle Ages, these episodes recur on the walls of Saint-Savin, on capitals from Cluny and Saint-Benoit-sur-Loire, in the mosaics of Monreale, on the façades of Notre-Dame-la-Grande at Poitiers and of Strasbourg cathedral, and in many other sanctuaries. However, the apex of the depiction of Adam and Eve's crime is reached during the fifteenth to seventeenth centuries, under the double influence of the multiplication of artworks and of the conjoined preoccupations of the taught and teaching church. One could spend a great amount of time listing the major artists of this period who portrayed the tragic disobedience, from Ghiberti to Rubens, from Hugo van der Goes to Titian, including Rizzo, Dürer, Lucas Cranach the Elder, Raphael, and Michelangelo. Lucas van Leyden devoted eleven engravings to Original Sin.[34] Above all, however, alongside the major works, how many stained-glass windows, and how many altarpieces featured the first offense in their full-color catechisms!

Certain landmarks indicate the growing diffusion of the doctrine. The *Jeu d'Adam* (twelfth century) was one of the first dramatic works performed outside the church. Nonetheless, until the fifteenth century, the texts concerning Adam and Eve were mainly the work of theologians writing at length for a restricted group of clerics. Things then changed with the success of the mystery plays and the arrival of printing. An ever-growing audience would henceforth contemplate the first sin and demand a variety of sensational works. The first day of Arnoul Greban's *Passion* (1452) opens with the history of creation until the murder of Abel and the death of Adam; then one sees Adam in limbo pleading for a Savior, while in Hell the demons sing and celebrate the demise of the human race. Finally, in Heaven, Redemption is decided upon. In another mystery, the *Vieil Testament*, printed about 1500, Eve dies before the spectators, and bids them these sad "adieus":

Alas! I see, my children, that I leave
You all bound to my maternal vice.
Adam sinned, I was his mediatrix,
For tempting him to eat of the apple;
To the false snake was I aid and accomplice.
Thus war was born betwixt God and man . . .[35]

The anonymous poem *Le mors de la pomme* (ca. 1470) has renewed interest here, since it reveals a certain link between the macabre and the dramatization of the doctrine of Original Sin (because Adam and Eve ate the apple, all power was given to death). This work inspired an iconography that must have led to Holbein's *Dance of Death*.[36]

During the late sixteenth and seventeenth centuries, interest in Original Sin reached its highest point among the cultivated elite. Literary texts from a variety of countries share an interest in evoking the glory and then the misery of the first man[37]: Du Bartas's *Seconde semaine* (1584), which was often imitated in England; Hugo Grotius's *Adamus Exul* (1601); the prolific playwright Giambattista Andreini's *Adamo* (1613); the prose poem *Adamo* (1640) by the founder of the most important Venetian academy, Francesco Loredan; *La Scena tragica d'Adamo e Eva* (1644), a prose drama by Troilo Lancetta; Serafino della Salandra's tragedy, *Adamo caduto* (1647); Samuel Pordage's long world history, *Mundorum explicatio* (1661); the great Dutch playwright Jost Van den Vondel's *Adam banni* (1664); and finally, a tributary of many of the preceding works, John Milton's *Paradise Lost* (complete edition, 1674). In France, Pascal's entire religious thinking is based on Original Sin, "which is a folly before men . . . But this folly is wiser than all man's wisdom . . . Because without it, how could one say what a man is? His entire estate depends on this imperceptible point."[38] Before the *Pensées*, the *Provinciales* (1656–57) had essentially comprised a treatise, sometimes ironic and sometimes vehement, on "sufficient" grace, which no longer suffices ever since Adam's breach of trust. In the wake of Augustine, Pascal argues that the ignorance of evil, the result of the first offense, does not excuse evil, and that the laxity of the Jesuits and other casuists puts "pillows beneath the elbows of the inveterate sinners" we all are and have been, from the time of the expulsion from Eden. The *Provinciales*, moreover, met with great success: eleven French editions between 1657 and 1700,[39] an English translation in 1657, and a Latin translation (by Wendrock, alias Nicole) in 1658, which was then reedited four times before 1700.

To discuss grace in a comic vein (at least in the first *Provinciales*) was an innovative step and explains the rapid diffusion of clandestine "brief writings." But this success can also be explained by the great interest the subject had for the public. Antoine Arnauld's austere *Fréquente communion* (1643, p. 490), inspired by the same anthropology as the *Provinciales*, had already made an impact. This first great book by the author called "a theologian of civil war," and "a living syllogism . . . , helmeted, fierce,"[40] went through six editions between 1643 and 1648. Four more followed between 1656 and 1703. Thus an entire civilization was constantly face to face with Original Sin. The child who opened a catechism, or was taught it orally, first encountered these lessons: "Question: What was this disobedience? (of Adam). Answer: He ate a fruit which God had forbidden him. Q: Was Adam's sin a truly great one? A: Yes, because it deserved God's malediction on all people."[41] In their turn, Christmas carols recounted, sometimes with humor, the story of the Fall. Those by Lucas Le Moigne, a priest of Poitou, describe the scene of the first sin with the following lines (from the first ed., 1521):

Adam bit into the apple,
He had no knife at all,
So he ate a little piece.[42]

When he had tasted
The bitter apple
It could not go down
Past his Adam's apple,
So he heaved it back up
Through his gargling mouth.[43]

When he had failed
By trying to please Eve,
He realized his deed,
And cutting a pitiable figure,
He became more milky-ugly
Than a lump of plaster,
As he found himself stark naked.
So he hid his behind
As well as his pecker.[44]

Before Original Sin, thought Bellarmine, man was naturally naked. Afterward, he felt himself undressed.

THE ORIGIN OF EVIL AND THE EARTHLY PARADISE

Pedagogical simplism and the spiciness of Le Moigne's Christmas carols should not disguise the importance of the doctrine they contain.

Is it possible for humanity not to inquire after the origin of evil? Various non-Christian systems of thought—religious myths or philosophies—attenuate, indeed suppress the responsibility of humans for the appearance of evil on earth: for example, an evil principle is opposed to the benevolent god; or one god has disturbed the work of other gods; or evil angels have taught human beings the perverse arts of civilization; or souls have sinned before their earthly existence and they are therefore willfully "fallen" into the punishment of inhabiting a transitory body. The German Idealists would say that evil is only one dialectical moment in the development of good. On the other hand, the Judeo-Christian tradition, without erasing the conniving intent of the tempting serpent, has emphasized man's free sin and the inevitable solidarity of Adam and his descendants. In certain respects, Kant remains faithful to the Christian explanation when he detects a "radical evil" in man, a natural inclination toward perversity.[45] All the same, the philosopher of Königsberg rejects any effort to locate the root of this evil in a past event. If the Bible speaks of a beginning of sin, this is not to be taken historically. Adam is each and every one of us. The diachronic dimension is reestablished by Freud who, while eschewing transcendence, identifies at the origin of guilt feelings a great traumatic event: the murder of the father of the horde.[46] Theodor Reik therefore rightly describes how "Christianity and psychoanalysis, in their attempts at elucidation, take off from the same premise, that is, that a prehistoric event is the cause of the feeling of collective guilt."[47] It is true, however, that Freud later modified his explanatory system with an element differing from hereditary crime: the "death drive," which connects to Kant's "radical evil."

If one attempts to sort out the main characteristics of traditional Christian doctrine regarding hereditary sin, four elements become especially prominent: (1) the assertion that evil has existed in all its forms throughout human history; (2) the immense theological effort to free God from responsibility for the above condition. As Saint Bonaventure writes:

> *If, in the beginning, God had created man beset with so many miseries, He would have neither pity nor justice; . . . if God had either filled us with so many miseries or allowed that we should be without any fault, divine providence would govern us without pity, without justice. Our present state, under the government of a just and good God, can only be the result of a punishment.*[48]

(3) The affirmation that human death is the consequence of the first sin; (4) the proclamation of salvation by a Redeemer. It is this "good news" that marks the difference between Christianity and certain African myths that explain in a very similar way how, at the beginning of the world, God became "distanced" from his children. The following is a Rwandese version of one of these myths:

> *Once upon a time, long long ago, God lived among men and women and spoke with them. But he had forbidden them, under pain of bringing on many misfortunes, to ever try to behold him.*
>
> *A young maiden had the task of placing water and firewood each night at the entrance of the great circular hut where God lived, out of human sight. One night, however, as she was carrying the gourd filled with spring water, the daughter of God succumbed to the desire that burned inside her: She resolved to spy upon her divine Father from a hiding place, in order that she might see him. She crouched behind the fence, hoping to glimpse at least the hand of her father. Then God came to take his gourd; he put out his wrist, richly adorned with shining brass rings. And she saw his sumptuously decorated divine arm. How her heart pounded at the sight of this splendor!*
>
> *But God knew the disobedience of his little daughter. The next night, he ordered the people to go back inside their huts, and he made them listen to his bitter reproaches. To punish them, he would go away, never to return; henceforth they would have to live without him. He disappeared beyond the lake. Ever since, no one has heard him. And with God there also disappeared peace and happiness; fruits, game, and all the foods that had before offered themselves up spontaneously, all these became rare and hard to obtain. Worse still, death and other afflictions entered the world.*[49]

It would be hard not to notice the similarities between this story and that of Genesis; both stress the curiosity of Woman, the necessary solidarity between human beings, punishment marked by God's departure, the loss of earthly paradise, and the arrival of death.

As for the text of Genesis, it did not hide from the keenest minds the mysterious character of sin and of inherited guilt. A twelfth-century theologian, Robert of Melun, giving particular attention to the fate of unbaptized children, declared: "Nobody should ask the question: how comes it that the soul of a child could be guilty before God, because of sin?" elsewhere adding, "One must admit with Hugh [of St-Victor] that the justice of God, if it is unimpeachable, is also incomprehensible."[50] Pascal unhesitatingly writes: "Nothing, to be sure, is more of a shock to us than such a doctrine . . . the tangled knot of our condition acquired its twists and turns in that abyss."[51] Saint Vincent de Paul announces in a lecture to his missionaries: "O Messieurs and my brothers, there must be some grand thing, that our understanding cannot grasp in our crosses and torments."[52]

Bayle was in particular obsessed with the problem of evil, an insoluble question for faith in a unique and good God.[53] For if God "foresaw Adam's sin, and did not take firm steps to sway him from it, He lacked good will toward mankind . . . If He did all He could to prevent the Fall of man, and did not succeed, He is not therefore all-powerful, as we have thought Him to be."[54] Bayle did remain Christian, as Jean-Pierre Jossua notes, citing this last declaration: "I die in Christian philosophy, imbued and persuaded with the blessings and mercy of God."[55] He did not, however, seek to deny the impossibility for reason to understand the existence of evil. Our intellect must humble itself before this mystery, which at once makes "man recognize his benightedness and impotence, and the need for another revelation."[56] In expressing this fideism, Bayle is not that distant, at a fundamental level, from Pascal and Bossuet. Nevertheless, he stresses the incomprehensible nature of evil and misfortune more than these two thinkers, who in the *Pensées* and the *Sermons* respectively make strong claims that the solution has been found.

Pascal shows how faith proposes two truths that are "of equal permanence: one, that man in his native state, or state of grace, is raised above the whole of nature and made like God, participating in his divinity; the other, that in his state of corruption and sin he has fallen from this estate and become like the animals."[57] As for Bossuet, he affirms, almost triumphantly, that "We have explained the enigma. Those remnants of greatness in man are left over from his first condition, . . . but by his depraved desire he has fallen in ruins."[58] Bayle would not have been prepared this confidently to saddle man with all the blame for the evil and misery that afflict the earth. He criticizes various Christian theologians—from Thomists to Socinianists—for trying to solve an enigma that passes human understanding. Explanation by Original Sin is unsatisfactory. "How evil could occur under the sovereign rule of an infinitely good, infinitely holy, infinitely powerful being is not only inexplicable but incomprehensible."[59] One does not clear God by attributing the crime to Adam: "To allow for it to happen, strictly speaking, left open a way which He could have removed."[60] Prudent twentieth-century individuals would readily agree with Bayle and Jean Nabert, who writes that it is necessary "to leave off asking why there is evil, and how evil is possible in a universe whose very existence has been assigned to a principle that guarantees its order and goodness."[61]

In contrast, for the vast majority of Europeans of the past, even those of the eighteenth century, there was really very little mystery to evil. They thought with Bossuet that "the enigma" had been clarified. An "insoluble question of human philosophy"[62] became clear, through a religion that indicated "the precise moment when [man] was deprived of justice."[63] For an entire civilization, Original Sin had become a sort of *deus ex machina*, constantly used as the final and definitive reason for all that goes bad in the universe. The reliance on this explanation is a historical fact of the first order and is justly observed by the contemporary theologian Gustave Martelet:

> . . . *Beginning with Augustine, and with the double support of the biblical story of the Fall and Paul's affirmations in Romans, the West adopted a type of rationale that satisfied both hearts and minds for a long time: if man suffers and dies, people reasoned, it is because man has sinned. In the beginning, it was not like this, it*

> *did not have to be like this. By his crime, however, Adam threw nature out of balance for man: he removed it from an economy, now gone forever, where suffering and death would not have existed.*[64]

With tremendous poetic force, Milton expressed the commonly held opinion of his time on this subject. He shows how, after the first offense, "with delight he [Death] snuff'd the smell / Of mortal change on Earth."[65] "The Sun / Had first his precept so to move, so shine, / As might affect the Earth with cold and heat / Scarce tolerable, and from the South to bring / Solstitial summer's heat."[66] The angels teach "the fixt [stars] / Their influence malignant," and "To the Winds they set / Their corners, when with bluster to confound / Sea, Air, and Shore."[67] Despairing, Adam wants to die. He laments, crying out: "But from mee what can proceed, / But all corrupt, both Mind and Will deprav'd . . . first and last / On mee, mee only, as the source and spring / Of all corruption, all the blame lights due."[68]

The historiography of mentalities must clearly strive to understand how a culture could accept the primarily Augustinian explanation that Milton, with and following so many others, invokes in *Paradise Lost.* First of all, almost no fifteenth- to seventeenth-century European knew that the biblical *adam* is far more often a collective noun that a proper name. People did not pay heed to Richard Simon's advice that "since . . . the greater part of words are equivocal, especially in the Hebrew tongue, one must know all their different meanings; then one will choose that meaning that best accords with the subject referred to by the word."[69] In Hebrew, the same root usually conveys both the general ("man") and the particular (Adam). Hence the ambiguities. The French *Bible de Jerusalem* translates Genesis 4:1 as "*L'homme* connut Eve, sa femme," and Genesis 4:25 as "*Adam* connut sa femme."* In fact, in the biblical texts *adam* is used 539 times in the collective sense of "man" and more precisely of "earthy," and less than 10 times as a proper name. "As for Jesus, he never speaks either of Adam or of Adam's sin."[70]

The attribution of a crime of cosmic dimensions to the first man was facilitated by the unanimously accepted notion that human history occupied only a short chronology (of six or seven thousand years), which was nearing its end. There was not the faintest idea of the vast length of the earth's geological, paleontological, and archaeological timelines. Nor was there the slightest inkling of the now obvious fact that "more than 99 percent of the history of the human species belongs to prehistory."[71]

Still, it needs to be pointed out that Saint Irenaeus had an intuition, if not of a long maturation of the universe—he also believed that the world was only a few millennia old—at least of the constructive value of time. Adam and Eve were like children: "God could have . . . given perfection to man from the very beginning, but man was incapable of receiving it, for he was no more than a little child."[72] This conception does not invest the first crime with the enormity it inevitably takes on when Adam and Eve are represented as full-grown, radiant adults, veritable gods on earth. Irenaeus writes that "Adam was inadvertently, not maliciously, disobedient."[73] For the Bishop of Lyon, "the history of humanity is not that of a painful ascent after a vertical fall; but rather a providential progress toward a future filled with promise."[74] Hence the current return toward Irenaean doctrine by all those who seek to reconcile evolutionary science with the Christian revelation.[75] However, Irenaeus's message was swept away on the one hand by Augustinian pessimism and on the other by the mental revolution that progressively hindered the diffusion of

*Translator's note: the King James version of the Bible gives the proper name "Adam" in both these cases.

any attempt to give up the short chronology of human history. This tendency appears in the general hostility that the theory of the pre-Adamites encountered in the seventeenth century. Its author, Isaac de la Peyrère (1594–1676), was a Huguenot. Convinced that biblical accounts were in contradiction with what was known of the history of the ancient Oriental and American peoples, la Peyrère proposed a bold hypothesis: Adam was not the first man, but only the ancestor of the chosen people; the Bible does not reveal the history of all mankind but only that of the Jews; before Adam lived the pre-Adamites. The work, the *Preadamitae* . . . (1655), pleased libertines but provoked the combined anger of both Catholics and Protestants. Its author was arrested in Belgium by order of the Archbishop of Malines and the book condemned by the Parliament of Paris. La Peyrère retracted his position and abjured Protestantism.[76]

The mental universe of preindustrial Europe included another key element, which was bound up with ideas concerning Adam and Original Sin: the general belief in the earthly paradise. Certainly Pascal counseled prudence in discussing it: "We cannot conceive either the glorious state of Adam or the nature of his sin, or the way in which it has been transmitted to us. They are things that occurred in conditions which were entirely different from our own, and which transcend our present powers of comprehension."[77] However, Pascal's contemporary Milton took delight in evoking Adam's "glorious state." Having gone blind, the poet compensated for his infirmity by giving such a highly colored and intoxicating description of the earthly paradise (in book 4) that it is generally regarded as the highpoint of his epic poem. Milton presents Satan arriving at the border of Eden. Beholding the lovely landscape, the animals living in fraternal harmony, and man and woman beautiful, pure, and naked, he almost repents his crime. "Blossoms and Fruits at once of golden hue, / Appear'd, with gay enamell'd colors mixt"; "now gentle gales, / Fanning their odoriferous wings dispense / Native perfumes," and so bring "Vernal delight and joy"; "from that Sapphire Fount the crisped Brooks, / Rolling on Orient Pearl and sands of Gold, / With mazy error under pendent shades / Ran Nectar." The serpent sees Adam and Eve, "the loveliest pair / That ever since in love's embraces met." In Eden, "Sporting the Lion ramp'd, and in his paw / Dandl'd the kid; Bears, Tigers, Ounces, Pards, / Gamboll'd before them."[78] Across the centuries, Milton's idyllic description refines Augustine's prolix discourse on the Garden of Eden.[79]

The belief in the "almost fairylike"[80] condition of newborn humanity continued to have a long and lively career in Western civilization. Although the first Christian writers had consistently rejected the golden age and the fortunate isles of Greco-Roman poetry, these pagan myths entered into commentaries on Genesis from the second century and the work of Saint Justin Martyr.[81] They were read as pagan versions of the Christian Eden. In the East, the *Hexameron* of Saint Basil (d. 379) and its anonymous source homilies greatly contributed to spreading the popular image of an earthly paradise situated atop a high mountain, in an always temperate climate, filled with fruits and flowers, streams of milk and honey, and perpetually docile animals. In such an environment, Adam and Eve lived like angels, lovely, immortal, and without unruly passions. Saint John Damascene (d. 749) completed this idyllic picture in specifying that paradise was located to the East, on a mountain higher than all others, and that it was bathed in marvelous light. All these details are still further improved upon in the *De Paradiso commentarius* [Latin trans., Antwerp, 1569 (Plantin)], originally composed in Syriac by the ninth-century Bishop of Mosul, Moses Bar Kepha. His work is a synthesis of all the previous writings on Eden.

In Latin Christianity, the great promulgators of the paradisiac image of Eden are Ambrose and Augustine. They integrate the golden age into the Bible story and conceive of a nature satisfying all the needs of an original couple, angelic and immortal, living without cares, and constantly face to face with God. Fifth- to seventh-century Western poets and encyclopedists would follow the lead of the two church fathers in describing the earthly paradise: Among the first were Prudentius, Saint Hilaire of Arles, and Avitus; among the second group, Isidore of Seville and the Venerable Bede. Isidore locates the now-forbidden "Garden of Delights" in Asia, and describes how it is surrounded by flames that cut like swords and leap as high as heaven. For Bede, the four rivers of paradise mentioned in Genesis pass beneath the earth and resurface as the Tigris, Euphrates, Ganges, and Nile. The belief then became widespread that the earthly paradise was now inaccessible, but that it still existed. Joinville's account of the Seventh Crusade has no doubt as to the source of the Nile:

> *It is now time to speak of the river that runs through Egypt, flowing from the earthly paradise . . . At the place where the Nile enters into Egypt, the river workers throw their open nets into the river, at nightfall; and when the morning comes, they find in them the precious commodities of that country—ginger, rhubarb, aloe wood, and cinnamon. They say that these spices come from the earthly paradise, falling in the wind from the trees of that place, like the dry wood the wind blows down in the forest.*[82]

Given his immense authority (from the sixteenth century on), Aquinas greatly contributed to affirming the "historical" and "realistic" image of paradise on earth. He also believed that it still existed, somewhere far away. He writes:

> *For whatever Scripture tells us about paradise is set down as matter of history; and wherever Scripture makes use of this method, we must hold to the historical truth of the narrative as a foundation of whatever spiritual explanation we may offer. And so paradise, as Isidore says [*Etym. *xiv. 3], "is a place situated in the east, its name being the Greek for garden." It was fitting that it should be in the east; for it is to be believed that it was situated in the most excellent part of the earth. Now the east is the right hand of the heavens, as the Philosopher explains [*De Coel. *ii. 2]; and the right hand is nobler than the left: Hence it was fitting that God should place the earthly paradise in the east.*[83]

He goes on to explain: "Augustine says [*Gen. ad lit.* viii. 7]: 'It is probable that man has no idea where paradise was, and that the rivers, whose sources are said to be known, flowed for some distance underground, and then sprang up elsewhere. For who is not aware that such is the case with other streams?' "[84]

Aquinas then asks whether paradise is located below the equator. His prudent conclusion is that "whatever the truth of the matter, we must hold that paradise was situated in a most temperate situation, whether on the equator or elsewhere."[85]

A number of medieval maps place the earthly paradise atop a mountain in Azerbaijan. Certain "geographers" confirm that it takes forty days to cross it. For others, paradise is only a few leagues in diameter. John Mandeville (d. 1372) wrote a fanciful narrative of a voyage he supposedly made through Asia, in which he devotes an entire chapter to the earthly paradise. He does admit that not even he has been there. For this place of happiness is inaccessible. Nonetheless, it is certainly the home of the true sources of the Ganges, Nile, Tigris, and Euphrates.[86] Mandeville's book was extraordinarily popular during the late Middle Ages. Three hundred manuscripts in six different languages have come down to us. Finally, the

Legend of Prester John's kingdom, widespread in Europe since the twelfth century, fortified the attempts to locate the earthly paradise: It was mapped as lying beyond the realm, already wonderful in itself, of this rich and pious Christian king.

Nonetheless, the ancient myths of the golden age and the Garden of the Hesperides gained renewed popularity. The *Roman de la Rose* revives them in both its first and second parts. Thus they became newly grafted onto the Christian earthly paradise, as especially in Canto 28 of Dante's *Purgatorio*:

> *These ancients who in poetry presented*
> *the golden age, who sang its happy state,*
> *perhaps, in their Parnassus, dreamt this place.*
> *Here, mankind's root was innocent; and here*
> *were every fruit and never-ending spring;*
> *these streams—the nectar of which poets sing.*[87]

Another significant association occurred in Henry VI's triumphal entry into London after his coronation: An earthly paradise was portrayed, with the four rivers of Genesis gushing forth. When they reemerged from an underground passage, their water had been changed to wine. Elias and Enoch appeared beside Bacchus and wished the new sovereign a long and prosperous reign.[88] In its ongoing development, the new interest in the golden age accounts for Armida's pleasure garden in Tasso's *Gerusalemme Liberata*, as well as the Arcadia of Guarini's *Il Pastor Fido* (1580–83).

Moreover, in their fabulous imaginings of the Orient, their quest for precious goods in far-off oceans, and their attempts to discover El Dorado, did not the Europeans more or less consciously desire to regain the earthly paradise, or at least some clues and fragments of it?[89] The great voyages of discovery were inseparable from the dream of a hidden Eden and an imaginary geography of distant countries that Original Sin had not polluted, where the golden age still continued. For a certain time—primarily the sixteenth century—reality strengthened these illusions.

As was mentioned in chapter 4,[90] the belief in the golden age was never so alive as in the Renaissance. It finds expression in various Utopias, in sometimes more mythical than faithful descriptions of a sweet and luxuriant America inhabited by happy people, in accounts of the Fountain of Youth and the Land of Cockaigne, and in the inexhaustible iconography of the first couple, luminous in a blessed land. The names of Bosch, Dürer, Michelangelo, and Brueghel are cited here as only the most influential figures in a thriving artistic production, which was sustained by this tenacious dream: a humanity free of sin in a garden of the Hesperides.

Between the end of the fifteenth and the middle of the seventeenth centuries, almost every major author wrote in some way or another about the earthly paradise. Catholics, Anglicans, Lutherans, and Calvinists all treated this subject, as did—according to their sectarian allegiance—commentators on the Bible, theologians, historians, geographers, travelers, moralists, politicians, mystics, and poets. Revealingly, Sir Walter Raleigh's *History of the World* (1616) opens with a description of man during the days just after his creation and with a study on the whereabouts of paradise. Although left unfinished, this work was highly popular in England and influenced Milton. The numerous commentaries on Genesis written as part of the Reformation could only have reinforced the collective belief that Adam and Eve enjoyed an idyllic life before their sin. It has been noted that between 1527 and 1633, thirty-five Latin and six English commentaries on Genesis appeared in Great Britain, most of them in large folio format.[91] In addition, the Renaissance promoted the works of Ambrose and Augustine, revived those of Saint Basil and Saint John Damascene, and translated (in 1569) Moses Bar Kepha's commentary on paradise from Syriac into Latin. The last-named book was reedited three times during the seventeenth century.[92] The period even produced works whose exclusive subject was the earthly paradise: the *Synopsis paradisi* (1593) by John Hopkinson, an Orientalist who located Eden in Armenia; the Anglican priest John Salked's *Treatise of Paradise* (1617), which describes the situation and nature of Eden and even the beauty of the tempting serpent; and the Sicilian Jesuit Agostino Inveges's *Historia sacra paradisi terrestris* (1651), which is the most comprehensive work in the genre and discusses the site of the wonderful garden, its characteristics, the occupations of Adam and Eve, and so on.[93]

In direct opposition to the hard European reality of the time, the increased belief in the idyllic aspects of paradise inevitably reinforced the symmetrical belief in the story of the Fall. Consequently, a close tie existed between the religious pessimism of early modern times and the new success of the Christianized golden age. The one fortified the other. Generally speaking (even beyond the period of the Renaissance), the more the first sin was made ugly, the more the prelapsarian state was embellished, and vice versa. As evidence—and as a special case—of this conviction, there is the account written by the visionary Antoinette Bourignon (1616–1680), who at the age of nineteen saw an apparition of Saint Augustine.[94] She imagines Adam as having a bisexual body before his transgression; an ambiguous horror of sexuality clearly explains the surprising anatomy given to the original man by a woman who was ill at ease first with Catholicism and then with Protestantism:

> *His body was more pure and transparent than crystal, all light and airy, as thus: one could see in and all over it ducts and streams of light that came and went through all his pores, ducts that carried in them liquids of all kinds and colors, most lively and entirely translucent, not only water and milk, but fire, air, and other things. His movements conveyed wondrous harmonies: all things obeyed him; nothing could resist him, nor injure him. His stature was greater than men of today; his hair short, wavy, and shading toward black; his upper lip covered with a wisp of hair: and, in place of the bestial parts one does not name, he was made as our bodies will be restored in eternal life, and in such a way that I do not know if I should tell of it. In this area, he had the structure of a nose in the same form as that on his face; and it was a source of wonderful scents and fragrances: from this place did men emerge, whose essential matter he possessed within him; for in his belly he had a vessel where little eggs were born, and another vessel full of liquid that made these eggs fertile. And when this man became heated with the love of his God, his desire that there would be other creatures to praise, love, and adore this Great Majesty caused this liquid, through the fire and love of God, to spill over one or several of these eggs, with inconceivable delight, and some time later this now fertile egg would leave the man's body by this means, in the form of an egg, and soon hatched into a perfect man.*[95]

This remarkable description illustrates in a grotesque but revealing way the opinion of the Augustinians, especially Baius and Jansen. If they overexaggerated the painful sequels to Original Sin, it was due to their extraordinarily optimistic conception of the rational creature shaped by God's hands. In Thomistic terms, one could say that they naturalized the supernatural. In 1972 André Chamson entitled one of his articles "We Have Lost Original Sin."[96] It would be more apt to write, "We Have Lost the Earthly Paradise," a dream that was once an article of faith. To the question "Where did God put the man whom he had created?" all the catechisms answered in a single voice "In the earthly paradise, a land of delights."[97] Today, instead of the radiant images of Adam and Eve amid a luscious and loving nature that received so many artists' fond attentions, our modern museums and school textbooks supply learned reconstructions of prehistoric peoples and their environments. We see pictures and models of Neanderthal man, slightly over five feet tall, with a bulky head, a flattened skull, a muzzled face, a projecting nose, large round eye sockets, superciliary arches forming heavy folds of flesh, a robust but chinless lower jaw, a roll-like occiput, and a massive torso resting on short legs. Other images evoke his life in caves: his diet, tools, clothing made from animal skins, and so on. Eden has vanished like a mirage. Adam and Eve have disappeared. Their tracks have been lost since the eighteenth century. Modern Christianity now finds itself constrained to muse upon Original Sin without placing it in a delightful landscape and a decidedly mythical golden age. Sixty years ago Teilhard de Chardin had already written of the difficulties confronting the traditional representation of the earthly paradise:

> *It is a doubly serious difficulty for us to retain the former representation of original sin, and this difficulty can be summed up as follows: "The more we scientifically revive the Past, the less we find any place for Adam or the earthly paradise."*
>
> *Today, the earthly paradise could not be conceived of as a privileged reserve of some acres. One sees now that everything is too physically, chemically, and zoologically held together* [illegible] *for there to be a* permanent *absence of death, of pain, of evil (even for a small fraction of things) to be thought of beyond the* general state *of a World different from our own. The earthly paradise can only be understood as a* different way of being *from that of the Universe (this conforms to the traditional sense of [Christian] dogma, which sees Eden as "another World"). Now, however much we have looked into the past, we see nothing resembling this wondrous state. Not the least trace on the horizon, nor the least scar, indicating the ruins of a golden age of our amputation from a better world. As far as the eye can see, looking back, the World, dominated by physical Evil, impregnated with moral Evil (sin is clearly "in power" at the appearance of the slightest indication . . .), reveals itself to us* in a state of original sin.
>
> *In truth, the impossibility of putting Adam back into the earthly paradise (imagined literally) within our scientific perspectives is such that I wonder if any single man, today, is capable of* simultaneously *keeping his eyes on the geological World evoked by Science, and the World commonly described by Sacred History. One can maintain the two portrayals only in moving from one to the other. Their association jars, it rings false. In uniting them on the same plane we are surely the victims of an error in our perspective.*[98]

THE AUTHORITY OF SAINT AUGUSTINE AGAINST ATTENUATED GUILT

Our Christian forebears believed in the earthly paradise. On the other hand, they had a lesser notion of extenuating circumstances, or rather of attenuated guilt. The casuists, whom Pascal excessively mocked, certainly contributed to elaborating and diffusing the idea. At the same time, the Augustinian conception of Original Sin impeded its formulation and growth. Augustine had in fact clearly asserted that we are all guilty in Adam because "we all were this unique man."[99] Hence ensues our misery: We are born guilty, and not only that, but the concupiscence released by the first sin lures us into committing more and more sins. Therefore the highly

Augustinian author of the *Imitation*, addressing himself to God, laments in these terms:

> *Even if I shed tears as abundant as the waters of the sea, I would still be unworthy of thy consolation. I deserve nothing but the rod of punishment because I have oft and grievously offended Thee, and my sins are numberless. Thus after a strict examination I know myself unworthy of the least consolation . . .*
>
> *I cannot remember having done any good; on the contrary, I was always inclined toward vice and slow to correct myself . . . What have I earned for my sins except hell and eternal fire?*[100]

Luther felt no less guilty. Also speaking to God, he tells Him: "You see how true it is that I am a sinner before You, because of the sins of my nature, my initial being, my conception, all the more for my sinful words, deeds, thoughts, and remaining life."[101]

People could certainly hope for divine pardon, but they still had no excuse. Drawing support from Saint Bernard, Bucer states: "If one were to consider all our justice (our good works) in the light of truth, it would look like underwear dirtied by a sick woman."[102] Although Abelard had emphasized the morality of intention, the Augustinian universe passed over this point in silence. Thus Pascal could write, "Our sins . . . are dreadful."[103] He cites Jesus' words, "If you knew your sins, you would lose heart."[104] A Jansenist position, one would say? Not exclusively. A sermon composed by de Paul or his secretary includes this frightful warning: "A Christian cannot rely on any excuse when he violates the commandments of his Lord."[105]

Even ignorance was an inexcusable sin. Seventeenth-century preachers never tired of lecturing on "criminal ignorance," though their relentlessness was often an urgent call for the faithful to follow the sermons of a mission. One of the Lazarists' standard homilies features this harsh dialogue between a damned soul and Christ in Judgment:

> *I was ignorant, and knew no malice; why then, my Lord, do you not forgive me as Saint Paul would? —But your ignorance is criminal; you did not lack enlightenment, you had enough of it, but you cared not to be instructed by so many preachers:* Noluit intelligere *(Psalms 35:4). Yours is a feigned ignorance, and therefore punishable.*[106]

This passage thus castigates guilty negligence. The condemnation of ignorance, however, went much farther. Augustine categorically teaches that ignorance, like concupiscence the daughter of Original Sin, is itself just as much a sin. Hence Pascal chides the Jesuit in his *Quatrième Provinciale*: "Father, no longer hold out against the prince of theologians, who thus decides this point, in Book I of his *Retractiones*, chap. 15,[107] 'Those who sin by their ignorance only do so because they want to, though they sin without wanting to sin.' "[108] Although Pascal and Augustine do allow for a hierarchy within the guiltiness of ignorance, this does not lessen its damnability, for as the Bishop of Hippo writes: "Ignorance does not excuse any man to the point of preventing his burning in the eternal fire, even if the cause for his ignorance is his not having fully understood that which he must believe; but it may be that he would be delivered to gentler flames."[109] Saint Vincent de Paul sometimes questioned the validity of such rigor. In a 1656 lecture to his missionaries "On the duty of catechizing the poor," he recalls "what Saint Augustine, Saint Thomas, and Saint Athanasius say, that they who do not explicitly know the mysteries of the Trinity and Incarnation will not be saved."[110] He adds, however, that

"I know well that other doctors are not so rigorous and maintain the contrary, because, they say, it is cruel to see that a poor man, for example, who has conducted himself well, might be damned for not having found himself someone to teach him these mysteries." Since there is "doubt," De Paul then concludes, "it will always be our great charity, if we teach these poor people, no matter who they are."[111] This lesson thus leaves a door open to the salvation of the ignorant. Two years later, however, de Paul closes it in another lecture to his missionaries:

> *You know the ignorance of poor people, which is almost beyond belief, and you also know that there is no salvation for people who are ignorant of the necessary Christian truths; such is the opinion of Saint Augustine, Saint Thomas, and others, who judge that anyone who knows not the Father, the Son, and the Holy Ghost, nor the Incarnation, nor the other mysteries, can save himself.*[112]

On this question, then, de Paul shared the frequently expressed views of the majority of contemporary churchmen. Saint Alexander Sauli declared in the synodal statutes of Aléria (1571) that "Nobody can be saved without believing the necessary articles of salvation: the *Pater Noster*, the *Ave Maria*, the *Credo*, the Ten Commandments, the seven sacraments, etc."[113] A widely used booklet, *La Science sacrée du catéchisme* (first ed., ca. 1675), by the Archdeacon of Evreux, Henri-Marie Boudon, also contains this explicit warning: ". . . Without clear faith in the fundamental truths of our Holy Church, it is impossible to please God and be saved, howsoever one may observe external ceremonies."[114]

This fostering of guilt about religious ignorance by numerous Augustinians thus clarifies a larger and encompassing fact: the relatively weak assimilation and diffusion, from the modern standpoint, of the notion of extenuating circumstances. Other confirmations of this phenomenon can be found in bygone enactments of justice, such as the execution of animals who had caused a person's death. In any case, there was a great lack of the distinction between sin and guilt that Jean Nabert[115] and Paul Ricoeur have clarified in recent times. The latter in fact writes: ". . . The sinful condition cannot be reduced to a notion of individual guilt, such as it had been developed by the Graeco-Roman legal spirit in order to give a foundation of justice to the administration of the tribunal penal system."[116] Ricoeur also considers the egalitarian experience of sin to be opposed to the diversified experience of guilt: People are entirely and radically sinful (a Protestant assertion), but guilty only to a greater or lesser extent.

It is indeed possible to ask whether the distinction between sin and guilt would have come into better and earlier use had not Augustine's authority been so undisputed and pervasive in Latin Christianity. In any event, the elite culture of early modern Europe can be understood only by allotting Augustine the full influence he held at that time. Nevertheless, this return to the interior of a mental universe elicits two remarks. First, the Augustinian message was never reduced to Augustinism, if this is taken to mean anti-Pelagian stances toward grace and justification. The work of the Bishop of Hippo was immense. It covered all the great dogmatic, moral, ascetic, and mystical problems of Christianity, and moved our civilization toward the awareness and thorough study of the human individual's inner workings. Until Montaigne's *Essays*, the *Confessions* were the most vivid personal testamonial in Western literature. To every Christian, *The City of God* remains the most powerful effort yet made to unravel the supernatural sense of history. The great Augustinian themes—cognition, love and wisdom, memory and presence—have fed European thought for many centuries. Throughout the years, every Christian renaissance has drawn from Saint Augustine as from an ever-flowing spring.

The second remark is that even if the height of Augustine's influence, in both extent and profundity, was reached between the fifteenth and eighteenth centuries, his prestige never ceased to dominate Latin theological speculation. While in the Christian East, the patristic tradition met with no break of continuity throughout the Byzantine epoch, the destruction of the Roman Empire left Augustine without any successors, and hence magnified the stature of the greatest of the Latin doctors,[117] the man who had given Western theology its autonomy. An early sixth-century fresco at Saint John Lateran in Rome, which is the most ancient portrayal of the saint, bears this significant text: "The divers Fathers explained divers things, but only he told all things in Latin, explaining the mysteries with the thunder of his great voice."[118]

Augustine thus always stood at the peak of Latin Christianity. Isidore of Seville places him above all other church fathers, Greek or Latin. Saint Caesarius of Arles (d. 543) and Gregory the Great (d. 604) perhaps too modestly presented themselves as the custodians and adaptors of the Bishop of Hippo. Bede (d. 735) ranks Augustine just after the apostles: *Maximus post apostolos ecclesiarum instructor.*[119] This appraisal is resumed by Gottschalk, the son of a Saxon count converted by Charlemagne, who also saw the great doctor as *post apostolos omnium ecclesiarum magister.*[120] The fecund work of Augustine inspired the Carolingians' religious advisors as well as the platonizing humanism of the twelfth-century School of Chartres. Throughout the Middle Ages, numerous groups of Canon Regulars entrusted their lives to Saint Augustine's teaching and to the rule attributed to him. In his turn, Saint Dominic gave his order the *regula sancti Augustini.* Until Aquinas, it is therefore possible to speak of an "almost obsessive presence of Augustinism"[121] in Christian theology. He is the privileged master, the authority *par excellence*, the uncontested philosopher.

The Thomist synthesis, by completing the Christianization of Aristotelianism, partially altered this situation, but only partially. For it integrated entire sections of Augustinism. It was not by chance that during the great debates over grace (sixteenth to seventeenth centuries), the Thomists came across as Antimolinists. In fact, the Augustinian current continued on its course, preparing for the imminent flood. The Franciscan order sought out Augustine for the inspiration of its theology. In 1256 Pope Alexander IV founded the Order of the Hermits of Saint Augustine, who soon became, after the Carmelites, the fourth of the mendicant orders, to whom Luther belonged. During the fourteenth and fifteenth centuries, in a notoriously increasing climate of unrest, the severe and pessimistic tendency of Augustinism then becomes explicit in the works of Gregory of Rimini (d. 1358), who damns unbaptized children, the English archbishop Bradwardine (d. 1349), the "profound doctor" and author of an anti-Pelagian treatise,[122] and John Wycliffe (d. 1384), who mingles anticlericalism and negation of free will.

This rise of theological pessimism coincided with the anti-Aristotelian reaction, the new interest in Platonism, and the desire to return to sources (including Christian sources, hence the writings of the church fathers), which characterized the Renaissance. This coincidence therefore involved a complex and apparently paradoxical situation: On the one hand, Augustine, especially through his *De Doctrina christiana*, was a guide and herald of humanism, from Petrarch to Erasmus[123]; yet on the other, now more than ever on the culture's "front page," he served as the standard-bearer and rallying point for all those who darkened the picture of the human condition. Thus no matter where one turns during the Renaissance and then Classicism, one finds Saint Augustine. He stimulated the Neoplatonic vogue, he promoted stripping ancient temples to adorn the Church of Christ (hence to integrate Greco-Roman culture into the Christian universe as far as possible), and, at the same time, he supported and encouraged the devaluation of sinning mankind.

The role that the author of *The City of God* played in the sixteenth century again demonstrates that one should not necessarily associate humanism with optimism. The great poet Luis de Léon, whose superb verses inspired by the *contemptus mundi* were cited above, belonged to the Augustinian order.

A vast number of converging signs confirms the enormous place held by Saint Augustine from the Renaissance on. He is the most frequently quoted church father in Erasmus's *Enchridion*.[124] The leading French expert on Thomas More writes, "If I were to name the single Latin author whose style and general manner appear the most in More's work, I would propose Saint Augustine."[125] This was the era of the publication and diffusion of the first great collected editions of the works of the Latin doctor[126]: that of Amerbach (Basel, 1506); of Erasmus (Basel, Frobenius, 1527–29, with reissues from 1531 to 1584 in Basel, Paris, Lyon, and Venice); the truly remarkable edition put together by sixty-four theologians from Louvain (Antwerp, Plantin, 1564–77, with six republications from 1586 to 1616 in Paris, Geneva, and Cologne). The Oratorian Viguier published a two-volume *supplementum* (Paris, 1654–55) to all the prior editions, notably including the sermons and the *Contra Julianum*. Finally, from 1679 to 1700 the Benedictines of Saint-Maur published their great eighteen-volume edition.

The name of Erasmus on this list may come as a surprise. It is true that deep down, the humanist of Rotterdam preferred Jerome and Origen to Augustine. Still, he admired the Bishop of Hippo and contributed to enlarging still further the latter's stature in sixteenth-century lettered opinion. He cries out in the preface to his edition of Augustine's works, "Does the Christian world possess anything more radiant and august than this writer?" Likewise, Saint Francis de Sales, who did not share the pessimism of anti-Pelagian authors, was nonetheless an avid reader of Augustine. The Archbishop of Annecy's treatises make seventy citations from twenty-four of the church father's works.[127] Thus the most confirmed Augustinians seem to have acted in accordance with the general opinion of the time, in taking renewed pains to praise their great inspiration and freely drawing from his work. Certainly Luther had the occasional feeling that he was going beyond the master. At one time he wrote significantly on both himself and his era, "Augustine did not quite reach the thought and sense of Saint Paul, although he came far nearer to it than the scholastics. But I keep Augustine with us, because of the high esteem he enjoys among all people, even if he did not adequately explain justification by faith."[128] All the same, Luther frequently voices his admiration for the adversary of the Pelagians. He praises Peter Lombard, "for in all things he drew on the Luminaries of the Church, and above all on the most illustrious and never enough praised star" (Saint Augustine).[129] In *The Duty of a Christian*, he lashes out at Erasmus by saying: "Augustine, whom you neglect to mention, is entirely with me."[130] In *Table-Talk*, he declares: "Except for Augustine, the blindness of the Fathers is great. After the Holy Scripture, one must read him, for his judgment is acute."[131] And again, "Augustine is the best interpreter of Scripture, above all others."[132]

Calvin similarly writes, "Augustine is indisputably superior to all dogmas."[133] In Calvin's work there are 4,100 citations to Augustine: 1,700 with and 2,400 without reference.[134] Naturally, the Jansenists showered praises on their mentor: "the foremost doctor," writes Jansen, "the first among the Fathers, the first of the ecclesiastical writers after the canonical doctors, Father of Fathers, doctor of doctors, discerning, solid, irrefutable, angelic, seraphic, most excellent and ineffably admirable."[135] The entire "opening book" of volume 2 of the Augustinus is an extended eulogy of the saint: Chapter 14 claims that his doctrine of grace is "evangelical, apostolic, and of irrefutable authority. He wrote for the entire Church, while other writers remained silent"[136]; meanwhile, chapter 23 asserts that Augustine is "unique." He is "equal to anyone," indeed he is "superior to all others"[137]; chapter 30 concludes that it it would be better to discard any theology that does not derive from him.[138] During the seventeenth century, however, not only strictly obedient Jansenists but a host of others considered Augustine to be "the eagle among doctors," the "doctor of doctors"—these are Bossuet's descriptions—and an infallible "oracle." Bossuet elsewhere wrote (against Richard Simon): ". . . The body of Augustine's doctrine, especially in his final works (that is, against the Pelagians), which the succeeding centuries have most fully approved, is beyond all reach . . . It would be accusing the entire Catholic Church of self-contradiction, to persist any longer in finding misguided innovations in his books."[139] In a chapter "*Esprits forts*," Bossuet's friend La Bruyère equals Augustine to Plato and Cicero:

> *What a pleasure it is to love religion, and see it believed, upheld, and explained by such firm minds and true genius! Especially when one recognizes that for breadth of knowledge, for profundity and penetration, for principles of pure philosophy, for their application and development, for just and fitting conclusions, for a dignity of discourse, for beauty of morality and feeling, there is nobody, for example, whom one could compare to Saint Augustine except Plato and Cicero.*[140]

Augustine's prestige during the Age of Reason was such that people strove, sometimes candidly and sometimes with a touch of jealousy, to find a correspondence between his doctrine and "the opinions of Monsieur Descartes." Regarding the notion of *cogito*, Pascal observes that Augustine "said the same thing twelve hundred years earlier."[141] Arnauld writes that in connection with Descartes, one finds Augustine to be "a man of a great mind and singular doctrine, not only in the field of theology but also of human philosophy."[142] It is revealing that the Oratorian Malebranche attempted to put contemporary Christian philosophy on firm footing by invoking both Augustine and Descartes. The church father and the philosopher of *cogito* did share the notion that God's existence is inherent in us as idea. Adolf Harnack thus correctly writes, "Where in the history of the west is there a man whose influence could be compared to that [of Saint Augustine]"[143]; and also: "The long series of Catholic reformers is Augustinian . . . until the Jansenists of the seventeenth and eighteenth centuries, and even after them."[144] This analysis pertains even more to the Protestant Reformers.

Nevertheless, and in possible opposition to the most commonly accepted historiography, it can be affirmed that Augustine's domination of Western culture did not culminate during the sixteenth century alone, nor during the seventeenth century alone. In this context the Renaissance and the ensuing period form a single ensemble, attested to by iconography. For three centuries, illuminated manuscripts of *The City of God*, paintings, and sculptures continually exalted the great doctor. Many famous artists depicted him, including Fra Angelico, Luca and Andrea della Robbia, Benozzo Gozzoli, Botticelli, Correggio, El Greco, Van Dyck, Rubens, Ribera, Murillo, and others. During the Baroque era, countless churches placed near the curves of their pediments the figure of the Bishop of Hippo, wearing his miter, beard, and wind-blown draperies. In the eighteenth century, the church of San Agostino de Mexico portrayed the *Triunfo del Santo sobre herejia* in a vast plateresque setting. Jeanne and Pierre Courcelle have studied and clarified a truly great subject of cultural history in their four rich volumes covering Augustinian iconography from 1300 to 1800. From the beginning, their project was to show "how this [iconography] was formed in the fourteenth century," became "flourishing in the fifteenth," held "an important place in the seventeenth, and adorned numerous Baroque ceilings in the eighteenth century."[145]

Augustine's primacy, even outside narrow theological circles, is thus a historical fact that attained its fullest dimensions in the first stages of European modernity. Only a synthetic study of past mentalities would allow his influence to regain full significance, through an analysis of its components (here the conjunction of humanism with pessimism) and through its exposition within a vast context. A network of reciprocal actions did in fact exist between the Renaissance exaltation of the Bishop of Hippo and the eschatological mood that washed over a great part of the contemporary religious elite. The author of *The City of God*, writing when the Roman Empire had been shook by invasions, greatly contributed to spreading the theme of the world's old age. This theme, moreover, regained currency between the fifteenth and seventeenth centuries, and many Protestants—both orthodox and extremist—interpreted their own struggle in terms of the Augustinian opposition of the two cities: that of God and that of the Antichrist,[146] any compromise with the latter being unacceptable.

In a still wider sense, an elite but increasingly diffuse culture exalted the great doctor—the common denominator of Catholicism and Protestantism—at the same time that it dreamed of the lost paradise, confused sin with guilt, almost enthusiastically darkened its image of humanity, and ceaselessly agonized over a free will just as ceaselessly besieged by Fortune, the stars, and Satan. With regard to the early sixteenth century, Marcel Bataillon has perceptively evoked this "vast international communion," the "Europe of justification by faith."[147] Neither should one think that learned Renaissance Italy was absent from this shared concern. Many Italian humanists inclined toward this doctrine to free themselves from anguish regarding sin.[148] Such a catechesis made Augustine sacrosanct and accounts for the drama of Jansenism within the Catholic Church. Indeed, how to simultaneously extol the Bishop of Hippo and condemn the extremist doctrines taken from his work? Cardinal Albizzi was rather exceptional when he stated in 1656 that rather than continuing to authorize the Jansenists by specifying that the bull *Cum occasione* did not condemn Saint Augustine's doctrine, "it would be better, if one could, to suppress Augustine."[149] For want of this clarification, the Jansenists could play the strong hand of taking shelter behind the doctor *par excellence* to justify their positions and to embarrass Rome; it would take until 1690 before a pope—Alexander VII—would condemn the following formula, which many theologians had either implicitly or explicitly adopted over the centuries: "If anyone finds that a doctrine is clearly based on Saint Augustine, he can defend and teach it without regard to any bull of the Sovereign Pontiff."[150]

ORIGINAL SIN AND OPINIONS ON CHILDHOOD[151]

Saint Augustine made a profound mark on generations of Westerners. Conversely, European culture saw itself in him and to some extent pushed him to the foreground. More generally, any theology is at once cause and effect: It shapes mentalities, but expresses them just as much. Hence an Augustinian conception of Original Sin led to misogyny. Contrariwise, however, an age-old misogyny, reactivated by the clerical milieu, found a perfectly timed justification in the story of the first crime. Among a thousand other examples, this passage from the *Malleus Maleficarum* is worth citing here:

> *And I have found a woman more bitter than death . . . For though the devil tempted Eve to sin, yet Eve seduced Adam. And as the sin of Eve would not have*

> *brought death to our soul and body unless the sin had afterward passed on to Adam, to which he was tempted by Eve, not by the devil, therefore she is more bitter than death. More bitter than death, again, because that is natural and destroys only the body; but the sin that arose from woman destroys the soul by depriving it of grace, and delivers the body up to the punishment of sin.*[152]

Similarly, clarifying the place of Original Sin in past mentalities also contributes to a better understanding of collective attitudes toward small children. Any doctrine, whether rigorist or not, striving to define the nature and consequences of the first sin, entailed a stance not only on the fate of babies deceased before baptism but also on the status of childhood in general. Again, society and religious doctrine were a mutual influence.

Late medieval and early modern Europe had inherited two opposed ancient views on the subject of childhood[153]: one, a certain tenderness, seen in numerous funerary inscriptions dating from the first four centuries A.D.; and two, feelings of severity, such as the exposure of abandoned children by decision of the *pater familias*. The Latin *puer* signified both "child" and "slave." Five hundred years ago, a lack of understanding about childhood appears to have been widespread. This lack involved two complementary aspects: People were not that sensitive to the freshness and innocence of the newborn, not much moved by their fragility; concomitantly, they tended to see school-age children (as they would be called today) as collections of defects, vicious and wicked beings who must be strictly trained to prevent their becoming bad adults. Here it must be added that generally harsh living conditions and a high mortality rate, among not only infants but older children and adolescents, almost inevitably hardened people's hearts: Dying young was much more common than it is today. Fifteenth- through seventeenth-century proverbs reveal this gamut of negative attitudes toward little men and women: "Happy they who have children, and not unhappy they who do not."[154] "A little child, a little mourning."[155] "See a child, see a naught."[156] "'Tis a great insult to call a man a child."[157] "Pigeons, chicken, and children soil and shit on your house."[158] " 'Tis good work to punish one's child."[159] "A father pitying and mild has a sad and lazy child."[160] "Tell no secrets to women, fools, or children."[161]

Although terse, this sampling still provides converging insights: Children were not recognized as such. Once trained, they became adults. These anonymous proverbs are in agreement with the remarks by Montaigne, La Fontaine, and La Bruyère that historians of childhood have so often and so aptly cited: "I have lost two or three nursing children, not without regret, but also without vexation"[162] (Montaigne). "This time of life is pitiless"[163] (La Fontaine). "Children are arrogant, disdainful, full of tantrums, envious, curious, selfish, lazy, flighty, timid, bad-tempered, liars, and deceivers; . . . they hate to suffer pain, but love to inflict it; they are already grown-ups"[164] (La Bruyère). As for Descartes, he has no doubt that the "mind, as soon as it enters the child's body, begins to think."[165] However, he qualifies this positive claim with statements to the contrary: "A child's faculties of thought are drowsy."[166] "If the body always hinders the soul's ability to think, it does so the most during one's first years." "The first and principal cause of our errors [as adults] . . . are the prejudices of our childhood."[167] The early stage of life is thus made of weakness and error.

The list of citations of this type could be easily extended, all of them tinged with misunderstandings of children. The following pages will make reference to others. At the same time, several corrections of this reading come to the fore. First, the following: The culture whose written and artistic records survive from this period is that of the elite, and this is at least partially true even of the proverbs. It therefore might be risky to emphasize, as complementary evidence for the general population's opinion, the allusions of Luther and Felix Platter to the harshness of their respective mothers. From the Middle Ages to the eighteenth century, stories of miracles permit a dive into a collective outlook adjacent to that of the elite and show how children occupy an important place. Parents seek and obtain the recovery and life of their ailing child. Miracles obtained by the intercession of Saint Helena at the abbey of Hautvillers (in Champagne) benefited young and adolescent children in 25 percent of the eleventh-century cases and 39 percent of seventeenth-century ones.[168] A third of those cured by miracles of Sainte-Anne d'Auray from 1634 to 1646 were children: 186 out of 541 cases. Of these 186, 147 were less than eleven years old and 103 less than five.[169] Thus any judgment regarding the whole of society would be mistaken. All the same, one can argue with nearly full assurance that at the highest level of early modern culture, there existed a strong bias against children.

Here, however, a second correction applies: The voice of high culture is primarily masculine. First and foremost, women could have better expressed a tenderness for their newborn and a gentleness for their growing children. Unfortunately, on this as on other subjects, they were rarely allowed to publicize their feelings. At the level of written culture, the women of the time often remain silent. They did not ordinarily compile the "*livres de raison*." But in the exceptional cases when they do recount their private lives, the happiness of being a mother or grandmother is readily apparent. Madame de Sevigné tried in vain to excuse herself, for she passionately loved her little daughter Pauline:

> *I love her with all my heart. I have trimmed her hair: she now has a harum-scarum coiffure, made just for her. Her neck, complexion, and little body are wonderful. She does a hundred little things, she talks, she caresses, she hits, makes the sign of the cross, asks for pardon, curtsies, kisses my hand, shrugs her shoulders, dances, flatters, takes me by the chin: finally, she is absolutely lovely. I am amused by her for hours on end. I pray she does not die . . . I can hardly understand how one could ever not love her daughter.*[170]

If French (and European) Renaissance and classic literature had included as many female as male writers, would not the current historiography of children be profoundly different?[171]

Finally, Philippe Ariès and Georges Snyders have thoroughly researched and established the point that Ancien Régime art and literature featured two conflicting but coexisting opinions on children: one that scorned and found them guilty, and another that valorized them and found them innocent. Over the course of decades, moreover, this second view attained greater prominence. From the fourteenth century on, Marian iconography and portrayals of the Virgin Mother and Nativity helped to spread a new sensibility toward children. A certain secularization of the baby Jesus made him a suckling child like any other, especially in works by Leonardo and Raphael: He snuggles close to his mother (*The Virgin of the Grand Duke*), plays with the little John the Baptist (*The Virgin of the Rocks*, the *Belle Jardinière*), and diverts himself with a flower or bird (*The Virgin of the Goldfinch*). Correggio, in the *Marriage of Saint Catherine* and the *Madonna with Saint Jerome*, takes pleasure in conveying the amused tenderness of the great figures who take part in the games of the holy infant. The latter is increasingly shown as naked: first as a baby in the paintings of Van Eyck and Fra Angelico, and soon thereafter as an already-walking toddler in works by Leonardo, Raphael, and Michelangelo. Religious art thus supported the expression of emotion toward children and more generally an improved regard for childhood and adolescence. The two *cantorie* carved by Luca della Robbia and Donatello for the cathedral of Florence together evoke the joy and value of the first years of life. These are contemporary with the growing number of choir schools, the appearance of choirboys, and the popular vogue for Christmas carols and presents.

This new sensibility tended to overflow the religious context. Triptychs whose compartments reserved for donors sometimes showed children with their parents give way, after the mid-sixteenth century, to family portraits no longer destined for churches or chapels. Even more numerous are the illuminations, and then engravings, calendars, and tapestries that highlight women and children in depicting the trades, labors of the months, and the ages of life. Another noteworthy innovation, again of the sixteenth century, is the appearance of funerary effigies of deceased children. Donors of altarpieces show themselves with their living and dead children, the latter holding little crosses; or a prematurely deceased child appears on a tomb, either beside his or her mother or at the feet of the parents' recumbent effigies. The beginning of the seventeenth century sees the first Western tomb exclusively dedicated to an early-dying child: an alabaster crib commissioned by James I for one of his daughters, who was born and died in 1606 (Westminster Abbey).[172] Some years earlier the greatest sixteenth-century Polish poet, Kochanowski, had dedicated his finest work, the *Nineteen Threnodies*, to his little Ursula, deceased at age four.

The Renaissance thus played a major role in rehabilitating the image of children; an improved knowledge of ancient art made this an easier task, for a close tie existed between this rehabilitation and the portrayal of infant nudity. The extraordinary fortune of the Italian *putto* owes a great deal to the contemporary taste for Roman sculpture. At the same time, this reuse of ancient cupids gave a new means of expression to a feeling that was struggling for release. The naked, plump, and smiling baby, from Donatello's *Eros Attis*, to the bas-reliefs of the Fontaine des Innocents, to the *Triumph of Bacchus and Ariadne* at the Farnese Palace, progressively conquered Western iconography. Soon it became inconceivable to paint paradise without filling it with chubby and big-bottomed little angels, and Louis XIV wanted "childhood everywhere"—meaning nude childhood—in the gardens of Versailles.

In early modern Europe, however, interest in children did not always mean admiration for their freshness or recognition of their otherness—far from it. The schoolmasters—Gerson, Melanchthon, the Jesuits, the heads of the "little schools" of Port-Royal, the Oratorians, and so on—did certainly place a high value on education and instruction, but they had only one objective: to shape grown men. Applying adult criteria, they did not reflect on the child's own gradual development. They could only see the child's future, and they conceived of their task as a strictly "medicinal" correction of the weakness and bad tendencies inherent in youth. Aristotle had written "Children who are deemed happy are thus called only for the promise they show."[173] Hence the need for enclosure, for isolation from the outside world, for silence, perpetual surveillance, discipline, and the rejection of any idleness, all of which are extolled by the educational treatises of the time. Fortin de la Hoguette's widely read *Testament ou conseils fidèles d'un bon père a ses enfants* (1648) teaches that "the neglect of the infancy of the body and soul begins all the defects" of body and mind.[174] The rule of the parish seminary of Saint-Nicolas-du-Chardonnet (certainly dating from the end of the seventeenth century) includes this statement: "Since man's spirit, itself being enclosed in flesh and darkness, is incapable of all dealings, all trades, all professions, if not enlightened, taught, and shaped with care, it is therefore needful to provide him with appropriate means for being trained for something."[175]

Here again Original Sin intervenes, especially in its Augustinian version, as a justification for such pedagogy and as a curb on any rehabilitation of the particular worth of childhood and innocence. The young child is bad. For Saint Augustine, this is self-evident: "Though little, he is already a great sinner." "I was conceived in sin . . . my mother carried me in sin . . . Oh, Lord . . . when and where was I ever innocent?"[176] The author of the *Confessions* also asks,

> *What then was my sin? was it that I hung upon the breast and cried? for should I now so do for food suitable to my age, justly should I be laughed at and reproved. What I then did was worthy reproof; but since I could not understand reproof, custom and reason forbade me to be reproved. For those habits, when grown, we root out and cast away.*[177]

If one lets a child grow up following his instincts, he will become a monster:

> *For who is not aware of the vast ignorance of the truth (which is abundantly seen in infancy) and the wealth of futile desires (which begins to be obvious in boyhood) which accompanies a man on his entrance into this world, so that if a man were left to live as he chose and act as he please, he would fall into all, or most, of those crimes and sins which I have mentioned—and others which I was not able to mention.*[178]

Georges Snyders astutely observes that for the Bishop of Hippo, childhood "is the most overwhelming proof of a condemnation of all men, because it cruelly shows how corrupted nature tends, indeed rushes on, toward evil."[179] Not surprisingly, Bossuet commends Augustine and confirms that "from our mothers' wombs, where the flesh submerges and dominates reason, our soul is crushed by this weight, and made its slave."[180] To the question "O Lord! why do you send down your anger on this newborn child? Whom has he wronged? What is his crime?" Bossuet answers: "He is a child of Adam, that is his crime. Hence he was made to be born in ignorance and weakness, his heart a source of all sorts of wicked desires."[181]

Sin, ignorance, and weakness: These three negative conditions are inseparable in early modern religious discourse. Thus weakness is found to be guilty as well as a failure. Even Saint Francis de Sales writes, "we come into this world in the greatest imaginable misery, because not only in our birth, but during our childhood, we are like beasts deprived of reason, speech, and judgment."[182] Bérulle is even more emphatic: "Childhood [is], after death, the most vile and abject state of human nature."[183] Childhood "is dependence, indigence, impotence: dependence to the degree of indigence, and indigence to the degree of impotence."[184] Condren, Bérulle's successor as the leader of the Oratoire, likewise opines: "[Childhood] is a state in which the spirit is wrapped in weakness, and where the senses of corrupt nature reign over reason. In this state, the grace even of our divine adoption and the spirit of Jesus are captives of impotence, and reduced to annihilation."[185] A dangerous weakness: "The devil attacks children, and they do not put up a fight," one reads in the *Entretien entre M. de Saint-Cyran et M. Le Maître.*[186] The Jansenist-leaning Claude de Sainte-Marthe goes still further, writing that

> *The dark night where we are born is such that we neither know the evil we must flee, nor the good we must embrace, and the sequel to our dark night is strangely mortal. For as it has no interest in enlightening us, the rest of our years makes our blindness all the more criminal; we always veer from the straight and narrow path whenever we ignore it, and we plummet into all the bottomless pits that surround us, just when we do not see them. The natural corruption of our hearts*

cleaves to every vice that can bring us perdiction, and make us despise every virtue . . .[187]

These pessimistic statements speak for themselves, clearly revealing not only a suspicion but a true and full condemnation of childhood.

Nevertheless, such viewpoints did sometimes give way to more positive and tolerant evaluations. Snyders is again right to make this observation, which is worth at least partially following. First, because there is weakness, the schoolmasters realize the need for patience: Claude Lancelot tells how M. de Saint-Cyran "wished that [the children] might be much tolerated in their failings and weakness, so that God might have mercy on our own."[188] The pedagogue Pierre Coustel gives the same advice: "Tolerate their inattention to their studies and all their other faults with great patience . . . Treat them most gently. Use encouragement more than rigor and threats."[189] Corrupted human nature being especially obvious in children, the profession of teaching is one of the hardest, though still less dreadful than that of the craftsman who becomes bored with his work or the merchant exposed to shipwrecks. Having made these comparisons, Father Jouvency (d. 1719), a Jesuit, ends a work addressed to teachers with this encouragement: Resigned that Original Sin will appear again and again:

I concede that it is painful and tiring to spend the finest hours of one's youth and to sometimes endanger one's health in the dust of classrooms; to sometimes grind this mill forever; to put up with the pranks and fooleries of children; still, everyone also understands that we were born to work, and that we are so condemned not so much for our sins as for the sin of our first parents. Work is that which is most useful for us; we must even seek it out. This work is hard, it is true, but as hard as it is, think of the eternal reward that awaits you: should not that consume a good number of worries?[190]

Jacqueline Pascal likewise considers it difficult to teach young girls, "since there is much to endure from these little creatures."[191] Since, however, the work involves reforming personalities ruined by sin, there can be no higher calling. Lancelot elsewhere notes that Saint-Cyran "so esteemed the charity of those who worked to give children Christian upbringing that he said that the Church afforded no worthier occupation for a Christian."[192]

Still, childhood not only gave adults the opportunity to surpass themselves and show charity. Lancelot again remarks that one "must be kind" to the feebleness of children, just as "Jesus Christ showed himself in our likeness, so that we might show ourselves like him."[193] Here Lancelot recalls Bérulle, who magnified the mystery of the infant Jesus. God deliberately appointed two highly cruel miseries, two humiliations: being a child and being crucified. He lowered himself to "flesh, swaddling clothes, and the manger. The "life of glory" hid itself "in childhood, impotence, and suffering." The All-Powerful God made Himself a nonentity. Hence the nonentity became exemplary. God chose "dullness" in order to abase human reason and to teach us docility.[194] "Let us be as little children before our Savior: children do not have their own will . . . , since they depend on the decisions of their parents; so too must we depend on the good will of God, through a complete submission of our will and reason."[195] Following Bérulle, the Sulpician Blanlo advises "surrender to God disfigured by childhood."[196] As for the Jesuit Saint-Jure, he states in *La Vie de M. de Renty*, "The spirit of childhood is a state in which one must be dead to all things."[197]

Berullian theology contributed to spreading the cult of the infant Jesus and thus, by a completely unparadoxical about-face, to partially favoring the valorization of childhood, after it had emphasized the insignificance of one's first years.

Moreover, this theology took part in an inquiry on the Gospel passage of Jesus' letting the children come to him, and inviting adults to become like them (Matt. 19:13–4; Mark 10:13–16; Luke 18:15–17). This episode was not easily integrated into a pessimistic conception of childhood. Reflecting on childlike "innocence," Augustine writes: "The weakness then of infant limbs, not its will, is its innocence. Myself have seen and known even a baby envious; it could not speak, yet it turned pale and looked bitterly on its foster-brother."[198]

Nor is Calvin tender toward children: "Their nature carries the seed of sin; therefore they can only be displeasing and abominable to God."[199] Nonetheless, he recalls the Gospel example and uses it to conclude—against the Anabaptists—that young children must be baptized.[200] It is significant that the scene of Jesus' asking the apostles to let the little (unbaptized) children come to him had rarely been represented during the Middle Ages.[201] In contrast, sixteenth-century prints brought it iconographic circulation and popularity, which reached a height in the nineteenth century. In addition, the seventeenth century saw the development of the theme of the guardian angel protecting each child, as well as the increase of portrayals of the young Jesus by himself, where before he had always been shown with Mary. The cult of the child Jesus was on the rise. In the church schools, the lives of model, indeed martyr, children were read to the students, and first communion grew more common and became, like Christmas, a festival of childhood.[202] Thus the early stage of life progressively gained new value, through a general tide that reached even as far as the most Augustinian groups. His Jansenist biographers record that Saint-Cyran "always showed children a kindness that bordered on reverence, to honor the innocence and Holy Spirit living inside them."[203] For her part, Jacqueline Pascal had included this prayer in the rule for the boarding-school girls at Port-Royal: "Lord, let it be that we are always children, in simplicity and innocence . . ."[204] Coming from a Jansenist, this last word is highly surprising.

Given the later evolution of Western sensibility, the preceding survey of textual and iconographic material remains significant. It has shown that within élite culture, and even at the heart of a discourse that found babies guilty, there were elements of a positive evaluation of children. At the same time, it would be hazardous to overrate the importance of more or less isolated facts. The period before 1760 is little more than a prehistory of children, involving the emergence of a new image that at once highlighted both their otherness and innocence. The enormously influential educational system was universally founded on a failure to recognize the originality and richness peculiar to childhood. The beginnings of a truly collective awareness of the freshness and singularity of the child seem rather to date from the mid-eighteenth century. This latter moment is precisely when the traditional—I stress this adjective—conception of Original Sin begins to slacken. There then emerged, despite a good deal of apathy, an outlook that not only found children innocent but was itself an integral part of a larger phenomenon.

SANCTUARIES OF RESUSCITATION: "A VAIN TENDERNESS"?

In the Catholic countries, the traditional and predominantly Augustinian conception of Original Sin goes far to explain the phenomenon of sanctuaries "of resuscitation," which have intrigued recent historians,[205] in particular Jacques Gélis, to whose definitive studies I am especially indebted.

To these sanctuaries, most frequently dedicated to the Virgin, but also to other saints, people would bring children who had died before baptism. The small, often bare dead body would be placed, according to the circumstances, on the altar, on its steps, on the stairway of the sanctuary choir, or even on a stone located beneath or to one side of the "miraculous image." Candles were lit, prayers were said, and masses celebrated. At a certain moment, those in attendance—the parents, friends, midwife, priest, or other religious—believed they saw signs of life appearing: "warmth" near the left breast, "distinct and visible redness" in the face, an opened eye, beads of blood in the nose or ears, a spurt of urine, a moved arm or leg, the tongue emerging from the lips, and so on. Any one of these signs sufficed for a miracle to be cried out and for the baby to be baptized as soon as possible. In the great majority of cases, the infant would quickly return to death. He or she would be saved, however, and people could sing out a *Te Deum* for the act of grace, or even ring the bells to tell the neighborhood of the happy tidings. The parents showed their gratitude with ex-votos, gifts of money to the sanctuary, or donations of masses. These gestures expressed relief: Mothers and fathers no longer felt a burden of guilt. They had succeeded in baptizing their child, who directly ascended to Heaven. How happy the fate of infants delivered from Original Sin, who never had any chance to lose their regained innocence! For them, the certainty of paradise was preferable to the risks of an earthly existence full of danger and misery. Had not Nicole taught "that baptized children who died before the age of reasoning comprised three quarters of the elect"?[206]

Despite the views of some theologians, for many centuries there was little concern with the fate of unbaptized children, judging by the often lengthy delays between birth and the administration of the sacrament.[207] The practice of group baptisms, often by immersion, is an index of this "negligence." But by the early fourteenth century, individual baptism by sprinkling of holy water had won the day. Not only the clergy, but soon the parents, became aware of the danger incurred by an unbaptized baby. Concurrently, the sanctuaries of resuscitation started to appear.

Jacques Gélis notes that "the frequenting of sanctuaries of resuscitation had a long history; the first recorded case (in France) dates from 1387, in Avignon, and these practices sometimes persisted into the early twentieth century."[208] So far, 220 sanctuaries have been identified in France, mainly in the north and east of the country. There were also thirty or more of them beyond French borders: in Belgium, Switzerland, and Germany, in Austria, and in the Italian Alps. Benedict XIV, who in the mid-eighteenth century categorically condemned the baptism of stillborn children, observed that "these sanctuaries exist above all in Germany," and he makes particular mention of "the most famous of them, at Ursperg in Swabia, in the diocese of Augsburg, belonging to the canon regulars of Prémontré."[209] The chance of archival preservation had passed on eighteen cases of these baptisms between 1450 and 1480 in Vienne, France, on the tomb of a pious layperson buried in the cloister of Saint-Maurice,[210] 489 at Faverney (in the Doubs region) between 1569 and 1593,[211] making for an annual average of twenty, and 135 at Avioth (in the Meuse region) from 1624 to 1673.[212] In the last example, however, the series is continuous only from 1657 to 1673, when there were thus seven or eight such baptisms per year. In these last two sanctuaries, these expositions of children were certainly more numerous, since, as everywhere, there were failures that have left no written trace.

Most often, the dead infant was brought to the shrine immediately after death.

People had to recognize, however, the distance between the place of death and the sanctuary, "as a general rule a two to four days' ride by horse or cart."[213] Still, there are cases of children "resuscitated" by baptism eight, even fifteen days after their birth. They were thus buried, then disinterred, for example upon the return of a father absent from the birth. Decomposition must have already begun. This process also occurred when the miracle was late in arriving, and the dead child was left in the sanctuary, awaiting resuscitation. At the end of the seventeenth century, the Protestant Gabriel d'Emiliane passed through Dijon, where

> *we went at ten in the morning to this church, that held the miraculous image of the Virgin, commonly known as the little Notre-Dame de Saint-Bénigne, and we saw two stillborn children who for two days had been all black and ashen, and almost entirely rotten. The parents, who were of the best families in Dijon, had for these two days commissioned the celebration of more than two hundred masses in this church, at one écu each, to obtain from God, by the intercession of this statue, and by the prayers of these clergymen, just so much life as would be needed for these poor children to receive holy baptism.*[214]

D'Emiliane malevolently claims that the priests, through their avarice, had purposefully delayed the miracle. The smell, however, became intolerable. A monk who was assisting the mass then placed himself where he could bump against the altar that held the two children . . . who moved. Whereupon they were baptized.

The Protestant narrator's irony, echoed by the early twentieth-century positivist Pierre Saintyves, need not be followed today. Rather, as Michel Bernos[215] and Jacques Gélis suggest, it is more worthwhile to rediscover all the ethnographic and religious dimensions of practices that may now seem disconcerting and that—it will soon be reiterated—the official church condemned. The current state of research has not yet fully explained the geographical distribution of sanctuaries of resuscitation: Why, in France, are they numerous to the east and north as well as in the Bourbonnais, Burgundy, and the Auvergne, but in contrast only sparsely scattered in the Parisian area, in Normandy and Brittany, and almost nonexistent in Languedoc?[216] One can only note a certain coincidence between the map of their establishments and that of the close network of monasteries on the Lorraine–Provence axis. This proximity again applies to the Germanic rim of the Alps. Early on, monks showed a special care for the washing and burial of their dead, for praying for the latter, and for the cemetery, blessed ground that was for them an anticipation of the celestial city. Cluny had a veritable predilection for the cult of the dead.[217]

It is therefore not unreasonable to posit a link between the diffusion of monasteries and the presence of sanctuaries where the gates of blissful eternity were opened to children who would be otherwise excluded. Moreover, the Benedictines could only favor a type of miracle that recalled Saint Benedict's resurrection of a deceased child. Other Christian elements may also have influenced the location of these sanctuaries; such was the motivation for bringing stillborn children to the church of Notre-Dame de Liesse, near Laon.[218] For one of the famous miracles performed by this church's image of the Virgin had been the resurrection of the son of a woman sentenced to death on the false accusation of infanticide. This miracle tale was dramatized in the fourteenth century as the *Miracle de l'enfant ressucité*, and performed by the Paris confrérie of goldsmiths.[219] In addition, certain miraculous sites attracted the bringing of stillborn children for their more general healing and liberating powers: places that had rescued pregnant women, captives, prisoners, epileptics, and so on.

Nonetheless, even if Christian piety and theology usually motivated requests for supernatural intervention, other subconscious demands can be perceived that date back a long way and that played a part in the explicit demand for baptism. Rural sanctuaries are most often found in isolated places, somewhat surprising for Christian sanctity: at the edge of the parish boundary, on an atmospheric height, at the base of a sheer cliff, or in a hollow valley. In most cases there was a well, a spring, a fountain, a stream, or a small lake within or near the sanctuary. In these rugged or forest surroundings, the gushing water established contact between the chthonic and human worlds. During the "resuscitation," water was the agent of salvation, as it had been in ancient rituals of purification at birth. Gélis notes that until the nineteenth century, the body of the child was placed near the spring; occasionally he or she was ritually dunked in a tub or basin full of spring water: This occurred at Vénasque (diocese of Carpentras), at Benoite-Vaux, at Meyronnes Saint-Ours, and at Froloy (diocese of Autun).[220] Furthermore, certain hollowed-out rocks or ruined megaliths played a role in the exposition of children. Finally, Gallo-Roman ex-votos or statues of mother goddesses have been found beneath these sanctuaries, or in the springs whose water was used for baptisms (for example at Roche d'Hys, diocese of Autun). All these details are convergent throwbacks to pre-Christian fertility cults.

Historical study should also address how parents experienced the death of their unbaptized children. Having failed in both their birth and death, and thus doubly frustrated from accomplishing their rites of passage, were not deceased children destined to become wandering beings, like those lost at sea? Would they not seek revenge on their parents, who had denied them access to the gates of blissful eternity? Burchard of Worms, in the early eleventh century, records and condemns the practice that involved driving a stake into dead unbaptized babies, to keep them from becoming troublesome goblins.[221] This custom partakes of the then-widespread belief in ghosts.[222] As late as the nineteenth century, Dorset peasants hastened to baptize their children, fearing that if they were to die without having received a name, they would wander aimlessly through the forests and desert places and never find any rest.[223]

The rule that unbaptized corpses had to be buried outside of sacred ground could have only increased the psychological discomfort of parents. The church refused to inter "in a holy and religious" place those "abortions" whose Original Sin had not been pardoned. "Only the faithful are to be buried with the faithful."[224] It is true that later diocesan rituals preferred to bury unbaptized children in "decent and honest ground," out of respect for the souls that had momentarily inhabited them and for their Christian parents. Still, their interment took place without the presence of any priest, and they remained barred from sacred ground, like other people branded with infamy: unbelievers, heretics, apostates, schismatics, excommunicated people, despairing or angered suicides, victims of duels, actors, comedians, conjurers, public sinners, and other notorious nonchurchgoers.[225] According to traditional canon law, the burial of an unbaptized child in Christian ground made the entire cemetery off-limits. It was then necessary to exhume the little corpse and "reconsecrate" the "polluted" graveyard.[226] On the importance of burial in sacred ground, Pierre Saintyves provides a revealing anecdote about Saint Francis de Sales:

> *There lived at Tonon, in the outskirts of Saint-Ber, a woman stubborn with Calvin's heresy, who had recently given birth to her husband's child. As the two differed on how to baptize it, the child then died without receiving baptism; whereat this extremely afflicted mother burst into tears, and filled the entire house with lamentations. However, seeing that there was no remedy, she resolved on seeking*

out Monsieur Pierre Bouverat, a priest, so that there would be a place for her child in the burial ground. On the way, she met the apostolic man [Saint Francis de Sales], who had worked hard to convert her; she threw herself at his feet, and renewing her tears she cried out: "O my father, I will return to being Catholic, if your prayers return my child to life, so he can be baptized." The blessed François then fell on his knees, and prayed God for the faith of this woman; and in the self-same hour the child came back to life. His parents gave thanks to God, and brought him to baptism, after which he lived for two more days.[227]

Here then is a demand for a "resuscitation," motivated primarily by the desire to secure the child's burial in sacred ground. That the latter was prohibited to stillborn children, and that these went unrecorded by Catholic parish registers—in France, until 1736—indicates their exclusion from the secure, sacred space of the church and their abandonment to a doubtful fate. The very word "limbo," coined in the thirteenth century by Albertus Magnus and Aquinas, meant "borders." What borders could these be except those of Hell? It is not surprising that as late as the eighteenth century, at Kintzheim in Alsace, a couple buried their unbaptized child below the roof-gutter of the church. Thus the rainwater, having run down the roof of the sacred building, would eventually baptize their little one.[228] In Orthodox lands, such as Romania, unbaptized children were also refused burial in Christian cemeteries; thus these countries also witnessed the baptism of little cadavers, which were believed to become reanimate.[229]

As these were marginal beings before their sacramental readmittance into Christian space, people readily turned to hermits for the administration of baptism, since they were themselves marginal figures in regard to human communities. Hermits undoubtedly found some material advantage in living near a sanctuary of resuscitation. Above all, however, living near isolated chapels, in touch with a savage and mysterious nature, they seemed to be privileged mediators between the everyday world of the living and the uncertain, disturbing universe from which parents had to wrench their unbaptized children. The general ordinances of the diocese of Toul (1658) "forbid all priests to baptize stillborn children, on pain of suspension, or hermits, on pain of expulsion from their hermitages and ecclesiastical censure."[230]

Keith Thomas has amply demonstrated how the late English Middle Ages, like other Christian societies, conceived of baptism as a magical rite procuring first and foremost some sort of earthly protection.[231] A 1975–76 survey taken by the clergy in a southern Brazilian province yielded similar results.[232] More profoundly, however, Catholic baptism guaranteed the automatic entry to paradise of the child who died before the age of reasoning. Protestant churches therefore had trouble getting their congregations to accept a less formalized practice of baptism and a more flexible theology, which admitted unbaptized children into paradise provided that their parents were Christian. In England, some of the early religious dissenters who had at first rejected the baptism of children later returned to the established church when they became parents. They too worried that their offspring might die without receiving the sign of Christianity.[233] The abbot de Vertot observed that in late seventeenth-century Sweden, "the greater part of women feared (even after the Reformation) that, without the use of salt and other common exorcisms, their children would not be well baptized."[234] During the forty-sixth "visit of consolation" of Charles Drelincourt, a pastor was shocked to see a Protestant woman crying because her child had died unbaptized. The pastor told her:

"Console yourself . . . for if death has taken your little one . . . he has been put into God's breast, and he drinks the milk of his eternal consolations."

> *But the mother answers: "If my child had been baptized, I would not doubt his salvation . . . but [he] died without baptism, and that is the true cause of my sorrow."*[235]

In 1674 the synod of Lower Languedoc had to prohibit pastors from interrupting their sermons to administer urgent baptism to sick children.[236] During the same period, in the Béarn region, Protestant parents preferred Catholic baptism to that given by their ministers. To them, it seemed more reliable.[237]

Despite all the ethnographic aspects of baptism, actual religious experience thus led back to theology. This process was at the heart of an acculturation: That is, it was subject to a doctrine that deployed ancient rituals but greatly transformed their final effect. Baptism certainly appeared to ensure the protection of the living child as well as the repose of the dead baby's body in sacred ground, which meant that the infant would not become a tormented wandering ghost. Above all, however, baptism's proper and fitting rituals opened the gate of paradise. It thus allowed the deceased to escape the discomfort of limbo and the surviving parents to stop torturing themselves about their child's eternal destiny.

Throughout Christian history, optimistic theologians refused to believe in the punishment of unbaptized children, or to follow Augustine's and Fulgentius's conviction that these children "will be punished by the eternal fire; for, although they have no personal sin, they have encountered Original Sin through their essential pollution."[238] The Thomist line of thought asserted that children dying with Original Sin do not deserve the penalty of hellfire. One of Gerson's sermons, and a commentary by Cardinal Gaetano on Aquinas's *Summa*, goes so far as to surmise that God fulfills the prayer of the unhappy parents whose babies die before baptism and that He admits the latter to blessed eternity.[239] In general, however, the teaching of the church remained more disturbing, even independent of the doctrine of the Augustinians who, from Isidore of Seville[240] to the Franciscan Conrius (d. 1629)[241] and Cardinal Noris (d. 1704),[242] by way of Saint Anselm[243] and Gregory of Rimini,[244] continued to consign unbaptized children to the flames of Hell. The Council of Florence (1439), echoing that of Lyon (1274), declared: "Those souls who die in the state of Deadly Sin, or with the sole Original Sin, will go down into Hell, there to be nonetheless punished with differing penalties."[245]

Although less rigid, the Council of Trent still cast "anathema" on those who "deny the necessity of baptizing children recently emerged from their mothers' wombs" under the pretext that the parents are themselves baptized.[246] These and other similar doctrinal statements made since the Council of Carthage (418) depend on a verse from the gospel of John (3:5): "Except a man be born of water and of the Spirit, he cannot enter into the kingdom of God." It is likely that the Council of Florence's dramatic interpretation of this text revived the collective anguish over the death of unbaptized children.[247]

At the same time, certain Thomists declared that in limbo, children may be deprived of the beatific vision (the penalty of the "dam"), but that they do not suffer, since they do not know they are deprived. Dante comes near to Aquinas when, describing "Hell's limbo,"[248] he presents it as a place without suffering, but also without joy:

> *Here, for as much as hearing could discover,*
> *there was no outcry louder than the sighs*
> *that caused the everlasting air to tremble.*
> *The sighs arose from sorrow without torments,*

out of the crowds—the many multitudes—
of infants and of women and of men.[249]

On the one hand, however, limbo was not officialized by the pontifical sovereign until Pius VI, at the end of the eighteenth century.[250] On the other, there was an obvious and troubling semantic relationship between "dam" and "damnation." It was widely taught that the "dam" (= deprivation, injury) was a dreadful suffering. The chapter on Hell in the 1604 edition of the *Doctrinal de sapience* tells its readers, "Consider then that the penalty of the dam is incomparably greater [than the penalty of the senses] and consists in being deprived forever of the vision of God and the pleasant company of the blessed."[251] Similarly, a *Mystère des Rameaux* performed at Embrun in 1529 assures its audience that unbaptized children "do not descend to the great abyss, where the other damned souls lie. But they are deprived of the true God and his divine essence." And if the parents were the cause of this "damnation and privation," on the Day of Judgment their children would be witnesses for the prosecution and appeal to God for "justice" against them.[252] "Damnation," "privation": There is a fearful ambiguity between these terms, here employed as synonyms. Early modern Catholic practice, at least in its rituals, continually emphasized the weighty sin that the unbaptized child would carry. Even in the 1940s, in Brittany and the Ardèche region (but no doubt elsewhere), pious mothers would not hold and kiss their baby unless it had been baptized.[253] This significant refusal, motivated by a traumatizing theology, bears comparison with a prohibition from the *Rituel de Toul* (1760):

> *Priests must at all costs prevent children from being led to baptism with violins or other instruments playing. For one should recall that these are criminals and children of anger who are being presented to God's mercy; that in this state they are captives of the devil; that therefore nothing is less fitting to their condition than these foolish celebrations.*[254]

After a boy's baptism, parents in Québec used to joke, "Now he can swear," since he had become a Christian.

The Catholic Church thus made a case of conscience out of any delay taken by parents in the administration of the first sacrament to their newborn. The *Roman Ritual* spells out that

> *This sacrament is of necessity so great, that nobody can partake of eternal life if he has not been regenerated by the waters of baptism . . . or at least if he has not wished for them with perfect charity.*
>
> *Baptism thus being so indispensable for salvation, priests will take care to frequently remind fathers and mothers not to delay that of their children, with the excuse of waiting for a godfather or godmother or whatever other reason they might give; they will show them how any human motive must yield before the danger of the* eternal perdition *[my emphasis]*[255] *which threatens any unbaptized child; that they should not put off baptism beyond twenty-four hours after the birth; that waiting for eight days was formerly punished by excommunication, and that if this penalty is no longer in effect, it at least indicates that such delay was considered grounds for deadly sin.*[256]

These dramatic recommendations bespeak the ecclesiastical discourse regularly addressed to the faithful. It is noteworthy that this passage makes no reference to limbo. Parents thus had good grounds for dreading the "eternal perdition" of their unbaptized baby, since he or she would remain "a child of anger," following the Pauline formula (Eph. 2:3), which was repeated thousands of times through the centuries, but completely out of context ("we all had our conversation in times past in the lusts of our flesh, fulfilling the desires of the flesh and of the mind; and were by nature the children of wrath, even as others"). These lines do not apply to children. Nevertheless, later times would make them do so.

A French royal ordinance of 1698 repeats the obligation of baptizing children within forty-eight hours of their birth. Moreover, rituals demanded increased guidelines to priests, both on the choice of midwives and how to perform baptism during difficult deliveries. It was normal to require that midwives were "taught to administer baptism," since they sometimes had a child's "eternal salvation in their hands."[257] A salvation, however, that misspoken works could jeopardize forever. The Lazarist Pierre Collet's *Abrégé* (1764) of Ponthas's *Dictionnaire des cas de conscience* (1715) recounts under the heading of "baptism" the case of an ignorant midwife who baptized a child *in nomine matris* instead of *in nomine patris*. This baptism was null and void, "because this variation utterly destroys the Catholic sense of the form of this sacrament."[258] On the other hand, a male bumpkin who used the words "*Ego te baptizo, in nomine patria, et filia, et spirittu sancta*" would be administering a valid baptism, since "*patria* spoken by a man who poorly speaks a language means what *patris* means when spoken by a man who speaks it well."[259]

There was a still more delicate question: At what precise moment, during a difficult delivery, should one confer baptism? In other words, at what precise moment did the baptized mother's spiritual protection no longer work for her child? The *Rituel de Blois* (1730) instructs: "One should not ordinarily baptize a child until a limb has appeared, whose movement gives a sign of life, and then one must perform the baptism on this part. If afterward all of the child emerges, alive, one will conditionally rebaptize."[260] But what would be the correct procedure if the woman were to die before the child appears? Consulted as a significant example, the *Rituel de Blois* gives this rather embarrassed answer:

> *It is not permissible to open a woman before her death in order to save her fruit and give it baptism. If she dies before being delivered, it is necessary to keep her mouth open, lest the child be suffocated, and promptly find a surgeon or some other to open the mother's womb, skillfully take out the baby, and baptize it if it shows the slightest sign of life. But if the baby is dead, before it could be baptized, it must not be buried in sacred ground; but in an unblessed place, appointed for unbaptized children. If the child remains in the mother's womb, one must bury it with her, without any fear that the sacred ground will be polluted, because in this state it is part of the mother.*[261]

Thus the baby was held to be baptized, Christian, and saved if he or she did not come out—or was not taken out—of the mother's womb. If, however, the baby thrust out merely its head or foot, or if the surgeon removed it from the mother's dead body, it was a "child of anger," and paradise was closed to it, for having died before baptism.

The Catholic Church thus diffused—but itself experienced—the fear of death without baptism. This fear was the main reason for Henri II's severe 1556 edict ordering pregnant girls to declare their condition, then their deliveries, to the authorities: Here the king acted in the context of Christianity, as responsible for the life but even more for the spiritual salvation of his subjects.[262] The edict's text proves that the sovereign and his advisors feared that seduced girls, in getting rid of their illegitimate children, would deprive them of baptism. Infanticide was especially grave, since it excluded the victim from paradise. The edict announces that as the child "had been deprived of baptism [and] accustomed public burial," the mother "will be held for the homicide of her child. And as reparation, she will be punished with death and extreme penalty, with such rigor as the particular qualities of the case will demand."[263] This draconian legislation was irregularly applied, depending on the time and place. By the end of the eighteenth century, it had fallen into disuse. What is relevant here, however, is that Henri II arranged for his edict to be published every three months, and obliged priests and vicars to read it in their sermons. In addition, it was renewed by Henri III in 1586, Louis XIV in 1708, and Louis XV in 1731. Many early eighteenth-century parliaments also ordered judges to see to it that priests would read it in their sermons.[264]

This sensational conception of baptism more or less survived within Protestantism, not only at the congregational level, as discussed above, but also, at least for a certain time, at the level of theological discourse and pastorship. Article 9 of the Augsburg Confession condemns the Anabaptists, who bestowed salvation on unbaptized children; Article 2 states that anyone not reborn through the sacrament of water will fall into eternal death.[265] In England, the first *Book of Common Prayer* stresses the need to confer baptism in the first days of life, and the later Elizabethan edition permits it to be administered on days other than Sundays and holidays, in case of "necessity." To be sure, the majority of late sixteenth- and early seventeenth-century Anglican theologians, while holding baptism to be "formally" in dispensable, refused to believe it as "absolutely" necessary for salvation. All the same, in 1569 the vicar of Ashford, Kent, declared that unbaptized children go to everlasting hellfire. French Protestantism would also debate this question for many years.[266]

To return to the sanctuaries of resuscitation, a sample of fragmentary evidence suggests first that parents and witnesses from all social milieus sought out these temporary resurrections, which were only expected to provide a brief grace period and thus allow baptism. In fifteenth-century Valence, two out of every eighteen families who obtained their child's resuscitation next to the tomb of the pious Philippe de Chantemilan were "noble." In the Church of the Annunciation in Aix-en-Provence, at a 1558 "resurrection," six out of the seven witnesses were merchants or artisans owning at least 200 florins' worth of property, the seventh being a fifteen-year-old boy.[268] The ironic Gabriel d'Emiliane, in late seventeenth-century Dijon, notes that the two children brought before the "little Notre-Dame" of Saint-Bénigne belonged to the town's "best families."[269] Jacques Gélis attests to the variety of social origins of the pilgrims at the santuaries of resuscitation: in Benoite-Vaux (diocese of Clermont) in the seventeenth century as at Ambert, at the tomb of Father Gaschon in the nineteenth. Moreover, resuscitations occurred not only at the rural sanctuaries: Valence, Aix-en-Provence, and Dijon have just been mentioned, and earlier, the miracle of Saint Francis de Sales at Thonon. The oratory of Notre-Dame de Loos, where, in the seventeenth century, resuscitations and other miracles took place, was located "at the first milestone after the town of Lille," thus in immediate proximity to a large city.[270] During this same period, however, it would seem that the most numerous and highly reputed of these sanctuaries were found in the countryside, far from the suspicious regard of the established hierarchy.

Another noteworthy conclusion, again reached by Gélis, is that the seventeenth century saw the "proliferation," indeed the "explosion," of these sanctuaries, which reached their height just before 1700. The phenomenon thus flourished during the golden age of the Counter-Reformation, when an unprecedented effort of Christianization was being directed at the rural world. This correlation allows one to suppose that the catechesis of the time increased peasants' anguish over the death of their unbaptized children. The "devotion to baptism" especially proposed by the French school of spirituality, the era's abundant baptismal literature, and the evangelical attempts to sanctify an annual day for baptisms[271] had the long-range effect, at the most everyday level, of reinforcing the public demand for this vital sacrament: Without it, a prematurely dying child would never attain an eternity of bliss.

Nonetheless, the official church was hostile to the sanctuaries of resuscitation. The priest Jean-Baptiste Thiers, at the end of the seventeenth century, cites in his *Traité des superstitions qui regardent les sacremens* . . . the principal texts condemning recourse to such sanctuaries. These condemnations were issued by the bishops of Langres in 1452 and 1455, in the synodal statutes of Sens in 1524, of Lyon in 1557 and 1566, of Besançon in 1592 and 1666, and in the general ordinances of the diocese of Toul in 1658. The Enlightenment Pope Benedict XIV, who did not believe in the resurrection of little corpses, cites in a passage on baptism the decree of the Holy Office, dated April 27, 1729, condemning the practice of carrying stillborn children to certain religious places, especially that of Ursperg in Swabia.[272] From the fifteenth century on, these texts display a striking critical spirit. In the synodal statute of 1452, the bishop of Langres Philippe de Vienne writes: "Children are often born without life or soul, and are baptized by certain ignorant people, who think that these children have life and soul, because they see them move in the flicker of firelight or because of the heat that is usually made around these children in certain churches or holy places in our town and diocese . . ."[273] At the other end of the period, Benedict XIV sounds the same note:

> *. . . The signs by which they vouch for the resurrection of these children are very ambiguous and . . . the witnesses who attest to these facts are for the most part untrustworthy and of little authority. For they take as certain signs of revival either the change from pale to reddish complexion, or the flexibility of members that had been rigid, or the blood that runs from the nostrils or some drop of sweat appearing on the forehead or stomach . . . The said physical effects can be easily attributed to the heat that comes from the torches held around the dead children's bodies, and from other fires lit to heat these sanctuaries.*[274]

The Pope goes on to observe that the accounts of these supposed miracles mention "neither cries, nor groans . . . which, in a case of resurrection, would have to be taken as having great importance. For these signs are less susceptible to fraud or falsehood."[275]

Throughout the period, this critical outlook is accompanied by a contemptuous tone toward overly hurried baptizers and credulous or biased witnesses. The first group are labeled "ignorant people"[276] or "ill-taught priests."[277] The second are generally branded as contemptible women: "There are certain women who for financial gain involve themselves in these abuses"[278] (Synod of Langres, 1455). "Various drunken women, of poor conscience, observe these children in the churches over two, three, or several days, and then bear witness that the signs of life have appeared"[279] (synodal statutes of Besançon, 1592 and 1656). "For the most part, uncultured young women are the witnesses of these events"[280] (Benedict XIV). These antifeminist accusations provoke two immediate qualifications: (1) The witnesses were not necessarily women. For example, at the Church of the Annunciation in Aix-en-Provence in 1558, they were all male; (2) while it is likely that women were often in the majority, what is abnormal in that? These rites involved newborn infants, and thus an appropriate sharing of the sorrow and hope by their mothers, aunts, and friends, who no doubt suffered more than men from the idea that the baby might never know the joys of paradise.

Thus masculine clericalism strove to prohibit sanctuaries of resuscitation and the burial in sacred ground of "abortions." Despite these efforts, some of these sanctuaries continued to function until the twentieth century, especially in rural areas. The anguish of parents was too strong: an anguish that might have been alleviated by another doctrine of baptism, and which early Christian parents did not feel. Their assurance appears in this late fifth-century Gallo-Roman inscription from La Cayole, in which the parents express their hope in the blessed destiny of their unbaptized little one:

> *This gracious child, armed with the sign of the cross*
> *whose innocence was not stained with any sin,*
> *little Theodosius, for whom his parents justly*
> *desired holy baptism,*
> *cruel death has carried off; but the master of heaven above*
> *will grant rest to his remains, which the noble sign*
> *of the cross had marked, and he will be called the Heir of Christ.*[281]

The sanctuaries of resuscitation thus comprised a limited but secularizing response to a depressing theology, for which the great Arnauld gives, as was his wont, a peremptory justification:

> *I would wish . . . that everyone would take to heart a most judicious consideration of Cardinal Bellarmine. It is that the pity we have for children cannot do them any good, and that likewise the sternness of our feelings does not in fact make their condition the more unhappy. Hence it is not by the human impulse of a vain tenderness for the dead that one should judge these things, as most men do; but by the light of Scripture, of the Councils, and of the Holy Fathers.*[282]

All the same, Arnauld concedes that "most men," despite the theologians, succumb to the "impulse" of this "vain tenderness."

CHAPTER 9

The Mass of Perdition and the System of Sin

"MANY ARE CALLED BUT FEW ARE CHOSEN"

The traditional conception of Original Sin explains the extraordinary importance that until the nineteenth century the most official Catholic doctrine—but also that of Protestants[1]—gave to the brief phrase in the Gospel of Matthew, "Many are called but few are chosen" (22:14). Aquinas clearly underlined this link, even while striving to react against Augustinian pessimism. He states in the *Summa Theologica* that

> *The good that is proportionate to the common state of nature is to be found in the majority and is wanting in the minority. The good that exceeds the common state of nature is to be found in the minority, and is wanting in the majority. Thus it is clear that the majority of men have a sufficient knowledge for the guidance of life; and those who have not this knowledge are said to be half-witted or foolish; but they who attain to a profound knowledge of things intelligible are a very small minority in respect to the rest. Since their eternal happiness, consisting in the vision of God, exceeds the common state of nature, and especially insofar as this is deprived of grace through the corruption of original sin, those who are saved are in the minority.*[2]

This text, frequently reused during the next few centuries, reveals both the general character of a conviction among theologians and a logical defect in the Thomist argumentation. Aquinas's distinction between the natural and supernatural should have led him to an analogous distinction between the paradise open to the few elect souls and a reception area, at the very least without suffering, for the mass of people who had accomplished "the good that corresponds to the common condition of nature." But the contemporary geography of the afterlife did not allow for this enlargement of the already vague realm of limbo.

The biblical references that formed the base for "the frightful and horrible" doctrine of the small number of the chosen—the adjectives are those of the great liturgist Cardinal Bona (d. 1674), who supported this idea[3]—are worth recalling.

First and foremost, there is the same line from Saint Matthew, "*multi sunt vocati, pauci electi*," which appears at the end of the parable of the wedding feast (22:1–14), then the two texts of Matthew (7:13–14) and Saint Luke (13:24) on the "strait gate." In the latter passage, someone asks Jesus, "Are there few that be saved?" and He answers, "Strive to enter in at the strait gate: for many, I say unto you, will seek to enter in, and shall not be able." To support these statements, theologians and preachers often added Deuteronomy 30:16, and line 1 of the Psalm 1—which both propose the choice between the two ways—as well as the Second Letter of Peter (2:5–8, with allusions to the Flood and the destruction of Sodom and Gomorrah), Corinthians I (9:24)—"they which runneth a race run all, but one receiveth the prize"—and a few verses from Isaiah (24:13–15). In the apocalyptic description of the ruined city, the prophet announces that the city will be left in desolation, "as the shaking of an olive tree, and as the gleaning grapes when the vintage is done." Bellarmine borrows these violent images, writing that

> *The number of the reprobate will be as the multitude of olives that fall to the earth, when the olive tree is shaken; and the tiny number of the chosen will be as the few olives that, having escaped the hands of the gatherers, remain in the highest branches and are picked separately. Likewise, the multitude of the reprobate will be as the wine harvest, which fills up many vessels with the grapes the peasants have gathered; and the tiny number of the chosen will be as the few grapes that, the harvest being finished, will be found by chance, still on the vine.*[4]

Saint Jerome had already employed these analogies,[5] and they reappear in the famous seventeenth-century *Cursus theologicus* of the barefoot Carmelites of Salamanca.[6]

Contemporary exegesis clarifies the Gospel phrases better than was formerly possible. Behind Matthew 22:14 lies a popular saying, whose closest parallel occurs in the nonbiblical *Apocalypse of Ezra* (8:3), without the image of the Banquet: "Indeed, many have been created, but few will be saved." The idea expressed by these two concordant texts (not everyone will have a place in the world to come) was banal by Jesus' time: A large number of surviving tannaitic allusions, part of the teaching of doctors of Torah in the second century A.D., attest to this fact and reflect Jewish religious ideas during the early Roman empire. In the Palestinian religious thought of the time, however, these questions were left to individual judgment and in no way provided any grounds for normative rules.[7] Moreover, in the parable of the "wedding feast," the saying "many are called, but few are chosen" does not fit in well with the preceding scene: The servants of the king "gathered together all as many as they found," and only one man is sent away, for not wearing a wedding garment. Finally, the most probable sense of the phrase itself is: All those who are called will not necessarily be chosen. As for the two Gospel texts on the "strait gate," the context of Jesus' preaching in Hebraic society makes it clear that these words signify the casting out of faithless Jews and the calling in of righteous pagans. Herein the sense is consonant with the vision of Saint John, who sees before the throne of the Lamb and beside 144,000 of all the tribes of the children of Israel "a great multitude, which no man could number, of all nations, and kindreds, and people, and tongues." This passage from the Book of Revelation (7:4–12) did not fail to embarrass classic theology.[8]

On the other hand, this theology frequently drew support from a sermon of Saint John Chrysostom to the people of Antioch, which asks, "How many saved souls do you think there are in this city? What I am going to say may offend many, but I will say it all the same. Of the many thousands of inhabitants here, there are no more than a hundred who will be saved, and I even doubt this figure."[9] A homily by Louis of Granada[10] and a retreat "meditation" by Louis Tronson[11] both refer to this Chrysostom sermon: two cases among many. Nonetheless, "until Saint Augustine, the Fathers gladly believed in a widely extended salvation, at the very least among the Christians, and some even, such as Origen and the Origenists, in universal salvation. After Augustine, a reaction set in . . ."[12]

This historical summary by Antonin Sertillanges invites reemphasizing the importance of Augustine, some of whose assertions regarding the doctrine of the "mass of perdition" now seem stupefying. He wrote to Optatus that

> *they whom He foresaw would not be fit to receive His grace, God made them so numerous that their multitude is incomparably greater than the number of the promised children to whom He has appointed the glory of His Kingdom. Thus the very mass of rejected souls shows that such a vast quantity of justly damned men does not at all involve the justice of God.*[13]

This remark is more clearly explained by the following famous lines from *The City of God*:

> *mankind is divided between those in whom the power of merciful grace is demonstrated, and those in whom is shown the might of just retribution. Neither of these could be displayed in respect of all mankind; for if all had remained condemned to the punishment entailed by just condemnation, then God's merciful grace would not have been seen at work in anyone; on the other hand, if all had been transferred from darkness into light, the truth of God's vengeance would not have been made evident. Now there are many more condemned by vengeance than are released by mercy; and the reason for this is that it should in this way be made plain what was the due of all mankind.*[14]

It is a historical fact that the most eminent Western Christian thinkers, from antiquity to the nineteenth century, agreed on the tiny number of the chosen. A Latin work published in Bruxelles in 1899, by one P. Godts, had no trouble in demonstrating this point, in citing "73 Fathers and Saints of the Church, "74 theologians, and 28 interpreters of Holy Scripture."[15] Aquinas, whose opinion on the matter was quoted above (and which next to Augustine's carried immense weight), thus found himself in agreement with the majority of church spokespeople. There are too many examples from which to choose. A homily of Saint Gregory the Great declares: "It should not frighten you that in the Church there are so many evil and so few good souls." Behold the ark, "amid the waters of the Flood: it was wide where it held the beasts, but narrow where it held the people." In the same way, "the Holy Church is vast in its flesh, but cramped in its spirituality." Hence it is necessary "to oft repeat and never forget that many are called, but few are chosen."[16]

One of Saint Bernard's sermons demands, "What Christian, no matter how modest, is not aware that the Lord will come to judge the quick and the dead, and to render to each according to his deeds? And yet not all, nor many, but only a few possess the knowledge that there are truly only a few who will be saved."[17] Innocent III explains:

> *Not everyone believes in the Gospel of Christ. Who does not believe, is already judged. Thus, since the unbelievers outnumber the believers, without a doubt "many are called but few are chosen." All the same, just as many of the faithful will be*

damned, for repudiating their faith by their works; for "it had been better for them not to have known the way of righteousness, than, after they have known it, to turn from the holy commandment delivered unto them." (II Pet. 2:21.).[18]

Saint Bonaventure repeats and elaborates on Augustine:

When God condemns and casts down, he works according to His justice; when He predetermines [to salvation], He acts by His grace and mercy, which do not exclude justice. For all those belonging to the mass of perdition should be condemned. There are thus more reprobate than chosen souls, so it may be manifest that salvation comes from special grace, while damnation results from ordinary justice . . .[19]

Ludolph of Saxony, whose fourteenth-century *Vita Christi* was soon to become one of the great successes of early printing, comments on the parable of the wages given to the grape pickers,

Even though everyone, in this parable, received a wage, we must not conclude that those who are called to the faith are saved; whence the terrible words: for many of the workers, at the first, third, sixth, ninth, and at the final hour are called but few are chosen and received into heaven. Many belong to the Militant Church who will never belong to the Triumphant Church.[20]

The archbishop of Florence San Antonino (d. 1459), friend of Fra Angelico and a humanist who had a casuist audience,[21] pondered how to reconcile the phrase *pauci sunt electi* with Revelation 7, which contrastingly features an enormous number of saved souls. He resolves the contradiction in the following way: It seems impossible to succeed in counting the number of the chosen; however, they are far fewer in number than the outcasts. "Likewise, the grains of sand in a sack are almost countless, but they hardly amount to anything compared to the sands of the sea's beaches!"[22]

Until recently it was a matter of "faith" in the Roman church that the greater part of humanity was destined to damnation. This was certainly the opinion of the rigorist school, and Pierre Nicole propounds it in claiming "there is no more surprising truth in the Christian religion than that which shows us just how few in number are the chosen; and it is no less true that the Holy Spirit had greater care to express in plain terms . . . Who will thus assure us that we are among those who run with success, rather than those who run in vain?"[23] Still more revealing is the dramatic sermon given by the Bishop of Vence in 1788, whose citation by Michel Vovelle I must here repeat.[24] The orator (Monsignor de Surian) aims not only to frighten, but he admits his own fear before the certainty that such a great number of souls will be cast out:

For, finally, when I envision the horrid aftermath of death, when I consider the dreadful ceremony of judgment, when in my mind I descend into hell, these diverse spectacles trouble me; however, if only a few people were to see all that, I would not be as afraid of the magnitude of evil, by there being only a few souls in misery. But when, as a result of Jesus Christ's oracle—few are chosen—I think that this death will be the eternal death of almost all the Christians who surround me; that this hell will be the permanent home of almost everyone with whom I live, with whom I speak; when I think that there is perhaps my fate and my abode, I admit that I am no longer the master of my fear. Everything afflicts me, everything on earth disgusts me, and I find myself complaining that I must speak to you, when I am only inclined to grieve and shed tears.[25]

Even a saint of great compassion, such as Vincent de Paul, professed a narrow conception of salvation. At one point he told his missionaries, ". . . great is the number of those who enter through hell's wide gate." The father superior of the Lazarists also draws on the tradition of the church and the classic scriptural arithmetic:

Let us beware, let us remember what the saints have said on this matter, and how they judge that only a few will be saved. Let us consider that in the ark of Noah, there were only seven or eight people, and that all the others perished, and that five of ten virgins were condemned, and that only one of the ten healed lepers returned to Jesus Christ. These examples are signs of the small number of the chosen.[26]

Another of de Paul's maxims on this subject was the following: "I believe that half the world, indeed even three-quarters, will be damned for the sin of sloth."[27] In a letter addressed to a limited audience (*Lettre circulaire aux Amis de la Croix*), Grignion de Montfort claims "to have recorded the tiny number of the chosen":

It is so tiny, so very tiny, that were we to know it, we would be stricken with grief. It is so tiny, so very tiny, that scarcely one in a thousand is chosen, as it has been revealed to many saints . . . It is so tiny that if God wished to assemble them [the chosen], he would cry out, as he once did through the mouth of a prophet: Congregamini unus et unus *(Isa. 17:12), meet together one by one, one from this province, one from this kingdom.*[28]

Responding to Malebranche's critiques, Fénelon also wrote: "So that the author will therefore no longer ask us why so many men die, since God who wishes to save all of them could wish on them, without impairing their freedom, all that pleased Him . . . like Augustine, I will answer you that I ignore it . . . Therefore, undertake, I say to the author, if you like, to fathom this mystery of divine judgments."[29] Saint Alphonsus Liguori (d. 1787), like de Paul a founder of a missionary congregation, strove to keep a fair middle course between rigor and laxity, and so came up against Jansenistic opponents.[30] On several occasions, however, he affirmed that "the number of the condemned is far greater than that of the chosen,"[31] in one instance stating: "The way to heaven is narrow, as they are wont to say, it cannot give passage to a carriage; those who wish to travel by coach will not be able to get there. Very few ever arrive there, because so few force themselves to resist temptations."[32]

Despite first impressions, it would be an error to suppose that from the sixteenth century the Jesuit movement brought an appreciable moderation of a potentially depressing conception of salvation. Many of the spokesmen of the Company shared the common opinion of the theologians on this topic. Godts, in his catalogue of authors favoring the doctrine of the chosen few, includes no less than thirty-one sixteenth- through eighteenth-century Jesuits. Certainly he sometimes relies on such a cutting and pasting of citations that the book's argument is impaired.[33] Nevertheless, it is hard not to be struck by the consensus among even the Jesuits, from Bellarmine to Bourdaloue, that advocated the notion of the limited effects of Redemption. For example, there is the (moderate) thinking of Suarez (d. 1617), which can be condensed in three propositions: (1) the "common and credible" view is that the majority of human beings will be damned; (2) if one now takes into account only the baptized people, given all the heretics, schismatics, and bad Christians among them, the majority of Christians will also perish; (3) at the same time, the majority of Catholics will arrive at salvation, because on the one hand, many children die before the age of reasoning, and on the other, adults often repent and receive the sacraments before dying.[34]

The doctrine of "the chosen few" was professed by the most eminent Jesuits: Canisius, Salmeron, Bellarmine, Suarez, Vasquez, Lessius, Bourdaloue, and so on. Jean-Baptiste Saint Jure (d. 1657), whose authority in the Company was great throughout the seventeenth century, having declared that "the number of those who cause their own damnation" is "incomparably greater than that of those who save themselves," resolved the primary objection in these terms: "For if you ask me how it is possible that God, who loves humanity so perfectly, who has such desire to save us and suffered so much for this end, could wish to condemn almost everyone, I answer you that He has still more love for them, and more desire for their salvation than we can either say or think . . ."[35] Finally, Bourdaloue in turn came to grips with the daunting subject: he writes that

> *It is a constant that the number of the chosen will be minute, and that there will be a far greater number of condemned souls . . . I declare! what is indeed more evident in the Gospels, than this small number of the chosen? what did the Savior of the World more authentically tell us in his divine instructions, more often remind us, and more expressly and clearly make us to understand?*"[36]

It is true that a Jesuit, Gravina, defended with unprecedented clarity the thesis that "the greater part of humanity will be saved"[37]—but only in the second half of the eighteenth century. A professor at the College of Palermo, Gravina published the work of one of his deceased colleagues, Father Plazza, entitled *Dissertatic anagogica, theologica, paraenetica de paradiso* (1762), and inserted a chapter on the number of the elect. Significantly, the book met with severe opposition in Palermo's ecclesiastic circles and was condemned by the Congregation of the Index in 1772. All the same, a movement henceforth took shape that, especially among the Jesuits and soon the ex-Jesuits, but also outside the Company, followed Gravina's lead. Father Perrin (d. 1767), addressing Jansenistic rigorists, told them: Could I love a "pitiless and barbaric tyrant, a God who would be worthy of my hate? Your God is not mine; I love One full of justice and mercy, and do not at all know that one whom your gloomy hearts have invented."[38] The Capuchin Ambroise de Lombez, in a meaningfully entitled work, the *Traité de la paix intérieure*, posed the question: If God revealed their predestined salvation to the saints, "did he ever let any condemned soul know of his condemnation?"[39] A pious noble of the Franche-Comté, Lezay-Marnésia, accused the Port-Royal disciples (but clearly various others) "of making Christianity almost impossible" and of reducing God "to filling heaven only with the youngest and most innocent children."[40] In the nineteenth century Lacordaire, Ravignan, Monsabré, Castellein, and others strove to reverse the standard opinion of over a thousand years. Lacordaire remarked, "The chosen few is not a dogma of faith, but a question freely debated in the Church," and he forcefully added: "Christ restored all, blessed all, overcame all, and his generous hands hold His beloved universe."[41] Thereafter, a theology that had effectively taught the failure of Redemption came to be discredited.

One can gauge the route traversed in less than two centuries by reading these words, written by Cardinal Marella in 1967 as part of a preface to a *Présentation de la foi catholique*, edited by the Roman secretariat for nonbelievers: ". . . No man can judge if anyone has incurred such misfortune [Hell]. Only God knows who these men are, and if there are any of them."[42]

CRIMINAL MAN AND TERRIBLE GOD

Lacordaire's above-cited, consoling statement would have received these answers from the great Arnauld and many others of his time: "Human nature is a woman, possessed by the devil."[43] "We are sick people, who must be healed, and sinners, who must be punished"[44] living in the "disgraceful necessity of being ashamed of the most natural deeds, even when they are permitted."[45] To late twentieth-century eyes these are extreme comments, but they do clarify the close tie commonly made by past theologians between the chosen few and the enormity of sin in general, and of each offense in particular.

From the Christian standpoint, human history is, clearly, a history of sin but at the same time a history of salvation. "It is by virtue of the supremacy of grace over the forces of evil that the Christian revelation has the right to call itself 'Good News.' "[46] In contrast, before the contemporary religious revolution, sin seemed to be the main point of existence, while the notion of extenuating circumstances was not clearly adumbrated, except by the casuists who received Pascal's excessive mockery. Since the time of Original Sin, God had become a fearsome creditor, presenting man with a debt that he could neither avoid nor repay.

L'Homme Criminel: This is the title of a work published in 1644 by Jean-François Senault, chaplain to Cardinal of Bérulle, later the fourth father superior of the Oratory, and generally reputed to be the finest preacher of his day—his sermons were sold in manuscript.[47] Hostile to Jansenism and favorable to the Formulary, Senault is an excellent representative of orthodox Augustinism within the Catholic Church. Through Original Sin, "criminal man" offended God. Ever since, "the sun that shines on the guilty is defiled . . . and light ceases to be innocent when it descends on criminals." This is but one of the aspects of the collective and general punishment determined by the Almighty:

> *For it seems that divine justice treats sinners as human justice treats the worst criminals. This justice is not content to punish only the guilty party in his own person, but it vents its anger against his children and servants, it believes that all that touches him is polluted; . . . it mixes the blood of the children with that of their father, it applies the same punishment to the innocent as to the guilty, and to make the crime more odious, it punishes all that which belongs to the criminal. It does not even spare inanimate things, it attacks the dead after it has punished the living: for it beats down its enemy's houses and ruins his castles, it makes the rocks and marbles feel its anger, it burns what it cannot overturn, and if the guilty one lives in each part of his works, it aims to give him as many deaths as ruined buildings . . . Thus does divine justice deal with the sinful man.*[48]

Senault goes on to assert that the "birth" of men "makes their entire crime. It is enough that Adam was their father for them to be guilty." God need not therefore wait "for them to break his commandments in order to punish them: He foresees how they will use their reason, and makes them miserable before they come of age, that one knows that they are guilty before their birth."[49]

In fact, the sinner is doubly criminal, since he brings death not only to himself but to God. Bérulle writes:

> *The grandeur of our sins [is a] pernicious and abominable grandeur, the grandeur of a ruinous and deadly efficacy, a powerful grandeur, capable of bringing death, not only to man, but to God Himself: a grandeur annihilating not only sinners but God Himself in a certain sense, for He, being a man of flesh when He wished to abolish sin, made himself commit sin; and a victim of sin, according to his apostle, subject, captive, and as a slave under the power of darkness.*[50]

This analysis differs considerably from the teaching of the Bible, which, to be sure, does not present an indifferent Aristotelian God but does present Him as out of the sinner's reach. Jeremiah (7:18–19) records that "[they] pour out drink offerings unto other gods, that they may provoke me to anger. Do they provoke me to anger? saith the Lord: do they not provoke themselves to the confusion of their own faces?" In Job (35:6), these words appear: "If thou sinnest, what doest thou against him? or if thy transgressions be multiplied, what does thou unto him?"

A revealing statistic: In a classic work such as the *De Perfectionibus moribusque divinis* (1620) by the Jesuit Lessius (d. 1623), an adversary of Michel Baius, the subject index includes more citations uner "sin" than under any other heading; moreover, books 11 and 12, which discuss the "kindness" and "mercy" of God, together amount to only 147 pages in the 1875 edition,[51] whereas book 13 ("On the justice and anger of God") alone covers some 214 pages. Aquinas had defined Deadly Sin as a desire to turn away from God. Lessius deduced that this *aversio* involved "contempt" and "injury" toward the supreme Lawmaker.[52] This injury is obvious, even if it is not expressed in a blasphemous remark or an act marked with hatred. If God did not exist, all faults would be venial.[53] Likewise, without divine prohibitions the mere transgression of natural law would no longer be a Deadly Sin.[54]

"Eternal Law" and its commandments do, however, exist. Deadly Sin is the "contempt" for these laws, and it is thus weighed down by "infinite malice." For a single deadly offense "contains the malice of all the sins together"[55] and is the same as the contempt for "the entire Law."[56] It therefore deserves eternal punishment,[57] and by its "weight alone," which is "immense," it leads into Hell.[58] "So great is the malignity of deadly sin that, placed on the divine scale, it outweighs all the good works of all the saints, even if these were a thousand times more numerous and a thousand times greater than they really are: a truly terrible consideration!"[59] Any Deadly Sin is thus "by its nature unpardonable, except through Christ's atonement."[60] No creature can ever atone for his or her sin.[61] No sorrow, no contrition can efface the offense, unless God's freely given pardon intervenes.[62] Finally, it is not unjust that "an entire multitude be punished (on earth) for the sin of a single man," as happened to the Israelites on account of David,[63] especially since the accumulation of sins "calls down divine vengeance."[64]

Not only must one avoid Deadly Sin, but also one must not add up venial sins. In this regard, Lessius recalls the unanimous agreement of the Doctors. The abuse of minor faults puts a chill on fervor, creates a barrier to divine assistance, and makes for a more deadly fall. The Jesuit author cites Augustine (*De Decem chordis*)[65]:

> *Venial sin is not a beast like the lion who, with a single blow, can tear your throat. But often a great many insects can kill. Throw someone into a place full of fleas, will he not die? Grains of sand are tiny, but fill a ship with them, and it will*

lurch to the point of sinking. How tiny are raindrops! But do they not fill up the rivers and knock down houses? Hence do not make light of venial sins.[66]

These considerations do not only tie in with the long-since classic theme and iconography of the solidarity between the sins, expressed by the tree or chain of vices[67]; they also seek to extend a verse of Saint James (2:10): "For whosoever shall keep the whole law, and yet offend in one point, he is guilty of all." As often, this phrase was taken out of context and sensationalized. For the apostle soon explains: "if thou commit no adultery, yet if thou kill, thou art become a transgressor of the law" (2:11). Aquinas therefore took pains to qualify the statement, "Whoever falls into one sin is subject to the rest." He explains that "the opposite virtue is not banished by every act of sin; because venial sin does not destroy virtue . . . yet one act, even of mortal sin, does not destroy the habit of acquired virtue; though if such acts be repeated so as to engender a contrary habit, the habit of acquired virtue is destroyed."[68] A bit farther in this same "question," the "angelic doctor" also deems that "the gravity of sins varies in the same way as one sickness is graver than another . . . and in each of these grades of sin, one sin will be graver than another according as it is about a higher or a lower principle."[69]

Despite these restrained analyses, the sensational tone most often had the upper hand in past religious discourse. For example, the Franciscan Olivier Maillard (d. 1502) preached a sermon at Bruges, telling his audience that

It is written in God's hand, says the blessed Saint James, that whoever has obeyed all the laws, but then fails in one of the commandments, will be guilty of breaking all the others. For, my lords, it is not enough for me to say: I am not a murderer, I am not a thief, I am not an adulterer. If you have failed in the least degree, you are guilty of every sin. [Here lies the overstepping of the Saint James text: "the least" is not synonymous with "one point."]

Maillard goes on to say: "Only one little leak is needed to sink the greatest ship on the seas. Only one faulty postern gate is needed for taking the strongest city or strongest castle in the world. Only one little open window is needed to rob from the greatest and richest merchant's boutique in all Bruges."[70]

In contrast, Gerson had written, one will recall,[71] a highly ambivalent treatise *Le Profit de savoir quel est péché mortel et véniel*, in which he observed that "the Seven Deadly Sins—pride, envy, anger, avarice, sloth, lust, gluttony—are not so-called because every instance of pride or envy, or any of the rest, is a deadly sin, for they are often venial . . ."[72] For Gerson, only "full consent" made for a Deadly Sin. But is this humane viewpoint that of God? Théodore de Bèze did not think so; in his *Chrétiennes Méditations* he cries out: "O God, You who have said that the means of not being judged is to judge one's self, behold this unfortunate who knows before You and your angels, before heaven and earth, that the least offense among a million is most worthy of your most dreadful wrath, that nobody can get away with it, seeing that nobody is your equal."[73] On this subject Bérulle echoes Calvin's friend and successor, by gathering these striking phrases: "The nothingness and the privation of grace to which sin reduces us, is much more damaging and deplorable than the pure and simple nothingness which was ours before creation."[74] "A light sin weighs more in God's scales than a harsh penalty,"[75] and again, "One cannot think that any sin for which Christ shed his blood may be slight."[76]

Similarly, Pascal speaks of the "terrible results and consequences . . . of the slightest offenses,"[77] and his sister Jacqueline gives this advice to the religious women in charge of children at Port-Royal: "It is good that they [the young girls]

do not make any distinction between the major sins and the most minor ones, and thereby have less fear of them. Thus one must tell them that for a soul who loves God, everything is of great consequence."[78] Maria-Teresa of Austria no doubt received this type of education in her native Spain, however far away she was from the halls of Jansenism. In the funeral oration that he gave in her honor, Bossuet remarked: "She did not understand how one could willingly commit any one sin, even if it was a minor one. She thus did not say: 'It is venial'; she said 'It is sin,' and her innocent heart was offended. But as some sin always slips past human fragility, she would not say: 'It is light'; again she would say, 'It is sin.' " Bossuet had earlier exclaimed, "Christian! You regard too much the distinction of the venial sins from the deadly ones."[79]

Inevitably, the perpetual stress on sin tended to enlarge the terrifying image of God as Judge. With the growing success of apocalyptic literature after the Black Death, this image assumed a remarkable stature in fourteenth- to sixteenth-century Europe. Tapestries, stained-glass windows, illuminated manuscripts, and engravings were filled with representations of the Son of God with a sword between his teeth.[80] Luther's confessed fears may be recalled: "I did not believe in Christ, but I took Him to be a severe and terrible judge, such as in paintings where He sits on the rainbow"[81]; and again: "my hairs stand on end when I think of the Last Judgment."[82] This judge had become a rigorous accountant, keeping a list of the deeds and acts of each and every person. Hence the portrayal, for example at Albi, of human beings appearing before the divine tribunal on the Final Day, with two-columned lists of all their good and evil actions hung from their necks.

Texts assured the long survival of these images. The Supreme Accountant determines when the "measure" of the sins of a community is "full." Lessius emphasizes this theme, making use of various Old Testament examples (the Flood, the destruction of Sodom and Gomorrah, and so on), and he warns his contemporaries: "This is worth considering: the more numerous are the impious people who, in whatsoever Christian republic, sin with impunity, the more rapidly is the measure filled up, and the heavier and swifter will be the inevitable vengeance."[83] Tronson, however, internalizes this notion of the "full measure," linked to the ancient idea that the Divinity punishes masses of guilty sinners on earth. One of the meditations he proposes to his audience of recluses is in fact "on the number of sins" and on the "measure of grace."[84] For one should remember, he says, "the three terrible words" that the proud Balthazar saw written on the wall of the chamber where "he went too far in his iniquities": *Mane, Tecel, Phares*, that is, "counted, weighed, divided." From this example, Tronson deduces five "truths." The first is that God, for all eternity, has counted the days and minutes of our life, a limit "which is impossible to overstep." Likewise, "He also knows the number of sins that He intends each man to suffer, and [of the] graces that He has resolved to bestow upon each man." Hence it follows—this is the second truth—that "on the final committed sin that fills this measure, or on the final rejected grace, which is the one that attains this number, depends the decision of your eternity." Therefore there are no more graces to wait for, and . . . "the mercy of God has been all used up." The third truth is that "this measure of sins is different in regard to each man; the same may be said for God's graces: because for some this measure is greater, and for others it is smaller." "Now, knowing how many [sins] it takes to fill this measure," Tronson tells his recluses, "is something you cannot know; perhaps after all those that you have committed, no more than one is required." The fourth truth is that the final sin "which fills the measure is of no other kind or nature from the rest; it is not even necessary that it be greater." Is life's final hour any longer than the preceding ones? The fifth truth follows on the first four: this final sin "which will fill your measure . . . perhaps it will come only twenty years from now; perhaps ten; perhaps this year; perhaps today." Hence fear any sin "as death, eternal death."

A sermon by Bourdaloue on "spiritual blindness" speaks of divine arithmetic in the same way:

> *Beware that this kindness [of the Lord] does not finally cease, and have fear of the patience of the same God who will strike all the more harshly, for having stopped His blows for so long. Who knows if He has decided to wait any longer? Who knows if after the first sin you will commit He will put out your light and blind you? Who cannot be seized with fear in thinking that there is a sin which God has marked out as the final limit of His grace, I speak of that powerful grace without which we will never be saved? What is it, this sin? I cannot know it; after so many sins will it come? That is what I do not know; of what sort, of what nature is it? Another mystery for me; is is a special or extraordinary sin? Is it a common or ordinary sin? An abyss, where I discover nothing. All I know—O my God!—is that I must not forget anything, not contrive anything to avert the misery with which You threaten me.*[85]

These striking warnings, whose effect on their audience may be imagined, are in keeping with an abundance of other documents that gave an alarming image of God. A rapid survey shows that fifty French sixteenth-century proverbs established a relation between sin and punishment, and only five between sin and pardon.[86] What had become of this paternal "mercy" that Pope John Paul II has recently stressed in the encyclical *God Rich in Mercy*? One of Tauler's sermons compared God to a hunter who tracks us down through punishments and temptations. It is true that it is for our own good:

> . . . *God does not wish to be the only one to punish us, He wishes that we may be punished by all creatures. Man is hunted like game offered to the Emperor; he is hunted, torn, and bitten by dogs, and he is thus more pleasing to the Emperor than if he had been taken gently. God is the Emperor who wants to eat the game taken by the hunt. He also has his hunting dogs; it is the Enemy who hunts man through temptations of all kinds; he slithers toward you from all corners, in all kinds of ways, and hunts you through diverse temptations; first through pride, avarice, and all sorts of vices, then through despair and excessive sorrow. Dear child, hold steady, that will not do you any harm; your needs must be hunted.*[87]

A biographer of Saint Jeanne de Chantal, whose work was published in 1653, writes that "God treated her as He treats these great souls, with a most divine thrashing, which is His recompense for long sufferings, these renewed tortures that make their faith the more pure, their service the more glorious, and their pains more worthy of crowns."[88]

Certain like-minded documents help to grasp the shift from an already severe image of the Supreme Judge ("God pays back all," a sixteenth-century proverb instructed), to that of a God "perverse" by dint of His justice.[89] Boaistuau, who launched the sixteenth-century French vogue of *Histoires prodigieuses*, also wrote a *Théatre du monde* . . .,[90] which owes much to medieval curses on the world. This work has renewed interest here, as the author uses the *danses macabres* to develop the idea that at death, everyone takes off his or her mask. At this moment there are no longer kings, nor counts, nor barons, but only men. "And then the Lord in heaven laughs at their follies, undertakings, and vanities (as David attests), but with such a horrible laugh, that it shakes the entire world, and makes us dumb with fear."[91] God roaring with huge and horrid laughter at human vanity conjures up a strange spectacle. Still, this portrayal of the Almighty has something in common with Tauler's Hunter, greedy to "eat game," and this claim by the famous blind preacher of the seventeenth century, Jean Lejeune, made in a sermon "On the Demoniac": "God's typical amusement is to see us bravely fighting the roaring lion."[92] Phenomena of possession rightly show how God uses Satan to test human beings and to manifest either His glory or His vengeance. Hence this statement, which is not so distant from the thought of Lejeune, put in the mouth of God by a "convulsionary" text of the eighteenth century: "Let me in my fury play a terrifying game."[93]

A God "completely given to revenging Himself" on the damned, making "eternal showers of fire and brimstone" fall down on them: Such is the description of an eighteenth-century expert on preaching.[94] The image of a terrible God had been familiar to the Western religious elite for some time. One proof among many is the seventeenth-century account by Monsieur de Quériolet, a counselor at the Parliament of Rennes, who was "converted" by the spectacle of the possessed persons of Loudun and became a priest and a renowned exorcist himself:

> *. . . New Saul, prostrate and lying on his back, [was] so terrified and quivering that he never dared raise his eyes above, except to contemplate the thunder and lightning that must destroy him, and reduce him to dust. But fear always kept his eyes staring at the ground; and he clung to it vigorously, to refresh his memory of the horrible vision he had had of hell, where his place had been reserved, and where he had been forever, if God had punished him for the enormity of his crimes . . . he greatly feared falling into the hands of a God incensed against him . . .*
>
> *He kept thinking and rethinking about what he had read and heard preached concerning the chosen few . . . He constantly pondered God's judgments, the horror of death, the rage of the damned, and the unthinkable pain of the souls caught in the flames of purgatory . . .*[95]

The pessimist Nicole, whose *Essais de morale* (widely read in the seventeenth century) devotes a "treatise" to "the fear of God," describes divine justice in haunting pages that would be hard to surpass.[96] Reflecting on the "fearful number" of condemned souls (for even within the church there is a "prodigious" amount of bad Christians), Nicole judges that "all these blind people, given over to their passions, are so many proofs of the rigor of God's justice." "It is that [God's justice]", he goes on, "which hands them over to the demons," who dominate them, who toy with them, deceive them, throw them into a thousand disorders, and burden them with an infinity of earthly miseries, in order then to hurtle them down into the eternal abyss. "Thus the world is a place of torments, where with the eyes of faith one sees only the dreadful effects of God's justice"; meanwhile, however, the "mouth of hell is always open, and the great and small, the rich and the poor go in pell-mell at all times." Echoing a verse of Jeremiah (47:6), Nicole cries out: "O sword of God's justice, will you never rest? Will you forever fill the earth with murders? Will you never cease ravaging even the Church Herself? . . ."

To thus re-create the image of God as it was proposed by theologians leads to the very heart of a history of mentalities, which reveals a link between the devaluation of a horribly sinful humanity and the rigor of the Supreme Judge. His anger was such that he did not even take pity on His only son.

Such a doctrine had the support of the most acute spiritual authors and the most authoritative bishops. Tronson puts it to use and explains it to his recluses to show them the enormity of sin. Since Jesus "gave himself as surety for sinners" and cloaked himself in "the semblance of sin,"

> *God the Father abandoned him, he gave him to the fury of the Jews, he treated him as the most abominable of men; and after an infinity of disgraces, of ignominies, and suffering, without any regard that the was His own Son, he caused him to die by the most shameful and cruel torture there ever was . . . He worked his vengeance on His Son, as if He had nothing to do with Him. Is it possible that sin is so horrible that it could cover the Son of God in horror, and make him abominable to the eyes of this tender Father? O sin, how black thou art, and how hideous!*"[97]

Bossuet maintains the same tone in a moving Good Friday sermon on "the divine leper." Original Sin had so offended the Creator that "it demanded an atonement worthy of God, one performed by a God; a vengeance worthy of God, and also performed by God." Having noted this crescendo from "atonement" to "vengeance," Bossuet does not hesitate to go to the extreme verge of a logic that obliges the Father to overwhelm his Son:

> *Indeed, it is only fitting for God to revenge His own injuries, and as long as He is not involved, sins are punished but feebly: He alone has the right to pass fitting justice on sinners; and He alone has an arm of sufficient power to treat them according to their deserts. "To me, to me," he says, "vengeance: eh! I will know well to give them their due"*—mini vindicta et ego retribuam. *It thus had to happen, my brothers, that He Himself brought all His condemnations against His Son: and since He had put our sins into Him, He also had to give Him His just vengeance. He did so, Christians, do not doubt it. That is why the same prophet teaches us that, not content with handing His Son over to the will of his enemies, He himself wished to join in the torture, and so bruised and broke Him with the blows of His almighty hand:* Et Dominus voluit conterere eum in infirmitate *(Isa. 53:10). He did so, he says, He wished to do so*—voluit conterere*; it was by a premeditated design . . .*"[98]

Bossuet continues by demonstrating that the Father turned the same face toward His Son as He presents to the condemned, as well as "that terrible glare which lights fire before Him." He moved against Jesus "with all the equipment of His justice."

The Jesuit Bourdaloue had no other image of God to present to the faithful than did the Augustinian Bossuet. His sermon on the Savior's Passion—a veritable anthology piece—describes the eternal Father who

> *with conduct as divine as it is rigorous, forgetting [that Jesus] is His Son and envisaging Him as His enemy (please forgive these expressions), declared Himself His persecutor, or rather the leader of His persecutors . . . ; the cruelty of the Jews did not suffice to punish a man such as He, a man wrapped in the crimes of the entire human race; it was necessary, says Saint Ambrose, that God took part, and this is what faith perceptibly shows us . . .*
>
> *For You Yourself, Lord, rightly turned to a cruel God, made not only Job, but Your only Son, feel the full weight of your arm. For a long time did you await this victim; it was time to restore your glory and satisfy your justice; you thought on it; but seeing only vile subjects in the world, only criminal minds, weak men, whose acts and sufferings could not have any merit before You, You found Yourself*

reduced to a powerless figure in which to avenge Yourself. Today You are enough to fully enact this vengeance; for here at last is a victim worthy of You, a victim capable of expiating the sins of a thousand worlds, a victim whom You would want as well as deserve. This Savior fixed to the cross is the subject for whom Your justice is itself prepared. Strike now, Lord, strike: he is ready to receive Your blows; without considering that it is Your Christ, cast Your eyes down on Him only to remind Yourself that He is ours, our victim, and that by killing Him, You will satisfy this divine hatred with which You hate sin . . .

It is not in hell that [the Lord] most authentically manifested Himself as the God of Vengeance, it is on Calvary: Deus ultionum Dominus *(Ps. 93). It is there that His retributive justice acted freely, without constraint, not being, as elsewhere, confined by the pettiness of the subject upon whom it came down:* Deus ultionum libere egit *[ibid]. For Him, all that the damned will suffer is only a half-vengeance: the gnashing of teeth, the groaning and crying, the fires that can never be put out, all of that is nothing, or almost nothing, compared to the sacrifice of the dying Christ.*[99]

If God had acted in this way against His so beloved Son, what would be our fate? This question quickly comes to mind, and Tronson did not fail to challenge his Saint-Sulpice recluses with it:

If sin is so horrible in itself that it could raise the fury of the Father against His Son, a Father so indulgent toward His so lovable, dear, and precious Son, a Son who was one with Him: what sort of horror will you give to God, you a creature already horrid in your birth, already banished and separated from Him, who have an accursed heritage, intolerable in the eyes of God? Finally, if our God worked His vengeance, if he put wood unapt to burn [Jesus] into the furnace, what will become of wood ready to be consumed by fire?"[100]

This bold relief given by high-level ecclesiastical discourse to divine "fury" and "vengeance" explains the thousandfold emphasis of the works of piety, catechisms, and sermons on the "sentences" of the "inflexible judge," the "accounts" that must be rendered to Him, the "condemnation" pronounced on humanity "since Original Sin," the "terrible" individual judgment, "the tribunal of penitence," and the priest-"judges," established to open or close Heaven by their verdicts.[101] Certain pedagogues, such as Pierre Coustel, also taught that "man's felicity on earth, as Saint Bernard says, consists of thoroughly fearing the Lord . . . whence one must let children know of the terrible effects of His judgments, as seen in the punishment of the rebel angels."[102] A small anthology of piety printed in 1730 for students at the Oratorian college of Angers recommends that one pray to God, trembling "exactly like the accused wretch who exposes himself to the gaze of the Judge."[103] Clearly the spirit of this recommendation is contrary to that of Pope John Paul II's meaningfully entitled encyclical, *God Rich in His Mercy*, in which the Pope especially affirms: "Thus, mercy is in a certain sense opposed to divine justice, and in many cases it shows itself not only to be more powerful, but also more fundamental . . . Love, as it were, is the condition of justice, and when all is said and done, justice is in the service of charity."[104] John Paul II's words mark a genuine rupture with the long and weighty "Augustinian" tradition.

The image of a terrible God, whose justice prevails over mercy, was matched by the removal of laughter from Christian experience. Tronson writes (without anticipating the ecology movement) that a Christian must be such that "it should not occur to him to gather flowers, nor to sniff any, just to have the pleasure of sniffing them."[105] There is also Nicole's astonishing claim regarding Jesus. Describing the "painful and laborious life of Jesus Christ during the time that He preached," he asserts that Christ, though He did not refuse to eat what was offered to Him, "nevertheless his eating was accompanied by a supreme mortification, which far surpassed that of all other men." Nicole then adds that the Lord "always had His cross before His eyes . . . by which one can imagine what sort of pleasure He could have had in this world." Moreover, He never laughed:

> *It has also been noted that He never laughed. Nothing has ever equaled the seriousness of His life: it is clear that He had no interest in pleasure, entertainment, and anything that can divert the spirit. Jesus' life was completely devoted, completely given over to God and the misery of men, without which His nature would have been such that He would have been able to shrink from it without destroying it.*[106]

Bossuet shared this opinion: He writes in the *Maximes . . . sur la comédie* that

> *Let us like Saint Paul consider Jesus to be both the author and consummator of our faith: this Jesus who, having sought to take on all our frailties, owing to His resemblance to us, except in sin, did take on our tears, our sorrows, our pains, and even our fears, but not our joys nor laughter, for He did not wish His lips, which poured out grace, to be distended even a single time by a movement that He would have thought showed a poverty unworthy of a God made flesh.*[107]

It is not surprising that Rancé, like Bossuet, believed that Jesus never laughed.[108]

A COLLECTIVE GUILT COMPLEX

A terrible God, more a judge than a father, despite the mercy with which He was almost accidentally credited; a divine justice connected to vengeance; the conviction that, despite Redemption, there would remain only a chosen few, all humanity having deserved hellfire because of Original Sin; the certainty that each sin is both insult and injury to God; the rejection of any amusement or concession to human nature, since these remove one from salvation: All these elements of a "primitive theology of blood," to use Rudolf Bultmann's expression,[109] involve a "Christian neurosis" that modern psychiatric research confirms beyond the shadow of a doubt. Two works are especially useful for clarifying this point. The first brings together the works of a symposium on obsessional neurosis.[110] Yves Pélicier's remarkable introduction establishes the conjunction between current medical analyses of this disorder and its interpretation by Christian moralists of the Age of Reason, who were anxious to fight against the torments of souls. Pélicier logically follows the symposium talks on Jacques-Joseph Du Guet's *Traité des scrupules* (1717). The second book is Antoine Vergote's *Dette et désir: Deux axes chrétiens et la dérive pathologique*.[111] I would like to express my recognition of this calm and lucid study, which integrates as well as goes beyond Freudian analyses, and takes a Christian look at Christian neurosis. Vergote's work again confirms the convergence between historiography and psychiatry that I stressed in the first chapter of *La Peur en Occident*. Psychoanalysis enables a discussion of files opened by history.

Regarding this subject, which will not admit of simplism, an entire series of important preliminary remarks must be made.[112] On the one hand, clinical experts recognize that the pathology of sin also pertains to nonbelievers and that religious obsession obeys universal psychological laws. On the other, it seems a utopia to believe that one could ever eliminate the consciousness of guilt. Contrary to André Hesnard's thinking, not all guilt feelings are morbid; it would be reductive to characterize sin only by the traits of pathological guilt. If one bluntly classifies guilt among morbid disorders, why not also include any affective or intimate experience, such as indignation, love, and joy? In reality, guilt belongs to that part of the conscious mind that concerns itself with moral conscience, and Freud was right to observe that "it is precisely those people who have carried saintliness farthest who reproach themselves with the worst sinfulness"[113]

A normal sense of guilt appears to act as a call not for the suppression but rather for the transformation and sublimation of impulses that are at odds with one's ideal self and relationship with God. More generally, to detach one of Freud's observations from his systematically negative judgment of religion, one can say that any civilization pays for its own moral demands and "cultural repressions."[114] Yet another observation extends the necessary qualifications: The frequency of self-accusation in obsessional neurosis does not inevitably coincide with the confession of sins for the sake of pardon. The admission aimed at moral improvement should not be confused with verbose "bean-spillings" that result from narcissistic introspection and do not always involve regret. Vergote again helps to clarify this preliminary focus: To stress a psychology of "massive normalization" in order to "strictly align masochistic perversion, neurosis, ascesis, and the spirituality that intends to participate in Christ's Passion, is a discourse . . . as futile as it is facile to hold."[115] In addition, it is difficult to trace a clear boundary between the normal and the pathological, "between the guilty conscience that darkens its own darkness, and that which leads to the clarity of a life of truth."[116]

Thus spelled out, these indispensable remarks make it impossible for either the clinician or the historian to deny that Christianity carries with it the risk of burdening the faithful with mistrustful and repressive guilt. There are in fact two sides to the Christian religion: On the one hand, it is reassuring, since God pardons all through Jesus and promises faithful love to mankind; on the other, however, it provokes an uneasy conscience. For nothing about the latter can escape the view of a strict and all-knowing judge. How to achieve a harmonious synthesis of the justice that justifies humans and that which judges them? This problem worsens, given that "sin" weighs more heavily than "fault," since the former includes the notion of personal responsibility, not only to other human beings but also to "one Other whom one cannot delude."[117] By making the confession of sin a fundamental requirement, part and parcel of the message of liberation, Christianity exposes the individual to morbid guilt.

Consequently and not at all surprisingly, these conditions lead to a development that in certain contexts takes on an almost collective quality, particularly during the period covered by this book. The documents that have and will be cited clearly demonstrate a pathological anguish before God's judgment, an escalation of doubts, a rumination on sin (original, deadly, and venial), and a fixation on death. Hence the diagnosis of a collective guilt complex, which is not to be judged but rather clarified and explained. This collective guilt complex is here defined as "the religious and pathological deviance of a Christianity that focuses its message on the evocation of sin and which narrows its aim to the fight against sinning."[118] Its obsessional character shows itself through psychic forces that "besiege" the spirit, take hold of the subject, and engage it in a debilitating battle against itself (sometimes with anorexic consequences). It struggles with itself in incessant examinations of conscience, surrenders to ever-increasing mortifications, and sets its internal sights on a contemplation of death. Objects appear unreal, the external world seems devoid of substance, and existence becomes a perpetual combat against the threats of a foul and decaying universe.[119]

Psychology perceives a repressed violence behind this exaggerated guilt: Freud's famous explanation still thrives. The guilty conscience, he argues, develops when an aggressiveness normally directed toward the outside, and proven to be destructive of the bonds of love and friendship, returns against the self.[120] Throughout history, but more precisely during the Counter-Reformation and in the most religious circles, excessively constraining education impaired and stigmatized with guilt the aggressivity—or rather, the "instinct for mastery"—that is essential to all human activity. The repression of aggressiveness, compounding that of sexuality, exalted the passive virtues of obedience and humility beyond all reasonable limits. As a result, there was a simultaneous turning against both one's self—the bad conscience and sickly scruples—and other sinners. One can only be struck by the violence and frequency of anathemas that churchmen leveled against every category of sinner: At work is a repressed aggressiveness that resurfaces in infinitely repeated diatribes against "criminal mankind."

In reviewing the innumerable statements regarding the chosen few and the harshness of divine "vengeance," one notes a striking mental coexistence of two contradictory images of God, the one stressing His justice and the other His mercy. Hence two distinct attitudes seem to have divided the conscience: a repressed but still-present hatred of the Persecutor and a loudly asserted love. Saint Francis De Sales admirably analyses this cohabitation of contrary attitudes in his *Traité de l'amour de Dieu*: "We must always adore, love, and praise the avenging and punishing justice of our Lord . . . and also kiss, with love and equal reverence, the right hand of His mercy and the left hand of His justice."[121] Psychiatrists interpret such affective ambivalence as the nucleus of obsessional neurosis. The simultaneous presence of self-denied hatred and love accentuated by the very denial, such is the conflict that provokes neurosis and can consume the subject in a ceaseless inner struggle.

This "malaise" of the divided soul itself stems from an overemphasis on two elements of the religious message: debt and defilement. Casting these notions as *idées fixes* tends toward a misunderstanding of the actual person. "The nostalgia for purity and the sense of an insolvent debt form part of the basis of the religious dilemma. When obsessive individuals reach the heart of their interrogations, they collide with the antinomies of the pure and the impure, of joy and of debt."[122]

The obsession with absolute purity transforms the examination of conscience into a hostile outlook on any connivance with spontaneous carnality. Any sin is labeled "impure" and becomes an almost material substance that "stains" the soul (to such a degree that the transmission of Original Sin is explained in terms of the biological inheritance of procreation). An excessive materialization of sin causes physical impurity to bring about religious and moral impurity. This degradation leads not only to the condemnation of any physical pleasure but to veritable revulsion at the obscenity of the world. At the core of psychosis lies the refusal to accept one's own body and desires. The obsessive subject wishes to take a direct route to purity without using any patience or instruction from his or her instinctual being. Emphasis has already been put on how far back this angelic idealism goes in Christian history (moreover, it is not exclusive to Christianity).[123] Saint Athanasius writes: "God's first objective was not for men to be born by marriage and corruption, but the breaking of His commandment led to sexual union, because of the iniquity of Adam."[124] Saint Gregory of Nyssa goes still further by explaining that this division between the sexes does not at all pertain to the divine archetype; sexual difference almost makes irrational beings out of humans. The Creator made man in His image, that is, neither male nor female. Since, however, "He saw in advance, in his 'prescient power,' the bent that the movement of human liberty in full possession of itself would and must take, in His knowledge of the future, He established the division of male and female in His own image, a division that no longer resembles the divine model, but . . . puts us in the family of irrational beings."[125] It would be impossible to more clearly contradict the text of Genesis. This tradition of angelism explains the disgust with the flesh experienced by Monsieur Olier, this "hero of Christian humility," whose following words, already cited by Ernest Renan,[126] are representative of a tenacious current of thought:

> *My God! What is the flesh? It is the result of sin, it is the principle of sin . . . All hatred, all malediction, the persecution that falls on the devil must fall on the flesh and its movements . . . One must do as did the saint of long ago who was led to torture for a crime he had not committed, and which he did not try to justify, telling himself that he would have committed it, and others still more grave, if God had not prevented him. —Men, the angels, and even God should therefore persecute us incessantly? —Yes, that must be so.*[127]

Jean-Jacques Olier thus inextricably links hatred of the flesh, the image of God "the persecutor" (his own word), and the desire for punishment.

The other element of the soul's condition that agitates both love and hate is "the sense of an insolvent debt." Since one received everything from God and one is a sinner, one remains in infinite debt toward this jealous creditor. Does this notion of a price to pay lie submerged beneath the *Vergeld* of Germanic law? In any case, the feeling that an order must be restored through expiation became widespread in the highest Catholic spirituality. Catherine du Bar held that the Benedictines of the Holy Sacrament were destined to "redress" the offenses Christ suffered in the Eucharist, and Bernières also spoke of "redressing the injury of God." This drama of atonement was clearly expressed in the monarchical models of the time, as the supreme Sovereign, offended by the failings of his ungrateful and rebellious subjects, would threaten them in his anger.[128]

The debt to pay was so heavy that the most saintly Christians were themselves convinced of their being great sinners. At one point Saint Marguerite-Marie Alacoque writes, "It seems that all things condemn me to eternal torture. All that I may do for good cannot atone for the least of my faults, without Your help. I am insolvent: You see it well, my divine Master. Put me in jail, I consent to it, as long as it is in Your Sacred Heart . . ."[129] Any earthly pleasure is henceforth an affront to God. Hence the merciless campaign of both Reformations against dances and other profane diversions. Protestant Swiss towns suppressed carnival; taking power in England in 1642, the Puritans closed the theaters. The unconscious certainty that underlies such attitudes is that there is only one vacant seat, and God and humanity cannot occupy it together.

> *By rights, this seat goes to the Father. To assert one's self, to succeed, to enjoy, even to exist, is to dispossess the Father, to kill Him in the imagination, to return to assassinate Him, as accords with the laws of psychology. It is therefore impossible not to contract an insolvent debt with Him, one forever renewed, at least in order to concede everything to Him.*[130]

An exaggerated and all-powerful Father overwhelms His child with a fantastic heritage, causing him to feel equal but at the same time condemning him to always remain on this side of an imaginary ideal.[131] At the extreme limit one again approaches the negation of the human, and one no longer sees the autonomy that the Creator gave mankind. There is a desire to confuse God with his creation, no matter how unattainable such a project would be.

Logically, God the jealous creditor became bloodthirsty once the sins on earth went beyond the measure and the debts owed to Him kept mounting. So his "angers" are terrible and lead on to "vengeance." Christian literature produced an almost infinite number of texts in this vein, concerning the earthly punishments of sinful communities as well as the torments assigned to the damned. There also appeared an equal number of categorical assertions on the death of the Son, the compensating "atonement" for sins. "Why did Jesus suffer so much and die?" asks a Sicilian "summary" of the *Roman Catechism* (1768). The answer: "In order to pay the penalty for the sins of all mankind."[132] To quote Antonie Vergote, "Can one imagine a more obsessional phantasm than that of a God who demands the torturing of His own Son to death as satisfaction for his anger?"[133] Nonetheless, it is precisely this God who inhabits the pages of Bossuet, Bourdaloue, Tronson, and thousands of other directors of Western conscience. The Lamb of God became a scapegoat, burdened with the sins of the entire world: His death was necessary to "satisfy" the wrath of a God whose honor had been wounded by a deadly conflict between Him and mankind.

One escapes from this neurosis-producing conception only via a different reading of the story of Redemption and a different interpretation of not only Jesus' "sacrifice" but more generally any sacrifice that offers God the best that man has to offer. By establishing a link between the human and the divine, the authentic sacrifice occurs "beyond the imaginary struggle for the same place . . . [It] is not automutilation as payment of an insolvent debt. It does not seek to pay a debt at all; rather it affirms that there is no debt to pay."[134] The present analysis at least partially concurs with that of René Girand.[135] Like this author, I believe, from reading the Gospels and especially that of Saint John, that Jesus, during his Passion, suffered "desacralized" violence at the hands of men and not of God: He arrived amid His own, and His own would not receive Him.

Paranoid fear of corruption, the consciousness of an insolvent debt, and the image of a destructive God, loved and hated at the same time, who does not allow His subjects any of their own desires and is content with their martyrdom: these are just so many factors that simultaneously induce perfectionism and narcissism. For the feeling of guilt combines two fears: that of losing the love of the other and that of being unworthy of oneself. When such an attitude develops, the price of gaining another's love never seems high enough. The impossible identification with the idealized father leads to self-inflicted castigations that sever the victim from his or her human destiny. The individual is seized with giddiness and the obsession to surpass all human limits. This escalation, however, does not provide relief. The more demanding the conscience, the more the consequent renunciations risk inspiring urges and temptations that in turn become sources of moral anguish. In this regard, it is worth recalling the endless debate on the guiltiness of temptation (in which Luther fully believed). Spiritual leaders frequently denounced the trap of perfectionism. They perceived a dangerous narcissism in this syndrome, as well as an incestuous concern with one's self, involving the impossible desire to be faultless. Moreover, a defense mechanism against oppressive guilt can lead not only religious communities but also individuals to instigate a legalism that works to emphasize the anguished conscience through meticulous observation of demanding rituals. All the same, to briefly renew the comments made at the beginning of this study of "the collective guilt complex," the above clinical portrait describes pathological behavior. It can be sustained only through qualifications and it does not underestimate the high religious value of the sublimation through which certain mystics went beyond "primary masochism." Among these individuals, a "sympathetic identification" (Saint Bernard's term) with the suffering Christ evolved into a nonnarcissistic decentering of the self, a participation in the life of the Beloved.

Given these points, can one deny the existence of a superego that the church overenlarged through the centuries, but more precisely at the moment of the respective triumphs of the Protestant and Catholic Reformations? In the West, the guilt-making process reached its height during the sixteenth and seventeenth centuries. In itself, this evaluation charts a major historical experience. Where, however, to locate the key or rather keys to this situation? At the individual level and in today's world, it sometimes seems that a family with a humble and self-effacing father—or without any sort of father at all—has an empty space, where children tend to put an all-powerful, vindictive, and persecuting God. At the same time, they receive a message of renouncement from this insufficient (or absent) father.[136] On the other hand, experience also proves that an obsession with guilt can arise in inverse circumstances and that an overauthoritarian father is liable to instill a morbid sense of moral failing in his child: Such was the case with Kafka. While these analyses are of great interest, they are difficult to apply to the past, even if the first hypothesis may apply to Saint Marguerite-Marie Alacoque (whose father died when she was eight) and the second to Luther.[137] Modern psychological dossiers on past individuals are inevitably incomplete. In addition, who could ever gather and catalogue the multitude of cases that together comprised the "collective guilt complex" of extensive sectors of Western culture? Thus the historian's role mainly consists in establishing connections that clarify, without any pretense of being exhaustive, a phenomenon of this importance.

Humanity has not always cared to relativize misconduct. For a long time, the now-familiar notion of attenuated guilt (absent in Luther) did not apply. Likewise, people tended and still tend to confuse justice with vengeance; a profound inertia causes it to remain at the level of Aeschylus' *Eumenides*.[138] This dire equation held a significant place in the religious discourse discussed above, as well as in Bandello's *Novelle* and the Elizabethan theater. The churchmen of the time considered themselves to be God's avengers, in the service of the more jealous than merciful Almighty. Similarly, an ancient pedigree belongs to the idea, frequently encountered in this study, that God wreaks His vengeance on living guilty souls and communities. The Old Testament often highlights this belief, though the example of Job runs in the opposite direction, since this just man is overwhelmed with suffering.

Jesus, it must be recalled, made three protests against the explanatory link between sins and misfortunes: regarding the man born blind (John 9:1–4), the victims of the tower of Siloam, and the Galileans massacred by Pilate (Luke 13:2–6). For a long time, however, this highly modern lesson of the Lord was forgotten. During the Age of Reason as in the Middle Ages, Christian preachers unanimously looked on mass catastrophes as God's enraged responses to excessive human wickedness. In the early nineteenth century, Joseph de Maistre revived this explanation. In *Les Soirées de Saint-Pétersbourg* (1821), he notes that Jesus healed sick people only after they had remitted their sins, and he has one of his spokesmen say that God is not the author of moral pain but rather "of the pain that punishes, that is of physical pain and affliction, just as a sovereign is the author of tortures that are legally inflicted."[139] In 1871 the French church saw the country's recent defeat as a divine punishment. Again, in 1897, a Dominican, preaching at Notre-Dame at the official service for the victims of the fire at the Bazar de la Charité, resumed the old theme: "Our tears [are] the price we pay for our readmission to mercy . . . France deserved this punishment for its new abandoning of traditions."[140] More recently, Léon Blum claimed in 1945 that "a national calamity—alluding to the debacle of June 1940—has been linked since the beginning of time to the idea of a sin or an offense, with its natural developments: contrition, expiation, redemption."[141] Thus, until the difficult challenges of recent years, past communities saw a definite causal link between sin and "just" divine vengeance here below. During the fifteenth to seventeenth centuries, the repeated trials of witches and heretics can make some sense only in the light of the ancient but then intensified conviction that God, angered by these individual crimes of "lèse-majesté," would not fail to avenge Himself on human populations who would tolerate such transgressions.

Why the "then intensified" conviction? The Europeans who lived between the advent of the Black Death and the end of the religious wars had an acute sense of an accumulation of misfortunes: epidemics, repeated famine, civil and foreign wars, denominational ruptures, the Turkish threat. They identified these events as punishments from on high and saw a proliferation of the monstrous as the forewarning of even heavier punishments. Divine vengeance only made the omnipresence of sin more evident.

Despite these fears and setbacks, or perhaps because of them, Western civilization went forward, driven by a profound dynamism. In the intervals left open by the many tests, this civilization invented, innovated, discovered, and grew wealthy, offering, at least to some, previously unknown possibilities for individual promotion. The era known as the "Renaissance" thus appears as a mixture of strong outbursts of life and descents toward death, of grand schemes, progress, and festivals, but also of disillusionment and morbidity. The will to push forward and the feeling of failure had a tight coexistence. Philippe Ariès rightly stressed this feeling of failure during the age of the "macabre."[142] My analyses connect with his remarks. A dynamic elite had a sharp perception of its limits and felt itself to be the prisoner of the stars, of Fortune, of predestination, and of sin. Hence its propensity for melancholy and meditation on death; and the need, in the reconstruction of a mental universe, to observe the links that then united the rise of individualism, the consciousness of human frailty, and an inclination toward sorrow.

The guilt-instilling discourse of the church met head on with this divided Western individual: a discourse elaborated by and for monks but aimed more and more toward laypeople, with a constant stress on sin. Very early on, monastic morality had assimilated a more Greek than Hebraic, a more Neoplatonic than Christian conception that devalued the body to the profit of the soul and led to the *contemptus mundi*. The evangelization of the masses worked toward a conversion to asceticism. Christian life inevitably came to model itself on that of the convents. The latter also inspired the style and discipline of the Counter-Reformation seminaries. In contrast, Protestantism categorically rejected convents, ecclesiastic celibacy, and salvation by good works. It held these views, however, because it saw just as strong a dose of sin outside as within the world. The situation was the constant drama of the immensity of evil and the radical impotence of the individual. Thus Western people, beginning with the Renaissance, had the choice between two concurrent emphases on sin, the more recent ultimately being the heavier. Within this latter, asceticism and ritualism managed to reemerge, thanks to the general cultural refinement of the West. In fact, Augustinian humanism, rediscovered Stoicism, the two religious Reformations, and their literary expression—preciosity—together contributed to a disgracing of the body. An increasingly abstract language then translated this voluntary trend with regard to instinctual expressions that had to remain under tight surveillance. "The constraints of social refinement were internalized as emotional constraints."[143]

Finally, the Roman church's slide into greater ritualism and rubricism during the Counter-Reformation translated, albeit in a different manner, the growing subordination of the instinctual body. In the age of ceremony, excessively ritualistic worship turned into sheer technique and barred the expression of spontaneous feelings. Undeniably, the Catholic hierarchy intended this reinforced liturgy to reaffirm a unity that the Protestant revolts had wounded. At the same time, as a "besieged citadel,"[144] Catholicism sought to cut off any internal conniving with outside enemies. Hence a double suspicion pushed it toward rigorous formalism, an integral part of the collective obsession this study aims to describe.

CHAPTER 10

Religious "Uneasiness"

THE DOCTRINE OF PAIN

Among the consequences of the Catholic guilt complex, two of the most notable were a penchant for pain and a "disease of scruple."

To fear God, the Christian must be quite courageous. The impious soul, states Massillon, is someone "who being unable to tolerate and firmly confront the terrors and threats of religion, seeks to become stupefied by ceaselessly repeating that these are childish fears."[1] In the same vein, an expert preacher, Hyacinthe de Montargon (d. 1770) tells his listeners: "Misfortune befall . . . these men who, disdaining to ponder what disturbs them, remove from their minds the fearful idea of God the Avenger; let them learn that only the fearing souls will have cause to hope on the day of judgment."[2] This religious theme was most often joined with that of the rejection of the world, specifically our universe, which coincides, to be sure, with that of Satan. Saint-Cyran writes: "Mathematicians hold that the earth is but a point, and Scripture speaks of it as no more than a desert, a prison, a hospital, and an image of hell. Therefore woe betide they who cling to this world, and do not strive to be dead to all things of this present life."[3]

The late seventeenth- and early eighteenth-century sermons given to missionary Lazarists included this statement: "The world is a prison, from which we escape only through death."[4]

These two unnatural ideas led, by reinforcing each other, to a devaluation of the self, a search for suffering, and a rejection of human joys; the human creature had to judge him or herself—according to Arnauld—"worthy of every kind of contempt, humiliation, and prostration."[5] The above-cited *Imitation* supplies these remarks: "I deserve naught but the rod and punishment . . . After . . . a strict examination I realize that I am unworthy of the slightest consolation."[6] Indeed, the most saintly individuals, as Freud rightly observes, were the most critical of themselves, and thus followed the example of the author of the *Imitation*. "In me there is only vice," claims Saint Catherine of Genoa.[7] Loyola writes to Ribadeneira: "I am but a dunghill," and wishes that at his death, his body be thrown to the dogs and birds. "Is not that what I should desire for the punishment of my sins?"[8] Saint Theresa of Avila calls herself "a miserable shelter of the Lord" and "an ocean of miseries."[9] Saint Vincent de Paul describes himself as an "abomination," and confesses at his death, "Alas! I see nothing in me which does not deserve punishment; all the things I have done are sins, and thus I have come to apprehend God's judgment."[10] One of the most striking saintly admissions of guilt comes from the pen of Marguerite-Marie (d. 1690). In her eyes, she was a "monster":

> *[during a religious retreat] the second day, it became clear to me, as in a painting, all that I had ever been and was then: but, my God! Could there be a monster more defective and hideous to behold? I saw in me not a single good, but so much evil that it was a torment to think upon. It seems to me that everything condemns me to eternal torture, for the great abuse that I made of so much grace, and to which I was wholly unfaithful . . . I can hardly wait for all the vengeance that it will please your divine justice to wreak on this criminal, except if you abandon her to herself, and by new relapses you do not punish me for my earlier sins.*[11]

For Marguerite-Marie, love most often, though not always, surpassed fear. The fear of damnation, however, as it was maintained by the "preparations for death," iconography, sermons, and spiritual writings certainly haunted numerous anxious souls at a very deep level. The painter Hugo Van der Goes (d. 1482), who became a lay brother in a monastery and died mad, spent the latter part of his life being obsessed with damnation. He finally had to be prevented from killing himself.[12] Torquato Tasso (d. 1595), afflicted by the fear of heresy, could not rid himself of the idea that he was damned. He sought relief in general confession, especially to the inquisitor of Ferrara, who absolved him. His doubts persisted: They had tricked him, they had sworn to destroy him . . .[13] The Jesuit Jean-Joseph Surin (d. 1665), who exorcised the excessively famous possessed people of Loudun, fell for twenty years into such terrible sadness that he was regarded as insane. In his hallucinatory book, *La Science expérimentale des choses de l'autre vie*, he explains the moral tortures of this long period. He had felt an irresistible sensation of being damned, and despite knowing that other mystics before him—Louis de Blois, Henry Suso, Saint John of the Cross, Saint Theresa of Avila—had undergone the same trials, he took no comfort. He struggled within a dark dilemma: Since he was irrevocably condemned to hellfire, logic demanded that he behave according to this decree. He thus had a duty to do evil. God wished it so. But he dared to disobey God. "My most dreadful crime was to go on hoping, and to keep trying to do good."[14] He was driven to thoughts of suicide, sent by Satan. All night long he would hold a knife against his own throat. On one occasion, he threw himself out the window and broke his knee, an injury that never healed.

A work such as Burton's *Anatomy of Melancholy* allows a passage from these famous cases to the religious anguish of ordinary people and thus a move from the singular to the plural. It is no accident that an early seventeenth-century author would put stress on religious melancholy. In his long treatment of this particular affliction, Burton does not omit the obsession with damnation.[15] Drawing on Felix Platter[16] and Pierre Forestus,[17] he cites the example of a painter's wife of Basel, who fell into despair after the death of her son. God, she thought, refused to pardon her sins. For four months she was seized with delirium, perceiving herself to be in Hell. The next example tells of a merchant who had wasted a small quantity of grain he had stored for too long. Although a pious and well-educated man, he oppressed himself with reproaches: Why had he not sold this grain on time? Why had he not given it to the poor? Nobody could rationalize it; he believed himself damned. A third case: A priest diligently observed Lenten fasting and sank into deep meditation. He ultimately fell into depression; he saw demons in his bedroom and despaired of his salvation. A final anecdote: Having committed a grave offense, a man wished to neither eat nor drink for an entire fortnight. The priests failed to cure his anguish and he died. From these case histories Burton moves to a conclusion, inspired by his predecessor Guatinerius: "many [note the adverb here] fall into despair through fear of the last judgment." Burton also observes that an excess of solitude, prolonged fasts, exhausting meditations, an imprudent "meditation" on God's judgments, and an incessant rumination of the mystery of eternity with its "innumerable infinite millions of years" can lead only to melancholy. This argument is clearly aimed at the Catholic Church, accused of encouraging abusive mortification and minute reckonings of good works. An Anglican pastor, Burton thanks Luther for having found a solution to these self-"tortures" and "crucifixions," and he cites Saint Bernard's advice that "we should not meddle the one without the other, nor speak of judgment without mercy."[18] Removed from both Catholicism and Puritanism, Burton finally remarks—this point will be discussed later[19]—that certain Protestant pastors also promote a fear of the otherworld among the faithful.[20]

The fear of God's judgments, a desperate search for perfection, the conviction that sins continue to crucify Jesus and that it is necessary to "repair" not only one's own failings but also those of the world, and the thirst for humiliation inspired, across the ages, a "Christian heroism" marked by stupefying feats. All the same, one need not take literally the overabundant and terrifying details regarding the penance of Henry Suso, author of his own *Life*, who died in 1366 at the age of seventy-one.[21] According to this account, the pious Dominican kept silent at table for thirty years, breaking this vow but once. For a long time he wore a hairshirt and an iron chain, removing them only when they drew too much blood. In secret, he made himself a horsehair shirt that clung to his body, and on to this he attached leather strips with 150 nails turned toward his flesh. This penitential garment, which he never took off, attracted vermin and often in the night he seemed "to be lying on an anthill, so much did the vermin crawl all over him."[22] The book called *Suso* describes still more inventions of the hero, which were just so many tortures he inflicted on himself. He thus would have worn, "constantly for eight years," "on his naked back, between his shoulders," a cross furnished with thirty iron nails and seven sharp needles, the latter in memory of Mary's sorrows.[23] The accumulation of horrible details makes it impossible that the holy monk could have simultaneously inflicted all these trials on himself. Moreover, how would he have kept secret so many mortifications that would have often stained his white clothing with blood? With the learned Madame Ancelot-Hustache, one must reasonably think that "the account of mortifications, such as we read in the *Life*, [is] absolutely suspect."[24] On the one hand, however, there is the fact that Suso was undeniably a man of penance, and on the other, that he was "one of the most popular of late medieval authors."[25] Printing then contributed to the dissemination of his works, which frequently included the *Life*.[26] Hence the contagion of such an example.

During the sixteenth and seventeenth centuries—to limit the discussion to this slice of history—ascetic exploits were often in the news. At Manresa, Loyola stayed up entire nights, spent a week without eating, whipped himself with studded chains, struck his chest with a rock, and said prayers for seven hours a day. Like the *poverello*, he gave the "Franciscan kiss" to an unfortunate individual whom all had abandoned, touching his lips to a sore and "sucking forth the rottenness to heal the sick person."[27] Peter of Alcantara astonished even Saint Theresa. He was so thin that he "seemed to be made of tree roots." He confessed to the Carmelite of Avila that "for forty years . . . he had slept only for one and a half hours per day, and that he never had known a more trying penitence; in the beginning, to overcome sleep, he remained seated, his head propped on a stick protruding from the wall . . . usually he only ate but once every three days."[28] When San Carlo Borromeo was stripped for his funeral preparations—he was forty-six years old—it was found that his shoulders were cut by whipping, his body torn by the sharp points of his hairshirt.[29]

A poor late sixteenth-century priest, perhaps ironically nicknamed the *Letterato*, would receive the orphans of Rome. His zeal, however, did not prevent him from feeling the temptations of the flesh. Finally, no longer able to keep these feelings in check, he took a pot from the fire and decided "to overcome the heat of temptation with that of boiling water." By doing so, "he so gravely injured his bodily parts that had refused to obey reason" that he was ill for many months. Dom Claude Martin, the son of Mary of the Incarnation, also used harsh remedies to fight against concupiscence. One night in Angers, imitating Saint Benedict, he stripped himself naked and rolled himself in sharp currant bushes, then covered his body with stinging nettles, and so put out the flames of desire that had tortured him for more than ten years. In 1608–09, Mother Angélique, then a young abbess at Port-Royal, devoted herself to extraordinary penitence. She dressed herself in the heaviest garments, chose to sleep on the hardest of cots, and would secretly get up in the night to pray. "She was surprised in the night, cauterizing herself, pouring hot wax on her naked arms."[30] Saint Francis de Sales made the Cistercian women of his diocese wear serge shirts, which caused them soon to complain to him, since these garments attracted vermin. He replied that "'tis no marvel that vermin eat vermin."[31] Thus there resurfaces both the macabre and the obligation of moral debt.

Another popular idea of the time was that the more that one suffered in this life, the less one would have to pay in the other. Alberto Tenenti clarifies this view with several striking texts, which must also be cited here. Marcello Mansio, in a work entitled *Documenti per aiutare al ben morire* (Bologna, 1607), writes: "Our body resembles a vine, against which Our Lord sends a tempest of infirmities and trials, which are just so many precious stones of paradise." "A man may [through sorrow] become the creditor of God, while at the same time remaining His debtor. For in suffering he gives to God his own welfare, while in other things he receives from God."[32] Such was also the view of one "Madonna Faustina" (d. 1562), who at the point of death engaged in a remarkable dialogue with Father Girolamo Cacciaguerra, the friend of Filippo Neri:

> *The father tells her: "Do you not have enough with that which you suffer already?" —"No," she answers, "because I want to suffer until there only remains the skin on my bones." "But you have indeed obtained this grace: only your skin does remain on your bones." Some days later, the sick woman's condition being still worse, Cacciaguerra tells her: "All your present sufferings must suffice, and you must be content with them." The dying woman retorts: "Oh, no, father, I am not content with them. I want to see with mine own eyes the vermin eating my flesh."*[33]

One could spend years enumerating the mortifications of Christian heroes in the age of *Polyeucte*. Saint Jeanne de Chantal, a new "Sunamite," had "the courage and nobility to take a burning hot iron, which served her as a burin, and so she herself engraved the sacred holy name of Jesus on her breast."[34] Monsieur Hamon, a doctor of Port-Royal, covered himself in rags and took delight in eating bread left to the dogs, giving his own to the poor.[35] The following account describes Margaret of the Holy Sacrament, who died at the age of twenty-nine in the Carmelite convent of Beaune:

As she had a most delicate nature, and loved cleanliness, she had a special remedy for subduing herself in this regard, which was not only to touch and smell things for which she felt repugnance: in order to mortify herself still further, she would put such things in her mouth and would find any filthy thing, such as spittle, pus, and the like, that she would not eat, and hold it on her tongue until she felt revulsion: this she did practice for the first three or four months that she was in the Holy Religion [i.e., in the convent].[36]

Marguerite-Marie likewise reveals a quenchless thirst for humiliation. An eighteenth-century writer, Monsignor Languet, records that "she so sincerely believed that all creatures had the right to treat her with contempt, that she chastised herself for not being held in enough contempt. She asked in all good faith that her superiors humiliate her often."[37] Her biographer adds that "sackcloth, hairshirts, bloody and frequent discipline, iron belts studded with sharp nails, and a thousand other inventions designed to afflict her body and make it suffer, were for her a daily practice, or at least the object of her desires, and of the continual requests she made to her superiors."[38] Languet goes on to cite a confession of the saint herself, which assimilates her to the Carmelite of Beaune:

I was so squeamish that the slightest uncleanliness would make me queasy. He [i.e., Jesus] reproved me so strongly about this, that one time, wishing to clean up the vomit of a sick person, I could not keep myself from doing it with my tongue, and I said to Jesus Christ: if I had a thousand bodies and a thousand lives, I would sacrifice them all in order to be your slave, O my Husband. I then discovered so much delight in this action, that I could have wished every day to meet with similar opportunities to learn to conquer myself, and have only God as my witness.[39]

Her biographer comments: "I shudder in recounting these pious excesses . . ." which Mme. Guyon also practiced. This woman engaged in extended discipline, wore studded belts, burned herself with candles, let molten wax drip all over her body, wrapped herself in nettles, extracted her own healthy teeth, walked with pebbles in her shoes, and ate filth. At one point she put her lips and tongue on a hideous lump of spit.[40] With such precedents as these, the "small" and "great reliefs" of eighteenth-century convulsive groups seem less surprising. These voluntary victims, for whom pain was the highway to salvation, struck their heads and stomachs with clubs, rocks, andirons, and heavy folio volumes. Certain individuals let themselves be nearly drawn and quartered, others had themselves crushed "by a machine that had been invented for this purpose." The exceptional apotheosis was crucifixion, sometimes with actual nails.[41] These bodily torments gave visionaries the right to prophesize, permitting them to announce the return of the Crucified Christ and the reinstatement of a purified church.

The less spectacular and more organized austerities that Rancé[42] established at La Trappe stirred up controversy. Rancé prescribed the curtailment of fish, eggs, spices, sugar, syrup, jellies, and vegetables of any flavor; increased hardness of cots; obligation of sleeping with the cowl; perpetual silence; prohibition of letters and visits; a ban on lighting fires before the hour of prime (that is, six in the morning, but the monks rose at three-thirty), and after compline. Cells were exclusively appointed for sleep; light was never to be brought into them. The statute for the sick henceforth barred any appeal to a doctor; the sick were not confined to their beds, but observed the rhythm of the community; they also slept with the cowl; they went to church to receive the final sacraments; no fire could be lit in the infirmary before prime. Another astonishing rule was the silence imposed even on the mourning of monks who had lost their mother or father: Even they "are dead to all the things of this world." It eventually became necessary to moderate some of the severe reformer's austerity measures. Nonetheless, and despite criticism, La Trappe attracted devotees—the community grew from ten to three hundred members between 1664 and 1700, the year of the death of "l'abbé Tempete"—and moreover, "the work of the abbé of Rancé has victoriously stood the test of time."[43] On the other hand, what has changed since the time of the order's foundation is the spirit of the mortifications.

Rancé's inexhaustible pen conveys the sharpest doctrine of pain as well as his own highly disturbing motivations. In his famous *Lettre sur le sujet des humiliations et autres pratiques de religion*,[44] the author constantly has before his eyes the angelic model, and the word "angel" frequently recurs in his writings. Thus one must "humiliate and . . . thwart the monks until they gain the mortification of the Crucified Christ, the sanctity of the Apostles, and the purity of the angels."[45] Monks, however, are always far from rectitude. They are "criminals." In this regard, the letter reaches a striking conclusion:

> *As for the monastic congregations, they are packs of criminals and public penitents, who, having failed in their fidelity toward God and having provoked Him through their disobedience, can only hope for His benevolence after having satisfied His justice through punishments fit for their sins.*[46]

Rancé proceeds to state that monks are "prodigal sons who abandoned the house of their fathers and squandered the goods they had received." Only "profound" humiliations and their "sincere self-degradation" can open "the gates of divine mercy" to them. Thus it is necessary that, "following the thinking of Saint Gregory, since they cannot peacefully acquire the heritage of the just by the sanctity of their lives, they must seize it through their sweat and their combat, God wishing that they force Him to pardon them, and they do violence to Him." Forever "criminal" man confronts God the Creditor who requires incessant "atonements": Such are the conjoined anthropology and theology that the reformer of La Trappe argues, with support from Saint John Climacus. One might ask whether there are righteous monks. Rancé unhesitatingly answers,

> *. . . a righteous man ceases to be considered as such at the moment when he becomes a monk . . . He loses his innocence by enclosing himself within the monastery, just as Jesus Christ in some way ceased to be holy the moment when he appeared in the world in the form and attire of a sinner; not only in the eyes of men, but also in the rigorous treatments he received from the hands of his Father.*

Once again, as with Bossuet, Bourdaloue, and Tronson, God the Judge no longer knows His own Son. Rancé concludes that "the cloister is a prison that makes for guilty men, both those who have preserved their innocence and those who have lost it." Citing Saint Bernard and Saint Gregory in turn, he asserts: "We seek refuge in cloisters only in order to beweep our own sins and those of other people." Hence the monks "continually keep their thoughts on death, their eyes lowered, their heads bent toward the ground, and they look upon themselves as criminals who are always prepared to appear before God's terrible judgment, to render Him the account of their sins . . ."

One might argue, however, that monasteries are "shelters and havens." The "hermits" who live there are "protected from the storms and troubles of the age." Their tranquility is never disturbed. They have nothing to suffer "from either the world or their brothers." "Nothing confronts them that could cause them the slightest pain."[47] How, therefore, to train them to the indispensable humiliations that they need in order to conquer the first of the deadly sins, pride? Rancé replies: "Their condition would be quite unhappy, if a superior did not have the exact remedy of procuring for them, through every means of mortification and humiliation that he deems the most useful and appropriate, that which God supplies to the people of the world [through the trials they undergo]."[48] This necessity of inventing occasions for humbling the monks is the primary theme of the *Lettre*: Rancé avers that "the intention of Saint Bernard was that monks would be trained through humiliations" and, the world no longer meaning anything to them, "it must needs be that their superiors give them the means, in consigning them to vile and humiliating occupations, or in disciplining them through humiliations and disgraces."[49]

Such a policy invited censure, from monastic as well as other milieus. The father-general of the Chartreux, Le Masson, was shocked that in 1689 one could assert "that people do not enter the monastery to live there, but to die there," and he refused to believe "that it might be necessary to undertake austerities by considering them as means to shorten life and lessen its health to the point where one loses it altogether."[50] Mabillon likewise protested Rancé's refusal to allow the monks intellectual endeavors under the pretext that "study destroys humility" and transforms houses of peace and seclusion into "tumultuous academies."[51] Henri Bremond is right in concluding that the excessive rigors of the abbé of La Trappe prevented his canonization. More generally, one becomes overwhelmed by perplexity and vertigo in looking at these examples of shocking mortifications extracted from the long annals of Christian sanctity. At this point there is a need for a moment of repose and calm reflection.

Georges Bataille wrote with despondency: "I hoped for the rending of heaven. I hoped for it, but heaven did not open itself."[52] Nostalgically, he cites this passage from Angelo Foligno's *Livre de la vie crucifiée de Jésus* (author died 1309; French trans. of 1604): "When God appears in darkness . . . all the kindnesses [he has shown me], so numerous and indescribable, and his gentleness, his gifts, words, and deeds, all of that is minuscule next to He whom I behold in the vast gloom."[53] There were some for whom the sky "did open itself": Foligno, Theresa of Avila, Saint John of the Cross, and so on. Having decided to "take the plunge," to "risk all for God," to avoid haggling with him, to "venture" their life, and to "depend only on His good pleasure,"[54] they attained mystical experience and could say with the poet of the *Cantique spirituel*: "Reveal your presence to me. For the vision of your beauty kills me."[55] Their itinerary inevitably passed through suffering, since "pain is the livery of lovers."[56] To immediately assign mystic experience with its inevitable hardships and terrible renunciations to a single category of pathological behavior would be to level out all human history, to imply that there are only plains, to deny the existence of the Himalayas.

Even at the more modest level of Mother Angelica and Rancé, is it reasonable to belittle in an overrationalist way their excess of self-denial? Rancé angered a good number of his contemporaries, but he also had his admirers: Bossuet, Saint-Simon, and so on, and his work has been lasting. In his *Port-Royal*, Saint-Beuve advises against any simplistic judgment of such behavior, however disconcerting it may be, which must be evaluated in the light of its results. "It is at the price of these particulars [mortifications such as those of Mother Angelica] . . . that the human soul attains . . . a certain fixed and invincible state, a truly heroic state whence it can then perform its greatest actions . . . One should not be too shocked by the peculiarity, whether repulsive or apparently futile, of these methods." To "break through" "the barrier between the world and God . . . any opening is good, as long as one penetrates through it."[57] The great historian of Saint John of the Cross, the agnostic Jean Baruzi, writes of his hero: "Despite limitations and poverty [of the philosophical kind], he overcame, beyond ordinary rules, his nervous defects"[58]; and Baruzi argues that "a forgetting and isolation from all worldly things," "a mortification of all tastes and appetites" allowed the saint to reach a "tranquility" and "consistent grace" that never left him.[59] The road toward the Crucified Christ passes through pain. "Whosoever seeks to enjoy divine love," proposes Suso, "will undergo much suffering."[60] Elsewhere Suso addresses Eternal Wisdom, or Jesus:

> *Suffering is an abjection for others, but for me it has immense dignity. Suffering quells my anger and gains my favor. Suffering makes mankind lovable to me, for he who suffers is like me . . . It makes a man of the earth a man of heaven. Suffering makes me no part of the world, and in exchange gives my faithful intimacy . . . he whom I receive in friendship must have completely renounced and abandoned the world.*[61]

The Christian ascetic suffers with Jesus, because of sins: his own and those of everyone else. This suffering, however, is provoked by love, and the ascetic goes beyond the pain. The Benedictine Rule enjoins the monk to conceive of his life as "a sharing of the sufferings" of Jesus.[62] Thus he will not prefer anything to the love of Christ. Against this rock, depression and temptation will shatter themselves. Saint John of the Cross affirms that "the pain or torments embraced for God are as precious pearls which, the larger their size, the higher their value and the more they inspire love, for both he who receives them and he who gives them."[63]

Loyola reveals that at Manresa "he was determined to perform great penance, not so much wishing to expiate his sins as to be acceptable to God and to please Him."[64] Saint Theresa of Avila's spiritual ascension began the day she saw an image that, she writes, "showed Christ covered with wounds in such an edifying way . . . that I was thoroughly disturbed by His suffering for us. My heart broke with remorse, in thinking of my ingratitude for these wounds. I fell down on my knees . . ."[65] This compassion for the Beloved explains all the incredible "kissing of lepers" of Christian history. A seventeenth-century biography of Margaret of the Holy Sacrament recounts that she "did not nor could not see anyone other than Jesus in the person of these poor folk, and in putting her mouth to their sores filled with ulcerous pus, she had the impression that these were the sacred wounds of Jesus Christ, and felt that her mouth was filled with His precious blood."[66] Certainly a doctrine of pain! All the same, it needs to be more carefully considered: At its root, there is mad love. Marguerite-Marie, who knew herself to be "insolvent"[67] vis-à-vis her divine lover, gives herself to Him in these terms: "To my beloved, I will forever be His servant, His slave, His creature, for He is everything to me. His unworthy spouse, sister Marguerite-Marie, dead to the world. All in God, and nothing in me. All to God, and nothing to me. All for God, and nothing for me."[68]

Another avenue of reflection on Christian ascetic exploits reveals that the most unusual excesses did not last entire lifetimes. They occur during phases, of varying lengths, of spiritual crisis. Afterward, though penitential exercises do not disappear, they take on a less inhuman character and also become more regular. At the same time, the saint returns to a more exterior mission. Suso had been fully devoting himself to mortifications for sixteen years, when a vision advised him to henceforth forsake the exercises by which "his entire being was ruined." God "showed him that this austerity and all these habits were but a good beginning and conversion of his untamed nature . . . He now had to push himself further, in another manner . . ."[69] Suso then threw all his instruments of torture into the Rhine. At

Manresa, Saint Ignatius inflicted the harshest penances on himself. Moreover, he made a vow of no longer eating meat. Finally, he often used his normal sleeping hours for dialogues with God. At the end of a year, however, he changed his outlook, concluded that it was better "to sleep during the time appointed for sleep," and decided to eat meat again and "to abandon the excessive measures that he had previously taken."[70]

Dom Martène, the disciple, friend, and biographer of Dom Martin (the son of Mary of the Incarnation), recorded the "fearful penitence" that his master inflicted on himself to stop the temptations of the flesh. He does also confirm that victory was finally achieved. Thenceforth the inhuman mortifications were no longer necessary. Dom Martène gives this fact as a more or less general rule. "After the Wisdom has held a faithful soul in chains and in servitude and . . . made it undergo certain necessary works, the soul is set free and . . . is only held by His eternal embraces, which in truth is a sort of extremely strong chain, but which one wears with a pleasure that surpasses all manner of speech."[71] Mme. Guyon explains in her turn that the passage through voluntary tortures should last only for a time, because "an excessive attachment to mortifications impedes the spirit and one's own will." The individual who is dead from the death of the senses and of personal will "no longer needs mortifications, but all that is in the past."[72]

Finally, the third element of this dossier: Spiritual masters continually warned against the abuse of mortifications. Suso, first and foremost, refused to be imitated and condemned the exaggeration of asceticism. He told nuns that their self-inflicted tortures were useless and dangerous.[73] Saint Theresa of Avila, addressing the mother superiors of convents she had founded, tells them:

> *What I have to say is very important, especially in regard to mortification. For the superiors will pay close attention to this matter, for the love of Our Lord. One cannot be too careful in this, nor work too hard to discern the nuns' diverse capacities. If the superiors are not extremely circumspect, they will, instead of being useful to their religious women, do great harm to them and throw them into much anxiety.*[74]

To the penitent devoting himself to "spiritual exercises," Loyola recommends the following dietary regime: "Become used to plain dishes," eat only delicate repasts "in small quantity," maintain in eating and drinking the "middle level . . . which is appropriate" to everyone. If the individual perceives that his abstinences deprive "him of the necessary physical strength and disposition for spiritual exercises, he will easily judge what is more proper to his bodily subsistence."[75] In a work addressed to nuns, Saint Alphonsus Liguori does recommend mortifications, but at the same time a measured practice of them: "Saint Basil," he writes, "also exhorted every monk to content himself as much as possible with ordinary and common things. That is a thousand times worthier than oppressing oneself with fasts, disciplines, hairshirts, and a conspicuously severe diet. The exceptions have actually been a point of departure for the laxity of many religious Orders."[76]

In a consistent and categorical way, the founders of orders always required monks and nuns to put obedience before bodily mortification. The Benedictine Rule demands—this is the eighth degree of humility—that a monk do nothing except "that which is prescribed by the common rule of the monastery or counseled by the examples of the elders."[77] Saint Theresa cites the case of a virtuous Bernardine who "was weakened by fasts and disciplines to such a degree that at each communion, and each time that her piety excited her, she fell to the ground and stayed there for eight or nine hours." The nun's confessor had reported this to Theresa, who diagnosed false rapture and advised "that he prohibit the nun from fasts, disciplines, and to divert her to other pursuits. The nun was obedient, and she submitted. When she had regained her strength, there was no longer any question of such raptures . . ."[78] An applicant to the Visitandines, Saint Marguerite-Marie, in her thirst to suffer for Jesus, resolved one day "to extend an austerity that had been allowed her farther than exact obedience would permit." Saint Francis de Sales appeared to her and severely scolded her: "What! Do you think," he told her, "you please God in going beyond the limits of obedience? The latter is the guiding principle of this congregation, and not austerities."[79] Some time later Jesus would tell her: "You will suspect all that hinders you from the exact practice of your rule; I desire that you prefer it to all the rest."[80]

These warnings resume the distinction proposed at the beginning of this work between "contempt for the world" and "removal from the world": One can retire from the world without throwing a curse on creation and, likewise, practice ascesis without destroying oneself. It is only too true, however, that over the course of Christian history these two lapses did in fact occur. It is also true, for example with Rancé, that the negation of the created world sometimes overtook impassioned love. It is especially true that religious pedagogy gave the exceptional as the model, the inimitable as example, and constantly emphasized such unlikely destines that these examples ended up causing depression or aversion among the faithful. Where to locate the transition between overpraised austerity and a normal life? The call continually addressed to nuns and monks to live with "downcast eyes" has become difficult to understand, when it leads to a contempt for beauty and creation. For even the smiling Monsieur Vincent requested the Sisters of Charity "not to look at beautiful things when curiosity compelled them to" and to mortify . . . their ears "which delight in listening to songs, music, the praises given to you, the singing of birds. The ears take joy in these things; but you must mortify yourselves and flee them, instead of seeking them out."[81]

Finally, the drama of atonement brought about so much ecclesiastical ink-spilling that it occasionally led to unbearable quantifications. Only fifty years ago, for example, in Switzerland, certain nuns read to children, during the procession of the cross, the list taken here from "the revelations" given by Jesus to the Saints Elisabeth, Bridget, and Metchilda, "who desired to know the number of blows He had received in His Passion":

> *Think, my sisters, that I shed 62,200 tears for you, and in the Garden of Olives 97,307 drops of blood. I received 1,667 blows on my sacred body:*
> *On my neck, 107.*
> *On my back, 380.*
> *On my chest, 43.*
> *On my head, 85.*
> *On my sides, 38.*
> *On my shoulders, 62.*
> *On my arms, 40.*
> *On my thighs and legs, 32.*
> *They struck me on the mouth 30 times.*
> *On my precious face they spat 32 rude and vile spits.*
> *They kicked me, as though I were a rebel, 370 times.*
> *They pushed and knocked me to the ground 13 times.*
> *They pulled me by the hair 30 times.*
> *They grabbed and pulled me by the beard 38 times.*
> *Thus your hearts may be inflamed.*

Their crowning me with thorns put 303 gashes in my head.
I groaned and sighed, for your salvation and conversion, 900 times.
Of torments apt to kill me, I suffered 162.
Of extreme agonies, as if I were dead, 19 times.
From the Praetorium to Calvary, carrying my cross, I took 320 steps.
For all that, I did not receive a single act of charity except from Saint Veronica, who wiped my face with a napkin, on which my features were and are imprinted by my precious blood . . .[82]

THE DISEASE OF SCRUPLE

The doctrine of pain often went hand in hand with exhaustive interrogations. When they gave themselves to the harshest excesses of penitence, Christian ascetics were tormented by a disease of scruple, a conviction that they were condemned, and by a temptation to despair. "He [Suso] was told that his acceptance into the Order [of Dominicans] had been procured through a material donation; in other words, through the sin of simony." For ten years Suso was tortured by this scruple and "could only see himself as one of the damned." He told himself: "No matter what you do, you are lost."[83] Finally, he confided in Meister Eckhart, "who delivered him from suffering." Saint Ignatius of Loyola also described the crisis of scruple he underwent at Manresa: His analysis of his own psychological conditions during this time is a model of shrewd observation, and worthy of a medical dossier:

But he [Loyola] began to have many difficulties about this [confession and communion] from scruples, for even though the general confession he had made at Montserrat had been made with enough care and had been completely written, as has been said, still at times it seemed to him that he had not confessed certain things. This caused him much distress, because although he confessed it, he was not satisfied. Thus he began to look for some spiritual men who could cure him of these scruples, but nothing helped him. At last a very spiritual man, a doctor of the cathedral who preached there, told him one day in confession to write down everything he could remember. He did so, but after confession the scruples still returned and each time in more detail so that he was very troubled. Although he realized that those scruples did him much harm and that it would be wise to be rid of them, he could not do that himself.[84]

The confessor then ordered him to only confess those past faults that seemed "absolutely clear." Ignatius, however, saw "all of them as most clear," and he remained "in perpetual pain." Thus he fell into complete crisis: He devoted seven hours a day to prayer on his knees, shouted to God "for help," considered throwing himself into a large hole near his praying area, and mortified himself in every possible way. Nothing worked. Recalling his sins and "treating them like objects that one arranges one after the other," he went "from the thought of one past sin to another" and believed it necessary to confess them yet again. Finally, with God's help, clarity filled his spirit, and he resolved "not to confess anything from the past anymore; from that day forward he remained free of those scruples."[85]

Loyola's crisis only lasted a few months, but Surin's dragged on for twenty years. Likewise, Marguerite of the Holy Sacrament seems to have repeated her childhood sins (?) throughout her adult life. At the age of three, she lied to excuse a servant's transgression. She held such remorse for this act that, after she had taken orders, she accused herself more than a hundred times, performing rigorous penance to expiate the crime. Her confessor reassured her, saying "My sister, you well know that children do not sin before the time they attain reason." To which she responded, "I know it well, but that only reveals my fundamental malice."[86] As for Saint Marguerite-Marie who even at the end of her life thought herself a "monster," she began her religious life being seized by deadly anxiety before each communion. Her eighteenth-century biographer records that

> *many times her examination of conscience was so rigorous that it threw her into agitation and fear, so much did she dread bringing the slightest stain to holy communion . . . She saw few or no sins to accuse herself of, and she believed that it was her own blindness and insensitivity that hid these sins from her. In this imagined blindness, she condemned all the sins that she could not see in herself, of which she thought she was guilty.*[87]

In our Western civilization, this spiritual malady touched not only exceptional characters. It was a relatively widespread and identifiable phenomenon, a field of study for scholars of melancholy.[88]

Emmanuel Mounier rightly notes that "this syndrome of scruple has historical boundaries. It was unknown in the Eastern church. Even in the Latin West, it does not receive any mention until the moral theologians of the later Middle Ages."[89] In fact, the Eastern church made no distinction between venial and Deadly Sin, and it never obliged its adherents to the detailed confession of their offenses. Thus it did not press on to the inexhaustible analysis of cases of conscience.[90] Conversely, the latter—while spurring an extraordinary development of introspection—flourished in the Latin church with the annual and mandatory confession of specific, comprehensively organized sins.

In Aquinas's era, the phenomenon had yet to assume its subsequent scale. The great doctor only discussed "conscience as a philosopher, asking whether or not it was a "force." He did not study scruple. Soon, however, there proliferated the "Summae" of cases of conscience and confessors' manuals,[91] since it was necessary to enlighten both priests and their congregations. By the fifteenth century, a scrupulous religious anxiety had already become a phenomenon of European civilization, at least at a certain social and cultural level. It reached its fullest dimension during the sixteenth to eighteenth centuries, but since then has ebbed, if only gradually. It has been estimated that from 1564 to 1663, six hundred Catholic authors—French, Italian, Spanish, Flemish, and so on—composed casuistic treatises.[92]

Certainly a primary function of these works was to guide confessors through the dense jungle of actual situations and thus to provide solutions to their interrogations of the faithful. Casuistry is inseparable from the history of conscientious scruple. The latter, however, goes beyond even the wide field of annotated catalogues of cases of conscience. For the preoccupation with scruple gains clearer focus in the specialized tracts that aimed to soothe troubled souls. Their full inventory would be lengthy indeed. Near the source one would find the *Consolatio theologiae* by the Dominican Jean von Dambach (fourteenth century), and above all the writings of Gerson: *Instructio contra scrupulosam conscientiam; Tractatus de remediis contra pusillanimitatem, scrupulositatem . . . ; Tractatus pro devotis simplicibus qualiter se in suis exercitiis discrete et caute habere debent,*[93] and so on. Downstream, there appear the *Lettres spirituelles sur la paix interieure* (1766) by the Capuchin Ambroise de Lombez.[94] Standing out between these landmarks are a number of works with revealing titles: the *Directeur pacifique des consciences . . .* by the Capuchin Jean-Francois de Reims (complete ed., 1634), the *Directeur des consciences scrupuleuses . . .*[95] by the Franciscan Colomban Gillotte (1st ed., 1697), the *Traité des scrupules* by the moderate Jansenist

Jacques Joseph Du Guet (1st ed., 1717), and so on. These works often met with a success that proves a popular demand: The bulky *Directeur pacifique des consciences* . . . (974 octavo pages) was already in its sixth edition by 1666. Gillotte's treatise was republished six times between 1698 and 1753.

Casuistic works and dissertations on scruple do not by any means exhaust the analysis of this subject, which is also present in numerous spiritual writings of the period. Among these, one can cite offhand a sermon by Suso,[96] "notes for assisting one to sense and judge scruples," inserted in the Spiritual Exercises,[97] Saint Francis de Sales's *Traite de l'amour de Dieu*,[98] diverse "lettres de direction" by Fenelon,[99] and Saint Alphonsus Liguori's *La Sainte religieuse*,[100] and so on. The above signposts demarcate the international space in which the Western "rack of conscience"[101] was constructed. Within this space, both historians and clinicians may make an almost laboratory investigation of the disease of scruple, which moralists carefully distinguish as a "holy anxiety,"[102] a "healthy fear of God" characteristic of "delicate" consciences.

"Anxiety, timidity, the doubts that make the soul uncertain about everything"[103] often develop in predisposed ground, that is, in obsessive or psychotic personalities. The first, who act in conflict with their pregenital impulses, tend toward meticulousness, to excessive cleanliness, to perfectionism, to obstinacy, thrift, and a fastidious observation of obligations.[104] The second group suffer from a feeling of imperfection, from numerous doubts, morbid reflections, introspective obsession, depressive tendencies, and thus they slide toward inhibition and impotence. The loss of love of one's self and the meditation on death lead them toward a melancholy that Freud compares to "mourning."[105] These dispositions belong to all periods of history. Certain cultural inducements, however, can accentuate their primary tendencies and, moreover, engender a disease of scruple among people who would not normally be so inclined.

From the fifteenth to the end of the eighteenth century, to keep the survey within limits, the ecclesiastical discourse on scruple maintains a striking homogeneity. More often than not the writers on this subject explicitly or implicitly refer to two great pioneers: Gerson and San Antonino di Firenze. The first, as has been noted, frequently addresses the question of scruple. The second, in his famous *Summa*, devotes a chapter of the word "scruple," originally an exact term, a diminutive of the Latin *scrupus* (pebble). Scruple, whether "a small rock" or one of "heavy weight," has become the "little ennui" that injures the soul.[106] San Antonino, who successively studies "good," "bad," and "scrupulous" consciences—observe the road taken since Saint Thomas Aquinas—defines scruple as "a doubt accompanied by a groundless fear which, arising from weak and uncertain conjectures, afflicts the spirit and makes it apprehend sin where none exists."[107] Gillotte specifies that all scruple is doubt, but that not all doubt is scruple, for one may have doubts that are well founded. In contrast, "the scrupulous conscience doubts without reason."[108] For San Antonino, "the disgust and sorrow" that besiege the soul to the point of paralysis are serious enough to be compared "to the storm which, raging in Egypt, destroyed every green and living thing in its path." Similarly, "the sadness caused by scruple destroys the strength and vitality of the soul."[109] For it is the nature of souls in good health "not to see sin where there is none."[110]

Read through ecclesiastical analysis, this scrupulous behavior of former times presents several predominant traits. First and foremost there emerges the importance of "filthy imaginations," since many pious souls were obsessed with sexual temptations. Gillotte is explicit in this regard: "As scruples that arise from wicked thoughts are the most frequent, and outnumber those that beset the spirit; spiritual authors go to great lengths to teach the remedies that must be employed to chase away such thoughts."[111] In Article 18 of his *Traité* . . . , Du Guet likewise specifies: "I have only one more category of scruples to examine, but it is more abundant than any other; its object is chastity."[112] It was especially in this domain that anxious souls tended to identify temptation with sin.

A second type of scruple, not exclusive of the preceding one, springs from the temptation to blasphemy. A number of converging paths lead to this dramatic situation that Du Guet prefers not to describe, since "it would be dangerous to frighten others' imaginations with a picture that might leave scars from its very images of horror."[113] A "saddened piety," a certain "disgust" with religion, the fear of divine punishment, "anguished thoughts . . . which cause one to doubt if one has faith"[114] induce a "spiritual melancholy, a troubling of the soul, a certain self-humiliation and despair."[115] Hence are stirred gusts of rebellion against an over-demanding God; these can become particularly violent and dangerous at the time of death.[116] This point connects to the second temptation described in the *Artes moriendi*[117] and thus to a classic theme of religious teaching. Father Gillotte writes in his *Directeur des consciences scrupuleuses* that these "temptations to blasphemy, that the devil sometimes makes dying Christians undergo, most often attack the scrupulous soul in the hour of our death." Quite logically, he incorporates long passages from the *Art de bien mourir* (1622), translated from the Spanish original of John of Jesus Mary, which discuss "the way to resist temptations to despair" at the approach of one's death.[118]

Another predeliction of numerous scrupulous souls was to confuse venial and Deadly Sin, despite the wise counsels given by Gerson on this matter in the early fifteenth century.[119] In Gerson's spirit, the Capuchin Jean-François de Reims edited his *Directeur pacifique des consciences* with the aim of helping devout people to "distinguish deadly from venial sin."[120] As for Du Guet, he reproaches certain scrupulous types for not knowing how "to distinguish that which they should correct from that which they are constrained to suffer; that which strains them, from that which is left to make them humble and keep them on guard."[121] Extending his analysis, he also indicts the tendency "to consider rather petty offenses almost as more important ones, so that one becomes persuaded that God will consistently inflict this horrible punishment on any manner of sin."[122]

Often both an accretion and a result of the above perplexities, one common habit of scrupulous personalities was to increase confession, sometimes even general confessions:[123] a spiritualized version of the washing mania described by psychiatrists.[124] Thoroughgoing examinations of conscience with compilations of lists of sins, the search for ever stronger contrition, incessant returns to the confessional, indeed a pilgrimage "from tribunal to tribunal" (of penitence): These habits were cited time and again in works seeking to "help" and "pacify" these disturbed souls, often "intolerable"[125] to others and especially their own confessors. Gillotte thus defines the typology of the person who can never be satisfied with his or her confessions:

> *When he thinks that the greater part of the confessions he has made are null, void, and sacrilegious, his pain and scruples grow still further that he perceives, by a false conviction, that his necessary remedy makes him more diseased than ever; and that which is prescribed for the elimination of sins is the cause for their increasing number. This occurs almost always; he spends not only the satisfactory amount of time, but a needlessly long period to examine his sins, which he writes down in extraordinary detail, in order to move himself with grace to a true and sincere sorrow for having committed them: nonetheless, once he has performed full confes-*

sion, not only does he read over the paper on which his sins were transcribed, but he undertakes a second examination of conscience, longer than the first, to decide if he has not forgotten anything, or if he has made every circumstance crystal clear; and since he acts so strictly, he imagines that he does not have the necessary contrition, because his contrition was not perceptible.[126]

A related behavior applies to the pious exercises that one repeats because one believes to have said them poorly. Due to her lack of attention, a nun is uncertain that she has properly recited the office. Hence she repeats the same words and the same verses without obtaining a better result. Another priest likewise recommences the reading of his breviary. This attraction for repetition, a classic syndrome in obsessional neuroses, is mentioned by several casuists[127] and well described by Du Guet:

The one cannot recite his breviary without being alarmed by the fear of distractions; and through this very fear he brings them on; he desperately wants to be attentive to everything . . . He repeats that which he thinks he has poorly said, and says it even worse in repeating it, and thus he turns an occupation that should console him into a torture which robs him of time, freedom, and peace.[128]

This mania for verification that lies at the base of both perfectionism and guilt[129] causes the anxiety-ridden priest to tremble at the moment of the consecration of the Host, "not in awe," notes Du Guet, "of the holy mysteries, but in fear of not quite distinctly or effectively pronouncing the words of the Savior." Moreover, once communion has been performed, he is left confounded and motionless, since he dreads that "some imperceptible particle [of the Host] may have escaped his hands and eyes."[130] The disease of scruple thus leads to a paralysis of activity, or to ritual procedures that serve as security blankets.

The spiritual directors of the West commonly perceived three types of "squalls and whirlpools of scruples" that assail the soul. The first come from God—Tauler's "God the Hunter"—who wishes to test His worthier subjects (all the same, San Antonino is silent on this point). The second are inspired by the devil who, with divine permission, "assaults man's spirit with dangerous scruples with the aim of disgusting him and turning him from the path of virtue:"[131] This is a spiritualized version of the trials of Job. Finally, the third derive from purely human causes. On this matter, every specialist in confession since Gerson and San Antonino evokes the "natural complexion"[132] of people who are of a "cold and melancholic" temper and therefore predisposed to fear and doubt.[133] Still, "the bad disposition of the brain occurs especially in its foremost part, which is the seat of the imagination and also the cause of scruples: For it is from the imagination that understanding receives its impression of sensible things. Thus it often happens that the spirit judges things badly, through the false impression of an imaginary evil that it receives from this force."[134] The doctors of souls also know that the pusillanimity and fears of the scrupulous can arise from an excess "of fasts, tears, vigils, disciplines, prayers, meditations, delusions involving subtle questions or divine things, and excessive thinking of the terrors of death, of the last judgment, of hell and other similar subjects": Thus spoke Gerson.[135]

This diagnosis engages an entire cultural environment. The casuists also did not refrain from incriminating certain directors of conscience, who provoked the disease of scruple. Jean von Dambach humorously explains that "if a scrupulous man were to confess himself exactly according to what he had written in his confession, he would need to have a confessor in his pocket."[136] The *Confessionale* (1518) of the Dutch humanist Rosemondt claims that certain zealous but ignorant confessors "impose a yoke and great burdens, which sinners cannot bear on their shoulders."[137] The Franciscan Benedicti still more sharply attacks "underexperienced or overscrupulous confessors who aspire, says a Spanish doctor (Bart. Medina, *De Poenitentia*, Book I, ch. 12) to hold the souls of penitents between their fingers like slaves, and especially poor and miserable women."[138] The Capuchin Jean-François de Reims also criticizes "certain directors who guide souls with too much fear, giving them scruples about nearly everything, in such a way that they cannot attempt to do anything except with fear."[139] In his turn, Du Guet believes it his duty "to warn that one can sometimes cast into temptation people of sincere piety but also vivid imagination, in exhorting them to see into their hearts, and to ask themselves if they would be in any state to overcome all the obstacles to their salvation."[140]

Along the same conceptual lines, Gillotte advises the scrupulous against reading works "that treat of predestination and grace, and those that, under the specious pretext of reforming the abuses of a lax doctrine that one should avoid [an allusion to the Jansenists and other contemporary rigorists], go to the opposite extreme, holding to excessively severe and exaggerated morals, and are entirely contrary to the spirit of Jesus Christ, which is a spirit of kindness and mercy."[141] More generally, spiritual directors of the early modern era observe that the disease of scruple is contagious. Already San Antonino had said, "One scrupulous person makes another."[142] Jean-François de Reims also asserts that "scruples can arrive from keeping company with scrupulous people,"[143] and Gillotte stresses this point, noting that scruples "are also caused by a bad habit: for example, when one too often associates with scrupulous people whom one esteems, [for] . . . one becomes scrupulous with the scrupulous, just as one becomes wicked with the wicked."[144] There is no better way to underline the collective aspect of this obsessional neurosis.

An entire literature strove to advise and reassure troubled souls, by pointing them to the best remedies against the paralysis of scruple: Avoid excessive mortifications, use medicine to treat melancholic disorders and sickened imaginations, know how to tell a Deadly from a venial sin and the temptation to consent, do not relive the past, do not resume confessions made with a sincere heart, do not repeat prayers made amid distractions ("our weakness is so great that we can hardly ever say a *Pater noster* without distraction,"[145] do not have a proud notion of one's self and know how to look on one's imperfections without anxiety,[146] confide in God directly and openly, obediently take the reasonable advice of a well-chosen director of conscience (this important person then being the necessary counterpart to the disease of scruple), and so on. Although rigorist, the fourteenth-century *Supplementum* to the *Summa pisanella* cautions against accusing oneself of sins one has not committed and to not take literally the too-famous formula of Gregory the Great: "[the pious man] recognizes his own guilt even when he is not guilty."[147]

All the same, the very mass of works that sought to be reassuring proves that the anxiety continued. For the religious language of the time was self-contradictory, and simultaneously blew hot and cold. It advised "loving and serving God not with a view to paradise and hell, but simply and purely because He Himself deserves to be loved and served";[148] yet how many sermons laid stress on Hell! The discourse advised against being upset by "dirty imaginings"; but the examinations of conscience proposed to the faithful, for instance in Saint John Eudes's *Le Bon Confesseur*, were able to bring about all manner of scruples regarding sexuality.[149] People were taught to "distinguish deadly from venial sin"; but contemporary preaching underlined the gravity of venial offenses, and the letters of spirituality urged the most devout souls to see themselves as sinks of iniquity. Jean-Jacques Olier, for example, exhorted the Bride of Christ "to see her inner self as excommunicated, worthy to be chased from the society and company of the saints . . . , in such sight unable to be sufficiently scorned, rebuked, and persecuted, so much is she worthy of not only contempt, oblivion, and being forsaken, but also of horror, condemnation, anathema, and execration, in herself deserving naught but hell."[150]

There was an effort to give a reassuring image of God; but there was an emphasis, even in ostensibly consoling works, on His more troubling side. Gillotte writes that

> *it often happens that God is the author of scruples, when, according to the wise decrees of His providence, it pleases Him not only to abandon a soul in pain, but also to Himself produce such deep-seated fears and anxieties that one suffers a sinful fall into the disgrace of God; thus this soul is left in a darkness where it has exceptional trouble in discerning the paths on which it moves, and what it must do or avoid for its salvation.*[151]

Here is God the persecutor.[152]

Likewise, the spiritual directors also warned avoiding "thoughts of predestination";[153] but they continued to teach that "the number of the condemned is much greater than that of the elect," because "few people observe God's commandments."[154] For Du Guet, the doctrine according to which "there is a certain measure of grace, after which God gives no more" leads to scruples in "timid or imperfectly instructed souls."[155] This doctrine, however, was taught at Saint-Sulpice.[156] Finally, there can be no denying that the rigorist warnings sent out by Antoine Arnauld and his spiritual cousins had a considerable impact on the most fervent Christians. Deferred absolutions[157] and the trembling before the Eucharist could only have engendered sorrowful scruples. Drawing support from Saint Francis de Sales, Arnauld's *De la Frequente communion* grants that those who have only venial sins may receive the Host every Sunday,

> *but with two extremely important conditions. One, before approaching this sacred altar, that [they] purify themselves of even their slightest offenses by prayers and tears. The other (which is of the highest importance for the conduct of souls . . .), that they did not willfully commit these venial sins. For there is a great difference, as M. de Geneve excellently teaches in his* Philothée, *between venial sins and the fondness for venial sins . . . This fondness is in direct opposition to devotion, and makes the soul extremely ill, though it does not kill it.*[158]

In the same spirit, how many sermons and catechisms presented the Eucharist as "the most dreadful and terrible"[159] of the sacraments!

At another level, the spiritual authors generally agree that women are more subject than men to the disease of scruple. San Antonino especially asserts that the pusillanimity of the soul, when it proceeds from a "frigid complexion," is highly frequent "among old and melancholic women."[160] His successors consistently repeated this statement, while their misogyny definitely underestimated masculine anguish. On the other hand, there was some debate and uncertainty regarding the social level of people troubled by scruple. Gerson had written his treatise against "indiscreet" mortifications for the sake of "simple folk," who were insufficiently educated to be able to distinguish the reasonable from the excessive.[161] Father Gillotte, however, explains "that excellent as well as feeble minds, the wise as well as the ignorant may become scrupulous." The general public, he adds, believes that only the simple and ignorant suffer from scruples, but this belief runs "contrary to reason, to everyday experience, and to the doctrine of the most famous spiritual authors."[162] The Franciscan here cites the best-known scrupulous individuals: Saint

Bonaventure, Saint Catherine of Genoa, Saint Mary Magdalene de Pazzi, Saint Angelo Foligno, Henry Suso, Saint Ignatius Loyola, the Fathers Balthazar Alvarez and Zanchez d'Avila (both confessors of the Great Theresa), Mother Chantal, Surin, Father John of Jesus Mary, the Father General of the Carmelites, and so on.

The author of the *Directeur des consciences scrupuleuses* was certainly right. In fact, spiritual writers sought above all to reassure relatively well-educated religious people. As a counterproof, it may be observed that the sermons for large audiences did not dwell much on scruple. Saint John Eudes's *Le Bon Confesseur* (1642), a classic work for use by Catholic missionaries, does not speak a word on this subject.[163] During the Age of Reason, the disease of scruple thus seems to have especially touched groups most involved with the Counter-Reformation, in other words the most pious and educated members of society; at the same time, it is true that within these limits the phenomenon grew to large proportions, enough to worry and irritate confessors. In his *Dictionnaire des cas de conscience*, Ponthas writes that scruple is "a disease of the soul occurring in the most tiresome of people, to whom one is never able to sufficiently attend, as I have realized through fifty-six years of experience."[164]

THE DIFFICULTY OF DEATH

The above material leads toward a wider and more telling conclusion. Today we have a tendency to stress how the church used to coerce people's consciences. We perceive better than our forebears the links between power and doctrine, how the latter props up the former. Just as the discourse of suffering tended to make the poor obediently accept the "miseries of this life,"[165] so too did a terroristic language effectively reinforce the authority of the governing ecclesiastical body. It would be impossible to deny this "shepherding of fear," an enormous historical trend that the following chapters will stress. It would be a mistake, however, to perceive only the "utilitarian" aspects of this pastorate and to believe that it was no more than a means of governing Christian society. The reality of the situation was richer and more complex, and even invites a reversal of perspective: Spiritual fear most deeply afflicted the Christian elites themselves. The "thoughtful" fears emphasized by the previous volume thus resurface, again more painful and more lasting than the "spontaneous" fears[166] felt at moments of sudden danger. Spiritual fears sometimes lasted a lifetime.

Not surprisingly, these fears primarily and most strongly affected people of the church. Priests (but nuns as well) were more conscious of guilt than laypeople. Their constantly invoked and exalted "supereminent dignity" had its counterpart in the continual encouragement of a guilty conscience. A single proof, which nevertheless applies to a span of centuries as well as the entire Catholic world, emerges from Tronson's words to the seminarians of Saint-Sulpice. Offering them a meditation on "the circumstances that make the sins of priests and churchpeople more monstrous and terrible,"[167] he develops three main points:

1. ". . . Of all sins, there is none so monstrous as that of a priest . . . It is the most hideous of all monsters, the most abominable ruin that could be." Because "the priest has received more of God's graces, he is also more obliged to thankfulness." Our Lord has confided in him to the point of revealing His secrets. "What more horrible treason than . . . of putting him to death, by consenting to sin!" The priest, having "more understanding and enlightenment, cannot claim that he sins through ignorance; likewise, having more grace, he cannot claim that

he sins through weakness; thus his sins . . . can only come from pure malice." "The sin of a priest is highly contagious in the Church, and is capable of losing an infinite number of souls." Moreover, what regard can one have for the mysteries of God, when "he who should have a constant care for them gives himself to sin so freely"?

2. "A priest must have a profound fear of sin," for when he falls, "it is extraordinarily difficult for him to get back up; that is most rare indeed." The reason: He falls from too great a height.
3. "The third consideration that should make us [we priests] tremble at the very thought of sin is God's completely devastating fury against the sins of priests and the dreadful punishments by which He punishes them."

Thus resounds a language of fear, addressed not to the masses but to the elite of Christian elites, in the context of priests who shared authentic spiritual terror. How could such meditations possibly fail to engender a disease of scruple among men and women of the church? Saints felt the fear of damnation far more sharply than did the common people. Even Francis de Sales experienced this fear, at the beginning of his spiritual journey. Bossuet recalls that "in the fears which had gripped him, black melancholy and convulsions . . . made him lose sleep and appetite, and pushed him so near death that nobody saw any cure for his sickness . . ."[168] Cardinal Bond (d. 1674), the former general of the Feuillants and an ascetic, wrote in his *Principes de la vie chrétienne*: "If I remember . . . the actions of my past life and examine them closely, I am horrified by having so often offended God's law . . . For if I turn my thoughts toward the future, I apprehend His judgment, and being assured neither of pardon for my sins nor of my salvation, my body shakes all over."[169]

Hence the difficulty of death, even for ascetics: "Until the middle of the thirteenth century," writes André Vauchez, "the last moments of God's servants does not seem to have drawn any special attention. At most, people note that after their decease their bodies are well preserved and emit a pleasant odor . . . After 1300, in contrast, people start thinking that the quality of a life is judged by the manner of one's death."[170] This fine death, however, is not necessarily peaceful. In his sermon "On the chosen few," Massillon evokes the frequent anguish of Christian heroes at their oncoming death:

> *O God Almighty! how little do we on earth know of the terrors of Your Law! The righteous of all centuries have withered with fear, contemplating the severity and depth of Your judgments on the destiny of men: solitary saints have been seen, after an entire life of penitence . . . to enter their deathbeds in such terror that they could not be calmed down; they made their poor bare cots shake with them in their fear, and they would ceaselessly ask their brothers, in a voice of death: "Do you think the Lord will have mercy on me?" They would have been ready to fall into despair had not Your presence, O Lord! quelled the storm and ordered the winds and sea to abate their rages.*[171]

Two concurrent readings of such a text are both possible and desirable. The first perceives a terroristic pastoral message, aimed at jolting dormant Christians. The second, however, detects a statement and confession: The fear of damnation does not always spare the most pious of Christians arriving at the portal of death. It is true that numerous testimonies run contrary to this assertion. Saint Theresa of Avila and many female nuns of the sixteenth to eighteenth centuries died in "bliss"[172]: They made haste to join their Beloved. Mary of the Incarnation, "toward the final days of her life, seemed to be in sweet ecstasies, joy on her brow, her gaze modestly lowered or fixed on the crucifix she kept holding; she spoke little, but always with reassuring grace."[173] Recent studies have been made of the last moments of several French Visitandines of the seventeenth and eighteenth centuries. One, from Autun, "trembled with joy the more that her illness increased. She received the good news that her yearned-for hour was approaching . . ."[174] The final words of another Visitandine, of Bourges, were the following: "The horrors of death and the grave, which once gave me so much pain, now give me joy. To me it is a pleasure to think that I will perish and that through my death I will pay homage to the immutable being of God."[175] A third member of the same order, from Auxerre, responded to the news of her imminent death by saying "O such good news, soon I will see my Lord, I will enjoy that which I have desired for so long."[176] Such death frequently occur in the numerous biographies of holy figures from the Age of Reason. The Oratorian Jean Hanant, with an evident concern for apologetics, evokes numerous serene, indeed desired, deaths of pious sixteenth- to eighteenth-century Christians.[177]

These accounts, however, mask others that make it clear that the final days of deeply Christian men and women were often tragic and were resolved for the better only at the very end of a lengthy struggle to gain confident serenity. Writing of today's Catholic experience, Paul Milliez, while noting that "I have seen priests and nuns, especially young ones, meeting death piously and joyfully," also observes: "I was always struck by the death of certain priests. Sometimes they died unhappily. They believed too much in hell or the void . . ."[178] To return to the seventeenth century, Rancé's best biographer Gervaise quite briefly writes of his hero: "After this sad moment, the holy man had no more good days, he wasted away before our eyes, he could only languish; a dark and sorrowful melancholy gradually diminished him, and finally led him, some months later, to the tomb."[179] In his last weeks, Bossuet was assaulted with anxiety. His secretary, Le Dieu (!), notes in April 1704: "[His] senses are keen and filled with the fear of God's judgments; he confesses to this."[180] After the great bishop's death, his grand-vicar also discusses the former's final illness: "I sometimes said to him that I was astonished that he wished to consult me, he whom God had given such great and vivid enlightenment. 'Do not believe that,' he would say; 'God only gives a man such light for the sake of others, often leaving him in darkness regarding his own conduct.' "[181]

It is not timely here to emphasize the extraordinary fear of death that Mme. de Sablé exhibited her entire life, during the second half of which she became a devout Jansenist as well as a gourmand. Tallemant des Reaux has left a malicious version of her story.[182] On the other hand, it is more edifying to discover, in a biography of Saint Jeanne de Chantal, that toward the end of her life she went through physical suffering and anguish over the afterlife. "God treated her," one reads in a work by Maupas du Tour,

> *as he treats all great souls of truly heavenly character, whose long suffering he recompenses with new torments [God the Persecutor still], in order to make their fidelity more refined, their services more glorious, and their pain more worthy of crowns . . . He even hid Himself from her mind's eye for the rest of her life, leaving her in such horrible and excruciating agony and desolation over His absence [here one thinks of Saint Therese de Lisieux] that she often said that as she had seen her inner self, she had died in the line of duty.*[183]

During her final illness she maintained perfect self-control. "When she regained some strength, we would see her smiling face, saying what she could to console . . . the sisters gathered around her,"[184] but telling her confessor, "Ah, my father, how terrifying are God's judgments!—Do they cause you pain? he responded. — No, but I assure you they are quite terrifying."[185]

Sainte-Beuve, who remarked that Nicole was unusually fearful,[186] often and movingly described the pangs of Mother Angélique in her final weeks (1661):

> *. . . This most pure person, who during the fifty-five years since she had received the holy veil never ceased keeping watch and strict control over herself, found herself gripped, near the end of her life, by unspeakable terror, and suffered all the anguish of true agony. She saw herself before God, in her own words "as a criminal in the dock, awaiting the execution of the edict of her judge"; and, in speaking these words, it seemed that she was crushed and paralyzed. Nothing else occupied her time. The idea of death, once it had entered her spirit, remained etched there, and did not leave her for a single minute. Everything else disappeared; she now only thought of preparing herself for this terrible hour. She had thought about it all her life: "but everything that I have imagined of it," she would say, "is less than nothing compared to what it actually is, to what I feel and understand at this time." She feared the Supreme Justice, and there were moments when she did not dare hope for mercy.*[187]

This is a far cry from the serene and edifying "fine death" that is usually and not unreasonably mentioned in accounts of the Age of Reason.[188] Henri Bremond has rightly underscored the tragic quality of several Christian deaths; as a test case, he gives the agony of the second Duchess of Luynes (d. 1684), as told by the abbé Jean-Jacques Boileau. Until the final instant, the pious duchess felt a horrible fear of God's judgments. "Four hours before her death, she seemed a prophet, desolate at the sight of the final day. She groaned, she drenched her bed in tears, her sight was dimmed by apprehending the fury of the Almighty."[189] Reflecting on this end, which filled all her companions with "desolation," Boileau remarks: "The history of the Church is full of such examples. And, on the whole, I think that the fear which occurred at her death, mixed with the confidence Madame [de Luynes] had, is the . . . most appropriate attitude for a penitent sinner, and the one least subject to dangerous delusions." Moreover, "Jesus Christ, God's own saint . . . , did he not die in this state of desolation?"[190]

The anguish of Mother Angélique and the Duchesse de Luynes helps to clarify other such cases. Three eighteenth century Visitandines of Auxerre died (in 1739, 1751, and 1757) in states of exceptional fear. Prayers and sacraments seemed incapable of pacifying them, and their lives ended in near despair.[191] Similarly, a group of eighteenth century nuns themselves describe the agony of a "chorister" of the Autun Visitation, in the most dramatic of terms:

> *She said that she had great need of help in the state she was in . . . , a state of panic and of extreme confusion . . . She cried out, "O such pain! there is no suffering like this in this world" . . . Her spirit had never been in such torment . . . She said she could not explain it, for it was nothing in particular, but rather some sort of confusion with which her enemy [Satan] meant to perplex her. Our most honored Mother, having sprinkled her with holy water, said, in blessing her with the sign of the cross, that our enemies [the demons] have no power over souls armed with the sacraments, as she now was. The nun responded: "In some sense*

that is true, but in another it is impossible to say or even think of the power that they have." "[192]

This Visitandine had assimilated all too well the religious literature that since the fifteenth century had been stressing the demons' all-out attack at the time of final agony. At the same time the deaths of most of the saints, both male and female, were far more edifying. To follow the biographies (and hagiographies) of the time, these final exemplary moments fall into two models: that of a death long wished for, which is accomplished in extreme "peace" and "joy,"[193] and that which first involves a crisis of anxiety before God's judgments but then gives way to consolation and confident surrender. Such was the experience of Mother Mary of Saint Joseph, an Ursuline who died in Canada in 1652 with a reputation for holiness. A contemporary report does not hide the fact that, during her final days, she felt "so extremely forsaken, that it seemed that God had completely abandoned her."[194] However,

> *Our Lord, who had ordained for His glory and for the sanctification of His servant that she would pass through so many internal and external afflictions for four and a half years, and had greatly increased them during her final illness, wished that she should end her life in the delights of His grace and charity. Three days before her death, He filled her soul with a peace that gave her a taste of the peace of Paradise, and which freed her from all worldly desires.*[195]

The death of the Jesuit Jean Rigoleuc (d. 1692), an admirable spiritual missionary, follows the same scenario. "Fifteen days before his death, after three days when he had been troubled by the apprehension of God's judgments, Our Lord showed him the grace of consoling him in his pain through an inner voice; . . . and suddenly all his fear vanished, and his spirit became calm in the sweet assurance of his salvation."[196] Saint Margaret also made the harsh passage through fear preceding the serene arrival. Bishop Languet recounts how

> *God willed that before her death she would undergo a final trial of internal suffering. The peace that her heart had enjoyed, and the consolation with which her soul was almost intoxicated, suddenly gave way to inconceivable fears of God's judgments. The desire for death, which until now had given her delight, brought her feelings of terror about divine justice. These terrors were so palpable that her entire body could be seen shaking and trembling: to reassure herself, she pressed her crucifix to her heart; she let out deep sighs, and often she was heard repeating these words, "Mercy, my Lord, mercy." One of the nuns who witnessed this behavior said that she told her that one of the causes of her fear was the loss of time, which she felt she had not fully employed for her salvation.*[197]

After receiving extreme unction, however, "she remained in full repose and, having uttered the sacred name of Jesus, she sweetly rendered up her spirit."[198] The final moments of a pious canon of Chartres, Paul Cassegrain (d. 1771), director of a congregation of religious women, also illustrate the fears of the afterlife felt by the best of Christians. This priest who lived only for God was seized by the fear "of being condemned" at the very moment of extreme unction. Just before giving up the ghost he shouted out his terror to a relative, who tearfully responded: "We know the life that you have led; we know our own: if yours cannot reassure you, what can remain to us but despair?" Finally, the tenderness of his nephew, the affection of the nuns in attendance, and the feeling that a community leader should not yield to despair brought serenity to the dying man.[199]

During his final years, the ascetic hero Saint Alphonsus Liguori was besieged with fear. At the age of eighty-two (he was ninety when he died, in 1787) he confessed: "I tremble to think of the account I must soon give to Jesus Christ." In 1784–85 he went through phases of spiritual despair. "Who knows," he would say through his tears, "if I am in the grace of God and if I will be able to save myself." He would then face the cross: "No, Jesus, do not allow me to be damned, for in hell one can no longer love you." "How are you?" a visitor asked him. "I find myself beneath the rod of God's justice," he answered. "You have a melancholy air," another told him, "you who always seemed so joyous." "Joyous?" Liguori replied. "I suffer a living hell." On the eve of his death, however, his face was resplendent as he smiled before an image of the Virgin.[200]

Thus, even for saints, death is sometimes difficult. During the period of this study, moreover, fear of the afterlife was the special as well as the tragic privilege of a Christian elite. As Tronson reminded his congregation: "There are few priests who fulfill all [their] obligations; whence I infer a most dreadful consequence: there are few priests who will be saved."[201]

PART THREE

An Evangelism of Fear in the Catholic World

C H A P T E R 1 1

The Diffusion of a Religious Doctrine

FROM CONVICTION TO TACTICS

In extending *La Peur en Occident*, which had stressed the fears experienced by early modern high culture, the preceding chapters stressed the fear of God the Judge, with all its consequences, among a Catholic elite comprised of priests, theologians, bishops, and pious laypeople. It is now necessary to follow the diffusion of this anxious religion at the level of the Catholic masses (a parallel survey will then be attempted for the Protestant context). Without a doubt, this diffusion had occasional recourse to terroristic tactics, and it no less clearly reinforced—at least for a time—the power of the clergy. This study has thus far shown, however, that the will and tactics for keeping parishioners in line were not primary considerations, in contrast to what an overly brief historiography might otherwise argue. In this regard, Emile Mâle provides convincing evidence: Cardinal Baronio's personal seal featured a figure of Death; Innocent IX, before making major decisions, would look at a painting of himself lying on his deathbed: Alexander VII kept a coffin beneath his bed, ate from earthenware plates with death's-head decorations, and sometimes received visitors in a chamber where he preserved actual human skulls; during the course of a day Cardinal Oliva would frequently gaze upon a casket in the shape of a sepulcher containing a skeleton.[1] This subject thus involves an anguish felt by the top echelon of society, an anguish that the church's evangelical program wished to convey to the general populace. As an inevitable result, there was resort to tactics; the most apt means of moving the public were sought out; and use was made of "*trucs*" (tricks, devices) designed to support the authority of preachers and to create a believable mixture of threats, consolations, and promotion of guilt: This blend would for centuries comprise the most common framework for preaching.

The movement from the fear one feels to that which one strives to share with others is highly perceptible in the already cited homily of Monsignor Surian, Bishop of Vence at the end of the Ancien Régime: ". . . Whenever . . . I think that . . . hell will be the permanent residence of almost everyone with whom I live . . . , whenever I think that perhaps such is my fate and allotment, I confess that I can no longer control my fear."[2] This was not an isolated confession. A well-known preacher, the Oratorian Loriot, once declared to his audience: "If my words strike fear into you, they also do the same to me. If my speech terrifies you, it is only after I myself have been terrified"; and the missionary gives the remarkable reason for his apprehensions:

> *In fact I have more grounds than Saint Paul (I Cor. 9:18–27) for saying that I fear damning myself in trying to save others, because I attend to them instead of attending to myself and demanding pardon for my own sins. This was also Saint Chrysostom's fear. But it is most unlikely that his fear was as well founded as mine. Yet this great prelate would say to his flock, "I am in great fear for my salvation, because in praying and weeping for you, I am not at leisure to weep for myself."*[3]

Passing over the way in which Loriot uses Saint Paul, it is definitely worth stressing his allusion to Saint John Chrysostom. For it leads back to the ascetic model that had such a profound impact on Christian pedagogy, especially during the Counter-Reformation. Many desert fathers were afraid of receiving damnation. After their example, what should ordinary Christians not fear? In another sermon, Loriot again asserts: "How can the sinner not be seized with fear thinking of what must happen to him, since the saints themselves were not free from this fear, and trembled when it was their turn to die." The orator evokes the agonies of Hilarion, Arsenius, and Agathon, all monks of the desert, at the time of their undertaking the "terrible passage."[4]

In *Le Pédagogue chrétien*, the Jesuit Philippe d'Outreman summons Saint Gregory and Pope Innocent III to justify, through the example of the saints' fear of death, the necessary fear that must be instilled in a sinning public. This author in fact states,

> *The righteous, says Saint Gregory, are afraid of everything they do, when they consider the judge before whom they must someday certainly appear. O! what dreadful terror [cries Pope Innocent III] will there be at that time! What tears and groaning! For if the columns of heaven shake before him, what will poor sinners do? If the righteous man will be saved by the skin of his teeth, what will become of a sinner?*[5]

In the same vein, Pierre de la Font's revised homily for the fifteenth Sunday after Pentecost affirms that the greatest saints "only ceased to fear dying badly when they ceased to live."[6]

This reminder of the religious fear felt at society's highest levels makes it difficult to maintain categorically a commonly held claim of current historiography, which opposes two domains of Counter-Reformation discourse: "to the missions, to the people, fulminations; to the devout elites, kindness and seduction."[7] In regard to this matter, Bourdaloue explains his position in the clearest of terms. He begins a sermon on Hell by saying

> *To preach of hell at the court is the duty of an evangelical minister; and the preacher does not please God if, by false prudence or cowardly catering to the depraved taste of his auditors, he passes over such an essential matter and fundamental point of our religion! But he must also be attentive to whom he speaks on this subject. To the common people, this truth may be expressed through tangible figures: lakes of fire, flaming pits, hideous ghosts, gnashings of teeth. To you, however, my dear listeners who, however fleshly and wordly, are in another sense the sages and Christian spirits of the world, these things must be explained in the simplicity of the faith, so that you are given an exact understanding of them, one apt to edify you.*[8]

There undoubtedly existed a temptation to preach a sugar-coated religion to the great and wealthy: Bourdaloue attests to this. On the other hand, the Counter-Reformation firmly rejected such a tendency. At the courts as well as in retreats set up for upper-class souls, the church spoke in a loud and clear voice. Sometimes less concrete than the sermons addressed to the general public, homilies for the use of the fortunate elites still conveyed the same vehement message, because they expressed the same theology: that of a God whose justice prevailed over His mercy.

Keeping the process of "objectification" in mind—he who is afraid may feel the need to be feared—it is impossible not to be struck by certain traits common to the majority of sermons. First, the use, perhaps most frequent in the preceding period,[9] of "you" or "ye" addresses to one's listeners, and more generally the vogue for formulas that emphasize the moral superiority of the preacher over his audience. In contrast, the "we" pronoun, which puts the cleric at the level of the sinners who listen to him, is less common. San Bernardino di Siena constantly employs the "you" singular, and attacks each of his listeners in a false dialogue where he is the only interlocutor.[10] Olivier Maillard often begins his sermons with guilt-instilling phrases such as "these words [of today's homily] are for they who are Christians in name only or who lead not the Christian life";[11] or "these words are for the miserable sinners with stained souls,"[12] or they are "for hardened sinners, who will thus be overcome (*ut conterantur*) and moved to act properly,"[13] and so on. The frequently used "ye" of seventeenth- and eighteenth-century preaching allowed for invectives of the following kind: "Fathers and mothers," says Bishop Godeau, "if ye have lost your children and ye seek them out, where will ye find them? In the church? No. Ye will find them at the cabaret, or gambling, or in some debauchery."[14]

The same Godeau, comparing his flock to the pagans, tells them quite bluntly: "What is in your mouths but tricks, lies, deceits, curses, and slanders?"[15] François Hébert declares in an Ascension Day address to the people of his Versailles parish: "Ye have much more cause, my dear brethren, of being gripped with fear and grief by this mystery of Christ's Ascension; for he could reproach you far more than he did his apostles when he left them . . ."[16] During his missions in Lower Brittany, Father Maunoir still more vigorously abused his audience in these terms: "Do ye see Him, this God/Man whom ye have crucified? 'Tis ye who have put this crown of thorns on this sacred head, the very home of God's wisdom. 'Tis ye who have placed on the Saviour's shoulders this heavy cross which crushes him . . . Behold this divine face that the angels themselves yearn to see: behold how ye have disfigured it."[17] Jacques Giroust, another famous Jesuit preacher of the seventeenth century, once invited those who listened to him to join him in a momentary descent into Hell. He told them: "Descend with your minds into this abyss, which God may soon open beneath your feet to engulf you. Go down there in advance. What will you find? Sacreligious people like you, blasphemers like you, voluptuaries like you, misers like you, slandering and vindictive people like you, in a word, sinners like you."[18]

The "you," the "ye," and the abuse hurled at the sinners of the audience—but who is not a sinner?—reveal an immensely important fact: The audience of this period's evangelizing discourse was constantly suspected, spied upon, accused, and made guilty. A case in point among thousands of others is a statement made by the curé Reguis in a Sunday sermon:

> . . . *My dear parishioners . . . when I see you here, attending our holy mysteries, listening to the word of God, singing His praises, I say 'Behold these Christians.' But if I follow you into your houses, if I examine your ways, and study your*

> *habits, these Christians disappear, and I see almost nothing but enemies of the Cross and the Gospels: drunkards, misers, slanderers, and immodest, envious, or vengeful people.*[19]

Thus these sacred orators often used the pulpit as a tribunal, where they assumed the role of prosecutor.

Playing this part, how could they not resort to the means most likely to cause fear? How could they avoid scare tactics? San Bernardino once told the citizens of Perugia that at his next sermon he would show them the Devil in all his flesh and blood. The Perugians rushed to attend this sensationally advertised event. Bernardino did indeed remember his promise, and then began to cry in a terrifying voice, "Do you wish to see the devil? Look but at one another! For you yourselves are the true devils," and he lashed out at the vices of his listeners.[20]

Numerous confessions prove that preachers, especially "missionaries of the interior,"[21] willingly used an evangelism of fear to more effectively convert sinners, above all rustic ones. Jean-Pierre Camus relates how in order to provoke this sacred horror [of sin], the custom existed [in the missions] of beginning with a sermon on the final days, death, particular and collective judgment, purgatory, hell; these were always frightening and horrible, and inspired the fear of God."[22]

In 1627 Bourdoise, who was on mission in the diocese of Chartres, asked himself if he should continue to hold large services, given the threat of a plague. He finally decided to carry on with his sermons, in thoughts that "the fear of this pestilence and the sight of the oncoming death to which everyone was exposed would leave salutary impressions on the entire populace, and would inspire feelings of true penitence."[23] For Louis Abelly, whose biography of Saint Vincent de Paul appeared in 1664, the Lazarist missionary must make it his first priority to stress

> *penitence, man's ultimate fate, the enormity of sin, the rigors of God's justice toward sinners, the hardening of the heart, final impenitence, false shame, relapses into sin, slander, envy, hatred and hostilities, perjury and blasphemy, intemperate drinking and eating, and other like sins that are commonly committed by countryfolk.*[24]

With regard to Father Maunoir's preaching, Antoine Boschet recounts how "During the first weeks of his mission he frequently preached on the subjects most apt to move the soul and encourage penance: death, judgment, hell, and paradise."[25]

The Italian Jesuit Paolo Segneri the Elder (d. 1694) proceeded in identical fashion. One of his biographers reveals that

> *the subjects of his sermons were among the harshest that the Holy Gospel offers us: the need for penitence, the great peril faced by those who defer penance until death, the gravity of deadly sin, the terrible quality of divine judgment, the inexpiable penalties of hell, and other arguments of this kind that were likely to wake up any sleepers or to put the brains of anyone who had accidentally lost them back in his head.*[26]

In this regard, missionary methods were much the same from one congregation to the next. It was said of Christophe d'Authier (d. 1667), who preached extensively in the Dauphiné region, that

> *His opening words concerned only God's terrible justice, the need for penitence, the means of good confession and the three final fates of man, which he spoke every*

night to the faithful by the light of numerous torches lit up all around the church. He kept them spellbound for forty straight days and softened their hearts, and caused them to have holy repentance of their sins. He then spoke to them of the infinite kindness of God, of his great mercy, and of his superabundant grace and divine love, to bring them all the more to His love, though he had previously made them apprehensive of His threats and punishments.[27]

As for the Capuchin Albert de Paris, he also spells out the habitual practice of his order in regard to missions:

He who preaches in the evening usually treats of the more remarkable subjects, such as hell, eternity, final unrepentance, of judgment and the like. Then he undertakes the great moral subjects, which are reconciliation, restitution, slander, and the like. He goes through them all, and at the end provides sweeter material, such as the practice of the virtues, and the methods to persevere in grace.[28]

Concerning Hell, the Jesuit Houdry specifies: "All the preachers have something to say about it; and they do not believe they have properly fulfilled their duty until they have spoken of this fearful subject." Houdry approves of this catechesis and even encourages it: "There is no need to warn that the exaggeration the Christian orator must usually avoid is to be feared in this; for the human spirit cannot even conceive of the extreme pains of hell."[29] Thus every superlative of horror is allowed on this theme, since one will always be far short of the truth. Likewise, Jean-Pierre Camus wrote several decades earlier: "One cannot possibly exaggerate these devouring flames, these everlasting fires of hell, nor the grandeur of God's judgments, which are deep mysteries."[30]

It was with the clear intention of providing missionaries and priests with a collection of shocking tales that Philippe d'Outreman gathered them in his *Pédagogue chrétien*, a work that borders on the macabre.[31] The Oratorian Loriot includes an astonishing anecdote in a sermon on "the shame that hides sins in confession": "a lady of quality, who had otherwise been most pious, having committed an indecent action all by herself, had so much shame of this, that she never dared to tell her sin to her confessor." To quell her remorse she entered into a convent, followed all its rules, and was elected mother superior, but without ever confessing her sin, even at the time of death. After her decease she appeared to one of the nuns and revealed that she had been damned. This *exemplum*, however, is not as revealing as Loriot's footnote: "the author has often told this story in his missions, with the most vivid colors that he could give it; and he has never told it but that it has soon had its effect."[32] Loriot's work, moreover, is comprised of model sermons for repetition. Large numbers of the faithful therefore must have heard this anecdote.

Missionaries stage-managed impressive spectacles. In the early seventeenth century, Michel Le Nobletz began his mission at Douarnenez by sounding the alarum bell. The townspeople ran to the church, thinking some disaster had occurred. The man of God indeed explained that they were in danger of losing their souls.[33] Julien Maunoir employed the same technique, ordering the church bells to ring at four in the morning the day he began his mission. Boschet writes:

All the same, they rang the bell at the church and everything was in turmoil in the streets, as is sometimes caused by fear. For since the mission had arrived in the town in the midst of winter, some visitors who did not know of its arrival or were ignorant of its purpose woke up with a start at the noise of the great bell, and hearing everyone at their inn getting up in haste, they believed there was a fire in the neighborhood, and they hurriedly joined the others. The noise in the street added to their fear and confirmed their supposition. Hence they put their heads out the window, and asked this crowd of people where they were running so early in the morning; they learned that it was not fire, but the mission that was causing this tumult.[34]

On numerous occasions, missionaries used the "prop" of a death's head. In 1608 Le Nobletz offered a noble penitent a skull, adorned with a blond wig that was curled in the latest fashion.[35] Ten years later the English Benedictine William Gifford preached a Lenten sermon at Reims "with incredible applause from those in attendance," to whom he wished

to leave as a present one of the most lovely flowers with which, he said, nature had ever embellished the earth . . . Everyone then thought of diverse kinds of flowers, whether carnations, or lilies, roses . . . behold what he then takes out of a cloth, a remarkable thing, this flower that the great king of Egypt Ptolemy Philadelphus displayed amidst his festive processions: a skull, so that with such a natural and palpable image, the memory and fear of death might remain vividly stamped on their hearts . . .[36]

Seventeenth-century Eudists apparently did not bring skulls into the pulpit.[37] On the other hand, the Capuchins, as well as others, made use of this procedure. A Capuchin historian has recently written of Father Honoré de Cannes: "[He] also used the classic stratagem of this period of the death's head, which he successively dressed with a judge's cap, a military headpiece, a 'Fontange' [that is, a Fontange-style headgear], a doctor's wig, an Academy member's crown, or an abbot's hair-grip"[38]: in short, a new adaptation of the *danse macabre.*

This pedagogy left a long-standing heritage. In the mid-nineteenth-century, the Neapolitan Redemptorians received as a sermon text, with the stage property of a skull (the *funzione del teschio*), the following script:

The missionary, having just concluded a dramatic peroration on the hideous death of sinners, suddenly interrupts himself and removes his headpiece. "But I perceive, my beloved brethren, that my preaching on death has not made any impression on you this evening. You sit there with dry eyes and hearts of stone. Do you know what I'm going to do? I am bringing another preacher here this evening. I am bringing one of your compatriots . . . from the other world. He will give you his own sermon on death. Who knows? Perhaps he will be able to move you? Perhaps he will make you cry and convert you to Jesus?

(Saying this, he takes a burning torch and adds):

"Quick, before this other preacher arrives, ask Jesus for pardon. Yes, run to Mary."

(At the same time he suddenly takes a death's head and, turning it toward the crowd, he illuminates it with his torch and begins a dialogue with it, making sure that when he speaks to the skull, he turns himself toward it, and when he speaks the skull's answer, he faces the audience . . .)

THE PREACHER: *—Speak, speak to your compatriots out there: what do you do in the other world?*

THE SKULL: *—Oh my friends! It goes badly before God's tribunal! Mad are they who love not God. Mad who do not become holy!*

THE PREACHER: *—What's happened to your eyes, with which you perhaps enjoyed* *looking at so many things you liked, with so many sinful glances, what's happened to them?*

THE SKULL: *—Mice ate them. Worms ate them. Mad are they who love not God. Mad who do not become holy.*

THE PREACHER: *—And this tongue, with which you perhaps sang many a love song, said many blasphemies, spoke so much idle chat, what's become of it?*

THE SKULL: *—Worms ate it . . . ! Mad who do not become holy.*

THE PREACHER: *—And this face that you made to look so fair, and for which you stayed so long before the mirror, what's become of it?*

THE SKULL: *—Worms ate it too, they consumed every bit of it. Mad are they who do not become holy.*

THE PREACHER: *—And your hair, which perhaps you lavished with many perfumes and delicious scents to make you beautiful to others' eyes and a hellish snare for so many poor souls, where is it now?*

THE SKULL: *—It has decomposed. It has returned to dust. Mad are they who do not become holy. Ah, my dear compatriots! I too lived in this land. Like you I walked these streets, through the squares of Naples . . . I was in your church, as you are now . . .*

THE PREACHER: *—And now?*

THE SKULL: *—And now everything is finished! The world will soon be finished for you too. Only those who love God are blessed. Blessed they who save their souls.*

THE PREACHER: *—Where is your soul, in heaven or hell? I do not know. If your soul is in heaven, pray to God for me and for your compatriots, that their hearts may be moved this evening and that they be converted to Jesus Christ. But if your soul is in hell, get on, I no longer wish to see you.*

(So saying, he makes the skull disappear, takes up the crucifix and shows it to the people, saying—in an exclamatory tone—"Raise your voices and say: "O Lord, I repent")."[39]

Other theatrical creations contributed to the success of various missions, especially those of the Jesuits. Ending a series of sermons at Phouhinec (Finistère, Brittany), Maunoir, at least according to Boschet, wished to confirm the inhabitants' "conversion" by "a spectacle that would be likely to inspire a healthy and lasting fear." This preacher had already composed a canticle, which would become famous, on the torments of Hell. The song featured a dialogue in which "the people still on this earth interrogate those who suffer in hell":

At the end of the general procession [of enclosure] . . . he gathered on a stage erected . . . in the middle of the field, some children [the reading is correct: some children] who were to ask questions in the name of the living, and he placed below the stage those who were to give the answers of the damned.

When the procession reached this place, the living began to interrogate the dead reprobates: the entire audience was moved by their questions, which concerned everyone, but the lugubrious voices, which expressed the tortures of the damned below the stage as from the depths of an abyss, so truly terrified this crowd of four thousand people that each of them beat their breasts and made new resolutions to do penance and avoid sin.[40]

In Italy the Jesuits integrated processions of flagellants into their processions, but they did control them. Paolo Segneri the Elder himself gives the example.[41] At the end of some sermons on the theme of "either penitence or hell," he was seen to be "transported with zeal and, to make an example," to place on his head a crown of sharp thorns, to put a rope around his neck, to raise his cassock and, standing with an undergarment that left his chest and shoulders exposed, to give himself a whipping. He even had invented a more refined device, made of a cork-oak cane set in a tin case and armed with fifty needles. He struck himself with this primarily in penitential processions or to overcome, by his own mortifications, the resistance of those who balked at pardoning their enemies. The priests and friars who sought to convert the New World peoples also used spectacular self-punishments that amazed onlookers.[42]

Due to the crowds, Paolo Segneri's sermons generally took place in squares or in fields. Once the homily was over, the throng headed for the church. The preacher then said to them, "Whoever is innocent should stay here, but whoever is a sinner come with me." The crowd would quickly rush to the church, which was closed as soon as it was full of men, since women had to stay outside. During the singing of the *miserere*, the people, "stripped to the waist," wildly flagellated themselves (*alla disperata*). Those who had not been able to obtain whips beat themselves with ropes, with nail-studded belts, even with rosaries. Others slapped themselves, or pounded on their chests. All would cry out, "Peace, pardon, live Jesus, better to be dead than ever sin again!" "The women would echo these voices from outside, clapping their hands and raising pitiable cries."[43] Then the missionary, as though inspired, would ask in a loud voice: "Who is the greatest sinner in this church?" and all would answer "Me, Me!" The tears and blows redoubled. They did not, however, last for more than a quarter of an hour.[44]

A still more dramatic variant of these penitential ceremonies was the great nocturnal, torchlit procession that would go through the streets at the end of a given mission. Paolo Segneri appeared in one of these with his torso naked, a rope around his neck, his black cowl over his face, chains around his feet, and a rod in his hand. He carried a cross and was followed by the clergy and congregation. Many of these followers were crowned with thorns or also carried crosses. Some had their arms pinioned behind their backs and attached to horizontal staffs, so that they looked like "walking victims of crucifixion."[45] Great chains bound others together like prisoners, while still others struggled beneath yokes, like oxen. These processions often included a cross borne on a black-draped stretcher, which represented the dead Christ.

This missionary program also had great success in seventeenth- and eighteenth-century Spain, where both Jesuits and Capuchins increased the number of nocturnal processions and spectacular rituals, to the point of causing mass fear.[46] In addition, these practices were exported into Catholic Switzerland and German-speaking areas, especially by the Jesuits.[47] The reports of Father Fulvio Fontana, a disciple of the elder Segneri, bear convincing witness of this trend. Accompanied by interpreters, Fontana made frequent visits to Switzerland, the Tyrol, and Austria between 1705 and 1710.[48] He sometimes attracted enormous crowds: At Innsbruck 40,000 people (?!) received the Host during general communion.[49] Whenever he arrived from a neighboring canton, hundreds of boats would escort the preacher across the Swiss lakes. Wherever he went, the great penitential processions were comprised of people wearing crowns of thorns, which were sold in the streets by young children.[50] "You could [then] only see spectacles of penitence, immense crosses on shoulders [carried even by the most delicate young women], chains around feet, and whips in hands. The onlookers were themselves part of the spectacle: all of them with faces stained by tears, which streamed from their eyes and thus showed their completely grief-stricken hearts."[51] Such was the favored mission of Italian Jesuits, usually shorter but more moving than the French version.

Michel Le Nobletz and Julien Maunoir, as well as New World missionaries, are known to have used tableaux to support words with images.[52] The mise en scène thus became an audiovisual pedagogy, without however losing, at least in most cases, the impressive theatrical dimension stressed by this analysis. Le Nobletz, sometimes called the "mad priest," who early in his career prescribed terrible mortifications for himself—his "madness," however, being perceived because of his recourse to catechizing women—commissioned some seventy "*cartes*" (ca. two by three feet in size), painted on lambskin. Fourteen of these survive at the bishop's palace in Quimper (*carte de Babylone, carte de la Croix, carte du Jugement, carte des coeurs*, and so on). Le Nobletz began painting such works at Landerneau in 1613, and Alain Croix rightly observes that these "tableaux"—*taolennou*—could not have been easy to "read," since they included series of scenes in miniature. The missionary therefore composed commentaries on these naïve posters, which he and his catechists would then explain with the help of a wooden pointer.[53]

Maunoir also employed the *taolennou*, though apparently to a lesser degree and in a simpler way than his predecessor. In any case, once this technique had been developed, it was soon adopted by the Lazarists and even by secular priests in the diocese of Vannes, in 1697.[54] Breton priests carried on this tradition until the early twentieth century; by this time, the mission tableaux had become progressively clearer and hence more directly accessible to the public. They had also come to convey a vehement and often terrifying message of "conversion." Louis Kerbiriou and Pierre-Jakez Hélias testify to this effect in recounting their childhood memories of certain missions. The first author states that horrific details definitely left a greater mark on the faithful than did "pious and consoling imagery": He writes that "all eyes immediately fixed on repulsive figures and terrifying colors."[55] The second relates, "the words of the priest went in one ear and out the other . . . But the tableaux were an entirely different matter. It was no use closing one's eyes, and barely shut eyelids opened wide as the successive images of our fate kept beating upon us like so many sharp blows." At night, these impressions turned into "seething nightmares," from which one awoke in "the odor, sweat and desire of contrition."[56]

These tableaux, moreover, depicted hearts. The first such depictions of Christ's or Mary's heart most likely date from the fifteenth century.[57] The rich emblematic literature of the sixteenth century, especially after 1570, then stimulated an increase in representations of the heart. The Flemish Antoine Wierix (late sixteenth–early seventeenth century), who did extensive work for the Jesuits, was the first great promulgator of pious images in which a heart was surmounted by a head. Wierix in turn influenced Le Nobletz, the creator of a picture composed of thirty hearts: a heart held in the nets of the devil, a heart enclosing a "worldly" man, a heart with each of the deadly sins, a heart expelled by Jesus, a heart where Jesus takes refuge, and so on, the general theme being "know thyself."[58] More of a teacher than his predecessor, Maunoir seems to have used mainly these images of Hell, Paradise, and hearts, schematizing each one in turn.

The symbolism of the heart had a decided vogue during the seventeenth century. A Breton rector, Quendu Le Gall, came to Italy and presented the Pope with an *Oratorio del cuore* (published in Rome in 1668), which depicts every day of the week with a large heart, above which appears the head of a man. This work met with widespread success: twenty-three editions, eleven of them dating from before 1700. A French translation was made in 1670. Contemporaneously, a Jesuit, Father Vincent Huby, the founder of a men's "House of spiritual retreat" at Vannes, issued his *Images morales*, which fully inherited the tradition discussed above. These depictions were frequently used as after-dinner conversation pieces. Their dimensions (roughly two by three feet) indicate that they could have been shown to fairly sizable gatherings. The series includes twelve prints, each of which features a heart surmounted by a head, whose expression matches the scenes depicted below.

The first print portrays a man unaware of the sin in which he dwells. His face is unhappy. In his heart, one can make out the star of faith and the eye of conscience, as well as animals that symbolize the Deadly Sins. In the second, a guardian angel implores the Holy Ghost and uses a death's head to help the "worldly man" reflect on his deeds. The demon and the animals of the Deadly Sins begin to flee. The third print evokes repentance. The Holy Ghost fully possesses the heart, where one can see the flames of grace and the tears of penance. The face now projects regained peace. The fourth depicts the life of the man who does penance and divides himself among prayer, almsgiving, and fasting. The fifth is devoted to the perfection of the man who has "purged himself of his sins." The heart, around which are inscribed the names of the seven virtues, is occupied by the Holy Trinity. Nonetheless, the battle for salvation has yet to be won: The sixth print illustrates the all-out return of the temptations of the world and of the flesh, and the seventh delineates the estate of man whose heart Satan and seven other demons have retaken. Logically, the eighth scene, in the tradition of the *Artes moriendi*, presents the "bad death" of the sinner. A great demon shows the dying man the book of his sins. Christ can only say to the unfortunate soul: "Get out, accursed wretch." The ninth print describes Hell, its grills and tortures, and the great numbers of damned souls who fall there. These people are being gnawed on by the worm of remorse. In contrast, the tenth print glorifies perseverance, which resists all temptations. The eleventh portrays the good death of the man who clutches a crucifix, while an angel presents the list of his good works. Finally, the twelfth evokes the joys of paradise. Anne Sauvy notes that copies of this last print are now the most difficult to find. Is this due to its being the most consoling to look at, and the one that people preferred to hang on their walls? In passing, it is also worth noting the absence of Purgatory from this comic strip devoted to the streamlined history of individual salvation.

The *Images morales* had both considerable impact and a lengthy posterity. Many of these prints illustrated the famous *Miroir du pécheur*, composed by the Capuchins at the end of the seventeenth century and simultaneously printed and reprinted by both a Le Mans printing house[59] and the "Bibliothèque bleue" of Troyes until the mid-nineteenth century.[60]

The potential support of an object—a skull or pictures—did not exempt the preacher from great vocal strain. Although the numbers reported for the audience size of San Bernardino di Siena and Giovanni di Capistrano are fantastical (80,000 people (!) supposedly heard the latter at Vienna in 1451[61]), it is nevertheless certain that they often spoke to large crowds, massed if necessary in the largest square of the town. Father de la Haye, who in 1635 edited the Latin works of San Bernardino, recalls in his preface:

> *The numbers of those who gathered to listen to [the great orator] were so consistently great that they hastened at dawn toward the preaching place, sometimes coming from thirty miles away . . . And this wonderful hero of Our Lord, filled with the Holy Spirit, exhorted his listeners in his great voice to do penance and use tears and fasts to placate an offended God.*[62]

A contemporary tells how at Vienna, during Pentecost of 1451, the coming of Giovanni di Capistrano attracted the people "as if it were Rome at the time of a great jubilee; all the inns and taverns were full."[63] Hence the necessity of a powerful voice and, moreover, of gestural skills, especially when an orator like Capistrano did not know German. He therefore spoke in Latin and an interpreter translated. The voice and gestures of the Italian preacher amazed his Austrian audience. One day, discussing as he often did the Last Judgment, and having loudly exclaimed, "Away from me, ye accursed!" he suddenly interrupted himself because of audience reaction and embarked on a rhetorical parenthesis:

> *If you have read [like San Bernardino, he addressed his listeners in the singular] Cicero and Augustine . . . you should know the importance of voice and gestures in the presence of the people . . . If I seek to bring them to devotion, I must raise my voice; and if you say "Away from me, you accursed!" you must yell with a terrifying voice, as is required by the sense of the words. On the other hand, one must lovingly pronounce the words, "O come all ye blessed children of Our Father."*[64]

Having made these remarks, Capistrano resumed his description of the Last Judgment. Many other missionaries and parish priests followed his example and believed it necessary to speak in a loud voice to awake sleeping Christians. Orders for this approach were sent from the hierarchy itself. Guillaume Briçonnet wrote to his clergy in 1520: "We order you . . . to make the clarion of God's word echo in the ears of those who pretend they cannot nor will not hear it."[65] This call to "ring out" the message of the church explains the title of a work—famous in the seventeenth century—of Father Yvan, *Trompette du ciel qui esveille les pecheurs et les excite à se convertir*.[66] This monk figuratively did what preachers accomplished literally. Thus the voice of the Dominican Father Antoine Le Quieu (d. 1676), the founder of a congregation of the Blessed Sacrament, "was rolling thunder, which brought the most obstinate sinners to tears; a strong and powerful voice that broke the pride and lowered the haughtiness of the tallest cedars; a voice that put out the hottest flame, that stopped the raging of fires, or of the most vehement wrath."[67] He retired, exhausted "by the strength and vehemence with which he preached."[68] In the mid-seventeenth century, a parish priest of the Savoy region gave the following praise of a Capuchin missionary: "God who takes special care of his creatures, brought to this world a most special and wondrous means of putting out the rage and fury of the infernal spirits, through the cries and thunder of a father, which resounded unto heaven."[69]

For many centuries the sermons of missionaries on death often took place in cemeteries, beside an open grave. Other homilies of the missions—on judgment or Hell—were generally given after nightfall, in churches dimly lit by flickering candles. Thus the sermons became even more emotive. Many times over they provoked astonishing reactions from the audience: groanings, tears, heart-rending cries ("pardon!" "mercy!"), faintings, and so on. Preachers often had to interrupt their sermons to allow the crowd thus to physically release the anguish that they themselves had provoked.[70] Some orators, such as Vincent Ferrer, Giovanni di Capistrano, and Fulvio Fontana caused these collective psychic discharges even among listeners who spoke a different language. Such effects pose a problem, which may be tentatively solved by citing the description of missions preached at the beginning of this century in southern Italy. Preachers in this area used, with a most exact technique, the art of the *cantilena*, or chanted lament, and the "third tone"—equivalent to the minor key, or "scenic modulation" of the ancients—by which one could mesmerize an audience. Francesco di Capua's childhood recollections best describe this phenomenon.[71]

The sermon, he relates, would begin with a confession pantomimed by two priests, who played the parts of priest and penitent; the latter sometimes imitated the voice of a woman reciting trivia and blaming her sins on her husband or neighbors. After this opening sequence, "another father ascended the dais and intoned, in a muffled voice, a sad cantilena." More than a chant, it was a lament. It evoked the episodes of Christ's Passion, to each of which the people responded with an even more lugubrious refrain: "I have been an ingrate. O my God, pardon, pity!" Following the cantilena, a third priest appeared on the platform and began the *Predica grande*. This was not an ordinary sermon but

> *a declaimed recitation, which at certain points naturally took on the melodic tone of a cantilena. The orator, slowly pacing the dais with an inspired air, in a languid voice and a slow, serious tone, recited his phrases and ended them on an almost musical cadence. It was a most simple cantilena, which proceeded from a single note; nonetheless, by means of crescendo, it sometimes rose from a tone. The inflected syllables, especially those of the final words of a phrase, became voluntarily elongated.*

The phrase begun in recitative thus ended on a rhythmic cadence. The effect produced by this *cantilena* "was so powerful that anyone who had not seen this spectacle can possibly imagine it. A wind of intense emotion blew through the truly delirious crowd, alternating with gusts of terror that caused tears and wailing."

The orator then cited the story of Elizabeth of England, who, having reigned for thirty years, asked the Devil for ten more in exchange for her soul. He recounted,

> *After her death, the royal specter appeared each night on the banks of the Thames. Amid the grating clank of her heavy chains, with a mournful desperate voice, she cried: "Forty years my rei-ei-ei-gn, and an eternity of pai-ai-ai-n." These last words were repeated several times, almost as a chant. The preacher spoke them in a deep and heavy voice, reinforcing stresses, separating syllables, and lengthening the vocal tonics of the final words.*
>
> *Upon this fantastic story, this melodic declamation, a tremendous quivering seized the entire crowd. Their nerves vibrated, their limbs leapt and shuddered. The current of a mysterious emanation unsettled the multitude, that was both unified and in flux. It sufficed for a woman to let out a moan, for a little girl to burst into tears, for the entire throng, as if it had only one single soul, to moan, to weep, to shout. These cries, these tears seemed to be a collective invocation for the spasms to stop. These moans and tears soothed their nerves. Little by little, the soul of the listeners was seemingly wrapped in an ecstatic, restful, and beneficial calm.*

Even people who had come to the church more out of curiosity than devotion were gripped by the collective emotion: The same occurrence is often described in tales of the missions. "There was nothing else to do: either leave at once, or groan and wail with everyone there." Commenting on this remarkable account, Father Bourdeau adds: "It was in the sermon on death that the 'third tone' was held the longest. This was the mandatory accompaniment to the notorious showing of the skull. Nothing lent itself so well to the *scenica modulatio* than these macabre theatrics."[72]

The use of the "third tone" further underlines the church's tactics. These also entered, but in a different way, into the sermons of the famous German Augustinian Abraham a Santa Clara. His collection of eleven sermons given at Graz in 1683, at the time of the last great Turkish threat, is an epitome of Baroque excess.[73] "The Imperial Preacher," who became famous for his sermons during the Vienna plague of 1679, Abraham knew that he was a hallowed orator, adored by the populace. Moreover, the impending danger exalted his talent. All the same, wishing to mobilize public opinion, he did not shy from gross exaggerations, alarming comparisons, plays on words, puns, streams of imagery, shocking enumerations, and terrifying statistics. The Christian West, he said, resembles the eyeless Samson; the Turkish army is the flooding Danube, a leech that stinks of onion. Mohammed, he asserts, had forty legitimate wives and countless mistresses. His father was a sorcerer, his mother Jewish. He bathed every day in mallow with his concubines. The Turks are the cruelest soldiers in the world. Abraham describes at length the tortures they inflict on their victims: impalement, pike-thrusts, hanging by the feet, disembowelment with the entrails given as fodder to their animals. Having been thwarted at Vienna in 1526, Suleiman the Magnificent put to death, in revenge, 400,000 Christians of the Viennese countryside, men, women, and children. Why should his successor Mehmet IV (1648–1687) be any better? The fight against the Porte is the fight against the Antichrist. This fight is thus no less than a crusade.

On the other hand—in a spectacular about-face of argumentation—if God is permitting the Turkish advance, it is because Christians are all sinners. They should take the Moslems as their example. They, at least, pray to God with humility and devotion. They neither swear nor blaspheme. They practice justice and charity. They fast and do not get drunk. They respect animals and human beings. In contrast, Christianity is like a hospital filled with weak and sickly people. The world has never been so corrupt—an old and frequently recurring theme—indeed, it is truly "upside down." No people are so cruel as the Christians. In the seventeenth century alone, they have killed 800,000 (!) of their religious kindred. There is thus an urgent need to repent and to pray.

It is now worth turning from this potent preacher, but not from the realm of tactics, to see the latter at work in ordinary sermons, at the level of weekly parish worship. Strange uses of biblical texts occasionally appear, leading to misreadings, indeed distortions, of their sense. Giving the homily for the eleventh Sunday after Pentecost, on the text of Mark 7:31–35 ("and the string of his tongue was loosed, and he spake plain"), the prior of Valabrége, Pierre de la Font, starts with a veritable pirouette: He says:

> *This indeed was a great miracle that our Gospel tells us, when the son of God untied the tongue of a mute man and, giving him free use of speech, made him speak well and clearly. But it would be a far greater miracle and infinitely more useful if God, through a contrary miracle, tied up the tongues of most men and, by putting a stop to their speech, prevented them from saying wicked things.*[74]

The orator then takes arms against the "sins of the tongue." N. Girard (Christian name unknown),[75] for the sixth Sunday after Epiphany, glosses the parable "the kingdom of heaven is like to a grain of mustard seed" (Matt. 13:31), and also overturns the sense of the text: "Allow me today," he asks his parishioners, "to give an entirely different sense to this parable, and say that the mustard seed, so tiny in itself yet which becomes so sizable a tree, may very well represent to us the vain regard for public opinion, which seems to be nothing in itself but nevertheless causes prodigious effects."[76] This "monster" will thus be the object of the sermon. Throughout its history, the church has read the Gospels according to its preoccupations of the moment, its mutable anthropology, and its projects of pastorship. During the period of this study, its prime objective was to instill guilt, in order to "save." Luke 8:19 relates how "his mother and his brethren [Jesus'] . . . could not come at him for the press," and so Godeau concludes that few people approach communion with good attitudes. "The number of communions oppresses Jesus Christ. The crowd tramps in to be with Him, but this same press of people then tramples on Him."[77] The same Godeau envisions Jesus as a child crying in his créche, and explains: ". . . As he infinitely hated sin, and as he was burdened with it, he felt and weeped for it most bitterly."[78] Jesus fasted for forty days in the desert, but he went to the feast at Cana, and he sometimes ate amid the publicans. Nonetheless, Beurrier assures his listeners at Saint-Etienne-du-Mont that the Lord was "forever fasting" and that he "never . . . ate any food for its flavor, but out of pure necessity."[79] With a certain ingenuity Pierre de la Font, on Palm Sunday, seizes on the text of Matthew 21:2 ("ye shall find an ass tied, and a colt with her: loose them, and bring them unto me") and explains that, just as the apostles untied the ass and the colt, so too the priest untie sinners by absolution. This Palm Sunday sermon thus applies to confession.[80] A final example from a list that could be extended: Girard, commenting on Luke 19:41 (Jesus weeping for Jerusalem), explains that the sinners for whom it is most necessary to weep are "those who are buried deep in filth and impurity: this shameful vice of which Christians should not have knowledge, not even of its name, but is nevertheless common in this world."[81]

Finally, it was not a rare occurrence for the preachers of former times to turn church festivals, in theory times for rejoicing, into occasions for menacing sermons. Regarding the "mystery of the Epiphany," Montargon composed a text with the following notable lines: "Let us tremble, Christians, before the sight of the crèche. However humble Jesus Christ may appear, he is terrible . . ."[82] These threats partake of the desire to combat "the pagan festivals" of the "Roi-boit." Likewise, Pierre de la Font, at Easter, and François Hébert, on Ascension Thursday, believed it necessary to strike fear into their flocks. The first announced to them that "the majority of you, at the resurrection, will not experience this blessed change, for which the righteous strive . . . Their resurrection . . . will only increase and aggravate the evils of your unfortunate condition."[83] The second tells his listeners, "You have far more reason, my most dear brethren, to be consumed with sorrow and fear before the mystery of Christ's ascension. For He can reproach you much more than He did His apostles in leaving them, and He can, not only through His angels but through the witness of your own conscience, threaten you with the rigors of His dreadful judgment."[84]

At the end of this treatment on the "tactics" of preachers, an alternate view becomes apparent. Whatever methods were used, this evangelical program did aim to "convert." An eighteenth-century Breton priest wished to justify his use of elaborate means to his listeners and said to each of them: ". . . Miserable ones . . . , if you are insensitive to my words, at least think upon the death that approaches you, fear a God who is a rigorous judge, tremble before the hell which is ready to swallow you. With these words, supported by the grace of God, I hope to convert the most impious among you."[85] Similarly and contemporaneously, Saint Alphonsus Liguori stated: "I can attest from experience that in those places where I have preached this sermon [on "actual" death] . . . it has caused a great sensation and left the congregation struck with terror. Concrete things make a far greater impression than speculative ones."[86] All the same, Saint Alphonsus was not a terrorist. Elsewhere he declares: "Conversions made in fear do not last long: One forgets, shrugs one's shoulders, and it is over . . . But if one is converted by the love of the crucified Jesus, the conversion is stronger and more lasting. What love does not do, neither will fear, and when one cleaves to the crucified Jesus, one is no longer afraid."[87] This assertion invokes a wider-ranging comment: Preaching, even of the most traumatic variety, has always sought to inspire hope.[88] In this respect, the Christian macabre is distinct from the Elizabethan theater's gratuitously morbid aspects and from a certain melancholic literature of the eighteenth century.[89]

During the course of the missions and throughout the liturgical calendar, other more joyful religious holidays strove to compensate for the disturbing effects of harsh religious messages. In addition, these latter elements had to give way, at least in principle and at the end of a time such as Advent or Lent, to a discourse of solace. Following Bernard Dompnier, it is worth citing the useful advice of the Capuchin Albert de Paris: "As soon as one has astounded the auditor, and made him nearly despair, in showing him the immensity of his crimes, the rigor of God's justice, and the nearness of punishment, one must promptly move on to the remedy, and prescribe the means for preventing all these misfortunes."[90] Hence the evangelism of fear indisputably went hand in hand with an "evangelism of seduction." Still, were not the faithful more touched by fear than by hope, the former often and inevitably being presented in more striking terms than the latter?

As for the aggressive approach outlined above, which is also the subject of the present work, it must be connected to a diagnosis churchpeople made of ordinary Christians throughout the centuries. The former considered the latter as great sinners, hard of hearing, and difficult to move; they felt that only a message with shock value could—perhaps?—unsettle or "convert" these recalcitrant people. This term must be understood in its full sense. The clergy believed they were pursuing in Europe a task comparable to that which overseas missionaries were attempting among the pagans. "Convert": The word implies that facing their religious project and the highly austere morality they were teaching, preachers of all orders found a great deal of inertia, a passive resistance all the more difficult to shake loose for its taking refuge behind an almost regular religious practice. The evangelism of fear, whether accompanied or not by "seduction," repelled an apparently docile yet restive public. Preaching on Hell, Bourdaloue once had to chide his listeners that "preachers have tried a thousand times in vain to make you understand [its] horror."[91] In November 1819 Laurence Balzac, age sixteen and living at a boarding school on the Rue des Francs-Bourgeois, wrote to his sister:

> *Today is Sunday . . . The preacher preached to us on the last judgment, and on the vicissitudes of the grandeurs of this world; after the sermon there was no individual who would not have thought himself burnt, damned. As for me, my legs were so cold that I perceived I was not yet in hell; thus you see me disposed to recommence my deadly crimes, going to the theater, to balls, concerts, in all these worldly and depraved places . . .*[92]

THE DOCUMENTS

To clarify the themes and impact of the evangelism of fear in the sixteenth- to eighteenth-century Catholic world requires that certain sources be consulted. Among the most clearly important are the "preparations for death," the "*Faut mourir*" and other "*Pensez-y bien*" publications that historians have recently studied, revealing their dominant themes,[93] their evolution, and their place in spiritual literature. Other types of documents, however, also and especially demand attention: specifically, sermons and hymns, the latter often being rhymed versions of the former. Grignion de Montfort bears witness to this syndrome, writing "Preacher, in my songs / You may find your sermons. / I have prepared their words / To help you and to please you."[94] Jacques Le Goff affirms that the sermon was "the consummate cultural product of the Middle Ages."[95] With Gutenberg's invention, the printed word gained massive ground. Nevertheless, oral communication retained its prestige and force of persuasion for a long time. At the end of the seventeenth century, only 21 percent of the French (mainly men) could sign their deed of marriage. Their numbers certainly rose through the course of the eighteenth century, but were still no more than 37 percent by the years 1786 to 1790.[96] It is true, however, that people can read without being able to write. Still, at the eve of the Revolution more than half of the kingdom's inhabitants were totally illiterate. Hence the importance of sermons to the spreading of Christian doctrine. The most up-to-date historiography will henceforth eagerly lean on this long neglected but essential source,[97] which conveys both the major themes and the importance of preaching. Here are perceived the sometimes strained relations between the teaching and taught churches. Here between the lines can be read the religious experience of former times.

The sermons themselves subdivide into two categories. The first includes those that were given on the occasion of missions, or during the offices of Advent and Lent. To these must be attached many of the hymns composed for missions, for example those of Saint Louis-Marie Grignion de Montfort. The missions again lead from San Bernardino de Siena to Saint Léonard of Port-Maurice, in particular via Father Maunoir, the seventeenth- and eighteenth-century Lazarists, the Capuchin François de Toulouse, Abbé Bridaine, the Jesuits Giroust, Vieira, Fontana, and Segneri, and the Oratorians Lejeune and Loriot. I have likewise drawn on the *Bouquet de la mission composé en faveur des peuples de la campagne par M. Jean Leuduger pretre . . . de St. Brieuc* (1st ed., 1700). The hymns are primarily by Grignion de Montfort,[98] but also include those that were brought together in 1746, in a *Manuel des retraites et missions á l'usage du diocése de Rennes*. The notable additions here are the hymns sung in the eighteenth century by the students of the Brothers of the Christian Schools[99] and those taught to the people of baroque Bohemia.[100] The second category of sermons is that of the weekly preachings strung out across the year, according to the march of the fifty-two Sundays of the liturgical calendar; this group also includes the homilies spoken at other obligatory holidays.

The inquiries of modern historiography decisively reveal the long-underrated role that missionaries "of the interior" played in Catholic countries from the seventeenth to the nineteenth centuries. While these men and women took the baton from the itinerant preachers of the Middle Ages, they had more method in their activities and a greater concern for the countryside. In all its forms, the missionary discourse thus furnishes a rich mine of information. Nonetheless, an even more important area for scrutiny will be the immense literature of the fifty-two Sunday sermons. Born in the Middle Ages,[101] illustrated in the fifteenth century by Olivier Maillard in his *Dominicales*[102] and in the sixteenth by Lefèvre d'Etaples,[103] these productions reached both a sizable volume and audience during the seventeenth and eighteenth centuries. A doctoral thesis "à la française" would not suffice fully to study this weekly preaching, which conveys the most ordinary pastorship of the period, the type that our ancestors would have heard from the age of catechism until death. Hence the fundamental question: Did this routine preaching, necessarily less intent than that of the missions, also transmit a message of fear?

The answer to this question must take into account the internal diversity of the corpus of material. I have purposely consulted collections of sermons that reflect a wide range of pastoral experiences and religious sensibilities. François Le Picart in the sixteenth[104] and Paul Beurrier[105] in the seventeenth century published sermons that had been addressed to the Parisians, the second, the abbot of Sainte-Geneviève, also being a priest of Saint-Etienne-du-Mont. The bishops Jean-Pierre Camus at Belley[106] and Antoine Godeau at Vence[107] shepherded congregations from small local towns. Pierre de la Font, the prior of Valabrège, who had formerly been an official of Uzès and published his sermons in 1701, also seems to have wished to reach this same sort of clientele.[108] The Oratorian Edmond Bourée had his Sunday homilies printed in 1703: These seem aimed at an undifferentiated audience.[109] This had already been the objective of François Bourgoing, the third Superior of the Oratory (d. 1662), whose *Homilies chrestiennes* . . . (1642) sought to be useful to both priests and simple laypeople, the latter being encouraged to read them either alone or to their families and servants.[110] On the other hand, François Hébert, having become Bishop of Agen, published sermons that he had given as priest of the "royal parish" of Versailles.[111] In the mid-eighteenth century, Symon was the priest of a central parish in Rennes, Saint-Germain, in whose district the Parliament of Brittany was located.[112] *Les Petits prosnes ou instructions familières* . . . of N. Girard (1st ed., 1753), the priest of Saint-Loup in the diocese of Lyon,[113] the *Missionaire paroissial*[114] (1st ed., 1753) of J. Chevassu, "former priest of the diocese of Saint-Claude," and the *Discours familiers* (1st ed., 1766) of L. Réguis,[115] "curé of the diocese of Gap and before curé of that of Auxerre," reflect the experience of the rural milieu.

The authors were themselves diverse. Their temperament, their religious situation, their spiritual families, and their objectives as pastors inform their language. François Le Picart composed vigorous polemics against the Protestants, but stressed divine mercy toward those who remained faithful. Jean-Pierre Camus, in the spirit of Saint Francis de Sales, overflows with tenderness for his flock, whom he calls "my most sweet lambs," "my most beloved," "my most dear brothers," and "my tender souls." Such formulas are not very common in the sermons. Godeau in particular hardly ever used them, and speaks in a stiff tone to his audience. Like Beurrier, he was a rigorist. Bourée is much less consoling than Bourgoing. Pierre de la Font and Girard have a threatening manner of speech. Symon, Hébert, Chevassu, and Réguis, for their part, are somewhat moderate. The third member of this group always hovers between threats and hope; so too the last one, but he found himself confronted, in the 1770s, by the rise of unbelief and he ceaselessly attacked the libertines, whose "venom" was spreading even into the fields around Auxerre. All the same, independent of individual temperaments, a claim of chronological nature can be made: The weekly sermons of Lefèvre d'Etaples, of Vigor and Le Picart in the sixteenth century, and of Jean-Pierre Camus in the early seventeenth, are less aggressive toward their listeners than those of the following period (1630–1770). It appears that the Counter-Reformation, once it had truly entered the field of combat, provoked a hardening of the language of pastors, who doubtless strove for maximum effect.

The above-proposed distinction between sermons of the missions and special occasions on the one hand and weekly preachings on the other, however pertinent it may be, cannot hide the links that joined these two types of discourses. In fact, they drew from the same sources. Joseph Chevassu entitled his sermon collection the *Missionaire paroissial*, at the end of which he indicates how to compose a series of sermons for missionary purposes by choosing from the panoply of his weekly preachings. Hence the necessity of also referring to works that sought to bring material, citations, themes, and sketches as much to missionaries as parish priests. Here one thinks especially of three great compilations that were still used by the nineteenth-century clergy. The first is *Le Pédagogue chrétien* (Saint-Omer, 1622) of the Valenciennes Jesuit Philippe d'Outreman. In the "new, revised, and augmented" version of 1650 that I consulted, the author, at the beginning of volume 2, does not conceal the fact that his first edition was a great commercial success, "as the more than fifty printings and translations into all languages testify."[116] In

Candide, Voltaire alludes to this large audience. Assuredly, the work is addressed to the general Christian reader, but d'Outreman seeks first and foremost to help the clergy to preach. He also puts at the end of each of the two volumes an "index for the use of preachers" and at the end of each chapter edifying and conclusive "histories," heirs to the *exempla* of Etienne de Bourbon (d. 1261)[117] and apt to rouse the attention of any listener.

A second compendium designed for preachers is *La Bibliothèque des prédicateurs* by another Jesuit, Vincent Houdry (1st ed., 1712). The edition I have employed, that of Lyon (1715–25), includes twenty-one quarto volumes, of which two are "supplements." At the head of these "supplements," the "bookseller" makes it known that "thc work entitled *La Bibliothèque des prédicateurs* was most favorably received by the public, since it has already gone through several editions during the space of five or six years."[118] The last reprint dates from between 1865 and 1869.

The third title on this more representative than exhaustive list is the *Dictionnaire apostolique à l'usage de MM. les curés des villes et des campagnes et de tous ceux qui se destinent à la chaire* (thirteen octavo volumes, Paris, 1752–53), by the Augustinian priest Hyacinthe de Montargon,[119] chaplain to the King of Poland before whom he preached an Advent service. Not only does this work include an entire volume of tables and index, but for each of its topics a doctrinal exposé, two "discourses" that are practically interchangeable and are addressed to a privileged audience, and finally a "familiar preaching," aimed at a more simple group of people. One can thus consult this pastoral encyclopedia to find both ready-made sermons and the elements for composing them. It was reprinted in 1822–24 and again in 1830–31. It is evident that the doctrine and emphases of these dictionaries and "apostolic" libraries were exploited by multiple sermons intended for different kinds of audiences. Provided that the social level is widened, one can add to the preceding works *La Manière de bien instruire les pauvres et en particulier les gens de la campagne*, composed by Joseph Lambert, a Sorbonne doctor and prior of Saint-Martin de Palaiseau.[120] In his preface, he notes that he has worked "primarily [for the] pastors of the countryside, who will find in this book the principal truths that they must teach to the poor folk entrusted to their care." Lambert thus attempts to provide the materials for an entire program of rural pastorship.

These four works doubled the influence of collections of sermons edited in their entirety, as they often themselves contained prepared sermons. Thus these experts in the field, endowed with both the word and writing, offered immediately usable texts to less educated and less astute priests and vicars. Pierre de la Font composed his sermons on the order of his bishop—of Uzès—"for the use of his diocese."[121] The Oratorian Loriot, who was sometimes satisfied "to put in order" the sermons of his blind colleague, Father Lejeune, writes his *Sermons sur les plus importantes matières de morale chrétienne* "for the use of those who undertake missions and those who work in parishes."[122] Girard specifies in his preface to his *Petits prones* that he composed them "for the benefit of numerous priests and vicars . . . of the country."[123] Moreover, these works were widely diffused. Lambert's *La Manière de bien instruire les pauvres* was republished six times in the eighteenth and five times in the nineteenth century. The sermons of Father Loriot went through ten editions between 1695 and 1853.[124] Those of Girard were translated into Latin in Augsburg (1766) and again reprinted in French in 1760, 1766, 1769, 1823, and 1839, and they appear in volume ninety-two of Migne's *Collection des Orateurs sacrés*. Thus these texts, first thanks to printing, but then because they were reused and repeated by obscure churchpeople, had an undeniably large impact; they may be rightly looked upon as essential sources for the most widespread doctrinal messages.

Via this documentation, which magnified the effect of the "preparations for death," the following chapters will follow the dissemination of religious fears. First, however, it will be necessary to individualize the main themes of this agonizing catechesis, before trying to assess its weight in the general discourse spoken by the church to the Catholic masses.

CHAPTER 12

"Think on It Well"

THE "PREPARATIONS FOR DEATH"

Among its terrifying themes, the evangelism of fear obviously includes death. Recent illuminating studies of this subject confirm, at least in the case of France, certain conclusions regarding the "preparations for death" and other "Think on it well" works; it will suffice to summarize them here.[1] First, it is now clear that the greatest success in France of the "preparations for death" occurred in the last quarter of the seventeenth century, in other words at the apogee of the French Counter-Reformation. During this era, religious works accounted for nearly 50 percent of all printed books,[2] and requests for masses for souls in purgatory reached their height in Parisian wills[3]; in Provence, this peak was attained somewhat later.[4] Following the ebb of the years 1530 to 1600, successively caused by humanism and the Wars of Religion, the Catholic discourse on death resumed its triumphant offensive: twenty-six new "preparations for death" from 1600 to 1624 (against ten for the entire fifty preceding years), thirty-two from 1625 to 1649, and more than sixty between 1675 and 1699. This production starts to run out of breath in the first part of the next century: only thirty-eight titles from 1700 to 1724. The deceleration then becomes even more evident: twenty unedited titles from 1725 to 1749, then thirteen for the second half of the century. Likewise, ordinations and requests for masses for the dead taper off after 1760, especially in the dioceses of Reims, Rouen, Troyes, Autun, Rodez, Grenoble, and Gap.[5]

"The pious invasion" thus came accompanied by a greatly intensified emphasis on death: Throughout Europe, the seventeenth century represented a high watermark in this regard. For example, Italian libraries overflow with revealing entitled works from this period: *De Bono mortis*, *De contemplatione mortis*, *De Arte bene moriendi*, *Atrium domus aeternitatis seu praxis praeparationis ad mortem sanctam obeundam*, *La Morte del giusto*, *L'Arte di ben morire*, *La Morte disarmata*, *Morte dolce e santa*, *Scuola della buona morte*, *La Morte felice a chi ben vive*, *Orologio della morte*, *La Preparazione alla morte*, *Vero apparecchio per la buona morte*, and so on. In France, along with the Italian Bellarmine's *De Arte bene moriendi* (1620) and the German Drexel's *Avant-coureur de l'éternité* (1636), certain books would become long-lasting best-sellers: Father Crasset's *Douce et saincte mort* (1680) and *La Préparation à la mort* (1689), with over forty editions; Father Coret's *L'Ange conducteur . . .* (1683), with twenty editions; Father de Barry's *Pensez-y-bien* (1654), with at least ten.[6]

In this religious literature of death, words gradually come to outstrip imagery —the reverse of the short versions of fifteenth-century *Ars moriendi*—the sense of the macabre grows more discreet, the place given to suicidal temptations diminishes, and the weight bears more and more on a lengthy preparation for death, one that lasts for an entire life. Consequently, these works also come to integrate invocational phrases and practices of piety that would be useful either in the usual course of life or toward its end. Finally, these writings exalt the importance of the viaticum and the role of the priest at the dying person's bedside. In describing this evolution,[7] Daniel Roche observes that an overwhelming number of the authors of the "preparations" were priests.[8] Of 190 named authors of the seventeenth and eighteenth centuries (excluding Protestants), a dozen are laypeople (Isaac Arnauld being one), ten belong to the high clergy and nineteen to the lower clergy. All the others are regular priests: For instance, the Oratorian Quesnel published an essay on *Le Bonheur de la mort chrétienne. Retrait(e) de huit jours* (1686). Among these regulars, however, Capuchins and Jesuits clearly stand out, the latter providing some sixty authors.[9] It is no accident that these two leading wings of the Counter-Reformation were invested with attending to death: The entire pedagogy of Rome was then centered on this subject. De Barry's *Pensez-y-bien*, Crasset's *La Préparation à la mort*, and Huby's *Miroir du pecheur* are all examples of successful Jesuit publications.

Both Michel Vovelle and Daniel Roche[10] propose a division of the authors of "preparations for death" and other similar works into partisans of gentleness and purveyors of terroristic messages. The first, such as Crasset and Lalemant—the latter the author of the *Saints désirs de la mort* (1673)—would appear to be the winners of the competition, if one goes by the reissues of their treatises. The group of "terrorists," on the other hand, is well represented by Father Antoine Yvan of the Oratory, founder of the Congregation of Mercy. The title of his *Trompette du ciel qui esveille les pécheurs et les excite à se convertir* (1661) sets the tone for the entire book. More generally, these authors would have stressed the disturbing side of the final days to their large audiences—who were not necessarily comprised of poor people—and reserved the reassuring aspects of death for Christian elites in retreats, whose success increased from the late seventeenth century. Resuming the earlier discussion on the two doctrinal campaigns of "fear" and "seduction,"[11] I would like to reemphasize the fact that the two discourses on death were more akin than opposed.

A priest of the Mission Saint Francis de Sales in the diocese of Vienne published a *Méthode pur finir saintement sa vie* (1741) that opens up certain perspectives on happiness. Access to the latter, however, is reached through "beneficial terrors."[12] Even the writers of consoling works stress the importance of the final moments. First, the phrase of Saint John Chrysostom, "one must not praise someone else before his death,"[13] so often reused in the seventeenth century,[14] remained current in the following period. The gentle knight De Lasne d'Aiguebelle, author of a sensitive essay on *La Religion du coeur* (1768), also speaks of "the fatal moment."[15]

The importance given to these dying moments since the fifteenth-century *Artes moriendi* explains the birth and development, during the Counter-Reformation, of lay foundations that took charge of either dying people or of individuals during the time between their death sentence and their execution.[16] During the course of the Middle Ages, a person condemned to death was seen as a future citizen of Hell and was renounced by society. An inverse viewpoint guided the foundations that were later formed to take care of such condemned people, for example in Rome from 1490 on.[17] All might be either saved or lost in the final moments of life, even if one is a criminal. Are we not all criminals, condemned to die for Original Sin? Thus he who faces execution is not fundamentally different from other sinners. The instructions given to *confortatori* to advise, comfort, and pray with "poor criminals" thus comprise only a chapter in the vast literature of the "art of dying well." The final moments of a condemned man are, even more than for others, the time of a decisive battle between the angels and the devils. Prayers and the presence of *confortatori* can only assist the victory of God in a particularly difficult case. For the success of such an enterprise, the foundations did not spare any action, any effort, any argument: They would kiss the feet of the condemned individual to beseech him to convert, they would frighten him with the prospect of Hell; if he remained obstinant, they would pray with him; they would not leave his side from between the gates of the prison and the scaffold.

Helping someone who faced hanging, burning, or decapitation was done not so much for the sake of giving comfort, but rather as a religious service. Such help did not involve getting the victim intoxicated to stun him and make him blind to his impending departure. On the contrary, it was necessary to relentlessly remind him of his presence at the gates of eternity. Lucidity is thus indispensable for this narrow journey. If, however, the condemned person was reconciled to God, he or she became an example. Having willingly accepted the sentence, such individuals could die in the firm hope of salvation. Better to die executed but repented than to be taken by sudden death, perhaps in a state of Deadly Sin.

This conclusion ultimately holds true for everyone. Crasset, whose *Préparation . . .* and *Douce mort* headed the field of French tracts on the subject in the eighteenth and even into the nineteenth century, writes: "[the time of death] is when the danger of being eternally dead most nearly threatens us."[18] He confesses that "I fear this eternal durance, whether good or bad, which depends on a single moment, unknown as yet to me, that I cannot avoid and must pass through to enter the house of eternity. I fear this final day, which will be the last of my earthly days, and the first of eternal happiness or unhappiness."[19] Farther on Crasset presents a Christian who cries out to the Lord: "Do not forsake me in the time when I will be deprived of all human aid, when all the demons will do their utmost to take my soul"[20]—an apparent evocation of the temptations of the *Ars moriendi*. "I beseech," the penitent prays, "that it may please you to strengthen me against the terrors of death[21] . . . Dissolve and drive away the fears of death that my weakness causes me to have."[22] Crasset's main objective in composing his works is to fight the anguish of people's dying moments. He judges that "fear is dangerous at the time of death" but "good during one's lifetime."[23]

Thus there again looms the need of lifelong self-preparation for the "fatal moment," the encouragement to do so being consonant with the emphasis on one's dying hour. The former Jesuit Jean-Nicolas Grou, discussing certain *Caractères de la vraie dévotion* (1788), concedes that in old age, "wan passions leave to the spirit all the clarity of its light, while infirmities bring useful warnings." In an opposite direction, however, he asserts that it is the age of "inertia," and concludes that to reach salvation one must "act against one's feelings and prepare for death throughout one's life."[24] Lalemant follows the lead of Saint John Climacus—the reference to the desert fathers continues—and says: "We cannot live piously a single day, unless we desire that it be the last day of our life, so as not to offend God. The continual thought of death ultimately quells all vices. And as perfect charity exempts man from falling into sin, so a perfect meditation on death makes it impossible to fear anything but God's judgments."[25] In this spirit, the "(Roman) Congregation of Good Death," created on the initiative of the Jesuits in 1646, devoted the last

Sunday of each month to a "retreat of preparation for death," since "each month may be the last of one's life." The members of the "congregation" undertook "to keep in mind as much as possible the thought of death, which seems to be a stimulant for removing oneself from vice."[26]

To become familiar with death necessarily entails confronting the macabre. According to Daniel Roche, references to skulls and tombs appear in 57 percent of the "preparations . . ." edited between 1750 and 1800.[27] Even authors who resist indulging morbid details recommend the sight of death. Hence this simultaneously strong and prudent advice, from Fénelon's *L'Education des filles*, which must be quoted here, following Robert Favre:

> *Get children into the habit of hearing talk of death, of seeing without anxiety a funeral shroud, an open tomb, even sick people on the verge of death and already dead people, if you can do so without exposing them to seizure by fear. There is nothing so annoying as seeing people who have spirit and piety not being able to think on death without trembling.*[28]

Going beyond Fénelon's advice, the *Formulaire de prières à l'usage des pensionnaires* (of the Ursulines) advised students to go to bed reciting the following prayer: "Alas! Thus will my body someday be put in the tomb, to be eaten by worms. O God, how mad is man, to work only for this body, which in so little time will be reduced to dust, and to neglect his soul, which is immortal."[29]

In the edition of Crasset's *Préparation* . . . that I have consulted, the first page includes the image of a victorious skeleton trampling on a grandee, musical instruments, various books, and military standards. Lalemant's *Saints désirs* . . . takes up one of Saint John Chrysostom's instructions, namely that "in order to be virtuous, one must constantly think on death, speak of it all the time, become familiar with it, visit tombs, and even attend to dying people, because nothing is so edifying and consoling as watching saints die; because nothing so discourages impiety as watching impious people die."[30] Thus, even the most consoling religious pedagogy had its gaze fixed on life's final days. The only path toward salvation goes through cemeteries. The Christian must live amid thoughts of death.

The necessary meditation on death forms a wide bridge between threatening evangelism aimed at the general public and that which gives individuals in retreats (and other such people) the holy aspiration for a liberating death. In the *Spiritual Exercises*, which the Christian elite practiced in the seventeenth and eighteenth centuries, there appears this advice: "We must imagine ourselves to be in a cemetery, looking at, touching the bones of the dead, now this head, now another; we must think that these bones were those of people like us, rich in honors, loaded with all the possessions of this world."[31]

Another similar line incites: "Portray me in the bed of death, crucifix in hand, a candle lit, and attendants praying for me."[32]

Grignion de Montfort also asserted that "the death of the righteous person is sweet and desirable," and to make it so, he invited his listeners—in this case, especially people on retreat—to

> *inspire them to follow certain practices of the saints for thinking on death, such as: 1) Sleep in the position of death. 2) Eat a piece of bread at each meal to feed the worms that will eat the body. 3) Consider illnesses as the companions of death. 4) Keep a death's head in one's room, and contemplate what it has been, what it is, and what it will be, and reflect on oneself. 5) Make one's reliquary and tomb, and kiss them every day.*[33]

Fénelon once gave this counsel to the Elector of Cologne: "You must constantly be dead to yourself, in order to bring others to follow this practice of death which is the foundation of Christianity."[34] Dom Jean-Paul Du Sault also addresses "religious people" and tells them that they must "make an alliance" with death: "O death," he writes, "I wish to ally myself with thee . . . I will take thee for my sister, for my wife, for my friend . . . I will live in thy house, which is the grave . . . I will divest myself from now on of all that I love and possess on this earth, in your favor."[35]

These remarks clearly speak the familiar language of followers of "the contempt for this world." For the great common denominator of all "preparations for Death," whether terrifying or reassuring, is the doctrine of the *contemptus mundi*. In this regard, a revealing comparison can be made between Yvan's *Trompette du ciel* and Lalemant's *Saints désirs de la mort*. The first work teaches fear: "He who lives without the fear of God and of himself is a great ignorant fool and a lost soul,"[36] and Lalemant logically encourages "renouncing the maxims and examples of the world." For "the way of the world [is] opposed to God's way, and is the enemy of Jesus Christ." "The business of this world is a great obstacle to the business of salvation, the most important of all." "To adhere to the spirit of God, one must strip oneself of the spirit of the world and of oneself." These statements are selected from the chapter headings of his book.[37] As for Father Lalemant, he seeks to show the reader how to learn "to desire death." He will thus demonstrate how "to have contempt for life": In fact, his entire book is a dissertation on the contempt for this world, with repeated citations of Saint Augustine, Saint Cyprian, Saint Jerome, the Greek fathers, Saint Gregory the Great, and Saint Bernard. One learns that "to the degree that the Christian feels his love of virtue increasing, so will he also feel the desire for death growing in him"; "Christians—a maxim of Saint Cyprian—should not love the world, since the world hates Christians, and they must be joyful when death delivers them from the traffic of the world"; "the principal character [of a Christian] is to desire and love death"—a phrase of Saint John Chrysostom; "the strongest virtue of Christians and the most visible character of the chosen, is to continually sigh and moan while waiting for death, and in the hope for another life"—a teaching of Saint Augustine. The author completes his treatise by recalling the "admirable feelings that Saint Theresa left us in her writings, concerning meditation on eternity and the desire for death."[38] In short, a monastic and mystical language would henceforth address tens and tens of thousands of readers.

The same analysis is at work in Crasset's book. The penitent whom the pious Jesuit momentarily allows to speak declares: "Having but a miserable life that I have nearly used up in offending [God], I say that I am delighted to lose it."[39] Crasset's work contains further advice, which could be that of a twelfth-century monk, an apostle of the *contemptus mundi*:

> *In reflecting that you are still alive on this earth, you must moan as if in exile, and constantly sigh for the happy eternity that is your true homeland, where you will have a life that lasts as long as that of God himself. You must completely detach your heart from the love of this world, since sin, death, and the domination of the devil have reigned here since Adam's sin, as Saint Paul teaches us: hence it follows that the earth we inhabit is called the region of shadow and death, and that our body is called the body of death. Finally, men living on the earth are not only mortal, but Jesus Christ confirms that they are just so many dead people, when he*

said to the young man who wished to inter his father before coming after him: "Let the dead bury the dead . . ."

Might we understand leaving an earth that is the land of death and the place of our banishment?[40]

In addition, the Bibliothèque Nationale in Paris preserves twelve different editions of Crasset's *Préparation* reprinted from 1689 to 1825. Such was the longevity of his audience.

Identifying the common basis of two types of works on Christian death leads to the observation that the horror and desire of death often existed in the same writings. There was no contradiction between the two attitudes. Death is horrible, being the worst of punishments inflicted on sinful man. At the same time, it is desirable, since it puts an end to our exile in this "vale of tears": It opens onto the light. Robert Favre recounts in his fine study *La Mort au siècle des Lumières* that in 1784 the inhabitants of Vitry-le-François saw for the first time against a pillar of their church a sculpture, still in place, representing "Religion trampling death." The latter is a grimacing skeleton whose shroud does not fully cover his skull and bodily extremities. This character is offset by two cherubs and the radiant figure of Religion, who carries the cross and smiles at the corpse. An inscription recalls a phrase from the *Imitation*: "Happy they who always keep death before their eyes, and who only live to learn how to die well."[41] The religious macabre of the fourteenth to sixteenth centuries discussed in earlier chapters also had this significance. It led to hope for resurrection, by way of the spectacle of the decomposing body. There was thus a repetition of an essential discourse on death.

In the mid-eighteenth century, two carefully chosen witnesses, Saint Alphonsus of Liguori and Caraccioli, together speak for both the disgust caused by the cadaver and the aspiration for death that any true Christian must feel; these two attitudes have their roots in the *contemptus mundi*. The founder of the Redemptorians' *Apparecchio alla Morte*, or Preparation for Death, appeared in 1758, while Caraccioli's *Le Tableau de la mort* came out in 1761. The first work was an enormous success—350 editions from 1758 to 1961, 128 of them Italian.[42] The second received a certain measure of contemporary esteem (three editions in 1761, one in 1765, and another in 1767). Saint Alphonsus had a profound knowledge of the literature of spirituality. Caraccioli, a layman, was only a "Christian moralist of the second rank." It is all the more remarkable to see the one (in France) and the other (in Italy) speaking the same language. Above all, the language of the macabre. Caraccioli:

I would like for man . . . to be shown lying between worms and putrefaction, successively losing his eyes, his ears, his lips, and becoming a hideous skeleton, apt to terrify the entire human race . . .

There is no more fearful spectacle than that of a dying man: all his features grimace, his eyes are lost, his mouth turns, his face goes to pieces, his limbs become twisted, his soul spills over in regrets and sighs, and all his nature seems to go unstitched . . .

It is necessary that this death be necessarily fearful, since it is a consequence of sin, that is to say a terrible punishment of our pride. And what punishment! . . .

At a gallery in Florence . . . a worker traced in wax all that rotting could do to the body. First one saw a body swell, become livid and greenish, get cut open by cuts, split wide open, fill with worms, and finally dessicate and decay into powder . . . at the end, a man loses even the name of corpse, says Tertullian; he dissolves into dust and vapor.[43]

At the beginning of his *Apparecchio*, Saint Alphonsus recommends:

> *Imagine that you are looking at someone who has just died. Behold this corpse, still lying in bed, with head slumped on chest: the disheveled hair, still bathed in the sweat of death; the sunken eyes, emaciated cheeks, skin the color of ashes, tongue and lips the color of iron, the entire body cold and heavy. Whosoever sees it grows pale and trembles. How many, upon seeing a dead friend or relative, have changed their lives and renounced the world!*
>
> *The cadaver causes an even greater horror when it begins to rot. Less than twenty-four hours have passed since the death of this young man; and already one can smell the stench. One must open the doors, burn much incense, and make sure to promptly send the body to the church and bury it, so that it will not stink up the entire house . . .*
>
> *To better see what you are, my Christian friend, says Saint John Chrysostom, "go to the graveyard, and contemplate the dust, the ashes, and the worms, and sigh."*[44] *See how this corpse first becomes yellow, then black. There then appears a white and repulsive coating all over the body, and a slimy, stinking putrefaction that infests the earth. From this pus there soon is born a great quantity of worms, which feed on the flesh. The rats then join in, and they also feed on this body, some attacking the outside, others gnawing through the mouth and entrails. Cheeks, lips, and hair fall off in pieces. The sides are the first to go hollow, then the arms and legs. The worms, after having eating all the flesh, eat themselves; and finally, all that remains of this body is a fetid skeleton, which comes undone over the course of time, its bones falling apart from each other and its head cracking off from the neck and shoulders.*[45]

This striking excerpt is clearly worthy of any anthology of the macabre. It must be taken, however, within the context not only of the *Apparecchio* but also the work of Saint Alphonsus. To be sure, the description commences this "preparation for death"; nonetheless, the book is not predominantly morbid. Only one of thirty-six meditations is on the corpse. Moreover, if the *Apparecchio* went through 350 editions, other works by the saint, which have nothing to do with the macabre, were far more successful: *Les Visites au Saint Sacrament*, 2,017 editions; the *Gloires de Marie*, more than a thousand; the *Pratica di amar Gesu-Cristo*, 535.[46]

The macabre opening of the *Apparecchio* belongs to an ancient tradition (in eighteenth-century France the "Bibliothèque bleue" continued to spread the *Grande danse macabre*),[47] but above all it can be understood only when linked to the explicitly cited Chrysostom and an entire monastic tradition; simultaneously, it must be connected to the *contemptus mundi*, itself a cause of the desire for death. In this regard as well, Caraccioli and Saint Alphonsus say basically the same thing.

Caraccioli:

> *It is remarkable that there are people so detached from the world that they can sequester themselves in Carthusian monasteries; but it is quite more remarkable that not all men run to such places . . .*
>
> *I would gladly say, like Job: "Why died I not from the womb? . . ."*
>
> *Death, according to the renowned Leibniz, is only an advantageous development of our faculties, which enlarges the sphere of our knowledge, of our activity, and our happiness . . .*
>
> *What a hideous moment must be that of our burial, to the eyes of a world accustomed to admiring only the body, to enjoying only the pleasures of the senses, and to feeding on naught but vanity! But what a blessed moment to the eyes of a*

religion that is entirely devoted to condemning the body, to see it as a sack of dust and corruption, and to esteeming only the life of our soul.

Saint Alphonsus:

David calls the happiness of our earthly life "dreams" (Ps. 73:20) . . . Who thinks on death cannot love the earth . . . Let us now remove ourselves from desiring the things of this earth before death inevitably snatches them from us . . . Life is like a vapor, that a breath of wind disperses . . .

The passions momentarily make the things of this world seem other than they are. Death reveals them, and shows them in their true form: vapor, filth, vanity, and misery . . . What purpose does the beauty of the body serve, if only worms, stench, and horror are left of it? . . .

Seen from the point of view of the senses, death horrifies and is to be feared; but for they who have faith, it comforts and is to be desired . . . Tertullian is right to say that when God cuts short someone's life, he also cuts short its torments . . . Death is certainly given to man as a punishment of sin, but the miseries of this life are so numerous that death (as Saint Ambrose says) seems granted to us as a support, and not as a punishment . . .

Saint Jerome prayed to death, and told her: "Open to me, my sister!" . . . San Carlo Borromeo, seeing a painting of a skeleton in his house, with scythe in hand, called the painter and ordered him to erase the scythe and replace it with a golden key. In this way, he wished to constantly inspire himself to wish for death, since it is death who must open paradise for us and allow us to see God.[49]

Emile Mâle attributes a decisive role to the *Spiritual Exercises* in the resurgence of the Christian macabre that accompanied the Counter-Reformation. "Death," he writes, "perpetually lent itself to the meditation of generations shaped by the commentaries on the *Spiritual Exercises* and pious retreats of the Company of Jesus."[50] He adds,

All the Counter-Reformation saints read this book. There is hardly an ascetic tract where one does not recognize its spirit. In reading L'Image de la vie chrétienne *by the Portuguese Hieronymite Hector Pinto, R. P. Charles Jouye Récollet's* Brève instruction pour méditer, *the Italian Theatin Scupoli's* Combat spirituel, *or Pierre de Bresse's* Héraclite chrétien, *death always comes across as the best remedy against the violence of the passions.*[51]

On the basis of Mâle's statements, one could emphasize the example of Bernini, who was the first artist to sculpt a grandiose skeleton on any tomb (that of Urban VIII) and who thereafter seems to have constantly had the figure of death in mind in his sculptures. Moreover, Bernini, who took communion twice a week, undertook an annual retreat along the lines of the *Spiritual Exercises*. He often went to pray, in Rome, in the Jesuit chapel of "Good Death," and the thought on his final end was familiar to him. Likewise, as discussed above, the Company (Jesuits) played a major role in the diffusion of scenes of martyrdom.[52]

All the same, the Spanish original of the *Spiritual Exercises* . . . does not mention the meditation on death.[53] Father Bourdeau, however, appositely demonstrates that Saint Ignatius himself accepted an amendment in this regard.[54] From its inception, the Company of Jesus made use of meditations on death and judgment. Before the death of Saint Ignatius, his secretary Father Polanco had already added the following lines to the fifth exercise of the first week in the *Versio vulgata* (1548): "If he who gives the *Exercises* deems it advantageous to the progress of the novices to add . . . other meditations, such as on death, on the other penalties of sin, on judgment, etc., he should not think that such is prohibited, even if they are not herein prescribed."[55] Likewise, the official rule book, *In Exercitia spiritualia B.P.N. Ignatii*, laid down by the Company in 1599 after the convening of the different provinces, gives this advice in chapter 20, part four: "To these five exercises of our blessed Father Ignatius one may add others, such as: on the other penalties of sin, of death, of judgment, and of the other tortures of hell. And, in truth, it seems that they should rarely be omitted." In practice, then, the *Exercises* . . . must almost always have included one if not several meditations on death.

It is therefore impossible to deny the contribution of the Jesuits to the new vogue for the macabre. This resurgence, however, also stimulated by the cruelty of the Wars of Religion, would no doubt have happened even without Saint Ignatius's Company. The *Meditaciones para todos los dias de la Semana* (1554) of the famous Dominican Louis of Granada offers an itinerary organized for meditating on death and one's final souls: Day 1, knowledge of ourselves and our sins; Day 2, the miseries of this life; Day 3, the hour of death; Day 4, Judgment; Day 5, the pains of Hell; Day 6, the glory of the chosen; Day 7, the blessings of God.[56] The *Tratado de la oracion y meditacion* (1556) by the Franciscan Saint Peter of Alcantara follows this work closely: Day 1, meditation on sins and self-knowledge; Day 2, the miseries of this life; Day 3, death; Day 4, Last Judgment; Day 5, the pains of Hell; Day 6, Heaven; Day 7, the blessings of God.[57]

It made sense for this period's Catholic evangelical program to place in the foreground both the thought and actual image of death. True, the terrifying depictions of the "Triumph of Death" disappear in the seventeenth and eighteenth centuries, with the exception of certain archaic scenes of the Apocalypse, such as in the *Grand Compost des bergers* of the "Bibliotheque bleue." Recumbent gisants and "*transi*" tombs gradually ceded the stage to skeletons and especially skulls, which in Michel Vovelle's words became thoroughly "aseptic." All the same, during the golden age of the Counter-Reformation, skulls and bones were "alive and well," and through iconography were frequently offered to a wider audience than that which could achieve the "preparations for death." Churches and hospitals, paintings of the death of saints, chapels and altars for souls in purgatory, charnal-house sculptures, costumes of the the penitential brotherhoods, the southern Capuchins' cemeteries, and saints' relics presented either as mummies with waxen masks or as clothed and bejeweled skeletons: These rueful images were given as opportunities for all Christians to meditate on their mortality.

Throughout the seventeenth-century Catholic world, the sense of the macabre induced by the *contemptus mundi* had led to a flourishing production of "vanitas" paintings and engravings. Bossuet's and Bourdaloue's sermons, as well as the numerous poems arguing that "life is a dream," have their counterparts in Georges de La Tour's *Mary Magdalene Meditating on a Skull*, Valdes Leal's *Three Coffins* at the Seville Hospital of Charity, and a great many other compositions that associate the skull, hourglass, and flower. When the seventeenth century presented a saint for admiration by the faithful—whether Bruno, Francis of Assisi, Francis-Xavier, Carlo Borromeo, and others—it preferred to show him or her meditating before a skull. For the death's head was "in France and throughout Europe, as well as in Italy, the emblem of saintliness."[58] All these Christian heroes had understood that on this earth "all is vanity."

Certainly the clerically inscribed macabre generally receded during the eighteenth century, at the same time that the Counter-Reformation was losing momentum. During sporadic outbursts of religious fervor, however, the skulls and bones would then reappear. A connection has been made between the return of these macabre images in late eighteenth-century Italy[59] and the Redemptorian missions, as well as the diffusion of the *Apparecchio alla morte* . . . Although this observation is correct, it is too narrow. In reality, the Counter-Reformation was making a strong comeback in southern Italy, not only with Saint Alphonsus's and the Redemptorians' preaching but also through the activity of bishops who sought to imitate San Carlo Borromeo: Giovanni-Angelo Anzani, Ignazio, and Nicola Monterisi, and so on.[60] Not surprisingly, therefore, the same evangelism gave rise to the same images.

To take hold of the audience of this evangelism thus leads on toward a more important source than the preparations for death: sermons. In primarily illiterate populations, Christian acculturation took place through oral means: specifically, through preaching. Hence the works of Father Crasset, Saint Alphonsus, and others were conceived and designed for wide oral diffusion, to be accomplished by preachers, by local priests, or even by laypeople who assembled their families and servants for lessons on how to die well.

In fact, the preparations for death and the sermons shared a reciprocal influence. Preachers had read works on the art of dying well. Other churchmen, such as Saint Alphonsus, were missionaries, who then composed manuals on death; these in turn supplied material for sermons. Consequently, these two documentary sources speak the same language.

SERMONS AND HYMNS

Throughout the remainder of this book's discussion not only of death but also of the evangelism of guilt, sermons and hymns will comprise the main documentary resource. Clearly, these works are rich in their diversity, due to their authors' widely ranging times, places, and outlooks. My thematic study, however, will strive to highlight the homogeneity and repetitivenes of the ecclesiastical discourse of this time. These two aspects appear to be of more consequence than the variations of detail from one text to another.

Regarding death, the sermons and hymns incline toward the previously identified double language, which alternately stressed the horror and desirability of death. One of San Bernardino di Siena's sermons offers a significant and quite early example, as he successively asserts that death is "most near," "most cruel," "most audacious," "most fierce," "most deceptive," "most hidden," and "is waiting for us everywhere," but that, "pitiless" as it may be, it is nevertheless a "blessing." For "it separates mutually incompatible elements, so that they will no longer attack one another (the soul and body), and it is the port for they who, worn out by life in this world, seek a place of rest."[61] In the sixteenth century, François Le Picart taught his Parisian listeners that "the day which should be most desired is the day of death, for it is the end of all sins and miseries."[62]

Philippe d'Outreman's *Le Pédagogue chrétien*, a veritable preacher's encyclopedia filled with macabre tales, accounts of sudden death, and phrases such as "fearful eternity"[63] and "God's dreadful tribunal,"[64] gives two counsels for fighting against the fear of death. First, one must think of it often and "await it patiently": "We must take this bull by the horns and not let it see us first, in fear that it would make us speechless through suddenly overwhelming terror." Then follows the second remedy:

Ardently desire to die, in order that you may sooner rejoice in God . . . They who gladly await and desire death . . . are like those who seek out veins of silver and gold, whose joy is never so great as when they finally find what they are seeking. What joy shall a good soul feel, when it receives the news that it will soon discover, through a happy death, veins of inexhaustible treasure that it will possess forever and ever![65]

In a homily for the fifteenth Sunday after Pentecost, François Bourgoing concedes that "in itself, death is hideous and terrifying" and that "among terrible things, it is the most terrible"; at the same time, he confirms that the death of saints "is for them sweet and lovely," and he concludes with this prayer: "O precious death, death saintly and happy! O that my soul may die the death of the Righteous, and that my final hour may be like theirs."[66] Another Oratorian, Julien Loriot, emphasizes in his ninth sermon on fear that even desert ascetics were distressed at the moment of death.[67] In his first sermon, however, he had exclaimed: "For how long, my Lord, will I live in this mortal body, where I can offend you and be cut off from you? When will that day come, that blessed day, when I, being completely united with you, will never be apart from you?"[68] Among the hymns that the Brothers of the Christian Schools published in 1703 for the use of their students, several are devoted to "death," to "judgment," to "the four ends of mankind," to "the sorrows of the damned soul"; but the one that treats of "the feelings of love for Jesus" includes these quatrains:

Blessed martyrs,
How I thee admire,
For having sacrificed
Your lives to Jesus . . .

When shall that day come
When in the angelic host
We shall give ye
Thousands upon thousands of praises?[69]

Likewise, the *Recueil des cantiques . . . durant les missions et retraites à l'usage du diocèse de Rennes* contains a number of macabre passages, evocations of the Last Judgment, and sharp invitations to penitence, but also verses that express a longing for death:

I languish
On this foreign Earth . . .
Comforting death,
Come to cut the cord
That impedes me,

That binds me
And drags me
Into the dangers
Of a thousand torrents.
O that I might die!
For I desire sweet rest.[70]

In another collection of hymns, published at Angers, one reads:

Heaven will be closed to me my entire life,
And only thee, O death, can open it to me.
Come, happy moment of infinite glory . . .[71]

The same coexistence of dreaded death and desired death appears in the hymnals of the Czech poet-editor Adam Michna (1600–1676), whose work of 1647 includes the following stanzas:

Sound out the final hour—
We shall die . . .

To heav'n, to heav'n, we haste
Most joyously

For so long have I thee desired, *Toward God we take flight*
Divine lodging! *In our piety.*[72]

So too do the sermons of the associate priest Réguis feared with wished-for death. Only three pages separate the following lines, which occur within the same homily (for the eighth Sunday after Pentecost): "What is death, after all? The end of a thousand miseries . . . [we should] desire the grave, as the place of our rest and the end of our pain"; "Come, come [it is Death who speaks] descend with me into the tomb: open this coffin, unfold this winding sheet. You tremble: it makes no difference."[73]

For the righteous, death gives access to an eternity of happiness. In itself, however, it is a punishment, the consequence of Original Sin. A Lazarist mission's sermon strongly expresses this conviction:

> *Oh, my dear brothers . . . remember that you are wretches, condemned to death, not by the courts, but by the irrevocable sentence of God's high justice. You are in the world; but you will be taken from it to be led to a torture whose gallows will be your own bed; for nobody dies a natural death, since this death is the execution of a decree of the Lord, who has condemned us to it; why not then prepare yourself for it?*[74]

This position is plainly distinct from Thomist doctrine, which sees death as a "natural" phenomenon and teaches that the immortality granted to our first parents in the earthly paradise was, on the contrary, "preternatural." In his *De Origine Mali* (1702), the Anglican archbishop William King followed Aquinas's line of thought: "[With his first sin] man rediscovered his original mortality."[75] Maintaining the spirit of his Lazarist predecessors, Hyacinthe de Montargon also notably explains:

> *You cannot see the state of man at his death without instantly thinking of his sin. The grave implies crime (*stipendia peccati mors, *Rom. 6:23); consequently, the time spent there can only be most shameful. Furthermore, one must regard the grave as the place where the final terms of our sentence are carried out: Divine Justice pursues men there, even after their death, and not content with having taken their lives, reduces them to ashes.*[76]

The students of the Brothers of the Christian Schools sang during the Christmas season:

Fallen from grace, Adam *The world became the victim*
Did change our fate. *Of Death and the Devil.*[77]

Another noël hymn of the *Manuel des retraites et missions à l'usage du diocèse de Rennes* concordantly declares:

The pride of our first parents
Lost the souls of all their children,
And each of them is born a criminal: Noël, Noël.
Heaven by a just destiny
Condemns us all to die—
'Tis a universal decree: Noël, Noël.[78]

A number of authors, however, also affirm that death is the deserved result of the personal sins of our earthly lives. Montargon, preaching on Assumption Day, develops this theme in a remarkable way. He asks his listeners,

> *O ye men, is your death, like Mary's, the glorious effect of a heart consumed with love? Alas! It is often in us only the sad effect of a temperament worn down by crime, of a body dried up by lust, burned by intemperance, scorched with anger, devoured by ambition. One dies every day, and from what? From the chagrin of a secret infidelity or a hurtful preference, of an overwhelming sorrow or the death of a loved one, etc. People die, and for some, it is the result of ever-insatiable greed; for others, it is the result of voluptuous delicacy; people die and for many it is the punishment for their immoderate desire for glory, which makes them face a thousand dangers, endure a thousand risks, engage in frequent quarrels of honor and finally succumb to their adversary's fire and fury.*[79]

Such an assertion speaks the logic of a doctrine that taught that death was "unnatural." In a sermon concerning the preparation for death, Bridaine could thus encourage the penitent to address God in these terms: "I grovel here before you, Lord, like a criminal, worthy of a thousand deaths . . . I consent to the separation of my soul and my body, as punishment for the sin with which I separated myself from you . . . O dust, o ashes, o worms, I cherish all of you, and regard you as the instruments of the justice of my Lord, punishing my vainglory, as well as the pride which made me rebel against your orders."[80]

Since death is punishment, it was to be expected that early modern evangelism, with its concern for "conversion," stressed its melodramatic aspects over the comforting notions that it offered the elect. Was it not taught that the latter were in the minority? Hence the long survival, at the level of a widely diffused oral discourse, of themes as time-worn as the "*Ubi sunt?*" Thus the numerous eighteenth-century students of the Brothers of the Christian Schools were made to sing:

> *Where be they now,*
> *The most powerful kings? . . .*
>
> *Where is the wise Israelite?*
> *Where the strong Samson?*
> *The lovely Jonathan*
> *And the fair Absalom*
>
> *And thou noble Caesar,*
> *Who sought to make the world*
>
> *Prostrate at thy feet,*
> *And burdened with thy chains—*
> *Admit that death*
> *With deadly ruin*
> *Did make of thee*
> *The food of worms.*[81]

The Franciscan Leonard of Port-Maurice, who was enormously popular in eighteenth-century Italy, also resumes the old refrain: "Where are all the famous warriors and scholars? Where an Alexander, a Cato? They are dead and gone, taking with them neither their brave deeds, nor their great knowledge."[82] The theme of Death the Leveler, closely linked to the "*Ubi sunt?*" topos and found in vivid form in the *danses macabres*, remains present in the hymns of the Brothers of the Christian Schools:

> *Death lays all things low*
> *And respects nothing,*
> *Nor rich nor wise,*
> *Nor those who are well spoken;*
>
> *Death strikes quietly*
> *In all places, at all times,*
> *The priest, the layman,*
> *The good and the bad,*

Be you young and healthy,
Be you old or infirm,
Today it is my turn,
Tomorrow yours.

Both night and day,
In town and field,
In autumn, winter,
Summer, spring.[83]

Similarly, Michna's *Musique mariale* observes:

Death destroys silver, wrecks gold,
And turns all riches into mud.
'Tis the end of every treasure . . .

Once the knell rings out,
Ashes and dust begin to stink.
The season without end commences.

It wipes out royal favors
And scoffs at lordly commands;
'Tis the end of all power . . .

Mankind, think upon this end,
Always think of that bell,
And sin ye shall not.[84]

Michna's hymn was reused by the Jesuit Steyer in his Czech *Cantionnaire* and occurs in all of its six editions, from 1683 to 1764.

Despite these tenacious survivals, can it be said that lugubrious images are truly present in the hymns and sermons of the seventeenth and eighteenth centuries? A distinction must be made between, on the one hand, sermons for the fifty-two Sundays of the liturgical year and, on the other hand, encyclopedias for the missions' preachers, hymns, and sermons. The sense of the macabre persists much more strongly in this second part of the corpus than in the first. Philippe d'Outreman's *Le Pédagogue chretien*, having first told tales of sudden deaths, presents twelve "examples of those who refrained from sinning by the remembrance of death." One of these concerns a priest of Hainaut, who could not stop thinking of a certain woman, even though she had been dead for more than three years. To overcome this temptation, he eventually paid a nocturnal visit to the dead woman's tomb and, "having lowered himself down, he put his nostrils to her carcass, for as long as he could bear its stench, and then finally fell on his back, as if half-dead. Coming to his senses, he emerged victorious, as he never again felt any goad of the flesh."[85] In another similar anecdote, a hermit, "unable to remove a dead woman from his imagination, descended into her tomb and cut off a piece of her flesh, which he then would put to his nostrils whenever the thought of this woman came back to him; each time, the stink of this rotten flesh would make him victorious."[86]

Citation has already been made of Saint Alphonsus of Liguori's frightening description of the corpse, from the time of death to its being devoured by worms in the grave.[87] In fact, he was not the author of this striking passage. His is a nearly word-for-word translation of a sermon by Leonard of Port Maurice, which predates the *Apparecchio* . . .[88] and is devoted to "the certainty of death"[89]: It thus seems to have become a topos in eighteenth-century Italian missionary preaching. The same holds true for the description of death throes that, in Port-Maurice's text but not in the *Apparecchio*, precedes the passage on the corpse. These same two sequences appear in a hymn on death included in the *Manuel des retraites et missions . . . de Rennes*. It is worth quoting several stanzas of this poem, which was sung to the faithful during the mid-eighteenth century and which brings together all the traditional components of macabre teaching, such as the "miroir" and the *contemptus mundi*:

Stanza 6: Behold the horrid ugliness
Disfiguring this lovely face,
As soon as a cold sweat

Covers the body with its gloom:
All these features and vain charms
Now disappear forever.

Stanza 7: *This wrinkled brow, these deathly eyes,*
This pale and ashen color,
These sighs of a dying man
Which strike fear into the most fearless soul
Ah! What a strange transformation
Death makes in a single moment.

Stanza 8: *Brought to the edge of his grave*
Consider him in the bier
See what a horrid new change
Before he returns to dust.
This is naught but a corpse of horror
Whose smell one cannot endure.

Stanza 9: *Behold this crawling mass of worms*
Which are born in the decay
See how they devour the flesh
Of the body, which is their fodder:
That which so charmed our eyes
Supplies delicious meals for them.

Stanza 10: *Contemplate this hideous skull,*
Listen to his sad speech;
Although he is mute, he speaks better
Than does the wisest man—
Ah! Could anyone so eloquently
Prove what our end is to be?

Stanza 11: *Alas, what hast thou become,*
Fine clothes, splendid coiffures?
A mass of filth and pus
Is what remains of your finery.
Is it not mad to so much cherish,
That which one sees will so soon perish?

Stanza 12: *Such is the fate that awaits you,*
Man of mud and dust;
Yes, this body you so adore,
Will soon rot within the earth;
And despite your divers cares,
It shall soon become the food of worms.

Stanza 13: *And that is where you shall someday be,*
Judged there for what you are:
A heap of decayed bones,
Like all these ghastly skeletons;
Learn at last what someday hence
You too shall become in your turn.

Stanza 14: *Contemplate this grisly object,*
See thyself there, ashes and dust,
Recognize in this portrait

That which you shall be in the coffin
You could not ever see yourself
In a mirror more faithful than this.

Stanza 15: Since you cannot doubt
So obvious a truth
Beware not to flatter
Such vile corruptible flesh;
To prevail over such a fate
One must die before one's death.[90]

This hymn, the collection specifies, was sung at the beginning of the mission and to the tune of "dites votre *confiteor*."

In seventeenth- and eighteenth-century France, weekly sermons for the liturgical year rarely feature both ample and polyvalent macabre details that are aimed at both the devout and the pious. On the other hand, Sunday sermons and missionary preaching together stress the death of the sinner, and in this context recover the terrors of the deathbed and the vermin off the tomb. The evidence suggests that Counter-Reformation evangelism, increasing the contrast between the death of the sinner versus that of the righteous, tended to concentrate the numerous elements of the macabre tradition on the former. One of the fifty-five Lazarist sermons of this period is indicative of this evolution. The missionary address his guilty audience in the following terms:

> *. . . You shall see yourself stretched out in your own bed, as you soon shall be in your grave. How sad is this vision! And how shattering your thoughts at that time! —"In a short while, I will be but a corpse; in a short while, they will put me in the ground!" . . .*
>
> *All that, however, is nothing next to the horror of the anguish that will seize you once you begin to see the approach of death: when you begin to feel your feet grow cold, your hands to lose their strength, your eyes to grow dark, your face and entire body covered with a chilling deathly sweat, your tongue stammering, and your bowels in a fearful state, which Holy Scripture compares to the pangs of a woman in labour:* Dolores parturientis venient ei *(Hos. 13:13); finally, when, during this final seizure, you will feel this vile breast, the seat of so many licentious feelings, to contract and palpitate in the last moments preceding the ultimate mournful sigh that puts an end to it all.*[91]

Likewise, in two interchangeable sermons on the death of the sinner, the priest Girard emphasizes how it is a "horrifying tragedy." He first invites his listeners to attend this overpowering spectacle:

> *[the sinner] will suffer extremest pain in his body; it will seem to him that his skull is constantly being opened. His eyes will gleam with the heat of his fever. His ears will let in a dreadful noise. His tongue will be entirely dried out. His mouth will burn like a furnace. He will have such aversion that meats and stews will seem like poison to him . . . It will be hard for this dying man to breathe, he will not have a minute of rest, for he will feel cramps, churning in his stomach, poundings in his heart, shivers and fainting fits. The pain will run through the very marrow of his bones. He will feel he is on fire, and that all his members are being ripped apart: in short, he will suffer, in the words of Holy Scripture, like a woman in childbirth (Ezek. 30).*[92]

The sinner, Girard adds, "will be deprived of all nature's blessings." What then shall become of his body? The answer:

> *Hideous sepulcher, horrible grave, you are the sole refuge of this abominable body, for after you he has only to wait for eternal flames. There his only company shall be worms; there pus and filthy decay shall be his bed, his blanket, and mattress, as is said in Holy Scripture (Ecclus. 10:10). "To a coffin, a grave, the snakes, the vermin, and corruption: such is the end, as the wise man says (Job 17:9), of the most flourishing youth, the most vigorous health, the most perfect beauty, dexterity, strength, and all other natural gifts. He will be stripped, this sinner, of all the blessings of fortune."*[93]

The climax of this excerpt reveals how the macabre is here employed in only one direction, as though it were henceforth to be reserved for the reprobate only.

The same arbitrary distinction occurs in a hymn by Grignion de Montfort on "the despair of the dying sinner." The soul, on its way down to hell, says to the body:

> *Adieu, accursed carcass,*
> *Adieu, food for worms.*
> *I shall await thee in the place*
> *Reserved for thee in hell.*
>
> *Ah! If I had tamed thee,*
> *Death would be my pleasure.*
> *But alas! I flattered thee—*
> *'Tis my cruel remorse.*[94]

The central idea behind these descriptions is that the sinner's death is especially painful due to his or her sudden moral afflictions. These agonies, however, are augmented by all sorts of macabre images. Réguis, contrasting the sinner's death throes to those of the Christian soul—who "sighs after the moment of his deliverance"—describes the former in the following way:

> *These listless eyes, or else unusually bright with the heat of a burning fever, will remind you, my dear child, of the sins that you yourself have committed through your miserable eyes. These pale and trembling lips, this dried-up palate, this thick or furred tongue will recall your curses, your swearing, your indecent speech, your lascivious kisses, your intemperance, your drunkenness, your excess . . . This body in pain from head to foot will be as a witness who will give evidence against you and will call to your memory all the iniquities of which you are guilty, and in which he also shared.*[95]

Nonetheless, the authors of hymns and sermons sometimes hinted that even sinners may have a peaceful end: a slight testimony to an actual experience of death that did not always correspond to the preconceived notions of official doctrine. A Lazarist sermon begins with the question: "Is there any Christian who does not shudder at the very thought of a bad death?" The text then presents two equally dreadful possibilities: "Either the sinner dies in the knowledge of his misery, and hence he dies in a kind of despair, which is very common; or he dies without hardly knowing himself, and hence in a horrible insensitivity."[96] In a long hymn on the "contempt for this world," Grignion de Montfort slips into self-contradiction. First he describes the hardened sinner who commits offense upon offense, then "dies without apprehension / and falls into damnation."[97] Only ten stanzas later, however, the classic scenario reappears: "But at his death, what despair / What rage, what stabbing pain."[98] An eighteenth-century Breton preacher thought it necessary to warn his congregation of an important distinction: Some people "have a good death in the eyes of the world, but a bad one in the eyes of religion."[99]

Having identified these fleeting hesitations, there remains the central discourse of the death of the sinner. This moment of passing is terrible, because it gives the dying person a glimpse of the tragic fate that lies waiting in the afterlife. Port-Maurice explains the matter quite well: "It is not so much the pains of the body, nor the agonies of the sickness that afflict the dying man, for since his physical nature begins to dissolve, it is less sensitive to the blows of suffering: thus if one asks the sick man at his last extremity, he will answer that he does not suffer." Thus an objective observation is made here concerning the natural process of dying. The preacher, however, goes on:

> *The true pain of dying belongs to the soul, to the interior, and not to the body . . . All the sins that you have committed since your first use of reason to the present time, in their number, kind, and circumstance, will come to assail you like an impetuous flood . . . [Your iniquities] will pierce your very heart, like so many sharp thorns.. You will wish to rid yourself of such thoughts: impossible.*[100]

These statements thus are part of a coherent, homogeneous, and incessantly repeated doctrinal program that can be seen in the work of San Bernardino at Siena[101] as much as in nineteenth-century sermons. Further corroboration: In a work familiar to preachers, Father Yvan's *Trompette du ciel* . . . , a nearly continuous series of twelve chapters is devoted to the tragic death of the sinner:

> *chap. 21: The obstinate sinner dies overwhelmed by the curses of his life.*
> *chap. 22: Horrible convulsions of the sinner dying impenitent.*
> *chap. 23: Fear and agitation of the sinner at the time of death.*
> *chap. 25: Hardened sinners die in horrible sorrow.*
> *chap. 27: Dejection of the sinner at the time of death.*
> *chap. 28: The impenitent sinner dies in desperation.*
> *chap. 29: Dismay of the sinner, dying without having done penance.*
> *chap. 30: Fright and horror of the sinner at the sight of Jesus Christ his judge.*
> *chap. 31: The impenitent sinner will have neither refuge nor excuse at the time of his judgment.*
> *chap. 32: The impenitent sinner is horribly tormented at his death by the memory of his sins.*
> *chap. 33: The presence of Jesus Christ is intolerable to sinners at the time of their death.*
> *chap. 34: The wounds of Jesus, which encourage sinners to do penance during their lifetime, will condemn those who have remained impenitent, at the exact moment of their death.*[102]

To clarify by comparison the horror of the sinner's death at the moment when he realizes the extent of his crimes, Loriot cites the case of a "saintly man" who was converted at the age of twenty. God made him see all his past sins "in the same way that He makes us see them at the hour of our death." All the same, specifies Loriot with the aim of further impressing his audience, "he had not committed these great horrific crimes, but only youthful pranks one would count for nothing." Who has not been in such a case? Still,

> *this vision [of his past] gave him so much pain that he became ill and nearly dead for three months. The marrows of his bones were practically boiling; his flesh was*

burned so severely that scars still remain in several places. The strain he endured was so violent that he sweated huge drops from every pore, even from his fingertips, to such a degree that he drenched his sheets, blanket, mattress, and pallet. When he touched burning coals, the heat seemed slight compared to the internal pain he felt. And he affirmed in all sincerity that if he had seen a blazing furnace and been told that he would have to stay there forever to be delivered from his consuming internal pain, he would have chosen this furnace as a great cooling refreshment.[103]

What then are the (moral) pains that the dying sinner feels? First, he has to bid farewell to "this miserable world," which will be forever vanished for him, to his "companions in debauchery," and to his "criminal pleasures."[104] He must literally "vomit" the things of this world. The priest Girard explicitly and forcefully announces:

The sinner will vomit, says Holy Scripture, the possessions, the pleasures that he has devoured, and God will tear them out from his gullet. Do not these words fill ye with terror, Christian listeners? What efforts do ye make to keep from vomiting? But what are the pains when one vomits up blood, and even lumps of flesh? If one tears out a wretch's heart, liver, and entrails, what more hideous torture could there be? If one were to tear a suckling child to shreds, who could endure the sight? Ah! All that, however, is but a faint picture of what the sinner will suffer when all that he has possessed in this life will be wrested from him with the most extreme violence.[105]

"The more you will have tightened the bond between your soul and body, the more trouble you will have in freeing yourself from it," Saint Leonard of Port-Maurice declares.[106]

However excruciating this tearing apart may be, it is not the only torment of the sinner upon death's threshold. Indeed, everything oppresses him. The prior of Valabrège, Pierre de la Font, employs Luke 19:43 ("For the days shall come upon you, when your enemies will cast up a bank about you and surround you") to describe the final misery of the sinner who dies impenitent. He bitterly recalls the time he has lost, the graces he has rejected. He is racked with remorse, and Hell opens before him. "No matter where he turns, he finds only new causes for dread and fear."[107] The Lazarist sermon on this theme compares the dying sinner to three things: first to a fish that has played with the bait and suddenly finds himself caught, taken from the water and prepared for slicing and eating; then to a thief "found guilty, and immediately pinioned and taken to the gallows"; and finally to a felon

on whom are suddenly thrown the heaviest chains, to make him a galley slave just when he thought only of his promotion[108] *. . . we therefore should not be surprised, my Brothers, to see sinners, arrived at this fearful moment, crying, shrieking, and saying that they are damned . . . They pull back one arm, throw out the other, seek to flee, turn themselves around and about with horrible shudders, and open their distracted eyes, where one sees, even though they have lost any power to communicate, the very painting of despair.*[109]

Thus the past, present, and future combine to overwhelm the poor wretch. One of Grignion de Montfort's hymns expresses this tragic convergence, in the voice of the damned soul:

Verse 1 What then! Must I die
And leave my belongings?
O cruel and accursed time
That takes from me all these things . . .

Verse 3 Ah! I am trapped in the snare
That Satan did hide from me,
Of my sacrilege I'm now 'ware
And all my sins I do see.

Verse 4 O graces abused!
O counsels refused!
O hours misused!
O gifts kicked and bruised! . . .

Verse 15 I see thee, fatal devil,
In wait beside my bed.
Take me away, hated evil,
'Twas thou seduced me and misled.[110]

Girard's "homilies" lay heavy stress on the despair of the dying sinner. "If he looks up, he sees an angry God, ready to strike him with the arrows of his vengeance." He sees the Holy Virgin "who refuses him any help," and the angels and saints "who see him as the enemy of their master." He sees "at the foot of his Judge's throne, a vast number of accusing witnesses, who testify against him." Finally, "he forever has in mind the frightful tortures prepared for him, which he deserves for so many crimes. He thinks he sees only fires, burning braziers, other outcasts, and horrid monsters. He feels he can already hear the blasphemies, screams, and wailing of the damned."[111]

More than half of the seventeenth-century preparations for death and almost as many eighteenth-century examples of this genre emphasize the dangers of sudden death. Sermons do not fail to echo these works. Neither did the missions omit the obligatory song on this subject. One finds in the corpus of Lazarist homilies, among other examples: "O death, you are a traitress! You strike us without warning, you carry us off when we least expect it . . . 'tis a proverb most true, 'with health he thinks he's blest, who carries death within his breast . . .' How many external means does death employ to quickly take away the healthiest of men? . . . Who can promise himself a minute of living, being in constant danger of dying by so many accidents?[112] . . ." and so on. In a preparatory sermon for a penitential procession, Port-Maurice, skull in hand, asks his companions the agonizing question: for whom does the bell toll?

> *Yes, surely, for many of you the bells will toll in only a few days; for many of you there shall be mourning; many of you shall soon die. Who will it be? . . . Take, my brother, take, my sister, this death's head, it shows you that it is you who must ceaselessly die. The world will soon be over for you.*
>
> *But how shall it be if some of you must die, not only in a few days, in a few hours, but rather of sudden death? O Jesus, what misfortune! And is this misfortune all that rare? Ah! How many, how many indeed have gone to a dance, to a party, to a vigil in the evening, and in the morning found themselves dead! How many have been attacked by apoplexy while sleeping! How many have been struck, in the very act of sin, by the bolts of divine malediction! How then to confess? How then to repent?*[113]

The Italian missionary's questions reveal how the stereotypical description of the sinner's death increasingly annexed the theme of sudden death, just as it tended to monopolize the macabre. There is an easy leap from the claims that "everyone is surprised by death,"[114] "we are all on the brink of death,"[115] to two other assertions of growing influence: (1) Many sinners die suddenly; (2) Death is always unexpected by the "worldly." Bridaine does not fail to describe how

> *many sinners whom we see every day are struck by death while they go about their dissipations; some suddenly snatched away by an unforeseen accident, without being able to say a word, others brought down, in the heat of debauchery or in the midst of a brawl, senseless and lifeless; these ones taken and slaughtered by cruel assassins, or struck by lightning in fair weather, those ones crushed beneath the rubble of a falling building, or drowned in a tragic shipwreck they could not avoid.*[116]

Father Yvan had written earlier: "The death of the impenitent and obstinate is always violent and fraught with execrations: for they almost always meet with sudden death, as punishment for their wickedness . . . Cruel and crafty men would not expire in the middle of the lives God had prepared for them, were they to live decently, or do penance in good time."[117]

One of Réguis's sermons also shows how the theme of sudden death became enclosed within the wider one of the death of the sinner. The priest compares Death to a vampire, who accosts the worldly, carefree man:

> *I like to surprise and suddenly strike him who does not expect me, and hardly thinks of me. While his spirit is fully bent on pleasure and the things of the world, I enter his house, I stretch him out on his bed, I suck the blood from his veins, I drink, I drain everything from him, I exhaust every well-spring of life in him, I spread pallor across his face, I freeze every part of his body, I snatch his soul, and just as a famished wolf will drag to his lair the prey he has just slaughtered, so I bring this cadaver here, or else I devour it in the shadows. Behold and consider: thus shall you be treated some day, and this day is not as far off as you might think . . . Go, madam, go spend two hours before your mirror, and see, not what you are, but what you soon shall be . . . Go, miser, go count your money and remember that I likewise count every second of your life, and that I will finish my counting before you finish yours. Go, drunkard, and you who make a god of your belly, go stuff yourself with wine, with meat, with debauchery, and know that I shall soon grow drunk with your blood and fat with the flesh of your corpse.*[118]

There is only one step from this hallucinatory description to the conviction that the death of the wicked is always sudden and violent. Port-Maurice, in a sermon on the "uncertainty of the the hour of death," solemnly warns the sinners in attendance: ". . . Before you may have begun to lead a Christian life, your halfhearted attempt at conversion will be cut off by death; death will preempt the completion of your imaginary plans to change your life." "The wrath of God thunders just when one thinks of it least."[119] Girard cast the obdurate sinner as "another Pharaoh": He was warned, rejoined, cajoled, and prodded to be converted. He resisted, however, the voice of the Lord. "What will happen to him? Death will surprise him. And when? In the middle of the night; amid the dark shadows of his conscience; when his soul will be blackened by a thousand crimes; when he will not have gone to confession, perhaps for a year; after having profaned the sacraments, perhaps for his entire life." His affairs, both temporal and spiritual, will be in disarray, he will have trials left to defend, debts to pay, he will not have time to make a will, he may leave behind young orphans, and so on.[120]

An eighteenth-century Breton priest, preaching in Breton, also explains to his flock that even the death of a sinner after a prolonged illness is "sudden." For he first deceives himself regarding his sickness, which he believes to be benign, and his relatives help to delude him in this way. They find "a thousand reasons for consoling him." The time comes, however, when the patient must learn the truth. He then panics. Disturbed by his illness, by "the sorry state of the business he has left unfinished," entrapped by "his bad habits," "terrified by the fear of death and the judgments of God," he no longer has "enough time to prepare himself for a good death."[121] Such accounts explain why sermons like the preparations for death constantly encouraged a daily kind of dying, in order "to avoid, in the surprise of this unforeseen and terrifying moment, the confusion and perturbations of an ill-governed conscience."[122]

Bridaine teaches that "when death shall come, there will be no more time for preparation."[123] Likewise, God refuses to let tardy repentance move him to pity. This final element of the scenario culminates the drama of the sinner's death, which is no longer necessarily described as a decisive combat, where all may still be saved. During the Age of Reason, many sermons tended to abandon this aspect of the medieval *Artes moriendi* and to erase the *in extremis* intervention of Christ, the Virgin, and the saints. Instead, they adopted another conception of life and death: One dies as one has lived. Last-minute conversions are rare. This is a far cry from François Le Picart's highly comforting sermon of 1555 "against the temptation to despair," which features this dialogue between the priest and the dying sinner:

> —*My friend, do not distrust yourself, when the hour of your death shall come, but lean upon the death and cross of Jesus.*
> —*O, I only have half an hour in which to repent! And I have done such evil that I could never say how much.*
> —*My friend, in the very short time you have, do not lose heart, but love God with all your heart and mind and strength, then confess yourself to God.*
> —*Yes, but I will forget half the sins I have to confess.*
> —*Undertake to accuse yourself of the slightest wrongdoing you can remember, and thus if it happens that you forget any, God will not fail to pardon you of all.*[124]

The retort to Le Picart is made, among others, by Father Yvan, who warns: "To defer penance is to wish to be abandoned by God." "He who is not converted when he can be, will not be able to do so when he wishes it." "The sinner's conversion, in itself difficult, becomes incomparably harder when deferred to the time of death." "The conversion of terminally ill sinners is often false and of no value." "Sinners who defer their conversion die in a worse state than they have lived." "Those who put off doing penance from one day to the next usually die without ever doing it at all." "The longer the sinner defers his conversion, the more pain, weakness, and terror he shall have at the hour of his death." These categorical statements are all nothing less than chapter headings from the *Trompette du ciel.*[125]

The evangelistic efforts of seventeenth- and eighteenth-century Catholicism sought less to fight the temptation to despair at the approach of death than to give a distant forewarning against a desperate death. In *Le Petit missionaire de la campagne*, Father Chesnois strikes a sharp note, while assuming the voice of Jesus: "Even though they [the sinners] will have the time to beseech this pardon, they will not think on it; when they will think on it, they will not beseech it; and when they do beseech it, they will not obtain it: you have abused my counsels, you have neglected my rebukes: and I in turn will laugh at you when you die. (Prov. 1, 28)"[126] Grignion de Montfort also presents a Jesus and a Mary who are insensitive to the dying man's prayers:

The sinner:	*"My Jesus, have mercy*
(Verse 5)	*On this wretched sinner;*
	Mother of mercy,
	Pray for me to the Savior."
Jesus:	*"You did laugh, wretch,*
(Verse 6)	*At the calls of my love:*
	'Tis just and reasonable
	That I now laugh at you."
	"I laugh at your fears
(Verse 7)	*And your false repentance.*
	I jeer at your tears
	You must die and perish."
Mary:	*"It was needful, in life,*
(Verse 8)	*For you to pray to me, and mend:*
	'Tis too late that you pray me
	For I no longer wish to help you."[127]

Similarly, Girard's sermons, first destined for Lyonnais peasants, explain at length the impossibility for the sinner to achieve an *in extremis* conversion. Still, the unfortunate man whom he describes does have some "semblance of religion." He has a priest called in, though mainly "out of fear of eternal tortures, perhaps even out of hypocrisy." For Girard, this dying man resembles Saul at his wit's end, uselessly summoning Samuel. The latter had rebuked the king, "Why then do you ask me, since the Lord has turned from you and become your enemy?" Like Samuel, the priest might say:

What need was there for me to come here now, and what could I do for you, since God has forsaken you? It will happen to you as I have oft told you. I warned you in my sermons, and in particular I told you that if you did not change your life, you would die . . .

The priest, however, because God did not reveal to him the condemnation of this sinner, encourages and exhorts him to seek God's infinite mercy; and having convinced him to confess, listens to him. But this confession is like the others he made during his life. He confesses in few words, he dissembles, he explains away, he apologizes for the violence of his sickness, that does not let him make a longer self-accusation . . . The confessor does not persist much, because he fears overtiring the sick man; he gives absolution, he gives extreme unction; it is by these two final sacrileges that this unfortunate soul puts the seal to his condemnation.[128]

Going still further in another sermon, Girard wonders how to explain the final failure of a sinner, despite his seeking to be converted at the approach of death. His answer, imbued with Jansenism: "He will not have grace." To be sure, he will receive "ordinary" graces. Since, however, he abused them his entire life, they will remain worthless at the hour of death.

As for strong and powerful graces, how could God give them to him, since he did everything possible to make himself unworthy of them? But that which makes me

> *most tremble for sinners, is this final grace, this final perseverance, without which one cannot be fully saved, which is so freely given that no one can truly deserve it. Now, how will God grant the gift of ultimate grace . . . , the grace of the saints and the chosen . . . to one who has been His enemy during his entire life? Will he give the same reward to a deserter as to a valiant soldier?*[129]

These remarks connect with those of Lessius and Tronson on "the extent of grace,"[130] and with them comprise a sort of small change for the general public. There comes a time when God, wearied by the sinner, no longer comes to his aid. Port-Maurice, concluding a jubilee year with a sermon on obstinate sinners, tells his audience: ". . . I may not be persuaded that a habitual sinner, after having laughed at God for so long, may then succeed, in exchange for so many infidelities, in wresting a miracle from the hands of God. No: I may not believe that God would wish to enact miracles to convert a sinner of this kind. Do not pile sin on top of sin, and do not say that God's mercy is great; for his wrath is forever fixed on sinners."[131]

All the same, one senses an objection to these declarations that arbitrarily limit divine mercy. Certain anonymous listeners, reacting to these sermons, could well have countered them with the case of the good thief. Bridaine takes full hold of this objection:

> *If it be true, as you claim, that God quite often gives the grace of conversion, why then would God, in all the sacred books, have denied you this hope? . . . I challenge you to produce any such examples. Alas! Saint Bernard, after combing through all of Scripture, found only one, that of the thief upon the cross . . . Do not be deceived about this; this could never be an example for you . . . [he] was quite a great sinner, I admit; but was he a sinner who had deferred until death his conversion and penance? Not at all . . .*[132]

Neither should one be impressed by the apparently good death of some great sinners. Bridaine again provides the questions and answers: "But you will tell me that every day we see many other sinners who finish their lives so well, after starting badly, who die like saints, after living in dissipation." Bridaine is never short of an answer. He swiftly retorts:

> *As for me, I'll tell you, with Saint Augustine, that most of them die as outcasts. O men, ignorant of God's terrible secrets, if you knew what then happened in the heart of these supposed penitents! O, you would clearly see how this death you call so saintly, so Christian, is in fact naught but wretched and disastrous! . . . You would see that they are loathsome Judases, who seek out priests and pontiffs, and give them money; but for all that, their eternal damnation is no less certain nor irrevocable.*[133]

An eighteenth-century Breton preacher's sermon (of which there is a French as well as Breton version) also sets forth—and at length—the same "terrible truth." "My aim," he tells his listeners, "is to make you see that the sinner who defers this conversion until death will never be converted, and for two reasons: (1) because he will not be prepared to be converted; (2) because God will refuse the sinner the necessary grace."[134] Some would object, however, that the sinner "is not left to only himself; there will be some charitable person who will help him to put his trust in God, and so he will die with profound religious feeling. We have seen several sinners die, who, after having forgotten God while healthy, nonetheless die with the finest of sentiments, and edified us in the hour of their death."[135] The preacher's response: These last-minute conversions are not sincere. When it chances that certain libertines believe themselves at the point of death and then give some signs of repenting, but afterward recover their health, as sometimes happens, they return to their vicious ways. Let us not then be fooled by appearances, even if certain great sinners die in "the finest religious feeling."[136] Saint Ambrose affirms that "only one in a hundred thousand who will have deferred their devotion to God until their final illness will be saved."[137] This lack of sincerity in conversion is compounded by the fact that God will refuse giving the necessary grace to the sinner, without which he will never be converted.[138] Certainly, God might give him grace. "Yet I fear that He will not grant it to him."

> *Let us learn that His kindness is not without wisdom and reason. Now, my brethren, to believe that God will always be ready to pardon the sinner who has scorned Him during health, and who only asks pardon for his offenses because he sees that he can no longer commit them, that is to presume in God a kindness without wisdom and reason . . . But if His glory and wisdom oblige Him to punish and forsake sinners to death, His justice obliges Him to do so all the more. It is certain that God takes as much glory from His justice as from His other perfections. I mean that it is as glorious for God to punish the sinner as to reward the righteous. Now, on whom will he work His justice, if not on these sinners who scorned Him during their lives . . . ?*[139]

A new objection arises, however: Even the laborers who worked at the eleventh hour were rewarded by the owner of the vineyard. This example, replies the preacher, is "not propitious" for you. For these "laborers" would have wished for nothing better than to go to work earlier. As soon as they were called, they came.[140] Let us therefore conclude: "The sinner will cry out to God in his last illness, and his wish will not be granted. He will swear the prettiest promises to God, but God will tell him that it is not the time."[141] With this categorical assertion comes an absence: the notion of extenuating circumstances. Had not the Jesuit Jacques Giroust given a collection of Advent sermons the meaningful title of *Le pecheur sans excuses*?[142]

CHAPTER 13

The Tortures of the Afterlife

HELL

The horrors of the deathbed and the decomposition of the dead body are the price of sin. Once this punishment had been accepted, even if death should lead on to eternal bliss, the former had to happen before one could aspire to the latter. On the other hand, if death should plunge the sinner into the gaping jaws of Hell, this misfortune is infinitely more dramatic than the end, however painful, of earthly life. The macabre pedagogy of the Catholic Church had always offered views of the other last ends. At the same time, the description of Hell is unequally present in the sermons. The professional preachers, from San Bernardino to the Lazarists and Leonard of Port-Maurice, during missions and the stations of Advent and Lent, willingly lingered over the terrifying evocation of the tortures of the beyond. Conversely, the collections of Sunday sermons are more reserved on this subject, especially those of Jean-Pierre Camus, François Bourgoing, and Edmond Bourée. Even rigorists such as Antoine Godeau and Paul Beurrier resist pouring out excessively shocking descriptions.

Nevertheless, it would be a mistake to think that parish priests left this theme only to visiting preachers who came to give "special features." On the first Sunday after Epiphany, Pierre de la Font told his flock: "Since that the apostolic preachers, who have made the most wondrous changes in the world, have most usually made the pains of hell the subject of their sermons, having recognized through experience that there is no other truth so apt to intimidate the greatest of sinners and bring them to penance, I have resolved to begin my necessary weekly sermons with this subject . . ."[1] A classic case is that of the priest Symon de Rennes, whose homily for the first Advent Sunday concerns the Last Judgment, that for the third Sunday of Lent "the harshness and fire of hell," and that for the twenty-fourth Sunday after Pentecost to individual judgment. Girard treats of Hell even more copiously, since he dedicates three entire sermons to it, namely for the second and third Sundays of Advent and the third Sunday of Lent. In the first two, he stresses the universality and incomprehensibility of the pains of Hell; in the third, their "infinite duration."

There is yet another convergent symptom: The "spiritual hymns" of the Brothers of the Christian Schools frequently evoke Hell, especially in the two songs on death, in that on the Last Judgment, in the "regrets of a damned soul"—a theme also favored by Maunoir and the "Bibliothèque bleue"—and in the "Commentary on the *dies irae.*" Hymn Ten, "On death," contains this notable verse:

> *O Death! O Judgment! O blazing fires! O forever!*
> *O condemnation! O reprobation!*
> *O final sentence! O Rage! O despair!*
> *O Separation! O desolation!*[2]

Finally, it is no surprise to find a heavy emphasis on Hell in works that provided material for both missionaries and parish priests. Philippe d'Outreman, writing of "the memory of hell and eternity," argues that there should only be two prisons in the Christian republic: one for the atheists and one for the "madmen." In the first should be placed those who do not believe that "there is a hell destined for the torture of sinners" and, in the second, "with its baubles and insane asylums," those who believe in Hell but become infatuated with "wallowing in deadly sin."[3] Vincent Houdry's chapter on Hell in his *Bibliothèque des predicateurs* considers this final destination to be "one of the principal articles of our faith."[4] In his turn, Montargon holds that it is an essential subject, treated by "almost all ancient and modern preachers, and all books of piety."[5] He also offers his readers and users an entire heap of references on Hell, drawn first from Scripture, then from the church fathers, and finally from more recent authors. It will now be useful to cite the principal authoritative texts on this topic, as a disturbed and disturbing evangelical program, though sometimes taking them out of context but always relating them to one another, succeeded in creating a traumatized mass conviction.[6]

To begin with, there is Matthew 25:31–46, or the description of the Last Judgment, with the lambs on the right hand and the goats doomed to "everlasting fire" on the left. In addition, Matthew 3:12, "he will throughly purge his floor, and gather his wheat into the garner; but he will burn up the chaff with unquenchable fire"; Matthew 10:28, "fear him which is able to destroy both soul and body in hell." Also Matthew 13:24–30, the parable of the sower; Matthew 13:47–50, the parable of the fisher; Matthew 22:1–14, the parable of the royal wedding with the the casting out of the man without the wedding garment; Matthew 25:1–fourteen, the wise and foolish virgins; Matthew 25:15–30, the parable of the talents. Mark 9:42–43 supplied the phrase: "It is better for thee to enter into life maimed, than having two hands to go into hell, into the fire that never shall be quenched." The most frequently used quotations from the rest of the New Testament are: Hebrews 10:31: "It is a fearful thing to fall into the hands of the living God"; II Thessalonians 1:9, "In flaming fire taking vengeance on them that know not God, and that obey not the gospel of our Lord Jesus Christ: Who shall be punished with everlasting destruction from the presence of the Lord"; Revelations 9:6, "And in those days shall men seek death, and shall not find it; and shall desire to die, and death shall flee from them"; and Revelations 20:15, "And whosoever was not found written in the book of life was cast into the lake of fire."

As for the Old Testament, use was generally made of selections from the chapters of Job (20, 22, 27) that describe the punishment of the wicked; of Psalm 11:6, "Upon the wicked he shall rain snares, fire and brimstone, and a burning tempest: this shall be the portion of their cup"; verses from the Wisdom of Solomon that discuss punishment, such as "wherewithal a man sinneth, by the same also shall he be punished" (Wisd. of Sol. 11:16), "For the creature that serveth thee, who art the Maker, increaseth his strength against the unrighteous for their punishment" (Wisd. of Sol. 16:24), and "they were scattered under a dark veil of forgetfulness, being horribly astonished, and troubled with apparitions" (Wisd. of Sol. 17:3). Also invoked were the fearsome threats of Ecclesiasticus, "Teeth of wild beasts, and scorpions, serpents, and the sword, punishing the wicked to destruction" (Ecclus. 39:30), and "Woe be unto you, ungodly men . . . if ye die, a curse shall be your portion" (Ecclus. 41:8–9). From Isaiah came this prophesy made to the haughty daughters of Zion: "And it shall come to pass, that instead of sweet smell there shall be stink" (Isa. 3:24), and from Jeremiah this speech of Yahweh: "I will make my words in thy mouth fire, and this people wood, and it shall devour them" (Jer. 5:14). Such explicit statements as these were ripe for embellishment by the sermon writers' inexhaustible imaginations.

Among the early Christian authors who discuss Hell, the most often cited are Tertullian, Saint Cyprian, Saint John Chrysostom, Saint Augustine, and Saint Gregory. Of the fire of Hell, Tertullian in fact wrote that "its nature is incorruptible, by a property for torture given to it by God" and that it "does not consume that which it burns, but mends it."[7] Saint Cyprian affirms that "these wretches [the damned] who are now immortal will live on amid these fires. Their bodies will be thrown there, and eternally burned, without being consumed."[8] For Saint John Chrysostom, "this torture of hell is dreadful, but you will there undergo a thousand more tortures that you would say nothing could equal the privation of this glory you have lost!"[9] He also describes more specific pains: "Let us think therefore what misery it is to burn without cease, to be plunged into darkness, to be stretched and torn by groaning, and to gnash one's teeth without being heard . . . If darkness alone is enough to trouble our own oppressed souls, what shall it be like . . . when this horror joins with the horror of such tortures?"[10]

As for so many other themes, Saint Augustine is an essential source for that of Hell's torments; *The City of God* is his most employed text here. With sometimes erroneous references, Montargon draws on this work on four occasions: (1) "To be eternally apart from God is a pain as great as God Himself is"; (2) "Such is their condition [the damned]: never alive, never dead, but forever dying amid torment"; (3) "Their pain will last to forever torment them, and their physical nature will last so that they shall always feel the pain"; (4) "It is the infinite power of God that punishes the damned, a punishment he carries out in an ineffable but real way."[11] From Saint Gregory the Great came the favored assertion, "the punishment is proportioned according to the nature of the crime, and each of the damned will be afflicted by hellfire according to the scale and enormity of his crime."[12] Six centuries later Saint Bernard makes his contribution: "It is right to always punish that which can never be expiated through any atonement" and "That which is done cannot be undone . . . That which goes beyond time does not go away with time: thus you must eternally suffer from the evil you will eternally know you have committed."[13]

Writing in the mid-eighteenth century, the recent authors whom Montargon cites as models for those who are to speak on Hell are primarily Bourdaloue, Giroust, Massillon, Dufay, Cheminais, and Pallu; to these there may usefully be added material taken from Father de la Colombiere's *Reflexions*, from Father Croiset's *Reflexions chretiennes*, and from Nicole's *Essais de morale* (vol. 4, treatise two, chap. 6).

Throughout the centuries, this ecclesiastical discourse on Hell met with certain objections, especially one that clearly resurfaced on numerous occasions: Why does God punish with eternal punishment an offense that was only temporal? From Saint Gregory the Great to the early twentieth century, the answer was the same. One of San Bernardino's sermons is an exemplary case in point.[14] The great preacher explains that the author of a Deadly Sin "prefers something unstable to the eternal and definite good. But the offense itself depends on He whom is offended. Since

He is infinite, the offense must also be judged as infinite; thus, as the penalty must needs fit the crime, it is necessary that deadly sin be rewarded with an eternal penalty." Does human justice proceed any differently? Does it not eternally exile from civil society and the human race an assassin whose crime lasted for only a second? There follows an argument on "duration" and "intention." It is true that sin is short-lived. In this sense, it is "finite." On the other hand, it can be said that its effects "last through the infinite," and thus it must be punished through eternity. Saint Gregory explained how, and San Bernardino resumes his demonstration: If they could, sinners would like to live forever, so they might always sin. For they conspicuously show that they desire to live forever in order to sin forever, since they never cease to do evil as long as they live. It therefore befits God's justice that those who wished to sin throughout their lives be punished by endless torture.[15] God looks into intentions more than deeds.

Three centuries later the priest Girard takes up San Bernardino's arguments in a sermon on Hell directed at peasants. He also draws support from Saint Gregory for "two incontestable principles":

> *The first is that sin must be punished as it deserves. The second is that sin must be punished according to its degree . . . For it is incontestable that deadly sin encloses infinite malice. Now, the damned being but creatures, limited and finite beings, they cannot be capable of suffering an infinite penalty of infinite majesty; consequently, their sin must be punished by the most fitting penalty; thus it must be infinite according to its duration: hence eternity.*
>
> *Sin must be punished insofar as it exists . . . God . . . must punish sin according to its degree: so it is that sin will remain forever in those who died in this deplorable state, and so it is that it will exist forever.*[16]

Girard immediately backs up these claims with the reference to Saint Gregory.

With greater vehemence, Montargon envisions that God will someday say to sinners:

> *. . . You have no cause for complaint, you are merely receiving what you deserve. During your life, you trampled on the laws of an eternal God, so the expiation for this crime must be eternal; you never repented of your crimes, so I shall never repent of your torments . . . You did not cease being rebels, I will not cease being an avenger. Nothing limited your outrages, so your pain will be without limit. Your soul that sinned was immortal, and it deserves a torture after its own nature, an immortal torture.*[17]

This highly scholastic logic, which greatly embroidered on biblical texts, led to the assertion that a single fleeting sin could merit an eternity of punishment—a banal theme of a purposefully brutal doctrinal campaign. One of de Montfort's hymns includes a damned soul's lament:

> *I dallied for a knickknack,*
> *A moment's idle pleasure,*
> *Life eternal I now lack,*
> *But have rages without measure.*[18]

Dramatizing in classic fashion the phrase of Saint James (2:10), another hymn by the same author thunders: "To disobey on a single point / Is the crime of all crimes."[19] A Lazarist sermon gives this exclamation to a condemned soul: "What!

For a glass of dirty water, I mean for an indecent pleasure, I lost the kingdom of heaven? What! For a bowl of lentils, I mean for excessive gluttony, I lost the blessing of my heavenly Father, I am the object of his execration, and chased out of paradise?"[20] The Jesuit Houdry advises preachers that "what is important to make well understood, is that a single deadly sin makes us worthy of this torture [Hell]."[21]

In one of the hymns appearing in the *Manuel des retraites et missions a l'usage du diocèse de Rennes*, a damned person states: "There are also a great number, who for a single crime / Are with us in this deadly place."[22] During a Sunday sermon, Girard asks each of his listeners: "What . . . you wish, for some glasses of wine, for the pleasing of your gluttonous appetite, to resolve yourself to suffer eternal hunger and thirst? You wish, for the sake of a moment's animal lust, to be swallowed up by the furnace of hell? . . . You wish, for a puff of honor, to be abused by demons and the damned, and become the dung of infernal prisons?"[23] Likewise, the priest Nicolas Le Gall, at the end of the Ancien Régime, teaches his Breton congregation: "Consider then how a single deadly sin enough to damn you, if you have the misfortune to die without having confessed and done penance. And thereby understand how you must take care to guard yourself from deadly sin, and even from venial sin, since the latter paves the way for the former."[24]

The almost invariable structure of these sermons on Hell reveals three major, sterotyped emphases concerning the pains experienced by the damned. They suffer both spiritually and physically, and this double punishment will last forever. The order in which these three elements are presented matters less than their constant presence. San Bernardino adheres to the scholastic penchant for divisions and subdivisions and distinguishes eighteen spiritual penalties that oppress the reprobate: (1) they are deprived bliss; (2) they know themselves to be cursed by God; (3) they contrast their fate to the glory of the blessed; (4) they are gnawed by the worm of remorse; (5) they are afflicted by spiritual fire; (6) by the eternal absence of happiness [a repetition of the first point]; (7) by continual fear; (8) by shame at knowing that their crimes are known to all; (9) they would like to harm (the chosen) but cannot do so; (10) they rebel against the punishment that strikes them down; (11) they are hateful to themselves; (12) they envy the chosen [a repetition of point 3]; (13) they despair of their salvation; (14) they are certain of damnation; (15) they are possessed with demonic fury; (16) they are spiritually blind, being deprived of grace; (17) they continually blaspheme; (18) they know that they can no longer redeem themselves.[25] Bernardino's finely distinguished spiritual tortures are more or less present in all later preaching on Hell, with perhaps a greater emphasis on the pain of damnation (the deprivation of beatific vision), also given first place by the great Italian preacher. It was not easy, however, to move an audience deeply on this topic. Hence seventeenth- and eighteenth-century Lazarist sermons explain that in this life "we only feel weak desires to possess God, since our soul is continually weighed down by its confinement to the body; but in the other world, being freed from all these impediments, it will feel desires and inexplicable impulses to be one with God, whom it will regard as its center, its end, and its sovereign happiness."[26] However, the anonymous missionary explains, the damned soul will try with all its might to go toward God but it will not be able; moreover, "this just and inexorable Judge will do Himself glory worthy of His justice by casting this damned soul into the deepest pit of hell."[27] A Breton sermon succeeded better, I feel, than many more elaborate ones in conveying to the listeners the extraordinary punishment of being cast far away from God:

> . . . *To lose his family, friends, fortune, health, oh! all these are great losses indeed! Still, they are nothing compared to the loss of which I speak. Yes, when you will*

> *have almost nothing, when you will be on a high dunghill like the saintly Job, you will have everything if God is with you. But if you have lost God . . . you have lost everything, both in this world and the next. You are worse than a woman without a husband, a man without a country, a child without a father.*[28]

The preacher Nicolas Le Gall extends his discourse by offering himself an objection: The damned will not know the loss that they have caused. Alas, replies the orator, they will only know it too well. Now we do not see our Lord, and we do not feel ourselves to be miserable. But after death, we will understand the sweetness, the pleasure, the happiness there is in being in the company and house of God. Then the Lord will say to the damned: "Behold this happy dwelling, and behold it well, it pleases you but it is not for you." Hence the rage and despair of the outcast. A young child who sees his father die does not realize his loss until much later. Similarly, at death the damned will realize the extent of his disaster and the blessing that is deprived him.[29]

Even sermons or parts of sermons that concern the "spiritual" tortures of the damned often take detours into concrete details, easier to describe than the pain of damnation: the hideous crowd of demons, the despair of the accursed who eat themselves, the torment of Tantalus that reminds them of their earthly feasts, and so on. In addition, the description of "corporeal" torments (even if they affect souls waiting for the Last Judgment) was always the *pièce de resistance* of sermons on Hell, the first and foremost torment being that of fire. As Gaston Bachelard says of fire: it is "a privileged phenomenon that can explain everything . . . and the only one which can as clearly receive two contrary values: good and evil. It shines in paradise. It burns in hell. It is sweetness and torture. It is cooking and the apocalypse . . . It is a protecting and terrible god, both good and evil."[30] Modern technological civilization, by increasing its mastery of fire, has removed its presence to the point that its revival is sought through the placing of chimneys in new homes. In past centuries, however, flames caused both true fascination and immense fear. They illumined, purified, heated, but they also destroyed. They obliterated the sin of heretics and witches, but they also frequently devastated towns and reduced farms and harvests to ashes. Today it is hard to grasp the justifiable fear people had of lightning before the invention of the lightning rod. In reading certain verses of the Capuchin missions' hymns that associate God with thunder and lightning, a real impact on people's minds must be imagined. "The God who hurls thunder / Today may deign to enter my house" runs a preparatory song for communion.[31] Another hymn alerts the "sleeping sinner," telling him: "You see him [God] arming himself / His arm takes up lightning / To reduce you to nothing."[32]

All the same, during the main period studied in this book, people had not entirely forgotten cold (Tertullian's *refrigerium*) as one of the tortures that beset the damned. It figures prominently in the third-century *Apocalypse of Paul.*[33] San Bernardino puts it in seventh place (*rigor frigoris*) among the eighteen "external pains" of the reprobate, "between the fire which does not consume" and "the hunger which drives one mad."[34] Breton plays, poems, and hymns of the fifteenth to seventeenth centuries yield over sixty references to "cold hell," "the cold abyss," and "cold death."[35] The infernal chill also appears in the Age of Reason in the Lazarists' sermons,[36] in those by Bridaine ("hunger, maddened thirst; bitter cold, scorching heat,"[37] in *Le Chemin du ciel* . . . diffused by the "Bibliothèque bleue" ("cold and icy waters will be thrown into these blazing fires"[38]) in Girard's sermons ("they will ceaselessly travel from an extremity of heat to an extremity of cold".[39]) To these authors' minds, the worst of tortures is neither cold nor heat but the passing from one to the other. It is noteworthy that to justify this passage from extreme cold to extreme heat, the Lazarist sermon writer and Girard both rely on Job 24:19, then translated as "He will suddenly pass from the snow to excessive heat, and his sin will lead him into hell,"[40] whereas the Revised Standard Version translates: "Drought and heat snatch away the snow waters; so does Sheol those who have sinned."

Nevertheless, cold remains only episodic in the hell of the sixteenth to eighteenth century. Recounting her vision of the places of eternal torment, Saint Theresa of Avila writes: "I felt my soul burning with such a horrible fire that I can scarce describe it, since I could not even imagine it . . . I felt myself burned and almost cut into a thousand pieces . . . To burn in this world is nothing in comparison to burning in the other."[41] In fact, everything that related to fire and heat was vitally important to preaching on Hell: "thick smoke," "molten lead," "boiling oil," "burning cauldrons,"[42] "lakes of fire . . . without end and bottomless,"[43] and so on. In such places, where the flames give no light, the damned weep scalding tears of fire. Thus speaks Godeau, who announces to future doomed souls: "Then you shall groan . . . , then you shall weep, then you shall sigh, but your tears shall be tears of fire that will burn you."[44]

Is the fire of Hell "metaphoric"? Nicole agrees with many others that there is "no need, following reason, to conceive of any other fire than that which we already know, nor any other pain than that which we undergo when it touches our bodies."[45] Bourdaloue also confirms that the infernal fire works on "both mind and body," in a "manner no less true than it is strange."[46] Metaphoric or not, this fire is a creation of God, who "stretches the laws of nature"—Bourdaloue's words still—to make them the instrument of his vengeance,[47] so that "the sharpest pains [on earth], the slowest tortures, the punishments, the torments, the most unheard-of kinds of death, compared to this fire do not even deserve the name of torment."[48] Hence its remarkable effects. "It will act," Nicole explains, "on every part of the body [of the damned], as it acts on every part of a hot blade; there will be not a nerve, fiber, or tendon that will not be distressed, and not cause a violent pain."[49] Thus a striking agreement between the Jesuit and the Jansenist.

The place fire held in people's imaginations doubtless explains the facile but nevertheless impressive tirades of preachers who spoke on Hell. On this subject, the Italians were unsurpassable, and some of their lengthy speeches must be cited. The sermon on Hell by the famous Jesuit Paolo Segneri the Elder includes the following notable passage:

> *Fire will be the sole occupation of all the executioners, and it will replace all the tortures that could be put together. It will cause one to feel all at once the heat of braziers, the cold of ice blocks, the bite of asps, the bile of dragons, the teeth of lions, the violence of the rack, the dislocation of nerves, the twisting of bones, the hail of rocks, floods of whippings, yokes, manacles, steel-toothed combs, gibbets, wheels, and torture benches, it will join, it will gather all that together.*[50]

Clearly, the increasingly urgent rhythm of this enumeration is designed to keep audiences riveted to their seats. The orator, however, has not yet put out this fire. Further on, he adds:

> *This fire will serve as their [the damned] shelter, clothing, furniture, bed, blanket, company, everything: it will become so tightly bound to their bodies, it will so thoroughly enter and penetrate to the bottom of their souls that it will be impossible to tell the damned soul from the fire, the fire from the damned soul . . .*[51]

As for Port-Maurice, he begins a sermon on Hell by employing repetitions that will stun the congregation:

> *Fire, fire: such is the reward for your perversity, you stubborn sinners. Fire, fire, the fire of hell. Fire in your eyes, fire in your mouth, fire in your bowels, fire in your throat, fire in your nostrils, fire within, fire without; fire below, fire above, fire all about. Ah wretches, you will be like burning embers in the middle of this fire.*[52]

This fiery proselytizing was also employed in France, for example in this sermon by Girard. He asserts,

> *The damned will see only fire; they will breathe only fire; fire will surround them on all sides and for miles. Fire will be their element; it will feed them; it will preserve them forever in order to torment them forever. It will penetrate to the marrow of their bones; it will roast all the parts of their bodies, and fill them entirely. Their tongues shall be like bars of burning iron; their lips like strips of burning copper; their palates like hot furnaces; their teeth like squares of burning steel; their lungs like bellows of fire; their stomach and abdomen like a crucible where the hardest metals are refined.*[53]

Were the directors of Western conscience thus expressing a collective, almost nightmarish fear of fire? Quite possibly. On the other hand, these preachers betray undeniably "pyromaniac" tendencies. As Bachelard observes, "modern psychiatry has elucidated the psychology of the pyromaniac. It has shown the sexual character of these tendencies . . . Fire smolders within the soul as surely as under the cinder . . . The pyromaniac is the most concealed of criminals . . . Dreams of fire . . . are among the clearest, the most distinct, for which a sexual interpretation is the most reliable."[54]

Hellfire is unbearable, "huge," and moreover, "wise." It is an ancient notion that the fire of the beyond is "intelligent." For instance, Clement of Alexandria distinguishes "devouring and consuming fire," which torments the incorrigible, from the "prudent" and "intelligent" fire that passes over the soul of a redeemable sinner.[55] Origen and Paulinus of Nola also speak of this "examining" and knowing fire, which burns only the evil part of the sinner, still allowing the latter to take flight toward eternal life.[56] By the seventeenth century, then, what has become of this "intelligent" fire? It has moved down one level, and it punishes rather than purges. The Lazarist sermon on "the corporeal pains of hell" explains, on the strength of Tertullian, Saint John Chrysostom, and Saint Augustine, that the "wise" and selective hellfire "can detect the malice of each sin, in order to more rigorously punish the part of the body and the faculty of the soul that conspired to commit a greater sin, and make them feel a livelier pain than those parts which were not as criminal . . . It will distinguish a parricide from a common killer, an incestuous person from an adulterer." Finally, it is "the deputy commissioner of God's justice, informed of the crimes of sinners and thereto administering the appropriate penalties that each sense, each part of the body, and each faculty of the soul will have deserved."[57] Only God can light this fire. Such is the opinion of Pierre de la Font, for whom "God Himself is the effective and immediate principle of the fire that burns them [the damned]; 'tis He who lights it with His breath, so that 'tis God who burns them with this fire, rather than the fire itself."[58]

During the seventeenth and eighteenth centuries, the sermons that detail the "bodily" sufferings of the damned abandoned the overabundant scholastic distinctions of San Bernardino. Instead, they prefer to organize infernal tortures in relation to the five senses: (1) Hell's prison is dark, but these "dreadful" shadows do not prevent the damned from seeing demons, specters, dragons, and instruments of torture[59]; (2) the sense of hearing has its own "special torture," since in Hell one hears only howling, blasphemies, taunts, and reproaches: in short, "tiresome" and "dreary" concerts; (3) smell is also tormented, Hell being the sewer for all the world's filth, while the damned themselves emit an "intolerable stench"; (4) taste becomes aggrieved by unimaginable thirst and hunger, for the only wine drunk by the damned is that of "God's anger, prepared in the chalice of his vengeance"; (5) as for touch, "the least noble of our physical senses," the "cause of an infinite number of most considerable sins," it will be attacked by "terrible pains," which obviously include the multifarious effects of fire.

Sermons on Hell do not always present their listeners with this logical partition into the five senses. Another topos—which eventually links up with the former—consists of explaining with the help of terrifying examples that infernal tortures surpass anything that one can suffer on earth through sickness, natural disaster, justice, or human depravity. The most ghastly torments are accumulated, and it is asserted that even when brought together they are but a "faint sketch" of the ones borne by the damned. Moreover, as stated by Joseph Lambert on the authority of Saint Augustine, "the tortures reserved for the wicked in the afterlife are infinitely greater than the punishments God uses in this life to punish those who have disobeyed His holy laws."[60]

In its turn, Father Loriot's sermon on Hell recalls Nashe's detailed, matter-of-fact descriptions of torture.[61] There is the same sadism in the portrayal of gruesome details, the same desire to "shock" readers and listeners, the same nightmarish visions, the same museum of horrors. Having amassed all sufferings whose theater is the hospital, Loriot invites his audience to ascend "this scaffold to see the diverse tortures that the spirit of cruelty, as Tertullian says, invented to torment the first Christians, which made the very executioners tremble, and which drew tears from the eyes of anyone who was present at these inhuman and barbarous spectacles."[62] There follows a hallucinatory list of tortures, each more hideous than the last, which ends with this conclusion: "Gather all these tortures together, commit them to your memory. Imagine that a single individual suffers them all at once—the sword, the flame, the beasts, all the rest—and even then you will have only a most vague and rough image of the tortures of hell." Such lists also appear in sermons by d'Outreman,[63] de la Font,[64] Bridaine,[65] Giroust,[66] Girard,[67] and many others. This morbid literature reveals these authors' violent aggressiveness, externalized in frenzied threats against sinners. "Can there be too great of a hell to punish them as they deserve?" asks the Oratorian Bourée.[68] He was not the only one to pose this question.

The final constant element of preaching on Hell is the emphasis on the eternity of its pains. "Appalling eternity" is a cliché in these sermons. It is so banal that one is tempted to give it no attention. At the same time, Gerson, Burton, and anyone who sought to cure the diseases of scruple and religious melancholy were alert to the danger of deep contemplation on this disturbing mystery, especially when linked to the depiction of infernal tortures. As this was a frequent association, it is not unreasonable to suppose that the idea of eternity traumatized a sizable number of early modern Christians. Bourgoing, an otherwise moderate author who opposed all exaggeration, meditates on Hell and eternity with a good deal of anguish:

> *As the third exercise [this advice comes in a sermon], I ponder the horror and eternity of the pains in hell's prison, which are due to a single sin, deadly, since the wretched damned will never be able to atone for this one sin, and so will never*

> *escape hell. O end of all miseries, which yet have no end! O beginning which will last forever! O life that will die and death that will live through eternity. O, whenever I shall be on the point or in danger of committing a deadly sin, may I think on this fearful eternity, and may I, like the Psalmist, always keep in mind the years everlasting.*[69]

Pious orators ran out of purposefully inadequate analogies for explaining "the infinite duration" of the evils of hell: a circle whose end is never found, centuries more numerous than drops of water in the sea, than grains of sand on a beach, than all the specks of dust on earth. For his part, however, Girard chose to stress two images that "seem to carry the imagination the farthest in this matter." The first is that of a globe a million times larger than ours, from which a bird would take a single speck of dust every hundred thousand years. The second is that of the same globe, but in bronze, which an ant would strive to wear down. The bird and ant would eventually finish after an enormously long time to "consume the globe of earth." But "this time would be ininitely different from eternity, because from the finite to the infinite, there is no ratio."[70] In the same spirit, the priest Le Gall assures the hardened sinner and future damned soul:

> *. . . After you will have been in hell for so many thousands of years, for as many hundreds of millions of years as there have been seconds since the beginning of time, as there are blades of grass on the earth, as there are grains of sand on the beaches . . . you will only begin [to suffer] . . . O eternity, eternity! I cannot understand you, but if we cannot understand it, we can at least give it some thought.*
>
> *Therefore, my brethren, contemplate . . . eternity, many times each day. Many sinners have been converted through such contemplation, and so may you, if you wish.*[71]

Such reflections and arithmetic are enough to make one dizzy: Indeed, this was the intended effect.

PURGATORY, OR TEMPORARY HELL

Toward the Infernal

In his outstanding study of Purgatory,[72] Jacques Le Goff demonstrates how the trials that purify the deceased—a notion dating back to early Christian times—were gradually moved to an intermediate place; by the late twelfth century, this place had been firmly defined and established. Le Goff also stresses the primary function of this intermediate afterlife: Rather than a black-or-white retribution, it now offered graduated penalties, adapted to each repentant sinner and to every type of "venial sin." It thus constituted a restriction of Hell, at least in theory, since it opened the path to Paradise to a range of petty though moderate offenders. There was thus an increased sense of security as well as of hope: The church assured that indulgences, masses, alms, and the prayers of the living had the power to diminish purgatorial suffering.

Pierre Chaunu, meanwhile, emphasizes the many "merits" of Purgatory. It was "highly pedagogical . . . this motivation for another world that avoided"—I would rather say "had to avoid"—"the paralyzing fear of hell." It contributed to social progress by favoring "the evolution" of Western Christianity. It brought together the living and the dead and stimulated an "interpenetration" of their fates. Purgatory "prolonged" the deceased individual's biography. It helped to promulgate casuistry, and therefore psychology as well.[73] As Chaunu also remarks, however, both Catholic and Protestant theologians, perhaps due to their shared Latin rationalism, did not understand the position of the Eastern church, which prayed for the dead without taking account of good works.[74]

Despite the above-noted intentions, Purgatory became "internalized." Le Goff rightly extends this observation of Arturo Graf,[75] and it is this aspect that most pertains to the current discussion of fear.

The discourse on the pains of Purgatory oscillated between two poles, one that sought to minimize and another that tended to dramatize the temporary punishments of the afterlife. The latter viewpoint drew largely on Saint Augustine's assertion that "this purgatorial fire is harsher than any pain which one can see, feel, or imagine here below."[76] To the Bishop of Hippo's authoritative polemic against the "merciful types," the "laxists" of his period,[77] there was added Aquinas's seconding of the tragic assertion.[78] On the other hand, Saint Cyril of Alexandria (d. 444) had written about those whose plantings were not entirely unproductive: "Through a small trial, abundance and fecundity shall be restored to them . . . the tribulation that purifies us is but slight; yet all the same, since its discipline is imposed from on high, it makes us blissful."[79]

Saint Augustine's opinion did not go uncontested. Dominic Soto, for example, tempers it in an unexpected way: The pains of Purgatory, he declares, are indeed terrible, but the prayers of the church are equally efficacious, so that any soul, no matter the debt, need not remain there for more than ten or twenty years.[80] Bellarmine rejected this relatively consoling estimate, but thought it likely that a part of Purgatory existed where "souls no longer feel physical pain, but only the pain of deprivation of bliss: a rather comfortable purgatory, an honorable, almost noble, prison, where nonetheless the soul is not happy and suffers even from the delay given its beatitude."[81] He also rejects Augustine's and Aquinas's statement that the slightest pain of Purgatory is more painful than the most dreadful earthly suffering. He explains that while privation from God is a severe penalty, it is "softened, and assuaged by the certain hope of possessing Him; this hope gives birth to an incredible joy, which grows all the more as the end of the exile approaches." The Jesuit theologian prefers to speak of "dilation" rather than the "dam," or deprivation. Moreover, how can one think that souls who die burdened with only a few light offenses would be punished by a torture more extreme than all the pains of this world?[82]

Bellarmine belongs to the group of commentators who strive to balance the pains and joys of Purgatory. A fellow member is San Bernardino di Siena, who adopts Augustine's tragic assertion but also specifies that posthumously saved souls undergo "external but not internal darkness." Furthermore, he enumerates the dozen joys that they feel, which "cause them to sing."[83] In its turn, a short sixteenth-century work concerning the apparition of a nun returned from purgatory brings reassuring news. The deceased woman does not suffer continual pain. She receives great comfort every Friday, during the Feasts of the Virgin, and on certain days such as Christmas, Easter, Ascension, Pentecost, All Souls', and the second of November. On occasion, she even partakes of the joy of the saints.[84]

Among the works that do not cast purgatory as a temporary hell, certainly the most important is that of Saint Catherine of Genoa (1447–1510). The "great lady of pure love" describes purgatory as she herself experienced it in her own lifetime. Her *Trattato*[85] recounts a mystic experience composed of both joy and pain. Significantly, she rejects certain imaginings that would depict souls in purgatory as being tormented by demons (Saint Catherine of Siena, *Dialogo*, chap. 81), as well as Brigid of Sweden's assertion (Revelations 4:8 and 6:66) that some of the souls there are not assured of salvation. On the other hand, she does not deny the sufferings of purgatory. Indeed, she affirms that the pain undergone in that place "is so extreme that no tongue could express it, nor no intellect grasp even its least glimmer, unless God were to reveal it through a most special grace."[86] She even adds: "purgatorial torments equal those in hell."[87] At the same time, she declares that "I think that there can be no happiness like that of a soul in purgatory, excepting that of the saints in paradise."[88] This "happiness" goes still further, by continually increasing as the soul nears God through purification. Furthermore, Catherine mentions the "physical" pains of purgatory only to say that they are less serious than the moral torment.[89] Herein the mystical experience is given expression. The soul in waiting suffers, because she realizes her imperfection in regard to the divine model, and also because she passionately aspires for an exact conformity between herself and God. She is moved by a powerful "flame of love." Her obstacle of sin, however, prevents her from opening herself to "this divine inclination." The impatience to be liberated is thus severe agony. "This burning and yet shackled instinct": in other words, Purgatory.[90]

Some years after Saint Catherine of Genoa, two optimistic theologians made their contributions to writings on Purgatory. Gaetano's *De Purgatorio* (1518) and Jean Eck's work of the same title (1523), both aimed at Luther, strive to minimize the potentially harsh aspects of the intermediate place. The first author states that souls in Purgatory are assured of salvation. They do not live in perpetual horror, since "they love divine justice, and gladly endure their penalties by submitting to this justice." Eck shows how suffering is not the same as fear and that Luther is wrong to assimilate the pains of Purgatory to those of Hell, at least in their length.[91]

Saint Francis de Sales and his disciple Jean-Pierre Camus agree with Saint Catherine of Genoa, and cite her in arguing that the thought of Purgatory can give us "more consolation than fear." Camus writes that the Bishop of Geneva "strongly recommends reading the admirable treatise on purgatory by the blessed Catherine of Genoa. I have often attentively read and reread her advice, but always with new pleasure and new insights; and I confess that in this matter I have never read anything which so satisfied me."[92] In Saint Catherine's spirit, Camus and Saint Francis de Sales explain the subject of Purgatory:

> *It is true that its torments are so great that the most extreme pains of this life cannot be compared to them [the obligatory reference to Saint Augustine] but also that there, the internal satisfactions are such that no earthly prosperity or happiness can match them. There, souls are in continuous union with God. They are perfectly obedient to his will . . . They gladly and lovingly purify themselves . . . They love God more than themselves . . . They are consoled by the angels. They are certain of their salvation . . . Their most bitter melancholy is now in the profoundest peace. If it is a kind of hell for its pains, it is a paradise for the sweetness with which divine love fills their hearts.*[93]

In the same line of thought, one of Fénelon's "spiritual letters" presents a comforting conception of Purgatory: "One must turn from this our earthly life," he writes, "like the souls in purgatory, placid and docile in God's hands, to abandon oneself, and be ready to be destroyed by the vengeful fire of love. Happy they who suffer thus."[94]

A problem, however, then arises: Why pray for souls in Purgatory? De Sales's and Camus's answer: "Because in spite of these advantages, the condition of these souls is most painful, and truly worthy of our compassion; moreover, the glory that they will give to God in heaven has been delayed."[95]

In contrast to these measured and reassuring messages, others put a tragic emphasis on the pains of Purgatory. During the seventeenth century, the Carmelites of Salamanca would write that

> *We think it not unfitting that a righteous soul, leaving this life with a considerable amount of venial sins, or with a heavy debt of deadly sins that have been remitted according to the guilt but not the temporal penalty, may suffer in purgatory a more atrocious, sensible pain that to be suffered by certain other souls, damned and punished eternally for one or two deadly sins.*[96]

If Purgatory was frequently made to be infernal, it was above all due to sermons by those whom Pierre Chaunu calls "the men of anger." De Sales had already identified this group: "most men who so greatly fear purgatory do so with a view to their own profit and self-love, more than for God's benefit; for they who speak of it from the pulpits usually evoke only the pains of this place, and not the joys and peace enjoyed by the souls therein."[97] In 1936 the author of the article "Purgatory" in the *Dictionnaire de Théologie catholique* would conclude: "It seems necessary above all to oppose the tendency of certain preachers who portray purgatory as a veritable hell, or at least an eternal state."[98]

Among those responsible for making a hell out of purgatory, Le Goff gives a prominent place to the Dominican Etienne de Bourbon, author of a *Traité de prédication (Tractatis de diversis materiis praedicabilibus)*, composed between about 1250 and his death in 1261.[99] In this treatise, Purgatory comprises the fifth section of the first gift of the Holy Spirit, the gift of fear (*De dono timoris*). Within this section, several chapters concern the reasons for fearing the suffering of purgatory: the sharpness (*acerbitas*) of the penalties, their diversity (*diversitas*), their duration (*diuturnitas*), sterility (*sterilitas* = the impossibility for souls to achieve merits after death), noxiousness (*dampnositas* = deprivation of the vision of God), the nature of the torments (*tormentorum qualitas*), and the low number of helpers (*subveniencium paucitas* = the living soon forget the dead). De Bourbon describes tortures taken from *The Apocalypse of Paul* via *The Purgatory of Saint Patrick* and tries to clarify the painful character of the penalty of deprivation by insisting that the saints would prefer to be in Hell but able to see God than to be in Paradise but unable to see Him. The author illustrates these negative considerations with thirty-nine separate anecdotes. Moreover, Le Goff confirms that De Bourbon's treatise met with great success and that his *exempla* were often reemployed.

Following De Bourbon, the "Preaching Friars" appear to have greatly contributed to spreading the notion of Purgatory as a provisional Hell, just as they also diffused the theme of the *danse macabre*: One telling example is the Florentine Dominican Iacopo Passavanti's *Lo Specchio della vera penitenza* (1354), which reached a wide audience.[100] The author calls anyone stupid who refuses to do penance in this life, thinking that Purgatory is made for that purpose. First, will one have the will or even the time to repent in the hour of death? When that time comes, however, "what madness to prefer the pains of purgatory, which Saint Augustine says surpass all that one can suffer on earth, to a little penance here below!"[101] Passavanti identifies two types of purgative expiations after death. The first will transpire in a place "which is near the center of the earth, or hell, where the souls shall purify themselves in the same fire that is in hell." The second are undergone on earth. In both cases, the expiations are "very great." To demonstrate his point, Passavanti uses a tragic *exemplum* set in the "Comté de Nevers" and borrowed from Hélinand de Froidmont. A married noblewoman fell in love with a knight and committed adultery with him. To sin more freely, she killed her husband. Having fallen ill, she repented, as did her lover. Thus they were not condemned to Hell. Their purgatorial "martyrdom," however, is striking. Every night, naked and with disheveled hair, the woman is pursued by a black rider carrying a knife. Both this rider and his horse spit flames from their eyes, mouth, and nose. The woman soon arrives near a wide ditch filled with burning coals, which she is unable to cross. The rider—her former lover—catches up with her, cuts her with his knife, throws her into the coals, then takes her back out, flings her over his horse, and rides off with her. Passavanti's technique is still somewhat archaic compared to later writings and sermons on this theme. Furthermore, he asserts that the horse in this account is an authentic "demon,"[102] an executor of divine justice. Finally, since the man and woman loved each other in the way of guilt, they are condemned to hate each other for the duration of their punishment.

In reaction, official doctrine attempted, not always successfully, to empty Purgatory of demons and teach that the souls who suffer there can no longer sin and are therefore incapable of hate. From another standpoint, however, the Dominican's *exemplum* connects with the numerous later evocations of the terrible hardships of Purgatory. The *Complainte des Trespassés* (d. 1507) of the canon and "rhétoriquer" Jean Molinet vividly testifies to the diffusion of a vision of Purgatory where the negative side largely overtakes the positive one. Addressing earthly individuals who loll in the pleasures of life, the prisoners of the temporary Hell tell them:

You rest on silken sheets,
While we in torment burn and roast;
The soothing lute lulls you to sleep,
Most sweetly, while we harshly and most
Hideously from bed are pressed
All naked, while you are well dressed;
We are tortured, and while you laugh, we weep.
So today there is only good and bad fortune . . .[103]

Burning in "the inhuman brazier," the souls of Purgatory therefore beg for instant prayers.

Temporary Hell in the Seventeenth and Eighteenth Centuries

Purgatory has only a sporadic presence in early modern preaching. As large a corpus of missionary sermons as that of the Lazarists does not give it any special attention. On the other hand, it receives heavy emphasis from the Capuchin François de Toulouse and the Jesuits Segneri and Fontana. It sometimes appears in Sunday sermons (as with Girard and Symon), and sometimes not (as with La Font, Hébert, Chevassu and Réguis).[104] In the latter case, the silence is doubtless explained by the fact that sermons on Purgatory were usually reserved for the second of November and that most collections of Sunday sermons do not include the homily for this day. In any case, the "libraries" and encyclopedias for preachers all contain a special chapter on Purgatory, which also plays a major role in the hymnals. Michna's *Svatoraná muzika* (Prague, 1661) provides revealing evidence:

1. *Hear, I prithee, hear my call,*
Hear O Lord eternal
My cry and my lament,
Release me from this torment!
Listen to these sinners—
Ah! Cast not out a single one
Who puts his hope in Thee.

2. *This prison where I stay,*
O Lord, is lasting far too long;
Yet still I'll not defend
My gross and heavy crime:
I only seek Thy grace,
Ah! May Thy generosity
Free me from this anguish!

3. *Cut short, sweet Lord, this long*
Moment of raging fire.
O please bestow on me
Thy gracious pardon,
Judge not according to my sin,
But rather to Thy Passion,
Do not prolong this salvation.

4. *Deliver me from this dark prison,*
From this most wretched hovel,
In heaven I shall give Thee glory
Abundant glory to my Lord.
Ah, cut short, cut short my woes.
To those for whom Thou deigned to suffer,
Give happiness without end!

5. *Behold me in my sorrow,*
In this my horrid punishment.
On my poor and humble soul,
Inflict no penitence
According to my deeds:
For desertless, in misery,
I am sustained by Thy love
And I fear Thy justice.

6. *O my Guardian, I implore Thee,*
Console one sore afflicted,
I trust in Thy support,
See how they torture me!
I cannot escape danger:
Thou, intercede with God,
That He may grant my rescue!

7. *That my thirst might cease at last,*
That my hunger might vanish,
That both this cold and heat might end,
That God might pardon my sins,

Committed long ago
In my weak and feeble youth.

8. *I call, always I call to Thee,*
All things constrain me,
So much that I shall not attain
That blissful rest.
Cry out, cry out my friends:
Your voice shall appease
And calm the wrath of God.

9. *In return, obtain from God*
Remission of torments
For souls so fiercely burning,
Give them sweet refreshment;
Thou can come to their aid,
Thou might succour them
If thou wouldst remember them![105]

Hence it is clear that many Europeans of the Age of Reason heard about Purgatory. Otherwise they would not have prayed so much, or had so many massess said for souls in this plight. The tone and style of this discourse would readily have incited people to make such spiritual offerings.

As it has been done for Hell, one could easily reconstruct the stereotypical components of this early modern discourse on Purgatory: a predominantly tragic discourse, which rarely stressed God's kindness. François Le Picart, however, a theologian who preached at Paris at the beginning of the Wars of Religion, both wrote and spoke in more positive terms. Although he does inevitably mention the all-too-notorious words of Saint Augustine, which he translates as "the pain of all the martyrs together is not so great as that of purgatory," it is mainly to affirm that solid faith and prayers for the dead can spare us even from Purgatory: "If you are without faith in the Church, [even] if you were to do all the good works possible in the world, still you will not be saved. Keep an entire (Catholic) faith, and you will escape every pain, of both hell and purgatory . . . And by praying for the dead we will guard ourselves against going to purgatory . . ."[106] Throughout the liturgical year, Le Picart stressed the "mercy of God . . . greater than our infirmity and sins."[107] He also declares: "God calls sinners his friends."[108] All the same, he hopes that heretics and schismatics will be burned.[109] His main objective is to keep Parisians within the Catholic faith. To those who remain faithful during this time of religious crisis, he almost guarantees a direct flight to Paradise. In the changed context of the seventeenth and eighteenth centuries, however, Catholic proselytizing sought above all to "convert" sinners. It tapped all its resources to dramatize the end of life and played up the gloomier aspects of Purgatory.

This place is thus a punishment more than a purification.[110] It is a scene of expiation, of the execution of "the judgments of God," who "avenges" Himself on guilty men, no matter if they have been pardoned. Monsignor de Fromentières, reciting a homily for the Day of the Dead to Louis XIV and the court, informs his illustrious listeners: "It is thus true that God, who is terrible in His judgments on mankind, brings horrible punishments on those who will not have atoned for their offenses with appropriate penance in their lifetime." The orator goes on to repeat that God does so "to take vengeance on these poor souls, in proportion to the sins which they have committed."[111] The terms "avenger," "vengeance," and "justice" were part of the contemporary vocabulary of Purgatory. In one of Grignion de Montfort's hymns, the prisoners of temporary Hell cry out to the living:

Friends, this Avenging God
Sets up our torture.
We feel the rigors
Of all His justice.[112]

Another missionary hymn requires the faithful to sing:

The justice of a watchful God
Holds them captive in the flames.
The justice of a watchful God
Makes them groan 'neath the weight of His blows.[113]

On All Saints' Day, the priest Symon de Rennes addresses God, telling Him that "[souls in Purgatory] satisfy Thy justice by the excess of their pains."[114] In giving models of sermons for preachers, Montargon asserts: "One must necessarily expiate the sin, either in this life or the next . . . Let us think on these underground places, where God's vengeance is deployed with all the more severity, because it punishes in order to pardon."[115] In contrast to many of his colleagues, Yves-Michel Marchais, a priest of Anjou, refuses to speak of "the anger of a vengeful God" at work in Purgatory. He describes only "the justice and omnipotence of an offended God," while specifying that Jesus Christ "takes all things into account, and exacts atonement down to the last penny."[116]

In the afterlife, payment is made for everything, even light offenses. One of D'Outreman's model sermons states that the torments of Purgatory are inflicted "for little vanities, idle words, white lies and other venial sins, which we judge so lightly and commit so readily."[117] François de Toulouse, giving a missionary sermon, presents God "as a pitiless debt collector," who "demands payment to the last detail." The preacher marvels at this divine strictness toward already saved souls. At the same time, he observes: ". . . He punishes them for a venial sin that may consist of a brief burst of anger or vain chatter, of a laugh, of a slight enjoyment of beauty; O God, how extreme are your rigours, and how unfathomable are your judgments."[118] Grignion de Montfort develops the same theme in his *Plaintes des âmes du purgatoire*. These title characters alert the living in these terms:

Keep yourself from sin,
And listen to no story,
That 'tis only but a pin
To burn in purgatory!

No tiny little fall,
Nor petty false desire,
Since God doth punish all
With His extremest ire.[119]

"The slightest stains / Do hold us in these flames": So too the suffering souls affirm in a hymn of the Capuchins.[120] The Jesuit Fontana, an expert in excessive speeches, stresses the length of the pains of Purgatory and teaches his audience that "Cardinal Paschage" must endure "a most long and dreadful Purgatory" for a fault that was only out of "ignorance" and for which he was only "slightly guilty." A "holy virgin," one Vitalina, was also condemned to an "extremely long Purgatory" for "being somewhat vain about her hair." A Franciscan was punished with "the lengthiest torments for the single fault of not having inclined his head during the *gloria patri*." With such examples, the preacher more or less declares, think of what things your friends and relatives must suffer, they who have sinned so greatly![121] Girard, meanwhile, confidently asserts that "[in Purgatory] the most trifling lies, the jokes, the idle gossip that pass in society for permitted recreation will be punished by horrid torments. There one shall see the madness of they who do not fear venial sin."[122] The same sermon contains a theologically correct but logically paradoxical statement: "Do you truly know for whom Purgatory is destined? To the saints, and God's chosen people, to they who, having observed the law and fulfilled a Christian life, have the happiness of dying in the state of grace."[123] "Horrid torments" for they who have "the happiness of dying in the state of grace": Such are Girard's "Good News."

Purgatory is a prison. Souls are there "held in captivity."[124] This view dates back to the Middle Ages and carries on for centuries. It was linked to the notion of God as accountant, judge, and jailer. In Jean Molinet's *Complainte des Trespassés*, the dead bid the living to look down toward the bottom of their "prisons."[125] At the beginning of a sermon on Purgatory, Fulvio Fontana gives his listeners the following advice: "Imagine . . . below your feet a deep prison that, because of its proximity to hell, though it has none of its impiety, still brings the same pains and torments."[126] An eighteenth-century French hymn invites Christians to listen to "these pitiful sounds" that the souls of Purgatory "utter in their dungeons."[127] De Montfort's suffering souls beseech their living friends and family, saying.

Free us from prison
Through all your justice.
Pay our ransom
Through your holy sacrifice.[128]

In his turn, the priest Symon evokes "the gloomy prisons where they (the suffering souls) finally satisfy divine justice."[129] The *Bouquet de la mission* also confirms that these souls "are detained in these prisons of divine justice for minor faults, or for not having fully satisfied sins that were remitted to them in this world . . ."[130]

This prison is a hell, if not an eternal one. De Fromentières speaks before Louis XIV: "To clarify the extreme violence of the ills endured by faithful souls in purgatory, I will first put forward a statement which will surprise you yet is most true, that these poor souls, as regards physical pain, suffer the same fire as do the damned; and as regards the pain of deprivation of bliss, they suffer even more than the damned."[131] The Jesuit Houdry's *Bibliothèque des prédicateurs* includes this declaration: "Only the pains of Hell can compare to those of purgatory; they are the same, but for the duration and despair."[132] In his *Dictionnaire apostolique*, Montargon ponders the difference between the pains of Hell and Purgatory and concludes: "There is no difference between these afflictions but their duration. There, as well as in hell, a soul will be wrapped, surrounded by fire . . . the same prison, the same captivity, the same tormentors, horrible specters, and gnawing worms."[133]

The contamination between Hell and Purgatory went still further. In this regard, revealing evidence comes from a note dictated by Pascal to his young nephew Louis Périer: "people of all ranks and even the martyrs have much to fear from Scripture. The greatest pain of purgatory is the uncertainty of judgment. *Deus absconditus*."[134] The undeniably heterodox sense of the second phrase has caused some to question the authenticity of this note. Jean Deprun, however, has skillfully and perceptively placed it within an entire theological current that for centuries had affirmed that the greatest torture for souls suffering in Purgatory was the uncertainty of their salvation, the ignorance or oblivion of the place where they actually were, indeed the fear of being damned forever.[135] Pascal undoubtedly drew on a tradition of "private revelations," from Saint Brigid of Sweden through Saint Lydwine of Schiedam and Denis the Carthusian to the account by Father Amelote in his *Vie de soeur Marguerite . . . de Beaune* (1654). According to Amelote, this nun frequently had the vision of a dead man, who told her that "his purgatory was terrible and hideous, that he suffered torments she could not express, that his spirit was in such great darkness that he knew not whether he was in hell or purgatory, and she could tell that this plight was so agonizing that all the other tortures of the righteous seemed to her slight in comparison."[136]

Margaret of the Holy Sacrament's revelation can be compared, I believe, to a passage from a sermon on Purgatory by François de Toulouse:

> *Our [earthly] pains are . . . lessened by the thought that they will soon reach their end, and that they will obtain us eternal glory, but the souls of purgatory have not this consolation. There are some doctors of the Church who say that these souls know not whether they are tormented by an enemy who makes them suffer tortures that must last for centuries, or whether they are being purged by a Father who will soon remove them from this place of misery.*[137]

In Purgatory as it is in Hell, fire reigns supreme. Once more, the pyromaniac phantasms of the afterlife are given free rein. "If we consider the instruments God uses to make them [the souls of Purgatory] suffer," François de Toulouse again asserts,

> *we will see that they are the most violent ones possible. It is true that God could torment them with roses, and purge them of their filth with perfumed waters, since all things in His hands take whatever stamp He pleases. But He uses fire, the most violent of the elements, and the most rigorous of tortures . . . and some doctors say that the same fire which torments the damned does purge the elect, and that it differs from that of hell only in its duration.*[138]

The ecclesiastical discourse on Purgatory excessively amplified and dramatized a verse from I Corinthians 3:13–15: ". . . and the fire [of the Day of Judgment] shall try every man's work of what sort it is . . . ; If any man's work shall be burned, he shall suffer loss: but he himself shall be saved; yet so as by fire." Commenting on this text and drawing support from Saint Augustine, Saint Caesarius of Arles had written: "May no one say: what does it matter to me to stay in purgatorial fire if I must thereafter attain eternal life? O! Do not speak thus, my dear brethren, for this purgatorial fire is more painful than any pain we can conceive, undergo, or feel in this world."[139]

During the Counter-Reformation, Bellarmine was convinced that the primary physical pain of Purgatory is that of fire. Like many experts, however, he wonders whether this fire is actual or metaphoric. Without formally committing himself, he argues that, on the general opinion of the theologians, it is a real fire.[140] Such also is the viewpoint of De Fromentières, for whom "these poor souls [of Purgatory] suffer the rage of a material fire that, being lit by God's justice and made miraculously capable of working on spiritual substance, causes them to feel a pain that no imagination could possibly conceive."[141] For Symon de Rennes, the "avenging fire" of Purgatory "surrounds" these souls,

> *penetrates them, and devours them. This miraculous fire, raised by a superior power, attains heights of activity and violence that it could never yet work on*

> *spiritual and immaterial substances [those in purgatory not yet being such] torments them in unutterable fashion; and though it may only be for a time, say Saint Gregory and Saint Augustine, it makes them suffer pains beyond all present afflictions.*[142]

Moreover, as in Hell, this fire is "intelligent." This "judicious" fire, teaches Paolo Segneri the Elder, "will extend its search even to sins already confessed, already pardoned, in order to remove, expiate, and efface the least vestiges of them, the tiniest remnants, the slightest blemishes."[143]

An actual but "inconceivable" fire: This is also Hyacinthe de Montargon's diagnosis: "Shall I agree with the theologians that there is in purgatory a fire which torments unfortunate souls in a manner that is as real as it is inconceivable?" The answer is yes: "There, as well as in hell, a soul will be wrapped, surrounded by this fire; this same element kindled by the same brimstone will make itself felt and penetrate to the marrow."[144] In fact, the majority of preachers and hymn writers—and certainly the faithful with them—did not question the nature of the fire that burned in either Purgatory or Hell. For them, unbearable flames consume both the temporary and permanent prisoners of these two places. The dead in Molinet's work alert the living, since they are "condemned to the fire of purgatory": They are "in torment, burned and roasted"; they blaze in "the inhuman brazier."[145] De Montfort's *Plaintes des ames du purgatoire* features in succession the words and phrases "furnace," "to burn in purgatory," "searing fire," "flaming coal," "lively fires," and "bed of fire."[146] Other eighteenth-century French hymns speak of "horrible fires,"[147] "consuming fires," "beds of flame," "heated braziers," and souls who are "captive in the flames."[148] The oft reedited *Bouquet de la mission* gives the period's official doctrine on the question, based on both Saint Paul and Augustine. The author, Jean Leuduger, declares that the physical pain

> *is none other than that of fire, as the Fathers confirm, but a fire so excruciating that they [the souls of Purgatory] suffer more than can be possibly imagined. So it is, as Saint Augustine says regarding Psalm 37. Because it is written that one will be* saved by fire, *one scorns the fire of purgatory. Yes, one shall surely be saved by fire (I Cor. 3:15), but by a fire more painful and excruciating than any that might be endured in this life.*[149]

This text typifies the way in which Saint Paul was read through the mediation of Saint Augustine.

The tortures of Purgatory provided further material for preachers on this theme of impressive escalations and accumulations. The sermon on Hell served as a copy text, and Saint Augustine's inevitable statement both authorized this plagiarism and licensed all manner of superlatives. For example, Girard assures his flock: "All the torments of this life, the crosses, diseases, afflictions, the harshest trials, the most cruel tortures, and even death itself, are nothing compared to the rigors of purgatorial fire; and one should not be surprised by this, since purgatory is a prison, filled with a fire lit by God's anger . . ."[150]

The Jesuit d'Outreman surpasses even the vast range of pains suggested by the Bishop of Hippo: "I cannot omit what Saint Thomas seems to profess, that the pains endured by these souls are more severe than the ones suffered by the Son of God in this life."[151] The sufferings of Purgatory, like those of Hell, are unimaginable. The Catholic mission, however, strove to give it some description *a minima*. For instance, Monsignor de Fromentières tells Louis's court:

Imagine all the tortures assigned to criminals for the gravest lèse-majesté, all the torments invented by the tyrants against the Christians; imagine a man who all at once has a violent migraine, an enormous gallstone, a cruel gout in his feet and hands, and a sharp fever that burns his insides: all that is nothing compared to the least ember of fire that attacks souls in purgatory."[152]

An eighteenth-century complaint of souls in Purgatory contains this plea to the living:

You cannot see criminals
Tolerate the gallows:
Know that we suffer sorrows
A thousand times more terrible:
Inhuman hearts, please help us—
Alas! We burn, haste to us.[153]

Other similar songs include words and lines such as "tortures," "excessive ills," "torments," "mournful sighs," "groanings," "inconceivable pain," and so on.[154] Some preachers and missionaries did wonder if these expressions might be excessive. In addition, the Twenty-Fifth Session of the Council of Trent had ordered bishops to prohibit any "popular preaching" on Purgatory to address "uncertain points, or to affirm evidently false things. They are to prohibit, as scandalous and offensive to the faithful, anything that may arouse pure curiosity, or attracts shameful profit."[155]

Montargon, who edited eighteenth-century model sermons, could not ignore this warning. He thus first restrains himself and states, "let us not exaggerate, and let us only speak of the fire of purgatory as it is told to us by Saint Augustine." Having taken this precaution, he then elaborates: "Who can show you these deep chasms, these dreadful dungeons, these burning cauldrons, these floods of fire and brimstone? . . ."[156] A few lines later, however, the author returns to prudence: "God would not wish me to deceive your piety, by offering to you as dogmas of faith statements that I believe to be true, but which the Church has not yet authorized: I know indeed that the way in which God purifies the chosen, the amount of time which they must suffer, are questions that have not been answered for us."[157] Does the orator stop at this point? Not at all. On the contrary, he opens the gates to a blistering harangue:

But although one may not exactly determine the extent of their sufferings [of the souls in Purgatory], I will venture to say that their torments surpass all those that can be borne in this life. Recall the most cruel tortures invented by the barbaric tyrants of the first centuries [A.D.] *Let your imagination bring together in a single torture the pain and grief of all the rest: a mere outline, a faint image of the piercing pains endured by the faithful in purgatory:* Umbrae sunt ad tua tormenta *[Saint Augustine, Sermon 41* De sanctis*]. No, the volcanoes that vomit burning floods, that throw fear and confusion all around, these diverse torments that the ingenious madness of persecutors can cull from the rigor of flames, these boiling baths that scalded the martyrs of ancient Rome are but dim sketches of the keen and fiery pains that the dead in purgatory feel:* Umbrae sunt . . ."[158]

"Ingenious madness": The description would suit the Jesuit Fulvio Fontana, preaching on Purgatory. As he proclaims in this excerpt from his anthology,

Know therefore that the souls of your friends, of your relatives, of those whom you most dearly loved, live in torments so excessive that neither Nero's barbarity nor Dionysius of Syracuse's cruelty invented anything worse . . . Imagine . . . below your feet a deep deep prison . . . there you will see the night fraught with gloomy mists, the air beset with deadly lightning, the ground shook by tremendous earthquakes. These caves continually echo with the disconsolate wailing of souls and the sharp whistling of monsters. Here the bulls of Phalaris [this tyrant burned his victims in a brass bull], the bodies filled with worms by Maxentius, Diocletian's cruellest wheels would all be a comfort to these souls in penance.[159]

The orator then recounts the case of "Saint Christine" (*sic*) who once died and then had the privilege of contemplating the "horrors" of Purgatory. Then conducted before Christ, she had the choice between a throne of gold, pearls, and all the jewels of Paradise, and a return to earth to suffer for the souls of Purgatory. Struck by that place's tortures, she opted for the more heroic alternative. She therefore rose from the stretcher where she had lain during the funeral service, came back to life, and thereafter sought out the most abominable tortures, knowing, alas! that she could not succumb to them:

Be gripped with fear, gentlemen: see how Christine lies down in fetid tombs to be eaten by worms, plunges into boiling cauldrons so the waters will destroy her—but by a miracle she comes out alive and intact. She lowers herself into frozen ponds so the cold will petrify her, places herself near a fire so the consuming flames will slowly diminish her.

She enters the most dreadful forests to be torn apart by wild beasts, throws herself into hot ovens to be reduced to ashes, throws herself off cliffs so that her brains will be dashed out on the jagged rocks, places herself under millstones to be ground into flour. In short, Christine was a living purgatory, miraculously surviving all these tortures . . . and that during twenty-five years. Deduce then, sirs, what chasms of pain, what horrible spectacles she must have seen in purgatory, if they put such measureless compassion in her heart![160]

Do the preachers then forget the penalty of privation of bliss? No. As in their descriptions of Hell, however, they place less emphasis on this sorrow, since it does not easily lend itself to horrific elaborations. On occasion, some concrete approximations do make it perceptible to the audience. Girard, for instance, describes "a most tender woman, whose truly lovable husband is far away on a long and dangerous voyage." He finally nears his home port. "But just when he is ready to touch land, a sudden squall throws his boat back out on the open sea, with the obvious danger of dying without help . . ."[161] While this is a theologically false image, since the inhabitants of Purgatory are not in "danger of dying without help," it is fully consistent with an ecclesiastical discourse where there is no longer any question of San Bernardino's "twelve joys" of Purgatory, nor of the "happiness," the "internal satisfaction," and the "most profound peace"[162] that Catherine of Genoa, Saint Francis de Sales, and Jean-Pierre Camus saw pervading repentant yet saved souls.

The sermon on Purgatory was becoming increasingly unbalanced, as its negative side gained more and more weight. Even when the testimony of Catherine of Genoa was recalled, suffering was stressed more than hope. The author of the *Bouquet de la Mission* writes: "Their pain is so great, says Saint Catherine of Genoa, that no tongue can express it, no mind can understand its least glimmer. For they have such an ardent desire to possess God that the least delay is a pestilent gall to them."[163] The priest Marchais, describing to his Angevin congregation the "terrible and dreadful tortures" of Purgatory, cites the following as the most serious: "To see one's self deprived of the possession of God and the entry into this blissful rest whose entire price and value they will then know; to constantly long for this object without being able to attain it and, despite all the ardor of the love and eagerness that it brings, to see one's self removed and cut off, like a prisoner from his country . . ."[164] It is no longer averred, however, that the souls of Purgatory "sing," as they do in San Bernardino's version. Instead, Segneri asserts that the pain of the deprivation suffered in Purgatory is in some ways worse than that of the damned. His reasoning: The damned

> *are deprived of possessing God, but a God whom they do not love whatsoever and of whom they have but imperfect understanding; whereas these chosen souls [of Purgatory] suffer the deprivation of a God whom they know, whom they love, and whom they desire in an infinitely passionate way. Wherefore, if the deprivation of God is as the hell of hells for those who hate this sovereign blessing, what effect will this deprivation have on those who love it much more than they love themselves?*[165]

In order to excite the compassion of the living and to provoke their prayers, both songs and sermons insist on the actual—or at least truly experienced—length of the pains of temporary Hell. In one of de Montfort's hymns, a soul in Purgatory cries out to the living in these terms: "I have been burning in fire / For more than a year. / By both Men and God / I am abandoned."[166] A year: perhaps it is not so long. May one think otherwise. In his enormously successful *Guia de los pecadores*, Louis of Granada tells the story of a "holy man, who by God's dispensation expiated in the chains of his body the pain of purgatory in a single instant." However, "he found this instant to be as excessively long as the pain was excruciating."[167] Two hundred years later Girard would affirm: "'Tis there [in Purgatory] that the hours will seem to last for years and that the years will seem like centuries."[168] Then again, are we sure that we will stay there for only a short while? If it is true, as Saint Augustine says, that its fire

> *surpasses all that one can suffer in this world, what will it be like to stay there for many years, and perhaps many centuries? And, when it will be necessary to endure the heat of this fire for a single day to expiate a single venial sin, how much time will be needed for so many thousands of venial sins that we will realize we have committed in our lifetime, and for which we will not have done penance?*[169]

To explain both the intensity and duration of Purgatory's tortures, the Sorbonne professor, missionary, and later seminary director Laurent Chenart employs a striking analogy:

> *. . . If one cannot help but be touched by some compassion to see a criminal burned alive, even though this torture may not last long, what a sorrow would it be therefore to see this cruel torment last an entire day! What would it be like to see this man, however criminal he is, amid these flames, not only for one day, but a month, a year, ten years, a hundred, God willing this wretched man's soul to stay inside his body, and not allowing its dissolution from the heat of the flames, as he also does by His power and justice to these poor souls who suffer in purgatory? Would not such a spectacle strike the utmost fear in the hearts of all those present?*[170]

Fontana's preaching also accentuates the quantitative aspects of Purgatory. He speaks first of the "millions of souls drowned in these torments, trapped in this brutal slaughterhouse, who let out the most pitiable screams that extreme pain could possibly cause." He then gives the above-cited examples of saintly people who suffered "extremely long" pain in the afterlife for their peccadilloes. He concludes:

> *I cannot guess how much time in purgatory is allotted to your dead friends and relations, who hurt their inferiors with stinging words and mockery, who laughed at their equals, muttered against their superiors, derided priests, railed against the nobility, and applauded the licentious. Alas, how infinitely will they suffer!. . . What mountains of offenses! When will they ever stop receiving these terrifying penalties?*[171]

Did the audience then feel a sense of incredulity? The Jesuit continues: "You think I exaggerate. But you are deceived." His proof: Sixtus V gave an indulgence of 11,000 years for the reciting of a certain prayer at Notre-Dame; Gregory XIII published one of 74,000 years in favor of the members of the Confraternity of the Rosary; the Holy Church allows for the principle of masses in perpetuity. Why? Because the popes "know the length of purgatory, which for unaided souls will last until the end of the world."[172]

For the audience, the most shocking aspect of the church's discourse on Purgatory was undoubtedly the cry for help that the prisoners of the temporary Hell aimed at the living, especially since it could bring about a nagging sense of guilt. De Toulouse tells his listeners: ". . . We are the cause of their misery! Yes, we have lit the fire that burns them; for most of them are in purgatory simply for having too much loved their children; they gave them many good things, but often with an eagerness that made them forget their own salvation. But the number of those who are in purgatory for having concealed, or too lightly corrected the faults of their children is much greater."[173] The suffering souls' call for help is all the more insistent because in this place of waiting they cry "worthless tears."[174] There one can cry and have merit for others, but not for one's self. Hence the constant recourse of the doctrinal campaign of the seventeenth- and eighteenth-century to the literary genre of the complaint of souls in Purgatory, in tandem with hymns on the pains of Hell. Molinet's verses are worth recalling:

> *Halt, ye who pass before us,*
> *And take heed to the pitiful story*
> *Of human bodies dead this past century . . .*
>
> *We cannot, nor this day nor another*
> *Lend a hand to neither cousin nor brother*
> *From this inhuman brazier where we burn;*
> *We await mercy, grace, and pardon*
> *And true repose through your giving deed:*
> *One knows his friends at times of need.*
>
> *You who keep our goods and wealth for us,*
> *So we may have prayers and masses,*
> *Spend now quickly, do not deceive us; . . .*
>
> *Pray for us, say the* De Profundis
> *Say seven psalms and vigils for the dead:*
> *Through your good deeds shall we reach paradise.*[175]

The *Bouquet de la mission* cites Job 19:12 and confirms: "These souls cry out to us from their tortures, 'Have pity on us, you who are our friends; have pity because the hand of the Lord is striking us.' "[176] In his hymns for missions, de Montfort inserted two lengthy complaints of souls in Purgatory, which both begin with the same reproaches:

O mortals, listen, all of you,
List to us, o brethren dear,
We deeply long for you
From the depths of misery drear.

Alas! How we suffer pain!
But who would understand such fear?
We weep and we complain
Though not a soul does care to hear.[177]

These complaints would have been all the more trying for those who heard or performed them—for example, one of de Montfort's complaints is a minidrama with twenty characters—since they were supposed to come from a father, mother, brother, and so on. Although on a lesser scale, such tactics inevitably call to mind the proselytizing directed at the Indians of South America ("Tell me now, my sons, of all these people born in this land before the Spanish preached the Holy Gospel, how many were saved? . . . Not a single one!"[178] In both cases, this frightful acculturation played on the ties of kinship and exploited them at the risk of damaging the listeners' psychological health. It was hard to listen to this reprimand from the beyond without feeling some uneasiness:

You amuse yourselves,
you play,
You live a life of ease
And make us longer stay
In burning agonies.

You waste, you foolishly
Misspend your precious
gain,
That could so easily
Relieve us in our pain.[179]

In de Montfort's playlet, which was performed during his missions, five living people reveal after hearing the cry "Bring to our terrible suffering":

1. 'Tis the voice of my father,
Moves pity in my breast!
2. 'Tis the voice of my mother,
I know her cry distressed!
3. 'Tis my sister or brother!
4. That dead man is my husband!
5. Alas! 'tis the prayer
Of my dear old friend.[180]

As usual, Fontana exploits to the full a theme that was bound to affect everyone in the audience. In his sermon the reproaches rain down thick and fast, and soon the dead are speaking through his voice, lashing out at the entire congregation:

> *It is you, parents, you, sons, you, daughters, who keep the fire lit that torments your loved ones, by not bringing water to put it out. It is you who keep them in fetters by not lending your hands to free them. It is you who refuse these good dead souls the grace of leaving their cruel slavery, by not lending them even a penny . . .*
>
> *(The relatives proving themselves to be wanting,) You, friends, bring us relief, since there no longer is any love in the hearts of my father and son. Friends, bring us relief, since my mother, my daughter only has the heart to hate me by making me suffer here below. Friends, bring me relief, since all my brothers and relatives forget that I burn in these flames.*[181]

Therefore one must immediately celebrate masses, visit churches, acquire indulgences, give alms, and take communion for the sake of souls in Purgatory, especially those of one's dearly beloved. Moreover, if the latter left money so the church would pray for them after their death, their heirs are all the more obliged to quickly execute the terms of their wills.

Good charity, however, begins with one's self. While it is well to pray for the eternal rest of friends and relatives, is it wise to forget one's self and not arrange for masses to be said for one's own deliverance from the flames of purgatory? D'Outreman here speaks for the prudent point of view:

> *Among the legacies that you arrange for your nearest and dearest, do not forget yourself, that is, remember to also leave something so that masses may be said for the eternal rest of your soul. For it is not right that your children, relatives, and friends should have the support and benefit of your wealth, while you would be burning for ten, twenty, thirty, and fifty years in the unspeakably raging fire of purgatory:* Miserere animae tuae, *says the sage (Ecclus. 3:24).*[182]

It would be foolish, however, to think that the heirs, even after giving formal but oral promises to the dying person, would deprive themselves of money simply to say masses for the latter's benefit. After the hallucinatory descriptions and vehement reproaches of his sermon on Purgatory, Fontana concludes with a witty but bitter story, designed to give pause to those individuals who would enjoin their heirs to pray for them. A peasant, nearing death, had only a lamb and a horse. He left them both to his son, under the obligation of selling the horse and having masses said for him with the profits from the sale. His son was lazy but cunning. He went to the market with the two animals and put them up for sale. Along came a farmer and horse trader. The son told him that he would not sell the one without the other. The farmer asked: How much do you want for the lamb?—Thirty écus.—And for the horse?—Half an écu." The deal was closed. The son used the half-écu for masses and kept the thirty écus for himself. Fontana then closes his sermon with the following advice from a man of experience: "Do not charge others to do that which you can and should do yourself, for in this world you cannot trust anyone. When you want to leave money for the sake of your soul, do so with the strictest clause that if your heirs do not punctually satisfy their obligations, the money will then go to the prince or sovereign."[183]

In the eighteenth century, the priest and scholar d'Artigny judged that the way in which Purgatory was depicted in the Low Countries was often "foolish." He succeeded in getting himself expelled from a monastic church in Malines because he had been seen laughing at a large painting "with the greatest absurdities in it." It showed a great many angels, looking like "fishermen," throwing an infinite number of scapularies, prayer beads, cords, belts, medals, and rosaries into the flames of Purgatory and pulling them back out "laden with a prodigious number of souls." At the Dominican monastery in Antwerp Artigny saw something even more shocking:

> *For in the little graveyard that adjoins one of the portals of their church, they have hollowed out certain underground chambers, which are indeed most dreadful to behold, for both their darkness and the hideous way in which purgatory is depicted therein.*
>
> *From top to bottom, everything is painted in the color of fire. A bit of daylight is let in to these dungeons by a few skylights, whose windows are also painted red; thus the idea of a burning furnace is fully achieved. Amid the painted flames one sees an infinite number of naked figures all chained together, who grimace and seem to shriek most dreadfully. An angel descends from heaven to console them, but they seek to do more than just listen to him. Another angel comes holding a huge rosary: these poor souls haste to leap onto it, and climb up the beads as if they were a ladder. When they finally reach the top, their chains fall away. Then the Holy Virgin, accompanied by Saint Dominic, takes them all by the hand and presents them to Our Lord, who gives each of these souls a place in heaven, according to their desert. Almost all the monastery churches of the Low Countries are filled with this sort of painting, yet with this difference, that each monastery presents the triumph of the particular colors and attributes of its Order.*[184]

This ironic document leads to several observations, For one, alas, it amply confirms the manifold, terroristic motifs of the hymns and sermons, and it invites comparison with the oratory of the *Sacro Cuore del Suffragio* at Rome, a veritable museum of Purgatory. This chapel, where one could see the prints of burning hands and feet, was not closed to the public until well after Vatican II. In addition, d'Artigny's text vividly conveys the Low Countries' predilection for the cult and iconography of souls in Purgatory. It thus corroborates Michel Vovelle's argument that this cult spread into France, and especially Provence, from both Italy and Flanders.[185] Provence, where altars of Purgatory abound, was located on the main Italy-to-Flanders itinerary.

On the other hand, Michelle Ménard's detailed study of the region of Le Mans finds no seventeenth- to eighteenth-century altarpieces portraying the souls of Purgatory.[186] Were they housed in now-destroyed monastic churches, or were they part of parish church side altars that have not survived? Ménard favors an explanation that takes two interrelated factors into account: (1) fewer missions visited this region than neighboring ones, and (2) the people of Le Mans resisted the overly pathetic iconography of Purgatory. Pictures are worth a thousand words. They remain long after speeches have vanished. This iconographic gap would involve an undoubtedly unconscious and collective refusal to conceive and depict the flames of Purgatory. Nonetheless, this local absence of images showing the intermediate place, which most likely is not an isolated case, does not in any way diminish the massive impact of the sensationalistic evangelism on the subject of Purgatory. A study of fear must stress this key historical phenomenon.

This emphasis, however, clarifies only one aspect of a much richer belief system. D'Artigny's account has the merit of recording the two corresponding sides of the question: on the one hand, unbearable suffering, and on the other, liberation by angels, scapularies, prayer beads, and the action of intercessors. Recent learned studies of wills and purgatory altars in Provence and Paris have illuminated the importance in these two places of donations for masses, religious confraternities, and altarpieces dedicated to souls in Purgatory. Moreover, they have underlined the iconographic role played by intercessors who appease the Eternal Father's justice: Jesus (and the baby Jesus), Mary, Saint Dominic, Saint Catherine of Siena, Saint Simon Stock, Saint Joseph, Saint Michael, and so on. All this spiritual—and financial—investment was the response to a Counter-Reformation mission that had darkened the picture only to more thoroughly incite demonstrations of a yearning for security.

CHAPTER 14

A "Lynx-eyed" God[1]

JUDGMENT OR VENGEANCE

An infinitely kind God, who nonetheless gives terrible punishments: Such is the image of the Almighty that Catholic preaching constantly offered the faithful until the end of the eighteenth century. As has been noted, this image conformed with the one that haunted the religious elite itself. Thus it would be a mistake to try to distinguish two fundamentally different ecclesiastical dialects: a consoling one addressed to the devout and a threatening one aimed at the masses. In fact, both threats and consolations coexisted in each of the discourses. It is true that ordinary Christians, with their relative apathy, were often spoken to more harshly than were others. This harshness, however, only expresses in a major key the fear that most directors of Catholic conscience felt, whether or not they were Jansenists.

At times God willingly curtails his kindness, as his "vengeance" is always inexorable: Such is the view of the Jesuits Bourdaloue and Giroust. The first explains that Purgatory is a "violent state," not only for the suffering souls but for God Himself, who

> *sees souls whom He loves with a sincere, tender, and paternal love, yet for whom He cannot do any good; souls filled with merit, saintliness, and virtue, whom He nevertheless cannot reward, souls who are of the elect and are his spouses, whom He is constrained to afflict and punish . . . He finds Himself in a kind of impotence to do any good for creatures who are dear to Him . . . He is almost obliged to treat them with more rigor than He does sinners on earth, His most overt enemies. Why? Because there is no sinner on earth, even in his dissipation, to whom God does not still give his graces for the sake of atonement and reform; whereas in purgatory, however saintly a soul may be, that soul is excluded from these kinds of graces. Therefore the state of these souls is violent for God.*"[2]

As for Giroust, he exclaims in a sermon on Hell: "Such a prodigy! A fire that burns forever, without ever consuming its victim, and without ever consuming itself . . . One would deem this impossible, if we did not know that all things are possible for an avenging God."[3]

Early modern preaching often portrayed both the end of the world and the Last

Judgment as the supreme "vengeance" of the Almighty against stubbornly sinful earth and all humanity. For Hébert, the priest of Versailles, the sins of men must be "quite great," if "such a patient, good and merciful" God finds Himself compelled "to order the destruction of His loveliest works in order to avenge Himself on the impious."[4] The final cataclysm is thus defined as a punishment, preceded by serious but less extensive disasters that Heaven periodically unleashes on a disobedient world. The preaching of this period typically invoked the age-old notion that God enacts His punishments here below and that great collective misfortunes are at once warnings and chastisements. This belief was one of the mental resources of the taught as well as teaching church.[5] In the late eighteenth century, Réguis forcefully expresses this conviction to his flock. The orator addresses God and says:

> *[God's creations] have become the instruments of your justice and you make use of them, whenever it pleases you, to spread fear, troubles, and confusion across the earth. Sometimes you call furious winds from the four corners of the world to knock down our fruits, uproot our trees, overturn our houses, stir up the depths of the sea, raise great waves, and sink all our ships; sometimes you send violent rains down from heaven, which swell our rivers, flood our fields, cover them with sterile sand, enter our houses, and sometimes carry people and animals away with them . . .*[6]

If such catastrophes happen, it is because mankind has somehow broken the order established by God. These punishments are just so many prefigurations of the general, final calamity.

Although eschatological sermons had always included a positive note—the entry of the elect into Paradise—the elaborate descriptions of the final cataclysm, of the scene of judgment, and of the condemnation of the damned were given much more space than the explanation of the reward given to the elect. In the Lazarists' *ad hoc* sermon, for example, sensationalistic elements occupy more than 70 percent of the text. Fontana's Lenten sermon on the same theme is summarized by the author himself, "The dreadful nature of the last judgment: because of the horrors that will precede it; because of the severity of the trial; because of the verdict that threatens us."[7]

Although visual representations of the Last Judgment nearly disappeared after Rubens, this was not the case with the theme as it was preached. These essentially repetitive sermons did not omit the impressive description of the Last Day of God. A number of Sunday sermons, however, do mix together individual and final judgment. Hébert explains to his parishioners that "the time of the Lord's judgment is not so far away as we think" and that God "waits not for the final day, the terrible day when all men will appear before His tribunal to serve as footstools for His enemies. This prophesy, says Saint Augustine, is fulfilled every day; thought it is carried out little by little, it is accomplished all the time with no interruption."[8] Réguis even more clearly says, in taking the place of each of his listeners, but also speaking for himself, "What makes me shiver, is that the end of the world will soon arrive for me; for as soon as my eyes shall be closed, the sun and moon shall be as eclipsed to me, nature herself shall be overthrown in this wretched body, which is a world of iniquity, and which shall be no more than a clod of earth and a mass of decay."[9]

Despite these examples of the contamination between the two judgments, sermons on the end of the world and the general rendering of accounts before the Great Judge remained prominent all the way to the nineteenth century. In *La Peur en Occident*, I showed how the Catholic Church came to increasingly distrust over-exact announcements of the dates of either the Antichrist's birth or of the end of the world. For instance, in the fifteenth-century, San Bernardino set himself off from such preachers as Vincent Ferrier and Saint John Capistran,[10] who were both eager to prophesize the final cataclysm. Bernardino's prudence, however, does not mean that he avoided preaching on the theme of the Last Judgment. On the contrary, both his Latin sermons and his *Prediche volgari* frequently take up this subject.[11] In many ways, Bernardino's attitude clarifies all later Catholic preaching.

Indeed, missionary homilies and sermon collections for either Advent or Lent most often include an exposé on the end of the world or the Last Judgment. Likewise, the hymnals almost always contain one or more songs on this theme. Neither is it missing from sermons for retreats.[12] As for the *Dominicales*, they consistently expound on it at either the first Sunday of Advent, the last Sunday after Pentecost, or even both at once. Girard, who sought to alarm his audience, did not shy from highlighting this theme on the Eighth Sunday after Pentecost.[13] Other concordant evidence further demonstrates the presence of the Last Judgment in Catholic preaching. Pierre de la Font opens the liturgical year by revealing these warnings to his listeners:

> . . . *As most are but mean-spirited souls, more sensitive to the horrible evils of the afterlife than to the ineffable blessings of heaven, God had to control such people by adding threats to His promises, and by astounding them through the fear of a judgment that must require of them so exact and rigorous an account of their entire life. Similarly, the Church, at the beginning and end of the ecclesiastical year, as well as at various other times, reminds the faithful of the terrible day of judgment, and orders Her ministers to give Her children a vivid and faithful picture of this day's terrifying circumstances.*[14]

Loriot also states that the Last Judgment is much talked of in churches, but to no apparent effect. "Hence we see through unhappy experience that these annual sermons at the beginning of Advent and Lent make no impression; and if people do react with some fear, it is so slight, so superficial and so ineffectual that it can hardly destroy sin."[15] Montargon, who cites Nicole, Croiset, Bourdaloue, Pallu, Dufay, Giroust, Massillon, Hébert, and Molinier as the finest authors of "modern" writings on the final disasters and the Last Judgment, adds this significant note: "Almost all the books of devotion discuss this matter."[16] Thus, even when the Catholic Church was strongly accentuating individual judgment, her spokespeople were far from silent on the end of time.[17] The catastrophic ingredient always remained a part of Catholic preaching, helping to express the process of the world. At times discreet but rarely absent, it encouraged forceful reappearances: Such was notably the case in the nineteenth century, immediately following the dissolution of the Pontifical State.[18]

Occasionally, however, a more soothing picture was given of the Great Day of God. For example, the Oratorian Edmond Bourée announces that "the intention of the Church in this first gospel of the ecclesiastical year is to console the righteous with the hope of their coming deliverance, rather than to frighten the wicked by preaching the ills that must seize upon them."[19] For his part, Hébert worries that the continual thought of judgment provokes "gloom" and "dejection" in pious souls. He also reminds them that "such was not . . . Christ's intention when He advised us to reflect on this terrible day." God seeks "to teach men the fear they must have of His judgments, but at the same time He gives us the confidence to rejoice in Him."[20] Nevertheless, this was not the most common way of characterizing universal judgment.

The classic sermon on this subject usually featured a description of the terrifying phenomena that preceded the appearance of the Judge. A list, dating back to Saint Jerome and the Venerable Bede, of the twelve or fifteen "signs" of the end of the world reappears in some seventeenth century sermons: for example, in texts by Jean-Pierre Camus[21] and François Bourgoing.[22] Even when this enumeration is absent, some mention is made of the world's final calamities. As Hébert effectively explains, these "will be the portents of the eternal revenge that Our Ever-Just Lord must wreak on the impious in hell."[23]

It would be profitless to linger over the countless paraphrases of Luke 21 and Matthew 24 elaborated by centuries of preachers. Even a Salesian-spirited bishop such as Camus (who did, however, write several sensational *Nouvelles*)[24], was caught up in the general current.

> *That shall be the day of the evil spirits' festival, their great harvest, their final trick . . . Then Satan shall be unleashed and allowed to unmercifully afflict the wretched Job, with the world at the point of death. There shall be only horrid specters, phantasma, howling and screeching . . . O people . . . what shall ye be except signs of death, living dead and dying in life, paralyzed phantoms! . . . Behold your portrait.*[25]

The Lazarist sermon on the Last Judgment lists all the "miseries" that will then occur: "cruel wars in every land"; kingdoms, towns, and peoples armed against one another; "general carnage, massacres, assassinations, poisonings, fires, famines, the plague. The raging sea will drown entire countries. The sun will no longer revolve, will no longer shine"; it will become "a black and hideous wreck." The moon will be "bloody and stand still." Stars will fall and drop "mountains of fire on the land." Violent earthquakes will crack the earth wide open . . .[26] A hymn by the Brothers of the Christian Schools includes these verses:

> *For then the moon and sun*
> *Shall stop the course they run,*
> *And all the world be split asunder*
> *With horrid, rumbling thunder.*
>
> *One shall see far and nigh*
> *Stars falling from the sky:*
> *Their heat all things, all places must*
> *Reduce to embers and to dust.*
>
> *The fire, and lightning's terror*
> *Shall chill all things with horror:*
> *A trumpet shall awake the dead*
> *And blaring loud shall raise their flesh.*[27]

The Jesuit Fontana, who doubled as actor and orator, reached a height in the apocalyptic genre. Although he is a special case, he was popular in Italy, Switzerland, and Austria. He begins his sermon with a bare-faced warning, designed to play on the psyche: "Sirs, prepare your hearts for spasms of terror, since I am going to show you the terrifying day of universal judgment." The preacher's hallucinatory descriptions deserve to be quoted in full. Lacking space, however, it will suffice to examine his most significant passages regarding the end of the world.[28] The descent from broad daylight to pitch-black night will take place in a single moment. Then the moon shall rain down blood; thunder and lightning shall strike the earth and ignite blazing fires. The roaring sea will overflow the highest mountains by forty cubits—a recollection of the "fifteen portents of the end of the world"—and then sink so low that it shall disappear. The waters shall turn into rotten blood. The fish and sea monsters, previously mute, shall make strange clamors. Ferocious and starving beasts will come howling from their lairs. Every blade of grass shall drip with blood. "Locusts" with the head of a man, teeth of a lion, and tail of a scorpion will attack all sinners. An eagle shall cry in a thundering voice: "Beware, you sinners!" Struck by an angel, stars will fall to earth in bits and pieces. Two million angels wearing impenetrable breastplates and mounted on monstrous horses will slaughter people by the thousands of millions.

All this, however, is no more than a "prelude." For God will then summon all the animals:

> *To arms, to arms! Bears, tigers, panthers, to arms! No longer submit to men, but come out of your forests and let loose your cruelty on sinners. Leopards, wolves, lions, to arms, to arms, out of the woods, follow the tracks of the wicked, unleash your savagery, kill them, tear them, devour them. Snakes, vipers, dragons, toads, basilisks, to arms against the offenders! . . . And ye earthquakes, do not stop at the devastation of Ragusa [Dubrovnik], the ruins of Rimini, or the extermination of Catania, but shake towns, villages, and castles to their very foundations, and make sure that all sinners be destroyed and buried in an instant.*

Fontana then predicts a plague far more deadly than the one that ravaged Genoa in 1656–57. That notwithstanding, "I have yet said nothing compared to what remains, since I must now speak of the annihilating fire." The preacher cites the 1631 eruption of Vesuvius: A wide gash in the mountain opened up and belched forth a flood of fire, sulfur, pitch, and bitumen that burned for twelve days in the nearby sea. This same furnace emitted sparks and huge rocks, which in a crash of thunder knocked down houses, killed livestock, and crushed men, women, and children. Before perishing, they cried "Mercy! 'tis the day of judgment!" Fontana, however, claims that

> *had I been present, I would have stopped these words in their throats, and I would have reproached them: fools, what do you mean, the last judgment? The last judgment will bring another fire, and another horror . . . You say, with regard to the eruption of Vesuvius, that the day of judgment was come. If so, what will happen to your towns, your palaces, your farms, when it truly comes? Ashes, ashes! What will become of your magnificent sepulchers, your glorious inscriptions, your pleasure gardens? Ashes, ashes! Of your books, learned men, of your statues, heroes, cities, princes? Ashes, ashes! . . .*

Systematic repetitions, exaggerated allusions to recent disasters, interjections, direct addresses to the audience, and a crescendo of horrors: These devices inhabit the realm of tactics but are also especially pertinent to the subject matter. Regardless of tactics, however, the preachers were convinced, in the manner of Chevassu, that "the total eclipse of the sun, the blood-red moon, the teetering earth, the disorder of the elements, and the overthrow of the entire universe, will be nothing compared to the presence of Jesus Christ which, according to Saint Basil, will be more intolerable to the wicked than all the torments of hell."[29] Furthermore, human life has only one purpose: to lead toward judgment. "The entire condition of man,"

Chevassu again teaches, "is contained in three words: to live, die, and be judged. We are born to die and we die to be judged . . ."[30] On this theme, sermons on individual judgment join up with those on the Last Judgment: Tirelessly repeating the same expressions over and over and over, they become fused together. We will have to "render accounts,"[31] undergo a test of "unthinkable rigor,"[32] appear before the Supreme "Tribunal," and hear the "terrible executioner,"[33] at the end of the "trial," pronounce the "dreadful sentence."[34]

In studying these sermons, I have come across the following line from the Letter to the Hebrews an almost countless number of times: "It is a fearful thing to fall into the hands of the living God" (Heb. 10:31). It recurs as a leitmotif, inducing and renewing an anguished homiletics. From the time of death, the meeting with the Judge can only be overwhelming: "What an interview!" cries Réguis. "What a fearful encounter!"[35] For the modern reader, living in a time of iron curtains, Father Yvan eloquently expresses what takes place upon arrival in the undiscovered country: "Finally you arrive at death, the border crossing to the other world; there the angels and the demons stop you, examine you, and inspect all that you carry with you: your spirit, your heart, your conscience, your thoughts, words, works, omissions . . . They will ask you for the passport of the Church, without which you are lost."[36] In his *Extrait du catéchisme du diocèse de Rennes* (1746), the anti-Jansenist vicar-general François de Guersans prescribes the following act of fear before making confession: "Lord, how terrible is your justice! Who will not fear it? I think of the severity of your judgments, and of the hideous punishments with which you reprimand impenitent sinners."[37]

A key assertion in many of the sermons on the two judgments is that once our earthly life is ended, so too is God's mercy. A Lazarist sermon expresses this theology in these words: "His omnipotence played its part in creation, His mercy in redemption; hence it is only fitting that His justice have its turn for the vengeance of outrages . . ."[38] From the time of death, redemption exits the scene. On the day of the "light" and "rigor" of "inexorable judgment," Godeau expostulates, "there shall no longer be any grace or mercy for us to hope for."[39] Loriot agrees, arguing that Scripture was right to call Jesus both a lamb and a lion: "In His first coming, He is a lamb; in the second, a lion."[40] The students of the Brothers of the Christian Schools sang a paraphrase of the *Dies Irae* that includes the notable lines: "The sovereign lord of heav'n on high / Indifferent to groans and tears / Shall judge us on earth when we die. / How his aspect shall strike deep fears!"[41]

In his turn, Hérbert informs his listeners at Versailles that someday Jesus will be "a severe, inflexible, and pitiless judge; then he shall no longer pardon." At the time of individual judgment, "the soul, abandoned by all, without help, without counsel, and without support, is examined with rigor and judged without either favor or mercy."[42] Chevassu tells those sinners listening to him that on the day of judgment they will see "God, made human for your salvation, who will match his vengeances to the vast scale of His blessings; and who, after having once loved you so much, shall present Himself once more, to no longer show you mercy."[43] Réguis likewise tells his parishioners:

> *Beware: if all is not acquitted, repaid, and redressed, your account shall not be in order . . . I will soon come before this terrible Judge, who will have tallied up even the most secret stirrings of my heart, who will fully reproach me, who will avenge Himself on everything I have done, who will be inexorable, pitiless, and without compassion: May this be your final thought before going to bed; may it trouble your sleep; may it waken you with a start; may it be your first thought when you rise.*[44]

Not only shall the Judge have neither pity nor compassion—Réguis prophesies that "He will laugh at sinners"[45]—but also the supporters of Christians on earth shall become assessors without any indulgence. Camus plainly teaches this lesson in his sermon on "the signs of judgment": ". . . All the saints, our protectors, who pray for us at times of need in our lives, on the great day of universal judgment which shall be a deluge of all the waters or rather of all the flames, they shall fall silent, breathing only His justice, as now they entreat only His mercy."[46] A century later Girard speaks the same language to his Lyonnais congregation:

> *To whom shall we address ourselves? The Holy Virgin shall no longer be a refuge for sinners, this lovely moon will be in total eclipse for them, and will no longer let them feel her tenderness. She shall no longer shed her sweet influence upon them. The angels shall be the executioners of the Supreme Judge's commands. The highest order of saints shall be seated on thrones, to serve as this dreadful Judge's assessors.*[47]

Fontana declares to his listeners:

> *Madman, what are you, who shall assist us* in die furoris Domini*? There will be no more saints, advocates, nor protectors for you. They will all side with God against you. Do you put hope in your guardian angel? Impossible. On that day he shall have a sword in hand to execute the sentence. Will you have recourse to the Virgin? Not anymore. This radiant moon shall hide her beams, and on that dismal day* non dabit lumen suum.[48]

Such tirades regressed from the iconography of medieval churches, which sometimes showed the Virgin playing the role of intercessor to her Son during the Last Judgment.

In addition, the preachers prophesied that priests, entrusted with the spiritual guidance of human beings, will become the accusers of those who did not listen to them: "I shall ask for punishment of your contempt and disobedience," Godeau promises them.[49] "If the damned," Girard adds, "plead ignorance, the pastors, confessors, and missionaries will shut them up and make them see that it was up to them to be instructed."[50] A missionary hymn on the Last Judgment appeals for the final punishment of the obdurate: "Blaze, fires, rage on you deadly storms / To serve the wrath of God. / Take what remains of guilty humans' forms / For none can hide from His fierce rod."[51]

On the Great Day of God, the cross—interpreted during this period as the "sign of the Son of Man"—will become the instrument of justice. Bourgoing explains that some "will see it as the fearful sign of their damnation, others as the triumphant standard of their salvation."[52] "The power of the cross," Beurrier likewise states, "will establish the tribunal of Jesus Christ."[53] "It will cry down vengeance / On its enemies, / But joy and indulgence / For all its worthy friends," sang de Montfort's missionary pupils.[54] The anonymous author of another missionary hymn has Christ make the following dramatic announcement to sinners:

> *[On that day] so terrible,*
> *Day of justice and of fear,*
> *This sign both bright and visible*
> *Will all destroy before me here.*
> *Then to the hills and mountains*
> *You will shout: please crush us.*

But across their remains
The cross shall deal its blows.[55]

Given the importance of individual judgment in catechesis, preachers definitely wondered if they should continue to hold forth once or twice a year on the Last Judgment. To the scriptural reason—the presence of eschatological texts in the Bible—they added two supplementary motives. First, universal judgment will be the great operation of truth. The wheat will finally be separated from the chaff,[56] for a father may then be taken from his children and a wife from her husband. All that had lain hidden shall be revealed: every good deed, but also every offense, especially every secret impurity, and every guilty omission. On that day of "light," "we shall not be able to hide our thanklessness."[57] Fontana predicts,

> *how greatly shall you be confounded that day, when not one but all of your sins shall be announced, not before a few people but the entire universe, before your friends, your compatriots, the noblemen, the knights, your family, your husband, father, elders, in short, everyone: all this, moreover, to the sound of infernal trumpets, amid the cries of demons, and from the mouth of God. Every wicked deed you will have done shall be made public.*[58]

Girard impresses on his audience the shame that sinners will feel when their concealed crimes are at last disclosed:

> *If an angel came down from heaven right now, and wrote on the walls of this church one of your shameful and secret crimes for all to see, how could one describe this wretched person's shame? Would he not choose to be consigned to some dungeon for the rest of his life rather than suffer such disgrace? Ah! How great shall be the shame of the damned on the day of vengeance, when the secrets of their conscience will be made manifest to the angels, saints, demons, and all other reprobates. Thus we read in Holy Gospel that these unhappy souls shall say to to the hills and mountains: fall upon us and hide us.*[59]

The second main justification of the Last Judgment, and the second main reason for expounding on it to the faithful, is that the Great Day of God will put everything in its proper place. The values of eternity will finally replace the values of the world. This reversal will be the occasion of a double "vengeance": God "will avenge" the injuries He has received from mankind, and the elect will be "revenged" of the abuse they suffered at the hands of sinners. These are the two aspects of the Last Judgment that Montargon gleans from Bourdaloue's Advent sermons on this subject, in giving these homilies as models for other preachers.[60] De la Font explains that God does not let "criminal attempts" against him go unpunished. "He is not so little jealous of His glory" that He will keep from showing His "resentment."[61] This feeling will appear not only in the sentence given to the damned, but also in the "public reparation" that Jesus "will provide for his saints . . . for all the indignities they will have received from the damned. Reparation for all the calumnies with which they were defamed. Reparation for all the insults, all the mockeries, and all the outrages they will have suffered."[62] This theme of the reversal of earthly conditions insistently recurs in both sermons and hymns on the Last Judgment. De Montfort writes:

One day, they [the damned] shall be startled to see
These wise souls and devout,

Whom they but contemptuously did see.
Filled all with rage, they'll then cry out:
What! There they are, whom we deride,
There they are, whom we despise?

What! There they are! Those things,
Whose lives we thought a folly,
Are God's children and are kings
Adorned with infinite glory?
O misery! Why did we, so cruel,
Decide to take the wise for fool?[63]

They who laugh one day will cry the next. The profiteers of the earth will be beggars beyond the grave. So it was sung by the Brothers of the Christian Schools:

Those who have such a pleasant time,
The drunkards and the gluttons,
Will have much to drink, but only tears,
For these bad souls will shake with painful fears . . .

The worldly and indecent,
So full of bad intent,
Their crimes shall bring them torment
In suffering the day of judgment.[64]

"Behold," Jesus will say to the damned on Judgment Day, according to a Lazarist sermon,

> *behold this saintly man! You said he lived dishonorably, you who cut such a fine figure; now he is here, crowned with glory, and you are overcome with shame. Behold this poor woman whom you scorned, these poor artisans, these poor servants whom you treated like slaves, those whom you ruined, those who were the target of your abuse . . . know that they will be in heaven forever, more powerful than kings, more honoured than all the princes and great ones of the world, while you with your evil wealth will scream in eternal flames.*[65]

Thus the Last Judgment will bring the end of the world turned upside down. It is not proper to rebel against injustices on earth. The sinfully rich, however, have nothing to look forward to. For in the end, one will see what true wealth was. Later sections of this book will reemphasize how the church never stopped protesting against the exploitation of the poor.[66] It reserved the punishment of social injustice, however, to the "Great Day of God." In the meantime, one must arm oneself with patience. In this regard, its discourse was "demobilizing." All the same, by threatening sinners—including the sinfully rich—with the thunder and lightning of the Almighty, it hoped to bring about conversions. The prophetic description of the Last Judgment seemed particularly apt to cause the desired transformations. Hence the vivid scenes depicted by Fontana:

> *. . . Who is this other woman? 'Tis she who had servants walk before her, their heads bare in the cold of winter . . . And that man over there, who appears before the Tribunal, shaking and terrified, who is he? 'Tis a knight, whose pride swelled up with the privileges of nobility . . . And that other, who was so rich on earth*

and now goes naked, what sentence shall he receive? A harsh one, because he refused to give even modest relief to the poor, and because he has no fund of good works.[67]

The logical consequence of this reversal of conditions and rehabilitation of the oppressed is that the elect will rejoice in the punishment of the damned. Out Girard's mouth, this inevitable reestablishment of justice takes on intimations of both social revenge and millenary feeling. His rural audience no doubt felt some satisfaction in hearing these prophesies of vengeance. Provided they be patient, they would someday triumph over their oppressors:

Poor children of the Lord, the sinfully rich oppress you, they fatten off your product, but there will come a day when you shall reap full satisfaction, for as the Psalmist saith, "The righteous shall rejoice when he seeth the vengeance: he shall wash his feet in the blood of the wicked" (Ps. 58:10).

What atonement would you have them make to you, God's chosen people? Do you wish that these reprobates ask your pardon, that they confess before heaven and earth that they have unjustly treated you? Do you wish them to be humiliated and placed beneath your feet, to be trampled on like mud and dust? All this shall happen; these wretches shall be reduced to this. O ye poor beggars, shepherds, laborers, you who are looked down on as nonentities, if you live piously, if you bear your hardships patiently, if you carry your cross well, if you endure your humiliations with love and resignation, on the day of judgment you will see at your feet these great lords, these arrogant men who will have misused their titles, wealth, and honors.[68]

THE LIMITS OF DIVINE BENEVOLENCE

In short, Girard gives hopes of the revolution. It will surely take place . . . at the end of time. Sermons on the Last Judgment do not always have such social overtones. On the other hand, taking special inspiration from the psalm cited by Girard, they frequently affirm that the heavenly court and the elect shall take shared pleasure in the punishment of sinners. In the Lazarists' late seventeenth–early eighteenth-century sermon on this matter, it is explained that the Virgin and saints "shall enjoy, as the prophet says, seeing God's justice satisfied, and the honor of God . . . restored by the punishment of the impious, just as in extreme heat one will wash one's hands in refreshing water: *Manus suas lavabit in sanguine peccatoris* (Ps. 58:11)."*[69] De Montfort similarly prophesies the feelings of the chosen ones: "What just pleasure shall they have . . . / To see condemned to hell / All the worldly of this world! / To hear them groan: / 'Alas! How we are wretched.' "[70] The Archbishop of Lyon Montazet (d. 1788) also asserts that the elect will perform the Last Judgment with Christ and will be its active instruments: "With him we shall judge the nations: we shall put to the sword all that was most great and most daunting. We shall execute the dreadful decree He shall pronounce against the ungodly." Such are the "comforting promises" made by the prelate to "faithful" souls.[71]

De Sales had already foretold that "the blessed will happily approve of the judgment and damnation of the reprobate, as much as the salvation of the chosen."[72] Centuries earlier, Aquinas considered whether "the blessed have compassion for

*Translator's note: Vulgate version, which gives "Manus" as "hands"; the King James and Revised Standard Versions translate the Hebrew as "feet."

the suffering of the damned" or "whether they rejoice in the pain of the impious." His answer includes the citation from Psalm 58, as well as the line from Isaiah 66:24, "And they shall go forth, and look upon the carcasses of the men that have transgressed against me." The "angelic doctor," however, misreads this passage. The actual sense, expressed a few lines later, is "they shall be an abhorring unto all flesh." In any case, although he takes a less extreme position than the two above-cited texts, his *Summa Theologica* concludes that the pains of Hell give the elect "the satisfaction of beholding therein the justice of God, and realizing that they have escaped this suffering."[73] Segneri the Elder, however, draws a far more startling text out of Aquinas's *Opusculum*, which he exploits in a sermon:

> *The more horrid the damned will seem to themselves for the foulness of their crimes, the more they will seem fair and lovely to God's eyes, for the justices of the penalties He will cause them to suffer. "They will be,"* says Saint Thomas, *"as so many stars set in this region of fire"; and their tortures shall make a more regular and more pleasing spectacle than does heaven with its innumerable glimmering stars. Indeed, the damned will be no less an ornament in hell than are the stars in the firmament.*[74]

All these texts that fix a limit to God's pity at the moment of death convey a crucial viewpoint one that was formerly taught to the Christian faithful: God's mercy can in no way encroach on His justice. In his frequently reedited *Guía de pecadores*, Louis of Granada tells sinners: "You keep repeating that you are counting on divine mercy: As for me . . . I repeat to you that divine mercy only lessens the number of the damned, and it will not put you among that number if you carry on in this way . . . [It] allows hell to grow fatter; it allows thousands of souls to descend there every day; may it not allow that your soul will also descend there, if you do not reform your conduct?"[75] Such assertions are more than tactical threats, since they partake of the clergy's deepest conviction: God is no less just than merciful. Hence San Bernardino's statements in a sermon on Hell:

> *God's glory is equal to the vast number of the reprobate . . . The demonstration of divine justice will be all the greater, the more clearly do appear the vices of the damned . . . Just as the infinite praises and thanksgivings of the elect will proclaim His mercy, so the tears, sighs, lamentation, roaring, shouting, and howling of the others will proclaim His justice. Therefore hell will resound to the chosen ones in glory with ineffable sweetness. The charm, the perfection of the paradisical concert would not be complete if the hymn proclaiming divine mercy lacked the counterpoint of the infernal song glorifying divine justice.*[76]

Following San Bernardino's example, later preachers strove to teach the faithful that they could not rely on God's kindness to the point of forgetting His necessary strictness: There are a countless number of attestations to this theme. Beurrier encourages the parishioners of Saint-Etienne-du-Mont to ponder how "God is the upright judge of His own children, just as He is their merciful father; He avenges crimes, the same way that He rewards good deeds, and He shows no personal preference in this matter."[77] An eighteenth-century missionary hymn enjoins the penitent to sing:

> *And should a father treat his child*
> *With tender kindness mild,*
> *If that one's life has not abated*

From doing evil that is hated?
Thus far more God the Father hath
Become enflamèd with His wrath.[78]

Bridaine declares: "God did not put you in the world to damn yourselves; but He also did not put you here to offend Him, to be drunkards, blasphemers, lewd and vindictive in your ways . . . God did not put the Turks and infidels in the world to damn them to hell: nonetheless, they damn themselves."[79] Saint Leonard of Port Maurice accosts "habitual sinners" in these terms: "How mad you are! . . . to make a mild and merciful God, you create an either injust or impotent God, who will not or cannot punish your outrages."[80] Still more emphatically, Girard puts his Lyonnais congregation on the lookout:

God is infinitely good, just, and merciful: do not doubt it, these are articles of our faith. Nevertheless, this good, just, and merciful God, this Father full of love and tenderness, condemns a person to hell for a single deadly sin, for a spontaneous impure thought, for a criminal desire, for a wicked deed that lasted but a second, for a willful omission of an essential duty. Yes, for this single sin, this single deadly offense that passed like lightning, which gave its perpetrator but a moment's satisfaction and left him with regret and pangs of conscience, God condemns this person who is His image, His creation, His child, His own work, the price of the Redeemer's sacred blood; He condemns him to hell.[81]

For his part, Montargon harps on the difficult reconciliation between divine justice and divine mercy, always tipping the balance in favor of the former: "God severely punishes those who do not love Him."[82] And again: "By claiming to raise up mercy, they discredit religion."[83] Another passage from the same work, the *Dictionnaire apostolique*, reads: "the patience with which God cares for the sinner must make him fear His justice . . . the more God will have been merciful, the more will He be severe." Montargon's most revealing statement, however, is the following: ". . . the extent we attribute to this poorly known kindness [of God] so diminishes the idea of justice that it makes but the slightest impression. And such, I dare say, is the swelling source, not only of the debauchery of sinners, but also of the straying of the righteous from the path of salvation."[84] Loriot's preaching, however, contains perhaps the most striking exposé on the mercy-justice dialectic. Like San Bernardino, the orator uses the second-person singular to address one of the hardened sinners in the audience:

Yes, you wretch, God is good, God is merciful, and infinitely better and more merciful than you imagine, or could possibly imagine. At the same time, learn that this same God, so good and so merciful, threw from the heights of heaven down to the lowest depths of hell the third part of the angels, these lovely and noble creatures, merely for a sinful thought, conceived in a moment, and without any other moment in which they might do penance. It is the same God who banished Adam from the earthly paradise for eating a fruit against His injunction; who condemned him to endless woes, and just as swiftly condemned his descendants to the flames of hell. This same merciful God condemned His own Son to die on the cross for the expiation of sins He had not committed; but especially, this good kind God will see throughout eternity an almost infinite number of poor souls languishing in blazing pits of fire, making horrible shrieks and eternal howls, and He will never even think to deliver them from their agony, nor be touched with the least compassion for them. Therefore

> *learn, if you do not know this already, that when you say that God is good, you speak true, but you have not spoken the entire truth, for you must add that He is just; that the extent of His kindness equals that of His justice; that just as He is infinitely good, so is He infinitely just, and that the strictness of His justice primarily touches those who will have abused His goodness, and that to offend Him; and so they will have to endure a wounded mercy, an angered justice.*
>
> *No, do not attribute God with a base mercy, one without intelligence and discrimination, as if He were like some injudicious fellow who treated all men indifferently, without telling the guilty from the innocent, or those whom He has made worthy of His grace from those who are unworthy.*[85]

Since the majority of Christians received such an image of God, it was only normal and logical that they should also hear of the chosen few. Nonetheless, some preachers wondered whether they should let the masses share the religious elite's tragic outlook on this subject. There was the undeniable risk of discouraging the main body of the faithful and of making them feel powerless through the inevitable reiteration of their misdeeds. Bourdaloue, for one, points to the Counter-Reformation's self-scrutiny regarding this difficult question. As part of his advice to sermon writers, he sweeps away the hesitations of timorous preachers:

> *. . . this is an issue that preachers sometimes make, namely, whether it is right to explain this truth [the chosen few] to the people, and to discuss it from the pulpit, because it might trouble certain souls, and throw them into despair. I would just as soon have someone ask me whether it were good to explain the Gospel to the people, and to preach it from the pulpit . . . Let us preach the Gospel, and preach it without at all suppressing or softening it; let us preach it in its entirety, in its purity, in its severity, in all its strength. Woe betide any who are scandalized by it; he will himself bear the penalty of his scandal.*[86]

"It is better to awaken [consciences] by disturbing them, than to let them sleep in idle and deceitful rest,"[87] Bourdaloue again says. This is also the opinion of another Jesuit, Vincent Houdry, whose *Bibliothèque des predicateurs* brings together advice and texts for the use of preachers. He thus begins his chapter "Predestination" with the forthright claims:

> *The number of the chosen is most small, and can accommodate only a few people. This is an oracle from Jesus Christ's own mouth. No Church Father has interpreted, softened, or taken it in any less rigorous sense; no heretic is advised to contest it; and no matter how one explains it to comfort the spirit concerning a fear that the Son of God Himself deemed necessary for Christians most confirmed in the truths of the religion and most steady in their doings, this oracle will be forever true, not only for men in general but even mature Christians.*[88]

In his chapter "Beatitude," near the beginning of his *Dictionnaire*, Montargon asserts that "very few Christians will reach heaven, because so few desire it, and effect the means to get there."[89] Later, in volume 5 of his encyclopedia, he treats the subject in detail, resuming Bourdaloue's arguments but also recalling his own experience as a preacher and the uncertainties of his colleagues:

> *. . . It is a question I have heard has been made, and one that I even once made to myself during a sermon on this subject: whether it is right to explain these truths*

to the people, since they might disturb souls and throw them into despair. I would just as soon have someone ask me whether it were good to explain the Gospel to the people, and to preach it from the pulpit. What is indeed more evident in our holy books than this dreadful truth, that there are but a chosen few? A truth that Jesus Christ so often and so clearly explained.[90]

Montargon then goes on to cite the usual scriptural proofs, while admitting an objection: In the parable of the wedding banquet, (Matt. 22:13), "only one is found who deserves to be cast into outer darkness." The solution to this problem: "This one individual, both Saint Chrysostom and Saint Augustine say, represents the entire body of the outcasts; and Jesus never claimed to make exact numerical comparisons; his speech would have been contrary to His thought, and He would have destroyed on the one hand what He had established on the other."[91]

These texts reveal definite positions: The men of the Catholic Church were convinced that few adult Christians achieve salvation. Listeners, however, were made visibly despondent by this alarming doctrine. Should it continue to be preached? Some preachers said yes, and this answer had a double function: It justified their mission in their own eyes, since they believed that both the Bible and the church fathers were on their side; and it allowed for conversion through "the bringing of fear." In a sermon on "the chosen few," Loriot clearly presents both the question and the answer:

And please do not tell me that these things are too terrible and too dreadful. For, gentlemen, they are not dreadful because I am preaching them, but because they are truly dreadful in themselves. They should not happen because I preach them, but I preach them because they invariably happen. —But you are throwing everyone into despair. —The same objection was made to Saint Augustine, and he answered: "Twas not I who wrote the Gospel, so it is not for me to efface it . . ."

—But what you tell us to justify the terror you put in our hearts makes us all the more afraid. —You are joking, to say that I put fear in your hearts. For where are the effects of this terror, the fruits of this fear? . . . I have been preaching for a long time, and for just as long I have cried, I have strained my lungs to entreat, to warn, to pray, to terrify, and do I make any progress? Are the cabarets any less busy, is debauchery any less than it was before? . . . Even were there no other proofs of the small number of the saved than what takes place here, this would suffice, since after so many sermons, so many exhortations, so many entreaties, the majority of you are the same as ever, if not even worse.[92]

The obvious fact must be acknowledged: These peremptory arguments did not convince all those who set out to preach. Not a single Lazarist sermon is exclusively concerned with the theme of the chosen few, even if it is acknowledged that "salvation is difficult."[93] Nor does Saint John Eudes's *Prédicateur apostolique* broach the subject. "He was not the one who gave the sermon of Massillon on the chosen few."[94] De Montfort expressed his private thoughts on the matter to small groups, but his hymns written for large congregations make no special mention of the tragic doctrine. The same absence applies to the hymnals of La Salle and the *Cantiques de missions . . . a l'usage du diocèse de Rennes*, which do however spend time on Hell, judgment, and the macabre. "Many are called but few are chosen" would be a harsh phrase for a hymn.[95] As for the widely diffused *Bouquet de la mission composé en faveur des peuples de la campagne . . .*, it contains no formal sermon on the subject. This lacuna, if one may call it that, is even more evident in the numerous collections of Sunday sermons. Even the inflexible Girard desists from giving a comprehensive account of this excessively disheartening topic. The priest of Rousses, Chevassu, is somewhat exceptional when he uses Luke 19 (Jesus crying over Jerusalem) to launch an entire homily on "the chosen few."[96] In the previous century, Bourgoing, commenting on Matthew 22 (the parable of the wedding feast), had devoted only the second and shorter part of his sermon to the line "many are called but few are chosen."[97]

Nevertheless, the relative absence of full-length sermons on this tragic theme does not therefore mean that the Catholic mission would have judged only the Christian elite capable of facing up to a terrifying truth that had to be kept hidden from the masses. Two relevant considerations, the one more significant than the other, must now be discussed: (1) a substantial number of Sunday sermons do allude to the notion of the chosen few in the context of other main points; and (2) Advent, Lent, and missionary sermons were rarely silent on a doctrine whose potential to shock an audience was also rarely overlooked.

A few examples will illustrate the first point. Olivier Maillard invites the "worldly" members of his flock to seriously reflect on the importance of the Eucharist by recalling the line from Luke 14:24, "none of those men which were bidden shall taste of my supper."[98] During a Good Friday sermon at Vence, Godeau explains that "the cross of Jesus is nothing else than that incomprehensible choosing forth, by which He culls the elect from the general mass of the condemned human race, and leaves behind the reprobate, through a most secret but also most just and wise judgment . . ."[99] Beurrier, glossing I Corinthians, cites God's extreme punishments on the ungrateful and rebellious Jews, certain proof that "the number of the saved is most small compared to the great number of the damned."[100] On Easter Sunday, Pierre de la Font announces that on the day of general resurrection "the majority of mankind will not enjoy this favorable change for which the righteous do so earnestly strive."[101] Hébert, who is usually less severe than La Font, nevertheless expresses his conviction that "hell has stretched its belly and opened its chasms to an infinite degree."[102]

Bourée is undoubtedly hostile to those who preach laxity—"these flesh-eating wolves."[103] All the same, he tells true Christians: "Banish your doubts . . . what have you to fear?"[104] On the other hand, the rest have everything to fear, and their numbers are great: "This particular man [the one cast out for not wearing wedding garments] represents the multitude who are destined to the eternal flames . . . ; the number of those who have not dirtied their clothing, or who, having had this misfortune, have washed them in the water of their tears and the blood of the lamb, however many they may be, their number is most small in comparison."[105] Joseph Lambert's *Manière de bien instruire les pauvres* . . . is restrained regarding Hell and generally speaks an unthreatening language. Nonetheless, among other complaints, the author publicly asked this question: "The life of countryfolk being in itself most hard, why do so few save themselves through a life-style that would by itself merit salvation?"[106] In the early nineteenth century, a priest in Montréal, Quebec, unhesitatingly informed his congregation: "The majority of people in the parish of Montréal will be condemned to eternal death."[107] Citations such as these frequently recur in ordinary homilies. In particular, the above selections show that the doctrine of the chosen few would briefly but tellingly resurface from the theological background, even in sermons whose major theme did not depend on the line "*multi vocati, pauce vero electi.*"

Turning now to missionary sermons and those given during retreats,[108] at Advent, and Lent, Maillard's Lenten message asserts:

I dare say that the majority will be damned. Therefore tremble . . . I might imagine that an angel would appear above this crucifix, and that he might unfold a great proclamation before you, saying, "People, I bring you good news: of all that are here, only one shall be damned." Who would not shudder at being that one sole person? But indeed! It is not just one of you, it is the greater part of all of you who shall be damned, for many are called but few are chosen.[109]

At the same time, these preachers most often opposed themselves to Jansenistic arguments on predestination, holding instead to an essentially "voluntarist" discourse. Bourdaloue speaks for a wider school of thought than the Company of Jesus, which affirms that God desires the salvation of all people, that He shed his blood for all people, and that to teach the contrary is "to scandalize an audience."[110] If the doctrine of the chosen few is presented with "unchecked zeal and strictness," it "provokes despair."[111] François de Toulouse, who performed missionary work in seventeenth-century Languedoc, is likewise most emphatic. He opens his missionary sermons on the theme "God seeks the salvation of all mankind."[112] He laments that certain melancholic souls "say that the Son of God died only for a small group of the predestined . . . [and] that the rest of mankind is a body of sin, a mass of reprobation, children of anger, and victims, on whom God will wreak the fury of His justice throughout all eternity." Such talk, he proclaims, "leads to despair and opens the door to all manner of crimes."[113]

Were these statements, however, as reassuring as they aimed to be? The Jesuit Antoine Vieira's explanation in a sermon at the cathedral of Salvador de Bahia in 1639 seems to me an exception to the rule. He notes that the link between the parable of the guests at the wedding feast and its conclusion (many are called but few are chosen) has been "a great topic of controversy," since there was only one who was turned away. For Vieira, however, the solution to this problem is "simple": Not everyone who was invited to the feast actually came. These absent people are in some sense symbolized by the guest who came, but without the nuptial garment. Hence Vieira's optimistic conclusion: "So it is a great reason of confidence for us, that all those who were called and came to the Last Supper with their nuptial garment were indeed chosen, except one."[114]

The Portuguese Jesuit seems to take an isolated stand on the subject. Even the Dominican Louis of Granada, who had a large international audience, not only makes frequent reference to the chosen few[115] but also employs "Augustinian" assertions to qualify the doctrine of free will he elsewhere professes. The following passage points to this doctrinal hesitation:

[God] calls all people to Him, for he wishes their salvation; but the extent of help that He grants them for cooperating with this calling depends on His divine will, and not on our own deserts: so His will is more generous to some than to others. It follows that there are many who are called, in other words many to whom God grants ordinary help, which their negligence puts to no good account; and a chosen few, in other words those who obtain extraordinary grace or make good use of the ordinary graces bestowed on them. Thus, brethren, the Lord distributes His graces to worthy souls after His own pleasure, or rather in a way that is disproportionate to their merits and desires.[116]

In fact, two alarming stipulations frequently reduced the strength of the argument that all people are called to salvation. First, the notion that it takes little to condemn one's self. Lovis of Granada again remarks, after affirming that "if I live as a Christian, I will enter the kingdom of heaven," that

> *all men are placed as on the scales: on one side lies eternal life, on the other hell, and we are free to choose the side that we prefer. Furthermore, this balance is so delicate that a single deadly sin, even of thought, is enough to make one of the scales descend all the way down to hell . . . [Who is not] seized with fear, finding such uncertainty in such an important matter [salvation], and seeing oneself in continual danger of being lost forever?*[117]

François de Toulouse sums up the second stipulation: "We receive abundant grace . . . but we make little use of it. We have not the will to save ourselves."[118] Hence the small number of the elect. Bossuet, meanwhile, claims that "the world is full of these called souls, who do not care to think on their calling or to remember that they are Christians."[119] In his famous sermon on "the small number of the elect," Massillon scolds his audience by telling them:

> *. . . as long as you live like the majority, it is certain that you should not aspire to salvation: for if by living in this way, you could be saved, nearly all men would be saved; . . . our Faith, however, prevents us from believing this to be true: therefore you have no grounds for presuming your salvation, since you cannot be saved if the majority of people are not.*[120]

Massillon's reasoning deserves attention: Since it is an article of faith that there are only a chosen few, one must therefore explain how this came to be. This supposedly certain article, once it was brought into the open, could lead only to traumatic sermonizing. Bourdaloue notably strives in vain to declare first "that we are all right to hope that we will be among the elect; . . . that there is not even any sinner who should not maintain this hope"; but he then asserts that "if there will be only a chosen few, even within Christianity, it is due to the failings and negligence of most Christians; it is due to their entirely pagan and worldly conduct, that runs contrary to the law they have embraced and the religion they profess."[121] "The apostle wants us to achieve our salvation through fear and trembling."[122]

Nonetheless, Bourdaloue confines his discussion within "reasonable limits."[123] Not all preachers, however, imitated his reserve when they held forth on a subject that lent itself to the most disturbing arithmetic and the most troubling phrases. De Toulouse is typical in this regard. At the outset of a sermon on Matthew 20 (the workers in the vineyard),[124] he dismisses the "reveries" of those who wonder whether there are as many saved people as there are fallen angels, or as many angels "in glory" as both blessed spirits and demons put together. For the Capuchin author, the Father of the family is the only one who knows the precise number of the elect, and it is "rash to enter into these counsels." A wise saying, which all the same quickly steers clear of any prudence.

For the author soon adds: "Nevertheless, we can, without rashness, with certainty, and for our edification, affirm that the number of the elect is most small, and that it cannot be compared to that of the reprobate, which is enormous and far outstrips it." Embarked on this route, the orator recalls the classic examples: the survivors of the Flood, the dead of Sodom and Gomorrah, the three or four Jews out of 600,000 who entered the Promised Land, the single house left standing in Jericho, the olives remaining on the tree and the grapes on the vine after the harvest.[125] He then develops the parable of the Foolish Virgins. Claiming that they were not great sinners, since they had "kept the integrity of their bodies," he elaborates his argument, and citing Gaetano, concludes:

> *Dreadful words, the cause for the greatest surprise that has ever been, since we therein find that half of the men who lead virtuous lives, such as priests, monks, virgins, and worthy people of all degrees and conditions, will be damned. There is no surprise that the impious, blasphemers, misers, murderers, the obscene, infidels, and heretics should be cast down into hell; but that at least half the monks, good priests, honest women, chaste maidens, poor sufferers, and generous, merciful rich people should also be damned: O Christians, such is grounds for true astonishment, and even for shuddering with fear! We know that the number of honest men is most small; for there are very few virtuous people in the world, and yet the half of this small number will be damned.*[126]

Such statements go beyond the mere will to convert, and express the fear of the speaker himself, which he seeks to share with his listeners. The tragic estimates that follow convey simultaneous tactics and panic. Since, De Toulouse explains with regard to the parable of the sower, only the fourth part will ripen, "we learn that the number of the chosen is tiny, and that only one fourth of humanity will be saved, and the rest most assuredly damned. For every four of you living in the same house, only one will be saved; there are forty of you here in this assembly, so only ten of you will be saved; the rest shall be damned."[127] Elsewhere, De Toulouse ventures into an even more demoralizing calculation:

> *There are ten people in your household, and only one of you will be saved; all the rest shall be condemned to eternal hellfire. There are a hundred people in this village, and only ten shall reach paradise, while the other ninety shall be damned. There are a thousand Christians in this audience, and it will be a high number if one hundred will be saved; the rest shall be thrown into the everlasting flames. Christians, are you not afraid? Do you not tremble?*[128]

The author of these lines had sufficient renown for a portion of his sermons to be reprinted in the nineteenth century in Migne's *Collection des orateurs sacrés* (vols 10 and 11).

Taking off from Bourdaloue, Massillon, and François de Toulouse, various well-known preachers loudly and clearly taught the doctrine of the chosen few to audiences of all social levels. One could cite Bridaine, Loriot, and others. Of special note, however, are the words of the blind Oratorian Jean Lejeune in a Lenten sermon: ". . . a hundred years from now, and even sooner, a great number of the infinity of people on earth shall be condemned to eternal death . . . This fearful truth . . . was made known to us by the Son of God, for of all the men who were living in His time, He chose only twelve to be His apostles, and of these twelve apostles He chose only three to have the blessing of seeing His transfiguration."[129] According to this logic, Lejeune would have to argue that three quarters of the apostles were damned. He does not go so far as that, but he does say that the sword of God "is sharp as a razor," that it "cuts and thrusts," makes "a horrible carnage," and "moves from one end of the universe to the other," so that "the revenge of heaven shall cover the greater part of the world with its punishments."[130]

The same dire predictions are made by one of the leading lights of Baroque preaching, Paolo Segneri the Elder. Does the violence of Italian preachers when verbally attacking their listeners imply that the latter were less receptive or more apt to forget than their Transalpine counterparts? In any case, Segneri aims to disillusion any of "those who too easily count on the hope of divine pardon." He intends to "wake them . . . by telling them the most awful truth that one can discuss in the most solemn of assemblies: whether the number of the elect is smaller or greater than that of the damned." He hopes to instill in them "the feelings of holy fear, such as one must have, and which however so few common Christians possess."[131]

Segneri undoubtedly read the treatise by Suarez analyzed above.[132] Like him, he explains that among Catholics there will be more saved than damned "because of those who die before the age of reason, and those who attain salvation through their faithfulness." Among heretics, baptized children who die young will also be saved. It is clear, however, that among adult Christians, many will be damned, especially because of ill-made confessions and sins of omission. What then to say to those who object that "God's mercy is infinite, that Christ's blood was not shed in vain, and that God did not make Christians in order to damn them to hell"? Segneri answers with a theology of redemption that displaces its finality: Jesus died first and foremost to redress the outrage done to His Father, and only then to save mankind:

> *Christ's blood was not shed in vain, I admit, but one must bear in mind that the first purpose of Jesus in His Passion was to satisfy divine justice for the injuries men had done to it, and to put an end to the great disorder that reigned throughout the world, where God suffered such great abuse, and received from no one a satisfaction worthy of Him and the greatness of His sovereign majesty. Now since the Redeemer most fully accomplished this redress of the glory of a God offended by His creatures, which was the first and principal goal of His Passion, it follows that when all mankind shall be damned the blood of Christ will not have fallen in vain, but that its fruit will be great and infinitely glorious to the majesty of God.*[133]

Segneri thus resumes the theme of an angry God who requires an exemplary atonement from His Son. Despite its cruel aspects, this conception, which was devised at the highest doctrinal level, was also expounded in ordinary sermons. It therefore establishes a bridge between a pointedly disquieting campaign of conversion and the intimate conviction of preachers who inevitably used brutal phrases to express the theologians' shared outlook.[134] The pedagogical intent of sermons that show God the Father implacable toward Jesus is clearly indicated by Father Yvan: "Divine justice punished the slightest failings of the saints, it punished Jesus Christ, the saint of saints, because He took on the marks of sin: so what will become of impious and abominable sinners?"[135] What strikes deeper, however, than the pastoral aim is the assertion that God hates sin and therefore Him who took upon Himself all human faults and offenses. On Good Friday, Godeau explains that if the Eternal Father "punished His Son with such severity, [it was] for the sins of mankind with which He was burdened." He "vented [on Him] the fury" of His "holiness" and "justice."[136] On the same holiday, Beurrier asks his listeners to consider

> *the rigorous judgment of the Eternal Father against His own Son . . . He had no regard for His true innocence . . . He treated Him like the greatest of criminals . . . He gave Him no relief from His torture, and as if He were not fully satisfied with His death and His Passion, which were enough to redeem a hundred thousand worlds, He let His body be pierced by a lance after it had expired, and Him to be treated as an impostor after His death.*[137]

Bourée observes that "all the torrents of His Father's anger swept over Him in His Passion; He was practically crushed beneath the Almighty's pressing fury."[138]

Pierre de la Font strikingly summarizes the debate that took place in God's heart. "I imagine," he declares,

> *that the heart of the Eternal Father, so to speak, was divided between two contrary impulses: between the love He has for His Son and the hate he has for sin. Love demands His life; hate His death; love pleads that He is His Son, that He is innocent; hate that He is the embodiment of sinners and that He consequently deserves all pains that are due them . . . We know, however, that hate finally wins this argument, and that God seems to divest Himself of His being a father, to put on only the garb of a judge.*[139]

During this period, divine justice nearly always prevailed over mercy. For Loriot, the proof is that "this most merciful God condemned His own Son to die on a cross, for the expiation of sins He did not commit."[140] In a sermon on penance, Saint Leonard of Port-Maurice enumerates the terrible demands of divine justice. Evoking the "crucified" and "slaughtered" Jesus, he asks this question:

> *Who condemned Jesus to such a horrible death? Was it Pilate? The scribes and pharisees? No, my brethren, no. But who then? It was divine justice, which did not ever wish to say: "enough," while the Son was not yet dead on this gallows. The Good Savior was in agony, suspended in midair on three nails, He shed tears of blood, His blood ran from His entire body: but inexorable justice said:* Nondum satis, *it is not yet enough. His loving mother cried at the foot of the cross, pious women were sobbing, all the angels and blessed spirits themselves groaned to see such a cruel spectacle; but God's justice was not moved, and repeated:* Nondum satis, *it is not yet enough. And for as long as Christ had not yet drawn His final breath, it would not say, "it is enough." What do you say now, brethren? If God's justice so severely treated the Father's only Son, only because He had taken upon Himself our sins, or rather the shadow of our sins, how will it treat us, we wretches who are the true sinners?*[141]

Under these terms, one perceives how there were but a chosen few, and why Montargon inserted similar statements into his model sermons for the Christmas season: "God required, the Fathers say, a victim worthy of Him: holy, who might be looked at without dimming the luster of His glory; sovereign, who might absorb the terrible blows of His revenge; infinite, who by the immense extent of His deserts might expiate the very outrage that sin had done to the infinite perfections of God." "God rightly needed a victim; and His own Son, innocent as He was, had to sacrifice Himself to pain, from the moment that his love caused Him to take on our iniquities."[142] In another Good Friday sermon, a Breton priest, after recounting Christ's Passion, asks the question: "Is that enough, Eternal Father, is your justice finally content?"[143]

A conspicuous fact emerges from the above quotations: The terrifying doctrine of the Father enraged against His Son was not confined to the upper echelon of the church. It descended to the ground level of everyday Catholics and was widely promulgated by a concerted theological campaign. Hymns (" 'Tis midnight, Christians") and catechisms[144] also confirmed that only the sacrifice of Jesus could have appeased His Father's "wrath."

The doctrines of the chosen few and God the Judge who punishes His own Son together reflect an image of fatherhood that men of the church no doubt shared with a substantial part of the public. This image is no longer applies. Today, "father" evokes above all "kindness," "affection," "tenderness," and "pardon," which, moreover, is the sense found in the Gospels. Despite the evangelists, however, "father" used to imply, at least for many of our ancestors, "majesty," "power," "justice," and "honor." The image of God and the image of fathers have evolved hand in hand. They have both progressively mellowed.

CHAPTER 15

Sin and Sins

DEADLY AND VENIAL SIN

The Christian God of early modern times was irritable, and it was sin that irritated Him: Preachers constantly harped on this theme, using a copious store of motifs. Salvation, the straying of sinners, delays in conversion, the end of life, the chosen few, the woes of a relapse, the particular kinds of offenses, and even Christ's Passion provided them with renewed opportunities to explain the how and why of "divine vengeance." They reiterated to their listeners that Christians will be more severely judged than Jews and idolaters, since they have received the grace of the Faith[1]; they regarded sin as eternal, as demons and the damned would never stop cursing God and man in endless tortures. This absolute definition of sin, the result of studied theological conceptualizing, was translated for the general public by an evangelical campaign that spoke in sensational phrases and striking analogies.

Maillard and San Bernardino did not fail to stress the "infinite malice" of deadly sin,[2] this "incurable leper [being without grace], whose contagion severs you from God."[3] However, for the quality of its images as well as its counterpoint on repentance, one of the finest texts on sin I have read is by Jean-Pierre Camus:

> *If sin is a winter . . . full of frosts, lack of devotion, freezing winds, insensitivity, ice, obstinacy, clouds, and fogs of blindness, removing all the freshness of our consciences, killing off the flowers, leaves, and fruits of our good desires and good works, how delicious must be repentance, which, like a lovely spring, restoring the zephyrs of sweet sighs, the dew of loving tears, the flowers of holy intentions, the warmth of saintly fervor, and the fruits of pious deeds, disperses all the rigors of the chilly and displeasing season.*[4]

Still, sermons on sin rarely have this Salesian freshness and optimism. Instead, they emphasize the enormity of Deadly Sin, and therefore of even a single Deadly Sin. Louis of Granada's *Guía de pecadores* informs its readers and listeners:

> *Christians must be fully convinced, and this is a most certain truth, that if all the calamities, disasters, and evils that ever visited the earth since its creation, and*

> *will visit it to the end of time, as well as all the tortures of hell, were all put together in one scale, and but one single deadly sin in the other, the latter would weigh more heavily.*[5]

D'Outreman may have been thinking of the above text, but certainly of Lessius's *De Perfectionibus* . . . when he wrote, for the sake of preachers: "The theologians . . . say that all pains, including the primary and eternal one, can never equal the harm of a single deadly sin, once one suffers all the penalties of the damned. The reason is that the harm of the sin is infinite, given the infinite Majesty that it offends."[6] At the beginning of Lent, Godeau invites his diocesans to think themselves "unworthy to avail themselves of any food of any living thing," and to recognize "the goodness and indulgence of the Church, which allows you to eat certain living things, such as fish and vegetables."[7] In another sermon Godeau, like many preachers, defines Deadly Sin as "the horror of desolation."[8]

Instructing countrypeople, Chenois gives them three reasons for the eternity of infernal penalties: "(1) as infinite malice is found in the least deadly sin, (2) as one cannot find an infinity of being in the most repentant of sinners, and (3) as each deadly sin deserves infinite torture," it is logical and necessary that the torments of hell must last forever.[9] Discussing "the injury God receives from sin," Loriot affirms that "if we knew what it [sin] were, the blood would freeze in our veins and our hair stand on end just to hear it named; we would seek out the loneliest places, the caves and grottoes of the desert, like the first Christians, in order to be far away from the great dangers and opportunities for sin that abound in this world."[10]

An ad hoc sermon, which the late seventeenth- and early eighteenth-century Lazarists kept in their traveling files, tells how sin is "a monster, such a horrid betrayal that only God can know its full enormity." The reason given to the educated audience is that sin is the gravest of all possible abuses, since it contemptuously attacks God Himself. Two comparisons made this argument more accessible. To insult a peasant in the streets of Paris is already a blameworthy action. If one derides "one of the leading citizens, the affront is still greater. But if one ridicules a king, it is unanimously agreed that this offense deserves capital punishment. To sin is to ridicule God, through the contempt one shows Him." To convey the depth of this contempt, the preacher uses a second analogy: At the sound of a trumpet, a king orders the inhabitants of a town to immediately surrender their arms on pain of death. Instead, "a quarter hour later, an hour later, a month later, all these people remain in arms; they do nothing but laugh, when warned that they disobey the prince's orders." So too do men, "maggots" who scorn the commands of God.[11]

Although preachers never tired of expounding on the major categories of sin, the above excerpts are from sermons concerning sin as such: not only did missions and retreats[12] highlight this subject, but also hymns on "Deadly Sin" and "the habit of sinning."[13] Moreover, parish priests sometimes employed an entire Sunday sermon to expose "the enormity of sin": Such was the case with the priests Hébert, Symon, Chevassu, and Réguis, among others.[14] Finally, preaching on venial sin demands attention. To be sure, it was always distinguished from Deadly Sin. It is serious, however, in that it shares the general wickedness of all sin; in addition, it weakens grace and thus comprises a step down the stairway toward deadly transgressions. In a Sunday homily on the theme "Avoiding the slightest faults." Camus encourages his listeners to hate "venial sins more than death."[15] For "even though they are not enough to make us lose all grace, they nevertheless greatly alter and weaken it."[16] "Therefore let us flee and hate venial sin, not because it leads us into hell, but because it does bring us to the gate."[17] Likewise, Fontana devotes a Lenten sermon to the "great and necessary vigilance against minor falls, which most often open the way to great disasters."[18] Loriot also composed an entire sermon on venial sin.[19]

The most prevalent doctrine agreed with Pascal that "the least offenses have the most horrendous consequences." A few examples will demonstrate this point. Girard teaches his parishioners that "venial sin is an evil greater than all others, excepting deadly sin itself; venial sin is an evil that outweighs any good that anyone can do; hence one must never commit a single one."[20] De Toulouse's sermon on "the enormity of venial sins" carries this ecclesiastical exaggeration of minor offenses still further. The Capuchin does protest against certain philosophers and heretics who make no distinction "between a great fall and a slight stumble" and who argue that all our offenses are "equally criminal." As has been seen regarding the chosen few, however, De Toulouse habitually extends one hand while pulling back the other. In this case he explains that it is difficult to say whether a sin is venial or deadly. To be absent from the Sunday mass is a Deadly Sin. But is it venial or is it deadly to speak during the mass? "To commit an indecent act with a woman is a Deadly Sin." However, "to hold hands, to give or receive kisses," are these venial sins? It is hard to tell. In any case, God punishes Deadly Sins here on earth: "For a minor slip, which could only have led to a venial sin," a prophet was eaten by lions.

> *Yet all these punishments, which are most severe and whose rigor reveals the enormity of venial sin and how much God detests it, are but a faint shadow of those which He enacts in the afterlife; 'tis there, as a prophet says, that He will weigh, not only mountains but low hills, not only great but small venial sins . . . 'Tis there . . . that He will exact payment for idle or disrespectful speech, for thoughtless smiles and glances, for a moment's angry word or action; all that will happen on the last day of our life, when we must appear before God, when those little sins so lightly regarded and so immoderately committed will cause us terror and look like great mountains.*[21]

The logical result of such dramatization was self-examination on venial sin: This was extolled by Saint Leonard of Port-Maurice during his missions. The preacher advises penitents:

1. *Consider whether you have always had a correct understanding of venial sin, seeing it as an inherently serious evil.*
2. *Thoroughly consider and assess the value of a venial sin, since under no circumstances may one be committed, even if it might save the world.*
3. *Consider whether you have adequately weighed the harm of a venial sin, whose expiation requires the precious blood of Jesus Christ, and which, in some sense, is a greater affliction than hell itself.*
4. *Consider whether you have ever understood the pernicious effects that venial sin sometimes causes.*
5. *Consider whether you have ever sought the most effective remedy for obtaining the pardon of the many venial sins you daily commit.*
6. *Consider whether you have ever thought of how venial sin may in some respects be called a deadly evil, because it both directly and indirectly predisposes one to deadly sin.*
7. *Consider whether you have ever realized how severely God punishes venial sin both in this life and the next.*

8. *Consider whether you have ever employed effective remedy to deliver you from venial sins.*[22]

This famous eighteenth-century preacher's model for self-examination on venial sin needs to be situated in the context of a vast ecclesiastical discourse, which tended toward the "guiltification" of faithful Catholics. The sermons of this period are replete with such phrases. Bridaine advises his listeners to count their venial sins:

> *Count them, if you can. O, you shall be surprised, you shall be frightened, and you will realize, like David, that the number of your iniquities is more than that of the hairs on your head (Ps. 40:12). Yes, if you look deep down into your conscience, you will find that it is a cavern, an abyss, a vast immense sea, filled with many upon many insects and reptiles, I mean venial sins, these "things creeping innumerable" (Ps. 104:25).*[23]

Furthermore, Father Yvan asserts, "the least faults are the source of great sins and great punishments."[24]

Catholic preaching consistently affirmed, against both Protestantism and Jansenism, that temptation is not sin. It just as clearly declared, however, that "mere temptations do not excuse the sinner" (Father Yvan).[25] The evangelical program often transmitted the message that a Christian has no excuse. Amazed by the "abominable" sins of his listeners, Godeau reminds them that God will someday "examine them with inconceivable severity," and that then "they will have no excuses to bring along."[26] A Lazarist sermon proclaims that "a Christian can make no excuse when he violates God's commandments."[27] Similarly, Réguis protects his parishioners against self-indulgence by telling them: "He who commits a deadly sin does not intend to lose grace. Does he therefore lose less, and is he less guilty? . . . Christians who are now in hell did not intend to be damned. Are they therefore less so?"[28] Thus one should not engage in cheap reassurance.

Montargon writes that "there is no earthly misery comparable to that of a false conscience." For the role of conscience, "in its capacity as judge," is to "gather up all that might terrify the sinner."[29] De la Font therefore concludes: "Keep whatever strict examination you have made of your life, whatever sharp pain you have felt for your sins, to obtain pardon thereby."[30] Such statements contradict the occasional warnings made by ordinary preachers against excessive scruples.[31] These men also adhered to Godeau's conviction that "everyone dwells in sin; men are sinners and are naught but sin."[32] Recalling the vision of Ezekiel, a Lazarist sermon explains that "these bones scattered here and there in a vast field" represent "the condition of most Christians living in villages, and often in towns, of all stations, who, through the deadly sin in which they have the misfortune to live, no longer act to gain eternal life."[33] Hence the need for the examination of conscience and for missionaries whose express purpose was to make people know "the gravity and multitude"[34] of their sins.

Our offenses are so grave and so numerous that they deserve every kind of punishment. "Confess," Chenois goads a group of countrypeople, "that your disgraces come only from your debauchery and impurity."[35] He then demonstrates (1) "that sinners are the living dead," (2) "that sinners are crazed animals," and (3) "that sinners are devils incarnate."[36] D'Outreman urges his readers and listeners to meditate on "the great evils we have done, and those that we deserve done to us . . . Even if we have committed but one single sin, the majesty of God, dishonored thereby, is such that the world does not have enough penalties to give Him legitimate atonement. There is no gallstone, no gout, no plague, war, or famine that can worthily atone for an offense to God, no matter how slight."[37] Such a viewpoint clarifies Pierre de la Font's advice "to overstate rather than belittle your offenses."[38] This instillation of excessive guilt also explains certain verses from missionary hymns in which converted sinners, realizing that they deserved the tortures of Hell and overjoyed to have escaped them, plead for their own earthly punishments:

I truly deserved my torture:
Hell, hell would not suffice.[39]

Since my crime knew no bound,
I should be punished on this ground.
'Tis not enough, a blood like mine.
To appease Him; there must be thine [Jesus'].[40]

O Lord! No more be indulgent.
Strike me now in Thy Mercy.[41]

In suffering your agony
Think on your offense.
You deserved from the Lord on high
Eternal vengeance.
Too lucky you are, that your sufferance
May appease His fury.[42]

Likewise, the students of the Brothers of the Christian Schools sang:

My pains could ne'er be too great,
Almighty God, increase thy blows;
The soul doth soon degenerate
Who follows not her spouse.[43]

As for Réguis, he assumes the voice of the repentant sinner and cries out: "Strike me, Lord Almighty, strike, strip me of my possessions, ruin my health, multiply my afflictions, slash, burn, give me no pardon here below, so that my iniquities will be washed away, and You will show me mercy in that other life."[44]

THE CLASSIFICATION OF SINS

The numerous generalizing sermons on sin, the sinner, confession, and penance do not always allow for the identification of which precise categories of sin the preachers had in mind. Nevertheless, this identification is highly pertinent. For it simultaneously clarifies the daily experience of the masses and the ethical grid with which the teaching church mapped and judged the behavior of the faithful. By analyzing the homogeneous documentation afforded by sermons on specific aspects of religious ethics, the following discussion will aim to achieve this clarification, or at least its rough outline. At the same time, a good number of sermons on other topics also castigated various types of sinful conduct. The ideal project—which would require a vast amount of time—would be to add up within a corpus of sermons all the lines concerning a particular sin. Despite the absence of such a costly enterprise, the following quantification will hopefully provide useful insights.

As a starting point, I have chosen both the Latin and Italian sermons of San

Bernardino on specific doctrinal emphases. These same themes then recur in: (1) six collections of sermons by seventeenth- to eighteenth-century missionaries (François de Toulouse, Lazarist sermons, Lejeune, Loriot, the *Bouquet de la Mission*, Segneri the Elder); (2) Hyacinthe de Montargon's encyclopedia for preachers; (3) four compendia of sermons for the fifty-two Sundays of the year, also dating from the seventeenth and eighteenth centuries (edited by Camus, Chevassu, Girard, and Réguis). This selection thus includes 70 sermons by San Bernardino and 259 by the later authors. Most of these latter examples were written by missionaries (198 out of 255). Moreover, sermons for the fifty-two Sundays of the year often concern appointed Gospel readings and rarely focus on a specific vice (lechery, slander, and so on). Hence the collections by Bourgoing, La Font, Bourée, Hébert, and Symon contain no full-length sermon on the Deadly Sins or related subjects. The following chart summarizes the results of this analysis.

This chart's imperfections of classification and therefore of quantification are readily apparent. The most considerable of these defects is to yoke under the same rubric sermons on lust and sermons on marriage. The latter are by no means exclusively preoccupied with questions of purity and impurity. They tend rather to propose the terms for a good match and the spouses' reciprocal duties. If one then removes from the first rubric the sermons relating to marriage, chastity, and widowhood, one obtains seven by San Bernardino (10 percent) and twenty-one by the other authors (8.1 percent). It might also be worth subtracting homilies on almsgiving from the range of sermons on financial problems. One then finds that San Bernardino devotes twenty-three sermons (33.3 percent) to avarice of all kinds, and the other preachers twenty-nine (10.1 percent). All the same, this statistical refinement only confirms the findings of a more rudimentary calculation:

1. Catholic evangelists dwelt on three sins above all others: the love of money, lust, and envy, the last often in the sense of slander. Pride, though listed as the first of the Deadly Sins, was only a secondary target of the preachers.
2. Despite his vociferous harangues against "rivalries," sodomy, and the excesses of feminine attire, San Bernardino primarily attacked usury. His sermons on this practice, in their modified Latin form, are veritable treatises on the various types of loans at interest. Although seventeenth- to eighteenth-century preaching remained on guard against greed and other financial matters, its preoccupations were more diverse, and it spent far more time than San Bernardino on slander, self-love, blasphemy, drunkenness, missing church on Sundays, regard for public opinion, and above all to the reciprocal duties of parents and children as well as of masters and servants. The great fifteenth-century Franciscan aimed all his verbal artillery at certain activities of his Italian contemporaries, especially usury, sodomy, women dressing luxuriously, and political feuding. His Baroque successors, particularly in France, sought more to oversee the entire scope of daily behavior. Hence they put great stress on the good example that parents and masters must give their children and servants. Moreover, they were confronted with the persistence of blasphemy, cursing, and rural drunkenness. Finally, they had to attend to an entire range of habits found suspect by the governing religious bodies: missing Sunday mass, apathy, hypocrisy, impiety inside churches, and so on.
3. It is clear that the seventeenth- to eighteenth-century sermon writers,

PASTORAL EMPHASIS ON . . .	SAN BERNARDINO		11 17TH- AND 18TH-CENTURY SERMON WRITERS	
	Number	%	Number	%
1. lust, physical beauty, feminine attire, dances and shows;/chastity, marriage, widows	17	24.3	45	17.5
2. greed, theft, financial problems;/almsgiving opposed to "avarice"	27	38.5	43	16.8
3. envy, slander, rash judgments	8	11.5	27	10.6
4. the reciprocal duties of parents and children	1	1.5	26	10.2
5. anger, hatred, rivalries	6	8.5	18	7.1
6. pride, ambition, self-love, ostentation	3	4.3	17	6.7
7. blasphemy, cursing, and swearing	2	2.8	15	5.2
8. honoring and dishonoring Sundays and church holidays	-	-	10	4
9. gluttony, intemperance, drunkenness	-	-	10	4
10. the reciprocal duties of masters and servants	-	-	9	3.6
11. lying, hypocrisy	2	2.8	8	3.2
12. regard for public opinion, apathy, the tyranny of habit	1	1.5	7	2.9
13. scandal	1	1.5	6	2.5
14. sloth, idleness	-	-	6	2.5
15. respecting and disrespecting places of worship	-	-	5	2
16. gambling	2	2.8	3	1.2
TOTAL	70	100	255	100

like San Bernardino, zeroed in on two main categories of behavior: the one pertaining to money and the use of material goods, the other to marriage and sexuality.

"AVARICE"

The threats made by Girard to those with ill-gotten gains aptly convey the dominant tone of commonplace preaching on the improper use of worldly possessions. To repeat his prophesies, the poor will see at their feet "these great lords, these arrogant men who will have misused their titles, wealth, and honors."[45] By tapping the entire corpus of sermons, one could compile an impressive anthology of sharp messages to the rich, which cover every kind of "larceny" (the preferred word of the time for "theft"). Discussion of the obligation to give alms, of necessary detachment from the world, of the impossibility of serving two masters, and of the words of Jesus, "render unto Caesar . . ." provided opportunities for harsh critiques of all forms of avarice.

Commenting on the miracle of the multiplication of loaves, Pierre de la Font tells his listeners: "All that you will leave here to your heirs will be lost to you; but all that you will give to the poor will be paid back to you with interest."[46] Riches are dangerous. Montargon, who sought to be a guide for preachers, is categorical: "Wealth," he writes, "no matter how honestly acquired, always remains deadly." "Wealth is opposed to religion." "Great wealth is almost always the fruit of great injustice, and fosters iniquity." "Seeing what happens today, one can say that Christians outdo the rich in luxury and opulence." "'Tis an ill-founded presumption to think that you will only be damned for great crimes. The damnation of the rich and wicked reverses this system."[47] De Montfort composed the following verses for singing by crowds of the poor, who must have derived some comfort from them:

While the rich shall groan
Amid a thousand woes,
The good poorfolk shall rejoice
Amid a thousand joys . . .

Since God confirms and proves it,
I believe the rich are miserable.
I believe it is a deadly blessing
To become rich like them . . .

'Tis this malice [avarice] that by itself
Makes so many rich people die,
That makes the yawning maw
Of hell open to swallow all.[48]

Blessed are the poor: These are also the tidings of the Angevin priest marchais, who congratulates his parishioners for escaping the "snares" of the world through their very poverty. His sincere and moving elegy of daily work and the health-giving strains of the peasant condition deserves lengthy citation:

> *When one task is finished, another begins; each hour is filled with labor; each minute has its exercise or hardship; unnoticed, the days go on, time passes in honest work. And if occasional rest or relaxation is needed, modesty and sobriety are the rule, for when in other places there might not be principles of religion or the love of God, here there are not the means to either spend lavish amounts or to engage in idle pastimes. O happy impotence of means, which becomes the most potent agent of sanctification, and makes poverty itself the direct way to salvation.*[49]

"The eminent dignity of the poor," Bossuet had earlier said. As for Réguis, he asks the rich this embarrassing question, which could well apply to present-day relations with the third and fourth worlds: "The rich, who otherwise seem so irreproachable, do they not make useless expenditures? Are there not in their parishes poorfolk who die of hunger, while their dogs and horses are well fed? Are the gold and silver that shine on their clothes and in their houses as necessary as they think? Do we not invent necessities?"[50]

Wealth is even more dangerous, since one does not commonly consider the true seriousness of the multiple "larcenies" that occur every day. For thievery is everywhere. An anonymous Lazarist preacher states, "'Tis a strange thing: Although the world condemns larceny, there is nothing so common; the very people who detest it in others do not see it in themselves, though they are indeed most guilty thereof."[51] Chevassu likewise says: "Nothing is as common as injustice or larceny; and if we closely examine the various conditions of humanity, we will find that almost everyone lives off someone else's property"[52]—a singularly strong assertion.

The men of the church courageously spared nobody in listing thefts and thieves. They may well have caused some bad feeling in their audiences. De la Font counts among "dangerous professions" (for salvation) not only that of soldier but also "buying and selling, the professions of lawyer, notary, attorney, baker, and butcher."[53] The Lazarist sermon on "larceny" carefully enumerates and subdivides every type of thief: Those who are guilty of "secret larcenies" and those who commit "public larcenies." The two lists are striking. In the first, children "who steal from their parents" are grouped with parents who steal from their children, servants and masters who do the same to one another, stock exchange brokers, and especially "certain trades that endanger [salvation] because they exploit another's property." The preacher goes on to cite the many cheating ways of millers, tailors, carders, weavers, haberdashers, merchants, innkeepers, and bureaucrats who put "trickery" atop "a throne." "I would never finish," the preacher declares, "if I tried to detail all the beguiling tricks of the bureaucrats."

Under the heading of "public thieves" are found not only highwaymen and soldiers but also "noblemen who require uncalled-for corvées from their vassals," tax collectors "who, when they are ungodly, are the most signal thieves of the parishes," merchants who pile up "monopolies," usurers of every stripe, and finally those who rob both God and the church ("since the beginning of the world, God has willed that we pay Him His tithe"[54]). In a Sunday sermon on "different specific larcenies," Girard speaks like the priest of the Mission.[55] He thunders against usurers and fraudulent traders, recalls the obligation to faithfully pay the tithe, and strongly emphasizes the injustices too frequently committed in the apportionment of taxes.[56]

All these sermons on theft reach the logical conclusion that restitution is a necessity. Recent studies of early modern preaching strongly accentuate this point.[57] "The reports of the missions are filled with victorious announcements regarding reconciliations, restitutions, and amiable settlements that suddenly put a stop to seemingly endless proceedings."[58] Sunday sermons on the subject clearly aim at the same target, especially when they refer to Jesus' words, "Render unto Caesar." De la Font explains that this advice applies not only to "the duties of submission, loyalty, and obedience to princes," but also to the just treatment we owe our neighbor. His entire sermon then addresses "the duty of amends and restitution."[59]

In the sequence of the fifty-five Lazarist sermons, the homily on "restitution" immediately follows that on "larceny," and does not stint on threats:

> . . . *It is the nature of larceny to continually hoard, and almost infinitely accumulate, by delaying restitution . . . You sin every time that you think of paying*

back, of restituting, of making compensation for this damage, and yet do nothing about it, even though you might have. If that thought comes to mind a thousand times a day, and you remain determined to hold on to another's property, you thereby commit a hundred deadly sins: calculate and add up, if you can, how many that will be by the end of the year.[60]

Like Girard, Chevassu spends an entire Sunday sermon on restitution, cajoling:

You must make restitution . . . you must, because it is impossible to go to heaven with another's belongings . . . [you must make restitution] to this widow; you, to this master; you, master, to that servant; you, businessman, to the town or parish that has chosen you as its steward; you, lawyer and attorney, to the party whose interests you have craftily betrayed; you, merchants, to this artisan or that partner whom you have deceived; you, usurer, to the family you have ruined through forbidden loans.[61]

A detached historical inquiry thus illuminates the full extent of this period's sermonizing on economic injustice. One of Girard's arguments provides a useful conclusion. Preaching on the danger of wealth and the need to give alms, the Lyonnais priest warns his audience that on the day of judgment Jesus "will not say: go, accursed ones, to eternal hellfire, because you were obscene, blasphemous, or drunken; but because I was hungry and you gave me nought to eat; I was thirsty and you gave me naught to drink; I was naked and you did not clothe me."[62]

MARRIAGE, A "DANGEROUS" SITUATION

Referring to the chart on page 428, one notes that in the sermons, of the seventeenth and eighteenth century, the advice, warnings, and reprimands pertaining to marriage, virginity, and sexuality come in first place (17.5 percent), ahead of monetary issues (16.8 percent). It is quite markedly the opposite in San Bernardino's output (24.3 percent for the first group, 38.5 percent for the second). This evolution is significant. At the same time that casuistry on lending at interest ran dry, ecclesiastical fear of sex increased. By leaps, if not by rights, lust ascended the rungs of the septenary. It had long since moved up from seventh place, where Aquinas and Dante had once put it.[63] In the following section, San Bernardino's sermons will serve as reference points, marking the degree to which later sermons approximated or deviated from them.

First, every preacher emphasized the sacramental nature of marriage. San Bernardino reminds his audience that this sacrament was instituted before all the rest, in the Garden of Eden, before Adam and Eve had sinned[64]: hence its eminent dignity. In the Age of Reason, numerous sermons on marriage used the episode of the wedding at Cana to show that Jesus Himself honored this important sacrament with both His presence and a miracle. Similarly, all preachers unanimously celebrated the union of man and wife as reflecting that of Christ and the church. Nevertheless, a few more touching and less stereotypical notes, though rare, call for attention. These are the work of Christian humanists. In the mid-sixteenth century, François Le Picart told his Parisian listeners on All Saints' Day: "You married people, on condition that you live and govern yourselves honestly in your condition, moderately tasting God's blessings, in good strength, you will go to paradise; but still do this that I tell ye: Be merciful."[65] With regard to the wedding at Cana, Camus gives spouses this moving compliment:

But what honor is thine, O fathers and mothers, to cooperate with God in the most excellent work of the world, the masterpiece of the universe, which is the human body, the most perfect and best organized of all bodies, in which God places, like a pearl in the shell, the soul He has created, an immortal soul, capable of loving, knowing, and adoring.

Thus you are to your children as vice-Gods, as little creators, terrestrial divinities, to whom honor and obedience are not only recommended by God, but enjoined under pain of damnation . . .

It is true that celibate chastity fills not earth but heaven; but marital chastity fills heaven from earth, and its fruits fill up both heaven and earth. It provides soldiers for the Earthly Jerusalem, conquerors for the Heavenly one.[66]

Such praise of the body, however, is unusual for a preacher. On the other hand, the praise of good marriage was a commonplace. Over truly Christian spouses there reigns a "holy tenderness," which is "the link, the charity, and the cement of their union": Thus speaks the severe Bridaine.[67] Once they have made these concessions, however, the preachers tend to treat marriage in extremely discouraging terms, liable to inspire a guilty conscience. At the same time, an evolution can be traced from San Bernardino to his Baroque successors. The former, who was familiar with the confession handbooks and manuals, gives specific details that the latter generally avoid. The great fifteenth century Franciscan prohibits intercourse during menstruation, advises against it during pregnancy, sets forth the conditions in which the conjugal debt should be paid, criticizes overfrequent sexual relations, the abuse of petting and stroking, and feathered beds. He also prohibits making love in public, and lists periods for abstinence: religious holidays, Lent, days of fasting, and every church-ordained vigil. At the same time, the preacher admits some compromises: Even on these days, no sin is committed if the couple's intention is to have a child. If the act involves the "conjugal debt," or extinguishes concupiscence, the sin is no more than venial. On the other hand, it is strictly forbidden to use marriage for the primary goal of gaining pleasure (*libidine*).[68]

For the most part, such details disappear from the seventeenth- to eighteenth-century sermons, whose speakers rely on generalities and leave more concrete questions to the confessors.[69] It is quite exceptional to find a Lazarist missionary asserting that it is "sinful" and "irreverent" to have marital relations "on those days . . . when one must take Holy Communion, on the principal religious holidays, and when one must do greater penance."[70] The more prudent Pierre de la Font informs his audience that "even the catechism of the Council of Trent does not offer to you as an exact precept, but rather as a most salutary practice that will bring heaven's blessing to your families, to be abstinent for a few days prior to communion, and especially during Lent."[71]

Like San Bernardino, these later preachers describe marriage as "a dangerous" situation. The Franciscan's dramatic announcement again comes to mind: "Out of a thousand marriages, I believe that 999 belong to the devil."[72] For de la Font, marriage is "a state hemmed in by immense danger," to be entered into only after close and careful consideration. If it is "a happy port for some, for many others it is a tragic shipwreck."[73] This sermon, which refers to the wedding at Cana, launches into a systematic attack on women using the most traditionally misogynistic terms: "The apostles rightly found it too difficult and onerous to have to keep a woman by one's side . . . a woman replete with defects and disorders; to live with this domestic enemy of one's rest; hence it was more tolerable to resist the natural inclination that leads to marriage, than to make oneself constantly suffer the mad and outlandish behavior of a woman."[74]

Marriage is "dangerous" because women, even when married, are perverse. This is the Jesuit Vieira's lesson in a sermon on the beheading of Saint John the Baptist:

> *Of all the miseries that overcome us, all bodily hardships, spiritual vices, all these woes of today and of eternity, these grievous consequences of original sin, what is the primary cause? A woman, a wife; and not an adulteress, but a lawful and innocent one, sprung from the hands of God Himself . . .*
>
> *All the sorrows, diseases, private and public disasters, plagues, famines, wars, the rises and falls of nations, some appearing as others disappear forever, all these catastrophes can only have their prime source in the disobedience of woman, who was given to man by God Himself:* mulier quam dedisti mihi *(Gen. 3:12).*[75]

Under these hard conditions, how could one not distrust marriage? Loriot states: "'Tis even more certain, that many who would be saved through celibacy are damned through marriage, because they have neither sufficient strength nor courage to conquer the great and continual temptations that surround this condition."[76] Similarly, Bridaine is convinced that "many horrible and hateful sins are daily committed in marriage; and you should be put to trembling by the fact that an infinity of Christians damn themselves daily by committing them . . . For such believe they are sound in spirit, though their souls are laden with a thousand hideous disorders, and they are ready to fall into hell, unless they reform . . ."[77] For the priest Symon de Rennes, there are in marriage "great dangers and impediments for salvation . . . most marriages are inspired only by the devil, who also presides over them."[78] In a hymn by de Montfort celebrating "the beauty of virginity," the wise virgins lament over those who marry:

> *Alas! So many foolish virgins,*
> *So many thoughtless lads*
> *Do sell for baubles*
> *This treasure of paradise!*
> *Though losing all, they revel*
> *In their beastly pleasures.*
>
> *What lose they who marry?*
> *Shall I speak truly?*
> *They put themselves in slavery,*
> *They lose tranquility,*
> *They kiss, they are polluted.*
> *And thus they often lose all grace.*[79]

Marriage not only carries the risk of leading one into Hell, but for many it is already a living Hell. Montargon claims that there are "few marriages without dissension,"[80] and for him, "the disorders that reign over married couples are pressing reasons for exhorting widows not to remarry."[81] As for Bridaine, he is "not at all surprised to see so many unhappy marriages, so many men and women who constantly grieve over their fate and misfortune, who moan and complain every day about the slavery to which they are reduced. For they have not received the grace of their condition; and they have not received it because they were not prepared for it."[82]

Girard paints a desolate picture of the most frequent matrimonial situations. He says:

> *Let us first suppose, as something only too certain, that the number of bad marriages is extremely high and consequently that of good ones low . . . What do we see all the time? Can one think on it without shaking? Poor wretches, ye have been ill conjoined, who have been married without God's calling . . . how ye have cause for lamentation! Is not your life a prefiguration of hell? The noise, the quarrels, confusion, crimes, and disorder that afflict your family, are they not the image of that terrible place where there is eternal confusion and disorder?*[83]

Réguis hints at the same complaints, and he also compares marriage to Hell: "How many mismatched marriages! And therefore how many miserable ones! How many households of trouble and discord! Ye know it better than I, my dear parishioners." A bad marriage is both "a glimpse and a first step into hell."[84]

These sermons constantly return to the themes that marriage is dangerous and that its many cares and turmoils take one away from God. This double deterrent was directed especially at virgins and widows. To the latter, San Bernardino argues that "if the true widow thinks on death, she will not dream of a second husband." The widow worthy of her name is already "half-saintly. She has felt the blows of this world, and does not wish to undergo the sorrow of mourning a husband once again." To discourage remarriage, the Siennese preacher explains all the worries and troubles it would bring. If she has children, they will have a potentially mean and jealous father. If he also has children, he will want his new wife to show them as much affection as she would her own. If, however, she starts to love her own children less, he will decide that she is a heartless mother. Finally, if she has no children but her new husband does, the difficulties are even greater. For "it is a general rule" that stepmothers and stepchildren "never like one another." San Bernardino then draws on Saint Jerome for a second rationale: He essentially tells the widow that she had a good husband and wept for him. If she marries a second good husband, she will be afraid of losing him. On the other hand, if the second spouse is bad, she will bitterly pine for the first. Again, if the first was bad and the second good, she will worry that the latter will die. Finally, if the second is as bad as the first, she will have the feeling of going from frustration to frustration. "Therefore it is better to remain a widow."[85] In the Latin version of this sermon, the widow is finally told that "if you have no children, you would be quite mad, you who are free, to enter into slavery for the sake of having children."[86]

San Bernardino's remarks are echoed by other lines from the above-quoted de Montfort hymn, proving the repetitive character of this doctrinal message:

> *My dear friend is*
> *married,*
> *O how I pity her! . . .*
> *I am free, she a slave.*
>
> *I am a maiden wise . . .*
> *No children, no*
> *household,*
> *Nor a jealous husband.*[87]

Even the most usual preaching, that of the parish priests, sought to steer young women toward religious life by employing the same arguments against marriage. With reference to the lepers healed by Jesus, Girard preaches on chastity and becomes, temporarily, "feminist":

Married women, behold your hardship; recall the cares and troubles that have bothered you since you set up house, the debts you have owed, the maintenance of your family, education of your children, worries about the future, the almost continuous illnesses and infirmities, the needs of people with different temperaments, their way of upsetting each other often, and you will realize that your situation is wretched . . .

Christians, know that a married woman enters into a kind of slavery, she leaves behind her joy and well-being; she cannot do anything of any importance without her husband's consent; even her work is not her own, and her livelihood depends on his means. I find this arrangement quite harsh; nevertheless, it is established by law, and it is criminal to stray from it. For all that, however, nearly all young maids willingly submit themselves to an evidently heavy yoke, and freely sacrifice their most valuable property, in order to have a husband; I mean their virginity, which is an inestimable treasure, their freedom and their belongings . . . their life and their health, in risking vexatious pregnancy and dangerous childbirth. But what am I saying, to have a husband? All too often, it is to have a scoundrel, a blasphemer, a lecher, drunkard, or brute.[88]

For the late twentieth-century reader, this speech—addressed to an audience composed mainly of married couples—is astonishing. Clearly, these preachers were trying to justify to themselves their own celibate life-style. The reasons, however, behind the rejection of the flesh and the devaluation of marriage—in opposition to what was said elsewhere about the nobility of this sacrament—involve a guilt complex about sexuality far more Neoplatonic than Judeo-Christian. In the religious discourse of the time, desire is always called "concupiscence" or "weakness." "Conceived and born in sin, such is mankind," Hyacinthe de Montargon repeats,[89] in the most traditionally monastic way.[90] Again, the centuries-old continuity of this doctrine is apparent. Another eighteenth-century missionary hymn sings out:

I am the child of that first rebel
Who ruined his posterity.
My mother, just as criminal,
Conceived me in iniquity.[91]

Sexual intercourse, even in the context of marriage, is thus only a last resort; a remedy, but only because there is disease. Bourée tells his Sunday listeners: "The principal purpose of marriage is the begetting of children, and not pleasure; if the latter is the case, for the sake of keeping clean from other more obviously illicit and criminal motives, then one is only opting for the lesser of two evils. Always remember that it is a remedy for your incontinence, and that you do not take a remedy without disgust and repugnance, but with moderation and precaution."[92] Loriot uses the same expressions to discuss the same subject:

There are those who marry to gain support for the common needs of life, comfort amid hardships, and mutual consolation amid afflictions . . . this aim is good, and can be legitimately endorsed.

There is another, which is not strictly bad, but is less perfect, when one's weakness is perceived as well as one's inability to resist temptation, and marriage is resorted to as a remedy to this infirmity. Saint Paul says that this remedy is allowed through condescension, but not by recommendation. True, remedies are useful to combat disease, but it is quite base to depend on them; at the very least, it is necessary in these encounters to recall that remedies are never taken without necessity, repugnance, and disgust, and only with precaution, moderation, circumspection, and the love of health. The true end of marriage, however, which one must keep uppermost in mind when marrying, is to have children.[93]

Warning young virgins against men who ask for their hands in marriage, de Montfort also discredits sexuality:

They promise the wonders
That marriage will bring,
And thus bring to your ears
A poisonous sting.
They are possessed by a devil
Who only wants you to be evil.[94]

In conclusion, most marriages make "honest" what is in itself "shameful." Such is a Lazarist preacher's viewpoint: ". . . If marriage does not completely stamp out the impulses of corrupted nature, and the actions of concupiscence, it at least turns these innately shameful things into honest ones, in a man and woman who marry for the reasons and purposes ordained by God."[95]

IMPURITY

The church had long feared the body. In the wake of Innocent III, San Bernardino teaches that the body "is so foul that it corrupts the pure and immaculate soul that is sent into it."[96] Hence the horror of nudity. The same preacher, speaking in Siena's main piazza, scolds anyone who too freely uses "the eye" during conjugal relations. His words are startling:

Look at me, do you see this eye? It was not made for marriage. What has the eye to do with marriage? Every time it desires to see obscene deeds, it is a deadly sin. For what is permissible to touch is not permissible to look at. In satisfying your dishonest eyes, you sin most greatly, for you desire to see that which is forbidden. Now tell me, have you confessed it? Go then, and confess!

Bernardino proceeds to insist on honor in marriage, as Saint Paul advises. "How some think there is no dishonor in wanting to see their wife entirely naked! O! 'Tis the greatest of shames! Wives, never consent to such a wish. Rather die than let yourselves be seen! If you are barefoot, not even your feet should be visible."[97]

The preacher also advises widows to always sleep with their clothes on.[98] Following his lead, the clergy ceaselessly warned the faithful against "nude necks," lascivious fashions, and enjoyment taken in removing one's clothes. One of de Montfort's hymns, entitled "The Discipline of a Man Converted by the Mission," includes these lines:

Out of my sight, these figures
Filled with Satan's fire,
These naked pictures
That fools do so admire.

I shatter them, overturn them,
Erase them and deface them.[99]

In the chapter of the *Bouquet de la mission* concerning remedies against lust, one is advised "to treat one's body as a sworn enemy, and subdue it through work, fasts, hairshirts, and other mortifications."[100] In addition, the same book carries on a long tradition by explaining that the best way to gain contempt for the human body is to remember "the woeful state to which death reduces it." As has been shown, this was the function of macabre preaching and imagery: to feel disgust for the living human body, a dangerous object one should neither look at or display to others. Réguis reminds his listeners that on the day of judgment, "this miserable body, which is like to a little world of iniquity, will then be no more than a heap of earth and a mass of decay."[101]

The *Bouquet de la mission* enjoins that in the morning, "you will dress yourself modestly, remembering that you put on your garments in the presence of God and your guardian angel who observe you. Therefore do no unseemly thing, and never appear naked to anyone else, especially members of the opposite sex."[102]

The fear of nudity led religious orders to allow priests and novices to take only medically prescribed baths. In 1734 Father Bonnet, the Superior of the Lazarists, interrogated the Jesuits, Trinitarians, Sulpicians, and others on this subject. The Jesuits gave him this response: We have no written law against bathing.

It is believed that religious modesty is enough to prohibit it. The peril risked by young men who would be more liable to this temptation than others would have been a reason for laying down a rule; but it was not thought needful, because we have had no difficulties in this matter, and the superiors would severely punish those whom modesty and decency would not restrain. A youth who dared to bathe at one of our country houses did drown there, perhaps by God's merciful judgment, for He may have wished this fearful example to serve as law.

The Superior of Saint-Sulpice replies:

We never allow our priests, nor even our seminary students to take baths, neither in public nor private, in streams, ponds, lakes, or pools, and consequently they are forbidden to go swimming; 2) when the sick are prescribed hot or cold baths for health reasons, they take them indoors, and with a cloth across the tub, and no servant is left in the bather's room, in order to prevent the potential incidents that you so wisely fear.

With this advice, Father Bonnet lays down the same rule for his religious community.[103]

There is no need to exaggerate the church's tenacious hostility toward dances and dancing, and that the same fear of the body was the reason, the same belief that Satan "slithers through the flesh / Of dancing men and dames / To hold them in the mesh / Of his hot and am'rous flames."[104] This is the analysis of de Montfort, whose hymns frequently attack dancing. To be sure, the vehement missionary concedes that in theory dancing is "indifferent." "In itself, it is not an evil / It may even be innocent." Just as quickly, however, he corrects this concession. For,

. . . To dance without sin
There wants such circumstance,
That one cannot keep one's skin
From offending God in dance.[105]

Hyacinthe de Montargon sums up the general thinking of the preachers when he declares: "Balls and dances attack purity from all sides."[106]

Catholic evangelism aimed the same condemnation, for the same reasons, against love songs—whose melodies were sometimes appropriated for use in hymns—against tales and romances "which spread like the plague . . . and corrupt so many people,"[107] and against shows and entertainments in general. It is somewhat surprising to find the latter being pilloried as late as the mid-eighteenth century. Montargon again expresses the preachers' common feelings, in a series of biting phrases: "Public performances are inherently opposed to the spirit of Christianity." "Plays give only dangerous lessons." "Plays are the source of our time's dissoluteness." "Even when plays are honest, they remain dangerous."[108] To the objection that the contemporary theater "is most chaste, and portrays passion as modestly as possible," Montargon responds: This is all the more reason to mistrust it. "I daresay that this semblance of modesty and suppression of indecencies make it all the more to be feared."[109] In essence, he writes elsewhere, "no matter what they say, there will always be the concupiscence of the flesh."[110]

Crimes of impurity are always serious. Entire sermons propound this belief of the teaching church to every social class. D'Outreman asserts that "among all sins, we must especially beware of this one . . . which delights the devil more than all the rest."[111] Having preached in the morning on Hell, Bridaine gives an evening sermon on impurity and connects his two texts in the following way: "There is a hell rife with sinners who died impenitent, blasphemers, false witnesses, thieves, slanderers, drunkards, and the vindictive; but the greatest number of sinners who fall into this place, and those who are most hideously tormented, are without doubt the lascivious."[112] The Lazarists of this period also assure their listeners that "this sin is the most common cause for the damnation of those who are addicted to it."[113] Resuming an old theme of the anti-Protestant polemic, as well as a stereotyped accusation against religious deviants, they add: "If you seek the source of heresies, you will find it in lewd and unclean behavior."[114]

"Accursed lewdness," Loriot cries, "deadly plague of the human race, cruel murderer of the soul, vile seed-bed of hell, is there anyone who hates and dreads you as they should?"[115] Moreover, the preacher is brought to "tears" by the fact that "often it is this sole sin that causes the damnation of so many, who are blameless of other major vices, or, if they are guilty of others, only feel the effects of this one, from which being delivered, they would lead entirely pure and innocent lives. Most wretched, deadly and hated sin, must thou so miserably bring to ruin people who without thee would most certainly be saved?"[116] In his turn, Joseph Lambert vigorously puts peasants on guard against "the huge and most fearful" sin of impurity. He reminds them of the "vengeance" God wreaked on those people of the Old Testament who were guilty of it; citing Saint Paul's all-too-famous maxim, he then explains: "It is a fearful thing to fall into the hands of the living God. But it is still more fearful to fall into His hands, guilty of a sin so deplored by God as impurity."[117] Furthermore,

you must not think that God is angered only by those who take such sinning to the extreme. For as regards impurity, no sin is minor. Thus you must regard every kind of touching of your own and others' bodies, every liberty, as the most serious of sins; although these lewd acts may indeed be secret, they are loathsome in God's sight, who sees them all, is offended by them, and never fails to punish them most severely.[118]

The *Bouquet de la mission* likewise observes that

as regards impurity, any sin of thought or desire, of word or action, is deadly if consented to; . . . and so one must not think oneself innocent, because this consenting to enjoy lewd pleasure lasted for a brief moment; for likewise one is guilty of murder, through the stroke of a sword or the shot from a gun that lasted but a second; thus, for your act to be unpardonable, it is enough that in this moment you knew what you were doing and that you wanted to do it.[119]

For Montargon, there can be no doubt whatsoever:

Impurity encompasses all other sins . . . This vice . . . is not only a sin like the rest, [it] is the epitome of all sins; it is sin itself . . . A sin is more weighty according to the extent to which it outrages and injures God. Now, the sin of lust is all the greater because the thing preferred to God is more vile and contemptible. For such is the voluptuary: he prefers the pleasures of the flesh, a moment of desire, to God and a blissful eternity . . . Impurity profanes the entire faith of a Christian . . . Those who have just a smattering of our holy books will note that God has always punished the sin of impurity more severely than all others.[120]

The idea that impurity is "the cause of all the world's disorders"—Montargon again supplies this phrase[121]—had become a commonplace by the eighteenth century. Le Maure and Chevassu give nearly the same tirade on the subject, as preachers in France as elsewhere[122] tend to copy one another's writings:

This sole crime creates a gap between the Lord and the sinner, filled with all the passions it so powerfully arouses: pride, envy, perjury, cruelty, lying, all these horrid branches stem from this root; the other vices do not so strongly distance the creature from the Creator, do not so violently attack all the infinite perfections of God, and are not so stubbornly opposed to the three divine entities . . .

The indecent person attacks God in all His perfections: indulging his blind conduct, he no longer wishes to depend on the Lord, therein lies his pride; feeling his own pleasures, he is unfeeling toward the misery of the poor, therein lies his hard-heartedness; accruing and applying his fortune only to his desire, he no longer acknowledges providence, thus is he blind; carried away by passion, he is no longer kind, thus is he vengeful; he persecutes whomever opposes him, therein lies his hatred; he corrupts the object of his lust, thus he wastes time idly; attacking God Himself if he finds obstacles in his path, thus he is blasphemous; living without religion, thus his impiety; not having faith, he is an unbeliever; ravishing another's most precious possession, he shows his envy, thievery, and criminality.[123]

These texts, which resemble passages from the 1604 version of the *Doctrinal de sapience*,[124] help to establish a conclusion: Although fifteenth- to eighteenth-century preachers did not give lust an inordinate place vis-à-vis other sins, especially "cupidity," they did come to overestimate its gravity and to see impurity no matter where they looked.

This "intensification of guilt" regarding impurity explains the presence of a solemn warning in many of the period's sermons on marriage: One should not get married without "a sense of vocation." The notion of marriage as a "dangerous situation" thus recurs here, dangerous because of its hidden uncertainties, the chief of these being impurity. As Girard affirms, "it is far easier to be completely chaste, than to be moderate in the practice of pleasures that are permitted only under extreme precaution, and that are fraught with so many dangers."[125] To set out on such a hazardous venture without the express call of God is to run straight into hell. Thus the emphasis on "vocation" is not surprising, during the time when the Catholic Church was privileging the role of the priest. Transposing the priestly model, preachers based their guidelines for married life on those for ecclesiastical celibacy.

These points lie at the heart of a clerical discourse. If there are "continual disorders" in marriage, and if these are "the most deadly source of the great and sundry evils that afflict the Church," it is due to "the fully profane and godless manner in which this contract is made." This is the diagnosis offered by Pierre de la Font in his sermon for the second Sunday after Epiphany.[126] In addition, this text includes the story of the wedding at Cana and was given during the high season for marriages that preceded Lent. Loriot states the Prior of Valabrège's point even more clearly: ". . . 'Tis most certain that to receive God's blessing for one's marriage, to be happy in this life and in the next, the vocation of God is necessary as much if not more than for the other states of secular life, because of marriage's greater perils and complications."[127] The sermons of Bridaine, Chevassu, Girard, and the Lazarists[128] discuss the vocation of marriage at length, and their counsels are almost interchangeable: Clearly, this message was widely diffused, in both town and country. Marriage is "sacred" and "honorable." "It was instituted, not to authorize licentiousness, but to prevent it; not to ignite concupiscence, but to restrain it; not to bring libertines into the world, but to give children to the Church and chosen souls to heaven."[129] If this sacrament is "venerable," it must be received with the right predispositions, and the first of these is to be called unto it[130]:

"It is a truth upheld by all the doctors and masters of Christian life, that it is morally impossible to achieve one's salvation in any walk of life if one has not been called thereto by God; for one must discharge the obligations of one's calling, and avoid the dangers that it entails." God will give His grace to each walk of life "only to those who have embraced a way of life after being called unto it. Says one Lazarist,

> *But for you, my dear listeners, "you who would proceed without consulting divine will, you would not receive such grace, and without it, you would do nothing that you should, and you would most certainly damn yourselves: This is the pure doctrine of the Church Fathers.*
>
> *"If this is true for all the stations of life, who can doubt that it is especially true of marriage, and for two reasons? (1) marriage is a difficult, dark, and tangled undertaking, and (2), this undertaking has consequences of the utmost importance for time and eternity."*[131]

The dissuasive side of the ecclesiastical discourse on marriage is thus made manifest. Did it cause impotence in some people, by disturbing the psychic state of anxious and scrupulous newlyweds through the fear of damnation? I have already posed this question in *La Peur en Occident.*[132]

The preachers of the Age of Reason unanimously advise against premarital relations. They desire that fiancés should never be left alone together. In short, they deny fiancés the chance to seriously know each other before their wedding day. Nevertheless, they deplore marriages between strangers: "In such cases, you would not know the spirit, character, and qualities of your partner until after your vows had been made, and when they could not be retracted."[133] The reality thus arrives too late:

> . . . *Wait a short while, let the marriage go on, and you shall see that this young woman [she is always the first to be singled out] only had the appearance of piety and sweetness; you shall see that this sham of a maiden has become a most truly malicious woman; you shall see that this young man, who seemed the most humble and submissive of slaves, has become a rude and insolent master; he was thought to be sober, but he is debauched; he was thought to be chaste, but he is adulterous.*[134]

Such is certain proof that marriage is "a dark and tangled business." It therefore requires the light of divine grace.

Since marriage conceals so many "obstacles," so many "dangers, hazards, and temptations," what "a perilous step it is to marry without vocation!"[135] "Let us deplore," Girard says,

> *the blindness of so many people who become married without vocation or preparation. Indeed, is it not astounding, the way that people get married every day? Can this be? When it is a question of entering the priesthood or embracing ecclesiastical life, one must go through numerous tests, entire years in the seminary, or of being a novice, even though these callings procure great succour and opportunities for salvation; but when it comes to marriage, this most dangerous situation, so filled with cares and sorrows, so exposed to the most dangerous temptations [note the repitition of this adjective], people proceed without caution, reflection, or preparation.*[136]

The priest then asks if all those who marry without vocation will be damned. "I do not say that their damnation is certain," he answers himself, "for I would be speaking against Holy Scripture, which says that one may reform a wicked calling, and which exhorts one to do so through sincere penitence. But I daresay that doing so requires strong and extraordinary grace, which God only gives rarely to those who go against His divine plans . . . Therefore beware, you who are still free, of entangling yourselves in such a dangerous state as that of marriage."[137] Was it wrong to speak of "dissuasion"? How could one know if God would wish one to marry, and with whom? For, Chevassu specifies, "it is not enough to be called to the state of marriage in general, but the marriage proposed between the two spouses must be made in heaven before it is contracted on earth."[138] One will know God's will through fasting, almsgiving, taking communion, consulting "a wise director," and obtaining the consent of the father and mother (and only if these latter do not make themselves "the masters and arbiters of their children according to their own interest, caprice, and folly").[139] Moreover, if God destines you for marriage, you must choose someone who agrees with you in age, humor, and condition, but without either money or carnal pleasure in mind. Yet what does one see? "It is clearly visible," Chevassu opines, "that the time's plague infects nearly everyone with precisely the opposite feelings: most people are led only by blind passions of self-interest, ambition, or impurity."[140]

Stressing the vocation of marriage, preachers also stressed the danger of mixed assemblies, as well as the necessary austerity of betrothal parties, which evidently were rarely austere. Lambert, whose main targets were "countryfolk," considers

> *mixed gatherings to be dangerous [again this adjective], because human weakness is so great that one runs great risk in getting close to things that are only too strong*

in lighting a flame, or arousing desire. A wise and modest maiden will not be found among young men; a young man of piety, fearing he may compromise his virtue, will regard the company of young women as very dangerous . . . Therefore one must assiduously avoid dances and parties, where people of the opposite sex poison each other. Upstanding and Christian parents will never allow, under any pretext, their children to be exposed to such great dangers.[141]

These dangers are even greater if the young couples take those very liberties that the priests and missionaries so vehemently denounce. "At this crucial time of life," cries one Lazarist preacher, "such hussies, whose dress and affectations reek with impurity! . . . Such immodest acts! Such criminal intimacy! Such dirty thoughts and filthy desires wantonly cramming the imagination!" Addressing parents, the missionary reminds them of their responsibilities: "Do you forget that there is no time less appropriate for allowing the two sexes to mingle than at these dangerous occasions? . . . Just wait . . . to see your children suffer a thousand disgraces and a thousand miseries, which will be the just punishment for their sins."[142] It may be guessed that audiences did not wholeheartedly accept such tirades. Some sermons yield evidence of objections that reached the preachers' ears. For example: Many couples who have committed "these sins before their marriage lead a good and happy life together, and on the contrary, many of those whose preparations for marriage were wise and Christian, live together like demons."[143] The Lazarist unhesitatingly responds that the former will receive their punishment in the next world and that the latter must not have had the proper vocation.[144]

The priests therefore continue repeating to fiancées that they must "avoid every kind of liberty contrary to Christian decorum and propriety."[145] Loriot is even more insistent than Chevassu, the author of the preceding advice: "If betrothed or affianced couples live together, they must do so with the greatest self-control, or far better yet, they should talk to each other as little as possible [but how then would they get to know each other?], and never by themselves. They must know that they have no more right than they did before to take the least liberty, and that a thousand indecencies arise from the criminal liberties that are only too often taken by fiancés."[146] Girard also deplores what goes on between betrothals and weddings: "They have been advised not to become overfamiliar with each other; they have been forbidden to visit each other; they have been shown that lewd offenses are capable of causing their damnation."[147] Clearly, however, the church was preaching in a desert. One illicit visit would lead to another, and so on. Bridaine analyzes this process of the decline into iniquity:

Under the pretext that they must someday be wed, or perhaps that they are already engaged, they see each other, at the beginning, with modesty; then they have little private interviews; finally, they spend rendezvous where nothing illicit occurs; they begin to like each other, and their meetings become more frequent; by means of constantly seeing each other, their mutual inclination and pleasure grows still more; they think of each other night and day, freely and willingly talk of each other, and can only part from each other with difficulty; whence are born criminal thoughts, filthy desires; such thought burns more and more; when they cannot speak, they make signs, and trade glances, everywhere, even inside the church; and when they can speak together, they say tender and affectionate things; they then proceed to phrases and suggestions that are an affront to decency; they spend two, three hours at night together; they allow themselves to touch and kiss each other; . . . soon they take the final liberties . . . What abomination! What scandal! And they wallow

> *without remorse in this wicked and shameful state for weeks, months, and entire years. Parents see it, they know it, applaud it, lend their house, give them support . . . My God! Did you not create a hell in the center of the earth? And why have you not ordered it to open and swallow up so many wicked and low-minded fathers and mothers who every day send the children you have given them to perdition and damnation!*[148]

Granted, this overdone admonition was spoken by an orator who thought damnation easy. Nonetheless, it clarifies more than Bridaine's own mental universe, since it echoes a suspicious and widely held ecclesiastical view of love: to be amorous is dangerous. At what point should fiancés stop showing each other affection? The best solution is to keep the couples apart from each other and never leave them alone together. The reader will have noted, however, that the guilty parties "have no remorse," that these premarital relations may last "entire years," and that parents "applaud" and "lend their house" to the lovers. This was the era of late age at marriage. Did couples wait for the church ceremony before they made love? The predominant strain in preaching makes this doubtful and confirms Jean-Louis Flandrin's diagnosis of this subject.[149] It also reveals a lay understanding of sexuality that diverged from that of the priests. The future spouses who took the "final liberties" did not feel they were doing evil, and their parents did not disapprove of them. Ecclesiastical language made threats and aimed to instill guilt, but it often fell on deaf ears. All the same, the church's policy was understood. For instance, Segneri the Elder begins the first of his sermons on impurity fighting "those who dare to maintain that impurity is the least evil to which a man can stoop."[150] Further evidence is provided by the questions Leonard of Port-Maurice inserts in his *Tratatto della confessione generale*: "Examine whether you are one of those who say that impurity is the least evil a man can do . . . ; if you are one of those who like to say that God has compassion for the sin of impurity . . . ; if you distort proper meaning by calling it a weakness instead of a failing."[151]

The obsession with purity on one side and the persistence of a practice on the other explain the preachers' repeated warnings against both diurnal and nocturnal pollution; there are echoes here of the confession manuals. Louis of Granada's *Memorial de la vida cristiana* questions the penitent: "Have you fallen into some kind of pollution? If it happened in your sleep, did you not enjoy it, or rather did you not already cause it to happen?"[152] In the following century, Saint John Eudes similarly encourages confessors to question "boys and unmarried men" on this matter, asking them "whether they have not touched themselves for the sake of carnal pleasure; if they have not fallen into voluntary pollution; if in sleeping they have polluted themselves because of a prior inclination, or if they have willingly taken such pleasure upon waking."[153] The two above cross-examinations thus cast suspicion even on nocturnal "pollution." François de Toulouse makes the interrogations of the confession manuals reverberate from the height of his pulpit: "Woe betide ye who think evil thoughts, who dwell on indecent things at night, and so give yourselves evil dreams and the impurities that happen in your sleep."[154] Not surprisingly, then, the men of the church felt they had to combat a widespread evil. The Jesuit *Pédagogue chrétien* voices this feeling quite clearly and makes a consequent threat:

> *There is yet another [type of lust] that I cannot leave out, to my great regret, a most filthy and abhorred sin, whose very name horrifies me: I must speak of it, for it is, alas, so common and widespread. It is the sin of voluntary pollution,*

> *of which the apostle says, writing to the Corinthians: the lax (in other words, those who willfully pollute themselves, whether youths, maidens, married, or unmarried) shall not inherit the kingdom of God (I Cor. 6–10).*
>
> *Listen to the doctors and theologians. Cardinal Tolète* [*sic*] *teaches that this sin is the most difficult to correct, because one always has the opportunity to commit it; and so widespread that he believes that the greater part of those who go to hell are damned for this sin.*
>
> *Thomas de Cantimpré is of the same mind. Jean Benedicti in his Somme, regarding the Sixth Commandment, writes . . . that those who practice this sin as many years as lived Our Lord Jesus Christ, in other words thirty-three, are incurable and have almost no hope for salvation, unless God relieves and converts them through rare, marvelous, and extraordinary grace.*[155]

The Lazarist sermon on impurity lists three sins against nature: masturbation, sodomy, and bestiality, and says of the first: "This sin is only too common. Alas, what is it? It occurs when a man has no other witness than God and his conscience, and excites himself to filthy and sterile pleasure through the detestable touching of his own body: a disordered passion that even the animals [so the preacher believes] are not capable of possessing."[156] Beurrier does not fear being challenged by his audience when he states: "It is rare to find truly continent Christians, and even rarer to find truly innocent virgins."[157] Lambert warns the poor and peasants against "secret lewd acts, which are loathsome in God's sight, who sees them all, is offended by them, and never fails to punish them most severely."[158] Finally, Girard groups under the same heading and condemnation "indecent songs and speeches, whether said or heard, shameful insinuations and touches, criminal actions committed with oneself or with different persons of either sex . . . or with other things, that I dare not name: O my Lord! What an abyss of horror."[159] These citations, which would be easy to multiply, clearly refute the thesis that identifies the repression of masturbation as an eighteenth-century novelty, whose impetus came from the medical world.[160]

Taking an extremely severe view of human sexuality, the teaching church believed that most Christians married only for reasons of greed or sensuality and did not respect necessary chastity. De Toulouse declares: "It is certain that most men who marry do so for this reason [to please their senses],"[161] and Saint John Eudes exhorts the missionaries of his order to ask spouses whether they "did not enter into marriage more for carnality or avarice than for the reasons laid down by God."[162] Such a question raises a disturbing ambiguity: Do not those who marry to overcome concupiscence—supposedly a permissible reason—do so "for reasons of carnality"? Marital relations would thus allow for a countless number of possible sins! San Bernardino identifies three main and "deadly" ones: "Unchecked affection" for one's spouse, "excessive use," and "spiritual dissipation," which makes one forget God through sensual pleasure.[163] During the reign of Louis XIV, this last point is vividly brought home by the blind missionary, Father Lejeune: "As soon as there is the least attachment to whatsoever creature, there is foulness, and God is displeased."[164]

Within San Bernardino's general scheme, there clearly enters the question of knowing whether the married couple has not illicitly tried to avoid childbirth. Explicit or not, this question lies at the heart of every sermon aimed at spouses. "Do married couples fulfill their marital duty?" asks Louis of Granada. "Or do they swerve from its purpose? Do they act according to nature? Or should they reproach themselves for some pollution committed beyond the use of their duty?"[165] Saint John Eudes's confessors also had to ask the same question of wives and husbands:

"[Have they practiced] excessive liberties, outrages, and disorders, which constitute venial and sometimes even deadly sins, namely when these things are the cause of pollution or when they prevent childbirth."[166]

Following several church fathers, these later ecclesiastics thus associated excessive love with blameworthy conduct. In this regard, a Lazarist missionary invokes the authority of Saint Ambrose and Saint Augustine, "against Julian, that wretched bishop who fell into Pelagian heresy, and who said that everything was permissible in marriage." The orator agrees with these two fathers that

> *he who abandons himself without either shame or restraint to his passion becomes a sort of adulterer, which happens whenever he does not fulfill his conjugal duty according to God's intentions and commits certain crimes that Scripture calls detestable [an allusion to Onan, Gen. 38:10]. In a word, one sins in this way when one lacks wisdom and decency: there may be debauchery of manners, indecency of speech, irreverence of daily activity . . .*[167]

Bridaine makes the conclusion to this analysis, and in doing so speaks for the entire range of Catholic preachers of his age:

> *Not all things are permitted, not all things are permitted, remember it well, and never forget it. Many horrid and hateful sins are daily committed in marriage: and you should tremble that an infinite number of Christians are daily damned for having committed them. It would not please God . . . that I speak of them in detail . . . I send you to your confessors, to your consciences: listen to them well, do not stifle your remorse [but was there "remorse"?], and you will no doubt be reproached for crimes of which you are only too guilty.*[168]

I have stressed this ecclesiastical campaign against impurity for two main reasons. First, as was said above, the preoccupation with sexuality was a growing feature of the teaching church's discourse. Significantly, Saint John Eudes's *Le Bon confesseur* devotes twenty-two passages (40 percent) to interrogations on the Sixth and Ninth commandments, and only thirty-three (or 60 percent) to the other eight.[169] Likewise, a work by the Bourbon Restoration missionary Father B. L. Enfantin treats of the "three most deadly sins" and devotes 172 pages (29 percent) to pride, 166 (27 percent) to avarice, and 264 (44 percent) to lust.[170] My main objective, however, is not so much to demonstrate the growing fear of sex as to emphasize the diffusion, through masses, of an anthropology that by its very definition could not oversee the daily life of ordinary people. San Bernardino, repeating Cardinal Lotario, states: ". . . For there to be conception, carnal union can never transpire without the itching of the flesh, the fever of desire, the infection of lust. Man is born in his parents' sin . . . O weighty necessity: before sinning we are forced to sin . . ."[171] The same rejection of the flesh inspires Beurrier when, discussing "the enormity of the crime of lewdness among Christians," he uses these highly revealing analogies: "Our bodies resemble glasses that break when they touch one another, and fruits that lose their blossom and beauty as soon as they are handled."[172]

CHAPTER 16

The Ascetic Model

"NOTHING SO PLEASES GOD AS A THIN BODY"

The distrust of sexuality involved several converging ethical values and attitudes: the Judaic concern with ritual purity, the rejection of the body by Neoplatonic pessimism, and the mistrust of worldly attachments common to Stoicism and the Book of Wisdom.[1] These three ancient traditions thus also involve the discourse of the *contemptus mundi*, which in fact had adopted, accumulated, and propagated them. The monastic model that then emerged was gradually imposed on the clergy, and later—with inevitable modifications—on laypeople as well. Chapters 1 and 2 traced this model's diffusion from monasteries and convents to educated secular circles.[2] The present chapter will go still further, arguing that preachers presented the *contemptus mundi* to the masses as Gospel truth and that they most frequently identified the world we live in as the realm of Satan.

San Bernardino's Latin writings contain at least six sermons against this world (*De Contemptu mundi, De Miseria conditionis humanae, De Vilitate hominis, De Mundi amore, De Adversitate mundi, De Calamitate et miseriis humanae vitae*).[3] True, this orator lived during the heyday of Cardinal Lothair's *De contemptu mundi*, when the mendicant orders were also spreading the monastically inspired iconography of the macabre. It is something of a surprise, however, to find Jean-Pierre Camus, in the early seventeenth century, also devoting six urgently phrased Sunday sermons to the same theme ("The ebbs and flows of the world"; "The blindness of the world"; "Against the world"; "Of not serving two masters"; "The goodness of affliction"; "Of fleeing the world").[4] This preponderance within a group of Sunday sermons is exceptional. On the other hand, seventeenth- and eighteenth-century priests frequently spent one or two entire sermons a year on the miseries of clinging to the things of this world. La Font,[5] Hébert,[6] Symon,[7] and Girard[8] all address this theme at least once.

These figures, however, are deceiving. In practice, the faithful often heard lectures on "the contempt for this world" far more than once a year. For this subject intersected with many others that were addressed in the pulpit: "the business of salvation," afflictions, the praise of chastity and virginity, penitence, death, judgment, and beatitude. Whether implicitly or explicitly, the *contemptus mundi* was omnipresent in ecclesiastical discourse. It is the primary theme of sixteen, or 10 percent, of Grignion de Montfort's 164 hymns.[9] Moreover, it shows up in at least another ten of the saint's verse compositions.[10] Similarly, the Rennes *Recueil des cantiques* (1746) contains thirty-seven entire hymns (9 percent) on the contempt for this world out of a total 401. Again, the theme recurs in seventy-one hymns on the conversion of the sinner and in eight others that exalt "the blessings of solitude."[11]

This long survival of endlessly repeated laments on deceptive beauty, the sinful world, ephemeral life, and the instability of all things that suffer time's strict law might seem unlikely. Nonetheless, certain seventeenth- and eighteenth-century Czech hymns, infinitely superior to de Montfort's, convey the undeniable poetic wealth of a subject that in Baroque Bohemia was enjoying a new golden age, at the same time that literary Europe proclaimed "life is a dream." Czech priests skillfully and sincerely exploited the resources of a topos that directly connected with melancholy, evanescent nature, mysticism, and the macabre. Despite their supposed optimism, the Jesuits joined in this evocation of the *contemptus mundi*. One of them, Steyer, included the following lines in his highly popular collection of religious songs, the *Kancional cesky* (1683):

Like as the wild winds blow from all sides,
Waging rabid war against each other,
Scattering ravaged leaves before them,
So do the world's delights pass quickly on!

Put more faith in the drift of fleeting clouds,
The sea's cruel impetuous waves,
Fluttering birds, ephemeral servants,
Than in the wretched world and its devices.[12]

Another Jesuit poet, Bridel, sings in a similar vein:

Land, wine, flowers, beauty—
Are they stable? No, not in the
least.
The land dies, withers like a leaf;
Love rather that which is to be
loved.

Love God, ye men here below,
Love that which never dies,
Love and pleasure are in Him
And all things else shall surely
die.

Ah, who is there shall lend to me
The wings of a sweet and humble
dove,
To fly unto eternal life?
I wish no more to stay on earth.[13]

The priest Bozan (d. 1716), author of the *The Nightingale of Paradise*, was in contrast protected by a resolute adversary of the Jesuits. He echoes them, however, in expressing the dying man's grief ("I bid thee farewell, frail stars . . . / I bid thee farewell, lovely orchards . . ."), and he renews the fifteenth-century spirit of the macabre:

Less than a year after burial,
The body is already all undone.
Something else lies within the coffin:
A handful of dust and rotting bones.

Where be the lungs, the intestines,
The heart, the eyes? Where be these cheeks?
Consumed, decayed, like bits of chaff
They vanish into nothing.[14]

Sin is the cause of the body's decay. Ever since the Original Sin that put an end to the golden age, both the body and the earth have been the targets of divine condemnation. This tendency to link Original Sin with the myth of the earthly paradise led to presenting the Christian public with an "antinatural" discourse and a model of sanctity that devalued human life. To his contemporaries, Charles de Blois (d. 1361), the epitome of the canonized layperson, seemed to be a priest who had missed his calling. He once declared: "If I had not had a wife and children, I would have gladly entered the Carthusian Order."[15] This husband was reluctant to pay his conjugal debt. In the eighteenth century, Girard, following Saint Paul, likewise instructs his male parishioners to live, if they "have wives . . . as though they had none."[16] However, he leaves out Paul's essential preceding phrase: "The time is short." In fact, the entire Christian discourse on the *contemptus mundi* hinged on an eschatological vision. It began amid the certainty of an imminent Apocalypse . . . which failed to happen.

The anathema cast on life by the most common preaching came across in such phrases as "miserable life" (Bourée[17]) and "accursed world" (La Font, Hébert, Grignion de Montfort[18]). A Lasallian hymn advises, "to obey God, renounce nature."[19] Hébert assures his Versailles audience that "you must detach yourselves from worldly things, neglect your wretched bodies and avoid treating them softly, refrain from indulging yourselves, and finally you must not let the fear of losing feeble health and transitory life keep you from fulfilling all the duties and obligations of a Christian."[20] Montargon repeats Ecclesiastes 7:1, "the day of death [is better] than the day of one's birth" and gives this formal warning:

Man carries within him the most dangerous of his enemies . . . O wretched man! The heir to the punishment of our first father, who then shall comfort your heart, torn apart by this internal warfare? Follow Our Lord's example, and hate your body; if you love it, strive to lose it, says Holy Scripture, in order to save it; if you wish to make peace with it, always go armed, always wage war against it; treat it like a slave, or soon you yourself shall be its unhappy slave.[21]

An eighteenth-century hymn "against the world" sung by the people of Rennes (but also by inhabitants of other French towns) features the assertion: "This body of decay deserves nothing but contempt."[22] A stanza from another hymn, on "chastity," declares:

Your body is a rebel
Which must be harshly treated.
With holy zeal forever

Arm yourself against it.
No one can be faithful
If he lives a life of ease.[23]

It is worth repeating Robert Bultot's apt description of this religious model as an "angelic anthropology."[24] This was indeed the case. San Bernardino and François de Toulouse both agree that God created mankind only in order to fill the seats left vacant by the rebel angels.[25] This widely held opinion of the teaching church explains the repeated praise of virginity and chastity. These states of being anticipate celestial life, when the elect shall live as angels. Saint Francis de Sales affirms that "chastity is the lily of all virtues; it makes men almost equal to the angels."[26] The humanistic Camus teaches the people of Belley that "just as nothing makes us more beastly than to always think of our appetites, so nothing makes us more angelic than forgetting them . . . The more something is removed from earthliness, the more is it perfect."[27] There was thus a shift from an appropriate concern with "the beast" and "the belly" to an upside-down anthropology that devalued man and exalted angels.

In a sermon on virginity, de Toulouse explains that Adam, having sinned and desiring heirs, "lay with his wife and lost that purity that made him like to the angels."[28] In other words, and strictly speaking, Adam remained "pure" until he slept with Eve, despite his disobedience. Loriot, also lecturing on virginity, first plays devil's advocate and wonders "whether it is a praiseworthy desire, or whether it is presumptuous boldness, to presume to live on earth as the angels do in heaven; to desire, so to speak, to trespass on eternity, and by happy impatience to wish to be elevated from this life to the condition of the angels and God Himself." His answer is clear. "[This] anticipation of the blessings of heaven . . . however transgressive it may be, is far worthier of the greatest praise . . . Virgins . . . by their very condition, place themselves above other people, and approach the angels . . . [they] leave earth for heaven . . . , [they] come near the state of the angels and . . . even God Himself."[29]

In the same spirit, and conveying the opinion of most men of the church, Montargon also clearly defines the angelic plane to which virginity leads. By this means, thousands

have raised themselves above their own natures, and become as angels . . . What is there more glorious in the Church than this virtue, which is the mistress over nature, and precedes all other virtues, which brings the state of heaven to earth, which turns a thing of iniquity into one of purity, a mortal human into an angel, a weak and fragile creature into the most noble image of Divinity, and returns to former glory a being fallen into the base desires of an unreasoning animal?[30]

The priest Louis de Rougemont's *Traité de la virginité* (1699) is most revealing. This work recognizes that marriage is "good" and advises virgins not to "hold married people in contempt," but "to place yourselves beneath them." "A humble married woman is better than a proud virgin." These concessions do not prevent the author from stating that "in itself virginity is preferable to any kind of marriage, and marital chastity is always inferior to virginal chastity." Married couples therefore will benefit from this treatise, which will teach them "the difference between virginity and marriage." "They will not be able to note the happy, joyful, and saintly freedom of virgins, without at the same time learning to feel the heavy chains of their own condition." Rougemont explains that "virginity is preferable to divinely sanctioned marriage" because "it is above nature." It "has been on earth longer than marriage." The fathers rightly believed that "no marriage or conception is made in the state of innocence. Virgins preserve the original state of creation."[31]

Imbued with the angelic anthropology of these treatises, preachers and hymn writers constantly extolled virginity and chastity. Father Lejeune composed no less than twenty panegyrics of the Virgin Mary.[32] One hymn proclaims:

If our Great Lord gives recompense
For the efforts of charity,
If He loves obedience,
The kindness of humility,
He cherishes by preference
The virtue of chastity.[33]

For his part, de Montfort exhorts young women to enter religious life by having them sing:

O! What a hideous end
To lose virginity!
This loss one cannot mend
In all eternity . . .
Let us carefully guard our lily,
With restraint and privacy . . .[34]

Loriot grudgingly allows marriage to those who are too cowardly to maintain continence, in hopes that at least their children will remain virgins. One of his sermons on the education of children expostulates:

> *[Parents], if you no longer have the glory of virginity, at least keep the blessing of being the father or mother of virgins, by attentively watching over your children's chastity: for their innocence and saintliness may appease God for the looseness of your lives, and offer Him the submission of their souls, as payment for your infidelities. Thus they may commend your spirits to God, and take your place to serve Him after your death.*[35]

Loriot would not let go of this theme, as two sermons later he returns to it, speaking as a father on the purposes of marriage:

> *When I die, or even in my old age, I will no longer be able to praise God, thank God, or serve Him. But I will have children who will take my place. I will have children, good priests or monks, who will sing day and night the praises of God and will serve Him in divers ways. I will have daughters, holy virgins, who will preserve in them the virginal integrity that I was too afraid to keep. I will have other children who will serve the State and the people in other divers ways.*[36]

Thus there is no question of children becoming themselves the parents of a family. These quotations help to clarify the tenacious Roman admiration for the "angelic" voices of castrati. Not until Pius X, at the beginning of the twentieth century, did the Sistine Chapel stop recruiting these celestial singers.

Fifteenth- to eighteenth-century clergymen clearly had no patience with elderly people who still pursued love interests. "Alas, we only see too many," laments Camus, "of these white swans who pull Venus' chariot, too many greybeards addicted to indecency, who are thus wicked and pernicious examples for our youth. O ye old stallions, can ye not, like Socrates, thank your years for having kindly delivered you from the fires of sensuality?"[37] Girard, referring to "what the chaste Suzanne went through," exclaims: "How many people hide the dark and detested flame of lust beneath their white hairs! . . . How many foolish old men, like those who assailed Suzanne . . . give themselves over, with final fury, to the greatest excesses of impurity."[38]

This astonishment—accompanied by curses—with persistent lust helps to demonstrate the preachers' constant attitude toward second marriages, though they more often targeted widows rather than widowers. To be sure, they never failed to mention that the church did accept remarriage: It is better to marry than to "burn." Once they have made this concession, these orators follow San Bernardino[39] in striving to persuade widows to retire from the world and become in some way secular nuns, serving God and educating children. De Toulouse directs an entire page of a sermon on virginity toward discouraging widows from remarrying.[40] Montargon, who obviously knew nothing of maternal feeling, gave a sermon "for the entire class of widows" in which he notably says:

> *Of what do mothers think when they desire to have children? Their needs interest heaven, but they perhaps also have some interest in their perdition. They want to have hostages, whom they will no doubt yield up to death, babies by whom they may suffer martyrdom; they desire something whose chances of survival are slim, and livelihood uncertain; they desire a series of vexations, whether they leave their children, or their children leave them.*[41]

A fine example of the antinatural discourse, which concludes: "The disorders that commonly reign over married couples are pressing reasons for discouraging widows from remarrying."[42] Clearly the model widows for the church were Jeanne de Chantal and Mary of the Incarnation, who entered the convent despite the tears of their children.[43]

At the very least, widows should leave the world behind. A lecture by Chevassu "on marriage and the state of widows" explains:

> *Although the state of widows is inferior to that of virgins, it is nonetheless certain that the honor and desert of this state surpass those of married people. A widow may remarry, says the apostle, but if she remains a widow, I judge she will be happier:* Beatior autem erit, si sic permanserit *(I Cor. 7:40). For widows have greater means and ability to work for their salvation. A married person has a divided heart; for it is quite difficult to be occupied with the things of the world and to please one's spouse, without dividing one's heart between God and nature. But they who live chaste lives have full liberty to occupy themselves only with God and their salvation (I Cor. 7:34) . . .*
>
> *You have lost your husband; you have lost your wife. What course should you take? That of retreat. While you lived together, union and society were your lot; now that death has broken this commerce, solitude is the lot of the surviving spouse. Death has stolen the husband from the wife's bosom; he is no longer in her company. What to do after such a sad separation? Remain within her family and with her children . . . preserve her widow's chastity; to this effect keep far from worldly society, and profane amusements, games, dances, festivals, etc. For a widow who lives amid soft pleasures is dead in the sight of God, however alive she may seem to men:* Nam quae in deliciis est, vivens mortua est *(I Tim. 5:6).*

With regard to the above exhortation, it is worth referring to the relevant Pauline text. The Apostle of the Gentiles asks Timothy, "Let not a widow be taken into the number under sixty years old, having been the wife of one man," and furthermore adds: "I will, therefore, that the younger woman marry, bear children, rule the house, give no occasion to the adversary to speak reproachfully" (I Tim. 5:9 and 14). As for Chevassu's two citations of I Corinthians, they are taken from a markedly eschatological letter ("The time is short"). These preachers lacked any trace of such exegetical concern, agreeing with Girard that "second marriages are not an evil. However, they commonly allow for such great abuses that one may truly say that God more often curses than blesses them."[44] Furthermore, "what can one say . . . of marriages between people who should only be thinking of the grave!" Finally,

> *I am amazed to see people, who for so long have experienced all that is most harsh and unpleasant about this state [of marriage]; husbands who have endured the bizarre humors of a wife; wives who have been treated in the most brutish way, and nonetheless forget all that, and think of it as a dream; forget their children; give up their tranquility, and risk their salvation, to expose themselves to the dangers and hindrances of a second marriage. Is it not a great yet all too common folly?*[45]

Girard and his colleagues' bewilderment should be taken seriously: They were confronting situations they simply did not understand. On the subject of sexuality, there was a misunderstanding and perhaps a wide moat between them and their audience.

Neither did they understand the beauty of the human body, at once a fleeting illusion and a trap laid by Satan. In *Le Pédaqoque chrétien*, Philippe d'Outreman attempts to console ugly and deformed women. To be loved for one's beauty, he says to one of them, is to be loved not for one's self but

> *for one's flesh, just as the boar is loved by the hunter and the horse by its master . . . ; those who would pursue and make love to you for your beauty love only their own pleasure, and would pursue it in your flesh, seeking neither you yourself nor your happiness, not caring that you would be eternally buried, body and soul, in hell, thereby making your mortal body their unsuspecting prey.*[46]

Extending the classic tradition of the *contemptus mundi*, the Jesuit of Valenciennes thus uses a macabre reminder to protect against the temptation of beauty. He then cites Ovid and Seneca to prove that "beauty and chastity have an eternal quarrel," that beauty brings the tyranny of the passions, that it is a "bait to perdition" and a siren "that has lured many to make a shipwreck of their honor and salvation."[47] De Toulouse resumes the same arguments in a sermon especially concerned with "the tomb of beauty." He teaches that "we must scorn beauty, because for all its supposed luster, imagined charms, promised satisfactions, and all the efforts to preserve it, it passes like smoke and shadows . . . It is vain . . . It is neither real nor stable." Finally, "it is fatal to those who behold it, because it gives birth to unclean thoughts and wicked desires."[48]

This excommunication of beauty lies at the antipodes of Renaissance Neoplatonism, which saw beauty as the image of God and a beautiful body as the sign of a beautiful soul. In contrast, the Jesuit and Capuchin's combined rationale expresses the double certainty that beauty is both dangerous and false. Like life itself, it is a dream. Only eternity matters. According to de Toulouse, anything ephemeral deserves "contempt."

When proposing models to the great mass of Christians, almost inevitable figures of speech irresistibly pushed bishops, priests, and missionaries toward the ascetics, or the apostles of antinature. Although some admitted that it would be hard to imitate such heroes, they could offer no other role models. In this regard, a sermon by Camus on "sobriety" is typical. "San Carlo Borromeo," he tells his listeners,

> *the marvel of prelates of our era, gradually limited himself to bread and water. O God, what can I say of the innumerable sobrieties and parsimonies of the ancient anchorites and desert fathers, like Saint Paul, Saint Anthony, Saint Hilarion, Saint Benedict, and a thousand others whose example calls more for astonishment than imitation. You can at least recognize how distant we are from the excellence of these great servants of God.*[49]

The seventeenth- and eighteenth-century church made great use of the *Vitae Patrum*, and preaching followed suit. A noteworthy text on this subject comes from an unexpected source, namely the Jesuit Fournier's famous *Hydrographie* (1643). Addressing sailors in the chapter entitled "On the devotion of seamen," the author gives them both an authentic sermon and a lovely eulogy (though perhaps somewhat removed from reality): By virtue of their trade, sailors are ascetics; they lead a retired and solitary life; they practice silence and abstinence; what better way to achieve salvation?

> *If sobriety and abstinence remove the log and put out the fire that ignites our passions and leads us into a thousand errors, your way of life is a perpetual fast; there are few people on land who would content themselves with a pound of biscuit, a little rancid water, and a piece of salt-pork, and you still remain happy when you lack even that much . . .*
>
> *Your daily sufferings surpass those of the most austere hermits, your customary beds are straw mats or hammocks. Your finest cabins are like coffins. You keep watch half the night exposed to the elements, on the bridge or on deck, amid all the rigors of heat, cold, rain, or tempest . . .*
>
> *If a life removed from the bustle of the world is necessary for having an innocent soul, and for becoming familiar with God, you are so perfectly removed that not only do you not converse with men, but not even with beasts or birds . . . In what other place are silence and obedience so well kept as on a boat? Faithfully keeping both, you will please God greatly.*[50]

The ascetic model resurfaces in a sermon by Pierre de la Font on the prodigal son. The orator contrasts this character to Saint Anthony and Saint Arsenius, "who, having renounced all the greatness of the world, condemned himself to never speaking or beholding anyone," and finally to "so many other saints made thin by fasting and other mortifications, who feared the sight and speech of a woman as a sharp and most fearful reef."[51]

Saintliness equals asceticism: This equation was an evident truth for these preachers and led them to simultaneously affirm that marriage is "saintly" (since it is a sacrament) and that saints must renounce marriage. This contradiction is immediately apparent in an All Saints' sermon given by the Jesuit Vieira:

> *Marriage being in itself so saintly, [since] Jesus elevated it to a sacrament, why then have saints abstained from it, and its consequences, such as the blessing of a*

> *large family, the pleasure of being encouraged in one's labors by the thought of working for one's children, and finally the solace of surviving through one's descendants; yes, why renounce such evident advantages?*

Having thus clearly and creditably explained the problem, Vieira solves it by referring to a necessarily antinatural model of sainthood:

> *Such a solution [as renouncing marriage] . . . will surprise only those who forget the grandeur of sainthood, and how great the desire for so great a blessing can be in those who know to appreciate it. All that pleases our nature, charms our senses, flatters our taste, ravishes our heart, the saints have trampled underfoot; in contrast, all that can mortify our senses and dearest affections, they have generously embraced; and why? Because they desired to be saints.*[52]

Montargon, however, goes even further: Everyone can practice mortification, otherwise Hell awaits us all. In a model sermon on observing Lent, he attacks "weak-hearted" Christians who refuse to fast because their "natural strength will diminish":

> *One must afflict the body to strengthen the spirit, which is never in better health than when the body is weak, says the apostle. —But fasting diminishes the strength of the body. —I wish it would do so all the more. Listen, however, to Tertullian: nothing so pleases God as a thin body; the more it is emaciated by sharp mortifications, the less will it be subject to corruption in the grave, and it will thus be resurrected all the more gloriously."*

Finally, "there is no middle ground between abstaining from the meats proscribed by the Church during this time and being condemned to ask for a single drop of water for all eternity."[53]

Two examples out of a thousand others demonstrate that these men of the church constantly had the ascetic model in mind. One is a hymn of the Brothers of the Christian Schools ("Saint John, the divine precursor / Was penitent in heart and deed; / He wore a camel-skin shirt / Ate only honey, and drank only water"[54]), the other a sermon by Réguis reprimanding his parishioners for their religious apathy:

> *Indeed, a Trappist monk, dressed in a hairshirt, sleeping on the ground, fasting all the days of his life, eating only tasteless vegetables, never leaving his solitude, speaking only to or of God, spending part of the day in prayer, the rest in digging soil or other hard labors, rising every night to sing the praises of God for hours on end, a Trappist monk, who leads the most austere and saintly life, still never stops groaning and praying: "I am a great sinner." The greatest saints have spoken the same language: all Christians who have the most piety and fervor share the same feelings and say the same things. And you, who lack both fervor and devotion, you who do nothing or almost nothing for your salvation, you who are to God as fruitless trees, useless servants, you have the temerity to say: I do no evil.*[55]

Penance is the consequence of sin. "What is a sinner?" asks Bridaine, and like Tertullian he answers: "A man born for penance and mortification . . . therefore, my brethren, since you are sinners, you must weep, you must groan, you must be afflicted."[56] Every missionary preaching book contained at least one sermon on this theme.[57] Their common argument is succinctly expressed by Saint Leonard of Port-Maurice, who started a procession of flagellants by announcing: "What a terrible choice! Either penance or hell, . . . let those who have sinned hear me well: either hell or penance!"[58]

THE REJECTION OF AMUSEMENT

The preceding threat represents the negative side of the ascetic model propounded to sinners. Its positive aspects were conveyed by the praise of retreat and refreshing solitude, where the world's sins and noise are forgotten, where one finds God, the only being who matters, far from "amusements," as Pascal called them. One of de Montfort's finest poetic achievements is a hymn "on solitude," which sings the charms of the cave of Mervent in the Vendée, a place where are heard "the sweet harmony / Of birds and echoes, / The cries of animals / But not those of impious man." Here, the woods and rocks "are wise and saintly masters. / The rocks preach constancy, / The woods fecundity, / The waters purity." The refrain would have gladdened the desert fathers: "Far from the crowd, in this hermitage / Let us hide ourselves to serve God."[59] In the Rennes *Recueil de cantiques*, eight bucolic songs likewise pay "homage to God in this solitude."[60]

Refuting oversimplifications, these excerpts reveal that the rejection of "amusement" and the praise of retreat outside the world were more than just a Jansenist preference, illustrated by Pascal's *Pensées* and the Port-Royal recluses. There was a deeper and more general attitude at work, spurred by the conviction that earthly things have no value with respect to God. A Jesuit poet, the Czech Bridel, expressed this feeling with exceptional talent. He tells God:

You are the store of honey . . .
You are the delight of gardens,
Balm, flower, greenery, paradise . . .

Why did I seek brightness
In the sun and moon?
Why did I seek my pleasures
In gall and bitter herbs,
In wine and other delights,
Dinners, good living, and
music? . . .

If I want milk, if I want cream,
Sweet-cakes and candied fruits,
I may find all things in your breast,
Coriander and sugar sweet.[61]

Catholic preaching, especially before carnival season, waged war against masks, "bacchanals," and "vulgar debauchery." It tirelessly condemned balls, parties, profane songs, theaters, cabarets, and gambling. All these amusements, in the usual sense of the term, brought with them sensual temptations, drunkenness, "swearing," waste of time and money, family disputes, and so on. A single sentence suffices to recall this constant theme of both Sunday and missionary preaching. On the other hand, it is worth extending the discussion to analyze the essential reasons for the rejection of festivity. Although Jesus did go to the wedding at Cana, it was surely because he knew that the guests would keep within the limits of proper decency. More generally, the church permitted relaxations, but only to recuperate weakened resilience. To go beyond this therapy made necessary by sin would be to prefer earth to Heaven, especially if an excessive pastime occurred on the Lord's Day.

Did one, however, have the right to laugh? Nicole's words, repeated by Bossuet and Rancé, again come to mind: "Jesus never laughed."[62] Was this remarkable assertion only the passing thought of morose, thoroughly Augustinian spirits, or did it also emerge in mainstream preaching? The answer is that it did make substantial inroads, though not without puzzling someone like Camus, who expresses his perplexity in a sermon on "the blindness of the world" and concludes by rehabilitating laughter:

> *Laughter is not a thing to be dismissed . . . it is the sugar of this life's bitterness, the sauce of honest recreation and, if we may believe philosophy, an integral quality of man.*
>
> *I know that Holy Scripture contains great maledictions against excessive and immoderate laughter, against those who laugh for worldly pleasures: Woe betide you who laugh, for you will later weep, your laughter will be mixed with sorrow. It is better to go to the house of tears than that of joy.*
>
> *I know that weeping is one of the evangelical beatitudes. I know that Our Lord cried many times, wept for Jerusalem, for Lazarus, and that nowhere does it say He laughed; and therefore if we wish to imitate this our perfect example, we must refrain from laughter and plunge ourselves in lamentation . . .*
>
> *[But I make] a great distinction between one laugh and another; for though I admit that a laugh for worldly reasons is deadly and abhorrent, I hold that to laugh for spiritual ones and in moderation, as much for inner peace . . . as for the feeling of grace and an assenting to glory, aptly shows a positive spiritual disposition, full of health and saintliness.*[63]

This moderate text thus stands well outside the discourse of the *contemptus mundi*, with which Camus himself was quite familiar. For this discourse logically led to the rejection of laughter. Vieira's "Defense of Heraclitus' Tears" is a case in point. To be fair, this "Defense" was part of a game that took place in Rome in 1674 before a group of cardinals and other prelates. Two speakers faced off in a contest, arguing for and against the laughter of Democritus. Chance determined that one Father Cataneo would praise Democritus, and thus Vieira had to plead Heraclitus' case. In contrast to his adversary's speech, the Portuguese Jesuit's apologia for tears was so persuasive that it eventually reached an international audience through several translations. Playing a game or not, Vieira did resume the countlessly repeated arguments in favor of the *contemptus mundi*. Hence his audience: He reiterated the collective belief of the majority of ecclesiastics, and no doubt of a good number of those who listened to them. He declares,

> *I concede that the ability to laugh is proper to a rational being; but I say that laughter is even more improper to reason. If laughter indicates a rational being, tears denote the use of reason. In support of this truth, which seems to me obvious, I could wish no other proof than the world; and this proof is as great as the wide world itself. Whosoever knows the world well can only weep over it; if one laughs, or if one does not weep, it is because one does not know the world.*
>
> *What is this world but the universal meeting-ground of all miseries, all suffering, all dangers, all accidents and manners of death? And beholding this great theater, this so tragic, sorrowful, and lamentable place where each kingdom, each town, each family continually comes on and off the scene, where every rising sun is a comet, every passing moment, a disaster, and every hour, every minute, a mine*

of misfortunes; yes, beholding such a sight, what man is there who would not be ready to weep? If he does not weep, he shows that he is irrational; if he laughs, he proves that brute beasts also have this ability.[64]

In other words: Man was endowed with the faculty of laughter. He sinned, however, and unhappiness burst down upon him and the world. There thus is no longer any reason for laughing. San Bernardino adopts one of Saint Jerome's phrases: "To laugh and rejoice in these times is to be not sensible but frenetic." In his *Monitoire sur la sanctification du dimanche et l'interdiction des danses publiques* (1520), Guillaume Briçonnet warns the people of Meaux that "holidays are not for the pleasure of the body, but for the salvation of the soul; not for laughter and frolic, but for weeping."[65] In the following century, Godeau teaches the people of Vence that "a true Christian takes joy in having some afflictions to suffer, because suffering is the badge of a true Christian."[66] These statements, spoken on the second Sunday after Easter, appear in a different guise the following week. The bishop then addresses the "too delicate" Christian and tells him: "You are senseless, if you seek pleasure in this world, if you think you will find it there and decide that what the world calls pleasure really is so. What greater pleasure is there than a distaste for pleasure?"[67]

Hébert, complaining of the excessively lenient education of daughters, cites Ecclesiasticus 7:24: "Hast thou daughters, keep their bodies, and show them not a pleasant countenance," and he continues:

Why do you think, my Brothers, that God advises parents not to appear merry before their daughters? To teach them how much they must inspire in them a grave, modest, and serious air, which is the chiefest ornament they can have, and which they must value infinitely more than their beauty, their wealth, their birth, and the other advantages of fortune.[68]

Can one have Christian gaiety? Camus thought so, and Saint Francis before him. When the first Franciscans arrived in England, their mirth was a source of wonder.[69] Briçonnet, Godeau, and Hébert, however, distrusted mirth, and so did Grignion de Montfort, who made potential future nuns sing:

Maidens, be wise virgins,
Flee from dances and from games
And a hundred tricks and engines
That can only light hot flames.
To drink, eat, sleep, and laugh
To us can only be great martyrdom.[70]

Indeed, the portraits of Counter-Reformation heroes such as San Carlo Borromeo and Grignion de Montfort reveal livid, emaciated faces that seem to have lost their ability to laugh.

At the beginning of his closing address for the Jubilee Year of 1750, Saint Leonard of Port-Maurice recalls that at the tomb of Lazarus there was seen crying "He who in His majestic gravity was never seen laughing."[71] Thus there were others who shared Nicole's, Rancé's, and Bossuet's opinion. Many centuries earlier, the great preacher Saint John Chrysostom had already expressed this view.[72] It was then repeated by Jonas of Orléans, Ludolph of Saxony, and Olivier Maillard, among others,[73] and was still commonly held as late as the eighteenth century. If Christ never laughed, could the devout Christian possibly imitate his or her master? Apart from "honest recreation," which then enhances one's ability to work and pray, any festive activity must be banished from the calendar. For "where there are dances, violins, and clapping of hands, there are the dark deeds of men and the perdition of women, the sorrow of angels and the rejoicing of devils." In the seventeenth century, Philippe d'Outreman revived this comment by Saint Ephrem.[74]

The Catholic Church of yesteryear taught that one could not "sway between the sacred and the profane."[75] Hyacinthe de Montargon passes this harsh judgment at the end of a homily on plays and entertainments. If Christians cannot do without such shows, what then could be a more "moving" image than "the works of the apostles, the suffering of the martyrs, their bodies crushed beneath heavy chains, their heads battered on scaffolds, their limbs torn by the cruellest tortures? What could be more tender than the chaste sighs of the pious, the tears of the repentant, and the saintly groans of so many faithful souls?"[76] The only earthly business that matters is that of salvation. It is therefore harmful to engage in any amusement that strays from this uniquely reasonable goal. To amuse one's self is, in the strongest sense of the word, "to waste one's time."

These preachers repeated time and again that the Christian must not waste his or her time: It is too precious to squander. It will soon lead into eternity. As for joy, we will know it in the afterlife, if we wish it. In our daily life, however, in this corrupt world we inhabit, all must be work, affliction, and straining toward the ultimate home. Hence the absurdity of festive revels, which are just so many victories of the devil. "Libertines" would beseech Leonard of Port-Maurice: "Do not string the bow so tightly." Poor laborers, busy the entire week washing the earth with their sweat, distracted by a thousand domestic worries, do they not have the right "to breathe for a moment on Sunday?" Must they be condemned to "willful abstinence from any sort of amusement, even honest and legitimate ones?" The Italian Franciscan responds, in a sermon given during carnival season: "Having worked for six entire days for the body, is anything more just than to work one day for the soul?" The preacher then hears the objection that it is impossible to live without a certain amount of pleasure. Saint Leonard retorts: Does not virtue have its delights? "Is there any joy more palpable than that which flows from fervent penance? What honey is sweeter than that which is gathered at the foot of the cross?" He therefore proposes the appropriate Christian Sunday:

> . . . *Spend the morning in churches, attending holy services, and just as importantly, thinking of how to assure your soul's salvation, to uproot your vices, to follow virtue, and to enact in the presence of Jesus Christ at communion various acts of piety and generous avowals of faith. After dinner, faithfully attend catechism, vespers, compline; and if you then still have the time, amuse yourself. How? In participating in carnival revels, in licentious talk and dancing, in idle schemes and drunknenness? Of course not, for all that is the plague of souls and the Catholic world. You can find no more delightful recreation than pious conversation with people of good sentiments.*"[77]

The orator then senses some disappointment in his audience. Some people are eager to ask him: ". . . If we must endure so much pain, who then will be saved? Who will be saved? Ah, my fellow Christians, you force me to sigh and show my feelings on this subject; I would rather have kept them hidden. Who will be saved? There are few, my dear listeners, yes, very few who will be saved."[78] This remarkable conclusion gives one the undeniable feeling of going around in circles: We are back at the Augustinian doctrine of the chosen few. Now, however, it assumes its full stature within early modern ecclesiastical thinking. For it becomes clear that this doctrine was linked to a monastic conception of all religious life. The model offered the faithful is an ascetic one, which does not take responsibility for the works and days of people of flesh and blood. In this life, one must strive toward angelic status, and this can be accomplished only through mortification. Anything else is a false step away from the true path. Since, however, many stumble, despair, or let themselves be "diverted," very few will be chosen for salvation.

Commenting on the Letter to the Romans ("if we have died with Christ" 6:8), Godeau expresses paradoxical thoughts that were not necessarily well understood by his Sunday listeners:

> *Christianity . . . is death itself. The essence of Christianity is death [an "old man's", of course] . . . , consider then, my brothers, that you are as dead people . . . and use this thought against all the temptations of the devil . . . The dead no longer trade with the living, they indeed are horrified by those whom they most loved. Therefore, Christians, you must have no trade or business with the people of the world . . . You must live according to the law of this land [that of Christ], which is the law of the dead.*[79]

This ambiguous emphasis on death could go a long way. Fléchier, who was not a rigorist, contrasts the Christian custom of honoring the memory of saints "on those dates when they entered heaven" with "the thoughtless vanity" of the pagans, who "would celebrate unhappy birthdays when sinning mortals enter the world to feel the infirmities of their bodies and souls.[80]

There thus is no cause to rejoice over one's arrival in this "vale of tears." Rather it is the departure that must be celebrated, especially if it leads into salvation. Godeau is amazed by the sorrow of parents who have lost their children at an early age. This premature death is in fact a lucky chance for a child who has preserved "baptismal innocence." "Happy those children who die before falling into this misery [Deadly Sin]! Happy are you, fathers and mothers, to lose them at this early age! You should thus not afflict yourselves as you die, crying, complaining, blaspheming against God, blaming His will when you lose them in the cradle or infancy. You know not what you do."[81] Did parents understand this message? Did they understand Pierre de la Font, when he spoke of Jairus's dead daughter? The preacher tells his listeners:

> *Without entirely condemning the tears that natural compassion produces on such occasions, the Son of God wished to teach us that there are fit reasons for crying. Do not deceive yourselves, says this Father [Saint John Chrysostom], all the woes, disasters, disgraces, worldly losses of this life are not worth our tears . . . Do you seek to know where you can most piously and usefully employ them? In shedding them, abundantly, with the heavy sadness of a contrite heart, on the sins which have brought death to your soul.*[82]

In the fifteenth century, Maillard had already taught that seven paths lead "to the world and sin: greed, the pursuit of pleasure, the desire for honors, the love of one's family (*amor parentum*), the neglect of God, self-ignorance, and apathy for judgment."[83] To be sure, Maillard meant excessive and uncontrolled familial love. His remarks, however, partake of a wide and long-lasting pastoral incomprehension of earthly affections.

. . . And of daily worries. As I noted above, the preachers of this period took a hard line on those with ill-gotten gains, who on the Day of Judgment would receive nothing and be forced to make restitution by the righteous Judge. If, however, a few priests encouraged and even led seditious movements, especially in seventeenth-century France,[84] it must be stressed that both sermons and hymns unvaryingly preached submission to power, no matter how oppressive. In this respect, the pastoral message was "demobilizing." A convenient explanation might be that the church delivered an ideology that in the nick of time was favorable to those in power, since it promised Paradise to the "good poor," that is, the docile underlings. The preceding analyses of the *contemptus mundi*, however, point to something deeper than this superficial explanation. Western directors of conscience, being privately convinced that earthly life was of no value with regard to eternity and that all afflictions are just punishments for sins, could do no other than encourage patience and obedience in situations of injustice. The logic of the *contemptus mundi* demanded the refusal of any sedition and, even more strongly, any revolution.

The coherence of this doctrine, which this study has striven to make clear, led Vieira, preaching at the Cathedral of Saint-Louis du Maragnan, to advise the poor—many of them black—not to envy the rich. Moreover, he gave this message amid other observations borrowed from the most classic repertoire of the macabre. The following passage comes from a sermon on the question *Quo Vadis*?:

> *Where are you [the poor] going? Is it not to the grave? Indeed. And the rich, the affluent, where are they going? To the grave as well. Ah! Rejoice therefore that you have but a small piece of bread to eat, for since the grave is the inevitable resting place of all people, you, having eaten less, will arrive there later, and will be less eaten once you are there . . . When the rich and the poor are both in the grave, will there be much difference between them? Yes, great difference, which is all to the advantage of the poor: by excessive feed, poultry is fattened to be eaten by men; by the same token, men fatten themselves, to be eaten by worms. Eat to be eaten, O, what a sad fate! . . . The bodies of the rich, being fat and fleshy, are veritable feasts for worms, while the bodies of the poor, which are but skin and bone, can only provoke these creeping feeders to abstinence.*[85]

The fat will be the first to be eaten in the tomb: a strange consolation! An even stranger assertion is that the malnourished will die later than the rich. Vieira was doubtless never hungry and was even less likely to have studied the ravages of malnutrition. Pastoral relapses into the macabre on the subject of social injustice do not, however, seem frequent during this period. On the other hand, preachers were constantly intersecting two convincing reasons: one, await the Day of Judgment, and two, suffer oppression as legitimate expiation. "If there are people," Godeau explains, "who abuse the authority of sovereigns and charge you unfair taxes, God allows it in order to enact His justice, to punish your sins and the ill use you make of your property."[86] In a homily on the same topic, Bourée even more categorically affirms:

> *Steadfast piety is inseparable from submission to legitimate authority. Neither the ruler's way of life nor religion should command our obedience, but only the will and order of God who has established them. The abuses of political power do not give you the right to rebel [an allusion to the many revolts of seventeenth-century France]; they will some day pay a terrible account, God will threaten them, and the mighty shall be tormented mightily. The part we must play is that of blind obedience, when it only works to our own benefit and we only stand to lose transitory belongings. We must generously earn merit by making earnest sacrifices to God, for no power can abduct our souls.*[87]

Discussing the Gospel statement that "No servant can serve two masters," François Hébert aims the main point of his speech at well-to-do listeners, who "sacrifice everything to money, to their business, to wealth, and to pleasures." Nevertheless, some of these ascetically inspired phrases encourage losing interest even in food: "Do not say, where shall we find something to eat."[88] In an eighteenth-century missionary hymn entitled "An exhortation for working people," there appear these "demobilizing" verses:

You who live by your labors,
Who suffer indigence,
Learn to make your ill favors
Worthy of recompense . . .

We were made for salvation,
The goal we all should plainly see.
No, it is not distressing
To be of low degree:
'Tis rather a blessing
When God makes us humble;
Too oft does temporal fortune,
Grandeur, abundance,
Make us treat eternal fortune
With naught but indifference . . .

Do not suffer to complain
Of life's arduous pain,
And harbor no envy
For those who dwell on high.[89]

De Montfort's hymns, which frequently harp on the theme of happy poverty,[90] provide the essential features of preaching aimed at the underprivileged. They promise the reversal of conditions in the afterlife. The Virgin assures:

Pray, poor ones, consumed
By endless taxes,
You will be discharged of them
Without facing trial.
Come, ye poor, ye laborers,
Ye shall have abundance.

The preacher himself proclaims to them:

Ye poor ones, tremble with joy,
Be happy, live in peace:
Ye shall amass riches
That shall never be taken from ye.[91]

Any pursuit of worldly possessions in suspect, indeed fatal:

Do you therefore seek
abundance,
An excess of the worldly?

First and last, and above
all
Seek treasures that are
eternal:

The Lord, and His justice,
His kingdom and His love;
Attain through this sacrifice,
Thy wholesome daily bread.[92]

"To be rich in this world? / O Lord, I would rather be dead!" cries the saint, speaking, it is true, for himself. Like the entire teaching of the church of his time, however, Grignion de Montfort sometimes identifies coerced poverty with voluntary poverty and sometimes urges that the one be transformed into the other. Too bad for those wicked poorfolk who fail to sanctify their condition by accepting it!:

But do not be mistaken, Brothers,
For many of the poor are damned;
Only the poor by choice
Are the poor who will be chosen.

Many of the poor, being so
perforce,
Complain of their destitution;
Only having the outer shell of
virtue,
They are the poorfolk of the devil.[93]

Hence the following conclusion, reached by a *contemptus mundi* that accepted all social injustices:

When you lack bare necessities,
Endure it joyfully,
Without saying anything
contrary
To the most perfect detachment.[94]

CHAPTER 17

The Difficulty of Obligatory Confession

SACRILEGIOUS CONFESSIONS

How the world is filled with sins and sinners of all kinds! Thanks to confession, however, pardon is always obtainable, as long as this confession is sincere. The Catholic Church was obsessed with confession, and its pastoral efforts, especially from the thirteenth century on, reflected this obsession. For example, at least five of San Bernardino's Latin sermons discuss this sacrament, as does his entire *Tractatus de confessione.*[1]

In the year 1700 the corpus of Lazarist sermons included no less than four express directives (out of fifty-five) on confession.[2] Two exceptions stand out from the generally brief chapters of the *Bouquet de la mission*: the chapter on pride (fourteen pages) and that on the sacrament of penance (twenty-nine pages).[3] Several collections of "Sunday homilies" also lay heavy stress on confession: Maillard gives at least three[4] and Camus, two.[5] On the other hand, La Font, Girard, and Réguis limit themselves to one annual lesson on the subject.[6] These figures, however, are deceptive simplifications, since most sermons on "sacrilege," "penance," and "delayed penance" include at least some mention of confession. François de Toulouse has left twenty-one sermons on penance[7]; Lejeune, twenty-seven[8] and Loriot, twenty-six.[9] Similarly, 71 out of the 401 hymns of the *Manuel des missions a l'usage du diocèse de Rennes* sing of "the conversion of the sinner,"[10] which could be achieved only through confession.

This emphasis involves a major historical trend that partially explains the success of the Reformation in the sixteenth century as well as the strength of anticlericalism in the nineteenth: public resistance to obligatory oral confession, especially when it had to be made, at least in theory, to one's all-too-familiar parish priest. Saint Vincent de Paul states that "shame prevents many of these good peasants from confessing all their sins to their priests, and thus they remain in a state of damnation."[11] The *Memoires* of Christophe Sauvageon, prior of Sennely-en-Sologne from 1676 to 1710, reveal what would often happen during confession:

> *[At confession] they almost never think of the time of their final confession, they almost never accomplish final penance, they claim to have done nothing, they accuse themselves of nothing, they laugh, they recount their misery and poverty, they make*

excuses . . . they blame their neighbor . . . , they only mutter their great sins, afraid that the priest will hear what they are, and hence they seek to deceive themselves in seeking to deceive him. Without a doubt, there are but a handful of good confessions.[12]

This account corroborates the cynical admission of a character in the *Confession Rifflart*, a farce that predates Sauvageon's *Memoires* by some two hundred years:

. . . Because my priest is deaf
I gladly seek him out
I tell him my tale, or just about,
Quickly, under my breath, and make it tall;
When I'm done, he asks me, "Is that all?"
I say "yes," and so he absolves me.
However that may be, it hasn't yet dissolved me.[13]

A text of this sort clarifies a popular notion that saw absolution as the touch of a magic wand, able to usher its beneficiary into the gates of paradise. The Roman church left no stone unturned in its quest to replace this popular formula with a sacramental practice of detailed confession, repentance, and voluntary self-correction.

We still lack a history of the actual experience of confession. Any attempt at this vast project, however, must recognize a basic psychological fact: namely, the inherent difference "between voluntary and spontaneous confession made by a troubled individual to someone whose friendly support, or even liberating pardon, he or she has requested, and obligatory confession to someone who though given the power of absolution has been imposed by ecclesiastical authority."[14] Having failed to make this distinction, the Catholic Church became embroiled in an extraordinary fight against the stubborn silence of the people. There was obvious awkwardness between the priest and his parishioners. In the mid-eighteenth century, Chevassu provides full clarification of this problem. Giving the answers to anticipated questions, he declares: "I am too familiar to my priest and the other priests of my parish: I must wait for a confessor from the outside. Waiting thus, you keep putting off your confession and, to hide the deplorable chains of a long habit you have no desire to stop, you change confessors . . . You want confessors who see but don't see, who listen but don't understand."[15]

Godeau refused to acknowledge this uneasiness of penitents before their confessors when he told his audience:

An outside confessor [for instance a visiting missionary] who knows neither you nor the bottom of your heart, except for what you have briefly revealed to him, can give you only blind and unrealistic advice; and experience shows us that those who flee their own pastor never do true penance and never reform themselves. The shame of always admitting the same sins to the same person is a curb that can restrain sinners. You cannot so easily deceive your priest as you can a stranger, nor hide from him your daily circumstances and temptations; and a stranger cannot so easily suggest the ways for avoiding these problems.[16]

At the same time, the expansion of congregations of "missionaries of the interior" proves that Godeau's argument had few contemporary adherents. These priests' main aim in visiting parishes was to obtain good confessions: All their efforts and energies were directed toward this purpose, as they would spend six hours and more each day in the confessional.[17] "Lions in the pulpit, they had to be as sweet and charming as lambs" when they listened to the penitent; if possible, they hid their faces to facilitate confessions.[18] These missionaries clearly believed that confession to a visitor, whom one might never see again, was less traumatic for the faithful than the complete admission of their most intimate secrets to a man they saw every day, yet in return did not admit his. Moreover, they took pains to specify in their first sermons that they had "the power to remit all manner of crimes, in respect to both guilt and penalty, even those that are the concern of the Pope and Holy See," and that they brought free dispensations for pledges and vows, rehabilitations of marriages, and plenary indulgence, which good confession and fervent communion could all obtain.[19]

To overcome the enormous psychological obstacles surrounding obligatory confession, preachers always stressed "the mercy of God that knows no bounds,"[20] as well as the certainty that "if we do penance we shall be saved."[21] Camus encouraged his listeners by telling them that "there is no music more melodious to God's ears than the piteous sounds of holy confession."[22] In a mid-eighteenth-century Breton sermon, the rector addresses his audience in engaging terms:

> *Come all ye parishioners of Irvillac, sinning men and women whose hearts are dry with thirst, hasten all of ye to the source of life, the fountain of grace; the gates of paradise are open, the bosom of Christ is open, come then and pay no price for milk and wine, in other words for the pardon of your sins . . . O how sweet, how pleasant, how beauteous, how charming, and how lovely it is to be invited by Jesus to wash away our sins in the fountain of life . . .*[23]

Another Breton priest undertakes a nearly word-for-word imitation of a sermon by Bourdaloue to demonstrate "the advantages of confession." He states that "they often preach to Christians of the horrible crime and dangers of a sacrilegious confession"—a noteworthy claim in itself—"but perhaps they do not adequately show them how useful a good confession can be for the reformation of their lives, and for their progress in the ways of God."[24]

With the same objective of helping the penitent make his or her difficult confession, centuries of sermons repeat that the "confessor is bound to keep a secret so inviolable that he can never reveal, either directly or indirectly, what is told him in confession,"[25] that he is thoroughly familiar with human fragility, that he is himself capable of "falling into the same excesses that he hears recounted in the confessional,"[26] and finally that "in the sacred tribunal of confession, [he] is your father, your brother, your friend, doctor, advocate, merciful judge, teacher, and pastor."[27]

These assurances of Girard are also given by many other churchmen, among them the canon-regular Jean-Baptiste Le Vray, prior of Saint-Ambroise de Melun: "By confessing your sins to a priest, you reveal them to your friend. What happiness, says Seneca, to meet loyal friends to whom you may confide your private thoughts and feelings." In addition, "you confess yourself to a sinner like yourself. Why do you fear telling him that which he might himself confess to another?"[28] Le Vray unconsciously put his finger on the great psychological difficulty of obligatory confession: One had to reveal everything about one's self to a person one had not chosen and who most often was not one's "friend." In any case, friendship is not imposed by decree. Moreover, it entails an exchange, a sharing of cares and weaknesses as well as mutual confidences. Father Rey-Mermet writes that in the Baroque era "carpenters, sculptors, and cabinet makers were more than glad to make the confessional a work of art. But not a place of dialogue!"[29] Without this open, candid dialogue, the most friendly and "tender" words of the priest in the confessional—whether "maternal" (the Lazarists)[30] or "paternal" (Girard)[31]—were liable to encounter profound silence, concealed behind a curtain of banalities and stale repetitions.

Furthermore, this silence was only increased by the official insistence on the inequality between the priest and the penitent, which cast the latter as a defendant before a judge sitting in the "tribunal." This judicial language was indeed apt and thus did not make confession any easier. The severe Pierre de la Font was not the only one to say that "the sacrament of penance is, according to the Fathers, a trial in which the penitent must be at once his own judge, prosecutor, witness, and even executioner."[32] The less rigorous Réguis nevertheless asked this question: "What is a Christian before Jesus Christ in the tribunal of penance? A criminal, who appears before his judge to accuse himself, in order to thereby obtain his absolution and grace."[33] Girard likewise confirms: "The priest in this tribunal holds the office of judge, and the penitent is at once his own prosecutor, criminal, and witness."[34]

This severity illuminates a far-reaching syndrome: The Counter-Reformation's doctrinal campaign spoke a double language, at once inviting and threatening, beckoning and forbidding. One of its most traumatic themes was that of "relapse." Who does not revert to the same sins? Godeau, however, could only threaten "with God's most extreme wrath, those sinners who always fall back into their sinning ways," and this same bishop stresses their "hateful ingratitude," their out-and-out insolence," and their "execrable treachery." "If we are so thankless as to return to sin, even after receiving God's pardon, the Host will no longer remit our sins."[35] Pursuing his own logic, Godeau then takes arms against priests who too readily give absolution.[36] With even more vehemence, the Oratorian Bourée calls these men "flesh-eating wolves" and accuses them of making "a cruel shambles of souls," since their laxity leads to damnation.[37] A Jansenist viewpoint? Perhaps. Bourée's diagnosis, however, was not an isolated one.

The Brothers of the Christian Schools' hymn "on the sacrament of penance" contains this order: "He [the sinner] must appear before the priest / Prostrate like a criminal . . ."[38] as well as the warning that "the tractable confessor / Hardly helps . . . the negligent!"[39] In fact, Jansenism comprised only a limited sector of a much wider rigorist discourse. In a *Discours pour des prêtres au sujet de la confession*, Girard warns his colleagues against excessive indulgence in granting pardons: "Is there any confessor," he says, "who does not shudder at such a thought? Where is the priest whose justified fear would not overwhelm the very fabric of his soul in awaiting the fearful judgments of the Lord, after he had given ten, perhaps a hundred thousand absolutions?"[40] This anxiety-ridden question harks back to the especially deep fears of the religious elites, while it also arises from the fears felt by the public at large.

Along with the theme of relapse, Catholic preaching emphasized the necessary humility of the penitent individual. In practice, this lesson was given to the faithful with large doses of unpleasant threats. Lambert asks, "if [sinners] cannot reveal their sins to their confessors, how will they be able to tolerate the world's wide face when, on the Day of Judgment, that which they hid from one single man will be made known unto all?"[41] The same argument recurs, in more elaborate form, in the Lazarists' model sermon on "misplaced shame": Saint Bernard cries:

> *My dear listener, why would you be ashamed to confess what you were not ashamed to do? Why do you blush at a sincere confession before God, you who know that you cannot hide yourself from His all-seeing eyes? If this wretched shame keeps you from confessing your offenses to a sinner like yourself, imagine the intolerable shame*

> *you will have to gulp down on the Day of Judgment, when these humiliating sins will be exposed to the eyes of all the world.*[42]

Although each orator brings his personal touch to the theme, banal repetition predominates: Chevassu cries,

> *What! You don't dare tell a priest what you weren't afraid to commit in the presence of God Himself, nor to confide in secret what you weren't ashamed to do in the presence of so many? . . . it's one or the other: either bring forth your sins in the tribunal of penance, or wait for God to reproach you for them through all eternity, and show them to the eyes of all the universe on the Great Day of His revelations and revenges.*[43]

The priest of Rousses then compares this irresponsible sinner to the young woman who, "having acted indecently," tries to hide her offense but is constrained to make it public knowledge through the pangs of childbirth.

"Be not ashamed to confess yourself to the priest." The above quotations repeatedly give this advice, which was also increased, surpassed, and contradicted by yet another exhortation: namely, that the penitent sinner must feel shame. Réguis complains of its frequent absence:

> *My Lord, you know it well, and we too have heard these once-a-year confessions that the false Christian regards as a torture, that he can make only with the most extreme disgust, and even then as a matter of form. It is not a criminal filled with shame and sorrow who humbles himself, who accuses himself, who seeks grace and believes himself unworthy of it; it is a man who tells his story, and tells it badly, who distorts the facts, belittles and varnishes his offenses, and forever tries to seem less guilty than he is.*[44]

Blessed shame of the sincere penitent! Le Vray recommends it to his listeners: "If it pains you to reveal your sins to a fellow sinner, you have well deserved it." The shame of penitents "removes . . . the embarrassment appointed them on the Judgment Day . . . [Their] tears extinguish the consuming flames of hell destined for sinners."[45] Therefore one must seek out shame, and priests must cultivate it. This is Bourdaloue's teaching:

> . . . *This shame that it [confession] causes you, humbles you before God; and that which humbles you before God is what you must seek in penance. What has ruined you, my brother, says Saint Chrysostom, what has been the source of your woes, is your very lack of shame . . . Therefore preachers and confessors must . . . themselves [inspire] this holy shame in those who do not already possess it.*[46]

The juridical, casuistic, and meticulous Roman church has believed that this salutary shame can spring only from a meticulous confession of faults. In contrast, the Eastern church, which places just as much importance on a humble sense of guilt before God, has never required the detailed confession that the Council of Trent[47] imposed as a sacred obligation (*de jure divino*). The *Roman Ritual* of 1614 explains:

> *To be beneficial and part of the sacrament of penance, it [confession] must be accompanied by sharp pain and deep humility, and it is* above all *necessary that*

> *it be as complete as possible, so that the penitent may distinctly tell his confessor the nature of the deadly sins he has committed since his baptism or his last confession, their number (to the best of his recollection), and the circumstances that have changed their kind and those that have substantially increased their degree of malice . . . He who would deliberately suppress a confession of any one of these things, through shame, fear, studied or careless negligence, commits a* sacrilege *that nullifies his confession and obliges him to recommence it.*[48] (My emphasis.)

This edict brings us to the heart of the drama of Roman Catholic confession, as the clergy was convinced that any incomplete confession that omitted a single Deadly Sin was a "sacrilege" and liable to cause eternal death. Especially from the fifteenth to the nineteenth century, there are innumerable texts on this theme. For San Bernardino, "the confession is not complete, when the sinner conceals some deadly offense, and therefore God will not pardon him . . . To hold a deadly sin in one's conscience is like protecting a traitor in one's house, who will deliver you to the hands of your enemies. It displeases God, it is abominable for Him to cohabit with the traitor of His friends."[49] The same saint devotes an entire sermon to *Taciturnitas*,[50] that diabolical trap which makes false penitents, like witches [my comparison], hold their tongues before the judge. Maillard also gives a Sunday sermon on *Taciturnitas* and declares: "You cannot hope that your crime will be pardoned, when you have concealed something in confession."[51]

Camus enumerates the seventeen characteristics of good confession: it must be "simple, humble, pure, pious, true, frequent, plain, discreet, honest, shameful, thorough, secret, tearful, brief, courageous, accusatory, and obedient." Regarding the fifth condition ("true"), he specifies that

> *truth is especially required [in confession], otherwise one piles burning coals on one's head, and converts judgment into wormwood, making for one's own damnation through abuse of divine mercy. It is a sacrilege that partakes of atheism to lie at this great tribunal . . . It is to deny God, the first truth of all, to thus disguise it to His face. It is to spit at heaven and have it fall back on one's nose.*[52]

Father Yvan's *Trompette du ciel* . . . confirms that "one cannot hide one's sins, since God sees and lets all other creatures see them"; "when one maliciously hides them, God takes extraordinary measures to reveal one's secret sins."[53]

Missionaries such as Loriot often spend an entire sermon discussing "the shame that hides sins in confession," and they tell stories of ghosts who rise from Hell to admit their silence about a single Deadly Sin that caused their damnation.[54] One of the Lazarists' special sermons addresses "misplaced shame," but others emphasize the necessary exactitude of confession: The preacher cries, "Ah! Such an important point, but so few perform this obligation as they should! How these sacrileges are made by Christians of every age, sex, and degree!"[55] These exclamations could be connected to almost any parish priest speaking on this question. Chevassu asks,

> *Why are this man and woman damned? At Easter they confessed themselves like the others, perhaps even more often; nevertheless, there they are in Hell, beneath the feet of the devil. Whence comes their terrible misfortune? From the wicked disposition with which they undertook the sacraments. Instead of doing penance with honest hearts, they did it with hearts full of hypocrisy, deceit, and false appearances.*[56]

How were churchmen to justify this strict obligation to tell all to the confessor? Closely following Bourdaloue, a Breton priest opposes human and divine justice. Men "punish only what they discover, but God has only punishment for what is hidden from Him." The rest of Bourdaloue's sermon (which the rector Omnes does not follow) stresses the need for "self-abasing discipline," a shame that brings salvation. On the Day of Judgment, God "will explore and penetrate the secret places of our souls." This is the

> *model that our confession should imitate . . . this confession that we make not only to God, but to a man whom we regard as His envoy; to a man who, of his own accord, may not know us, but to whom we expose all our weaknesses, all our cowardice, all our hypocrisies, all that is spoiled and corrupt in our hearts: we shall submit ourselves to listen to that which his zeal will dictate to him, to undergo all the penalties he will impose on us, and to observe all the rules of life he will prescribe us. For what is all this, if not the heroic practice of that self-abasing discipline described by Tertullian.*[57]

Bourdaloue astutely perceived that the Catholic Church proposed, at least once a year, a "heroic exercise" to its millions of adherents, one whose "model" was the confession made at the Last Judgment. Another imperative reason for complete confession to the confessor is given by a Lazarist preacher, who invokes Aquinas to affirm that "one must obtain remission for all one's sins together, because one cannot be at once God's friend and foe, acceptable and unacceptable, in grace and in sin."[58]

Therefore, watch out for incomplete confessions caused by negligent self-examination! A Lasallian hymn teaches children "to carefully examine your conscience . . . surveying the deeds and omissions of our conduct."[59] De Montfort, speaking for Jesus, asks "good children" to go "each month to confession."[60] Thus it will be harder to "conceal anything" from the confessor. To be sure, "involuntary neglect or ignorance . . . after sufficient self-examination" do not cause any guilt.[61] "Confession is not a torture session for the soul."[62] On the other hand, "you should know, my Brothers," warns a priest of the Mission, "that if it is a horrible sacrilege to willfully hide a deadly sin which one does remember, it is also one not to confess something one has forgotten through not using the necessary means for remembering it."[63] Likewise, Girard requests his parishioners to examine themselves "at length and with extraordinary exactitude." He exclaims,

> *what presumption, then, do so many sinners have when they go to the sacred tribunal of penance without hardly any preparation! How many sinners are there who, seeing a priest in the confessional, think it expedient to take the opportunity and confess themselves without prior examination? How many others there are who, instead of examining themselves, simply say their credo, recite prayers, or engage in readings that have nothing to do with the examination that must precede confession.*[64]

A historian cannot be indifferent to the repeated warnings, reprimands, and threats that the clergy addressed to the Catholic faithful. On the contrary, they clearly reveal the fact that a majority of Christians have regarded obligatory confession, with the detailed admission of offenses, as a heavy burden. The teaching church was aware of this public inertia and frequently denounced it. "Vicious modesty" impeded confession. Hence this statement by a Capuchin missionary who visited Sixt (Savoy region) in 1644:

After all these kind warnings given to the penitent during confession, to instill in them great confidence that their confessors will help them to be saved, and finally after an infinite number of means employed toward this end, there still are found sinners who, even in the missions, against confessors whom they have never seen and may never see again, commit sacrilege by hiding sins during confession, which they dare not confess from a pernicious shame of their enormity.[65]

Réguis obviously did not fear being contradicted by his parishioners when he gloomily asserted that confessions were delayed to the very end of the Easter season. He asks,

What does this mean? Do not flatter yourselves, do not blind yourselves, look at things as they are, do yourselves justice! What does all this mean? It means that if the Easter season lasted until Pentecost, I would not confess myself until Pentecost; that if Easter fell only every ten years, I would only confess myself once every ten years; that if the Church did not expressly order at least one annual confession, I would only confess myself on my deathbed.[66]

Like the rest of his colleagues in the clergy, Réguis confused Christian faith with obedience to the precept of a yearly, detailed confession of sins. This confusion had extensive ramifications. How many people, when Christendom tore itself apart, abandoned Catholicism because of the obligation of giving an "exact" confession of their sins to someone they had not chosen to consult!

The investigation must now be taken a step further, with a look at what most hindered confession. One answer to this question might be that people no doubt feared being constrained, after a stringent confession, to reconcile themselves with a former adversary or to return ill-gotten gains. Nevertheless, the main reason for willful silence in the confessional was the shame of admitting to sexually related sins. When preachers indicate the penitents' motives for recalcitrance, they generally give priority to breaches of purity. Le Vray writes, "How, this hypocrite says to herself, can I reveal my impurity to my confessor, who thinks me so chaste and reserved? In what way, says this parishioner, dare I say to my priest that I stole or retained someone else's belongings? that I sold at false weights and measures? that I loaned at interest?"[67] The same precedence of sexuality appears in a Lazarist sermon on the "fear of the confessional": The preacher opines that "we see so many people, of every sort, damned for having hidden their dirty and dishonest sins during confession. They gladly confess their minor disorders, their white lies, but do they speak of these bestialities, these incests, sodomies, adulteries, thefts, and usuries?"[68] Sauvageon also cites the difficulty of admitting sexual sins as the primary cause of his flock's horror of confession: "A youth who has abused a maiden before marriage will wait for death, and so will she, before confessing; thieves, perjurers, arsonists, and most people who have committed shameful and punishable crimes wait until the last minute to tell priests of them, claiming that it is unwise to trust anyone else."[69]

Loriot's sermons frequently refer to the case of a "lady of quality" who became a nun but never dared to confess a certain sin, by means of which she was damned. The preacher goes on to specify that this sin consisted of "an immodest act" she had committed "all alone."[70] Moreover, another of Loriot's sermons points to a subject that calls for further attention: Women more than men, he affirms, are restrained by a "vicious modesty" when trying to reveal sexual offenses during confession. He in fact says: "They usually receive the sacrament of marriage in a state of deadly sin, because they do not confess these sins [the "intimacies" and other "criminal liberties" of betrothals], especially maidens whose misplaced shame keeps them silent . . ."[71] Lejeune had already said nearly the same thing in a sermon on "the sacrament of marriage":

> *. . . the fiancée allows her fiancé sensual liberties, impure fooleries, persuading herself that since he is to be her husband, she need not say anything to the priest when she confesses herself before the wedding, and so she takes communion unworthily, being poorly confessed. She receives the sacrament of marriage in this wicked state; and how can they then have God's blessing for a marriage that they have started with three sacrileges?*[72]

One is prompted to object: Did not many women face an insurmountable obstacle in having to speak to a man of their most intimate experiences?

Thus, for a number of reasons, a large proportion of early modern Catholics evaded the obligation of making truly personal confessions. Priests were well aware of this evasion, and many would have certainly chimed in with Girard's lament to his colleagues:

> *If reason would suggest that it is a paradox to say that there is hardly any place where one less knows a man than in the tribunal [of confession], experience shows us otherwise. Indeed, where are the priests who are not often swindled there? Vanity, hypocrisy, shame, fear, regard for public opinion [in passing, note these three last terms], sometimes self-interest, and always prejudice, all these things impede the sinner who wishes to confess the state of his conscience.*[73]

Does this imply the failure of oral confession? In my opinion, there can be no doubt of it, at least at the collective level.

The obsession with "exact" confession was one of the main and most definite causes for the Roman church's use of an evangelism of fear. There was an urgent need to make the faithful understand the gravity of their silences and halfhearted confessions, which made them guilty at the "tribunal of penance." If one disguised a Deadly Sin, this voluntary omission constituted a "sacrilege," punishable by hellfire. Moreover, a tragic consequence of this system was that a bad confession marred every preceding one, even if these had been thorough and sincere, as long as the secret offense had not been admitted. Thus one would ride down an entire toboggan of "sacrileges." Lambert admonishes his audience, "behold for a moment, the fatal effects of your criminal delays. How many confessions have you made since you began to hide your sin? Just so many sacrileges!"[74] "What strange corruption and horrid blindness!" lament the priests of the Mission, speaking of those who conceal their faults during confession; "for you speak to Jesus Christ, who knows all the secret places of your heart."[75] In another sermon, they announce: "Scripture, the church councils, the Fathers and theologians all teach us that we will never obtain pardon for our deadly sins if we willfully hid some of them in the tribunal of penance, and that this concealment suffices to damn us forever."[76] The rector of Irvillac in Brittany entreats his parishioners to "make an inquisition" of their lives during the trial of penance and to there "open up their consciences." He reminds them, however, that "there are sinners, both men and women, quite blind, quite wretched, and quite miserable for having denied or hidden some sin through their shame or confusion, even though they knew that, if they did not declare their sins, they were committing sacrilege. Ah, ah, ah! Why then, poor sinning men and women, have you committed so many sacrileges?"[77]

For Chevassu, bad confession, especially when the result of "shame for sin" and "fear of the confessor," puts poison in the remedy. The sinner "finds death in that which should give him life, and his damnation in that which should work toward his vindication."[78] Réguis also attacks Christians who "every year add a sacrilege to their sins, the more they think themselves pleasing to God in fulfilling a duty [pascal confession] that religion imposes on them."[79] "Sacrilege" and "damnation": These were the keynotes of sermons devoted to confessions in which "vicious modesty" attempted to deceive God. Le Vray complains, "Behold this shame, that the devil removes from the act of sin, but gives to confession in order to keep men enslaved and take them away with him forever."[80] There was thus a direct connection between the ruling authorities' somber diagnosis of numerous ill-made confessions and the ecclesiastical belief that many are called but few are chosen.

It is no exaggeration to confirm that the primary motive for the foundation of missionary congregations (within France), as well as for the proliferation of missions, was the desire to overcome the obstacles to complete confession at the "tribunal of penance." The impetus for Saint Vincent de Paul's calling is a case in point.[81] If missionaries ceaselessly harped on the need to make a general confession, it was due to their recognition of the great number of "sacrilegious" confessions. In 1641 a Capuchin preaching in Savoy wrote to his Provincial:

> . . . *One can scarce find four or five out of a hundred commoners who do not need to make a general confession, as we know from experience. This shows us that the greatest plague and misery of our times consist in sacrilegious confessions. It is the most common cause of the damnation of Catholics, for which we beseech Divine Mercy to bring instant remedy to such a bloody, deadly slaughter of souls, which costs him so very dearly.*[82]

Although I have cited this text elsewhere,[83] I think it worthwile to quote it again, insofar as it strikingly demonstrates the convictions of the missionaries, their actual experiences, the motives of their activity, and the rationale behind their methods. Their mission was to stop, or at least diminish, the "slaughter of souls" caused by ill-made confessions. They also knew that as confessors they were far less intimidating than parish priests. "When [the Capuchins preaching in the region of Gex in 1642] would ask the penitent why they had remained so long in such enormous, incestuous, sacrilegious, and other similar sins, the latter would answer that they put no trust in other confessors"—in other words, their local priests.[84] All the same, even missionaries sometimes met with a wall of silence. Another Capuchin, who preached in the Savoy in 1644, complained of this resistance.[85] Hence the need to inspire fear. Threats abound in the collection of Lazarist sermons. Having reached the forty-sixth sermon in his sequence of fifty-five, the preacher finally mentions Paradise and, alluding to his previous homilies, he declares: "It is enough, my brethren, to have made this pulpit resound with the thunder, lightning, and swift arrows of God's justice. It is enough that I have terrified and religiously disturbed you with the rigors of His wrath; one need not always speak of death, judgment, and the pains of sin . . ."[86] Once the parenthesis on Paradise ends, however, the missionary's listeners are treated to more threats and terrors in his last nine sermons.

The reports of the Capuchins who preached in the Savoy region during the 1640s supply precious documentation of the impressive anecdotes—the descendants of the medieval *exempla*—that various missionaries recounted and of the intense emotions they aroused in their audiences through both word and gesture. Their accounts help to convey the visions, nightmares, and hallucinations of several restive penitents, who could free themselves from their anguish only through general confession. The Capuchin editor himself underlines the link between their phantasms and the terrifying as well as edifying tales told during these sermons:

> *Some others as well, who had followed us in other parishes, being asked why they were more disposed to make a good and thorough confession in a foreign parish than in their own, after so many saintly exhortations and* examples that must have struck terror in the most obstinate sinners, *they told us how they had been scared out of their wits by nocturnal visions which made them shiver with fear, leaving them half dead.*[87]

A woman from Saint-Julien who had not revealed a sin of "larceny" in confession saw in a dream "black and horrible officers of justice" who pursued her "to confine her in prison."[88] One of the "principals" of Taninges was possessed by "hate and rancor." During a mission, however, as he tossed and turned in his bed, demons suddenly entered his room, making "leaps, jumps, tumbles, and somersaults." Their leader then seemed ready to grab the sinner by his feet: He quickly invoked all the saints of paradise and was converted.[89]

A peasant of Nuz (in the Val d'Aosta) "at the mere sound of the mission" despaired over the "abominations of her life" and was "haunted" by an evil spirit who tempted her to drown herself. Happily, her husband brought her to the missionaries and she confessed herself.[90] A farmhand of Lugrin (in the Chablais district) felt himself "for days and nights on end being tormented by small visible rocks, thrown by an invisible goblin,"[91] an event that made him confess all his sins. A peasant of Normandy, during a Eudist mission in 1650, dreamed that two thousand wolves were attacking him, for each one of his sins.[92]

These cases bear comparison with the "visions" of Mexican Indians, recorded in Jesuit reports from the years 1580 to 1620. The hallucinations of these Indians directly involve the missionaries' sermons, as the visionaries certainly relived scenes and *exempla* they had heard in church, made even more palpable by audiovisual devices[93] (this technique, however, was not altogether absent from European missions, such as those of Father Maunoir in Brittany). There was a remarkable parallel of methods on either side of the Atlantic and, consequently, a similar set of reactions. The Jesuit accounts observe that during sermons the guilt-ridden Indians would burst into sighs, tears, and sobbing; they could be soothed only through confession. The same scenario was enacted in Europe.

In this respect, Abelly's writings are very sober and only incidentally mention sermons that had to be interrupted to stop "all the crying and sighing."[94] On the other hand, the Capuchins' reports are filled with observations of this kind, so much so that they appear as a topos. One highly revealing quotation will stand for the rest. Regarding the village of Massanger in the Chablais, visited by missionaries in 1642, we learn:

> *Here there had to be repeated what had been said earlier in sermons interrupted by weeping, moaning, and the clamor of these poor people, so prodigiously moved by the horror of sin, the pains of hell, and the love of God. Which meant that many people, being prevented by their sobs, sighs, and tears, could not come to the end of their confessions, sprawled out on the ground in the middle of the church, deploring their sins, with so much grief that they inspired everyone else to compassion and similar feelings, and so well that it seemed, in seeing such sights, that the time of the primitive Church had returned . . .*[95]

General confession was thus tremendously difficult! To surmount the obstacles, preachers had to create, through numerous sermons and verbal violence, an extraordinary state of excitation in their audience, to stir in them such "piercing pangs of conscience" that they were literally "beside themselves."[96] In this exceptionally intense psychological atmosphere, confession became possible and brought about great liberation. And hence the scenes recounted in contemporary chronicles: public confessions, sudden and spectacular reconciliations, restitutions of ill-gotten gains, promises to "tame the body through stringent fasting,"[97] requests for extraordinary penance, and so on.

SACRILEGIOUS CONFESSIONS AND SHAMEFUL COMMUNIONS

If one continues to withhold a serious offense, a sacrilegious confession brings the risk of leading to others and also of performing sacrilegious communions, given the obligation of the Easter sacrament. Through a series of lapses, one arrives at this supreme crime.

For centuries, preachers laid particular stress on this tragic sequence. Having cried, "How many confessions have you made since you started hiding your sin? Just so many sacrileges!" Lambert logically proceeds: "How many communions? Just so many sacrileges, to give you even more grounds than the prophet David for assuring yourself that 'mine iniquities are gone over mine head; as an heavy burden they are too heavy for me.' "[98] In a Lazarist sermon on "shameful communion," there appears this solemn warning to those who outrage God: "If, by some mischance, you allow yourself to approach the sacred table after having hidden or disguised a single deadly sin, or I should rather say, a single important circumstance that a misplaced shame caused you to omit in confession, you are guilty of this horrible boldness."[99]

"Are any of you, my dear children," asks Girard at a first communion, "a demon and a Judas, who will be abandoned for coming to eat Christ's body on this holy table, for taking communion with a crime-laden conscience, or for having hidden your sins in confession?"[100] On Passion Sunday, Chevassu discusses "sacrilege": This topic leads him to speak of "shameful communions," a "crime . . . more common than is usually thought." Will he mention the "impious" who "in cold blood . . . come to trample down the blood of the new covenant"? No, this is not his purpose. "Against those monsters, one would need lightning bolts and not instructions." He therefore aims "only at those who do not entirely confess their sins, who have no wish to correct themselves, nor to do penance."[101] The rector of Irvillac, Pierre Le Gentil de Quelern, is even more unequivocal in a lesson on confession "that can be given at any time." He states:

> *Shame, sinners, shame and embarrassment, it would have been good to have felt them in order to keep you from sinning; but since you have had, wretches, the shame of having committed sins, you must reveal them without shame. Otherwise, you will be like Judas, who took communion in the state of sin, wherewith the devil entered his heart,* post buccellam introivit in eum Satanas. *Think then and consider, sinners, what woes they have who are in this case, reflect on your unnatural hearts, tremble then, yes tremble, poor and miserable sinners, tremble at your own blindness, tremble at woes of this sort. The greatest disgrace of all disgraces, to seek to put both God and the devil within the same heart; beware then, my brothers*

> *and sisters, of bad communion, beware of denying or hiding some sin. For the greatest disgrace of all disgraces is bad communion,* post bucellam . . .[102]

This dreadful warning must indeed have moved and disturbed a great many consciences, since annual communion was mandatory, but secret offenses were not always revealed to the confessor. Therefore one became a Judas.

Nonetheless, when these sermons target ill-made confessions, they aim not only at those that hide a Deadly Sin. They also attack failure of repentance by Catholics subject to the rule of annual confession, who obey, but without any real resolution to mend their ways. They will also take communion at Easter; they will also commit the sacrilege of "shameful communion," even if they have not "hidden" their grave offenses. A Lazarist missionary, having asked his listeners whether they have "hidden or disguised a single deadly sin" before taking communion, pursues his investigation and assures them that they are guilty of "horrible boldness" if they draw near the sacred altar without having "sincerely pardoned" their enemy, or "before having returned another man's belongings or . . . restored the reputation [of their] . . . neighbor." Sacrilege again occurs if one dares "to take communion with the firm wish to return to some habitual deadly sin, or to any of these opportunities" that are sure to bring about an offense to God. The preacher elaborates:

> *If this is so, what ought we to say of these maidens and women who forever go out to these parties, to these promenades, these secret conversations, these rendezvous where they are most apt to say or to hear with pleasure things that are a grave affront to God, and yet they still take communion, wishing all the while to revert as before to these opportunities for sin, or at least without having made any definite plans for abandoning them?"* [103]

How many occasions, then, for committing sacrileges! The preacher logically concludes: "Is this crime of bad communion so rare as you perhaps have imagined?"[104] Such words speak from the center of a vast enterprise of "guiltification." Should one equate the failure to return another's property or the failure to restore a lost reputation with the act of going to parties or promenades to listen to idle talk?

In his Palm Sunday sermon, Girard distinguishes two kinds of sacrilegious communion. "The first are spiteful sacrileges, the second deceitful ones." There is "spite" when one comes to the altar in the state of Deadly Sin that has not been confessed, or after having made a knowingly incomplete confession. There is "deception," however, as well as sacrilege, if a penitent gives full confession but while knowing "that he is neither changed nor converted; while not seeking to leave either the habit or the nearest opportunity for sinning . . ." Moreover, "there are deceitful sacrileges when one comes to the altar thinking that one is good, although one actually is not." The Lyon priest's conclusion echoes that of the Lazarist missionary: ". . . My brothers, the number of sacrilegious communions is almost infinite, and nothing should give us more cause to shudder."[105]

Contrary to what one might initially think, the emphasis on "shameful communion" does not necessarily contradict the call for "frequent communion." In Montargon's *Dictionnaire apostolique*, twenty-six pages are concerned with the former and ten with the latter, and more precisely those people who "abstain from frequent communion out of false reverence, indifference, baseness, lack of time, apathy, or disgust."[106] On the other hand, on the eve of the Revolution, a pastor like Réguis, however clear he was on his congregation's indifference, also castigated "those who protest with more pride than zeal, more bitterness than charity . . . the abuses of the sacraments and sacrilegious communions."[107] This is the first step toward a new language. All the same, in the sermons I have analyzed—whether Jansenist or not—the discourse on communion is by and large intimidating, if not disheartening.

San Bernardino promises that God's justice will be "extremely severe" against "three types of men who dare to shamefully receive the body of Christ": the *curiosi*, who go beyond the limits of the faith by asking questions about the sacrament, the *praesumptuosi*, who receive communion in a state of Deadly Sin, and the *malitiosi*, "whose weakness turns them toward obstinacy (in evil)." The author again affirms that "the nature of this sacrament is to harden the hearts of those who do not receive it, or of those who receive it in a bad way."[108] Godeau recommends approaching the Host "with fear and trembling."[109] One of Father Lejeune's sermons is entitled: "The sacrifice of the Eucharist and that of the Cross oblige us to great reverence."[110] Bourée and many others speak of the "fearful mysteries" of the mass.[111] Loriot is particularly explicit on this subject: ". . . deadly sins make communion harmful, and the addition of venial sins makes it useless . . . In the apt words of Cardinal Gaetano . . . , we must receive holy communion with the same circumspection, the same reverence, and the same trembling we would have were we surrounded on all sides by drawn swords, all pointed at our throat."[112] Finally, Chevassu encourages his parishioners to receive communion "with saintly fear."[113]

These preachers repeatedly asserted that anyone who receives communion shamefully is a deicide, a new Judas and worse than the Jews. Woe betide such a criminal! "Think well, my brethren," Godeau declares, "that when you receive communion shamefully and for a second time you betray Jesus as Judas did, you condemn him as Pilate did, you crown him with thorns, you flagellate him as the soldiers did, you nail him to the cross, you pierce his side, and finally you kill him." When someone is taken to execution, the bishop again explains, it suffices to read him his sentence. "But those who shamefully receive communion eat their sentence, and receive it . . . in their stomach." Thus it "becomes mixed with every part of their body, it runs through all their veins, enters their bones and thus becomes a part of them." It therefore requires "God's exceptional mercy"[114] to retrieve them from such a false step.

Among other threats, Lambert makes the following one, which occurs frequently in sermons on sacrilegious communion: "Shameful communion is a crime that God punishes through griefs and diseases in this life. If God hastens to punish this crime in your own lifetime, how will He punish it on the terrible Day of His vengeance? You have shamefully received communion, which means that you are a true Judas, the living image of that treacherous disciple."[115] In his turn, the Lazarist missionary lashes out at wicked communicants. These people, he claims, are worse than those who stick daggers in their enemies' hearts, since they stab God Himself. Their crime is thus worse than murder. To kill a man is "only" to destroy the image of God, but to shamefully receive communion is to offend "the greatness of God Himself," it is "to attack Him every minute of the day."[116] It is thus a "greater sacrilege than that of Judas," "greater than that of the Jews who crucified Jesus."[117] The same theme recurs in a missionary hymn that simultaneously encourages communion and discourages receiving it shamefully:

Take then this nourishment
If you seek to die not.
But be sure your soul is pure
Before you try to eat of it . . .

How a sacrilege is detestable!
Great God, how his breath is deadly!

Judas, that hideous traitor
Was far less criminal.[118]

Saint Leonard of Port-Maurice laments, "How many outrages are committed each day against this divine sacrament!" He then pretends to be amazed at the patience of God . . . a patience, however, that will not last:

Why has heaven not rained down thunder and lightning against these impious wretches who dare to treat God so shamefully? How many times has the Host been thrown to the dogs, to fish, crows, on the dungheap, in the most polluted sewers, like worthless mud! How many times has it been stabbed by daggers or needles, or fouled with spittle, trampled under foot, thrown to the flames! How many unclean magicians have used it as an instrument of death, when it should be the source of life! O wondrous patience of Jesus in the sacrament of the altar! Softly, however, speak softly, for God has never failed to punish such a horrible sacrilege.[119]

The Franciscan missionary here exploits the age-old repertory of accusations, which feature both anti-Semitism and hostility to black magic. I wish, however, to call special attention to his belief that sacrileges involving communion are frequent and that they have even been committed by his listeners, when they "have laughed, gossiped, or played in the presence of the most Holy Sacrament."[120] Pastoral teaching thus laid incessant stress on "the dangers that accompany this act [of receiving communion]."[121] One of these risks is to approach the holy mysteries without being in a state of grace. Réguis tried in vain to advocate frequent communion, as he could not prevent himself from berating those who perform their Easter duty but then persist in their habitual sins. In this case, the pastor was himself the accomplice of his unhappy flock. To his more conformist than guilty parishioners he cries:

You make us assist you in your sacrileges. This ministry of life is for you a ministry of death and damnation. Good Lord! How this thought terrifies me! It troubles my spirit, tears at my heart and fills me with bitterness. To receive Easter communion and never reform one's ways: O what profanation, what shameful communion! And I myself may have contributed to this sacrilege, out of too much kindness and condescension, too much fear that I might reject you sinners.[122]

It would be a distortion to depict early modern preaching on communion as universally discouraging and threatening. On the contrary, it never failed to emphasize that the Host bestowed spiritual blessings on whoever received it with piety and repentance. The preachers, it must be recalled, were never exclusively negative. They always offered hope to those who sought to practice sanctity. At the same time, being strongly conscious of sin, they were obsessed with sacrilegious communions and convinced that these sacrileges were frequent. Hence the clergy raised their voices and turned to superlatives to dissuade the faithful from this treason. A sermon on "shameful communion" by the Breton rector Gilles-Baptiste Le Hars (eighteenth century) typifies this pattern. He expostulates that "of all the crimes, of all the horrors that are committed in the world, there is none that compares with bad communion which, according to the Fathers, is a deicide, a murdering of God, and consequently a crime whose malice and scale surpass all other sins combined." He goes on:

What would you say, Christians, about a wretch who would take the cross from the altar and trample on it out of the darkest spite, or would angrily smash a communion cup to pieces or, if you like, would pull the Host from his mouth just to stomp on it? . . . All the same, my brothers and sisters, this person would not do as much injury and outrage to Jesus Christ as he who receives communion in a state of deadly sin.

The Breton priest also says that this guilty party is a new Judas, that he "tolls the knell for Jesus," and that he throws pearls to swine.[123]

Texts of this type enlarge the field of inquiry and clarify the dramatic overtones that this period's preaching willingly gave to the reception of the Host. This dramatization is especially apparent in sermons on first communion that, although they include touches of tenderness and religious effusion, mainly tend to make labored threats and warnings. Since they were given to twelve- and thirteen-year-olds, these messages would be all the more astounding to an audience of today. I conclude this chapter with two revealing examples. The first is by Girard, and repeats to students completing their catechism the warnings given to adults on the subject of sacrilegious communion:

Are there any of you here today in this sacred place, whom Our Holy Savior might reproach in the same manner that He once reproached his treacherous disciple in the Garden of Olives, to whom He would be obliged to say from the bottom of his heart: my friend, my child, what do you come here to do? What, the first time that you come to receive Holy Communion, you come to betray me, to deliver me to the devil, to profane and defile my divine body and precious blood! What have I done to you that you would treat me this way? I have chosen you to be a plant in my heavenly garden; and the first fruit you bear is the fruit of death! I have cultivated you like a stock of my mystical vine, in other words, of my Church; and you give me wormwood and gall! I sprinkle you with my graces and my holy word; and you bring forth thorns and brambles. What is to follow, since these beginnings are so bad? If there are any of you, my dear children, who feel yourself to be in a wicked state, may he not be so bold as to approach the Lord's sacred table; but may he go home, to weep for his sins: may he dread the exterminating angel and the just punishment for such a horrible outrage.[124]

One can imagine how a child, not necessarily worse than another, having concealed a fault that was difficult to admit, would experience internal traumas after such a sermon. Would he go and rest in his bed while his comrades received their first communion? It was psychologically impossible, for he had committed "a horrible outrage," and could now dread the exterminating angel.

The other excerpt is by Loriot. In this case, the stress is no longer on the sacrilege of shameful communion but on the moral dangers that await children in their future life. The ceremony of first communion was the occasion for highly sensational speeches. The orator first exalts the courage that the Host brought to the first Christians, making them indifferent to their torments. Thus Saint Lawrence

was laid out on a burning bed, so that half of his body was slowly burned and, shedding his blood drop by drop over a brazier, his death was deferred and his torture prolonged. He saw his nerves and veins contracting, his bones growing black, his marrow melting; and amid all these agonies he did not complain, instead he resisted . . . this extreme pain and never succumbed to impatience.

Was this description of torture all that healthy? The following lines are even more dubious:

> *You are about to enter, my dear children, the age when you will meet with great temptations, and just as many fierce combats. All your enemies, I mean the devil, the flesh, and the world, will join together to lay you to waste and combine forces to engage you in perilous battles . . . The devil . . . will use your flesh that is his dear friend, and will there ignite the flames of concupiscence and the hellish braziers of sensuality, which will wreak terrible havoc, if you do not strive to put them out. The world, which is in league with him, will attack you even more fiercely than the two others; by the world I mean your relatives, friends, and all those who would lead you into sin, either by their examples or their words . . .*
>
> *But you above all, my dear daughters, you will have the most arduous attacks to undergo, there will be flatterers who will woo you, who will praise your beauty, your elegance, who will bring you presents and soften your hearts. You may even meet these friends who will openly solicit you to do evil, and will assault your chastity. Perhaps you will be so unlucky to have mothers who, instead of preserving your innocence, will make you lose it . . . So you shall face, my dear children, these harsh attacks and great combats, and you will need extraordinary courage and rare strength to resist them.*[125]

This text brings together a number of elements, which makes it both disturbed and disturbing: the exclusively negative sense given to the word "world," the obsession with impurity, the confusion of sensuality with sexuality, as though the latter were not a normal component of human nature, and the distrust children are encouraged to have of their parents, especially their mothers. Could not such a speech have given a feeling of uneasiness to young listeners and stimulated curiosity in more than one of them, curiosity that would soon be stigmatized with guilt?

In short, fear and intimidation pervaded sermons on "the bread of life."

CHAPTER 18

The Catholic Doctrinal Campaign: An Attempt at Quantification

The preceding discussion has identified and analyzed the main themes of a guilt-instilling discourse, as well as its frequent links and associations with fear. What is the place of these themes within the entire scope of preaching? A historian cannot avoid this essential question, which should allow for a reassessment of the material as well as a balanced effect of light and shadow. At the same time, one quickly realizes the difficulty of measuring the relationship between the different elements of the church's doctrinal campaign. Undeniably, quantitative analysis is necessary for this study, in order to appraise the implications of its qualitative aspects. Yet how does one arrive at an accurate estimate? One would have to supply a machine with a guide and charts for reading, and then feed it all the sermons preached over a period of fifty to one hundred years in carefully chosen regions. This machine would then analyze the words and phrases of this corpus of sermons and would classify them by their content, whether on the side of threats or of hope. Moreover, a coefficient would have to be assigned to each sermon, indicating both the extent of its oral transmission and its eventual diffusion in printed form.

These methodological exigencies serve to illustrate the wide gap between them and the approximate estimates that appear in the following pages. It is necessary not only to attempt these imperfect calculations, but also to beware their deficiencies. I can thus only refer to what the canon Ernest Sevrin wrote over thirty years ago in the conclusion of his detailed thesis on the *Missions religieuses en France sous la Restauration*: "I have presented my documentation conscientiously and in all honesty; may I then draw a conclusion? Perhaps, but an uncertain one, full of ambivalence doubts, and reservations, as befits a man who cannot flatter himself that he knows his subject in depth and who constantly perceives, behind the apparent facts, realities that escape him."[1]

First, it must be noted that the theme of death is only one of the elements of the evangelism of fear. This point inevitably evokes the diverse "preparations for death" that publishers consistently put on the market. In quantitative terms, what audience did they reach? For the seventeenth century, Henri-Jean Martin has determined an average number of 1,350 copies per edition.[2] This figure no doubt also applies for the eighteenth century. The *Apparecchio* . . . of Saint Alphonsus went through twenty-one editions in Italy between 1758 and 1796.[3] During these thirty-eight years, therefore, it would have been printed in some 28,350 copies.

Daniel Roche's calculations, which relate to 236 preparations for death sold in France between 1600 and 1800, yield the following global estimates: between 400,000 and 500,000 copies printed in the seventeenth century, between 250,000 and 400,000 during the first half of the eighteenth century, and again 250,000 or 300,000 during the second half.[4] One might be surprised by the eighteenth century continuation of comparable and even higher figures than those for the preceding century, especially since the number of new titles was steadily dropping.[5] This apparent anomaly is explained by the reissues of best-sellers, such as Crasset's treatise. It is true, however, that the curve of Parisian editions descends after 1750. On the other hand, the growing diffusion of the cheap publications of the "Bibliothèque bleue," along with the new freedom gained by provincial booksellers after 1775, maintained the output of ascetic works, as the regional centers then dipped into reserves that had previously been controlled by the Parisian monopoly.[6]

What was the place of the preparations for death within the entire economy of French printed works, as well as in regard to the French production of religious books? To reproduce Daniel Roche's findings: (1) The surviving titles represent no more than 1 percent of the total French production for the seventeenth and eighteenth centuries. "With a significant drop after 1725, when French bookstores could order more than 500 new titles per year." If one now considers the fluctuations in editions, one arrives at roughly 2 percent for the first half of the seventeenth century, 5 percent for the second, and less than 0.5 percent on the eve of the Revolution: Thus for two hundred years, a general proportion of between 1 and 2 percent of the national production. (2) Within French religious literature, the preparations for death account for 2 to 3 percent in the seventeenth century and less than 1 percent in the eighteenth, if one calculates by new titles. In terms of editions, there is an oscillation between 7 and 10 percent for the years 1600 to 1670, 3 to 5 percent for 1725 to 1775, and 5 to 10 percent for 1775 to 1790 (due to the stimulus from provincial publishing during this last period). To clarify these figures, it must be remembered that at the end of the seventeenth century, 21 percent of all French people (especially men) could sign their act of marriage, and 37 percent in the years 1786 to 1790.[7] Finally, the kingdom had 19 million inhabitants in 1700 and 27 million by 1789. Hence, even at the time of the Revolution, more than half of all French people did not have their own direct access to religious writings on death.

First and foremost, these were readings designed for priests, nuns, and monks. They appeared in the list of "good books" recommended by bishops to their clergy. Nonetheless, the authors sought to reach beyond the clerical audience. Saint Alphonsus hoped that his *Apparecchio* . . . would be useful "to preachers for preaching, and to everyone for meditation."[8] As for Father Crasset, he declares in the "preface" to his *Double Préparation* . . .:

> *There are priests in the countryside who once a month gather the local peasants into their church to recite some of these Preparations to them. This practice cannot be too highly recommended, and can only be of great benefit, for thus these poor people learn to live and die well . . .*
>
> *Once a month or even more often, fathers and mothers can also assemble their children and servants in the evening, and after having advised them to consider themselves ready to die, can read one of the Preparations, kneeling in their presence. Every individual can do the same once or several times a month in church or at home, before confession or communion.*[9]

These suggestions prompt the historian to also reach beyond the frame of individual readings and attempt a sketch of the collective audience of the discourse on death. In fact, the latter reached the public through a variety of media: masses and funerals for the dead, iconography, "spiritual exercises" performed by pious laypeople, preaching, and works such as the *Imitation*, which were not strictly speaking preparations for death. The success of the *Imitation* did not diminish in the eighteenth century: Nineteenth editions appeared in France between 1735 and 1789, and 25,000 copies were sold between 1780 and 1790.[10]

All the same, while recognizing this multiplicity of means, what place did the emphasis on death occupy within the totality of religious discourse? Philippe Ariès and Michel Vovelle both note that the "*transi*" tombs and macabre *gisants* of the fifteenth century never amounted to more than 5 percent of all mortuary monuments.[11] Statistically speaking, they were almost a marginal phenomenon. To briefly return to Daniel Roche's calculations, I would concur with him that the preparations for death supplied less than 3 percent of the titles and 5 to 7 percent of the editions of French religious publications between 1600 and 1790. The question must now be posed as to the stature of the sermon on death within the body of preaching discussed in this book. Houdry and Montargon devote less than 2 percent of their speeches and model sermons to this theme; the sum of the Sunday sermons of Camus, Symon, Girard, Chevassu, and Réguis, about 3 percent; missionary sermons (by François de Toulouse, Loriot, the Lazarists, and the *Bouquet de la mission . . .*), about 4 percent; Lenten sermons (Fontana, Delarue, Lejeune, Grignion de Montfort), in the neighborhood of 7 percent. These figures corroborate the 5 to 7 percent of preparations for death in the French religious literary output of the seventeenth and eighteenth centuries.

Have we thus been the victims of a thematic study that, by overemphasizing content, has exaggerated the importance of the evangelism of fear, for want of assessing it by evaluating its diffusion and its place within the entirety of religious discourse? One can surmise the stakes of such a question. The answer, however, soon stands out. Sermons on death were but one element of a vast ensemble of moral pedagogy. Witness the cycle of weekly mediations proposed in the eighteenth century to the Ursulines' boarding-school girls: Sunday, eternal rest; Monday, the Nativity; Tuesday, death; Wednesday, the Last Judgment; Thursday, the Passion; Friday, the Crucifixion; Saturday, "they will descend in their minds into hell, where the damned are stretched out on braziers burning with eternal fire."[12] The "evangelism of fear" emerged from an intense "guiltification," as well as an urgent call for a consciousness of pain and sorrow. I have therefore grouped under this general heading cumulative emphases:

- on the enormity and variety of sins, and on confession;
- on death, judgment, God's justice, the difficulty of salvation, the chosen few, Purgatory (as a temporary Hell), and Hell;
- on the necessity of restorative penance ("calvary or Hell"), the sufferings of Christ in His passion[13] portrayed as the result of our own personal sins, and the intermediate and necessary afflictions of restoration and sanctification;
- on the "contempt for the world," with the confusion of the two senses of the word "world," the rejection of dances, shows, parties, carnival, profane songs, and fancy dress.

Based on these four groups, I have attempted to measure the extent of fear and "guiltification" in the hymns and sermons that have provided my essential documentation, as synthesized in the following table.

The figures in the table are verified by calculations based on Migne's index,

17TH–18TH-CENTURY AUTHORS	NUMBERS OF SERMONS, ARTICLES, AND HYMNS	PREDOMINANTLY MELANCHOLIC OR GUILT-INSTILLING SERMONS	
		Number	Percent (%)
V. Houdry (*Bibliothèque des predicateurs . . .*)	Articles: 197 on morals 199 on saints and mysteries 396	102 – 102	51 – 25
H. de Montargon (*Dictionnaire apostolique*)	Articles: 64 on morals 27 on saints and mysteries 91	32 – 32	50 – 35
François de Toulouse (*Le Missionnaire apostolique . . .*)	Sermons: 158 for missions and on virtues and vices 52 for Sundays 210	108 22 130	68 42 61
P. Segneri the Elder (*Works*)	Sermons: 53 for the missions	39	73
Loriot (*Sermons sur les plus importantes matières de morale chrétienne*)	Sermons: 120 on Christian morals (missions) 18 on mysteries 138	72 2 74	60 11 53
Lazarist Sermons (edited by Jeanmaire)	Sermons: 55 for missions	31	60
Bouquet de la mission . . .	Chapters: 72	31	43
F. Fontana	Lenten sermons: 38	32	84
J. Lejeune (*Sermons*)	Lenten sermons: 62	35	56
Delarue (S.J.)	Lenten sermons: 32	18	56
L. Grignion de Montfort (*Oeuvres*)	Lenten sermons: 74 (list of subjects for Lenten sermons)	19	39

		Number	Percent (%)
J.-P. Camus (*Homélies dominicales*)	Sunday and holiday sermons: 44	15	34
P. de la Font (*Prosnes* . . .)	Sunday and holiday sermons: 52	38	73
E. Bourée (*Homélies* . . .)	Sunday and holiday sermons 52	23	44
F. Hébert (*Prosnes* . . .)	Sunday and holiday sermons: 53	32	60
J. Chevassu (*Le Missionnaire paroissial: Prônes pour tous les dimanches*)	Sunday and holiday sermons: 52	29	55
Symon (Prônes)	Sunday and holiday sermons: 52	24	46
N. Girard (*Les Petits prônes*)	Sunday and holiday sermons: 70[1]	47	67
Réguis (*La Voix du pasteur*)	Sunday and holiday sermons: 52	24	46
Brothers of the Christian Schools	Hymns: 53	12	22
Grignion de Montfort	Hymns: 164	36	21
Manuel des retraites et missions	Hymns: 373	180	48
M.V. Steyer (S.J.) (*Kancionál česky*, Czech Hymnal, 1683, 1712)	"General hymns": 132	57	43
J.J. Bozan (*Slaviček rajsky*, The Nightingale of Paradise) 1719	"General hymns": 123	28	21
A. Konias (S.J.) (*Citara Nového zákona*, The Cittern of the New Testament, 1727)	"General hymns": 63	11	19

[1]Girard, however, offers several sermons for the same Sunday.

the *Collection . . . des orateurs chrétiens.*[14] This collection includes ninety-nine volumes of all types of French sermons dating from the seventeenth to the nineteenth centuries. Four hundred twelve themes have been identified, providing 8,956 references:

	THEMES IN THE INDEX	REFERENCES IN THE SERMONS	PERCENTAGE OF REFERENCES (%)
Predominantly guilt-instilling or disturbing	264	3,428	38.3
Predominantly reassuring	90	3,119	34.8
Divided between both of the above	58	2,409	26.9
Total	412	8,956	100

By dividing the third percentage (26.9 percent) in half, one arrives at a 51.75 percent/48.25 percent ratio, which more or less agrees with the half-and-half evaluation suggested by the above-studied Sunday sermons. At the same time, some imbalances arise from Migne's index. The headings "Sin(s)-Sinners" and "Bad Conscience" account for 448 references. In contrast, "Pardon-Mercy-Redemption" only add up to 90. "Hell," "Deprivation (of grace)," "The Damned," "Damnation," "The Chosen Few," and "Judgment (the Last or individual)" consist of a total of 344 references, "Beatitude-The Blessed-Happiness-Heaven-Glory-Immortality-Paradise-The Chosen (for Salvation)" consist of only 207. Finally, Christ's Passion appears 156 times, but His Resurrection and the Easter Holiday appear only 135 times.

These estimates, however rough, do provide certain insights. At the very least, they show the shortcomings of any method that would measure the weight of the evangelism of fear only on the basis of hymns and sermons exclusively devoted to the theme of death. In fact, sermons that used excessively guilt-instilling messages as a source of intimidation far surpassed the 5 to 7 percent of seventeenth- to nineteenth-century French editions of preparations for death; this is not to discredit Daniel Roche's remarkable article, which studies only these works and does not in any way seek to accomplish the "global assessment" I am attempting.

These estimates reveal that none of the consulted collections includes less than 19 percent of sensational emphases and that most often this mark was far outstripped. Nonetheless, the under-50 percent totals deserve comment. They occur above all in the hymns. On the one hand, the faithful of yesteryear were made to sing hymns that were likely to induce trauma and guilt: A number of such compositions have been cited. On the other, the hymns generally tend toward the side of hope, confidence, and love. In this second category must be placed all the hymns by Grignion de Montfort and from Bohemia that exalt the bliss of retreats and of solitude, the positive counterpart to anathemas on the world. Elizabeth Ducreux notes that only one of some three thousand Catholic Czech hymns published between 1588 and 1764 dwells on the "infernal tortures." In addition, in the main vernacular hymnals that she has studied, the sum total of insistences on tragic and guilt-oriented themes is about 30 percent.[15] These percentages confirm those determined for the hymns of de Montfort and the Brothers of the Christian Schools, and make the 48 percent of the *Manuel des retraites et missions* exceptional. In passing, it must be observed that de Montfort's hymns (as well as his list of Lenten sermons) fall less on the side of guilt, threats, and melancholy than one might be led to believe by his above-cited complaints of the dead and severe texts for the use of preachers. Thus an even sketchy quantitative analysis adjusts the impressions given by the thematic one.

A worthwhile consideration regarding the function of hymns, which were often sung during processions and pilgrimages and include frequent praises of the saints and especially the Virgin, is the fact that they had to inspire hope and confidence. Moreover, Christmas carols naturally appear in these hymnals. All these reasons together explain the relative absence of the evangelism of fear in songs written for congregational singing: If their content had been primarily tragic, the congregations would have had trouble singing them. Furthermore, it cannot be doubted that hymns provided sustenance for the religious life of the people and that many illiterates knew them by heart, especially in Bohemia. The hymn collections thus occupy "both written and oral territory," though the latter must not be confused with "folkloric."[16]

Jean Quéniart has shown that in 1759 the shops of a single Rouen printer contained some 15,000 hymnals. He adds: "This single exact figure allows one to imagine the extent of a diffusion which for 250 years, in a few centers—such as Troyes and Rouen—located in areas of fledgling literacy, contributed to popular culture."[17] In the same article, Quéniart rightly proposes a systematic study of the content of these hymns and hypothesizes that their image of God would come across as generally more comforting and reassuring than that promulgated by official sermonizing: He thus echoes Elisabeth Ducreux's impression.

This sermonizing, however, is diverse, due not only to the individual dispositions of the orators and their respective theological camps, but also to the nature of the sermon collections themselves. The percentages of guilt-instilling, melancholic, or threatening sermons vary according to whether they pertain to preachers' encyclopedias, Sunday sermon collections, or instructions for Lent and missions. Uncontestably, Houdry's and Montargon's articles on Christian morality spend considerable time on restraint, sin, and punishment (at least 50 percent). Nevertheless, the *Bibliothèque des predicateurs* . . . and the *Dictionnaire apostolique* . . . also furnish models for sermons on the Christian mysteries and praises of the saints. This type of religious discourse moves away from fear and thus appreciably reduces its presence in these two books.

All the same, the "moral" sections of these encyclopedias were the ones most often used by priests and missionaries. In addition, the nine collections of Sunday sermons (including François de Toulouse's) analyzed here yield a figure of 52 percent for strongly guilt-instilling sermons, or ones that offer dark views of their listeners' eternal future. This 52 percent average redresses the balance between primarily soothing messages (for instance, by Camus) and primarily demoralizing ones (de la Font and Girard). The approximately fifty-fifty split between threats and encouragement accurately conveys the priests' habits of preaching. They definitely had to alarm their parishioners and occasionally give them sharp reprimands, but at the same time they had to be aware of their audiences' reactions and neither discourage nor antagonize them. Bourée speaks for the common priest in a homily for the first Advent Sunday: ". . . In this first gospel of the ecclesiastical year, the Church intends more to console the righteous through the hope of their coming deliverance than to terrify the wicked through predicting the evils that must befall them."[18]

On the other hand, Lent and the missions afforded opportunities for the more stern preachers to make hard-hitting attacks. They sought to "convert," to transform their listeners' life-styles and moral habits, and to shock them into making sincere confessions (if possible, general ones), reconciliations, and restitutions. To remove every obstacle that "regard for public opinion" placed on the road to conversion, they resorted to the weapon of intimidation. Hence the percentages of slightly less than 60 for Lent and slightly more for the missions. The abnormally low figure of 43 percent for the *Bouquet de la mission* is explained by the fact that this text was specially designed for already "converted" Catholics on religious retreat. At the other extreme beyond the 60 percent median, two Italian preachers—Fontana and Segneri the Elder—reach disturbingly high levels (84 and 73 percent), which no doubt indicate a southern European penchant for excess.

One cannot neglect the importance of missionary discourse in early modern Catholic Europe. A good deal of research is currently being undertaken on the missions that were organized in areas still loyal to Rome between the second half of the sixteenth to the middle of the twentieth century.[19] This research has produced quantitative results that help to clarify the Vatican's campaign. The career of Saint John Eudes included 117 missions; of Father Maunoir, 439 (in forty-three years), of Bridaine, 256 (also in forty-three years), in the Cévennes, Languedoc, Provence, the Comtat and Dauphiné, without counting his visits to other parts of France; and the Montfort father Pierre-François Hacquet carried out 274 in western France between 1740 and 1779. The Blessed Antonio Baldinucci (1665–1717), a Jesuit, preached 448 missions in thirty dioceses in the districts of Frascati and Viterbo. Saint Leonard of Port-Maurice (1676–1751) accomplished 344; the Jesuit Charles Maillardoz (1675–1735), 312 in Switzerland and Germany; and another Jesuit, Georges Laferer (1680–1756), 1,187 in Styria, Carinthia, and the Tyrol.

These star performances were augmented by humble and methodical team efforts. Recent research has especially shed light on the Lazarist missions. It was hitherto believed that due to the work of the indefatigable Father Maunoir, Lower Brittany was far more touched by missionary propaganda than the rest of France. François Lebrun, however, demonstrates that in fifty-six years (1645–1700), the Lazarists of Saint-Méen in the diocese of Saint-Malo gave 127 missions in eighty-six parishes of this diocese and 35 others in neighboring dioceses. Of the thirty-two seminaries founded in France by the Lazarists between 1641 and 1683, twenty-three supported teams of missionaries. The house of Montuzet in the Gironde sent out between 800 to 1,000 missions during one century, while that of Fontenay-le-Comte approximately 500 between 1699 and 1789. In Italy, the Lazarists were also intensely active: 952 missions in the papal states from 1649 to 1699, of which 79.9 percent were in Latium. Other orders that performed the same tasks attained similarly high levels. For example, the Jesuits of Jülich-Berg undertook 440 missions in the Lower Rhineland between 1690 and 1695, and the Doctrinaires visited 1,100 different French parishes during the seventeenth and eighteenth centuries. From 1751 to 1790 the priests of Beaugé were responsible for 400 missions.

Leaving behind the reports of victory and of mass confessions and communions, the actual results of these missions remain controversial. How long did such transformations last? In any case, it is certain that a vast number of Catholics between the mid-sixteenth and mid-twentieth century were exposed to terroristic sermons (for Lent, Advent, and the missions), in which threats and "guiltification" were predominant, even if words of comfort and hope, along with elaborate ceremonies, strove to offset the alarmist phrases. The canon Sevrin, in his study of French religious missions during the Bourbon Restoration, admits to his feelings on this subject: "Let us acknowledge that this preaching is founded more on fear than love."[20]

It is particularly revealing that a number of nineteenth- and twentieth-century writers have conveyed the traumatic aspects of missionary sermons. In *Lamiel*, Stendhal writes that Monsieur Le Cloud "spoke like one of Mme. Radcliffe's novels: he gave a repulsive description of hell. His menacing phrases echoed through the Gothic colonnades, for they had carefully refrained from lighting the lamps."[21] In his "Story Without a Name," Barbey d'Aurevilley presents the following dialogue between the young Lasthenie de Ferjol and the aged Agatha regarding the Capuchin Riculf, a Lenten preacher who has just departed the scene: Lasthenie: "That man put a kind of fear in me that I'd never felt before." Agatha: "He only talked of hell! Hell was forever on his lips! . . . No one's ever preached on hell so much as he. He damned us all . . ."[22] James Joyce devotes an entire section of *A Portrait of the Artist as a Young Man* to a retreat preached by a Jesuit at the Irish college of his youth. The theme is that of "the last things, death, judgment, hell and heaven":

> *The next day brought death and judgment, stirring his soul slowly from its listless despair. The faint glimmer of fear became a terror of spirit as the hoarse voice of the preacher blew death into his soul. He suffered its agony. He felt the deathchill touch the extremities and creep onward towards the heart, the film of death veiling the eyes, the bright centres of the brain extinguished one by one like lamps, the last sweat oozing upon the skin, the powerlessness of the dying limbs, the speech thickening and wandering and failing, the heart throbbing faintly and more faintly, all but vanquished, the breath, the poor breath, the poor helpless human spirit, sobbing and sighing, gurgling and rattling in the throat. No help! No help! He, he himself, his body to which he had yielded was dying. Into the grave with it! Nail it down into a wooden box, the corpse. Carry it out of the house on the shoulders of hirelings. Thrust it out of men's sight into a long hole in the ground, into the grave, to rot, to feed the mass of its creeping worms and to be devoured by scuttling plumpbellied rats.*[23]

Although this passage refers to a retreat prior to the festival of Saint Francis Xavier, it also records the missionary mode of preaching. Even weekly sermons, however, sometimes strike their listeners with the effects of an evangelism of fear. Wincenty Witos (1874–1945), the founder of the Polish Peasants' Party, writes in his "Recollections":

> . . . *Usually the ardent and voluble preacher, knowing the level of his audience's intelligence and understanding, and seeking to prove them guilty beyond the shadow of a doubt, almost every Sunday would demonstrate, in a simplistic way, that everyone there had violated many commandments and prescriptions. As these violations were serious sins, they would be punished not only on earth but would undoubtedly lead to hell. Thus the poor people would see themselves in that place, and would tremble at its description. This exaggeration would transport a great many of the more sensitive listeners into a nearly pathological trance, for the hell which awaited all sinners, portrayed in all its horror, could only cause shock and dismay. Everyone knew that the devils who reigned there would roast unhappy sinning souls through all eternity, turning them over on glowing grills after they had impaled them on skewers. The women were especially prone to sobbing, and lost heart, not only during the sermon but for the rest of the week.*
>
> *There were some reasons for this reaction. For example, the preacher would declare that the sin of theft would not be absolved so long as the stolen object was not returned; no act of penance could make up for it. Now, in the village everyone had at some time filched something from the woods without intending to return it,*

or to improve in the future, saying, "the wood, he is our grandfather, and we are his children, so we go to him."[24]

All the same, one should not judge all Sunday preaching in Catholic Europe on the basis of these few "recollections," which no doubt simplify a far more complex reality. Moreover, one cannot ignore the reassuring aspects of pastoral service, from the standpoint not only of its words but also its liturgy and songs. Nor can one neglect the churchmen's constantly announced intention to balance kindness and severity in their sermons and writings, so that in their catechesis, fear of God and trust in Him, would form "two complementary more than contradictory sides."[25] One must also take into consideration the fact that catechism, itself a component of the doctrinal campaign, greatly emphasized (and increasingly privileged) the duties of a Christian, but without speaking a language of threats. Finally, there is Marcel Bernos's double observation: (1) those who were "lions" in the pulpit proved to be "lambs" in the confessional, and (2) the overinstillation of guilt was more a product of preaching than a deliberate intention on the part of the teaching church.[26]

Given these necessary correctives, is the considerable number of guilt-oriented themes in Sunday sermons (ca. 50 percent) to be regarded as secondary? This percentage agrees with the advice of the Lazarist Pierre Collet (1693–1770) regarding the choice of a good confessor. Let him be, he recommends, "a wise and enlightened man, and let him be neither too soft nor too severe. Excess counts for nothing, but I would prefer a touch of severity to the softness that ruins all."[27] For the most part, seventeenth- to nineteenth-century preaching seems to have obeyed this guideline. Moreover, whether rightly or wrongly, listeners most likely retained sensational and gruesome passages more than calm and soothing ones. And while it is true that no matter how accusatory they were, every sermon included reassuring elements and sounded a final note of hope, it is no less certain that many sermons, even Sunday ones, whose subjects were not supposedly melodramatic (marriage, the duties of parents, respect for churches, communion) and therefore do not appear in the negative column on pages 483–485, nevertheless contain threat-laden incitements to feel guilt. Finally, the positive language of catechism was offset by the liturgy of funerals. Death was frequent in the seventeenth and eighteenth centuries, so much so that by the end of his or her lifetime, the average Catholic had spent more time in church for funerals than for the lessons of catechism. The excellent liturgist Father Gy notes that the *Roman Ritual* of 1614 reduced or suppressed the texts in the office of the dead that inspired trust in God, hope in heaven, and the peace of the soul. Conversely, extra attention was given to passages that expressed fear. The entire equilibrium of this ceremony was thus undermined.[28]

The study I have conducted of the Catholic countries dovetails with the shared observations of several historians who have noted that the Jesuits and Jansenists bandied about the accusation of excessively using the evangelism of fear: The former reprimanded the latter for depressing the faithful by insisting on the notion of the chosen few, while the latter rebuked the former for talking too much of Hell. In reality, each side—and with them most preachers—widely enlarged on these two themes, which were both attached to that of God the Supreme Judge. I think I am not deceiving myself, distorting the material, or exaggerating the percentages in concluding that during the Age of Reason (that is, the seventeenth- and eighteenth-centuries), the pastoral efforts of the Roman church, taken in their entirety as well as in their tendency to both mix and alternately stress seduction and intimidation, opted more for this latter approach.

My impression, which I have attempted to support with statistical evidence, is confirmed by the findings of the majority of researchers who, in the last few years, have addressed the same documentation. The first part of Robert Favre's outstanding book is entitled "A Religion of Death," and it ends with these words: "Christian literature [of the eighteenth century] was addressed, one might say, to the sick and the dying . . . Everything transpired as if the masters of spiritual life had decided in favor of death . . . An entire fund of spiritual energy turned its gaze on death, and became won over to the concept and practice of mortification, within the terms of an individualist vision."[29] In his study on Breton preaching at the end of the Ancien Régime, François Roudaut accepts François Lebrun's earlier opinion regarding the Anjou region: "The Church constantly used the fear of death, judgment, and hell as a pastoral instrument, and a way to keep the faithful on the straight and narrow."[30] In his edition of the selected sermons of an Angevin priest, Lebrun also confirms: "The entirety of the speeches [of the priest Marchais] . . . rests on a fundamental pessimism, aggravated by unshakeable certainty and impelled toward a religion not of joy, but of sorrow and fear."[31] At the end of his remarkable essay on *Les Hommes, L'Eglise et Dieu dans la France du XVIIIe siècle*, Jean Quéniart expresses a similar viewpoint: "Through its obsessive emphasis on the inevitable consequences of sin and on the chosen few, the severe post-Tridentine Church only offered hard or barely reassuring answers."[32] Assessing the Jesuit missions in the *Mezzogiorno* of the sixteenth to eighteenth centuries, an Italian historian describes "a religion of intimidation and punishment, apt to provoke a sense of sin in individual consciences, who could only achieve expiation through prayer and penitence."[33]

Are all these concordant judgments erroneous? If so, how does one explain the extraordinary success, at the zenith of the Counter-Reformation, and even later, of masses for the dead and impressively large legacies made for this purpose? What reason for these donations, other than the fear of Purgatory? Pierre Chaunu rightly explains: "500,000 Parisian wills demonstrate how imperative was the need to attenuate the pains of purgatory for tens of millions of people (from 1517 to 1800), and how it inspired personal conduct before death."[34] Judging by late nineteenth-century encyclopedias (though these may be somewhat malicious), Purgatory would have brought the French clergy over 32 million francs per annum.[35] Without being overly amused by this almost ludicrous assessment, it can be concluded that there was strong and genuine fear, also and especially in directors of Catholic conscience, and that this fear was something altogether different from the reverential "fear" of the Father.

PART FOUR

In the Protestant World

CHAPTER 19

"You Are a Terrifying Word, Eternity"

MUST ONE INSTILL FEAR?

The Reformers of the sixteenth century and, in their wake, all leading Protestant thinkers saw in the doctrine of justification by faith the only theology capable of reassuring sinners that we all are, and will remain so until our death. Many texts corroborate this idea. Here one needs only mention some of them, in particular those that might be considered the earliest and most important examples. Luther, in his *Introduction* (1522) to *The Letter of Paul to the Romans* wrote that he considered chapters 9, 10 and 11 of this letter by Saint Paul on predestination to be "consoling."[1] Previously he had explained his sixty-second thesis of 1517 in the following terms: "The light of the Gospel illuminates those who have been crushed by the law and tells them 'Courage! Do not be afraid.' (Is. 35:4), 'Console my people, console them' says your God' (Is. 40:1) . . . When the conscience of the sinner hears this good news, it comes back to life, it exults, it is full of confidence, it longer fears death and, having become the friend of death, it no longer fears any punishment, not even hell."[2] This then is the reason for which Luther expressed his sense of relief in the *De Servo arbitrio* when he wrote that: "God has now separated my salvation from my will. He has promised to save me not because of my good works and not because of my efforts but because of his grace and his mercy. Thus I am sure and certain that he is faithful and will not lie and that he is sufficiently powerful that no demon and no adversity will be able to impose on him or tear me from him."[3] This theology explains why Luther's preface to a collection of funeral hymns (1542) called death "a deep sleep that is strong and sweet," and the grave "a bed to rest in."[4]

Calvin is just as categorical as his German predecessor, though his tone is less personal. As he points out: "[The Scriptures tell us] that since God has been reconciled to us [by the death of Jesus], we are no longer in danger that things will not turn out well . . . God will never desert us. The basic assurance of faith rests on waiting for the future life that was promised to us by the Word of God and this beyond any incertitude."[5] Elsewhere, in the *Institutes of the Christian Religion*, he pointed out again that: ". . . If we look for a way in which the soul can come to rest and happiness in front of God, we will not find any other way than that in which he confers on us by the justice of his free benignity."[6] Why, then, should true

Christians fear the Last Judgment? It is not meant for them. In fact, Calvin asserted in one of his sermons that: ". . . We know that Our Lord Jesus Christ will not come to consume the members of his body through rigors, but rather he will come to show the fruit of the redemption he has gained for them . . . and therefore he will not come with terrible and fearsome majesty to treat us according to our demerits, rather he will see that our sins will be pardoned . . . we will love his coming."[7]

The reader will have noticed the use made by the two Reformers of significant words such as *consoling, sure and certain, no longer in danger, beyond any incertitude, rest and happiness* (of conscience). John Whitgift, Archbishop of Canterbury from 1583 on, added the following statement to the Lambeth Articles: "The truly faithful, that is the one who has received the justifying faith, is certain through the assurance of faith that his sins will be forgiven and that he will achieve eternal salvation through Christ."[8]

Why be fearful with such a reassuring doctrine? Why should fear be instilled? All the same, it is a fact that fear also slipped into Protestant souls and preaching, though in differing degrees according to the time, place, and different denominations. Czech Protestants of the nineteenth century were still singing a hymn, translated from the German, whose words reminded the singers that:

You are a terrifying word, eternity,
A sword that pierces the bones! . . .

As long as the God Above will be alive
And He will rise above the clouds,
The torments [of Hell] will persist;
. . . Hunger, cold, anguish, and chagrin . . .
All of these torments will come to an end
With the eternity of God.[9]

Ann Sauvy, who has studied the "longue durée" of the rather traumatizing iconography of hearts touched with either God or the Devil,[10] was surprised to find that nineteenth-century Protestants also used these striking Catholic images. Hundreds of thousands of such images were distributed in Protestant overseas missions.[11] *The Scarlet Letter*, one of the most famous American novels, was written in the middle of the nineteenth century. Its author, Nathaniel Hawthorne, lets his readers relive the incredible sense of guilt and fear that oppressed the seventeenth-century inhabitants of Salem under the Puritan sway. At the time he wrote his novel, the author was actually living in Salem, a town in which some of the same conditions had lingered on. Hawthorne received many letters from people who identified with the story and who discovered a liberating sensation in reading it. The novel enjoyed "an immediate success both in the United States and in England despite the harshness with which North American works were usually judged."[12]

The great writer August Strindberg also evoked in his *Son of a Servant* (1886–1887) the stifling atmosphere of the Swedish society of his time, with its rigid hierarchical ordering, its image of an almighty, severe, as well as distant God, and its refusal to give children some freedom and affection.

When his mother prayed to God in the evening, the child—the author himself—could not picture him clearly except that he certainly had to be much taller than the king . . . The child only heard about his duties, never about his rights. Any other person wanting to be heard was able to, while he was ignored. He could not do anything that was not bad, he could not go anywhere without getting in someone's way, he could not say a word without it disturbing someone . . . His supreme duty and his greatest virtue was to sit on a chair and to stay there quietly. He was perpetually afraid to do something bad.[13]

Yet another example of fear in Protestant countries is the one shown to the French and Swiss television public in 1982. The program, alas, was based on a true story. In Calvinist Switzerland at the end of the last century, an unruly and somewhat turbulent little orphan by the name of Merette could not understand very well the mercifulness of God, that all-powerful figure that had taken her mother from her. As a consequence, she was sent to a pastor known for his ability to convince the hardheaded, who forced her to write "God" . . . by hitting her hands with a ruler.

The main reason for mentioning these relatively recent accounts is to draw attention to the fact that it is necessary to study religious fear in the Protestant realm. I do not hope to cover this immense subject entirely. On the other hand, and more modestly, I would like to outline the work that could be more fully done by English- or German-speaking historians. My discussion will focus on Lutheran Germany in the sixteenth and seventeenth centuries and the Puritan movement in England and North America. However, I will not entirely exclude the Anglican church, the church of Sweden, or the French and Swiss Calvinists. I would especially like to thank Francesco Chiovaro, who looked in Germany for some of the texts that I will quote, as well as Angela Armstrong and Annie Becker, who undertook the same work in England and the United States.

The basic documentation is made up of the most widely read devotional literature and sermons, as was the case for my study of the Catholic realm. It might be added that this kind of literature was even more important for the Protestants than for the Catholics, since their creed was so much based on them. The Protestant Thomas Becon (1512–1567), in his catechism, asserted that "the first and most important duty of a bishop and a minister is to teach and to preach" and that "there is no greater jewel in the Christian community than a fervent, faithful, and constant preaching of the Word of the Lord."[14] Many well-known Puritans declared that they were "converted" by sermons.[15] However, the request for sermons did not remain confined to the Puritans. During periods of calamity the demand for sermons was very great indeed. During the 1625 plague in London the Parliament decided on a solemn fast. The king and the lords attended a mass that lasted six hours. The mass attended by the members of the House of Commons lasted nine consecutive hours, seven of which were devoted to sermons. None of the members of the House of Commons fainted on this occasion.[16] Some important figures of the Anglican church, such as Andrewes, Hooker, and Donne, were well-known preachers. Furthermore, it has been possible to show the influence of fifteenth- and sixteenth-century preaching on English poetry and theater.[17]

Since the sermon took on a greater importance in the Protestant world than other forms of pastoral activity, especially liturgy and sacramental symbolism, it is hardly surprising that much thought went into developing the structure and form of preaching.[18] Lutheran Germany soon witnessed the appearance of certain models of sermons, at first quite schematic, then increasingly complex, that progressively stifled the spontaneity and prophetical quality that had characterized Luther's sermons. One has to wait for Philipp Jakob Spener (1635–1705) and the Pietist movement to see the rebirth—though not everywhere—of a vigorous inspiration. Meanwhile, Lutheran homiletics became a rhetorical science and acquired an increasingly rigid set of rules that turned the sermon into a kind of lesson. After Johannes Gerhardt (1582–1637), a champion of orthodoxy, a large production of *Loci theologici* provided the preachers with a treasure of erudition. In fact, Lutheran sermons had a fondness for erudition. Furthermore, as in the Catholic world, specialized publications offered pastors collections of maxims and texts ordered in terms of subject matter, in which they could find materials to compose and order their sermons.[19]

Lutheran homiletics were shaped by the rhetorical mold that had been outlined by Melanchthon (*De Officio concionatoris*, 1537)[20] and given a more concrete shape some years later by Andreas Hyperius (*De Formandis concionibus sacris* . . . , 1533).[21] The latter work was translated into French some ten years later. According to Hyperius, "sermons are meant to instruct, exhort, reprimand and console."[22] This was the reason for the classical Lutheran subdivision of sermons into: (1) *Lehre (doctrina)* sometimes followed by a refutation (*Widerlegung*) of the opposite position; (2) *Mahnung (exhortatio)*; (3) *Strafe (objurgatio)*, or reproaches and menacing chastisement; (4) *Trost (consolatio)*. In this ordering of things the pair menace and consolation (*Strafe-Trost*) seem to be quite inseparable. The preacher was asked to make a doctrinal statement in such a way that it would inspire four different sentiments, coupled two by two, in the public he was to address: the love of God and the hatred of sin, the fear of chastisement and the trust in the Savior. The preachers' manuals thus suggested the use of *amplificatio*, exaggeration, when a subject was meant to move the public. This tactic was a suggestion that came from antiquity, and it is not surprising that, to a certain extent, it was followed by Lutheran pastors. However, as had been the case in the Catholic world, menace was counterbalanced by consolation. The latter was always the final note. The following discussion of the pastoral dissemination of fear in the Protestant world should be seen in this light. I have already discussed this idea in my analysis of this process in the Roman Catholic world.[23]

This essential corrective measure must not, however, hide the fact that threats were frequently used and that, more seriously, the stress on consolation evoked in itself a pessimistic and negative conception of man and the triad *Teufel, Sünde, Tod* (Devil, Sins, Death) that were omnipresent in the discourse and theology of Protestant spokesmen.

More often than not, Protestant preachers answered the question as to whether one should have recourse (up to a certain extent) to a terroristic language with a yes. An example of this was the advice to preachers given by Christophe Schrader in a book based on Aristotle, *De Rhetoricorum Aristotelis sententia et usu commentarius* (1674). Schrader explained that the orator could not forgo the art of impressing (*ars commovendi*) since he has to push his public toward goodness and make them shrink from evil. The author, in quoting Clement of Alexandria and Saint Basil, affirmed that the fear of God chases out sinfulness, that he who is not afraid will not be justified, and that a constant meditation as to the "formidable mysteries of the terrible judgment" is the mistress of piety. The preacher must therefore use this pedagogical tool when the occasion demands and must "frequently" punctuate his sermon with references to "God the Father, to Christ the Savior, to the good angels, to Satan, to the magistrates, to the laws, to sin, to the society of the wicked, to the last judgment, and to all that which will inspire fear and horror." He must not only threaten eternal punishment but also, as did the prophets, apostles, and church fathers, evoke the imminent calamities that menace impenitent men and women.[24] Schrader goes on to declare the necessity of having "a very great fear of the all-powerful and excellent God who chased the rebel angels from heaven and our first ancestors from paradise, destroyed practically the whole universe with the deluge, and overthrew whole kingdoms and cities."[25]

Protestant pedagogy on preaching thus called for a double approach: a menacing one and a consoling one. An order of 1659 in the county of Hanau-Lichtenberg called for all pastors to "present [to the faithful] the main articles of the Christian faith . . . so as to frighten the impious with the announcement of God's wrath, and console the uneasy hearts of those that have sinned reminding them of God's grace."[26] This two-part counsel was the outcome of thoughts devoted to the "fear of God." A good example of this can be found in a sermon of Pierre du Moulin. The preacher reflected on Proverbs 3:7, "Do not think of yourself as wise, fear Yahweh and turn your back on evil." His sermon explained that one must not have a "servile fear" of God and obey his commands only because one fears him. "The real motive for piety is not the fear of hell but the love of God." Du Moulin added, however, that one should not condemn all fear of being punished. In fact, Jesus Christ told his disciples whom he called friends (Luke 12:4): "Fear him who, after he has killed, has the power to cast into hell." The pastor of Sedan went on to say that:

> *It was a good thing for the Ninevites to be scared by the menace of a future ruin and Saint Paul to have been converted when he was struck by lightning that caused great anguish and fear. It is not only useful at the beginning of the conversion of a sinner but also when and if we let up and become negligent in our good works. It is expedient that we be told about the horrors of hell and the armed hand of God that is lifted against those who are slow or draw away from his call and let both the time and occasions go by that would make them get closer to the Kingdom of God. Saint John said in the fourth chapter of the first epistle that "perfect charity chases fear." But where is the man endowed with perfect charity? In short, Solomon's declaration in Proverbs 28 is still true, "Happy the man who is never without fear, he who hardens his heart will fall into distress.*[27]

Du Moulin believed that as the love of God grew in a soul, the fear of punishment diminished, since the conscience slowly settled in "peace and tranquility." This was, without a doubt, the general feeling of all Protestant and Catholic spiritual leaders of the past. What was not yet cleared up was the exact dosage that was required in mixing threats and comforts. The mix was subject to the temperament of the preacher and the spiritual movement to which he belonged. John Pilkington (d. 1576), Bishop of Durham, asserted in his *Exposition upon Nehemiah* that a kindly method of preaching wins over weak-hearted spirits more effectively than the terrible thunder of vengeance. While it is necessary to teach the Law in order to disconcert rebellious souls and lead them to self-knowledge, love can make men willingly strive to do good, rather than simply flee from evil. Therefore Pilkington argues, preachers should use kindness more than severity, promises more than threats, the Gospel more than the Law, and love more than fear. Fear restrains the flesh, but love comforts the soul.[28]

THEOLOGY AND PEDAGOGY

Pilkington's advice stresses kindness and consolation. At the same time, it contains an opposition between the Law and the Gospel that lies at the heart of Protestant theology. Consequently, this opposition dominated preaching in the countries that broke with Rome during the sixteenth century.

With its strict demands, the Law can cause despair, as it reveals both innate human corruption and the damnation that this corruption inevitably causes. It is worth recalling that the Reformers arrived at justification by faith via the path of "despair." Luther observes that a clear-sighted and exacting conscience cannot help but be "overwhelmed"[29] by the number and gravity of one's sins. When compared to such offenses, good works "vanish like a breath of wind." Like Lorenzo Valla, whom he considered to be on his side,[30] Luther opposed scholasticism and rejected the Thomist distinction between the natural and supernatural orders, more so than Calvin. He had no time for talk of the superadded privileges God gave our first parents, which raised them above their original condition. The Reformers argued that before the Fall, Adam and Eve maintained supreme control over their senses: "each and every one of [their] organic parts," writes Calvin, "were ready and inclined to obey, in all innocence."[31] Original sin did not make them lose any supernatural status, it rather debased their fundamental essence. The *Smalcald Articles* puts the case in plain terms:

> *Original sin is so profound and pernicious a corruption of human nature that no effort of reason can comprehend it . . . Therefore the Scholastics' teaching to the contrary is but error and blindness: namely, their claim that after Adam's Fall, man's natural forces remained intact and that man naturally retained clear reason and good will, as the philosophers also taught.*[32]

The *Articles* label the scholastic position as "pagan," since it makes the Savior's death of no use. In his *Commentary on the Letter to the Romans*, Luther had already written:

> *What then is original sin? . . . According to the subleties of the theologians, it is the deprivation of original justice, but according to the Apostle and Jesus Christ's own straightforward meaning, it is not only the deprivation of a quality of the will, nor of the light of understanding, nor of the powers of memory, but a deprivation of rectitude in all human capacities, both of the body and soul, in the external as well as internal man. It is the readiness to do evil, the nausea with the good, disgust with enlightenment and wisdom, the love of error and darkness, the disdain and utter contempt for good works, the uncontrolled racing toward evil.*[33]

The Augsburg Confession does not take a stand on the nature of Adam and Eve before their sin; in an Augustinian manner, however, it does accentuate the catastrophic effects of the first offense:

> *After the Fall, all men born after nature are conceived and born in sin; that is to say that all, from the breast of their mother, are filled with evil cravings and inclinations and that, by their nature, they can possess neither true fear of God, nor true faith in God. We also hold that this innate corruption, this original sin, is well and truly a sin, and that it dooms to damnation and the eternal wrath of God all those who are not reborn in baptism and the Holy Spirit.*[34]

During the sixteenth century, Lutherans engaged in heated debates over the degradation of human nature by sin. The Formula of Concord (1580), which brought reconciliation, recognized objections in man's favor: "We affirm that human nature, after the Fall, has remained God's creation, and that between it and original sin there is as much difference as between a work of God and a work of the devil."[35] Against the Thomist tradition, however, it adds: "Far from being a superficial corruption original sin is such a profound corruption of human nature that every sound part of the human body and soul is yet somehow corrupted."[36]

Luther notably reinforces this anthropology of fallen man by fully adopting Saint Augustine's cherished thesis that the sexual act is, without exception, sinful. The Reformer closely links the assertions that "man is so corrupt through Adam's fall that he carries innate execration,"[37] and "the flesh is enflamed and corrupted by wicked desires. The natural work of the flesh, conception, cannot occur without sin; that which is sown and impregnated by the act of the flesh produces carnal and sinful fruit. Therefore Saint Paul says, in Ephesians 2:3, that 'we were by nature the children of wrath.' "[38] The *Institutes of the Christian Religion* express a similar view: "Therefore all of us, who have descended from impure seed, are born infected with the contagion of sin. In fact, before we saw the light of this life we were soiled and spotted in God's sight. 'For who can bring a clean thing from an unclean?' as the Book of Job says [Job 14:4]."[39] The *Tetropolitan Confession* (1530), presented to Charles V at the same time as that of Augsburg and signed by Zwingli, declares: "I acknowledge that this original sin is transmitted through birth, by condition and contagion, to all those who have been engendered by the joining of man and woman . . ."[40] The almost-constant Augustinian position recurs, with its accusation against a carnal act that spreads the "contagion" of a deadly affliction. It might be objected, however, that Protestant theology does not equate flesh and sensuality[41] and that it also exalts the "sanctity of marriage," an institution decreed by God. It sees continence as an exceptional "gift," granted to only a few people, which one should not rashly think one possesses. All the same, it maintains the ancient ecclesiastical tradition by calling sexual desire a "vice of incontinence." In the form it has taken since Original Sin, this desire is nothing other than "lewdness." Its remedy is, of course, marriage, which channels "our concupiscence."[42]

Moreover, the Protestants develop the long-standing Augustinian notion that temptation is sin, since it expresses the general concupiscence that has marked all humanity since the original transgression. This is one of the deepest convictions of classic Protestantism and the point of departure for Luther's thinking. In 1515–16, commenting on Saint Paul's statement, "Blessed is the man to whom the Lord will not impute sin" (Rom. 4:8), he wrote:

> *It is not only a question of sins committed in deed, word, and thought, but also of the inclination toward evil . . . And it is a mistake to think that this evil can be cured by works, since experience proves that, despite good works, this desire for evil persists, and that no one is free from it, not even a newborn child. But divine mercy is such that, though this evil persist, it does not count as a sin for those who invoke God, and with tears beg their deliverance.*[43]

These lines speak from the heart of the doctrine of justification by faith and its motivations. Luther again affirms that "in baptized Christians, the impulses of nature are always deadly, but God regards them as no more than venial."[44] Calvin is likewise convinced that our temptations are sins. God forbids that the heart be "tempted to anger, hatred, lechery, thievery, deceit . . . [just as] He forbids that it be moved or provoked to actually do these things."[45]

Therefore, why distinguish between sin and sins, the Original Sin and everyday sins, between temptation and action? Since Adam and Eve's first disobedience, all our acts have been wicked (unless God takes possession of us). Indelible and indestructible, sin remains after both baptism and justification, but is no longer imputed to us. The *Profession de la foi de La Rochelle* teaches that "even after baptism, it is still sin in regard to guilt, even though its condemnation is removed for the children of God . . . More than that, it is a perversity, still bearing the fruits of spite and rebellion."[46] This argument sweeps away Saint Augustine's subtle distinction, which determined that only the temptations of the unbaptized were sinful. The Bishop of Hippo had found disciples who were even more logical than he.

The necessary horror of one's self and the certainty of deserved punishment should throw the believer on the mercy of God. It becomes impossible to move toward the Savior without a preliminary pilgrimage to the land of fear. This "despair" in both the spirit and discourse of the pastors was the only way to obtain the final goal of pardon. When asserted in overly harsh terms, however, this doctrine may well have taken on traumatic overtones. Erasmus prudently warned: "Do not tell the crowd that all human action leads to sin. Although this is in some ways true, the ignorant tend to interpret it in ways that do them no good."[47] Many sixteenth-century Lutheran pastors refused such advice. Caspar Aquila, superintendant of Saalfeld in Saxony during the 1530s, put Sunday school children through a series of questions and answers, such as these notable examples:

> Question: "*What do the ten commandments teach you?*
> Answer *[by the child]: I learn from them that we lead a life of damnation and sin, and that God can find nothing in us of any good." The ten commandments make us see, "as in a looking-glass," that which we are without grace, namely "idolaters, miscreants, blasphemers and violators of God's holy name, accursed wretches who rob from His sacred temple and scorn His eternal word; rebels who insult our parents and kill our children, envious dogs, cutthroats, debauchees, adulterers, thieves, knaves, cheats, hypocrites, liars, perjurers, false witnesses, wretched and insolent braggarts."*[48]

The same dramatic lessons appear in Andreas Osiander's *Kinderpredigten* ("Sermons for children") (1533). The famous Nuremberg theologian affirms that our parents filled us with sin "just as a leprous mother contaminates the child in her womb." "For each of our fellow creatures is as bad as the next, and no one is better [except those who believe]; we are surrounded on all sides by envy, hatred, anger, disputes, deceit, pillaging, theft, insults, calumnies, assaults, murders, lies, duplicity, fraud, war, and all kinds of iniquity. Such horrid sins must needs be punished by God."[49] Osiander's sermons were compulsory reading in all the churches of Nuremberg, as well as in those of the neighboring margraviate of Brandenburg-Ansbach. They were especially meant to be read prior to first communion. Finally, they had an even wider diffusion, since at least fifty-four editions of these *Kinderpredigten* appeared between 1533 and 1567.[50]

In England, these Lutheran texts are matched by thousands of Puritan ones. In a sermon on disobedience, Samuel Hieron (1576–1617) comments on Paul's Letter to the Romans and concludes that "the nature of man is nothing but even a compound, a thing made of these two, Corruption and Death . . . our understanding [is] nothing but ignorance and dullnesse, our will nothing but obstinacy, our affections nothing but disorder."[51] Hieron's sermons were published at least six times between 1614 and 1634. For Richard Sibbes (1576–1635), a Puritan whose preaching was also popular with many non-Puritans, "Our righteousness is as a menstrous cloth that is spotted and stained and defiled."[52]

> *First by the sin of Adam, in whose loynes we were all damned; there was a sentence of death upon all Adams rotten race, as we say,* damnati ante quam nati, *we were damned before we were borne, as soon as we had a being in our mothers wombe, by reason of our communion with Adam in that first sinne . . . if we had*

no actual sinne it were enough for the sentence of death to passe upon us, but this aggravates the sentence.[53]

A sermon by another Puritan, Christopher Love (1618–1651), contains this reason for being a diligent Christian:

Should you pray till you can speak no more; and should you sigh to the breaking of your loynes; should every word be a sigh, and every sigh a tear, and every tear a drop of blood, you would never be able to recover that grace which you lost in Adam; you obliterated the beautiful image of God; you lost that knowledge by the commission of one sin, which you cannot regain by ten thousand sermons, or doing ten thousand Duties.[54]

This theology, which constitutes the nucleus of Protestantism, clarifies how preachers were asked to convey a double emphasis, beyond any mere tactical considerations. In his famous *Sermon of the Plough*, preached in London on January 18, 1548, Bishop Hugh Latimer—later burned at the stake on Mary Tudor's orders—explains that the preacher "hath first a busy work to bring his parishioners to a right faith, . . . and then to confirm them in the same faith: now casting them down with the law and with threatenings of God for sin; now ridging them up again with the Gospel and with the promises of God's favor."[55]

In the seventeenth century, some Puritans gave more severe instructions for preaching. "The word in preaching," Samuel Hieron expounds,

must not be fitted to the pleasing of mens Eares, but to the stirring up and affecting of their hearts . . . a man must go to the roote, and knock at the door of every mans conscience, that everie soul may tremble, and men at the least may be convinced against the day of reckoning . . . This is the right use of the word . . . preaching was not ordained to be a tale sounding well in the eare, but to be a sharper cutting instrument, searching deepe into the heart.[56]

Hieron's pedagogy leads him to draw sizable conclusions regarding the power of the preacher, with which Catholic orators would have concurred: "Those whom the ministry of the Word heweth downe now, the justice of God at the last day shall send them to the fire. Let men imagine as they list, and say of the preaching of the word, that it is but a blast, and the threatenings thereof but wind; yet to their eternall woe, they shall one day find it otherwise."[57] Christopher Love, who was accused of plotting against the commonwealth and was executed, could also be speaking for Catholic missionaries when he explains that

sermons of terrour have done more good upon unconverted souls, then sermons of comfort ever have done. Sermons of hell may keep many out of hell . . . Were all our hearers converted, doctrines of grace might be most for edification. But feeling we have to deal with a mixt people, our doctrines must be mixt also, else we shall never profit . . . Some mens natures are rather led then drawn, yet others are so stout and knotty that nothing but flashes of hellfire will make their conscience startle.[58]

Hieron's and Love's harsh phrases met with the same sort of objections that Loriot and Montargon allude to in France.[59] Like their French counterparts, the Puritan pastors recognize these critiques only in order refute them to more effectively. In a dialogue between a minister and a layman, Hieron has the latter say: "Your manner of preaching is too austere; you have nothing in your mouths but hell and condemnation, and the judgment of God, which (as some say) is the next way to bring men unto despaire." To which the minister retorts, citing the classic progression from the Law to faith: "The fallow ground of our hearts must first be broken up with the sharpness of the law, and the very terror of the Lord, before we can be fit to entertain the sweet seed of the Gospell."[60] People also reproached Love for practicing a "legal" style of preaching, for preaching the Law rather than the Gospel through his emphasis on the flames of hell. No less than Hieron, Love is equipped with a reply:

> *If preaching of Terrour be legal preaching, then the Law was more preacht in the new Testament than ever it was under the old. It is a note of Chrysostome that in all the Old Testament, the word* damnation *was never used, but it is used thirteen times in the New . . . Therefore it is cleare to every eye, that the Gospell is more backt with terrour, and with the doctrines of hell and damnation, than ever the law was.*[61]

Love was an extremist, and his sermons should not be seen as typical of all Protestant preaching. The Anglicans, for example, tended to be far more comforting and reassuring. At the midway point of the seventeenth century, Love specifically complains of "these new teachers" who moderate doctrine, "pretend more light than their Brethren," and have not converted a single soul. "How can a Minister discharge his conscience to God . . . if in the course of his Ministry he shall run only upon strains of free grace?"[62] However excessive he may be, Love exemplifies how a pedagogy of fear undeniably existed in certain Protestant times and places. For instance, religious "awakenings" periodically activated this terroristic brand of teaching: in North America of the 1730s and '40s, to cite one case, "Revivalists" such as Samuel Finley and Gilbert and John Tennent stirred up debates and shock-waves. With the aim of leading their listeners toward a "new birth," the apostles of the Great Awakening employed violent rhetoric; they thus touched off polemical criticism,[63] which they were compelled to echo in their own sermons. Hence Gilbert Tennent, the first Presbyterian minister without European college training, described in 1734 the thoughts of an imaginary interlocutor: The pastor is a strange sort of man, who talks only of Hell and damnation. Tennent's character goes on to say that he fears being led into despair, since one of the preacher's sermons put so much fear in him that his blood curdled in his veins, and he could not keep from trembling.[64] An anonymous poem of 1741 warns Gilbert Tennent against his own terroristic pedagogy, cajoling him to pray that his scare tactics and fierce harangues will not entrap his listeners in dark despair over their accursed nature, guilty conscience, and a menacing God.[65]

Also in 1741 John Thomson, a Presbyterian minister who was hostile to the methods of Tennent and his colleagues, wrote that they sought to terrify their listeners with talk of horrors and damnation. He also claims that these preachers refuse to sound any comforting notes until their listeners have suffered through a certain amount of terror.[66] The preacher thus assumes the dreadful power of being the only judge of the medicine he administers! In another contemporaneous publication, Thomson attacks preachers of the Gospel who emphasize only avenging justice, who downplay pity and thus bring their audiences to hate God and to despair of their salvation.[67]

The Moravian Brothers of America were among those who opposed the terrorism of the "Revivalists." According to Samuel Finley, the Moravians argued that Christ was a good, loving, and powerful King and that the Revivalists dishonored Him by saying that He left His people, overcome by sins, in darkness, doubts, sorrow, and vexation.[68] Finley vigorously replies that he does not wish to make "religious peace" with such "heretics." Coming to the rescue, Tennent reprimands them, above all for giving up belief in Hell. They are worse than papists in trying to turn Hell into Purgatory, Hell being one of the main deterrents against vice, without which the floodgates of all immorality and anarchy would open.[69]

Even more important than this response to the Moravians was the Revivalists' frequently expressed conviction that their tactics were especially vital to conversion. Tennent preached that we are children of anger and that this terrible inheritance made us born only to be reborn.[70] Luther and Calvin could both have signed their names to such a statement, which returns us to the heart of the most essential Protestant theology. Taken to the limit, the latter could logically support Finley's pedagogical viewpoints. He argued that the demands and terrible threats of the Law should be phrased in such a horrifying way that they would convince those who comfortably dwell in sin.[71] Tennent therefore scolds the "Anti-Revivalists" for prematurely comforting their listeners and thereby reinforcing their carnal security. They have neither the courage nor the honesty to drive the nail of terror into slumbering souls.[72] Tennent's sermon at Nottingham, Pennsylvania, caused a "schism" among the Presbyterians at the 1741 Philadelphia Synod.

Tennent's supporters observed that the harsh preacher convinced his listeners less through explanations of the terrors of the Law, the wrath of God, and of damnation than through an exposure of their vain and secret refuges, their mistaken idea of grace, and their idle hopes: All these were roads toward damnation.[73] Tennent and his closest adherents, however, placed their primary stress on the notion that only a trying journey could lead to spiritual assurance. Thus they constantly explained the necessary dialectic of fear and faith. Gilbert Tennent preached that man's degeneration since the apostasy [of Adam] has thoroughly wrecked his sense of love and sincerity, and therefore men must be aroused by the stimulants of fear and awe, in order to be converted.[74] Tennent was tireless on this subject, and elsewhere asserts that belief in the threats of God brings fear of God and fear of His threats brings greater belief in God. In another sermon, Tennent proposes that Christians work in fear and trembling, in a reverential fear for God's majesty; for the fear of God is the foundation of all religion. Tennent cites Augustine and adds that faith produces fear and fear confirms faith. Love without fear becomes irreverent, and fear without love becomes anguished. Fear authorizes joy, and joy sweetens fear, making it pleasing and delicious.[75]

A fear that becomes pleasing and delicious! Did the Revivalists' sermons actually spread this phrase, which could aptly characterize the feelings aroused by horror movies? In any case, these orations provoked reactions similar to those caused by various Catholic missionaries. Beyond the confessional ruptures, these "convertors" proved to be close cousins. Gilbert Tennent gives a striking description of the "conversion" of his brother John, of which he himself had been the instrument: He writes that John cried out that his soul was nearly lost and that he was on the extreme verge of despair. He was in such distress that he made public confession of his sins to everyone he would meet, looking as fearful and dejected as a criminal about to be tortured or hanged. Gilbert also affirms that his brother's wound was so deep that only the hand of God could cure it, and that this cure was indeed effected after four days and nights spent in extreme agony and spiritual distress.[76]

A friend and colleague of Tennent similarly described the tribulations of a young woman who had been stricken by forceful sermons. For a while she became deaf and blind. She then spent several weeks in extreme distress, seeking pity but finding no comfort, until one Sunday evening when her soul was filled with strong hopes of reconciliation with God through Christ. Her heart then became possessed with joy.[77]

The interest of these individual agonies is surpassed by the collective reactions to such sermons. They inevitably bring to mind the scenes that attended the Catholic missions. John Tennent, one of his brothers relates, deeply moved his audiences. He testifies that he saw his brother and the latter's congregation bathed in tears, and that some of them were carried out in a trance.[78] Anglicans as well as moderate Presbyterians did not fail to reproach the Revivalists for acting on the "devil's insinuation," for using methods that caused "desperate" terror and fears in their listeners,[79] and for teaching that "regeneration" had to be accompanied by howling, weeping, and bodily contortion.[80] The Revivalists defended themselves as "enthusiasts." A thematic index, however, based on the letters of pastors who described the "Great Awakening" of the 1730s and '40s (in the periodical *The Christian History*), spotlights such terms as "shouts," "disorders," "distress of the heart," "fervor," "fainting," "ecstasies," "terrors," and "trembling."[81] Tears, sobbing, and sighs were the listeners' most common symptoms,[82] though these were often compounded by shouts, convulsions, and fainting fits.[83]

CHAPTER 20

Shared Aspects of the Protestant and Catholic Doctrinal Programs

THE EMPHASIS ON DEATH

The theological as well as pedagogical inquiry into the relationship between fear and love, and their relative weight within particular sermons, calls for an extended investigation of the shared aspects of Protestant and Catholic preaching and spirituality.

First, it would be a mistake to see the Reformation as a complete break with the religious history of the preceding centuries. It would be equally mistaken to believe that Protestants did not read sixteenth-century Catholic spiritual publications. For example, Swedish historians have recorded a continuity between the piety of the Catholic Middle Ages and that which prevailed in their country until at least 1700. In the seventeenth century, Jesuit books were being distributed in Sweden. In 1650 a professor of Uppsala advised his students to buy Catholic ascetic works during their travels abroad. Moreover, Swedish historiography has located the survival of the Catholic pastoral tradition precisely in sermons and devotional works on the preparation for death, Hell, Satan, and the wrath of God toward sinners.[1]

Furthermore, Protestants and Catholics had a common taste for Saint Augustine. Stuart readers had access to two English versions of the *Confessions*, one by the Catholic Sir Tobie Matthew (1620), the other by the Protestant William Watt (1631). The latter remained a British classic until the twentieth century. In fact, from 1570 to 1640 the British Isles witnessed a vogue for translations of works attributed to Augustine: *An Introduction to the Love of God*, *The Glasse of vaine-glorie*, *Select Prayers gathered out of St. Augustines Meditations*, *A pretious Booke of Heavenlie Meditations*.[2] All these books conveyed Augustinian pessimism. John Donne was an avid reader of Augustine . . . and of Saint Bernard. The latter was only slightly less popular in England than the Bishop of Hippo. The English public would have been especially familiar with the Saint Bernard of the *memento mori*, due to the 1616 translation by the Puritan pastor William Crashaw—the poet's father—of "The Complaint or Dialogue, Betwixt the soul and The Bodie of a damned man."[3]

The third major work of medieval devotional literature that survived in Great Britain was *The Imitation of Christ*, whose success persisted and crossed confessional boundaries. Two English versions had been published in the early sixteenth century and five more would appear between 1567 and 1639. The one by Thomas Rogers, who also translated Saint Augustine's *Prayers*, went through at least fourteen editions between 1580 and 1640.[4] These Protestant translations were quick to correct the *Imitation*'s strongly Catholic passages, but they retained those that argued for the *contemptus mundi*. As for Catholic influences on English Protestantism after the Council of Trent, they arrived mainly via the work of the Dominican Louis of Granada. A first translation of his *Libro de la Oracion y meditacion* was officially approved and published in 1569. It was a Catholic version by the exile Richard Hopkins, however, published first in Paris in 1582 and then reprinted with corrections in London (ca. 1592), that established this book's popularity in Great Britain. The famous *Guía de pecadores* reached the London bookstalls in 1598, under the title of *The Sinners Guyde*. This best-seller of Catholic spirituality succeeded in meeting the spiritual needs of Anglo-Saxon Protestants, to the extent that it stressed divine perfection, the priceless value of predestination, and both the fight and preventive measures against sins, especially the Deadly Sins.[5]

Have historians adequately underlined this interpenetration of Catholicism and Protestantism during a period of intense religious conflict? In any case, the points of contact between two determinedly adverse religious parties become strikingly apparent, especially when studied in the context of fear and intensifying guilt. Hence Protestant sermons echo their Catholic counterparts in reproaching parents. Johann Brenz (1499–1570), the Reformer of Wurtemberg, tells his Sunday audience:

> *Among many parents there is neither civil honesty nor Christian piety. At home parents only speak blasphemies, curses, ugly and obscene words, railings or slanders against their neighbors . . . They never say a word about God or Christ His only begotten son. If they do mention the true religion, it is to curse it . . . [parents] are not ashamed to say in public and to their families that everything spoken in church sermons is of no importance. Thus they neither listen to nor care about the Word of God, nor would they make their children hear it.*[6]

Likewise, Caspar Aquila, the ecclesiastical administrator of Thuringia, in a commentary on the Fifth Commandment, identifies as murderers those parents who neglect "to raise their children in good discipline and the fear of God."[7]

I would accentuate yet another, more methodological connection between the Protestant and Catholic discourses, involving the fear that must be felt before communion. At the beginning of a collection of sermons, Pierre du Moulin warns:

> *When one must appear before God to hear His word and partake of His table, a thousand considerations will mingle in the hearts of those who fear God, that will touch them with religious fear and keep them in respect and reverence. One must remember that we appear before God, who is a consuming fire, who sees into our hearts and justly weighs our deeds, and from whom nothing is hidden . . . One must recognize that we are weak creatures, fragile vessels, sinners, spiritual invalids who seek to be healed, criminals guilty of the ultimate lese-majesté, who beg their sovereign's grace.*[8]

How could "criminals guilty of the ultimate lese-majesté" help being seized with "fear" before Him who "justly weighs our deeds"?

"One must be horrified by the slightest nudity," Louis Tronson recommends in his *Manuel du séminariste*.[9] It is no surprise that there also developed, at least in Puritan circles, a true hostility toward the body, which had its basis in shame. Cotton Mather, one of the most influential pastors of late seventeenth—early eighteenth-century New England, lamented to observe the close resemblance between the natural functions of men and beasts. He writes in his *Journal*: "I was once emptying the *Cistern of Nature*, and making *Water* at the Wall. At the same time, there came a dog, who did so too, before me. Thought I: 'What mean, and vile Things are the Children of Men, in this mortal state! How much do our natural Necessities abase us, and place us in some regard, on the same level with the very Dogs!' " In such a case, Mather consoles himself with an edifying lesson: "when my natural Necessities debase me into the Condition of the Beast, my Spirit shall (I say, at theat very Time!) rise and soar, and fly upward, toward the Employment of the Angel"[10] This last term evokes the same "angelic anthropology" so frequently encountered in Catholic preaching.

Not only the most severe Presbyterians but also every "evangelical"[11] who strove to "wake up" and "convert" the masses shared and confirmed the belief that the body is in some way the proof of our corruption. John Wesley wrote, and preached: "there is in every man a carnal mind, which is enmity against God, which is not, cannot be subject to his law, and which so infects the whole soul, that there dwelleth in him, in his flesh, in his natural state, no good thing; but all the imagination of the thoughts, of his heart, is evil, only evil, and that continually."[12] It is worth noting that Wesley married late—at the age of forty-eight—and was never happy with married life. Like many preachers of Protestant "awakenings," he was convinced that the guilty body must be mortified. Another Methodist leader, George Whitefield, who was especially active in America, wrote: "mortification itself, when once practiced, is the greatest pleasure in the world . . . there is really more pleasure in these formidable duties of self-denial and mortification, than in the highest indulgences of the greatest epicure upon earth."[13] These words could have been penned by Rancé.

Another theme common to both Protestant and Catholic homiletics was the affirmation that Jesus, through the "punishment" he suffered, paid his Father "the debt" contracted by sinful humanity. One of Brenz's Sunday sermons asserts that "God's anger became manifest through Our Lord Jesus Christ. Indeed, God flung him into the greatest afflictions, even to the point of making him the last of the living, obliged to descend into hell like the most damned soul of all . . . Such a cruel punishment, which touched the Son of God, should teach us the severity and gravity of God's anger toward sins."[14] Johann Arndt (1555–1621) expresses the same doctrine in a short popular tract devoted to the "regeneration" or "new birth" of the Christian. He writes, "dragged down by ambition and pride, disobedient man turned away from God and, having fallen, his apostasy or fall could only be punished and at the same time corrected by the entire humiliation, abasement, and obedience of the Son of God."[15] Arndt's writings will be cited again, especially his *De Vero Christiano* (first German edition, 1606–10). Studies made of private libraries in eighteenth-century Speyer reveal that Arndt, in 1780 to 1786, as in 1744 to 1750, was by far the most widely read spiritual author in this particular town. He was also at the top of the list for mid-eighteenth- and early nineteenth-century Tübingen.[16]

Still another shared and simultaneously preached doctrine was the belief that God's mercy ends at the same time as an individual's life. Many Roman Catholic priests would have agreed with the Puritan pastor Samuel Hieron: "The reason why there must be a resolution of present entrance is, because, as there is a time of grace, in which the gate of Mercy stands open, so there is a time of judgment, in which this gate will be shut up, and all hope of entry utterly removed."[17]

The focus on disease and death, however, formed an even tighter bond between the two doctrinal campaigns, though it remains true that the evangelism of fear cannot be reduced to this theme alone, which in any case aimed to reassure as well as disturb. Regarding the insistence of death, Margaret Spufford writes: "The main themes of popular sermons may have changed less at the Reformation than is at first supposed."[18] First, many sectors of the Protestant world either perpetuated or revived the *contemptus mundi*-inspired Christian macabre. As Jean-Claude Margolin has aptly shown,[19] the work of the Zeeland poet Jacob Cats (1577–1660) is a case in point. The life of this fervent Calvinist was one long meditation on death and a constant preparation for its coming. "For a long time," he confessed in his later years, "since my youth, I have never ceased learning how to die. The tomb and all it brings have always been familiar to me . . . ; no matter where I have gone, whatever I have seen has awakened the thought of death in my soul."[20] Accustomed to staring death in the face, Cats discovers in a "dried-out skeleton all the beauty of a freshly blown rose, sparkling with dew."[21] He is also a spokesperson for the contemporary message of consolation: Death, he argues, is falsely terrifying. Before it, "the fool starts to flee, but the wise man laughs."[22] Although this statement is more Stoic than Christian, Cats elsewhere addresses Death: "When one lives for God, in virtue and humility, one has nothing to fear and no cause for trembling at your threats."[23] Therefore, why be afraid of deathly sights?

If one does not fear them, however, one risks enjoying them, and so it is with Cats. His Baroque realism, if one may call it that, forges a Protestant link between the funereal poetry of the fourteenth and fifteenth centuries and the nauseating descriptions made by deeply Catholic eighteenth-century authors.[24] Like the latter, he evokes the passage from life to death, predicting with disturbing detail the changes that his dying breath will work on him:

> . . . *These eyes, which today enable me to read, will suddenly close and turn into sunken cavities. My hand, which now writes poetry and other more important things, will instantly freeze at death's touch. My tongue, which has spoken for so long in the Dutch Parliament,*[25] *will fall limp, mute, a lifeless organ. My breast, this center of life, where I now feel the beating of my heart, will be but a wretched fragment, crushed beneath a mass of earth.*[26]

Still more revealing is the following text, which Margolin likens to the *Anatomy Lesson*. It appears in the meaningfully entitled work *A Coffin for the Living*, whose lessons resemble those of Saint John Chrysostom. When a man expires,

> *his mouth dribbles thick saliva, which remains stuck to his cheeks or his pallid lips. Now that the soul has departed it, this once lively body is no more than a shameful wreck. Its lifeless eyes are a cause for horror, and they shall never open again. A man is so hideous when he is dead that his nearest relatives turn away from him. Behold this cadaver: there it lies, a shapeless mass . . . These remains stink, and that is all: for they belong in the grave.*[27]

Such descriptions encourage the historian to examine the macabre even in Calvinist countries. On the other hand, Lutheran preachers usually seem to have avoided gruesome images of death and decomposition. This avoidance, however, was not universal, as witness several homilies by Johannes Gerhardt, one of the main representatives of "evangelical" orthodoxy. In the first sermon of a series, this orator distinguishes "spiritual" death from "natural" death and "eternal" death, explaining that the "natural" death of a true Christian does not deserve this name, since it is "a pleasant sleep, and a journey to true life." He who has put Jesus' teaching into practice will not fear death, will not taste its bitter gloom.[28] A later sermon, however, on the son of Nain's widow, emphasizes the death of young people. "Neither a pink complexion, bodily strength, nor pleasant surroundings could protect him from death." Death does not spare a child in the womb: He finds his tomb even there, in the supposed source of life.

Gerhardt then demonstrates the "atrocity" of death, preceded by countless "ushers," those illnesses that "so torment and torture the patient that he comes to yearn for death." At its approach, "his ears grow deaf, his eyes cloud over, his tongue stiffens, and a cold sweat breaks out over his entire body." Ought one to refer to Cats?

> *Once the soul is gone, the body begins to rot, so much so that his best friends cannot tolerate his corpse's fetid stench . . . Why then so much care to feed and adorn the body? Tomorrow it will be the food of worms. Why scorn one's neighbor? Tomorrow the tomb will make you equals. Why indulge in idle pleasures? Those who reveled with us yesterday are gone today to render their accounts to the Lord.*[29]

Thus drones this repetition of an old theme. Another sermon, however, contains a more surprising assertion, which involves the doctrine of Original Sin. Gerhardt claims that "no animal rots so quickly as man. No corpse emits such a foul odor. Wherefore? Because of the poison of sin . . . for in the beginning, 'God created man for incorruption' (Wisdom 2:23). Since death is contrary to man's essential nature, his body reeks malodorously."[30] As a visual reference, Gerhardt points to the famous "*transi*" tomb of William II of Hesse (d. 1509) in the Church of Saint Elisabeth, Marburg.

Without a doubt, Great Britain and her American colonies provide the richest ground for studying macabre themes in the seventeenth- and eighteenth-century Protestant world. Margaret Spufford's study of English popular literature, which compares the inventories of seven London booksellers to Samuel Pepys's collection of cheap books and pamphlets, offers pertinent conclusions for the present discussion.[31] In the seven inventories, religious works comprise 45 percent of the titles (compared to 19 percent in the library of Pepys, who preferred less austere writings). This figure is quite respectable, especially in regard to those that Daniel Roche has established for the catalogues of seventeenth-century booksellers in Paris, Lyon, Troyes, and Bordeaux: 28 percent, 42.5 percent, 73 percent, and 39 percent respectively, for devotional works.[32] In France, these same inventories are relatively lacking in preparations for death: 0.25 percent in Paris, 1.55 percent in Lyon, 5.20 percent in Troyes, and 2.60 percent in Bordeaux, out of the entire range of religious books. In contrast, Spufford finds that 20 percent of such publications in England specifically discussed death and judgment.[33] She remarks that "the most striking thing about the religious chapbooks is their domination, both in words and woodcuts, by the skeletal figure of Death."[34] She argues that after 1650, British printers flooded the market with treatments of a theme that had permeated oral culture for centuries. In any case, it is fair to conclude that during the third quarter of the seventeenth century, this macabre literature made a strong impact on the popular imagination.

Spufford also writes that low-cost books favored visual images of death and judgment over any other type of Christian iconography. For instance, the engraved frontispiece of *Heaven's Messengers* leaves out any New Testament figure, but does show Death blowing a trumpet, while Time stands nearby. In *Penny Godlinesses*, there are two images of Christ's resurrection, two of the Trinity, and one of the crucifixion, but nine of death, judgment, and the general resurrection. In English books of piety, skeletons appear even more often than the nevertheless frequent as well as striking image of the Divine Shepherd, which itself was vastly preferred by editors (and readers?) to portrayals of Christ's own life. Death, the grimacing antihero of these cheap publications, launching his arrows at both the young and the elderly and, carrying a banner with the words "I kill you all," was thus depicted as an Anticupid, as the unstoppable conqueror of the world.

It is likely that the plague of 1665 and the Great Fire of London in the following year reinforced the credibility of such images.[35] Spufford therefore wonders "whether the Puritans of New England were really more preoccupied with death than their English counterparts."[36] I would only add that, during the "Great Awakening" of the 1730s, Gilbert Tennent delivered a terrifying speech to the students of the "Little School" of Princeton, which invites them to consider that they may not outlive their teens. For the great majority of boys die when they are little; and death may strike even the members of his audience in just a few days, if not hours. Tennent asks the students if they have not witnessed the interment of short coffins, and reminds them that their small size and tender youth will not keep them out of Hell, nor free from the clutches of the Evil One, unless they behave well before dying.[37]

Like their Catholic counterparts, the Protestants of this period were encouraged constantly to think on death. In a 1618 sermon Donne advises his listeners to remember their last ends: "and fear will keep them from sinning; *Memorare praeterita*, remember the first things which God hath done for thee, and love will keep thee from sinning."[38] Another of his sermons—for Easter 1619, when King James I was, it is true, gravely ill—reminds the audience that life is a circle, which soon joins the grave with the cradle.[39] As he nearly always does, Donne ends this sermon on an optimistic note. Nonetheless, the preoccupation with death is frequent in this period's Protestant discourse, even if the main point is to guard against the fear of one's final departure. Charles Drelincourt's famous "Preparation," *Les Consolations de l'âme fidèle contre les frayeurs de la mort* (1651), went through some forty editions.[40] As the second remedy against death, the author recommends "awaiting it at all times."[41] In 1665, at the Protestant academy of Die, the winner of the second prize for piety in the junior class received a book entitled *The Terrors of Death*.[42] In fact, this would have been none other than Drelincourt's *Consolations*. It is revealing that such a book would be given as a prize to sixteen seventeen-year-old adolescents.

Back across the English Channel, the Puritan Thomas Becon's *The Sicke mannes Salve* (1561) was published seventeen more times by 1632.[43] The Puritan Michael Sparke's preparation for death, *The Crumbs of Comfort*, first appeared in 1623, then nine more times by 1629, and another thirty by 1652. Sparke himself notes that by this latter date 60,000 copies of his book had been sold.[44] The success of these prayers and meditations designed to help one toward a good death was surpassed, however, by Jeremy Taylor's *The Rule and Exercises of Holy Dying* (1650), the most famous in a long line of seventeenth-century English works in this genre (at least forty-four editions are known).[45] Taylor would have agreed with the great theologian and moderate Puritan Richard Baxter that "preparation for Death is the whole work of Life, for which many hundred years are not too long . . . the *best*, the *surest*, the Wisest *Preparation*, is that which is made by the whole course of a holy obedient heavenly Life."[46]

"Salvation," "security," "consolation," "good death": These terms convey the authors' intention, which was to reassure those who were brave enough to continually think on death. For them, death will bring "joy." Such is Donne's viewpoint:

> *I joy, that in these straits, I see my West;*
> *For, though theire currants yeeld returne to none,*

What shall my West hurt me? As West and East
In all flatt Maps (and I am one) are one,
So death doth touch the Resurrection.[47]

Donne was seriously ill when he composed these lines, and he goes on to affirm that suffering is the surest way toward salvation.[48] Thus even those authors who, like Donne, offered comforting visions and readied themselves for entry to "the sacred room," where, with the saints, they will sing "God's music forever," linger over the drastic consequences of Original Sin and the power it gave to death. Hence Christ's final victory over these forces will be all the greater.

Meanwhile, however, death will be the last enemy to be destroyed (I Cor. 15:26), after having been the enemy not only of men but also of Heaven. Until it is destroyed, full peace shall not reign over Heaven. On earth, it is man's most intelligent enemy. Death waits for the time when its certain victim "shall be able to stir no limbe in any other measure than a Fever or a Palsie shall shake them, when everlasting darknesse shall have an inchoation in the present dimnesse of mine eyes, and the everlasting gnashing in the present chattering of my teeth, and the everlasting worme in the present gnawing of the Agonies of my body."[49] Thus, even in the era's most optimistic sermons and spiritual writings, the macabre infiltrates discussion of death as punishment. In a similar sermon, Donne extends a tradition of commentary on Job 17:14—"[I] must say . . . to corruption, thou art my father, and to the Worme thou art my mother and my sister"—and elaborates with subtlety: "Miserable riddle, when the same worme must be my mother, and my sister, and my selfe. Miserable incest, when I must be married to my mother and my sister and bee both father and mother to my own mother and sister, beget and beare that worm which is all that miserable penury; when my mouth shall be filled with dust, and the worme shall feed, and feed sweetely upon me."[50]

The spirit of both the *danses macabres* and the *contemptus mundi* also inspire Jeremy Taylor's preface to his famous *Holy Dying*:

A man may read a sermon, the best and most passionate that ever man preached, if he shall but enter into the sepulcher of kings. In the same Escurial where the Spanish princes live in greatness and power, and decree war or peace, they have wisely placed a cemetery where their ashes and their glory shall sleep till time shall be no more; and where our kings have been crowned, their ancestors lay interred, and they must walk over their grandsire's head to take his crown. There is an acre sown with royal seed, the copy of the greatest change from rich to naked, from ceiled roofs to arched coffins, from living like gods to die like men. There is enough to cool the flames of lust, to abate the heights of pride, to appease the itch of covetous desires, to sully and dash out the dissembling colors of a lustful, artificial, and imaginary beauty.[51]

Thus the ghastly meditations of seventeenth-century English directors of conscience could not escape the vertigo of the macabre. Having explained that death is a release, Samuel Hieron then corrects himself:

this death as a release cannot but sweeten the remembrance of death, which is in itself full of bitterness; and to the nature of man, the very King of Feare.[52] *Let it be thought upon simply, the torture of a fervent sickness, the pangs of death, the violent renting asunder of two so well liking and agreeing friends as the soule and bodie, I speak of them naturally . . . the lying in the grave, there to embrace corruption, and there to become a a prey to stench and rottennesse, who can but abhorre to remember these things?*[53]

OTHER LAST ENDS AND THE *CONTEMPTUS MUNDI*

It is almost banal to observe that seventeenth- and eighteenth-century Protestants rivaled Catholics in associating fear and the Judgment that will lead to either Hell or Paradisc. Hence the ongoing success of Saint Bernard's *Memorare novissima*. For example, Gilbert Tennent preached that one should think often and deeply on death, on judgment and the torments of Hell. Such meditation would be the only way to endure the cruel dart of death.[54] One could thus align a number of interchangeable sermons from different countries and sects, in which churchmen intimidated their listeners with the wrath and judgment of God. What causes, wonders Johann Brenz, the predilection for sin that one sees all about? He answers that it results from "the fact that men do not know—or knowing, do not believe—that God is a cruel and strict tyrant toward sin, a terrible avenger who is not content to punish it with mere physical pain, but also with eternal tortures . . . If God's love cannot move us to refrain from evil, at least let us avoid it because of the extreme tortures that threaten us."[55]

In a sermon at Charenton in 1660, Drelincourt follows many of his Catholic colleagues by citing the famous phrase from the Letter to the Hebrews, which he uses as the basis for this warning: "Sinners, be not deceived, God cannot be mocked. His aggrieved patience will turn to fury. The more He waits to punish, the more hideous will be His punishments. "It is a fearful thing to fall into the hands of the living God." For He shall rain fire and brimstone on the wicked, and tempestuous winds shall be their portion."[56] Two years later Drelincourt explains that given our sins, it is dangerous not to be punished on earth. God punishes us for our own good. Indeed, what father would not punish his children? Conversely, woe betide those whom God does not punish here below: He often "abandons them to the devil, to be eternally tormented in hell."[57] All the same, if one's sins cross a certain threshold, will not the Almighty accumulate both earthly and afterlife punishments? "Destruction is at thy door," Drelincourt announces to a Protestant congregation in Paris, whose internal conflicts had increased. Penitence is therefore of the utmost necessity. "To prevent this terrible judgment, and to escape the lightning bolts God is prepared to hurl at our heads, this fast [of March 25, 1660] has been ordered, and we ask of you sighs, groans, and tears . . ."[58]

Protestant preachers frequently warned their various audiences not to forget God's judgments. Baxter, for one, poses the question: "Is not that man every worse than mad, that is going to God's Judgment, and never thinks of it?"[59] Hence the following advice: "Use frequently to think of the Certainty, nearness and dreadfulness of that day."[60] Furthermore, the moderate Puritan Daniel Featley affirms, "Observe ye not the heavie judgments of God lighting daily upon presumptuous sinners? See ye not before your eyes continual spectacle of Gods justice?"[61] In 1530s Saxony, the Lutheran superintendant made children learn the following dialogue by heart, which they recited in church on Sundays:

The child: "Tell me what Scripture says will happen to ingrates who scorn the word of God.

Another child answers:—. . . God will scorn and mock such a man, even if he will suffer intolerable anguish (Prov. 3). He will not hear him, but terribly punish him with numerous torments and disasters (Lev. 26), fevers, consumption, boils, plagues, swellings, war, fire, destruction, hailstorms, epidemics, and utter ruin. In short, God will pour on him so many terrors, miseries, sufferings, failures, and misfortunes that he will sink to the bottom of despair."[62]

This type of admonition returns with a vengeance during times of collective misfortune. Samuel Hieron recommends the following prayer "in time of death and famine":

Cleaness of teeth (O Lord) and scarcenesse of bread, have been anciently threatened by thee, as judgements upon the sonnes of men for their sinnes. Many waies also thou hast to turn a fruitfull land into barrennesse for the wickednesse of the inhabitants: Thou canst make the heaven over our heads as brasse, and the earth under us as iron, by bringing a drought upon the land . . . O Lord, thou hast even store-house of punishments.[63]

Hieron composed another prayer, "applied to the time of great contagion," which censures frivolous Christians for their disdain of the preachers' warnings:

Heavy at this time is thy hand upon us, and fearfull is the disease with which thou hast afflicted us . . .

It is just with thee, to smite us with botches and scabbes that cannot be healed, and to make the pestilence even to cleave unto our loins, and to sweep us away from the earth . . . For, how have we multiplied our iniquities before thee, and to what a shameless and intolerable measure are our sins increased? Many warnings have been given by thy Ministers, thou hast risen early and late, and sent unto us by them: yet we have made our hearts as an Adamant stone, and have put from us the evil day, persuading ourselves, that their sermons were but wind, and that they did but commend unto us their own fancies.[64]

"What is the plague and other judgements," Richard Sibbes asks his audience, "but so many messengers sent to everyone of us to knocke, and our answer must be, Lord I will repent of my evil ways . . . but when there is no answer, God will add plagues upon plagues till we give our answer, till we repent and turn from our wicked ways."[65] The London plagues of 1603, 1625, and 1665, to name only a few, credibly supported such observations, which clearly appealed to a widespread belief in an omnipresent God, always ready to use His own creations against sinful mankind.

In this regard, the verse and prose writings of George Wither (1590–1667) are conclusive. Although Wither was of a surly and melancholic disposition, he placed his theological views on the side of the "Arminians." This notwithstanding, he interpreted the plagues of 1625 and 1665, the comet of 1664, and the Great Fire of 1666 as obvious signs of the wrath of God.[66] One day in 1625 he saw "God's dreadfull Angell" (the plague) entering his room.[67] He also describes "The King of Gods; and from about / His eye-lids, so much terror sparkled out / That every circle of the Heav'ns it shooke, / And all the World did tremble at his looke."[68] When one adds this image of God to the classic doctrine of the chosen few, the result, though it may only be a limited case, is the extremist type of sermon that the Puritans of New England willingly used to terrify children: "remember Death; think much of Death; think how it will be on a deathbed"; "after the Judgment, children shall see their Father going with Christ to Heaven, but themselves going away into Everlasting Punishment."[69] Contemporary memoirs record that seven-year-old children would scream upon hearing that they might join the damned in Hell.

The attention paid to judgment explains how death was difficult even for the most devout Protestants. As in the Catholic realm, "fine deaths" did occur: for example, that of Charles Drelincourt, as told by his son. The famous pastor of Charenton devoted himself to his flock and visited the sick to the last limit of his strength. He then met his end with serenity and confidence.[70] The dying moments of a Poitou Calvinist, Anne Fontaneau, who died in 1664, were imbued with the same feelings. Her daughter describes her "wishing to be set free to become one with Christ her Savoir."[71] A seventeenth-century biographer likewise affirms that a friend, visiting the pious Robert Bolton (d. 1631) in his extreme illness,

> *found him wonderously desirous to be dissolved and to be with Christ: He said, Oh this vile Carcass of mine! When will it give way that my Soul may get out and go to my God? When will this rotten Carcass be consumed, that I may mount up to Heaven? And when he saw any probable Symptoms of Death (which he called, the Little Crevises and from which his Soul did peep out) he was exceedingly joyful.*[72]

Earlier chapters of this book have shown how some seventeenth- and eighteenth-century nuns died in this same fashion.

At the same time, just as certain others felt apprehension at the approach of death because of the "judgments of God," so too did devout Protestants, touched with an identical anguish, become alarmed at the prospect of the unknown country. Bernard Vogler, an expert on the German Reformation, argues that only a small minority experienced a calm, quiet death.[73] In a Sunday sermon, the Lutheran theologian Tileman Heshusius (d. 1588) made the following claim: "Of all afflictions, death is the most grievous. One must submit to this tyranny with fear and trembling . . . It is the glimpse of eternal damnation that causes the fear and anguish of death."[74]

Even people who had lived their entire lives convinced of their salvation succumbed to doubts at the last moment. Thomas Brooks writes that the Elizabethan theologian Richard Hooker lost confidence on his deathbed, after almost thirty years of close communion with God.[75] On the other hand, a pastor who was generally reputed to be one of the finest and most saintly in all England only became calm but one hour before his death. Again, this *in extremis* pacification resembles that of pious Catholics, as part of a larger syndrome of "difficult death."[76] Another such Protestant case occurred in Lancashire in 1601. A young noblewoman, Katherine Brettergh, fell deathly ill and became panic-stricken by the thought of judgment. From all accounts, however, her life had been "most saintly." She was thus seized by the fear of damnation. Her relatives tried in vain to reassure her. They sent for the minister of the parish, who still had no success, and therefore called in one of his neighboring colleagues. The affair became so upsetting that the woman's anguish affected her entourage and risked giving the local papists a chance to turn this metaphysical distress into an attack on the new religion. Happily, five hours before the end, Katherine was pacified and found "internal joy," praying and thanking God until the last second.[77] If one of the clerics present at her bedside believed it necessary to publish the story of this death, it was apparently due to its not being an isolated case: The public needed to be informed that the spiritual agony of a pious woman had ended happily.

Before leaving the subject of death, it is worth noting yet another similarity between the pastoral efforts of Rome and the Reformation, namely the stress on the horrific death of sinners. This was the logical outcome of a sensationalistic theology of Original Sin, pushed to the limit by Protestantism. The Lutheran preacher Heshusius declares in a Christmas sermon: "Alas, men here on earth keep not the peace of God in their conscience. Their hearts are filled with cares, anguish, and fear because they know that God is angry with them."[78] The antidote to this "fear" is faith. For those, however, who refuse this mainstay of salvation, there remains only the horrid certainty of their internal decay. Thus, Heshusius asserts, "many cannot bear the anguish [of sin] and kill themselves like Judas and so many others."[79] As for other impious folk, behold "the anger and agitation in which they die: they bellow like wild beasts, move and shake their hands and feet. Their eyes gleam as if they were filled with fire, and strike fear into any onlooker. This is the sign that the worm (of remorse) is gnawing at their hearts, and that the eternal fire, which will never go out, is already burning inside them."[80] In a New Year's Day sermon, Johann Gerhardt confirms this description by implying that the death of the righteous is always tranquil. He thus contrasts the "sweet slumber" of the devout to the tragic dying moment of the impious. The latter, he says, "end their days amid fears, and their words and gestures betray the torture within their hearts. Such is their just death, which is the beginning of that other, eternal death."[81]

In the next century Drelincourt echoes these German Lutherans. His famous *Consolations* . . . feature a running commentary on the bad conscience of the sinner. He writes, "it can be said of such wretches, that hell comes to them before they go to hell, and that in their own lifetime they are already racked by the dreadful torments of the life to come. Whence it happens that some of them despair to the point of committing detested suicide, as though they had feared that no other hand would be wicked enough to kill them."[82] This international language, which had not yet taken agnosticism into account, resurfaces in seventeenth-century England. Richard Sibbes maintains that

> *there is a noise of fear in the unrepentant persons heart; wheresoever he goes, he is afraid of the plague, affraid of sicknesse, affraid of death, affraid of everybody; he knows he hath his heaven here . . . therefore he is affraid he shall go from the terrors of conscience to the torments of hell, his conscience speaks terrible things to him, what a cursed state is this? If he look to Heaven, God is ready to pour down his wrath . . . If he look to the Earth, he knowes not how soone he shall be laid there, or that the earth may swallow him up. If he thinke of death it strikes terror to him; every thing is uncomfortable to an unrepentant sinner.*[83]

The Puritan Christopher Love also avers that one of the proofs of the existence of Hell lies in "those horrors and terrors of Conscience that are in wicked men when they are dying . . . The very terrors of Conscience declare, there is a hell, a place of torment provided for wicked men."[84] Similarly, the Anglican Donne describes both the tragic death of the wicked rich man and the tortures of the dying sinner enmeshed in the agony of despair.[85] In his turn, the Baptist John Bunyan evokes the deathbed of the godless person, around whom swarm a crowd of demons.[86]

Regarding predestination, we will again find the temptation to despair that the *Artes Moriendi* had made familiar. For the moment, emphasis must be placed on a consequence of the discourse on the sinner's bad conscience and tragic death: One must not delay one's conversion. Like Catholics, Protestants stressed the dangers of "delaying penance." Brenz teaches:

> *Since we must die, we must also prepare ourselves for death by our own conversion. If there were no other life, or if one could not obtain the privilege of immortality, one might perhaps conceive of living according to one's pleasures, without making any effort to be godly. But nothing is more certain: there is life after death, and one cannot prevent death from cutting men down. One cannot negotiate with death so that it will not come. There never yet was a king so powerful who could abrogate this custom in his land . . . Therefore one must resign oneself to suffering death, and especially to preparing for it in good time . . . One must not defer penitence until one's final breath . . . In this matter, any delay is dangerous.*[87]

Gerhardt gives the same advice in the seventeenth century:

> *We must not put off our conversion to the hour of our death, but do penance during that very time when we can sin. It is perilous to delay penance until the end of one's life: first, because of the uncertainties of this moment, but also because of the uncertainties of our being converted at that time. For then penitence comes less from the love of God than from the fear of punishment, and a man seems not so much to leave his sins behind as to be left behind by them.*

This was a traditional phrase in this type of discourse. "Moreover, the sharpest pains are often joined to death. At the end, we see our relatives, wife, and children. Their sorrow and their pity grieve us so much that, unless we already be detached from them, we can only raise our hearts to God with great difficulty."[88]

English preachers spoke in the same terms. One example among many is a sermon by Henry Smith (d. 1591) on Jacob's ladder. Although Smith's leanings were Puritan, his audience was large. He was nicknamed "silver-tongue," to signify that he came just below Saint John Chrysostom. From 1592 to 1632, his sermons (mainly given in London) went through fourteen editions. On the subject of Jacob's ladder, he says:

> *It is an old saying, Repentance is never too late; but it is a true saying, Repentance is never too soon; for so soon as ever we sin, we had need to ask forgiveness. Besides, Repentance is a gift, and therefore it must be taken when it is offered . . . The time past is gone, and thou canst not call that to repent in; the time to come is uncertain, and thou canst not assure that to repent in: the present time is only thine, and thou mayest repent in that, but anon that will be gone too.*[89]

In 1634 *The Mystery of self-Deceit* by the English Puritan Daniel Dyke (d. 1614) was translated into French and published at Geneva under the title *La Sonde de la conscience*. This treatise appeared in ten English editions before 1645, in two German versions (1652 and 1739), and one Hungarian translation (1670). One of its main preoccupations is the delaying of repentance. Three of its thirty-one chapters address the "deceit," "fraud," and "woes" of the "temporizer," in other words the person who puts off repentance.[90]

Preaching on the terrors of death, Sibbes describes, like Hieron, the coming of the "King of fear," and beseeches the listener not to delay repentance until the day of His terrible visit. "What sort of man will you be then?" Sibbes asks. The child of wisdom must always take every opportunity for asking pardon, for accepting the inspiration of the Holy Spirit, for examining his conscience and for self-correction.[91] At the funeral of the Bishop of Norwich, Joseph Hall, in 1656, John Whitefoote assures his listeners that "we should so spend every day, as considering it may be the last"; on the other hand, "what a desperate wretched thing it is to put off the time of repentance still, when our time to diē is so near." How can we put our trust in tomorrow? "Whether he that puts off his repentance till his deathbed, doth not he run the evident hazard of at least a hundred to one never to repent at all?"[92]

It is not surprising that the preachers of "awakenings" insisted on the need to hasten one's penitence. One of John Wesley's sermons is specifically entitled "Awake, thou that sleepest." The orator vehemently exhorts each of his listeners, saying: "[awake] lest thou 'drink at the Lord's hand the cup of His fury . . . Stand up this moment . . . Hast thou put off the old man, and put on the new? . . . [God] hath given us long space to repent. He lets us alone this year also: but he warns and awakens us by thunder. His judgments are abroad in the earth; and we have by reason to expect the heaviest of all."[93] All of the above warnings, as well as those that appear in Donne's sermons,[94] could have as easily been spoken by Catholic priests and missionaries. On either side of the confessional barrier, the same message was delivered to the faithful: Death and judgment threaten you, therefore make haste to be converted.

This pressing and constant plea makes any lengthy study of the Protestant Hell unnecessary, since such a warning implies another widely and obviously perceived threat: that of the eternal torments. Confirmed by the Augsburg Confession,[95] although not mentioned in the thirty-nine Articles of the Anglican Church, Hell was a belief shared by Catholics and most Protestants. Jurieu chided Nicole for finding this "dogma"—to which Arnauld's friend naturally adhered—to be in contradiction with "ordinary human understanding" and that it had to be accepted solely on the authority of biblical references. Jurieu's counterargument is that "reason, custom, and all the laws of the world" prove the existence as well as the necessity of Hell.[96]

Nonetheless, it appears that apart from Puritan circles, the stress on eternal tortures was less heavy than in Catholic countries. Out of Donne's 160 surviving sermons, only ten specifically accentuate divine punishments and Hell. Still, more than a third of his homilies (at least fifty-five) make sin their dominant theme (original as well as daily sin), and thus they indirectly allude to the punishments that await the obdurate. This implication would have been increased by the fact that Donne, like almost all Protestant and Catholic theologians of his time, adhered to the Augustinian conception of the "mass of perdition."[97] This doctrine prods the usually reassuring Dean of Saint Paul's toward a spirit of pessimism. In any case, Donne's notoriety helped to spread the fame of several of his passages on Hell. The most famous appears in a sermon spoken in 1622 before the Count of Carlisle. Donne therein discusses the nature of damnation and explains in the most orthodox manner that the physical pain of the afterlife is nothing next to being deprived of God. Although this text is indeed rhetorical, it is mixed with evident conviction and true poetic force. It is also significant that Donne speaks in the first person, and hence gives his speech a highly intimate as well as eloquent sense of anguish:

> *That God should let my soule fall out of his hand, into a bottomless pit, and roll an unremoveable stone upon it, and leave it to that which it finds there . . . and never thinke more of that sould, never have more to doe with it. That of that providence of God, that studies the life and preservation of every weed, and worme, and ant, and spider, and toad, and viper, there should never, never any beame flow out of me; that that God, who looked upon me, when I was nothing, and called me when I was not, as though I had been, out of the womb and depth of darknesse, will not looke upon me now, when, though a miserable, and a banished, and a damned creature, yet I am his creature still, and contribute something to his glory,*

> *even in my damnation . . . That that God should loose and frustrate all his owne purposes and practises upon me, and leave me, and cast me away, as though I had cost him nothing, that this God at last, should let this soule goe away, as a smoake, as a vapour, as a bubble, and that then this soule cannot be a smoake, nor a vapour, nor a bubble, but must lie in darknesse, as long as the Lord of light is light it selfe, and never a sparke of that light reach to my soule; What Tophet [the dung-hill near Jerusalem] is not Paradise, what Brimstone is not Amber, what gnashing is not a comfort, what gnawing of the worme is not a tickling, what torment is not a marriage bed to this damnation, to be secluded eternally, eternally, eternally from the sight of God?*[98]

Outside the Anglican Church, the Baptist John Bunyan is the epitome of the preacher alarmed and fascinated by Hell. In his *Treatise of the Fear of God* (1679), he teaches that if the fear of God is motivated only by the apprehension of his judgments, it is "an ungodly fear" and brings "no change of heart."[99] At the same time, one gains "reverential fear" of God only via a road strewn with fears. Bunyan's *A Holy Life* (1684) agrees with many other contemporary preachers that the cries of the damned, the eternity of punishment, the impossibility for the outcast to repent, and the host of demons are subjects that must be frequently impressed on people, so that they will change their evil ways.[100] The famous *Pilgrim's Progress* (1678–84) not coincidentally begins by mentioning the flames that threaten sinners. In the first chapter, the Pilgrim, named "Christian," warns his wife and children that their city "will be burned with fire from heaven" and that they must escape from it as quickly as possible.[101] It is possible, however, to err on the road of escape. "Christian" lets himself be deceived by "Mr. Worldly-Wiseman," who treacherously steers him toward a high mountain. From its height "came also flashes of fire . . . that made Christian afraid that he should be burned."[102] It was thus a great struggle for the Pilgrim to escape hellfire in both his town and the outside world.

Nevertheless, Bunyan most thoroughly explores Hell in his other writings. *The Life and Death of Mr. Badman* (1680), *The Greatness of the Soul* (1683), *A Holy Life* (1684), and above all *A few Sighs from Hell* (1658) are highly revealing in this regard. In the last-named work, the parables of Lazarus and Dives provide renewed relations with the Dantesque tradition, and describe the damned "surrounded with fears, with terrors, with torment and vengeance."[103] One of the damned seems to have his belly crammed with pitch, which sets him on fire. There are swords reddened by bellows, burning pincers that rip flesh to tiny shreds, demons busy filling the bodies of the damned with molten lead, roasting spits, and so on. Those abandoned by God are seen to "fry, scorch and broil, and burn for ever" but are not consumed[104]: Bunyan thus renews the obsession with fire analyzed by Bachelard. "Thou hadst better have been plucked one limb from another; thou hadst better have been made a dog, a toad, a serpent; nay, any other creature in the visible world, then to die unconverted."[105] This evangelism of fear fully and freely operates in *The Life and Death of Mr. Badman*, a dialogue between Attentive and Wiseman. The latter, impressed by the alarming statements of his neighbor, does not fail to exclaim: "But if, as you say, and that truly, the very name of hell is so dreadful, what is the place itself, and what are the punishments that are there inflicted, and that without the least intermission, upon the souls of damned men, for ever and ever?"[106] To briefly return to *A few Sighs from Hell*, it must be noted that this treatise, which apparently developed from an actual sermon, met with tremendous success. At least thirty-five editions of it came out between 1658 and 1797, two of which were published in Boston in 1708 and 1731.[107]

In the opening pages of *Grace Abounding to the Chief of Sinners* (1666), Bunyan makes an admission as telling as it is disturbing:

> *These things, I say, when I was but a child nine or ten years old, did so distress my soul, that when in the midst of my many sports and childish vanities, amidst my vain companions, I was often much cast down and afflicted in my mind therewith, yet could I not let go my sins. Yea, I was also then so overcome with despair of life and heaven, that I should often wish either that there had been no hell, or that I had been a devil—supposing they were only tormentors; that if it must needs be that I went thither, I might be rather a tormentor, than be tormented myself.*[108]

Excessive feelings of guilt in early childhood, despair, sadistic temptations: Such are the dark vistas opened by this exceptionally loaded text. For whatever his personal equation may have been, when Bunyan eagerly described Hell he was drawing on the Puritans' standard preaching repertoire. As we have seen, many Puritans were convinced that "Threatnings and Punishments, Hopes and Fears of the State of another life are necessary to the well governing of this world," as Baxter has said.[109] William Perkins repeats the saying that "the right way to go unto heaven is to sail by hell."[110] Edmund Calamy urges the saints themselves to contemplate the Day of Judgment and hell, that place of enless and unalleviated torments.[111] Others, in the manner of Donne, placed more emphasis on the psychological aspect of the infernal punishment, namely the deprivation of God. For example, Thomas Goodwin argues that the "knowledge" of this immense loss brings "horrors, yellings, groans, distractions."[112]

The majority, however, of Puritan preachers—Keach, Sibbes, Bromley, Love, and so on—dwell on the physical sufferings and the action of fire in hell, on sulfur and quicksilver.[113] Samuel Hieron claims that the "unspeakable" torments of the beyond are "not to be comprehended, much lesse to be endured."[114] Hieron also takes the line of Catholic preachers in showing his listeners how "the word 'never' is exceeding fearfull."[115] During a funeral oration, Daniel Featley encourages the wise to listen well and think on their final ends before it is too late, so that they may choose between God's never-ending springtime and "the lake of fire and brimstone," where the damned wallow with the Devil and his minions, "the smoake of whose torment ascendeth up for ever and ever, and they have no rest day or night."[116] The rigorous Christopher Love reached new heights in this type of sermon: "If a man had the tongues of Men and Angels, he is not able to unfold the extreme misery of a tormented soul . . . If all the land were paper, and all the water in the sea were ink, as many pens as grass upon the ground, and as many writers as sands upon the sea shore, all would be too little to set forth the torments of hell.[117] There is an obvious drawback to the thematic discussion of these selections: The focus is narrowed on a limited subject, isolated from its context. It would be wrong to think that even among the Puritans Hell was a preferred theme for preaching. Reacting against earlier historical work on this subject, Babette M. Levy notes: "Considered in relation to the mass of sermon literature produced in New England between 1620 and 1670, such horrific descriptions of the fate of the unelect are infrequent, at least in the printed sermons."[118] Later, things changed somewhat when the preachers became aware that the settlers' moral rectitude had abandoned the style of the "Pilgrim Fathers." Finally, a study of the evangelism of fear in the Protestant as well as Catholic world should not be chained to texts exclusively devoted to Hell and death.

Just as important and tragic are the repeated calls to undertake the necessary "contempt for this world." This was further common ground for Catholics and Protestants, who together constantly referred to the primal catastrophe of Original Sin. In sixteenth-century Germany, the *Sententiae pueriles* taught schoolchildren such phrases as "*Homo ad calamitatem nascitur*" (Man is born to misfortune), "*Hominis cor ex natura sua malum*" (The heart of man is naturally wicked), and "*Homo sibi ipsi calamitatum auctor*" (Man is the author of his own misery).[119] In a Sunday sermon on Luke 7:11–17—the ostensibly comforting episode of the widow's son at Nain —Gerhardt starts preaching on death, in the respect that it itself is preceded by "the miseries of life." An entire section of his homily thus addresses this latter point, with all the traditional baggage of the *contemptus mundi*, as well as the usual quotations from Job, Ecclesiasticus, and Saint Bernard. Man is born to suffer; he lives in fear; he is overcome by his infirmities. A heavy yoke weighs down the sons of Adam from the womb to the tomb, the common mother of all. We are subject to work, to accidents, to disease, poverty, cares, anxieties, and fear: "How miserable, how disastrous is this our life!"[120]

Johann Arndt, after Luther the most widely read of the "evangelical" theologians, frequently insists on the "contempt for the world." In his popular pamphlet, "On Regeneration," he shows the reader that "the inheritance man receives from Adam by ancient, or natural descent is the greatest of all evils, namely sin, which brings us hatred, anger, suffering, death, the devil, hell, and damnation . . ."[121] The *De Vero Christiano*, Arndt's best-known tract, invites the faithful soul "to imitate Christ and scorn the world, to hate one's life in this world."[122] Significantly, one of the chapters of this book is comprised of an "*Oratio pro contemptu mundi*," stitched together from various biblical phrases: ". . . O how much did I love the vanity of this world, which fades like a flower, grows dry as hay, and passes like a shadow! O, why did I give my love and my heart to that which is feeble and fleeting, to shades without life, to nothing? O how many pains, sorrows, cares, and troubles did I give myself for petty profitless things, in exchange for my immortal soul! Where are Solomon's glory and magnificence now? They are withered, like the flower . . ."[123] The "*Ubi sunt?*" returns here with renewed vigor. These reminders clarify another of Arndt's striking expressions: "Those who meditate not on death and the misery of the world cover themselves in theories, like mud-laden pigs."[124]

"Vanity of vanities . . .": This belief pervades seventeenth-century French Protestantism. Both Drelincourt and Jean Daillé remind the Charenton congregation that "the gales and whirlpools of this raging sea of the world carry our vessel toward destruction . . . All that is under the sun is but vanity and vexation of spirit . . . all flesh is like the grass, and all man's glory is like the flowers of a field . . . The finest of our days is but vexation and torment."[125]

Even more eloquent testimony comes from an anonymous speech in *Le Mépris du monde* (1612; place of publication unknown), which is followed by a "meditation on the grief at the death of a loved one."[126] A hand-written annotation attributes the entire work to Drelincourt. This attribution, however, cannot be correct, since in 1612 Drelincourt was only seventeen. Moreover, "the meditation on death . . ." was composed by the husband of Marie Perrin, who died in 1610. Whatever the case may be, the author is Protestant, though capable of having written the *Imitation of Christ*. The opposition of the soul and body, the certainty that all earthly things turn out for the worst, the message that "we hasten *en masse* toward our ruin,"[127] are commonplaces of this text, which repeats the age-old belief that life is "nothing . . . but perpetual misery."[128] "The principal benefit of virtue is (thus) the contempt for this life."[129] The "angelic anthropology" of the desert fathers and medieval monks resurfaces here. The author castigates those who, "instead of transforming themselves into angels, transform themselves to beasts,"[130] and strongly advises:

"Know then . . . let us no longer debase our spirits among these mortal things, let us divorce ourselves from the earth: only breathe that which is eternal,"[131] and let us make "war against the body."[132] "Let us not love the world, nor the things of the world . . . the world and its covetousness doth pass."[133] This last phrase again demonstrates the classic slippage between one sense of the word "world" and the other. On the whole, this discourse tends to recognize not the relative, the transitory, nor the physical: "What is man? A weak body, subject to a thousand diseases, in which the soul is housed only as a visitor, put there by force. It is a rented lodging, which must be left vacant when the lease runs out."[134] Like Godeau, the text reaches the logical conclusion that there is no point in pitying the death of children:

> *You have lost your children; was it not God who gave them to you, who now takes them from this world? Were they not born but to die? . . . Were they less mortal than so many others who are taken each day to the grave? . . . Is it something new that death should carry off a child? Could you, who are mortal, have immortal children? . . .*
>
> *Is there not shame in shedding so many tears for happy souls who are now enjoying eternity, who died to the world to live with God? . . . True, they gave you pleasure; you had hopes that they would support you in your old age, and that they would inherit your belongings. But God did not create them for such vain, low, and earth-bound purposes.*[135]

Such a citation makes it no surprise to find the *contemptus mundi* in puritanical preaching. One preacher declares: "it is a common proverbe: *Homo bulla*, Man is but a bubble of water, soone up, soone downe. Man is but grasse, soone withered away: but a flower soone faded away: but a smoke soone vanishing away: but dust soone puffed away: but a shadow suddenly carried away"[136]: The repetition of the same analogies goes on *ad infinitum*. Henry Smith is at pains to resume the "*Ubi sunt*?" anthem,[137] and he also compares life to the fleeting wind and dissolving vapors.[138] The pessimistic Hieron sees human nature as a "thing made of these two, Corruption and Death: there is nothing in it but Evill, and there is nothing due unto it but destruction."[139] Sibbes adopts the hallowed saying "Better is the day of death than the day of birth"[140] and argues "let us consider wee are not for this lefe, we are not to live here alway: the child in the wombe is not for that life, and when it is in the world, it is not for this life; there is a third life that we are for."[141]

Featley provides a rather remarkable passage on the vanity of life: "man, like a Tennis-ball, is beat from wall to wall, and as it were racketted from one trouble to another, from one care to another." The ancients called man the sport of the gods (*ludus deorum*). The vanity of youth follows the foolishness of childhood, the ambition of maturity succeeds the madness of youth, and then the terrors of death rapidly approach. The course of life is a succession of miseries; we fall from external to internal woes, from sickness to sin and vice versa; we go "from feares to cares, and from cares to feares."[142] Finally, Richard Baxter—though the list could be expanded—closely links the pessimistic view of man to the observation of his inconstancy and mutability:

> *truly the sad experiences of these times, have much abased my confidence in man, and caused me to have lower thoughts of the best, then sometimes I have had. I confess I look on man, as such a distempered, slippery and unconstant things, and of such a natural mutability of Apprehensions and Affections, that I shall never*

> *more call any man on earth, My friend, but with a supposition that he may possibly become mine enemy.*[143]

These lines appear in a text composed especially for "poor women, and Country people." This misanthropy, however, followed the logic of a *contemptus mundi* based on a firm belief in man's utter depravity.

Arthur Dent's *The Plaine Mans Pathway to Heaven* (1601) was one of the most famous books of devotion in seventeenth-century England. Speaking in the voice of a theologian, the author provides a tirade reminiscent of Pleberio's in *La Celestina*[144]:

> *The world is a sea of glasse, a pageant of fond delights, a Theatre of vanity, a labyrinth of errour, a gulfe of griefe, a sty of filthiness, a vale of misery, a spectacle of woe, a river of tears, a stage of deceit, a cage full of owls, a den of scorpions, a wilderness of wolves, a cabin of bears, a whirlwind of passions, a feigned Comedie, a delectable frenzy, where is false delight, assured grief, certain sorrow, uncertain pleasure, lasting woe, fickle wealth, long heavinesse, short joy.*[145]

Did the Puritans have a monopoly on such language in sixteenth- and seventeenth-century Britain? Not entirely. The Anglican Donne delivered several sermons on the "afflictions" of life and "the miserable condition of all mankinde." In one, he identifies man as "the Receptacle, the Ocean of all misery. Fire and Aire, Water and Earth, are not the Elements of man; inward decay, and outward violence, bodily pain and sorrow of heart may be rather styled his Elements; And though he be destroyed by these, yet he consists of nothing but these." The orator continues by asserting that man is no more than "misery" and "crying"; hence he cries that he is come to this great stage of fools.[146] Like Donne, the Methodist John Wesley rejects the Calvinists' dramatic conception of predestination. He also offers relatively optimistic prospects to the faithful, on condition that they convert themselves; his sermons, however, prove that he still partook of the traditional discourse on the contempt for this world. Two of his orations ask the question: "What is man?" Another explains "In What Sense We Are to Leave the World." A fourth discusses "Worldly Folly," while a fifth affirms that life is a dream.[147]

CHAPTER 21

Eschatology and Predestination

THE END IS NEAR

The preceding pages have located, within the evangelism of fear, shared aspects of Catholic and Protestant preaching. This chapter will now survey two more distinctly Protestant preoccupations: eschatology and anxieties concerning predestination. Certainly the aim is not to suggest that the Reformation had sole rights to these topics. As this study has already shown, Catholic preachers also made much of the Last Judgment and the chosen few. In the century and a half that followed Luther, however, the Protestant ministers' eschatological message that the end is near became all the more urgent, especially in Germany and England. Furthermore, the doctrine of the bondage of the will that soon became a universal Calvinist belief brought with it a heavy burden of anxiety: Who could be certain of their election?

In *La Peur en Occident*, I examined the theme of Protestant eschatology.[1] I now want to bring special attention to the siege mentality that permitted the resurgence of already ancient hopes and fears and also stimulated a discourse mixed of fears, threats, and expectations. When a siege mentality takes hold of either an individual or a group, there is the risk of feeling more exalted and powerful the more one senses one's growing weakness in a losing battle against the enemy. In sixteenth-century Germany, this was especially the case with the words and actions of both Thomas Müntzer (between 1520 and 1525) and Johann van Leyden in 1534–35. Filled with millenary spirit, believing themselves to be prophets newly-inspired, convinced that in the Christianity of their time "the eels madly fornicate with the serpents," each of them sought to establish the kingdom of God on earth, and so end all corruption, constraint, and discord. They also realized that the immensity of their project entailed the radical overthrow of the entire social and political order. They therefore believed that the "elect" must have recourse to violence. They cited Deuteronomy (13:6) to proclaim that "the enemies do not have the right to live," and literally interpreted Luke 19:27: "But those mine enemies, which would not that I should reign over them, bring hither, and slay them before me." The disparity between ends and means thus becomes a source of both exaltation and violence. These sixteenth-century "Elijahs" announce—and seek to accelerate—the devastating chaos that will lead to the new earthly Paradise. They did not doubt God's effective aid, which "has thrown the mighty from their thrones and raised the humble."[2] These extremist ideologies serve as magnifying glasses through which one discerns, as if in a laboratory, the workings of an eschatological discourse: Fear is driven out—or masked—by aggressivity and makes up for the gloom of the present with the brightness of the future.

This analysis clarifies the numerous Protestant sermons that announce the coming end of the world: a terrifying prospect for sinners, an exalting one for the elect. More often than not, this type of preaching (with some notable exceptions) departed from the millenarian model and did not prophesy any kingdom of God on earth. Instead, it directly indicated the sudden arrival of the Last Judgment. What lurks behind these threats, compounded as they are by great expectations for the "predestined"? In short, a great fear, sprung from a dark diagnosis of the present.

Current historiography now more keenly perceives this eschatological aspect of the Reformation, which nevertheless continues to cause surprise. As noted above, humanists such as Guillaume Budé combined praise for the renaissance of arts and letters with the conviction that all was going from bad to worse and that the end of the world was at hand.[3] A parallel observation can be made regarding most Reformers. Luther, Melanchthon, the geographer Carion, and a great many Lutheran preachers throughout the sixteenth century and afterward affirmed that history was reaching its end and that the Day of Judgment was soon coming. At the same time, they actively devoted themselves to the education of young people.[4] One might try to resolve the contradiction between these two attitudes by saying that the founders of Protestantism wanted to keep busy while awaiting the final day, an event for which they intended to give children the proper moral and religious formation. Should the historian, however, be so Cartesian? Should one rather concede the coexistence of contraries within communities as well as individuals? To a greater or lesser extent, each of us is self-contradictory: this exciting it is that makes human beings rich in their complexity, and history an occupation.

Luther and his German disciples experienced two inseparable types of fear. On the other hand, they were horrified by the state of affairs in their contemporary Christian world and therefore concluded that the compounding of sins could lead only to catastrophe and final deliverance. On the other hand, they were aware, more than Müntzer and the Westphalian Anabaptists, of the precariousness of their status as Reformers within their social milieu: They felt themselves hemmed in by numerous enemies. They blamed Satan for these two categories of danger and saw him as the master of the game, who moved his various pawns across the world's chessboard in order to capture as many possible souls before the end of time. He was aiming to achieve the final checkmate before being eternally imprisoned, powerless within the depths of Hell. A Berlin pastor told his listeners: "The devil, seeing the world grow old, does all he can to lull the conscience of men, so that they will die fully secure in their sins."[5]

Having done so already,[6] I will not repeat my emphasis on the strong sense of uneasiness felt by the sixteenth-century German elite. On the other hand, it is necessary to recall that the prominence in Protestant literature of the demon, "the prince of this world," of witchcraft, blasphemy, of the endless descriptions of contemporary vices, monstrous phenomena, disturbing omens, and the like, can be understood only when connected to eschatological pronouncements, to the belief that the Antichrist had already come, and to the certainty that human history was nearing its conclusion. Sinners therefore had to be awakened, by being shown the terrible consequences that would soon face them. This terroristic discourse did have its consoling side: The righteous would soon see the end of their fears and anxieties.

Bearing these points in mind, I especially wish to highlight the fragility of the Reformation in Germany—and throughout Europe—during the sixteenth and early seventeenth centuries. Hindsight allows us to see that Protestantism succeeded in establishing itself throughout half of Europe. Luther's contemporaries, however, as well as his later successors, were in no way certain of this partial victory. For a long time Protestants had good reason to fear the silencing of "evangelical" voices. The preservation of the Lutheran Reformation in Germanic Europe was not secured until the treaties of Westphalia (1648). Early on, it appeared that a Catholic counterattack was developing—hence the panic over the Jesuits. While Germany was at peace in the second half of the sixteenth century, the Roman reconquest was targeting nearby France and the Low Countries, while Spain asserted itself as the world's superpower. Then, during the Thirty Years' War, circumstances frequently seemed to favor the Catholic armies. In addition, there were the Turkish threats, the dissensions between Protestants, and returns to the traditional religion: in short, myriad reasons for Lutherans to fear the failure of their efforts.

This persistence of the "besieged city" explains the unbridled attacks of writers and "evangelical" preachers against the diverse enemies of God. Among other insults, Luther called the Pope "the devil's swine," the mass "an invention of hell," and the sacrament of holy orders "the sign of the beast of Revelations." Songs, pamphlets, farces, and sermons constantly resumed the same accusations, which mingled the Pope, Antichrist, and devils within an eschatological discourse. Their satires were not only propagandistic, but also expressed a belief in the imminence of the final catastrophe. The comedy "Tug-of-War" (ca. 1525) features Luther pulling a rope against his enemies Eck, Murner, and others. The Reformer cries: "I want to play tug-of-war with the Antichrist. To support my cause I have only you, Lord; your passion is my only strength. The Pope has many soldiers, for he commands the army of hell. I risk everything in fighting such a battle. But always, Lord, you will be with me."[7] Thomas Kirchmaier, nicknamed Naegeorgius, was a preacher of Thuringia and also the most prolific of the Protestant dramatists. His *Pammachius* (1538), translated into German the following year, exposes the treason of the Pope Pammachius, who renounces Jesus Christ, puts himself in Satan's service, and tries to draw the Emperor into his heresy. Jesus, however, saves the day by sending Paul and Truth to Wittenberg. The preface to the German translation states that "the doctrine of the Pope is an abomination, a hellish and diabolical blasphemy" and that the Pope is "the accursed and damned Antichrist."[8]

In 1555 the former Franciscan Burckhard Waldis published *Burlesque Verses*, a German version of another Latin work by Kirchmaier on the "Papist kingdom" and the "habits of the Pope." Notably, it affirms that "the cult of the Turks is far superior to that of the Papists" and that "the Turk has more reverence for God than all the Papists combined."[9] These *Burlesque Verses* were published five times in twenty years (1555–75). Johann Fischart's polemical pamphlets of the 1570s are no less violent toward "the Papacy, founded by the devil" and toward the "*Jesuit's Little Square Cap*." The Pope is labeled as "a vile charlatan" and a "coarse puller of teeth." At a time when monstrous prodigies abounded—a certain sign of both evil and an irate God—Fischart affirms that the "true arch-marvel" is "that sea-lamb, that beast seated on a throne, the Great Whore of Babylon established in Rome from hell . . . that poisonous spider and deadly magician."[10] Within the same accusation, Fischart associates papism, Jews, and witches: This was typical of contemporary Protestant eschatology.

At the end of the sixteenth century, the preacher Bartholomew Ringwaldt eloquently speaks for Lutheran pastors who lamented the world's general corruption, denounced the papacy, and announced the end of the world. In his poem, *Die lauter Wahrheit* (1585) ("The True Truth"), the author perceives "the last days of the world . . . We can no longer hope for relief." Fourteen editions of this work appeared between 1585 and 1610. In another text, *Christliche Warnung des trewen Eckarts* (1588) (*The Christian Warning of the Faithful Eckart*), Ringwaldt sadly admits, "no, my verses will not succeed in freeing people from the glue of the devil." He attempts to impress sinners with a horrifying picture of Hell, wistfully describes the good Catholic "times of yore," and yet inveighs against the Antichrist of Rome, "that hideous shell of Satan."[11]

The preacher Erasmus Alber's *Das Buch von der Tugent und Weisshait* (*The Book of Virtue and Wisdom*) (1550), a collection of fables, opens with bold attacks against the host of enemies assailing the Lutheran city. In fact, the author of this book for schoolchildren explains that "the devil also has his fables: those invented by Papist monks and preachers, by Mohammed's Koran, and the Jews' talmudic fables: these only serve to increase the devil's empire, and to make people stray from God and the truth."[12] In Luther's wake, "evangelical" preachers waged war against both Jews and Turks. In a Sunday sermon published in 1564, Johann Spangenberg proclaims: "Indeed, Jews are wretches, always ready to speak slander . . . They have no fixed residence, no land, and every thread they wear is the product of their accursed greed and usury . . . Their greatest desire is that no Christian will survive . . . There is no race in the world as accursed, as malevolent, as cruel, and as dangerous as theirs."[13]

During the same period, Regius Urbanus's Latin writings were published in Nuremberg. One of his sermons invites the listener "to see Satan's image in the Turks, who are his dear and loyal instruments, because they bend to his every will." Such is their hatred for Christians that they are "ready to undergo every misery and disaster: hunger, thirst, injury, cuts, blows, pain, and even death—to harm them." After their victories "they pierce and massacre the young and the old, women and children, they disembowel pregnant women, impale and run stakes through fetus and little babies."[14]

The enemies of the New Testament are thus legion, and, moreover, they have never been so numerous: This is the oft-repeated belief of sixteenth- and early seventeenth-century Lutheran preachers. Dietrich Veit's sermons (published in 1549) point to the papacy as the first of Christ's adversaries, but he also lists Jews, Anabaptists, and Calvinists.[15] Urbanus is likewise convinced that Satan sends all sects against the Lutherans, especially that of the Anabaptists.[16] Heshusius uses the parable of the tares to identify all the weeds that have shot up within the church: Zwingli, Calvin, and the Anabaptists appear in this list, and the preacher cites the proverb: "When God builds a church, the devil puts up a chapel next door."[17] In the Latin comedy *Phasma*, presented at Tübingen before an audience of lords and princes and then twice translated into German, Luther and Brenz dispute with Zwingli, Bèze, and Carlstadt. The devil drags into Hell not only the Pope but all those who stray from "evangelical" orthodoxy.[18] A "spiritual comedy" by the deacon Martin Rinckhart, performed by his students in 1613 and entitled *The Christian Knight of Eisleben* portrays Luther as a valiant warrior, overwhelming all of God's enemies: the Pope, the "Sacramentarians, the Zwinglians, the Calvinists," and all "false-brethren." These pseudo-Christians are called "vipers" and are accused of vomiting "a flood of infernal fire" on Jesus and Mary.[19]

These evocations, which could be multiplied, show that even in Germany Lutherans did not feel they were in a position of strength. This feeling increased when, after the initial shock and early enthusiasm for the Reformation, the weight of the past and the Catholic counterattack brough a number of people back to the traditional faith. This infrequently stressed aspect of the religious situation deserves attention: One of Brenz's sermons observes that "among those who have accepted the Gospel, there are some who, seeing the prosperity of Papist idolatry, run back to it."[20] The former priest Urbanus strove in the 1560s to bring back to Lutheranism people who had been loosened by Catholic arguments: "We must hold fast to our doctrine. If Papists succeed in spreading doubt, we are lost. It has already happened that some who had joined us have lapsed to their former ways."[21] As for Heshusius, he laments of the defections of some of the German nobility, in a text dated 1581:

> *One could name some nobles who have studied at Wittenberg, listened to Martin Luther and Philip [Melanchthon] for an entire year, and accepted the truth of the New Testament. But hardly did they acquire a canonry, a rich abbey, or a powerful bishopric—in Augsburg or Wurzburg—than they freely renounced the New Testament, received communion with the Antichrist and fell back under the yoke of Satan.*[22]

Finally, the preachers sadly note that the doctrine of justification by faith has encouraged some people to misbehave—no matter what, they believe, they will be saved—and that religious indifference is on the rise. Having castigated those who return to papistry, Brenz adds: "Others run straight to atheism. They claim that both the old and the new priests should go hang."[23] Elsewhere, he attacks parents who "are not ashamed to say in public and to their families that everything spoken in church sermons is of no importance."[24] Heshusius launches a pell-mell diatribe against all those who "abandon the Church, return to paganism and godlessness, or to the Papist blindness, or start new sects: madness!"[25] In another sermon, this assertion gains focus from a remark that might surprise but should also instruct the historian: "The majority of the people do not believe in the resurrection of the dead."[26]

The accumulation of signs and dangers led Lutheran thinkers to see Satan everywhere. Veit acts as their spokesman when he warns children against the power and proximity of the devil: "Because you have been baptized and have put your trust in your Lord Jesus Christ, do not therefore think that you are secure; think not that the devil is a thousand miles away. No, he is always near at hand, because the enemy knows he has the right to hunt us down . . . Because of sin the demon has become the prince of this world, the god of this world."[27] Regius confirms this statement: "Satan is a master technician, the inventor of a thousand devices . . . The more he promises, the more he threats and terrifies. He attacks us from the front, the rear, and on all sides."[28]

With Satan so violently on the rampage, there can be no doubts: "the great torture draws nigh," and Germany in particular "shall be the example to the entire world of the wrath of God."[29] Brenz makes this prophesy in a homily given between 1537 and 1552. Throughout the sixteenth century, Lutheran discourse was laced with eschatological forecasts.[30] Osiander wrote an entire book (published in 1544) to demonstrate that by any method of calculation, the end of the world can be fixed for no later than 1672.[31] Heshusius observes that "fear infects men more than ever; it is the worst of the signs that the last judgment draws near."[32] The preacher Gigas, whose sermons were published in 1582, asserts that the final millenium is come and that it will not reach completion "because, as Christ, or truth itself, says, the time grows short . . . The final flood, that of fire, cannot be too far removed from the passion of the new Adam, Jesus Christ . . . without a doubt, Doctor Luther is the third and final Elijah."[33]

These statements are neither exceptional nor surprising. In particular, they clarify the Protestants' indignant refusal of Gregory XIII's calendrical reform, which to them proved that the Pope did not believe in the end of the world.[34] On the other hand, it is less well known that eschatological tensions persisted in early seventeenth-century Germany. The jubilee year of the Reformation (1617) and the Thirty Years' War (1618–48) were two main reasons for this persistence, or reactivation. Although Janssen[35] had already cited the 1617 jubilee, its role has been more fully elucidated by Bernard Vogler, who stresses how along with feelings of happiness, this occasion prompted an outburst of violent anti-Papism and blatant chauvinism, especially in the forty-six sermon collections published in the empire in 1617–18. These works make abundant reference to the Antichrist's Roman tyranny, the Pope as the "devil's insect," the bondage in Egypt, to Moloch and the Great Whore of Babylon. Centennial parades and demonstrations triggered an atmosphere of civil war in mixed localities, which soon escalated into the Thirty Years' War. More than ever, the Apocalypse was the order of the day.[36]

This prevailing mood illuminates Gerhardt's words in a sermon for the second Sunday of Advent: "Just as an old man's faculties weaken and deteriorate—his eyes grow dim, his feet tremble, his strength diminishes, his spirit is agitated—so at the approach of the world's end, the sun and moon will grow dim, the earth will tremble, the strength of heaven will be diminished, and men will dwindle away in their sorrow." One might think that these rather banal predictions would not necessarily announce a coming dénouement. Pursuing his argument, however, and having detailed the different signs of the end of the world in Heaven, earth, and sea, Gerhardt specifies that

> *all these signs occur each day to make us understand that the Day of the Lord is at hand. Have we not seen horrible eclipses? Did not a new star appear in 1572? Who can doubt that it announces Christ's last coming, just as a new star also announced His birth? Are not all things dismal and disturbed? Are not men filled with anguish? Does not their strength wither under their afflictions? The sky is dead to us. A fertile earth: that is more our wish than experience. Therefore let us beware of saying, like that evil servant, "My lord delayeth his coming" (Matt. 24:48). Rather let us remember that "the judge standeth before the door" (James 5:9).*[37]

This sermon appears in a collection dated 1634. A few years earlier—in 1625—Johann Arndt's (d. 1621) *De Vero Christiano* had first appeared, a treatise that would have lasting success in Germany and deeply impress Spener. The preface presents the reader with the evidence of the world's imminent ruin:

> *Today's way of life, corrupt and godless, is not only diametrically opposed to Christ and his teachings, but continually calls down upon us the wrath of God and His punishments, which almost the entire universe—heaven, earth, fire, and water—enacts in order to avenge our injuries to the Creator. The very fabric of the world, as if shook with righteous indignation, threatens ruin. Therefore we are punished with crop failure, whipped by the scourge of war, tortured finally by famine and pestilence. But the limit has not been reached. For soon there will be plagues that will usher in the total annihilation of the world. They will erupt with violence, like an army, so thick and fast that few creatures shall be spared. Before the exodus from Egypt and the liberation of the Jews, the impious and unbelieving were afflicted with terrible plagues; likewise before the final liberation of God's children from this world, the unprecedented impiety of mankind will be punished by extraordinary and unheard-of punishments. The time of repentance is therefore come.*[38]

Arndt's work was soon followed by Alsted's *Diatribe de mille annis apocalyptis* (1627), a commentary on Revelations whose translation had a strong impact in

England. One wonders to what extent readers and listeners put credence in such announcements. In fact, German Catholic preachers, as part of their anti-Lutheran polemic, sometimes offered an exactly opposite view.[39] Moreover, there is evidence, sometimes coming from the preachers themselves, that reveals irony and skepticism among certain people. A 1581 broadsheet declares that "people can only laugh at the last judgment and those who predict it. They've talked so much about it, people say, and nothing's happened! What ever became of the Day of the Lord? Did it get lost on the way?"[40] Another broadsheet, dated 1594, states that if one wants to be considered a "man," one must "have no fear of the last judgment, of the devil, or of hellfire; one must think of all these as old wives' tales."[41] "When one speaks of the last judgment to our Epicureans," opines the Tubingen professor Johann Sigwart in 1603, "they begin to grumble and say: 'They've been announcing it to us for a long time now. When will it finally happen? As far as we're concerned, we'll never see it. Meanwhile, if we eat, drink, and make merry, so much the better.' "[42]

These reactions approximate those that have also been glimpsed in the Catholic world. It is likely that a certain number of listeners, especially men, remained impervious to the evangelism of fear in all its forms. On the other hand, it is undeniable that intimidating sermons made a lasting mark on the most religiously "motivated" people. It is impossible to think that the apocalyptic antipapism of Lutheran preachers did not have lingering effects. There would otherwise be no explanation for the strong confessional tensions that continued in Germany well after 1648. Mutual tolerance at the level of daily interaction did not come about until the late eighteenth century.[43]

The case of France supplies further proof of the links among an endangered community, Protestant eschatology, and the discourse of intimidation, the latter being alternately directed against the enemies of the Reformation and against lukewarm or Nicodemite Huguenots. *La Peur en Occident* highlighted the Zwinglian-Calvinists' sharp accusations against the Roman Antichrist during the sixteenth and early seventeenth centuries.[44] Daneau's *Tractatus de Antechristo* (1576), Vignier's *L'Antechrist romain* . . . (1604), and Duplessis-Mornay's *Le Mystère d'iniquité* (1611) are only the best known titles in a long and plentiful series. All goes from bad to worse; sin increases its ascendancy; men grow smaller; nature runs dry; the papacy nears the end of its contract; the terrible judgment of God draws nigh but the dawn will soon rise on the select flock: These are all components of an eschatologically based literature, even when this eschatology is more implicit than explicit. Such is the case with Chassanion's *Des Grands et redoutable jugements de Dieu* (Morges, 1581), whose sole topic is the sin-punishment dialectic. The book opens by citing the obviousness of "the corruption and perversity of the present world" (chap. 1). It is clear—at least now—that the expected vengeance of God symbolically expressed the aggressive impulses of a beleaguered minority. It is no coincidence that Chassanion's text was a source for Agrippa d'Aubigné's *Tragiques*.

The same analysis holds true for the Protestant eschatological writings that followed the Revocation of the Edict of Nantes. Of particular note is Pierre Jurieu's famous treatise, *L'Accomplissement des prophéties* (1686), composed in a resolutely millenarian spirit. This tract links hopes and threats more closely than ever. The author first proves that papism is the Antichristian empire and then foretells its coming ruin. The persecution of the true believers (that is, the French Protestants) will end in three and a half years. "The Reformation will rise up again in France in just a few years; it will then be established by royal authority. France will renounce Papistry and the kingdom shall be converted."[45] The Antichrist's reign will end between 1710 and 1715. The reunion of all Christians will take place in 1740. "All pagans shall then flock to the Church, along with the Jews, and in 1785 there shall commence the glorious reign of Christ on earth."[46]

This cascade of exact predictions will surprise only the person who forgets how common they were in the sixteenth and seventeenth centuries. Amid his prophesies, Jurieu pauses to reflect that "it is a vexed question, to determine if the antichristian empire of papistry will be destroyed by fire, the sword, and the spilling of blood."[47] He concedes that Revelations "does not oblige us to believe it." At the same time, he wants "to acknowledge the universal agreement of the doctors of either communion, who hold that in the demise of the antichristian empire there will be great bloodshed, and that this empire's capital, Babylon [that is, Rome] will be reduced to ashes."[48] There are two good reasons for accepting this view. First, it "is not clear that the Pope and his followers will go down without a fight." Second, it seems "fitting that the city of Rome which, for two thousand years, has been the mistress of the world, the tyrant of the universe, which has shed so much blood and which has swum in such impurity should be destroyed, and the entire world avenged."[49]

"Vengeance": This word was inseparable from the eschatological predictions of the time. Jurieu had earlier declared that "the harvest is . . . past, and the *vendange* (grape-gathering) will soon begin." "*Vendange*" is synonymous with "vengeance." Jurieu explains that "the corn harvest can mean something good; but we never see the *vendange* being positively interpreted"—an astonishing phrase for a Frenchman. "The juice of the grape is of the color of the blood that runs from the veins of murderers. Therefore the *vendange* always signifies anger, wrath, destruction, vengeance, and bloodshed."[50]

To turn now to the contemporaneous preaching in the wilderness, high exaltation and powerful eschatological expectations are therein offset by a double accusation: the one against the Roman Babylon and her supporters, the other against the cowardice and apostasies of frightened Protestants.[51] Repentance was preached to these individuals, through an evangelism of fear. The former Cévennes wool-carder Antonie Rocher was arrested in August 1686. He was found to be carrying five notebooks stuffed with sermons, whose long and articulate texts so astounded the commissioner Baville that he could scarcely believe that a simple artisan could have composed them. Yet Rocher was indeed their author. One of his sermons threatens the apostates:

> *. . . Remember that Jesus Christ said that many are called but few are chosen . . . "He carries his winnowing basket, he comes to clean his threshing floor and gather his wheat into his storehouse," but "he will burn the chaff in everlasting fire." Do you wish to be of that chaff or of that bale that must be burned? So you shall be if you do not come out of the midst of these infidels . . .*
>
> *I warn you today on God's behalf, in order to take you out of the fire, that you may be saved through fear.*[52]

The former lawyer Brousson also became an itinerant preacher and spoke the same language as Rocher. In his sermon *Les Démons servis par les idoles* (1690), which he delivered on twelve separate occasions, he renews the attack on the apostates:

> *. . . Do you not shudder with horror when you think how you have left the communion of your Lord and Savior, and have entered that of the devil and Antichrist? Are you not terrified when you think that whenever you have bowed down before the gods of dung and offal, or before other idols, you have adored the devil, who invented such idolatry to make himself adored.*[53]

This is a typical speech from a leader of the "besieged city," attacked by far more numerous forces, but putting all its hope in the Almighty, who would not fail, on the day of His triumph, to take revenge on the renegades.

Without a doubt, however, sixteenth- and seventeenth-century Britain offers the prime example of a mental system that brought together danger, fear/expectation, and the language of intimidation. To those who lived in them, the dangerous times also seemed to be "times under pressure," which hurriedly ran toward the great cataclysm.[54] The latter—the rupture of the world and its history—will give a sensational victory to the righteous. But woe betide those who will not have joined the ranks of the victors over the Antichrist. The day of radiant truth will also be the day of their damnation. More than their French or German counterparts, British historians have rightly tended to emphasize the eschatological aspects of the Reformation. Christopher Hill, Bryan Ball, and Paul Christianson have all vividly clarified this dimension of British Protestantism from the time of Henry VIII to the Stuart Restoration.[55]

It is worth repeating that in general, the Reformation constituted both the resurgence and the outcome of an eschatological ferment that had been gaining momentum ever since the fourteenth century.[56] The coming end of the world, or the impending thousand-year reign of the righteous (before the Last Judgment): These were the two main outlooks on the future that countless early modern prophets tended to repeat, drawing above all on the books of Daniel and Revelations. From the outset, Protestantism took arms against the Pope-Antichrist and the modern Babylon (Rome), and thus was inevitably launched on an eschatological trajectory. Thus the apocalyptic elements of British Protestantism originated on the continent. As early as 1519, Luther had affirmed that his times were drawing to a close and that the end of the world was not far off.[57] He never lost this conviction. Melanchthon was of one and the same mind. He spoke of "these perilous final days," of the coming return of Jesus, indeed of his advent "now only a hand's breadth away." Not only Melanchthon's, but also Ecolampadius's and others' commentaries on Daniel were translated into English in 1545.[58] Although Calvin never clearly stated his own expectation of the great final event, his contemporaries read it between the lines of his work.[59] As for Bucer, his *De Regno Christi* (posthumously published in 1557 but dedicated to Edward VI) exhorted the Christian princes to fight against the kingdom of the Antichrist. The English translation of the Geneva Bible, sold at a low price and widely read before and during the Civil War, could only have reinforced this vision of history. Its marginal notes on Thessalonians 2 and Revelations 13 affirmed that the Pope was "a man of sin," "the son of perdition," and "the second beast" described by the Book of Revelations.[60] Throughout the sixteenth and seventeenth centuries, an uninterrupted stream of translated continental publications stoked the eschatological fire in England. The most notable of these were:

A. Osiander, *Vermutung von den letzten Zeiten und dem Ende der Welt aus den heiligen Schrift gezogen* (Nuremberg, 1545); translated by Joye, *The Conjectures of the ende of the world* (Antwerp, 1548).

S. a Geveren, English translation by Rogers, *Of the ende of this worlde and the second comming of Christ*, 1577; five English editions from 1577 to 1589.

Ph. Duplessis-Mornay, *Traité de l'Eglise*, 1578; English translation by J. Field, *A Notable Treatise of the Church*, 1579. *Le Mystère d'iniquité* (1611), English translation by S. Lennard, *The Mysterie of Iniquitie*, 1612.

Fr. Junius, *Apocalypsis methodica analysis notisque illustrata*. (Heidelberg,

1591); English translation *Apocalypsis, a Brief and Learned Commentarie upon the Revelation of St. John*, 1592.

P. du Moulin, *L'Accomplissement des propheties*, English translation by J. Heath, *The Accomplishment of the Prophecies*, 1612.

D. Pareus, *In Divinam Apocalypsim . . . Commentarius* (Heidelberg, 1618), English translation by E. Arnold, *A Commentary Upon the Divine Revelation*, 1644.

J. H. Alsted, *Diatribe de mille annis apocalyptis* (Frankfurt, 1627), English translation *The Beloved City, or, The Saints Reign on Earth a Thousand Years*, 1643.

This less-than-exhaustive list shows that a regular influx of writings by German, Dutch, and French Protestants brought the prophetic beliefs of the Continental Reformation to the British Isles. Moreover, this importation conveyed precisely the two leading apocalyptic options: the announcement of the imminent end of the world and the vision of the thousand-year reign of the righteous. If, however, the eschatological discourse met with such success in Britain, and not only among extremists and revolutionaries, it was due to the British Protestants' feelings of fragility and isolation. It perhaps is not sufficiently known that the Anglican Church also had its index[61] and that a translation of the *Introduction à la vie dévote* was burned at the stake in 1637.[62] This index reveals that 294 books "printed or published in England" were censored between 1530 and 1683, clear proof of a siege mentality. The Saint Bartholomew's Day Massacre (1572); the assassination of William the Silent (1584); the invasion of the "Invincible Armada" (1588); the "capitulation of Henry IV to the Antichrist" (1593) (in other words, his recantation); the Gunpowder Plot (1605); the arrival in 1625 of the bride of Charles I, Louis XIII's sister Henrietta, with a train of monks and Catholic advisors; the Protestant defeats in Germany before the intervention of Gustavus Adolphus; and the massacre of the English in Ireland (1641) had the cumulative effect of increasing the fear of final chaos as well as the notion of the besieged city and confirmed the apocalyptic interpretation of the Reformation. The most extreme Antipapists saw the actions of Charles I, Laud, and the "Arminians" as evidence that a diabolical conspiracy was brewing even in their own country. Fear of the Antichrist and the exaltation caused by hopes for imminent victory over him reached their climax during the twenty years between the calling of the Long Parliament (1640) and the return of the Stuarts (1660). The two civil wars—1642 to 1646 and 1648—and the execution of Charles I in 1649 were a "traumatic experience" for the English, especially for those who regarded England "as the elect nation, favored by God, and destined by Him as an instrument, perhaps the chief instrument, for the final accomplishment of the divine purpose."[63] For them, theirs was a "Labor of Hercules," a combat of "cosmic" dimensions[64] that could end only with the defeat of Satan.

It was no accident that James VI of Scotland—the future James I of England—composed in 1588, while the Spanish fleet closed in on the English coast, his "Ane fruitfull Meditatioun . . . [on] the Revelation."[65] Napier was still exulting over the defeat of the Armada when he published (in 1593) and dedicated to King James *A plaine Discovery of the whole Revelation of St. John*, a work read and reread by Scottish and English people and translated into Latin, French, Dutch, and German.[66] The period from 1640 to 1660 was, in terms of sheer quantity, the high watermark of eschatological publications, particularly of the millenarian kind, as brochures, almanacs, and broadsheets came to double the output of sermons. According to Grotius, eighty prophetic works were published in English in the year 1649 alone. This estimate, however, does not take into account the various polemical tracts, commentaries, and treatises that, though not exclusively eschatological, were at least partially so.[67] During the twenty crucial years opened by the Long Parliament, everyone in Great Britain could hear the voice of the Antichrist. The belief resurfaced, in an echo of the *Malleus Maleficarum*, that "Satan knows his time is short, he stirs up all his instruments" (Stephen Marshall).[68] Likewise, Thomas Goodwin claimed that "The Devil, the shorter his time is, the more he rages and . . . seeing these are the last daies . . . the more should we endeavour to do God service."[69] This mission was imperative, even if one's enemies rose up on all sides. A Presbyterian text of 1645, 'The Triumph of Truth over Heresy,' attacks ten categories of Satan's agents who conspire against the true church: Papists, Familists, Arians, Arminians, Anabaptists, Separatists, Antinomians, Fifth Monarchists, Millenarians, and Independents.[70]

Apparently, the battle raging on all fronts did not frighten the partisans of the Long Parliament and a strictly Calvinist church. On the contrary, these visions of combat filled the most fanatic with "divine impatience": The victory over the forces of evil was at hand. This period's eschatology thus carried with it a strong sense of hope. True, it was "late" and getting "dark." All the same, it was still "the last midnight."[71] The light of dawn would soon break through. It would thus be unfair to portray these eschatological expectations as solely alarming and traumatic. The more or less precise dates frequently proposed for the end of the world or the advent of the thousand years' peace were undoubtedly perceived as a calendar of hope. John Napier fixed the final day at sometime between 1688 and 1700.[72] In his *Ruine of Rome* (1603)—one of the most popular prophetic works of the time—Arthur Dent recommends waiting "every hour" for the sound of the seventh trumpet of the Apocalypse.[73] In 1614 Thomas Brightman calculated that the 1,335 days of Daniel, construed as years, would end in 1695 or 1700.[74] The Anglican Joseph Mede, whose *Clavis apocalyptica* (1627) earned him the name of "the father of English millenarianism," avoids exact dates but still asserts that the time which "shall finish the days of the Man of Sin" would come before 1715.[75] For Thomas Goodwin, another leading light of British eschatology, 1666 would mark the end of the reign of the Antichrist, while the second coming of the Savior would take place during the 1690s.[76]

The above forecasts, selected from thousands that contemporary English people read and heard, indicate a mass feeling of greatly excited expectation. Many individuals aspired to this great climax, which would bring the Lord's final victory. Richard Baxter cried, "Oh, fellow Christians, what a day will that be?" "O blessed day, when I shall rest with God!" "Hasten, O my Savior, the time of thy return."[77] The Independent pastor John Durant, a moderate millenarian, alludes in his *Salvation of the Saints* (1653) to the story of a poor man who saw all his neighbors overcome by an earthquake, thinking it was the Last Judgment. In contrast, he was happy and said, "Is the day come? Where shall I go, upon what mountain shall I stand to see my Savior?"[78] In these hopes, the Christian soul must be as a bride awaiting her husband.[79] There is thus no need to fear the inevitable calamities preceding the great liberation. The founder of the Quakers, George Fox, wrote in 1659 that "an Earthquake is coming upon you that hath not been since the foundation of the world . . . but the Lamb and the Saints shall get the victory."[80] Another Quaker, Edward Burrough, impatiently asked: "How long, Lord? how long? . . . Is it not the fulness of thy time which thou hast promised?"[81] Since the conversion of the Jews was to precede the downfall of the Antichrist, according to the shared belief of the Geneva Bible, the Presbyterians, and the Independents, many people in the 1640s and '50s thought that this conversion was imminent. This belief at least partially explains Cromwell's decision in 1656 to let Jews return to England.[82]

One therefore cannot underestimate the optimistic element in the "divine impatience" of the English, who before 1660 leaned toward great eschatological extremes. Bryan Ball rightly stresses this aspect of their expectations.[83] His analysis also applies to pre-1648 Germany and to French Protestants, whose hopes were raised by the opening of the War of the League of Augsburg. On the other hand, one can no less emphasize the release of aggressivity that gave rise to the era's prophetic discourse. In England, the Antichrist became a veritable myth, the scapegoat in which one perceived one's sworn enemy. From this standpoint, these eschatological statements appear to be both the result of fear and the cause of further threats.

Having already discussed the sensation that "all goes worse"—a conviction common to all sixteenth- and seventeenth-century prophets—I will not reexamine this diagnosis, which perceived "excesses of iniquity" everywhere and culled from them an equal sensation of fear. It is more pertinent here to focus on the "named" enemies who stand out from this general background of disaster. The first was the papacy. With the exception of William Laud and his circle, who debated the question whether the Pope was indeed the Antichrist, English theologians—Episcopalians, Presbyterians, and Independents—almost unanimously made this equation. It was the confirmed opinion of the founders of Anglicanism.[84] During the period of the present study, it remained the view of most English people, who customarily grouped both Spain and the Turk with the leader of the modern Babylon.

Laud's religious politics, however, and his sympathies for Arminian doctrine, which accepted the Catholic conception of free will, succeeded in enlarging the notion of Antichrist. Laud's opponents perceived a "Papist plot" in the authoritarian attitude and decisions of the Archbishop of Canterbury. To them he seemed a "Babylonian," an apostate, and a "Counter-Christ" who was reviving pagan cults.[85] He was also called the Antichrist's "pander and broker."[86] A trail had been opened that would lead to countless elaborations on the myth of the Antichrist. Soon, and particularly after 1640, the entire episcopate was lumped under this heading. Were not bishops a by-product of the papacy? During the two civil wars, the king's adversaries called his army that of the Antichrist. The rebellious Irish were also the disciples of God's enemy. This escalation of accusations soon caused everyone to turn into the Antichrist of his enemy. The Independents accused the Presbyterians of worshipping the Dragon and the Beast. To which orthodox Calvinists responded by labeling all types of "sectaries" as Antichrists.[87] The tidal wave of insults made Cromwell himself seem to the Baptist John Canne like "the little Horn of the Beast." The "Fifth Monarchist" John Rogers went further and thought that the Protector was the Antichrist himself.[88] Baptists regarded baptism as "a chief part of antichristianism."[89] The Leveler John Lilburne affirmed that choral singing and organs had been introduced by the Antichrist.[90] Others thought that Latin was the language of the Antichrist.[91] As for the Digger Winstanley, he associated the gentry, private property, and the Antichrist.[92]

The eschatological discourse of this period was thus highly charged with violence. It either proclaimed the punishment of sinners in general, or it mobilized the saints against clearly designated enemies. It therefore summoned a crusade against them. It covered them in accusations of murder. It allayed the fears of the besieged, by sending out threats and gathering forces aimed first to terrorize the besiegers, then to bring them down. At the time of his invasion of Scotland, Edward VI had already launched an offensive against the Antichrist. Later, Sir Frances Drake proposed attacking this enemy—Spain, in this case—in the New World.[93]

In 1588 James VI called for armed resistance against the enemy of God. "It is all our duties in this Ile at this tyme," he says, to "concur one with another as warriours in a camp, and citizens of a beloved citie."[94] One of the first English Independents, Robert Browne, asserted that Rome, the seat of the Antichrist, should therefore be burned.[95] The Scots who rebelled against Charles I in 1638 were convinced that "our Lord Jesus [was] on horseback, hunting and pursuing the Beast."[96] The Irish revolt of 1641 prompted inflammatory speeches, such as the Puritan Cornelius Burges's sermon before a meeting of Parliament in Saint Margaret's chapel at Westminster, in which the speaker says that the Irish rebellion is the continuation of the Antichrist's actions against the Church of England, after the Armada and the Gunpowder Plot. Burges therefore urges Parliament to use all its power "to destroy property, and to reduce (if possible) those many thousands of poor seduced souls, that, having not known the *depths of Satan*, are miserable, hoodwinked by antichrist to withstand the light and their own salvation. For, till then, they will never be at an *end* of their *rage* against us."[97]

This sermon can be grouped with the bellicose homilies given before Parliament in the years 1640 to 1643. In February 1642 Stephen Marshall implores the deputies to enlist in the battle of the final days and to join the legions of the Lord. Parliament is persecuted by Royalists and neutralists, who are just so many agents of the Antichrist. England must expect troubles comparable to those of Ireland if the saints do not take up arms. Their duty is "to revenge God's church against Babylon."[98] The member of Parliament Joseph Caryl, preaching on the Apocalypse to his Westminster colleagues, calls for purging England of any vestige of Babylon: "Not to bear evil is mercy not only to the good, but to the evil. You cannot be more cruel to them, than in sparing them." Hence God will topple and destroy Babylon wherever he finds it.[99]

In the same year another Puritan, William Sedgwick, explains that the Devil is attempting to prevent Parliament from reforming the church. One cannot wait for the dragon to run out of breath. On the contrary, "he raves and tears and foams and blasphemes, shakes the very pillars of the kingdom, cracks the foundation of government, and threaten confusion to the whole; but we hope by the help of Christ's hands, the issue will be good." The supporters of Christ need not fear the final combat against the captains of Babylon. "Yea, may not a strict observer see the beginnings of the dissolution and breakings in the kingdom of the beast itself?" The millennium was on its way. Then the wicked, like dogs, "crouch and bow to the soles of the feet of God's children." "You should carry the blood of the lamb always about you, wear it in your hearts, and think you have to do with the enemies of that Christ that shed his blood for you."[100]

The Long Parliament also heard less militaristic sermons,[101] but the ones quoted above are representative of a threatening eschatology that pushed for definitive measures against enemies who had been tolerated for too long. They tended to make terror the order of the day and thus hooked up, at least through their intentions, with those preachers who foretold hardened sinners of the worst punishments that would come on the judgment day. The millenarian English revolutionaries, like those of Munster in 1534–35 and like Müntzer in 1525, of course affirmed the right of the elect to engage in "fighting against the enemies of Christ with the material sword."[102] A *Sermon of the Fifth Monarchy* proclaimed that the present Fourth Monarchy would have to be destroyed "by the Sword of the Saints."[103] A seditious ballad (dated 1649?), "A Penny Thrown in the common treasury," prophesies from a millenarian perspective that the poor, oppressed for so long by both the nobility and clergy, will rise up to overcome these and other filthy property owners. They will then behold a glorious communism and the leveling of valleys and mountains.[104]

Eschatology can be put to good use. Especially in Protestant countries, however, it has often served both to express and cause fear.

PREDESTINATION AND ELECTION

Apart from these eschatological tensions, the doctrine of predestination caused an anxiety that formed another major dimension of the Protestant drama. A close reading of sixteenth- to seventeenth-century English sermons, which frequently ask troubled questions about salvation, makes it hard to maintain the argument that "once the Protestant is freed from all his *post mortem* anguish, he is given renewed strength and enthusiasm for the accomplishment of his earthly life."[105] The facts of the matter would rather support the well-known theory that "the Puritan (the primary figure in question here), uncertain of either election or damnation, clings to his works and the success of his enterprises as signs of his election"—although he would never consider these works as the cause of his salvation.[106]

Calvin constantly affirms that "man is in himself naught but concupiscence."[107] Stemming from a "rotten root," we are "rotten branches," which carry our "rottenness into all the sprigs and leaves we produce."[108] In these conditions, how can our will retain any of its former strength against evil? Luther states that "free will" is "a beast of burden, Satan's prisoner, which cannot be freed unless the devil is first cast out by the finger of God."[109] The denial of free will is thus fundamental to both Luther and Calvin. The former writes that in the natural domain, free will still exists: People can decide to eat, drink, procreate, command.[110] In the domain of grace, however, free will is nothing, less than nothing.[111] Similarly, Calvin teaches that "in his essential nature, man had free will, by which he would have obtained eternal life, had he wanted to." "In corrupting and ruining himself," however, he wasted this essential blessing. Hence the error of those who "still seek free will" in a creature "spoiled and decayed by spiritual death."[112] " 'Whosoever committeth sin is the servant of sin' (John 8:34). We are all sinners by nature: it thus follows that we live beneath the yoke of sin. Now, if all men are held captive by sin, the will, which is man's primary characteristic, must needs be clasped and enclosed in tight fetters (by Satan) . . . We are nothing but sin,"[113] unless the sovereign grace of God frees us from ourselves. In their turn, the *Smalcald Articles* condemn those who believe that man possesses a free will to do good and abstain from evil or conversely, to abstain from good and do evil.[114]

The denial of free will logically leads to affirming predestination. In this regard, Protestant thinkers follow Bradwardine and Wycliffe, and Luther, in contrast to Melanchthon, proves to be as categorical as Calvin. Although Melanchthon had written that "God clearly makes all things happen, not in permitting but in enacting them, so that Judas' betrayal was as much His work as the calling of Paul," he then omits this remark from post-1525 editions of the *Loci communes*.[115] Luther, however, held fast to the position he had taken in his *Bondage of the Will*, which repeats some famous and already-quoted phrases: "Human will is not free to choose a master: the two knights contend over who will take possession of him."[116] Calvin labels as "follies" the "daydreams" that some "have invented to refute predestination." The latter is "the eternal principle, by which [God] has determined what He will do with each man. For He does not create them equal, but appoints some to eternal life, and others to eternal damnation."[117] Mercy to the former, justice to the latter: "The damned . . . became slaves to this perversity, in as much as . . . they were created to manifest the glory of God in their damnation."[118]

Both Luther and Calvin were aware of the shocking as well as paradoxical character of this doctrine. Hence they laid stress on the "incomprehensible" side of this mystery. God is His own separate entity. Does one summon Him to a trial, as if He were a rope maker or a tanner? Luther also posed the question, Does one ask Him why He is God? Does one conceive of Him as a mere figurehead, indifferent to human debates and decisions?[119] On the contrary, it is true that He hardened Pharaoh's heart. Luther explains that it is one of "the secrets of His Majesty." Nonetheless, "Why did God let Adam fall, and why did he create us all tainted with the same sin? . . . [because] God is He for whose will no cause or ground may be laid down as its rule and standard; for nothing is on a level with it or above it."[120] In his chapters on predestination, Calvin constantly draws on Saint Augustine and borrows his analogy of the vase and the potter. "But why is it this way with one man, another way with another? Far be it from us to say that judgment belongs to the clay, not to the potter!"[121] Addressing those who dare "to bark like dogs" against predestination, Calvin lashes out: " 'Who are you, miserable men, to make accusation against God?' [Rom. 9:20] Why do you, then, accuse him because he does not temper the greatness of his works to your ignorance? . . . Now consider the narrowness of your mind, whether it can grasp what God has decreed with himself."[122]

Like Melanchthon, however, the French Reformer advises against sinking oneself in a mystery that risks bringing on despair and reminds his audience that if one has indeed heard the Word, this should bring certainty of election.[123]

It might come as a surprise that Zwingli's writings include as harsh a doctrine of predestination as those of Luther and Calvin, even though, at least until 1522, he was strongly influenced by Erasmus and indeed continued to hold humanist views on several points. In fact, Zwingli's doctrine[124] at times precariously associates mutually contradictory elements. For the Zurich Reformer, "nothing happens without God's decision and providence."[125] Predestination is nothing other than His providence. Man's superiority over the rest of creation does not give him any independence in regard to God. All that pertains to us, body and soul, "comes from God as its true and only cause." He governs not only the external course of our life but also the innermost workings of our thoughts, ideas, and decisions, even to the inspiration of our dreams.[126] It is therefore true that the outcast are "traitors and homicides" by virtue of divine providence. "They are destined to eternal torture to serve as examples of His justice." "God makes His vessels, that is to say men, as He wishes; He chooses one to be a finished vessel, and does not care for another. He can maintain His creatures in their integrity, or break them, as he pleases." God is above the Law. The Law is for men, and condemns him, even if it was decreed by the Almighty. "This very felony—adultery or murder—in that God is its author, agent, and initiator, is not a crime; but in that it is the deed of a man, it is a heinous crime." Men sin against the Law "not as authors, but as instruments." God uses them according to His pleasure "more freely than a father of a family, either to drink water or throw it on the ground."[127]

Removed from their original context, these are almost stupefying comments. While this removal does not alter their sense, they are better understood when returned to an entire system of thought; the same holds true for the statements of other leading Protestants. Zwingli, Luther, and Calvin aimed more to inspire confidence than fear. The elect need no longer worry about the salvation that has already been granted to them. God gives faith, but this is itself a sign of election, "for faith," writes Zwingli, "remains firm, even though an elect soul might fall into crimes as enormous as those of the impious and outcast, except that for the elect they are an opportunity for edification, and for the outcast a cause for despair."[128] Like all the Reformers, Zwingli affirms that grace is "irremovable." One cannot lose it. Once He has appointed it, God does not take back election.

In the nineteenth and early twentieth centuries, there was a tendency to regard double predestination (some to Paradise, the others to Hell) as the key to Calvinist teachings. Although some still adhere to this view, most scholars now agree that Calvin did not make this concept the basis for his theology.[129] In the 1560 edition of *The Institutes*, the main discussion of predestination occurs in book 3 (chaps. 21–24), after extended consideration of sanctification and justification (chaps. 3–20). Moreover, Calvin suggests that one should not too much inquire as to God's secrets in such a difficult matter. We must be guided by the teaching of the Revelation. At the same time, this doctrine should not be hidden away, as is done by some who think "that it unsettles faith, that it troubles and wears down hearts."[130] In fact, Calvin's sermons do not give any lengthy treatment of reprobation. His main objective was instead to accentuate the reassuring aspects of election: "Therefore when we doubt if our inheritance is laid up for us in heaven, it is though we renounce the death and passion of Our Lord Jesus Christ, says Saint Paul."[131] If Calvin was constrained in his polemical works to insist on double predestination, it was due to the attacks of his opponents.[132]

For the history of mentalities, it is not so important to know whether Calvin put predestination at the center of his theology or not, but rather to observe that this doctrine was hotly contested within Protestantism itself, while Calvin's successors tended to magnify this aspect of Protestant theology. Has Theodore de Bèze's role in this latter process been exaggerated? Karl Barth argues that it is erroneous to see predestination as the keystone of Bèze's theology.[133] J. S. Bray concurs with Barth. He argues that taken in its entirety, the theological work of this champion of Protestantism at the Poissy Debates, who succeeded Calvin as moderator of the Geneva company of pastors, does not give center stage to the theme of predestination. Bèze's references to "God's eternal decree" do not explain his entire outlook, nor does he organize his doctrine around this single concept.[134] All the same, he did contribute to reinforcing the place of predestination within the ensemble of Protestant beliefs. Several of his works focus on this particular subject: the *Tabula praedestinationis* (1555), the *De la Predestination, contre Castellion* (1558), and the *De Praedestinationis Doctrina* (1582).[135]

While Bèze did not distort Calvin's thinking on predestination,[136] he systematized it and integrated it into a new scholasticism. He devised the famous diagram that divides humanity into two separate groups, between whom there exists no bridge. God's "eternal resolution," in other words the decree of predestination, placed at the top of the chart just below the word "God," appears as the source of two rivers that will never again meet. The first is marked by "vocation" (= the calling of the elect), mercy, faith, justification, and a conclusion at "glorification in eternal life." The second runs through "no vocation" or "ineffectual vocation," obstinacy, ignorance or contempt of the Gospel, injustice, and "pollution," and inevitably empties out at "damnation in eternal death"[137]

Bèze may have first circulated this striking diagram without any accompanying text. Then, at the request of Peter Martyr Vermigli, he composed the *Tabula praedestinationis* as its commentary.[138] In any case, the clear and simple graphics of this chart started a fashion. Whether directly or indirectly, both Perkins and Bunyan were inspired by Bèze, and drew diagrams portraying the double destiny of humanity, half being eternally loved by God and the other half eternally hated.[139] At the top of his outline, Perkins clearly indicates that it is an "*ocular Cathechism* to

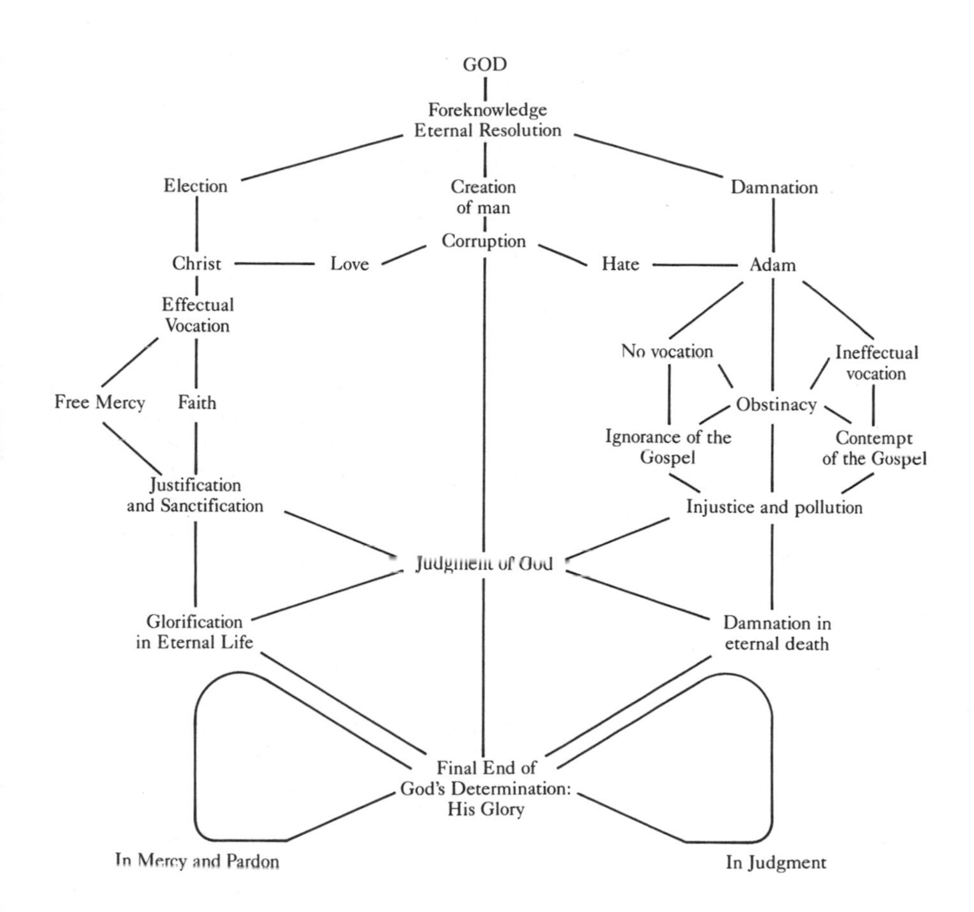

From Theodore de Bèze, *Tabula praedestinationis*, 1555.

them which cannot read: for by the pointing of the finger they may sensibly perceive the chief points of religion, and the order of them." Bèze thus initiated an audio-visual pedagogy, which both disseminated and focused religious lessons on predestination.

Bèze's influence was matched by that of Heironymous Zanchius. The Italian was an Augustinian monk who converted to Protestantism. He taught at Strasbourg, then at Heidelberg and Neustadt, where he died in 1590. His principal work, *De tribus Elohim* . . . (1572), greatly contributed to the foundation of Protestant scholasticism. Like Bèze, Zanchius was a firm adherent to supra-lapsarianism (God's decree of election and damnation preceded that which determined the Fall of Adam). In addition, he was heavily influenced by Aristotelianism—both Aquinas's and that of Padua

University. Seeking to give full weight to the revelation of God's name in Exodus 3:14 ("I am that I am"), Zanchius cloaked the Bible in metaphysics and made God the universal cause of all things. Thus the Trinity "chooses" the elect. The latter are not saved because Jesus died for them. On the contrary, Jesus died because it had been decided for all eternity that he would sacrifice himself for them. Election is thus prior to justification, and the strongly Christocentric tone of Calvinist theology is replaced by harsh statements regarding the order of God's decrees. A rigid orthodoxy that insisted on predestination came to overtake the religious effervescence of the early Reformation, as well as simple trust in the Savior.[140]

It has been said that William Perkins (1558–1602), like Bèze, distorted Calvin's doctrine,[141] especially because of his emphasis on predestination. Conversely, other recent commentators have revealed Perkins's more humane qualities.[142] Even if he was undeniably influenced by Bèze and Zanchius, Perkins in fact had pastoral preoccupations and casuistic interests that the former Italian Augustinian lacked. If one compares his diagram to Bèze's, one notes that it includes a long central column devoted to the action of Christ, which is missing from his predecessor's chart. For Perkins, the *ordo salutis* originates in Christ and is accomplished by Him.[143] Finally, the diagram appears in *A Golden Chaine*, a work that is not presented and should not be read as a complete theological synthesis (the same thing is also true of Bèze's writings on predestination). The book contains no formal church doctrine, nor none of the Holy Spirit, and only a very incomplete explanation of the Last Supper.[144]

In what remains his most notable book, Perkins is primarily interested in questions concerning individual salvation. All the same, there is no debating the role played by Perkins, along with Bèze and Zanchius, in steering international Calvinism—and soon the Dordrecht Synod (1618–19)—toward a growing polarization on the issue of the ways and means of predestination. This subject was a constant preoccupation of the Cambridge preacher. In 1589 he published a *Treatise tending unto a declaration wether a man be in estate of damnation or in estate of grace*; in 1590 his great work on the question *Armilla aurea*, translated into English as *A Golden Chaine: Or, the Description of theologie*; then in 1592 *A Case of conscience, The Greatest that ever was: how a man may know wether be he the Child of God, or no*; in 1598, *De Praedestinatione*; and finally, in 1602, *A Treatise of God's Free Grace and Man's Free Will.* Perkins's evident piety and his success as a preacher helped to popularize his writings. In 1612 *A Golden Chaine* had already appeared in three Latin and nine English editions. Furthermore, at least eleven editions of his collected works were printed between 1600 and 1635.[145] Perkins thus played a large part in putting the question of predestination at the heart of English people's religious preoccupations.

The later evolution of Anglicanism makes it possible to forget that the *Thirty-Nine Articles* of 1563 were of largely Calvinist inspiration, even if the church service kept its own Catholic appearances. These articles thus affirm justification by faith alone, which, in the formulation of the time, was necessarily linked to the bondage of the will and predestination. Article X confirms that "the condition of man after the fall of Adam is such that he cannot turn and prepare himself, by his own natural strength and good works, to faith and calling upon God: wherefore we have no power to do good works pleasant and acceptable to God without the grace of God by Christ preventing us, that we may have a good will, and working with us, when we have that good will."

According to Article XIII, of Works before Justification, "works done before the grace of Christ and the inspiration of His Spirit are not pleasant to God, forasmuch as they spring not of faith in Jesus Christ; neither do they make men meet to receive grace, or (as the School-authors say) deserve grace of congruity: yea rather, for that they are not done as God hath willed and commanded them to be done, we doubt not but they have the nature of sin."[146]

This doctrine is consonant with the positions of the first English Reformers. In his *Prologue to the Epistle to the Romans*, Tyndale states that he wrote this commentary "to prove that a man is justified by faith only; which proposition whoso denieth, to him is not only this epistle and all that Paul writeth, but also the whole Scripture, so locked up, that he shall never understand it to his soul's health."[147] Cranmer was even more definitive: He writes that justification by faith "is the strong rock and foundation of Christian religion . . . this whosoever denieth is not to be reputed for a true Christian man, nor for a setter-forth of Christ's glory, but for an adversary of Christ and His Gospel, and for a setter-forth of men's vain-glory."[148] In a *Sermon on Repentance*, John Bradford entreats his audience to "abhor this abomination, even to think that there is any other satisfaction to God-ward for sin than Christ's blood only. Blasphemy it is, and that horrible, to think otherwise."[149] Preaching on the Lord's Prayer, Hugh Latimer also affirms that "as touching our salvation, we must not go to working to think to get everlasting life with out own doings. No, this were to deny Christ. Salvation, and remission of sins, is His gift, His own and free gift."[150] Furthermore, this was the doctrine taught by the Geneva Bible, which, in its English translation, was far and away the most widely read version of Holy Scripture in Elizabethan England. This text not only included Calvinist-flavored explanatory notes, but also a typically Genevaesque catechism entitled *Certaine Questions and Answers Touching the Doctrine of Predestination*. In 1595 Archbishop Whitgift's *Articles of Lambeth*, though they did not become an offical text, clearly promulgated Calvinist dogma.

Episcopalians and Presbyterians did not so much fall out over predestination as over religious service and the ecclesiastical hierarchy. Nonetheless, a rejection of the bondage of the will emerged within the official church during Elizabeth I's reign and continued to gain strength afterward. From the 1580s on, an anti-Calvinist opposition, in league with certain continental Lutherans, developed at Cambridge. This development provoked response from Perkins, who was alarmed by a doctrine that operated like a bad doctor, putting on the plaster before having cured the injury.[151] Richard Hooker's great work, *Of the Laws of Ecclesiastical Polity* (1594), which many have seen as one of the foundations of the Anglican Church, was in some ways a counterresponse to Perkins's Calvinist options. It not only defended the Anglican hierarchy against Puritan attacks, but also took a position regarding predestination that Hooker's adversaries called "Lutheran," meaning to them crypto-Catholic. The agitation at Cambridge between "Pelagians" and "Anti-Pelagians" led to the drafting of the *Articles of Lambeth*, a move that pleased Perkins and his friends. Whitgift approved them, though Elizabeth refused to sanction them. The most conspicuous "Pelagians," however, had to leave Cambridge. The affair took an international turn when, from the United Provinces of the Netherlands, Arminius decided to answer Perkins's *De Praedestinatione*. His *Examen modestum libelli* . . . (1612) accused Perkins of adding his own ideas to Holy Scripture. In turn, this critique of the English theologian provoked the meeting of the Dordrecht Synod, to which the Anglican Church sent its official representatives; the synod confirmed strict Calvinist positions on predestination.

This debate continued to rage and, as in the Catholic world, split the Protestants into two opposed camps. In his discussion of religious melancholy, especially regarding each individual's doubts over salvation, Burton logically groups together "our late Arminians . . . our late Lutherans and modern Papists," who "have revived that plausible doctrine of universal grace.[152] An Anglican pastor, Burton had adopted Donne's position, which gradually became that of the Anglican Church. For the most part, it follows that of "double justification" by both faith and works, established in 1541 at the Conference of Regensburg: We are saved by faith, which is a free gift from God, but we will not be saved without works, which depend on our doing. This moderate doctrine explains how Donne gave at least seven sermons[153] in which he criticizes the excessively severe Calvinist conception of predestination and clarifies how God's judgments are not irrevocable.

One of these sermons, dated 1622, makes specific reference to the king's recently given guidelines concerning sermons on this theme. James in fact prohibited anyone, except for bishops and deans, from preaching on predestination, election, or reprobation, as well as on the universality, efficacy, and inevitability of grace.[154] Paul V had enacted a very similar measure, which banned any publication on grace without the express permission of the Holy Office. Both Paul's and James's edicts had little effect. In the 1638 edition of *The Anatomy of Melancholy*, Burton alludes to a new prohibition and declares: "I might have said more of this subject [predestination]; but inasmuch as it is a forbidden question, and in the Preface or Declaration to the Articles of the Church, printed 1633, to avoid factions and altercations, we that are university divines especially, are prohibited 'all curious search, to print or preach, or draw the article aside by our own sense and comments, upon pain of ecclesiastical censure.' "[155] This statement, however, follows a good twenty pages focusing on the anxieties caused by overly strict doctrines of predestination. This subject could not be hidden beneath the bushel. The Anglo-Saxon religious community thus became divided between two diverging sensibilities: the "Arminian," which was more relaxed, more confident in mankind, and more extroverted, versus the "anti-Arminian," which was more anxious, pessimistic, and introspective.[156] This latter theology will be the primary subject of the following pages, though it will not exclude some further citation of Donne's preaching.

Following the precedent of the first Reformers, English preachers of the following two centuries filled their sermons and treatises with phrases mixing justification by faith and exhortations to have confidence. This is a significant emphasis. Like other Protestant leaders, they were addressing an audience who had come to reject earlier means of security: patron saints, Purgatory (to the extent that it allowed an escape from Hell), indulgences, and various forms of intercession. It was no easy feat to fill this suddenly opened gap.[157] The increase in the number of reassuring statements is a certain sign of a collective anxiety: all the more so, since the rejection of earlier protective measures was compounded by a theology of election that urged each individual to examine his or her own particular case.[158] Launching a direct assault on this problem, Puritan pastors accused both Catholicism and "Arminianism" of enmeshing the faithful in doubts over their salvation, since these two latter systems suggested that grace could be successively lost, regained, and lost again. Thomas Becon writes that some individuals "doubt of their salvation" and that "this is the doctrine of the papists, both wicked and damnable."[159] Burton attacks papists who "terrify men's souls with purgatory, tales, visions, apparitions" and "crucify their mind with superstitious observations."[160] The spate of prayer-books for all social categories, designed for use at all times of the day and of one's life, doubtless served to replace these Catholic observations. The Puritan Michael Sparke's best-selling *The Crumbs of comfort* (1623) typifies this genre.

To many English Protestant preachers, the conviction that grace, once given, cannot be withdrawn, was a strong reason for reassurance. John Bradford writes to Mary Honywood that "above all things, of this I would have you to be most assured, that you are beloved of God, that you are his dear child, and shall be for evermore."[161] "When we believe in Him [Christ]," Latimer affirms, "it is like as if we had no sins."[162] The bishop John Hooper, executed in 1555 on Mary Tudor's orders, writes in a *Brief and Clear Confession of the Christian Faith*: "I do believe and confess that Christ's condemnation is mine absolution; that His crucifying is my deliverance; His descending into hell is mine ascending into heaven."[163] Number 17 of the Thirty-Nine Articles states that "predestination to life is the everlasting purpose of God, whereby (before the foundations of the world were laid) He hath constantly decreed by His counsel secret to us, to deliver from curse and damnation, those whom He hath chosen in Christ out of mankind, and to bring them by Christ to everlasting Salvation, as vessels made to honor." The article goes on to confirm that "the godly consideration of predestination, and our election in Christ, is full of sweet, pleasant, and unspeakable comfort to godly persons". Likewise, Archbishop Whitgift's *Articles of Lambeth* include the declaration that the true believer, that is to say the person who has received justifying faith, is certain through the assurance of faith to have remission of sins and eternal salvation through Christ.[164]

The doctrine of the "Covenant," which was above all codified by Bishop Jewel (d. 1571), by Perkins, by the ardent Puritan John Preston (d. 1628),[165] and by another Puritan, Thomas Brooks (d. 1680), is quite clearly offered as a reassuring message. According to Perkins's definition, the pact ("Covenant") of grace comprises two agreements: God's promise to man and man's promise to God. God freely promises Christ and his blessings, and in return He requires that man receives Christ through faith and repents of his sins. The "Covenant" is sealed by the sacraments, which bring confirmation of faith.[166] It goes without saying that man does not himself make this pact with God, but God alone makes it with His elect. Thus no one can possibly wrest the elect from God's hands. Salvation is certain, because it depends on God and not on us.[167]

Elsewhere, Calvinists were also speaking words of comfort. In a sermon at Charenton, the pastor Jean Daillé told his listeners that "if you pronounce your belief in Lord Jesus and believe in your heart that God resurrected him from the dead, you will be saved."[168] A catechism from Berne, translated into French in 1655 for the people of the Vaud region, teaches that faith, even if "extremely weak," suffices to obtain pardon, just as a trembling hand is no less worthy than a steady one to receive alms from the rich."[169] Daniel Featley, a Puritan within the Anglican Church, preached at Lambeth (in 1619) that "hee (Christ) came not to quench, butt to kindle; not to destroy, but to save; not to launce, but to plaster; not to revenge; but to reconcile; not to punish, but to suffer; not to breake the bruised reed, but to be beaten and bruised with reeds and whips, yea and to be broken also upon the crosse."[170]

For his part, Richard Sibbes told his audience: "let us not be over much discouraged with our infirmities and corruptions; if God be with us, who can be against us? . . . The Spirit of God is stronger in us, than corruption in us, or the world without us . . . If you bee under the Spirit and under grace, sinne shall not have dominion over you."[171] In another sermon, Sibbes makes this urgent exhortation: "And (to conclude with a word of comfort) if there be any poore distressed soule frightened in conscience with the sight of his sinnes and Satans temptation, O let such consider the love of God in Christ . . . let not Satan abuse thee by setting God before thee as a terrible judge, and Christ as one that would not save thee . . . wherefore hath the father Sealed Christ but in love to thee?"[172] In the same spirit, Baxter exclaims: "Sinners, there are none of you shall have cause to go home, and say I preach Desperation to you . . . ; tell me if you can when did you ever hear any sober Man say, that there is no hope for you, though he repent and be Converted? . . . whoever is born again, and by Faith and Repentance doth become a new Creature, shall certainly be saved." This excerpt comes from the twenty-third edition (1685) of this well-known instruction.[173]

FEAR OF REPROBATION

A reading of these consolations, which echo those of the first Reformers, might tempt one to ignore unsettling notes sounded by these same preachers. Like their Catholic counterparts, Lutheran and Puritan theologians taught the doctrine of the chosen few. While it would be easy to cite many others, a few key texts will demonstrate this point.

On the Sunday of the Sexagesima, Johann Spangenberg (d. 1550) discusses the Parable of the Sower (Luke 8:1–15) and asks,

> *What does the Evangelist wish to teach us? Two things. First, that there are more damned souls than saved ones. Wherefore? Because only a tiny group acts upon the word of God . . . The second matter: although a great number of men must be damned, it is still worthwhile to preach the word of God . . . Granted, it is horrible to think that only a quarter of one's seed will fall on good soil, and that the other three quarters will go to waste . . . But an evangelical preacher must not ask whether a great many or only a few will receive the Word, but rather preach and offer it to everyone, as Christ commanded at the end of the Gospel of St. Mark.*[174]

In a sermon collection that includes Melanchthon's *De officio concionatoris*, Antoine Corvinus (d. 1553) also asserts that true Christians have always been "very few in number" and that many people who "pride themselves in the name and gospel of Christ" are nevertheless "subjects of Satan."[175] Perkins's *De Praedestinatione . . .* (1598) answers critics of Puritan preaching with the comment that "strictly speaking, many men will be saved; but if their number is compared to that of those men who will be justly damned, then one must admit that there will be only a very few elect, as is clearly said in Scripture."[176] At the time of another Sexagesima, Johann Gerhardt claims that the Word will be profitable only to a select number of people.[177] Finally, on the prefatory page of his *De Vero Christiano*, Arndt gives priority to the phrase from Matthew 7:14: "Because strait is the gate, and narrow is the way, which leadeth unto life."[178]

Seventeenth-century English Puritans speak the same language. Hieron also comments on the "strait gate," saying that "the fewer to enter in by the strait gate to Heaven there be that are partakers of the true happinesse, the more we should labour to be in that number."[179] Christopher Love asks the question, "Whether all shall be damned?" and he answers: "Most shall be damned."[180] Baxter is generally more moderate than Love. All the same, he requests the "converted" to consider "that the faithful servants of Christ are few; and therefore if those few dishonor him, and prove not just to him; what do you but provoke him to forsake all the World, and make an end of all the Sons of men. It is but a little flock to whom he will give the kingdom, Luke 12:32. It is but a few from whom God expecteth any great matter: And shall those few prove deceitful to him?"[181]

This type of speech inspired counterarguments from those who feared the discouragement of congregations. On many occasions, Donne beseeches his listeners not to sink into despair. God does not leave his children dark and comfortless. One need not attend to sermons on predestination. God's mercy effaces our sins, just as the sea washes away the wake of a ship. It touches all people, even Christians of other confessions, and even the Jews. It has the power to save those who could not hear its word. No one can know the number of the elect. God's judgments are not irrevocable. He wills that all men be saved.[182] Studying the causes of religious "despair," Burton takes to task "the very inconsiderate reading" and "misinterpretation" of several passages of Scripture, notably "Many are called, few are chosen," "Fear not, little flock" (the emphasis here being on "little"), and "Strait is the way that leads to heaven, and few there are that enter therein." "These and the like places terrify the souls of many," Burton affirms—an observation that the historian of mentalities must take into full account.[183]

The doctrine of predestination included a highly positive point: Once He gives grace, God does not take it back. At the same time, it is impossible to know on what criteria He chooses those to whom grace is given and those to whom it is not. His plans are "impenetrable," "inscrutable," and only the proud seek to fathom them. It follows that any decision of God is irrevocable. Two disquieting conclusions derive from this theology:

1. The election or damnation of an individual "inevitably" transpires at the moment God issues His decree. Scholars have rightly noted the "determinism" which characterizes discussions of predestination, such as those by Bèze. His writings on this subject often return to the expressions *Necesse est* and *oportet*.[184] This fearsome logic could only have disturbed the public at large; so too for the rationalism that denied all endeavours to gain security.
2. Since God has eternally fixed one's salvation or damnation, regardless of one's acceptance of the faith (contrary to Lutheran positions, especially after 1580), or of one's works (contrary to Catholic and "Arminian" positions), it follows that He has always willed the sins of the impious. Zwingli and Bèze, it must be recalled,[185] were explicit on this matter. By force of circumstances, this conception gradually descended from the level of erudite speculation to that of everyday preaching. Among others, Perkins's *Golden Chain* testifies to this process. This work of the second Protestant generation, inspired by "practical" considerations, aimed to diffuse a coherent soteriology among its author's contemporaries.

These two key aspects are concentrated in the following lines:

The decree of God is that by which God in himself hath necessarily, and yet freely, from all eternity determined all things. Therefore the Lord, according to his good pleasure, hath most certainly decreed every thing and action, whether past, present, or to come, together with their circumstances, of place, time, means, and end. Yea, he hath most justly decreed the wicked works of the wicked. For if he had nilled them, they should never have been at all. And albeit they of their own nature are and remain, wicked, yet in respect of God's decree they are some ways good, for there is not anything absolutely evil. The thing which in its own nature is evil, in God's eternal counsel is respectively good, in that it is some occasion and way to manifest the glory of God in his justice and mercy . . .

God is not only a bare permissive agent in an evil work, but a powerful effecter of the same; yet so as he neither instilleth an aberration in the action, nor yet supporteth or endureth the same, but that he most freely suffereth evil and best disposeth of it to his own glory.[186]

The diagrams of Bèze, Perkins, and Bunyan are popularizing illustrations of this theology, which allowed for no cross-over between the universe of the elect—that of mercy—and the universe of the reprobate—that of justice. Before we were born, it was determined that we would be either on the side of Abel or on the side of Cain. To be of the reprobate, as Bunyan's chart proclaims, is to be outside of God's election. But everyone already knew that there were only a few who were chosen by God. With this in mind, how could one not feel terrible anxieties? This type of questioning clarifies why Laud reproached the Puritans for teaching that "God from all eternity reprobates by far the greater part of mankind to eternal fire without any eye at all to their sin. Which opinion my very soul abominates. For it makes God, the God of all mercies, to be the most fierce and unreasonable tyrant in the world."[187]

This portrayal of God grew all the harsher since, as has been shown,[188] a religious pedagogy already advocated by the first Lutherans and later amplified by all preachers of predestination shipped the faithful on a pilgrimage of "conversion," whose route bordered on a hell of despair. It was precisely at those moments when they asked sinners to assess the gravity of their condition that Puritan preachers laid heavy stress on the wrath of God and the flames of Hell. An eye- (or in this case ear-) witness tells how Perkins, who was renowned for the simplicity and directness of his speeches, uttered the word "damned" with such force that he left a painful lingering echo in the ears of his listeners.[189] Not surprisingly, late sixteenth- and seventeenth-century English literature has a fascination for heroes pushed by their sinning condition into despair: Among these are Spenser's Redcrosse Knight, Marlowe's Faust, and Milton's Samson. As Richard Bolton eloquently perceives,

> *Alas! when a poor, polluted wretch, upon some special illumination by the word, or extraordinary stroke from the rod, doth once begin to behold God's frowning face against him in the pure glass of his most holy law, and to feel Divine justice, by an invisible hand, taking secret vengeance upon his conscience, his heavy heart immediately melts away in his breast and becomes as water. He faints and fails both in the strength of his body and stoutness of his mind.*[190]

On the one hand, Puritan preachers did advise that one must escape from this "legal terror" (the fear provoked by the gap between the Law and our deeds). Did some individuals, however, remain in a state of despair? Or having left it, might they not later return to their anxieties? The spiritual itinerary lived and recommended by Bunyan,[191] which corresponds to the classic religious teaching of the Puritans, reveals four stages. The first is that of blindness, the sinner being unaware of his corruption; the second is marked by "terror," or the sinner's discovery of sin within himself and his deserved punishment. In a third phase—illumination—this despair suddenly turns into comfort and reassurance. Finally, life, if I may put it this way, recommences; the "convert" now leads a Christian existence, but is still subject to struggles and temptations. Crises of despair can recur. Therefore one must stick to the certainty that the decree of election can never be repealed.[192]

The psychological behavior induced by such messages finds concrete expression in alternating fears and expectations. Calvin was the first to understand and explain that the certainty of the believer could never ensure the total peace of the soul: "When we teach," he writes,

> *that faith must be firm and certain, we do not conceive of a certainty that is untouched by doubt, nor a firmness that is unassailed by anxiety: on the contrary, we say that the faithful are in perpetual combat with their own distrust; far be it from us to so much assuage their conscience that no storm may trouble them! Nevertheless, however much they may be afflicted, we deny that they ever give up or fall from their trust, which they once thought entirely certain, in God's mercy.*[193]

Thus the elect are in theory certain of their salvation, though in practice they continue to go through fits of anxiety.

Protestant preachers constantly emphasized the two proofs that should persuade true believers of their election: faith in Christ the Savior and the good deeds he accomplishes through his followers. Perkins expresses a general conviction of the Protestants in arguing that the individual predestined to glory is also predestined to having the means to salvation, namely union with Christ through both faith and good works.[194] In one's deeds, however, faith can be obscured and one's bad tendencies come to the fore. What then becomes of the assurance of election? Pierre du Moulin answers that "the peace of conscience" is neither profane drowsiness nor material security.[195] Numerous Puritan leaders in Great Britain likewise strove to soothe their congregations by distinguishing objective certainty from subjective assurance. Only the first is given to the elect; the second is subject to eclipses.[196] Thomas Brooks wrote that grace and assurance are not an inseparable couple: "There are thousands of Christians that are in a state of grace, and shall be saved, that want assurance, and the proper effects of it, as high joy, pure comfort, glorious peace, and vehement longings after the coming of Christ. Assurance is requisite to the well-being of a Christian, but not to the being; it is requisite to the consolation of a Christian, but not to the salvation of a Christian."[197]

Puritan spiritual writings contain a number of concordant analyses that recall Catholic descriptions of mystical experience. Henry Smith observes that "there is nothing in our life which suffers so many eclipses and changes as our devotion."[198] In another sermon, he states that "in respect of God, our election standeth certain from all eternity . . . But in respect of ourselves it is uncertain, and therefore we must strive to make the same sure by good works."[199] Perkins recommends adhering to the light of faith even in the darkest tunnel. "It is the principal art of a Christian to believe things invisible, to hope for things deferred, to love God when he shews himself to be an enemy and thus to persevere unto the end."[200] Significantly, on the "saved" side of his diagram Perkins includes elements that do not appear in Bèze's chart, namely: "Doubting of Election," "Despair," "Doubting of Faith," and "Doubting of justification." One must continually overcome these obstacles in order to reach "sanctification" and "glorification."[201]

Hieron asks "whether it be such an assurance [of election] which is so certain, that it is never intermixed nor over-clouded, nor disturbed with doubtings?" His answer: "I . . . am assured, that they which never doubted of their adoption, did never beleeve it."[202] Sibbes explains to his audience that "God hath a double face, a face that shines on our soules in peace and joy and comfort, when he saith to the soul, I am thy Salvation," and another, when He "takes his face away from us in regard of the inward man, when he gives us no peace: but leaves us to spiritual desertion."[203] Featley also describes the *deliquium spiritus* (the spiritual eclipse) that can affect the believer. God sends him this trial, either to humble him so that he will not grow proud with his spiritual favors or to make him even more strongly desire the comfort of the Gospels. In any case, this desertion causes the individual to "swoon, feeling no motion of the spirit, as it were the pulse beating, taking no breath of life by hearing the Word."[204] Although writing a work designed to bring peace to the conscience, Baxter concedes that "it is but very few Christians that reach to Assurance of Salvation" and that even "those few who do attain Assurance, have it not either perfectly or constantly but mixt with imperfection, and oft clouded and interrupted." Hence this useful advice: "You may be saved though you never get Assurance here, but you cannot be saved without Christ and Grace. God hath not made Assurance the Condition of our Salvation . . . It is better to go sorrowful and doubting to Heaven, than comfortably to Hell."[205]

The believer then faces the question of knowing how to interpret the misfortunes that can oppress one in this life. In this context, two contradictory discourses were offered, which risked increasing already great perplexity of the "convert." Drelincourt, speaking in 1662 on the Apocalypse, argues that God punishes Christians for their own good. "The punishment of this heavenly Father is no less necessary to us than our daily bread." Conversely, "God does not punish [on earth] most of those people who should be the object of His justice, since He abandons them to the devil to be eternally tormented in hell."[206] Two years earlier, however, Drelincourt had intimidated his flock by telling them that "the clamor [of our sins] ascends into heaven. And so the Almighty takes arms, and prepares to take His vengeance, our sins bringing destruction to our door."[207] Likewise, Featley consoles people beset with misfortune, affirming that "God afflicteth them whom he affecteth, [and therefore] we have just cause to feare, because wee are not under his rod we are out of his care." Later, however, Featley acknowledges that "afflictions in some sort are common to all sorts of men." How then to distinguish between different misfortunes? The answer lies in the fact that those that befall the virtuous are for their correction and improvement, while those that befall the wicked are punishments incapable of edifying them whatsoever.[208]

One of Christopher Love's sermons confirms that this diagnosis of the afflictions of life was a definite source of anxiety for faithful Protestants: "Men do doubt of their election, because God pursues them with continuall afflictions, and layes the continued strokes of his heavy wrath upon them; and this makes many a godly man thinke, that he is not in the number of Gods elect ones."[209] In this case, Puritan pastors responded that resignation to one's trials is a sign of election. Even if he possesses the objective assurance of his election, the Christian must follow his religious itinerary in "fear and trembling."

Puritan writers and preachers unanimously referred to this phrase from Scripture, which, Burton notes, called forth traumatic misinterpretations.[210] Furthermore, they were joined by Donne, whose sermons frequently stress the necessary fear of God. For "no man may be so secure in his election, as to forbear to work out his salvation with fear and trembling."[211]

Man will have no assurance and no rest before his judgment.[212] These same words that come from an orator hostile to Calvinist predestination could also have been spoken or written by Catholic or "Arminian" theologians. They also coincide, however, in fact if not theological intention, with the Puritan discourse that simultaneously taught that the elect are assured of salvation but that they must nevertheless "fear and tremble" their entire lives.

Love explains that "the holy ghost here presseth, that men should pass their time in feare [cf. I Peter 1:17], is not meant of a fear about our election; but it is meant of a feare of sinne." The rest of this sentence, however, contradicts the first part, since Love adds: "we must not sinne against God, but fear God, and fear to provoke God by our sinne."[213] To what else can He be provoked than punishment? Henry Smith specifies the permanent anxieties the believer should feel:

> *It is not enough to run, but we must know how we run; it is not enough to hear, but we must care how we hear; it is not enough to believe, but we must care how we believe; it is not enough to pray, but we must care how we pray; it is not enough to work, but we must care how we work . . . Cain offered, and God abhorred.*[214]

Drelincourt asked his Charenton audience: "Are you prepared in humility, and do you complete your salvation with fear and trembling?"[215] The verb "complete" [*achevez* in the French original] must be emphasized. For the "fear and trembling" of this and other similar texts are not those of the phase of terror and despair that the future convert must undergo. On the contrary, they characterize the religious experience of those who have already "converted" and are "completing" their salvation. If one is already saved, why "tremble"?

This objection was indeed raised to the preachers, often enough that Featley says in one of his sermons: "To what end doth David advise, Serve the Lord with feare: and Saint Paul admonish, Be not high minded but feare: and work out your salvation with fear and trembling: and Saint Peter exhort, passe the time of your sojourning here in feare? If all true believers are so assured of their salvation, that they are in no danger of forfeiting their estate of grace here, or losing their crowne of glory hereafter?"[216] Featley responds that bad fear is opposed to "spirituall confidence," but that good fear counteracts "carnall security."[217] In the eighteenth century, Gilbert Tennent similarly declared that love without fear brings too much certainty, and fear without love too much servility.[218]

Calvinist preaching thus fought against "carnal security." In doing so, did it not give constantly renewed impetus to spiritual anxieties? One is justified by faith; but is our faith good? Are we not "hypocrites"[219] if our works contradict the faith we profess? It is obvious that we continue to sin. Do not our bad deeds therefore derive from a faith God does not recognize? In short, an endless spiral of introspective interrogations. Cranmer asserted:

> *That faith which bringeth forth [without repentance] either evil works, or no good works, is not a right, pure, and lively faith, but a dead, devilish, counterfeit, and feigned faith, as St. Paul and St. James call it. For even the devils know and believe that Christ was born of a virgin, that He fasted forty days and forty nights without meat and drink, that He wrought all kinds of miracles, declaring Himself very God . . . It pertaineth to a Christian man to have this true Christian faith, and to try himself whether he hath it or no . . . Therefore, as you profess the name of Christ, good Christian people, let no such fantasy and imagination of faith at any time beguile you; but be sure of your faith: try it by your living.*[220]

Similarly, Henry Smith teaches that "there is a zeal without knowledge, a love without singleness, a prayer without faith, and a faith without fruits. Therefore the Apostle doth warn us to *examine ourselves whether we be in the faith* (II Cor. 13:5) not, whether we have a kind of faith, but whether we be in the faith—the true faith."[221] The orator goes on to declare that one does not reach Heaven merely by being a conformist Protestant ("*Statute-Protestant*") going to church, listening to sermons, and receiving annual communion. Faith requires far more. A troubling question and an equally troubling assertion then follow: "Who hath so much faith as the Apostles? yet how oft doth Christ say, *O ye of little faith* (Matt. 6:30), complaining that their faith was too little."[222] One can imagine the effect of such reasoning on an audience. If faith is necessary to salvation, what happens when one's faith is soft or weak? When we are both sincere and "hypocritical"? The preachers' double-talk on predestination is clearly revealed by Jean Daillé: "If you proclaim your faith in Lord Jesus, and believe in your heart that God has resurrected the dead, you shall be saved. Only beware that your faith is ardent and sincere; that it is not a dream, an illusion, or an idol, but a firm conviction, a total assurance in the truth of the Gospel. That it is a faith like unto that of Abraham, or of the Apostle."[223] But who could be certain of having the faith of Abraham?

Preaching on the theme that "each man makes trial of himself," Pierre du Moulin likewise urges examining "whether we have faith," and he warns against "false faith," which he calls "profane slumber" as well as "lethargy and carnal security, by which a man convinces himself that God will show him mercy while he serves his own belly and his money. Sleeping in this vain confidence, he becomes corrupted."[224] Some years later Spener, the founder of German Pietism, would give this lesson on damnation: "All who will not have had true faith shall go to hell. They who let sin predominate in themselves do not have true faith. If they remain in this state, they will be most certainly damned. Ah my well-beloved ones, faithfully examine in the sight of God our present condition, in what state we live, and if, after this investigation, we can count ourselves among the reprobate or among the blessed."[225] In the same spirit, Baxter is amazed that one can think on God the Almighty without feeling fear and wonder, since one is "unsure" whether God is our "father or enemy" and whether he will aim all His power at us. "How dost thou think without trembling upon Jesus Christ? When thou knowest not whether his blood hath purged thy soul or not? and whether he will condemn thee or acquit thee in Judgment?"[226] Furthermore, do we truly have faith when we let our friends and relatives sink themselves in sin?[227]

The call for questioning one's own faith was part of a larger insistence on the examination of conscience, which was not a monopoly of Catholic preaching. Even if it does not involve private, detailed, and obligatory confession, it appears with the same degree of urgency in Protestant discourse. Donne argues that the most dangerous condition for a sinner is happiness, happiness here being synonymous with the sleep of the conscience.[228] Donne explains that it is a condition in which one forgets one's sin and the damnation that it brings. He returns to the same theme in several other sermons, asking the Christian to be his or her own judge, in order not to be judged later.[229]

The emphasis on the necessary examination of conscience became, especially during Perkins's time, a leitmotif of Puritan preaching and theology. According to the Puritans, the self-knowledge acquired in the second phase of conversion (that of "legal terror") had to be maintained for the rest of one's life, through a never-ending investigation of one's self, recorded if necessary in private diaries.[230] Bunyan's copious detail on the various conditions of his soul is thus only one example of a more or less collective phenomenon, set in motion by a strongly guilt-instilling discourse. "When thou hast any particular occasion of renewing thy repentance,"[231] Perkins observes, "make catalogues and bills of thine own sins, especially of those sins that have most dishonored God and wounded thine own conscience. Set them before thee often . . . that thy heart by this doleful sight may be further humbled."[232]

It is revealing that a 1648 broadsheet bears the title of *The Daily Examination and Araignment of Sins: gathered out of the most Reverend the Primate of Ireland's Sermon at Lincoln's Inne, Dec. 3, 1648.*[233] Daniel Dyke offers his *The Mystery of Self-Deceit* as a means for discovering "the infinitely intricate windings, and turnings of the darke labyrinths of mans heart." The dedication to the Countess of Bedford, which praises her dead husband, contains this notable passage: "Yet may I not altogether passe over in silence his holie and religious course; which was, to keepe a catalogue or diary of his sinnes against God: and every night, or the next morning, to review the faults of the day past."[234]

Similarly, Dyke's contemporary Samuel Hieron declares: "every man, when he is alone by himself, should retire his thoughts, should look back into the day past, to see what he hath done . . . that no sinne should bee suffered to lodge all night with us."[235] For his part, Sibbes advises listening to one's conscience because "God hath erected a tribunall in every man; he hath set up conscience for a register, and witnesse, and judge etc. There are all the parts of judiciall proceedings in the soule of man."[236] Sibbes elsewhere affirms that "conscience is Gods vicar . . . What conscience saith, God saith; and what it forbids, God forbids, especially when it is enlightened by the word."[237] Featley recommends that we "examine daily our spirituall estate, and to informe our selves truly how we stand in the Court of Heaven, in Gods favour or out of it."[238] After the fashion of Catholic preachers, Featley posits that it is in our own interest to judge ourselves, for "God will certainly call all men to a most strict and particular account of every moment of time they have spent, of every particular grace they have received, of every particular duty they have omitted, of every particular sinne they have committed in deed, word, or thought, nay of the first motion and inclination to evill."[239]

These warnings help to clarify how Puritans could feel pangs of conscience similar to those that tormented many devout Catholics. Perkins's casuist writings prove that there was a need to reassure anxiety-ridden souls. He was an innovator in this field, as he started a tradition that hitherto had been absent from Protestant England.[240] In evident response to anxious popular demand, Perkins successively brought out *A Case of Conscience . . .* (1592), *A Discourse of conscience* (1595), and the posthumous *The Whole Treatise of the Cases of Conscience . . .* (1606). More thoroughgoing manuals then appeared, notably Jeremy Taylor's *Ductor Dubitantium* (1660) and Richard Baxter's *Christian Directory* (1673). As with the disease of scruple in the Catholic world, the cause-and-effect relationship between spiritual fears and reassuring messages inevitably resurfaces. Is it going too far to suggest that English authors have left us the most striking descriptions of the afflicted conscience? One of these comes from the pen of Henry Smith, at the end of the sixteenth century:

> *If there be any hell in this world, they which feel the worm of conscience gnawing at their hearts, may truly say, that they have felt the torments of hell. Who can express that mans horror but himself? Nay, what horrors are they which he cannot express himself? Sorrows are met in his soul as at a feast: fear, thought, and anguish divide his soul between them. All the furies of hell leap upon his heart like a stage, Thought calleth to Fear: Fear whistleth to Horror: Horror beckoneth to Despayre, and sayth: come and help me to torment this sinner . . . he goeth through a thousand deaths and cannot die. Irons are laid upon his bodie like a prisoner. All his lights are put out at once: he hath no soul fit to bee comforted. Thus he lieth, as it were upon the rack and sayth, that he beares the world upon his shoulders, and that no man suffereth that which he suffereth. So let him lie (sayth God) without ease, untill he confesse and repent, and call for mercie.*[241]

Smith's description clearly applies to the second leg of the road to conversion, located between initial blindness and illumination. This latter phase, however, was subject to eclipses, and in any case a daily examination of conscience was highly recommended. Delicate souls were therefore liable to periodic lapses into "religious melancholy," that great threat to the Christian that "will make him think himself an Hypocrite, when he is a Saint, and therefore take heed of a Melancholy, lumpish and sad temper; it is a very great hindrance to this grace of assurance" (Christopher Love).[242] Love's admission says a great deal, but did not Puritan preaching itself encourage melancholy? Such was Burton's view, expressed in his vivid description of the individual made ill by scruples:

> *it is the conscience alone which is a thousand witnesses to accuse us,* Nocte dieque suum gestant in pectore testem *(night and day they carry the accusing witness in their own breast). A continual testor to give in evidence, to empanel a jury to examine us, to cry guilty, a persecutor whith hue and cry to follow, an apparitor to summon us, a bailiff to carry us, a serjeant to arrest, an attorney to plead*

against us, a gaoler to torment, a judge to condemn, still accusing, denouncing, torturing and molesting.[243]

A good many of Burton's compatriots would have recognized their own experience in this portrait of the conscience, at once policeman, prosecutor, judge, jailer, and executioner, confining its victim in the prison of scruple. Burton also describes how these unhappy souls "can think of naught that is pleasant, 'their conscience will not let them be quiet,' in perpetual fear, anxiety . . . They are generally weary of their lives, a trembling heart they have, a sorrowful mind, and little or no rest: *Terror ubique tremor, timor undique et undique terror.*" They refuse to eat and drink —mental anorexia. They see sins where there are none, or aggravate those which they may have committed. "God's heavy wrath is kindled in their souls, and notwithstanding their continual prayers and supplications to Christ Jesus, they have no release or ease at all."[244]

Despite the fact that Puritan preachers did aim to reassure their audiences, they did not succeed in doing so, insofar as they themselves provoked the tragic question, "Shall I be saved?" A close reading of sixteenth- and seventeenth-century English sermons identifies this reaction of anguish: These texts regularly integrate the question of supposed interlocutors who ask, "Shall I be one of the elect?" The repetition of the same interdictions implies the stubborn disobedience of the churchgoers: analogously, the preachers' reiterated anticipation of their readers' and listeners' nagging question indicates the latter group's heavy and persistent burden of anxiety.

The problem of salvation and its attendant uncertainties were of extreme consequence to seventeenth-century English people.[245] Two of Perkins's above-cited works, in both their titles and contents, convey this deep concern: *A Treatise tending unto a declaration whether a man be in the estate of damnation or in the Estate of grace* (1589),[246] and *A Case of Conscience, the Greatest that ever was: How a man may know whether he be the Child of God, or no* (1592).[247] Likewise, Arthur Dent gives *The Plain Mans Path-way to Heaven* this revealing subtitle: "Wherein every man may clearly see, whether he shall be saved or damned." In addition to his sermons, Henry Smith transcribes questions that clearly bespeak a pastor's consternation before his audience. These include "whether predestination, election, etc. are to be preached unto laymen? What free-will had Adam? And what free-will remaineth unto us? . . . Whether heretics, living to themselves, without corrupting others, are to be punished with death?"[248]

In one of his sermons, Hieron imagines a listener asking "how shall I know that I am one of Gods people?"[249] Meanwhile, Sibbes observes that four questions disturb the peace of the Christian: sin and guilt; the effects of corruption; the miseries of life; and the most suffocating of all, death and damnation.[250] Love acknowledges that "many men will think these Doctrines [of the chosen few] will lead men to despaire: and they are so uncomfortable, they will make a man never have a glad day all his life."[251] Love also devotes no less than sixteen sermons to the problem of knowing "whether yet he [a Christian] be effectually called and elected,"[252] and he confronts the difficulty by clearly echoing his audiences' own questions. He formulates these as "whether may a Christian in this life be assured of eternall Salvation, for as much as Election was done in the decree of God, before ever he had a being, or the world was? Therefore weening we are not privy to Gods decree and counsell, how can it be said, that we may know and be assured of our Eternal Election?"[253] Among others, Baxter strove to resolve this case of conscience: "How a Sinner may attain a settled Peace of Conscience, and some competent measure of the joy of the holy Ghost, who hath been conceived of Sin and Misery, and long made a Profession of Holiness, but liveth in continued doubting of their sincerity, and fears of Gods wrath because of an exceeding Deadness of Spirit."[254] This repeated question of Puritan sermons clarifies Burton's description, borrowed from Luther, of melancholics who "doubt of their election, how they shall know it, by what signs and . . . with such nice points, torture and crucify themselves, that they are almost mad, and all they get by it is this, they lay open a gap to the devil by desperation to carry them to hell."[255]

Burton's use of "desperation" and "despair"—words that frequently recur in the contemporary diagnosis of religious anxiety—deserves reemphasis. These words play a crucial role in the reconstruction of past psychologies. According to the analyses of both Catholic and Protestant churchmen, metaphysical despair was simultaneously linked with blasphemy and suicide, or at least the temptation to suicide. Heshusius notes that "many cannot tolerate the anguish of sin, and kill themselves like Judas and so many others."[256] Despite indications to the contrary, however, suicides seem to have been rare in sixteenth- and seventeenth-century Western Europe.[257] All the same, one fact is certain: The Catholic directors of conscience who composed the *Artes moriendi* or fought against the disease of scruple, as well as Protestant religious authors and speakers, were frequently faced with the religious despair of their congregations. The phenomenon assumed a prominent position in early modern civilization.

The Anatomy of Melancholy features important discussions of this topic. Burton describes melancholic individuals who believe that they are damned, abandoned by God, and accuse themselves night and day, trembling and thinking on the wrath of God or their impending doom. They construe their least fault as an unpardonable crime.[258] Some, suffering "a most intolerable torment," resort to blasphemy: "Who is that God that I should serve Him, what will it help me if I pray to him? If he exists, why does He not help me? . . . Far be from me such a God." He does not exist. Many of these desperate souls then become violent, either toward their good friends or themselves.[259] If this type of illness had not been at least relatively widespread, Burton would not have taken the trouble, no doubt for the sake of preachers as well as his other readers, to provide a long list of reassuring scriptural citations[260]; these were intended to counteract the disturbing or misinterpreted passages used by many sermon writers. In the same way, Donne frequently sought to quell the "despair" that tormented overscrupulous souls.[261]

On the one hand, the Puritan doctrinal campaign encouraged the "disheartened" to study their case from a medical point of view (were they not overcome by the melancholic humor?), and on the other, to alert these same people to the traps laid by Satan. Indeed, the Enemy first seeks to give the sinner excessive confidence in his own merits and God's pardon, and then to plunge him into despair once he perceives the darkness of his sinful deeds. He takes malignant pleasure in crushing these wretches beneath "the horror of sinne, the terror of the law, the fearfulnesse of Gods majesty."[262] "The devil," writes Perkins in a first-person narrative of a specific case, "cried in my ears that I was a reprobate, his child: that none of God's children were as I am, that this grief of my Soul was the beginning of hell."[263] Perkins elsewhere describes the "fearful" temptation of blasphemy.[264] Featley, in his turn, comes to the aid of the sould whose "fit of despair more and more groweth on him."[265] Bunyan, however, offers by far the most striking account of the double temptation to despair and blasphemy that infected scrupulous Puritans. This famous passage from *Grace Abounding to the Chief of Sinners* captures the apogee of the crisis:

> *one morning, as I did lie in my bed, I was, as at other times, most fiercely assaulted with this temptation, to* sell and part with Christ; *the wicked suggestion still*

> *running in my mind, which also in my mind, as at other times, I answered, No, no, not for thousands, thousands, thousands, at least twenty times together; but at last, after much striving, even until I was almost out of breath, I felt this thought pass through my heart,* Let him go if he will*! and I thought also that I felt my heart freely consent thereto. Oh, the diligence of Satan! Oh, the desperateness of man's heart!*
>
> *Now was the battle won, and down I fell, as a bird that is shot from the top of a tree, into great guilt and fearful despair; thus getting out of my bed, I went moping into the field; but God knows with as heavy a heart as mortal man, I think, could bear; where for the space of two hours, I was like a man bereft of life, and as now past all recovery, and bound over to eternal punishment.*[266]

While this is an extreme case, it illuminates a psychological syndrome that would have had a certain collective dimension in seventeenth-century England. There can be no doubt that the theology of predestination and its pastoral diffusion were largely responsible for this religious melancholy. Burton attests to this point, as he accuses "those thundering ministers, a most frequent cause they are of this malady."[267] It was reported that the preacher William Vetch once cried from the pulpit that eighty of the two thousand people in attendance would definitely not be saved. Upon hearing this news, three of his listeners were seized with despair and eventually killed themselves.[268]

Such an anecdote cannot be given too much scope. At the same time, it would be wrong to neglect several facts of wide-ranging implication: for example, Perkins was the most frequently read British preacher of his time.[269] Later, Bunyan's writings, especially *The Pilgrim's Progress*, were enormously successful. In 1792 this work was in its 160th edition.[270] Finally, Puritanism influenced people who did not fully subscribe to it, and left its mark on a certain number of Anglicans.

The areas of research that the three preceding chapters have explored converge toward the same conclusion: The evangelism of fear undeniably existed in the Protestant world, despite the positive aspect that the Reformers sought to impart to the doctrine of justification by faith. First, Protestant preaching adopted a number of unsettling themes from traditional Catholic discourse (the chosen few, the horrible death of sinners, the last ends, contempt for the world, and so on). Subsequently, it also gave way to tactics for the sake of conversion. Nevertheless, it added its own original touches. At least during the sixteenth and seventeenth centuries, its eschatological preoccupations mingled threats and anxieties in expectation of impending deliverance. This double language pertained especially to bondage of the will and predestination. After a traumatic spiritual journey, the elect soul attains the objective certainty of salvation. Subjective assurance, however, may elude this soul throughout his or her lifetime. Moreover, he or she is constantly urged toward self-interrogation regarding "true faith." Hence the possibility of lapses into despair, even after "conversion." Eventually, both Lutheranism, after the 1580 Formula of Concord, and Anglicanism distanced themselves from the theology of the bondage of the will. One might therefore suppose that in these two major sections of the Protestant world disquieting sermons became more and more subdued and finally much less significant than in the Catholic countries. Given, however, the influence of Puritanism beyond its own boundaries, the impact of its discourse cannot be underestimated. The work of Catholic missionaries and Puritan pastors bore close resemblances and provoked the same reactions from their audiences. Their doctrinal messages, first cousins to each other, have weighed heavily in Western history.

Conclusion

Fear has two sides. According to the particular case, it can be either salutary or destructive. As a modern philosopher wittily puts it, "*Timeo, ergo sum,*"[1] and it is true that, when viewed in clear focus, fear is a "call to being." It is "creative of being," for "the control of fear provides access to the world." The concept of sin can itself engender a potentially fruitful fear of one's self. Experienced positively, guilt creates tensions that can redeem the elite. These tensions can actively foster well-being, stimulate creative anxiety, help to develop a sense of responsibility, and also, thanks to introspection, open treasures locked deep within ourselves.

On the negative side, however, excessive fear as well as an excessively promoted language of guilt can paralyze, discourage, and alienate. Time and again the present study has revealed, among Catholics as much as Protestants, this temptation to despair, which especially afflicted individuals on their deathbeds. These people, after all, had heard more talk of sin than of pardon. It is necessary to fear real danger. It is useful to warn others when they are imminently threatened. The weapon of fear, however, cannot be wielded without its own risks and dangers. Too great an emphasis on death and the macabre, on the tortures of the afterlife, on ill-made confessions and communions proved dangerous to the psychological health of a certain number of listeners. The aggressivity toward sinners was suspect. Throughout my presentation, I have shown the religious discourse's slide from the moderate to the excessive, as well as its astonishing misuse of biblical quotations, whether ripped from their context or taken to the limit of their sense. The discourse of fear most often leaned on garbled references or misunderstood texts.

Yet why this propensity to sensationalize the message of Holy Scripture? This book has attempted to answer this enormous question, by considering sin as a "historical object." It was, I believe, a new enterprise to undertake a cultural history of sin in the West. The choice of this study has had the advantage of providing access to a kind of observatory, from where we have been able to survey more than six hundred years of guilt-instilling efforts.

Across the "*longue durée,*" this aerial view has revealed previously ill-distinguished facts and clarified historical ensembles of which only a few scattered elements had been given rudimentary attention. Thus have emerged the continuity and the extraordinary cultural importance of the *contemptus mundi* doctrine, first highlighted by Robert Bultot. The world is a "vale of tears": This was the general belief of Western directors of conscience, from the church fathers to Anglo-Saxon Puritans. Thus from one end of this period to the other, the discourse of the church was predominantly pessimistic. Moreover, the ideology of the *contemptus mundi* claimed to have universal value and made a critique of all human destiny in this vile world. It devalued sexuality, was disgusted by procreation and childbirth, laid heavy stress on our miseries and diseases, had a strong taste for the macabre, and pronounced the human mind incapable of any true knowledge. For the most part, then, medieval and early modern preachers taught their congregations a monastic ethics and a philosophy of "denial."

If the diverse components of the *contemptus mundi* discourse formed a coherent whole—the coherence of pessimism—it was primarily due to the belief in a myth. This myth was that of the golden age, known in the Christian lands as the "Earthly Paradise": that Eden where Adam and Eve lived like "angels." The consequence of the Original Sin, whose dimensions were truly cosmic, was the extraordinary wrath of God who, in His just "vengeance," condemned mankind to suffering, death, and damnation. True, the sacrifice of the Son would someday appease the wrath of the Father. Some would therefore escape the "mass of perdition." This assessment, at one time accepted by nearly all Western theologians, inevitably engendered dramatic pastoral messages and activities and pushed the entire teaching church toward strict severity.

In this light, it comes as no surprise that the Renaissance appears far gloomier than is ordinarily taught. This less sunny complexion should not be perceived without qualification. Should one dismiss Manetti's and Pico della Mirandola's praise of man, or Raphael's serene paintings, or the festivals of the Renaissance? This is not my aim. All the same, I have wished to demonstrate that humanism does not necessarily mean optimism (for example, in Machiavelli, Budé, and Montaigne), that several eminent figures of the Renaissance moved toward religious anxiety (the same Pico della Mirandola and Michelangelo), and above all that the most representative people of the fifteenth and sixteenth centuries hardly felt Promethean. Instead, they most often felt fragile and sinful, susceptible to melancholy, and anguished by the rapid decline of an aging, decrepit world. It has been said that Neoplatonism was the principal philosophy of the Renaissance. It would be equally accurate—though not contradictory to the preceding statement—to see Augustinism as the predominant philosophical system of this period of Western history, especially during the sixteenth century—the birth date of Protestantism.

There are many equally valid ways of conducting the historiography of "mentalities." The road taken here has been to clarify the expansion and dissemination, from the level of elite groups, of a discourse of fear and intimidation. How and why did it gain credibility? The answer would seem to lie in a coincidence, which might otherwise not have occurred, between a pessimistic brand of preaching that was rapidly widening its appeal and a series of vast collective disasters that besieged Europeans from the Black Death to the end of the Wars of Religion. The preachers seemed to have good reason to say that mankind was guilty and to foretell punishments in both this world and the next. In the eighteenth century and after, the alleviation of serious threats to daily life encouraged challenging the validity of these dire pronouncements.

Circumstances helped to steer this type of pastoral discourse toward tactical measures as well as toward dramatic devices that impressed audiences. At issue, however, was something far more serious. In *La Peur en Occident* I emphasized the fear of the elites. This fear is the key to the investigations I have made in the present book. The most saintly individuals were often those who most deeply feared themselves. The death of the devout was never easy. Tronson, for one, was convinced that even among priests there would only be a chosen few. Can there be much surprise that people haunted by truly metaphysical fear would divulge it in their preaching? Augustinism, which must be cited once more, could only have brought on fears among both the instructors and pupils of the church (or at least among the most motivated of these people). In any case, the result was a type of preaching that spoke more of the Passion of the Savior than of His Resurrection, more of sin than of pardon, of the Judge than of the Father, of Hell than of Paradise. There was thus a true deviation from Saint Paul's tidings that "where sin abounded, grace did much more abound" (Rom. 5:20). Hence one might consider whether the rejection of an oppressive doctrinal campaign was one of the causes of the "de-Christianization" of the West.

NOTES

Titles of books that are known to English-language readers in a form different from that familiar to French readers have been translated and placed in brackets where first mentioned. Page references refer to the work originally quoted by Jean Delumeau.

TRANSLATOR'S PREFACE

1. Robert Burton, *Anatomy of Melancholy, volume 1* (London: G. Bell), p. 138.
2. Sigmund Freud, *Civilization and Its Discontents* (New York: Norton, 1961), p. 9.

INTRODUCTION

1. J. Delumeau, *La Peur en Occident: Une cité assiégée* (Paris: Fayard, 1978), in particular part II.
2. Edited by G. Bedouelle and Father Giacone (Leyden: Brill, 1976), p. 302. See also J. Boisset, "Les Epistres et Evangiles . . . par Lefèvre d'Etaples," in *Platon et Aristote à la Renaissance* (Paris: Vrin, 1978), p. 89. I fully agree with France Quère, *Les Pères apostoliques* (Paris: Seuil, 1980), p. 30, when she says that: "Of course Christianity did not invent the concept of conscience or of culpability nor did it invent the prodigious dynamics of the soul and its efforts to reach beyond itself. However, it did direct the efforts of the soul in an unprecedented direction . . . The existence of man became the theater of a continous battle between the love of Christ and that which is known as sin."
3. Bourdaloue, *Oeuvres complètes*, 16 vols. (Paris: 1830), vol. 14, pp. 128–129 ("Pensées diverses sur le salut").
4. Delumeau, *La Peur*, pp. 136–137.
5. Quoted in Father Ponthieux, "Prédictions et almanachs du XVIe siècle," (Master's diss. University of Paris I, 1973), pp. 85–86.
6. "Dialogue de l'âme et du corps," part I, chap. 12, quoted in *Choix de lectures ascétiques: vie de Sainte Catherine de Gênes*, (Clermont-Ferrand: 1840), pp. 145–146.
7. Agrippa d'Aubigné, *Oeuvres* (Paris: Pléiade, 1969), pp. 376 and 538.
8. Francis de Sales, "Introduction à la vie dévote," in *Oeuvres* (Paris: Pléiade, 1969), chap. 12, pp. 53–54.
9. M. Gendrot, *Saint Louis-Marie Grignion de Montfort. Oeuvres complètes* (Paris: Seuil, 1966), p. 1667.
10. See J. G. Arapura, *Religion as Anxiety and Tranquillity* (The Hague: Mouton, 1975).
11. G. B. Segni, *Trattato sopra la carestia e fame: sue cause, accidenti, provvisioni, reggimenti* (Bologna: 1602). See D. Zanetti, "L'Approvisionnement de Pavie au XVIe siècle," *Annales E.S.C.* (January–February 1963), p. 62.
12. S. Freud, *Malaise dans la civilisation [Civilization and Its Discontents]* (Paris: P.U.F., 1973) p. 93.
13. C. G. Jung, *L'Ame et la vie* (Paris: Buchet-Chastel, 1963), p. 59.
14. H. Gouhier, "La Tyrannie de l'avenir," *Archivio di filosofia* (1977): p. 178, quoting *Les Deux sources de la morale et de la religion*.
15. On this subject see also the illuminating work of J.-C. Sagne and, in particular, *Péché, culpabilité,*

pénitence (Paris: Cerf, 1971); *Conflit, changement, conversion* (Paris: Cerf, 1974); and *Tes Péchés ont été pardonnés* (Lyon: Chalet, 1977).

16. P. de Boisdeffre, *Goethe m'a dit. Dix entretiens imaginaires* (Paris: Luneau-Ascot, 1981), p. 230.

CHAPTER 1

1. Plutarch, *Traités de morale [Opera moralia]*, Budé series, VII, 1, p. 214. *The Iliad*, 17, V. 446–447.
2. Cappadocian church doctors such as Basil the Great, Gregory of Nazianzus and Gregory of Nyssa. Boethius' (480–524) *Consolation of Philosophy* is also impregnated with Neoplatonism. Regarding the influence of classical pagan thought on the doctrine of *contemptus mundi*, see R. Bultot, "Les Philosophes du paganisme. Docteurs et exemples du *contemptus mundi* pour la morale médiévale," *Studia Gratiana* 19 (1976), Mélanges G. Fransens, 1, pp. 101–122. See also note 3.
3. This idea, and the discussion that follows it, were inspired by the penetrating work of R. Bultot, *La Doctrine du mépris du monde* (Louvain: Nauwelaerts, 1963–1964), IV, 1 and 2. See in particular IV, 1, pp. 18, 23, 39, and 136–139. See also, by the same author, "La Doctrine du mépris du monde chez Bernard le clunisien," *Le Moyen Age* 70 (1964): 179–204 and 335–376; "Grammatica, ethica et contemptus mundi aux XIIe et XIIIe siècles," in *Arts libéraux et philosophie au Moyen Age* (Montreal: 1969): 815–927; "Bonté des créatures et mépris du monde," *Revue des sciences philosophiques et théologiques* (1978): 361–394; "Cosmologie et contemptus mundi," *Recherches de théologie ancienne et médiévale* 1 (1980), Mélanges H. Bascour, pp. 1–23. I also owe much to B. Roy, "Amour, Fortune et Mort: la danse des trois aveugles," in *Le Sentiment de la mort au Moyen Age* (Montreal: Univers, 1979), pp. 121–137.
4. Bultot, *La Doctrine*, IV, 1, p. 40.
5. Ibid., pp. 67–70.
6. Bultot, "Cosmologie et contemptus mundi," pp. 1–23.
7. Bultot, *La Doctrine*, IV, 1, pp. 113–115.
8. C. Tresmontant, *La Métaphysique du Christianisme et la naissance de la philosophie chrétienne* (Paris: Seuil, 1961), p. 457.
9. *Cité de Dieu [City of God]*, vol. 37 of the Combès edition of Saint Augustine's *Oeuvre* (Paris: Desclée de Brouwer, 1960), XV, chap. 15. See also P. Brown, *Augustine of Hippo* (London: Faber and Faber, 1967), which I consulted in the Italian translation *Agostino d'Ippona* (Turin: Einaudi, 1974), p. 325.
10. *Cité de Dieu*, XXX, 24, pp. 670–672.
11. H. I. Marrou, "The Resurrection and Saint Augustine's Theology of Human Values," *Revue des études augustiniennes* 12 (1966): 287–299.
12. Brown, *Agostino d'Ippona*, pp. 287–299.
13. *Cité de Dieu*, XXII, 22, p. 645, quoted by P. Sellier, *Pascal et saint Augustine* (Paris: A. Colin, 1970), p. 234.
14. Delumeau, *La Peur en Occident*, pp. 252–253.
15. The following analysis is based on the *Dictionnaire de théologie biblique* (Paris: Cerf, 1971), cols. 784–791.
16. See T. Rey-Mermet, *Croire*, 3 vols. (Limoges: Drouet-Ardant, 1976–1977), and in particular vol. 1, pp. 281–282.
17. See H. Spitzmuller, *Poésie latine du Moyen Age* (Paris: Desclée de Brouwer, 1971) pp. 1798–1800; J. Le Goff, *La Civilization de l'Occident médieval* (Paris: Arthaud, 1964; reprint ed. 1972), p. 236.
18. See M. Loos, *Dualist Heresy in the Middle Ages* (The Hague: Nijhoff, 1974), passim and in particular pp. 67–72 and 252–254.
19. *Conf. Théol.*, III, 5, in A. Wilmart, ed., *Auteurs spirituels et textes dévots du Moyen Age latin* (Paris: 1932), pp. 145–146. See also Bultot, *La Doctrine*, IV, 2, p. 13.
20. A. Wilmart, "Jean de Fécamp, la complainte sur les fins dernières," *Revue d'ascétique et de mystique* 9 (1928): 395–398. See, in addition, Bultot, *La Doctrine*, IV, 2, p. 22.
21. Spitzmuller, *Poésie latine*, pp. 577–579.
22. *Patrologiae cursus completus: series graeca*, ed. by J.-P. Migne (Paris: 1857–1866), hereafter cited as *PG*, vol. 60, col. 724.
23. See in particular L. J. Friedman, "The 'Ubi sunt'; the regrets and effictio," *Modern Language*

Notes 72 (1957): 497–505; M. Liborio, "Contributi alla storia dell' 'Ubi sunt,' " *Cultura neolatina* 20 (1960): 141–209; Bultot, *La Doctrine*, IV, 2, p. 36, note 20; A. Costanzo, "Time and space in Villon: les trois ballades du temps jadis," in G. Mermier and E. Dubruck, *Fifteenth Century Studies* (Ann Arbor: University of Michigan Press, 1978), pp. 51–69.

24. Spitzmuller, *Poésie latine*, p. 969.
25. Ibid., p. 1383.
26. *Patrologiae cursus completus: series latina*, ed. by J.-P. Migne (Paris: 1841–1864), hereafter cited as *PL*, vol. 159, col. 163, and Bultot, *La Doctrine*, IV, 2, p. 113.
27. *PL*, vol. 144, col. 534 CD. See also Bultot, *La Doctrine*, IV, 1, p. 77.
28. Spitzmuller, *Poésie latine*, p. 1425.
29. See Bultot, *La Doctrine*, IV, 1, p. 37.
30. Ibid., IV, 2, p. 22.
31. Ibid., pp. 35–36.
32. Ibid., pp. 66–67. Regarding the existing manuscripts of this poem, see again Bultot, *La Doctrine*, IV, 2, pp. 50–52.
33. *PL*, vol. 217, col. 702.
34. *PL*, vol. 50, col. 917. For a translation of the same see Bultot, *La Doctrine*, IV, 2, pp. 17–18.
35. Spitzmuller, *Poésie latine*, pp. 1365–1367.
36. The Book of Wisdom, in particular 2:1–24. All biblical quotations, unless otherwise specified, are from the King James Bible.
37. Quoted by Bultot, *La Doctrine*, IV, 1, p. 37. Letter edited by J. Leclercq, *Studia Anselmiana* 18–19 (1947): 287.
38. Bultot, *La Doctrine*, IV, 1, p. 51.
39. Ibid., p. 32.
40. Ibid., p. 55.
41. Ibid., p. 56.
42. Ibid., p. 48.
43. Ibid., p. 59.
44. Ibid., p. 35.
45. Ibid., p. 80.
46. Ibid., IV, 2, p. 82.
47. *Cité de Dieu*, XIV, 24, pp. 450–451.
48. Ibid., XXII, 24, p. 660.
49. See C. Tresmontant, *La Métaphysique*, pp. 462–464.
50. Bultot, *La Doctrine*, IV, 1, pp. 100–111.
51. *PL*, vol. 217, col. 702–704. With respect to the church's suspicious attitude toward sexuality, see F. Chiovaro, "Le Mariage chrétien en Occident," in J. Delumeau, ed., *Histoire vécue du peuple chrétien* (Toulouse: Privat, 1979), vol. 1, pp. 231–241; J. L. Flandrin, *Un Temps pour embrasser. Aux origines de la morale sexuelle occidentale* (Paris: Seuil, 1983). Concerning the *De Contemptu* of Innocent III, see C. Martineau-Genieys, *Le Thème de la mort dans la poésie française de 1450 à 1550* (Thèse d'Etat, University of Montpellier, 1978), pp. 97–106. I would like to thank E. Le Roy Ladurie for drawing my attention to the abovementioned Ph.d. dissertation, which was published by Champion, Paris, in 1977.
52. Spitzmuller, *Poésie latine*, pp. 401–403.
53. Ibid., p. 443.
54. Ibid., p. 479.
55. Ibid., p. 493.
56. Ibid., p. 515.
57. Ibid., p. 565.
58. H. Spitzmuller, *Poésie italienne du Moyen Age (XIIe–XVe siècle)* (Paris: Desclée de Brouwer, 1975), vol. 1, pp. 723–725.
59. See the discussion between R. Bultot and his critics in the *Revue d'ascétique et de mystique* (1964): 185–196, 481–492, 493–494; ibid., (1965): 233–304; F. Vanden-Broucke, *La Morale monastique du XIe au XIVe siècle* (Louvain: Nauwelaerts, 1966), in particular pp. 18–20; L. J. Bataillon and J. P. Jossua, "Le Mépris du monde. De l'intérêt d'une discussion actuelle," *Revue des sciences philosophiques et théologiques* 51 (1967): 23–28; R. Grégoire, "Il Contemptus mundi: ricerche e problemi," *Rivista di Storia e letteratura religiosa* 5 (1960): 140–154; F. Lazzari, *Mistica e ideologia tra XI e XIII secolo* (Milan: 1972), pp. 9–14.
60. See M. de Gandillac and T. Jeauneau, eds., *Entretiens sur la Renaissance du XIIe siècle* (Paris:

Mouton, 1968), above all pp. 53–69, 147–160, 296–308; H. Schipperges, *Die Benediktiner in der Medizin des frühen Mittelalters* (Leipzig: 1964), pp. 57–58.
61. See A.-J. Festugière, *Les Moines d'orient*, vol. 1: *Culture et sainteté* (Paris: Cerf, 1961), passim.
62. *Revue d'ascetique* (1964): 489. See also C. Duquoc, "Eschatologie et réalités terrestres," *Lumière et vie* 9 (1960): 4–22.
63. Translated by J. Ancelet-Hustache, *Maître Eckhart et la mystique rhénane* (Paris: Seuil, 1956), p. 106.
64. Ibid., p. 94.
65. H. Suso, *Oeuvres complètes*, trans. and introduced by J. Ancelet-Hustache (Paris: Seuil, 1977), p. 350.
66. Tauler, *Sermons*, trans. by Hugueny, Théry, and Corin, 3 vol. (1927–1935), vol. 2, p. 237.
67. *Dialogue de Sainte Catherine de Sienne*, trans. by J. Hurtaud (Paris: 1913), vol. 1, p. 190.
68. Ibid., vol. 1, p. 109.
69. *Le Chateau de l'Ame [The Interior Castle]*, in *Sommets de la littérature espagnole* (Lausanne: Rencontres, 1961), vol. 3, p. 41.
70. Ibid., p. 71.
71. Ibid., p. 72.
72. Ibid., p. 62.
73. Ibid., p. 61.
74. *Oeuvres complètes*, trans. by M. Auclair (Paris: Desclée de Brouwer, 1964), p. 51.
75. *Le Chateau de l'Ame*, p. 250.
76. *La Montée du Carmel [The Ascent of Mount Carmel]*, in *Oeuvres spirituelles*, trans. by Father P. Grégoire de Saint Joseph (Paris: Seuil, 1972), I, chap. 3, p. 34.
77. Ibid., all of chap. 3 and 4.
78. Ibid., chap. 12, p. 84.
79. Ibid., p. 45.
80. Madrid, National Library, MS 6624, translated and published in J. Baruzi, *Saint Jean de la Croix et le problème de l'expérience mystique* (Paris: Alcan, 1924), p. 411.
81. *La Montée du Carmel*, I, chap. 4, p. 38.
82. Baruzi, *Saint Jean de la Croix*, p. 408. The expression "volatilized" is Barrès's.
83. J. Baruzi, "Luis de Léon interprète du Livre de Job," in special issue (*Cahiers*) of the *Revue d'histoire et de philosophie religieuse*, no. 40 (1966): 8.
84. The following discussion and the translations used are from A. Guy, *La Pensée de Fray Luis de Léon* (Paris: Vrin, 1943), pp. 292 passim. The quotations are translated from Luis de Léon, *Obras*, ed. by Muinoz Saens. However, I have also used the article quoted in note 83.
85. *Obras*, vol. 1, *Exposicion de Job*, XIV, 2, p. 244.
86. Ibid., IV, 19, p. 70.
87. Ibid., III, 22, p. 48.
88. Ibid., VII, 1, p. 120.
89. Ibid., VII, 1, pp. 120–121.
90. Ibid.
91. *Obras*, vol. 4, *Poesias*, Oda: "De la avaricia," stanza 1, p. 308.
92. Ibid., Oda: "Del moderato y costante," stanza 1, p. 308.
93. Ibid., "Del mundo y su vanidad," stanza 14, pp. 356–357.
94. *Opera*, M. Gutiérrez, ed. (Salamanca: 1891), vol. 1, p. 301.
95. *Obras*, vol. 4, *Poesias*, Oda: "Noche serena," stanza 3, p. 314.
96. Ibid., Oda: "El aire se serana," stanza 9, p. 302.
97. M. Maccarone, *Lotharii cardinalis. De miseria humanae conditionis* (1955), pp. ix–xxii. A new edition of *De contemptu mundi* of Cardinal Lothair, ed. by R. E. Lewis, published by University of Georgia Press, 1978, may now be consulted.
98. B. Giamboni, *Della miseria dell'uomo*, ed. by G. Piatti, (Florence: 1836), p. 6.
99. See A. Tenenti, *Il Senso della morte e l'amore della vita nel Rinascimento (Francia e Italia)*, 2nd ed. (Turin: Einaudi, 1977) whose book is entirely devoted to this subject. See also G. Di Napoli, "Contemptus mundi et dignitas hominis nel Rinascimento," *Rivista di filosofia neo-scolastica* 48 (1956): 9–41.
100. Tenenti, *Il Senso*, p. 450.
101. Petrarch, *Africa*, 6, lines 879–900 quoted by Tenenti, *Il Senso*, p. 192.
102. E. W. Kohls, "Meditatio mortis chez Pétrarque et Erasme," in *Colloquia erasmiana turonensia* (Paris: Vrin, 1972), vol. 1, pp. 303–304.
103. Erasmus of Rotterdam, *Opera omnia*, with an introduction by S. Dresden (Amsterdam: 1977),

vol. 5, pp. 1–87 (introduction covering pp. 3–36). A concise summary of Erasmus's text may be found in R. R. Post, *The Modern Devotion: Confrontation with Reformation and Humanism* (Leyden: Brill, 1968), pp. 660–670. One should also consult the essential article by R. Bultot, "Erasme, Epicure et le *De Contemptu mundi*," *Scrinium erasmianum* 2 (1969): 205–238.

104. Ronsard, *Oeuvres complètes*, ed. by P. Lemonnier (Paris: 1914–1919), vol. 6, pp. 10–44.
105. E. Delaruelle, E. R. Labande, and P. Ourliac, *L'Eglise au temps du Grand Schisme* tome XIV, vol. 2 of Fliche and Martin, *L'Histoire de l'eglise*, p. 937. See also *Dictionnaire de Spiritualité*, vol. 7, cols. 2338–2368.
106. See A. de Backer, *Essai bibliographique sur le livre "De Imitatione Christi"* (Liège: 1864).
107. Delaruelle, Labande, and Ourliac, *L'Eglise*, p. 935.
108. All of these quotations are adapted from the translation done by F. de Lamennais (Paris: Seuil, 1979), pp. 13, 23, 45, and 127.
109. H. J. Martin, *L'Apparition du livre* (Paris: Albin Michel, 1958), p. 381.
110. *Dictionnaire de Spiritualité*, vol. 7, col. 2342 quoting a French translator of the *Imitation* (Jehan de Graves) whose translation was published in Antwerp in 1544. Concerning Thomas à Kempis see Post, *The Modern Devotion*, pp. 521–551.
111. [Ludolph of Saxony] Ludolphe le Chartreux, *La Grande vie de Jésus-Christ*, trans. by Marie-Prosper Augustin, 6 vols. (Paris: 1864), vol. 3, p. 132.
112. Ibid., p. 80.
113. Ibid., p. 79.
114. Ibid.
115. Ibid., vol. 1, p. 427.
116. Ibid., p. 433.
117. *Dictionnaire de Spiritualité*, vol. 9, col. 1135.
118. *Exercices spirituels*, trans. by Father Courel (Paris: Desclée de Brouwer, 1960), p. 51, section 63.
119. Ibid., pp. 28–29, section 23.
120. F. Luis de Granada, *Guida de pecadores*, ed. by M. Burgos (Madrid: Espasa Calpe, 1953), p. viii. See also *Dictionnaire de Spiritualité*, vol. 9, cols. 1043–1054.
121. de Granada, *Guida de pecadores*, p. 114.
122. Ibid., p. 148.
123. Ibid., p. 161.
124. Ibid., p. 156.
125. Ibid.
126. M. Luther, *Commentaire de l'Epitre aux Galates [Commentary on the Epistle to the Galatians]*, in the Labor and Fides edition, *Oeuvres* (Geneva: 1957–), vol. 15, pp. 224–225.
127. Ibid.
128. M. Luther, *Propos de table [Table talk or Tischreden]*, ed. by G. Brunet (Paris: 1844), p. 84.
129. Ibid., p. 85.
130. Ibid., p. 87.
131. Ibid., p. 217. See also *De la vie conjugale [Vindication of Married Life]* (1522) in the *Oeuvres*, vol. 3, pp. 225–226.
132. M. Luther, *Une manière simple de prier [A Simple Way of Praying]* (1535), in *Oeuvres*, vol. 7, p. 213.
133. J. Calvin, *Institution de la religion chrétienne [Institutes of the Christian Religion]*, 4 vols. (Geneva: Labor et Fides, 1955–), I, V, 1, pp. 17–18.
134. Ibid., I, XIV, 21, p. 130.
135. Ibid., II, II, 15, p. 37.
136. Quoted by R. Stauffer, *Dieu, la création et la providence dans la prédication de Calvin* (Berne: Peterlang, 1978), p. 203. Concerning the *Imago Dei* in the sermons of Calvin, see chap. 5.
137. Quoted by R. Stauffer, *Dieu*, pp. 199–200.
138. M. Luther, *De la vie conjugale*, in *Oeuvres*, vol. 3, p. 226.
139. Ibid., p. 251.
140. Ibid.
141. M. Luther, *Controverse contre la théologie scolastique [Against Scholastic Theology]* (1517), in *Oeuvres*, vol. 2, p. 96.
142. M. Luther, *Commentaire de l'Epitre aux Galates*, in *Oeuvres*, vol. 15, pp. 30, 36, and 63.
143. Ibid., p. 55.
144. Ibid.
145. Ibid.

146. Ibid. Did Luther understand Saint Paul? See D. Olivier, *La Foi de Luther* (Paris: Beauchesne, 1978), pp. 136–139.
147. See J. V. Pollet, *H. Zwingli et la Réforme en Suisse* (Paris: P.U.F., 1963), pp. 39–54. One may also consult the following article by the same author, "Zwingli—Zwinglianisme," in *Dictionnaire de théologie catholique*, XV, 2, cols. 3728–3928 and in particular cols. 3788–3790. See also R. Stauffer, "L'influence et la critique de l'humanisme dans le 'De vera et falsa religione' de Zwingli," in *L'Humanisme allemand (1480–1540)* (Paris: Vrin, 1979), pp. 427–440.
148. See J. Rilliet, *Zwingli. Le troisième homme de la Réforme* (Paris: Fayard, 1959), p. 105.
149. I consulted the German edition of *De vera et falsa religione*, in *Zwingli Hauptschriften*, ed. by F. Blancke, O. Farner, and R. Pfister (Zürich: 1941), vol. 9, pp. 42–58.
150. Rilliet, *Zwingli*, pp. 98–99.
151. M. Bucer, *Resumé sommaire de la doctrine chrétienne*, trans. by Father Wendel (Paris: P.U.F., 1951), pp. 43 and 61.
152. These accusations against man are collected by P. Imbart de la Tour, *Les Origines de la Réforme*, 4 vols. (Paris: 1905), vol. 4, p. 72.
153. J. Calvin, *Institution*, II, I, 9, p. 19.
154. Ibid., I, I, 1, p. 3.
155. Ibid., p. 5.
156. Ibid., I, IV, 1, p. 12.
157. Ibid., II, VI, 1, p. 97.
158. Ibid., II, II, 10, p. 31.
159. Ibid., I, I, 1, pp. 3–4.
160. Ibid. III, IX, 1, p. 179.
161. Ibid.
162. Ibid.
163. T. Beza, *Chrestiennes méditations*, text ed. and introduced by M. Richter (Geneva: Droz, 1964), p. 9. The first edition of this text is of 1582.
164. Ibid., p. 42.
165. Ibid., p. 52.
166. Ibid., p. 60.
167. Ibid., p. 76.
168. Ibid., p. 74. See also J. S. Bray, *Theodore Beza's Doctrine of Predestination* (Nieuwkoop: de Graaf, 1975), who points out the similarities between the doctrine of predestination of Theodore Beza and that of Calvin.
169. J. Knox, *The Work of John Knox*, ed. by D. Laing, 6 vols. (Edinburgh: 1846–1864), vol. 5, p. 144.
170. J. Knox, *John Knox's History of the Reformation in Scotland*, ed. by W. Croft-Dickinson, 2 vols. (ed. by Nelson, 1949), vol. 2, art. 12, p. 262.
171. J. Séguy, "Non-Conformismes religieux," in *Histoire des religions* (Paris: Pléiade, 1972), vol. 2, pp. 1264–1268.
172. E. Troeltsch, *Die Soziallehre der christlichen Kirchen und Gruppen*, in *Gesammelte Schriften* (Tübingen: 1923), vol. 1. English translation: *The Social Teaching of the Christian Churches*, 2nd ed. (London: 1949). See also J. Lecler, *Histoire de la tolérance au siècle de la Reforme*, 2 vols. (Paris: Aubier, 1955), vol. 1, p. 201; J. Séguy, *Les Assemblées anabaptistes-mennonites de France* (Paris: Mouton, 1977), pp. 20–27.
173. See Delumeau, *La Peur*, pp. 153–154.
174. Quoted by Séguy, *Les Assemblées*, p. 303.
175. Ibid., p. 299.
176. Quoted in Leclerc, *Histoire*, vol. 1, p. 207.
177. Quoted by Séguy, *Les Assemblées*, p. 236.
178. Ibid., p. 238.
179. Quoted in Leclerc, *Histoire*, vol. 1, p. 218.
180. Ibid, vol. 2, p. 394.
181. Quoted in Séguy, *Les Assemblées*, p. 310.
182. Ibid., p. 317.
183. Ibid., p. 316.
184. Ibid., p. 318.
185. Ibid., pp. 244–245.
186. Ibid., p. 237.

187. Ibid., p. 253.
188. Ibid., p. 831.
189. Séguy, "Non-Conformismes," in *Histoire des Religions*, vol. 2, pp. 1286–1287.
190. Ibid., p. 1295.

CHAPTER 2

1. The bibliography on this subject is, of course, immense. I would like to draw special attention to the following books that are to be added to the works mentioned in the course of this chapter: E. Male, *L'Art religieux de la fin du Moyen Age en France* (Paris: A. Colin, 1925); A. Tenenti, *La Vie et la mort à travers l'art du XVe siècle* (Paris: A. Colin, 1952 and 1977); A. Tenenti, *Il Senso della morte e l'amore della vita nel Rinascimento*, 2nd ed. (Turin: Einaudi, 1977); J. Huizinga, *Le Déclin du Moyen Age [The Waning of the Middle Ages]* (Paris: Payot, 1967); F. Lebrun, *Les Hommes et la mort en Anjou aux XVIIe et XVIIIe siècles* (Paris: Mouton, 1971); M. Vovelle, *Piété baroque et déchristianisation en Provence* (Paris: Plon, 1973); by the same author, *La Mort et l'occident de 1300 à nos jours* (Paris: Gallimard, 1983); P. Chihaia, "Les Idées de pérennité et de décomposition dans la sculpture funéraire occidentale" Ph.D. diss., University of Paris IV, 1973 (A. Tenenti kindly let me borrow his notes on this dissertation); P. Ariès, *Essais sur l'histoire de la mort en Occident du Moyen Age à nos jours* (Paris: Seuil, 1975); by the same author, *L'Homme devant la mort* (Paris: Seuil, 1977); L. V. Thomas, *Anthropologie de la mort* (Paris: Payot, 1976); P. Chaunu, *La Mort à Paris* (Paris: Fayard, 1978); R. Favre, *La Mort au siècle des Lumières* (Lyon: Presses Universitaires de Lyon, 1978); J. Wirth, *La Jeune fille et la mort. Recherches sur les thèmes macabres dans l'art germanique de la Renaissance* (Geneva: Droz, 1979); *Le Sentiment de la mort au Moyen Age*, conference held at the University of Montreal, ed. by C. Sutto (Montreal: Univers, 1979).
2. M. Montaigne, *Les Essais*, 3 vols., ed. by Thibaudet (Paris: Livre de Poche, 1965), vol. 1, chap. 20, pp. 118–122.
3. Ibid., p. 119.
4. Ibid., p. 115.
5. Ibid., vol. 3, chap. 12, p. 281.
6. Ibid., vol. 1, chap. 20, pp. 124–125.
7. Ibid., vol. 3, chap. 12, p. 294.
8. Ibid., p. 293.
9. Ibid., p. 281.
10. Ibid., p. 290.
11. Ibid., p. 294.
12. Ibid., p. 295.
13. Ariès, *L'Homme devant la mort*, pp. 29–30.
14. Delumeau, *La Peur*, p. 75–87.
15. J. Soustelle, *La Vie quotidienne des Aztèques* (Paris: Hachette, 1953), p. 233. *Les Rites de la mort*, catalogue of the exhibition held at the Musée de l'Homme, Paris, 1979–1980, p. 38.
16. E. Le Roy Ladurie, *Montaillou, village occitan de 1294 à 1324* (Paris: Gallimard, 1975), pp. 576–607.
17. See in particular E. Morin, *L'Homme et la mort* (Paris: Seuil, 1970), pp. 132–156, and Thomas, *Anthropologie de la mort*, pp. 152, 182–187, 301, 511–518.
18. One example out of thousands may be the apparitions of the damned and of their souls in J. Passavanti, *Lo Specchio della penitenza* (Milan: 1808), in particular pp. 75–77 and 82–83.
19. Quoted by R. Kanters and M. Nadeau, *Anthologie de la poésie française* (Lausanne: Rencontres, 1972), vol. 4, part 2: *Le XVIe siècle*, pp. 339–340.
20. Inquiry done by L. Stomma, results of which are cited in Delumeau, *La Peur*, pp. 86–87.
21. P. Jacob, *Les Revenants de la Beauce* (Montreal: éd. du Boréal Express, 1977), p. 16.
22. Ibid., p. 21.
23. Ibid., pp. 66–71.
24. One must not, however, confuse ritualized ancestor cults and the feeling that the dead were "living beings" of a particular type.
25. See R. Decary, *La Mort et les coutumes funéraires à Madagascar* (Paris: Maisonneuve, 1962), p. 73.
26. Ibid.

27. This custom is also a tradition in Spain where *huesos de santos*, "saints' bones," were eaten. Such pastry was made of marzipan, had the shape of a bone, and was filled with a yellow cream meant to be the marrow. See Decary, *La Mort*, p. 17.
28. J. Descola, *Le Mexique* (Paris: Larousse, 1968), pp. 102–104. See also Decary, *La Mort*, pp. 34–36.
29. Ariès, *L'Homme devant la mort*, pp. 73–76.
30. Ibid. and A. Le Braz, *La Légende de la mort chez les Bretons armoricains* (Paris: Champion, 1902), vol. 1, p. 123.
31. Ariès, *L'Homme devant la mort*, pp. 75–76.
32. Ibid., pp. 74–75.
33. M. Luther, *Si l'on peut fuir devant la mort [Can One Flee Before Death]*, in *Oeuvres*, vol. 5, p. 257.
34. *Encyclopaedia Universalis*, s.v. "Macabre."
35. See *Gli Scritti di San Francesco d'Assisi*, ed. by V. Facchinetti (Milan: Vita e Pensiero, 1954), pp. 168–169.
36. See below, end of chap. 3.
37. Ronsard, *Oeuvres complètes*, vol. 6, pp. 10–44.
38. Rabelais, *Pantagruel* (Paris: Pléiade), chap. 8, pp. 224–225.
39. Paris, Bibliothèque nationale, MS fonds fr. 1654, fol. 149.
40. Aimé de Montgesoye, *Complainte de très haulte et vertueuse dame . . . Ysabel de Bourbon*, printed in *Medium Aevum* 2 (1933): 1–33.
41. J. Molinet, *Faits et dictz*, ed. by N. Dupire (Paris: 1936), vol. 2, pp. 670–680. See C. Martineau-Genieys, *Le Thème de la mort*, p. 247.
42. C. Marot, *Oeuvres complètes* (Paris: A. Garnier, 1920), vol. 1, "Déploration de messire Fl. Robertet," p. 544.
43. Ariès, *L'Homme devant la mort*, p. 114.
44. See A. M. Malingrey, "Sentences des sages chez Chrysostome," in *Jean Chrysostom et Augustin. Actes du colloque de Chantilly, 22–24 septembre 1974*, ed. by C. Kannengiesser (Paris: Beauchesne, 1975), pp. 204–206.
45. *PG*, vol. 60, col. 727.
46. *Collectio selecta SS Ecclesiae Patrum*, ed. by Caillau-Guillon (Paris: 1833), vol. 38, pp. 23–24. I must thank Father F. Bourdeau both for finding this reference and for the translation he provided.
47. Migne included this text among the works of Saint Augustine, *PL*, vol. 40, col. 987. Concerning the Neoplatonic sources of Christian pessimism up to the twelfth century see, above all, P. Courcelle, *Conais-toi toi-même, de Socrate à St Bernard*, 3 vols. (Paris: Etudes augustiniennes, 1974–1975).
48. In actual fact, the biblical reference concerns the debauched.
49. *De vita humana et de defunctis*, in *PG*, vol. 97, col. 1291, quoted by A. Tenenti, *La Vie*, p. 86, n. 20.
50. *De meditatione mortis*, in *PL*, vol. 171, col. 361, quoted in ibid.
51. *Sermo XXXIII*, in *PL* vol. 198, col. 308, quoted in ibid., p. 87.
52. *PL*, vol. 184, col. 1178. Again I must thank Father F. Bourdeau for this reference.
53. *Aliud carmen de contemptu mundi*, in *PL*, vol. 158, cols. 705–707. See R. Bultot, "Sur quelques poèmes pseudo-anselmiens," *Scriptorium* 18 (1965): 36–41.
54. I am quoting from B. Roy, "La Danse," in *Le Sentiment de la mort*, p. 124. See Saint Anselm, letter 169 in the Schmitt edition, vol. 4, pp. 47–48. See also A. Wilmart, "Une lettre inédite de saint Anselme," *Revue bénédictine* 10 (1928): 319–332.
55. *PL*, vol. 184, cols. 485–508.
56. *Dictionnaire de Spiritualité*, vol. I/II, col. 1500 (article on Saint Bernard).
57. One must not confuse this *Meditatio* with Saint Bernard's original work. His authentic writings also express *contemptus mundi* but in a much more restricted way. See F. Lazzari, "Le *contemptus mundi* chez saint Bernard," *Revue d'ascétique et de mystique* 41 (1965): 291–304. See also R. Bultot, "Saint Bernard, la Somme, le Roi et le double idéal antique de la magnanimité," *Citeaux* 15 (1964): 247–253.
58. The modern translation would be *amnion*, the innermost membrane enveloping the fetus.
59. *PL*, vol. 184, cols. 487–490.
60. *PL*, vol. 217, col. 736.
61. J. C. Payen, "Le *Dies irae* dans la prédication de la mort et des fins dernières au Moyen Age", *Romania* 86 (1965): 61. C. Martineau-Genieys, *Le thème de la mort*, is wholly in agreement

with J. C. Payen. My feelings are quite different. See also R. Morris, *Old English Homelies of the XIIth century (London: 1873), pp. 180–183.*

62. *Die henige Regel für ein volkommenes Leben*, ed. R. Priebsch (1909), vol. 16 of *Deutsche Texte des Mittelalters*, p. 29.
63. B. Roy, "La Danse," in *Le Sentiment de la mort*, p. 127. *PL*, vol. 210, cols. 111–198.
64. Ariès, *L'homme devant la mort*, pp. 73–76.
65. Huizinga, *Le Déclin*, p. 143.
66. Maccarone, *Lotharii cardinalis*, pp. ix–xxii; B. Roy, "La Danse," in *Le Sentiment de la mort*, pp. 125–126.
67. See L. Guerry, *Le Thème du "Triomphe de la mort" dans la peinture italienne* (Paris: Maisonneuve, 1950), pp. 46–47.
68. *PL*, vol. 145, col. 968.
69. The *Disciplina* was translated into French verse in the second third of the thirteenth century with the title *Chastiment d'un père à son fils*.
70. *PL*, vol. 184, col. 488.
71. *PL*, vol. 217, col. 742. Concerning the earlier uses of Sophonias, see P. A. Février, "La Mort chretienne," in J. Delumeau, ed., *Histoire vécue du peuple chrétien*, 2 vols. (Toulouse: Privat, 1979), vol. 1, p. 85. Concerning the *Dies irae*, other than that of Thomas of Celano, see Payen, "Le *Dies irae*," in particular pp. 59–60.
72. See chap. 1.
73. Delahaye, *Le Problème*, pp. 23–24.
74. See below, chap. 3.
75. *Der Ackermann aus Böhmen [The Plowman of Bohemia]*, 2 vols., ed. by K. Burdach (Berlin: 1926), vol. 2, p. 55, quoted and translated in J. Wirth, *La Jeune fille et la mort*, p. 29. See also R. M. Kully, "*Dialogus mortis cum homine.* Le laboureure de Bohème et son procès contre la mort," in *Le Sentiment de la mort*, pp. 141–167.
76. Delumeau, *La Peur*, p. 313. See also G. J. Engelhardt, "The *Contemptu mundi* of Bernardus Morvalensis," *Medieval Studies* 22 (1960): 108–135; ibid., 26 (1964): 109–142; ibid., 29 (1967): 243–272; R. Bultot, "La Doctrine du mépris du monde chez Bernard le Clunisien," *Le Moyen Age* 70 (1974): 179–204 and 355–376.
77. It is worthwhile noticing that, in quoting the pseudo-Bernard text, Torini's translation actually reinforces the text.
78. E. Deschamps, *Oeuvres*, Anciens textes français (Paris: 1878), vol. 2, p. 262. For the following remarks see Martineau-Genieys, *Le Thème de la mort*, pp. 111–245.
79. The passages quoted are from P. Champion, *Histoire poètique du XVe siècle*, 2 vols. (Paris: Champion, 1966), vol. 1, p. 203.
80. Ibid.
81. Deschamps, *Oeuvres*, "Double Lay," vol. 2, p. 256–257.
82. See Delumeau, *La Peur*, p. 313.
83. Deschamps, *Oeuvres*, "Double Lay," vol. 2, p. 261.
84. Champion, *Histoire Poètique*, vol. 1, p. 210.
85. Deschamps, *Oeuvres*, "Double Lay," vol. 2, p. 283.
86. Champion, *Histoire Poètique*, vol. 1, p. 201.
87. Ibid., p. 205.
88. Ibid., p. 204.
89. See C. Martineau-Genieys, *Les Lunettes des princes de Jean Meschinot* (Geneva: Droz, 1972), pp. cxiii and 38.
90. Champion, *Histoire Poètique*, vol. 1, p. 212.
91. See H. Martin, "Prédication et masses au XIVe siècle," in *Histoire vécue du peuple chrétien*, 2 vols., ed. by J. Delumeau, (Toulouse: Privat, 1979), vol. 2, p. 38.
92. G. Chastellain, *Oeuvres*, 6 vols., ed. by Kervyn de Lettenhove (Brussels: 1863–166), vol. 6, pp. 49–65.
93. Ibid., p. 50.
94. Ibid., p. 57.
95. Ibid., p. 59.
96. Ibid., p. 57.
97. Ibid., p. 62.
98. Ibid., p. 63.
99. Cicero *Philipp.* 8, 23; *Oratio pro C. lancio* 83; Tibullus II, 3, 27; Ovid *Met.* 13, 92; Plutarch *Consol. ad Appollonium* 110, D.

100. Gilson, *Les Idées et les lettres*, pp. 9–38. My approach leads me to many of the same conclusions as E. Gilson with respect to the *Ubi sunt* theme. I here follow the general outline of Gilson's above-mentioned book.
101. *De Divinitiis*, published among the works of Saint Augustine (*PL*, vol. 45, cols. 1897–1898) and collected by Prosper of Aquitaine.
102. *Synonimes*, in *Patr. Lat.*, vol. 83, col. 865.
103. *De Arte predicatoria*, in *Patr. Lat.*, vol. 210, col. 189.
104. *Soliloquium* (Florence: Franciscan Fathers of Quaracchi), chap. 2, 3, pp. 96–97.
105. Deschamps, *Oeuvres*, respectively vol. 1, p. 181; vol. 3, pp. 34–35 and 113; vol. 6, p. 123; vol. 8, p. 149.
106. F. Villon, ed. by A. Mary (Paris: Garnier, 1970), p. 26.
107. Ibid., p. 31–32. In Villon's time, Alcibiades was thought to be a woman.
108. Champion, *Histoire Poètique*, vol. 8, pp. 278–279.
109. Chastellain, *Oeuvres*, vol. 6, pp. 51–54.
110. Tenenti, *Il Senso*, pp. 144–146 and 165–166. In 1266 Robert de l'Orme had already composed *Miroir de la vie et de la mort*, which has been published in *Romania* 47:511–531 and in 50:14–53.
111. Champion, *Histoire Poètique*, vol. 2, pp. 229–230.
112. Chastellain, *Oeuvres*, vol. 6, p. 64 (8).
113. K. Cohen, *Metamorphosis of the Death Symbol* (Berkeley: University of California Press, 1973), pp. 77–78, 93–94, pl. 31 and 32.
114. Ibid., pp. 103–104 and pl. 1 and 2; Male, *L'Art*, pp. 347–348.
115. Cohen, *Metamorphosis*, pp. 33–38 and pl. 5 and 6; Male, *L'Art*, pp. 347–348.
116. Male, *L'Art*, pp. 434–435.
117. Cohen, *Metamorphosis*, pl. 93. This monument was never finished as it was refused by Catherine and was replaced by one signed by Germain Pilon. See E. Panofsky, *Tomb*, p. 80.
118. Cohen, *Metamorphosis*, pl. 111–113.
119. Ibid., pp. 189–196. K. Cohen's list is not meant to be complete. For this reason, the transept of the North Italian Cathedral of Merano (dedicated to Saint Nicolas) is not included. See E. Panofsky, *Tomb*, pl. 260 and p. 64.
120. Champion, *Histoire Poètique*, vol. 1, p. 279.
121. Deschamps, *Oeuvres*, vol. 2, pp. 295–298.
122. Chastellain, *Oeuvres*, vol. 6, p. 64 (6).
123. See Champion, *Histoire Poètique*, vol. 2, p. 367; R. Deschaux, *Les Oeuvres de Pierre Chastellain et de Vaillant* (Geneva: Droz, 1982), pp. 160–164.
124. Martineau-Genieys, *Les Lunettes*, p. xxxviii.
125. Ibid., p. 419.
126. Ibid., p. 237.
127. Chastellain, *Oeuvres*, vol. 6, pp. 64 (6) 64 (7).
128. Of course there were some Christian reactions to this traumatic pedagogical tool.
129. In the following pages I make much use of a work by Father Bourdeau and A. Danet, "Fiche de prédication missionaire: la mort," written in 1954 for the use of Redemptorians. Father Bourdeau kindly loaned me this study. From now on I will refer to it as Bourdeau, *La Mort*. Material contained in this study has been partially used in Father Bourdeau and A. Danet, "Faut-il prêcher la crainte de la mort," *Vie Spirituelle* 492 (March 1963): 281–297, and Father Bourdeau, "Les Origines du sermon missionaire sur la mort," in ibid., 319–338.
130. *Vita sti Pacômi abbatis*, In *PL*, vol. 73, col. 265.
131. N. S. Guillon, *Bibliothèque choisie des Pères de l'Eglise* (Brussels: 1829), vol. 8, p. 113.
132. *Vita sti Basilii*, in *PL*, vol. 83, col. 297.
133. Ibid., vol. 84, col. 909.
134. *Epistola sti Macarii ad filios*, in *PL*, vol. 67, col. 1163.
135. *Verba seniorum. III, "De compuctione,"* in *PL*, vol. 73, col. 966 passim.
136. *Enarratio in Ps 144*, in *PL*, vol. 37, col. 1876–1877.
137. *La Règle de saint Benoît* [The Benedictine Rule], trans. by H. Rochais (Paris: Desclée de Brouwer, 1980), pp. 24–25. See also *Règles des moines*, ed. by J.-P. Lapierre (Paris: Seuil, 1982), p. 67.
138. *Scala Paradisi; gradus VI*, in *PG*, vol. 88, cols. 794–798.
139. *De primordiis mediis et novissimis*, sermon 12, in *PL*, vol. 183, col. 572.
140. *De Vita heremitica*, in *PL*, vol. 32, cols. 1465–1474. See also Tenenti, *Il Senso*, p. 66.
141. François d'Assise [Francis of Assisi], *Ecrits* (Paris: Cerf, 1981), p. 241.

142. Ibid., p. 195.
143. Bonaventure, *Soliloquium*. I consulted the translation by E. Mézière in the "Bibliothèque des âmes chrétiennes" (Paris: 1859), p. 128.
144. Tenenti, *Il Senso*, esp. pp. 32–34.
145. H. Suso, *Oeuvres complètes*, presentation, translation and notes by J. Ancelet-Hustache (Paris: Seuil, 1977), chap. 21 "Livre de la sagesse," pp. 391–392.
146. Tenenti, *Il Senso*, p. 65.
147. Suso, *Oeuvres*, pp. 82 and 381.
148. See below, beginning of chap. 3.
149. Vincent Ferrier, *Oeuvres* (Lyon: 1555), pp. 559 passim.
150. Tenenti, *Il Senso*, pp. 69–73.
151. Bernardino of Siena, *Opera Omnia*, 4 vols., ed. by J. de la Haye (Paris: 1635). This edition includes only the Latin sermons. Respectively, vol. 3, "Extraordinary sermons" XIV, XVI, XVII, XVIII, XIX, and XX, pp. 498–530. Sermon XV is consecrated to "satisfaction."
152. Bourdeau, "Les origines," p. 238. I would like to remind the reader that I am following Father Bourdeau's reasoning very closely.
153. See *Dictionnaire de Spiritualité ascétique et mystique*, s.v. "Cisneros," 2 (1), pp. 910–921.
154. *L'Imitation* [Imitation of Christ] (Paris: Seuil, 1961), vol. 1, chaps. 19, 22, 23, 24, pp. 36–54.
155. Father Bourdeau's translation of *"Bis duo sunt, quae cordetenus sub pectore misi. Mors mea, judicium, barater nox, lux paradisi"*.
156. See below, chap. 12.
157. This is Sister M. C. O'Connor's hypothesis, *The Art of Dying Well. The Development of the Ars Moriendi* (New York: Columbia University Press, 1942), pp. 61–112.
158. R. Chartier, "Les Arts de mourir, 1450–1600," *Annales E.S.C.* (January–February, 1976): 51–75 and the bibliography thereof, which directs the reader above all to Tenenti, *Il Senso*, and O'Connor, *The Art* (see previous note).
159. This painting is now in Washington, D.C.
160. O'Connor, *The Art*, pp. 131–171.
161. Tenenti, *La Vie et la mort*, pp. 92–95, suggests a total count of 97.
162. See below chap. 3.
163. Chartier, "Les Arts de mourir," p. 63; J. M. Lenhart, "Pre-Reformation Printed Books: A study in statistical and applied bibliography," *Library: A Quarterly Review of Bibliography and Library Lore* (1903–1907).
164. Tenenti, *La Vie et la mort*, p. 60.
165. Tenenti, *Il Senso*, pp. 80–81.
166. Chartier, "Les Arts de mourir," p. 55.
167. L. Dacheux, *Les plus anciens écrits de Geiler* (Colmar: 1882), pp. ii–iv.
168. Chartier, "Les Arts de mourir," p. 57.
169. T. Lupset, *A Compendious and very fruteful treatyse teachynge the way of Dyenge well* (1534); see Tenenti, *Il Senso*, pp. 109–111.
170. T. Bacon, *The Sicke Mannes salve*.
171. J. Polanco, *Methodus ad eos adjuvandos qui moriuntur: ex complurium doctorum ac piorum scriptis, diu diuturnoque usu, et observatione collecta*.
172. Chartier, "Les Arts de mourir," pp. 63 and 73; C. Sommervogel, *Bibliotèque de la Cie de Jésus* (Paris: 1909), vol. 10, tables pp. 510–519.
173. *L'Agonia del transito* may be found in tome 43 of the *Coleccion de los majores autores espanoles: Tesoro de escritores misticos espanoles* (Paris: 1847), vol. 2, p. 1.
174. Ibid., p. 14.
175. Ibid., pp. 44–45.
176. Ibid.
177. Ibid.
178. Ibid.
179. Ibid., pp. 52–107.
180. Ibid., pp. 83–87. Regarding Peter of Lucca, see also Tenenti, *Il Senso*, p. 315.
181. Tenenti, *Il Senso*, pp. 95 and 114.
182. Erasmus of Rotterdam, *La Préparation*, p. 9.
183. Montaigne, *Essais*, vol. 1, chap. 19: 1, p. 111.
184. J.-P. Camus, *Homélies dominicales* (Rouen: 1624), p. 381 (5th Sunday after Whit Sunday).
185. Clichtove, *De Doctrina moriendi* (Paris: 1520); see Tenenti, *Il Senso*, p. 103.

186. I am using P. Sage's recent translation (Montreal: Paulines, 1976), pp. 78–87.
187. Ibid., p. 79.
188. I consulted the Latin edition of Paris (1620), part 2, chaps. 9–13.
189. See below, chap. 12.
190. Suso, *Livre de la sagesse éternelle [Das Büchlein der ewigen Weisheit]*, in *Oeuvres*, p. 389 (chap. 21).
191. Bernardine of Siena, *Quadragesimale de religione christiana*, in *Opera*, vol. 1, sermons 13 and 14, pp. 64–71 and 71–76.
192. Tenenti, *Il Senso*, p. 314.
193. Ibid., pp. 323–324.
194. P. Collenuccio, *Operette morali, poesie latine e volgari*, ed. by A. Saviotti (Bari: Laterza, 1929), pp. 115–118. I would like to thank Dr. Jettaz for drawing my attention to the writings of Collenuccio, who was executed in 1504.
195. Collenuccio, *Operette*, pp. 324–325.
196. B. D'Angelo, *Ricordo del ben morire* (1589), chap. 7, pp. 152–153, quoted in Tenenti, *Il Senso*, p. 349. Concerning B. D'Angelo, see M. Metrocchi, *Storia della spiritualità italiana. Il Cinquecento e il Seicento* (Rome: 1978), p. 13.
197. Bremond, *Histoire littéraire*, vol. 9, especially the last chap; Vovelle, *Mourir autrefois*, pp. 96–102; ibid., *La Mort et l'Occident*; Ariès, *L'Homme devant*, pp. 306–307.
198. Savonarola, *Predica dell'arte del ben morire* (Florence: 1496), fols. A(VI)–B(II) quoted in Tenenti, *Il Senso*, pp. 94–95.
199. Pietro da Lucca, *Dottrina del ben morire* (n.p.: 1540), fols. 6v°.–9v°. quoted in Tenenti, *Il Senso*, pp. 313 and 340.
200. C. Musso, *Prediche* (Venice: 1576), vol. 1, p. 89.
201. I. Ringhieri, *Dialoghi della vita e della morte* (Bologna: 1550), vol. 1, pp. 310 quoted in Tenenti, *Il Senso*, pp. 309–310.
202. G. Le Menn, "La Mort dans la littérature brettone du XVe au XVIIe siècle," *Mémoires de la Société d'Histoire et d'Archéologie de Bretagne* 56 (1979): 24–25.
203. Ibid., p. 24. See also, for Brittany, H. Martin, *Les Ordres mendiants en Bretagne* (Paris: Klincksieck, 1975), pp. 350–351.
204. Pietro da Lucca, *Dottrina*, fols. 2v°.–3, quoted in Tenenti, *Il Senso*, p. 312, and A. Croix, *La Bretagne au XVIe et XVII siècles. La vie, la mort, la foi*, 2 vols. (Paris: Maloine, 1981), vol. 2, pp. 1169–1177.
205. Pietro da Lucca, *Dottrina*, fol. 7, quoted in Tenenti, *Il Senso*, p. 313.
206. Doré, *La Déploration*, fol. 109 v°.
207. Michelangelo, *Le Rime di Michelangelo*, ed. by C. Guasti (Florence: 1863), p. xxxi, quoted in Tenenti, *Il Senso*, p. 299.
208. Erasmus of Rotterdam, *La Préparation*, p. 13.
209. Ibid., p. 15.
210. Ibid.
211. Ibid., p. 17.
212. Bellarmine, *De Arte*, book 2, chap. 2, p. 208.
213. Ibid., p. 210.
214. Michelangelo, *Le Rime*, p. xxxi.
215. B. Arnigio, *Discorso intorno al disprezzo della morte* (Pavia: 1575), fols. 17r°.–v°., quoted in Tenenti, *Il Senso*, p. 317.
216. Dupuy-Herbault, *Mirroir de l'homme chrestien* (1557), fol. 24, quoted in Tenenti, *Il Senso*, p. 320.
217. B. D'Angelo, *Ricordo del ben morire* (1589), chap. 9, p. 177.
218. See above, chap. 1.
219. Erasmus of Rotterdam, *La Préparation*, p. 28.
220. Ibid., p. 29.
221. Ibid., p. 16.
222. Bellarmine, *De Arte*, part 1, chap. 2, pp. 5–17 of the Paris, 1620, edition.
223. The 1620 edition is incorrect in referring to I Cor. 7.
224. See below, chap. 9.
225. T. Batiouchkoff, "Le Débat de l'âme et du corps," *Romania* 20 (1891): 1–55 and 513–578. See also R. W. Ackerman, "The Debate of the Body and the Soul and Parochial Christianity," *Speculum* 37 (4) (1962): 541–565.

226. Concerning this, see *PL*, vol. 73, cols. 1109–1119 in particular.
227. *Contentione anime et corporis*, quoted in Batiouchkoff, "Le Débat," pp. 566–567.
228. *Contrasto fra l'anima e'l corpo*, quoted in ibid., p. 568.
229. Ibid., p. 575–576.
230. *Disputacione betwyxt the Body and Wormes*, quoted in P. Tristram, *Figures*, p. 160.
231. See I. Siciliano, *François Villon et les thèmes poètiques du Moyen Age* (Paris: Nizet, 1967), pp. 493–496.
232. L. Bréhier, *La Civilisation byzantine* (Paris: Albin Michel, 1970), pp. 312–314; S. Der Nersessian, *L'Illustration du roman de Barlaam et Joasaph* (Paris: de Boccard, 1937), see especially the Introduction and pp. 1–15, 67–68.; Chihaia, *Les Idées de perennité*, p. 30; J. Baltrusaitis, *Le Moyen Age fantastique* (Paris: Armand Colin, 1955), pp. 235–248. I would like to thank Paul Lemerle who suggested readings in this direction.
233. The story of Barlaam and Josaphat is printed *in extenso* in *PL*, vol. 73, cols. 446–604.
234. P. Vigo, *Le Danze macabre in Italia*, 2nd ed. (Bergamo: 1901), p. 82 passim; K. Künstle, *Die Legende der drei Lebenden und der drei Toten und der Totentanz* (Freiburg: 1908), p. 33; L. P. Kurtz, *The Dance of Death* (New York: 1934; reprint ed., Geneva: Slatkine Reprints, 1975), pp. 16–18; H. Rosenfeld, *Der mittelalterlichen Totentanz* (Münster: Böhlau Verlag, 1954), p. 317. Attributed to Saint Bernard by G. Ferraro, *Poesie popolari e religiose* (Bologna: 1877), p. 14.
235. S. Glixelli, *Les Cinq poèmes des trois morts et des trois vifs* (Paris: 1914), p. 35; L. Guerry, *Le Thème*, p. 41.
236. See, above all, Mâle, *L'Art réligieux*, pp. 355–358; Tenenti, *La Vie et la mort*, pp. 12–15 with bibliography and pp. 21–28; P. Tristram, *Figures*, above all pp. 159–167.
237. J. A. Herbert, *Catalogue of Romances in the Department of Manuscripts in the British Museum* (London: 1910), vol. 3, p. 693, no. 13 above all. See also p. 125, no. 57; p. 232, no. 30; p. 445, no. 9; p. 621; and p. 193. Three young people, while walking in the desert, are converted at the sight of corpses being devoured by worms. I would like to thank Jacques Le Goff for this information. Other inquiries did not turn up any further examples even though they were carried out in both *An Alphabet of Tales: an English 15th century translation of the "Alphabetum narrationum" of Etienne de Besançon*, ed. by Mcleod Banks, 2 vols. (London: 1904–1905), especially the articles on *Mors* and *Contemptus mundi*, and Father C. Tubach, *Index exemplorum*, Communications edited for the Folklore Fellows (Helsinki: 1969), pp. 117–121.
238. Jacques de Voragine [Jacopo de' Varazze], *Légende dorée [The Golden Legend]*, French translation of 1843, vol. 1, p. 80.
239. Guerry, *Le Thème*, pp. 175–176.
240. The five poems were published by Glixell, *Les cinques poèmes des trois morts*. The Guyot Marchand publications of 1485 and 1486 of the *Dict des trois morts* begins: "Se nous vous aportons nouvelles, qui ne soient ne bonnes ne belles, a plaisance ou a desplaisance prendre vous fault en patience . . ." [If we bring you a tale that is neither good nor beautiful, whether you like it or not, you must listen patiently]. These words are said by the "first dead man."
241. Tristram, *Figures*, pp. 163–164.
242. Ibid., pp. 56–57; Tenenti, *La Vie*, p. 15.
243. Ibid., p. 92; Tenenti, *La Vie*, p. 15.
244. A. Van Marle, *Iconographie de l'art profane au Moyen Age et à la Renaissance*, 2 vols. (The Hague: 1932), vol. 2, pp. 385–389; Guerry, *Le Thème*, pp. 163–167; Tenenti, *Il Senso*, pp. 412–413.
245. G. Monaco, *I Frammenti del Trionfo della Morte di Melfi* (Potenza, n.d.) incorrectly identifies the fresco as being an example of the triumph of death.
246. Paris, Arsenal, MS no. 3142, fol. 311; vo. Mâle, *L'Art*, pp. 355–356.
247. Tenenti, *Il Senso*, p. 413; *Bulletin de la Sociéte des Antiquités de France* (1905): 133.
248. British Museum, *Arundel Psalter*, fol. 127 in Tristram, *Figures*, pp. 163 and 264.
249. Tenenti, *La Vie*, p. 14, and Tenenti, *Il Senso*, p. 414.
250. *Summa Theolo.*, Ia-IIae, 1, 7 ad. 3.
251. Pascal to Mr. and Mrs. Perm, 17 Oct. 1651, in *L'Oeuvre de Pascal* (Paris: Pléiade), p. 272.
252. Much the same opinion as that expressed by Roy, "La Danse," in *Le Sentiment de la mort*, p. 272.
253. Tenenti, *Il Senso*, pp. 412–413.
254. Mâle, *L'Art*, pp. 355–358.
255. Ibid.
256. P. Tristram, *Figures*, pp. 15–16 and 163.

257. Ibid., pp. 163–167.
258. Tenenti, *Il Senso*, p. 413; Künstle, *Die Legende*; G. Servières, "Les Formes artistiques du Dict des trois morts et des trois vifs", *Gazette des Beaux Arts* (January 1926): 19–36.
259. Wirth, *La Jeune fille et la mort*, p. 38.
260. Tristram, *Figures*, pp. 163–164.
261. *Religious Lyrics of the 15th Century*, p. 241, quoted in Ibid., p. 166.
262. Quoted in Rosenfeld, *Der mittelalterlichen Totentanz*, pp. 37–38.
263. J. Saugnieux, *Les Danses macabres de France et d'Espagne et leurs prolongements littéraires* (Paris: Belles Lettres, 1972), esp. pp. 14–17 and 323–326. See also Ariès, *L'Homme devant la mort*, p. 118.
264. Saugnieux, *Les Danses macabres*, pp. 14–17, 323–326. See also "La Danse macabre" in *Mélanges de linguistique offerts à A. Sauzat* (Paris: 1952), pp. 307–311.
265. *Roman van Melegijs*, ed. by N. de Pauw (Gand: 1889), p. 67, verses 14–16; Father G. Huet, *Le Moyen Age* 29 (1917–1918): 162 passim; Rosenfeld, *Der mittelalterlichen*, pp. 48–49 and 180–181; A. Corvisier, "La Danse macabre de Meslay-le-Grenet," *Bulletin des sociétés archéologiques d'Eure-et-Loir* (1969–1970): 45.
266. Rosenfeld, *Der mittelalterlichen*, p. 49.
267. L. Lavater, *Trois livres des apparitions des esprits, fantosmes, prodiges* (n.p.: 1571); W. Fehse, *Der Ursprung der Totentänze* (Halle: 1907), esp. p. 41 passim. See also Wirth, *La Jeune fille et la mort*, pp. 20–25.
268. Mâle, *L'Art*, pp. 362–363.
269. W. Stammler, *Die Totentänze*, Bibliothek der Kunstgeschichte, no. 4 (Leipzig: 1922). An English version of this legend may be found in R. Brunne, *Handlynge Synne*, ed. by F. J. Furnivall (London: Early English Text Society, 1903), vol. 2, p. 283. A story very much the same became an *exemplum* and may be found in *An Alphabet*, ed. by Mcleod Banks, p. 151.
270. Vienna, National Library, MS no. 2827, fol. 252 r°.; Clark, *The Dance*, p. 110–111. I do not agree with J.M. Clark who thinks that the word "dance" is only to be understood in a symbolic sense.
271. Mâle, *L'Art*, pp. 361–361.
272. Saugnieux, *Les Danses*, pp. 50–51; N.D. Shergold, *A History of the Spanish Stage* (Oxford: 1967), p. 119.
273. *Réserve* of the Montserrat Library, MS 1, fol. 27 r°. and 28 v°. See *Analecta montserratensia* (1917), vol. 1, pp. 184–192. O. Martorell, "Les danses i els cants del Libre Vermell de Montserrat," *Serra d'Or* (December 1978) with bibliography. I must thank both Mrs. Dominique de Courcelles and Mr. Henri Gachet who found the documentation concerning this "dance of death."
274. Saugnieux, *Les Danses*, pp. 49–52; J. M. Sòla-Sole, "Entorno a la dança General de la Muerte," *Hispanic Review* 36 (4) (1968): 303 passim.
275. It could be danced either in a straight line or in a star shape.
276. R. P. Helyot, *Histoire des ordres monastiques, religieux et militaires* (Paris: 1850), vol. 3, pp. 145–147. Apparently the order was dissolved by Urban VIII in 1637.
277. *Speculum historiale*, XXIX, 108; Saugnieux, *Les Danses*, p. 28.
278. *Les Vers de la mort par Hélinant, moine de Froidmont*, ed. by F. Wulff and E. Walberg (Paris: 1905).
279. Robert Le Clerc, *Li vers de la mort*, published by C. A. Windahl, *Litteraturblatt* 8 (1887).
280. Paris, Bibliothèque Mazarine, no. 80; Mâle, *L'Art*, p. 361, thought it to be of the beginning of the fourteenth century. The poem has thirty-five stanzas of two lines each. Every stanza ends with the words *vado mori*.
281. Quoted in Rosenfeld, *Der mittelalterliche*, pp. 323–325.
282. Mâle, *L'Art*, p. 389.
283. *Le Respit de la Mort par Jean Le Fèvre*, ed. by G. Hasenor-Esnor (Paris: Picard, 1969), p. 113, verses 3078–3079.
284. Quoted in L. P. Kurtz, *The Dance of Death*, p. 215, and by Wirth, *La Jeune fille et la mort*, p. 25.
285. Rosenfeld, *Der mittelalterliche*, pp. 60–66 and 89–92. Texts on pp. 307–323. Documents at the Library of the Heidelberg University (Cod. Pal. 314). The theory of a German origin is refused by W. Stammler, *Der Totentanz* (Munich: 1948), pp. 9–18, and by E. Dubruck, *The Theme of Death in French Poetry of the Middle Ages and the Renaissance* (London: Mouton), pp. 22–23.

286. Saugnieux, *Les Danses*, pp. 42–52. However, it can hardly be denied that there are striking similarities between the *Dança general* and the *Innocents* as transmitted by Guyot Marchant.
287. These figures are obtained by combining the data furnished by Kurtz, *The Dance*, pp. 70–154; Tenenti, *Il senso*, pp. 90–91, and Rosenfeld, *Der mittelalterliche*, pp. 347–363.
288. See M. Martins, *Introducao històrica a vidência do tempo e da morte*, 2 vols. (Braga: Cruz, 1969), vol. 1, pp. 171 passim as to the influence of the *danse macabre* on Gil Vincente; ibid., vol. 2, p. 32 concerning Juan de Pedraza; and ibid., p. 225 passim concerning the later influence on Antonio Vieira.
289. Kurtz, *The Dance*, pp. 116–117.
290. It is kept at the University Library of Heidelberg, Codex. Pol. germ. 438. Reproduced in W. L. Schreiber, *Der Totentanz, Blockbuch von etwa 1461* (Leipzig: 1900).
291. Clark, *The Dance*, pp. 85–87; Rosenfeld, *Der mittelalterliche*, pp. 93–95.
292. Paris, Bibliothèque Nationale, *fonds latin*, MS 14904; Mâle, *L'Art*, p. 363, n. 5.
293. Concerning this (in the Eure-et-Loire), see the remarkable monographic work by A. Corvisier mentioned above.
294. Clark, *The Dance*, pp. 28–29. Saugnieux, *Les Danses*, from which comes the erroneous attribution to Gerson.
295. Paris, Bibliothèque Nationale, *fonds latin*, MS 14904; Mâle, *L'Art*, p. 363, n. 5.
296. Concerning these two *danses macabres*, see the catalogue of the exhibition *Der Tod zu Basel* (1979), published by the *Gesellschaft Schweizerischer Zeichenlehrer*. Recent research seems to have inverted the order of these works as compared to what has been thought the correct order up to now. The fresco of the cemetery next to the Dominican church seems to have been the model for the Klingental painting and not the other way around.
297. On this subject, see Rosenfeld, *Der mittelalterliche*, pp. 151–152.
298. *Niklaus Manuel Deutsch. Maler. Dichter. Staatsmann* (Bern: Kunstmuseum, 1979), pp. 252–267 and plates 57–71. The *danse macabre* of Niklaus Manuel Deutsch is known to us only from copies since it has been destroyed.
299. Rosenfeld, *Der mittelalterliche*, p. 18. A card game of 1392, known to have belonged to Charles VI of France, also features some macabre themes. See also H. R. d'Allemagne, *Les Cartes a jouer du XIVe au XVIe siècle* (Paris: 1906).
300. Clark, *The Dance*, pp. 82–83.
301. Kurtz, *The Dance*, pp. 25–69; Saugnieux, *Les Danses*, pp. 123–128.
302. Tenenti, *Il Senso*, p. 162.
303. Also the author of the *Vigiles de Charles VII* and of the *Arrêts d'amour*.
304. Saugnieux, *Les Danses*, pp. 184–185.
305. This was the opinion of E. Mâle, *L'Art*, pp. 365–366, later taken up by Huizinga, *Le Declin*, p. 150; by Corvisier, "La Danse," p. 46; Saugnieux, *Les Danses*, p. 20; qualified by Rapp, "La Réforme religieuse," p. 59; and refuted by Clark, *The Dance*, pp. 109–110. Personally I agree with Clark.
306. Concerning the *Ackermann aus Böhmen*, consult the well-informed article by R. M. Kully, "*Dialogus mortis cum homine*. Le laboureur de Boheme et son procès contre la mort," in *Le Sentiment de la mort*, pp. 141–167. The *Plowman* remains a relatively unknown work in the French-speaking world although it is well known abroad.
307. See quotation chap. 2.
308. L. P. Kurtz, ed. (New York: 1957) and studied by A. Monteverdi, "Le *Mors* de la pomme," *Archivum romanicum* (1921): 110–134.
309. Rosenfeld, *Der mittelalterliche*, pp. 64–65.
310. All of this in Mâle, *L'Art*, pp. 378–380.
311. Kurtz, *The Dance*, pp. 195–200.
312. Concerning the *Danse macabre* of Bern see, above all, C. A. Beerli, *Le Peintre poète N. Manuel et l'évolution sociale de son temps* (Geneva: 1953) and P. Zinsli, *Der Berner Totentanz des N. Manuel* (Bern: 1953).

CHAPTER 3

1. Mâle, *L'Art*, p. 366 passim; Huizinga, *Le Declin*, p. 150. A more restricted outlook is to be found in Saugnieux, *Les Danses*, p. 20, and above all in Corvisier, "La Danse," p. 51.

2. Strassburg, *Musée de la ville*. Painting of the Rhenish school reproduced in Tenenti, *Il Senso*, plate 17.
3. Delumeau, *La Peur*, p. 187.
4. See below, chap. 7.
5. Mâle, *L'Art*, p. 380.
6. Huizinga, *Le Declin*, p. 144.
7. Tenenti, *La Vie*, pp. 37, 38, and 88; Tenenti, *Il Senso*, pp. 135, 141, and 147.
8. Ariès, *L'Homme*, p. 131.
9. Saugnieux, *Les Danses*, pp. 97, 108, 118.
10. Corvisier, "La Danse," p. 40.
11. Wirth, *La Jeune fille et la mort*, p. 166.
12. Mâle, *L'Art*, pp. 354 and 362.
13. I would like to thank Josef Macek for this reference and the following one. J. Hus, *Sermones in Bethleem* (1410–1411), ed. by V. Flajshans (Prague: 1941), vol. 4, p. 16.
14. A sermon delivered in 1416 and printed in Prague in 1951, fol. 64.
15. In Ariès, *L'Homme*, there are only allusions to this pedagogical aspect: pp. 112, 113, 116, 125 and 139.
16. This is still the opinion of Father Rapp, "La Réforme religieuse," p. 59.
17. Rosenfeld, *Der mittelalterliche*, pp. 65–67, 323, and more generally pp. 308–323.
18. See above, chap. 2.
19. This might be an addition to the work of Niklaus Manuel Deutsch. It would seem quite likely that an "actor" preceded the dance in Ker-Maria.
20. See John Lydgate, *The Dance of Death*, in *English Verse Between Chaucer and Surrey*, ed. by Eleanor P. Hammond (Durham, NC: 1927), p. 140.
21. Saugnieux, *Les Danses*, p. 166.
22. Ibid., p. 167.
23. This is the the theory on which *Der mittelalterliche Totentanz* is based.
24. The one of the cemetery, next to the cloister, was the model for the one in the Dominican nunnery of Klingental.
25. *Fioretti de Saint François* [*Little Flowers of St. Francis*], trans. by A. Masseron (Paris: Seuil, 1953), p. 88.
26. Chihaia, *Les Idées de pérennité*, p. 56.
27. *Journal d'un bourgeois de Paris à la fin de la guerre de Cent ans* (Paris: éd. 10/18, 1963): 106.
28. Mâle, *L'Art*, p. 362. Du Cange, *Supplément*, s.v. *Macchabaeorum chorea*.
29. Rosenfeld, *Der mittelalterliche*, esp. pp. 203 and 252.
30. Ibid., pp. 176 and 212.
31. Florence, Biblioteca Riccardiana, MS. no. 1510, published by P. Vigo, *Le Danze macabre in Italia*, 2nd ed. (Bergamo: 1901), appendix.
32. Vigo, *Le Danze*, pp. 112–114. Clark, *The Dance*, p. 59.
33. P. Chaunu, *La Mort à Paris, XVIe, XVIIe, XVIIIe siècles* (Paris: Fayard, 1978), pp. 246–249.
34. Ariès, *L'Homme*, p. 109.
35. Expression used by Chaunu, *La Mort*, p. 246.
36. A. Gurevič, "Conscience individuelle et image de l'au-delà," *Annales E.S.C.* (March--April 1982): 255–275.
37. See above, chap. 2.
38. Rosenfeld, *Der mittelalterliche*, pp. 14–15.
39. See chap. 6, "L'Attente de Dieu," of *La Peur en Occident*.
40. J. Fournée, *Le Jugement dernier d'après le vitrail de Coutances* (Paris: 1964), pp. 166–167.
41. G. and M. Vovelle, *Vision de la mort et de l'au-delà en Provence* (Paris: A. Colin, 1970), p. 14; M. Roques, *Les Peintures murales du Sud-Est de la France* (Paris: 1965); R. Mesuret, *Les Peintures murales du Sud-Ouest de la France du XIe au XVIe siècle* (Paris: Picard, 1967).
42. Cohen, *Metamorphosis*, p. 194.
43. In Italy one must speak of a relative absence since there are some such representations, in particular the one by F. Uebler (Merano 1509) and that of Antonio Amati (end of the fourteenth century) in the Church of Santa Trinità in Florence.
44. See below, chap. 21.
45. See X. Léon-Dufour, *Face à la mort: Jésus et Paul* (Paris: Seuil, 1979), pp. 293–302.
46. G. and M. Vovelle, *Vision*, p. 20 and plate II, 2 (Fragonard Museum, Grasse).
47. Mesuret, *Les Peintures murales*, pp. 72, 109, 230, and 248 respectively.
48. Now at the Kunsthistorisches Museum of Vienna.

49. Cohen, *The Metamorphosis*, p. 111 and plate 56.
50. Ibid., pp. 100–103 and plates 44 and 45.
51. Ibid., pp. 104–112 and plates 48 and 51.
52. Ibid., p. 109. Louvre (Cabinet des dessins), Notebook of G. Bellini, fol. 18a.
53. Ibid., plates 64–67.
54. Mâle, *L'Art*, p. 432. I would like to thank Marc Venard for having helped me to find this stained-glass window, now reconstructed in the church of the *Vieux Marché* after the destruction of the church of Saint-Vincent. See the special issue (1978–1979) of the *Amis des Monuments roueannais* bulletin.
55. Cohen, *Metamorphosis*, p. 111 and plate 56.
56. In particular, Tenenti, *La Vie*, plate 10 and pp. 38–39; Cohen, *Metamorphosis*, p. 113 and plates 58–60; Wirth, *La Jeune fille et la mort*, pp. 42–43 and plates 27–28.
57. Cohen, *Metamorphosis*, pp. 113–114.
58. Dom Calmet, *Bibliothèque lorraine* (1751), col. 825.
59. Mâle, *L'Art*, p. 433.
60. See Chihahia, *Les Idées*, pp. 32, 121–123, 127–130, 132, 141, 170; Cohen, *Metamorphosis*, pp. 77–83 and 93–95.
61. Scholars are not yet agreed as to the exact date to be attributed to this monument. H. Reiners, *Burgundisch-allemanische Plastik* (Strassburg: 1943), p. 70, suggests 1360; E. Panofsky, *Tomb Sculpture* (New York, 1964), fig. 257–258 and E. Kantorowicz, *The King's Two Bodies* (Princeton: Princeton University Press, 1957), p. 453, both suggest 1370; while R. Nicolas, "Les monuments funéraires des seigneurs de Neuchâtel et de la Sarraz", *Musée neuchâtelois* nouvelle série, 10 (1923): 160, suggests the 1390s.
62. Cohen, *Metamorphosis*, p. 83 and p. 77
63. Wirth, *La Jeune fille et la mort*, pp. 40–41 and plate 27–28.
64. Chihaia, *Les Idées*, in particular p. 145.
65. See, on this subject, the article of M. Vovelle, "La Mort et l'au-delà dans la bande dessinée," *L'Histoire* 3 (July–August 1978): 34–42.
66. J. Heers, *Annales de démographie historique* (1968): 44; Ariès, *L'Homme*, pp. 126–127. However, Chaunu (*La Mort à Paris*, pp. 176–184) fully recognizes the importance of this phenomenon. Other contemporary historians still stress the importance of the plague (for example, Rosenfeld, Cohen, Tristram in the books already mentioned).
67. See, of course, J. N. Biraben, *Les Hommes et la peste en France et dans les pays européens et méditerranéens* 2 vols. (Paris: Mouton, 1976), in particular vol. 1, pp. 155–190 and the comments on this book by M. W. Flinn, "Plague in Europe and the Mediterranean Countries," *Journal of European Economic History* 8 (Spring 1979): 131–148.
68. This is the central theme of my book *La Civilisation de la Renaissance*, 2nd ed. (Paris: Arthaud, 1973).
69. M. Meiss, *Painting in Florence and Siena after the Black Death* (Princeton: Princeton University Press, 1951), p. 73.
70. Ibid., p. 74, but see also Cohen, *Metamorphosis*, p. 107. The portrayal of the Virgin with stars around her head and the moon at her feet makes her become the celestial woman of the *Apocalypse*. This is yet another example of the link between eschatology and the macabre.
71. Meiss, *Painting*, pp. 76–77 and plates 87–90.
72. Ibid., p. 77.
73. Guerry, *Le Thème*, pp. 232–233.
74. Cohen, *Metamorphosis*, pp. 63–67.
75. Rosenfeld, *Der Mittelalterliche*, pp. 76–77, 311, and 323.
76. A. S. Piccolomini, *Commentaria de gestis basiliensis concili*, book 2, German trans. by D. Hay and W. K. Smith, p. 191 passim.
77. Rosenfeld, *Der mittelalterliche*, p. 185.
78. Biraben, *Les hommes*, vol. 1, pp. 378–379.
79. Ibid., vol. 1, p. 401.
80. Tristram, *Figures*, p. 13.
81. Biraben, *Les Hommes*, vol. 1, p. 396.
82. Rosenfeld, *Der mittelalterliche*, p. 184.
83. On this subject, see *La Peur en Occident*, esp. pp. 100–108.
84. Guerry, *Le Thème*, pp. 115–117.
85. Ibid., pp. 118–119.
86. Ibid., pp. 146–161. The fresco is now at the Abatellis Palace.

87. Tenenti, *Il Senso*, p. 420 and plate 7.
88. Ibid., pp. 144–145.
89. F. Russel, *Dürer et son temps* (New York: Time Life, 1972).
90. Van der Meer, *L'Apocalypse dans l'art*, pp. 212–213 and plate 143.
91. Ibid., p. 271, plate 175, Hospital of Saint John in Bruges.
92. Ibid., p. 281, plate 189.
93. See Tenenti, *La Vie*, pp. 20–21.
94. Paris, Bibliothèque Nationale, ms. it. 548, fol. 29 vo., Italian MS dated 1476. See Tenenti, *Il Senso*, p. 452 and plate 42.
95. Royal Palace, Madrid. See Guerry, *Le Thème*, p. 215.
96. C. Marot, *Oeuvres Complètes* (Paris: Garnier, 1920), vol. 1, p. 533.
97. Guerry, *Le Thème*, p. 99.
98. Vasari, *Vite Scelte*, ed. by A. M. Brizio (Turin: U.T.E.T., 1948), pp. 278–279, quoted in ibid. pp. 100–101 (Weiss translation).
99. Ibid., p. 101.
100. See Rosenfeld, *Der mittelalterliche*, p. 175 and plate 12.
101. Tenenti, *Il Senso*, p. 462 and plates 3 and 4. Wood inlay work by Giovanni da Verona, Abbey of Monte Oliveto Maggiore, Siena.
102. Tenenti, *La Vie*, p. 27 and plate 6, *Heures à l'usage de Rome* (end of fifteenth century-beginning of sixteenth century), Paris, Bibliothèque Nationale, ms. lat. 1354, fol. 160 v°.
103. Tenenti, *La Vie*, p. 34 and plate 8, *Heures à l'usage de Rome* (second half of the fifteenth century), Paris, Bibliothèque Nationale, ms. lat. 1160, fol. 151 r°.
104. Wirth, *La Jeune fille et la mort*, p. 63 and plate 58.
105. Tenenti, *Il Senso*, p. 216 and plate 23, p. 43 and plate 45. Respectively S. Brant, *Stultifera navis* (Bâle: 1497), fol. 94, and MS at Paris, Bibliothèque Nationale, ms. lat. 9471, fol. 196.
106. Wirth, *La Jeune fille et la mort*, pp. 17–20 and plate 1. See J. C. Hutchinson, *The Master of the Housebook* (New York: 1972).
107. Chambéry, Musée des Beaux Arts.
108. Wirth, *La Jeune fille et la mort*, p. 39.
109. Rosenfeld, *Der mittelalterliche*, plate 1 and p. 13. This is the card game said to have belonged to Charles VI of France, dated 1392.
110. Wirth, *La Jeune fille et la mort*, p. 32 and plate 14; BR Master of the Anchor.
111. Ibid., p. 28.
112. Deschamps, *Oeuvres*, vol. 1, ballade XLVIII, p. 136.
113. Ibid., vol. 5, ballade DCCCCLXXXII, p. 226.
114. Ibid., vol. 5, ballade DCCCCXIV, p. 113.
115. Ibid., vol. 1, ballades LXV and CV, pp. 161 and 217.
116. Ibid., vol. 1, ballade LXV, p. 161.
117. *Fortunes et adversitez* quoted in Champion, *Histoire poétique du XVe siècle*, vol. 1, pp. 243–244.
118. Quoted in ibid., vol. 2, p. 337.
119. *Continuation du discours des misères de ce temps*, ed. by Laumonier (Paris: 1914–1919), vol. 5, p. 337.
120. S. Castellion, *Conseil à la France désolée* (n.p.: 1562), p. 3.
121. A. D'Aubigné, *Les Tragiques*, ed. by A. Garnier and J. Plattard (Paris: Didier, 1966), vol. 1, pp. 97 and following.
122. See C. Anderson, *Dirnen, Krieger, Narren. Ausgewälte Zeichnungen von Urs Graf* (Bâle: G.S. Verlag, 1978) with bibliographical indications. The illustrations discussed below are reproduced in the above-mentioned book.
123. Reproduction also to be found in Wirth, *La Jeune fille et la mort*, p. 117.
124. Ibid., plate 38.
125. Ibid., plate 45.
126. J. Bousquet, *La Peinture maniériste* (Neuchâtel: Ides et Calendes, 1962), p. 252.
127. Kunsthistorisches Museum, Vienna.
128. Berne Art Museum.
129. Louvre, Paris.
130. Latin edition 1587, French edition 1588. This information and all the other information in this paragraph is taken from E. Mâle, *L'Art*, pp. 109–116.
131. P. Gallonio, *Trattato degli instrumenti di martirio* (Rome: 1591). Latin translation, 1594 and 1602, with a summary of the *Théâtre des cruautés des hérétiques*.

132. These frescos are known to us thanks to the engravings made by J. B. de Cavaleriis in 1584. One of these engravings is to be found in the University Library of the Sorbonne.
133. Huizinga, *Le Déclin*, p. 27 and III p. 487.
134. Molinet, *Chroniques*, ed. by Buchon (1828), vol. 3, p. 212.
135. Vovelle, *La Mort et l'Occident.*
136. H. Boos, *Thomas und Felix Platter, zur Sittengeschichte des sechzehnten Jahrhunderts* (Leipzig: 1878), pp. 152–153, quoted in J. Janssen, *La Civilisation en Allemagne depuis la fin du Moyen Age* (1902), vol. 6, p. 406.
137. Quoted in ibid.
138. Thomas Nashe, *The Unfortunate Traveller, or the Life of Jacke Wilton*, ed. by J. B. Steane (Harmondsworth: Penguin, 1972), p. 359. I would like to thank André Rannou for having called my attention to this play as well as for his useful suggestions in the domain of sixteenth- and seventeenth-century English literature.
139. F. Howson, "Horror and the Macabre in Four Elizabethan Tragedies," *Cahiers élisabéthains* (1976), published by the University of Montpellier: pp. 1–12; E. Cuvelier, "Horror and cruelty in the works of three Elizabethan novelists," *Cahiers élisabéthains* (1981): 39–52. See also P. Messiaen, *Théâtre anaglais. Moyen Age et XVIe siècle* (Bruges: Desclée de Brouwer, 1948), for a translation of *La Tragédie du vengeur* [*The Revenger's Tragedy*] and extracts of *La Duchesse d'Malfi* [The *Duchess of Malfi*].
140. In *Le Massacre à Paris* [*The Massacre at Paris*] (French translation published by Gallimard, 1972), Marlowe complacently lists the thousand and one ways of killing and being killed. The massacre he is referring to is, of course, the Saint Bartholomew massacre. Concerning sadism in Mannerist art and literature see Bousquet, *La Peinture*, pp. 206–207 and 246–252.
141. Florence, Biblioteca Nazionale Centrale, Fondo Palatino, E, 5, 6, n. 65, end of the fifteenth century; Paris, Bibliothèque Nationale, fonds ital. ms. 545, 1466; London, British Museum, two "suites" of the end of the fifteenth century. See Guerry, *Le Thème*, pp. 205, 209, 220, 221.
142. Florence, Biblioteca Nazionale Centrale, Fondo Magliabechiano, 1478. See ibid. (last), p. 205.
143. See ibid., fig. 9 and pp. 200–201.
144. Marot, *Oeuvres*, vol. 1, pp. 539–543.
145. Paper delivered by J. Wirth, "Hans Baldung Grien et les dissidents strasbourgeois," Proceedings of the Congress on *Croyants et sceptiques au XVIe siècle*, Strassburg, June 9 and 10, 1978 (Strassburg: Istra, 1981), p. 136.
146. I am fully in agreement with Wirth, *La Jeune fille et la mort*, pp. 9, 21–26, and 94–95 on this point.
147. Ibid., p. 95 and plate 78.
148. Ibid., pp. 97–98 and plates 79–80. See M. J. Friedländer and J. R. Rosenberg, *Lucas Cranach* (Paris: Flammarion, 1978), pp. 127–128.
149. Ibid., (last), pp. 36–37 and plates, 17, 61, 83. See also R. Bernheimer, *Wild Men in the Middle Ages* (Cambridge: Harvard University Press, 1952); E. Dudley and M.E. Novack, eds., *The Wild Man Within. An Image in Western Thought from the Renaissance to Romanticism* (Pittsburgh: 1972).
150. Ibid. (last), p. 132 and plate 115.
151. See esp. *La Vie*, pp. 14–15.
152. Wirth, *La Jeune fille et la mort*, pp. 158–167.
153. Ibid., pp. 135–145 and plates 121–142.
154. Ibid., plate 70.
155. *Croyants et sceptiques*, p. 129; also F. G. Parizet, "Réflexions à propos de Hans Baldung Grien," *Gazette des Beaux Arts* (1979): 1–8. Much the same opinion is expressed in the catalogue of the exhibition *Hans Baldung Grien in Kunstmuseum Basel* (Bâle: 1978), p. 27.
156. *Le second livre des sonnets pour Hélène*, ed. by P. Laumonier (1914–1919), VI, p. 10.
157. *Pièce retrancée des Amours*, ibid., p. 249.
158. *Troisième livre des Odes*, XXV: stanza 2, p. 303.
159. *Les Amours*, 1st book, I, p. 11.
160. *Amours diverses*, ibid., p. 343.
161. *Les Hymnes*, 2nd book, IV, p. 372.
162. Bion of Smyrna, a poet who lived in the third century B.C.
163. *Troisième livre des Odes*, XXV, stanza 2, p. 303.

164. *Les Hymnes*, 2nd book, IV, p. 366.
165. Ibid., p. 368.
166. *Derniers vers, Stances*, IV, p. 5.
167. See the *Quatrième livre des Odes*, IV, stanza 2, p. 315, and *Cinquième livre des Odes*, XXXII, stanza 2, pp. 454–457.
168. *Derniers vers*, Sonnet 1, stanza 6, p. 6.
169. *Troisième livre des Odes*, XXV, stanza 2, p. 303.
170. *Les Hymnes*, 2nd book, VI, p. 372.
171. Ibid., pp. 367–368.
172. E. Battisti, *L'Antirinascimento* (Milan: Feltrinelli, 1962), esp. pp. 126–133. Concerning the fasination for the monstrous, see J. Céard, *La Nature et le prodige. L'insolite au XXIe siècle en France* (Geneva: Droz, 1977).
173. See Delumeau, *La Peur*, pp. 119–120.
174. See Baltrusaitis, *Le Moyen Age fantastique*, pp. 236–237.

CHAPTER 4

1. Tauler, *Sermons*, vol. 2, p. 94 (second sermon for the Holy Sacrament).
2. Spitzmuller, *Poésie latine*, pp. 997–999.
3. I consulted a Dutch edition (Leyden: Elzevir, 1613) of *Nicolaï de Clamangis . . . opera omnia*, which is subdivided into two parts; each part has its own page numbering. The letters and the *De Antichristo* . . . are in the second part.
4. Letter no. 15.
5. Letter no. 28.
6. Letter no. 90.
7. *De Corrupto ecclesiae statu*, chap. 2, p. 5 of the first part in the 1613 edition.
8. Ibid., chap. 3, p. 6.
9. Ibid., chap. 25, p. 23.
10. Ibid., 2nd part of the book, pp. 357–358.
11. Certainly an allusion to the Hussites.
12. See Delumeau, *La Peur*, pp. 335–336. Concerning the pessimism of the period, see esp. Huizinga, *Le Déclin*, pp. 35–40.
13. Deschamps, *Oeuvres*, vol. 2, ballad CLXXXIX, pp. 6–7.
14. Ibid., vol. 1, ballad XII, pp. 86–87.
15. Ibid., vol. 1, ballad XCVI, pp. 204–205.
16. Ibid., vol. 3, ballad CCCXLIII, pp. 60–62.
17. Delumeau, *La Peur*, pp. 223–225.
18. Deschamps, *Oeuvres*, vol. 5, ballad MLXXXVIII, pp. 394–395.
19. Ibid., vol. 3, ballad CCCXXXIX, pp. 51–53.
20. Ibid., vol. 5, ballad DCCCLVIII, p. 35.
21. Ibid., vol. 6, ballad MCCXL, p. 248.
22. Ibid., vol. 6, ballad MCLXVII, p. 109.
23. Ibid.
24. Ibid., vol. 5, ballad MDCCCCLXXXVIII, p. 235.
25. Ibid., vol. 5, ballad MV, p. 261.
26. Ibid., vol. 5, ballad DCCCCXLVI, pp. 162–163.
27. Ibid., vol. 2, pp. 1, 10, 75, and 93 respectively.
28. Ibid., vol. 3, pp. 131–132.
29. Ibid., vol. 5, ballad DCCCLVIII, p. 34.
30. Ibid., vol. 5, ballad DCCCCXLII, pp. 157–158.
31. Ibid., vol. 5, ballad DCCCCXLVIII, pp. 165–167. Concerning the nefarious influence of the moon, see Delumeau, *La Peur*, pp. 92–93.
32. Deschamps, *Oeuvres*, vol. 3, ballad CCCLXII, pp. 118–120.
33. Ibid., vol. 1, ballad LII, pp. 142–143.
34. Ibid., vol. 1, ballad CXXVI, p. 247.
35. Ibid., vol. 1, ballad CLII, p. 279.
36. Ibid., vol. 1, ballad CLXII, p. 292.
37. Ibid., vol. 4, *rondeau* DCXIX, p. 78.

38. Ibid., vol, 3, ballad CCCLXV, p. 107.
39. Ibid., vol. 1, ballad DCCCCLXXXII, p. 226.
40. See ibid., vol. 1, p. 142.
41. C. de Pisan, *Oeuvres poétiques*, ed. by M. Roy (Paris: 1891), vol. 2, pp. 296–297.
42. *L'Espérance ou consolation des trois vertus* quoted in Champion, *Histoire poétique de XVe siècle*, vol. 1, p. 137.
43. See H. Zahrnt, *Dans l'attente de Dieu* (Paris: Castermann, 1970), pp. 33 and 41.
44. Ibid., p. 33. See *Nicolae Cusae cardinalis opera* of which the Paris, 1514, edition has been reprinted (Frankfurt: Minerva, 1962) in three volumes. Here, vol. 3, chaps. XXIX–XXXIII of the *De Concordantia catholica*. The French translation is by J. Doyon and J. Tchao of the Center for Renaissance Studies of the University of Sherbrooke, 1977, pp. 280–371.
45. Quoted in Zahrnt, *Dans l'attente*, p. 33. Concerning Geiler, see L. Dacheux, *Un Réformateur catholique à la fin du XVe siècle: Jean Geiler de Kaysersberg* (Paris: 1876). F. Rapp, *Dictionnaire de spiritualité*, vol. 67, pp. 174–178; *Réformes et Réformation à Strasbourg* (Paris: Ophrys, 1974). The *Vita Geileri* of Wimpheling has been edited by O. Herding (Munich: 1970).
46. S. Brant, *La Nef des fous* [*The Ship of Fools*], trans. by M. Horst (Strassburg: Nuée-bleue, 1977), pp. 167–168.
47. Ibid., chap. XCV, p. 371.
48. Delumeau, *La Peur*, pp. 400–403.
49. Brant, *La Nef des fous*, chap. LXXXVII, pp. 343–344.
50. Ibid., chap. XCIX, p. 387.
51. Ibid., chap. LXXXVIII, p. 347.
52. Ibid., chap. CVIII, p. 434.
53. Ibid., chap. CIII, p. 410.
54. Ibid., chap. CVIII, p. 438.
55. Ibid., chap. XCIX, p. 394.
56. Ibid., chap. CVIII, p. 437.
57. Ibid., chap. CIII, p. 408.
58. Ibid., p. 409.
59. Ibid., p. 411.
60. Ibid., p. 412.
61. Ibid., p. 414.
62. Delumeau, *La Peur*, pp. 222–225.
63. See in particular M. Luther, *Oeuvres*, vol. 10, p. 116 (Sermon on the Gospel of the second Sunday of Advent, composed in Wartburg).
64. M. Luther, *Propos de table*, p. 275. See also ibid., pp. 238–239.
65. Ibid. p. 109.
66. Ibid.
67. Luther, *Oeuvres*, vol. 8, pp. 188–189 (letter to J. Propst).
68. M. Bucer, *Traité de l'amour du prochain*, trans. introduction, and notes by H. Srohl (Paris: P.U.F., 1949), p. 53.
69. H. Estienne, *Apologie pour Hérodote* (1566), pp. 110–125.
70. G. Budé, *De Transitu Hellenismi ad Christianismum*, trans. by M. Le Bel (Sherbrooke: Paulines, 1973), pp. 44, 66 and 93.
71. Ibid., p. 132.
72. Quoted in R. Muchembled, *Culture populaire et culture des élites* (Paris: Flammarion, 1978), p. 200.
73. Delumeau, *La Peur*, pp. 385–386 and 402–403.
74. A. D'Aubigné, *Vengeances*, ed. by A. Garnier and J. Plattard (Paris: 1932–33), vol. 4, p. 28.
75. *La Semaine* (imitation of the one of Du Bartas), pp. 246, 249 and 361. See C. G. Dubois, *La Conception de l'histoire de France au XVIe siècle (1560–1610)* (Paris: Nizet, 1977), pp. 359–361.
76. E. Sandys, *The Sermons*, ed. by J. Ayre (Cambridge: 1841), p. 439, quoted in B. W. Ball, *A Great Expectation: Eschatological Thought in English Protestantism: 1660* (Leyden: Brill, 1975), p. 18. Concerning the link between eschatology and menacing discourse, see below, chap. 21.
77. T. Adams, *A Commentary . . . upon the Divine Second Epistle . . . written by St. Peter* (1633), pp. 1138–1139, quoted in ibid. (Bell), p. 97. On English eschatology of the end of the sixteenth century and the beginning of the seventeenth, see C. Hill, *Antichrist in Seventeenth Century England* (Oxford: University Press, 1971), esp. pp. 1–41.

78. *I Diari di Girolamo Priuli*, ed. by A. Segre, vol. 1, p. 14 in Muratori, *Italicarum rerum scriptores*, new edition, vol. 24, part 3.
79. N. du Fail, *Oeuvres facétieuses*, ed. by J. Assézat (Paris: 1874), esp. "*Propos rustiques*," chaps. 2 and 6, "*Contes et discours d'Eutrapel*," chaps. 1 and 22, and the "*Discours sur la corruption de notre temps*."
80. Boaistuau, *Histoires prodigieuses* (Paris: Club Français du livre, 1961), p. 91.
81. Boaistuau, *Le Théâtre du monde où il est faict un ample discours des miseres humaines*, 1572 edition at the Bibliothèque Nationale (Paris), preface (without page numbers). A recent edition of the same is that edited by M. Simonin (Geneva: Droz, 1981).
82. E. Pasquier, *Lettres politiques (1566–1594)* (Geneva: Droz, 1966), p. 109.
83. Ibid., p. 394.
84. Montaigne, *Essais*, vol. 3, chap. 2, 3, p. 28.
85. T. Cornhert, *A l'aurore des libertés modernes. Synode sur la liberté de conscience*, Introduction, trans. and notes by J. Lecler and M.F. Valkhoff (Paris: Cerf, 1979), p. 65.
86. Quoted in A. Redondo, "Monde à l'envers et conscience de crise chez Graciàn," in *L'Image du monde renversé et ses représentations littéraires de la fin du XVIe siècle au milieu du XVIIe* (Paris: Vrin, 1979), p. 91. This sentence is from the *Memorial de la politica necessaria y util restauraciòn de Espana* (Valladolid: 1600).
87. L. Febvre, *Le Problème de l'incroyance. La religion de Rabelais* (Paris: A. Michel, 1968), p. 329.
88. G. Rucellai, *Zibaldone quaresimale*, ed. by A. Perosa (London: Warburg Institute, 1960), p. 61, quoted in A. Chastel and R. Klein, *L'Age de l'humanisme* (Paris: ed. des Deux Mondes), p. 30.
89. Quoted in J. Norström, *Moyen Age et Renaissance* (Paris: 1935), p. 18.
90. Letter to W. Pinckheimer (November 1518), quoted in Chastel and Klein, *L'Age*, p. 30.
91. *Pantagruel* (Paris: Pléiade), p. 227.
92. See H. Levin, *The Myth of the Golden Age in the Renaissance* (Bloomington: University of Indiana Press, 1969). See also Tenenti, *Il Senso*, p. 64.
93. Brant, *La Nef des Fous*, chap. XLVI, p. 168.
94. Erasmus, [*The Praise of Folly*], trans. by Hoyt H. Hudson (New York; 1941), p. 44.
95. C. Marot, *Oeuvres complètes* (Paris: Garnier, 1951), vol. 1, pp. 438–439.
96. Cervantes, *The Adventures of Don Quixote*, trans. by J. M. Cohen (Harmondsworth: Penguin, 1968), pp. 85–86.
97. J. Bodin and P. Mesnard, eds, tome 5, vol. 3 of the *Corpus général des philosophes français* (Paris: P.U.F., 1951), pp. 428–429.
98. Ibid.
99. Ibid., p. 430.
100. Ibid.
101. E. Garin, "L'Attesa dell'età nuova e la '*renovatio*,' " in *L'Attesa dell'età nuova nella spiritualità della fine del medioevo*, Congress of the Centro di Studi sulla Spiritualità della Fine del Medioevo, October 1960 (Todi: 1962), vol. 3, pp. 16–19.
102. With respect to the spring of eternal youth and the belief in its existence among alchemists, see B. Le Trevisan, *Le Livre de la philosophie naturelle des métaux* (Paris: Trèdaniel, 1976), pp. 63–75.
103. Levin, *The Myth*, p. 55. See also J. C. Schmitt, "Christianisme et mythologie," in *Dictionnaire des mythologies* (Paris: Flammarion, 1980), pp. 1–9. Concerning the land of plenty (*pays de Cocagne*) as a consolatory dream compensating for reality, see A. Graf, *Miti, leggende e superstizioni del Medio Evo* (Turin: 1897), p. 235 passim; G. Cocchiara, *Il Paese di Cuccagna e altri studi di folclore* (Turin: 1956), especially, p. 187; and J. Tazbir, "Entre le rêve et la résignation: l'utopie populaire dans l'Ancienne Pologne," *Annales E.S.C.* (March–April 1982): 146–153.
104. Contribution of Chantal Couteaud to the collective volume, *La Mort des Pays de Cocagne*, ed. by J. Delumeau (Paris: Sorbonne University, 1976), pp. 11–14. See also F. Delpech, "Aspects des Pays de Cocagne. Programme pour une recherche," in *L'Image du monde renversé*, pp. 35–48.
105. Concerning this point, I would like to draw the reader's attention to my own *Civilization de la Renaissance*, 2nd ed. (Paris: Arthaud, 1973), esp. pp. 299–305 and 355–371. One may also consult *Les Utopies à la Renaissance* (1961 conference) (Brussels and Paris: P.U.B. and P.U.F., 1963) and *Le Soleil à la Renaissance* (1963 conference) (Brussels and Paris: P.U.B. and P.U.F., 1965).
106. See R. Ruyer, *L'Utopie et les utopies* (Paris: P.U.F., 1950).

107. G. Chinard, *Les Réfugiés huguenots en Amérique* (with an introduction on the "American mirage") (Paris: Les Belles Lettres, 1925). I would also like to draw the reader's attention to a remarkable study by Father Lestringant, "Millénarisme et âge d'or: Réformation et expériences coloniales au Brésil et en Floride (1555–1565)," Paper presented at the 1982 Tours Congress on *Enracinement de la Réforme* (forthcoming).
108. J. Servier, *Histoire de L'Utopie* (Paris: Gallimard, 1967), p. 376. See also M. I. Finley, "Utopianism Ancient and Modern," in *The Critical Spirit* (Mélanges H. Marcuse, ed.) (Boston: 1967), pp. 3–20.
109. What follows owes much to G. Atkinson, *Les Nouveaux horizons de la Renaissance française* (Paris: Droz, 1935), pp. 137–168 and 348–358. See also Levin, *The Myth*, pp. 58–83.
110. P. Bembo (pseudonym ?), *L'Histoire du Nouveau Monde* (Lyon: 1556), pp. 11–13.
111. J. Macer, *Les Trois livres . . . Histoire des Indes* (Paris: 1555), p. 61.
112. Montaigne, *Essais*, vol. 1, chap. 31, p. 263.
113. M. Lescarbot, *Histoire de la Nouvelle France* (Paris: 1609), pp. 759–760.
114. Ronsard, *Oeuvres*, vol. 5, p. 154 (*IIe livre des Poèmes*). See also ibid., pp. 157–163 ("Les iles fortunes").
115. Ibid., vol. 5, p. 154.
116. See Atkinson, *Les Nouveaux*, pp. 15 and 163.
117. See the bibliography in the work of Father Lestringant mentioned above in note 107.
118. M. Foucault, *Madness and Civilization* trans. by R. Howard (London: 1967), pp. 13–15.
119. J. C. Margolin, "Devins et charlatans au temps de la Renaissance," publication of the *Centre de Recherches sur la Renaissance* of the University of Paris-Sorbonne, 1979, p. 52. See also R. H. Marijnissen, "Bosch and Brueghel on human folly," in *Folie et déraison à la Renaissance* (Brussels: University of Brussels, 1976), p. 42.
120. E. R. Curtius, *Europäische Literatur und lateinisches Mittelalter*, 2nd ed. (Bern: 1951), p. 106.
121. E. Castelli, "Quelques considérations sur le Niemand . . . et personne," in *Folie et déraison*, p. 112.
122. On this theme, see *Folie et déraison* and *L'Image du monde renversé* where individual articles contain the necessary bibliographical materials. See also R. Chartier and D. Julia, "Le monde à l'envers," *L'Arc* 65 (1976): 43–53.
123. On all of these aspects consult Y. M. Bercé, *Féte et révolte* (Paris: Hachette, 1976), esp. pp. 13–53, and J. Caro Baroja, *Le Carnaval* (Paris: Gallimard, 1979), esp. part 1.
124. Quoted in *PL*, vol. 207, col. 1171, and, more recently, by M. Bakhtine, *L'Oeuvre de François Rabelais et la culture populaire au Moyen Age et sous la Renaissance* (Paris: Gallimard, 1970), p. 83. See also M. Grinberg, "Le Carnaval à la fin du Moyen Age et au début de la Renaissance dans la France du Nord et de l'Est," Thesis, University of Paris IV, 1974) and, by the same author, his article in the third volume of *Fêtes de la Renaissance* (Paris: C.N.R.S., 1975), pp. 547–554. See also C. Soland's contribution to *La Mort des Pays de Cocagne*, pp. 14–29.
125. C. de Rubys, *Histoire générale de la ville de Lyon* (Lyon: 1604), pp. 499–501 quoted in N. Z. Davis, *Les Cultures du peuple. Rituels, savoirs et résistances au XVIe siècle* [*Culture and Society in Early Modern France*] (Paris: Aubier, 1979), p. 159.
126. Caro Baroja, *Le Carnaval*, esp. pp. 28 and 157.
127. Bercé, *Fête et révolte*, p. 36.
128. Caro Baroja, *Le Carnaval*, pp. 320–325 on the *obispillo.*
129. Ibid., particularly pp. 32, 51, and 132.
130. Davis, *Les Cultures*, p. 170 and, more generally for what follows, pp. 159–209.
131. Bercé, *Fête et révolte*, p. 36 and, more generally for what follows, pp. 28–41. N. Z. Davis speaks of an "inversed rule."
132. Davis, *Les Cultures*, pp. 168–173.
133. Bakhtine, *L'Oeuvre*, passim and, esp., pp. 87–90.
134. See for example the "*ordonance*" issued January 19, 1539 in Nice that calls for the election of four "abbés des fous" mentioned in A. Sidro, *Le Carnaval de Nice et ses fous* (Nice: éd. Serre, 1979), pp. 22–23. In a more general way, see Grinberg "Le Carnaval," passim.
135. Caro Baroja, *Le Carnaval*, p. 321.
136. The complete translation of this title is *Carnival, or book introducing the real piety beloved by God, by means of a pleasant meditation on the twelve sons of Carnival, or infernal patriarchs, which teaches in a healthy way the reason for which it is best that we avoid their company* (Prague: 1580). This information has been kindly provided by M. E. Ducreux.
137. See, in particular, the Garnier edition, pp. 23, 33, 73, and 163.

138. See, esp., ibid., pp. 173–181 and 303 (note 543).
139. Quoted in Christopher Hill, *The World Turned Upside Down* (London: 1972), p. 225.
140. S. Brant, *La Nef des fous*, chap. 110, pp. 458 and 462.
141. By following the idea of "culpabilisation" I arrive at the same conclusions as those exposed in the collective work *Visages de la folie (1500–1650)*, ed. by A. Redondo and A. Rochon, (Paris: Public. de la Sorbonne, 1981).
142. A. Gerlo, "Badius Ascenius' *Stultiferae Naves* (1501), a Latin addendum to S. Brant's *Narrenschiff* (1494)," in *Folie et déraison*, pp. 119–127.
143. H. Plard, "Thomas Murner contre Luther," in ibid., p. 201.
144. This is the French title of the 1610 edition. The Italian title is *Il Mondo al rovescio e sosopra* (Venice: 1602). See "Le Monde renversé sens dessus-dessous de Fra Giac. Affinati," in *L'Image*, pp. 141–152.
145. *Le Monde renversé*, pp. IIa-b.
146. Ibid., p. 63a.
147. Ibid., p. 10b.
148. Ibid., pp. 84a and b.
149. J. Riandère la Roche, "La satire du 'monde à l'envers' chez Quevedo," in *L'Image*, pp. 55–71.
150. A. Redondo, "Monde à l'envers et conscience de crise dans le *Criticon* de Baltazar Gracian," in *L'Image*, pp. 83–97.
151. I use here both the analysis of A. Redondo and his translations, which are based on the *Criticon* published in *Obras completas de Gracian*, ed. by A. de Hoyo (Madrid: Aguillar, 1960), I, 6, pp. 564a–b.
152. Ibid., I, 6, pp. 572b–573a and III, 3, 864b.
153. *L'Image*, pp. 89–90.
154. Much the same opinion in J. A. Maravall, *La Cultura del Barrocco* (Barcelona).
155. J. Donne, *Satire V*, V, verses 35–38 quoted in M. T. Jones-Davies, *Victimes et rebelles. L'Ecrivain dans la société élisabéthaine* (Paris: Aubier, 1980), p. 37.
156. See R. Chartier and D. Julia, "Le Monde à l'envers," *L'Arc* 65 (1976): 43–53 (with bibliography).
157. See H. Adhemar, *Corpus de la peinture des anciens Pays-Bas* (Brussels: 1962), pp. 20–32; R. H. Marijnissen, "Bosch and Brueghel on human folly," in *Folie et déraison*, p. 46.
158. Marijnissen, "Bosch and Brueghel," pp. 41 and 43.
159. Ibid., p. 47.
160. Ibid., p. 42.
161. Ibid.
162. Ibid., p. 49.
163. Ibid., illustration 5, pp. 48–49.
164. Ibid., p. 45 and illustration 10, pp. 48–49. See also E. Castelli, "Quelques considérations sur le Niemand," in ibid., and R. Klein, "Le Thème du fou et l'hironie humaniste," in *Umanesimo e Ermeneutica*, special issue of the *Archivio di Filosofia* (1963).
165. "*Nemo non quaerit passim sua commoda. Nemo non quaerit sese cunctis in rebus agendis. Nemo non inhiat privatis undique lucris. Hic trahit, ille trahit; cunctis amor unus habendi est.*"
166. I have adopted the entire conclusion of R. H. Marijnissen, "Bosch and Brueghel," in *Folie et déraison*, pp. 45 and 47.
167. See H. F. Grant, "Images et gravures du monde à l'envers," in *L'Image*, pp. 17–33. See also R. Chartier and D. Julia, "Le Monde à l'envers."
168. Quoted and translated in ibid., p. 28.
169. Ibid., plate II, pp. 32–33.
170. H. Plard, "Folie, subversion, hérésie: la polémique de Thomas Murner contre Luther," in *Folie et déraison*, p. 200 and more generally pp. 197–208.
171. J. Lefebvre, *Les Fols et la folie, étude sur les genres du comique et la création littéraire en Allemagne pendant la Renaissance* (Paris: 1968), pp. 44–47.
172. P. Viret, *Le Monde à l'empire et le monde démoniacle* first edition 1561 but reference is to the 1580 edition, pp. 4 and 249 quoted in J. Céard, "Le Monde à l'envers chez d'Aubigné," in *L'Image*, pp. 117–127. The quotations below are also taken from Céard.
173. The *Tragiques* are published in vol. 4 of the *Oeuvres complètes* of A. d'Aubigné, ed. by E. Réaume and Caussade (Paris: 1887).
174. *Satire Ménippée*, ed. by C. Read (Paris: 1876), pp. 120–121.

175. I add this observation to those made by C. Hill, *Le Monde à l'envers*.
176. On this subject see M. Rouch's excellent *Thèse d'Etat*, "Les Communautés rurales de la campagne bolonaise et l'image du paysan dans l'oeuvre de Giulio Cesare Croce (1550–1609)," 4 vols., Ph.D., diss., Aix-en Provence, 1982, vol. 1, pp. 263–264.
177. Y.-M. Bercé, "Fascination du monde renversé dans les troubles du XVIe siècle," in *L'Image*, p. 13. See also A. Fletcher, *Tudor Rebellions* (London: 1968).
178. See C. Ossola, "Métaphore et inventaire de la folie dans la littérature italienne du XVIe siècle," in *Folie et déraison*, pp. 171–196.
179. See A. C. Fiorato, "La Folie universelle, spectacle burlesque et instrument idéologique dans l'*Hospedale* de T. Garzoni," in *Visages de la Folie*, pp. 131–145. See also J. Fuzier, "L'Hopital des Fous: variations européennes sur un thème socio-littéraire de la fin de la Renaissance," in *Hommage à J. L. Flecniakoska* (Montpellier: University of Paul Valéry, 1980), pp. 157–183.
180. Garzoni, *L'Hospital*, pp. 163 passim.
181. Ibid., pp. 170 passim.
182. Ibid., pp. 68 passim.
183. Ibid., pp. 109 passim.
184. Ibid., pp. 228–232.
185. Ibid., p. 2.
186. Ibid., p. 3.
187. Affinati, *Le Monde renversé*, esp. pp. 105b, 106a, 203a, quoted in Céard, "Le Monde renversé," pp. 143–147.
188. For what follows see J. Céard's important book, *La Nature et les prodiges*. The next few pages owe much to Céard's work. See also G. Matore, " 'Monstre' au XVIe siècle. Etude lexicologique," *Travaux de linguistique et de littérature* 18 (1980) 1: 359–367.
189. I would like to thank J.-Cl. Margolin for having sent me, before publication, the text of his paper delivered at the *Centre de la Renaissance* of the University of Paris IV. The title of his paper was "Sur quelques prodiges au temps de la Renaissance, ed. by M. T. Jones-Davies (Paris: Jean Touzet, 1980), pp. 42–55.
190. See R. Schenda, "Die französische Prodigien literatur in der zweiten Hälfte des 16. Jahrhunderts," *Münchner romanistische Arbeiten* 16 (1962).
191. Belleforest using Sorbin, Boaistuau, and so on, as well as some original material, published a book in 1580 entitled *Histoires prodigieuses extraites de plusieurs fameux auteurs*.
192. Respectively: Weinrich, *De Ortu monstrorum commentarius* (1595); J. Riolan, *De monstro nato Lutetiae a. D.* (1605); F. Liceti, *De Monstrorum causis, natura et differentiis, libri duo* (1616); U. Aldrovandi, *Monstrorum historia* (1642).
193. J. P. Seguin, *L'Information en France avant le périodique. 517 canards imprimés entre 1529 et 1631* (Paris: Maisonneuve, 1964), p. 14.
194. J. Grünpeck, *Speculum naturalis, coelestis et prophaeticae visionis* (Nüremberg ed. of 1508), chap. 1, fols. a iii v°.-a iv r°. quoted in Céard, *La Nature*, p. 77.
195. M. Luther, *Oeuvres*, vol. 10, p. 116 (Sermon on the Gospel for the second Sunday of Advent).
196. J. Camerarius, *De Ostentis* (1552 edition) quoted in ibid., p. 170.
197. C. Peucer, *Les Devins, ou commentaires des principales sortes de divinations* (French trans. of 1584), p. 574, quoted in ibid., p. 184.
198. J. Fincelius, *Wunderzeichen, Wahrhafftige Beschreibung and gründlich Verzeichnis schrecklicher Wunderzeichen* (1557), pp. 2–3, quoted in Janssen, *La Civilisation en Allemagne depuis la fin du Moyen Age*, 6, pp. 382–383.
199. Janssen, *La Civilisation*, 5, pp. 383–390, and 6, p. 376.
200. Belleforest, *Histoires prodigieuses*, p. 353, quoted in Céard, *La Nature*, p. 335.
201. Janssen, *La Civilisation*, 5, pp. 383–390, and 6, p. 376.
202. This information and the following observations are taken from Janssen, *La Civilisation*, 6, pp. 377–381.
203. J.-G. Schenk von Grafenberg, *Wunder-buch von menslischen unerhörten Wunder und Missgeburten* (Frankfurt: 1610).
204. C. Irenaus, *De Monstris. Von Seltzamen Wundergeburten* (1585).
205. See Céard, *La Nature*, pp. 71–75.
206. Ibid., p. 373. C. Gemma, *De Natura divinis characteris*, 1, pp. 62–63.
207. M. Luther, *Oeuvres*, vol. 10, p. 116 (Sermon on the Gospel of the second Sunday of Advent).
208. Sorbin, *Histoires prodigieuses*, p. 628, quoted in Céard, *La Nature*, p. 271.
209. Céard, *La Nature*, p. 272.

210. J. Nauclerus, *Chronica* (Cologne ed. of 1579), pp. 1121–1122, quoted in ibid., p. 77.
211. M. Luther, *Werke* (Weimar edition), *Briefwechsel*, vol. 3 (1933), p. 17, quoted in ibid., p. 81.
212. Ronsard, *Oeuvres complètes*, vol. 5, pp. 157–163 ("Les Isles fortunées").
213. Ibid., p. 392 ("Prognostiques sur les misères de nostre temps").
214. See Delumeau, *La Civilisation de la Renaissance*, pp. 96–98.
215. Budé, *De Transitu*, p. 94.
216. Luther, *Oeuvres*, vol. 10, p. 109 (Sermon on the Gospel of the second Sunday of Advent, 1522).
217. Ibid.
218. Ibid.
219. Le Roy, *De la vicissitude* (1576 ed.), fol. 15b, quoted in Céard, *La Nature*, p. 380.
220. Le Roy, *De la vicissitude*, fol. 96b, quoted in ibid.
221. Le Roy, *De la vicissitude*, fol. 114b, quoted in ibid.
222. Seguin, *L'Information en France*, pièce 149.
223. Belleforest, *Histoires prodigieuses*, p. 385.
224. Quoted in Jones-Davies, *Victimes et rebelles*, p. 165. [English original from *Marlowe's Doctor Faustus 1604–16*, ed. by W. W. Greg (Oxford: 1950.)]
225. These proverbs were gathered by M. Le Roux de Lincy, *Le Livre des proverbes français*, 2 vols. (Paris: 1859), vol. 1, pp. 252–257.
226. F. de Rojas, *La Celestina*, trans. by James Mobbe (1631), and ed. by H. Warner Allen (London, n. d.), pp. 259–60.
227. N. Machiavelli, [*The Prince*], trans. and ed. by R. M. Adams (New York: 1977), pp. 47–48.
228. Machiavelli, *L'Ane d'or* [*The Golden Ass*], trans. by E. Barincou (Paris: Pléiade, 1952), pp. 91–92. See esp. E. Massa, "Egilio da Viterbo, Machiavelli, Lutero e il pessimismo cristiano," *Archivio di Filosofia* (1949): 75–123; L. Huovinen, *Das Bild vom Menschen im Politischen Denken Niccolò Machiavelli's* (Helsinki: 1951), pp. 73–77.
229. A. S. Piccolomini, *De Ortu et auctoritate imperii romani* (Frankfurt ed. of 1658), p. 4. In this edition the Piccolomini text has been added to the Golden Bull issued by Charles IV.
230. L. B. Alberti, *Della Tranquillitate dell'anima*, in *Opere volgari*, ed. by A. Bonucci (Florence: 1843–49), vol. 1, p. 56. The same opinion is to be found in the dialogue *Fatum et fortuna*, Ital. trans. Bibliothèque Nationale (Paris), R 24687, p. 26.
231. C. Curcio, *La Politica italiana del '400* (Florence: 1932), pp. 163 and following.
232. The following ideas are inspired by Haydn, *The Counter-Renaissance* (New York: Scribner's, 1950), esp. pp. 410–412.
233. P. Pomponazzi, *De Immortalitate animi*, trans. into English by W. H. Hay (Haverford College, 1938), pp. 50–51.
234. F. Guichardin [F. Guicciardini], *Pensées et portraits* [*Maxims and Portraits*], trans. by J. Bertrand (Paris: 1935), p. 14.
235. Machiavelli, *The Prince*, pp. 49–50. See also A. Renaudet, *Machiavel* (Paris: Gallimard, 1956), pp. 267–272.
236. I. Gentillet, *Discours contre Machiavel*, ed. by A. d'Andrea and P. D. Stewart (Florence: Casalini Libri, 1974), pp. 11 and 14.
237. See the bibliography on this subject in ibid., p. xii–xiii.
238. For the following see C. G. Nauert, Jr., *Agrippa and the Crisis of the Renaissance* (Urbana: University of Illinois Press, 1965), esp. pp. 309–311.
239. C. Agrippa von Nettesheim, *De Incertitudine et Vanitate scientiarium declamatio invectiva* (Cologne: 1531), chaps. 68–71 and 80.
240. Ibid., chap. 62.
241. Ibid., chaps. 72–73.
242. Ibid., chap. 95.
243. Ibid., chap. 72.
244. C. Agrippa von Nettesheim, *De Occulta philosophia libri tres* (Cologne: 1533), book 3, chap. 65, pp. 345–346.
245. C. Agrippa von Nettesheim, *De Beatissimae annae monogamia* (1534), fols. a6 r°. and v°.
246. C. Agrippa von Nettesheim, *De Vanitate*, chap. 91.
247. Ibid., chap. 78.
248. Ibid., chaps. 80–81.
249. On this subject see Haydn, *The Counter-Renaissance*, pp. 405–409.
250. Jones-Davies, *Victimes et rebelles*, p. 60.
251. T. Hobbes, *Leviathan*, ed. by M. Oakeshott (Oxford: 1957), p. 64.

252. Ibid., p. 82. See also *Histoire des idéologies*, ed. by F. Chatelet (Paris: Hachette, 1978), vol. 2, pp. 317–319.
253. R. Favre, *La Mort au siècle des Lumières*, pp. 349–353.

CHAPTER 5

1. On the subject of Occamism, see esp. J. H. Randall, Jr., *Making of Modern Mind* (New York: 1940), pp. 101–102, and the articles "Occam" and "Occamism" by P. Vignaux, *Dictionnaire de Théologie catholique*. See also Haydn, *The Counter-Renaissance*, pp. 88–89.
2. Nauert, *Agrippa*, pp. 146 and 302; R. Stadelmann, *Vom Geist des ausgehenden Mittelalters: Studien zur Geschichte der Weltanschauung von Nicolaus Cusanus bis Sebastian Franck* (Halle: 1929).
3. Nauert, *Agrippa*, pp. 148–149; Imbart de la Tour, *Les Origines de la Réforme* (Paris: 1909), vol. 2, pp. 568–572; F. Strowski, *Montaigne* (Paris: 1906), pp. 124–130; P. Villey, *Les Sources et l'évolution des Essais de Montaigne*, 2nd ed. (Paris: 1933), vol. 2, pp. 154–155.
4. Nauert, *Agrippa*, pp. 140–141; T. Greenwood, "L'Eclosion du scepticisme pendant la Renaissance et les premiers apologistes," *Revue de l'Université d'Ottowa* 17 (1947); R. H. Popkin, *The History of Scepticism from Erasmus to Descartes* (Assen: 1960).
5. Erasmus, [*The Praise of Folly*], chap. 32, pp. 65–67. See above, chap. 3.
6. For the following discussion my guide is Nauert, *Agrippa*, esp. pp. 214–220 and 293–300. See also the books by Stadelmann, *Vom Geist*, and E. Cassirer, *Das Erkenntnisproblem in der Philosophie und Wissenschaft der Neuzeit*, 3 vols. (Berlin: 1906–20), vol. 1, pp. 162 and 181; G. Rossi, *Agrippa di Nettesheym e la direzione scettica della filosofia del Rinascimento* (Turin: 1906); Haydn, *The Counter-Renaissance*, esp. pp. 146–147.
7. C. Agrippa, *Opera*, 2 vols. (Lyon (?): 1620–30), vol. 2, pp. 554–555; *De originali peccato*, vol. 2, p. 491; *De triplici ratione*, chap. 5.
8. See Villey, *Les Sources*, vol. 2, pp. 166–170.
9. Haydn, *The Counter-Renaissance*, p. 90. One may mention, among the variety of books published at the time concerning a critique of knowledge, Francisco Sanchez, *Quod nihil scitur* (1581) and Fulke Greville, *Treatie of humane learning* (1632).
10. *Essais*, vol. 2, chap. 12, 2, p. 81. The sublunar sphere of corruption according to the Aristotelian and Ptolomaic conception of the world.
11. Ibid., p. 201.
12. Ibid., p. 136.
13. Ibid., p. 164.
14. Ibid., p. 121.
15. Ibid., p. 89.
16. Ibid., p. 93.
17. Ibid., p. 94.
18. Ibid., p. 117.
19. Ibid., p. 109.
20. Ibid., pp. 243 and 251.
21. Ibid., p. 240.
22. Ibid., p. 244.
23. Ibid., p. 246.
24. Ibid., p. 223.
25. Ibid., p. 180.
26. Ibid., p. 183.
27. Ibid., p. 210.
28. Ibid., p. 245.
29. Ibid., p. 207.
30. Ibid., p. 199.
31. Ibid., p. 181.
32. Ibid., pp. 139–143.
33. Ibid., p. 145.
34. Ibid., p. 256.
35. Ibid., pp. 215–216.
36. Ibid., vol. 2, chap. 1, 1, pp. 402–403.
37. Ibid., vol. 2, chap. 12, 2, p. 256.

38. Ibid., p. 231.
39. Ibid., p. 230.
40. Ibid., p. 230–231.
41. Ibid., p. 234.
42. Ibid., pp. 81 and 124.
43. Ibid., p. 127.
44. Ibid., pp. 137–138.
45. Sainte-Beuve, *Port-Royal*, 3 vols., ed. by M. Leroy (Paris: Pléiade, 1972), vol. 1, pp. 836, 841, and 853.
46. Ibid., p. 845.
47. For example, M. Conche, *Montaigne* (Paris: Seghers, 1966).
48. A. Gide, *Essai sur Montaigne* (Paris: 1929).
49. H. Friederich, *Montaigne*, French edition (Paris: Gallimard, 1968), esp. pp. 104–155. This was first published in 1949 (2nd ed., 1967).
50. See *The Complete Works of Montaigne* trans. by D. M. Frame (Stanford, CA: Stanford University Press, 1958), p. 320.
51. Ibid., p. 67.
52. Ibid., p. 145.
53. Pascal, *Entretien avec M. de Sacy*, in *Oeuvres complètes*, F. Strowski, ed. (Ollendoy, 1931), p. 40.
54. The authors responsible for rehabilitating the religiousness of Montaigne are, among others, Strowski, *Montaigne*; J. Plattard, *Montaigne et son temps* (1936); M. Dreano, *La Pensée religieuse de Montaigne* (1936); by the same author, "L'Augustinisme dans l'Apologie de Raymond Sebond," *Bibliothèque d'humanisme et Renaissance* (1962), pp. 559–575; M. Citoleux, *Le Vrai Montaigne, théologien et soldat* (Paris: 1937); C. Sclafert, *L'Ame religieuse de Montaigne* (1951). A recent bibliography may be found in F. S. Brown, *Religion and Political Conservatism in the Essais of Montaigne* (Geneva: Droz, 1963), and in B. Croquette, *Pascal et Montaigne. Etude des réminiscences des Essais dans l'oeuvre de Pascal* (Geneva: Droz, 1974).
55. P. Charron, *De la Sagesse*, in *Choix de moralistes français*, J. Buchon, ed. (Paris: 1836), book 1, chap. 14, p. 40.
56. Ibid., p. 41.
57. Ibid., p. 42.
58. Ibid.
59. Ibid.
60. Ibid., p. 43.
61. Ibid., p. 41.
62. Ibid., p. 44.
63. Ibid.
64. Concerning G. Bruno see esp. I. L. Horowitz, *The Renaissance Philosophy of Giordano Bruno* (New York: Colemann-Ross, 1952), and H. Vedrine, *La Conception de la nature chez Giordano Bruno* (Paris: Vrin, 1967).
65. See esp. *La République* (Darmstadt: Scientia Aalen, 1961), 5, 1, pp. 663–664; his introduction to the *Théâtre de la nature universelle* (French trans. of 1597) and L. Le Roy, *De la vicissitude ou variété des choses en l'univers* (1575).
66. Luther, *Oeuvres*, vol. 10, p. 399 (Sermon on the gospel for the High Mass of Christmas, written in Wartburg).
67. Calvin, *L'Institution chrétienne*, 2, 2, 14: 2, p. 37.
68. Ibid., 1, 5, 2: 2, p. 18.
69. Ibid., 2, 2, 18: 2, p. 40.
70. Ibid., 3, 21, 1: 3, p. 394.
71. Luther, *Oeuvres*, especially vol. 9, pp. 250 and 259; vol. 10, pp. 189, 254, and 357.
72. Ibid., vol. 10, p. 339 (Sermon on the Gospel for the High Mass of Christmas).
73. Calvin, *L'Institution*, 2, 2, 12: 2, p. 33.
74. Luther, *Oeuvres*, vol. 10, p. 351.
75. Ibid., vol. 10, p. 351.
76. Ibid., vol. 3, p. 243 (*Vindication of Married Life*).
77. Ibid., vol. 9, p. 345 (Sermon on the second Sunday after Epiphany, 1546).
78. Ibid., vol. 10, p. 189 (On the Gospel for the fourth Sunday of Advent, written in Wartburg).
79. Martin Luther, *Luther's Works*, vol. 51, ed. and trans. by J. W. Doberstein (Philadelphia: 1959), pp. 376–377.

80. Haydn, *The Counter-Renaissance*, pp. 272 and 165–166.
81. F. Bacon, *The New Organon and related Writings*, ed. by F. E. Anderson (New York: Liberal Arts Press, 1960), p. 91 (I, XCII).
82. J. Davies, *Poems*, ed. by C. Howard (New York: 1941), lines 114–115, quoted in Haydn, *The Counter-Renaissance*, p. 113.
83. Ibid., lines 173–180.
84. J. Donne, *Works*, ed. by H. Alford (London: 1839), vol. 5, p. 577, quoted in ibid., pp. 113–114.
85. J. Donne, *The Complete English Poems*, ed. by A. J. Smith (London: 1971), *The First Anniversary*, lines 205–215, p. 276.
86. Concerning pessimism in Elizabethan England and under the reign of the first Stuarts, see the mimeographed pamphlet, "*La Mort, le fantastique, le surnaturel du XVIe siècle à l'époque romantique*," ed. by M. Plaisant (Lille: University of Lille III, 1980), which gathers the results of a meeting on the same subject held in 1979.
87. Concerning this subject see, in particular, A. Warburg, "Zu den Wandlungen des Fortuna Symbols in der bildenden Kunst der Renaissance," in *Kunstwissenschaftliche Beiträge, A. Schmarsow gewidmet* (Leipzig: 1907), pp. 129 passim; A. Doren, "Fortuna im Mittelalter und in der Renaissance," in *Vorträge der Bibliothek Warburg* 1 (1922–1923): 72–144; H. R. Patch, "The Tradition of the Goddess Fortuna in Roman Literature and in the Transitional Period," in *Smith College Studies in Modern Languages*, 3(3) (April 1922): 131–187; by the same author, "The Tradition of the Goddess Fortuna in Medieval Philosophy and Literature," in ibid., 3(4) (July 1922): 1–45; by the same author, "Fortuna in Old French Literature," in ibid. 4(4) (July 1923): 1–45; E. Cassirer, *Individuum und Kosmos in der Philosophie der Renaissance* (Leipzig: Teubner, 1926); R. Von Marle, *Iconographie de l'art profane* (Brussels: 1931), vol. 2, pp. 181–202; E. Panofsky, *Essais d'Iconologie* [*Essays in Iconology*] (Paris: Gallimard, 1967); F. P. Pickering, *Literatur und Darstellende Kunst in Mittelalter* (Berlin: 1966). The above-mentioned basic bibliography on the subject will be expanded in the course of the following discussion on Fortune.
88. Cassirer, *Individuum*, p. 80.
89. E. Garin, *Moyen Age et Renaissance* (Paris: Gallimard, 1969), p. 164.
90. *PL*, vol. 6, cols. 437–440 (*De Falsa sapientia philosophorum*, 3, 28–29).
91. *Cité de Dieu* [*The City of God*], Combès ed. of the *Oeuvres*, 33, pp. 583–585.
92. I here follow the example of H. R. Patch, "The Tradition in Medieval Philosophy," in putting together two texts of Saint Augustine, namely *De Libero arbitrio*, 3, 2, in *PL*, vol. 32, col. 1273, and *Quaest in Hept.*, 1, 91, in *PL*, vol. 34, col. 571.
93. *Opera*, 3, 461, in *PL*, vol. 23, col. 1083.
94. Lactance [Lactantius], *De Vera religione*, 3, 29, in *PL*, vol. 6, col. 443; Augustine, *Cité de Dieu*, 4, 18, (see note 91); Saint Jerome, *Opera*, 4, 783, in *PL*, vol. 24, col. 639.
95. *Commentaria physicorum Aristotelis*, in *Opera*, ed. of Leo XIII, 2, p. 86 (13).
96. Calvin, *Institution*, 1, 5, 11 (Against "Fortune"): 1, p. 27.
97. See Doren, "Fortuna," p. 104, note 70.
98. G. Budé, *De Transitu hellenismi ad christianismum*, trans. by E. Lebel, pp. 139 and 249–250.
99. Ibid., p. 249.
100. Boèce [Boethius], *De Consolatione philosophiae*, 4, part 6. I consulted the English translation by R. Green (Indianapolis: Bobbs-Merril, 1962), p. 92.
101. Ibid., pp. 93–96.
102. Ibid., 1, Poem 1, p. 3.
103. Ibid., 2, part 1, p. 22.
104. Ibid. The importance of the wheel of fortune from Boethius on is discussed in Doren, "Fortuna," p. 82.
105. Ibid., 2, part 2, p. 24.
106. Now in the Munich Library. See H. Spitzmuller, *Poésie latine chrétienne du Moyen Age*, p. 1727; J. A. Schmeller, *Carmina Burana* (Breslau: 1904).
107. The cathedrals of Basel, Lausanne, Amiens, Trent, and the churches of Saint-Etienne (Saint Stephen) in Beauvais, Saint Zeno in Verona, and Saint Francis in Parma.
108. *Roman de la Rose*, ed. by F. Lecoy, 3 vols. (Paris: Champion, 1958–75).
109. Ibid., lines 4858–4861.
110. Ibid., lines 6168 and following.
111. Ibid., line 6189.

112. Ibid., line 5356 and following. Examples of the power of Fortune may also be found in lines 6717–6720, 7139–7141, and 7171–7174.
113. *Enfer* [Inferno], canto 7, lines 67–96, in the Pléiade ed., pp. 923–924.
114. *Le Banquet*, [*Il Convivio*] 4, 11, ibid., p. 471.
115. Cecco d'Ascoli, *Acerba*, ed. by Rosario (1916), 2, chap. 1, lines 19–22. See G. Boffito, "Il *De principiis astrologiae* di Cecco d'Ascoli," *Giornale storico della letteratura Italiana* supplement number 6 (1906), p. 28; Patch, "The Tradition in Medieval Literature," p. 202.
116. Petrarch, *Opera quae exstant omnia* (Basel: 1581), pp. 923–926.
117. For example, sonnets 228, 232, 234 and 256. The edition I used is the Basel, 1554, one, fourth part, pp. 165, 166, 168, and 170.
118. I am now quoting the 1581 edition, which does not number the sonnets but includes the foreword of the *De Remediis* that is not in the 1554 edition. The reference is, then, vol. 1, p. 1 passim.
119. *Esposizioni sopra la comedia di Dante*, in *Tutte le Opere di Giovanni Boccaccio*, ed. by V. Branca (Milan: Mondadori, 1965), vol. 6, pp. 398–399.
120. Boccaccio, *De casibus . . .* , book 6, chap. 1. See the previous note for the translation used.
121. Boccaccio, *Des nobles malheureux* [*De casibus virorum illustrium*] (Paris: 1538), book 6, chap. 1, fol. XXIII r°.
122. Boccaccio, *De Amorosa visione*, in *Opere*, vol. 14. See chap. 31, pp. 125 passim.
123. See A. Warburg, *La Rinascità del paganesimo antico* (Florence: La Nuova Italia, 1966), pp. 234–237 and plate 68.
124. Patch, "The Tradition of the Goddess Fortuna," p. 224.
125. Van Marle, *Inconographie*, vol. 2, p. 186.
126. The *Hypnerotomachia Poliphili* of Francesco Colonna published in Venice in 1499 had an international success. See E. Kruetzulesco-Quaranta, *Les Jardins du Songe. "Poliphile" et la mystique de la Renaissance* (Paris: Belles Lettres, 1976), pp. 90–91.
127. J. Macek, "La Fortuna chez Machiavel," *Le Moyen Age* 77 (1) (1974): 310.
128. Concerning this, see Haydn, *The Counter-Renaissance*, pp. 435–442.
129. S. C. Chew, "Time and Fortune," *Journal of English Literary History* 6 (June 1939): 89.
130. The original edition is of 1522.
131. I would like to thank Sara Matthews-Grieco for having given me these figures. The five volumes referred to are: G. de La Perrière, *Théâtre des bons engins* (Paris: 1539); G. Corrozet, *Hécatomgraphie* (Paris: 1540); A. Alciati, *Emblèmes* (Lyon: 1549); H. Junius, *Les Emblèmes* (Antwerp: 1567); J. J. Boissard, *Emblèmes* (Metz: 1588). The thesis of S. Matthews-Grieco, *L'Iconographie de la femme dangereuse dans l'estampe et les livres d'emblemes du XVIe siècle français*, was defended at the E.H.E.S.S. in February 1983.
132. Macek, "La Fortuna," p. 306.
133. A. Piaget, *Martin Le Franc, prévôt de Lausanne* (Lausanne: 1888), pp. 192–195. *L'Estrif de Fortune et de Vertu* [*The Debate of Fortune against Virtue*] is from 1447–48 and was commissioned by Philip the Good.
134. A. Chartier, *Oeuvres*, ed. by A. Du Chesne (1617), p. 267, quoted in Patch, "Fortuna," p. 31.
135. *Disputationes adversus astrologos*, ed. by E. Garin, 2 vols. (Florence: 1946–52), book 3, chap. 27, and book 4, chaps. 2 and 3.
136. P. Sidney, *Arcadia*, 3, 10; see Haydn, *The Counter-Renaissance*, pp. 436–437.
137. E. Spenser, *Faerie Queen*, 8, 3; see Haydn, *The Counter-Renaissance*, pp. 436–437.
138. E. Dolet, *Les Gestes de Françoys de Valois Roy de France* (1540), quoted in Céard, *La Nature*, p. 107.
139. H. Busson, *Le Rationalisme dans la littérature française de la Renaissance (1533–1601)* (Paris: Vrin, 1959), p. 115.
140. Baudoin and Jean de Condé, *Dits et contes*, ed. by A. Scheler, 3 vols. (Brussels: 1866–67), vol. 3, p. 151 passim, quoted in Patch, "Fortuna," pp. 17–18.
141. Charles d'Orléans, *Poésies complètes*, ed. by C. d'Hericault, 2 vols. (Paris: 1896), vol. 1, pp. 129–132 (Ballads 13–15). See Patch, "Fortuna," pp. 27–28.
142. Pickering, *Literatur*, p. 61.
143. A. Chastel, *L'Europe de l'humanisme et de la Renaissance* (Paris: ed. Des Deux Mondes, 1963), table 48 and p. 320.
144. Catalogue of the Dürer exhibition, Paris, Biliothèque Nationale, 1971, p. 78.
145. *Le Livre de la mutacion de Fortune par Christine de Pisan*, ed. by S. Solente, 4 vols. (Paris: Picard, 1959), vol. 1, p. xxxv, and vol. 2, lines 7171–7172.

146. Quoted in ibid., vol. 1, p. xxxv, and lines 2218–2220.
147. Quoted in Patch, "Tradition," pp. 224–225.
148. MS 1460 of the Leningrad Library, reproduced in A. Chastel, *Le Mythe de la Renaissance, 1420–1520* (Geneva: Skira, 1969), p. 6.
149. *Timon of Athens*, act 1, scene 1.
150. *The Contention between Liberality and Prodigality*, see Chew, "Time and Fortune," pp. 90–91.
151. C. Ripa, *Iconologie* (Paris: 1644), pp. 184–185.
152. Chew, "Time and Fortune," p. 80. The image goes back to classical antiquity and is also found in the *Roman de la Rose.*
153. Ibid., p. 87. See also Van Marle, *Iconographie*, vol. 2, p. 194, and plate 27.
154. Ibid., p. 99. See also R. Greene, *Arbasto, The Anatomy of Fortune. Prose Works*, vol. 3, pp. 171 passim.
155. Ibid., p. 98.
156. Concerning this subject, see Cassirer, *Individuum und Kosmos*, p. 81; Wartburg, *La Rinascità del paganesimo antico*, pp. 236–238; Chastel, *Le Mythe de la Renaissance*, p. 11; Van Marle, *Iconographie*, vol. 2, p. 189.
157. Budé, *De Transitu*, p. 169.
158. Panofsky, *Essais d'iconologie*, pp. 168–169.
159. Respectively: act 2, scene 1, and act 4, scene 6.
160. See the various references provided by Patch, "Tradition," pp. 216–217. Concerning 'Occasio,' which must be seized, see G. Corrozet, *L'Hécatomgraphie*, emblem number 83; J. J. Boissard, *Emblèmes*, plate number 26, pp. 60–61. This information was provided by Sara Matthews-Grieco.
161. H. Politien [Poliziano], *Stanze*, in the *Opera Omnia*, ed. by I. Maïer (Turin: Bottega d'Erasmo, 1971), vol. 3, pp. 58–59.
162. G. Manetti, *De Dignitate et excellentia hominis* (Bâle: 1532), p. 129.
163. *Disputationes adversus astrologos*, book 3, chap. 27. Concerning Pico della Mirandola, see *L'Opera e il pensiero di Giovanni Pico della Mirandola nella storia dell'Umanesimo*, 2 vols. (Florence: 1965).
164. See E. Garin, *La Renaissance. Histoire d'une révolution culturelle* (Verviers: Marabout, 1970), p. 193, as well as *Charles de Bovelles en son cinquième centenaire 1479–1979*, Proceedings of the Noyon, 1979, meeting, (Paris: Trédaniel, 1982), esp. pp. 101–109.
165. This print is reproduced in Cassirer, *Individuum und Kosmos*, pp. 302–303. The entire book of C. de Bovelles is reproduced, as an appendix, in Cassirer's book, pp. 301–412. Concerning C. de Bovelles see also J. M. Victor, *Charles de Bovelles, 1479–1553. An Intellectual Biography* (Geneva: Droz, 1978).
166. Ibid. (last), p. 321.
167. Ibid., p. 329.
168. J. Bodin, *Methodus ad facilem historiarum cognitionem*, trans. by Mesnard (Paris: 1951), book 1, chap. 1, in vol. 1, p. 115. See also Garin, *Moyen Age et Renaissance*, p. 151.
169. L. B. Alberti, *I Libri della famiglia*, ed. by R. Romano and A. Tenenti (Turin: Einaudi, 1969), p. 3.
170. Garin, *Moyen Age et Renaissance*, p. 77.
171. The letter is published in A. Warburg, *La Rinascita*, pp. 233–235.
172. L. B. Alberti, *I libri*, p. 4–11.
173. L. B. Alberti, *Della Tranquillità dell'animo*, book 3 in the *Opere Volgari*, ed. by A. Bonucci (Florence: 1843–45), vol. 1, pp. 113–114.
174. See Warburg, *La Rinascità*, p. 235.
175. Machiavelli, *The Prince*, Adams trans. pp. 70, 72.
176. Verse 13609.
177. Quoted in Le Roux de Lincy, *Le Livre des proverbes*, vol. 2, p. 490.
178. See Warburg, *La Rinascita*, p. 235.
179. Ibid., pp. 236–237.
180. Erasmus, *Eloge de la folie*, ed. by M. Rat (Paris: Garnier, 1953), chap. 51, p. 155.
181. *The Prince*, Adams trans., p. 70.
182. See Delumeau, *La Civilisation de la Renaissance*, pp. 397–402.
183. See Garin, *Moyen Age et Renaissance*, pp. 120–134.
184. L. Aurigemma, *Le Signe zodiacal du scorpion* (Paris: Mouton, 1976), pp. 81–82. The above-mentioned book also contains the recent bibliography on Renaissance astrology.
185. Quoted in ibid., p. 92.

186. Ibid., p. 82.
187. Ibid.
188. *Crònica dos feitos de Guiné*, trans. by L. Bourdon (Dakar: 1960), chap. 28, pp. 116–117.
189. Alberti, *I Libri della famiglia*, book 2, p. 178.
190. I used the Italian translation (Paris, Bibliothèque Nationale, MS 24687 to 24693) inserted in various *Opuscula de nobilitate*, 1544, pp. 23 r°.–23 v°.
191. Ibid., p. 26 r°.
192. Ibid., p. 9 r°.
193. Warburg, *La Rinascita*, p. 235.
194. Machiavelli, *Discours* [*I Discorsi*] (III,9)(Paris: Pléiade), pp. 640–642.
195. Ibid., *Capitolo della fortuna*, p. 85.
196. Ibid., *Discours*, III, 31, p. 686.
197. Ibid., *Capitolo della fortuna*, p. 82.
198. Ibid., *Discours*, II, 29, pp. 596–597.
199. Reproduced in Van Marle, *Iconographie*, vol. 2, p. 188.
200. Budé, *De Transitu*, p. 248.
201. Calvin, *Institution*, I, 5, 11, p. 27.
202. Machiavelli, *Le Prince*, chap. 25, pp. 364–365.
203. G. Meurier, *Trésor des sentences*, quoted in Le Roux de Lincy, *Le Livre des proverbes*, vol. 2, p. 301.
204. *Trésor des sentences*, quoted in ibid.
205. Gruther, *Receuil*, quoted in ibid., p. 300.
206. G. Meurier, *Trésor des sentences*, quoted in ibid., p. 277.
207. *Trésor des sentences*, quoted in ibid.
208. *Proverbes communs gothiques*, quoted in ibid., p. 293.
209. See Montaigne, *Essays*, Frame trans., p. 209 (from chap. 47, "Of the uncertainty of our judgment").
210. Ibid., I, chap. 45, I, p. 350 (Manilius, *Astronomiques*, IV).
211. Ibid.
212. See esp. R. von Albertini, *Das florentinische Staatsbewustsein im Ubergang von der Republik zum Principat* (Bern: Francke, 1955), pp. 222–260; F. Gilbert, *Machiavelli and Guicciardini. Politics and History in Sixteenth Century Florence* (Princeton: Princeton University Press, 1965, pp. 251–255, 267–279, and 289–291.
213. Text published in Gilbert, *Machiavelli and Guicciardini*, p. 266.
214. Published by A. Reumont in the *Appendice no. 22* of the *Archivio Storico Italiano* 6 (1848): 263–387.
215. See ibid., pp. 284–285, and 287.
216. Ibid., p. 289.
217. Ibid., p. 339.
218. Ibid., p. 348.
219. F. Guicciardini, *Storia d'Italia*, ed. by Panigada, 5 vols. (Bari: Laterza, 1929), book 1, chap. 1, which in this edition is in vol. 1, p. 1.
220. For example, book 10, chap. 14 (vol. 3, p. 197), book 14, chap. 7 (vol. 4, p. 116), book 16, chap. 5 (vol. 4, p. 288).
221. Gilbert, *Machiavelli and Guicciardini*, p. 289, note 4.
222. These two texts are quoted in ibid., p. 281, and are respectively *Scritti autobiografici*, "Consolatoria" of 1527, and *Ricordi*, "Ricordo" no. 138.
223. Shakespeare, *Henry V*, act 3, scene 6.
224. Ibid., *King Lear*, act 2, scene 6.
225. Ibid., *Antony and Cleopatra*, act 4, scene 15.
226. Ibid., *Timon of Athens*, act 1, scene 1.
227. Marston, *Antonio and Mellida*, ed. by H. Wood (London: 1934), act 3, p. 32. Concerning this point and the following discussion, see Haydn, *The Counter-Renaissance*, pp. 440–441.
228. Chapman, *All Fools*, ed. by T. Parrot (London: 1914), act 5, scene 1.
229. Ibid., *Bussy d'Ambois*, act 5, scene 2.
230. Ibid., act 1, scene 1.
231. For this and the following discussion I am using again the third-cycle dissertation of Sara Matthews-Grieco, "L'Image de la femme dangereuse."
232. G. de La Perrière, *Théâtre*, emblem number 20.

233. G. Corrozet, *Hécatomgraphie*, p. 27.
234. Here again I am basing myself on the dissertation of Sara Matthews-Grieco.
235. M. Luther, *Oeuvres*, vol. 5, p. 53.
236. The essential book by H. Heger, *Die Melancholie bei den französischen Lyriken des Spätmittelalters* (Bonn: 1967), proves that the recurrence of the theme of melancholy (and of Fortune) increases spectacularly in French poetry after the time of the Black Death.
237. Huizinga, *Le Déclin*, pp. 32, 36–40.
238. E. Deschamps, *Oeuvres*, vol. 1, p. 311.
239. Ibid., vol. 4, p. 18.
240. A. de La Borderie, *Jean Meschinot, sa vie et ses oeuvres* (Paris: 1895), p. 277, quoted in Huizinga, *Le Déclin*, p. 38.
241. G. Chastellain, *Oeuvres*, vol. 1, p. 10, quoted in ibid.
242. O. de La Marche, *Mémoires*, ed. by Béaune and d'Arbaumont, 4 vols. (Paris: 1883–88), vol. 1, p. 186.
243. E. de Monstrelet, *Chroniques*, ed. by Douët D'Arq, 6 vols. (Paris: 1857–62), vol. 4, p. 430.
244. See A. Chastel, "La Mélancolie de Laurent de Médicis," in *Fables, formes, figures* (Paris: Flammarion, 1978), vol. 1, p. 154.
245. Concerning melancholy at the end of the Middle Ages, see D. Jacquart, "Le Regard d'un médecin, sur son temps: Jacques Despars (1380?–1458)," *Bibliothèque de l'Ecole des Chartes* 138 (July–December 1980): esp. 61, 68–76.
246. Chap. 7 of the Carmelite edition (Paris: Desclée de Brouwer, 1952), pp. 46–50.
247. See C. G. Dubois, *Le Maniérisme* (Paris: P.U.F., 1979), pp. 200–203.
248. Redondo, "La Folie du cervantin licencié de verre," in *Visages de la folie*, pp. 35–38.
249. J. Starobinski, *Histoire du traitement de la mélancolie des origines à 1900* (Bâle: Geigy, 1960) (*Acta psychosomatica*, n. 3), p. 38. For the matter at hand, see chap. 1 of the book by H. Tellenbach, *La Mélancolie* (Paris: P.U.F., 1979). On the other hand, a fundamental book on the subject is by R. Klibansky, E. Panofsky, and F. Saxl, *Saturn and Melancholy. Studies in the History of Natural Philosophy* (London: Nelson, 1964 reprint ed.). Mrs. E. Berriot-Salvadore kindly let me consult her third-cycle dissertation (Montpellier, 1979), "Images de la femme dans la médecine du XVIe siècle et du début du XVIIe siècle."
250. In French, the essential book on Robert Burton is that of J. R. Simon, *Robert Burton (1577–1640) et l'Anatomie de la mélancolie* (Paris: Didier, 1964). I would like to thank André Rannou for having drawn my attention to it.
251. Starobinski, *Histoire*, p. 38.
252. Modern presentations of this explanation may be found above all in ibid., pp. 9–45; E. Panofsky, *The Life and Art of Albrecht Dürer* (Princeton: Princeton University Press, 1955), pp. 157–160; L. Thorndike, *A History of Magic and Experimental Science* (New York: Columbia University Press, 1941), vols. 5 and 6.
253. J. Fernel, *Universa medicina* (1554), book 6, chap. 3. French translation, *Les Sept livres de la thérapeutique universelle* (1648).
254. A. Paré, *Oeuvres*, ed. by P. de Tartas (based on the 1585 ed.), 3 vols. (Paris: 1969), vol. 1, intro. to chap. 8, pp. xi–xv. Similar explanations are given by a seventeenth-century doctor, in R. Mandrou, *Possession et sorcellerie au XVIIe siècle, Textes inédits* (Paris: Fayard, 1979), pp. 201–218.
255. T. Bright, *A Treatise of Melancholie* (1586).
256. Paré, *Oeuvres*, vol. 1, intro. to chap. 8, pp. xi–xv.
257. L. Lemne (Lemnius) *Les Secrets miracles de nature*, French translation of 1566, p. 249.
258. It was thus understood that hysteria was a sickness of nervous origin, caused by malfunctioning of the uterus. See I. Veith, *Histoire de l'hystérie* (Paris: Seghers, 1973).
259. An excellent presentation of the medical theories concerning melancholy may be found in L. Babb, *The Elizabethan Malady. A Study of Melancholia in English Literature from 1580 to 1642* (East Lansing: Michigan University Press, 1951), pp. 21–72. See also Klibansky, Panofsky, and Saxl, *Saturn*, pp. 67–126.
260. Starobinski, *Histoire*, p. 41.
261. Quoted in ibid., p. 40, from L. Vanini, *Dialogi de admirandis naturae reginae deaeque mortalium arcanis* (Paris: 1616).
262. Paré, *Oeuvres*, vol. 1, intro. to chap. 8, pp. xi–xv.
263. R. Burton, *The Anatomy of Melancholy*, ed. by H. Jackson, 3 vols. (New York: Dent, 1964), vol. 2, p. 103.

264. See A. Chastel, "La Tentation de Saint Antoine ou le songe du mélancolique," in *Fables, formes, figures*, pp. 137–146.
265. See Thérèse d'Avila, *Livre des Fondations*, chap. 7, pp. 48–49.
266. The essential book on this subject remains that of Klibanski, Panofsky, and Saxl, *Saturn*. See also Panofsky, *The Life of Dürer*, pp. 166–167; Delumeau, *La Civilisation de la Renaissance*, pp. 394–397; Seznec, *La Survivance des dieux antiques* (London: 1939, 1980 reprint), pp. 59–74.
267. Erfurt, Städtisches Museum, third quarter of the fifteenth century. Reproduced in Panofsky, *The Life of Dürer*, plate 213.
268. Waldburg-Wolfegg collection at Waldensee. See Seznec, *La Survivance*, p. 67; V. Lippmann, *Les Planètes et leurs enfants* (Paris: 1895).
269. Modena, Biblioteca Estense. Reproduced and commented in Delumeau, *La Civilisation*, plate 145 and p. 390.
270. Lisbon, Museo nacional de arte antigua. Painted between 1506 and 1509.
271. E. Panofsky and F. Saxl, *Dürer's "Melancolia I"* (Leipzig: 1923). See also R. Marcel, *Marsile Ficin* (Paris: Belles Lettres, 1956); A. Chastel, *Marsile Ficin et l'art* (Geneva: Droz, 1954).
272. See in particular book 1, chap. 6, of *De Triplici vita*.
273. Pico della Mirandola, *Opere di Giov. Benivieni fiorentino . . . con una canzona dello amore celeste e divino, con commento dell'ill. s. conte G. Pico Mirandolano* (1522), I, 7, fol. 10, quoted in Panofsky, *Essais d'iconologie*, p. 293.
274. These ideas owe much to the article of A. Chastel, "La Mélancolie," in *Fables, formes, figures*, vol. 1, pp. 149 passim.
275. Ibid., p. 152.
276. Quoted in ibid. and in A. Lipari, "The *dolce stil nuovo* according to Lorenzo dei Medici," *Yale Romanic Studies* 12 (1936). This is Lorenzo's commentary on one of his sonnets in Lorenzo de'Medici, *Opere*, ed. by A. Simioni, "Scrittori d'Italia" (Bari: Laterza, 1913), vol. 1, *Rime*, p. 31.
277. Starobinsky, *Histoire*, p. 73.
278. Marsilio Ficino, *De Triplici vita*, book 3, chaps. 22, 23 and 24. I have used the French translation done by Guy Le Fèvre de la Borderie (1581).
279. Ibid., book 3, chap. 22, p. 172 v°.
280. My discussion here follows Panofsky, *The Life of Dürer*, in particular p. 169. C. Agrippa, *De Occulta philosophia*, 1531 ed., book 1, chap. 60, pp. 78–80. In the manuscript of 1510 (Würzburg University Library), the first version of this book, book 3, chaps. 31–32. See also Klibansky, Panofsky, and Saxl, *Saturn*, pp. 241–276. Review article on this book by R. Klein, *Mercure de France* (1964): 588–594. K. Hoffmann, "Dürer's Melancolia I," in *Kunst als Bedeutungsträger. Gedenkschrift für Günter Bandmann* (1979): 251–277 and F. Anzelewsky, *Dürer. Vie et Oeuvre* (Fribourg: Office du Livre, 1980).
281. Quoted in Panofsky and Saxl, *Dürer's "Melancolia I,"* p. 31.
282. *De Triplici vita* was known in Germany as of the end of the fifteenth century, and it was Dürer's godfather who published Ficino's correspondence in 1497. See Klibansky, Panofsky, and Saxl, *Saturn*, p. 277.
283. Panofsky, *Essais d'iconologie*, pp. 293–296.
284. *Essays*, book I, chap. 2 ("of Sadness"), Frame trans., p. 6.
285. See J. B Bamborough, *The Little World of Man* (London: 1952), p. 107. See also Babb, *The Elizabethan Malady*.
286. *As You Like It*, act 2, scene 5.
287. Ibid., act 2, scene 7.
288. Ibid., act 4, scene 1.
289. Babb, *The Elizabethan Malady*, p. 74.
290. Burton, *The Anatomy*, vol. 1, p. 120.
291. Ibid., vol. 2, p. 70; Simon, *Robert Burton*, pp. 164–165.
292. Babb, *The Elizabethan Malady*, pp. 76–101.
293. *Titus Andronicus*, act 2, scene 3.
294. Burton, *The Anatomy*, vol. 1, pp. 305–333 ("The miseries of scholars").
295. Ibid., vol. 3, pp. 310–311.
296. Babb, *The Elizabethan Malady*, p. 157.
297. J. Ferrand, *De la maladie d'amour, ou mélancholie érotique* (1612). Jacques Ferrand was a doctor of Agen.
298. Burton, *The Anatomy*, vol. 3, pp. 311–432.
299. M. Ficin [Marsilio Ficino], *Théologie platonicienne* [*Theologia platonica de immortalitate animorum*],

trans. by R. Marcel, 3 vols. (Paris: Belles Lettres, 1964–70), vol. 2, pp. 272–273 (book 14, chap. 7).

300. In particular sonnets 12, 15, 16, 19, 56, 60, 63, 64, 65, 73, 74, 76. See also in *Le Viol de Lucrèce* [*The Rape of Lucrece*], the invectives against Time and Chance.
301. P. de Lancre, *Tableau de l'inconstance et instabilité de toutes choses* (1607), p. 100. I would like to thank Mr. Jean Lhérété for sending me his article, in manuscript form, "Portrait d'un juge. Pierre de Lancre. De l'angoisse baroque à l'ordre classique." The quotations from P. de Lancre come from this article.
302. Ibid., p. 42.
303. Bremen, Kunsthalle. Concerning melancholy in the cultivated upper classes, see Bousquet, *La Peinture*, pp. 215–224.
304. J. Du Bellay, *Oeuvres poétiques*, ed. by H. Chamard (Paris: 1934), vol. 4, pp. 92 and 106.
305. L. de Camoens, *Obras completas*, ed. by H. Cidade (Lisbon: 1946), vol. 2, p. 295.
306. A. d'Aubigné, *Le Printemps*, ed. by Desornoy (Geneva: n.d.), Stances 1.
307. M. Régnier, *Oeuvres complètes*, ed. by J. Plattard (Paris: Belles Lettres, 1954), "Poesies spirituelles: stances," p. 221.
308. Jean le Bon called l'Hétropolitain (a doctor), *Adages et proverbes de Solon* (1576), book 2, number 741, and book 4, number 64. This book is dedicated to Ronsard. I would like to thank Daniel Rivière for having sent me the above-mentioned proverbs as well as the one mentioned in the next note.
309. *Recueil de sentences notables, dicts et dictons communs* (Antwerp: 1568), number 46. This warning is among a whole series of similar ones concerning laziness, pride, judgments, hate, wine, and "women."
310. (Rouen: 1600). The edition I consulted is the 1616 one, pp. 19–27.
311. Panofsky, *Essais d'iconologie*, p. 113.
312. Corrected in Klibansky, Panofsky, and Saxl, *Saturn*, pp. 277–279.
313. Panofsky, *Essais d'iconologie*, p. 115. For all of the following I consulted the print reproductions Sara Matthews-Grieco kindly sent me.
314. Reproduced in Klibansky, Panofsky, and Saxl, *Saturn*, illustration no. 52.
315. See ibid. and Conrad Celtis, *Libri Amorum* (Nuremberg: 1502), folio IX r° and v°.
316. Klibansky, Panofsky, and Saxl, *Saturn*, p. 278.
317. Reproductions of these engravings may be found at the Cabinet des Estampes of the Bibliothèque Nationale (Paris).
318. P. Charbon, *De la Sagesse*, in *Choix de moralistes français*, ed. by J. Buchon (Paris: 1836), book 1, chap. 31, and book 3, chap. 39, which in this edition is pp. 59–61 and 284–285.
319. L. Lemne, *De Habitu et constitutione corporis* (Antwerp: 1561). I consulted the Italian edition *Della Complessione del corpo humano* (Venice: 1564), p. 115.
320. See below, pp. 255–264.
321. Text to be found in C. Pascal, *Poesia latina medievale* (Catania: 1907), p. 120. See Klibansky, Panofsky, and Saxl, *Saturn*, p. 78.
322. *PL*, vol. 176, col. 1000 passim; Klibansky, Panofsky, and Saxl, *Saturn*, p. 78.
323. Dante, *Oeuvres complètes*, trans. by A. Pézard (Paris: Pléiade, 1965), *Enfer* [*Inferno*], canto 7, lines 115–124, pp. 924–925.
324. J. Dupin (1302–74), *Le Roman de Mandevie ou les mélancolies sur la condition de l'homme*, chap. 29, Paris, Bibliothèque Nationale, MS Y2761 in 4°.
325. *Musae reduces. Anthologie de la poésie latine dans l'Europe de la Renaissance*, poems chosen, commented, and trans. by P. Laurens and C. Balavoine, 2 vols. (Leiden: Brill, 1975), vol. 1, pp. 93–95.
326. Klibansky, Panofsky, and Saxl, *Saturn*, pp. 89–90. Concerning the relationship between melancholy and acedia, see also B. G. Lyons, *Voices of melancholy. Studies in Literary Treatments of Melancholy in Renaissance England* (London: Routledge and Kegan Paul, 1971), pp. 6, 63, 87–90, and 127.
327. L. Joubert, *Seconde partie des erreurs populaires et propos vulgaires touschant la médecine* (Lyon: 1601); first edition 1578, pp. 352–354.
328. See below, chap. 7. G. de Tervarent, *Attributs et symboles dans l'art profane 1450–1500* (Geneva: Droz, 1958–64), vol. 1, cols. 28–29.
329. In the *Iconologia* see the representation of *Pigritia*.
330. L. Lemne [Lemnius], *Della complessione*, p. 116.
331. He is referring to the *Liber de anima* (1540) of Melanchton (vol. 13 of the *Ph. Melanchtonis opera quae supersunt omnia*, ed. by C. E. Bretschneider (Halle: 1834–40).

332. Burton, *The Anatomy*, vol. 1, p. 249.
333. G. de Tervarent, *Les Enigmes de l'art: l'art savant* (Paris: 1946), pp. 13–20; Lyons, *Voices*, pp. 6 and 163.
334. *Hamlet*, act 2, scene 2 and act 3, scene 4; Lyons, *Voices*, pp. 88–89.
335. Thérèse d'Avila, *Le Livre des fondations*, pp. 46–48.
336. St. Teresa of Avila, *The History of Her Foundations* trans. by A. Mason (Cambridge; 1909), pp. 56–57.
337. Luther, *Werke*, Weimar ed., *Tischreden* [*Table-Talk*], 1, number 832.
338. Ibid., *Tischreden*, 1, number 122.
339. Ibid. See also D. Koepplin and T. Falk, *Lukas Cranach*, 2 vols. (Bâle: Birknaüer Verlag, 1974), vol. 2, p. 292.
340. *Hamlet*, act 2, scene 2.
341. Lemne, *Les secrets miracles*, pp. 254–255.
342. Chastel, "La Tentation," p. 146.
343. J. Wier, *Histoires, disputes et discours des illusions et impostures des diables* (Paris: 1885) vol. 1, chap. 6, p. 300. See also M. Préaud, "De Melencolia D (la mélancolie diabolique)," *Cahiers de Fontenay* 9–10 (March 1978): 129.
344. H. Institoris and J. Sprenger, *Le Marteau*, trans. by A. Danet, p. 182.
345. Ibid., p. 279.
346. Ibid., p. 76.
347. Préaud, "De Melencolia," p. 124.
348. See Koepplin and Falk, *Lukas Cranach*, vol. 1, pp. 269–270 and 292, plate 13 and graph 133; Klibansky, Panofsky, and Saxl, *Saturn*, pp. 383–386, plates 128–130.
349. The title of all three is *Melencolie*. They are, respectively, in the Crawford collection (1528 version), Royal Museum of Copenhagen (1532 version), and in a private collection of The Hague (1533 version).
350. *Histoire du docteur Faust* [*The History of the Damnable Life and Death of Dr. John Faustus*] (1587), notes and glossary by J. Lefebvre (Paris: Belles Lettres, 1970), in particular pp. 72–73.
351. Ibid., p. 172.
352. Ibid., pp. 160 and 179.
353. See J. C. Schmitt, "Le Suicide au Moyen Age," *Annales E.S.C.* (January-February 1976): 14–16.
354. Ibid., p. 16.
355. "Lettre d'un médecin anonyme à M. Philibert de La Mane, conseiller au parlement de Dijon" (1647), in Mandrou, *Possesion*, p. 212. Montaigne, *Essais*, vol. 2, chap. 3, 1, p. 424, and Burton, *The Anatomy*, vol. 1, p. 439, both evoke this memorable event.
356. See Panofsky, *The Life of Dürer*, pp. 194–195 and gravüre 242.
357. See, for example, Mandrou, *Possesion*, p. 119.
358. See Institoris and Sprenger, *Le Marteau*, pp. 577–581.
359. Ibid., p. 23.
360. Burton, *The Anatomy*, vol. 3, p. 394.
361. These ideas are developed in ibid., pp. 395–397.
362. Ibid., p. 408.
363. Quoted in R. Mandrou, *Introduction à la France moderne* (Paris: Albin Michel, 1961), p. 328. The colloquium *Funus* is to be found in *Opera omnia D. Erasmi* (Amsterdam: 1969–), book 1, vol. 3.
364. Mandrou, *Introduction*, p. 328.
365. Concerning this subject, see the excellent article by J. C. Schmitt, "Le Suicide au Moyen Age," p. 5, and the discussion in B. Paulin, *Du couteau à la plume. Le suicide dans la littérature anglaise de la Renaissance (1580–1625)* (Lyon: l'Hermès, 1977), pp. 151–152.
366. Paulin, *Du Couteau*, p. 151.
367. Ibid., p. 4; A. Bayet, *Le Suicide et la morale* (Paris: 1922), p. 588.
368. Paris, Bibliothèque Nationale, Nlles acq. lat. 730. I would like to thank Jacques Le Goff for letting me use the results of this inquiry.
369. R. Chartier, "Les Art de mourir, 1450–1600," *Annales E.S.C.* (January-February 1976): 51–75.
370. Tenenti, *La Vie*, esp. pp. 104–105.
371. Montaigne, *Essays*, vol. 2, chap. 3, 1, Frame trans., p. 255.
372. Shakespeare, *The Rape of Lucrece*, lines 1723–1726.

373. Edition of 1619, vol. 1, p. 145. For much of this I am indebted to the book of Raulin, *Du Couteau.*
374. Charron, *De la Sagesse*, vol. 2, chap. 11, p. 190.
375. Paulin, *Du Couteau*, pp. 106–121. *Biathanatos* is the contraction of *Biaithanatos*, which means "violent death."
376. J. Donne, *Biathanatos*, (New York: The Facsimile Text Society, 1930), p. 47.
377. Paulin, *Du Couteau*, p. 264.
378. Ibid., pp. 565–575.
379. Quoted in ibid., p. 119; J. Donne, *Biathanatos*, pp. 17–18.
380. Ibid. (Paulin), p. 592; G. Deshaies, *La Psychologie du suicide* (Paris: P.U.F., 1947), p. 247.
381. Garzoni, *L'Hospital*, p. 31.
382. Burton, *The Anatomy*, vol. 1, pp. 39–40 (Democritus to the Reader).

CHAPTER 6

1. *Oedipe at Colonnus* trans. by R. Fitzgerald, in *Sophocles I* (Chicago: University of Chicago, 1958), ll. 962–972.
2. Plato, *Menon*, trans. by B. Jowett in *The Works of Plato*, vol. 2 (New York: Macmillan, 1940), p. 22. See M. Bouchez, *La Faute* (Paris: Bordas, 1971), esp. pp. 85–93.
3. A discussion on this point may be found in M. Simon, *La Civilisation de L'Antiquité et le Christianisme* (Paris: Arthaud, 1972), pp. 83–94.
4. For the following I am basing myself on the *Vocabulaire de Théologie biblique*, ed. by X. Léon-Dufour (Paris: Cerf, 1971), cols. 932–946, and the *Dictionnaire de Théologie catholique* (hereafter cited as DTC) (Paris: Letouzey, 1933), vol. 12, cols. 140–624.
5. See above all *DTC*, book 1, article on Augustine (cols. 2440–2442); book 2, vol. 2, article on "Capital" (cols. 1688–1692); book 12, vol. 1, articles on "Péché" (sin) (cols. 140–624) and "Pénitence" (penitence) (cols. 722–1138).
6. *De Spectaculis*, chap. 39, in *PL*, vol. 1, col. 735.
7. E. Mâle, *L'Art religieux du XIIIe siècle en France* (Paris: A. Colin, 1958), pp. 99–102.
8. Prudence [Aurelius Clemens Prudentius], *Psychomachia*, Budé series, 15iii, trans. by M. Lavarenne (1963), pp. 52 and 57–61.
9. See J. Houlet, *Les Combats des vertus et des vices: les psychomachie dans l'art* (Paris: Nouvelles Editions Latines, 1969).
10. *Contra faustum*, book 22, chap. 27, in *PL*, vol. 42, col. 418.
11. In the Desclée edition and then Le Cerf, 2 vols. on sin and 3 vols. on penitence.
12. *Summa Theol.*, I–IIae, quest. 71, art. 2.
13. Ibid., quest. 71, art. 6.
14. Ibid., quest. 72, art. 6.
15. Ibid., quest. 71, art. 3.
16. Ibid., quest. 72, art. 4.
17. The *Didachê*, in F. Quéré, *Les Pères apostoliques* (Paris: Seuil, 1980), pp. 93–95. *Adv. Marcionem*, 1, 4, chap. 9, in *PL*, vol. 2, col. 375. I mentioned earlier that Tertullian, toward the end of his life, considered idolatry, lewd behavior, and homicide as unforgivable sins.
18. *In Levit.*, 8, 10, 11, in *PG*, vol. 11, col. 502b–506a.
19. See *Dictionnaire de spiritualité ascétique et mystique* (Paris: Beauchesne), book 4, vol. 2, col. 178. Concerning the history of the seven deadly sins, see O. Zöckler, *Das Lehrstück von den sieben Hauptsünden* (Munich: 1893); M. W. Bloomfield, *The Seven Deadly Sins* (Ann Arbor; Michigan University Press, 1952), which was reprinted in 1967; and the work of Mrs. Vincent-Cassy quoted below from note 32 on.
20. *De Coenobium institutis*, 1, 4, chap. 1, in *PL*, vol. 49, col. 202 passim, and *Collatio*, book 5, chap. 10, in *PL*, vol. 49, col. 621 passim.
21. *Scala Paradisi*, 22, in *PG*, vol. 88, col. 948 passim.
22. *Moratium Libri*, 1, 31, chap. 45, in *PL*, vol. 76, col. 620 passim.
23. *Differentiarum*, 1, 2, number 161 and following ones, in *PL*, vol. 83, cols. 95–98.
24. *Liber de virtutibus et vitiis*, chap. 27 and following ones, in *PL*, vol. 101, col. 632 passim.
25. *Sententiarum libri quatuor*, 1, 2, dist. 42, in *PL*, vol. 192, cols. 753–754.
26. *Summa Theol.*, Ia–IIae, quest. 84, art. 4.

27. Ibid., quest. 71, art. 4 and quest. 73, art. 1.
28. Ibid., quest. 72, art. 7.
29. Ibid., quest. 75, art. 4 and esp. quest. 84, art. 4 *De Malo*, quest. 8–15.
30. *Homiliarum in Ezechielem*, book 1, in *PL*, vol. 76, col. 930.
31. *Expositio moralis in Abdiam*, in *PL*, vol, 175, col. 400.
32. M. Vincent-Cassy, "L'Envie en France du XIIIe au XVe siècle," University of Paris IV, typescript, 1974, pp. 37–39. See also by the same author, "L'Envie au Moyen Age," *Annales E.S.C.* (March–April 1980): 253–271; Mâle, *L'Art religieux en France au XIIIe siècle*, p. 44; and Mâle, *L'Art religieux à la fin du Moyen Age* (Paris: Armand Colin, 1925), p. 103.
33. Houlet, *Les Combats*, esp. pp. 14, 18, 44, 53, 57–58, 61, and 69.
34. *Summa Theol.*, 1a–2ae, quest. 87, art. 1.
35. *De Libero arbitro*, book 3, chap. 15, 44, in *PL*, vol. 32, col. 1293.
36. H. Institoris and J. Sprenger, *Le Marteau des sorcières*, trans. by A. Danet (Paris: Plon, 1973), p. 260.
37. *Summa Theol.*, 1a–2ae, quest. 87, is entirely devoted to this subject.
38. See *DTC*, vol. 1, article on Augustine, col. 2440–2442; vol. 12, 1, article on "*Peché*" (sin), cols. 225–226.
39. See above all *Enchridion*, chaps. 69–81, in *PL*, vol. 60, col. 265; *De Symbolo*, chap. 7, n. 15, in ibid., col. 636; *De Fide et oper.*, chap. 36, in ibid., col. 228; *De Civit.*, 1, 19, chap. 27, in *PL*, vol. 41, col. 657, and 1, 21, chap. 26, n. 4, ibid., col. 748.
40. See above all in Saint Thomas the *De Malo*, quest. 7, art. 1, and *Summa Theol.*, 1a–2ae, quest. 72, art. 5; quest. 73, art. 8; quest. 74, arts. 3, 4, 8, 10; quest. 77, art. 8; quest. 78, art. 2.
41. Concerning this subject, see C. Vogel, *Pécheur et pénitence dans l'Eglise ancienne* (Paris: Le Cerf, 1966); ibid., *Le Pécheur et la pénitence au Moyen Age* (Paris; Le Cerf, 1969); and ibid., *Les "Libri paenitentiales"* (Tournai: Casterman, 1978) which has a very good bibliography; J. Van Laarhoven, "Een Geschiedenis van debiechtvader" (A history of confessors), *Tijdschrift voor Theologie* 7 (1967): 375–422 (P. W. Ritters presented a critical analysis of this article in my seminar); F. Rekkinger, "Die Geschichte der Beichte in Stichwörter," *Die Anregung* (1970): 3; Z. Herrero, "La Penitencia y sus formas. Examen de su evolucion historica," *Estudios Augustinos* (1972): 38–71, 222–225. For a more general approach to the history of penitence, see esp. H. C. Lea, *A History of Auricular Confession and Indulgences in the Latin Church*, 3 vols. (Philadelphia: 1896); O. D. Watkins, *A History of Penance*, 2 vols. (London: 1920); P. Anclaux, *La Théologie du sacrament de pénitence au XIIe siècle* (Paris: 1949); P. Poschmann, *Penance and the Anointing of the Sick* (New York: 1964); as well as the already-mentioned works by O. Zöckler and M. W. Bloomfield; M. F. Berrourard, "La Pénitence publique durant les six prmiers siècles. Histoire et sociologie," *La Maison-Dieu* 118 (1974): 92–130.
42. Concerning this see J. C. Payen, *Le Motif du repentir dans la littérature française médiévale (des origines à 1230)* (Geneva: Droz, 1968).
43. Ibid., pp. 33–34.
44. Ibid., pp. 36–69.
45. J. Le Goff, "Au Moyen Age: temps de l'Eglise et temps du marchand," *Annales E.S.C.* (1960): 429, now in *Pour un autre Moyen Age* (Paris: Gallimard, 1978).
46. P. Delahaye, *Le Problème de la conscience morale chez saint Bernard* (Louvain: 1957), *Analecta mediaevalia namurcensia*, number 9, esp. chap. 3; Payen, *Le Motif du repentir*, pp. 63–66.
47. Payen, *Le Motif du repentir*, p. 38, n. 92. *De Panibus*, 12, in *PL*, vol. 202, cols. 983–986.
48. Ibid., p. 76.
49. Canon 21, *proprio sacerdoti*, translated into French by R. Foreville, in *Histoire des conciles oecuméniques* (Paris: Editions de l'Orante, 1965), VI, p. 357; P. M. Gy, "Le Précepte de la confession annuelle et al nécessité de la confession," *Revue des sciences philosophiques et théologiques* 73 (4) (October 1979): 529–548.
50. *Summa Théol.*, IIIa, quest. 84 and 85.
51. Ed. by Lecoy (Paris: H. Champion, 1966–70), vol. 2, lines 11556–11558.
52. This information and the following in P. Michaud-Quantin, *Sommes de casuistique et manuels de confession au Moyen Age (XIIe–XVIe siècle)* (Louvain: 1962), (*Analecta mediaevalia namurcensia*, number 13). See also below note 60.
53. Ibid., p. 40.
54. Ibid., pp. 41–42.
55. Ibid., pp. 98–106.
56. M. Luther, *Oeuvres*, "The Babylonian captivity of the Church," vol. 2, pp. 226–230.
57. See E. J. Arnould, *Le Manuel des péchés. Etude de la littérature anglo-normande* (Paris: Droz,

1940), esp. pp. 245–246; Michaud-Quantin, *Sommes de casuistique*, pp. 27–28; Payen, *Le Motif du repentir*, p. 563, continues to attribute it to William of Waddington.
58. E. Brayer, "Contenu, structure, et combinaisons du *Miroir du monde* et de la *Somme le Roi*," *Romania* 79 (1958): 1–38.
59. Michaud-Quantin, *Sommes de casuistique*, p. 74.
60. T. N. Tentler, *Sin and Confession on the Eve of the Reformation* (Princeton: Princeton University Press, 1977), pp. 37–38. See also, by the same author, "The Summa of confessors as an instrument of social control" and the answer by L. E. Boyle, "The Summa of confessors as a genere and its religious intent," both in *The Pursuit of Holiness*, ed. by C. Trinkaus and H. A. Obermann, (Leiden: Brill, 1974), pp. 103–137. An interesting analysis of Tentler's *Sin and Confession* is by H. Martin, *Annales E.S.C.* (November–December 1979): 1260–1262.
61. Arnould, *Le Manuel des péchés*, pp. 34–35.
62. Michaud-Quantin, *Sommes de casuistique*, pp. 95–97.
63. Ibid., p. 76.
64. Ibid., pp. 74, 75, and 90. J. Le Goff, "Métiers et profession d'après les manuels de confesseurs du Moyen Age," in *Pour une autre histoire* (Paris: Gallimard, 1977), pp. 162–180.
65. Tentler, *Sin and Confessions*, pp. 141–142.
66. For what follows see ibid., esp. pp. 69, 82–83, 87–90.
67. M. Luther, *Oeuvres*, "The Babylonian captivity," vol. 2, p. 228.
68. J. Gerson, *De Modo audiendi confessiones*, ed. by E. Du Pin (Antwerp: 1706), vol. 2, col. 446–453.
69. J. Gerson, *Examen de conscience*, ed. by E. Du Pin (Antwerp: 1706), vol. 2, pp. 446–453.
70. J. Gerson, *Traité des diverses tentations de l'Ennemi*, ed. by Glorieux, book 7, pp. 343–359.
71. Ibid., pp. 370–389.
72. Brayer, "Contenu, structure," p. 2.
73. For this information and the following, see Tentler, *Sin and Confession*, pp. 35–41. See also L. Febvre and H. J. Martin, *L'Apparition du livre* (Paris: Albin Michel, 1958), p. 382.
74. Ibid. (Tentler), pp. 42–43.
75. Ibid., pp. 47–48. H. Martin, *Annales E.S.C.* (November–December 1979): 1261, stresses the interest of studying the confessor's manuals that are in manuscript form. He had one of his students study such a manual for his master's degree at the University of Haute-Bretagne at Rennes. R. Libeau, "Edition et commentaires du ms B.N. 944. Analyse d'un manuel de confesseur," typescript, Rennes, 1979.
76. Arnould, *Le Manuel*, pp. 292–355. See also M. M. Dubois, *La Litterature anglaise au Moyen Age* (Paris: P.U.F., 1962), p. 107.
77. See C. Amalvi-Mizzi, "Le 'Doctrinal aux simples gens' ou 'Doctrinal de Sapience,' " critical edition and commentary, Thesis for the Ecole des Chartes, 1978.
78. The *Compost et Kalendrier des bergiers*, facsimile reprint of the G. Marchant ed. (Paris: 1493), with an introduction by Pierre Champion, (Paris: éd. des Quatre-Chemins, 1926).
79. Fol. 32 v°.
80. R. Mandrou, *De la culture populaire au XVIIe–XVIIIe siècles*, 2nd edition (Paris: Stock, 1975), p. 44; G. Bollème, *Almanachs populaires aux XVIIe et XVIIIe siècles* (Paris: Hague: Mouton, 1969).
81. See D. O'Connel and J. Le Goff, *Les Propos de Saint Louis* (Paris: Gallimard, 1974), pp. 142–144.
82. Arnould, *Le Manuel*, pp. 569–576. A text ed. of the *Dîme de pénitence* was done by H. Breymann (Tübingen: 1874).
83. Ibid. (Arnould), pp. 579–586. See, C. Foulon *L'Oeuvre de Jean Bodel* (Paris: P.U.F., 1958).
84. A resume of the *Voyage de paradis* in J. Dufournet, *Rutebeuf. Poésies* (Paris: H. Champion, 1977), pp. 74 passim.
85. Febvre and Martin, *L'Apparition du livre*, pp. 388–389; P. Renucci, *Dante* (Paris: Hatier, 1958), p. 225.
86. Geoffrey Chaucer, *The Canterbury Tales*, ed. by J.H. Fisher, *The Complete Poetry and Prose of Geoffrey Chaucer* (New York: Holt, 1977). "The Parson's Tale" appears on pp. 347–.
87. *Peter Idley's Instructions to His Son*, ed. by C. D'Evelyn (Boston: 1935), p. 109.
88. J. Pichon, ed., 2 vols. (1846).
89. Ibid., vol. 1, p. 62.
90. Ibid., vol. 1, p. 28.
91. Ibid., vol. 1, pp. 40–41, 49–50, and 52.
92. F. Chiovaro, "Le Mariage chrétien en Occident," in J. Delumeau, ed., *Histoire vécue du peuple*

chrétien, 2 vols. (Toulouse: Privat, 1979), vol. 1, p. 240. Much the same conclusions, and even worse ones for the High Middle Ages, appear in J.-L. Flandrin, *Un Temps pour embrasser* (Paris: Seuil, 1983), esp. pp.112–116.

93. Paris, Bibliothèque Sainte-Geneviève, MS n. 2734, fols. 3 passim, quoted in Champion, *Histoire poétique du XVe siècle*, vol. 1, pp. 410–411.
94. *The Complete Works of François Villon*, trans. by A. Bonner (London: 1960), p. 27 (stanza 14 of Villon's *Testament*).
95. Quoted in S. Brant, *La Nef des fous*, preface by P. Dollinger.
96. Sebastian Brand, *The Ship of Fools*, trans. by E. H. Zeydel (New York:, AMS Press 1944), introduction.
97. Ibid., p. 204–205.
98. Ibid., p. 344.
99. Ibid., p. 336.

CHAPTER 7

1. Vincent-Cassy, *L'Envie en France*, p. 52.
2. Quoted in ibid., p. 53. See *Statuts synodaux français du XIIIe siècle*, vol. 1: *Les Statuts de Paris et le Synodal de l'Ouest*, vol. 8 of the *Doc. inédits de l'histoire de France*, p. 221.
3. Ibid. (Vincent-Cassey), p. 78. See the *Summa Theol.*, Ia, quest. 63, art. 2, and IIa–IIae, quest. 36, art. 2.
4. Ibid. (Vincent-Cassey), pp. 71–73. Mrs. Vincent-Cassy refers to the text and the miniatures of the MS 1130 of the Bibliothèque Sainte-Geneviève (Paris).
5. Ibid., pp. 115–120.
6. Ibid., pp. 121–131.
7. Ibid., pp. 161–249.
8. *Eruditorium penitentiale* (1490 ?), Hòb-I1a. The references on the subject of lewdness are all to Tentler, *Sin and Confession*, unless mentioned otherwise.
9. Institoris and Sprenger, *Le Marteau des sorcières*, esp. pp. 55–56, 100, 219, 465 and 467.
10. *Le Doctrinal* (Troyes: 1604), pp. 57–58.
11. In the following pages I will use above all the book of Tentler, *Sin and Confession*, pp. 161–273. Of utmost importance on this subject are J. T. Noonan, *Contraception et Mariage* [Contraception and Marriage] (Paris: Le Cerf, 1969), pp. 141–398, and J.-L. Flandrin, *L'Eglise et le contrôle des naissances* (Paris: Flammarion, 1970), pp. 39–61.
12. Formulation of Ocellus Lucanus, Neo-pythagorian, in his treatise *Of the Nature of the Universe*, quoted in Flandrin, *L'Eglise*, p. 26.
13. *PL*, vol. 40, cols. 374–396; Noonan, *Contraception*, pp. 166–172.
14. *Raimundina seu summa . . . de poenitentia et matrimonio cum glosis*, reprint of 1603 ed. (Farnborough: 1967), vol. 4, pp. 519–520.
15. *PL*, vol. 77, cols. 1196–1197; Noonan, *Contraception*, pp. 193–196. This *Responsum beati Gregorii* is now attributed to Nothelm of Canterbury.
16. N. de Osimo, *Supplementum summae pisanellae* (1489), "Debitum conjugale," 4.
17. *Raimundina*, pp. 519–520.
18. Butrio (Anthony of), *Directorium ad confitendum* (Rome: 1474), "De pecatis contra sacramentum matrimonii."
19. Denys le Chartreux [Denis the Carthusian], *Speculum conversionis peccatorum* (1473), X6a.
20. G. Rosemondt, *Confessionale* (1518), 5 (6), fol. 94 v°.
21. De Osimo, *Supplementum*, "Debitum conjugale," 4.
22. See Tentler, *Sin and Confession*, pp. 186–204.
23. J. Nider, *Expositio preceptorum* (1482), book 6, 4 B2a-b. Concerning the taboo linked to impurity see Flandrin, *Un Temps pour embrasser*, esp. pp. 72–114.
24. J. Gerson (?), *Le Confessional autrement appelé le Directoire des confesseurs* (1547 ed.), 2b–3b.
25. De Osimo, *Supplementum*, "Debitum conjugale," 7.
26. This is the general feeling produced by Noonan's book.
27. Saint Albert [Albert the Great], *Summa Theologica*, in *Opera*, ed. by Borgnet (Paris: 1890–199), XXXIII, 2, 18; Noonan, *Contraception*, pp. 368–369.
28. Thomas d'Aquin [Thomas Aquinas], *Praeclarissima commentaria in quatuor libros sententiarum P. Lombardi*, J. Nicolas, ed. (Paris: 1659), IV, dist. 31, quest. 1, vol. 2, p. 501.

29. Ibid., quest. 2, answer to objection 3.
30. Noonan, *Contraception*, pp. 375–377.
31. Ibid., p. 378.
32. Gerson, *Regulae morales*, ed. by E. Du Pin, in *Opera Omnia* (Antwerp: 1706), book 3, 95B–C.
33. Antonin de Florence [Antonio, bishop of Florence], *Summula confessionis (Confessionale-Defecerunt)* (1499), p. 30.
34. *Summa Angelica* (1534 ed.), "Debitum conjugale," 4.
35. *Sylvestrina*, "Debitum conjugale," quest. 4, section 4.
36. Noonan, *Contraception*, pp. 390–398.
37. M. Le Maistre, *Questiones morales* (1490), vol. 2, "De temperantia," fol. 51 volume.
38. J. Mair, *In quartum Sententiarum* (1519), 4, 31.
39. Gerson, *Opus tripartitum*, ed. by E. Du Pin, vol. 2, pp. 444C–445A. See also *Regulae morales*, ed. by Du Pin, vol. 3, p. 106A.
40. *Compendium theologiae*, vol. 1 of the E. Du Pin ed., pp. 292D–293A.
41. Berthold de Fribourg, *Summa Joannis, deutsch* (1472), quest. 179.
42. *Summa angelica*, "Debitum conjugale," 25, fols. 191b–192b.
43. Tentler, *Sin and Confession*, pp. 200–211.
44. See ibid., p. 209.
45. See ibid., p. 205.
46. *Sylvestrina*, "Debitum conjugale," quest. 12, section 14.
47. Raymond de Capoue [Raymund of Capua], *Vita de s. Catharina senensi*, 2, 7, 215, in *Acta Sanctorum* (Antwerp: 1675), April 30, p. 906 (section 215); see Noonan, *Contraception*, p. 290.
48. Bernardin de Sienne [Bernardin of Siena], *Le Prediche volgari*, ed. by P. Bargellini (Milan: 1936), p. 100; see Noonan, *Contraception*, p. 291.
49. See note 47 above.
50. Tentler, *Sin and Confession*, pp. 214–215.
51. J. Foresti, *Confessionale seu interrogatorium* (1497), pp. 17b–18a.
52. D. De Soto, *Commentarium in quartum Sententiarum* (Salamanca: 1574), IV, 32; 1, 1.
53. Gerson, *De confessione mollitiei*, Glorieux ed., vol. 1, p. 49; P. Ariès, *L'Enfant et la vie familiale sous l'Ancien Régime* (Paris: Seuil, 1973), pp. 109–111.
54. R. Libeau, "Edition et commentaires du ms 944 de la B.N.," fol. 57 v° of the manuscript, lines 4 to 11. I would like to thank Hervé Martin for having drawn my attention to this text edition and for having sent me a copy.
55. See Noonan, *Contraception*, p. 478.
56. Tentler, *Sin and Confession*, pp. 223–224.
57. Ibid., p. 223.
58. M. Foucault, *Histoire de la sexualité*, vol. 1: *La volonté de savoir* (Paris: Gallimard, 1976), in particular pp. 21 and 82–84.
59. M. Le Maistre, *Questiones morales*, II, "Temperantia," fol. 50 r°, translated in Noonan, *Contraception*, pp. 394–395.
60. Tentler, *Sin and Confession*, p. 220.
61. A general survey in J. Delumeau, *La Civilisation de la Renaissance*, 2nd ed. (Paris: Arthaud, 1973), pp. 229–282. In the next few pages I will use above all the *Dictionnaire de Théologie catholique*, XV2, article on "*Usure*" (usury) (G. Le Bras), cols. 2316–2390; R. De Roover, *L'Evolution de la lettre de change*, 2nd ed. (Paris: A. Colin, 1953); J. T. Noonan, *Scholastic Analysis of Usury* (Cambridge: Harvard University Press, 1957); R. De Roover, *La Pensée économique des scolastiques* (Paris: Vrin, 1971). See also T. P. McLaughlin, "The Teaching of the Canonists on usury (XII–XIV c.)," *Medieval Studies* 1 (1939): 81–147, 2 (1940): 1–22; and B. Nelson, "The Idea of Usury, From Tribal Brotherhood to Universal Otherhood," Center for Medieval and Renaissance Studies, University of California, 1979, pp. 25–52.
62. G. Fourquin, *Histoire économique de l'Occident médiéval* (Paris: A. Colin, 1969), p. 260.
63. *Summa aurea*, III, 21, fol. 225 v°; see Noonan, *Scholastic Analysis*, pp. 43–44. J. Le Goff, "Au Moyen Age: temps de l'Eglise et temps du marchand," in *Pour un autre Moyen Age* (Paris: Gallimard, 1978), pp. 46–47.
64. Le Goff, "Au Moyen Age," pp. 46–47.
65. *Summa Theol.*, IIa–IIae, all of quest. 78.
66. Ibid., in particular art. 1 and sol. 5.
67. Ibid., in particular art. 1 and sol. 3.
68. Ibid., in particular art. 1, conclusion.
69. Ibid., in particular art. 2, sol. 7.

70. J. Lefèvre d'Etaples, *Politicorum Libri octo, Economicorum duo . . . , Economicarum publicarum unus* (Paris: 1506); R. De Roover, *La Pensée économique*, p. 20.
71. *Summa Theol.*, IIa–IIae, quest. 78, art. 2, sol. 1–4, 6. See also *De Malo*, quest. 13, art. 4, sol. 5, 10, 12, 13.
72. Ibid. (*Summa Theol.*), quest. 78, art. 2, sol. 5.
73. *Conciliorum oecumenicorum decreta*, ed. by G. Alberigo (Bologna: Instituto per le scienze religiose, 1973), pp. 384–385.
74. See J. T. Welter, *L'Exemplum dans la littérature religieuse et didactique du Moyen Age* (Paris: 1927), pp. 246, 251, 288, 311, and 382.
75. The following references are to the *DTC*, R. De Roover and J. T. Noonan give the exact references.
76. *Bullarium . . . Rom. Pontificum* (Turin: 1860–), vol. 7, pp. 1 passim. G. Mandich, *Le Pacte de Ricorsa et le marché italien des changes au XVIIe siècle* (Paris: A. Colin, 1953), esp. pp. 145–146; J. Delumeau, *Vie économique et sociale de Rome dans la seconde moitié du XVIe siècle*, 2 vols. (Paris: De Boccard, 1957–59), vol. 2, pp. 867–869, condensed in J. Delumeau, *Rome au XVIe siècle* (Paris: Hachette, 1975), p. 210.
77. See F. Melis, *Origini e sviluppi delle assicurazioni in Italia (XIV–XVI s.)* (Rome: Istituto Nazionale delle Assicurazioni, 1975), vol. 1, *Fonti*.
78. See R. Marcay, *Saint Antonin, archevêque de Florence* (Paris: 1914), esp. pp. 366–376.
79. The so-called Besançon fairs were no longer held in that city at the end of the sixteenth century and in the beginning of the seventeenth century but rather in the city of Piacenza.
80. An excellent resumé of this practice in Mandich, *Le Pacte de ricorsa*, p. 147, n. 106.
81. D. De Soto, *De Justitia et jure* (Salamanca: 1563), book 6, quest. 8, art. 1. R. De Roover, *La Pensée économique*, p. 36.
82. See, among others, Fourquin, *Histoire économique*, pp. 222–224; P. Goubert, *L'Ancien Régime* (Paris: A. Colin, 1969), vol. 1, pp. 127–128.
83. *Bull. rom.*, vol. 7, pp. 736–738.
84. Delumeau, *La Vie économique*, vol. 2, p. 870; Delumeau, *Rome au XVIe siècle*, pp. 210–211; M. Ulloa, *La Hacienda real de Castilla en el reinado de Felipe II*, 2nd ed. (Madrid: 1977), pp. 118–123.
85. Same references as in note 84, pp. 783–823 and 192–198 respectively. See also Delumeau, *La Civilisation de la Renaissance*, pp. 263–266.
86. Bernardin of Siena, *Opera*, ed. by J. de La Haye, 2 vols. (Paris: 1635), vol. 1, sermon number 41 delivered during Lent, pp. 725–740, quoted in Marcay, *Saint Antonin*, pp. 360–361.
87. Antonino bishop of Florence, *Summa*, vol. 2, title 1, chap. 11.
88. See esp. M. Mollat, *Les Pauvres au Moyen Age* (Paris: Hachette, 1978), pp. 337–338.
89. Concerning the pontifical offices, see Delumeau, *Vie économique*, vol. 2, pp. 772–782, and Delumeau, *Rome au XVIe siècle*, pp. 189–192.
90. In his *Commentaria super libros decretalium*, vol. 5, "De usuris," 16; see Noonan, *Scholastic*, pp. 118 passim. For the following discussion I am also using Noonan work.
91. *Commentaire sur Moïse* quoted in A. Bieler, *La Pensée économique et sociale de Calvin* (Geneva: Georg, 1959), p. 464.
92. *Commentaire sur Ezéchiel* quoted in ibid., p. 464.
93. Luther, *Oeuvres*, vol. 4, p. 123 (*Du commerce et de l'usure*).
94. Ibid., vol. 7, p. 69 (*Grand Catéchisme*).
95. Ibid., vol. 2, pp. 152–153 (*A la noblesse chrétienne*).
96. *Propos de table*, ed. by G. Brunet, p. 358.
97. Luther, *Oeuvres*, vol. 4, p. 135 (*Du commerce*).
98. Ibid., pp. 142–144.
99. J. A. Goris, *Etude sur les colonies marchandes méridionales . . . à Anvers de 1488 à 1567* (Louvain: 1925), pp. 503–545.
100. L. Guichardin, *Description de tous les Pays-Bas* (Antwerp: 1567), p. 320.
101. See the Littré and other dictionaries of Old French, such as the ones of F. Godefroy and of A. Hatzfeld.
102. See J. Burckhardt, *La Civilisation de la Renaissance en Italie* [*The Civilization of the Renaissance in Italy*], 3 vols. (Paris: Plon Club du Meilleure Livre, 1966), vol. 2, pp. 258–360; J. Delumeau, *L'Italie de Botticelli à Bonaparte* (Paris: A. Colin, 1974), p. 145.
103. I would like to thank J. Le Goff for sending me the results of an analysis he did on the *Alphabetum narrationum*. This text is to be dated 1308–1310 and was composed by Arnold of

Liège, a Dominican monk. The *Alphabetum* is made up of some 550 headings, which go from the word "abbas" to "zelotypa."

104. *Summa theol.*, Ia–IIae, quest. 84, art. 4.
105. Dante Alighieri, *Inferno*, trans. by A. Mandelbaum (Berkeley: University of California Press, 1980), p. 67.
106. Ibid., *Purgatoire*, canto 18, lines 103–145, pp. 1245–1247.
107. G. Chaucer, *Contes de Canterbury* [*The Canterbury Tales*], trans. by 21 authors (Paris: Alcan, 1908), pp. 513–523. It is uncertain whether this tale was actually written by Chaucer.
108. J. Gerson, *Oeuvres complètes*, ed. by Glorieux, vol. 7, no. 328, pp. 376–377.
109. The 1493 edition consulted is not paginated.
110. Proverbs 6:6–12.
111. Ibid., 12:27.
112. Ibid., 14:23.
113. Ibid., 19:15.
114. Ibid., 24:33–34.
115. G. Meurier, *Recueil de sentences notables* (Antwerp: 1568), nos. 2605, 2628 and 3218. I would like to thank Daniel Rivière for having drawn my attention to these proverbs.
116. D. Cavalca, *Disciplina degli spirituali*, ed. by Bottari, (Milan: 1838), p. 128.
117. Ibid., p. 129.
118. Ibid., p. 131.
119. The *Ménagier de Paris*, vol. 1, pp. 39–40.
120. Delumeau, *La Peur en Occident*, p. 315. See also P. Monnier, *Le Quattrocento*, 2 vols. (Paris: 1924), vol. 2, p. 198.
121. L. B. Alberti, *I Libri della famiglia*, ed. by A. Tenenti and R. Romano (Torino: Einaudi, 1969), pp. 57–58. See M. Auscher, "L'Education de la femme bourgeoise en Toscane au XIVe et XVe siècles: de la jeunne fille à l'épouse," Diplôme dissertation, E.H.E.S.S., 1978, pp. 16–17, 24, 162–163.
122. L. B. Alberti, *The Family in Renaissance Florence*, trans. by R. N. Watkins (Columbia, SC: University of South Carolina Press, 1969), p. 63.
123. For the following discussion see Mollat, *Les Pauvres au Moyen Age*, pp. 266–316.
124. J. Dupin, *Le Roman de Mandevie ou les mélancolies sur la condition humaine*, Paris, Bibliothèque Nationale, Rés. Y2761, in 4°, vol. 8, chap. 29, "Des paresseux."
125. G. de Lorris and J. de Meun, *The Romance of the Rose*, trans. by H. W. Robbins (New York: AMS Press, 1962), part 46, ll. 34–35, p. 192.
126. The *Ménagier de Paris*, vol. 2, p. 3.
127. Ibid., vol. 2, p. 17.
128. The reader may consult, above and beyond the work of M. Mollat mentioned above and the notes to the last chapter of my *Peur en Occident*, *Les Marginaux et les exclus dans l'histoire*, Cahiers Jussieu number 5 (Paris: 10/18, 1979). More specifically on the subject of acedia, see R. Ricard, "Pour une histoire de l'acédie," *Nouvelles Etudes religieuses* (1973).
129. "Gaufridi declamationes ex s. Bernardi sermonibus," in *PL*, vol. 184, col. 465; J. Le Goff, "Le Temps du travail dans la crise du XIVe siècle: du temps médiéval au temps moderne," in *Pour un autre Moyen Age*, p. 77.
130. Le Goff, "Le Temps du travail," p. 77.
131. Cavalca, *Disciplina*, Bottari, ed., pp. 132–133.
132. *Ménagier de Paris*, vol. 1, p. 3.
133. Le Goff, "Le Temps du travail," p. 78; Y. Lefèvre, *L'Elucidarium et les Lucidaires* (Paris: De Boccard, 1954), p. 279, note 1.
134. Le Goff, "Le Temps du travail," p. 78; Muratori, *Rerum italicarum scriptores*, vol. 20, p. 582.
135. Antonino bishop of Florence, *Summa*, part 2, title IX, "De acidia."
136. Ibid., chap. 14.
137. Ibid., chap. 13.
138. Ibid., chaps. 3–12.
139. Ibid., part 2, title IX, chap. 14.
140. Alberti, *I Libri*, p. 165.
141. Ibid., introduction by R. Romano and A. Tenenti, p. IX. The *Libro di buoni costumi* has been edited by A. Schiaffini, (Florence: 1945).
142. Ibid.
143. Albertini, *I Libria*, p. 172.

144. Ibid., p. 205. Other sources in much the same spirit are quoted in Tenenti, *Il Senso*, pp. 44–45.
145. Albertini, *I Libri*, p. 253.
146. Ibid., p. xii; F. Guicciardini, *Ricordi*, ed. by R. Spongano, (Florence: 1951), p. 157.
147. S. Brant, *La Nef des fous*, pp. 378–380.
148. Ibid., pp. 226–231.
149. Luther, *Oeuvres*, vol. 6, p. 220 (Commentary on psalm 117). See also vol. 3, p. 63.
150. Ibid., vol. 6, p. 211 (Commentary on psalm 117).
151. Luther, *Oeuvres*, vol. 7, p. 49 (*Le Grand Catéchisme*).
152. *Essais*, vol. 1, chap. 8 and vol. 2, chap. 21.
153. *The Complete Essays of Montaigne*, trans. by D. Frame (Stanford; Stanford University Press, 1957), p. 21.
154. Ibid., p. 513.
155. Ibid., p. 263, from the essay "Let Business Wait Till Tomorrow."
156. J. Calvin, *Institution*, book 2, chap. 1, 1 (I, p. 23); chap. 25, 7 (I, p. 444).
157. J. Calvin, *Commentaires sur le Nouveau Testament* (John 9:4) quoted in Bieler, *La Pensée*, p. 407.
158. J. Calvin, *Sermon sur le Deutéronome*, in *Calvini Opera* (Brunswick: 1863–1900), vol. 28, pp. 379–380, quoted in R. Stauffer, *Dieu la création et la providence dans la prédication de Calvin* (Bern: P. Lang, 1977), p. 269.
159. J. Calvin, *28° Sermon sur Isaïe* (*Supplementa calviniana*, vol. 2, p. 262), quoted in ibid., p. 273.
160. J. Lavalleye, *Lucas van Leyden. Pieter Brueghel l'ancien. Gravures* (Paris: Arts et Métiers graphiques, 1966), part 2, plate 42.
161. *Doctrinal de Sapience* (1604 ed.), pp. 66–69.
162. Geneva, 1478 ed. fol. 44 v°.
163. E. de Monstrelet, *Chronique* (Paris: Société d'histoire de France, 1866), vol. 5, p. 302.
164. The references are in Mâle, *L'Art religieux de la fin du Moyen Age*, pp. 336–337.
165. The following passage owes much to the oral report "Le Système des péchés capitaux dans l'art de la fin du Moyen Age" given by Mrs. Mireille Vincent-Caussy in my seminar. The houses of Orléans and du Blanc have been destroyed.
166. *De Fructibus carnis et spiritus*, in *PL*, vol. 176, col. 999.
167. J. Wall, *Medieval Wall Painting* (London: 1920), p. 193; E. W. Tristran, *English Wall Painting of the Fourteenth century* (London: 1955), p. 102.
168. Paris, Bibliothèque Nationale, Ms. fr. 9220, and Bibliothèque Sainte-Geneviève, Ms. 2200.
169. *PL*, vol. 175, cols. 405 passim.
170. The references, as given by Mrs. Mireille Vincent-Caussy, are: A. Kisa, "Die gravierten Metalschüsseln des XII und XIII Jahrhunderts," *Zeitschrift für Christliche Kunst* (1905): 374; E. Schwedeler-Meyer, "Die Darstellung von Tugenden und Lastern auf einem gravierten Bronzebecken des XII Jahrhunderts," *Bulletin de la Société pour la conservation des monuments historiques d'Alsace* 18 (1896):203–221.
171. Paris, Bibliothèque Sainte-Geneviève, Ms. 246.
172. At Ingatestone (Essex), see Wall, *Medieval*, p. 195, plate 85; at Hurstbourne-Tarrant (Hampshire), see Tristran, *English*, p. 183.
173. W. L. Schreiber, *Handbuch der Holz und Metallschnitte des XV Jahrhunderts* (Leipzig: 1862), vol. 4.
174. See Baltrusaitis, *Le Moyen Age fantastique*, p. 252.
175. See F. Van der Meer, *L'Apocalypse dans l'art*, (Paris: Chêne, 1978).
176. Wall, *Medieval*, pp. 196 passim.
177. See V. H. Debidour, *Le Bestiaire sculpté* (Paris: Arthaud, 1961), plate 4489, p. 324.
178. *Opera omnia*, Quaracchi ed. vol. 10, pp. 24 passim.
179. Debidour, *Le Bestiaire sculpté*, p. 323.
180. Mâle, *L'Art religieux de la fin du Moyen Age*, p. 331; Bibliothèque Nationale, Ms. 400.
181. Mâle, *L'Art religieux de la fin du Moyen Age*, pp. 329–332.
182. Ibid., p. 333.
183. Ibid., p. 335.
184. Formerly in the Royal Palace of Madrid.
185. Mâle, *L'Art religieux de la fin du Moyen Age*, pp. 336–337.
186. Delumeau, *La Peur*, vol. 1, p. 341.
187. This information is also from the work of Mrs. Vincent-Caussy mentioned above.

188. Mâle, *L'Art religieux de la fin du Moyen Age*, p. 328.
189. *Le Doctrinal de sapience* (1604 ed.), pp. 46–48.
190. R. H. Marijnissen et al., *Jérôme Bosch* (Brussels: Arcade, 1972), pp. 126, 150–152. See also C. de Tolnay, *Hieronymus Bosch* (London: Methuen, 1966), esp. pp. 58–69.
191. Lavalleye, *Lucas van Leyden*, plates 41–47.
192. See, among others, the painting of Tobias Verhaecht (1561–1631) exhibited at the Musée Royal des Beaux Arts of Antwerp, which depicts a large tower of Babel dominated by a threatening storm; see also a 1433 miniature kept in London and reproduced in F. Cali, *L'Ordre flamboyant* (Grenoble: Arthaud, 1967), p. 87.
193. For example, room 32 of the Barcelona Museum of Fine Arts. Concerning cruelty, see the last part of chap. 5 in this book.
194. F. Cali, *L'Ordre flamboyant*, pp. 104–105.
195. *Le Doctrinal* (1604 ed.), p. 45.

CHAPTER 8

1. B. Spina, *Quaestio de strigibus et lamiis* (Venice: 1523), p. 9. This book was often printed together with the *Malleus maleficarum*, as for example in the Lyon, 1669, Bourgeat ed. of the *Malleus*.
2. Malebranche, *Recherche de la verité*, 2 vols., in *Oeuvres complètes*, ed. by G. Rodis-Lewis (Paris: Vrin, 1963), IV, IX, section 3: II, p. 104. See also V, III, pp. 142–157. I would like to thank Jean Mellot for having drawn my attention to the syllogism of Malebranche.
3. See A. Rannou, "George Wither critique et témoin de son temps," Thèse D'Etat dissertation, University of Paris IV, 1981, p. 485.
4. L. Tronson, *Manuel du séminariste*, in *Oeuvres complètes*, 2 vols, ed. by J.-P. Migne (Paris: 1857), vol. 1, pp. 44–45.
5. S. Vigor, *Sermons catholiques sur les dimanches et fêtes* (1597), p. 28. Vigor was the archbishop of Narbonne and the king's preacher. The sermon in question was composed sometime around 1597 (third Sunday after Easter). He refers to Tertullian, *Contra Marcionem*, 1, II.
6. J. Basnage, *Histoire de l'Eglise*, 2 vols. (Amsterdam: 1699), vol. 1, chap. 1 ("Dessein de cet ouvrage" ["Outline of this book"]).
7. Hildegarde of Bingen, *Causae et curae*, ed. by Kaiser (Leipzig: 1903), p. 143, quoted in Starobinski, *Histoire de la mélancolie*, p. 35.
8. Burton, *Anatomy of Melancholy*, vol. 1, pp. 130–131.
9. R. Mentet de Salmonet, *Histoire des troubles en Grande-Bretagne*, Paris, 1661, ed. consulted, foreword, quoted in R. Mousnier, *Fureurs paysannes* (Paris: Calman-Lévy, 1967), pp. 307–308.
10. *Sermons de saint Vincent-de-Paul, de ses coopérateurs et successeurs immédiats pour les missions des campagnes*, 2 vols., ed. by Jeanmaire (Paris: 1859), vol. 2, pp. 86–87. Hereafter the notes referring to this edition will begin with "Jeanmaire."
11. The literature on original sin is enormous. I have used esp. N. P. Williams, *The Ideas of the Fall and Original Sin* (1929); J.B. Kors, *La Justice primitive et le péché originel d'après saint Thomas* (Paris: Vrin, 1930); A. Gaudel's article on original sin in the *Dictionnaire de Théologie Catholique*, vol. 12 (1933); A. M. Dubarle, *Le Péché originel dans l'Ecriture* (Paris: Cerf, 1958) and by the same author "Le péché originel: recherches récentes et orientations nouvelles," *Revue des Sciences philosophiques et théologiques* 53 (1969): 81–114; *Théologie du péché* (Paris: Desclée, 1960); P. Ricoeur, *Finitude et culpabilité*, 2 vols. (Paris: Aubier, 1960), vol. 1: *L'Homme faillible*, vol. 2: *La Symbolique du mal*; P. Schoonenberg, *L'Homme et le péché* (Tours: Mame, 1967); H. Rondet, *Le Péché originel dans la tradition patristique et théologique* (Paris: Fayard, 1967); P. Grelot, *Réflexions sur le problème du péché originel* (Paris: Casterman, 1968); P. Guilly, *La Culpabilité fondamentale. Péché originel et anthropologie moderne* (Gembloux: Duculot, 1975). I would also like to mention *Une introduction à la foi catholique* (the Dutch catechism) (Idoc-France, 1968), pp. 337–348, and T. Rey-Mermet, *Croire*, 3 vols. (Limoges: Droguet-Ardant, 1976–79), vol. 1, pp. 150–158.
12. Rondet, *Le Péché originel*, p. 47.
13. Ibid., pp. 86–87.
14. This is the formula used by Father J. M. Pohier in his article on "*Péché*" (Sin) in the *Encyclopaedia Universalis*, vol. 12, p. 663.

15. Ricoeur, *Le Conflit des interprétations* (Paris: Seuil, 1969), p. 267.
16. *Contra Julianum*, book 4, chap. 5, in *PL*, vol. 44, col. 757.
17. *Opus imperfectum contra Julianum*, book 3, chap. 147, in *PL*, vol. 45, col. 1307.
18. *De Correptione et gratia*, chap. 12, n. 34, in *PL*, vol. 44, cols. 936–937.
19. *Cité de Dieu*, book 14, chaps. 10 and 26, vol. 35 of the Combes ed., pp. 399–401 and 457–459.
20. *De vera religione*, book 1, chap. 20, in *PL*, vol. 34, col. 139. See, concerning the time we must live out as a "hidden wound," H. I. Marrou, *L'Ambivalence du temps de l'histoire chez saint Augustine* (Paris: 1950), pp. 47 and 54.
21. Rondet, *Le Péché originel*, p. 141.
22. *Contra Julianum*, book 3, chap. 21, n. 42, in *PL*, vol. 44, col. 723. See also *De Nuptiis et concupiscentia*, book 1, chap. 25, n. 38, in *PL*, vol. 44, cols. 429–430.
23. *De Nuptiis*, book 2, chap. 5, n. 15, col. 444–445 and *De Peccatorum meritis et remissione*, book 3, chap. 7, n. 13, col. 193, both in *PL*, vol. 44.
24. *Contra Julianum*, book 3, chap. 18, n. 35, cols. 720–721, and book 5, chap. 14, cols. 812–813, in *PL*, vol. 44.
25. Augustine, *Letter 217*, 5 (16–17), in the Péronne ed. quoted in H. I. Marrou, *Saint Augustin et l'augustinisme* (Paris: Seuil, 1965).
26. Ibid.
27. The third canon of the Council of Carthage (according to some manuscripts); H. Denziger and C. Bannwart, *Enchiridion symbolorum, definitionum et declarationum de rebus fidei et morum*, 1922 ed., p. 47, n. 3.
28. Luther, *Oeuvres*, vol. 5, p. 235 (*Du Serf arbitre*). I have used the translation done by A. Godin, "Une lecture sélective d'Origène à la Renaissance," *Origeniana, Quaderni di Vetera christianorum* 12 (1975): 87, n. 15.
29. R. Bellarmin, *De Amissione gratiae et statu peccati*, book 5, chap. 5, Vivès ed. (Paris: 1870–74), vol. 5, p. 401.
30. The translation of the *Augsburg Confession* in G. Casalis, *Luther et l'Eglise confessante* (Paris: Seuil, 1962), p. 141, and in P. Jundt, *La Confession d'Augsbourg* (Paris: Centurion and Labor et Fides, 1979).
31. Fifth session: "Decree on the original sin" (June 17, 1546); sixth session: "Decree on justification" (January 13, 1547. See G. Alberico, ed., *Conciliorum . . . decreta*, pp. 665–667 and 671–681.
32. See his article on the original sin in the *Dictionnaire philosophique*.
33. L. Réau, *Iconographie de l'art chrétien* (Paris: P.U.F., 1956), vol. 2, 1, pp. 77–93; *Lexikon der christlichen Ikonographie* (Bale: Herder, 1968), vol. 1, pp. 42–70.
34. See Lavalleye, *Lucas Van Leyden*.
35. Concerning this mystery play, which in actual fact is put together from several different and distinct mysteries, see L. Petit de Julleville, *Les Mystères*, 2 vols. (Paris: 1880), vol. 2, pp. 352–378.
36. Mâle, *L'Art religieux de la fin du Moyen Age*, pp. 379–380.
37. E. Duncan, *Milton's Earthly Paradise: A Historical Study of Eden* (Minneapolis: University of Minnesota Press, 1972), p. 100.
38. Pascal, *Pensées*, no. 445 in the L. Brunschvicg ed.
39. After the publication of his *Provinciales*, there follows brochure after brochure.
40. This is the expression of J. Carreyre, "A. Arnauld," in *Dictionnaire de spiritualité*, vol. 1, p. 882.
41. Quoted from *Catéchisme du diocèse de Bayeux* (1700), pp. xxvii–xxviii (third lesson).
42. J. Benesse and M. Darrieu, "Noëls français du XVIe siècle," in *La Mort des pays de Cocagne*, ed. by J. Delumeau, pp. 62–63, Christmas no. 6 of Lucas Le Moigne.
43. Ibid., Christmas no. 5.
44. Ibid.
45. Above all in *La Religion dans les limites de la Raison*, ed. by L. Gibelin (1952), pp. 50–60.
46. S. Freud, *Totem et tabou* (Paris: Payot, 1976), pp. 162–165.
47. T. Reik, *Mythe et culpabilité. Crime et châtiment de l'humanité* (Paris: P.U.F., 1979), p. 166.
48. Saint Bonaventure, *Breviloquium*, Latin text of Quaracchi, French translation (Paris: éd. franciscaines, 1967), vol. 3, p. 75.
49. Quoted in P. de Meester, *Où va l'Eglise d'Afrique* (Paris: Cerf, 1980), pp. 83–84. It is possible that this myth was influenced by Christianity, but it does not lead to redemption.

50. R. Martin, "Les idées de Robert de Melin sur le péché originel," *Revue des Sciences philosophiques et théologiques* 9 (1920): p. 115.
51. Pascal, *Pensées*, number 246 (p. 170).
52. Vincent de Paul, *Entretiens spirituels aux missionnaires*, ed. by A. Dodin (Paris: Seuil, 1960), p. 129.
53. Concerning Bayle, see the remarkable work of E. Labrousse, *Pierre Bayle*, vol. 1: *Du Pays de Foix à la cité d'Erasme*, vol. 2: *Hétérodoxie et rigorisme* (The Hague: M. Nijhoff, 1964), in particular vol. 2, pp. 346–387. See also J.-P. Jossua, *Pierre Bayle ou l'obsession du mal* (Paris: Aubier, 1977), and by the same author, *Discours chrétiens et scandale du mal* (Paris: Chalet, 1979).
54. *Réponses aux questions d'un provincial*, part 2, chap. 81, in *Oeuvres diverses* (The Hague: 1731), vol. 3, p. 663, quoted in Jossua, *Discours*, p. 18.
55. Jossua, *Pierre Bayle*, p. 167; Labrousse, *P. Bayle*, vol. 1, p. 269.
56. Bayle, *Dictionnaire historique et critique*, article on Diogène, Rem. N.; article on Manichéens, Rem. N.
57. Pascal, *Pensées*, no. 246 (pp. 170–171)
58. Bossuet, *Sermon sur la profession de Mme de la Vallière*, in *Oeuvres complètes* (Rennes: éd. des Prêtres . . . de Saint Dizier, 1863), vol. 3, p. 85.
59. Bayle, *Oeuvres diverses*, vol. 3, answer to the question of a "Provincial" 2, section CXLIX, p. 807 b, quoted in Labrousse, *Pierre Bayle*, vol. 2: *Hétérodoxie et rigorisme*, p. 386.
60. Ibid., vol. 2, section LXXV, p. 654 b, quoted in Labrousse, vol. 2, p. 369.
61. J. Nabert, *Essai sur le mal*, reprint ed. (Paris: Aubier, 1970), pp. 56–57. I would like to deeply thank the daughter of Jean Nabert for this reference. See also M. Adam, "Le Sentiment du péché," Dissertation, Paris, 1967, p. 127.
62. A. de Montazet, *Instruction pastorale . . . sur les sources de l'incrédulité et les fondements de la religion* (1776), p. 136; B. Groethuysen, *Origines de l'esprit bourgeois* (Paris: Gallimard, 1956), p. 136. Montpazet, archbishop of Lyon, was favorable to the Jansenists.
63. J. J. du Guet, *Explication du livre de la Genése* (1732), vol. 1, p. 382; Groethuysen, *Origines de l'esprit bourgeois*, Du Guet was a friend of Antoine Arnauld.
64. G. Martelet, *Vivre aujoud'hui la foi de toujours: relecture du credo* (Paris: Cerf, 1977), p. 19. Text of the speeches held at Notre-Dame (Paris).
65. Milton, *Le Paradis perdu* [Paradise Lost], book 10, lines 272–273.
66. Ibid., book 10, lines 651–656.
67. Ibid., book 10, lines 661–666.
68. Ibid., book 10, lines 824–833.
69. R. Simon, *Histoire critique du vieux Testament* (Amsterdam: 1685), p. 376.
70. Rey-Mermet, *Croire*, vol. 1, p. 156. I would like to thank Jean Deloffre for the note he sent me to explain the two meanings of the word "adam."
71. Reik, *Mythe et culpabilité*, p. 144.
72. Irenaeus of Lyon, *Adversus haereses*, IV, 38, 1, ed. and trans. by A. Rousseau (Paris: Cerf, 1965), vol. 2, pp. 946–947. Also quoted in H. Rondet, *Le Péché originel*, p. 52.
73. Ibid., IV, 40, 3, ed. by A. Rousseau, vol. 2, p. 981.
74. Rondet, *Le Péché originel*, p. 49.
75. The most recent large-scale study of Irenaeus of Lyon is that of H. Lassiat, *Création, liberté, incorruptibilité. Insertion du thème anthropologique de la jeune tradition romaine dans l'oeuvre d'Irénée de Lyon*, 2 vols. (reproduction des thèses de Lille III: 1972), vol. 2, pp. 487–538.
76. Rondet, *Le Péché originel*, pp. 259–261; *DTC*, vol. 8, cols. 2615–2616, "La Peyrère"; ibid., vol. 12, cols. 2793–2796, "Préadamites"; Haag, *La France protestante*, vol. 6, p. 305–307, "La Peyrère"; R. Pintard, *Le Libertinage érudit* (Paris: 1943), p. 362.
77. Pascal, *Pensées*, no. 14 (pp. 110–111).
78. Milton, *Le Paradis perdu* [Paradise Lost], book 4, lines 130–358.
79. Concerning the glorious state of Adam before the fall, according to Augustine, see esp. *De Genesi ad litteram*, VI, XXIV–XXVII, 35–38, in *PL*, vol. 34, cols. 353–355; ibid., IX, X–XI, 18–19, in *PL*, vol. 34, cols. 399–400; ibid., XI, I, 3, in *PL*, vol. 34, col. 430; *De Nuptiis et concupiscentia*, II, XIII, 26, and II, XIV, 29, in *PL*, vol. 44, cols. 451, 453, 458, 467–469; *De Peccatorum meritis et remissione*, I, XVI, 21, in *PL*, vol. 44, cols. 120–121; *Contra Julianum*, IV, V, 35, in *PL*, vol. 44, cols. 756–757; *Opus imperfectum*, V, 16–17, in *PL*, vol. 45, cols. 1449–1451; *De Peccato originali*, XXXV, 40, in *PL*, vol. 44, col. 405; *De Civitate Dei*, XIV, XXIII–XXIV, 1, in *PL*, vol. 41, cols. 430–432.

80. Formulation used by P.A.M. Dubarle in his article on original sin in *Encyclopaedia Universalis*, vol. 12, p. 667.
81. For this discussion of earthly paradise I relied heavily on J. E. Duncan, *Milton's Earthly Paradise*, esp. pp. 25–100.
82. Joinville, *Histoire de Saint Louis*, in *Historiens et chroniqueurs du Moyen Age* (Paris: Pléiade, 1952), pp. 247–248, quoted in J. Le Goff, *La Civilisation de l'Occident médiéval*, p. 177.
83. St. Thomas Aquinus, *Summa Theological*, part I quest. 102, art. 1 (vol. 4, p. 365).
84. Ibid., art. 2(vol. 4, p. 366).
85. Ibid., p. 369.
86. *Mandeville's Travels*, ed. by P. Hamelius, 2 vols. (London: 1919–23), vol. 1, pp. 200–204.
87. Dante Alighieri, *Purgatorio*, trans. by A. Mandelbaum (Berkeley: University of California Press, 1980).
88. J. Lydgate, *The Minor Poems*, ed. by H. N. MacCracken (London: Early English Text Society, no. 192, 1934), pp. 641–643.
89. See B. Penrose, *Travel and Discovery in the Renaissance, 1420–1620* (Cambridge: Harvard University Press, 1952), pp. 10–12.
90. See above, pp. 141–143 of French original.
91. A. Williams, *The Common Expositor: an account of the Commentaries on Genesis, 1527–1633* (Chapel Hill: 1948), pp. 3–19; J. E. Duncan, *Milton's*, p. 91.
92. Duncan, *Milton's*, p. 50.
93. Ibid., pp. 95–96.
94. Concerning Antoinette Bourignon, see L. Kolakowski, *Chrétiens sans Englise* (Paris: Gallimard, 1969), pp. 640–718.
95. P. Poiret, *Vie continuée de Mlle Bourignon*, in *Oeuvres de Mlle Bourignon* (Amsterdam: 1679–86), vol. 2, pp. 315–316. This passage was also used by Bayle in the article on Adam in his *Dictionnaire*, vol. 1, p. 203, in the 1820 ed.
96. *Le Figaro*, 15 March 1972.
97. This is in the *Petit Catéchisme* of Bayeux (1700), p. xxix.
98. P. Teilhard de Chardin, *Oeuvres*, vol. 10: *Comment je crois* (Paris: Seuil, 1969), pp. 62–63 (written before Easter 1922).
99. *Cité de Dieu*, XIII, chap. 14 (vol. 35, p. 285, in the Combès ed.).
100. *L'Imitation*, book 3, chap. 52 (Paris: Seuil, 1961), pp. 183–184.
101. Luther, *Oeuvres*, vol. 1, p. 52 (*The seven psalms of penitence*).
102. Bucer, *Résumé sommaire*, p. 45.
103. Pascal, *Pensées*, no. 506 in the Brunschvicg ed.
104. *Pensées* ("Le Mystère de Jésus"), no. 553.
105. Jeanmaire, *Sermons*, vol. 1, p. 389.
106. Ibid., vol. 1, p. 214.
107. *Retractationum libri duo*, book 1, chap. 15, in *PL*, vol. 32, col. 609. See also *Contra Julianum*, book 4, chap. 6, n. 49, in *PL*, vol. 44, cols. 850–851. Important points concerning the culpability of "religious ignorance" in P. Sellier, *Pascal et saint Augustin* (Paris: A. Colin, 1970), pp. 265–268.
108. Pascal, *Provinciales* (Paris: Garnier and Pléiade, 1950), pp. 471–472.
109. Saint Augustine, *De Gratia et libero arbitrio*, chap. 3, 5, in *PL* vol. 44, col. 885, quoted in Sellier, *Pascal*, p. 267.
110. A. Dodin, *Entretiens spirituels aux missionnaires* (of Vincent de Paul) (Paris: Seuil, 1960), p. 347.
111. Ibid.
112. Ibid., pp. 496–497.
113. Quoted in M. Venard, "Le Catéchisme au temps des Réformes," *Les Quatre fleuves* 11 (1980): 43.
114. Quoted in ibid., p. 45. H. M. Boudon, *La Science sacrée du catéchisme* (1749 ed.), p. 29. Concerning him, see J.-C. Dhotel, *Les Origines du catéchisme moderne* (Paris: Aubier, 1967), esp. pp. 156–159.
115. Nabert, *Essai sur le mal*, pp. 70–72.
116. Ricoeur, *Le Conflit*, p. 278.
117. Concerning this point, see the illuminating remarks of H. I. Marrou, *Saint Augustin et l'augustinisme* (Paris: Seuil, 1955), pp. 149–180.
118. Quoted in ibid., p. 154.

119. *Epist. ad Bernardum abbatem*, in *Opera s. Bernardi*, epistle 221, no. 13, in *PL*, vol. 182, col. 405.
120. Quoted in Marrou, *Saint Augustin*, p. 154; Gottschalk, *Oeuvres théologiques et gramaticales*, ed. by D. C. Lambot (Louvain: Spicilegium sacrum Lovaniense, 1945), p. 327.
121. Expression used by Marrou, *Saint Augustin et l'augustinisme*, p. 160.
122. Concerning this topic, see G. Leff, *Bradwardine and the Pelagians* (Cambridge: 1957); H. A. Oberman, *Archbishop Thomas Bradwardine, a Fourteenth Century Augustinian* (Utrecht: 1958).
123. See C. Béné, *Erasme et saint Augustin ou l'influence de saint Augustin sur l'humanisme d'Erasme* (Geneva: Droz, 1969), esp. pp. 136–147.
124. Ibid.
125. G. Marc 'Hadour, *Thomas Moore et la Bible. La place des livres saints dans son apologétique et sa spiritualité* (Paris: Vrin, 1969), p. 537.
126. Concerning these editions and the influence exercised by Augustine, see the article "Augustinisme" in *DTC*, vol. 1, col. 2398–2554.
127. W. Marceau, *L'Optimisme dans l'oeuvre de saint François de Sales* (Paris: Lethielleux, 1973), p. 96.
128. M. Luther, *Werke* (Weimar, 1883–), vol. 3, p. 181. Concerning Luther's augustinianism, see esp. A. V. Müller, *Luthers Werdegang bis zum Turmerlebnis* (Gotha: 1920); P. Vignaux, *Luther commentateur des "Sentences"* (1935), pp. 6–30; L. Cristiani, "Luther et saint Augustin," in *Augustinus magister* (Paris: 1954), vol. 2, pp. 1029 passim; M. Bendiscioli, "L'Agostinismo dei riformatori protestanti," *Revue des études augustiniennes*, 1 (1955): 203 passim; P. Courcelle, "Luther interprète des *Confessions* de saint Augustin," *Revue d'Historie et de philosophie religieuse* 3 (1959): 235–251.
129. Luther, *Werke*, vol. 9, p. 29.
130. Luther, *Oeuvres*, vol. 5, p. 57 (*Du Serf arbitre*).
131. Luther, *Werke*, vol. 4, p. 380.
132. Ibid., vol. 5, p. 664.
133. Calvin, *Opera omnia . . . (Corpus Reformatorum)* (Brunswick: 1863–), vol. 9, p. 835.
134. L. Smits, *Saint Augustin dans l'oeuvre de Jean Calvin*, 2 vols. (Assen: 1957–58). See also J. Cadier, "Calvin et Saint Augustin," in *Augustinus magister* (Paris: 1954), vol. 2, pp. 1039 passim.
135. C. Jansénius, *Augustinus* (1643 ed.), vol. 2, chap. 18, p. 17.
136. Ibid., p. 14.
137. Ibid., p. 17.
138. Ibid., p. 98.
139. Bossuet, *Défense de la tradition et des saints Pères*, vol. 6 of the *Oeuvres complètes* (Rennes: 1862 ed.), p. 442.
140. La Bruyère, *Les Caractères*, ed. by A. Destailleur, 2 vols. (Paris: 1854), vol. 2, pp. 264–265 (chapter on "Des esprits forts"). This significant passage is quoted in Marrou, *Saint Augustin*, p. 169.
141. Pascal, *Opuscules*, "De l'Esprit géométrique," p. 383 in the Pléiade edition.
142. *Objections contre M. Descartes*, vol. 28, p. 9 of the *Oeuvres* of A. Arnauld (Paris: 1775–82).
143. A. Harnack, *Lehrbuch der Dogmengeschichte*, 3rd ed. in 3 vols. (Freiburg: 1894–97), vol. 3, p. 95.
144. A. Harnack, *L'Essence du christianisme* (Paris: 1907), p. 311.
145. J. and P. Courcelle, *Iconographie de Saint Augustin* (Paris: public. des études augustiniennes, 1965–), vol. 1: *Les Cycles du XIVe siècle* (1965), quotation from p. 14; vol. 2: *Les Cycles du XVe siècle* (1969); vol. 3: *Les Cycles du XVIe et XVIIe siècles* (1972); vol. 4, part 1: *Les Cycles du XVIIIe siècle: L'Allemagne* (1981).
146. See P. Christianson, *Reformers and Babylon. English Apocalyptic Views from the Reformation to the Eve of the Civil War* (Toronto: University of Toronto Press, 1978), p. 15.
147. M. Bataillon, *Erasme et l'Espagne* (Geneva: 1937), p. 555.
148. C. Ginzburg, "Folklore, magia, religione," in *Storia d'Italia* (Turin: Einaudi, 1972), vol. 1, pp. 635–642. Concerning the interest for religious books in Italy during the fifteenth century, see A. J. Schutte, "Printing, Piety and the People in Italy: the first thirty years," *Archiv für Reformationsgeschichte* 71 (1980): 5–19.
149. Quoted in B. Neveu, "Juge suprême et docteur infaillible: le pontificat romain de la bulle *In Eminenti* (1643) à la bulle *Auctorem Dei* (1794)," in *Mélanges de l'ecole française de Rome* (M.A.T.M.) 1 (1981): 239. Neveu's article gives examples of other such texts.

150. Denzinger, *Enchiridion*, no. 1320, p. 366.
151. This section of the book had already been written when the remarkable volume 2 of the *Histoire générale de l'enseignement et de l'education en France* (Paris: Nouvelle Librairie de France, 1981) appeared. The authors, F. Lebrun, M. Venard, and J. Quéniart, have come to conclusions that are quite similar to the ones here; see in particular their conclusion, pp. 601–606.
152. Institoris and Sprenger, *Le Marteau*, pp. 207–208. See Delumeau, *La Peur*, pp. 305–340.
153. I am using here the classical works of P. Ariès, *L'Enfant et la vie familiale sous l'Ancien Régime*, 2nd ed. (Paris: Seuil, 1973); G. Snyders, *La Pédagogie en France aux XVIIe et XVIIIe siècles* (Paris: P.U.F., 1965); ibid., *Il n'est pas facile d'aimer*, 2nd ed. (Paris: P.U.F., 1982), esp. pp. 64–75; R. Chartier, M.-M. Compère, and D. Julia, *L'Education en France du XVIe au XVIIIe siècle* (Paris: S.E.D.E.S., 1976). These four books contain the necessary bibliography for this subject. See also the chapter "L'Enfant et l'instruction" in my own *Civilisation de la Renaissance*, pp. 403–420.
154. *Anthologie ou conférences des proverbes* (15th cent.), quoted in Le Roux de Lincy, *Le Livre des proverbes*, vol. 1, p. 217.
155. G. Meurier, *Trésor des sentences* (16th cent.), quoted in ibid.
156. *Proverbes communs* (Lyon: 1539), quoted in ibid., p. 218.
157. *Proverbes gallicans* (15th cent.), quoted in ibid., p. 217.
158. Meurier, *Trésor*, quoted in ibid., p. 216.
159. *Anciens proverbes* (13th cent.), quoted in ibid., p. 216.
160. *Proverbes communs*, no. 732. I would like to thank Daniel Riviére for having found this proverb for me.
162. Montaigne, *Essais*, I, chap. 14, vol. 1, p. 90.
163. La Fontaine, *Fables*, ed. by J. P. Collinet, 2 vols. (Paris: Gallimard, 1974), "Les deux pigeons," vol. 1, p. 55.
164. La Bruyère, *Les Caractères*, ed. by A. Destailleur, vol. 2, p. 62 ("De l'homme).
165. Descartes, *Méditations et réponses* (1641, French trans. 1644), "Quatrièmes réponses: de Dieu" (Paris: Garnier, 1979 ed.), p. 333.
166. Ibid., "Quatrième réponses: de la nature de l'esprit humain," p. 319.
167. *Conversations avec Burman sur la Première Méditation*, in Descartes, *Oeuvres et lettres* (Paris: Pléiade, 1953), p. 1360.
168. P. A. Sigal, "Les Miracles de sainte Hélène à l'abbaye d'Hautevillers au Moyen Age et à l'époque moderne," *Actes du 97e congrès des sociétés savantes* (1972): 499–513. See also R. Finucane, *Miracles and Pilgrims. Popular Beliefs in the Medieval Church* (London: Dent, 1977), pp. 109–110.
169. S. Janssen-Peigné, "Les Miracles de sainte Anne d'Auray," in *La Mort des Pays de cocagne*, ed. by Delumeau, p. 175, and J. Delumeau, *Un Chemin d'histoire*, p. 199. However, only 17 percent children in three "sacred places" between Picardy and Burgundy in the seventeenth century: H. Barbin and J.-P. Duteil, "Miracle et pèlerinage au XVIIe siècle," *Revue d'Histoire de l'Eglise de France* 167 (July–December 1975): 246–256.
170. Mme. de Sévigné, *Lettres, 1646–1696*, Les Grands Ecrivains de France, vol. 3, p. 79 (20 May 1672).
171. The book of C. Fouquet and Y. Knibiehler, *L'Histoire des mères* (Paris: Montalba, 1980), esp. pp. 12–13, goes in the same direction by evoking stories of miracles. Same idea followed by Favre, *La Mort au siècle des Lumières*, p. 126.
172. Reproduced in my *Civilisation de la Renaissance*, illustration 150, pp. 412–413.
173. Aristote, *Ethique à Nicomaque* [*Nicomachean Ethics*], ed. by J. Voilquin (Paris: Garnier, n.d.), 1, chap. 9, 10, p. 33. See also 3, chap. 12, p. 141, and 5, chap. 6, pp. 225–227.
174. Fortin de la Hoguette, *Testament ou conseils fidèles d'un bon père à ses enfants* (1648), part 3, chap. 3, p. 394. In the following discussion I used several quotations taken from G. Snyders, *La Pédagogie*.
175. A. N. (MM. 474). *Reglements du séminaire paroissial de Saint Nicolas-du-Chardonnet*, p. 225.
176. Saint Augustine, *Confessions*, 13, chap 12, in *PL*, vol. 32, col. 670.
177. St. Augustine, *Confessions*, trans. by E. B. Pusey (New York: 1961), book 1, chap. 7, p. 15.
178. St. Augustine, *The City of God*, trans. by H. Bettenson (Harmondsworth: Penguin, 1972), book 22, chap. 22, p. 1065.
179. Snyders, *La Pédagogie*, pp. 181–182.
180. Bossuet, *Elévations sur les mystères*, 7th week, 3rd elevation, in *Oeuvres* (Rennes: 1863), vol. 9, p. 53.

181. Ibid., 4th elevation, p. 54.
182. François de Sales, *Sermon pour le jour de la nativité de Notre-Dame*, vol. 4 of the *Sermons* (Paris: 1833), p. 504.
183. Bérulle, *Oeuvres de piété*, no. 47, in *Oeuvres complètes* (1644 ed.), p. 839.
184. Ibid., no. 48, p. 846.
185. C. de Condren, *Discours et lettres* (1648 ed.), p. 312.
186. N. Fontaine, *Mémoires pour servir à l'histoire de Port-Royal*, 2 vols. (1736), vol. 1, p. 195.
187. C. de Sainte-Marthe, *Lettres sur divers sujets de piété et de morale* (1709), vol. 1, letter no. 44, pp. 390–391.
188. C. Lancelot, *Mémoires touchant la vie de M. de Saint-Cyran* (1738; reprint ed.: Geneva, Slatkine reprints, 1968), vol. 2, p. 334 (and all of chapter 40).
189. P. Coustel, *Les Règles de l'éducation des enfants* (1710) vol. 1, chaps. 7, 8 and 9, pp. 175–182.
190. P. de Jouvency, *Christianis litterarum magistris, de ratione discendi et docendi* (1693), trans. by H. Ferté (1892), part 3, chap. 3, art. 3, p. 136.
191. J. Pascal, *Règlement des enfants. Constitutions de Port-Royal* (1665), chap. 16, "De l'Instruction des petites filles," in *Lettres, opuscules et mémoires de Mme Périer et de Jacqueline, soeurs de Pascal*, ed. by M. P. Faugère (Paris: 1845), p. 102.
192. C. Lancelot, *Mémoires*, vol. 2, p. 334.
193. Ibid.
194. Bérulle, in particular *Oeuvres de piété*, nos. 47 and 48, and quotations from an unpublished manuscript cited by P. Cochois, *Bérulle et l'Ecole française* (Paris: Seuil, 1963), pp. 119–120. See also J. Orcibal, "Les oeuvres de piété de cardinal de Bérulle."
195. Other unpublished material quoted in Cochois.
196. J. Blanlo, *L'Enfance chrétienne* (first ed. 1650; reprint Lethielleux, n.d.), p. 43.
197. J. B. Saint-Jure, *La Vie de M. de Renty*, 2nd ed. (1652), p. 258.
198. St. Augustine, *Confessions*, book 1, chap. 7 p. 15.
199. Calvin, *Institution*, 2, chap. 1, 1, vol. 2, p. 18.
200. Ibid., 4, chap. 16, 7.
201. Ariès, *L'Enfant*, p. 128.
202. Ibid., pp. 127–133.
203. Lancelot, *Mémoires*, vol. 2, p. 332.
204. Pascal, *Reglement pour les enfants*, p. 102.
205. Jacques Gélis kindly presented the results of his research in the course of my seminar. See also his contribution "Le Retour temporaire à la vie des enfants morts à la naissance" to the *Colloque des Chercheurs du C.N.R.S. en Hist. Mod. et Cont.* held in 1979, which was devoted to the subject of *Le Corps, la santé, la maladie* (Body, health, and sickness). His contribution was an attempt to analyze and interpret the phenomenon of "sanctuaire à répit" (sanctuaries of resuscitation). Other work published by the same author: "Les Miracles du bon père Gaschon," *Actes de la journée d'étude de la Societé d'Ethnologie française* (1979); "De la mort à la vie. Les sanctuaires à répit," *Ethnologie française* 11 (1981) 3: 211–224; "Miracles et médecine aux siècles classiques: le corp médical et le retour temporaire à la vie des enfants morts à la naissance," in *Historical Reflexions* (Ontario: University of Waterloo, 1982); and *L'Arbre et le fruit* (Paris: Fayard, 1984). See also J. Corblet, *Histoire dogmatique, liturgique et archéologique du sacrement de baptême*, 2 vols. (Paris: 1882), esp. vol. 1, pp. 160–169; P. Saintyves, "Les Résurrections d'enfants morts-nés et les sanctuaires à répit," *Revue d'Etnographie et de sociologie* 2 (1–2) (1911): 65–74; A. Van Gennep, *Manuel de folklore français contemporain* (Paris: 1943–), vol. 1, part 1, pp. 123–124 (with bibliography); H. Platelle, *Les Chrétiens face au miracle, Lille au XVIIe siècle* (Paris: Cerf, 1968); J. C. Didier, "Un Sanctuaire à répit du diocèse de Langres. L'Eglise de Fayl-Billot, Haute-Marne, d'après les actes notariès du XVIIIe siècle," in *Mélanges de sciences religieuses* (1968), pp. 3–21; R. Sauzet, "Miracles et Contre-Réforme en Bas-Languedoc sous Louis XIV," *Revue d'Histoire de la spiritualité* 48 (1972): 179–192; P. Paravy, "Angoisse collective et miracles au seuil de la mort: résurrections et batêmes d'enfants morts-nés en Dauphiné au XVe siècle," in *La Mort au Moyen Age* (Colloque de la Société des Historiens Médiévistes, 1975) (Strasburg: Istra, 1977), pp. 87–102; M. Bernos, "Réflexions sur un miracle à l'Annonciade d'Aix-en-Provence. Contribution à l'étude des sanctuaires à répit," *Annales du Midi* (January-March 1980): 87–93.
206. P. Nicole, *Essais de morale*, 14 vols. (1725 ed.), vol. 12, p. 144.
207. *Histoire générale de l'enseignement*, vol. 2, pp. 602–603.
208. Gélis, "Miracle et médecine," p. 86.
209. Benedictus XIV, *De Synodo diocesana*, in *Operum editio novissima* (Prato: 1844), chap. 6 of book

7 (vol. 11 in the above-mentioned edition), pp. 204–205. I would like to thank Father W. Witters for this reference.
210. Paravy, "Angoisse," p. 92.
211. Archives of the Haute-Saône, quoted in Saintyves, "Les Résurrections," p. 70.
212. Location studied by Jacques Gélis.
213. Van Gennep, *Manuel*, vol. 1, part 1, p. 124.
214. G. d'Emiliane, *Histoire des tromperies* (Rotterdam: 1963), vol. 1, pp. 17 passim, quoted in Saintyves, "Les Résurrections," p. 72.
215. Bernos, "Réflexions," pp. 5 and 17.
216. Saintyves, "Les Résurrections," pp. 66–70.
217. These are the remarks Father W. Witters made in the course of my seminar of 1980 in response to a talk by Jacques Gélis.
218. Concerning N.-D. de Liesse, see Aubert, *Histoire admirable de Nostre Dame de Liesse* (Troyes: 1602); the Duployé brothers, *Notre-Dame de Liesse: légende et histoire*, 2 vols. (Reims: 1862).
219. G. A. Runnals, *Le Miracle de l'enfant ressuscité* (Geneva: Droz, 1972), pp. XLIV-XLIX.
220. See J.-C. Schmitt, *Le Saint lévrier. Guinefort guérisseur d'enfants depuis le XIIIe siècle* (Paris: Flammarion,), pp. 192–193 concerning the immersion of sick children in the Chalaronne.
221. Book 19, chap. 5 of the *Decree* of Burkhart of Worms, in *PL*, vol. 140, cols. 974–975. This information is from Father W. Witters.
222. Delumeau, *La Peur*, pp. 75–87.
223. Thomas, *Religion*, p. 56.
224. Concerning this subject, see the texts of statutes of various French synods quoted in J. B. Thiers, *Traité des superstitions* (1741 ed.), vol. 2, p. 58–65.
225. *Rituel du diocèse de Blois* (1730 ed.), p. 14.
226. Corblet, *Histoire du baptême*, vol. 1, p. 167.
227. C. A. de Sales, *Histoire du bienheureux François de Sales* (Paris: 1870), vol. 1, p. 202 quoted in Saintyves, "Les Résurrections," p. 68.
228. Anecdote told by J. Gélis, "Miracle et médecine," p. 99, and taken by him from A. Lamb, *Uber den Aberglauben in Elssas* (Strasburg: 1880).
229. P. H. Stahl, "L'organisation magique du territoire villageois roumain," *L'Homme* (July–September 1973): 160.
230. Quoted in Thiers, *Traité des superstitions*, vol. 2, p. 64. The Latin edition is quoted by A. Artonne, *Répertoire des statuts synodaux de l'ancienne France* (Paris: 1963), p. 436.
231. Thomas, *Religion*, pp. 36–38. The author of this book mentions also baptisms of cats, dogs, lamb, and horses.
232. This inquiry, the results of which are not published, at least to my knowledge, were presented in my seminar at the University of São Paolo (1976). Seventy percent of the people who answered the questionnaire stated that baptism protected children from sickness and accidents.
233. Thomas, *Religion*, p. 56.
234. R.A. de Vertot, *Histoire des révolutions de Suède*, 2 vols. (1695), vol. 1, p. 108.
235. C. Drelincourt, *Les Visites charitables ou les consolations chrétiennes pour toutes sortes de personnes affligées* (Geneva: 1669), part 4, pp. 260 passim, quoted in Bernos, "Réflexions," p. 8.
236. R. Sauzet, "La Religion populaire bas-languedocienne au XVIIe siècle. Entre la Réforme et la Contre-Réforme," in *La Religion populaire* (Paris: C.N.R.S., 1979), p. 107, n. 21.
237. Talk by Miss Lallart in my seminar at the University of Paris I (1972).
238. Fulgentius of Ruspe, *De Veritate praedestinationis*, book 1, chap. 12, 27, in *PL*, vol. 65, col. 616–617.
239. I follow the example of M. Bernos and P. Paravy in referring to Gerson, *Opera* (Antwerp ed.), vol. 3, *Sermo in Nativitate Mariae*, p. 1350, and for T. Cajétan, *Commentaires sur la Somme*, part 3, quest. 68, arts. 1 and 2. See Pallavicino, *Histoire du Concile de Trente*, book 9, chap. 8, which is p. 348 in the Migne ed.
240. Isidore de Séville, 1. *I. Sentent.*, chap. 22, in *PL*, vol. 83, col. 588.
241. The French editions of the *Augustinus* included, as an appendix, the severe treatise of the Franciscan monk Florent Conry, known as Conrius, who rejected the existence of a limbo and thus relegated unbaptized children to hell.
242. H. Noris, *Vindiciae Augustinianae* chap. 3, section 5 (Verona: 1729), vol. 1, p. 981.
243. Saint Anselme, *Liber de conceptu virginali*, chap. 27, in *PL*, vol. 158, col. 460–461.
244. Grégoire de Rimini [Gregory of Rimini], *Lectura in II Sentent.*, dist. 33, quest. 3.
245. Denziger, *Enchiridion*, no. 464.

246. *Conciliorum . . . decreta*, ed. by J. Albergio, 5th session, c. 4, p. 666.
247. This is the opinion of Paravy, "Angoisse collective," p. 89.
248. Dante, *Purgatoire*, canto 22, line 13.
249. Dante Alighieri, *Inferno*, trans. A. Mandelbaum (Berkeley: University of California Press, 1980), canto 4, lines 25–30, p. 31.
250. *DTC*, article "*Limbes*" (Limbo), vol. 9, cols. 760–772. See also articles "*Baptême*" (Baptism), vol. 2, cols. 364–378; "*Dam*" (Damnation), vol. 4, cols. 6–27; and "*Sein d'Abraham*" (Bosom of Abraham), vol. 1, cols. 111–116.
251. *Doctrinal de sapience, revu et corrigé* (Troyes: 1604), p. 105.
252. Quoted in Paravy, "Angoisse collective," pp. 89–90. See *Les Rameaux. Mystère du XVIe siècle en dialecte embrunais*, ed. by L. Royer (Gap: 1928), pp. 84–86; J. Cocheyras, *Le Théâtre religieux en Dauphiné du Moyen Age au XVIIe siècle* (Geneva: Droz), pp. 75–77.
253. I have heard this said by several priests of the Ille-et-Vilaine and of the Côtes du Nord. One of them told me in 1945 that he had a brother sixteen years younger than himself who was baptized only eight days after birth. His mother made it a point not to kiss the child until it was baptized. Similar reports may also be gathered in the Ardèche region.
254. *Rituel de Toul* (1760 ed.), p. 25.
255. The italics are mine.
256. *Rituel romain à l'usage du diocèse de Bordeaux* (first ed., 1624; slightly modified ed. in 1728, and reprint in 1829), p. 6.
257. Ibid., pp. 76–77.
258. M. Collet, *Abrégé du Dictionnaire des cas de conscience*, 2 vols. (1764), vol. 1, pp. 128–129. This example is quoted in Knibiehler and Fouquet, *L'Histoire des mères*, pp. 82–83.
259. Ibid.
260. *Rituel de Blois* (1730), p. 14.
261. Ibid., p. 15.
262. M. C. Phan, "Les déclarations de grossesse en France (XVIe–XVIIIe siècle). Essai institutionnel," *Revue d'Histoire moderne et contemporaine* (1975); ibid., "Les Amours illégitimes à Carcassone, 1676–1786; d'après les déclarations de grossesse et les procédures criminelles," (third-cycle diss., University of Paris I, 1979).
263. This edict, issued in February 1556, is published in Isambert, Crusy, and Arnet, *Recueil des anciennes lois françaises*, 28 vols. (Paris: 1827), vol. 23, edict ratified 4 March 1556 by the Paris Parliament. See also *Edit du Roy sur le faict des femmes grosses et des enfans mors-naiz* (1556), Paris, Bibliothèque Nationale, F 46814(2).
264. Knibiehler and Fouquet, *Histoire des mères*, pp. 125–126.
265. Casalis, *Luther et l'Eglise confessante*, p. 141.
266. See Thomas, *Religion*, pp. 55–56 (includes bibliography on the subject).
267. Paravy, "Angoisse collective," p. 97.
268. Bernos, "Réflexions sur un miracle," p. 12.
269. See above, (p. 305 of French original).
270. Platelle, *Les Chrétiens face au miracle*, pp. 26 and 69–70.
271. Bremond, *Histoire littéraire*, vol. 9, esp. pp. 1, 21, and 37 but also, more generally, pp. 1–42.
272. See note 209.
273. Thiers, *Traité . . . sacremens* (1741 ed.), vol. 2, p. 61, and Artonne, *Répertoire*, p. 260.
274. Benedictus XIV, *Operum editio*, vol. XI, pp. 204–205.
275. Ibid.
276. In the text of the archbishop of Langres mentioned in note 273.
277. In the statutes of the synods of Besançon from 1592 to 1656, quoted in Thiers, *Traité . . . sacremens*, vol. 2, pp. 63–64, and Artonne, *Répertoire*, p. 129.
278. Thiers, *Traité . . . sacremens*, vol. 2, p. 61 and Artonne, *Répertoire*, p. 260.
279. Thiers, *Traité . . . sacremens*, vol. 2, pp. 63–64, and Artonne, *Répertoire*, p. 129.
280. Benedictus XIV, *Operum editio*, vol. 11, pp. 204–205.
281. Quoted in J. C. Didier, "Un sanctuaire à répit", p. 3. Diehl, *Inscriptiones latinae christianae veteres*, no. 1512. The inscription is now to be found in the church of Brignoles.
282. Arnauld, *Apologie pour M. l'abbé de Saint-Cyran*, in *Oeuvres complètes* (Lausanne: 1778), vol. 29, p. 263.

CHAPTER 9

1. See below.
2. St. Thomas Aquinas, *Summe*, I, quest. 23, art. 7, pp. 335–336.
3. J. Bona, *Principia vitae christianae*, chap. 49, in *Opera omnia* (Venice: 1764), p. 52.
4. R. Bellarmine, *De Gemitu colombae*, in *Oeuvres* (Vivès ed.), vol. 8, pp. 404–405.
5. Saint Jérôme, "Comm. in Isaiam," in *PL*, vol. 24, col. 294.
6. Salmanticenese, *Cursus theologicus: De praedestinatione*, disp. X, dub. 2, annotations concerning art. 7.
7. I owe this information to my friend and colleague André Caquot, professor of Hebrew and Aramaic at the *Collège de France*.
8. Concerning this point see, "Le premier sermon pour la Toussaint" of Louis of Granada, in *Oeuvres complètes* (Paris: Vivès, 1865), vol. 8, pp. 352–353.
9. *PG*, vol. 60, col. 189 (homily 24).
10. Louis of Granada, "Sermon II pour le 24e dimanche après la Pentecôte," in *Oeuvres*, vol. 6, p. 323.
11. L. Tronson, *Retraite ecclésiastique suivie de méditations* (1823 ed.), p. 262.
12. Commentary of Father A. D. Sertillanges to his translation of the *Somme théologique*, p. 328.
13. *Epist 157 (alias 190) ad optatum*, in *PL*, vol. 33, col. 860, no. 12.
14. St. Augustine, *The City of God*, book 21, chap. 12, p. 989.
15. F. X. Godts, *De Paucitate salvandorum quid docuerunt sancti*? 3rd ed. (Brussels: 1899). This book, whose doctrine seems antiquated today, is nevertheless very useful for its references and quotations. For this reason I have used it very often.
16. *PL*, vol. 76, cols. 1286 and 1290 (homily 38).
17. *Sermo tertio in vigilia nativitatis Dei*, in *PL*, vol.
18. *Sermo X in Septuag.*, in *PL*, vol. 217, col. 357.
19. Saint Bonaventure, *Breviloquium*, part 1, chap. 9, vol. 1, p. 119, in the French translation, éd. franciscaines, 1967.
20. Ludolphe le Chartreux, *La Grande vie de Jésus-Christ*, trans. by M. P. Augustin (Paris: 1865), vol. 3, p. 384.
21. See above p. 228 in the French ed.
22. Saint Antonin, *Summa*, part 1, title 4, chap. 7 (vol. 1, p. 93 in the Venice, 1581, ed.)
23. Abbot Cerveau, *L'Esprit de M. Nicole* (Paris: 1765), pp. 490–491.
24. Vovelle, *Mourir autrefois*, p. 120.
25. See *Sermons de M. de Surian, évêque de Vence . . . Petit carême* (Paris: 1778), pp. 278–279.
26. Saint Vincent de Paul, *Entretiens spirituels*, p. 542.
27. Ibid., p. 103. However, Vincent did not agree with the teaching of the doctrine of "the mass of perdition." See P. Coste, *Saint Vincent de Paul. Correspondance. Entretiens. Documents*, 14 vols. (Paris: 1920–25), vol. 3, pp. 318–336, 362–374; vol. 4, p. 633; and vol. 13, p. 650.
28. L. Grignion de Montfort, *Oeuvres*, p. 229 in the (Paris: Seuil, 1961) ed.
29. Fénelon, *Réfutation de P. Malebranche*, chap. 36, in *Oeuvres* (Paris: 1848), vol. 2, p. 157.
30. T. Rey-Mermet, *Le Saint du siècle des Lumières, Alfonso Liguori* (Paris: Cité Nouvelle, 1982), esp. pp. 433–450.
31. See the various quotations in Father X. Godts, *De Paucitate*, pp. 49–51.
32. Saint Alphonse de Liguori, "Sermon pour le 3e dimanche de l'avent," in *Oeuvres complètes*, 29 vols. (Paris: 1843), vol. 14, p. 43.
33. The book of Father Godts is meant as an attack on the book of Father Castelein (a Jesuit) entitled *Le Rigorisme, le nombre des élus et la doctrine du salut*, which was published in 1898.
34. Father Suarez, *Tractatus de divina praedestinatione et reprobatione*, book 6, chap. 3, "Sitne major numerus praedestinorum an reproborum?" in *Opera omnia*, ed. by L. Vivès (Paris: 1856), vol. 1, pp. 524–552.
35. J.-B. Saint-Jure, *De la conaissance et amour du Fils de Dieu* (1634), book 3, chap. 9, sect. 2. Personally I consulted the Paris, 1666 ed., p. 709. As it turns out, the edition I consulted is the tenth edition of a 935-page folio volume! Concerning this "berullian" Jesuit, see Bremond, *Histoire*, vol. 3, pp. 258–279.
36. Bourdaloue, *Pensées sur divers sujets de religion et de morale*, in *Oeuvres complètes* (Paris: 1830), vol. 14, pp. 110–111.

37. Roughly at the same time, in France, various people (in particular some Jesuits) began to argue in favor of the salvation of virtuous pagans and of a God that was not "a pitiless and barbarous tyrant." See R. Favre, *La Mort au siècle des Lumières* (Lyon: P.U.L., 1978), pp. 99–103.
38. C. J. Perrin, "Sermon sur l'amour de Dieu," in *Collection des orateurs sacrés*, ed. by Migne, vol. 53, col. 1048, quoted in Favre, *La Mort*, p. 100. For the following development I owe much to the book of R. Favre.
39. Ambroise de Lombez, *Traité de la paix intérieure*, 5th ed. (1776), pp. 239–242.
40. Lezay-Marnesia, *Pensées*, in *Plan de lecture pour une jeune dame*, p. 155.
41. Lacordaire, *Conférence de Notre-Dame* (1851), in *Oeuvres complètes* (Brussels: 1854), vol. 4, p. 121.
42. See *Documentation catholique* (2 April 1967), no. 1491. The title of the article was "L'Espérance qui est en nous. Brève présentation de la foi catholique" written by the Secretariat for non-Christians, with a foreword by Cardinal Marella.
43. A. Arnauld, *Seconde apologie de Jansénius*, in *Oeuvres* (Lausanne: 1775–83), vol. 17, p. 331, quoted in Groethuysen, *Origines*, p. 140.
44. *Réponse de M** à l'évêque de** sur cette question: y a-t-il quelque remède aux maux de L'Eglise de France* (1778), quoted in Groethuysen, *Les Origines*, p. 136.
45. A. Arnauld, *Seconde apologie de Jansénius* (vol. 17 of his *Oeuvres*), p. 140, quoted in Groethuysen, *Origines*, p. 135.
46. *Une Introduction à la foi catholique. Le Catéchisme hollandais* (Toulouse: Privat, 1968), p. 345.
47. See Bremond, *Histoire*, esp. vol. 3, pp. 218–219.
48. J.-F. Senault, *L'Homme criminel ou la corruption de la nature par le péché selon les sentiments de saint Augustin* (Paris: 1644), pp. 854–855.
49. Ibid., pp. 855–856.
50. Bérulle, *Oeuvres complètes* (Paris: 1644), p. 762 (*Oeuvres de piété*, XII, 4).
51. Published in Paris by Lethielleux, 1875.
52. L. Lessius, *De Perfectionibus*, book 13, pp. 484–485.
53. Ibid., pp. 485–486.
54. Ibid., pp. 486–487.
55. Ibid., pp. 487–488.
56. Ibid.
57. Ibid., pp. 467–468 and 502–503.
58. Ibid., p. 251.
59. Ibid., p. 488.
60. Ibid., p. 251.
61. Ibid., pp. 488–489.
62. Ibid., p. 494–495.
63. Ibid., p. 380.
64. Ibid., p. 381.
65. *PL*, vol. 38, col. 88 (sermon 9).
66. Text quoted in Lessius, *De Perfectionibus*, p. 389.
67. See above pp. 265–72 (of original).
68. St. Thomas Aquinas *Summa*, II, I quest. 73, art. 1, p. 294.
69. Ibid., p. 298.
70. O. Maillard, *Sermons et poésies* (Paris: A. de la Borderie, 1877), pp. 6–7.
71. See above, p. 256 of French original.
72. Gerson, *L'Oeuvre française* (Glorieux edition), no. 328, p. 371.
73. T. de Bèze, *Chrestiennes méditations* (meditation on psalm 6), p. 54.
74. Bérulle, *Oeuvres*, p. 443 (foreword to *La Vie de Jésus*, XI).
75. Ibid., p. 27 (*Traité des énergumènes*, chap. 7, 2).
76. Ibid., p. 902 (*Oeuvres de piété*, LXXXV, 1).
77. Pascal, *Pensées*, no. 506 in the Brunschvicg ed.
78. J. Pascal, "Règlement pour les enfants de Port-Royal," in *Lettres, opuscules*, p. 285.
79. Bossuet, *Oeuvres complètes* (Rennes: 1862), vol. 1, p. 453.
80. One might mention, among others, the tapestry of Angers, the Flemish Apocalypse of about 1400 kept at the Bibliothèque Nationale, Paris (B.N. néerl. 3), and the one of Dürer, and so on.
81. Luther, Explanation of John 14:16 (1537), in *Werke*, Weimar ed., vol. 45, p. 482, quoted in Strohl, *Luther jusqu'en 1525*, p. 52.

82. Luther, Explanation of I Cor. 15 (1534), in *Werke*, Weimar ed., vol. 36, pp. 553 passim, quoted in ibid., p. 53.
83. Lessius, *De Perfectionibus*, no. 65, p. 381.
84. Meditation IV of the 3rd day, in *Retraite*, pp. 129–131.
85. Bourdaloue, *Carême*, Sermon 22 on "spiritual blindeness," in *Collection des orateurs sacrés*, ed. by Migne, vol. 14, col. 709.
86. This information was given to me by Daniel Rivière.
87. Tauler, "2e sermon pour le saint sacrement," in *Sermons*, vol. 2, p. 93.
88. H. de Maupas du Tour, *La Vie de la vénérable Mère Jeanne Françoise Fremiot de Chantal* (Paris: 1644), p. 443.
89. See M. Bellet, *Le Dieu pervers* (Paris: Desclée de Brouwer, 1979), esp. pp. 168–175.
90. See above, p. 137 of French original.
91. P. Boaistuau, *Le Théâtre du monde* (1572 ed.), dedication, IIb.
92. J. Lejeune, *Sermons*, 12 vols. (Lyon: 1825–26), vol. 11, p. 348 (sermon 323 "De la possession").
93. R. Kural, "Etude de deux manuscrits de convulsionnaires jansénistes du milieu du XVIIIe siècle," (*Memoire de maîtrise*, University of Paris I, 1971), pp. 127–128.
94. H. de Montargon, *Dictionnaire apostolique* (1768), vol. 2, p. 382, quoted in Groethuysen, *Origines*, p. 88.
95. Dominique de Sainte-Catherine, *Le Grand pécheur converti représenté dans les deux estats de la vie de M. de Quériolet, prestre, conseiller au parlement de Rennes* (1677), pp. 358–362.
96. P. Nicole, *Essai de morale*, 14 vols. (1725 ed.), vol. 1, pp. 125–135 (3rd treatise, chap. 5).
97. Tronson, *Retraite* (3rd day, 2nd meditation), pp. 109–110.
98. Bossuet, *Oeuvres* (Rennes: 1862 ed.), vol. 2, p. 448. Sermon pronounced between 1656 and 1658.
99. Bourdaloue, *Mystères*, sermon 4: "Sur la passion de J.C.," in *Collection des orateurs sacrés*, ed. by Migne, vol. 14, cols. 1033–1034.
100. Tronson, *Retraite* (3rd day, 2nd meditation), pp. 111–112.
101. The latter formulation may be found in the *Catéchisme de Bayeux* (1700), p. 143. See also Groethuysen, *Origines*, pp. 67–88.
102. P. Coustel, *Les Règles de l'éducation des enfans*, 2 vols. (Paris: 1687), book 2, chap. 2, section 10, pp. 224–225.
103. *De Quibusdam officiis pietatis scholasticorum* (Angers: 1730). See J. Maillard, *L'Oratoire à Angers au XVIIe et XVIIIe siècles* (Paris: Klincksieck, 1975), p. 155.
104. Jean-Paul II [John Paul II], *Dieu riche en miséricorde* (Paris: Le Cerf, 1980), pp. 22–23. J. Ratzinger, *Foi chrétienne hier et aujourd'hui* (Paris: Mame), p. 197, and Father Varillon, *Joie de croire, joie de vivre* (Paris: Centurion, 1981), pp. 69–79, are in opposition to the traditional view of God the Father as requiring the death of his Son.
105. Tronson, *Examens particuliers sur divers sujets* (1811 ed.), vol. 2, p. 208, quoted in Groethuysen, *Origines*, p. 150.
106. Nicole, *Essais de morale*, vol. 13, pp. 285–288, quoted in Groethuysen, *Origines*, pp. 150–151.
107. C. Urbain and E. Lévesque, *L'Eglise et le théâtre. Bossuet. Maximes et réflexions sur la comédie* (Paris: Grasset, 1930), p. 273.
108. A. de Rancé, *Eclaircissement de quelques difficultés que l'on a formées sur le livre . . . de la Vie monastique* (Paris: 1685), p. 233; Urbain and Lévesque, *L'Eglise et le théâtre*, pp. 258–259.
109. R. Bultmann, *Kerygma und Mythos* (Hamburg: Evangelischer Verlag), vol. 1, p. 42.
110. Y. Pélicier, *Colloque sur la névrose obsessionnelle, suivie de l'intégralité du Traité des scrupules de J.J. Du Guet:* Cahier Vapeur 2 (Paris: Pfizer, 1976). I shall be using this volume farther on, pp. 352 passim.
111. Published by Seuil in 1978. See also P. Solignac, *La Névrose chrétienne* (Paris: éd. de Trevise, 1976), esp. pp. 82–114. The book by A. d'Hesnard, *L'Univers morbide de la faute* (Paris: P.U.F., 1949), now seems too simplistic an approach to the subject.
112. For the following passages, see esp. A. Vergote, *Dette et désir*, in particular pp. 20–22, 64–137, 153–161, and 253–254.
113. S. Freud, *Civilization and Its Discontents*, trans. by J. Strachey (New York: Norton, 1961), p. 73.
114. S. Freud, *Moïse et le monothéisme* [*Moses and Monotheism*] (Paris: Gallimard, 1948), pp. 150–155.
115. Vergote, *Dette et désir*, p. 252. A. Hesnard, *L'Univers*, p. 259: "There are any number of

intermediate states between the extremes constituted on the one hand by the endogenous guilt of normal individuals and, on the other hand, the entirely unreal sense of guilt of the mentally ill."

116. Ibid. (Hesnard), p. 117.
117. Ibid., p. 64.
118. Ibid., p. 97.
119. See H. Ey, P. Bernard, and C. Brisset, *Manuel de psychiatrie*, 5th ed. (Paris: Masson, 1978), pp. 490–505; L'Emperière, A. Féline, et al., *Abrégé de psychiatrie de l'adulte* (Paris: Masson, 1977), pp. 112–115; article "obsession et névrose obsessionnelle" in *Encyclopaedia Universalis*, vol. 11, pp. 1025–1027.
120. Freud, *Civilization and its Discontents*, p. 73.
121. François de Sales, *Traité de l'amour de Dieu*, book 9, chap. 8, in *Oeuvres* (Paris: 1833), vol. 7, p. 144.
122. Vergote, *Dette et désir*, p. 88.
123. See above, p. 275 (of original)
124. Quotation without reference in P. Solignac, *La Névrose chrétienne*, p. 97. The thoughts of Saint Athanasius concerning this are expressed in his *Contra gentes*, in *PG*, vol. 15, cols. 876–879.
125. Grégoire de Nysse [Gregory of Nyssa], *La Création de l'homme*, trans. by J. Laplace (Paris: Le Cerf, 1943), p. 159. See J. Daniélou, *Plantonisme et théologie mystique. Essai sur la doctrine spirituelle de Saint Grégoire de Nysse* (Paris: Aubier, 1944), pp. 50–65.
126. E. Renan, *Souvenirs d'enfance et de jeunesse* (Paris: Calman-Lévy, n.d.), pp. 117–118.
127. J.-J. Olier, *Catéchisme chrétien pour la vie intérieure*, in *Oeuvres complètes* (Paris: Migne, 1856), cols. 472–474.
128. Concerning this subject, see the *Dictionnaire de spiritualité*, fasc. 64–65, cols. 319–395.
129. J.-J. Languet, *La Vie de la vénérable mère Marguerite-Marie* (1729), I used the (Paris: 1860 edition), p. 364.
130. Vergote, *Dette et désir*, p. 156.
131. Ibid., p. 126.
132. G. di Fazio, "Salvatore Ventimiglia e il rinnovamento della catechesi nell'Italia del Settecento," *Orientamenti sociali* 351 (January–April 1981): 88.
133. Vergote, *Dette et désir*, p. 161.
134. Ibid.
135. R. Girard, *Des Choses cachées depuis la fondation du monde* (Paris: Grasset, 1978), esp. p. 263. See also "Quand ces choses commenceront," a discussion with P. Murray in the review *Tel Quel* 78 (Winter 1979): 49.
136. Vergote, *Dette et désir*, pp. 85–86.
137. This is one of the themes of the book by E. H. Erikson, *Luther avant Luther* (Paris: Flammarion, 1968).
138. See G. de Greef, *Les Instincts de défense et de sympathie* (Paris: P.U.F., 1947), p. 40.
139. J. de Maistre, *Les Soirées de Saint-Pétersbourg*, 2 vols. (Paris: 1831), vol. 1, pp. 27 and 49 (1st conversation); J. P. Jossua, *Discours chrétiens et scandale du mal* (Paris: Chalet, 1979), pp. 88–89.
140. Jossua, *Discours*, pp. 132–133.
141. L. Blum, *A l'Echelle humaine*, in *Oeuvre de Léon Blum* (Paris: Gallimard, 1945), vol. 5, p. 412; Hesnard, *L'Univers*, p. 438, n. 1.
142. Ariès, *L'Homme*, pp. 138–140.
143. Vergote, *Dette et désir*, p. 98. See N. Elias, *La Civilisation des moeurs* (Paris: Calman-Levy, 1973); M. Foucault, *Histoire de la sexualité*, vol. 1: *La volonté de savoir* (Paris: Gallimard, 1976), pp. 25–30.
144. This is the subtitle of my previous volume: *La Peur en Occident*.

CHAPTER 10

1. Massilon, "Sermon sur les doutes de la religion," in *Oeuvres*, vol. 1, p. 349. See Groethuysen, *Origines*, p. 74.
2. H. de Montargon, *Dictionnaire apostolique* (1768), vol. 3, pp. 234 passim; Groethuysen, *Origines*, p. 84.

3. Saint-Cyran, *Instructions chrétiennes* (Arnauld d'Andilly, 1678), p. 118; R. Tavenaux, *Jansénisme et politique* (Paris: Armand Colin, 1965), p. 18.
4. Jeanmaire, *Sermons*, vol. 1, p. 224.
5. A. Arnauld, *Apologie pour les religieuses de Port-Royal*, in *Oeuvres*, vol. 23, p. 266; Groethuysen, *Origines*, p. 74.
6. *Imitation*, book 3, chap. 52, pp. 272–273.
7. See above, p. 8 (of original).
8. Ignatius of Loyola, *Scripta de sto Ignation*, vol. 1, p. 379 of the *Monumenta Ignatiana* of the *Monumenta historica societatis Jesu*. See Father Ribadeau-Dumas, *Grandeur et misères des Jésuites* (Paris: 1963), p. 153.
9. Thérèse d'Avila, *Vie*, in *Oeuvres complètes*, ed. by M. M. Polit (Paris: 1907–10), vol. 2, pp. 155 and 117.
10. Vincent de Paul, *Entretiens spirituels*, pp. 774 and 786.
11. Languet, *La Vie de Marguerite-Marie*, pp. 363–364.
12. Klibansky, Saxl, and Panofsky, *Saturn*, p. 80. See also the H. G. Sander's article in *Repertorium für Kunstwissenschaft* 35 (1912): 519 passim.
13. See the article by G. Getto, "Torquato Tasso," in *Letteratura Italiana*, vol. 1: *I Maggiori* (Milan: Marzorati, 1916), pp. 459–495.
14. J.-J. Surin, *Lettres spirituelles*, ed. by L. Michelet and F. Cavallera, 2 vols. (Toulouse: 1926–1928), vol. 2, pp. 20, 32 and 54. See Bremond, *Histoire*, vol. 5, pp. 148–310; J.-J. Surin, *Correspondance*, ed. by M. de Certeau (Paris: Desclée de Brouwer, 1966), esp. pp. 15 and 133; L. Kolakowski, *Chrétiens sans Eglise*, pp. 443–491.
15. Burton, *The Anatomy*, vol. 3, pp. 396–399.
16. For this note and the following two, see again Burton, *The Anatomy*, vol. 3, pp. 398–399. F. Platter, *Observationum libri tres* (1614), chap. 3.
17. P. Forestus (Pierre Van Forest), *Observationes* (1602), book 10, chap. 12.
18. Burton, *The Anatomy*, vol. 3, pp. 396–399.
19. See below, pp.
20. Burton, *The Anatomy*, vol. 3, pp. 399–400.
21. H. Suso, *Oeuvres complètes*. Mme. Ancelot-Hustache's introduction is excellent; see, esp., pp. 59–60 concerning the mortifications of H. Suso. On the same subject see also A. J. Festugière, "Miscellanées sur la Vie d'Henri Suso," *Revue d'Histoire des religions* 194 (2) (1978): 159–180.
22. H. Suso, *Oeuvres*, p. 182.
23. Ibid., p. 183.
24. Ibid., p. 60. A similar conclusion is reached by L. Cognet, *Introduction aux mystiques rhéno-flamands* (Paris: Desclée de Brouwer, 1968), pp. 160–164.
25. Ibid., p. 122.
26. Ibid., pp. 122–132.
27. Ignatius of Loyola, *Autobiographie*, ed. by A. Guillermou (Paris: Seuil, 1962), pp. 70–72.
28. Thérèse d'Avila, *Oeuvres complètes*, vol. 1, p. 347–348.
29. Concerning the ascetic life of Charles Borromeo, see, esp., C. Orsenigo, *La Vita di San Carlo Borromeo* (Milan: 1929), and A. Deroo, *Saint Charles Borromée, cardinal réformateur. Docteur de la pastorale* (Paris: ed. Saint-Paul, 1963).
30. Saint-Beuve, *Port Royal* (Paris: Plèiade, 1952), vol. 1, p. 159.
31. Quoted in J. Orcibal, *Origines du Jansénisme*, vol. 1: *Jean Duvergier de Hauranne, abbé de Saint-Cyran et son temps* (Paris: Vrin, 1947), p. 57, note referring to the *Mémoires d'Utrecht* (1742), vol. 1, p. 316.
32. M. Mansio, *Documenti per aiutare al ben morire* (Bologna: 1607), pp. 33–34; Tenenti, *Il Senso*, pp. 302 and 337, n. 19.
33. G. Cacciaguerra, *Lettere spirituali* (Venice: 1584), vol. 1, p. 187 (translated into French by 1610); Tenenti, *Il Senso*, p. 302.
34. H. de Maupas du Tour, *La Vie de Jeanne-Françoise Frémiot* (1644), p. 170.
35. Saint-Beuve, *Port-Royal*, vol. 2, pp. 297 and 792; G. Gazier, *Ces Messieurs de Port-Royal* (Paris: 1932), pp. 181–182; R. Taveneaux, "Port-Royal ou l'héroïsme de la sainteté," in *Héroïsme et création littéraire sous les règnes d'Henry IV et de Louis XIII* (Paris: Klincksieck, 1974), p. 105.
36. Quoted in J. Rolland-Gosselin, *Le Carmel de Beaune* (Rabat: 1969), p. 71.
37. Languet, *La Vie de Marguerite-Marie*, p. 70. 38. Ibid., p. 94.
39. Ibid., p. 100–101.

40. *La Vie de Mme J.M.B. de la Mothe Guyon, écrite par elle-même*, 3 vols. (Köln: 1720), pp. 88–90; Kolakowski, *Chrétiens sans Eglise*, p. 523.
41. I use here a *Master's thesis* done at the University of Paris I in 1971 by R. Kural, "Etude de deux manuscripts convulsionnaires jansénistes du XVIIIe siècle," pp. 45–48 and Ph.D. diss. of Cottret, "Les Représentations mythiques de l'Eglise primitive dans les polémiques entre les Jansénistes et les Jésuites (1713–1760)," 2 vols., University of Nanterre, 1979, vol. 1, pp. 70–74.
42. The two best early works on Rancé, which are of value as documents, are those of R. P. Le Nain, *La Vie de Dom Armand-Jean de Rancé . . . abbé de la Trappe* (1715 and 1719); Dom Gervaise, *Jugement critique mais équitable des vies du feu M. l'abbé de Rance écrites par les sieurs Marsollier et Maupeau* (London [actually Reims]: 1742). The *Rancé* of Chateaubriand can hardly be considered a real biography. Very useful is H. Bremond, *"L'Abbé tempête" de Rancé* (Paris: Hachette, 1929).
43. Bremond, "*L'Abbé tempête*," p. 245, quoting Dom Canivet.
44. Published in 1677.
45. A. J. de Rancé, *Lettre sur le sujet*, p. 7.
46. Ibid., p. 212 and, for what follows, pp. 212–217.
47. Ibid., p. 13.
48. Ibid., p. 14.
49. Ibid., p. 124.
50. *Explication de quelques endroits des anciens statuts de l'Ordre des Chartreux avec des éclaircissements sur le sujet d'un libelle qui à été composé contre l'Ordre et qui s'est divulgué secrètement* (1689), quoted in Bremond, "*L'Abbé tempête*," p. 193.
51. Mabillon, *Traité des études monastiques* (1691), quoted in ibid., p. 165.
52. G. Bataille, *La Somme athéologique*, vol. 1: *Le Coupable*, in *Oeuvres complétes* (Paris: Gallimard, 1973), p. 248.
53. Ibid., p. 251. The first French translation of the *Livre de la vie* is of 1604. Bataille used the E. Hello translation, chap. 26.
54. This is the way P. Lallemant puts it, quoted in Bremond, *Histoire littéraire*, vol. 5, pp. 24–28.
55. Saint Jean de la Croix, *Oeuvres complètes* (Paris: Desclée de Brouwer, 1959), p. 748.
56. Quoted in Y. Pelle-Douel, *Saint Jean de la Croix et la nuit mystique* (Paris: Seuil, 1960), p. 43.
57. Saint-Beuve, *Port-Royal*, vol. 1, pp. 161–162, but see also pp. 1058–1059.
58. Baruzi, *Saint Jean de la Croix*, p. vii.
59. Ibid., p. 669.
60. Suso, *Oeuvres complètes: Sentences*, p. 535.
61. Ibid., *Livre de la Sagesse éternelle*, chap. 13, p. 362.
62. "La Règle de saint Benoît," in *Règles des moines*, ed. by J. P. Lapierre (Paris: Seuil, 1982), pp. 57, 65, 138–139 (end of foreword and rules 4, 5, and 72). See J.-Cl. Jean-Nesmy, *Saint Benoît et la vie monastique* (Paris: Seuil, 1967), p. 34.
63. Quoted in Y. Pelle-Douel, *Saint Jean de la Croix*, p. 43.
64. Ignatius of Loyola, *Autobiographie*, p. 56.
65. Thérèse d'Avila, *Oeuvres: Vie*, 1960 ed.
66. See J. Roland-Gosselin, *Le Carmel*, p. 70.
67. J.-J. Languet, *La Vie de Marguerite-Marie*, p. 364.
68. Ibid., p. 67.
69. H. Suso, *Oeuvres complètes: Vie*, chap. 19, p. 191; Cognet, *Introduction*, pp. 163–164.
70. Ignatius of Loyola, *Autobiographie*, pp. 72–74.
71. E. Martène, *La Vie du vénérable père Dom Charles Martin* (Tours: 1967), p. 82; Bremond, *Histoire littéraire*, vol. 6, pp. 91–92.
72. *La Vie de Madame Guyon*, vol. 1, pp. 97–99.
73. Suso, *Oeuvres complètes*, pp. 57–58; Cognet, *Introduction*, pp. 163–164.
74. Thérèse d'Avila, *Oeuvres complètes*, vol. 3, pp. 243–244.
75. Ignatius of Loyola, *Exercices spirituels*, trans. by Father Courel (Paris: Desclée de Brouwer, 1960), 3rd week, 3rd and 4th rule, pp. 116–117.
76. Alphonse de Liguori [Alphonsus Liguori], *La Vraie épouse de Jésus-Christ ou la sainte religieuse*, trans. by F. Delerue (Paris: 1926), p. 116.
77. *Règles des moines: Pacôme, Augustin, Benoît, François d'Assise*, ed. by J.-P. Lapierre, p. 77.
78. Thérèse d'Avila, *Le Livre des fondations*, chap. 6, p. 42.

79. J.-J. Languet, *La Vie de Maguerite-Marie*, pp. 51–52.
80. Ibid., p. 61.
81. P. Coste, *Correspondance. Entretiens. Documents* (Paris: 1923), vol. 2, p. IX-X, speech 72 (2 November 1655), which is speech no. 1439 of the Italian edition done by L. Mezzadri, *Conferenze spirituali alle Figlie della Carità*, pp. 945–946.
82. This "Key to Paradise" and the "Road to Heaven" are printed (n.d., n.p.) on four pages along with a "Cantique à N.D. de Bon-Secours" and an oration in honour of Saint Hubert.
83. Suso, *Oeuvres complètes: Vie*, chap. 21, pp. 199–200.
84. *The Autobiography of St. Ignatius Loyola*, trans. by J. F. O'Callaghan (New York:———, 1974), pp. 34–35. p. 68.
85. Ibid., p. 36.
86. J. Roland-Gosselin, *Le Carmel de Beaune*, p. 60.
87. J.-J. Languet, *La Vie de Marguerite-Marie*, p. 91.
88. See below, pp. 619–22 (of orginal).
89. E. Mounier, *Traité du caractère*, in *Oeuvres* (Paris: Seuil, 1961), vol. 2, p. 694. I would like to thank Father F. Bourdeau for having drawn my attention to this text.
90. He concludes that it is an "act," *Summa theologica*, Ia, quest. LXXIX 13 (Desclée de Brouwer, 1961), 9, pp. 260–264.
91. See above, chap. 6.
92. R. Tavenaux, "Le Catholicisme posttridentin," in *Histoire des religions* (Paris: Pléiade, 1972), vol. 2, p. 1083.
93. These three treatises are to be found in *Opera*, ed. by Du Pin (Antwerp: 1704), vol. 3, cols. 242–243, 579–589, and 605–618. Concerning "scruples" at the end of the Middle Ages and in the sixteenth century, see Tentler, *Sin and Confession*, esp. pp. 75–78, 113–115, 156, and 348.
94. See Y. Pélicier, *Colloque sur la névrose*, pp. 15 and 147.
95. The complete title is as follows: *Le Directeur pacifique des consciences où les personnes dévotes tant religieuses que seculieres pourront connoître clairement l'état de leur conscience, s'éclaircir de toutes leurs difficultés, discerner le péché mortel d'avec le véniel, découvvrir plusieurs abus et tromperies, se délivrer de leurs scrupules et tentations et apprendre à se confesser sans inquiétude.*
96. Suso, *Oeuvres*, "sermon no. 1," pp. 542–548.
97. Ignatius of Loyola, *Exercices spirituels*, pp. 181–183. See also his *Regulae de scrupulis*.
98. Above all chap. 14 of book 8. See Y. Pélicier, *Colloque sur la névrose*, p. 16.
99. Fénelon, *Lettres de direction*, ed. by M. Cagnac (Paris: 1902), pp. 195, 198, 205, 207, 261–263, 270, 272, 282.
100. Alphonse de Liguori, *La Vraie épouse ou la sainte religieuse*, ed. by F. Delerue, esp. chap. 13 ("La Patience"), pp. 260–286.
101. Expression quoted in Dhotel, *Les Origines*, p. 341.
102. Concerning this, see J. Deprun, *La Philosophie de l'inquiétude* (Paris: Vrin, 1979), esp. chaps. 9 and 10 and, specifically, pp. 154–156 (as well as the notes).
103. See, among others, G. Vauge (Oratorian), *De l'Espérance chrétienne contre l'esprit de pusillanimité et de défiance, et contre la crainte excessive* (Paris: 1732), chap. 8, sect. 2, p. 224 in the 1777 edition.
104. Lemprière, *Psychiatrie de l'adulte*, pp. 126–128; Ey et al., *Manuel de psychiatrie*, pp. 490–505; Pélicier, *Colloque sur la névrose*, pp. 13–14.
105. Ibid., plus, *Revue de Médecine* 2 (12 January 1980): 77–102; and "Le Noyau dépressif," in ibid., 14 (7 April 1980): 673–704.
106. C. Gilotte, *Le Directeur* (1723 ed.), p. 1. See Pélicier, *Colloque sur la névrose*, p. 13.
107. Antonin de Florence, *Summa*, part 1, title 3, chap. 10, section 9 and 10 (vol. 1, pp. 67–71 of the Venice, 1581–82 ed. in four volumes). The *Summa* of Sylvestre Prierias also has a heading for "scrupulus."
108. Gillotte, *Le Directeur*, p. 5.
109. Antonin de Florence, *Summa*, vol. 1, p. 68.
110. Ibid., p. 70.
111. Gillotte, *Le Directeur*, p. 5.
112. Ibid., p. 112.
113. J.-J. Du Guet, *Le Traité des scrupules*, ed. by Y. Pélicier *Vapeurs* 2 (1976): 198.
114. Ibid., p. 190.
115. Benedicti, *La Somme des pechez et remedes d'iceux* (Paris: 1595), p. 621.
116. See, among others, V. Regnault (S.J.), *Praxis poenitentialis ad directionem confessarii in usu sacri*

sui numeris (Mainz: 1617), book 2, chaps. 9 and 10, pp. 88–94; G. Loarte and M. Fornario (both S.J.), *Enchiridium seu instructio confessariorum* (Paris: 1653), chap. 18, pp. 180–189; de Reims, *Le Directeur pacifique*, part 2, book 1, art. 3, pp. 222–227.

117. Tenenti, *La Vie et la mort*, pp. 104–105.
118. Gillotte, *Le Directeur*, pp. 180–195.
119. Gerson, *Le Profit de savoir quel est péché mortel et véniel*, in *Oeuvre françaíse*, ed. by Glorieux, pp. 370–389.
120. This indication is in the explanation of the title. See also in the same book part 2, book 3, instr. 5, art. 1, pp. 636 passim.
121. Du Guet, *Le Traité des scrupules*, p. 156.
122. Ibid., p. 188.
123. Benedicti, *La Somme*, p. 621.
124. Pélicier, *Colloque sur la névrose*, pp. 16–17.
125. Benedicti, *La Somme*, p. 621; Gillotte, *Le Directeur*, p. 131.
126. Gillotte, *Le Directeur*, pp. 198–199. A similar description is to be found in the anonymous *Traité de l'espérance chrétienne*, chap. 8, quoted in Pélicier, *La Névrose*, pp. 15–16.
127. For example, J. Ponthas, *Dictionnaire des cas de conscience*, 3 vols. (Paris: 1730), vol. 3, pp. 755–771 (article on "scrupules").
128. Du Guet, *Traité des scrupules*, pp. 170. See also de Reims, *Le Directeur pacifique*, part 3, book 2, instr. 2, pp. 842–873.
129. See Ey et al., *Manuel de psychiatrie*, pp. 490–491.
130. Du Guet, *Traité des scrupules*, pp. 170–173.
131. Gillotte, *Le Directeur*, pp. 6–7.
132. De Reims, *Le Directeur pacifique*, p. 9.
133. Antonin de Florence, *Summa*, vol. 1, pp. 68–69; Gillotte, *Le Directeur*, p. 9.
134. Ibid. (Gillotte), pp. 10–11.
135. Gerson, *Tractatus pro devotis simplicibus*, in *Opera*, vol. 3, col. 606.
136. J. von Dambach, *Consolatio theologiae* (Strasburg: 1478), XIV, 8, 9; Tentler, *Sin and Confession*, p. 114.
137. G. Rosemondt, *Confessionale* (Antwerp: 1518), I, 7, pp. 77–78; Tentler, *Sin and Confession*, p. 338.
138. Benedicti, *La Somme*, p. 621.
139. De Reims, *Le Directeur pacifique*, p. 7. The same feelings are expressed by Gillotte, *Le Directeur*, p. 25.
140. Du Guet, *Le Traité des scrupules*, p. 180.
141. Gillotte, *Le Directeur*, p. 12.
142. Saint Antonin, *Summa*, vol. 1, p. 68.
143. De Reims, *Le Directeur pacifique*, p. 8 (the formulation he uses is nothing but a translation from Antonino, Bishop of Florence).
144. Gillotte, *Le Directeur*, p. 1.
145. De Reims, *Le Directeur pacifique*, p. 861.
146. See, for example, Fénelon, *Lettres de direction*, p. 207.
147. N. De Ausimio, *Supplementum summae pisanellae* (Venice: 1489) ("Confessio," 1, 9); Tentler, *Sin and Confession*, p. 156.
148. De Reims, *Le Directeur pacifique*, pp. 9–10.
149. Eudes, *Le Bon Confesseur* (1642), pp. 273–290 in the 1669 ed.
150. J.-J. Olier, *Lettres spirituelles* (Paris: 1672), letter no. 12, p. 36.
151. Gillotte, *Le Directeur*, pp. 6–7.
152. See above.
153. De Reims, *Le Directeur pacifique*, pp. 216–222.
154. Gillotte, *Le Directeur*, p. 169.
155. Du Guet, *Traité des scrupules*, p. 188.
156. See above, p. 317 (of original).
157. See G. Plante, *Le Rigorisme au XVIIe siècle. Mgr de Saint-Vallier et le sacrement de pénitence* (Gembloux: Duculot, 1971), esp. pp. 73–97 concerning postponed absolution.
158. Arnauld, *De la fréquente communion*, part 1, chap. 22, in volume 27 of the Lausanne 1779 ed., pp. 238–239.
159. Dhotel, *Les Origines*, p. 419. See below.
160. San Antonino, Bishop of Florence, *Summa*, vol. 1, p. 68.
161. Gerson, *Opera*, vol. 3, pp. 605–618.

162. Gillotte, *Le Directeur*, pp. 21–23. Same list in Ponthas, *Dictionnaire*, vol. 3, p. 758.
163. I consulted the Lyon 1669 ed.
164. Ponthas, *Dictionnaire*, vol. 3, p. 755.
165. M. Lagrée, "Le Langage de l'ordre. La souffrance dans le discours d'un évêque français au XIXe siècle," *Concilium* 119 (1976): 27–37.
166. Delumeau, *La Peur*, pp. 24 and 197.
167. Tronson, *Retraite*, 3rd day, 3rd meditation, pp. 114–128. I would like to remind the reader that the edition I consulted is of 1823.
168. Bossuet, *Etats d'oraison*, in *Oeuvres* (Rennes ed.), vol. 9, p. 564.; H. de Maupas du Tour, *La Vie du vénérable serviteur de Dieu François de Sales*, 2 vols. (1655–1658), vol. 1, chap. 5, pp. 25–26.
169. J. Bona, *Principes de la vie chrétienne*, vol. 1, chap. 4, in *Choix d'ouvrages mystiques*, ed. by J. Buchan (Paris: 1860), p. 491.
170. A. Vauchez, *La Sainteté en Occident aux derniers siècles du Moyen Age* (Paris: De Bocard, 1981), p. 598.
171. Massilon, *Petit carême suivi de sermons* (1824 ed.), p. 320.
172. See Thérèse d'Avila, *Le Livre des fondations*, pp. 68–71 (death of Beatrix of the Incarnation).
173. Marie de l'Incarnation (1599–1672), *Correspondance*, ed. by G. Oury (Solesmes: 1971), p. 1029.
174. I am here quoting the article of Geneviève Baudet-Drillat, "Regard à l'intérieur des congrégations religieuses," which was first published in J. Delumeau, ed., *La Mort des Pays de Cocagne*, pp. 189–206, and then in Delumeau, *Un Chemin d'histoire*, pp. 227–229.
175. D. Dinet, "Mourir en religion au XVIIe et XVIIIe siècles. La mort dans quelques couvents des diocèses d'Auxerre, Langres et Dijon," *Revue Historique* 259 (1978): 47.
176. Ibid.
177. P. Hanart, *Les Belles morts de plusieurs séculiers* (Douai: 1662). I consulted the 1667 ed.
178. P. Milliez, *Médecin de la liberté* (Paris: Seuil, 1980), pp. 317–318.
179. Father A. Gervaise, *Jugement critique mais équitable des vies de feu M. l'abbé de Rancé écrites par les sieurs Marsollier et Maupeou* (London [really Reims]: 1742), p. 551.
180. Abbé Le Dieu, *Mémoires et journal sur la vie et les ouvrages de Bossuet*, 4 vols. (Paris: Guettée, 1857), vol. 3, p. 95.
181. Ibid., vol. 2, p. 266 (speech of the abbé de Saint-André).
182. Tallemant des Réaux, *Historiettes*, 2 vols. (Paris: Pléiade, 1960), vol. 1, pp. 515–521.
183. H. de Maupas du Tour, *La Vie de Françoise Fremiot*, pp. 443–444.
184. Ibid., p. 503.
185. Ibid., p. 508.
186. Saint-Beuve, *Port-Royal*, book. 4 (vol. 2, p. 489, of the Pléiade ed.).
187. Ibid., pp. 647–648.
188. Vovelle, *La Mort en Occident* and *Mourir autrefois*, pp. 89–100; Ariès, *L'Homme*, pp. 306–307. A remarkable example of Christian death may be found in M. Czapska, *Une Famille d'Europe centrale* (Paris: Plon, 1972), pp. 205–207.
189. Quoted in Bremond, *Histoire*, vol. 9, p. 341.
190. Ibid., p. 343. *La Vie inédite de la duchesse de Luynes par J.-J. Boileau* was published by P. Tamizey de Larroque (Paris: 1880).
191. Dinet, "Mourir en religion," p. 47.
192. This undated report of the eighteenth century was pointed out to me by Geneviève Baudet-Drillat. The report is to be found at the Bibliothèque Nationale of Paris (4° Ld 173,2 [16]. It describes the final moments of Simone Madeleine Tixier, choir singer at Autun. Much the same information in M. T. Notter, "Les Ordres religieux féminins blésois. Leurs rapports avec la societé," Ph.D. diss., University of Tours, 1982, vol. 2, pp. 504–505.
193. Dinet, "Mourir en religion," p. 49.
194. Marie de l'Incarnation, *Correspondance*, p. 462.
195. Ibid., p. 464.
196. *La Vie du père J. Rigoulec de la Cie de Jésus*, by anonymous author (Paris: 1698), pp. 118–121, quoted in Vovelle, *Mourir autrefois*, p. 97.
197. Languet, *La Vie de Marguerite-Marie*, p. 367.
198. *Vie et oeuvres de la bienheureuse Marguerite-Marie Alacoque* (Paris: Paray-le-Monial 1876), vol. 1, p. 331 (tale of a nun). Sister Marguerite of the Holy Sacrament was also subject to great fear, which began to calm down only toward the end of her life (see Roland-Gosselin, *Le Carmel de Beaune*, p. 477).

199. F. Berriot, "Directeurs de consciences et confesseurs dans la tradition tridentine d'après la *Vie* et les *Oeuvres* manuscrites de l'abbé Cassegrain (1693–1771)," in *Intermédiares culturels*, Actes du coll. d'Hist. soc. des mentalités et des cultures, Aix-en-Provence, 1978, (Paris: H. Champion, 1981), pp. 46–47.
200. This information is from Rey-Mermet, *Le Saint du siècle des Lumières*, pp. 623–625.
201. L. Tronson, *Entretiens ecclésisastiques*, in *Oeuvres complètes*, 2 vols. (Paris: Migne, 1857), vol. 1, p. 698 (16th "entretien" on the small number of priests who will be saved).

CHAPTER 11

1. E. Mâle, *L'Art religeux après le concile de Trente* (Paris: A. Colin, 1932), p. 209.
2. Vovelle, *Mourir autrefois*, p. 120.
3. J. Loriot, *Sermons sur les plus importantes matières de morale chrétienne à l'usage de ceux qui s'appliquent aux missions et de ceux qui travaillent dans les paroisses* (new ed. of 1725), vol. 2, sermon 16, p. 564. Loriot's sermons were reprinted by Migne, *Collection des orateurs sacrés*, vol. 31, cols. 125–131.
4. Ibid. (Loriot), vol. 2, sermon 9, pp. 306–308.
5. P. d'Outreman, *Le Pédagogue chrétien* (Saint Omer: 1622). I consulted the 1650 ed., vol. 1, p. 200.
6. P. de la Font, *Prosnes pour tous les dimanches de l'année* (composed in 1693–94). I have consulted the 1701 ed. in four volumes, vol. 4, pp. 136–137.
7. D. Roche, "La Mémoire de la mort XVIIe–XVIIIe siècle," *Annales E.S.C.* 1 (1976): 109.
8. Bourdaloue, *Oeuvres*, vol. 3, p. 48 (Sermon on the second Friday of Lent). Bourdaloue's sermons are also in Migne, *Collection*, vols. 14–16.
9. H. Martin, "Les Procédés didactiques en usage dans la prédication en France du Nord au XVe siècle," in *La Religion Populaire* (Paris: C.N.R.S., 1979), p. 74.
10. For the sermons translated back into Latin, see *Opera Omnia*. Insofar as the *Prediche volgari* (Italian sermons) of 1427 are concerned, see the 3-vol. ed. by L. Blanchi (Siena: 1880–1888) and the 5-vol. ed., by C. Cannarozzi (Pistoia: 1939–1940). I have used the Blanchi edition available at the Sorbonne Library.
11. O. Maillard, *Sermones dominicales*, ed. by J. Petit (Paris: 1507), sermon 9, p. 20 r°.
12. Ibid., sermon 24, p. 49 r°.
13. Ibid., sermon 15, p. 34 v°.
14. A. Godeau, *Homélies sur les dimanches et fêtes de l'année* (1681). I had recourse to the 2-vol. Rouen ed. of 1755, vol. 1, p. 191 (Homily for the Sunday after Epiphany). Godeau's sermons may also be found in Migne, *Collection*, vol. 1, cols. 87–362.
15. Ibid. (Rouen), vol. 2, p. 154 (Homily for the fifth Sunday after Easter).
16. *Prosnes de messire Fr. Hébert évêque et comte d'Agen, cy-devant curé de Versailles, pour tous les dimanches de l'année*, 4 vols. (Paris: 1725), vol. 2, p. 198.
17. A. Boschet, *Le Parfait missionnaire ou la vie du R.P. Julien Maunoir de la Cie de Jésus, missionnaire en Bretagne* (Paris: 1697), p. 303.
18. J. Giroust, *Sermons pour le carême* (1700). I made use of the 3-vol., 1737 ed., vol. 2, p. 12 (sermon on Hell). Giroust's sermons are also in Migne, *Collection*, vol. 13, cols. 9–690.
19. L. Réguis, *La Voix du Pasteur. Discours familiers d'un curé à ses paroissiens pour tous les dimanches de l'année*, 2 vols. (Paris: 1771), vol. 1, pp. 19–20 (first Sunday of Advent).
20. This anecdote is in G. Hofer, *Giovanni da Capistrano. Una vita spesa nella lotta per la riforma della Chiesa*, trans. into Italian by G. di Fabio (L'Aquila), p. 134.
21. Concerning the missions to the interior, see the most important article "Missions paroissiales," in the encyclopedia *Catholicisme*, vol. 9.
22. J.-P. Camus, *Des Missions ecclésiastiques* (Paris: 1643), quoted in B. Dompnier, "Le Missionnaire et son public," in *Bossuet. La Prédication au XVIIe siècle* (Paris: Nizet, 1980), p. 115.
23. R. Sauzet, "Prédications et missions dans le diocèse de Chartres," *Annales de Bretagne* 81 (1974): 498.
24. L. Abelly, *La Vie du vénérable serviteur de Dieu, Vincent de Paul*, 2 vols. (Paris: 1664), vol. 2, pp. 12–13.
25. Boschet, *Le Parfait missionnaire*, p. 291. Same in Albert de Paris, *Manuel de la mission à l'usage des Capucins de la province de Paris* (Troyes: 1702), p. 48. See B. Dompnier, "Pastorale de la peur et pastorale de la séduction. La méthode de conversion des missionnaires cap-

ucins," Paper delivered at the Marseille 1982 Colloquium on Conversion in the Seventeenth Century.

26. G. Massei, *Vita del venerabile servo di Dio, il Padre Paolo Segneri* (Venice: 1727), p. 39.
27. N. Borely, *La Vie de messire Christophe d'Authier de Sisgau* (Lyon: 1703), pp. 79–80. I would like to thank B. Dompnier for this reference as well as the one contained in the following note.
28. Albert de Paris, *Manuel de la mission*, p. 48.
29. V. Houdry, *La Bibliothèque des prédicateurs*, of which I used the Lyon ed. of 1715–25, vol. 3, p. 526 (article on hell).
30. Camus, *Des Missions ecclésiastiques*, p. 393, quoted in B. Dompnier, "Le Missionaire et son public," in *Bossuet*, p. 115.
31. P. D'Outreman, *Le Pédagogue chrestien*, vol. 1, pp. 197–202, for example.
32. Loriot, *Sermons sur la morale chrétienne*, vol. 1, part 2, pp. 222–223.
33. F. Renaud, *Michel le Nobletz et les missions bretonnes* (Paris: 1955), p. 205.
34. Boschet, *Le Parfait missionnaire*, p. 280. Concerning the missions to Brittany, see A. Croix, *La Bretagne aux XVIe et XVIIe siècles. La vie, la mort, la foi*, 2 vols. (Paris: Maloine, 1981), esp. chap. 18 as well as the work of A. Croix and F. Roudaut, "La Mort Bretonne," which is still in manuscript form. The latter should be consulted for all that concerns Brittany in general.
35. Renaud, *Michel le Nobletz*, p. 128; Croix, *La Bretagne*, vol. 2, p. 1231.
36. The text of Dom Guill. Marlot is quoted in Y. Chaussy, *Les Bénédictins anglais réfugies en France au XVIIe siècle (1611–1669)* (Paris: Lethielleux, 1967), pp. 187–188.
37. C. Berthelot du Chesnay, *Les Missions de saint Jean Eudes* (Paris: Procure des Eudistes, 1967), p. 71.
38. J. Mausaise, *Le Rôle et l'action des Capucins de la province de Paris dans la France religieuse du XVIIe siècle*, 3 vols., University of Lille III (Paris: H. Champion, 1978), vol. 2, p. 1020.
39. Here I am making use of the work of F. Bourdeau and A. Danet, *Fiche de prédication missionnaire: la mort*, written in 1954 for the Redemptorians. F. Bourdeau kindly gave me a copy to consult and I am referring to pp. 62–63. From now on I will refer to this text as Bourdeau, *La Mort*. This report has been summarised in F. Bourdeau and A. Danet, "Faut-il prêcher la crainte de la mort," *La Vie Spirituelle* 492 (March 1963): 281–297, and in F. Bourdeau, "Les origines du sermon missionaire sur la mort," in ibid., pp. 319–338. Concerning the Redemptorian missions to the north of France in the nineteenth century, see Y.-M. Hilaire, *La Vie religieuse des populations du diocèse d'Arras (1840–1914)*, 3 vols. (University of Lille III, 1976), vol. 2, pp. 782–783.
40. Boschet, *Le Parfait missionnaire*, pp. 164–165; Croix, *La Bretagne*, vol. 2, p. 1221.
41. See C. Faralli, "Le Missioni dei Gesuiti in Italia (sec. XVI–XVII): problemi di una ricerca in corso," *Bollettino della Società di Studi Valdesi* 138 (1975): pp. 97–116, with necessary bibliography. In the following discussion I will combine the biography of Massei, pp. 39–45, with the document at the end of Carla Faralli's article. It must be pointed out that there are two people by the name of Paolo Segneri and both of them were preachers. The most famous one is the first (died in 1694).
42. Delumeau, *La Peur*, p. 258; S. Gruzinski, "Délires et visions chez les Indiens du Mexique," *Mélanges de l'Ecole française de Rome (M.A.T.M.)* 86(2) (1974): 336–480.
43. Massei, *Vita (di) P. Segneri*, p. 42.
44. Ibid., p. 45.
45. Faralli, "Le Missioni," p. 109.
46. See the encyclopedia *Catholicisme*, vol. 9, article on "Missions paroissiales," cols. 416–417, and the bibliography.
47. Ibid., cols. 417–418.
48. *Quaresimale del P. Fulvio Fontana della Cia di Gésu con l'aggiunta della serie delle missioni da lui fatte nell'Italia e nella Germania* (Venice: 1727). I have consulted the 1739 ed., pp. 319–348.
49. Ibid., p. 342.
50. Ibid., p. 324.
51. Ibid.
52. For the following discussions see Croix, *La Bretagne*, vol. 2, pp. 1222–1231 and illustrations 185–195; Lebrun, *Les Hommes et la mort en Anjou*, pp. 439–440 and illustrations 398–399; J. Quéniart, *Les Hommes l'Eglise et Dieu dans la France du XVIIIe siècle* (Paris: Hachette, 1978), pp. 116–118. I have also used some notes I took of a report that Anne Sauvy gave in my seminar.

53. Bremond, *Histoire littéraire*, vol. 5, p. 95.
54. C. Langlois, *Le Diocèse de Vannes au XIXe siècle* (Paris: Kliencksieck, 1974), p. 93.
55. L. Kerbiriou, *Les Missions bretonnes* (1933), p. 247; F. Roudaut, "La Prédication en langue bretonne," Third cycle dissertation; University of Paris I, vol. 1. p. 256.
56. P.-J. Hélias, *Le Cheval d'orgeuil* (Paris: Plon, 1975), p. 144.
57. I am summarizing the report Anne Sauvy gave in my seminar.
58. Reproduced in Croix, *La Bretagne*, vol. 2, illustration 190. See also Roudaut, "La Prédication en langue bretonne," vol. 1, p. 253–256.
59. Lebrun, *Les Hommes et la mort*, p. 440 and illustration pp. 398–399; P. J. Van Shaik, "Le Coeur et la tête. Une pédagogie par l'image populaire," *Revue d'histoire de la spiritualité* (1974): 447–478.
60. Bollème, *La Bibliothèque bleue* (Paris: Julliard, 1971), pp. 247–250 and 274.
61. Hofer, *Giovanni da Capistrano*, p. 345. See also p. 480 for Erfurt.
62. Saint Bernardino of Siena, *Opera omnia*, vol. 1, p. 12.
63. Ibid., p. 346.
64. Ibid., p. 365.
65. M. Veissière, "Monitoire de G. Briçonnet," *Revue d'histoire et d'art de la Brie* 27 (1976): 41.
66. This text by Father Antoine Yvan, "Prestre et instituteur des religieuses de N.D. de Misericorde" was published in 1661.
67. Archange-Gabriel de l'Annonciation, *La Vie du vénérable Antoine Le Quieu* (Avignon: 1682), vol. 1, p. 475, quoted in Dompnier, "Le Missionnaire et son public," p. 115.
68. Ibid. (LaVie), p. 414, quoted in ibid (Dompnier).
69. Charles de Genève, *Les Trophées sacrés ou missions des Capucins (1642–1643)*, 3 vols. (Lausanne: 1976), vol. 3, pp. 287 and 292, quoted in Dompnier, "La Pastorale de la peur."
70. See esp. Delumeau, *Un Chemin d'histoire. Chrétienté et christianisation*, pp. 178–179; Dompnier, "La Pastorale de la peur."
71. F. di Capua, "La *Predica Grande* dei Redentoristi e la *Modulatio* oratoria degli antichi," *Spicilegium historicum congregationis Ssmi Redemptoris* 1 (1–2) (1953): 234–240. See also Bourdeau, *La Mort*, pp. 23–24, whose translation I am quoting here.
72. Bourdeau, *La Mort*, p. 24.
73. Abraham a Santa Clara, *Werke in Auslese* (Vienna: 1905), vol. 3. See also B. Gorceix, "Le Turc dans les lettres allemandes au XVIe et XVII siècles: Johannes Adelphus et Abraham a Santa Clara," *Revue d'Allemagne* 13(2) (1981): 216–236.
74. De la Font, *Prosnes*, vol. 3, p. 532.
75. The complete name of N. Girard is not given in the editions I consulted.
76. N. Girard, *Les Petits prônes ou instructions familières principalement pour les peuples de la campagne*, 4 vols. in the Lyon 1766 ed., vol. 1, pp. 418–419. N. Girard's sermons are also contained in Migne, *Collection*, vol. 92, cols. 483–1362.
77. Godeau, *Homélies*, vol. 2, pp. 410–411 (twenty-third Sunday after Pentecost).
78. Ibid., vol. 1, p. 110 (third sermon for Christmas).
79. P. Beurrier, *Homélies, prosnes ou méditations sur les épistres de tous les dimanches et principales festes de l'année prêchées en l'eglise paroissiale de Saint-Etienne-du-Mont* (Paris: 1675). I consulted the 1688 ed. pp. 536–537.
80. De la Font, *Prosnes*, vol. 2, pp. 250–304.
81. Girard, *Les Petits prôsnes*, vol. 3, p. 348 (ninth Sunday after Pentecost).
82. Montargon, *Dictionnaire apostolique*, 1755 ed., vol. 8, art. 4, p. 267.
83. De la Font, *Prosnes*, vol. 2, pp. 346–347.
84. Hébert, *Prosnes*, vol. 2, p. 198.
85. Translated from the Breton by F. Roudaut, *La Prédication en langue bretonne*, vol. 1, p. 199 (A.D., Côtes du Nord, série i, B8, p. 12). Sermon of 1779, preached almost certainly in the diocese of Tréguier.
86. Alphonse de Liguori, *Sermons abrégés pour tous les dimanches de l'année* (Paris: 1840), nos. 38 and 44, vol. 2, pp. 172 and 235–251.
87. Said by Saint Alphonsus to P. L. Negri. See *Summarium super virtutibus* (Rome: 1806), p. 270. Translation by Rey-Mermet, *Le Saint du siècle des Lumières*, pp. 466–467.
88. See above, pp. 102–108, (of original) on the macabre and on resurrection.
89. Favre, *La Mort*, pp. 415–438.
90. Albert de Paris, *La Véritable manière de prêcher selon l'esprit de l'Evangile*, 3rd ed. (Paris: 1701), p. 212; Dompnier, "La Pastorale de la peur."

91. Bourdaloue, *Oeuvres*, vol. 3, pp. 75–76 (Sermon on the second Friday of Lent).
92. M. Fargeaud, "Laurence la mal-aimée," *Année balzacienne* (1961): 7. I would like to thank M. Gachet for this reference.
93. One might add, above and beyond the bibliography mentioned in note 1 of chapter 2, the essential article by D. Roche, "La Mémoire de la mort, XVII–XVIIIe siècle," *Annales E.S.C.* (January–February 1976): 76–120.
94. Grignion de Montfort, *Oeuvres*, p. 872.
95. This is the formulation Jacques Le Goff used during a talk he gave in my seminar.
96. Lebrun, Quéniart, and Venard, *Histoire générale de l'enseignement et de l'éducation*, vol. 2, pp. 458–459.
97. I would like to mention the articles concerning preaching done by J. Le Goff and J.-Cl. Schmitt, H. Martin, and F. Lebrun, in *Histoire vécue du peuple chrétien*, vol. 1, pp. 257–280; vol. 2, pp. 9–42; and vol. 2, pp. 43–66. See also F. Lebrun, *Parole de Dieu et Révolution. Les sermons d'un curé angevin avant et pendant la guerre de Vendée* (Toulouse: Privat, 1979); F. Roudaut, *La Prédication en langue bretonne au XVIIIe siècle*; H. Dansey Smith, *Preaching in the Spanish Golden Age* (reign of Philip III) (Oxford: University Press, 1978); P. Bayley, *French Pulpit Oratory (1598–1650)* (Cambridge: 1980). I might add that J. Le Goff's seminar was devoted above all to the *exempla* of the Middle Ages and that the *thèse d'Etat* of H. H. Martin's will be on the sermons of the end of the Middle Ages. The University of Warwick (Coventry) is collecting any information on medieval sermons and publishes regularly, since 1977, a *Medieval Sermon Studies Newsletter*.
98. Grignion de Montfort, *Oeuvres*, pp. 853–1694.
99. In *Cahiers lasalliens* (1965) 22, part 4, pp. 1–120.
100. M.-E. Ducreux, "De la Tradition médiévale aux recueils des XVIIe et XVIIIe siècles," in *Histoire vécue du peuple chrétien*, ed. by Delumeau, vol. 1, pp. 405–430.
101. See H. Barre, *Les Homéliaires carolingiens de l'école d'Auxerre* (Vatican City; 1962); *Quatorze homélies du IXe siècle d'un auteur inconnu de l'Italie du Nord*, ed. by P. Mercier (Paris: 1970). E. Brayer, "Manuscrit 574 de Cambrai," in vol. 43 of the *Notices et extraits des manuscrits de la Bibliothèque nationale et autres bibliothèques* (Paris: Imprimerie nationale and Klincksieck, 1965), pp. 145–341.
102. O. Maillard, *Sermones dominicales* (Paris: Jehan Petit, 1507).
103. J. Lefèvre d'Etaples (and his disciples), *Epistres et Evangiles pour les cinquante et deux dimanches de l'an* (1525). Reprint ed. with a commentary of G. Bedouelle and F. Giacone (Leyden: Brill, 1976).
104. Father Le Picart, *Les Sermons et instructions chrestiennes pour tous le dimanches* (Paris: 1567).
105. P Beurrier, *Homélies, prosnes ou méditations*.
106. J.-P. Camus, *Homélies dominicales* (Rouen: 1624). Camus's sermons are also in Migne, *Collection*, vol. 1, cols. 9–86.
107. Godeau, *Homélies sur le dimanche*. Concerning Godeau, see M. Bernos, "Tradition et modernité dans la moitié de Godeau," in *Antoine Godeau. De la galanterie à la sainteté* (Congress of Grasse, 1972), *Actes et Colloques* no. 17 (Paris: Klincksieck, 1976). Concerning the spread of the "instructions dévotes" (devoted instructions) of Godeau, one may turn to C. Sorel, *La Bibliothèque Française* (1664), pp. 41, 133, 141, and 182 (information given to me by E. Berriot-Salvadore).
108. De la Font, *Prosnes pour tous les dimanches de l'année*.
109. E. B. Bourée, *Homélies sur les evangiles de tous les dimanches de l'année pour l'instruction des fidèles*, 4 vols. (Lyon: 1703). Bourée's sermons are also printed in Migne, *Collection*, vols. 39 and 11.
110. Father Bourgoing, *Homilies chrestiennes sur les evangiles des dimanches et des festes principales de l'année*. I used the 1648 ed. I am quoting from the unpaginated introduction.
111. *Prosnes*.
112. *Prosnes de Me Symon, curé de Saint-Germain-de-Rennes*, 3 vols. (Rennes: 1748–52).
113. Girard, *Les Petits prônes*.
114. J. Chevassu, *Le Missionnaire paroissial*. I consulted the Lyon, 1802 edition in 4 vols. Reprint in Migne, *Collection*, vol. 94, cols. 9–839.
115. L. Réguis, *La Voix du pasteur*, in Migne, *Collection*, vol. 95, cols. 939–1802.
116. Foreword to vol. 2 in the Mons 1650 ed.
117. A great Dominican preacher whose sermons and *exempla* were studied in Jacques Le Goff's seminar.
118. Beginning of vol. 1 of the *supplements* (n.p.).

119. Two reprints were done in the nineteenth century: 1822–1824 and 1831–1839.
120. The approval of the chancellor is dated 1716 but the first edition is of 1721.
121. This is specified in the beginning of the first volume of his *Prosnes pour tous les dimanches de l'année*.
122. This indication appears, as can be seen, in the title. First published 1695. I have consulted the seven-volume 1725 ed., which is divided into eight books.
123. Girard, *Les Petits prônes*, preface to vol. 1.
124. *Dictionnaire de spiritualité*, fasc. 52, col. 1012. See also the *Dictionnaire portatif des predicateurs françois, dont les sermons, prônes, homélies, panégyriques et oraisons funèbres sont imprimés* (Lyon: 1757), pp. 109–111 (for Girard) and pp. 154–155 (for Loriot).

CHAPTER 12

1. Here I will use esp. Roche, "La Mémoire de la mort," pp. 76–119; Favre, *La Mort au siècle des Lumières*, esp. pp. 69–160; Vovelle, *Mourir autrefois* and *La Mort en Occident* (2 vols.). All of these authors mention, at one point or another, vol. 9 of Bremond's *Histoire littéraire*. Concerning Italy, see V. Paglia, *La Morte confortata. Riti della paura e mentalità religiosa a Roma nell'età moderna* (Roma: ed. di Storia e Letteratura, 1982).
2. H. J. Martin, *Livre, pouvoirs et societé à Paris au XVIIe siècle*, vol. 1, p. 89.
3. Chaunu, *Mourir à Paris*, esp. pp. 409–417.
4. M. Vovelle, *Piété baroque et déchristianisation en Provence au XVIIIe siècle* (Paris: Plon, 1973), pp. 122–126.
5. See ibid. and the figures (with bibliography) in J. Delumeau, *Le Catholicisme entre Luther et Voltaire*, 2nd ed. (Paris: P.U.F., 1979), pp. 317–327. See also T. Tackett, *Priest and Parish in Eighteenth Century France* (Princeton, NJ: Princeton University Press, 1977), pp. 43–53.
6. Roche, "La Mémoire de la mort," pp. 83–84.
7. Ibid., pp. 77–85.
8. Ibid., p. 94.
9. Ibid., pp. 94 and 114 (n. 49).
10. Ibid., p. 109, and Vovelle, *Mourir autrefois*, pp. 84 passim, and *La Mort en Occident.*
11. See above, p. 384 of French original.
12. Favre, *La Mort*, pp. 143 and 577.
13. *PG*, vol. 50, col. 597 (The Compliments of Saint Eustache); Favre, *La Mort*, p. 84.
14. J. Crasset, *La Double préparation à la mort.* I consulted the Brussels 1727 ed. (said to be the fifteenth ed.), p. 31.
15. Lasne d'Aiguebelle, *La Religion du coeur* (Paris: 1768), pp. 344 and 350; Favre, *La Mort*, p. 84.
16. For Rome, see Paglia, *La Morte confortata*. 17. Ibid., p. 34.
18. Crasset, *La Double préparation*, p. 31.
19. Ibid., pp. 33–34.
20. Ibid., p. 54.
21. Ibid., p. 101.
22. Ibid., p. 115.
23. Ibid., p. 56.
24. J.-N. Grou, *Caractères de la vraie dévotion* (Paris: 1788), pp. 108–109; Favre, *La Mort*, p. 132.
25. P. Lalemant, *Les Saints désirs de la mort.* I have used the Paris 1692 ed., pp. 285–286.
26. Paglia, *La Morte confortata*, pp. 57–62.
27. Roche, "La Mémoire," p. 105.
28. Fénelon, *L'Education des filles*, chap. 13, in *Oeuvres complètes*, 1851 ed., vol. 5, p. 583; Favre, *La Mort*, p. 98.
29. *Conduite chrétienne ou formulaire de prières à l'usage des pensionnaires*, 1734 ed., quoted in M. Sonnet, "L'Education des filles à Paris au XVIIIe siècle," *third cycle* dissertation, E.H.E.S.S., vol. 1, p. 289.
30. Lalemant, *Les Saints désirs*, pp. 120–121.
31. F. Veran (S.J.), *Manuale sodalitatis beatae Mariae Virginis* (1609), p. 568.
32. A. Vatier (S.J.), *La Conduite de Saint Ignace de Loyola* (Lyon: 1665), p. 128.
33. Grignion de Montfort, *Oeuvres complètes*, p. 1775 (sermons); Vovelle, *Mourir autrefois*, pp. 66–67.

34. Fénelon, *Oeuvres* (Paris: Leroux-Gaumé éd., 1845–52), vol. 8, p. 439; Favre, *La Mort*, p. 145.
35. Dom J.-P. du Sault, *Le Religieux mourant ou préparation à la mort pour les personnes religieuses* (1706), pp. 15–16; A. Alletz, *L'Art de toucher le coeur* (Paris: 1783), vol. 3, p. 290; Favre, *La Mort*, p. 145.
36. Yvan, *La Trompette du ciel*, p. 359 (book 3, chap. 9).
37. Ibid., book 2, chap. 6, p. 208; chap. 8, p. 215; chap. 10, p. 224; book 3, chap. 25, p. 435.
38. Lalemant, *Les Saints désirs*, respectively articles 2, 7, 12, 26, and 43.
39. Crasset, *La Double préparation*, p. 32.
40. Ibid., pp. 113–114.
41. Favre, *La Mort*, p. 142.
42. Liguori, *Apparecchio alla morte e opuscoli affini*, in vol. 9 of the *Opere Ascetiche* (Rome: Ed. di Storia e Letteratura, 1965), notes and introduction by O. Gregorio, pp. xxxv–lii.
43. L. A. Caraccioli, *Le Tableau de la mort*. I consulted the Liège, 1765 ed., pp. 78–79, 101–102, and 104–105.
44. *Paraenesis ad Theodorum lapsum*, 1, n. 9, in *PG*, vol. 47, col. 288.
45. Liguori, *Apparecchio*, 1st consideration, points 1 and 2, ration. points 1 and 2.
46. Rey-Mermet, *Le Saint du siècle des Lumières*, pp. 7 and 467.
47. Bollème, *La Bibliothèque bleue*, p. 247.
48. Caraccioli, *Le Tableau*, pp. 22, 109, 129, and 169.
49. Liguori, *Apparecchio*, pp. 24–25, 27, 29–30, 68, 70, 76.
50. Mâle, *L'Art religieux après le concile de Trente*, p. 208.
51. Ibid.
52. See above, (p. 121 of French original).
53. See the translation done by Father F. Courel, *Saint Ignace de Loyola. Exercices spirituels* (Paris: Desclée de Brouwer, 1960).
54. Bourdeau, "Les Origines," pp. 320–322.
55. This addition may be seen in the 1615 ed., p. 41.
56. Louis de Grenade, *Oeuvres complètes* (Paris: Vivès, 1866), vol. 18, pp. 7–31; Vovelle, *La Mort en Occident*.
57. Saint Pierre d'Alcantara [Peter of Alcantara], *Oeuvres spirituelles*, trans. by M. Bouix (Paris: 1862), pp. 13–101.
58. Mâle, *L'Art religieux après le concile de Trente*, p. 210.
59. See, for example, the Church of the Purgatory in Matera (1747) and its wooden portal with skulls and below it a stone skeleton.
60. G. De Rosa, *Vescovi, Popolo e magia nel Sud* (Naples: Guida, 1971), esp. pp. 18 passim and pp. 205 passim.
61. Bernardino of Siena, *Opera*, 2 (3–4), vol. 1, pp. 510–511 (sermon fifteen on death).
62. Le Picart, *Les Sermons*, pp. 2B–3A.
63. D'Outreman, *Le Pédagogue chrétien*, vol. 1, p. 190.
64. Ibid., p. 200.
65. Ibid., vol. 2, pp. 647–648.
66. Bourgoing, *Homélies*, pp. 780–781.
67. See above, (p. 360–363 of French original). J. Loriot, *Sermons sur les plus importantes matières*, vol. 2, p. 305.
68. Ibid., vol. 2, p. 29.
69. *Cahiers lasalliens*, 22, p. 89 of the canticles.
70. *Recueil des cantiques*, vol. 2 of *Manuel des retraites*, p. 201.
71. M. A. Y***, *Cantiques spirituels sur les principaux points de la religion* (Angers: P.M., 1737), vol. 2, pp. 103–104.
72. A. Michna, *Ceskà marianskà muzika* [Czech Marian music] (Prague: 1647), pp. 138–139. I would like to thank M.-E. Ducreux for her translation of this passage.
73. Réguis, *La Voix du Pasteur*, vol. 2, pp. 196–199. The sermons of Y. M. Marchais (a priest from the Anjou) also contain references to "wished-for death" according to Lebrun, *Parole de Dieu*, p. 79.
74. Jeanmaire, *Sermons*, vol. 2, p. 217.
75. W. King, *De Origine mali* (1702). The English translation of this book is entitled *An Essay on the Origin of Evil*. I am quoting from the fourth ed. of the translation (Cambridge: 1758), p. 152. See B. Cottret, "Hégémonie du discours et discours hégémonique. Le *De Origine mali* de William King," in *Recherches sur le XVIIe siècle*, vol. 4 (Paris: C.N.R.S.), p. 145–155.

76. Montargon, *Dictionnaire apostolique*, vol. 9, art. 2, p. 101.
77. *Cahiers lasalliens*, no. 22, p. 77 of the canticles.
78. *Cantiques*, vol. 2 of the *Manuel des retraites*, p. 242.
79. Montargon, *Dictionnaire apostolique*, vol. 9, art. 4, p. 265.
80. Bridaine, *Sermons*, of which I consulted the seven-vol. edition published in Paris in 1867, vol. 7, pp. 406–408.
81. *Cahiers lasalliens*, no. 22, pp. 27–28 of the canticles.
82. Léonard de Port-Maurice, *Sermons pour les missions* (Paris: 1860), vol. 2, p. 350.
83. *Cahiers lasalliens*, no. 22, pp. 28–29 of the canticles.
84. Translated into French by M.-E. Ducreux.
85. D'Outreman, *Le Pédagogue chrétien*, vol. 1, p. 197 (the author has taken the story from Thomas of Cantimpré).
86. Ibid. (story taken from the *Lives of the Church Fathers*).
87. See above, (pp. 395–396 of French original).
88. Léonard de Port-Maurice died in 1751 and the *Apparecchio* is of 1758.
89. Léonard de Port-Maurice, *Sermons pour les missions*, vol. 2, pp. 352–353.
90. *Manuel des retraites*, pp. 33–34.
91. Jeanmaire, *Sermons*, vol. 1, p. 274.
92. Girard, *Les Petits prônes*, vol. 1, pp. 171–173. The reference given by Girard is not the right one. He too should have referred to Hosea 13:13. The two sermons were delivered the third and fourth Sundays of Advent.
93. Ibid., p. 133. The reference to Job should actually be 17:14.
94. Grignion de Montfort, "Canticle no. 20," in *Oeuvres*, p. 1498.
95. L. Réguis, *La Voix du Pasteur*, vol. 2, pp. 492–493 (sermon on the fifteenth Sunday after Pentecost).
96. Jeanmaire, *Sermons*, vol. 1, pp. 267–268.
97. Grignion de Montfort, "Canticle no. 29," in *Oeuvres*, p. 1123.
98. Ibid., p. 1125.
99. Sermon by Graveran, translated by F. Roudaut, *La Prédication*, vol. 2, p. 221.
100. Léonard de Port-Maurice, *Sermons pour les missions*, vol. 2, pp. 371–373.
101. Bernardino of Siena, *Opera*, vol. 1, pp. 64–76. The two sermons are: no. 13, *De duodecim periculis quae superveniunt peccatoribus in ultima fine* and no. 14, *De duodecim doloribus quos patitur peccator in hora mortis*.
102. Yvan, *Trompette du ciel*, part 1, pp. 94–153.
103. Loriot, *Sermons*, vol. 2, pp. 288–290 (sermon no. 9 on "the death of the sinner").
104. Jeanmaire, *Sermons*, vol. 1, p. 269 (sermon no. 14 on "the death of the sinner").
105. Girard, *Petits prônes*, vol. 1, p. 131 (sermon on the the third Sunday of Advent).
106. Léonard de Port-Maurice, *Sermons*, vol. 2, p. 376 ("Pensées salutaires sur la mort" [Salutary thoughts on death]).
107. De la Font, *Prosnes*, vol. 3, p. 437 (sermon on the ninth Sunday after Pentecost).
108. Jeanmaire, *Sermons*, vol. 1, p. 277 (sermon no. 14 on "the death of the sinner").
109. Ibid., pp. 278–280.
110. Grignion de Montfort, "Canticle no. 120," in *Oeuvres*, pp. 1490–1498.
111. Girard, *Les Petits prônes*, vol. 1, pp. 174–175 (sermon for the fourth Sunday of Advent).
112. Roche, "La Mémoire de la mort," p. 105.
113. Jeanmaire, *Sermons*, vol. 1, pp. 220–221 (eleventh sermon, "on death").
114. Bridaine, *Sermons*, vol. 7, p. 400 ("In preparation for death").
115. Hébert, *Prosnes*, vol. 3, p. 41 (sermon for the eighteenth Sunday after Pentecost).
116. Bridaine, *Sermons*, vol. 1, p. 139 (sermon "on the death of sinners").
117. Yvan, *Trompette du ciel*, part 1, p. 99.
118. Réguis, *La Voix du pasteur*, vol. 2, pp. 200–201 (sermon on the eighth Sunday after Pentecost).
119. Léonard de Port-Maurice, *Sermons*, vol. 2, p. 359.
120. Girard, *Les Petits prônes*, vol. 1, pp. 128–129 (sermon on the third Sunday of Advent).
121. Sermon of Graveran trans. by Roudaut, *La Prédication*, vol. 2, pp. 222–225.
122. Montargon, *Dictionnaire apostolique*, vol. 4, p. 176 (art. 2, "On Death in general").
123. Bridaine, *Sermons*, vol. 7, p. 401 ("On preparing death").
124. Le Picart, *Les Sermons et instructions chrestiennes*, p. 233A (sermon exalting the Holy Cross).
125. Yvan, *Trompette du ciel*, part 2, chaps. 15–18, 20–22, 24–26, pp. 248–290.
126. A. Chesnois, *Le Petit missionnaire de la campagne ou l'instruction chrétienne pour les peuples de la campagne* (Caen: 1672), pp. 117–118 of the 1675 ed.

127. Grignion de Montfort, *Oeuvres*, p. 1497 (canticle no. 120).
128. Girard, *Les Petits prônes*, vol. 1, pp. 178–179 (sermon on the fourth Sunday of Advent).
129. Ibid., vol. 3, p. 320 (sermon on the seventh Sunday after Pentecost).
130. See above, (pp. 325–366 of French original.)
131. Léonard de Port-Maurice, *Sermons*, vol. 2, pp. 434–435 (sermon delivered in Sant Andrea della Valle, Rome, on December 20, 1750).
132. Bridaine, *Sermons*, vol. 1, pp. 92–93 ("On the delay of conversion").
133. Ibid., vol. 1, p. 145 ("On the death of sinners").
134. Sermon of Graveran trans. by Roudaut, *La Prédication*, vol. 2, pp. 217–218.
135. Ibid., vol. 2, p. 227.
136. Ibid., vol. 2, p. 234.
137. Ibid., vol. 2, p. 232.
138. Ibid., vol. 2, pp. 234–235.
139. Ibid., vol. 2, pp. 238–240.
140. Ibid., vol. 2, pp. 244–245.
141. Ibid., vol. 2, p. 248.
142. The first edition is of 1704.

CHAPTER 13

1. De la Font, *Prosnes*, vol. 1, p. 229 ("Sermon on the first Sunday after Epiphany").
2. *Cahiers lasalliens*, 22, p. 30 of the canticles. Many canticle collections contain one or more canticles on Hell. See, for example, an extract of a canticle on Hell taken from the *Recueil de cantiques (québécois) de Mgr de Capsa* (1794), manuscript quoted by J.-P. Pichette, *Le Guide raisonné des jurons* (Montreal: Quinze, 1980), p. 131.
3. D'Outreman, *Le Pédagogue chrétien*, vol. 1, p. 218.
4. Houdry, *Bibliothèque des prédicateurs*, vol. 3, p. 526.
5. Montargon, *Dictionnaire apostolique*, vol. 2, art. 6, p. 393.
6. Insofar as concerns the sources for preaching about hell, I have used the work of Montargon, ibid., pp. 387–391. The references he provides are not always correct.
7. Tertullian, *Apologeticus adv. gentes*, chap. 48, in *PL*, vol. 1, col. 596. This text and the following one are translated in Montargon.
8. Saint Cyprian, *Liber ad Demetr.*, in *PL*, vol. 4, cols. 581–582; *Liber de laude martyrii*, in *PL*, vol. 4, col. 829.
9. Saint John Chrysostom, *Hom. 23 (alias 24) in ch. 7 Matt.*, in *PG*, vol. 62, col. 317.
10. Ibid., *Commentary on the espistle to the Jews*, chap. 1, homily no. 1, in *PG*, vol. 63, col. 18.
11. The second and the third quotations are taken from *The City of God*, book 13, chap. 11, and book 19, chap. 28 (book 35, p. 281, and book 37, p. 173 in the Desclée de Brouwer ed.). On the other hand, the first and fourth quotations are not to be found where H. de Montargon refers to them (book 2, chap. 4, and book 12, chap. 10). However, they do express the general spirit of book 21, which is about the punishments of Hell and their eternal nature (book 37, p. 364 passim of the Desclée de Brouwer edition).
12. Saint Gregory, *Moralia*, book 9, chap. 10, in *PL*, vol. 75, cols. 913–914 (Montargon refers to book 20 of the *Moralia* without specifing anything else).
13. Saint Bernard, *De consid.*, 55, chap. 12, in *PL*, vol. 182, col. 803.
14. Saint Bernardino of Siena, *Opera*, vol. 2, 3, sermon 18 of the *Sermones extraordinarii: De Poenis inferni*, p. 518. See also sermon no. 11 on the Last Judgment, pp. 506–515.
15. Saint Gregory, *Dialog.*, book 4, chap. 44, in *PL*, vol. 77, col. 404.
16. Girard, *Les Petits prônes*, vol. 2, pp. 182–183 (sermon on the third Sunday of Lent).
17. De Montargon, *Dictionnaire apostolique*, 11, art. 2, pp. 199–200 ("Sur le mauvais riche").
18. Grignion de Montfort, *Oeuvres*, canticle 118, p. 1489.
19. Ibid., canticle 10, p. 922.
20. Jeanmaire, *Sermons*, vol. 1, p. 357 (sermon 18, "on the spiritual pains of Hell").
21. Houdry, *Bibliothèque des prédicateurs*, vol. 3, p. 526 (article on Hell).
22. *Manuel*, vol. 2, *Cantiques*, p. 325.
23. Girard, *Les Petits prônes*, vol. 2, p. 191 (sermon on the third Sunday of Lent).
24. Sermon translated by Father Roudaut, *La Prédication*, vol. 2, p. 280.

25. Bernardine of Siena, *Opera*, vol. 2, part 3, sermon 18 of the *Sermones extraordinarii*, "De poenis inferni," pp. 519–523.
26. Jeanmaire, *Sermons*, vol. 1, p. 348 (sermon 18, "on the spiritual pains of Hell").
27. Ibid., p. 349.
28. Translated by Father Roudaut, *La Prédication*, vol. 2, pp. 259–260 (sermon of Nicholas Le Gall).
29. Ibid., pp. 261–262.
30. G. Bachelard, *La Psychanalyse du feu* (Paris: Gallimard, 1949), pp. 19–20.
31. *Prières du matin et du soir avec l'abrégé de la doctrine chrétienne . . . suivies des cantiques spirituels à l'usage des missions des RR. PP. Capucins* (Rennes: 1747), p. 7 (canticle no. 6).
32. Ibid., p. 47 (canticle no. 23).
33. J. Le Goff, *La Naissance du purgatoire* (Paris: Gallimard, 1981), p. 57.
34. Bernardino of Siena, *Opera*, vol. 2, part 3, pp. 523–526 (sermon 18 of the *Sermones extraordinarii*).
35. Croix, *La Bretagne*, vol. 2, p. 1056. The same theme is developed by this author in his forthcoming *La Mort bretonne*.
36. Jeanmaire, *Sermons*, vol. 1, p. 346 (sermon 18, "on the spiritual pains of Hell").
37. Bridaine, *Sermons*, vol. 1, p. 230 ("on Hell").
38. G. Bollème, *La Bibliothèque bleu*, p. 257, in the 1723 edition.
39. Girard, *Les Petits prônes*, vol. 1, p. 61 (sermon on the second Sunday of Advent).
40. Same references as in notes 36 and 39.
41. Thérèsa of Avila, *Autobiographie*, in *Oeuvres complètes*, pp. 155–156, in the 1960 ed.
42. This is the formulation used by Bridaine, *Sermons*, vol. 1, p. 230 ("on Hell").
43. Bollème, *Bibliothèque bleu*, p. 257.
44. Godeau, *Homélies*, pp. 62–63 (eighth homily, on the fourth Sunday of Advent).
45. Nicole, *Essais de morale*, vol. 4, p. 132 (book 2, chap. 10).
46. Bourdaloue, *Oeuvres*, vol. 3, p. 76 (sermon on Friday of the second week of Lent).
47. Ibid.
48. Ibid., p. 77.
49. Nicole, *Essais de morale*, vol. 4, p. 134.
50. P. Segneri, *Sermons* (Avignon: 1836), vol. 5, p. 169 (forty-ninth sermon: "on the pains of Hell").
51. Ibid., p. 150.
52. Léonard de Port-Maurice, *Sermons*, vol. 2, p. 141 ("second procession: Hell").
53. Girard, *Les Petits prônes*, vol. 1, pp. 60–61 (sermon on the second Sunday of Advent).
54. Bachelard, *La Psychanalyse*, pp. 31–32.
55. Le Goff, *La Naissance*, pp. 81–83, who refers to the *Stromateis*, 5, 14 and 7, 6 of Clement of Alexandria.
56. Ibid., p. 91.
57. Jeanmaire, *Sermons*, vol. 1, pp. 334–335 (seventeenth sermon).
58. De la Font, *Prosnes*, vol. 1, p. 344 (sermon on the third Sunday after Epiphany).
59. I am here following the Lazarists' sermon mentioned in note 57, pp. 322–338. However, the same grouping according to the five senses may also be found in Louis of Granada, *Oeuvres*, vol. 11, p. 152 (*Mémorial de la vie chretienne*).
60. Lambert, *La Manière*, p. 73.
61. See above, (p. 122 of French original).
62. Loriot, *Sermons*, vol. 2, pp. 437–439 (sermon XIII "on Hell").
63. D'Outreman, *Le Pédagogue chrétien*, vol. 1, pp. 213–224 ("De la mémoire de l'enfer et de l'éternité").
64. De la Font, *Prosnes*, vol. 1, p. 327 (third Sunday after Epiphany).
65. Bridaine, *Sermons*, vol. 1, pp. 230–232 ("on Hell").
66. Giroust, *Sermons pour le carême*, vol. 2, p. 17 (sermon on Hell).
67. Girard, *Les Petits prônes*, vol. 1, pp. 101–118 (sermon on the second Sunday of Advent on the subject of "the hardening of the sinner").
68. Bourée, *Homélies*, vol. 3, p. 359 (sermon on the ninth Sunday after Whit Sunday).
69. Bourgoing, *Homilies*, p. 546 (on the twenty-first Sunday after Whit Sunday).
70. Girard, *Les Petits prônes*, vol. 2, p. 180 (sermon on the third Sunday of Lent).
71. Translated by Father Roudaut, *La Prédication*, vol. 2, p. 279.
72. Le Goff, *La Naissance du purgatoire*.

73. Chaunu, *Mourir à Paris*, pp. 141–158.
74. Ibid., p. 145.
75. A. Graf, "Artù nell'Etna," in *Legende, miti e superstizioni del Medio Evo* (Turin: 1925) quoted in Le Goff, *La Naissance du purgatoire*, pp. 416–423.
76. Saint Augustine, sermon 104 (former 41) "De sanctis," in *PL*, vol. 39, col. 1947, which is confirmed, among others, by *Enarratio in ps. XXXVII*, in *PL*, vol. 36, col. 397, and by the *Liber de vera et falsa penitentia*, in *PL*, vol. 40, col. 1128. J. Ntdedika, *L'Evolution de la doctrine du purgatoire chez saint Augustin* (Paris: Etudes augustiniennes, 1966), has collected the writing of Saint Augustine on this subject.
77. Le Goff, *La Naissance du purgatoire*, pp. 92–118 (Saint Augustine as the "father of Purgatory").
78. Thomas Aquinas, *In IVum Sent.*, dist. XXI, q. 1, a. 1, qu. 3; see *DTC*, article on "Purgatory" by A. Michel, cols. 1163–1326 but here cols. 1240–1241; Le Goff, *La Naissance*, pp. 357–372.
79. *In Johannem*, 15, 2, in *PG*, vol. 74, col. 352.
80. D. Soto, *In IVum Sent.*, dist. 19, quest. III, a. 2; *DTC*, article on "Purgatory," col. 1289. The following discussion owes much to this article.
81. Bellarmine, *Controversiae. De Purgatorio*, book 2, chap. 7, in *Opera*, vol. 3, p. 112.
82. Ibid., chap. 24, p. 121.
83. Bernardino of Siena, *Opera*, vol. 1, pp. 956–964 (sermon LXIII, *De statu purgatorii*).
84. This information is taken by Tenenti, *Il Senso*, pp. 303–306, from A. Montalambert, *La Merveilleuse histoire de l'esperit qui depuis n'agueres c'est apparu au Monastère de St Pierre à Lyon* (Paris: 1528).
85. Katherine of Genoa, *Trattato del purgatorio*, translated with her *Vita e dottrina* by P. Debognie, *Sainte Catherine de Gênes* (Bruges: Desclée de Brouwer, 1960), pp. 199–215.
86. Ibid., p. 204.
87. Ibid., p. 208.
88. Ibid., p. 203.
89. Ibid., pp. 208–209.
90. Ibid., p. 211.
91. *DTC*, vol. 13, cols. 1272–1277; Chaunu, *Mourir à Paris*, pp. 146–147.
92. M.P.C. "doctor of the Sorbonne," *L'Esprit de st Fçois de Sales evêque et prince de Genève, receuilli de divers écrits de M. Jean-Pierre Camus, evêque de Belley* (Paris: 1747 ed.), p. 408.
93. Ibid., pp. 406–407.
94. Fénelon, *Oeuvres*, vol. 8, "Lettres spirituelles," n. 189, p. 573.
95. M.P.C., *L'Esprit de st Fçois de Sales*, p. 408.
96. Salmanticenses, *De Vitiis et peccatis*, disp. 18, dub. 2, section 6; *DTC*, article on Purgatory, col. 1293.
97. M.P.C., *L'Esprit de st Fçois de Sales*, p. 406.
98. *DTC*, article on Purgatory, vol. 13, part 1, col. 1318.
99. Le Goff, *La Naissance*, pp. 416–426.
100. I. Passavanti, *Lo Specchio della vera penitenza*, 2 vols. (Milan: 1808), book 1, dist. 3, chap. 2, pp. 78–83.
101. Ibid., p. 78.
102. Ibid., p. 83.
103. J. Molinet, "Complainte," in *Faictz et dictz*, 3 vols. (Paris: 1937), vol. 2, pp. 434–435. I would like to thank G. H. Dumont for having drawn my attention to this text.
104. It is absent from the Sunday homily collection of J. Lefèvre-D'Etaples, *Epistres et evangiles*; however, it is certainly the doctrine of the justification of belief that is responsible for his not talking about this.
105. A. Michna, *Svatorana muzika* [Music for the Holy Year] (1661), pp. 246–248. Translation by M.-E. Ducreux.
106. Le Picart, *Les Sermons*, part 2, pp. 187a and b (sermon for All Souls' Day).
107. Ibid., part 1, p. 184 a (sermon for the nineteenth Sunday after Trinity).
108. Ibid., part 1, p. 200 a (sermon for the twentieth Sunday after Trinity).
109. Ibid., part 1, p. 123 a (sermon for the fourteenth Sunday after Trinity).
110. This despite the text of Saint Paul (I Cor. 3:10–15), which has served as the basis for believing in Purgatory.
111. *Sermons de Mire Jean-Louis de Fromentières, évêque d'Aire et prédicateur ordinaire de Sa Majesté*, 3 vols. (Paris: 1688–89), vol. 3, p. 195 (sermon on All Souls' Day).
112. Grignion de Montfort, *Oeuvres*, canticle 119, p. 1493.

113. *Cantiques spirituels sur les sujets les plus importants de la religion, l'usage des retraites, des missions et des congrégations* (n.d., but eighteenth century), pp. 213–214.
114. Symon, *Prosnes*, vol. 2, p. 424–425 (sermon on All Saints' Day).
115. Montargon, *Dictionnaire apostolique*, vol. 5, art. 4, pp. 348 and 351.
116. Lebrun, *Parole de Dieu*, pp. 80–81.
117. D'Outreman, *Le Pédagogue chrétien*, vol. 1, p. 417.
118. François de Toulouse, *Le Missionnaire apostolique* (Paris: 1679), vol. 3, pp. 241–242.
119. Grignion de Montfort, *Oeuvres*, canticle 119, p. 1493.
120. *Prières . . . suivies de cantiques*, p. 29.
121. Fontana, *Quaresimale*, pp. 156–157 (twenty-second sermon: delivered on the fourth Sunday of Lent).
122. Girard, *Les Petits prônes*, vol. 4, p. 357 ("Discours pour le jour des morts").
123. Ibid., p. 351.
124. Lebrun, *Parole de Dieu*, p. 81.
125. Molinet, *Les Faictz*, p. 425 ("Complainte," line 53).
126. Fontana, *Quaresimale*, p. 155 (twenty-second sermon, delivered on the fourth Sunday of Lent).
127. *Cantiques spirituels*, pp. 213–214.
128. Grignion de Montfort, *Oeuvres*, canticle 119, p. 1495.
129. Symon, *Prônes*, vol. 2, p. 426 (sermon on All Saints' Day).
130. *Le Bouquet de la mission*, pp. 415–416.
131. *Sermons de Mire . . . de Fromentères*, vol. 3, p. 198 (Sermon on All Souls' Day).
132. Houdry, *Bibliothèque des prédicateurs*, vol. 7, p. 755, article on Purgatory.
133. Montargon, *Dictionnaire apostolique*, vol. 5, art. 5, p. 352.
134. Pensée n. 518 in the Brunschivcg ed.
135. J. Deprun, "Pascal et le purgatoire," in *Missions et démarches de la critique. Mélanges J. Vier* (Paris: Klincksieck, 1973), pp. 209–216.
136. D. Amelote, *La Vie de soeur Marguerite du Saint-Sacrement, religieuse carmélite du monastère de Beaune* (Paris 1655 ed.), pp. 274–275.
137. François de Toulouse, *Le Missionnaire apostolique*, vol. 3, p. 246 (sermon on Purgatory). This preacher's sermons are also to be found in Migne, *Collection*, vol. 10, cols. 892–1134, and vol. 11, cols. 9–900.
138. Ibid.
139. See Caesarius of Arles, sermon 104, n. 1, in *PL*, vol. 39, cols. 1946–1948.
140. Bellarmine, *Controversiae. De Purgatorio*, in *Opera*, vol. 3, book 2, chap. 10 and 11, pp. 118–119.
141. *Sermons de Mire . . . de Fromentières*, vol. 3, p. 199 (sermon on All Souls' Day).
142. Symon, *Prônes*, vol. 2, p. 426 (sermon on All Souls Day).
143. Segneri, *Oeuvres*, vol. 5, p. 23 (sermon 51, on Purgatory).
144. De Montargon, *Dictionnaire apostolique*, vol. 5, art. 5, pp. 351–352.
145. Molinet, "Complainte," in *Les Faictz*, pp. 433–535.
146. Grignion de Montfort, *Oeuvres*, canticle 199, pp. 1492–1496.
147. *Prières . . . suivies de cantiques*, p. 29.
148. This formulation and the previous three are all from the *Cantiques spirituels*.
149. Leuduger, *Bouquet de la mission*, pp. 415–416.
150. Girard, *Les Petits prônes*, vol. 4, p. 357 ("Discours sur le jours des morts").
151. D'Outreman, *Le Pédagogue chrétien*, vol. 1, p. 417 (refers to Thomas Aquinas, *In IVum*, qu. 46, art. 6, ad. 3).
152. *Sermons de Mire . . . de Fromentières*, p. 199 (sermon on All Souls' Day) with reference to Saint Augustine, *Confessions*, book 13, chap. 10. François de Toulouse also encourages his listeners to visit "hospitals" and "gallows" so that one can contemplate suffering and torture. Adding all this cannot be compared to "the slightest pain" felt in Purgatory, see *Oeuvres*, vol. 3, pp. 239–240 (sermon on Purgatory).
153. *Cantiques spirituels*, p. 141.
154. Ibid., pp. 213–214 and 388–389.
155. L. Denziger-Schonmetzer, *Enchiridion symbolorum* (1963), n. 983. Father de la Ruë (S.J.) refuses to go beyond the strict official teachings on Purgatory (*Sermons*, 1st ed. 1718, of which I consulted the Lyon 1751 ed., vol. 1, p. 74).
156. De Montargon, *Dictionnaire apostolique*, vol. 5, art. 4, pp. 349–350.
157. Ibid., p. 350.
158. Ibid., pp. 350–351.

159. Fontana, *Quaresimale*, p. 155 (twenty-second sermon, delivered on the fourth Sunday of Lent).
160. Ibid., p. 156.
161. Girard, *Les Petits prônes*, vol. 4, p. 355 (sermon on All Souls' Day).
162. See above, pp. (See pp. 428–429 of French original).
163. *Le Bouquet de la mission*, pp. 415–416.
164. Lebrun, *Parole de Dieu*, p. 80.
165. Segneri, *Oeuvres*, vol. 5, pp. 238–239 (sermon 51, on Purgatory).
166. Grignion de Montfort, *Oeuvres*, canticle 127, p. 1519.
167. Louis of Granada, *Oeuvres*, vol. 2, p. 33 (chap. 2 of the *Guide des pécheurs*).
168. Girard, *Les Petits prônes*, vol. 4, p. 357 ("Discours pour le jour des morts").
169. Ibid., vol. 3, p. 304 (sermon of the sixth Sunday after Whit Sunday).
170. L. Chenart, *Discours sur divers sujets de morale* (1696), I consulted the 1703 ed., vol. 3, p. 331 (on the pains of Purgatory). Chenart's sermons are also to be found in Migne, *Collection*, vol. 90, cols. 705–1402.
171. Fontana, *Quaresimale*, pp. 155–157 (twenty-second sermon, delivered on the fourth Sunday of Lent).
172. Ibid., p. 157.
173. François de Toulouse, *Le Missionnaire*, vol. 3, p. 233 (sermon on Purgatory).
174. Girard, *Les Petits prônes*, vol. 4, p. 358 ("Discours pour le jour des morts").
175. Molinet, *Les Faictz*, pp. 433–435.
176. *Le Bouquet de la mission*, pp. 415–416.
177. Grignion de Montfort, *Oeuvres*, canticles 119 and 127, pp. 1492 and 1516.
178. P. Du Viols, *La Lutte contre les religions autochtones dans le Perou colonial* (Lima: 1972), p. 40.
179. Grignion de Montfort, *Oeuvres*, canticle 119, p. 1492.
180. Ibid., canticle 127, p. 1519.
181. Fontana, *Quaresimale*, pp. 157–158 (twenty-second sermon, delivered on the fourth Sunday of Lent).
182. D'Outreman, *Le Pédagogue chrétien*, vol. 2, p. 654.
183. Fontana, *Quaresimale*, p. 162 (twenty-second sermon, delivered on the fourth Sunday of Lent).
184. Quoted in C. Leber, *Collection des meilleures dissertations . . . relatives à l'histoire de France* (Paris: 1838), vol. 9, pp. 271–272. *The Deliverance of the Souls from Purgatory* of Rubens in the cathedral at Tournai gives only a slight place to the flames of Purgatory.
185. G. and M. Vovelle, *Vision de la mort*, pp. 19–21.
186. M. Ménard, *Une histoire des mentalités religieuses aux XVIIe et XVIIIe siècles. Mille retables de l'ancien diocèse du Mans* (Paris: Beauchesne, 1981), pp. 295–299.

CHAPTER 14

1. The expression is taken from J.-P. Camus, *Homélies dominicales*, p. 262 (sermon on the fifth Sunday after Whit Sunday).
2. Bourdaloue, *Oeuvres*, vol. 11, pp. 493–494 (sermon for All Souls' Day).
3. Giroust, *Sermons pour la carême*, vol. 2, p. 27 (sermon on Hell).
4. Hébert, *Prosnes*, vol. 4, p. 400 (sermon for the last Sunday after Whit Sunday).
5. See, for example, Beurrier, *Homélies*, p. 675 (sermon on the ninth Sunday after Whit Sunday); Bourée, *Homélies*, vol. 2, p. 428 (sermon on the second Sunday after Whit Sunday).
6. Réguis, *La Voix du pasteur*, vol. 1, p. 218 (sermon on Septuagesima).
7. Fontana, *Quaresimale*, pp. 30–37 (fifth sermon delivered on Tuesday after the first Sunday of Lent).
8. Hébert, *Prosnes*, vol. 4, p. 31 (sermon of the seventeenth Sunday after Whit Sunday).
9. Réguis, *La Voix du pasteur*, vol. 1, pp. 25–26 (sermon on the second Sunday of Advent).
10. Delumeau, *La Peur en occident*, pp. 211–231.
11. Bernardino of Siena, *Opera*, vol. 1, pp. 54–60 (eleventh sermon on Lent, *De Religione christiana*); pp. 496–509 (eleventh sermon of Lent, *De Evangelia aeterno*); vol. 2, pp. 292–295 (twenty-first sermon on the *Canciones de tempore*); and by the same author, *Prediche volgari*, vol. 1, pp. 307–332 (thirteenth sermon).
12. For example in P. Collet, *Sermons pour les retraites*, 2 vols. (Lyon 1763 ed.), vol. 1, pp. 262–302.
13. Girard, *Les Petits prônes*, vol. 1, pp. 5–25; vol. 3, pp. 328–347; vol. 4, pp. 207–227. It may

be assumed that since Girard composed two different sermons for the first and the last Sunday of the year, he would hardly discuss the same subject on two successive Sundays.

14. De la Font, *Prosnes*, vol. 1, p. 3 (sermon on the first Sunday of Advent).
15. Loriot, *Sermons*, vol. 2, p. 353 ("Du jugement universel").
16. De Montargon, *Dictionnaire apostolique*, vol. 3, pp. 199–201 (art. 3, on the Last Judgment).
17. Concerning the continued fascination with eschatological expectations in Marie des Vallées and Grignion de Montfort, one may now turn to the articles of J. Séguy, "D'une jacquerie à une congrégation religieuse," *Archives des Sciences sociales des Religions* 59 (1) (1981): 37–67, and, by the same author, " 'Millénarisme' et 'ordres adventistes': Grignion de Montfort et les 'Apôtres des derniers temps'," in ibid.
18. Paper delivered by C. Prandi at a C.N.R.S. symposium on millenarism in history, April 1982.
19. Bourée, *Homélies*, vol. 1, p. 8 (sermon on the first Sunday of Advent).
20. Hébert, *Prosnes*, vol. 1, pp. 14 and 18 (sermon on the first Sunday of Advent).
21. Camus, *Homélies*, pp. 1–12 (sermon on the first Sunday of Advent).
22. Bourgoing, *Homélies*, pp. 3–4 (sermon on the first Sunday of Advent).
23. Hébert, *Prosnes*, vol. 4, p. 426 (sermon on the last Sunday of Whit Sunday).
24. J.-P. Camus, *Trente nouvelles* (Paris: Vrin, 1977).
25. Camus, *Homélies*, p. 10 (sermon on the first Sunday of Advent).
26. Jeanmaire, *Sermons*, vol. 1, pp. 305–308 (sermon no. 16).
27. *Cantiques*, in *Cahiers lasalliens* 22 (1965): 32 (canticle no. 11 on the Last Judgment).
28. Fontana, *Quaresimale*, pp. 30–33 (sermon on Monday of the first week of Lent).
29. Chevassu, *Prônes*, vol. 1, p. 5 (sermon on the first Sunday of Advent).
30. Ibid., vol. 2, p. 10 (sermon on the eighth Sunday after Whit Sunday).
31. Fontana, *Quaresimale*, p. 34 (sermon on the first Sunday of Lent).
32. Godeau, *Homélies*, vol. 2, p. 132 (sermon on the fourth Sunday after Whit Sunday).
33. Loriot, *Sermons*, vol. 2, p. 35 (sermon no. 11, on the Last Judgment).
34. Ibid.
35. Réguis, *La Voix du pasteur*, vol. 1, p. 39 (sermon on the second Sunday of Advent).
36. Yvan, *Trompette du ciel*, p. 103 (book 1, chap. 23).
37. Article by M. Lagrée, in *Le Diocèse de Rennes* ed. J. Delumeau, (Paris: Beauchesne, 1979), p. 141.
38. Jeanmaire, *Sermons*, vol. 1, p. 305 (sermon 16).
39. Godeau, *Homélies*, vol. 1, p. 72 (sermon on the fourth Sunday of Advent).
40. Loriot, *Sermons*, vol. 2, p. 411 (sermon on the Last Judgment).
41. *Cantiques*, in *Cahiers lasalliens* 22 (1965): 111.
42. Bourée, *Prosnes*, vol. 3, p. 419 (sermon on the fifteenth Sunday after Whit Sunday).
43. Chevassu, *Prônes*, vol. 1, p. 2 (sermon on the first Sunday of Advent).
44. Réguis, *La Voix du pasteur*, vol. 1, pp. 33–39 (sermon on the second Sunday of Advent).
45. Ibid., vol. 1, p. 516 (sermon on the Sunday before Whit Sunday).
46. Camus, *Homélies*, p. 12 (sermon on the first Sunday of Advent).
47. Girard, *Le Petits Prônes*, vol. 1, p. 7 (sermon on the first Sunday of Advent).
48. Fontana, *Quaresimale*, p. 35 (sermon on Monday of the first week of Lent).
49. Godeau, *Homélies*, vol. 1, p. 387 (sermon on Passion Sunday).
50. Girard, *Les Petits prônes*, vol. 3, p. 341 (sermon on the eighth Sunday after Whit Sunday).
51. *Cantiques*, in *Manuel des retraites et missions*, vol. 2, p. 48.
52. Bourgoing, *Homélies*, pp. 7–8 (sermon on the first Sunday of Advent).
53. Beurrier, *Homélies*, p. 352 (sermon on Easter Monday).
54. Grignion de Montfort, *Oeuvres*, p. 1426 (canticle no. 1012).
55. *Cantiques*, in *Manuel des retraites et missions*, vol. 2, p. 74.
56. Jeanmaire, *Sermons*, vol. 1, p. 311 (sermon n. 16).
57. Godeau, *Homélies*, vol. 1, p. 72 (sermon on the fourth Sunday of Advent).
58. Fontana, *Quaresimale*, p. 35 (sermon on Monday of the first week of Lent).
59. Girard, *Les Petits prônes*, vol. 1, p. 19 (sermon on the first Sunday of Advent).
60. Montargon, *Dictionnaire apostolique*, vol. 3, art. 3, pp. 199–201.
61. De La Font, *Prosnes*, vol. 4, p. 560 (sermon on the twenty-fourth Sunday after Whit Sunday).
62. Girard, *Les Petits prônes*, vol. 1, p. 11 (sermon on the first Sunday of Advent).
63. Grignion de Montfort, *Oeuvres*, p. 1169 (canticle no. 34).
64. *Cahiers lasalliens* 22 (1965): 33 (canticle no. 11).
65. Jeanmaire, *Sermons*, vol. 1, p. 317 (sermon no. 16).
66. See below (p. 478 passim of French original).

67. Fontana, *Quaresimale*, p. 33 (sermon on Monday of the first week of Lent).
68. Girard, *Les Petits Prônes*, vol. 1, p. 11 (sermon on the first Sunday of Advent).
69. Jeanmaire, *Sermons*, vol. 1, p. 279 (sermon no. 14).
70. Grignion de Montfort, *Oeuvres*, pp. 1168–1169 (canticle no. 34).
71. A. Malvin de Montazet, *Instruction pastorale . . . sur les sources de l'incrédulité et les fondements de la Religion* (Lyon: 1776), pp. 258–259, quoted in Favre, *La Mort*, p. 116.
72. Francis de Sales, *Traité de l'amour de Dieu*, book 9, chap. 8, in *Oeuvres complètes* (Paris: 1833), vol. 7, p. 144.
73. Thomas Aquinas, *Summa Theologica*, suppl. quest. 99, art. 1, tome 64, pp. 542–543. See also ibid., quest. 94, art. 3, pp. 248–249.
74. Segneri, *Sermons*, vol. 5, p. 161 (forty-ninth sermon, "on the rigors of the pains inflicted in Hell"). He refers his readers to the *opusculum* 63, where I did not find the passage Segneri is speaking about.
75. Louis of Granada, *La Guide des pécheurs*, in *Oeuvres complètes*, vol. 10, pp. 359–360.
76. Bernardino of Siena, *Opera*, vol. 1, pp. 514–515 (sermon no. 12 of Lent, *De Evangelio aeterno*).
77. Beurrier, *Homélies*, p. 675 (sermon on the ninth Sunday after Whit Sunday).
78. *Cantiques spirituels*, in *Manuel des retraites*, vol. 2, p. 114.
79. Bridaine, *Sermons*, vol. 3, p. 343 (sermon on the subject of how few are the elect).
80. Léonard de Port-Maurice, *Sermons pour les missions*, vol. 2, p. 435 (sermon on the end of the jubilee year of 1750).
81. Girard, *Les Petits prônes*, vol. 4, pp. 247–248 (sermon on the twenty-fourth Sunday after Whit Sunday).
82. Montargon, *Dictionnaire apostolique*, vol. 2, art. 1, p. 48.
83. Ibid., vol. 2, art. 2, p. 107.
84. Ibid., vol. 5, art. 5, p. 353.
85. Loriot, *Sermons*, vol. 2, pp. 26–27 ("De l'injure que le péché fait à Dieu").
86. Bourdaloue, *Pensées sur divers sujets de religion et de morale*, in *Oeuvres complètes*, vol. 14, pp. 110–111.
87. Ibid., p. 111.
88. Houdry, *Bibliothèque des prédicateurs*, vol. 7, p. 422.
89. Montargon, *Dictionnaire apostolique*, vol. 1, p. 425.
90. Ibid., vol. 5, pp. 66–67 (art. 2, "Sur la prédestination et le petit nombre des élus").
91. Ibid., p. 76.
92. Loriot, *Sermons*, vol. 2, pp. 562–566 (sermon no. 16).
93. Jeanmaire, *Sermons*, vol. 1, p. 52 (sermon no. 2).
94. Quoted from A. Pioger, *Saint Jean Eudes* (Paris: Bloud and Gay, 1940), p. 170. However, this author thinks that the Jansenists and the pro-Jansenists were the only ones to teach the doctrine of the elect few.
95. It is surprising that a hymn printed in Angers in 1737 should contain the following verses: "Despite the cares of divine goodness / That the elect be so few / God just finds two Jews / Worthy of the good that he has sent upon them" (*Cantiques spirituels sur les principaux points de la religion*, p. 80).
96. Chevassu, *Prônes*, vol. 2, pp. 118–130 (sermon on the ninth Sunday after Whit Sunday).
97. Bourgoing, *Homélies*, pp. 813–824 (sermon on the nineteenth Sunday after Whit Sunday).
98. Maillard, *Sermones dominicales*, f° 8r° (sermon on the second Sunday after Whit Sunday).
99. Godeau, *Homélies*, vol. 2, p. 17 (sermon on Good Friday).
100. Beurrier, *Homélies*, pp. 675–766 (sermon on the ninth Sunday after Whit Sunday).
101. De la Font, *Prosnes*, vol. 2, p. 436 (sermon on Easter Sunday).
102. Hébert, *Prosnes*, vol. 3 p. 269 (sermon on the eleventh Sunday after Whit Sunday).
103. Bourée, *Homélies*, vol. 3, p. 285 (sermon on the seventh Sunday after Whit Sunday).
104. Ibid., vol. 2, p. 212 (sermon on Easter Sunday).
105. Ibid., vol. 4, p. 249 (sermon on the nineteenth Sunday after Whit Sunday).
106. Lambert, *La Manière*, p. 171.
107. Quoted in L. Rousseau, *La Prédication à Montréal de 1800 à 1830. Approche religiologique* (Montréal: Fides, 1976), p. 184, note 86. Montreal had only one Catholic parish at the time.
108. Thus the *Sermons pour les retraites*, 2 vols., of the Lazarite Father Collet (Lyon, 1763) contain an entire homily on the subject of "the small number of the elect," vol. 1, pp. 128–169.
109. Quoted in A. Samouillan, *Oliver Maillard et son temps* (Paris: 1891), p. 92.
110. Bourdaloue, *Oeuvres*, vol. 14, p. 113 ("Pensées . . . sur le petit nombre des élus").
111. Ibid., p. 112.

112. François de Toulouse, *Le Missionnaire apostolique*, vol. 2, pp. 1–23 (first sermon).
113. Ibid., p. 3.
114. A. Vieira, *Sermons* (Lyon: 1869), vol. 3, p. 531 (sermon on a Sunday devoted to the Holy Sacrament).
115. Louis of Granada, *Oeuvres*, vol. p. 497 (sermon on the Sunday of Septuagesima); vol. 2, p. 168 (sermon on Wednesday following Passion Sunday); vol. 4, p. 141 (sermon on the nineteenth Sunday after Whit Sunday); vol. 8, p. 353 (sermon on All Saints' Day).
116. Ibid., vol. 1, p. 497.
117. Ibid., vol. 2, p. 168 (sermon on the Wednesday following Passion Sunday).
118. François de Toulouse, *Le Missionnaire apostolique*, vol. 8, p. 303 (sermon no. 13).
119. Bossuet, *Meditation sur l'Evangile. Dernière semaine du Sauveur*, 34th day, in *Oeuvres* (Rennes: 1861 ed.), vol. 9, p. 233.
120. Massillon, "Sur le petit nombre des élus," in *Oeuvres complètes* (Paris: 1824), vol. 13, p. 316. Concerning Massillon, see J. Ehrard and A. Poitrineau, ed., *Etudes sur Massillon* (Clermond-Ferrand, 1974).
121. Bourdaloue, "Pensées . . . sur le petit nombre des élus," in *Oeuvres*, vol. 14, p. 117.
122. Ibid., p. 111.
123. Ibid., p. 112.
124. François De Toulouse, *Le Missionnaire apostolique*, vol. 7, pp. 257–271 (sermon on Septuagesima).
125. See above, (p. 316 of French original).
126. François de Toulouse, *Le Missionnaire apostolique*, vol. 7, p. 263 (sermon no. 7).
127. Ibid., p. 265.
128. Ibid., vol. 8, p. 311 (sermon on the thirteenth Sunday after Whit Sunday).
129. J. Lejeune, *Le Missionnaire de l'Oratoire, ou sermons pour l'avent, le carême et les fêtes* (Lyon: first 1826), vol. 9, p. 127 (sermon no. 311 delivered on Saturday of the first week of Lent). Lejeune's sermons are also printed in Migne, *Collection*, vols. 3, 4, and 5.
130. Ibid., p. 129.
131. Segneri, *Oeuvres*, vol. 1, p. 118 (sermon on the elect few and on those who are refused).
132. See (p. 320 of French original).
133. Segr :ri, *Oeuvres*, vol. 1, p. 144 (sermon on the elect few . . .).
134. See above (pp. 328–329 of French original)
135. Yvan, *Trompette du ciel*, p. 362.
136. Godeau, *Homélies*, vol. 2, pp. 18–20 (homily delivered on Good Friday).
137. Beurrier, *Homélies*, pp. 294–295 (homily delivered on Good Friday).
138. Bourée, *Homélies*, vol. 1, p. 116 (sermon on the fourth Sunday of Advent).
139. De la Font, *Prosnes*, vol. 1, p. 370 (sermon on the first Sunday after Easter).
140. Loriot, *Sermons*, vol; 2, p. 26 ("De l'injure faite à Dieu").
141. Léonard de Port-Maurice, *Sermons pour les missions*, vol. 2, p. 169 (sermons on the penitential processions).
142. Montargon, *Dictionnaire apostolique*, vol 7, art. 2, pp. 35 and 106.
143. Quoted in Roudaut, *La Prédication*, vol. 2, p. 305.
144. See J.-Cl. Dhotel, *Les Origines du catéchisme moderne d'apres les premiers manuels imprimés en France* (Paris: Aubier, 1967), p. 382.

CHAPTER 15

1. On this theme see esp. Yvan, *Trompette du ciel*, part 1, chaps. 8 and 9, pp. 32–39; Beurrier, *Homélies*, p. 673 (sermon on the ninth Sunday after Whit Sunday); Bridaine, *Sermons*, vol. 3, p. 326 (sermon on the sins of Christians).
2. Bernardine of Siena, *Opera*, vol. 1, pp. 509–515 (sermon no. 12, *De Evangelio aeterno*).
3. Maillard, *Sermones dominicales*, sermon 24, f° 59r° (sermon on the thirteenth Sunday after Whit Sunday).
4. Camus, *Homélies*, p. 239 (sermon on the third Sunday after Whit Sunday).
5. Louis of Granada, *La Guide des pécheurs*, in *Oeuvres*, vol. 10, pp. 411–412.
6. D'Outreman, *Le Pédagogue*, vol. 1, p. 26.
7. Godeau, *Homélies*, vol. 1, p. 335 (sermon on the first Sunday of Lent).
8. Ibid., vol. 3, p. 412 (sermon on the twenty-fourth Sunday after Whit Sunday). See also

Bourgoing, *Homilies*, p. 884 (sermon on the same Sunday as above) and Hébert, *Prosnes*, vol. 4, p. 410 (sermon on the same Sunday).

9. Chenois, *Le Petit missionnaire*, p. 115.
10. Loriot, *Sermons*, vol. 2, pp. 28–29 ("De l'injure faite à Dieu").
11. Jeanmaire, *Sermons*, vol. 1, pp. 122–126 (sermon no. 6).
12. Concerning the spiritual retreats, see, for example, Collet, *Sermons pour les retraites*, 2 vols. (Lyon: 1763).
13. *Cantiques*, in *Manuels des retraites et missions*, vol. 2, pp. 88–89.
14. Hébert, *Prosnes*, vol. 4, pp. 396–432 (sermon on the twenty-fourth Sunday after Whit Sunday); Réguis, *La Voix du pasteur*, vol. 1, pp. 147–163 (sermon on the third Sunday after Epiphany); Symon, *Prosnes*, vol. 2 (sermon on the eleventh Sunday after Whit Sunday); Chevassu, *Missionnaire paroissial*, vol. 2, pp. 307–319 (sermon on the twenty-fourth Sunday after Whit Sunday).
15. Camus, *Homélies*, p. 259 (sermon on the fifth Sunday after Whit Sunday).
16. Ibid., p. 262.
17. Ibid., p. 265.
18. Fontana, *Quaresimale*, pp. 37–44 (sermon on Tuesday of the first week of Lent).
19. Loriot, *Sermons*, vol. 2, pp. 198–235.
20. Girard, *Les Petits prônes*, vol. 3, p. 291 (sermon on the sixth Sunday after Whit Sunday).
21. François de Toulouse, *Le Missionnaire apostolique*, vol. 1, pp. 431–450 (sermon no. 21).
22. Léonard de Port-Maurice, "Examens particuliers sur les principaux sujets traités pendant la mission," in *Sermons pour les missions*, vol. 2, p. 342.
23. Bridaine, *Sermons*, vol. 3, p. 254 (sermon on venial sins).
24. Yvan, *Trompette du ciel*, pp. 425–428 (part 3, chap. 23).
25. Ibid., pp. 192–196 (part 2, chap. 2).
26. Godeau, *Homélies*, vol. 2, p. 132 (sermon on the fourth Sunday after Whit Sunday).
27. Jeanmaire, *Sermons*, vol. 1, p. 389 (sermon no. 20).
28. Réguis, *La Voix du pasteur*, vol. 1, p. 158 (sermon on the third Sunday after Epiphany).
29. De Montargon, *Dictionnaire apostolique*, vol. 2, art. 1, pp. 34 and 52.
30. De la Font, *Prosnes*, vol. 4, p. 139 (sermon on the fifteenth Sunday after Whit Sunday).
31. See, for example, De Montargon, *Dictionnaire apostolique*, vol. 12, art. 8, p. 439, and Girard, *Les Petits prônes*, vol. 2, pp. 155–160 (sermon on the second Sunday of Lent).
32. Godeau, *Homélies*, vol. 2, p. 125 (sermon on the fourth Sunday after Easter).
33. Jeanmaire, *Sermons*, vol. 1, pp. 25–26 (first sermon).
34. Ibid., vol. 1, p. 80 (sermon no. 4).
35. Chenois, *Le Petits missionnaire*, pp. 95–96.
36. Ibid., pp. 5, 61 and 72.
37. D'Outreman, *Le Pédagogue chrétien*, vol. 2, p. 396.
38. De la Font, *Prosnes*, vol. 2, p. 283 (sermon on Palm Sunday).
39. *Cantiques*, in *Manuel des retraites*, p. 109.
40. Ibid., p. 74.
41. Ibid., p. 417.
42. Ibid.
43. *Cantiques*, in *Cahiers lasalliens* 22 (1965): 10.
44. Réguis, *La Voix du pasteur*, vol. 2, pp. 538–539 (sermon on the twenty-third Sunday after Whit Sunday).
45. See above, (pp. 456–457 of French original).
46. De la Font, *Prosnes*, vol. 3, p. 335 (sermon on the sixth Sunday after Whit Sunday).
47. Montargon, *Dictionnaire apostolique*, vol. 11, art. 2, pp. 102, 105, 122, 123, and 207.
48. Grignion de Montfort, *Oeuvres*, pp. 1031–1032 (canticle no. 20).
49. Lebrun, *Parole de Dieu*, p. 62.
50. Réguis, *La Voix du pasteur*, vol. 2, pp. 518–519 (sermon on the nineteenth Sunday after Whit Sunday).
51. Jeanmaire, *Sermons*, vol. 2, p. 220 (sermon no. 40).
52. Chevassu, *Missionnaire paroissial*, vol. 2, p. 281 (sermon on the twenty-second Sunday of the year).
53. De la Font, *Prosnes*, vol. 2, p. 107 (sermon on the third Sunday of Lent).
54. Jeanmaire, *Sermons*, vol. 2, pp. 220–235 (sermon no. 40).
55. Girard, *Les Petits prônes*, vol. 1, pp. 366–389 (sermon on the fourth Sunday after Epiphany).
56. Concerning this, see ibid., pp. 383–388.

57. Fr. Lebrun, "Les Missions des Lazaristes en Haute-Bretagne au XVIIe siècle," *Annales de Bretagne et des Pays de L'ouest* 1 (1982): 31, and Delumeau, *Un Chemin d'histoire*, esp. pp. 181–183.
58. Delumeau, *Un Chemin d'histoire*, p. 182.
59. De la Font, *Prosnes*, vol. 4, pp. 489–505 (sermon on the twenty-second Sunday after Whit Sunday).
60. Jeanmaire, *Sermons*, vol. 2, pp. 244–245 (sermon no. 4).
61. Chevassu, *Missionnaire paroissial*, vol. 2, pp. 282–284 (sermon on the twenty-second Sunday after Whit Sunday).
62. Girard, *Les Petits Prônes*, vol. 4, p. 433 (sermon on the twelfth Sunday after Whit Sunday).
63. See above, (p. 238 of French original). Concerning the following discussion, see P. Darmon, *Mythologie de la femme dans l'Ancienne France* (Paris: Seuil, 1983), esp. pp. 33–47 and 74–77.
64. Bernardine of Siena, *Prediche volgari*, vol. 2, pp. 96–97 (sermon no. 19).
65. Le Picart, *Les Sermons et instructions*, p. 177 r° (sermon on All Souls' Day).
66. Camus, *Homélies*, pp. 66–67 (sermon on the second Sunday after Epiphany).
67. Bridaine, *Sermons*, vol. 5, p. 140 ("Instructions sur le mariage").
68. Bernardino of Siena, *Prediche volgari*, vol. 2, pp. 156–172 (sermon no. 21).
69. Much the same opinion in Fr. Lebrun, "Démographie et mentalité: le mouvement des conceptions sous l'Ancien Régime," *Annales de démographie historique* (1974): 46–67. See also Foucault, *La Volonté du savoir*, pp. 27–31, who refers to Segneri, *L'Instruction du pénitent*, and to Liguori, *Pratique des confesseurs*. See also, Léonard de Port-Maurice, *Le Traité de la confession générale*, French translation (Avignon: 1826), pp. 343–344.
70. Jeanmaire, *Sermons*, vol. 2, p. 27 (sermon no. 28).
71. De la Font, *Prosnes*, vol. 1, p. 317 (sermon on the second Sunday after Epiphany).
72. See above, (p. 244 of French original) Bernardino of Siena, *Prediche volgari*, vol. 2, p. 95 (sermon no. 19).
73. De la Font, *Prosnes*, vol. 1, pp. 287–289 (sermon on the second Sunday after Epiphany).
74. Ibid., p. 289. See the anonymous publication, *De l'Excellence des hommes contre l'égalité des sexes* (Paris: Antoine Dezallier, 1679), which is surprising if one considers its late date. The copy I consulted is to be found in the Capuchin convent of Rouen.
75. Vieira, *Sermons*, vol. 4, pp. 63–65 (sermon on the beheading of John the Baptist).
76. Loriot, *Sermons*, vol. 4, pp. 271–317 (sermon no. 9, "Des devoirs des personnes qui se marient").
77. Bridaine, *Sermons*, vol. 5, pp. 142–153 ("Instruction sur le mariage").
78. Symon, *Prônes*, vol. 1, pp. 120–125 (sermon on the second Sunday after Epiphany).
79. Grignion de Montfort, *Oeuvres*, p. 949 (canticle n. 12).
80. De Montargon, *Dictionnaire apostolique*, vol. 10, art. 7, p. 401.
81. Ibid., vol. 10, art. 6, p. 351.
82. Bridaine, *Sermons*, vol. 5, pp. 137–138 ("Instruction sur le mariage").
83. Girard, *Les Petits prônes*, vol. 1, pp. 330 and 335 (sermon on the second Sunday after Epiphany).
84. Réguis, *La Voix du pasteur*, vol. 1, pp. 128 and 134 (sermon on the second Sunday after Epiphany).
85. I have presented a summary of sermon no. 22 of the *Prediche volgari*, vol. 2, pp. 187–201. A Latin version of this sermon may be found in the *Opera* of Bernardino of Siena, vol. 2, *Sermones extraordinarii*, pp. 464–469 (*De Viduitate*).
86. See p. 469 of the Latin sermon mentioned in the previous note.
87. Grignion de Montfort, *Oeuvres*, p. 949 (canticle no. 12).
88. Girard, *Les Petits prônes*, vol. 3, pp. 449–462 (sermon on the thirteenth Sunday after Whit Sunday).
89. De Montargon, *Dictionnaire apostolique*, vol. 3, art. 2, p. 118.
90. See above, (pp. 23–24 of French original).
91. *Cantiques*, in *Manuel des retraites*, vol. 2, p. 127.
92. Bourée, *Homélies*, vol. 1, pp. 210–211 (sermon on the second Sunday after Epiphany).
93. Loriot, *Sermons*, vol. 4, pp. 290–291 (sermon no. 9, "Des devoirs des personnes qui se marient").
94. Grignion de Montfort, *Oeuvres*, p. 952 (canticle no. 12).
95. Jeanmaire, *Sermons*, vol. 2, pp. 5–6 (sermon no. 28).
96. Bernardino of Siena, *Opera*, vol. 2, p. 526 (sermon no. 18, *Sermones extraordinarii: De miseria conditionis humanae*).
97. Bernardino of Siena, *Prediche volgari*, vol. 2, p. 168 (sermon no. 21).

98. Ibid., p. 182 (sermon no. 22).
99. Grignion de Montfort, *Oeuvres*, p. 1578 (canticle no. 139).
100. *Bouquet de la mission*, p. 82.
101. Réguis, *La Voix du pasteur*, vol. 1, p. 26 (sermon on the second Sunday of Advent).
102. *Bouquet de la mission*, p. 425.
103. *Recueil des principales circulaires des supérieurs généraux de la congrégation de la Mission* (Paris: 1877), vol. 1, pp. 427–432. I would like to thank D. Julia for having sent me this information.
104. Grignion de Montfort, *Oeuvres*, p. 1933 (canticle no. 31).
105. Ibid., p. 1934 (canticle no. 31).
106. De Montargon, *Dictionnaire apostolique*, col. 12, art. 10, p. 599.
107. Grignion de Montfort, *Oeuvres*, p. 1578 (canticle no. 139).
108. De Montargon, *Dictionnaire apostolique*, vol. 12, art. 10, pp. 611, 620, 622, and 627.
109. Ibid., p. 596.
110. Ibid., p. 593.
111. D'Outreman, *Le Pédagogue chrétien*, vol. 1, p. 141.
112. Bridaine, *Sermons*, vol. 5, p. 7 ("Conférence sur l'impureté").
113. Jeanmaire, *Sermons*, vol. 2, p. 425 (sermon no. 51).
114. Ibid., p. 423.
115. Loriot, *Sermons*, vol. 5, p. 428 (sermon no. 14).
116. Ibid., p. 427.
117. Lambert, *La Manière de bien instruire*, p. 248.
118. Ibid., pp. 245–246.
119. *Le Bouquet de la mission*, p. 52 (chap. 11, on venial sins).
120. De Montargon, *Dictionnaire apostolique*, vol. 3, art. 2, pp. 91–100.
121. Ibid., p. 99.
122. See R. P. Lessenich, *Elements of Pulpit Oratory*, p. 12.
123. Le Maure, *Sermons sur les évangiles de l'avent et du carême et sur divers sujets de morale*, new ed. in 3 vols. (Trévoux: 1740), vol. 2, pp. 10–11 (sermon on Saturday of the second week of Lent); Chevassu, *Missionnaire paroissial*, vol. 2, pp. 174–175 (sermon on the thirteenth Sunday after Whit Sunday).
124. See above, (p. 239 of French original).
125. Girard, *Les Petits prônes*, vol. 3, p. 256 (sermon on the thirteenth Sunday after Whit Sunday).
126. De la Font, *Prosnes*, vol. 1, p. 275 (sermon on the second Sunday after Epiphany).
127. Loriot, *Sermons*, vol. 4, pp. 271–307 (sermon no. 9).
128. For Bridaine, "Instruction sur le mariage," in *Sermons*, vol. 5, pp. 113–160; for the corpus of Lazarist sermons, see Jeanmaire, *Sermons*, vol. 2, pp. 1–20 (sermon no. 28); for Girard, *Les Petits prônes*, vol. 1, pp. 318–342 (sermon on the same Sunday); for Chevassu, *Missionnaire paroissial*, vol. 3, pp. 73–87 (sermon on the second Sunday after Epiphany).
129. Bridaine, *Sermons*, vol. 5, p. 116 ("Instruction sur le mariage").
130. Ibid., p. 117.
131. Jeanmaire, *Sermons*, vol. 2, pp. 12–13 (sermon no. 28).
132. Delumeau, *La Peur*, vol. 1, p. 58.
133. Bridaine, *Sermons*, vol. 5, p. 119 ("Instruction sur le mariage").
134. Ibid., p. 14
135. Girard, *Les Petits prônes*, vol. 1, p. 328.
136. Ibid., pp. 326–327.
137. Ibid., p. 328.
138. Chevassu, *Prosnes*, vol. 1, p. 75 (sermon on the second Sunday after Epiphany).
139. Ibid., p. 78. On the instilling of a sense of guilt concerning sexuality during the early modern period, see J. Solé, *L'Amour en Occident* (Paris: Albin Michel, 1976), esp. pp. 72–96.
140. Chevassu, *Prônes*, vol. 1, p. 78 (sermon on the second Sunday of Epiphany).
141. Lambert, *La Maniére de bien instruire*, p. 131. Concerning the "veillées" (the evening meetings), see J.-L. Flandrin, *Familles* (Paris: Hachette, 1976), pp. 104–109.
142. Jeanmaire, *Sermons*, vol. 2, p. 11 (sermon no. 28).
143. Ibid., p. 12.
144. Ibid.
145. Chevassu, *Missionnaire paroissial*, vol. 1, p. 79 (sermon on the second Sunday after Epiphany).
146. Loriot, *Sermons*, vol. 5, pp. 427–428 (sermon no. 14).
147. Girard, *Les Petits prônes*, vol. 1, p. 332 (sermon on the second Sunday after Epiphany). The

same complaint may be found in Lebrun, *Sermons*, vol. 8, p. 159 (sermon no. 215, on the sacrament of marriage).
148. Bridaine, *Sermons*, vol. 5, pp. 134–136 ("Instruction sur le mariage").
149. J.-L. Flandrin, *Le Sexe et l'Occident* (Paris: Seuil, 1981), pp. 251–278.
150. Segneri, *Oeuvres*, vol. 3, p. 42 (sermon no. 23).
151. Léonard de Port-Maurice, *Traité de la confession générale*, p. 343.
152. Louis of Granada, *Mémorial de la vie chrétienne*, in *Oeuvres*, vol. 11, 2nd treatise, chap. 3, p. 587.
153. Jean Eudes, *Le Bon confesseur* (Lyon: 1679 ed.), p. 28.
154. François de Toulouse, *Le Missionnaire apostolique*, vol. 5, p. 233 (sermon no. 9, on chastity).
155. D'Outreman, *Le Pédagogue chrétien*, vol. 1, pp. 148–150.
156. Jeanmaire, *Sermons*, vol. 2, pp. 435–436 (sermon no. 51).
157. Beurrier, *Homélies*, p. 680 (sermon on the ninth Sunday after Whit Sunday).
158. Lambert, *La Maniere de bien instruire*, p. 245.
159. Girard, *Les Petits prônes*, vol. 3, p. 370 (sermon on the ninth Sunday after Whit Sunday).
160. J. Van Ussel, *Histoire de la repression sexuelle* (Paris: Laffont, 1972), pp. 198–205. The author writes: "It was at the beginning of the 18th century that masturbation was discovered" (p. 198). P. Ariès had already proven the contrary in speaking of Gerson and concerning the fifteenth century in his *L'Enfant et la vie famille sous l'Ancien Régime*, new edition (Paris: Seuil, 1973), pp. 109–112.
161. François de Toulouse, *Le Missionnaire apostolique*, vol. 4, p. 411 (sermon no. 16, on marriage).
162. Eudes, *Le Bon confesseur*, p. 301.
163. Bernardino of Siena, *Prediche volgari*, vol. 2, pp. 157–168 (sermon no. 21).
164. Lejeune, *Sermons*, vol. 8, p. 159 (sermon no. 215, on the sacrament of marriage).
165. Louis of Granada, *Mémorial de la vie chrétienne*, in *Oeuvres*, vol. 11, 2nd treatise, chap. 3, p. 587.
166. Eudes, *Le Bon confesseur*, pp. 285–286.
167. Jeanmaire, *Sermons*, vol. 2, p. 27 (sermon no. 27).
168. Bridaine, *Sermons*, vol. 5, p. 152 ("Instruction sur le mariage").
169. Eudes, *Le Bon confesseur*, pp. 255–303.
170. B.-L. Enfantin, *Les Sept péchés capitaux* (Valence: 1821–23) (3 books in one volume).
171. Bernardino of Siena, *Opera*, vol. 2, p. 527 (sermon: "De miseria conditionis humanae" in the *Sermones extraordinarii*).
172. Beurrier, *Homélies*, pp. 543–544.

CHAPTER 16

1. Concerning this last theme, see the forthcoming book by P. D'Iribarne on "l'homme de bien" and "l'amant de l'être" as well as his article, "L'Occident, l'Evangile et 'l'homme de bien'," *Etudes* (July 1981): 87–95.
2. See chaps. 1 and 2.
3. Bernardino of Siena, *Opera*, vol. 1, sermon 49 ("De Religione christiana"); vol. 2, sermons 19, 20, 23 of the *Sermones extraordinarii*, and sermons 9 and 14 of the *Sermones diversi*.
4. Camus, *Homélies* (sermon on the fourth Sunday after Epiphany; on Quinquagesima; on the fourth Sunday after Easter; on the fourteenth Sunday after Whit Sunday; on the twentieth Sunday after Whit Sunday; and on the twenty-fourth Sunday after Whit Sunday).
5. De la Font, *Prosnes*, vol. 1, pp. 612–664 (sermon on Quinquagesima), vol. 2, pp. 453–504 (sermon on the third Sunday after Easter).
6. Hébert, *Prosnes*, vol. 1, pp. 359–395 (sermon on the sixth Sunday after Epiphany); vol. 3, pp. 220–258 (sermon on the fourteenth Sunday after Whit Sunday).
7. Symon, *Prônes*, vol. 2 (sermon on the fourteenth Sunday after Whit Sunday).
8. Girard, *Les Petits Prônes*, vol. 3, pp. 3–26 (sermon on the third Sunday after Easter).
9. Grignion de Montfort, *Oeuvres*, canticles 29–39 included, 106, 107, 114, 150, 157.
10. Ibid., lines 1, 2, 7, 17, 79, 90, 93, 125, 139, 141 and 156.
11. *Recueil de cantiques*, in *Manuel des retraites*. I added the canticles of the first seven chapters to those of chapter 8 (supplement).
12. H. Jehova and M. F. Vieuille, eds., *Anthologie de la poésie tchèque* (Lausanne: L'Age d'homme, 1981), p. 41.

13. Ibid., pp. 83–85.
14. Ibid., p. 56.
15. Quoted in A. Vauchez, *La Sainteté en Occident aux derniers siècles du Moyen Age* (Paris: De Boccard, 1981), p. 423.
16. Girard, *Les Petits prônes*, vol. 3, p. 446 (sermon on the thirteenth Sunday after Whit Sunday), I Cor. 7:29.
17. Bourée, *Homélies*, vol. 1, p. 398 (sermon on Sexagesima).
18. De la Font, *Prosnes*, vol. 2, p. 471 (sermon on the third Sunday after Easter); Hébert, *Prosnes*, vol. 1, pp. 296–297 (sermon on the second Sunday of Lent); Grignion de Montfort, *Lettre circulaire aux amis de la croix*, in *Oeuvres*, p. 241.
19. *Cahiers lasalliens* 22 (1965): canticle no. 14, p. 39.
20. Hébert, *Prosnes*, vol. 4, p. 370 (sermon on the twenty-seventh Sunday after Whit Sunday or the 6th after Epiphany).
21. De Montargon, *Dictionnaire apostolique*, vol. 10, art. 3, p. 153.
22. *Cantiques*, in *Manuel des retraites*, vol. 2, p. 145.
23. Ibid., p. 219.
24. See above, (p. 16 of French original).
25. Bernardino of Siena, *Opera*, vol. 2, pp. 526–527 (sermon no. 18 of the *Sermones extraordinarii*) with a reference to Saint Bernard; De Toulouse, *Le Missionnaire apostolique*, vol. 4, p. 409 (sermon on marriage).
26. Francis de Sales, *Introduction à la vie dévote* (Paris: Seuil, 1962), pp. 304–305.
27. Camus, *Homélies*, pp. 272–273 (sermon on the sixth Sunday after Whit Sunday).
28. François de Toulouse, *Le Missionnaire apostolique*, vol. 5, p. 254 (sermon no. 10).
29. Loriot, *Sermons*, vol. 4, pp. 372–374 (sermon no. 12).
30. De Montargon, *Dictionnaire apostolique*, vol. 10, art. 5, pp. 276 and 279.
31. L. De Rougemont, *Traité de la virginité* (Paris: 1699), esp. pp. iv–v, 101–107, 301–305, 339–347, 354, and 364–371.
32. Lejeune, *Le Missionnaire de l'Oratoire*, vol. 4, sermons 101–118; vol. 5, sermons 114 and 120.
33. *Cantiques*, in *Manuel des retraites*, vol. 2, p. 219.
34. Grignion de Montfort, *Oeuvres*, pp. 950 and 952.
35. Loriot, *Sermons*, vol. 4, p. 201 (sermon no. 7, on the education of children).
36. Ibid., vol. 4, p. 293 (sermon no. 9, on marriage).
37. Camus, *Homélies*, p. 466 (sermon on the twenty-third Sunday after Whit Sunday).
38. Girard, *Les Petits prônes*, vol. 3, p. 355 (sermon on the ninth Sunday after Whit Sunday).
39. See above, (p. 484 of French original).
40. François de Toulouse, *Le Missionnaire apostolique*, vol. 5, p. 251 (sermon no. 10).
41. De Montargon, *Dictionnaire apostolique*, vol. 10, art. 6, p. 343.
42. Ibid., p. 351.
43. Bremond, *Histoire littéraire*, vol. 2, p. 506, and vol. 6, pp. 3–72.
44. Girard, *Les Petits prônes*, vol. 1, p. 322 (sermon on the second Sunday after Epiphany).
45. Ibid., pp. 322–323.
46. D'Outreman, *Le Pédagogue chrétien*, vol. 2, pp. 481–482.
47. Ibid.
48. François de Toulouse, *Le Missionnaire apostolique*, vol. 8, pp. 549, 551, and 557 (sermon on the second Sunday after Whit Sunday, "Le tombeau de la beauté").
49. Camus, *Homélies*, pp. 278–279 (sermon on the sixth Sunday after Whit Sunday).
50. G. Fournier, *Hydrographie* (Paris: 1643), book 10, chap. 3, p. 673. I would like to thank A. Cabantous for having drawn my attention to this book.
51. De la Font, *Prosnes*, vol. 2, p. 143 (sermon on the third Sunday of Lent).
52. Vieira, *Sermons*, vol. 4, p. 100 ("Sermon pour la fête de tous les saints").
53. De Montargon, *Dictionnaire apostolique*, vol. 3, art. 1, pp. 6 and 62.
54. *Cantiques*, *Cahiers lasalliens* 22 (1965): 50.
55. Réguis, *La Voix du pasteur*, vol. 2, pp. 153–154 (sermon on the seventh Sunday after Whit Sunday).
56. Bridaine, *Sermons*, vol. 3, p. 365 ("Sur la pénitence").
57. See, for example, Jeanmaire, *Sermons*, vol. 1, pp. 55–75 (sermon no. 3).
58. Léonard de Port-Maurice, *Oeuvres*, vol. 2, p. 121 (sermon on penitential processions, first procession).
59. Grignion de Montfort, *Oeuvres*, pp. 1641–1644 (canticle no. 157).
60. *Cantiques*, in *Manuel des retraites*, vol. 2, pp. 19–30.

61. Jehova and Vieuille, eds., *Anthologie de la poésie baroque tchèque*, p. 104.
62. See above, p.
63. Camus, *Homélies*, pp. 140–141 (sermon on Quinquagesima).
64. Vieira, *Plaidoyer en faveur des larmes d'Héraclite*, in *Sermons*, vol. 4, p. 551.
65. M. Veissière, "Monitoire de Guill. Briçonnet," *Revue d'histoire et d'art de la Brie et du pays de Meaux* 27 (1976): 40.
66. Godeau, *Homélies*, p. 100 (sermon on the second Sunday after Easter).
67. Ibid., p. 110 (sermon on the eighth Sunday after Easter).
68. Hébert, *Prosnes*, vol. 4, pp. 231–232 (sermon on the twenty-third Sunday after Whit Sunday).
69. I obtained this information from J. Le Goff, who in turn has taken it from Thomas of Eccleston, *De Adventu fratrum minorum in Anglia*.
70. Grignion de Montfort, *Oeuvres*, p. 951 (canticle no. 12).
71. Léonard de Port-Maurice, *Sermons pour les missions*, in *Oeuvres*, vol. 2, p. 418.
72. John Chrysostom, *In Matth. Homil.* VI, 6, in *PG*, vol. 57, cols. 69–70.
73. O. Maillard, *Opus quadragesimale*, sermon no. 18, quotes Ludolph of Saxony. See the article by M. Vigouroux in *Bessarione*, VII, vol. 4, fasc. 72. Insofar as Jonas of Orleans is concerned, see J. Chelini, *Histoire religieuse de l'Occident médiéval* (Paris: A. Colin, 1970), pp. 149–150. See also T. More, *The Dialogue of Comfort* (1534), chap. 13, p. 42 in the Yale ed. This data was sent to me by G. Marc'Hadour.
74. D'Outreman, *Le Pédagogue chrétien*, vol. 1, p. 103.
75. Montargon, *Dictionnaire apostolique*, vol. 12, art. 10, p. 638.
76. Ibid., p. 637.
77. Léonard de Port-Maurice, *Sermons pour les missions*, in *Oeuvres*, vol. 2, pp. 402–405.
78. Ibid., p. 405.
79. Godeau, *Homélies*, pp. 201–203 (sermon on the week of Epiphany).
80. E. Fléchier, *Panégyriques et autres sermons* (Paris: 1696), preface.
81. Godeau, *Homélies*, pp. 138–139 (sermon on the day of the Holy Innocents).
82. De la Font, *Prosnes*, vol. 4, p. 507 (sermon on the twenty-third Sunday after Whit Sunday).
83. Maillard, *Sermones dominicales*, f° 16 v° (sermon on the fourth Sunday after Whit Sunday).
84. See Delumeau, *La Peur*, pp. 186–187.
85. Vieira, *Sermons*, vol. 3, pp. 387–389 (sermon on the fourth Sunday after Easter).
86. Godeau, *Homélies*, vol. 2, p. 393 (sermon on the twenty-second Sunday after Whit Sunday).
87. Bourée, *Homélies*, vol. 4, p. 319 (sermon on the twenty-second Sunday after Whit Sunday). See also ibid., vol. 4, p. 91 (sermon on the fourteenth Sunday after Whit Sunday).
88. Hébert, *Prosnes*, vol. 4, p. 345 (sermon on the fourteenth Sunday after Whit Sunday).
89. Cantiques, in *Manuel des retraites*, vol. 2, p. 419.
90. Grignion de Montfort, *Oeuvres*, esp. pp. 1030–1038 (canticle no. 20); p. 1100 (canticle no. 28); p. 1370 (canticle no. 91); p. 1456 (canticle no. 108); p. 1602 (canticle no. 144); and p. 1655 (canticle no. 159).
91. Ibid., p. 1036 (canticle no. 20).
92. Ibid., p. 1100 (canticle no. 28).
93. Ibid., p. 1037 (canticle no. 20).
94. Ibid., p. 1038 (canticle no. 20).

Chapter 17

1. Bernardino of Siena, *Opera*, vol. 1, pp. 76–88, fifteenth sermon on Lent (*De Religione christiana*); pp. 117–125, nineteenth sermon on Lent; pp. 605–617, twenty-seventh sermon on Lent (*De Evangelio aeterno*) and sermon 57 on the same Lent; vol. 2, sermon 15 of the *Sermones diversi*.
2. Jeanmaire, *Sermons*, vol. 1, nos. 5, 9, 10 and 19.
3. *Bouquet de la mission*, part 2, pp. 304–333.
4. Maillard, *Sermones dominicales*, sermons no. 15, 16, and 19.
5. Camus, *Homélies*, pp. 20–31 and 327–339 (sermons on the third Sunday of Advent and the eleventh Sunday after Whit Sunday).
6. De la Font, *Prosnes*, vol. 2, pp. 250–304 (sermon on Palm Sunday); Chevassu, *Prônes*, vol. 1, pp. 88–89 (sermon on the third Sunday after Epiphany); Girard, *Les Petits prônes*, actually two interchangeable sermons, vol. 2, pp. 198–221 (sermon on the third Sunday of Lent) and

pp. 244–271 (sermon on the fourth Sunday of Lent). To this, one might add Girard, *Discours pours les prêtres au sujet de la confession*, in *Les Petits prônes*, vol. 4, pp. 465–486; Réguis, *La Voix du pasteur*, vol. 1, pp. 356–376 (sermon on Easter Sunday).
7. François de Toulouse, *Le Missionnaire apostolique*, vol. 2, sermons 4–24.
8. Lejeune, *Le Missionnaire*, vol. 1, sermons 6–32.
9. Loriot, *Sermons*, vol. 1, part 1, sermons 4–14; part 2, sermons 1–11.
10. *Cantiques*, in *Manuel des retraites*, vol. 2, chap. 3, and section 4 of the "supplement."
11. L. Abelly, *La Vie du vénérable serviteur de Dieu, Vincent de Paul* (Paris: 1664, reprint ed. 1839), vol. 1, p. 32.
12. G. Bouchard, *Le Village immobile. Sennely-en-Sologne au XVIIIe siècle* (Paris: Plon, 1972), pp. 291–292. I am here using the ideas that I previously developed in my own, *Un Chemin d'histoire*, pp. 173–180.
13. E. Droz, *Le Recueil Trepperel*, 2 vols. (Paris: 1935), here no. 27, lines 94 passim, quoted in Delumeau, *Un Chemin d'histoire*, pp. 35–36.
14. I am here using the distinction that I already formulated in my own *Un Chemin d'histoire*, p. 174.
15. Chevassu, *Missionnaire paroissial*, vol. 1, pp. 91–92 (sermon on the third Sunday after Epiphany).
16. Godeau, *Homélies*, vol. 2, pp. 92–93 (sermon on the second Sunday after Easter).
17. Concerning this point, see the rules given by Grignion de Montfort to his missionaries in *Oeuvres*, pp. 709–710.
18. See C. Berthelot du Chesnay, *Les Missions de saint Jean Eudes*, (Eudist Press, 1967), pp. 85–86.
19. Jeanmaire, *Sermons*, vol. 1, p. 2 (sermon no. 1).
20. Ibid., vol. 1, p. 64 (sermon no. 3).
21. Ibid., vol. 1, p. 67 (sermon no. 3).
22. Camus, *Homélies*, p. 339 (sermon on the eleventh Sunday after Whit Sunday).
23. Departmental Archives of Finistère, 6J49, quoted in Roudaut, *La Prédication*, vol. 2, pp. 19–20.
24. Departmental Archives of the Côtes-du-Nord, sermon B1a, série 1, quoted in ibid., vol. 2, pp. 40–41.
25. Girard, *Les Petits prônes*, vol. 2, p. 254 (sermon on the fourth Sunday of Lent).
26. Ibid., p. 248.
27. Ibid., p. 247.
28. J.-B. Le Vray, *Homélies ou explication literale et morale des Evangiles de tous les dimanches de l'année*, 5 vols. (Paris: 1701), vol. 1, pp. 223–226 (sermon on the fourth Sunday of Advent).
29. T. Rey-Mermet, *Laissez-vous réconcilier* (Paris: Le Centurion, 1972), p. 52. This book has been very useful to all historians who have tried to reconstruct what it meant to undergo confession.
30. Jeanmaire, *Sermons*, vol. 1, pp. 32–33 (sermon no. 1).
31. Girard, *Les Petits prônes*, vol. 2, p. 247 (sermon on the fourth Sunday of Lent).
32. De la Font, *Prosnes*, vol. 2, p. 255 (sermon on Palm Sunday).
33. Réguis, *La Voix du pasteur*, vol. 1, p. 365 (sermon on Easter Sunday).
34. Girard, *Les Petits prônes*, vol. 2, p. 200 (sermon on the third Sunday of Lent).
35. Godeau, *Homélies*, pp. 66–71 (sermon on the fourth Sunday of Advent).
36. Ibid., p. 87.
37. Bourée, *Homélies*, vol. 3, p. 285 (sermon on the seventh Sunday after Whit Sunday).
38. *Cantiques*, in *Cahiers lasalliens* 22 (1965): 49.
39. Ibid., p. 47.
40. This sermon is in Girard, *Le Petits prônes*, vol. 4, pp. 476–477.
41. Lambert, *La Maniére de bien instruire*, p. 265.
42. Jeanmaire, *Sermons*, vol. 1, p. 383 (sermon no. 19)
43. Chevassu, *Missionnaire paroissial*, vol. 1, pp. 93–94 (sermon on the third Sunday after Epiphany).
44. Réguis, *La Voix du pasteur*, vol. 1, pp. 366–367 (sermon on Easter Sunday).
45. Le Vray, *Homélies*, vol. 1, pp. 227–228 (sermon on the fourth Sunday of Advent).
46. Bourdaloue, *Oeuvres* (Noyon: 1830 ed.), vol. 7, pp. 19–20 (sermon on the thirteenth Sunday after Whit Sunday). This sermon inspired the sermon of an eighteenth-century priest of Brittany. See Roudaut, *La Prédication*, vol. 2, pp. 38–55.

47. Denzinger, *Enchiridion*, p. 402, session no. 14 of the council, canon 7. See Rey-Mermet, *Laissez-vous réconcillier*, p. 62.
48. I consulted the 1829 ed. of the *Rituel à l'usage de Bordeaux*, pp. 121–122. I have added the italics.
49. Bernardino of Siena, *Opera*, vol. 1, pp. 81–82 (sermon no. 15 on Lent, *De Religione christiana*).
50. Ibid., vol. 2, sermon no. 15.
51. Maillard, *Sermones dominicales*, f° 38 r° (sermon on the eighth Sunday after Whit Sunday).
52. Yvan, *Trompette du ciel*, pp. 495–505 (part 3, chaps. 41 and 42).
53. Yvan, *Trompette du ciel*, pp. 495–505 (chaps. 41 and 42 of part 3).
54. Loriot, *Sermons*, vol. 1, part 2, sermon 8, pp. 208–227.
55. Jeanmaire, *Sermons*, vol. 1, p. 721 (sermon no. 4).
56. Chevassu, *Missionnaire paroissial*, vol. 1, p. 93 (sermon on the third Sunday after Epiphany).
57. Bourdaloue, *Oeuvres*, vol. 7, pp. 16–17 (sermon on the thirteenth Sunday after Pentecost).
58. Jeanmaire, *Sermons*, vol. 1, pp. 183–184 (sermon no. 8).
59. *Cantiques*, in *Cahiers lasalliens* 22 (1965): 47.
60. Grignion de Montfort, *Oeuvres*, p. 965 (canticle no. 13).
61. Chevassu, *Missionnaire paroissial*, vol. 1, p. 90 (sermon on the third Sunday after Epiphany).
62. Ibid.
63. Jeanmaire, *Sermons*, vol. 1, p. 81 (sermon no. 4). This warning is repeated in sermon no. 10, p. 202.
64. Girard, *Les Petits prônes*, vol. 2, p. 206 (sermon on the third Sunday of Lent).
65. Charles de Genève, *Les Trophées sacrés (Missions des Capucins en Savoie, dans l'Ain, la Suisse romande et la vallée d'Aoste à la fin du XVIe et au XVIIe siècle)*, 3 vols. (Lausanne: Felix Tisscrand), vol. 3, p. 237. I have already used this book in my *Un Chemin d'histoire*, p. 176.
66. Réguis, *La Voix du pasteur*, vol. 1, pp. 362–363 (sermon on Easter Sunday).
67. Le Vray, *Homélies*, vol. 1, pp. 218–219 (sermon on the fourth Sunday of Advent).
68. Jeanmaire, *Sermons*, vol. 1, p. 72, (sermon no. 3).
69. Bouchard, *Un village immobile*, p. 291; Delumeau, *Un Chemin d'histoire*, pp. 174–175.
70. Loriot, *Sermons*, vol. 4, p. 222 (sermon no. 8).
71. Ibid., vol. 4, pp. 299–300 (sermon no. 9).
72. Lejeune, *Sermons*, vol. 8, p. 159 (sermon no. 215).
73. Girard, *Les Petits prônes*, vol. 4, pp. 476–477 ("Discours pour les prêtres au sujet de la confession").
74. Lambert, *La Manière de bien instruire*, pp. 264–265.
75. Jeanmaire, *Sermons*, vol. 1, p. 190 (sermon no. 9).
76. Ibid., p. 369 (sermon no. 19).
77. Sermon of 1752 quoted by Roudaut, *La Prédication*, vol. 2, pp. 22 and 31.
78. Chevassu, *Missionnaire paroissial*, vol. 1, p. 90 (sermon on the fourth Sunday of Advent).
79. Réguis, *La Voix du pasteur*, vol. 1, p. 357 (sermon on Easter Sunday).
80. Le Vray, *Homélies*, vol. 1, p. 220 (sermon on the fourth Sunday after Advent).
81. Abelly, *La Vie*, vol. 1, chap. 8, p. 32 (in the 1839 ed.).
82. Charles de Genève, *Les Trophées*, vol. 3, p. 237.
83. Delumeau, *Un Chemin d'histoire*, p. 175.
84. Charles de Genève, *Les Trophées*, vol. 3, p. 167.
85. See above, (p. 524 of French original).
86. Jeanmaire, *Sermons*, vol. 2, p. 328 (sermon no. 46).
87. Charles de Genève, *Les Trophées*, vol. 3, p. 164.
88. Ibid., pp. 164–165.
89. Ibid., pp. 182–183.
90. Ibid., p. 216.
91. Ibid., p. 229.
92. Berthelot Du Chesnay, *Les Missions*, p. 207. See also B. Dompnier, "Le Missionnaire et son public," in *Bossuet. La prédication au XVIIe siècle*, Proceedings of the Dijon 1977 Symposium, pp. 118–119.
93. S. Gruzinski, "Délires et visions chez les Indiens du Mexique," *Mélanges de l'Ecole française de Rome (M.A.T.M.)* 86 2 (1974): 446–480.
94. Abelly, *Vie*, book 2, section 2, vol. 1, p. 326 of the 1839 ed.
95. Charles de Genève, *Les Trophées*, vol. 3, p. 172, but see also pp. 171, 178, 181, 185, 188, 191, 211.

96. Ibid., p. 237.
97. Ibid., p. 203.
98. Lambert, *La Manière de bien instruire*, p. 265, refers to Psalm 38, line 5.
99. Jeanmaire, *Sermons*, vol. 2, pp. 354–355 (sermon no. 47).
100. Girard, *Les Petits prônes*, vol. 2, p. 347 ("Discours pour la communion des enfants").
101. Chevassu, *Missionnaire paroissial*, vol. 1, p. 223 (sermon on Easter Sunday).
102. Quoted in Roudaut, *La Prédication*, pp. 31–32.
103. Jeanmaire, *Sermons*, vol. 2, p. 355 (sermon no. 47).
104. Ibid., p. 356.
105. Girard, *Les Petits prônes*, vol. 2, pp. 339–340 (sermon on Palm Sunday).
106. Montargon, *Dictionnaire apostolique*, vol. 1, art. 7, pp. 465–544.
107. Réguis, *La Voix du pasteur*, vol. 2, pp. 35–36 (sermon on the second Sunday after Whit Sunday).
108. Bernardino of Siena, *Opera*, vol. 1, pp. 857–858 (sermon no. 54 of Lent, *De Evangelio aeterno*).
109. Godeau, *Homélies*, vol. 1, p. 264 (sermon on the fifth Sunday after Epiphany).
110. Lejeune, *Le Missionnaire de l'Oratoire*, vol. 12, sermon no. 353, pp. 307–317.
111. Bourée, *Homélies*, vol. 2, p. 105 (sermon on the fourth Sunday of Lent).
112. Loriot, *Sermons*, vol. 7, pp. 148 and 163 (sermon no. 4).
113. Chevassu, *Missionnaire paroissial*, vol. 1, p. 233 (sermon on Palm Sunday).
114. Godeau, *Homélies*, pp. 189–191 (sermon on Sunday of the Octave of the Holy Sacrament).
115. Lambert, *La Manière de bien instruire*, p. 266.
116. Jeanmaire, *Sermons*, vol. 2, pp. 351–354 (sermon no. 43).
117. Ibid., p. 358.
118. *Cantiques*, in *Manuel des retraites*, vol. 2, p. 282.
119. Léonard de Port-Maurice, *Sermons pour les missions*, vol. 2, p. 19, (sixth exhortation, profanation of the Holy Sacrament).
120. Ibid., p. 22.
121. Chevassu, *Missionnaire paroissial*, vol. 1, p. 234 (sermon on Palm Sunday).
122. Réguis, *La Voix du pasteur*, vol. 1, p. 414 (sermon on Easter Sunday).
123. Sermon translated by Roudaut, *La Prédication*, vol. 2, pp. 56–81.
124. Girard, *Les Petits prônes*, vol. 2, pp. 347–348 ("Discours pour la communion des enfants").
125. Loriot, *Sermons*, vol. 7, pp. 20–21 (sermon no. 6).

CHAPTER 18

1. E. Sevrin, *Les Missions religieuses en France sous la Restauration*, 2 vols. (Paris: Vrin, 1948–59), vol. 2, p. 503.
2. Martin, *Livre*, vol. 1, pp. 377–379.
3. Liguori, *Apparecchio*, introduction by O. Gregorio, p. xxxv.
4. Roche, "La Mémoire de la mort," pp. 83–84.
5. See above, (pp. 382–389 of French original).
6. Roche, "La Mémoire de la mort," pp. 83–84. See also J. Brancolini and M. T. Bouissy, "La Vie provinciale du livre à la fin de l'Ancien Régime," in *Livre et société dans la France du XVIIe siècle* (Paris: Mouton, 1970), vol. 2, pp. 3–37. Insofar as the *Bibliothèque bleue* is concerned, see G. Bollème, "Littérature populaire et littérature de colportage au XVIIIe siècle," in ibid., vol. 1, esp. pp. 79–80, and *La Bibliothèque bleue*, pp. 247–266. See also A. Morin, *Catalogue descriptif de la Bibliothèque bleue de Troyes* (Geneva: Droz, 1974).
7. See Lebrun, Quéniart, and Vénard, *Histoire générale de l'enseignement*, vol. 2, pp. 458–459.
8. Liguori, *Apparecchio*, p. 3.
9. Crasset, *Double préparation*, foreword, unpaginated.
10. Favre, *La Mort*, p. 154, n. 256; article "France" in the *Dictionnaire de spiritualité*, vol. 5, cols 785–1004.
11. Ariès, *L'Homme*, p. 116; M. Vovelle, *Idéologies et mentalités* (Paris: Maspero, 1982), p. 47.
12. *Conduite chrétienne ou formulaire de prières à l'usage des pensionnaires des Ursulines* (1734), quoted in Sonnet, *L'Education des filles*, vol. 1, p. 229.
13. Concerning the traumas that a "punishing God" or an "eternally crucified God" might produce in children, see M. Joz-Roland, *Qu'as-tu fait de ton Dieu?* (Paris: Seuil, 1970).
14. This *Collection* ran from 1844 to 1892.

15. I would like to thank Marie-Elizabeth Ducreux for the information she provided me. This specialist on Czech hymns is also the author of a Ph.D. dissertation "Hymnologia Bohemica" (University of Paris III, 1982) and of an article, "De la tradition médiévale aux recueils des XVIIe et XVIIIe siècles: les cantiques en pays tchèques," in J. Delumeau, ed., *Histoire vécue du peuple chrétien*, vol. 1, pp. 405–430.
16. Ducreux, "Hymnologia Bohemica," pp. 133 and 198.
17. J. Quéniart, "Les Représentations de Dieu dans les cantiques des XVIIe et XVIIIe siècles," *Daphnis, Zeitschrift für Mittlere deutsche Literatur* 3/4 (1979): 52. A systematic study of French hymns would have to begin with A. Gastoue, *Le Cantique populaire en France. Ses sources, son histoire, augmentées d'une bibliographie générale des anciens cantiques et noëls* (Lyon: 1924). See also the articles by J. D'Ortigue, "Cantique" and "Noël" (Christmas) in the *Dictionnaire . . . du plainchant* (Paris: Migne, 1853), and the article "Cantique spirituel" in the *Dictionnaire de Spiritualité*, vol. 2, cols. 109–116.
18. Bourée, *Homélies*, vol. 1, beginning of the sermon on the first Sunday of Advent.
19. The bibliography I am about to suggest is not meant, of course, to be exhaustive. See B. Dompnier on the missions to the Dauphiné in the eighteenth century, and Croix, *La Bretagne*, pp. 1212–1240, as well as, by the same author, *La Mort Bretonne* (forthcoming). One may also consult the article on "Missions paroissiales" in the encyclopedia *Catholicisme*, vol. 9, pp. 401–403, and the article by F. Lebrun, "Les Missions des Lazaristes en Haute-Bretagne," pp. 15–38. For Italy, I used L. Mezzadri, "Le Missioni popolari della Congregazione della Missione nello Stato della Chiesa (1642–1700)," *Rivista della Storia della Chiesa in Italia* 3 (1979): 12–44; G. F. Rossi, "Missioni Vincenziane, religiosità e vita sociale nella diocesi di Tivoli nei secoli XVII–XIX," *Atti e Memorie della società tiburtina di storia e d'arte* 53 (1980): 143–210; E. Novi-Chavarria, "L'Attività missionaria dei Gesuiti nel Mezzogiorno d'Italia tra XVI e XVIII secolo," in G. Galasso and C. Russo, eds., *Per la Storia sociale e religiosa del Mezzogiorno d'Italia*, vol. 2 (Naples: Guida, 1982). For German-speaking countries, see esp. B. Duhr, *Geschichte der Jesuiten in den Ländern deutscher Zunge*, 4 vols. (Freiburg-in-Breisgau: 1907–28). For Portugal, see E. Dos Santos, "Les Missions des temps modernes au Portugal," in Delumeau, ed., *Histoire vécue du peuple chrétien*, vol. 1, pp. 431–454.
20. Sevrin, *Les Missions*, vol. 1, p. 183.
21. Stendhal, *Romans* (Paris: Pléiade, 1947), vol. 2, p. 873.
22. Barbey d'Aurevilly, *Oeuvres romanesques* (Paris: Pléiade, 1966), vol. 2, p. 290.
23. J. Joyce, [*A Portrait of the Artist as a Young Man*], (Harmondsworth: Penguin, 1977), p. 112.
24. W. Witos, *Moje wspomnienia* [*My Recollections*], 3 vols. (Paris: Institut Literacki, 1964–65), vol. 1, p. 94. I owe this translation to Mrs. Nitecki, whom I would like to thank here.
25. See M. Bernos, "La Pastorale des laïcs dans l'oeuvre de Pierre Collet, Lazariste," in *Actes du Colloque international d'études vincentiennes* (1981), pp. 289–309.
26. J. Armogathe, "Les Catéchismes et l'enseignement populaire en France au XVIIIe siècle," in *Images du peuple au XVIIIe siècle* (Aix symposium) (Paris: A. Colin, 1973), pp. 103–122. Quéniart, *Les Hommes, l'Eglise et Dieu*, pp. 99–102.
27. P. Collet, *Sermons pour les retraites*, in Migne, *Collection des orateurssacrés*, vol. 55, vol. 522, quoted in Bernos, "La Pastorale," p. 304.
28. P. M. Gy, "Les Funérailles d'après le Rituel de 1614," *La Maison-Dieu* 44/1 (1955): 70–85; ibid., "Le Nouveau Rituel romain des funérailles," in ibid. 101/1 (1970): 15–32; Favre, *La Mort*, p. 79.
29. Favre, *La Mort*, p. 157.
30. Lebrun, *Les Hommes et la mort en Anjou*, p. 494 (conclusion).
31. Lebrun, *Parole de Dieu*, p. 24.
32. Quéniart, *Les Hommes, l'Eglise et Dieu*, p. 276.
33. E. Novi-Chavarria, "L'Attività missionaria," in *Per la Storia*, vol. 2, pp. 13–14.
34. Chaunu, *Mourir à Paris*, p. 149. See also Croix, *La Bretagne*, vol. 2, pp. 1132–1154.
35. Vovelle, *Vision de la mort*, p. 50.

CHAPTER 19

1. French translation by D. Olivier, *La Foi de Luther* (Paris: Beauchesne, 1978), pp. 132–133, here p. 130.
2. French translation by H. Strohl, *Luther jusqu'en 1520*, p. 262.

3. Luther, *Oeuvres*, vol. 5, p. 229 (*Du Serf arbitre*).
4. Luther, *Werke* (Weimar: 1923), vol. 35, p. 478. B. Vogler, "Attitudes devant la mort et cérémonies funèbres dans les Eglises protestantes rhénanes vers 1600," *Archives de Sociologie des Religions* 39 (1975): p. 139.
5. Calvin, *Institution*, book 3, chap. 2, 28 (vol. 3, p. 49).
6. Ibid., book 3, chap. 13, 3 (vol. 3, p. 229).
7. Calvin, *Sermons sur les deux epistres de sainct Paul à Timothée et sur l'epistre à Tite* (Geneva: 1563), p. 504.
8. *The Works of John Whitgift*, The Third Portion, Parker Society (1853 ed.), p. 622. See L. Carrive, "L'Assurance du salut, doctrine de la Réforme en Angleterre," *Etudes Anglaises* 31 (3–4) (July–Sept. 1978): 259–272. W. Haller, *The Rise of Puritanism (1570–1643)*: (Pennsylvania Paperbacks, 1st ed., 1938; reprint ed., 1972), pp. 65–67.
9. This hymn is found in the collection called that of Elsner, Brno, 1783, p. 865. This canticle is also to be found in the nineteenth-century editions of the *Cithara sanctorum* (the most important Czech collection of canticles). The translation and the above information are all from Elisabeth Ducreux.
10. See above, (p. 378 and p. 379 of French original).
11. Talk by Anne Sauvy in my seminar. The Orthodox Church also made use of this iconography.
12. Introduction of J. Green to the translation of *La Lettre écarlate* [*The Scarlet Letter*] (Paris: La Nouvelle Edition, 1947), p. 13.
13. I used the English translation of A. Strindberg, *The Son of a Servant* (London: Jonathan Cape, 1967), pp. 18–19, 30–33. See M. Douglas, *Natural Symbols* (New York: Pantheon Books, 1970), pp. 108–109.
14. T. Becon, *Works* (1563), vol. 2, p. 320, and vol. 3, p. 598. P. E. Hughes, *Theology of the English Reformers* (Grand Rapids, MI: W. B. Eerdmans, 1966), pp. 123–124.
15. P. S. Seaver, *The Puritan Lectureship. The Politics of Religious Dissent, 1560–1662* (Stanford: University Press, 1970), pp. 25 and 32.
16. Ibid., p. 38.
17. J. W. Blench, *Preaching in England in the Late Fifteenth and Sixteenth Centuries. A Study of English Sermons, 1450–c. 1600* (Oxford: Blackwells, 1964), p. 320, as well as all of chapter 6.
18. The following discussion is the outcome of research that E. Chiovaro did for me. Concerning Lutheran preaching, see esp. W. Beste, *Die Bedeutesten Kanzelredner der lutherichen Kirche*, 3 vols. (Leipzig: 1856–86); Caspari, "Homiletik, in *Realencyclopädie für protestantische Theologie und Kirche* (3rd ed., Leipzig, 1900), vol. 8, pp. 295–308; M. Schian, "Geschichte der christlichen Predigten," in ibid., vol. 15, pp. 623–747.
19. See, for example, the book by G. Walter (Georgius Walterius), *Regulae vitae christianae* (Wittenberg: 1572).
20. This dissertation by Melanchthon can be found in A. Corvinus, *Postilla in evangelia dominicalia* (Strassburg: 1537), fols. 73–79.
21. A. Hyperius, *De Formandis concionibus sacris, seu de interpretatione scriprurarum populari libri duo* (Basle 1562 edition consulted), French ed. Geneva 1963. See P. Denis, "L'Evangile à pleine bouche," *La Vie spirituelle* 63 (May–Aug. 1981): 469.
22. Ibid., p. 1.
23. See above, (p. 546 in French original).
24. Schrader, *De Rhetoricorum*, pp. 262–263.
25. Ibid., p. 266.
26. Quoted in M. Lienhard, *Foi et vie des Protestants d'Alsace* (Strassburg: Oberlin, 1981), p. 60, and taken from the Ph.D. diss. of C. C. Schildberg, "Le Pastorat du comté de Hanau-Lichtenberg de 1618 à 1789," 2 vols. (University of Strassburg, 1980).
27. P. Du Moulin, *Décade de sermons* (Sedan: 1637), pp. 115–116.
28. Pilkington, *Works* (Parker Society, 1842) pp. 354 passim; Hughes, *Theology of the English Reformers*, pp. 131–132.
29. Luther, *Oeuvres*, vol. 6, p. 252 (Commentary on Psalm 117).
30. On Lorenzo Valla and the attitude that the reformers had concerning him, see F. Gaeta, *Lorenzo Valla. Filologia e storia nell'umanesimo italiano* (Napoli: Istituto Italiano per gli Studi di Storia, 1955), pp. 70–71.
31. Calvin, *Institution chrétienne*, book 1, chap. 15, section 8, vol. 1, p. 143.
32. Luther, *Oeuvres*, vol. 7, pp. 240–241 (*Articles de Smalkalde*).
33. J. Picker, *Luthers Vorlesungen über den Römerbrief* (4th ed., 1930), vol. 2, pp. 143–144. Translation in Rondet, *Le Péché*, p. 202.

34. The Latin text is to be found in B. J. Kidd, ed., *Documents illustrative of the Continental Reformation* (Oxford, Clarendon Press, 1967), p. 262. See also "The Augsburg Confession: Perceptions and Receptions," in the special issue of the *Sixteenth Century Journal* (1980). A French translation can be found in G. Casalis, *Luther et l'Eglise confessante* (Paris: Seuil, 1962), p. 141.
35. A. Jundt, *La Formule de Concorde* (French trans, 1948), p. 7.
36. Ibid., p. 8.
37. Luther, *Oeuvres*, vol. 3, p. 71 (commentary on the *Magnificat*).
38. Ibid., vol. 4, p. 58 (*That Jesus Christ was Born a Jew*).
39. Calvin, *Institution*, book 2, chap. 1, section 5, vol. 2, p. 15. An editiorial note points out that "Here there is no discredit meant concerning the act of procreation." I believe, quite on the contrary, that the discredit is very obviously meant to come through. [Translation by F. L. Battles in Calvin, *The Institutes of the Christian Religion*, ed. J. T. McNeill (Philadelphia: 1960), vol. 1, p. 248.]
40. See Niemeyer, *Collectio Confessionum in ecclesiis reformatis publicatarum* (1840), pp. 16–35, section 4.
41. Calvin, *Institution*, book 2, chap. 1, section 2, vol. 2, pp. 18–19.
42. See esp. ibid., book 2, chap. 8, sections 41–44, vol. 2, pp. 163–166.
43. Luther, *Werke* (Weimar ed.), vol. 56, p. 271, trans. in H. Strohl, *Luther jusqu'en 1520*, pp. 133–134.
44. Luther, *Werke*, vol. 4, p. 343.
45. Calvin, *Institution*, book 2, chap. 8, section 49, vol. 2, p. 172.
46. R. Mehl, *Explication de la Confession de foi de La Rochelle* (Paris: Les Bergers et les Mages, 1959), art. 11, p. 59. Actually this confession was developed in Paris in 1551 and was "confirmed" at La Rochelle in 1571.
47. Erasmus, *Liber de sarcienda ecclesiae concordia* (n.p.: 1533), p. 84, quoted in G. Strauss, *Luther's House of Learning. Indoctrination of the Young in German Reformation* (Baltimore: Johns Hopkins University Press, 1978), p. 212.
48. C. Aquila, *Des Kleinen Catechismi Erklerung*, in J. M. Reu, *Quellen zur Luthers Haus*, p. 209.
49. A. Osiander, *Catechismus oder Kindferpredig*, in E. Sehling, *Institut für evangelisches Kirchenrecht* (Tübingen: 1955), vol. 11, part 1, pp. 265–266, quoted in Strauss, *Luther's House*, p. 210.
50. G. Seebass, *Bibliographia Osiandrica* (Niewkoop: 1971), pp. 67–97; Strauss, *Luther's House*, p. 365.
51. S. Hieron, *Sermons . . . Formerly Collected Together by Himselfe* (London: 1620), p. 330.
52. R. Sibbes, *The Churches Complaint and Confidence in Three Sermons* (1639), p. 304.
53. R. Sibbes, *The Dead Man, or the State of Every Man by Nature in One Sermon* (1619), pp. 143–144.
54. C. Love, *A Treatise of Effectual Calling and Election. In XVI Sermons on 2 Pet. 1:10* (London: 1653), p. 15.
55. H. Latimer, *Works* (Parker Society ed.), vol. 1, pp. 59 passim; Hughes, *Theology*, pp. 127–128.
56. Hieron, *Sermons*, p. 237.
57. Ibid., p. 249.
58. C. Love, *Heavens Glory, Hells Terror (17 sermons)* (London: 1653), pp. 8–10.
59. See above, (pp. 461–462 of French original).
60. Hieron, *Sermons*, p. 535.
61. Love, *Heavens Glory*, p. 7.
62. Ibid., p. 10.
63. All of the documentation concerning the Great Awakening comes from the research done by Annie Becker. The translations into French were also done by her. See also P. Greven, *The Protestant Temperament*, chap. 3, pp. 62–150.
64. G. Tennent, *A Solemn Warning to the Secure World, from the God of Terrible Majesty* (Boston: 1735), pp. 70–135.
65. *General Magazine*, ed. by B. Franklin (Philadephia: 1741), p. 281.
66. J. Thompson, *The Government of the Church of Christ* (Philadelphia: 1741), p. 44.
67. J. Thompson, *The Doctrine of Conviction Set in a Clear Light* (Philadelphia: 1741), p. 35.
68. S. Finley, *Satan Stripped of his Angelick Robe* (Philadelphia: 1743); p. 41.
69. G. Tennent, *The Necessity of Holding Fast the Truth Relating to the Errors lately Vented by some Moravians* (Boston: 1743), p. 12.
70. Tennent, *A Solemn Warning*, p. 132.

71. Finley, *Clear Light*, p. 8.
72. G. Tennent, *The Danger of an Unconverted Ministry*, ed. by B. Franklin (Philadelphia: 1740), p. 9.
73. T. Prince, *An Account of the Revival of Religion in Boston in the Years 1740–1743* (Boston: 1744), p. 17.
74. G. Tennent, *The Late Association for Defence* (Philadelphia: 1748), p. 2.
75. G. Tennent, *For a Provincial Thanksgiving* (Philadelphia: 1750), p. 15.
76. Preface by G. Tennent to a short book by his brother John, *The Nature of Regeneration Opened* (Boston: 1735), pp. ii–v.
77. T. Prince, *The Christian History* (the oldest religious periodical published in the American colonies). At this period, it was composed of letters from various pastors describing the action of the *Revival*, 2 vols. (1743–44), here vol. 2, p. 254.
78. Ibid., vol. 2, p. 300.
79. Thompson, *The Government*, p. 33.
80. Letter of an Anglican pastor published in W. S. Perry, *Historical Collections relating to the American Colonial Church* (Hartford: 1871), p. 230.
81. Prince, *The Christian History*, 2 vols. each 416 pages.
82. Ibid., vol. 1, p. 255.
83. Ibid., vol. 2, p. 240.

CHAPTER 20

1. I owe this information to Professor S. Göransson of Uppsala. The main works on the subject are G. Lizell, *Svedberg och Nohrborg. En homiletisk studie* (Uppsala: 1910); G. Lindberg, *Johannes Rudbeckius som predikant* (Uppsala: 1927); D. Lindovist, *Studier in der svenska andaktslitteraturen under stormaktstiden* (Uppsala: 1939); I. Kalm, *Studier i svensk predikan under 1600-talets göra hälft* (Uppsala: 1948); O. Nordstandh, *Den äldre svenska pietismus litteratur* (Lund: 1951); ibid., *Den svenska pietismen och Katolsk andakts litteratur* (1952).
2. H. C. White, *English Devotional Literature (Prose) 1600–1640* (Madison: 1931), pp. 75–78.
3. Ibid., pp. 79–80.
4. Ibid., pp. 81–83.
5. Ibid., pp. 105–107.
6. J. Brenz (Brentius), *Pericope evangeliorum, quae singulis diebus dominicis publice in Ecclesia recitari solent* (Frankfurt: 1559), pp. 149–150.
7. Aquila, *Des Kleinen Catechismi* in Reu, *Quellen*, p. 173, quoted in Strauss, *Luther's House*, p. 46. Concerning the English sermons of the same period, see the introduction of R. L. Greaves to vol. 9 of the *Miscellaneous Works of John Bunyan* (Oxford: 1981), pp. xli–xlii.
8. P. Du Moulin, *Decade de sermons* (Sedan: 1637), p. 1. Concerning P. Du Moulin, see L. Rimbault, *Pierre du Moulin 1568–1658 un pasteur classique à l'âge classique* (Paris: Vrin, 1966).
9. L. Tronson, *Manuel du séminariste*, in *Oeuvres complètes* (Paris: Migne, 1857), vol. 1, p. 42.
10. C. Mather, *Diary*, ed. by Worthington Chauncery Frod, 2 vols. (New York: n.d.), vol. 1, pp. 30–32, quoted in P. Greven, *The Protestant Temperament. Patterns of Child Rearing, Religious Experience and the Self in Early America* (New York: A.A. Knopf, 1977), p. 67.
11. I am here using the expression used by P. Greven in the above-mentioned book.
12. J. Wesley, *Works* (Oxford: 1975), p. 359 ("On Self-denial"); Greven, *The Protestant*, p. 60.
13. G. Whitfield, *The Works of. . .*, 6 vols. (London: 1751), vol. 1, pp. 5 and 8, quoted in Greven, *The Protestant Temperament*, p. 73.
14. Brenz, *Pericope evangeliorum*, pp. 438–439.
15. J. Arndt, *De la Régénération ou nouvelle naissance*, French trans. (Strassburg: 1836), p. 16.
16. E. François, "Livre, confession et société urbaine en Allemagne au XVIIIe siècle: Spire," *Revue d'Histoire moderne et contemporaine* 29 (July–September 1982): 364–365.
17. Hieron, *Sermons* (London: 1620), p. 6.
18. M. Spufford, *Small Books and Pleasant Histories* (London: Methuen, 1981), p. 203.
19. J.-Cl. Margolin, "L'Inspiration érasmienne de Jacob Cats," in *Commémoration nationale d'Erasme. Actes* (Brussels: 1970), pp. 114–151.
20. Quoted in ibid. as well as in G. Derudder, *Etude sur la vie et les oeuvres de Cats* (1898), p. 355.
21. J. Cats, *Werken* (Amsterdam: 1658), vol. 2, p. 405, quoted in Margolin, "L'Inspiration," p. 145.

22. Margolin, "L'Inspiration," p. 144.
23. Cats, *Werken*, vol. 2, p. 505 (*Dialogue between Death and an Old Man*), quoted in Margolin, "L'Inspiration," p. 145.
24. See above, (pp. 395–396 of French original).
25. Cats had a political career.
26. Cats, *Werken*, vol. 2, p. 283 quoted and trans. by Derudder, *Etude sur la vie*, p. 358, and also quoted by Margolin, "L'Inspiration," p. 146.
27. Cats, *Werken*, vol. 2, p. 345 quoted and trans. by Derudder, *Etude sur la vie*, p. 357, and also quoted by Margolin, "L'Inspiration," p. 148.
28. J. Gerhardt, *Sacrarum homiliarum in pericopas Evangeliorum dominicalium et praecipuorum totius anni festorum, libri duo*. The letter-preface is of 1634. The edition I consulted is the Iena 1647 one, vol. 1, p. 636 (*Dominica judica*, homily no. 4).
29. Ibid., vol. 2, pp. 688–689 (*Dominica XVI post Trinit.*, homily no. 1).
30. Ibid., pp. 693–694 (*Dominica XVI post Trinit.*, homily no. 2).
31. Spufford, *Small Books*, esp. pp. 129–147 and 102–208.
32. I have taken out the data concerning the seventeenth-century from the tables provided by D. Roche, "La Mémoire de la mort," pp. 91–93.
33. Spufford, *Small Books*, p. 203.
34. Ibid., p. 138. Concerning the Protestant *Artes moriendi*, see D. W. Atkinson, "The English Ars moriendi: its Protestant Transformation," *Renaissance and Reformation* 6 (1982): 1–10.
35. Ibid., p. 203–204.
36. Ibid., p. 204.
37. G. Tennent, *18 Sermons on important subjects adapted to the perillous State of the British Nation* (Philadelphia: 1758), p. 115.
38. J. Donne, *Sermons*, 10 vols., ed. by G. R. Potter and E. M. Simpson, eds. (University of California Press, 1955), vol. 2, p. 74.
39. Ibid., vol. 2.
40. M. Tuchle, C. A. Bouman, and J. Lebrun, *Nouvelle Histoire de l'Eglise* (Paris: Seuil, 1968), vol. 3, p. 428.
41. Drelincourt, *Les Consolations*, vol. 1, p. 81 in the 1734 ed.
42. F. Breuillaud and B. Urien, "Scolarisation et religion dans le diocèsede Die aux XVIIe–XVIIIe siècles," Master's thesis, University of Paris I, 1975, p. 43.
43. White, *English Devotional Literature*, p. 13, quoted in Chartier, "Les Arts de mourir," p. 73, n. 47.
44. White, *English Devotional Literature*, p. 13. This success explains why Sparke wrote a sequel to his book In 1652.
45. Ibid., esp. p. 158, 164, 263.
46. R. Baxter, *The Catechizing of Families: A Teacher of Householders how to teach their Households* (London: 1683), pp. 432–433.
47. J. Donne, "Hymne to God my God in my sickness," quoted in W. R. Mueller, *John Donne Preacher* (Princeton, NJ: Princeton University Press, 1962), p. 197.
48. Ibid., p. 176.
49. Donne, *Sermons*, vol. 4, pp. 45–56, quoted in Mueller, *John Donne*, pp. 195–196.
50. Donne, *Sermons*, vol. 10, p. 238, quoted in Mueller, *John Donne*, p. 196.
51. J. Taylor, *The Rule and Exercises of Holy Dying*, ed. by A. R. Waller (London: 1901), pp. 28–29, quoted in White, *English Devotional Literature*, pp. 268–269.
52. "King of fear" is an expression that can also be found in Robert Bolton's, *A Discourse about the state of true happinesse delivered in certaine Sermons* (1638), chap. 7, pp. 7–8.
53. Hieron, *Sermons*, pp. 645–655.
54. Tennent, *18 Sermons*, p. 132.
55. Brenz, *Pericope evangeliorum*, pp. 436–437.
56. C. Drelincourt, *Recueil de sermons* (sermons delivered at Charenton) (Geneva: 1664), p. 360.
57. Ibid., p. 512. Another very powerful text describing the wrath of God "the generous lion" and "the untamed ox" can be found in *Mespris du monde* (Protestant) (1612), pp. 139 v° passim.
58. Ibid., p. 310.
59. Baxter, *A Sermon of Judgement* (of 1654), (London: 1668), p. 235.
60. Ibid., p. 265.
61. D. Featley, *Clavis mystica . . . seventy sermons* (London: 1634), pp. 611–612.
62. Aquila, *Des Kleinen Catechismi Erklerung*, in Reu, *Quellen*, vol. 1, 2 (2), pp. 178–179, quoted in Strauss, *Luther's House*, P. 208. Pr. 3:34, says, quite simply, "He mocks those who mock,

but accords his favour to the humble." On the other hand, it is true that Lev. 26 abounds in descriptions of the chastisements wrought by Yahweh. The conclusion, however, ends on a note of reconciliation.

63. Hieron, *Sermons*, p. 740.
64. Ibid., p. 741.
65. R. Sibbes, *Gods Inquisition in two sermons* (1619), p. 89.
66. See Rannou, *George Wither*, vol. 1, pp. 45, 105–111 and 143; vol. 2, pp. 200–208, 253, and 258.
67. G. Wither, *Britain's Remembrancer*, 18 vols. (Manchester: Spencer Society, 1871–85) quoted in Rannou, *George Wither*, vol. 1, p. 45.
68. Rannou, *George Wither*, vol. 2, p. 253.
69. This information is from Vovelle, *La Mort en Occident.*
70. His last months and his death are told by his son in an annex of the *Consolations* published after his death.
71. Death mentioned by Vovelle, *La Mort en Occident.*
72. S. Clark, *The Lives of sundry Eminent Persons in this Later Age* . . . (London: 1683), p. 44.
73. See the already-mentioned article by Vogler, "Attitudes devant la mort . . . ," *Archives de Sociologie des Religions* 39 (1975).
74. T. Heshusius, *Postilla, das ist Auslegung der sontaglichen Evangelien durchs gantze Jahr* (Helmstadt: 1581), fols. 342 v. and 343 r.
75. Brooks, *Heaven on Earth* (1654), p. 57; Carrive, "L'Assurance du salut . . . ," p. 263.
76. See above (p. 362 in French original).
77. W. Harrison, *A Brief Discourse of the Christian Life and Death of Mistris Katherin Brettergh* (London: 1602), 2nd ed., pp. 28–29; White, *English Devotional Literature* . . . , pp. 54–56.
78. Heshusius, *Postilla, das ist Auslegung* . . . , fol. 33 r.
79. Ibid., fol. 164 v.
80. Ibid., fol. 343 r.
81. Gerhardt, *Predigt am Neujahrtage*, quoted in Beste, *Die Bedeutesten Kanzelredner* . . . , vol. 3, p. 132.
82. Drelincourt, *Les Consolations* . . . , vol. 1, ch. 1, p. 7.
83. Sibbes, *Gods Inquisition* . . . , pp. 97–98.
84. Love, *Heavens Glory* . . . , pp. 13–14.
85. Donne, *Sermons* . . . , vol. 3, no. 1, and vol. 7, no. 16.
86. J. Bunyan, *The Works of that Eminent Servant of Christ, Mr. John Bunyan*, ed. by C. Doe (London: 1692), Folio, p. 189 ("Paul's departure and crown").
87. Brenz, *Pericope evangeliorum* . . . , pp. 948–951.
88. Gerhardt, *Sacrarum homiliarum* . . . , vol. 2, p. 698.
89. Smith, *Sermons* . . . , London ed. of 1866, vol. 2, p. 76.
90. D. Dyke, *La Sonde de la conscience* . . . , trans. from English by Jean Verneuil (Geneva: 1634), pp. 148–209.
91. R. Sibbes, *A Sermon preached at Lent Assises* (1630), pp. 81–82.
92. J. Whitefoote, *Deats alarum, or the Presage of approaching Death: given in a Funeral Sermon* . . . (1656), pp. 52–60.
93. Wesley, *Sermons* . . . , (Paris 1888 ed.), vol. 2, pp. 8 and 20.
94. See Donne, *Sermons*, vol. 2, no. 11.
95. The seventeenth article states that "Christ . . . will condemn the impious and demons to being tortured endlessly." See Walker, *The Decline of Hell*, pp. 22–23.
96. P. Jurieu, *Traité de l'unité de l'Eglise et des points fondamentaux* (Rotterdam: 1688), pp. 378–380.
97. The seventh sermon in volume 1.
98. Donne, *Sermons*, vol. 5, n. 13, pp. 266–267.
99. J. Bunyan, *A Treatise of the Fear of God*, in *Miscellaneous Works*, vol. 9 of the R. L. Greaves ed. (Oxford: 1981).
100. J. Bunyan, *A Holy Life*, in ibid., pp. 341–342.
101. I used a French translation of 1869, *Le Voyage du Chrétien vers l'éternité bienheureuse*, p. 12.
102. Ibid. p. 33 (chap. 4).
103. J. Bunyan, *Some Gospel-Truths Opened; A Vindication of some Gospel-Truths opened; A few sighs from Hell*, T. L. Underwood ed. (Oxford: Clarendon Press, 1980), p. 276.
104. Ibid., pp. 273–300.
105. Ibid., p. 280.

106. J. Bunyan, *Grace abounding* and *The Life and Death of Mr. Badman*, G. B. Harrison ed. (London: Dent, 1969), p. 152.
107. Bunyan, *Some Gospel-Truths* and *A few sighs*, p. 227.
108. Bunyan, *Grace abounding* . . . , section 7, p. 8.
109. R. Baxter, *A Saint or a Brute* (1662), p. 143; Bunyan, *Some Gospel Truths* . . . , p. xlix.
110. W. Perkins, *A Dialogue of the State of a Christian Man*, in *The Work*, intro. and notes by I. Bredward (Appleford: Sutton Courtenay Press, 1970), p. 366.
111. E. Calamy, *The Art of Divine Meditation* (1680), p. 126. Bunyan, *Some Gospel-Truths*, p. xl. See M. M. Kappen, *Tudor Puritanism* (Chicago: University of Chicago Press, 1965), p. 504.
112. T. Goodwin, *Aggravation of Sinne* (1643), p. 17, and by the same author *Aggravations of Sinning against Knowledge* (1643), pp. 80–81.
113. See also Smith, *Sermons*, vol. 2, p. 89.
114. Hieron, *Sermons* . . . , p. 249.
115. Ibid.
116. Featley, *Clavis mystica* . . . , p. 289.
117. Love, *Heavens Glory* . . . , p. 39.
118. B. M. Levy, *Preaching in the First Half Century of New England* (Hartford, CT: The American Society of Church History, 1945), p. 25.
119. See G. Strauss, *Luther's House* . . . , p. 203 and notes 1–4 on p. 364.
120. Gerhardt, *Sacrarum Homiliarum* . . . , vol. 1, pp. 690–691.
121. Arndt, *De la Régénération* . . . , p. 10.
122. Arndt, *De Vero Christiano* . . . , pp. 76–83.
123. Ibid., pp. 783–784.
124. Ibid., p. 124.
125. Daillé, *Mélange de sermons* . . . , p. 241; Drelincourt, *Recueil de sermons* . . . , pp. 37–38.
126. *Le Mépris du monde* (1612).
127. Ibid., p. 2 v°.
128. Ibid., p. 113 r°.
129. Ibid., p. 42 r°.
130. Ibid., p. 18 r°.
131. Ibid., p. 23 v°.
132. Ibid., p. 25 v°.
133. Ibid., p. 26 v°.
134. Ibid., p. 115 r°.
135. Ibid., pp. 111 v°–114r°.
136. H. B., *A Verie profitable sermon*, p. 18, quoted by Blench, *Preaching in England* . . . , p. 315.
137. See also Blench, ibid.
138. Smith, *Sermons* . . . , vol. 2, p. 98.
139. Hieron, *Sermons* . . . , p. 330.
140. R. Sibbes, *The Spiritual Iubile in two sermons* (1638), p. 55.
141. R. Sibbes, *The Churches Eccho* (1638), pp. 125–126.
142. D. Featley, *Clavis Mystica* . . . (1624), p. 243.
143. R. Baxter, *The Right Method for a settled Peace of conscience and Spiritual Comfort*, 3rd ed. (London: 1657), nonpaginated dedicatory letter.
144. See above (p. 158 of French original).
145. A. Dent, *The Plaine Mans Pathway to Heaven* (London: 1601), p. 97. White, *English Devotional Literature* . . . , p. 210.
146. Donne, *Sermons*, vol. 2, no. 2, pp. 78–79. See esp. volume 2, no. 13; vol. 3, no. 1 and 8; vol. 9, no. 1 and 2; vol. 10, no. 9 and 11.
147. See J. Deschner, *Wesley's Christology. An Interpretation* (Dallas: South Methodist University Press, 1960), pp. 199–203, sermons no. 81, 103, 104, 119, and 121.

CHAPTER 21

1. In particular pp. 213–230.
2. See the introduction by J. Lefebvre of T. Müntzer (1490–1525), *Ecrits théologiques et politiques* (Lyon: Presses Universitaires de Lyon, 1982), esp. pp. 33–38.
3. See above all (p. 152 of French original).

4. These two parallel attitudes are well defined by Strauss, *Luther's House* . . . , pp. 31–33.
5. Quoted by Dollinger, *Die Reformation, ihre innere Entwiklung und ihre Wirkungen im Unfange des lutherischen Bekentnisses* (Regensburg: 1846–48), vol. 2, p. 541, and in J. Janssen, *La Civilisation en Allemagne*, vol. 8, p. 457.
6. R. Urbanus, *Opera latine edita* (Nüremberg: 1562), fol. 431.
7. Janssen, *La Civilisation en Allemagne*, vol. 6, p. 263, and vol. 3, p. 364. The following pages owe much to Janssen's work.
8. Ibid., vol. 6, pp. 273–279.
9. Ibid., pp. 204–205.
10. Ibid., pp. 215–216.
11. Ibid., pp. 210–215.
12. E. Alberus, *Das Buch von Tugent und Weisshait* . . . , ed. by W. Braune, in *Neudrucke deutscher Literaturwerke des XVI und XVII Jahrhunderts*, series no. 104–107 (Halle: 1893). See P. Carnes, "The Fable in service of the Reformation" forthcoming in *Renaissance and Reformation*.
13. J. Spagenberg, *Explicationes evangeliorum et epistolarum* . . . (Basle: 1564), fols. 17 r°–v°.
14. R. Urbanus, *Opera latine edita*, fol. 274 v° ("Homilia de bonis et malis angelis").
15. D. Veit, *Kinder Postilla über die Sonntags und der fürnembsten Festen Evangelia durch des gantzen Jahr* (Nüremberg: 1549), fols. 165–177.
16. H. Regius, *Opera latine edita* (Nürenberg: 1562), fol. 431 ("Consolatio in omni genere afflictionis").
17. Heshusius, *Postilla, das ist Auslegung* . . . , fol. 80v°.
18. K. Goedeke, *Grundriss zur Geschichte der deutschen Dichtung* (Dresden: 1886), vol. 2. See Janssen, *La Civilisation en Allemagne*, vol. 6, pp. 296–298.
19. Janssen, *La Civilisation en Allemagne*, vol. 6, pp. 296–298.
20. Brenz, *Pericope evangeliorum* . . . , p. 372.
21. Régius, *Opera latine edita*, fol. 427 r°.
22. Heshusius, *Postilla, das ist Auslegung* . . . , fol. 102 r°.
23. Brenz, *Pericope Evangeliorum* . . . , p. 372.
24. Ibid., p. 150.
25. Heshusius, *Postilla, das ist Auslegung* . . . , fol. 82 r°.
26. Ibid., fol. 129 r°.
27. Veit, *Kinder Postilla* . . . , fols. 83 v°, 91r°–95v°.
28. Urbanus, *Opera latina edita*, fol. 426 r° ("Consolation . . .").
29. Brenz, *Pericope Evangeliorum* . . . , p. 372.
30. See what I already said in *La Peur en Occident*, pp. 215–217.
31. A. Osiander, *Conjectura de ultimis temporis ac de fine mundi ex sacris literis* (Nürenberg: 1544).
32. Heshusius, *Postilla, das ist Auslegung* . . . , fol. 8 r°.
33. J. Gigas, *Postilla, das ist Aufklerung der Evangelien durchs ganze Jahr* . . . (Frankfurt am Main: 1582), fols. 15 r°–15 v°.
34. Janssen, *La Civilisation en Allemagne*, vol. 6, pp. 394–395.
35. Ibid., pp. 291–295.
36. B. Vogler, *Le Monde germanique et hélvétique à l'époque des Réformes, 1517–1618*, 2 vols. (Paris: SEDES, 1981), vol. 2, pp. 516–517.
37. Gerhardt, *Sacrarum homiliarum in pericopas evangeliorum dominicalium et praecipuorum totius anni festorum*, vol. 1, pp. 35–36. I used the two-volume 1647 ed.
38. Arndt, *De Vero Christiano*, first preface, nonpaginated.
39. Delumeau, *La Peur en Occident*, p. 216.
40. Janssen, *La Civilisation en Allemagne*, vol. 6, p. 396, and vol. 8, p. 458.
41. Ibid.
42. Sigwart, *Eilff Predigten* . . . (1603), pp. 123a–123b. Quoted in Janssen, *La Civilisation en Allemagne*, vol. 6, p. 396.
43. See E. François, "De l'Uniformité à la tolérance. Confession et société urbaine en Allemagne, 1650–1800," *Annales ESC* 37 (July–August 1982): 783–800.
44. Delumeau, *La Peur en Occident*, pp. 228–229.
45. P. Jurieu, *L'Accomplissement des prophéties ou la délivrance prochaine de l'Eglise* (Rotterdam: 1686), p. 182.
46. Ibid., pp. 18–36.
47. Ibid., p. 151.
48. Ibid., p. 152.
49. Ibid.

50. Ibid., p. 141.
51. See *Le Théâtre sacré des Cévennes* (1707), reprinted in 1978. H. Plard, "L'Apocalypse des Camisards: prédicants et inspirés," in *Problèmes d'histoire du Christianisme*, G. Gambier ed. by (Brussels: 1979), p. 65 (all of this article is of interest for my analysis); and D. Vidal, *Le Malheur et son prophète. Inspirés et sectaires en Languedoc calviniste* (Paris: Payot, 1983).
52. C. Post, *Les Prédicants protestants des Cévennes et du Bas Languedoc, 1684–1700*, 2 vols. (Paris: 1912), vol. 2, p. 534.
53. Quoted by Joutard, *Les Camisards*, p. 46.
54. Vidal, *Le Malheur et son prophète*, p. 30; M. Hamon, *La Prophéties de la fin du temp* (Paris: 1945); H. Lilje, *L'Apocalypse, le dernier livre de la Bible* (Paris: Payot, 1959), p. 30.
55. C. Hill, *Antichrist in Seventeenth-Century England: The World Turned Upside-Down* (1972), I consulted the Penguin Books ed. 1976. Br. W. Ball, *A Great Expectation. Eschatological Thought in English Protestantism to 1660*. P. Christianson, *Reformers and Babylon. English Apocalyptic Visions from the Reformation to the Eve of the Civil War* (Toronto: University Press, 1978).
56. See the chapter entitled "L'Attente de Dieu" in *La Peur en Occident*.
57. Luther, *Werke*, Weimar ed., vol. 1, p. 307.
58. G. Joye, *The Exposicioun of Daniel the Prophete gathered out of Philip Melancthon, Johan Ecolampadius, Chonrade Pellicane and out of Johan Draconite* (Geneva: 1545).
59. Ball, *A Great Expectation*, p. 16.
60. Hill, *Antichrist*, pp. 3–4.
61. W. H. Hart, *Index . . . anglicanus: or a Descriptive Catalogue of the Principal Books Printed or Published in England wich have been suppressed or burnt by the Common Hangman, or Censured, or for wich the Authors, Printers or Publishers have been Prosecuted*, vol. 1 (London: 1872), reprint 1969. See also "Censure romaine et censure genevoise au XVIe siècle," in *Les Eglises et leurs institutions au XVIe siècle* (Montpellier: 1979), pp. 169–191.
62. White, *English Devotional Literature*, pp. 133–134.
63. Ball, *A Great Expectation*, p. 101.
64. Christianson, *Reformers and Babylon*, p. 8.
65. James I, *Ane fruitfull Meditation contening ane plane and facill expositioun of ye 7, 8, 9 and 10 versis of the 20 Chap. of the Revelation* (Edinburgh: 1588).
66. Ball, *A Great Expectation*, pp. 59–61; Christianson, *Reformers and Babylon*, pp. 97–98. Hill, *Antichrist*, pp. 24–26.
67. G. F. Nuttall, *Visible Saints: The Congregational Way, 1640–1660* (Oxford: 1957), p. 157. Ball, *A Great Expectation*, p. 33. Hill, *Antichrist*, all of chap. 3, pp. 78–145.
68. S. Marshall, *A Sermon* (1641), pp. 34 passim. Christianson, *Reformers and Babylon*, p. 185.
69. T. Goodwin, *Works*, 5 vols. (1681–1704), vol. 1, p. 133. Ball, *A Great Expectation*, p. 218.
70. See O. Lutaud, *Les Niveleurs, Cromwell et al République* (Paris: Julliard, 1967), reproduction on pp. 128–129.
71. Expression used by W. Bridge in a sermon delivered in 1648 to the House of Commons; Ball, *A Great Expectation*, p. 93. I have used the latter work for much of the following paragraph.
72. J. Napier, *A Plaine discovery of the whole Revelation of S. John* (Edinburgh: 1593), p. 21.
73. A. Dent, *The Ruine of Rome* (1603), pp. 124 and 144.
74. T. Brightman, *Exposition . . . of the Prophecie of Daniel*, in *Works* (1644), p. 954.
75. J. Mede, *Remaines on some Passages in the Apocalypse* (1650), in *Works* (1672), p. 600.
76. Goodwin, *Revelation . . .*, in *Works*, vol. 1, p. 184.
77. R. Baxter, *The Saints Everlasting Rest* (1650), pp. 47, 791, 837.
78. J. Durant, *Salvation of the Saints* (1653), p. 302.
79. Love, *Heavens Glory* p. 50.
80. G. Fox, *The Great Mystery of the Great Whore unfolded: and Antichrists Kingdom Revealed unto destruction* (1659), p. 44.
81. E. Burrough, *A Trumpet of the Lord sounded out of Sion . . .* (1656), p. 41.
82. Hill, *Antichrist*, p. 155; Ball, *A Great Expectation*, p. 146.
83. Ball, *A Great Expectation*, pp. 91–92.
84. For all of what follows see, generally speaking, C. Hill, *Antichrist*.
85. Ball, *A Great Expectation*, esp. pp. 136–141.
86. Hill, *Antichrist*, pp. 37, 68, 70–71.
87. Ibid., p. 92. Anon., *Heretiks, Sectaries and Schismatikes, Discovered to be the Antichrist yet remaining* (1647), p. 8.
88. Ibid., pp. 121–122.
89. Ibid., p. 58.

90. Ibid., p. 75.
91. Ibid., p. 138.
92. Ibid., p. 141.
93. Ibid., p. 14.
94. James I, *Fruitfull Meditation . . .*, sig. Bivr. See Ball, *A Great Expectation*, p. 187.
95. Hill, *Antichrist*, p. 18. See *The Writings of R. Harrison and R. Browne*, ed. by A. Peel and L. Carlson. (1953), pp. 152 and 524.
96. Ibid., p. 72.
97. C. Burges, *Another Sermon* (5 November 1641), p. 35. For all that follows, see P. Christianson *Reformers and Babylon*, pp. 224–230.
98. S. Marshall, *Meroz Cursed* (23 February 1642), pp. 8 and 20.
99. J. Caryl, *The Workes of Ephesus explained* (1642), pp. 1, 32, 40, 41, 47, 50, 54.
100. W. Sedgwick, *Zions deliverance and her friends Duty* (1642), pp. 10, 11, 26, and 35.
101. See J. E. Wilson, *Pulpit in Parliament* (Princeton, NJ: Princeton University Press, 1969).
102. M. Cary, *The Little Horn's Doom and Downfall . . .* (1651), p. 122. Ball, *A Great Expectation*, p. 187.
103. Ball, *A Great Expectation*, p. 185.
104. Quoted in O. Lutaud, *Les Niveleurs, Cromwell et la République*, pp. 230–231.
105. J. Garrison-Estèbe, *L'Homme protestant* (Paris: Hachette, 1980), p. 95.
106. L. Carrive, "L'Assurance du salut . . . ," p. 270.
107. Calvin, *Institution*, book 2, ch. 1, 8; vol. 2, p. 19.
108. Ibid., book 2, ch. 1, 7; vol. 2, p. 17.
109. Luther, The Bondage of the Will, trans. by J. I. Packer and O. R. Johnston (London: 1957), p. 262.
110. Ibid., p. 188.
111. Ibid., p. 190.
112. Calvin, *Institution*, book 1, ch. 15, 8; vol. 1, p. 144.
113. Ibid., book 2, ch. 2, 27; vol. 2, p. 5.
114. Luther, *Oeuvres*, vol. 7, p. 239 (*Les Articles de Smalkalde*).
115. E. Leyser (1615), p. 173. Concerning the much more qualified outlook of Melanchthon during the rest of his life see J. Boisset, *Mélanchthon* (Paris: Seghers, 1967), above all pp. 36–56.
116. See above (p. 189 of French original) (*Du Serf Arbitre*).
117. Calvin, *Institution*, book 3, ch. 21, 5–7: pp. 399–404.
118. Ibid., book 3, ch. 24, 14: pp. 451–452.
119. Luther, *Oeuvres*, vol. 5, p. 136 (*Du Serf arbitre*).
120. Ibid., p. 143. [Trans. by Packer and Johnston, p. 285.]
121. Calvin, *Institution*, book 3, ch. 23, 14; vol. 3, p. 432. A Reference to S. Augustine, *De la Correction et de la grâce*, chaps. 5, 8. [Trans. from *The Institutes*, Battles trans., vol. 2, p. 963.]
122. Ibid., vol. 3, ch. 23, 5; vol. 3, p. 425. [Trans. ibid., pp. 952–953.]
123. Ibid., vol. 3, ch. 24, 4; vol. 3, pp. 439 passim. Advice analogous to that of Melanchthon, see J. Boisset, *Mélanchthon*, p. 56.
124. The following ideas on Zwingli were inspired by the article "Zwingli, Zwiglianisme" by J.V.M. Pollet in the *Dictionnaire de Théologie catholique*, vol. 15, cols. 3716–3928.
125. *Corpus Reformatorum*, vol. 96; Zwingli, vol. 9, letter no. 580 (dated 1527), p. 30.
126. *Ulrich Zwingli opera*, ed. by M. Schuler and J. Schultess (1828–42), vol. 4, *De Providentia Dei*, p. 139.
127. Ibid., p. 112.
128. Ibid., p. 140.
129. Concerning this subject and the following development, see Bray, *Theodore Beza's Doctrine of Predestination*, pp. 44–63.
130. Calvin, *Institution . . . chétienne*, book 3, ch. 21, 4; vol. 3, p. 397.
131. Calvin, *Sermons . . . sur les deux epistres de saint Paul à Timotée . . .*, p. 504.
132. P. Jacobs, *Prädestination und Verantwortlichkeit bei Calvin* (Neukirchen: 1937), pp. 142–152. Bray, *Theodore Beza's Doctrine*, pp. 50–51. The allusion here is to the *Congrégation sur l'élection éternelle*, (1551) written by Calvin in relation to the Bolsec affair and the *De aeterna Dei Praedestinatione* (1552) against Pighius.
133. K. Bath, *Dogmatique*, 2 vols. (Geneva: Labor et Fidès, 1958), p. 80.
134. Bray, *Theodore Beza's Doctrine*, pp. 82–84.
135. See F. Gardy, *Bibliographie des oeuvres . . . de Théodore de Bèze* (Geneva: Droz, 1960).
136. See the bibliography regarding this topic in Bray, *Theodore Beza's Doctrine*, p. 66, no. 193.

137. Reproduced in Gardy, *Bibliographie* . . . , p. 49.
138. Bray, *Theodore Beza's Doctrine*, p. 71.
139. Perkins's scheme is to be found in W. Perkins, *The Work*, pp. 168–169.
140. See O. Gundler, *Die Gotteslehre Girolamo Zanchis* (Neukirchen: 1965), esp. p. 159. See also J. Moltmann, *Prädestination und Perseveranz* (Neukirchen: 1961).
141. B. Hall, "Calvin against the Calvinists," in *John Calvin*, ed. by G. E. Duffield (Appleford: Sutton Courtenay Press, 1966), pp. 29–30.
142. R. A. Muller, "Perkin's *A Golden chaine*: Predestinarian System or schematized *Ordo salutis*," *Sixteenth Century Journal* 9 (1) (1978): 69–81; L. B. Wright, "William Perkins: Elizabethan Apostle of 'Practical Divinity,' " *Huntingdon Library Quarterly* 3 (2) (1928): 171–196.
143. Muller, "Perkin's *Golded chaine*," p. 76.
144. Ibid., p. 70.
145. Wright, "William Perkins," p. 192.
146. See E. G. Léonard, *Histoire générale du Protestantisme* (Paris: P.U.F., 1961), vol. 2, p. 59. See *The Text of the Thirty-Nine Articles of 1553, 1563, 1571*, W. M. Meredith ed. (London: 1889).
147. Tyndale, *Works*, Parker Society ed., vol. 1, p. 508. Hughes, *Theology*, p. 48.
148. Cranmer, *Works*, Parker Society ed., vol. 2, p. 129 ("Homily on Salvation"). Hughes, *Theology*, p. 50.
149. Bradford, *Works*, Parker Society ed., vol. 1, p. 48. Hughes, *Theology*, p. 54.
150. Latimer, *Works*, Parker Society ed., vol. 1, p. 419. Hughes, *Theology*, p. 54.
151. Perkins, *The Work*, p. 84.
152. Burton, *The Anatomy of Melancholy*, vol. 3, p. 421.
153. Donne, *Sermons*, vol. 3, no. 16; vol. 4, no. 7; vol. 5, nos. 1 and 15; vol. 7, nos. 9, 14 and 18.
154. Ibid., vol. 4, n. 7.
155. Burton, *The Anatomy of Melancholy*, vol. 3, p. 424.
156. Concerning this see D. Ebner, *Autobiography in Seventeenth-Century England* (Paris: Mouton, 1971) who draws attention to the differences between Anglican and Puritan autobiographies of the seventeenth century.
157. See Thomas, *Religion and* . . . , pp. 472–503.
158. See Ebner, *Autobiography*, p. 87, n. 32.
159. T. Becon, *The Sicke Mannes Salve* (1591), Parker Society ed., pp. 174 and 176. Carrive, "L'Assurance du salut," pp. 261–262.
160. Burton, *Anatomy of Melancholy*, vol. 3, p. 399.
161. J. Bradford, *Letter to Mistress Mary Honywood*, Parker Society ed., p. 132. Carrive, "L'Assurance du salut," p. 260.
162. Latimer, *Works*, vol. 1, p. 329. Hughes, *Theology* . . . , p. 47.
163. Hooper, *Works*, Parker Society ed., vol. 2, p. 4. Hughes, *Theology* . . . , p. 65. Concerning Hooper, see Knappen, *Tudor Puritanism*, pp. 59–109.
164. Whitgift, *Works* (The Third Portion), p. 622. Carrive, "L'Assurance du salut," p. 261.
165. Concerning Preston, see Haller, *The Rise of Puritanism*, esp. pp. 70–75.
166. Perkins, *The Work*, vol. 1, pp. 32, 70, 72.
167. Carrive, "L'Assurance du salut," p. 264, who refers to Jewel, Bradford, Preston, and Brooks.
168. J. Daillé, *Exposition des 3e et 4e ch. de l'Epitre aux Philippiens* (Paris: 1647), p. 169 (fourth sermon).
169. See H. Vuilleumier, *Histoire de l'Eglise réformée du pays de Vaud*, 4 vols. (Lausanne: 1928–32), vol. 2, p. 688 (*Instruction familière*).
170. D. Featley, *The still small voice* (1619), p. 20.
171. R. Sibbes, *Saint Pauls Challenge in one sermon* (1638), p. 85.
172. R. Sibbes, *The Fruitful Labour for eternal foode in two sermons* (1630), p. 215.
173. R. Baxter, *A Call to the Unconverted to Turn and Live* . . . , 23rd ed. (1685), p. 31.
174. J. Spangenberg, *Predigt am Sonntage Sexagesima*, Beste ed., vol. 1, p. 145. Same development is to be found in Brenz, *Pericope evangeliorum*, pp. 234–235 and 251.
175. A. Corvinus, *Postilla in evangelia domininicalia* . . . (Strasburg: 1537), fol. 69 v°.
176. See the Latin translation by W. Perkinsius, *De Praedestinatione modo et ordine, et de amplitudine gratiae divinae* (Basel: 1559 ed.), p. 32.
177. Gerhardt, *Sacrarum homiliarum*, vol. 1, pp. 494–495.
178. J. Arndt, *De Vero Christiano*, on the cover page of the Frankfurt 1658 ed.
179. S. Hieron, *The Christian Iournall. Three Sermons on Matth. 7: 13–14.*
180. Love, *Heavens Glory*, sermon 5 ("on Hells Terror"), p. 76.

181. R. Baxter, *Directions for weak distempered Christians* . . . (London: 1669), p. 80. Sermon delivered the preceding year.
182. I have collected here the themes that appear in the following sermons: vol. 1, no. 3; vol. 2, nos. 1, 6, 18; vol. 3, no. 16; vol. 5, no. 16; vol. 6, no. 7; vol. 7, nos. 2 and 12; vol. 9, no. 11.
183. Burton, *The Anatomy of Melancholy*, vol. 3, p. 398. The same theme is treated on p. 419.
184. See Bray, *Theodore Beza's Doctrine*, p. 70.
185. See above (pp. 602–604 of French original).
186. *A Golden Chain*, in W. Perkins, *Work*, ed. by I. Breward, pp. 183–185.
187. Laud, *Works*, vol. 6, p. 133; quoted in E.C.E. Bourne, *The Anglicanism of W. Laud* (London: Soc. for Prom. Christ. Knowledge, 1947), p. 61, and in Ebner, *Autobiography* . . . , p. 75.
188. See above (pp. 554–555 of French original).
189. T. Fuller, *The Holy and the Profane State* (1642), ed. by M. G. Walter (New York: 1938), vol. 2, p. 90.
190. R. Bolton, *Instructions for a Right Comforting (of) Afflicted Consciences* (London: 1631), p. 79; Ebner, *Autobiography* . . . , p. 40.
191. In particular in *Grace abounding to the Chief of Sinners*, no. 815 of the Everyman's Library ed. (London: Dent, 1969).
192. These steps are well shown in Ebner, *Autobiography* . . . , pp. 42–47.
193. Calvin, *Institution* . . . , III, 2, 17: vol. 3, pp. 36–37.
194. See the introduction by I. Breward to *The Work* of W. Perkins, p. 95.
195. Du Moulin, *Decade de Sermons*, pp. 32–33.
196. This illuminating distinction comes from Carrive, "L'Assurance," pp. 259–260.
197. Brooks, *Heaven on Earth*, pp. 45 and 59. Carrive, "L'Assurance," p. 263.
198. H. Smith, *Sermons* (1866 ed.), vol. 2, p. 80.
199. Ibid., p. 96.
200. W. Perkins, *A Grain of Mustard-Seed* (1597), p. 409.
201. This diagram is reproduced on pp. 168–169 of the I. Breward ed.
202. S. Hieron, *The Spirituall Sonne-ship* (1619), pp. 358–359.
203. R. Sibbes, *The Churches Complaint and confidence in three Sermons* (1639), p. 322.
204. Featley, *Clavis mystica* . . . , p. 25.
205. R. Baxter, *The Right Method for a settled Peace of Conscience and Spiritual Comfort* (1652), pp. 120, 160, and 181 of the 1652 ed.
206. Drelincourt, *Recueil de sermons*, pp. 512–513 (sermon no. 10).
207. Ibid., p. 309 (sermon no. 6).
208. Featley, *Clavis mystica* . . . , pp. 311–312.
209. Love, *Heavens Glory*, p. 245 (sermon no. 15).
210. Burton, *Anatomy of Melancholy*, vol. 3, p. 398.
211. Donne, *Sermons*, vol. 1, no. 6, p. 201.
212. See ibid., vol. 5, no. 9; vol. 6, no. 4; vol. 9, no. 14.
213. Love, *Heavens Glory*, p. 202 (sermon no. 12).
214. Smith, *Sermons*, vol. 2, p. 77.
215. Drelincourt, *Recueil de sermons*, p. 40 (sermon no. 1).
216. Featley, *Clavis mystica* . . . , p. 355 ("The New Name").
217. Ibid., p. 358.
218. G. Tennent, *For a Provincial Thanksgiving* (Philadelphia: 1750), p. 15.
219. A frequent term in Puritan preaching. See Levy, *Preaching* . . . , p. 54.
220. Cranmer, *Works*, Parker Society ed., vol. 2, pp. 133 and 136. Hughes, *Theology* . . . , pp. 55–57.
221. Smith, *Sermons*, vol. 2, p. 77.
222. Ibid., p. 79.
223. J. Daillé, *Exposition des 3e et 4e chapitres de l'épître de saint Paul aux Philippiens* (Paris: 1647), p. 169 (fourth sermon).
224. Du Moulin, *Decade de sermons*, pp. 23–27 (first sermon).
225. P. Spener, *Die evangelische Glaubenslehre* (Frankfurt: 1717), p. 1313 (sermon of 1687 for the Sunday after Trinity).
226. R. Baxter, *The Saints Everlasting Rest*, 1652 ed., part 3, pp. 134–135.
227. Ibid., pp. 294–295.
228. Donne, *Sermons*, vol. 1, no. 4.
229. Ibid., vol. 3, no. 5, and vol. 5, no. 2.

230. Ebner, *Autobiography* . . . , esp. pp. 19, 21 and 41.
231. Perkins, *A Grain of Mustard-Seed*, pp. 406–407.
232. Ibid.
233. *The Daily Examination and Araignment of Sins: gathered out of the most Reverend the Primate of Ireland's Sermon at Lincoln's Inn, Dec. 3, 1648*, at the British Museum. See White, *English Devotional Literature*, p. 163.
234. Dyke, *La Sonde de la conscience*, dedication, unpaginated.
235. Hieron, *Sermons*, p. 17 ("The Christians Journale").
236. R. Sibbes, *Gods Inquisition in two sermons* (1619), p. 101.
237. R. Sibbes, *St. Pauls Challenge in two sermons* (1638), p. 89.
238. Featley, *Clavis mystica* . . . , p. 286 ("Philip his Memento mori").
239. Ibid., p. 273 ("The Stewards Account").
240. See the introduction by Breward to *The Work* of W. Perkins, pp. 62–67.
241. Smith, *Sermons*, p. 426 (1594 ed.).
242. Love, *Heavens Glory*, p. 125 (sermon no. 8).
243. Burton, *The Anatomy of Melancholy*, vol. 3, p. 401. Translation by J. R. Simon, *Robert Burton* . . . , p. 559.
244. Ibid., vol. 3, pp. 405–406.
245. See White, *English devotional Literature*, esp. pp. 165–167.
246. *A Treatise tending unto a declaration whether a man be in the estate of damnation or in the Estate of Grace* (1589).
247. *A Case of Conscience, the Greatest that ever was: How a man may know whether he may be the Child of God, or no* (1592).
248. Smith, *Sermons*, vol. 2, pp. 419–420 ("Questions out of his own Confession").
249. Hieron, *Sermons*, pp. 103–104 ("The Abridgement of the Gospel").
250. R. Sibbes, *The Spiritual Iubile* . . . (1618), p. 2.
251. Love, *Heavens Glory*, p. 115 (sermon no. 7).
252. Love, *Treatise of effectual Calling and Election. In XVI Sermons on Pet. 1: 10* . . . (1653).
253. Ibid., p. 201 (sermon no. 12).
254. Baxter, *The Right Method for a settled Peace of Conscience*, p. 2.
255. Burton, *The Anatomy of Melancholy*, vol. 3, p. 399.
256. Heshusius, *Postilla, das ist Auslegung*, fol. 164 v°.
257. See above (p. 206 of French original).
258. Burton, *The Anatomy of Melancholy*, vol. 3, pp. 395–404.
259. Ibid., pp. 406–407.
260. Ibid., pp. 409–413.
261. Donne, *Sermons*, esp. vol. 2, nos. 6 and 18; vol. 3, no. 5; vol. 6, nos. 4, 7, 8, 16; vol. 7, no. 2.
262. Hieron, *Sermons*, p. 16 ("The Christians Journale").
263. Perkins, *A Dialogue of the State of a Christian Man*, pp. 367–368.
264. Ibid., *A Grain of Mustard-Seed*, p. 409.
265. Featley, *The Smoking Flax*, p. 25.
266. J. Bunyan, *Grace Abounding* . . . , Everyman's Library ed., pp. 43–44 (sections 139 and 140).
267. Burton, *The Anatomy of Melancholy*, vol. 3, p. 399.
268. H. Buckle, *Introduction to the History of Civilization in England* (London: Routledge, 1907), p. 770.
269. Wright, "W. Perkins . . . ", p. 196.
270. I. Watt, *The Rise of the Novel. Studies in Defoe, Richardson and Fielding* (London: Chatto and Windus, 1957), p. 51. See M. Brousseau, "Essai sur les livres de spiritualité et de dévotion populaire en Angleterre de 1680 à 1760, third cycle dissertation, University of Paris III, 1979, 3 vols.

CONCLUSION

1. Comment made by M. Vienne during the symposium "La peur en Angleterre des Tudors et des Stuarts," Lille, March 1983.

INDEX